Y0-EMC-228

WITHDRAWN

REFERENCE
INDIAN VALLEY COLLEGES
LIBRARY USE ONLY

ATLAS
OF THE
HISTORICAL GEOGRAPHY
OF THE
UNITED STATES

ATLAS
OF THE
HISTORICAL GEOGRAPHY
OF THE
UNITED STATES

BY

CHARLES O. PAULLIN
Carnegie Institution of Washington

Edited by

JOHN K. WRIGHT
Librarian, American Geographical Society of New York

GREENWOOD PRESS, PUBLISHERS
WESTPORT, CONNECTICUT

Library of Congress Cataloging in Publication Data

Paullin, Charles Oscar, 1868 or 9-1944.
    Atlas of the historical geography of the United
States.

    Reprint of the 1932 ed. published jointly by
Carnegie Institution of Washington and the American
Geographical Society of New York, which was issued as
no. 401 of Carnegie Institution of Washington.
Publication.
    1. United States—Historical geography—Maps.
2. United States—Historical geography. 3. United
States—Description and travel. 4. Cartography—
America. 5. Maps, Early—Facsimiles. I. Wright,
John Kirtland, 1891-1969. II. American Geographical
Society of New York. III. Title. IV. Series:
Carnegie Institution of Washington. Publication
no. 401.
G1201.S1P3 1975   911'.73   75-14058
ISBN 0-8371-8208-5

PUBLISHER'S NOTE

Charles O. Paullin's *Atlas of the Historical Geography of the United States* was the first major historical atlas of the United States to be published. It is reproduced here as a nearly identical facsimile. Although all the plates are included in the reprint edition, the color plates which appeared in the original edition are reproduced in black and white.

For the convenience of readers who require the color identification to interpret those respective plates, all color plates have been reproduced on color microfiche at a reduction ratio of 24:1. These microfiche are included in a pocket in the back of this edition.

CARNEGIE INSTITUTION OF WASHINGTON

PUBLICATION No. 401

Copyright 1932
By
Carnegie Institution of Washington

Originally published in 1932 jointly by Carnegie Institution of
Washington, and the American Geographical Society of New York

Reprinted in 1975 by Greenwood Press,
a division of Williamhouse-Regency Inc.

Library of Congress Catalog Card Number 75-14058

ISBN 0-8371-8208-5

Printed in the United States of America

CONTENTS[1]

1 This table of contents follows the order of topics in the text; occasionally this order differs from that of the maps. Where page references to maps are omitted no specific discussion of the individual maps is given under separate heading.

CONTENTS

CONTENTS

PREFACE

THE *Atlas of the Historical Geography of the United States* may be described as a composite work, since many scholars have coöperated in its making. In 1903, soon after the Carnegie Institution of Washington was organized, its Bureau of Historical Research considered the project and received suggestions in the form of a plan from Dr. J. F. Jameson, then professor of American history in the University of Chicago. Nine years later, when work on the enterprise was begun, and after Dr. Jameson had become director of the Department of Historical Research of the Institution, this plan was taken as the basis of the contents of the *Atlas*. Until 1927 Dr. Jameson closely supervised the enterprise, chose the collaborators, decided on the maps to be included, and in many other ways gave to it the benefit of his wide knowledge and expert judgment. For more than a decade the *Atlas* has had the advantage of the counsel and support of Dr. John C. Merriam who in 1921 became president of the Carnegie Institution.

The Institution is exceedingly grateful for the assistance rendered by numerous scholars and institutions who in one capacity or another had a share in making the *Atlas*. The work of several research associates and assistants of the Institution deserves especial mention. The late Professor Frederick J. Turner contributed many valuable suggestions respecting plans and maps. Professor Orin G. Libby of the University of North Dakota assisted in planning the maps illustrating states and territories; and Professor Frank H. Hodder of the Kansas State University, those illustrating Presidential Elections and Congressional Measures. Professor Max Farrand, now director of research in the Henry E. Huntington Library, made the initial plans for the series on economic and social history. Professor Jesse S. Reeves of the University of Michigan worked upon problems connected with the peace negotiations of 1779-1783 and the subsequent disputes over international boundaries. Professor R. H. Whitbeck of the University of Wisconsin first planned the maps relating to physical geography, mineral resources, railroads, and water transportation, executed them, and wrote the corresponding text (for later modifications see Introduction, p. xv). Professor James A. Robertson of the the John B. Stetson University and of the Florida State Historical Society first planned the division Cartography, 1492-1867, chose the maps, arranged them on plates, and wrote the text (this series was later reduced in size and otherwise modified, see Introduction, p. xv). Professor M. W. Jernegan of the University of Chicago assisted in planning the maps illustrating educational and church history, listed and located the churches for 1775-1776, and prepared the text relating to them.

Some disputed points respecting international boundaries were cleared up at a conference participated in by Dr. Otto H. Tittmann, for many years chief of the Coast and Geodetic Survey; the late John E. McGrath of that establishment; and the late James White, geographer of the Dominion of Canada and editor of its official atlas. The late E. C. Barnard, U. S. commissioner for defining the boundary between the United States and Canada, rendered similar service; Miss Louise Phelps Kellogg of the State Historical Society of Wisconsin made helpful suggestions respecting the map illustrating French Exploration in the West, 1673-1794; information relating to the Indians was supplied by Professor A. L. Kroeber of the University of California, and by Dr. John R. Swanton, Mr. J. N. B. Hewitt, and Dr. Truman Michelson, all of the Bureau of American Ethnology. The map illustrating English and Welsh Emigration to Virginia, 1607-1700, is based upon lists of emigrants supplied by Dr. W. G. Stanard, secretary of the Virginia Historical Society; and the similar map for New England, upon lists supplied by Mr. George Francis Dow, secretary of the Essex Institute, the late J. Gardner Bartlett, and Mrs. Elizabeth French Bartlett of Cambridge, Mass.

The Carnegie Institution is under many obligations to Dr. Herbert Putnam, librarian of the Library of Congress, to the late P. Lee Phillips and his successor, Colonel Lawrence Martin, chiefs of the Division of Maps. These officials provided the collaborators with special facilities for pursuing their researches and at the same time gave them access to the extensive collections of maps, manuscripts, and books of the library, without which it would hardly have been possible to have made the *Atlas*. The cartographic resources of the American Geographical Society and of the New York Public Library were frequently drawn upon, and maps or other information were supplied by the William L. Clements Library, Boston Public Library, Harvard College Library, John Carter

Brown Library, New York Historical Society, Department of the Interior of Canada, British Museum, Archives of the Indies (Seville), and Biblioteca Mediceo-Laurenziana (Florence).

For permission to reproduce maps thanks are due to Dr. E. L. Stevenson of Yonkers, N. Y.; Professor Charles M. Andrews of Yale University; Mr. W. E. Peters of Athens, Ohio; Dr. Joseph Schafer of the Wisconsin State Historical Society; the Russell Sage Foundation; the Western Reserve Historical Society; the Public Archives of Canada; the Sangamon Abtract Company of Springfield, Ill.; Geo. A. Ogle and Co., Chicago, Ill.; Geo. Philip and Son, Ltd., London; the Lewis Historical Publishing Company, New York; and the Burrows Brothers Company, Cleveland, Ohio.

Statistics respecting dates or other information relating to the political maps were supplied by Professor W. E. Dodd of the University of Chicago; Miss Elizabeth Donnan, now of Wellesley College; Dr. Worthington C. Ford, now of the Library of Congress; Mr. George S. Godard, librarian of the Connecticut State Library; Mr. Otis G. Hammond, director of the New Hampshire State Library; Professor Edgar E. Robinson of Stanford University; Professor St. George L. Sioussat of the University of Pennsylvania; Dr. Earl G. Swem, librarian of William and Mary College; Professor David Y. Thomas of the University of Arkansas; Mrs. Jessie P. Weber, librarian of the Illinois State Historical Society; the secretaries of state of Georgia, Kentucky, Nevada, Oklahoma, Tennessee, Vermont, and Washington; the state archivist of Maine; the Massachusetts Archives Division; the North Carolina Historical Commission; and the state libraries of Indiana, Louisiana, New Jersey, Rhode Island, and Vermont.

Information, chiefly relating to lands, was received from Professor Herbert E. Bolton of the University of California; Mr. A. S. Salley, Jr., secretary of the Historical Commission of South Carolina; Mr. G. W. Littlehales, hydrographic engineer of the Hydrographic Office; Professor T. C. Pease of the University of Illinois; and the University of Chicago Library. Aid was received from the departments of State, Treasury, War, Navy, Post Office, Interior, Agriculture, Commerce, and Labor, and especially from the following bureaus and offices in them: Agricultural Economics, Forest Service, Weather, Chemistry and Soils, Geological Survey, General Land Office, Indian Affairs, Education, National Park Service, Census, Foreign and Domestic Commerce, Coast and Geodetic Survey, Chief of Engineers, and International Boundary Commission.

The services of Mr. James B. Bronson of the Bureau of Construction and Repair, who drafted many of the maps, and of Miss Cornelia M. Pierce of the Division of Historical Research, who assisted with the manuscript and proofs, should be especially mentioned. The Institution is grateful to Mr. A. B. Hoen of A. Hoen and Company for interest and care taken in lithographing the maps.

The relations of the American Geographical Society to the enterprise and its specific contributions are set forth by Dr. Wright in the Introduction, page xv. By reason of the number and importance of these contributions the Society has had a large share in the production of the *Atlas*, notably in respect to geography and to economic and military history. Dr. Isaiah Bowman, director of the Society, has taken a lively interest in the enterprise and since 1929 has employed a considerable staff on the work of the *Atlas*. Much use has been made of the rich cartographical resources of the Society.

In carrying out its part of the enterprise the American Geographical Society has received assistance from many persons, to all of whom acknowledgment is gratefully made. Assistance rendered in connection with particular maps or series of maps is in general specifically acknowledged in the text. Special mention, however, should be made here of the following: Doctors O. E. Baker and O. C. Stine of the U. S. Department of Agriculture, for advice regarding the maps relating to agricultural history; Colonel Lawrence Martin of the Library of Congress, for help in connection with maps reproduced from originals in that library; the late Professor R. DeC. Ward of Harvard University and Professor C. F. Brooks, now of Blue Hill Observatory, for climatic data; Dr. John B. Andrews, for assistance with the maps illustrating the history of labor legislation; Professor N. M. Fenneman of the University of Cincinnati, for the text describing the physical divisions of the United States;

Dr. L. R. Hafen of the State Historical and Natural History Society, Denver, Col., for information respecting overland mail routes; Dr. G. O. Smith, formerly director of the Geological Survey, for data relating to mineral resources; Mr. Carl Snyder and his associates of the Federal Reserve Bank of New York, for suggestions concerning the maps relating to economic history; Mr. T. H. Thomas of Cambridge, Mass., for suggestions concerning the series of military maps; Mr. S. W. Boggs of the Department of State, for criticism of certain maps and portions of the text; and Messrs. L. B. Siegfried, editor of *The American Printer*, M. W. Davis formerly of the Yale University Press, and G. R. Grady of the George Grady Press, New York, for advice in matters of typography.

The publication has profited from the technical knowledge and skill of Mr. John Philip of the American Geographical Society in the preparation of the maps for the engraver. Many of the maps are based upon research carefully executed by Miss Margaret Warthin, Miss Lois Olson, and Miss Nordis Felland. Miss Marion Hale has efficiently handled complex details connected with the publication of the *Atlas*. To these and many others who have given aid to the Society the Carnegie Institution is under many obligations.

CHARLES O. PAULLIN.

March 25, 1932.

INTRODUCTION

THIS is the first major historical atlas of the United States and probably the most comprehensive work of its kind that has yet been published for any country. Its aim is to illustrate cartographically, in manageable compass, and yet with considerable detail, essential facts of geography and of history that condition and explain the development of the United States. There are, of course, no absolute criteria by which we may measure the relative importance of historical events. Historical judgment, however, must rest on the recognition of fundamental relationships in space as well as in time, and these are often made intelligible through the medium of maps.

Scope of the Atlas

In many respects the history of the United States reflects our European origins. In other respects our national development has been distinctive and exceptional if not unique. These two sides of American history are well represented in the *Atlas*. While the maps show how world-wide forces have operated on American soil, they also lay emphasis upon what is characteristic of the United States. In Europe the foundations of national life were laid far back in the Middle Ages or earlier. America is nearer its beginnings. The chronicle of material expansion is a large part of its record. The nation has just emerged from the pioneer epoch, and it is fitting that stress should be laid upon the frontier aspects of its history: the story of the exploration and charting of mountains, rivers, lakes, and plains, of the spreading tide of settlement into vacant lands; of the friendly and hostile contacts between settlers and Indians; of the progress of settlement as it was fostered here and thwarted there by the great facts of nature; of the use made of natural resources; of the apportioning of land among individuals; of the adjustment of conflicting political claims to territory; and of the marking out of new administrative units. The sections of the *Atlas* dealing with the Natural Environment, Cartography (1492–1867), Explorers' Routes, Indians, Settlement and Population, Lands, and Boundary Disputes illustrate these topics and fill more than half of the plates. In the following table, which shows the amount of space devoted to each of the major subdivisions of the *Atlas*, the topics just mentioned are listed first.

	Number of half plates	Per cent of total space
(1) Cartography, 1492–1867, and explorers' routes....	38	16.8
Settlement and population......................	28½	12.7
Lands..	27	11.9
Boundary disputes.............................	19	8.4
Natural environment...........................	9	4.0
Indians..	7	3.1
Total......................................	128½	56.9
(2) Agriculture, transportation, manufactures, and commerce....................................	31	13.7
Political maps.................................	28	12.3
Reform movements............................	14	6.2
Churches, colleges, and universities..............	11½	5.1
Military history, etc............................	9	4.0
Plans of cities.................................	5	2.2
Total......................................	98½	43.5
Grand total...............................	227	100.0

Function of the Text

The text gives references to the sources of information upon which each map is based. Wherever necessary critical comment is made upon the accuracy of the sources. How the maps were compiled and what the symbols show are pointed out where not self-evident—for the conventional signs are explained on the maps themselves and so far as possible made to tell their own story. Limitations in the method of representation are stated and explanations are made when necessary to avoid misconceptions. Some parts of the text run to considerable length, particularly the

parts relating to lands and boundary disputes. Here the negotiations respecting disputed limits and areas are outlined and selections from the original documents quoted in full. Without such extensive comment the maps would be meaningless, but no attempt is made to interpret or explain the maps in broader historical terms. To have done so would have expanded the text beyond all reasonable measure. It would have been equivalent to writing a history of the United States from a geographical point of view, and the *Atlas* does not purport to be a "history." It is, rather, an aid to historians and to teachers and students of history. Not only will it be used as a reference book by those who wish to look up particular points, but original studies will undoubtedly be based upon the data that it presents. Each map is a refinement, as it were, of the raw materials for historical research, comparable to a document carefully edited with textual criticism but without historical interpretation. The text gives enough information to enable the reader fully to understand what the maps show, but often he must go farther afield if he would know what they really mean.

Contents of the Atlas

The main purpose of this Introduction is to give a rapid survey of the *Atlas* as a whole and to point out some of the relations between maps that deal with closely allied topics. In addition, a few suggestions will be made about the interpretation of some of the maps.

The Natural Environment. The first seven plates illustrate the natural environment in relation to American history. Natural circumstances have at all times offered to the American people tremendous material advantages. They have also placed definite limitations upon the range of man's activity. These plates have been introduced to illustrate environmental advantages and limitations rather than to prove any thesis that physical geography is either more or less effective than inherited tradition in shaping institutions and character.

Position, topography, climate, soils, vegetation, and mineral wealth are the outstanding elements of the natural environment directly affecting human endeavor. The five maps on Plate 1 show the *position* of the area comprising the United States, especially with reference to the Atlantic Ocean and Europe. A projection was chosen that seems well adapted to make this clear. Incidentally the maps also show where the United States lies in relation to certain natural regions into which the earth's surface may be divided, to winds and ocean currents, and to the limits within which some of the world's principal crops are grown. Plate 1 enables the reader directly to compare the environments of the Old and New Worlds. It seems appropriate that the *Atlas* should begin and end on a broad theme. The opening plate discloses some of the larger physical relationships of the area of the United States and the closing plate (Pl. 166) shows far-flung interests that the United States has acquired in many outlying parts of the world.

Plates 2–7 deal with the natural environment within the limits of the continental United States (excluding Alaska). *Topography* is the subject, first, of a simple relief map (Pl. 2A) showing altitudes. Indispensable in itself, this would be insufficient if allowed to stand alone, for a mere relief map does not tell enough about the forms of the earth's surface. These forms are likely to mean much more to the dwellers on the land than their elevation above sea-level. All plains, all plateaus, all mountain ranges are not alike in their sculpturing. For this reason a map (Pl. 2B) showing physical divisions, or physiographic provinces, has been placed alongside the relief map. As the physiographic map shows merely the boundaries of the divisions, a concise description of each division has been contributed by the compiler, Professor N. M. Fenneman, and will be found in the text.

Climate is so complex and bears so directly upon nearly everything man does that no less than sixteen maps (Pls. 3E–5) are devoted to the climate of the United States. Although geographers and climatologists have marked out climatic provinces on the earth's surface, it was believed that several maps representing separately a variety of climatic elements would be more expressive than a single map of climatic provinces with the necessarily long and technical explanation that would have to accompany it. From the included maps the student may draw up for himself a statement summarizing most of the essential facts about the climate of any place in the United States; he may determine whether it is warm or cold, rainy or dry; and he may also learn something of special climatic elements—such as winds, length of growing season, droughts, snowiness, and cloudiness—each closely correlated in one way or another with farming, transportation, and manufactures.

The maps for *soils* (Pl. 2C), *vegetation* (including forests) (Pls. 2D-3D), and *mineral resources* (Pls. 6 and 7) require no special comment.

Cartography, 1492–1867, and Exploration, 1535–1852. The historical part of the *Atlas* opens with a series of reproductions of old maps intended to illustrate the gradual widening of geographical knowledge of North America. The first (Pl. 8), a reproduction of the gores of Martin Behaim's globe, 1492, shows us geographical concepts of the western hemisphere prevalent in Europe on the eve of the discovery of America. Of course it was well known at the time that the earth is a sphere, but so far as America is concerned the Behaim globe is a blank. On it a broad, uninterrupted ocean spreads from western Europe to eastern Asia. Nearly four centuries were to pass before this blank was completely filled in with the outlines of coasts, river systems, lakes, and mountain ranges in the forms with which we are now familiar. Plates 8–32 show how these forms took shape.

The format of the *Atlas* and the sizes and shapes of the original maps reproduced have rendered it impossible to arrange these reproductions of early maps in strictly chronological order. By classifying the maps in groups we may often study them to somewhat better advantage than when we examine them in the order in which they actually appear on the plates. For example, the maps illustrating Cartography, 1492–1867, might be grouped in two primary categories: (1) general maps summarizing how much was known of large areas at different times, and (2) special maps of more limited areas.

1. *General maps.* The six earliest maps in this category, all dating from before 1540, show the West Indies and portions of the Atlantic coasts of North and South America. They are as follows: La Cosa, 1500 (Pl. 10), the first map showing the results of Columbus' discoveries and those of John Cabot; Cantino, *ca.* 1502 (Pl. 9); Maggiolo, *ca.* 1519 (Pl. 11A); Turin, *ca.* 1523 (Pl. 17B); Verrazano, 1529 (Pl. 13); and Harleian, *ca.* 1536 (Pl. 14A). The Verrazano and Harleian maps both depict a vast inland sea in the interior of North America, and the Harleian map, in addition, shows the estuary of the St. Lawrence in some detail.

The maps of the next group in the first category date from 1546 to 1600 and cover either the whole or the major part of the North American continent. On the Gastaldi map, 1546 (Pl. 12B), North America is drawn as a great southeastward continuation of Asia. Mercator in 1569 (Pl. 15) separated the continents by a narrow passage, the mythical Strait of Anian. On Mercator's map, however, North America is still much too broad from east to west. By the time of Hakluyt, 1587 (Pl. 14B), and Ortelius, 1589 (Pl. 11B), the distortion has been largely eliminated and the passageway between North America and Asia is much broadened. On the Molineaux-Wright map of 1600 (Pl. 17D) the cartographer frankly recognized that he knew nothing of the northwest coast and did not attempt to continue it north of California. The Molineaux-Wright map is also the earliest map reproduced in the *Atlas* giving any indication of the Great Lakes. The Tattonus map, 1600 (Pl. 17E), is one of the earliest maps with the name California on the peninsula of Lower California.

For the seventeenth, eighteenth, and nineteenth centuries eight general maps are shown: Hondius, 1630 (Pl. 20A), Delisle, 1700 (Pl. 22A); Delisle, 1718 (Pl. 24); Popple, 1733 (Pl. 27), Bellin, 1743 (Pl. 23C); Delisle, *ca.* 1750 (Pl. 23B); Arrowsmith, 1814 (Pl. 29). Delisle's map of 1700 (Pl. 22A) summarized knowledge acquired during the preceding century by French and Spanish explorers of the Great Lakes and the course of the Mississippi. Arrowsmith's map of 1814 incorporates the results of the Lewis and Clark expedition (1804–1806). It also shows how little was then known of the southwestern states.

2. *Special maps of relatively restricted areas.* These may be further subclassified into six groups: (1) early maps of the coasts of the Gulf of Mexico and southeastern United States, 1520–1700—Cortés, 1520 (Pl. 17A); De Soto, *ca.* 1544 (Pl. 12A); Lemoyne, 1591 (Pl. 16); Gentil, *ca.* 1700 (Pl. 22B); (2) seventeenth and eighteenth century maps of northern and eastern North America, 1612–1755—Smith, 1612 (Pl. 18A); Champlain, 1612 (Pl. 18B); Smith, 1616 (Pl. 19A); De Laet, 1630 (Pl. 21); Champlain, 1632 (Pl. 19B); Sanson, 1656 (Pl. 20B); Delisle, 1703 (Pl. 23A); Evans, 1755 (Pl. 26); Mitchell, 1755 (Pls. 89–90); (3) seventeenth century maps of the Great Lakes—Jesuit, 1672 (Pl. 20C); Raffeix, 1688 (Pl. 20D); (4) seventeenth and eighteenth century maps of the Pacific coast—Vizcaino, 1603 (Pl. 17C); Müller, 1754 (Pl. 25A); Vancouver, 1798 (Pl. 25B); (5) maps showing in some detail the results of early nineteenth century explorations west of the Mississippi, 1810–1811—Clark, 1810 (Pl. 32A); Pike's map of the Rocky Mountain region, 1810 (Pl. 30A); Pike's map of the Mississippi River (Pl. 31C); and (6) more general maps showing the progress of geographical knowledge of the United States west of the Mississippi, 1804–1867—Lewis, 1804 (Pl. 28); Humboldt, 1811 (Pl. 30B); Bonneville, 1837 (Pl. 31A); Chapin, 1839 (Pl. 32B); Greenhow, 1840 (Pl. 31B); Smith, 1843 (Pl. 32C); Colton, 1867 (Pl. 32D).

For the progress of exploration in those parts of the United States lying west of the Mississippi the *Atlas* includes not only the reproductions listed above but also three maps showing the routes of Spanish, French, and American explorers, 1535–1852 (Pls. 38–39). Ninety-one routes are marked, and the route of each of the French and American

expeditions is described briefly in the text. The series for explorers' routes comes down to 1852; that for Cartography closes with a map for 1867. By this time the major topographical features of the United States—mountains, rivers, plains, deserts, lakes—were known, at least in their outlines.

Indians. The North America of the explorer and pioneer was not an uninhabited wilderness. The Indians were often an obstacle—at times a serious one—in the way of the advancing settler. The four maps on Plate 34 show the locations of hostile encounters with the Indians from 1521 to 1890, and, thereby, the progressive movement of the zone of Indian warfare westward with the advance of the frontier. More peaceful contacts with the aborigines are recorded on maps covering Christian missions to the Indians, 1567–1861 (Pl. 37), lands ceded by the Indians to the government, 1750–1890 (Pl. 47A), and Indian reservations, 1840–1930 (Pls. 35–36). The Indians differed greatly among themselves in character, language, customs, and degree of civilization, and these differences often meant much in the relations of the settlers and government to the several tribes. A map on which are marked the areas occupied by Indian tribes and linguistic stocks about 1650 has therefore been included (Pl. 33). During the succeeding centuries many of the tribes shown on this map were exterminated, and others were forced to migrate as hunting-ground after hunting-ground was taken from them.

Lands. A supremely important chapter in American history deals with questions of land. Except for the Indian's shadowy claims, which in the long run were easily swept aside, a boundless domain until recently lay open for governments, companies, and individuals to seize and subdivide and use. In the process divergent policies, practices, and conflicting interests arose, affecting in some degree the entire social, economic, and political history of the nation. Questions of land are treated in three separate parts of the *Atlas*, the sections entitled "Lands, 1603–1930" (Pls. 40–59), "States, Territories, and Cities, 1790–1930" (Pls. 61E–66), and "Boundaries, 1607–1927" (Pls. 89–101).

As in the case of the history of cartography, the maps for lands and territorial questions may be classified systematically.

1. *Territorial questions of international significance.* This group includes maps showing the possessions of European states in North America after 1763 (Pl. 41A), British possessions after 1774 (Pl. 46A), territorial claims and limits on the northwest coast, 1790–1846 (Pl. 49), and territorial acquisitions of the United States, 1783–1853 (Pl. 46C). These are all in the section "Lands, 1603–1930." However, the maps in the section "Boundaries, 1607–1927," covering the negotiations for peace, 1783 (Pls. 89 and 90), and the more important international boundary disputes to which the United States has been a party (Pls. 91–96) belong logically in this category, as well as the concluding map of the *Atlas* (Pl. 166), on which are shown possessions, claims, and dependencies of the United States in various parts of the world.

2. *The evolution of the boundaries of the colonies, states, and territories.* Land grants of European sovereigns to trading and colonizing companies and to great proprietors in the colonial period laid the foundations for the subdivision of territory between the several colonies and later between the states. The limits of the more important colonial grants are drawn on two general maps (Pls. 42 and 43A) and the boundaries between the colonies are indicated on Plate 61A-D. More detailed illustrations of two great colonial land grants, one in Maine, the other in Virginia, are given on Plates 44C and 51A. In the royal charters the lands granted were frequently described as extending indefinitely to the west or as reaching to the Pacific Ocean. This meant conflicting claims to the western territory as soon as settlement was pushed beyond the Appalachian barrier. The adjustment of these claims forms the topic of Plate 47B-E. Certain colonies and states proposed or organized west of the mountains, 1775–1802, but not destined permanently to survive are shown on Plates 41C and 46B. On Plates 61E–66 the general evolution of the boundaries of the states and territories, 1790–1920, is recorded, and on Plates 97–101 some of the more troublesome disputes over boundaries between the colonies and states, 1607–1927, are analyzed in detail.

3. *Lands ceded by the Indians* to the British, colonial, state, and United States governments, 1750–1890. These Indian cessions are summarized on a single map of the United States (Pl. 47A).

4. *The disposition of federal lands.* This group comprises maps of the whole United States showing the public lands in 1790, 1810, 1830, 1850, 1870, 1890, 1910, and 1929 (Pls. 57–59), as well as lands granted to the states for educational and other purposes, 1785–1919 (Pl. 50A), military reserves (Pl. 45B), and federal land grants for the construction of railroads and wagon roads (Pl. 56D). In this group, also, belong certain detailed maps illustrating surveys, divisions, and grants of government land in different parts of the country at different times (Pls. 50B, 41A, 48A, 48C, 50E, 55D, 55C, and 56E, noted in chronological order).

5. *The details of typical grants, surveys, divisions, and holdings of land,* not otherwise covered under paragraphs 1–4, above. These miscellaneous reproductions may be grouped according to whether the originals date from (1) colonial period (Pls. 41D, 43B, 44B, 53C, 40, 51A, 44C, 44D, 50D, and 51B) and (2) the national period (Pls. 50C, 53A, 45A, 53B, 48B, 44A, 53D, 41E, 52A, 52B, 56C, 55A, 55B, 54, 56A, and 56B). For each period the maps are listed in chronological order.

Population and Settlement. After the section entitled "Lands, 1603–

1930," comes a series of plates devoted to the history of population. Three movements are here shown: (1) the progress of settlement as a whole, 1660–1930; (2) the rise of towns and cities, 1650–1930; and (3) the changing composition of the population, 1790–1930. Settlement as a whole is treated differently for the period 1660–1775 than for the subsequent period. The five maps on Plate 60 show settled areas in 1660, 1700, 1760, 1775, and 1790, but owing to the lack of detailed statistics it was not feasible to map the density of population for any but the last of these dates. The five maps, however, indicate by globe symbols the approximate total population of each colony. For the period 1790–1930 the United States government has taken a census of population every ten years, and it was possible to include a map for each census year showing the density of population by counties (Pls. 76B–79D). The lines on these maps between areas having more and those having less than two persons per square mile mark—very roughly to be sure—the successive positions of the "frontier" in its march across the continent. The steady, almost due-westward course of the center of population from the vicinity of Baltimore in 1790 to southwestern Indiana in 1930 is shown on Plate 80A.

On Plates 61–67A space was economized by marking on the same maps both colonial and state boundaries and the locations of towns and cities. These maps cover the years 1650, 1700, 1750, 1775, 1790, and every tenth year after the last-named date. The towns and cities on the maps for 1790–1930 are represented by dots of two sizes, smaller dots for places of 5000–100,000 inhabitants and larger ones for places of over 100,000. Perhaps a somewhat more graphic effect might have been achieved had it been practicable to separate the two elements—political units and cities—and to employ a greater range and variety of symbols to distinguish the towns and cities according to size. These maps will repay careful comparison with the maps showing relief, physical divisions, climatic factors, and mineral resources, all circumstances upon which the location and grouping of cities are closely dependent. As regards the composition of the population, maps are included for negroes and foreign-born. The percentages of slaves in the total population are shown for every census year from 1790 through 1860 (Pls. 67B–68B), and the percentages of colored persons in the total population for 1880, 1900, and 1930 (Pls. 69B–70B). The number of free negroes is mapped for 1810 and 1860 (Pls. 68C–69A). Plate 70 E-O shows how many immigrants came to the United States from the different countries of Europe decade by decade from 1831 through 1929. Plates 71–76A reveal where the foreign-born have settled since 1860 and, more specifically, where Germans, Irish, and Swedes and Norwegians have settled since 1880. Based upon statistics by counties, the maps for densities, negroes, and foreign-born give a detailed picture of the distribution of these elements in the population.

Politics and Reforms. The political maps (Pls. 102–122) are the results of a far more exact and detailed type of research than their clear and simple appearance would at first suggest. They set forth the shifting alignments of political sentiment in different sections and show where local interests have often diverged from the prevailing sectional interests. They express the geographical distribution of parties and political opinion in terms of the smallest feasible territorial units—counties in the case of the maps of Presidential elections (with some exceptions) and Congressional districts for the maps representing the votes in the House of Representatives. All Presidential elections are mapped, as well as the votes on no less than thirty-six important Congressional measures. Close study of these maps will undoubtedly disclose significant relationships between politics on the one hand and physical and human geography on the other. It will also serve to correct many false ideas and unfounded generalizations. The maps, for example, make it quite clear that the Solid South has not always been as "solid" in voting for presidents as was once thought to be the case. The consistent opposition of the Southern congressmen to high tariff measures as revealed by a quick survey of the Congressional series is striking indeed. Curiosity is aroused by the detail on these maps. One would like to know what accounts for certain distinctive patterns on successive maps of Presidential elections and why these patterns break up to give way to new patterns at later dates.

The political maps are followed by a series illustrating political and social reforms as brought about chiefly by state legislation: the abolition of slavery (Pls. 123–124A), the elimination of property qualifications for suffrage (Pls. 124B–126B), woman suffrage (Pls. 126C–128A), prohibition (Pls. 128B–131A), labor legislation (Pl. 132), and primary and secondary school education (Pl. 131B-E). On the maps for woman suffrage and prohibition it is impressive to see how these great movements have swept across the country—woman suffrage like a giant wave rolling from west to east; prohibition in two successive tides, the tide of local prohibition spreading eastward and westward from a central tier of states, followed by a dry tide flowing from the South and West.

Cultural Development. There is available for the educational and religious institutions of the United States a large quantity of statistical material much of which lends itself to cartographic treatment. The series of dot maps showing the distribution of churches by denominations in 1775–1776, 1860, and 1890 (Pls. 82–88), and of colleges and universities in 1775, 1800, 1830, 1860, and 1890 (Pls. 80B–81) represent a selection from among a very wide range of topics that might have been mapped to illustrate the cultural life of the nation. Expenditures for schools by states indicate roughly (as shown on Plate 131B-D) nation-wide tendencies and sectional divergencies in primary and secondary teaching, but it should be remembered that the efficiency of schools is not measured by per capita expenditures, compulsory attendance, and minimum term laws (Pl. 131E) alone.

Economic History. The economic history of the United States is covered in part by the maps already mentioned in connection with the section "Lands, 1603–1930." The maps recording Congressional votes on the tariff, transportation, finance, and other economic measures also throw light on this broad subject. On Plates 133–155 maps will be found for industries, foreign trade, and wealth.

Under the general heading "Industries" about equal space is given to manufacturing (Pls. 133–137), transportation (Pls. 138–141), and agriculture (Pls. 142–147). The aim is to illustrate the general progress of each of these three groups of industries and incidentally to show something of the development of certain of the leading individual industries that compose each group.

For mapping the general progress of manufacturing (Pls. 133–134D) two criteria were chosen: (1) the growth of the principal manufacturing cities, 1839–1919, as measured by the number of wage earners; and (2) the increase in value added by manufacture, by states, in 1849, 1880, and 1927. The history of individual manufacturing industries is illustrated on Plates 135–137, where maps will be found for different dates showing iron and steel works, number of cotton spindles, and manufacture of motor vehicles. Improvements in the mechanism of transportation are reflected on the maps showing the length of time taken in 1800, 1830, 1857, and 1930 for passengers to reach different parts of the country from New York by the ordinary means of travel in use at each date (Pl. 138A-E). More detailed maps follow for canals and navigable rivers, the widening network of post routes, railroads, and air mail routes (Pls. 138F–141J). The rapid rise of motor travel and transportation during the last two decades may be inferred from two maps (Pls. 141K and L) indicating for each state the number of persons per motor vehicle in 1913 and in 1930. The general progress of agriculture from 1850 to 1930 is to some degree summarized in a series (Pls. 144C–146M) revealing the total acreages and the changes in the acreages of improved land and of land in harvested crops, decade by decade. Maps will also be found showing the production of individual crops since 1839 (Pls. 142B–144B), farm tenancy since 1880 (Pl. 146N-Q), and farm values since 1850 (Pl. 147).

To the subject of foreign trade two series are devoted. One (Pls. 148–151C) shows the value of exports and imports as they have flowed through the ports of entry of the colonies and the United States. The mapping, however, is by states and colonies rather than by ports. Exports and imports from England are shown for 1701–1710 and 1765–1774, imports from England for 1791–1800, all exports for 1791–1800, and all exports and imports for the decades 1821–1830, 1851–1860, 1871–1880, and 1901–1910, and for the nine years 1921–1929. The second series (Pl. 151D–G) comprises four maps of the world on which globe symbols depict the values of exports to and imports from the United States by continents and larger subdivisions of the continents, decade by decade from 1821 through 1920 and for the nine years 1921–1929.

As a basis for mapping the distribution of wealth the following sources of information were used: statistics by states, of wealth in terms of the value of houses and lands in 1799, of taxable property in 1850, and of all property in 1880, 1912, and 1922; statistics by states, of federal income taxes in 1866 and 1928, and of bank capital in 1801, 1830, 1850, 1880, 1910, and 1928; and a variety of documents relating to banks. From these sources maps were compiled showing total and per capita wealth (Pls. 152–153), income taxes (Pl. 155), and bank capital by states (Pl. 154B, D, F, H, K, and L), and also a series showing distribution of banks (Pl. 154A, C, E, G, and J).

Plans of Cities. On Plates 156–159 are reproduced plans of the seven principal cities of the United States at the close of the colonial or beginning of the national period. They furnish a means of identifying places where events of historical importance occurred, and are of interest as illustrations of different systems of early town planning.

Military History. Plates 160–165 cover the colonial wars and military history of the United States. Most maps illustrating wars and campaigns are confused and difficult to follow, especially when a tangle of lines on them is intended to show troop movements. Particular care was taken in arranging the maps of military history and in devising for them a scheme of conventional signs that so far as possible would render them self-explanatory.

World Relationships. The concluding plate (Pl. 166), as we have seen, like the first, takes us beyond the boundaries of our country. It shows the United States in some of its larger world relationships—its possessions, claims, and dependencies in various regions, as well as the locations of certain military engagements in which American forces have taken part, and grounds formerly visited by American whaling vessels.

Statistical Maps and Their Interpretation

History is a record of movement and change. Most maps represent static conditions—the earth's surface at a given moment. A large problem in any atlas of historical geography is how best to record movement and change by means of the somewhat unadaptable medium of the map. The ideal historical atlas might well be a collection of motion-picture maps, if these could be displayed on the pages of a book without the paraphernalia of projector, reel, and screen.

To illustrate movement and change cartographically three devices are used in this *Atlas*. The simplest is the sequence of maps revealing progressive stages in a process—as, for example, the series showing density of population or votes in Presidential elections. Another device is to show on a single map conditions that prevailed or events that occurred at different dates—for example, the maps of boundary disputes, foreign trade, and military history.

It is to the third device that we should like to draw particular attention at this point. This device is used on one series, the maps showing increase and decrease in acreage of improved lands (Pls. 145C–146M). Each map here summarizes a process of change during a decade. The student's attention is focused directly upon the fact of change and upon regional differences in its amount rather than upon a total quantity or a ratio of one to another total, as on most statistical maps. While maps showing processes of change cannot in any way take the place of those representing static conditions, they may be effectively used to supplement the latter, since they often bring out in sharp relief the vital movements with which the historian is likely to be most immediately concerned.

Many of the maps in the *Atlas* are based upon statistical tables. Everyone who has critically studied such tables knows that statistics are often tricky. They may be misleading when used for comparing conditions prevailing at different dates, because they are not always equally accurate and their compilers are tempted to change the definitions of categories without adequate explanation. Furthermore, in interpreting maps based on statistics given in terms of monetary values it should be remembered that the price level—or, in other words, the value of the dollar—has constantly fluctuated. On several series of maps the symbols showing values have been standardized with reference to the value of the dollar at a given date, but this could not be done consistently. Though faith may be placed in the main outlines of the statistical maps, hasty conclusions should not be drawn from a scrutiny of their minutiae. Too refined comparisons should be avoided between different small areas on the same map and especially between the same area as shown on different maps.

Although no distinction in the text is made between maps and cartograms, several of the so-called "maps" are not strictly maps in the geographer's sense of the term. A cartogram is a cartographic outline upon which are drawn statistical symbols that do not conform closely to the actual distribution of the phenomena represented. Discs, for instance, are used on some of the "maps" on Plate 154 to indicate bank capital in the several states. These "maps" are cartograms. Had data been available for showing bank capital in each county by a separate disc the picture would have been more realistic and would have resulted in a series of genuine maps.[1]

Some Cartographic Desiderata

In the preliminary plans and suggestions made by several scholars (see Preface) many maps were proposed for inclusion that for one reason or another had to be omitted. Since cartographical simplicity was regarded as a desideratum no complicated map illustrating many kinds of information was included. Furthermore, room was found for maps that illustrate only the most basic and essential parts of American history, and not for all of these. In all divisions maps were excluded because of the limits of space. Owing to inadequate statistics many desirable maps for the colonial period could not be made. Other maps were not made because of the great labor required to assemble the necessary information.

A few examples, however, may be given of avenues of research that

---

[1] It is sometimes difficult to draw a hard-and-fast line between maps and cartograms. Much depends on the scale. For a map, the larger the scale, the smaller must be the area represented by each symbol. So far as this *Atlas* is concerned, all "maps" where statistical data are shown in terms of units as large as a state may perhaps be regarded as cartograms; and those "maps" where the data are plotted by towns, counties, Congressional districts, etc., may be regarded as maps.

---

might well be followed further in directions already marked out in the *Atlas*. While every phase of American history offers alluring possibilities of cartographic interpretation, special attention is here directed to the subjects of exploration, population, education, and economic development.

The series for the history of exploration closes, as we have seen, with the year 1852, but the mid-nineteenth century by no means marked the end of exploration. The period of intensive work that followed and is still in progress has yielded results of hardly less scientific and economic value than the period of pioneer mapping. During the sixties, seventies, and eighties of the last century the federal government conducted important topographical and geological surveys in the Far West. These were supplemented by the private ventures of transcontinental railroads and by state geological and natural history surveys. Out of the work of the federal government in the Far West developed the nation-wide work of the United States Geological Survey. More recently the federal and state governments have pushed far the mapping of soils, minerals, and forests, and beginnings are being made in the field of land classification maps. Were it not for unrivaled natural resources the United States could hardly hold the position it now occupies among the nations. The progress of the systematic exploration of these resources deserves to be illustrated by maps showing the routes followed by some of the more notable exploring parties and the areas covered by surveys of different types at different times, as well as by specimens of the large-scale maps published on the basis of these surveys.

The *Atlas*, as has been seen, provides a substantial foundation for the history of the peopling of the United States. Welcome, however, would be maps showing the more recent currents of immigration from southern and eastern Europe and from Mexico, or a series depicting movements of different elements in the population from one part of the country to another—as, for example, the filtration of settlers from the eastern seaboard colonies and states into the lands beyond the Appalachians, or the recent migrations of negroes to the northern cities and of white people from the north-central and northeastern states to southern California and Florida. The social and economic characteristics that differentiate the newer sections of the country are due in part to geographical circumstances but also in large measure to marked differences between the older sections from which the settlers came. The Census, unfortunately, assists us little in tracing these internal migrations. In order to follow them satisfactorily, deep delving into local history is needed.

An important combination of forces during the last century has brought about the rapid growth of cities as contrasted with the slow growth of rural districts and actual decline of the latter in many sections. On the maps in the *Atlas* a county with one or two large towns surrounded by a desert waste is in general represented by the same symbol as a county in which an equal number of people is scattered evenly among farms and small villages. Had unlimited space been available, separate maps might conceivably have been included for rural and for urban population, or, possibly, for rural, urban, and farm population. The steady growth of a single manufacturing or commercial town may completely obscure, on the existing maps, the fact that the surrounding rural areas lost population. Different cities grow at different rates, and there are large cities that have become smaller during recent decades. Progress or recession region by region or locality by locality might be recorded on maps making clear these differential rates of growth and decline, much as differential increases and decreases in the acreage of improved farm lands are shown on Plates 144C–146M.

The history of education in the United States offers a particularly attractive field for further cartographic study. Maps in the *Atlas* present certain details regarding colleges, universities, and secondary schools. Statistical data, however, exist upon which maps could be based showing other equally significant factors, such as the age limits within which children are required to attend school or the number of pupils per teacher. The most important element of all, classroom standards, is hardly capable of measurement in statistical terms, but criteria could doubtless be discovered by which this factor might be estimated and mapped. Higher education should ultimately be illustrated in greater fulness, as, for example, percentages of college graduates in the total population above the age of twenty-one and of women among all college graduates. The cultural status of different parts of the country could be compared on maps showing the number of public libraries per capita, the prevalence of illiteracy, and the distribution of talent and of leadership in science, in the arts, in business, and in public affairs. More or less successful attempts have already been made to estimate and map some of these things, but there is a genuine need for further studies of the same sort.

In the almost boundless field of economic history there are many cartographic desiderata. For example, maps are needed illustrating in more detail than was possible in the *Atlas* the history of production in the agricultural and manufacturing industries, the volume and direction of domestic commerce, and the exchange of goods in trade between different parts of the United States and between the country as a whole and other parts of the world. Maps differentiating railroads and waterways according to the amount of freight and passenger traffic, showing the geographical structure of freight rates and freight differentials, and routes taken and ports visited by ships of the American merchant marine would also be of value. The agricultural series covers certain material bases of farming, crop production, and improved land, as well as property values. The whole subject of farmers' organizations, however, offers almost virgin soil to the map-minded historian. The national and state granges, the farm bureaus and farmers' institutes, and coöperative selling and buying organizations have often been powerful agencies in promoting the welfare of the farmer or in giving voice to his political aspirations. The industrial destiny of the nation is in the hands of labor no less than of capital. The distribution of capital and some of the interests of labor, as they have found protection in reform legislation, are illustrated in the *Atlas* (Pl. 132); but organized labor has had to be passed by, in the main because of lack of available statistics. Maps covering membership in the American Federation of Labor, the Knights of Labor, the Industrial Workers of the World, and similar units; maps for particular industries—such as coal mining—showing where labor has been organized and where not, and where there have been strikes and other conflicts—all might help to illumine much that is still obscure in the industrial history of the nation. But it is hardly profitable to add to these examples. Another atlas could scarcely do full justice to the economic history of the United States from a geographical standpoint if anything approaching a detailed presentation of the subject were to be attempted. The present atlas attempts to cover the essentials.

The Making of the Atlas

In the preparation of the *Atlas of the Historical Geography of the United States* two disciplines have been represented, history by the work of the Department of Historical Research of the Carnegie Institution of Washington, and geography by the work of the American Geographical Society of New York.

The making of the *Atlas* was authorized by the Carnegie Institution in 1911, and work was begun in the following year when Dr. Paullin was employed for four months on a survey of possibilities and on other preliminary tasks. In 1913 he was placed in charge and from 1914 until 1927 gave all his time to the work, with the exception of a few intermissions caused by the World War and other exigencies. He was aided by numerous scholars of history and geography whose names and services are, for the most part, mentioned in the Preface.

In order that the *Atlas* might be further strengthened geographically and might benefit from the experience and technical skill of the American Geographical Society in editing and publishing maps, an arrangement was made in 1929 whereby the Society accepted the responsibility of bringing the enterprise to a close. Besides editing and seeing the publication through the hands of lithographer, printer, and binder, the Society has rearranged the material and has added, with the approval of the Carnegie Institution, a considerable number of new maps with corresponding text.

As first conceived the *Atlas* was to have been a bulkier and much more costly volume than the present one. A layout was planned for the entire *Atlas* on the assumption that the plates would measure rather more than half again as much in height and width as the present plates. Most of the maps were actually drawn on this basis. After very careful consideration it was decided that the size of the plates should be reduced and that space should be economized by printing maps on the backs of the plates. Accordingly, a new layout was prepared for all the maps. Under this new plan it has been possible to reproduce nearly all of the maps on approximately the scales first contemplated. Only a few large reproductions of old maps had to be substantially reduced, and these have suffered little, if at all, from reduction. In the sections on Cartography, Lands, and Boundary Disputes some rearrangement of the order of the maps was necessary. Otherwise the adoption of the new format has not altered the content of the *Atlas* in any way, though the economy of space effected has made publication possible at a price within the means of every scholar.

The American Geographical Society is also responsible for a few minor departures from the original plan in the sequence of topics and for the discarding of certain maps in order to leave space for new ones that for various reasons it seemed desirable to add. Some of the new maps were included to bring as nearly up to date as possible the several important chronological series already compiled by Dr. Paullin—for example, the series for population, agriculture, trade, Presidential elections, and votes in Congress. Others were introduced to round out somewhat more fully

the treatment of particular topics. Many of the new maps were compiled on the basis of original investigations. Others are either reproductions or adaptations of existing manuscript and printed maps. A classified list of the items added by the Society follows.

1. *Maps compiled by the American Geographical Society from statistics, other maps, or miscellaneous sources, and drafted at the Society:*
   a) To complete chronological series: Plate 36B, Indian Reservations, 1930; 59B, Distribution of Public Lands of United States, 1929; 67A, States and Cities, 1930; 70B, Colored Population, 1930; 72B, Foreign-Born Population, 1930; 73C, Foreign-Born Population, German, 1930; 74B, Foreign-Born Population, Irish, 1930; 76A, Foreign-Born Population, Swedish and Norwegian, 1930; 79D, Density of Population, 1930; 111D, Presidential Election, 1928; 122B, Smoot-Hawley Tariff Act, June 13, 1930; 151B, Imports, 1920–1929; 151C, Exports, 1920–1929; 155C, Federal Income and Profits Taxes, 1928, Total Taxes per state.
   b) Illustrating new topics not covered under the original plan: Plate 1, North America in Relation to the Atlantic Ocean and Europe; 60, Settlement and Population, 1660–1790; 101A, Michigan-Wisconsin Boundary; 101C, Oklahoma-Texas Boundary along the Red River; 131B-E, Schools; 134B-D, Value Added by Manufacture, 1849–1927; 134E, Wholesale Prices, 1791–1930; 137B-C, Manufacture of Motor Vehicles, 1909, 1927; 141K-L, Persons per Motor Vehicle, 1913, 1930; 146 N-Q, Tenant Farmers, 1880–1930; 147A-D, Average Value of Farm Lands and Buildings per Acre of All Lands in Farms, 1850–1930; 147E-H, Average Value of Farm Implements and Machinery per Acre of All Land in Farms, 1850–1930; 151D-G, Imports from and Exports to the United States, 1821–1929; 152B, D, 153A, D, Wealth per Capita, 1799–1922; 154B, D, F, H, K, L, Banks, Capital, 1800–1928; 155B, D, Federal Income Taxes per Capita, 1866, 1928; 166, The World, Showing Possessions and Territorial Claims of the United States, etc.
   c) Illustrating topics covered under the original plan but compiled on the basis of different data or with different symbols: Plate 7A, Oil and Gas Fields; 70E-O, Sources of Emigration to the United States, 1831–1929; 138A-E, Rates of Travel, 1800–1930; 160–165, Military History.

2. *Maps drafted but not compiled by the Society:*
   a) Based wholly or in large part on maps prepared or used by Dr. Paullin: Plate 2A, Relief; 33, Indian Tribes and Linguistic Stocks, 1650; 34, Indian Battles, 1521–1890; 38–39, Explorations in the West and Southwest; 138F, Navigable Rivers, 1930; 138G, Canals and Canalized Rivers, 1930; 148–151A, Imports and Exports, 1701–1910.
   b) Based on other maps: Plate 2B, Physical Divisions; 4–5, Climate; 6A, Coal Fields; 132, Reforms; 141H, J, Air Mail Routes in Operation, 1920 and 1927, 1931.

3. *Maps drafted under Dr. Paullin's direction to which the Society has added data:* Plate 6B, Distribution and Production of Iron Ore; 7B, Gold, Silver, and Copper Districts; 36B, Indian Reservations, 1930; 37, Indian Missions, 1567–1861; 139A, B, Railroads, 1850, 1860, and Overland Mail, 1850–1869.

4. *Maps added by the Society as reproduced from other sources:* Plate 8, Behaim Globe, 1492; 30B, Humboldt Map, 1811; 31B, Pike's Map of the Mississippi River, 1810; 142A, Agricultural Regions; 142B–144B, Agricultural Production (selected topics); 144C–145C, Improved Land, Acreage, 1850–1910, Land in Harvested Crops, 1919, 1929; 145D–146M, Improved Land, Increase in Acreage, 1850–1920, Improved Land, Decrease in Acreage, 1850–1910, Land in Harvested Crops, Increase and Decrease in Acreage, 1909–1929; 159B, Baltimore, 1801.

———————

It is hoped that the foregoing paragraphs make sufficiently clear the general concept of the *Atlas*, some further avenues of research that its plates suggest, and the circumstances under which it has been produced. Unless one is much mistaken the *Atlas* will be a dynamic force in historical and geographical studies in this country for many years to come.

JOHN K. WRIGHT.

Note: No scales are shown on the diagrammatic maps in the *Atlas*. Scales applicable to most of these maps are given below.

Sixteen maps of the U. S. to a double plate (as on Pl. 146):

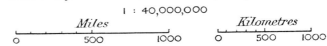

1 : 40,000,000

Nine maps of the U. S. to a double plate (as on Pl. 132); also four maps of the U. S. to a single page with tops to the left (as on Pl. 152):

1 : 30,000,000

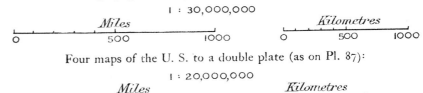

Four maps of the U. S. to a double plate (as on Pl. 87):

1 : 20,000,000

PART I. TEXT

THE NATURAL ENVIRONMENT

[PLATES 1-7]

ESSENTIAL to an understanding of the history of the United States is some acquaintance with the natural environment that has conditioned and modified the growth of the nation. For this reason the present series of maps illustrating important aspects of the natural environment precedes the more strictly historical parts of the *Atlas*.

NORTH AMERICA IN RELATION TO THE ATLANTIC OCEAN AND EUROPE

[PLATE 1]

The institutions and population of the United States are predominantly of European origin. The Atlantic Ocean has been the passageway over which the peoples and civilization of the Old World have come to the New. The very first maps, therefore—those of Plate 1—show North America in relation to the Atlantic and to Europe and furnish a means of comparing the geographical setting of life on the two continents. The maps were specially compiled for the *Atlas* on a polar zenithal equidistant projection.[1]

Natural Regions, Glaciated Areas, Ocean Currents, and Maritime Explorers' Routes [*Plate 1A*]. This map shows, in the first place, the natural regions into which the late Professor A. J. Herbertson of the University of Oxford divided Europe[2] and North America as outlined on a wall map entitled "The World: Natural Regions," Oxford University Press, 1912. As is made clear by the legend, regions having similar types of environment are shown on the map by the same colors. "In the determination of natural regions," wrote Herbertson, "climate and configuration must both be considered. Climate, because it not merely affects the physical features, but also because it best summarizes the various influences acting on the surface. Climate even more than configuration, for the great barriers of the land are climatic—wastes of arid desert or ice mountains—for it is the climate more than the configuration which renders lofty mountains effective barriers. Only when minor forms are taken into consideration does configuration become the all-important factor. On the accompanying map I have ventured to outline the regions which the consideration of all factors seems to me to determine" (A. J. Herbertson, "The Major Natural Regions," *Geogr. Journ.*, Vol. 25, 1905, p. 309).

Herbertson points out the historical significance of such natural regions as follows: "The recognition of natural regions gives the historian a geographical foundation for his investigations into the development of human society ... By comparing the histories of the same race in two different regions, or of a succession of races in the same region, it should be possible to arrive at some knowledge of the invariable effect of a type of environment on its inhabitants, and permit some estimation of the non-environmental factors in human development" (*loc. cit.*). A comparison of the historical development of regions in Europe and in North America having similar or dissimilar types of environment may be extremely suggestive.

The great merit of Herbertson's work on natural regions lay in the clear and definite manner in which the concept was formulated. It is mainly for this reason—but also because his regions are large, simple, and easy to understand—that Herbertson's regions have been shown on map A. During the last fifteen or twenty years, however, the regions as he actually marked them out—if not the underlying idea—have been subjected to a good deal of criticism, and other attempts have been made to subdivide the earth's surface according to more refined and precise criteria. An example is shown on map B. Similar synthetic maps of physiographic and agricultural regions within the United States will be found on Plates 2B and 142A respectively.

The southern boundaries of the areas in North America and Europe covered by continental ice sheets and the more extensive areas covered by mountain glaciers during the Pleistocene period—or last ice age—are also shown on map A. Glaciation brought about many alterations of the earth's surface. Where glacial deposits have dammed streams,

making lakes and swamps, or where glacial drift is spread over broad tracts in the form of boulders, gravels, clays, and sand, much land that might otherwise have been of agricultural value has been rendered relatively unproductive. This also is true of areas where the ice has removed the soil, leaving ledges of bare rock. On the other hand, some of the most fertile fields in Europe and North America are found on the beds of old glacial lakes; and glaciated regions are often regions of abundant water power. Obviously, former glaciation has been an important factor in the economic development of certain parts of the United States, although its effects have varied widely from place to place. The outlines are based, with slight modifications, on maps by Ernst Antevs, "Maps of the Pleistocene Glaciation," in *Bull. Geol. Soc. of America*, Vol. 40, 1929, pp. 631–720.

The ocean currents as shown on map A are adapted from maps by Gerhard Schott; for the Atlantic from his *Geographie des atlantischen Ozeans*, 2nd edit., Hamburg, 1926, Pl. 15; and for the Pacific from his *Weltkarte zur Übersicht der Meeresströmungen und Schiffswege*, Kaiserliche Marine, Deutsche Seewarte, 1917. The currents are those that prevail during the northern winter. During the summer the trends of the currents in the equatorial regions differ somewhat from the trends depicted on map A.

A few of the more important Transatlantic and Transpacific explorers' routes appear on map A. The routes of the Norsemen are of course extremely conjectural. Comparison of the routes with the ocean currents and prevailing winds (maps D and E) reveals the superior advantages to sailing vessels of the southerly routes taken by Columbus over the northerly routes. The routes are adapted from the following sources—Norsemen: Matthias Thórdarson, *The Vinland Voyages* (Amer. Geogr. Soc. Research Ser. No. 18), New York, 1930, maps on pp. 8 and 17. Columbus: G. E. Nunn, *The Geographical Conceptions of Columbus* (Amer. Geogr. Soc. Research Ser. No. 14), New York, 1924, Pl. 1; Gerhard Schott, *Geographie des atlantischen Ozeans*, 2nd edit., Hamburg, 1926, Pl. 1. Verrazano and Drake: W. R. Shepherd, *Historical Atlas*, 7th edit., New York, 1929, Pls. 107–108. Bering: generalized from map by E. P. Bertholf in F. A. Golder, *Bering's Voyages* ..., Vol. 1 (Amer. Geogr. Soc. Research Ser. No. 1), New York, 1922, Pl. 1.

Major Geographical Regions, or "Landschaftsgürtel," according to Passarge [*Plate 1B*]. This map shows in part the "Landschaftsgürtel" marked out by Professor Siegfried Passarge on a map of the world in his volume *Die Landschaftsgürtel der Erde: Natur und Kultur*, 2nd edit., Breslau, 1929. "Landschaftsgürtel" means literally "landscape zones," but "major geographical regions" seems a closer approximation to the true sense of the term. Passarge takes into account not only the elements of the natural environment but the works of man. His "Landschaftsgebiete" ("landscape regions") are thus geographical regions in a wider sense than Herbertson's natural regions (see above). His major geographical regions ("Landschaftsgürtel"), however, are determined essentially on the basis of natural criteria: climate and vegetation. The fundamental division is according to climatic zones: cold, intermediate (divided into subpolar and temperate), and warm (divided into subtropical and tropical). Each climatic zone is in turn split up into major regions according to the prevailing types of vegetation-cover.

The following brief explanation of map B is based mainly on Passarge's book cited above. Two points should be particularly noted. Though it may appear so on the map, there are of course no sharp dividing lines between the regions: each one merges into its neighbors. Each region, moreover, presents wide variations within itself. Variations due to altitude are particularly notable though they cannot be shown on a small map.

The lands are colored on map B. Lands within the cold zone are shown in blue. For the most part they are treeless tundras ("cold steppes and deserts"). The Alaska Peninsula, southern Greenland, and Iceland, where the cold is not so extreme and the moisture is great, constitute what Passarge calls regions of subpolar meadowlands, though natural meadowland by no means predominates in these areas.

Forests and cultivated regions originally forested are shown in green. The oceanic forests (marked "O") along the northwest coasts of Europe and North America receive much rain and have mild winters and cool

¹ Scale of map A, 1:75,000,000; of maps B-E, 1:150,000,000.
² Although map A also includes parts of Asia and Africa, Herbertson's Baikalia, China, Mongolia, and India are cut off by the upper border. Their American equivalents, however, are shown.

summers. The trees grow luxuriantly and remain green the year round, and the underbrush is thick. Passarge differentiates the oceanic forests from the "coniferous forests of the continental interiors" (marked "C"). The latter occur over tracts where climates of the continental type prevail, characterized by extreme variations of temperature. In North America and Asia these forest regions extend eastward to the Atlantic and Pacific coasts respectively. The subpolar coniferous forests, immense wildernesses of larch, spruce, and fir, lie mostly beyond the limits of agriculture (see map C). The regions of temperate coniferous forests, however, enjoy longer and warmer summers than their northern neighbors, and wheat and oats can be grown within their limits. North-Central Europe and a part of Russia constitute a region of mixed (*i. e.* coniferous and deciduous) forests (marked "M") that has been largely cleared and settled and has no strict counterpart in North America. Our northeastern states, which have a hotter summer and forests generally of a more subtropical character, Passarge designates as a region of subtropical-temperate forests. Mixed woodlands cover the highlands, but much of the lower ground is given over to cultivated fields. A corresponding region lies along the northern fringes of the Mediterranean basin. Our southeastern states are classified as a region of subtropical rain forests, resembling the eastern borderlands of the Black Sea. Heavy growths of blossoming trees and bushes—such as the magnolia, tulip tree, and rhododendron—as well as pine barrens and savanas are typical.

The regions of "steppes with woodlands of the temperate zone" are shown by buff and green stripes. Including the great wheat-growing areas of the world, they are transitional belts between the forests on one side and drier treeless steppes on the other. Their cover varies from woods broken by patches of prairie to open plains with isolated groves, copses, and strips of woodland along the stream valleys.

The "regions of sclerophyllous vegetation of the subtropical zone" are likewise shown by buff and green stripes but with black crosses. Sclerophyllous trees and shrubs have thick, succulent leaves capable of withstanding long, dry summers. Within these regions, which comprise California and the Mediterranean countries, the surface presents many local variations, ranging from forests and *maquis*, or chaparral, to grassy or bush-covered plains, salt steppes, and even sandy deserts.

True steppes are in buff. In the warm zone Passarge classifies them as humid (lower Mississippi basin and eastern Texas) and dry (western Texas).

The dry regions *par excellence* are shown in red; they may include sandy or rocky deserts, *salars* (or the salt-incrusted beds of dried-up lakes), saline steppes, sagebrush plains, etc., as well as irrigated oases.

Cultivated Crops [*Plate 1C*]. This map shows the areas in North America and Europe in which the following crops are raised in considerable quantities: potatoes, oats, wheat, corn, cotton, and citrus fruits. The first four, listed in the order of bushels produced 1911–1913, are, with rye, barley, and rice, the principal food crops of the world. Associated with each of these and with the cultivation of cotton and citrus fruits is a distinctive type of agricultural régime. Furthermore, to varying degrees each crop requires a particular combination of climatic circumstances. This is especially true in the case of citrus fruits and cotton but less notable in that of the great staple food crops. The map is based upon maps in V. C. Finch and O. E. Baker, *Geography of the World's Agriculture*, U. S. Department of Agriculture, 1917. The boundaries shown are not the extreme limits within which environmental conditions permit the raising of these crops but the limits within which the crops are actually grown on a substantial scale. The maps of Finch and Baker are dot maps on which each dot represents 5000 acres in the case of corn, oats, wheat, and cotton (except for Egypt, where one dot represents 1000 acres), 2000 acres in the case of potatoes, 100 acres for citrus fruits in the United States and 1250 acres in Europe. Lines were drawn connecting the outermost dots of each major cluster. Only the northern limit of citrus fruit culture is shown, owing to lack of sufficiently complete statistical data for the more southerly areas.

Winds and Sailing Routes [*Plate 1D and E*]. These maps show the prevailing winter and summer winds over the Atlantic and a part of the Pacific. They also illustrate the customary routes taken by sailing vessels from the English Channel and North Sea to American ports. The winds for the Atlantic are adapted from Gerhard Schott, *Geographie des atlantischen Ozeans*, 2nd edit., Hamburg, 1926, Pls. 20, 21; the sailing routes from Fig. 101 on p. 304 of the same publication; for the Pacific the winds are adapted from Deutsche Seewarte, *Stiller Ozean: ein Atlas . . .*, Hamburg, 1896, Pls. 18 and 19.

THE UNITED STATES: PHYSIOGRAPHY, SOILS, VEGETATION, CLIMATE, AND MINERAL RESOURCES

[PLATES 2–7]

Relief

[PLATE 2A]

This map is based upon the colored Relief Map of the U. S. Geological Survey (edition of 1916). The information on the Survey map has been somewhat generalized, and some of the minutiae of that map omitted.

Physical Divisions

[PLATE 2B]

This map is adapted from a map entitled "Physical Divisions of the United States," prepared by Nevin M. Fenneman in coöperation with the Physiographic Committee of the U. S. Geological Survey, accompanying N. M. Fenneman, "Physiographic Divisions of the United States, Third Edition Revised and Enlarged," *Annals of the Association of American Geographers*, Vol. 18, 1928, pp. 261–353, where a full description of each division will be found. Professor Fenneman has contributed the following summary description of the several divisions. The numbers correspond to the numbers on the map.

1. **The Superior Upland** is an area of very old hard rocks in which mountains have been worn down to a plain that was again raised up and subjected to valley cutting. Glaciers covered the whole, leaving numerous lakes and extensive swamps. Forests cover the surface except where cut or burned.

2. **The Continental Shelf** is a sloping submarine plain of sedimentation.

3. **The Atlantic and Gulf Coastal Plain** is an emerged sea bottom underlain by sand, gravel, clay, and marl; low and generally flat near the shore; rising and becoming more diversified inland. Only minor parts have fertile soil; but the topography favors agriculture, and most of the soil is easily worked and responds to fertilizers.

3A. THE EMBAYED SECTION has been affected by renewed subsidence which submerged the seaward margin and converted the major valleys into sounds and estuaries, navigable for small boats and producing a few deep harbors.

3B. THE SEA ISLAND SECTION shows submergence limited to a narrow zone, isolating a line of islands.

3C. THE FLORIDIAN SECTION in its southern part has been raised so little above sea level as to be imperfectly drained except for a low swell along the eastern shore, including Miami and other towns. The northern part, though still low, is pitted by lake basins due, in part, to solution.

3D. THE EAST GULF COASTAL PLAIN is a broad plain with alternating belts of higher (unproductive) and lower (fertile) land, the innermost lowland of central Alabama being the famous Black Belt, so called from the black soil formed on the outcrop of Selma chalk. This is one of the great cotton districts of the United States.

3E. THE MISSISSIPPI ALLUVIAL PLAIN consists of the delta of the Mississippi and of the coalescent flood plains of that river and its tributaries. In large part it is below the level of floods, the drier parts being natural levees, like the site of New Orleans. This is another of the great cotton districts of the United States.

3F. THE WESTERN GULF COASTAL PLAIN is a very broad plain somewhat belted. On its western side is the "Black Prairie," another great cotton district, corresponding to the Black Belt of Alabama. In general the Gulf Coast is slightly drowned; but, of the harbors of the great ports, Galveston harbor is largely artificial, and New Orleans harbor is in the river.

4. **The Piedmont province** is a plateau (with some lowland) lying between the Coastal Plain and the first of the Appalachian ranges. The rocks, except for the lowlands, are old and hard. The soils are only locally rich.

4A. THE PIEDMONT UPLAND is a plateau on hard rocks of moderate relief and slopes except where trenched by streams or surmounted (near the Blue Ridge) by isolated mountains.

4B. THE PIEDMONT LOWLANDS are several small but important districts in the narrow northern end of the Piedmont province. They are lower and smoother than the Piedmont Upland and are largely on Triassic sediments as in New Jersey, or on limestone as in Lancaster County, Pa.

5. **The Blue Ridge province** consists of mountains of resistant rock once almost completely worn away except in the southern half, where they were very much subdued. The range was renewed by uplift and the wearing down of adjacent provinces. Slopes are moderate and generally forested.

5A. THE NORTHERN SECTION shows the old lowland, now again uplifted, forming the crest, which, when seen from a distance, is fairly smooth, and is generally between 1500 and 3000 feet high.

5B. THE SOUTHERN SECTION shows the old subdued mountains surmounting the uplifted lowland, forming uneven crests 3000 to 6000 feet high. Here is the finest hardwood (and mixed) forest of the United States.

6. **The Valley and Ridge province** is a continuous belt 1200 miles long and 30 to 90 miles wide, in which parallel, narrow, even-topped ridges alternate with smooth-floored valleys. By a process of folding, complete wearing down, later uplift, and still later wearing away of the softer rocks, ridges have been made from the upturned edges of the strong sandstones. The less enduring rocks (limestone and shale) underlie the valleys, some of them being distinctly fertile.

6A. THE TENNESSEE SECTION has broadly developed valley belts predominating over the ridges. The major streams are longitudinal.

6B. THE MIDDLE SECTION has closely crowded ridges predominating over the valley belts except for the broad continuous valley (Shenandoah, etc.) on the eastern side. Master streams cross the province, alternately following the valleys and crossing the ridges through watergaps. Smaller streams follow the general trend. Travel crosses the province by taking advantage of the water-gaps.

6C. THE HUDSON VALLEY is practically free from the longitudinal ridges that characterize the province elsewhere. Soil and details of relief are influenced by glaciation. Subsidence has drowned the Hudson River, making the harbor of New York and permitting tides as far north as Albany.

7. **The St. Lawrence Valley** is a broad lowland, in large part flat; elsewhere are low hills.

7A. THE CHAMPLAIN SECTION is a glaciated rolling lowland, only its lower parts being marine plain.

7B. THE NORTHERN SECTION is chiefly a marine plain, with only occasional rock hills.

8. **The Appalachian Plateau** has a relatively high surface on horizontal rocks (except locally). Sandstone predominates at the surface, and most of the soil is not of high grade. The plateau is so cut by valleys as to leave little flat ground except near the southern end. In New York altitude and relief decrease toward the north, elsewhere toward the west.

8A. THE MOHAWK SECTION includes on its southern margin the valley of the Mohawk River. This is the lowest strip in the province, affording easy communication between the seaboard and the interior.

8B. THE CATSKILL SECTION is a plateau of very strong, nearly horizontal, rocks. Deep valleys carve the surface into mountains.

8C. THE SOUTHERN NEW YORK SECTION is completely dissected by valleys several hundred feet deep. Glaciation has somewhat rounded the forms and improved the soil. It is one of the great dairy districts of the United States.

8D. THE ALLEGHENY MOUNTAIN SECTION is mildly affected by the folding of the earth's crust in the New England province. Low anticlines were thus made in the eastern margin of the Appalachian Plateau. This folding and deep erosion have made this section truly mountainous. Much of it is still forest.

8E. THE KANAWHA SECTION is carved into hills and valleys, the relief decreasing westward from 500 feet (locally 1000 feet) to a few hundred feet in central Ohio. It embraces the larger part of the great Appalachian coalfield.

8F. THE CUMBERLAND PLATEAU is the least dissected part of the province. Some broad uplands more than 2000 feet high remain between valleys. They are capped by thick strata of sandstone, and the soil is poor. Toward the southern end the distinctive character is lost.

8G. THE CUMBERLAND MOUNTAINS are similar in character to the Allegheny Mountain section.

9. **The New England province** has for its dominant feature an upland above 1000 feet in the interior and sloping seaward. Narrow valleys in the strong rocks dissect the surface incompletely. Several broader lowlands occur on belts of weak rocks. Residual mountains surmount the upland in the west and north. Glaciation has left a stony drift, also numerous lakes, swamps, and rapids.

9A. THE SEABOARD LOWLAND, though hilly, is rolling rather than angular. Subsidence and drowning of valleys have fringed the shore with bays, headlands, and islands and afforded numerous small harbors.

9B. THE NEW ENGLAND UPLAND SECTION is of the type described for the province, its northern part being forested and its southern margin much like the Seaboard Lowland. A narrow southwestward extension into Pennsylvania constitutes the Highlands of New York and New Jersey. Isolated residual mountains, of which Mt. Monadnock is the type, increase in abundance toward the White Mountains.

9C. THE WHITE MOUNTAIN SECTION is that part in which monadnocks predominate, or in which large areas consist wholly of residual mountains with many summits above 5000 feet.

9D. THE GREEN MOUNTAIN SECTION is a low, somewhat even-crested, linear range with a granite axis.

9E. THE TACONIC SECTION consists of closely folded and metamorphosed rocks outcropping in longitudinal belts, the stronger ones making mountains. On its eastern side a belt of limestone (or marble) makes a continuous valley from northern Vermont to Connecticut.

10. **The Adirondack province** is an area of upland, similar to that of New England, on igneous and metamorphic rocks, surmounted by a group of subdued mountains near the eastern border.

11. **The Interior Low Plateau** is fairly described by its name.

11A. THE HIGHLAND RIM SECTION derives its name from its contrast with the Nashville Basin. Higher and flatter on the eastern side, it declines toward western Kentucky, where it is completely carved into hills.

11B. THE LEXINGTON PLAIN has at its center the Kentucky blue grass district, an area in which a slight doming of the crust has brought to the surface certain limestones which have been eroded down to a gently rolling plain with a very fertile soil.

11C. THE NASHVILLE BASIN is likewise cut out by erosion on limestone beds brought up by gentle doming. It is surrounded by the Highland Rim which breaks off at places abruptly in an escarpment 500 to 700 feet high.

12. **The Central Lowland**, described by its name, is divided into sections on the basis of features determined by glaciation. Its rocks are nearly horizontal sediments, limestone and shale greatly predominating over sandstone.

12A. THE EASTERN LAKE SECTION has all the features of recent glaciation—moraines, till plains, outwash deposits of all kinds, lakes, swamps, lacustrine plains, etc. Over considerable areas the glacial drift is several hundred feet thick. West of Lake Michigan, and extending into neighboring sections, is one of the two leading dairy districts of the United States.

12B. THE WESTERN LAKE SECTION may be described in the same general terms as the Eastern Lake section; but morainic features, lakes, swamps, and outwash deposits are less abundant, and the proportion of rolling till plain is greater. The lacustrine plain of glacial Lake Agassiz in the valley of Red River is very important.

12C. THE WISCONSIN DRIFTLESS SECTION was missed by the glacial ice, though its northern half was veneered by a sandy outwash that made extensive swampy and unproductive plains. The southern part is a dissected limestone upland probably showing the preglacial appearance of extensive areas.

12D. THE TILL PLAINS SECTION is distinguished by the extraordinary development of nearly flat ground moraine and by the relatively subordinate position of features associated with terminal moraines. Lakes and swamps are wanting, though much of the land is so flat as to require artificial drainage. No section in the United States is richer agriculturally.

12E. THE DISSECTED TILL PLAINS are like the Till Plains except that the drift sheet is much older. Valleys have had time to develop, and four-fifths of the area is now valley-side. The fertile soil, as in parts of adjacent sections, is derived not from the glacial drift but from loess deposited by wind.

12F. THE OSAGE SECTION lies south of the limit of glaciation. Most of it is smooth plains in northeast-southwest strips, separated by low ridges of outcropping harder strata which dip gently from the Ozark Plateau and under the Great Plains. The Brazos and other streams at the southern end have cut down sharply into these lowlands. Some moderately rough areas result from this erosion and from the outcropping stronger beds.

13. **The Great Plains province** is a semiarid to semihumid grass-covered plateau, sloping eastward from an altitude of 5000 feet or more at the foot of the Rocky Mountains. As a natural grazing land it has few equals. It has a very rich soil, lacking only water. Only a small part of it can be irrigated. Much of it is now devoted to dry farming.

13A. THE GLACIATED SECTION OF THE MISSOURI PLATEAU differs from the same plateau farther south only in the details of its topography and drainage.

13B. THE UNGLACIATED SECTION OF THE MISSOURI PLATEAU has a surface of rather large relief, though not generally within short distances. The surface is, in a rude way, terraced by repeated uplifts and concurrent erosion.

13C. THE BLACK HILLS are an isolated mountain uplift in the form of a dome truncated by erosion. Ridges on the stronger formations, and valleys on the weaker, almost surround the uplift. The greater rainfall due to altitude favors forests (hence the name "Black") and feeds streams which are used for irrigation on the adjacent plains.

13D. THE HIGH PLAINS are remnants of an almost featureless plain made by the spreading of alluvium by overloaded streams breaking up and interlacing as on a delta. Characteristically this section is covered by short grass that makes a tight sod, but in Nebraska there are some drifting dunes and a large area in which old dunes are now grassed.

13E. THE PLAINS BORDER is the eastern margin of the former High Plains and is now eroded, having several hundred feet of relief. Being on the more humid side of the Great Plains, the native vegetation resembles that of the prairies on the east.

13F. THE COLORADO PIEDMONT is likewise an eroded country, though for different reasons. It resembles the Missouri Plateau.

13G. THE RATON SECTION consists of more elevated plateaus, partly on a strong sandstone trenched by canyons and partly on sheets of lava, preserved only in remnants capping the mesas.

13H. THE PECOS VALLEY is a trough 500 to 700 feet lower than the High Plains on the east. A minor part of this section, near Pecos River, is a smooth plain on recent sediments. Here also is a well-known artesian basin and a famous irrigated district.

13I. THE EDWARDS PLATEAU is a limestone plateau continuous with the High Plains but lacking the fluviatile cover. It is high and level in the western half but declines eastward. Its steep edges fronting the Coastal Plain and the Central Texas section are much frayed by stream erosion.

13K. THE CENTRAL TEXAS SECTION is an area of varied relief embracing high mesas and other remnants of strong rock and interspersed with lowlands on the weaker rocks and near the main streams.

14. The Ozark Plateau consists of horizontal rocks, gently domed, stripped of their uppermost formations, and incised by abrupt valleys except on the western margin.

14A. THE SPRINGFIELD-SALEM PLATEAUS have a substratum of resistant limestone, locally stripped away near the eastern side and exposing the igneous rocks that constitute the St. François Mountains. For general farming the soil is poor. The western margin is more like the adjacent Osage plains.

14B. THE BOSTON MOUNTAINS are a remnant of thick, strong, southward-dipping sandstone beds rising above the limestone plateau and deeply carved by steep valleys. This section is comparable to the Cumberland Mountains in the Appalachian Plateau province.

15. The Ouachita province consists of folded strata deeply eroded and is comparable to the Valley and Ridge province of the Appalachian Highland.

15A. THE ARKANSAS VALLEY is underlain by gently folded rocks and has a floor of moderate relief. It corresponds in a general way to the Shenandoah Valley.

15B. THE OUACHITA MOUNTAINS consist of closely folded strata and have undergone the same history as the Valley and Ridge province. The topography is similar in plan.

16. The Southern Rocky Mountains are for the most part granite-cored ranges flanked by hogback foothills of sedimentary rock. They enclose extensive basins, some of them known as "parks." Much of the granite area is either plateau-like at elevations of 8000 to 10,000 feet or is again carved into mountains by stream work. The highest peaks and ranges rise above these granite uplands. The San Juan Mountains in southwestern Colorado consist of lava flows and other eruptive rocks.

17. The Wyoming Basin is a plateau similar to the neighboring Great Plains separating the Southern from the Middle Rocky Mountain province. Like the Northern Great Plains it contains isolated mountains and a few short ranges.

18. The Middle Rocky Mountains are similar to those farther south, the major ranges being separate structural uplifts caused by folding or faulting. Exceptions are found in the smaller ranges on both sides of the Wyoming-Idaho boundary. The Yellowstone Plateau is included in this province, though most of it is without mountains. The same is true of the Big Horn Basin.

19. The Northern Rocky Mountains differ from those farther south in having few "ranges" properly so called. A large part (especially in Idaho) is a vast highland of strong rocks deeply carved. Single groups or lines of mountains have been outlined by erosion, not raised up separately. Irregularly scattered through the province are basins, some of them ten to fifteen miles wide and generally elongated. Their floors are plains. Some of them, like the Three Forks district and the Bitterroot Valley, are favored agriculturally.

20. The Columbia Plateau province consists essentially of lava plateaus. Its type of stream valley is the canyon (not always narrow), and the typical vegetation is sagebrush and bunch grass.

20A. THE WALLA WALLA PLATEAU has a rolling surface, due to hills of loess and other loose material that cover the lava. The eastern part is largely devoted to wheat raising by dry farming.

20B. THE BLUE MOUNTAIN SECTION is an area of exceptional altitude, partly old mountains never buried by lava flows and partly a low dome in the lava surface carved into mountains by streams. The altitude (maximum above 7000 feet) causes larger rainfall and hence forests. Water for irrigation is thus provided in adjacent sections.

20C. THE PAYETTE SECTION is an area in which lava flows are interbedded with easily eroded lake sediments. The streams therefore have wider valleys than elsewhere in this province. Agriculture by irrigation is important in the valleys.

20D. THE SNAKE RIVER PLAIN is a typical young lava plain, having very little local relief except near the Snake River canyon (maximum depth 700 feet) and a few small tributary canyons. Where the lava flows are youngest there is almost no soil.

20E. THE HARNEY SECTION drains only to lakes that have no outlet. The streams have not enough fall to cut canyons. The surface is an arid plain partly covered with alluvium on the eastern side and volcanic ash elsewhere. Small volcanic cones are found in increasing numbers toward the west.

21. The Colorado Plateaus are distinguished by their height (generally 5000 to 10,000 feet) and by a tabular style of topography in which the several units are separated either by cliffs, sometimes due to faulting, or by canyons. Here and there are isolated mountains of volcanic origin or eroded domes like the Black Hills but smaller. A scrubby growth of trees is common above 6000 feet and forests above 7000 feet.

21A. THE HIGH PLATEAUS OF UTAH are a remarkable group of nine plateaus 7000 to 11,000 feet high, for the most part sloping eastward. The north-south lines of separation are faults or flexures, generally with upthrow on the east. The entire section lies south of and in line with the Wasatch Mountains and has sometimes been incorrectly mapped as a continuation of that range.

21B. THE UINTA BASIN is a dissected plateau of Tertiary rocks dipping north to the foot of the Uinta Range where the beds again turn up. To the south this terrace-like plateau terminates in south-facing escarpments, the Roan Cliffs and Book Cliffs.

21C. THE CANYON LANDS are a region of many steep escarpments, sometimes facing each other from opposite sides of a canyon, sometimes separating a higher from a lower plateau. Most of the area is below the level of trees.

21D. THE NAVAJO SECTION differs from the Canyon Lands chiefly in having fewer and shallower canyons.

21E. THE GRAND CANYON SECTION is traversed by one great canyon and not dissected by many, as are the Canyon Lands. Much of its surface is rolling rather than angular. Elevations above 7000 feet, and hence pine forests, are rather widespread. North of the Grand Canyon the surface rises in four great steps from less than 6000 feet on the west to 9500 feet in the Kaibab plateau opposite El Tovar. In the southern part (Flagstaff) is a large volcanic area, much of it reaching the level of pine forests.

21F. THE DATIL SECTION is marked by volcanic features. Lava flows are either widespread or survive in remnants as the capping of mesas. Volcanic necks are numerous.

22. The Basin and Range province is an extensive region in which short mountain ranges, commonly parallel, alternate with desert plains. In the larger part the plains are high, 4000 to 6000 feet, but the level declines toward the Gulf of California. A relative altitude of 2000 to 4000 feet for the ranges is common. In most of the northern half the feeble drainage terminates in enclosed basins with or without salt lakes. In much of the southern half stream courses lead to the sea but rarely carry water.

22A. THE GREAT BASIN is about half mountains. Vigorous streams from the Wasatch and Sierra Nevada afford water for irrigation on the borders. The Humboldt is the only considerable stream originating in the Great Basin. All the basins between the ranges are filled or covered with sand, gravel, and silt washed down from the mountains.

22B. THE SONORAN DESERT (which includes the Mohave) declines almost to sea level on the Lower Colorado. Its mountain ranges are smaller and occupy little more than one-fifth of its area. About half of the desert plains have a rocky floor or are covered by several feet of detritus. The annual rainfall on the Lower Colorado is only two to three inches, but this is likely to come in torrents.

22C. THE SALTON TROUGH drains toward the Salton Sink several hundred feet below sea level. This inclosed basin is separated from the Gulf of California by the delta of the Colorado River. The northern slope of this delta is known as the Imperial Valley, a famous irrigated district deriving its water from the Colorado River and having a semitropical climate.

22D. THE MEXICAN HIGHLAND, like the Great Basin, is about half mountains; but most of its valleys, at least in Arizona, are drained by through-flowing streams. In New Mexico this is true only near the Rio Grande.

22E. THE SACRAMENTO SECTION, like the rest of the province, has highlands tilted by faulting, but here the tilt is gentle and the highlands are more plateau-like, though most of them are completely dissected by erosion.

23. **The Sierra-Cascade province** is composed of unlike mountains described below but constitutes a continuous barrier between the inter-montane plateaus and the Pacific Border.

23A. THE NORTHERN CASCADE MOUNTAINS are composed of strong rocks much deformed but remarkable for the nearly uniform height of their sharp crests. The general level of these crests at 6000 to 8000 feet is surmounted by occasional volcanic cones—Mt. Baker, Glacier Peak, and others.

23B. THE MIDDLE CASCADE MOUNTAINS consist of beds of volcanic rocks forced up, though toward the southern end mere piling up by eruption becomes more important. As in the Northern Cascades, the moderately level horizon is surmounted by great volcanic cones—Mt. Rainier, Mt. Hood, and others.

23C. THE SOUTHERN CASCADE MOUNTAINS are due entirely to accumulation of erupted material. Several hundred centers of eruption have been located. As these are of all ages and sizes, there is no regularity of height. Lassen Peak and Mt. Shasta are among the volcanoes.

23D. THE SIERRA NEVADA MOUNTAINS, consisting of strong igneous and metamorphic rocks, have been at least once worn down almost to a lowland. The very short and steep eastern slope indicates faulting, by which the great mass was raised on the eastern side and tilted westward. Glaciation has caused the extreme ruggedness of the High Sierra and the vertical-walled valleys like the Yosemite.

24. **The Pacific Border province** embraces many ranges and groups of mountains called Coast Ranges and several deep and extensive troughs associated with them.

24A. THE PUGET TROUGH is a long depression stretching from the coast of British Columbia to central Oregon. Puget Sound is a system of stream-carved valleys submerged by the sea. The flat-floored Willamette Valley in Oregon has but recently risen above sea level.

24B. THE OLYMPIC MOUNTAINS are much like the Northern Cascades. A narrow strip of lowland surrounds the mountains on all sides. Here is the heaviest annual rainfall of the United States, more than 120 inches.

24C. THE OREGON COAST RANGE is due to gentle upfolding of rather weak rocks at a relatively recent time, though not so recent as to preclude the cutting down of the range to a lowland. It is that lowland, again uplifted, which makes the present even crest.

24D. THE KLAMATH MOUNTAINS, on the other hand, are perhaps the oldest feature on the Pacific Coast. Their rocks are ancient and resistant and have been subjected to repeated wearing down. Remains of old surfaces thus produced are now seen at various levels.

24E. THE CALIFORNIA TROUGH is for the most part remarkably flat and less than 400 feet above sea level. Its rivers have too little fall to transport their loads of sediment. The Sacramento, Feather, and other rivers have accordingly built up their beds and banks, and the present slope is from the rivers. The southern part is arid.

24F. THE CALIFORNIA COAST RANGES comprise many relatively low ranges inclosing long valleys. Sea cliffs and terraces up to 1500 feet on the seaward slope show recent rising of the land which extended far to the north and south of this section. San Francisco Bay is exceptional, being the result of recent sinking and drowning of a transverse river valley.

24G. THE LOS ANGELES RANGES are uplifted or tilted fault blocks more or less dissected by stream erosion. The intervening lowlands are covered with sand, gravel, and silt washed down from the mountains.

25. **The Lower California province** is a granite upland, lower than the Sierra Nevada and not glaciated, but otherwise similar.

Soil Regions

[PLATE 2C]

This map is a generalization of the information collected by the soil surveyors of the Bureau of Soils, Department of Agriculture, during more than a quarter of a century. On a map of this size many details are necessarily omitted. The "light colored soils" are usually the forest and less fertile soils and the "dark colored soils" are the grassland and more fertile soils.

Vegetation Regions

[PLATE 2D]

This is adapted from Plate 2 of B. E. Livingston and Forrest Shreve, *The Distribution of Vegetation in the United States, as Related to Climatic*

Conditions (Carnegie Instn. Publ. No. 284), Washington, 1921. The original title is "Generalized Vegetation Map of the United States, Showing Nine General Types or Subdivisions of the Vegetation."

Forests, 1620–1930
[PLATE 3A–D]

Area of Virgin Forests, 1620, 1850, 1926 [*Plate 3A–C*]. These maps are reproductions of original drawings found in the Forest Service, Department of Agriculture. Map C and the part of map B east of the longitude of western Kansas are based upon statistics. Map A and the western part of map B are generalizations from less specific information.

National Forests [*Plate 3D*]. This map is based upon a map entitled *National Forests, State Forests, National Parks, National Monuments, and Indian Reservations*, published by the Forest Service in 1927. The map was corrected to 1930 from maps of individual forests published by the Forest Service.

Climate
[PLATES 3E–5]

This series includes the following maps:

Length of the Growing Season [*Plate 3E*], or average number of days each year between the last killing frost in spring and the first killing frost in autumn;

Snow Cover: Average Annual Number of Days [*Plate 4A*]

Droughts: Frequency [*Plate 4B*];

Relative Humidity: Average at Local Noon for January and July [*Plate 4C and D*];

Cloudiness: Daytime Average for January and July [*Plate 4E and F*];

Winds and Pressure for January and July: Frequency Wind Roses and Average Pressure [*Plate 4G and H*];

Temperature: Average for January and July and Average Annual Maximum and Minimum [*Plate 5A–D*];

Rainfall: Average for January and July and Average Annual [*Plate 5 E–G*].

The climatic elements that have been selected for illustration in this series may all be directly correlated with regional divergencies in the conditions and circumstances of human life, particularly in the fields of economic, social, and political enterprise.

The following maps are adapted from maps in Sections 1, A, and B of the *Atlas of American Agriculture*, Part II, *Climate*, published by the U. S. Department of Agriculture: Plate 3E from Section 1, *Frost and the Growing Season*, by W. G. Reed, Washington, 1918, Fig. 29, pp. 10-11; Plate 4A from Section A, *Precipitation and Humidity*, by J. B. Kincer, 1922, Fig. 78, p. 43; Plate 4B from the same, Fig. 69, p. 40; Plate 5A from Section B, *Temperature, Sunshine, and Wind*, by J. B. Kincer, 1928, Fig. 12, p. 10; Plate 5B from the same, Fig. 42, p. 16. The remaining maps of the series, Plates 4C–H and 5C–G, are based on manuscript maps drawn under the direction of Professors R. DeC. Ward and C. F. Brooks for the *Handbuch der Klimatologie*, edited by Professors W. Köppen and R. Geiger and now in course of publication by the firm of Gebrüder Borntraeger, Berlin, Germany. The maps were redrawn for and reproduced in the *Atlas* with the courteous permission of the authors, editors, and publishers. They are based on records taken over longer periods and for more stations than are the corresponding maps in the *Atlas of American Agriculture*, which previously had constituted the most nearly complete and up-to-date series of climatic maps of the United States.

Mineral Resources
[PLATES 6–7]

These plates illustrate the distribution of the principal minerals. Many small "fields," such as the bog-iron region of eastern Massachusetts, much exploited during the colonial era, are not shown.

Coalfields [*Plate 6A*]. This map is based upon a map entitled *Coal Fields of the United States*, compiled by Marius R. Campbell, geologist in charge of mineral fuels, U. S. Geological Survey, and published in the *Proceedings of the International Conference on Bituminous Coal*, Carnegie Institute of Technology, Pittsburgh, Pa., 1926.

The bituminous and anthracite fields lying east of the Mississippi River are delimited with considerable precision. The other fields, for which the information is less complete, are approximately correct. The workable beds are distinguished from other beds by means of differences of shading.

Distribution and Production of Iron Ore [*Plate 6B*]. The distribution of iron ore is based, with revisions as of 1930 suggested by Dr. G. O. Smith, former director of the U. S. Geological Survey, upon a map prepared by E. C. Harder of the Survey and published by the Survey in *Mineral Resources of the United States*, 1908 (Part I, Pl. 1). The production of iron ore, which is shown for the eight states that lead in production, is based upon statistics published by the Bureau of the Census in *Mines and Quarries, 1909* (*Reports of Thirteenth Census*, Vol. 11, p. 240), and for 1929 upon a preliminary estimate of the U. S. Bureau of Mines for 1930 furnished by courtesy of Dr. G. O. Smith. In 1909 these eight states produced more than 96 per cent of the entire production.

The distribution of iron ore and that of iron-ore production differ greatly. High-grade accessible ores are mined first. In 1922 a small area in Minnesota produced more than 60 per cent of all the ore mined in the United States, while the relatively large iron-ore area in Ohio produced little or none. This map should be compared with the maps illustrating iron and steel works (Pl. 135).

Oil and Gas Fields [*Plate 7A*]. The oil fields as shown on this map are generalized, with permission of the publisher, from a recent undated map entitled *Oil Fields and Pipe Lines of the United States*, published by the International Map Company, New York. The original was compiled on the basis of data found in the publications of the U. S. Geological survey, General Land Office, and Bureau of Mines, and from information furnished by oil and pipe-line companies and by state officials.

The gas fields are based upon maps of the individual states showing oil and gas fields published by the U. S. Geological Survey between the years 1924 and 1930 inclusive, supplemented by a map of the United States, showing oil and gas fields, 1922, also published by the Survey.

Gold, Silver, and Copper Districts [*Plate 7B*]. The distribution of gold and silver districts west of the meridian passing through the eastern boundary of New Mexico is based in the first instance upon the maps and text of James M. Hill, *The Mining Districts of the Western United States* (U. S. Geol. Survey Bull. 507), 1912. Hill divides this region into mining districts and classifies each district according to the predominant metal produced therein. The "predominant metal" is the metal whose value exceeds that of any other produced in the district.

The gold and silver districts to the eastward of the meridian described above are regions in which small quantities of these metals are produced. The distribution of the districts in the Southern States is based in the first instance upon an unpublished map prepared by the Geological Survey in 1912. There are still other districts, unmapped, in which negligible quantities of these metals are occasionally obtained.

The distribution of copper districts is based in the first instance upon a map showing "copper-producing districts," published by the U. S. Geological Survey in *Mineral Resources of the United States*, 1910 (Part I, Pl. 1). Only the leading districts are shown. They, however, produce all but two or three per cent of American copper. The Survey map shows one hundred and seventy-one districts in twenty states. Sixty-six per cent of all the copper produced in the United States up to the close of 1910 had come from the Butte (Montana) and Lake Superior districts.

From data furnished by Dr. G. O. Smith of the U. S. Geological Survey the map as first drawn from the sources of information referred to above was corrected to represent, so far as possible, the situation prevailing in 1930.

CARTOGRAPHY, 1492-1867
[PLATES 8-32]

THIS series begins with the famous globe of Martin Behaim, constructed on the eve of Columbus' first voyage, and ends with a map of 1867—a date more or less arbitrarily chosen—by which year the general features of the cartography of the United States had been determined. Forty-eight maps have been selected for reproduction, to illustrate some of the more important landmarks in the history of the mapping of what is now the United States. They depict on the whole a progressive increase in the extent and accuracy of geographical knowledge and a progressive improvement in the cartographical art. The earlier maps reveal the misconceptions of their makers, who often filled up the gaps in their knowledge with conjecture.

While in some instances the whole of the original map is shown, more frequently only a significant part was chosen for reproduction. Many of the early maps are world maps (*mappemondes*), and obviously the whole map could not be used. Several maps which were published or are preserved in sections are reproduced as units.

The earliest maps of America were either hand-drawn or engraved. The engraving of maps began in 1460. Before this date all maps were in manuscript, and not until more than a hundred years after this date did cartographic engraving become general. The early manuscript maps had a wide circulation, and their geographical information not infrequently is more exact than that of contemporary engraved maps. In recent years many of the manuscript maps have been reproduced. Some of the maps in the *Atlas* are from these reproductions, and a few are from the original manuscripts. Many of the reproductions in the *Atlas* of engraved maps are from the original engravings. Some of the early delineations of America are on globes. The maps from this source are always from reproductions. Attempts made to obtain prints of manuscript maps were not always successful, owing to the fragility of the manuscripts or the difficulty of finding them.

Most cartographers derive their information for new maps largely from old ones. They follow the prevailing models. Occasionally a cartographer, more enterprising than the generality of his craft, by utilizing new information or making a new use of old produces a map that is a decided improvement over its predecessors. His map in turn becomes a model for less original and enterprising cartographers. It thus follows that maps may be classified according to types or classes. A type may be named for one of the early maps of its class—often for the first of these, the so-called "mother map." The originator of many of the early types, however, is not known, and the type may take its name from a later map. When it is stated in this text, for example, that "Map B" is of the "A type," it is understood that "Map B" may be derived from "Map A," or from some other map of the "A type." Often one cannot be more definite than this.

An effort was made to include mother maps and other representative type maps. These alone, however, would not adequately illustrate cartographical development. Maps were sometimes chosen because of their popularity or because of their great influence upon cartography. Many maps were rejected not because they were unworthy of inclusion but for want of space.

Some of the maps that were reproduced are without original titles on them. These have been designated for the purposes of this series by the titles that have been applied to them by recognized authorities. Such titles are usually derived from the name of the maker or publisher, from the depository in which the map is found, from some distinguishing feature, or from some combination of these. Occasionally when the authorities differ a choice had to be made. Other maps have original titles on them. These sometimes show on the reproductions but more frequently do not. In either case the titles that have been given them in the *Atlas* were derived after the manner for untitled maps described above.

In dating maps the best authorities were followed. Most of the originals have dates on them. These may be either the date of the manuscript drawing, the date assigned to the map in the title or elsewhere on it, or the date of publication. When the date of publication was long subsequent to the date on the manuscript, the earlier date was always chosen. When the dates were nearly the same, the date of publication was sometimes chosen because it could be ascertained with certainty.

The dates of some of the early maps can be fixed only approximately. The early maps differ widely from the later ones in general appearance. Many of them have no meridians or parallels or but a few of the one or the other. Often they are not graduated for latitude and longitude, or they are graduated for one and not the other. Graduations are often erroneous. The latitudes are likely to be close approximations. The longitudes are often wide of the truth, since the chronometer was not invented until the eighteenth century. The longitudes are often measured eastward from a prime meridian for three hundred and sixty degrees. Whether they are measured eastward or westward may be determined from the sequence of the graduation numbers. The prime meridians of some of the early maps are difficult to identify. The principal ones are those of Greenwich and the Island of Ferro (about eighteen degrees west of Greenwich).

Many of the early maps, notably the sea charts, or portolans, with which modern cartography begins, have a network of lines, known as loxodromes, radiating from various centers or crossing points, at which wind roses are often drawn. Such maps are sometimes described as "projectionless," since they have no system of points or lines laid down according to mathematical rules of projection. Some of the early maps are based upon estimates of the bearings of the principal ports and capes and of the distances between these and upon a more detailed survey of the intervening coast, others upon a rather careful determination of positions and measurement of distances.

On the early maps the interiors of continents, the geography of which was unknown, are sometimes left blank. It was the fashion, however, to fill up the interiors with legends describing their inhabitants, products, and natural features; with conventional pictures of these and of other things, real or fabulous; and with ornamental designs. The seas were filled up with similar materials, including pictures of ships and marine animals. Intricate scrolls and elaborate cartouches were common. Most of the maps of the series, including all the later ones, were laid down according to mathematical rules of projection. In the descriptions given below some of the unusual projections are identified.

Most of the original maps are in black and white, but some are partly colored. An attempt was made to eliminate the effect of color. On a few reproductions, however, some lines are accentuated by reason of the color on the original.

The following liberties have been taken: legends and scales have sometimes been transferred to the parts reproduced and graduation numbers added in brackets. To each reproduction a title has been added. Occasionally a name mutilated in cutting the reproduction has been removed. Where maps have been reduced or enlarged the amount of linear reduction or enlargement is indicated approximately in the text (for example, if the reproduction is six inches wide and the reduction is stated to be one-third, the portion of the original map reproduced would be about nine inches wide.)

The order of arrangement of the maps is roughly chronological. A strictly chronological arrangement was not possible because of differences between the size and shape of the maps and the size and shape of the available spaces on the plates.

Among the general authorities that were found most useful in preparing the following descriptions given below are the following:

Henry Harrisse, *Discovery of North America*, London and Paris, 1892; idem, *Jean et Sébastien Cabot*, Paris, 1882; Justin Winsor, *Memorial History of Boston*, Boston, 1881-1883; idem, *Narrative and Critical History of America*, Boston and New York, 1884-1889; idem, *Cartier to Frontenac*, Boston and New York, 1894; idem, *Kohl Collection of Maps relating to America*, Washington, 1904; E. L. Stevenson, *Maps Illustrating Early Discovery and Exploration in America, 1502-1530*, New Brunswick, N. J., 1903-1906; A. E. Nordenskiöld, *Facsimile-Atlas to the Early History of Cartography*, Stockholm, 1889; idem, *Periplus: An Essay on the Early History of Charts and Sailing Directions*, Stockholm, 1897; K. Kretschmer, *Die Entdeckung Amerika's*, Berlin, 1892; S. Ruge, *Die Entwickelung der Kartographie von Amerika bis 1570*, Gotha, 1892; J. G. Kohl, *History of the Discovery of Maine*, Portland, 1869; Woodbury Lowery, *Maps of the Spanish Possessions within the Present Limits of the United States, 1502-1820*, Washington, 1912, edited by P. Lee Phillips; P. Lee Phillips, *A List of Maps of America in the Library of Congress*, Washington, 1901; idem, *A List of Geographical Atlases in the Library of Congress*, 4 vols., Washington, 1909-1920; C. H. Coote, *Autotype Facsim-*

iles of Three Mappemondes, Aberdeen, 1898; Alexander Brown, *Genesis of the United States*, Boston and New York, 1890; R. G. Thwaites, *Jesuit Relations*, Cleveland, 1896–1901.

Behaim Globe Gores, 1492

[PLATE 8]

At the request of the town council of his native city, Martin Behaim of Nuremberg (1459–1507) constructed, in 1492, a terrestrial globe, the original of which is now in the Germanic Museum at Nuremberg. A portion of the globe is shown on Plate 8 in the form of gores, reproduced with a reduction of about five-twelfths from a full-sized colored reproduction accompanying E. G. Ravenstein, *Martin Behaim, his Life and his Globe*, London, 1908.[1] The globe measures 20 inches in diameter: upon it the equator is graduated in 360 degrees, a line shows the inclination of the ecliptic, and a meridian drawn 80° west of Lisbon passes from pole to pole. There are many place names and other legends written in the South German dialect of the period. The globe has suffered at the hands of time and of would-be restorers. Ravenstein on his reproduction deleted certain names added by restorers, and himself restored a few names that earlier reproductions show to have been once legible.

Behaim's geography as depicted on his globe represents usual fifteenth-century opinions, derived mainly from the writings of Ptolemy, Pliny, Isidore of Seville, Marco Polo, and Sir John Mandeville. Some use was made of the portolan coast charts. His concept of the distribution of land and water was probably much the same as that which is said to have led Columbus to seek a westward route from Spain to the East Indies, although there is no reason to believe that Behaim himself exercised "any influence upon the projects of Columbus" (*ibid.*, p. 41). Ptolemy had estimated the length of the then-known world from Spain to eastern Asia at 183°. Behaim accepted this figure, so far as it went, and followed contemporary interpreters of Ptolemy in his delineation of the coast lines of eastern Asia. However, eastward of the Ptolemaic Far East he added a broad expanse of territory to allow room for the regions described by Marco Polo, thus reducing the width of the ocean supposed to intervene between Europe and Eastern Asia to about 126° of longitude. A similar misconception may have induced Columbus to seek a westward route to the Indies, though it is probable that Columbus even exceeded Behaim in his under-estimate of the distance west from Spain to Asia. See G. E. Nunn, *The Geographical Conceptions of Columbus* (Amer. Geogr. Soc. Research Series No. 14), New York, 1924.

Cantino Map, ca. 1502

[PLATE 9]

This map is named for Alberto Cantino, envoy of the Duke of Ferrara to the court of Portugal, who ordered it for his ducal master from a map maker in Lisbon, probably an Italian. The information on it was probably derived from an earlier map or maps, although certain supplementary information in cursive writing may have come from Amerigo Vespucci (see Harrisse, *Discovery of North America*, pp. 422–425). The original map is now in the Reale Biblioteca Estense, Modena, Italy. It is a planisphere, manuscript, world map on vellum, colored and gilt. It is now faded, and the left-hand margin is missing. It is not graduated for latitude and longitude.

The section reproduced is from a photograph made for E. L. Stevenson, *Maps Illustrating Early Discovery and Exploration in America, 1502–1530*, New Brunswick, 1903–1906, map No. 1. The reduction is about ten-seventeenths.

The *Atlas* reproduction shows part of the northern coast of South America, the West Indies, part of the coast of what is now the United States, and a detached land mass labeled "Terra del Rey de portuguall" (only the first word showing on the reproduction), to the northeastward, which is thought to represent Newfoundland. The tropic of Cancer (heavy line) and the Line of Demarcation of the Treaty of Tordesillas (double lines) are readily identified, as are also Cuba, Jamaica, Haiti, and Porto Rico. On the North American mainland are twenty-two names.

About no other early map on which North America is depicted has there probably been so much controversy as about the Cantino Map. It has been suggested that its prototype was based in part upon the results of one or more clandestine Portuguese voyages. It is certainly based in part upon the Cortereal voyages. The Cantino Map and the family of maps to which it belongs undoubtedly portray a new land distinct from Asia, and they had much influence upon early American cartography.

[1] The American Geographical Society of New York possesses and has on exhibit a reproduction of the globe made by pasting Ravenstein's gores on a sphere of the correct size.

La Cosa Map, 1500

[PLATE 10]

The La Cosa Map is the earliest known map on which is depicted any part of the Western World. Obviously it is of prime importance for the history and cartography of America. It was found in 1832 by Baron Walckenaer in a Paris shop. It was acquired by the Spanish government in 1853 and is now in the Museo Naval, Madrid. It is a manuscript map of the world in colors and is drawn on parchment. Its size is about 71 by 38 inches (see Harrisse, *Discovery*, pp. 90–92 and 412–415).

La Cosa was regarded as the best map maker and as one of the best navigators of his time. He accompanied Columbus on the first voyage as master of the flagship. On the second voyage he was the official cartographer. In 1499 he accompanied Ojeda as chief pilot and made his map soon after his return from that voyage. The American features of the map are therefore based in large part upon La Cosa's own experiences.

As on many other early maps, the northeastern coast of North America is unduly prolonged. The map is not graduated for latitude and longitude. Harrisse expressed a doubt whether this is the original La Cosa map or a copy by a contemporary.

The section reproduced is from Jomard's *Les Monuments de la Géographie*, Paris, 1864, Pl. 16, Nos. 1–3, which is an excellent and slightly reduced facsimile, partly redrawn. The reduction is about four-sevenths. It shows the North American coast and outlying islands and portions of South America, Africa, and Europe. The white spots in North and South America are caused by holes in the original map.

The tropic of Cancer, the equator, and the prime meridian are easily recognizable by their prominence and by their designations. The lighter lines parallel to these, although they connect rose-compass centers, may be parallels and meridians. It has been suggested that the prime meridian was intended to coincide with the Line of Demarcation of the Treaty of Tordesillas, 1494. The main rose compass of La Cosa's map is cut by the tropic of Cancer. Off the coast of South America and the West Indian Islands are flags of Castile, and off the coast of North America is the English flag.

The attempts made to identify points on the North American coast are unsatisfactory. The inscription "mar descubierta por ynglese" (sea discovered by the English), together with other evidence, proves that La Cosa knew of Cabot's discoveries. Most of the names along the American coast do not appear on later maps. The islands of Cuba and "laespanola" (Haiti) are laid down with fair accuracy.

La Cosa's map is not a type or mother map; indeed, its effect on the cartography of the period appears to have been slight. It is, however, of great importance in the cartographical history of America, whether its maker intended to depict a part of Asia or a new continent.

Maggiolo Map, ca. 1519

[PLATE 11A]

The original manuscript of this anonymous Portuguese map, about 49 by 24 inches, is preserved in the Königlichen Bayerischen Hof- und Staatsbibliothek, Munich. It is neither signed nor dated. The equator and the Line of Demarcation are indicated by lines composed of circles (see Harrisse, *Discovery*, p. 508).

The section reproduced, reduction about five-elevenths, is from Plate 4 of Kunstmann, Spruner, and Thomas, *Atlas zur Entdeckungsgeschichte Amerikas*, Munich, 1859, which is a reproduction in colors of the western part of the original manuscript. It is noteworthy for its somewhat detailed representation of the eastern coast of North America. To the northward of the Florida region, which is called "Tera Bimini," there is a northeast extension of coast, then a break, then the coast of "Bacalnaos," corresponding in part possibly to the Maine coast, and, lastly, the coast of "Do Lavrador." The deep indentation on the coast of Bacalnaos may correspond to the Gulf of St. Lawrence. This is the first known map to note Balboa's discovery of the Pacific Ocean, which it does by means of the inscription "Mar visto pelos Castelhanos" (sea seen by the Castilians). The Spanish and Portuguese flags show the claims of these nationalities. Harrisse attempts to trace some of the information on this map to Columbus.

Ortelius Map, 1589

[PLATE 11B]

The original of this map, about 19 by 13 inches, was engraved on copper in 1589 and first published, in colors, in Ortelius, *Additamentum IV, Theatri Orbis Terrarum*, Antwerp, 1590. It is described in its title as the "most recent delineation of the Pacific Sea [which is commonly called the South Sea], with the neighboring regions and the islands scattered in various places in it." It is the first map to designate the two Americas by the names "North" and "South." The prime meridian passes near the west coast of Africa.

The section reproduced, with a reduction of about four-sevenths, is from Ortelius, *Theatrum Orbis Terrarum*, Antwerp, 1595, in which is a copy of the map, uncolored. Since the nomenclature is Spanish, doubtless the sources also are Spanish. The west coast is rather well depicted. The sharp turn to the west and then to the north above California is found on the maps of this region for many years and is a characteristic of the Mercator-Ortelius type.

De Soto Map, ca. 1544
[PLATE 12A]

The original of this map, about 23 by 17 inches, is in the Archives of the Indies, Seville. It is an anonymous, undated, manuscript map and was made to exhibit the explorations of De Soto and Moscoso, 1539–1543 (see Harrisse, *Discovery*, pp. 634–644).

The entire map is reproduced from Harrisse's *Discovery of North America*, p. 644, with a reduction of rather more than one-half. It shows the coast and interior of the Southern States between Georgia and Texas, and possibly part of some of the states bordering on this region. Many new names make their appearance. Twenty-one rivers are represented as emptying into the Gulf or the Atlantic. Among these is the "R del espiritu Santo," which is either the Mississippi or the Mobile. The large lake in the northeast may be the Okefenokee Swamp, in southern Georgia. Indian villages within the present United States are mapped for the first time. In the Texas region the inscription "en estas," etc., may be translated "In these mountains there are silver mines"; and the longer inscription to the northward thereof, "From Quivira to this point there are numerous herds of cattle"—probably the first mention on a map of buffalo.

This map marks an epoch in the history of the cartography of the United States, for it is the first graphic representation of any part of the interior of that country.

Gastaldi Map, 1546
[PLATE 12B]

The original of this map, about 21 by 13 inches, entitled "Universale," is by the celebrated Italian cosmographer Giácomo Gastaldi. It is a copperplate map of the world and was published in Venice in 1546. A copy in the Vossius Collection, library of the University of Leyden, was reproduced by Frederik Muller in Part IV of his *Remarkable Maps*, Amsterdam, 1897. The prime meridian cuts the west coast of Africa.

The section reproduced, original size, is from Muller's reproduction. Its chief feature is the blending of North America with Asia. On the west coast the Gulf of California is shown, with a "Colorado River" penetrating Asia. In this region are found the "Seven Cities" of the early Spanish explorers. Spanish sources of information were doubtless used for this part of the map. In the St. Lawrence region a knowledge of Cartier's explorations is indicated. The Gastaldi Map served as a model for many years.

Verrazano Map, 1529
[PLATE 13]

The original of this map, about 102 by 51 inches, a sea chart of the world on parchment, much faded and stained, is in the Museo Borgia, Propaganda Fide, Rome. It was drawn by Hieronymo Verrazano, brother of the navigator. The tropics and the equator are laid down. The degrees of latitude are along a line passing through the Canary Islands, which may have been intended for a prime meridian. Their position is so erroneous they may be disregarded. There are no degrees of longitude on the map (see Harrisse, *Discovery*, pp. 575–577).

The larger reproduction (approximately same scale as original), entitled "Verrazano Map, 1529," is from a photographic copy of the original made for E. L. Stevenson, *Maps Illustrating Early Discovery and Exploration in America, 1502–1530*, New Brunswick, 1903–1906, map No. 12. It shows many stains, notably the large one extending northward from western Florida. Some of the fainter place names of the original do not appear on the reproduction. The inset, which omits many details, is from a map based on photographs of the original and published in H. C. Murphy's *Voyage of Verrazano*, New York, 1875, p. 186. It is valuable for its outline of the coasts.

The Atlantic coast line of this map, which extends northeastward as far as Labrador, is of the Sevillan type (so called because the first maps of this type were made at Seville), and the Pacific coast line (best seen on the inset) is of the type of the Maggiolo Map (Pl. 11A). This is the first Italian map on which the designation "America" appears (see inset, northern part of South America). The language of the map is

Italian. The relative excellence of the delineation of the region of the Isthmus of Panama is worthy of note. The delineation of Verrazano's discoveries is one of the most important features of the map. Thirty-three new names are found on the Newfoundland and northeast coast. Newfoundland ("Terra nova sive Limo Lve"—see inset) is part of the mainland. The map had an important influence on American cartography.

Harleian Map, ca. 1536
[PLATE 14A]

The original of this map, about 98 by 47 inches, is preserved in the British Museum (Additional Manuscripts 5413). It is supposed to be the work of Pierre Desceliers and is the earliest known map of the Dieppe school (see C. H. Coote, *Autotype Facsimiles of Three Mappemondes*, Aberdeen, 1898, pp. 8–10).

The section reproduced, reduction about eleven twentieths, is from the reproduction in H. P. Biggar, *The Voyages of Jacques Cartier* (Publications of the Public Archives of Canada No. 11), Ottawa, 1924, Pl. 8. Its most significant feature is its representation of the St. Lawrence region, where an attempt is made to portray the discoveries of Cartier. The names "Canada" and "Sagne" (Saguenay) make their appearance. With the exception of this region the map is mainly after the Verrazano model (Pl. 13). The peculiar shape of the large "continental" land area northeast of Florida is characteristic of the Dieppe school. The nomenclature is mainly French.

Hakluyt Map, 1587
[PLATE 14B]

This map, about 8 by 6 inches, entitled "Novus Orbis," was first published in Hakluyt's annotated edition of Peter Martyr, *De Orbe Novo*, Paris, 1587. As the prime meridian passes through Toledo, Spain, it may be inferred that the map was drawn by a Spaniard or after Spanish models.

The section reproduced, enlargement about two-thirds, is from the reproduction of this map, in Richard Hakluyt, *The Principal Navigations*, etc. (Hakluyt Soc. Publs., Extra Ser., Vol. 8), Glasgow, 1904, opp. p. 272. Part of Asia is shown near the left-hand border. The northwestern coast line of North America is left unfinished, which indicates uncertainty. The mainlands of North America and Asia are continuous but devoid of nomenclature. The shape of North America and the trend of its coasts are well depicted. The east coast is of the Mercator type.

Mercator Map, 1569
[PLATE 15]

The original of this map, about 79 by 52 inches, was engraved by Gerard Mercator and published by him at Duisberg, Germany, in 1569. It is one of the most celebrated maps in the history of cartography. Mercator broke with Ptolemaic tradition and employed a new projection, the increased-cylindrical, or Mercator, projection. It is especially well adapted to marine charts. The parallels and meridians are straight lines and cross each other at right angles.

The Mercator Map is a sea chart of the world and is, according to its title, "A new and enlarged delineation of the land of the globe, perfectly adapted for the use of pilots." The prime meridian passes through the Island of Ferro.

The section reproduced, reduction about one-half, is from the facsimile of a copy of the original in the Stadtbibliothek, Breslau, Germany, which was published in *Drei Karten von Gerard Mercator*, Berlin, 1891. Parts of six sheets have been reproduced and joined together. The heavy line near the right-hand margin is the Line of Demarcation.

Among the important features of this map, apart from its projection, is its delineation of the form of North America (fairly good), of a great interior valley lying between the Atlantic and Pacific slopes, and of the St. Lawrence River system. There is a hint of the Great Lakes in the "fresh-water sea" and the three small lakes near thereto. Mercator did not slavishly copy his sources of information but used them constructively. They included maps showing the results of French exploration in the northeast and Spanish exploration in the southwest. The long inscription entitled "Inspectori S." describes the objects of the author in making the map and especially its unusual projection.

Mercator's map together with maps of Ortelius established a type which long prevailed and exercised great influence upon the cartography of North America.

Lemoyne Map, 1591
[PLATE 16]

The original of this map, about 18 by 14 inches, is found, opposite p. 1, in Theodor de Bry's *Brevis Narratio eorum quae in Florida Americae Provin-*

cia Gallis acciderunt, Frankfort-on-Main, 1591, which is the second part of his *Grands Voyages*. It is by Jacques le Moyne de Morgues, who accompanied Laudonnière's expedition to Florida. It shows the results of this expedition. The nomenclature is Latin. The original title appearing in the cartouche may be translated, "Recent and most exact delineation of Florida, a province of America." The map is not graduated for longitudes.

Plate 16, reduction about five-seventeenths, is from the reproduction found in Richard Hakluyt, *The Principal Navigations*, etc. (Hakluyt Soc. Publs., Extra Ser., Vol. 9), Glasgow, 1904, opp. p. 112. It is a map of the coast and interior of what is now Florida and the adjacent regions. The Appalachian Mountains receive their proper designation. The lake labeled "Sarrope" may be Lake Okeechobee; the larger lake to the northward, Lake George, and its outlet, St. Johns River. The royal arms of Spain and France are shown at the top of the map.

The Lemoyne Map became an important type map and served as a source for many later cartographers.

Cortés Map, 1520
[PLATE 17A]

The original manuscript of this sketch map, about 7 by 8 inches, was sent to Spain with the second letter of Cortés, dated October 30, 1520. It is now lost. A woodcut of it (on a plate with a plan of the City of Mexico), with a Latin edition of the letter entitled *Praeclara Ferdinandi Cortesii de Nova Maris Oceani Hyspania Narratio*, was printed at Nuremberg in 1524, without title, date, or name of author.

The reproduction, reduction three-sevenths, is from a copy in the Library of Congress (Lowery Collection, map 21). On the original South is at the top (see P. L. Phillips, *Lowery Collection*, pp. 26–28).

This map shows the entire Gulf coast and the western end of Cuba. It is rich in nomenclature. Twenty-one of its twenty-five names are also found on the Turin Map (Pl. 17B). It had considerable influence upon the cartography of the Gulf of Mexico.

Turin Map, ca. 1523
[PLATE 17B]

The original of this world map, about 79 by 39 inches, drawn on parchment, in colors, is preserved in the Royal Library of Turin. Its legends and names are in Spanish, Latin, and Portuguese. Its author and date are unknown. It is graduated for latitude and longitude, but the parallels and meridians are not drawn. The prime meridian if drawn would pass near the Island of Ferro. The North American coast above Florida is not shown (see Harrisse, *Discovery*, pp. 528–533).

The section reproduced, reduction from original about three-fifths, is from Harrisse's reproduction, which is not a facsimile. Florida is represented as an island. Westward of the mouth of the Mississippi River the coast line of the Gulf of Mexico is continuous. For richness and exactness of nomenclature this is one of the best of the early maps, and Harrisse says that many names are taken from early and authentic sources. The line near the bottom is the equator.

Vizcaino Map, 1603
[PLATE 17C]

The original of this map of Upper and Lower California, about 14 by 14 inches, is No. 4 of the *Atlas para el Viage de las Goletas Sutil y Mexicana*, Madrid, 1802, by N. F. de Navarrete. In 1602–1603 Sebastian Vizcaino surveyed this region and made plans of it, thirty-two in number. From these Navarrete made his map, a faithful, reduced copy of the originals. They were at one time in the archives of New Spain. Copies of them made in 1603 are now in the Archives of the Indies at Seville.

The section of the above-mentioned map that is reproduced, reduction about two-sevenths, extends from a point north of Cape Mendocino to a point south of San Diego. The coast is rather accurately delineated. The indentation at "Pto. de los Reyes" is San Francisco Bay. The nomenclature is similar to that on earlier maps of this region. The complete word of which four letters are shown is "Californias."

Molineaux-Wright Map, 1600
[PLATE 17D]

This map, about 25 by 17 inches, is found in Richard Hakluyt's *Principal Navigations*, London, 1600, Vol. 1. It is engraved on copper and is without title and date. It may have been first published in 1599 as a loose map. The map is here named for Emerie Molineaux, its maker according to some authorities, and Edward Wright, who improved

Mercator's projection and to whom also the map has been attributed. It is the first world map on the Wright-Mercator projection that was engraved in England. The map is also known as the "New Map of Shakespeare," as it is supposed to be the "new map with the augmentation of the Indies," mentioned by the poet in *Twelfth Night*, Act III, Scene 2. The prime meridian passes near the eastern part of the Cape Verde Islands. It is graduated for longitude.

The section reproduced, with a slight reduction, is from Richard Hakluyt, *The Principal Navigations*, etc. (Hakluyt Soc. Publs., Extra Ser., Vol. 1), Glasgow, 1903, opp. p. 356. The Strait of Anian is omitted (on the authority of Francisco de Gali, a Spanish captain, who made a voyage in the Pacific in 1583), and the west coast is stopped at New Albion, which was visited by Drake. The northern discoveries of Frobisher and Davis, which are shown, may have been delineated by Davis himself. "The Lake of Tadouac" suggests the Great Lakes. The sources of information appear to be numerous. The following comparisons between this and other maps should be made: the region of the Gulf of Mexico, with the Lemoyne Map (Pl. 16); the Great Lakes region, with the Mercator of 1569 (Pl. 15) and Hakluyt of 1587 (Pl. 14B); and the west coast, with the Hakluyt Map of 1587.

Tattonus Map, 1600
[PLATE 17E]

The original of this map, about 21 by 16 inches, was engraved on copper, in 1600, by the English engraver Benjamin Wright and was published by the famous hydrographer M. Tattonus. According to its title, it is a "New and recent delineation of the lands and kingdoms of California, New Spain, Mexico, and Peru, together with an exact and accurate delineation of the shores of the Gulf of Mexico to the Island of Cuba and of the seacoast as far as the South Sea."

All the upper part of the map is reproduced, reduction about one-third. The coast of the Gulf of Mexico, the drainage to the northward thereof, and the western part of the map are from Spanish sources. The map is noteworthy for its delineation of the western country. It is one of the earliest maps with the name "California" on the peninsula and one of the earliest engraved by an Englishman.

Smith Map, 1612
[PLATE 18A]

The original of this map, about 16 by 13 inches, is in Dr. William Simmonds, *A Map of Virginia, with a Description of the Countrey, the Commodities, People, Government and Religion, written by Captain Smith, sometimes Governour of the Countrey*, Oxford, 1612. It is probable that Smith furnished the manuscript drawing for this map, but did not make it himself. The map has been frequently republished, with additions and corrections. The prime meridian is probably that of the Island of Ferro (see Alexander Brown, *Genesis of the United States*, Vol. 2, pp. 596–597; Winsor, *Narrative and Critical History*, Vol. 3, pp. 167–168).

The whole map is reproduced from a reproduction in *The Works of Captain John Smith*, edited by Edward Arber, Birmingham, 1884, opp. p. 384. The reduction is about three-tenths. West is at the top. The map shows Chesapeake Bay and the surrounding region and is based largely upon Smith's explorations. The rivers emptying into Chesapeake Bay from the west, beginning with the James ("Powhatan"), will be readily identified. Beneath the original title, "Virginia," are the English arms; and near the lower right-hand corner, Smith's arms. In the upper right-hand corner is a legend explaining the symbols on the map.

Smith's map is a mother map for Virginia.

Champlain Map, 1612
[PLATE 18B]

This map, about 30 by 17 inches, was published in *Les Voyages du Sieur Champlain Xaintongeois*, Paris, 1613. It is a sea chart, dated 1612, and made, as Champlain explains, "for the greater convenience of those who navigate on these coasts" (inscription in upper left-hand corner) and "according to the compasses of France, which vary to the northeast." It is a map of prime importance, since for the first time the New England coast and the St. Lawrence region are delineated with fair accuracy. For this region there is no map of equal significance since Cartier's discoveries were laid down.

The section reproduced, reduction about five-eighths, is from C. H. Laverdière, *Oeuvres de Champlain*, Vol. 3, Quebec, 1870, opp. p. 326. It shows the coast line between Labrador and Vineyard Sound (northwest of Marthas Vineyard). Among the identifications that have been made are the following. On the Maine coast the four rivers west of

"R de St. Iehon" (St. John) are, respectively, the St. Croix, Penobscot, Kennebec, and Saco. On the Massachusetts coast, "baeu [sic] port" is Gloucester; "R du gas," the Charles River; "C. blan," Cape Cod; "Malle barre," Nauset Harbor; and "soupsonnouse," Marthas Vineyard. In the St. Lawrence basin one can readily identify Richelieu River, Lake Champlain, the Thousand Islands, and Lake Ontario. For the western and southwestern part of his map Champlain depended upon reports of the Indians, and for this reason the delineation of this region is more or less conjectural. The two lakes in southern New York correspond to two of the finger lakes. The large lake on the western margin corresponds to Lake Huron, although it is wrongly connected by a river with Lake Ontario. Lake Erie is not delineated. The words "sault de au" (waterfall) near an unnamed river are believed to refer to Niagara Falls. If so, this is the first indication of the falls on any map.

This map marks the beginning of the delineation of the interior of North America along the line of the St. Lawrence basin. It was considerably used by map makers, serving as the prototype for a part of De Laet's map of 1630 (Pl. 21).

Smith Map, 1616
[PLATE 19A]

The original of this map, about 14 by 12 inches, engraved on copper, is found in *A Description of New England: or the Observations, and Discoveries, of Captain Iohn Smith (Admirall of that Country), in the North of America, in the year of our Lord, 1614*, London, 1616. This map is based upon Smith's explorations and surveys. It was frequently republished, with changes, and is known to exist in ten states of the plate (see Winsor, *Memorial History of Boston*, Vol. 1, pp. 52–56).

The reproduction is of the whole map, reduction about five-fourteenths, and is from the reproduction in *The Works of Captain John Smith*, edited by Edward Arber, Birmingham, 1884, opp. p. 694. The coast between the region of Cape Cod and the mouth of the Penobscot River is shown with considerable detail and accuracy. Many New England names appear for the first time on a map. The reproduction should be compared with the Champlain Map, 1612 (Pl. 18B).

Smith's map was a considerable improvement over all previous delineations of the New England coast and for many years served as a mother map. It was used as a source for maps as late as the second quarter of the eighteenth century.

Champlain Map, 1632
[PLATE 19B]

This map, about 34 by 21 inches, was first published in Champlain, *Les Voyages de la Nouvelle France Occidentale, dicte Canada*, Paris, 1632. It was prepared for publication as early as 1629. It is described as a "Map of New France, with additions since the last map, useful for navigation, made on its true meridian" (inscription in lower left-hand corner). The prime meridian is about five degrees west of that of the Champlain Map of 1612. The map of 1632 extends much farther to the west and southwest than the map of 1612. It is generally more detailed, but the delineations are not always improvements.

In reproducing this map (from reproduction in C. H. Laverdière, *Oeuvres de Champlain*, Vol. 5, Quebec, 1870, opp. p. 1385) the original is cut on the north and is reduced about seven-thirteenths. The chief feature of the reproduction is the delineation of the Great Lakes region, based, westward of Lake Ontario, largely upon reports of the Indians and upon conjecture. Champlain had explored as far west as Georgian Bay. "Mer douce" is Lake Huron; and the lake northeast thereof, Lake Nipissing. "Grand lac" corresponds to Lake Superior; and the broad river south of "Mer douce" to Lake Erie. Niagara Falls is pictured near the figure "90."

The Atlantic coast east of the Penobscot is rather accurately delineated. Champlain had explored that coast as far south as "Rivière de Champlain." Farther south he depended entirely on the work of others. Chesapeake Bay, Delaware River, Hudson River (with the Mohawk running in from the north), Long Island ("Isle de l'Ascension"), and the three Connecticut rivers to the northward thereof will be readily identified. The adjoining Rhode Island coast may be distinguished, although poorly delineated. As on most early maps, the proportions are bad. Thus the St. Lawrence River and Lake Champlain are too near the New England coast, Lake Champlain is too large, etc.

The figures and letters on the map refer to an extensive legend which will be found in the above-mentioned book following the map, pp. 1–7.

The importance of Champlain's maps of 1612 and 1632 for the study of the cartography of the Great Lakes region is evident. The map of 1632 appears to have circulated more widely and therefore to have had greater influence. It was used by Sanson and many other cartographers.

Hondius Map, 1630
[PLATE 20A]

This map of America, about 10 by 7 inches, by Henricus Hondius was published in Mercator's *Atlas*, Amsterdam, 1630, p. 19. The prime meridian passes through the Cape Verde Islands. The section reproduced, enlarged about one-third, is from the above-mentioned *Atlas*. The craftsmanship of the map is crude. In the lake sources of the St. Lawrence River there is a suggestion of the Great Lakes.

Sanson Map, 1656
[PLATE 20B]

This map, about 21 by 16 inches, entitled "Le Canada ou Nouvelle France," was published in Paris in 1656 as a loose map. It is by Nicolas Sanson, royal geographer and the leading French cartographer in the latter half of the seventeenth century. Beneath the title is an explanation, which may be translated thus: "The part farthest north is taken from various relations of the English, Danes, etc. Toward the south, the coasts of Virginia, New Sweden, New Netherland, and New England, are taken from relations by the English, Dutch, etc. The Great River of Canada, or the St. Lawrence, and all its environs are from the relations of the French." The prime meridian is probably that of the Island of Ferro.

In reproducing this map the original is cut on the north and east and reduced rather more than three-tenths. The chief feature of the reproduction is the delineation of the Great Lakes (including Lake St. Clair and Georgian Bay), now for the first time mapped in approximately their correct position. Lake Superior and Lake Michigan ("Lac de Puans") are unfinished for lack of information. The territory in the vicinity of the Great Lakes is mapped either from Indian reports or from conjecture. The names of tribes are numerous, some of them appearing on a map for the first time. Worthy of note are the Atlantic coast line and drainage, the boundary lines separating colonial possessions, and the delineation of the New York lakes. Niagara Falls is correctly placed. The blank area west of the Great Lakes is suggestive of the limits of contemporary geographical knowledge.

The influence of Champlain on Sanson is evident. Sanson generally improved on the work of his predecessor but not always. His map became a type map and greatly influenced cartographers. He remained an authority until superseded by Delisle (see Pls. 23A, 24).

Jesuit Map, 1672
[PLATE 20C]

This map, about 19 by 14 inches, was first published in the *Relation* of 1670–1671, Paris, 1672. It was drawn to illustrate the Jesuit missions in the northwest "by two Fathers of considerable intelligence, much given to research, and very exact, who determined to set down nothing that they had not seen with their own eyes" (R. G. Thwaites, *Jesuit Relations*, Vol. 54, p. 255). These two fathers were probably Marquette and Allouez. They may have drawn their map as early as 1669, and additions may have been made up to the date of publication.

The reproduction, reduction a little more than one-half, is from the reproduction in Thwaites, *Jesuit Relations*, Vol. 55, opp. p. 94. It is the earliest map of a complete Lake Superior. Details are delineated with considerable accuracy, and the engraving is excellent. Most of the places may be easily identified. The most southerly lake in Wisconsin is Lake Winnebago, and the large island in Lake Huron is Grand Manitou Island.

This map became the type for succeeding maps, many of which are inferior to it. A long period elapsed before the region to the westward of the Great Lakes was equally well mapped.

Raffeix Map, 1688
[PLATE 20D]

The manuscript original of this map, about 24 by 15 inches, is in the geographical section of the Bibliothèque Nationale, Paris. It is a rough sketch map, which has the appearance of having been cut along the upper and lower margins.

This map is reproduced, reduction from the original rather more than one-half, from Marcel's atlas, *Reproductions de Cartes et de Globes*, Paris, 1893, No. 36. The river courses are generalized, and the main eastern tributaries of the Mississippi are drawn roughly parallel to each other. The two upper tributaries may be the Rum and St. Croix rivers; and the river flowing into the western end of Lake Superior, the Brule River. Lake Michigan is of the pointed type, and Lake Erie of the flat type (in contradistinction to the tilted type). The New York tributary of

Lake Ontario is supposed to be the Genesee. The results of the French explorers are shown by means of letters, which are explained by the "Remarques" at the bottom of the map.

De Laet Map, 1630
[PLATE 21]

The original of this map, about 14 by 11 inches, engraved on copper, is in Joannes de Laet, *Beschrijvinghe van West-Indien*, Leyden, 1630, p. 88. The entire map, including an inset of Bermuda, is reproduced from this book, reduction about one-eighth. The southern coast shows the influence of Smith's map (Pl. 18A); and the northern that of Smith and Champlain (see Pls. 18B, 19A, 19B). The central region is evidently copied from Dutch charts. The Delaware River ("Zuyd Rivier"), Lake Ontario ("Grand Lac"), Lake Champlain, and the Bay of Fundy are easily identified. The nomenclature of the map is a mixture of English, Dutch, French, and Indian. Many Indian settlements are named.

This map presents an excellent general view of the geographical knowledge of 1630. Other contemporary maps, however, are better for details. The general features of the coast between the Gulf of Mexico and Newfoundland were well known by this time.

Delisle Map, 1700
[PLATE 22A]

This map, about 24 by 18 inches, partly colored, was published at Paris in 1700 as a loose map. Its author, Guillaume Delisle, was the royal geographer of France and the foremost cartographer of his time. It is entitled "L'Amérique Septentrionale, dressée sur les Observations de Mrs. de l'Académie Royale des Sciences et quelques autres et sur les Mémoires les plus Récens." It marks an epoch in the history of American cartography. The prime meridian passes to the eastward of the Azores.

The section of this map reproduced (from reproduction published in connection with the *Report of the Labrador Boundary Committee*, London, 1927), reduction about one-half, presents both the coasts and the interior more correctly than does any previous map. It long served as a mother map. No attempt was made to delineate the then-unknown northwest. The delineation of the St. Lawrence and Mississippi basins should be compared with the delineations of these regions shown on Plates 18B, 19B, 20B, and 20C. Rivers, such as the Missouri and Colorado, will be readily identified from their positions.

The delineation of the Great Lakes, which is good, is based partly on Sanson (Pl. 20B). The rather unusual location of "Quivira" may be noted. The attempt to lay down interior boundary lines was relatively new.

Gentil Map, ca. 1700
[PLATE 22B]

The manuscript original of this map, about 11 by 9 inches, is in the Département des Cartes, Bibliothèque Nationale, Paris. It is attributed to the Abbé Gentil, who may have drawn it from manuscript "relations" and other information in his possession. Latitudes may be roughly calculated from the position of the tropic of Cancer.

The entire map is reproduced, reduction of the original about one-fourth, from Marcel's atlas, *Reproductions de Cartes et de Globes*, Paris, 1893, No. 17, first map. It delineates with considerable detail and fair accuracy the region of the lower Mississippi and of the coast of the United States between the Rio Grande ("Bravo ou del Nord") and a point on the Carolina coast. The mouths of the Mississippi and the Mobile ("Mobila") are well placed with respect to each other. The large western tributary of the Mississippi corresponds to the Red River. The large black spot near its mouth is apparently an ink stain. The dotted parallel lines in the southwest show La Salle's route.

Delisle Map, 1703
[PLATE 23A]

The original of this map, about 25 by 20 inches, partly colored, was first published at Paris in 1703. It is found as a loose map and also in bound collections of Delisle's maps. It is entitled "Carte du Canada ou de la Nouvelle France et des Découvertes qui y ont été faites." It is based on many printed and manuscript "relations." The prime meridian is probably that of the Island of Ferro.

The reproduction, reduction about one-fourth, is of the southern part of the original. Its most important features are its wealth of details and nomenclature and its delineation of the interior west of the Great Lakes. The delineation of the Mississippi River is superior to that of Delisle's map of 1700 (Pl. 22A). For the Minnesota region, Hennepin's map of

1683, Le Sueur's explorations, and reports of the Indians were used. Most of the principal tributaries of the Mississippi are readily identified, and with these determined the lesser ones may be conjectured. The "R. des Panis," a tributary of the Missouri, is the Platte. The southwestern part of the map is based upon the fictions of La Hontan, reports of the Indians, and conjecture. The "Riviere longue" or "Riviere Morte" is from La Hontan. The mountain range and the salt lake are suggestive, respectively, of the Rocky Mountains and the Great Salt Lake.

The Great Lakes are an improvement over Delisle's map of 1700. In general the Atlantic coast is well depicted. The English colonies are delineated with more detail than on earlier French maps. The Merrimac River is given an erroneous source in Lake Champlain. Dotted lines represent boundary lines or routes of travel.

In many respects the Delisle Map is an improvement on earlier maps. It is a mother map, and because of its excellence and the reputation of its distinguished author it served as a model long after new discoveries and explorations had rendered some of its information obsolete.

Delisle Map, ca. 1750
[PLATE 23B]

This map by Guillaume Delisle, about 23 by 19 inches, is found in Covens and Mortier, *Nieuwe Atlas*, Amsterdam, *ca.* 1750, No. 59. It is undated and is here dated approximately from the undated *Atlas* in which it appears. Its French title may be translated "America accurately divided into its Empires, States, and Peoples, for the use of Louis XV, King of the French." The map may be a revision of Delisle's "Carte d'Amérique" of 1722. The prime meridian passes through the Island of Ferro.

The section reproduced, reduction about one-ninth, is from the above-mentioned *Atlas*. It shows the central and southern part of North America. The geography of the Far West of the United States was still almost unknown.

Bellin Map, 1743
[PLATE 23C]

This map, about 14 by 11 inches, entitled "L'Amérique Septentrionale," was first published in Charlevoix's *Histoire et Description Générale de la Nouvelle France*, Paris, 1744, Vol. 1, p. 1, for which work it was drawn. Bellin was one of three leading French cartographers of the eighteenth century, the other two, Delisle and d'Anville, being rather the more celebrated. The prime meridian is that of Paris.

The section reproduced, approximately original size, is from the edition of Charlevoix which bears the imprint "Chez la Veuve Ganeau." It is based in large part upon Delisle and later information. The California peninsula follows Kino's map of 1705. In showing a water connection between Hudson Bay and the Pacific Ocean, Bellin accepted a current belief. He doubtless was influenced by the explorations of the Vérendryes. His delineation of the Ohio River is an improvement over the work of earlier cartographers.

Bellin's map is one of the mother maps of the middle of the eighteenth century. Carefully drawn and possessing much merit, it had a wide circulation.

Delisle Map, 1718
[PLATE 24]

This map, about 26 by 19 inches, partly colored, was published at Paris in 1718 as a loose map. An inset in the lower right-hand corner gives a more detailed delineation of the region of the lower Mississippi and lower Mobile rivers. Le Maire, who is referred to in the title, was a Parisian priest of the Maison et Séminaire des Missions Étrangères. One of his "relations" is accompanied by a map which was used by Delisle. The prime meridian probably passes through the Island of Ferro.

The entire map is reproduced from a copy in the Library of Congress, reduction five-ninths. It is notable for the many details that are delineated and their relative accuracy. Attention may be called to the improvement in the delineation of the region of the lower Mississippi and Gulf of Mexico, of the Atlantic coast line, and of the Missouri River and its tributaries. Many streams are well drawn in respect to their lower courses and poorly in respect to their upper courses, which are based upon conjecture. The absence of precise information respecting the upper Ohio, Cumberland, and Tennessee rivers is most obvious. The routes of explorers and the other historical information that are found on the map possess considerable interest. The route in the southwest near the coast is that of Alonso de León, 1689. For the region of the Gulf of Mexico the Delisle Map long remained a model for cartographers.

Müller Map, 1754

[PLATE 25A]

This map, about 25 by 18 inches, entitled "Nouvelle Carte des Découvertes faites par des Vaisseaux Russes aux Côtes Inconnues de l'Amérique Septentrionale avec Pais Adiacents," was published by the Imperial Academy of Sciences at St. Petersburg in 1754. Its author, unnamed on the map, is Gerhard Friedrich Müller, a German scientist, long a resident of Russia and a member of Bering's second expedition. The map is drawn on a polar projection. Its prime meridian passes through the Island of Ferro.

The section of this map reproduced, with a reduction of about one-half, is from the reproduction in *Voyages from Asia to America, for completing the Discoveries of the North West Coast of America*, transl. and edited by Thomas Jefferys, London, 1761, opp. title page. It shows the Alaskan region and the adjacent part of Asia. For the Alaskan region Müller depended chiefly upon the discoveries of Bering's second expedition, 1741-1742. The part of the coast line that is based upon conjecture is dotted. The author rejected the so-called discoveries of Admiral de Fonte. The inscription on the northern coast of Siberia relates to another fictitious exploration. The date "1730" on the American side of Bering strait should, it is believed, be 1732.

Müller's map had considerable influence on the cartography of Alaska.

Vancouver Map, 1798

[PLATE 25B]

This map, about 24 by 31 inches, entitled "A Chart shewing Part of the Coast of N.W. America ... prepared ... by Lieut. Edwd. Roberts," was published in the *Atlas* (Pl. 14) accompanying Captain George Vancouver, *A Voyage of Discovery to the North Pacific Ocean and round the World*, London, 1798. It is laid down on Mercator's projection. The prime meridian is that of Greenwich.

The section reproduced, reduction about three-eighths, is from the upper part of the map and covers the most northwesterly part of the North American coast that was surveyed by Vancouver. The lines indicating the route of the expedition are scarcely distinguishable on the reproduction. The route for 1793 comes from the south and passes around the Prince of Wales Archipelago (near the southeastern margin of the map). The route of 1794 begins at Tscherikows Island (on the western margin of the map) and passes northward and thence eastward.

The coast covered in the reproduction is based largely upon Vancouver's explorations. The extreme southwestern portion, however, is partly from Russian authorities, and the extreme southeastern portion partly from Spanish authorities. Vancouver changed somewhat the earlier nomenclature of this region and added to it. His explorations made evident that no water passage between the Pacific Ocean and Hudson Bay existed. On account of its many accurate details and of its wide use this map marks a distinct advance in the development of Alaskan cartography.

Evans Map, 1755

[PLATE 26]

This map, about 26 by 19 inches, is found in Lewis Evans, *Analysis of a Map of the Middle British Colonies in America*, 2nd edition, Philadelphia, 1755. The prime meridian passes through Philadelphia. The figures on the bottom margin indicate the longitude west of the meridian of London.

The entire map is reproduced from the reproduction in H. N. Stevens, *Lewis Evans: his Map of the Middle British Colonies in America*, London, 1920, map No. 2 at end of volume. The reduction is about one-third. The main map shows the northeastern part of the present United States, between a meridian passing through a point west of the falls of the Ohio and one passing through a point east of Narragansett Bay, together with the adjacent part of Canada. An inset map near the northwest margin, on a smaller scale, extends the territory in the northwest to the Mississippi River. The tables in the lower right-hand corner give distances between towns or places. It is conjectured that the figures along routes of travel indicate relative elevations.

In the *Analysis* (pp. 1-11) Evans gives with considerable detail the sources of information for this map. He used "actual surveys," astronomical observations, maps, notes, journals, books, and reports of traders and travelers. The information for the settled areas of the east was much more detailed and reliable than that for the unsettled areas of the west. Some of the imperfections of his map resulted from its "premature publication" and from the want of full and correct information. Evans said that Maryland was poorly executed.

The Evans Map is notable for its large scale, its wealth of details and their relative accuracy, and its wide influence on cartography.

It was frequently printed in regular and pirated editions. Its first publication was hastened on account of the impending conflict between the English and the French, and a copy was sent to Braddock. It is one of the best of the maps of its period and was long accepted as an authority for settling boundaries and purchases. In a few respects it is superior to its chief rival, Mitchell's map (Pls. 89, 90). It marks a considerable advance over Popple's map (Pl. 27).

The map's most novel contribution to cartography is its delineation of the region of the Ohio River and its tributaries, based upon the explorations of Gist, Walker, and others. The nomenclature is essentially modern, with slight variations in spelling; thus Miami appears as "Mineami," the Wabash River is the "White River," and the river "falsely called Wabash" is the Wabash. The courses of the western rivers are generalized.

Popple Map, 1733

[PLATE 27]

This map, about 19 by 20 inches, is the index map of Henry Popple's large map of America of twenty sheets, London, 1733, which at the time of its publication was the largest published map of America. The index map, which is a reduced copy of the large map with a few changes, is entitled "A Map of the British Empire in America with the French and Spanish Settlements adjacent thereto." According to a statement on the index map, Popple undertook his work with the approbation of the Lords Commissioners of Trade and Plantations and made use of the records and surveys in the office of their Lordships and of other maps and observations. It appears, however, that Popple alone was responsible for his map and that it was thought by the British government to be incorrect. It is based partly on Delisle's maps but is less accurate. It is a retrograde map. The prime meridian passes through London.

The section of this map reproduced, reduction about three-twentieths, shows the Mississippi Valley and adjacent regions. It should be compared with Delisle's maps (Pls. 22A, 23A, 24). The upper sources of the larger tributaries of the Mississippi were imperfectly known and are therefore poorly delineated. The heavy lines on the map mark the limits of the sections of the main map. Popple's map, while occasionally used as an authority, had much less influence upon cartography than the maps of his most noted contemporaries, Delisle, Bellin, Mitchell, and Evans.

Mitchell Map, 1755

[PLATE 89]

While this reproduction of the John Mitchell Map serves as a base map for illustrating the "Negotiations for Peace," it also serves as one of the maps of the series illustrating "Cartography, 1492-1867," and consequently a description of it is introduced at this point. The original is entitled "Map of the British and French Dominions in North America, with the Roads, Distances, Limits, and Extent of the Settlements"—size about 76 by 52 inches. It is the second edition of 1755 that is reproduced, reduction about two-thirds. (Plate 90 is a reproduction of the northeastern part of the Mitchell Map, original size.)

The Mitchell Map has a most important place in the history of American cartography. It is the second large-scale map of North America made by the English in the eighteenth century and is much superior to the first—the Popple Map (Pl. 27). In some respects it is superior to the maps of the great French cartographers of this century, the Delisles, Bellin, and d'Anville. Freeing himself from many traditional delineations and drawing upon fresh sources of information, Mitchell produced a mother map which for forty years served as a model, until it was succeeded by Arrowsmith's map (Pl. 29). Used by the commissioners who negotiated the Treaty of Peace of 1783, it was the basic map in the disputes over the northeastern boundary of the United States.

The map was constructed in the interest of the British and "with the approbation and at the request of the Lords Commissioners for Trade and Plantations." Its first drawing was made in 1750. It was executed chiefly from drafts, charts, and actual surveys of the British colonies in America, many of which had been made recently under the orders of the commissioners. Statements omitted on the reproduction, giving clues to sources, will be found on the original map. In addition to contemporary English and French maps, Mitchell drew upon newer and less known sources. His delineation of Maine and the adjacent region owes something to the work of Captain Cyprian Southack. For the Ohio Valley the reports of Christopher Gist and other traders were found valuable. For Virginia and Maryland, Fry and Jefferson's map of 1751 appears to have been used.

Mitchell's delineation of the drainage of the Atlantic seaboard is generally good with the exception of the upper river courses. The drainage of Texas, compared with earlier maps, is poor. The Great Lakes are somewhat after the Bellin model (Pl. 23B) but are an improvement on it, though many inaccuracies in their delineation still remain. West of the Mississippi River the map adds little to our knowledge. The delineation of the Ohio River basin, one of the noteworthy features of the map, is superior to all that preceded it.

Previous to the publication of his map Mitchell had lived for a time in America, and this may have had something to do with the excellence of his work. His map was highly regarded on both sides of the Atlantic. It was frequently reprinted, with changes; and French, Dutch, and other foreign editions were issued. In one form or another it was widely circulated and gained great popularity.

Lewis Map, 1804
[PLATE 28]

This map, about 8 by 10 inches, entitled "Louisiana," is found in Arrowsmith and Lewis, *A New and Elegant General Atlas*, Philadelphia, 1804, No. 55. The figures at the bottom of the map give the longitude west from Philadelphia.

The entire map is reproduced, enlarged about one-seventh. The reproduction shows the present United States west of the Mississippi River as it was depicted before Lewis and Clark's expedition of 1804–1806. Of special interest is the delineation of the upper waters of the Platte and Missouri rivers, which doubtless was based upon the reports of traders and explorers. The unnamed river flowing into the Pacific Ocean near the forty-fifth parallel is the Columbia. The "Red R." near the sources of the Mississippi is apparently intended for the Red River of the North. Lakes Michigan and Superior are well drawn.

Arrowsmith Map, 1814
[PLATE 29]

Arrowsmith's map, in six sheets, about 57 by 49 inches, partly colored, and entitled "A Map Exhibiting all the New Discoveries in the Interior Part of North America," was first published in 1795 and was republished in 1802, 1811, and 1814, with additions on each republication. The map for 1814 is chosen for reproduction because it is the first of the Arrowsmith maps to make use of the Lewis and Clark and the Pike explorations. The prime meridian is that of Greenwich.

The reproduction, reduction about one-third, is of the southern part of the map, with cuts on the east and west.

For the region east of the Mississippi Arrowsmith appears to have depended chiefly upon d'Anville, Mitchell, and Evans. West of the Mississippi his chief sources were the maps and explorations of Lewis and Clark and of Pike, as well as Humboldt's general map of New Spain. As little was known of the territory between the Columbia and the Colorado rivers, the map is there left for the most part blank. The mythical Buenaventura appears but without an outlet into the Pacific Ocean. West of the Mississippi many geographical details are still lacking, and some of those delineated are quite faulty.

In his delineation of the territory east of the Mississippi Arrowsmith made some advances over his predecessors. It is, however, his delineation of the territory west of that river that constitutes his principal contribution to American cartography. He is ranked as one of the most eminent map makers of his time, and his map of North America served as a model for many cartographers in the first half of the nineteenth century. He is said to have been a skillful cartographer but an indifferent geographer. He followed closely his sources, and his maps rank as "honest" maps.

Pike Map of the Rocky Mountain Region, 1810
[PLATE 30A]

This map is a reproduction of Plate II (about 15 by 17 in.) of "A Chart of the Internal Part of Louisiana," published by Major Z. M. Pike in *An Account of Expeditions to the Sources of the Mississippi, and through the Western Parts of Louisiana . . . during the Years 1805, 1806, and 1807*, etc., Philadelphia, 1810. Plate I of the same map, to which the last seven lines of the "Reference" and the note in the lower left-hand corner of Plate II refer, shows the area between the Mississippi and the eastern edge of the area covered by Plate II. The longitude is reckoned from Washington. The reduction is about nine-sixteenths. For Pike's expeditions see Plate 39 B, and p. 19, below.

In the course of his expedition of 1806–1807 Pike explored the upper waters of the Arkansas and Rio Grande (Rio del Norte). The Spanish cavalry sent in search of Pike preceded him up the Arkansas. Pike, who followed them, marks their camping places on his map. The upper waters of the Red and other rivers not yet explored are poorly delineated.

Notwithstanding its imperfections, the Pike map, which had a fairly wide circulation, made a considerable contribution to the cartography of the region between the Mississippi River and the Rocky Mountains. The mountain designated "Highest Peak" was subsequently named for Pike.

Humboldt Map, 1811
[PLATE 30B]

During a sojourn in Mexico City in 1803 the great geographer and naturalist, Alexander von Humboldt, compiled a large map of New Spain between the parallels of 16° and 38° north latitude ("Carte générale du royaume de la Nouvelle Espagne," in 2 sheets, in A. de Humboldt, *Atlas géographique et physique de la Nouvelle Espagne*, Paris, 1812). The map was based upon an extended study of all the information then available, including manuscript and printed maps, travelers' journals, and records of geodetic measurements and of astronomical determinations of positions. In all his work Humboldt set himself a high scientific standard, and the map of New Spain was unquestionably the best that had hitherto appeared. In keeping with his critical spirit, Humboldt gives a full description of the map, its sources, and the method of compilation in his *Essai politique sur le Royaume de la Nouvelle-Espagne* (Voyage de Humboldt et Bonpland, Part III), Vol. 1, Paris, 1811, pp. ii–li. As regards the northern part of the map, which covered a large portion of the area subsequently to become the southwestern United States, he writes as follows: "For the portion of New Spain situated north of the 24th parallel of north latitude, in the provinces called *internas* (New Mexico, the government of Coahuila, and the intendancy of New Biscaya) the geographer is reduced to making combinations based on travelers' notes (*journaux de route*). Since the sea is far distant from the most densely populated parts of these regions, he has no means of tying in positions situated in the interior of a vast continent with better known points on the coast. Also, beyond the city of Durango one wanders, as it were, in a desert; for these regions, despite the collections of manuscript maps that are available, the geographer finds no better resources with which to work than were at the disposal of Major Rennel when he prepared his maps of the interior of Africa" (*ibid.*, pp. iii-iv).

Owing to the large scale it was impracticable to reproduce Humboldt's map of New Spain in the present *Atlas*. Instead, there is shown on Plate 30B a reproduction, with reduction of about one-half, of a portion of a smaller map, which Humboldt asserts to be a faithful copy of the larger map in so far as New Spain is concerned. This map, entitled "Carte du Mexique et des pays limitrophes situés au nord et à l'est, dressée d'après la grande carte de la Nouvelle-Espagne de Mr A. De Humboldt et d'autres matériaux, par J. B. Poirson, 1811," will also be found in Humboldt's *Atlas géographique et physique de la Nouvelle Espagne* (cited above), as well as at the back of the book in some copies of his *Essai politique* (cited above). Like the larger map, the smaller one is on Mercator's projection; and, on both, longitudes are measured from the meridian of Paris. In compiling the smaller map Humboldt writes: "as to the countries adjoining New Spain, use was made for Louisiana of the beautiful map of the engineer Lafond; for the United States of Arrowsmith's map [see Pl. 29] corrected from the observations of Rittenhouse, Ferrer, and Ellicott . . ." (Humboldt, *Essai politique*, p. liv).

Bonnneville Map, 1837
[PLATE 31A]

This map, about 16 by 17 inches, was published in Washington Irving, *The Rocky Mountains, or Scenes, Incidents, and Adventures in the Far West*, Philadelphia, 1837, Vol. 2, frontispiece. It is based on a sketch map by Captain B. L. E. Bonneville, who explored the region of the map in 1832–1835. The entire map is reproduced, reduction about three-fifths, with the exception of a small cut on the lower margin. The prime meridian is that of Greenwich.

The map is remarkable for being the first to give a fair delineation of the territory between the present states of Colorado and Wyoming and the Pacific Ocean. "Lake Bonneville" is Great Salt Lake; "Ashley's Lake," Sevier Lake; "Battle Lake," Humboldt Lake; "Mary or Ogden's River," Humboldt River. "Eutaw L." is too far north. The "Buena Ventura" (Sacramento) is for the first time confined to California. The delineations of the Willamette and Snake rivers are decided improvements. The "Claymouth R." in Oregon appears to correspond to the present Rogue River.

The influence of the Bonneville map upon contemporary cartography appears to have been slight, for the old errors which this map corrects were repeated on many succeeding maps.

Pike Map of the Mississippi River, 1810
[PLATE 31B]

This map, about 29 by 8½ inches, is found in Z. M. Pike, *An Account of Expeditions to the Sources of the Mississippi*, etc., Philadelphia, 1810. The reduction is about two-thirds, and the prime meridian that of London.

The map shows the results of Pike's observations made during the winter of 1805-1806 in the course of an expedition from St. Louis to the headwater region of the Mississippi and return (see Pl. 39B). Pike believed that he had reached the "main source" of the Mississippi at Leech Lake, on the shore of which stood a Northwest Company post at the time of his visit. The actual source lies just south of Lake Itasca, some twenty-five miles northwest of Leech Lake (see Elliott Coues, *The Expeditions of Zebulon Montgomery Pike*, Vol. 1, New York, 1895, pp. 150-167).

The map is one of the earliest detailed maps of the upper Mississippi. The legend states that it was based upon Pike's notes "reduced, and corrected by the astronomical observations of Mr. Thompson," at the sources of the river, "and of Captain M. Lewis, where it receives the waters of the Missouri." The "Mr. Thompson" mentioned was David Thompson, the "great explorer and surveyor" of the Canadian Northwest, who for many years was in the service of the Hudson's Bay and the Northwest companies. Thompson had visited Cass Lake (Pike's Upper Red Cedar Lake) and is mentioned in Pike's narrative (*ibid.*, p. 168). Lewis was, of course, Captain Meriwether Lewis of the Lewis and Clark expedition.

The work of Coues cited in the preceding paragraphs is accompanied by an "Historico-geographical Chart of the Upper Mississippi River" (above Minneapolis, Pike's Falls of St. Anthony), on which points shown on Pike's map and mentioned in his narrative are identified with modern localities.

Greenhow Map, 1840
[PLATE 31C]

This map, about 22 by 16 inches, entitled "The North-West-Coast of North America and Adjacent Territories," was published in Robert Greenhow, *Memoir, Historical and Political, on the Northwest Coast of America*, Washington, 1840, p. 20. It was compiled from the "best authorities," and was drawn by David H. Burr, an American cartographer of note. The western part of the United States and its environs are reproduced, reduction about one-fourth. The longitude is measured west of Greenwich.

The most significant feature of the reproduction is the delineation of the territory between the Columbia and Colorado rivers. For Utah the influence of Bonneville's map is apparent, but there are improvements. The draining of a part of Nevada into the Pacific through the Sacramento and Inconstant rivers is a survival of erroneous conceptions. The "Clamet R." of Oregon corresponds to the present Rogue River. Both James Peak (an early name for Pikes Peak) and Pikes Peak are laid down as if they were different peaks. The line marked "Soublette Route" is the route followed by the fur trader William L. Sublette.

Clark Map, 1810
[PLATE 32A]

This map, about 28 by 12 inches, was drawn by Captain William Clark at St. Louis in 1810 (Elliott Coues, *History of the Expedition under the Command of Lewis and Clark*, New York, 1893, Vol. 1, pp. lxxxvi-lxxxvii) and was published in Paul Allen, *History of the Expedition under the Command of Captains Lewis and Clark*, Philadelphia, 1814, Vol. 2, frontispiece—a work promoted by Nicholas Biddle of that city. The whole of the map is reproduced, reduction about one-fourth, from the reproduction in Coues, *op. cit.*, Vol. 4, pocket.

For the territory covered by the two explorers (see Pl. 39B) Clark depended upon the information gathered by the expedition during 1804-1806, and especially upon his own detailed maps and sketches made at that time. For reproductions of these see R. G. Thwaites, *Original Journals of the Lewis and Clark Expedition*, 7 vols. and Atlas,

New York, 1904-1905. For other territory his sources were more various. John Colter, who separated from the expedition in 1806 and did not return to St. Louis until 1810, gave him much information relating to the region of the present Yellowstone Park. The headwaters of some of the tributaries of the Missouri and Columbia are based upon the reports of Indians and others and upon conjecture. For the region of the upper Mississippi Clark had the advantage of information collected by Pike in 1805-1806 (see Pl. 31B). This region is covered in one of Clark's sketch maps (Thwaites, *op. cit.*, Atlas, No. 3).

The map's chief contribution to the cartography of the United States is its delineation of the Missouri and Columbia river systems and of the Rocky Mountains. In 1804 only the lower courses of these two rivers were known. It fell to Lewis and Clark to fill in the gap extending along their upper waters and over the continental divide. This they did with considerable accuracy. Many of the names given by them to the tributaries of the rivers still survive. The promoter of the publication of the *History*, Nicholas Biddle, was honored in the naming of Lake Biddle, one of the Wyoming lakes. By stimulating an interest in the newly acquired territory of Louisiana and in the Oregon country Clark's map became a factor in the Westward Movement.

Chapin Map, 1839
[PLATE 32B]

This map, about 8 by 9 inches, entitled "The Western Possessions of the United States, including Texas and Part of Mexico," is an inset of "Chapin's Ornamental Map of the United States," New York, 1839. A section of the western part of the inset is reproduced, reduction about one-fourth. The prime meridian is that of Washington.

Uninfluenced by Bonneville's exploration (Pl. 31A) this is a typical map of its period.

Smith Map, 1843
[PLATE 32C]

This map, about 19 by 21 inches, entitled "Map of North America," is an inset of J. Calvin Smith's "Map of the United States including Canada and a Large Portion of Texas," New York, 1843. The portion of the map covering all of the present United States, with the exception of the northeastern part, is reproduced, reduction about three-eighths. The longitude is measured from the meridian of Washington. The heavy black line at the north is the line of division between the sheets of the original in the Library of Congress.

In making his maps Smith used the surveys of the General Land Office in Washington. He doubtless also was able to avail himself of the results of some of the recent explorers, possibly those of Frémont of 1842.

The territory east of the Mississippi is well delineated, and that between the Mississippi River and the Rocky Mountains shows a considerable advance over earlier maps, notably in respect to the upper waters of the Platte and Kansas rivers. For the territory west of the Rockies the Bonneville and Greenhow maps (Pl. 31A, C) have been used, but with changes and additions. The Colorado and Rio Grande regions are doubtless copied from contemporary maps.

Colton Map, 1867
[PLATE 32D]

This map, about 13 by 8 inches, is an inset of Colton's large map of the "United States of America, showing the Country from the Atlantic to the Pacific Ocean," New York, 1867. The map is named for its publishers, G. W. and C. B. Colton and Company, one of the best American publishers of maps in the second half of the nineteenth century.

All of the map showing the western United States is reproduced, reduction somewhat less than two-fifths. The reproduction illustrates this part of the United States after surveys and explorations had accurately ascertained all the general features of its geography. It remained only for future surveyors and explorers to correct the details and supply omissions. With a few exceptions, such as the use of "Nicollet" for Sevier (lake and river in Utah), the nomenclature of this map has not changed.

INDIANS, 1567-1930
[PLATES 33-37]

THE maps of this division of the *Atlas* and Plate 47A, "Indian Cessions, 1750-1890," of the division "Lands" illustrate the history of the Indians.

Indian Tribes and Linguistic Stocks, 1650
[PLATE 33]

The names and locations of tribes were derived in the first instance from a map in Clark Wissler, *The American Indian*, 2nd edit., New York, 1922, Fig. 81, and those of the linguistic stocks, with one exception, from a map entitled "Linguistic Families of American Indians North of Mexico, by J. W. Powell, revised by Members of the Staff of the Bureau of American Ethnology," published in 1915 by the U. S. Bureau of the Census in its volume entitled *Indian Population in the United States and Alaska, 1910*, Washington, 1915, facing p. 9. The exception is the several small linguistic groups of California and Oregon, which were united. The first draft of the map as thus compiled was thoroughly revised in 1930 and 1931 by Dr. John R. Swanton of the Bureau of American Ethnology, at whose suggestion many changes were made.

As it is not certain that the Ais, Tekesta, and Calusa tribes of southern Florida belonged to the Mushkogean stock the symbol for the latter is here shown in bands of color. In 1650 the Arawak had been swept off the Bahama Islands and had been destroyed in Cuba, with the exception of a small number living at the eastern end of the island. Hence their name and the number referring to them are shown in brackets. The Hurons had been destroyed and driven from their native region in 1648-1649 and the Tobacco Nation in December, 1649.

Indian Battles, 1521-1890
[PLATE 34]

These maps show the location of 198 Indian battles fought within the limits of the present continental United States between 1521 and 1890. The battles are shown on four maps covering successive periods (1521-1700, 1701-1800, 1801-1845, 1846-1890) in order to reveal the gradual westward movement of Indian warfare with the advance of the frontier. These battles include only those between Indians (aided or unaided by whites) fighting under Indian leadership on the one side, and whites (aided or unaided by Indians) fighting under white leadership on the other side. They have been chosen, out of a great number of actions, because of their relative magnitude and historical importance. A few battles were excluded for lack of definite information. As an Indian siege was usually of an informal character, sieges are included under the designation "battles." Before 1775 engagements were between the Indians and the English, French, or Spanish (chiefly in the Southwest), and after 1775 they were between the Indians and the Americans. Unnamed battles are designated by the names of the combatants.

The maps are based upon information derived from official reports, accounts of Indian wars, general and local histories, biographies and reminiscences of Indian fighters, maps, etc.

Indian Reservations, 1840, 1875, 1900, 1930
[PLATES 35-36]

These four maps illustrate the history of Indian reservations from the close of the Revolutionary War in 1783 until the present time (1930). Plate 35A shows the reservations in 1840 after the reservation policy of the federal government had been in operation for half a century and after the Indians to the eastward of the Mississippi River had been removed to their reserved lands, which lay chiefly to the westward of Arkansas, Missouri, and Iowa, and extended from the Red to the Little Nemaha River. In 1840 the area of the "Indian Territory" was at its maximum. Plate 35B shows the reservations in 1875 when their total area, 166,000,000 acres, was at a maximum. Plate 36A shows the reservations after a considerable reduction in area had been effected, notably by the application of the Dawes act of 1887, which provided for the allotment of the lands to the Indians in severalty. In 1900 the

acreage of the reservations was 78,000,000 acres. Plate 36B shows the reservations in 1930, forty-three years after the passage of the Dawes act, when their area had been reduced to 39,000,000 acres.

The date accompanying each reservation is the date of its origin as given by the most trustworthy authority. It may be the date of a treaty, executive order, act of Congress, or other official action. Information respecting reservations is often conflicting. The chief sources that were used are as follows: Plate 35A and B, Charles C. Royce, *Indian Land Cessions in the United States* (Eighteenth Annual Report of the Bureau of American Ethnology, Washington, 1899), Part II, pp. 648-949, with accompanying maps; Plate 36A, Royce's *Indian Land Cessions*, "Schedule showing the Names of Indian Reservations," in *Annual Report of Department of Interior*, 1900, pp. 601-618, and Map showing Reservations, Washington, 1900; Plate 36B, *General Data Concerning Indian Reservations*, Washington, 1930, with manuscript additions made by the officials of the Office of Indian Affairs, and Map of the United States west of the Mississippi River showing Activities of Bureau of the Department of the Interior, Washington, 1929. The maps on Plate 36 do not always show small tracts reserved for agency, school, burial, or religious purposes, or other small areas difficult to depict. Small reservations whose boundaries cannot be accurately marked owing to the small scale of the maps are shown by means of rectangles approximately proportional to the areas. This is also true of the following somewhat larger reservations on the map for 1930: Washington: Yakima, Colville, Spokane; Oregon: Warm Springs, Klamath; Montana: Crow; South Dakota: Pine Ridge.

Indian Missions, 1567-1861
[PLATE 37]

This map illustrates the Indian missions established within the present continental United States between 1567, when the first permanent Florida mission was founded, and 1861, the year of the outbreak of the Civil War—a year which roughly marks the end of the period of pioneer Indian missions. The missions that are illustrated are religious missions, although many of them in addition to inculcating religion conducted secular schools and gave industrial training. The missions were variously named. Many of them bore names derived from religious history. Frequently they bore the name of the Indian tribe that they served or the name of the place in which they were located. Some of them bore several names. When a choice of name had to be made, the more inclusive name was often preferred; and of inclusive names, the one derived from the name of the tribe was usually chosen. When, however, a name otherwise derived had acquired much historical importance it was regarded as preferable. Missions that served more than one tribe are often designated by the name of the principal tribe.

The missions that are mapped are permanent missions; temporary or visiting missions are disregarded. The stationing of a missionary within a tribe for a considerable period was regarded as a test of permanency. This usually resulted in a mission station consisting of one or more buildings used for religious, educational, industrial, or residential purposes.

The date following the name is the date of the establishment of the mission. In a few cases, owing to the lack of precise information, this date is only approximate. The name of the denomination founding or supporting a mission is indicated by an appropriate abbreviation. Those missions marked "Pr." (Protestant) were founded by organizations representing several denominations, such as the American Board of Commissioners for Foreign Missions, or, in a few cases, by Protestant ministers independent of denominational aid. When several denominations have missions of the same name near one another the name of the mission is given but once.

Owing to limitations of space and of information the following rules of inclusion were adopted: In those cases in which a denomination had more than one mission to an Indian tribe in a given state, only the earliest one is as a rule mapped. The later ones, however, are mapped when they have considerable historical importance. It is for this reason that all of the Catholic and Moravian missions in several of the states are shown. On the other hand, following the general rule, only the earliest Protestant missions in several of the Southern States to the Cherokees and other tribes are shown. When a mission moves from one location to another within a state only the first location is mapped. The case of the Kaskaskia mission in Illinois, however, is an exception to this rule. Each "X" marks the location of a missionary establishment. In the case, however, of the Guale, Timucua, Apalache, and Pueblo missions, owing to the absence of precise information respecting the first mission, the center of the mission field is marked; and in the case of some itinerant Methodist missions the chief preaching station is marked.

The sources of information for this map are diverse. Of the special histories of missions, the following were most serviceable:

J. G. Shea, *History of the Catholic Missions among the Indian Tribes of the United States, 1529-1854*, New York, 1855; A. C. Thompson, *Protestant Missions*, New York, 1894, pp. 59-147; William Gammell, *History of American Baptist Missions*, Boston, 1894, pp. 313-343; Isaac McCoy, *History of Baptist Indian Missions*, Washington and New York, 1840; Nathan Bangs, *An Authentic History of the Missions under the Care of the Missionary Society of the Methodist Episcopal Church*, New York, 1832; W. P. Strickland, *History of the Missions of the Methodist Episcopal Church*, Cincinnati, 1850, pp. 71-159; Ashbel Green, *Historical Sketch of Domestic and Foreign Missions in the Presbyterian Church*, Philadelphia, 1838; W. H. Hare, *Hand-Book of the [Episcopal] Church's Mission to the Indians*, Hartford, 1914; A. C. Thompson, *Moravian Missions*, New York, 1882, pp. 267-341; G. H. Loskiel, *History of the Mission of the United Brethren among the Indians in North America*, London, 1794; R. W. Kelsey, *Friends and the Indians, 1655-1917*, Philadelphia, 1917; Albert Keiser, *Lutheran Mission Work among the American Indians*, Minneapolis, 1922; Z. Engelhardt, *Missions and Missionaries of California*, San Francisco, 1908-1915; Joseph Tracy, *History of American Missions to the Heathen from their Commencement to the Present Time*, Worcester, 1840; *Annual Report of the American Board of Commissioners for Foreign Missions*, Boston, 1810-1861; *Baptist Missionary Magazine*, Boston, 1817-1861; *Foreign Missionary Chronicle*, Pittsburgh, 1833-1849; *Minutes of the General Assembly of the Presbyterian Church*, Philadelphia, 1802-1861; *Minutes of the Annual Conferences of the Methodist Episcopal Church*, New York, 1773-1861; *Report of Commissioner for Indian Affairs*, Washington, 1834-1861; *Catholic Almanac*, Baltimore, 1837-1861; H. E. Bolton, *Texas in the Middle Eighteenth Century*, Berkeley, 1915, and other books and articles by the same author treating of the Southwest; F. W. Hodge, *Handbook of American Indians*, Washington, 1912; R. G. Thwaites, *Jesuit Relations*, Cleveland, 1896-1901, and *Early Western Travels*, Cleveland, 1904-1907. Use was also made of state and county histories, church histories, Indian tribal histories, lives of missionaries, and the publications of state historical societies and of the Bureau of American Ethnology.

EXPLORATIONS IN THE WEST AND SOUTHWEST, 1535-1852

[PLATES 38-39]

THESE plates show the routes of the chief Spanish, French, and American explorers in the region of the Mississippi River and to the westward and southwestward thereof to the Pacific Ocean.

Spanish Explorations in the Southwest, 1535-1706

[PLATE 38]

This map is adapted from one compiled by Herbert E. Bolton, largely from original data, and published in 1916 in his *Spanish Explorations in the Southwest, 1542-1706* (Original Narratives of Early American History, edited by J. F. Jameson), frontispiece. The legend has been added, and the routes of a few French explorers have been omitted.

French Explorations in the West, 1673-1743 (1794)

[PLATE 39A]

This map illustrates the chief explorations made by the French in the region of the Mississippi River and to the westward thereof during the years 1673-1743, and the exploration of Truteau in 1794 (see below, p. 19). Several explorations were omitted because of a lack of specific information respecting them or because they followed routes for the most part explored. The homeward journeys were not mapped when relatively unimportant. The information respecting several routes was not sufficient to admit of minute precision in locating them.

The principal source of information for the French Explorations in the West is Pierre Margry's *Découvertes et Établissements des Français dans l'Ouest et dans le Sud de l'Amérique Septentrionale, 1614-1754,* Paris, 1876-1886, referred to below as Margry. In the references, translations are cited in preference to Margry when their annotations are an important source of information.

A brief account of each exploration is given below:

Jolliet and Marquette, 1673. These explorers made the first voyage on the Mississippi River of which there is now a detailed account, and they were regarded by their contemporaries as the discoverers of that river (Louise Phelps Kellogg, *Early Narratives of the Northwest, 1634-1699,* New York, 1917, p. 223). They left the mission of St. Ignace on the Straits of Mackinac on May 17, 1673, and reached their farthest south at a point on the Mississippi near the mouth of the Arkansas River about the middle of July. They began their return voyage on July 17 and reached Green Bay at the end of September. Jolliet and Marquette's account of their voyage will be found in Kellogg, *op. cit.,* pp. 229-257.

Hennepin, 1679-1680. This is the first voyage on the Mississippi River to the northward of the mouth of the Wisconsin River of which we have a detailed account. Hennepin left St. Ignace on September 2, 1679. On April 11, 1680, he was captured on the Mississippi River near the mouth of the Des Moines and was taken by his captors to the village of Issati near Mille Lac, where he arrived early in May. Hennepin's account will be found in J. G. Shea, *Description of Louisiana by Father Louis Hennepin,* New York, 1880, pp. 104-226.

Duluth, 1680. Duluth left the mouth of the Brule River, in what is now northwestern Wisconsin, in the midsummer of 1680. On July 25 he liberated Hennepin, who was then with his captors on the Mississippi, probably near the mouth of the Black River. Thence the two explorers ascended the Mississippi, going northward as far as the village of Issati near Mille Lac. On the return trip they reached Green Bay late in 1680. Duluth's account of this exploration is found in Kellogg, *op. cit.,* pp. 331-333; and Hennepin's in Shea, *op. cit.,* pp. 253-258.

La Salle, 1681-1682. La Salle was the first explorer to descend the Mississippi to its mouth. He left the St. Joseph River in December, 1681, and reached the Gulf of Mexico on April 9, 1682. One day later he began his return voyage, which ended with his arrival at the mouth of the St. Joseph in September.

This exploration is described by La Salle's companions, Tonty and Father Membré, who accompanied him. Tonty's account is found in Kellogg, *op. cit.,* pp. 296-304; and Father Membré's in J. G. Shea, *Discovery and Exploration of the Mississippi Valley,* New York, 1852, pp. 165-178.

La Salle, 1686. La Salle left Fort St. Louis, near Lavaca Bay, for the Illinois country in April, 1686. Several months later, in what is now eastern Texas, probably not far from the Neches River, he was compelled to return to Fort St. Louis. The narrative of this expedition, by Father Douay, is found in I. J. Cox, *Journeys of Réné Robert Cavelier, Sieur de La Salle,* New York, 1905, Vol. 1, pp. 222-236.

La Salle—Joutel, 1687. In 1687 La Salle made another attempt to reach the Illinois country and was murdered on the Brazos River. Joutel was the historian of the expedition and continued with it after the death of its leader. It left Fort St. Louis, near Lavaca Bay, on January 7 and arrived at Fort St. Louis on the Illinois River on September 14, 1687. Douay's account of this expedition is found in Cox, *op. cit.,* Vol. 1, pp. 238-261; and Joutel's account is in H. R. Stiles, *Joutel's Journal of La Salle's Last Voyage, 1684-7,* Albany, 1906, pp. 116-188.

Tonty, 1689-1690. In 1689 Tonty made an attempt to rescue La Salle's colonists at Fort St. Louis, near the Gulf of Mexico. He left Fort St. Louis on the Illinois River on December 3, 1689, and arrived at a village of the Asinai near the Neches River on April 24, 1690. At this point he turned back. Tonty's narrative is found in Kellogg, *op. cit.,* pp. 312-316.

Le Sueur, 1700. In 1700 Le Sueur ascended the Mississippi River to the mouth of the Minnesota River and thence up the Minnesota to the mouth of the Blue Earth River, where he arrived on October 1. For an account of this expedition see *Wisconsin Hist. Soc. Colls.,* Vol. 16, Madison, 1902, pp. 177-186.

Bienville, 1700. In 1700 Bienville made an expedition from a village of the Taensas Indians near the Mississippi River to the Red River and thence up that river into what is now northwestern Louisiana. An account of this expedition is found in Margry, *op. cit.,* Vol. 4, pp. 432-443.

St. Denis, 1715. Early in 1715 St. Denis went up the Red River on a trading and exploring expedition to Natchitoches, thence westward to the Asinai Indians near the Neches River, and thence southwestward to the mission of San Juan Bautista on the Rio Grande. Accounts of this expedition are Margry, *op. cit.,* Vol. 6, pp. 193-194, and B. F. French, *Hist. Colls. of Louisiana,* Part III, New York, 1851, p. 46.

La Harpe, 1719. In 1719 La Harpe was sent up the Red River to establish a post above Natchitoches. After performing this task he explored the country to the northwestward as far as the villages of the Toucaras. La Harpe's account is found in Margry, *op. cit.,* Vol. 6, pp. 248-290. La Harpe's explorations, 1719 and 1722, are mapped and described in Maria Anna Wendels, French Interest in the Activities of the Spanish Border of Louisiana (unpublished thesis of the Univ. of California). See also *Chronicles of Oklahoma,* Vol. 2, Oklahoma City, 1924, pp. 331-349.

Du Tisné, 1719. In the spring of 1719 Du Tisné went up the Missouri River to the village of the Little Osage Indians near the mouth of the Grand River. Accounts of this expedition are in Margry, *op. cit.,* Vol. 6, pp. 309-310 and 313, and *Kansas State Hist. Soc. Colls.,* Vol. 9, Topeka, 1906, pp. 251-254.

Du Tisné, 1719. Returning from the village of the Little Osage Indians to Kaskaskia, Du Tisné in the summer and fall of 1719 made a journey overland to the Great Osage and Pawnee Indians. The terminus of his journey was a village of the last-named tribe in what is now northeast Oklahoma. Accounts of this expedition are in Margry, *op. cit.,* Vol. 6, pp. 309-315, and *Kansas State Hist. Soc. Colls.,* Vol. 9, Topeka, 1906, pp. 251-255.

La Harpe, 1722. Early in 1722 La Harpe went up the Arkansas River on an exploring expedition and reached what is now central Arkansas before turning back. His narrative is found in Margry, *op. cit.,* Vol. 6, pp. 361-379.

Bourgmont, 1724. On September 20, 1724, Bourgmont set out from Fort Orleans on the Missouri River on a trading and exploring expedition and on October 18 reached a village of the Padouca Indians in western Kansas, the terminus of his journey. A journal of this expedition is found in Margry, *op. cit.,* Vol. 6, pp. 422-433.

Mallet Brothers, 1739-1740. This was a trading expedition which left the Pawnee villages in what is now central Nebraska on May 29 and arrived at Santa Fé on July 22, 1739. On May 1, 1740, it left Santa Fé, and some weeks later the main party arrived at New Orleans. An account of this expedition is found in Margry, *op. cit.*, Vol. 6, pp. 455-456.

Fabry, 1741-1742. In 1741 Governor Bienville sent Fabry up the Arkansas River to open a trade route to New Mexico and to explore the West. He reached a point on the Canadian River in what is now Oklahoma before returning. His expedition is described in Margry, *op. cit.*, Vol. 6, pp. 466-485.

La Vérendrye Brothers, 1742-1743. This was an exploring expedition which set out on April 29, 1742, from Fort La Reine on the Assiniboine River some seventy miles north-northeast of the point at which it entered the territory of the present United States, and returned there on July 2, 1743. Since wide differences as to its route exist among authorities, a choice of interpretations was made. The route shown on the map is that of Mr. Doane Robinson, secretary and superintendent of the South Dakota Historical Department (see map in *South Dakota Hist. Colls.*, Vol. 7, Pierre, 1914, p. 90). A narrative of the expedition by one of the brothers is found in Margry, *op. cit.*, Vol. 6, pp. 598-611, and a translation thereof is in the *South Dakota Hist. Colls.*, Vol. 7, pp. 349-358.

Truteau, 1794. This was a trading expedition, which is included here since Truteau was of French extraction. He left St. Louis on June 7, 1794, reached the villages of the Arikara near the mouth of the Cheyenne River on October 9, and thence descended the Missouri River and went into winter quarters in what is now southern South Dakota on November 4. Truteau's journal is printed in the *American Hist. Rev.*, Vol. 19, New York, 1914, pp. 301-320. A translation of a part of this journal will be found in the *South Dakota Hist. Colls.*, Vol. 7, Pierre, 1914, pp. 412-433.

American Explorations in the West, 1803-1852
[PLATE 39B]

This map illustrates twenty-seven American explorations made west of the Mississippi River during the years 1803-1852, when that region was more or less unknown. These are a selection from a long list of such explorations. In making a choice, consideration was given to the historical importance of the exploration, to its priority in visiting new regions, and to the value of the geographical or other scientific facts discovered. Those expeditions whose principal object was exploration and those that were conducted under the auspices of the United States government were regarded as most worthy of illustration. Private expeditions, of a trading or other character, that visited regions unknown or little known were, however, often chosen. Of the explorations that were excluded some were rejected because the route traveled had been previously explored, and others because the information was too slight to permit of the mapping of routes.

In locating routes the absence of detailed information occasionally prevented the exercise of minute precision. Sometimes a route is slightly displaced on the map because of a congestion of lines. A route that follows a river valley is not always shown on the right side of the stream, nor are all of its crossings indicated. The homeward route is not shown when it is identical with the outward route or when for other reasons it is unimportant. Deviations from the main course are not as a rule shown. When they are of importance the routes of minor parties that separated from the main expedition are mapped.

A brief account of each of these explorations is given below:

Dr. John Sibley, 1803-1804. In 1803-1804 Dr. John Sibley explored the Red River from its mouth to a point some seventy or eighty miles above Natchitoches. Sibley's exploration was a private adventure. In 1805, when he sent a report of it to the Secretary of War, Henry Dearborn, he was acting as an Indian agent under that official. His report will be found in *Amer. State Papers, Indian Affairs*, Vol. 1, Washington, 1832, pp. 725-730.

William Dunbar and Dr. George Hunter, 1804. Soon after the purchase of Louisiana, President Jefferson formulated extensive plans for its exploration. In accordance therewith he chose William Dunbar of Mississippi and Dr. George Hunter of Philadelphia to explore the Red and Arkansas rivers. Threatening movements of the Indians caused a change of plans, and a preliminary expedition to the Hot Springs in Arkansas was decided upon. Dunbar and Hunter left St. Catherines Landing (fifteen miles below Natchez on the Mississippi River) on October 16, passed up the Red, Black, and Ouachita rivers, and arrived at Hot Springs on December 9. For an account of this expedition, see Dunbar's "Journal" in *Documents relating to the Purchase and Exploration of Louisiana*, Boston, 1904, pp. 7-101, and I. J. Cox, *Early Explorations of Louisiana*, Cincinnati, 1906, pp. 39-51.

Captain Meriwether Lewis and Lieutenant William Clark, 1804-1806. This expedition, which originated with President Jefferson, was organized to explore the Missouri River and its headwaters, the portages between its headwaters and the headwaters of the rivers flowing into the Pacific Ocean, and the principal river flowing into that ocean. The expedition was commanded by Captain Meriwether Lewis and Lieutenant William Clark, both officers of the U. S. Army. It left Camp River Dubois (in Illinois near the mouth of the Missouri) on May 14, 1804, spent the winter of 1804-1805 near the site of the present Bismarck, N. Dak., and finally reached the mouth of the Columbia River in November, 1805, where it remained during the winter of 1805-1806. The homeward journey began on March 23 and ended with the arrival at St. Louis six months later, September 23, 1806. Through Montana it traveled eastward in two parties, the northern party under the command of Lewis and the southern under the command of Clark.

The principal sources of information for this exploration are R. G. Thwaites, *Original Journals of the Lewis and Clark Expedition*, 8 vols., New York, 1904-1905; Milo M. Quaife, *Journals of Captain Meriwether Lewis and Sergeant John Ordway*, Madison, 1916; and Olin D. Wheeler, *Trail of Lewis and Clark, 1804-1809*, New York and London, 1904. All of these books contain valuable maps.

Lieutenant Zebulon M. Pike, 1805-1806. This expedition was sent out by General James Wilkinson of the United States Army from his headquarters at St. Louis to explore the Mississippi River northward of that city. Pike left St. Louis on August 9, 1805, and reached his most northerly point in what is now northern Minnesota early in February, 1806. A narrative of the expedition is found in Elliott Coues, *Expeditions of Zebulon Montgomery Pike*, New York, 1895, Vol. 1. There is a map of the expedition in Vol. 3.

Thomas Freeman, 1806. In 1806 President Jefferson sent out a second expedition to explore the southern part of Louisiana, under the command of Freeman, a surveyor. On April 19 Freeman left Fort Adams, Miss., under instructions to explore the Red River to its source. He proceeded up that river until July 29, when, having reached a point near the present western boundary of Arkansas, he was turned back by a detachment of Spanish troops sent out for that purpose. A report of his expedition was contemporaneously published under the title, *An Account of the Red River in Louisiana, drawn up from the Returns of Messrs. Freeman and Custis to the War Office of the United States, who explored the same in the year 1806*, Washington, 1806 (?).

Lieutenant Zebulon M. Pike, 1806-1807. This expedition was sent out by General Wilkinson, who directed Pike to visit the Osage and other Indians, including the Comanches on the headwaters of the Arkansas and Red rivers, and if possible to explore those rivers. On July 15, 1806, Pike left Belle Fontaine, Mo. (near the mouth of the Missouri River). On November 28, at the Great Bend of the Arkansas, he divided his forces into two parties. One of these, under the command of Lieutenant James B. Wilkinson, went down the Arkansas, arriving at Arkansas Post, near the mouth of the river, on January 9, 1807. The other, under the command of Pike, went up the Arkansas, visited the region of Pikes Peak, explored the headwaters of the Arkansas, and passed southward to the Rio Grande, where it was captured by the Spaniards. It was taken to Santa Fé and thence to Chihuahua, Mexico, from which city it was escorted to the United States through Texas, arriving at Natchitoches, Louisiana, July 1, 1807. The narrative of this expedition is found in Coues, *Expeditions of Zebulon Montgomery Pike*, New York, 1895, Vol. 2. Some maps illustrating the expedition are in Vol. 3.

The Astorians, 1811-1813. The term "Astorians" is used to designate the men who went overland to the Northwest Coast and took part in the founding of Astoria and the establishment of the fur trade of John Jacob Astor. As this expedition was much divided at one time or another, the routes of only the two principal parties, one bound westward and the other eastward, are mapped. The westward party was commanded by W. P. Hunt, and the eastward party by Robert Stuart, both partners of Astor.

Hunt left St. Louis on March 12, 1811, and arrived at Astoria on February 15, 1812. Stuart left Astoria on June 29, 1812, spent the following winter on the Platte River, in what is now southern Wyoming and western Nebraska, and arrived at St. Louis on April 30, 1813.

There is no narrative of the entire expedition written by one of its participants. Parts are covered by John Bradbury, Alexander Ross, and Ross Cox. The principal source of information is *Astoria*, Philadelphia, 1836, by Washington Irving, who had access to "all the papers relative to the enterprise." Use was also made of a recent account found in H. M. Chittenden, *American Fur Trade of the Far West*, New York, 1902, Vol. 1, pp. 196-213, and Vol. 3, map in rear pocket, showing the route, and of J. Neilson Barry, "Trail of the Astorians," in *Quarterly of the Oregon Hist. Soc.*, Vol. 13, Portland, 1912, pp. 227-239.

Major Stephen H. Long, 1817–1818. Long, who was a topographical engineer in the army, went up the Arkansas River late in 1817 as far as the mouth of the Canadian River, retraced his course to the Poteau River, turned southward and went overland to the Red River, thence crossed Arkansas by way of Hot Springs and Little Rock, and finally reached St. Louis early in 1818.

There is no published narrative of this expedition. References to it are found in Edwin James, *Account of an Expedition from Pittsburgh to the Rocky Mountains, performed in the Years 1819 and '20*, Philadelphia, 1822–1823, Vol. 2, pp. 290–291, 296, 305, 315, and 319–320. James maps the route of the expedition in the Atlas accompanying his book.

Major Stephen H. Long, 1819–1820. This expedition was sent out by the Secretary of War, John C. Calhoun, "to explore the country between the Mississippi and the Rocky Mountains." Major Long left St. Louis on June 21, 1819, and spent the following winter near the present site of Omaha; thence he passed up the South Fork of the Platte River and, after discovering Long's Peak, crossed Colorado to the Arkansas River, explored that river, and near the site of the present town of Rocky Ford divided the expedition into two parties. One of these, under Captain John R. Bell, went down the Arkansas to Fort Smith, where it arrived on September 9, 1820. The other, under Long, passed southward to the Canadian River and down that river, joining the first party at Fort Smith on September 13. Thence the expedition crossed Arkansas and southeastern Missouri to Cape Girardeau, where it arrived early in October.

The official narrative of the expedition, consisting of two volumes and an Atlas, was compiled by Edwin James and published under the title *Account of an Expedition from Pittsburgh to the Rocky Mountains, performed in the Years 1819 and '20*, Philadelphia, 1822–1823. The route of the expedition is mapped in the Atlas accompanying this work.

Lieutenant Colonel Willoughby Morgan, 1820. This was an army expedition sent out from Camp Missouri, near the site of the present city of Omaha, to open up an overland route to Camp Cold Water (later Fort Snelling, near the present St. Paul) at the mouth of the Minnesota River. The best account of the expedition is found in the "Journal of Stephen Watts Kearny," a captain in the army and one of the officers under Morgan. This, with a map of the route, is published in the *Collections of the Missouri Historical Society*, Vol. 3, St. Louis, 1908, pp. 14–29 and 99–104.

Jacob Fowler, 1821–1822. This was a trapping and trading expedition of twenty men. The route shown is that of Fowler, second in command and journalist of the expedition. Fowler left Fort Smith, Ark., on September 26, 1821, and arrived at the Missouri River near the present town of Sibley, Mo., July 5, 1822. This expedition is one of the earliest American expeditions to ascend the Arkansas River, explore the headwaters of the Rio Grande, and return thence to the Missouri River. Information respecting it is derived from the *Journal of Jacob Fowler*, edited by Elliott Coues, New York, 1898.

Major Stephen H. Long, 1823. This expedition was sent out by President Monroe, under orders from the War Department, to explore "the river St. Peter's [Minnesota] and the country situated on the northern boundary of the United States between the Red River of Hudson's Bay and Lake Superior." Major Long left Prairie du Chien, Wis., on June 25 and, after extensive explorations in what is now Minnesota, passed into Canada, visited Lake Winnipeg, and reached Lake Superior on September 13. The narrative of the expedition, in two volumes, together with a map showing the route, was compiled by W. H. Keating, *Narrative of an Exploration to the Source of St. Peter's River . . . performed in the Year 1823*, Philadelphia, 1824.

William H. Ashley, 1824–1825. This was an exceedingly important fur-trading expedition. Ashley was a St. Louisan who in 1824 ran for governor of Missouri. He left Fort Atkinson, not far from the site of the present city of Omaha, on November 3, 1824, and arrived there on his return on September 19, 1825. He went out by the central overland route, crossed the Rockies, explored part of the Great Basin, and returned by the northern route. Ashley's narrative of his expedition, together with an excellent account thereof, is found in Harrison C. Dale, *Ashley-Smith Explorations*, Cleveland, 1918, pp. 59–164. This book also contains a map showing the route of the expedition.

U. S. Commissioners, 1825–1827. During the years 1825–1827 three United States commissioners, Benjamin H. Reeves, George C. Sibley, and Joseph C. Brown, surveyed a road from a point on the Missouri River near Fort Osage (a few miles east of Kansas City) to Taos, N. Mex., north of Santa Fé. The Santa Fé Trail, with a few exceptions, followed this road. The best account of this survey is found in the "Santa Fé Trail," published in the *Eighteenth Biennial Report of the Kansas State Historical Society*, Topeka, 1913, pp. 107–125, with map.

Jedediah S. Smith, 1826–1827. This was a fur-trading expedition commanded by Jedediah S. Smith, a companion of Ashley and one of the most adventurous of the early fur traders. Smith left Great Salt Lake on August 22, 1826, and after visiting California returned to Great Salt Lake about the middle of June, 1827. Smith's narrative and a journal by one of the members of his party are found in Dale, *op. cit.*, pp. 179–228.

Jedediah S. Smith, 1827–1828. In July, 1827, Smith set out to return to California, following the same route taken by him thither in the previous year. By November he had reached Monterey; thence he went northward, finally reaching Fort Vancouver in August, 1828. As the details respecting the earlier parts of this expedition are lacking, only the route from Monterey to Fort Vancouver is mapped.

The best account of this expedition, which includes a journal covering part of it, is found in Dale, *op. cit.*, pp. 229–274. Smith's routes are shown on the map appearing as the frontispiece to this book.

James O. Pattie, 1827–1829. This was a trapping and fur-trading expedition of the two Patties, father and son. Inasmuch as the father died during the expedition, it is designated by the name of the son. From 1824 to 1827 the Patties were trapping and trading in the West with Santa Fé as headquarters. On September 22, 1827, they left Santa Fé on an expedition that took them down the Gila and Colorado rivers and into lower and upper California. At San Diego they were imprisoned, and the elder Pattie died during his imprisonment. In the latter part of June, 1829, the son reached his farthest north, the Russian settlements near Bodega Bay. For Pattie's account of this expedition, see R. G. Thwaites, *Early Western Travels*, Vol. 18, Cleveland, 1905, pp. 180–286.

Henry R. Schoolcraft, 1832. This expedition was sent out by the War Department to visit the Indian tribes in Minnesota and to explore the regions visited. Schoolcraft was the United States Indian agent at Sault Ste. Marie, Mich. The expedition left Lake Superior at the mouth of the St. Louis River on June 23 and returned to the lake at the mouth of the Brule River in Wisconsin on August 4. It is distinguished by the discovery and naming of Lake Itasca, one of the sources of the Mississippi. Narratives of the expedition are found in H. R. Schoolcraft, *Discovery of the Sources of the Mississippi River*, Philadelphia, 1855, pp. 223–274, and in *House Doc. No. 323, 23rd Cong., 1st Sess.*, 1833–1834, Vol. 4. A map of the region explored accompanies this document.

Nathaniel J. Wyeth, 1832–1833. This was a trading expedition that followed the Oregon Trail on its westward journey. Wyeth left Independence (near Kansas City), Mo., on May 3, 1832, and reached Liberty (also near Kansas City) on his return, September 28, 1833. Part of the homeward route was unusual.

With the exception of the first thirty-four days, this expedition is covered by Nathaniel J. Wyeth's "Journal," which has been edited by F. G. Young and published in *Sources of the History of Oregon*, Vol. 1, Eugene, 1899, Parts III–VI, pp. 155–219. A narrative of the first part of the expedition is found in John B. Wyeth's "Oregon" in Thwaites, *Early Western Travels*, Vol. 21, Cleveland, 1905, pp. 47–74.

Joseph R. Walker, 1833–1834. This was a trapping and fur-trading expedition consisting of some forty men and commanded by Joseph R. Walker. It left Green River, in what is now southwestern Wyoming, on July 24, 1833, reached Monterey in November of that year, spent the winter in California, and on its return reached the Bear River, in what is now southeastern Idaho, early in July, 1834. This is one of the first American expeditions to enter California by way of the Humboldt River.

An account of this expedition was written by Walker's clerk, Zenas Leonard (W. F. Wagner, *Adventures of Zenas Leonard*, Cleveland, 1904, pp. 146–243). The best secondary sources of information respecting it are Washington Irving, *Adventures of Captain Bonneville*, New York and London, 1898, Vol. 2, pp. 92–98; H. M. Chittenden, *American Fur Trade of the Far West*, New York, 1902, Vol. 1, pp. 411–417; and H. H. Bancroft, *History of California*, Vol. 3, San Francisco, 1885, pp. 389–391.

Joseph N. Nicollet, 1838. This expedition was sent out by the War Department to collect materials for a map of the hydrographic basin of the upper Mississippi River. It left Fort Snelling, near the present site of St. Paul, in June, 1838, proceeded up the Minnesota River, passed over into what is now South Dakota, and reached its farthest north at Lake Traverse. Its route is shown on a map prepared by Nicollet and published by the U. S. government in 1843 (*Senate Doc. No. 237, 26th Cong., 2nd Sess.*, 1840–1841).

Joseph N. Nicollet, 1839. This expedition was sent out under the same auspices and for the same purpose as that of 1838. It left Fort Pierre (now Pierre, S. Dak.) on July 2, 1839, explored the eastern part of the Dakotas and the western part of Minnesota, and descended the Minnesota River to Fort Snelling.

No narratives of Nicollet's expeditions have been published. Their routes are mapped on "A Map of the Hydrographical Basin of the Upper Mississippi made by J. N. Nicollet," published by the United States Government in 1843 (republished in 1845). Information respecting them will be found in the report which accompanied this map (*Senate Doc. No. 237, 26th Cong., 2nd Sess.*, 1840–1841), in *Reports of Explorations and Surveys ... Mississippi River to the Pacific*, Vol. 11, Washington, 1855, pp. 40–42 (in *House Ex. Doc. No. 91, 33rd Cong., 2nd Sess.*, 1854–1855), and in the manuscript papers of Nicollet now in the Library of Congress. Nicollet, who was a Frenchman, was accompanied both in 1838 and 1839 by John C. Frémont.

Thomas J. Farnham, 1839. This expedition consisted of seventeen men bound for Oregon and seeking health, adventure, or a future residence. It followed in part an unusual route, notably through what is now western Colorado. Farnham left Independence (near Kansas City), Mo., on May 21, 1839, and reached Fort Vancouver in the latter part of October. The narrative of the expedition was written by Farnham and published in 1843 (Thwaites, *Early Western Travels*, Vol. 28, Cleveland, 1906).

Captain John C. Frémont, 1843–1844. Frémont's instructions, signed by the chief of the corps of topographical engineers, directed him to connect his reconnaissance of 1842, which extended to the Rocky Mountains, "with the survey of Commander Wilkes on the coast of the Pacific Ocean, so as to give a connected survey of the interior of our continent." He left Kansas (now Kansas City), Mo., on May 29, 1843, crossed the Rockies through South Pass, Wyoming, and reached Fort Vancouver early in November. Thence he proceeded southward through Oregon and Utah and crossed the Sierra Nevada into California. Returning eastward through Nevada, Utah, Wyoming, and Colorado, he arrived at Kansas on July 31, 1844. Frémont's narrative is found in *Senate Doc. No. 174, 28th Cong., 2nd Sess.*, 1844–1845, pp. 105–290. In 1845 the government published a map showing the route of the expedition.

Captain John C. Frémont, 1845–1846. This expedition continued the work of that of 1843–1844. Its objects, according to Frémont, were to explore "that section of the Rocky Mountains which gives rise to the Arkansas River, the Rio Grande del Norte of the Gulf of Mexico, and the Rio Colorado of the Gulf of California, to complete the examination of the Great Salt Lake and its interesting region, and to extend the survey west and southwest to the examination of the great ranges of the Cascade Mountains and the Sierra Nevada" (Frémont, *Memoirs of my Life*, Chicago and New York, 1887, p. 422). Its point of departure was Bent's Fort on the Arkansas River, in what is now southeastern Colorado. Leaving this place on August 16, 1845, Frémont passed through Colorado, Utah, and Nevada and again entered California, where he spent the winter of 1845–1846. In the spring of 1846 he ascended the Sacramento River and on May 8, while he was exploring Klamath Lake in southern Oregon, his explorations were brought to an end by the arrival of a message from Washington directing him to return to California as a war with Mexico was threatening. An account of this expedition is found in Frémont, *Memoirs of my Life*, pp. 422–487. See also "Map of Oregon and Upper California from the Surveys of John Charles Frémont" (1848).

The Mormons, 1846–1847. This was the migratory expedition of the Mormons, of which Brigham Young was the chief person in authority. The Mormons began leaving Nauvoo, Illinois, early in February, 1846. The following winter was spent on the Missouri River near Council Bluffs, and on July 22, 1847, the first party of the emigrants reached what is now Salt Lake City. The principal sources of information for this expedition are W. A. Linn, *Story of the Mormons*, New York and London, 1902, pp. 362–391, and H. H. Bancroft, *History of Utah*, San Francisco, 1889, pp. 216–262.

Captain Randolph B. Marcy, 1852. Inasmuch as all the early attempts to explore the upper course of the Red River had failed, the War Department in 1852 ordered Captain Marcy to explore the sources of that river. His route from the mouth of the Little Wichita River in Texas to Fort Arbuckle in what is now Garvin County, Oklahoma, is shown on the map. The exploration was made in May-July, 1852. The principal source of information is *Exploration of the Red River of Louisiana* (*Senate Ex. Doc. No. 54, 32nd Cong., 2nd Sess.*, 1852–1853), with accompanying map.

THE existence until recent years of a vast tract of unoccupied land is one of the greatest factors in American history. The division of the *Atlas* which illustrates Lands is therefore an exceedingly important one, and a large number of maps have been included in it. That the inclusion was not larger is owing to limitations of space and to the impossibility of illustrating certain phases of the subject because of a lack of information. The principal subjects illustrated are (1) divisions of land, (2) disposition of the land by the government, and (3) varieties of landholdings. For a detailed list of subjects, see Contents, pp. *vi–viii*.

Plates 41A, 41C, 42, 43A, 45-46, 47, 48A, 49, 50A, 57, 58, and 59 are new. For Plate 56 D-E two published maps were redrawn. The remainder of the maps are reproductions. While the arrangement is roughly chronological, a strictly chronological order has not been possible owing to the necessity of fitting maps of varying sizes and shapes into the available spaces. In the text below the maps are described in the order in which they are arranged in the *Atlas*. These maps may be classified by subjects as follows:

Land grants and divisions during the colonial period: Plates 40, 42, 43, 44B–D, 50D, 51.

Land grants and divisions during the period 1785–1919: Plates 41B, 44A, 48B–C, 50A–C, 50E, 55C–D, 56C–E.

Varieties of landholdings, 1651–1919: Plates 41D–E, 52A–B, 53, 54, 55A–B, 56A–B.

Public Lands of the United States, 1790–1930: Plates 48A, 57–59.

Miscellaneous maps showing: territorial possessions of European states in eastern North America, 1763: Plate 41A; British possessions in eastern North America, 1774: Plate 46A; proposed colonies and states 1775–1785: Plates 41C, 46B; military reserves, 1778–1842: Plate 45B; Indian cessions, 1750–1890: Plate 47A; territorial claims on the northwest coast of America, 1790–1846: Plate 49; claims and cessions of western lands, 1776–1846: Plates 45A, 47B–E; territorial acquisitions, 1783–1853: Plate 46C.

DIVISIONS OF LAND NEAR PHILADELPHIA, ABOUT 1730

[PLATE 40]

This is a reproduction of the southern and central portion of "A Mapp of the Improved Part of Pensilvania in America divided into Counties, Townships, and Lotts," surveyed by Thomas Holme and dedicated and presented to William Penn by John Harris. The date of publication of Harris' map is not known. It is a copy on a reduced scale of Thomas Holme's large wall map published about 1730.

This map and Plate 44A were chosen to illustrate early land divisions in America. It should be said, however, that the divisions shown on these maps are more regular than those generally found in the southern states and in some parts of the northern states. Plate 40 shows farms (with names of owners), townships, towns, manors and other large holdings, counties, and the city of Philadelphia with its Liberty Lands (the part of the city not originally laid off into streets and squares). Two racial settlements are shown, German Township (later Germantown), settled by Germans, and "the Welch Tract," settled by Welsh. In the upper left-hand quarter of the map is a tract labeled "The Free Society of Trade," a possession of the Free Society of Traders in Pennsylvania, a joint-stock company chartered in 1682. The base lines of the original surveys are either rivers or range lines.

POSSESSIONS OF EUROPEAN STATES IN EASTERN NORTH AMERICA AFTER THE TREATY OF PARIS, 1763

[PLATE 41A]

The provisions respecting colonial limits found in the treaty of Paris of 1763, the royal proclamation of 1763, and the commissions to the governors of Nova Scotia, Georgia, and West Florida, 1763-1773 (see pp. 23, 33, 53, below), constitute a veritable landmark in the history of boundaries on the North American continent. Previous to 1763 there were no settled limits between the American possessions of European states nor between the territorial claims of those states. Governments were not disposed to set specific limits to their claims when

leaving the limits indefinite better served their purpose. Such official or unofficial claims as were made from time to time varied in accordance with the policy of the government or the temperament of the person advancing the claim (R. G. Thwaites, *France in America, 1497-1763* (The American Nation: A History, Vol. 7), New York and London, 1905, p. 155). It is for these reasons that this *Atlas* contains no maps illustrating territorial claims during the colonial period.

Of the boundary lines shown upon this map those that were established by the treaty of 1763 or as a result of that treaty will be specifically described, as will also those of the Hudson's Bay Company. Most of the intercolonial lines bounding the thirteen original colonies are described in connection with "Colonial Grants, 1603–1732" (see pp. 25–30, below), and "Colonial and State Boundary Disputes" (see pp. 72–87, below). Those that are not described are relatively unimportant. The parts of these lines which were in dispute in 1763 are shown as finally settled. The westward extension of several of the colonies as set forth in their charters has been cut off by the Royal Proclamation Line of 1763. The colonies that were affected never accepted this limitation of their territorial rights. The boundary line between New York and New Hampshire is that established by the King in Council in 1764 (see Pl. 97B and p. 73, below). The province of Maine belonged to Massachusetts. Its northern boundary was fixed by the establishment of the southern boundary of Quebec in 1763, and its eastern boundary by the establishment of the western boundary of Nova Scotia in the same year.

The first undisputed international boundary line on the continent of North America was the Mississippi River (north of 31°N.). By the treaty of 1763 France lost all of her continental possessions, and Spain lost the Floridas and received as a compensation part of France's former possessions. The boundary line between Spain's new possessions and the British possessions is thus described by the treaty:

"... a line drawn along the middle of the river Mississippi from its source to the river Iberville, and from thence by a line drawn along the middle of this river and the lakes Maurepas and Pontchartrain to the sea" (George Chalmers, *Collection of Treaties between Great Britain and other Powers*, London, 1790, Vol. 1, p. 473).

The gap between the source of the Mississippi River and the possessions of the Hudson's Bay Company has been filled by a line drawn due north from the source of the river to the possessions.

Since the southern boundary of the territory of the Hudson's Bay Company was long disputed and never fixed, the line claimed by the company in 1750 is shown as the boundary. The company described this line as follows:

... "to begin from the Atlantic Ocean on the east side of an island called Grimington's Island, otherwise Cape Perdrix, in the latitude of 58½° on the Labrador coast, and to be drawn from thence southwestward to the great lake Miscosinke, otherwise called Mistoseny, and through the same, dividing that lake into two parts, down to the 49th degree of north latitude ... and from thence to be continued by a meridian line of the said latitude 49° westwards."[1]

The royal proclamation of October 7, 1763, established the boundaries of three new British colonies, Quebec, East Florida, and West Florida, the territory of which was acquired or mostly acquired under the treaty of that year. Quebec was bounded as follows:

... "on the Labrador coast by the river St. John, and from thence by a line drawn from the head of that river, through the lake St. John, to the South end of the lake Nipissim; from whence the said line, crossing the river St. Lawrence and the lake Champlain in 45 degrees of North latitude, passes along the High Lands, which divide the rivers that empty themselves into the said river St. Lawrence, from those which fall into the sea; and also along the North coast of the Baye des Chaleurs, and the coast of the Gulph of St. Lawrence to Cape

---

[1] David Mills, *Report on Boundaries of Province of Ontario*, Toronto, 1877, p. 176. This line was also proposed by the company in 1714, and the proposal (with an important condition) was incorporated by the British government in its instructions of 1719 to the British commissioners appointed to settle limits under the tenth article of the Treaty of Utrecht (*ibid.*, pp. 173 and 175). The northern part of the line was proposed by the company in 1712 (*ibid.*, pp. 156–157). In 1857 this line was again proposed as a boundary (*Report from Select Committee on Hudson's Bay Company*, London, 1857, p. 217).

Rosieres, and from thence crossing the mouth of the river St. Lawrence by the West end of the island Anticosti, terminates at the aforesaid river St. John" (*Annual Register*, London, 1763, p. 209).

The gap in the line of the description between the eastern end of the "High Lands" and the western end of the Bay of Chaleurs has been filled by a straight line joining the highlands and the bay.

The boundary of East Florida is thus described:

... "bounded to the Westward by the Gulph of Mexico and the Apalachicola river; to the Northward, by a line drawn from that part of the said river where the Catahouchee and Flint rivers meet, to the source of St. Mary's river, and by the course of the said river to the Atlantic Ocean; and to the East and South by the Atlantic Ocean, and the Gulph of Florida" (*ibid.*, p. 209).

The Gulf of Florida included the Bahama Channel, or the water between Florida and the Bahamas, and the Florida Straits, or the water between Florida and Cuba.

The description of the boundary of West Florida is as follows:

... "bounded to Southward by the Gulph of Mexico ... to the Westward by the said lake [Pontchartrain], the lake Maurepas, and the river Mississippi; to the Northward, by a line drawn due East from that part of the river Mississippi which lies in thirty-one degrees North latitude, to the river Apalachicola, or Catahouchee; and to the Eastward by the said river" (*ibid.*, p. 209).

The royal proclamation of 1763 also established an important line on the western frontier between Quebec and Georgia as part of the eastern boundary of a vast Indian Reserve extending northward from Georgia to the Great Lakes and thence northwestwards to Labrador. This reserve is thus described:

... "all the land and territories not included within the limits of our said three new governments, or within the limits of the territory granted to the Hudson's Bay company; as also all the land and territories lying to the westward of the sources of the rivers which fall into the sea from the west and northwest" (*ibid.*, p. 211).

By "our said three new governments" is meant the governments of Quebec, East Florida, and West Florida. The Indian Reserve did not include the coast of Labrador, since this was placed under the government of Newfoundland, as were also several islands. The provision of the proclamation on this subject is as follows:

"And to the end that the open and free fishery of our subjects may be extended to, and carried on upon the coast of Labrador and the adjacent islands, we have thought fit ... to put all that coast, from the river St. John's to Hudson's Streights, together with the islands of Anticosti and Madelaine [Magdalen] ... under the care and inspection of our governor of Newfoundland" (*ibid.*, pp. 209–210).

With the cession of Acadia or Nova Scotia to the English by the treaty of 1763, a long dispute between England and France over the boundaries of that country came to an end. In a commission dated November 21, 1763, to Montague Wilmot, as governor of Nova Scotia, the boundaries of the colony were fixed as follows:

... "to the Northward ... by the Southern Boundary of our Province of Quebec as far as the western Extremity of the Bay des Chaleurs; to the Eastward, by the said Bay and the Gulf of St. Lawrence ... to the Southward, by the Atlantick Ocean ... and to the Westward ... by the said river [St. Croix] to its source and by a Line drawn due North from thence to the Southern Boundary of our Colony of Quebec" (*North-Eastern Boundary Arbitration Papers*, Washington, 1829, Appendix, pp. 139–140).

As the identity of the St. Croix River was disputed in 1763, the river that was decided to be the true St. Croix in 1798 (see Pl. 91C and p. 58, below) is shown as the St. Croix of the description.

The royal proclamation of 1763 enlarged Georgia by an addition that was described somewhat indefinitely as "all the lands lying between the rivers Attamaha [Altamaha] and St. Mary's" (*Annual Register*, 1763, p. 209). In the commission of James Wright as governor of Georgia, dated January 20, 1764, the bounds of the enlarged colony are definitely described in the following language:

... "on the north by the most northern stream of a river there commonly called Savannah river as far as the head of the said river, and from thence westward as far as our territories extend; on the east by the sea coast from the said river Savannah to the most southern stream of a certain other river called Saint Mary ... and on the south by the said river Saint Mary as far as the head thereof, and from thence westward as far as our territories extend by the north boundary line of our provinces of East and West Florida" (*Amer. State Papers, Public Lands*, Washington, 1832, Vol. 1, p. 66).

The key to the possessions of the European states will be found at the bottom of the map. Islands that are too small to take color have their names underscored with the appropriate color. As the northern part of the island of St. Martin belonged to the French and the southern part to the Dutch, the name of this island is underscored with the colors of both nationalities. The division line between the French and Spanish parts of Santo Domingo is that of the treaty of Aranjuez, negotiated in 1776. Previous to this date the line was disputed.

THE SEVEN RANGES OF TOWNSHIPS, ABOUT 1795
[PLATE 41B]

This is a map of the first systematic survey of the federal government (see below, p. 36). Provision for the survey was made by the ordinance of May 20, 1785, according to which seven ranges of townships in eastern Ohio were to be surveyed (*Journs. Cont. Cong.*, Washington, 1823, Vol. 4, pp. 520–522; P. J. Treat, *National Land System, 1785–1822*, New York, 1910, pp. 396–397). Each township, which was to be six miles square, was to be divided into "lots" one mile square, which were to be numbered from south to north in ranges, beginning on the east side of the township. The survey was begun in 1786.

Plate 41B is a reproduction of a map found in *Carey's American Atlas*, Philadelphia, 1809, No. 23.

COLONIES OR STATES PROPOSED OR ORGANIZED BY SETTLERS WEST OF THE ALLEGHENY MOUNTAINS, 1775–1785
[PLATE 41C]

During a period beginning about 1750, when the westward movement of population passed the crest of the Alleghenies, and ending about 1787, when the first of the territories in the western country was organized, various proposals for new colonies or states in this country were made. The earliest of them were proposed by land companies, private speculators, or other makers of paper states residing in the seaboard colonies east of the Alleghenies or in the mother country. More frequently than otherwise these early proposals cannot be illustrated precisely on a map because the boundaries are left more or less indefinite.[2] In the latter part of the period the proposals are for the most part of a different kind. They emanated not from easterners but from settlers on the lands west of the Alleghenies, and they largely grew out of the actual needs of the settlers for governments more easy of access than the remote ones they had left behind on the tidewater. The private interests of the settlers, the unsettled conditions of frontier life, the conflict of jurisdiction caused by uncertain boundary lines, and the separatist tendency aroused by the philosophy of the Revolution were also causal factors in this movement for independent statehood. After the Revolution the cession of western lands to the federal government accelerated the movement. In several cases the settlers did not stop with proposing a new government, but proceeded to organize one. As a rule they describe with much precision the boundaries of their proposed states.

Plate 41C illustrates the second class of colonial scheme, that is, the colonies or states proposed or organized by settlers west of the Allegheny Mountains. These colonies or states, with the dates of proposal or organization, are described in the following paragraphs.

Transylvania, 1775. Transylvania was organized as a proprietary colony by the Transylvania Land Company, composed of North Carolinians, of whom Colonel Richard Henderson was the leading spirit. In May, 1775, the House of Delegates of the colony held its first and only meeting at Boonesborough in central Kentucky. The inhabited part of the colony then consisted of Boonesborough and three other settlements near thereto. The company purchased two tracts from the Cherokee Indians, the larger of which comprised Transylvania. Its boundaries are as follows:

... "beginning on the said Ohio River at the mouth of Kentucky, Chenoca, or what by the English is called Louisa River, from thence running up the said River and the most northwardly branch of the same to the head spring thereof, thence a south east course to the top ridge of Powel's mountain, thence westwardly along the ridge of the said mountain unto a point from which a northwest course will hit or strike the head spring of the most southwardly branch of Cumberland River, thence down the said River, including all its waters, to the Ohio River, thence up the said River as it meanders to the beginning" (Mann Butler, *History of Commonwealth of Kentucky*, Louisville, 1836, p. 504; G. H. Alden, *New Governments West of the Alleghanies before 1780*, Madison, 1897, pp. 50–51; *North Carolina Colonial Records*, Vol. 9, Raleigh, 1890, p. 1276). Powell Mountain, now called Powell Ridge Mountain, is east of the Cumberland range in southwestern Virginia (James Madison, "Map of Virginia," 1807).

---

[2] Many of them are mapped in C. W. Alvord, *Mississippi Valley in British Politics*, Cleveland, 1917, Vol. 1, frontispiece and pp. 97, 317; Vol. 2, frontispiece. See also G. H. Alden, *New Governments West of the Alleghanies before 1780*, Madison, 1897, pp. 9, 13, and 33; F. J. Turner, "Western State-Making in the Revolutionary Era," *Amer. Hist. Rev.*, Vol. 1, 1896, p. 74.

The limits of Transylvania are represented on the map by *line 1*—a short-dash blue line.

The territory of Transylvania lay mostly within what is now Kentucky, and partly within what is now Tennessee. The governors of Virginia and North Carolina denounced the company and continued to exercise jurisdiction over its lands. Congress failed to comply with the request of the company to make Transylvania one of the united colonies and to admit its delegate to a seat in that body. By the end of 1776 all prospect that the company would succeed in establishing a new government had vanished (for accounts of Transylvania see F. J. Turner, "Western State-Making in the Revolutionary Era," *Amer. Hist. Rev.*, Vol. 1, 1896, pp. 78–81; Butler, *op. cit.*, pp. 506–515).

Westsylvania, 1776. The settlers of southwestern Pennsylvania, disturbed by the conflicting claims of that state and of Virginia to jurisdiction over them and by the claims of land companies and private persons to ownership in their lands, memorialized Congress in 1776 to create "a distinct and independent province and government" to be called Westsylvania. The bounds of the new province were thus described:

... "beginning at the Eastern Branch [bank] of the Ohio opposite the Mouth of the Scioto, and running thence in a direct Line to the Owasioto Pass [Cumberland Gap], thence to the Top of the Allegheney Mountain, thence with the Top of the said Mountain to the Northern Limits of the Purchase made from the Indians in 1768 at the Treaty of Fort Stanwix aforesaid, thence with the said Limits to the Allegheney or Ohio River, and thence down the said River ... to the Beginning" (G. H. Alden, *New Governments West of the Alleghanies before 1780*, Madison, 1897, p. 68; for the line of the Treaty of Fort Stanwix see E. B. O'Callaghan, *Documents relative to the Colonial History of the State of New York*, Vol. 8, Albany, 1857, p. 136).

The limits of Westsylvania are represented by *line 2*—a short-dash red line.

Congress took no action on the memorial.[3]

Kentucky, 1782. In 1782 a number of the inhabitants of a "tract of Country called Kentuckey" petitioned Congress "to erect them into a separate and independent State and admit them into the federal Union."[4] Kentucky comprised the part of Virginia that lay south of the Ohio River and west of the Big Sandy River and the Cumberland Mountains—the territory of the present state of Kentucky. The limits of the proposed state are represented by *line 3*—a short-dash yellow line.

The movement for separate statehood for Kentucky lasted until 1792, when Kentucky was separated from Virginia and admitted into the Union (W. W. Hening, *Virginia Statutes at Large*, Vol. 12, Richmond, 1823, pp. 37–40).

Franklin, 1784. In June, 1784, North Carolina ceded its western lands to Congress. Left without a government, the settlers in that part of the ceded territory comprising what is now northeastern Tennessee organized the state of Franklin. The boundaries of the new state were never officially described. They may be derived, however, with considerable precision from the acts of the state organizing counties and from its claims to the ownership of lands (J. G. M. Ramsey, *Annals of Tennessee*, Charleston, 1853, pp. 294–295 and 344–345). They were as follows: on the north by the Virginia boundary line, on the east by the summit of the Alleghenies, on the south by the Little Tennessee and Tennessee rivers, and on the west by the Cumberland Mountains. The limits of this state are represented by *line 4*—a dotted yellow line.

Congress declined to recognize the new state. In November, 1784, North Carolina passed again the act ceding her western lands to the federal government and henceforth until 1790, when she passed the second act of cession, she asserted her right to the whole of Tennessee. The state of Franklin survived in a fashion until March 1, 1788, when the last term of its governor expired. (For an account of Franklin see *ibid.*, pp. 282–444; *Amer. Hist. Rev.*, Vol 1, 1896, pp. 257–259; Vol. 8, 1903, pp. 271–289.)

States Proposed by the Settlers of Washington County, Virginia, 1784–1785. Washington County, formed in 1777, comprised a large territory lying for the most part west of the Allegheny Mountains in what is now southwestern Virginia. It was drained by the Powell, Clinch, Holston, and Big Sandy rivers. During the years 1784–1785 the settlers of this county, led by Charles Cummings and Arthur Campbell, were exceedingly active in the state-making movement. In 1784 they memorialized Congress to form a state with limits as follows:

... "bounded by a Meridian line that will touch the confluence of Little River near Ingles Ferry; thence down the Kanhawa to the Ronceverte or Green Briar River; thence Southwest to latitude 37° North; thence along the same to the meridian of the rapids of the Ohio; South along that meridian untill it touches the Tenesee or Cherokee river; down the same to the part nearest of latitude 34°; South to the same; and eastwardly on that parallel to the top of the Apalachian mountains; and along the highest parts of the same and the heights that divide the sources of the waters that fall into the Mississippi from those that empty into the Atlantic, to the Beginning."[5]

The limits of the proposed state are represented by *line 5*—a solid blue line.

Congress received this petition on January 13, 1785. It took no action thereon.

On April 7, 1785, the settlers of Washington County addressed Congress, objecting to the artificial lines of division provided for in the resolution of Congress of April 23, 1784 (see below, p. 33) and proposing the erection of two states westward of the Alleghenies, bounded largely by natural lines. The first of these states, which included the settlements in Kentucky, was to have the following limits:

... "bounded on the East by the great Kanhawa as high as the confluence of the Ronceverte [Greenbrier River]; the Ohio, on the north; and on the West and South, by a Meridian line drawn from the mouth of Salt river until it intersects the Shawanoe or Cumberland river, up that river to the mouth of that branch of it called Rock-Castle, up the said river Rock-Castle to the Ausioto or Bush Mountain [Cumberland Mountain], thence a direct line to the confluence of the Ronceverte."[6]

The second of these states, which included the settlements in western Tennessee and southwestern Virginia, was given the following limits:

... "bounded by a line extended due South from that part of the Cumberland river where the Meridian line drawn from the mouth of Salt river will touch it, until it reaches Elk river, down that river to the Tenasee, thence South to the top of the Apalachian [Allegheny] Mountain, eastwardly along the same to a point from whence a north line extended would meet the Kanhawa at the mouth of Little river near Ingles Ferry, and down that River to the Ronceverte [Greenbrier River], westwardly along the boundary as above described for the Kentuckey Country."[7]

The limits of these two states are represented by *lines 6*—solid yellow lines.

Congress took no action on this communication.

In 1785 some of the settlers of Washington County under the leadership of their county lieutenant, Colonel Arthur Campbell, proposed that their county should join the new state of Franklin. Campbell drew up a constitution in which he proposed limits for a greatly enlarged Franklin. These are as follows:

... "beginning at a point on the top of the Alleghany or Appalachian mountains, so as a line drawn due north from thence will touch the bank of New river, otherwise called Kenhawa, at the confluence of Little river, which is about one mile above Ingle's ferry; down the said river Kenhawa to the mouth of the Rencoverte, or Green Briar river; a direct line from thence to the nearest summit of the Laurel mountain, and along the highest part of the same to the point where it is intersected by the parallel of thirty-seven deg. north latitude; west along that latitude to a point where it is met by a meridian line that passes through the lower part of the rapid of Ohio; south along the meridian to Elk river, a branch of the Tennessee; down said river to its mouth, and down the Tennessee to the most southwardly part or bend in said river; a direct line from

[3] For accounts of Westsylvania see Alden, *op. cit.*, pp. 64–68; Boyd Crumrine, *History of Washington County, Pa.*, Philadelphia, 1882, pp. 187–188.

In 1780 the settlers in southwestern Pennsylvania sent a second petition to Congress, in which the petitioners designated themselves "the Inhabitants on the West side of the Laurel Hill and Western Waters," Laurel Hill being the most westerly range of the Alleghenies in southwestern Pennsylvania. They petitioned Congress "to lay off a New State upon these Western Waters of such Extent of Territory as in your Judgment shall seem meet" (Papers of Continental Congress, Division of Manuscripts, Library of Congress, No. 48, f. 251). Pennsylvania answered this petition by passing an act making high treason the erection of a state within its borders, the advising of the erection of such a state, or the calling of a meeting for such a purpose (*Pennsylvania Acts*, 1782, Ch. 45).

[4] *N. Y. Hist. Soc. Colls.*, Vol. 11, New York, 1879, pp. 145–146; *Journs. Cont. Cong.*, Vol. 23, Washington, 1914, p. 532. On May 15, 1780, the "people" of Kentucky and Illinois counties petitioned Congress to form them into a separate state, or to grant them such rules and regulations as Congress in its wisdom should think most proper. Kentucky County comprised the territory of what is now the state of Kentucky. Illinois County lay north of the Ohio River and east of the Mississippi River, without definite bounds on the north and east (Papers of Continental Congress, No. 48, f. 237; *Journs. Cont. Cong.*, Vol. 17, Washington, 1914, pp. 760 and 763–764).

[5] Papers of Cont. Cong., No. 48, f. 281. In the memorial the settlers of Washington County are described as the "Freemen inhabiting the Country Westward of the Allegany or Apalachian Mountain and Southward of the Ouasioto" (Cumberland Mountains). The memorial is signed by Charles Cummings and seventeen other settlers. A second memorial from Washington County sent to Congress about the same time as the first described the boundaries less specifically, as follows: "bounded by the Kanawa on the East, the Apalachian and Ausioto Mountains on the south and North; Tenasee and Mobile Rivers on the West and South West" (*ibid.*, No. 48, f. 285). Little River is in southwest Virginia and is a branch of the Great Kanawha River (for its location and the location of Ingles Ferry see James Madison, "Map of Virginia," 1807). Since the crest of the Alleghenies and the watershed dividing the waters that flow into the Mississippi from those that flow into the Atlantic do not correspond precisely, the former is chosen for delineation. As the meridian of the mouth of Little River passes to the eastward of the Alleghenies, the provision respecting it is disregarded and the line is bent slightly eastward in order to connect the crest of the mountains with the mouth of the river.

[6] Papers of Cont. Cong., No. 48, f. 298. This communication was signed by Charles Cummings, chairman, representing "the Deputies of the good people of this County." Since the Rockcastle River does not rise in the Cumberland Mountains, the gap in the description is filled by extending the boundary from the source of the river eastwardly to the mountains.

[7] *Ibid.*, No. 48, f. 299. Respecting the meridian of the mouth of Little River see note 5, above.

thence to that branch of the Mobile called Donbigbee [Tombigbee]; down said river Donbigbee to its junction with the Coosawatee [Coosa] river, to the mouth of that branch of it called the Hightower; thence south to the top of the Appalachian mountain, or the highest land that divides the sources of the eastern from the western waters; northwardly along the middle of said heights and the top of the Appalachian mountain to the beginning."[8]

The limits of the enlarged Franklin are represented by *line 7*—a solid red line.

A COLONIAL TOWN: WETHERSFIELD, CONNECTICUT, 1641
[PLATE 41D]

This map is a reproduction of one made by Professor Charles M. Andrews entitled "Early Allotments in Wethersfield" and published in his *River Towns of Connecticut* (Johns Hopkins Univ. Studies No. 7), Baltimore, 1889, p. 4. The village with its home lots, buildings, and streets is shown below the southward bend of the river (the Connecticut). The small blank square near the center of the village is the church, and the blank area on the river in the northeastern part of the village is the common or green. The village was laid out and allotted in 1635-1636, and the outlying districts in 1636-1639, in about the following order: Great Meadow (to the right of the village), the Plains (below and to the right of the village), Wright's Island (within the river), West Fields (to the left of the village), and Naubuc Farms (to the right of the river). The home lots were used chiefly for residential purposes and contained from two to seven acres. The outlying lots were used for tillage or grazing or as woodland. The larger lots in the West Fields were a mile and a half long, and the lots in Naubuc Farms were three miles long (S. W. Adams and H. R. Stiles, *History of Ancient Wethersfield, Connecticut*, New York, 1904, Vol. 1, pp. 44 (map) and 88-99; Andrews, *op. cit.*, pp. 42-47).

SPECIMEN SURVEYS IN THE VIRGINIA MILITARY RESERVE, ROSS COUNTY, OHIO, 1799-1825
[PLATE 41E]

This map illustrates the surveys made according to the indiscriminate location or haphazard plan which was followed in parts of the eastern United States and especially in the Virginia Military Reserve of Ohio and in Kentucky and Tennessee. The systematic plan of surveys is illustrated by Plate 48A and is described below, p. 36. An extract from the description of "Survey No. 8842" will illustrate the method followed in giving the metes and bounds of a survey made according to the haphazard plan:

"Surveyed for Ann Garrett, 130 acres of land on part of a Military Warrant No. 5901, on Upper Twin Creek, a branch of Paint Creek.

"Beginning at two beeches, west corner to Abraham Shepherd's survey No. 4710; thence N.73° E. 170 poles, crossing the creek to a poplar, east corner to said survey; thence N.89°W. 93 poles to two beeches; thence S.55°W. 40 poles to a sugar tree, hornbeam, and white oak; thence West 110 poles, crossing the creek at 95 poles to two buckeyes and an elm; thence S.28°W .97 poles to two poplars ... thence N.64½°E. 122 poles to a beech and sugar tree in the line of Shepherd's survey; thence with said line, N.45°W. 20 poles to the beginning."

"Surveyed August 30, 1816, by Cadwallader Wallace, D. S." (W. E. Peters, *Ohio Lands and Their Subdivision*, 1918, Athens, pp. 22-23; plate 41E is based upon a map of Peters, between pp. 24 and 25).

COLONIAL GRANTS, 1603-1732
[PLATES 42, 43A]

These two maps illustrate the twenty-seven most important grants respecting lands within the present continental United States or the territory contiguous thereto that were made during the colonial period. In making a choice of grants, consideration was given to (1) the historical significance of the grant, (2) the quality of the granting authority, and (3) the permanence of the boundary established. All the grants emanate from the king or other high granting authority. A few grants of considerable importance were rejected because they are expressed in terms so indefinite, obscure, or inconsistent as to defy successful

representation by maps. Minor difficulties of this sort, however, in respect to some of the grants that are illustrated have been resolved by supplying obvious omissions, ignoring inconsistencies, making a choice of interpretations, or approximating locations. Grants of islands and of parts of the sea are not shown when they can be separated from grants of the mainland.

The base maps upon which the lines are drawn have been derived from enlargements of parts of the Map of North America published by the U. S. Geological Survey in 1912. Some details from these enlargements have been omitted, and a few details derived from other sources have been added. The use of a base showing modern drainage and projection is necessary for comparison of the lines of one description with those of another. It must be remembered, however, that the lines as conceived by those contemporary with the grants may vary considerably from those shown upon the maps. It is obvious that by relating the language of the grants to the more perfect cartographical representations of the present time, when that language was based on the geography of America as understood in the seventeenth and eighteenth centuries, serious misconceptions may arise. Occasionally the language of grants has an even less reliable basis than contemporary geography and must be traced to the carelessness or conjecture of those who drafted the descriptions of boundaries.

Of the twenty-seven grants all but two, those to De Monts (1603) and to Providence Plantations (1643), granted territory; and all but one, that to Lord Hopton and others (1649), granted powers of government. All the grants are of British origin with the exception of that to De Monts, which is of French origin. The period covered is 1603-1732. The grants often overlap, owing either to the grantors' ignorance of the geography of America or to their disregard of the rights of previous grantees.

To facilitate mapping, the twenty-seven grants were divided into two classes. The first class, consisting chiefly of grants for large tracts extending from sea to sea, may be illustrated adequately on a base of relatively small scale. The second class, consisting of grants for relatively small tracts lying chiefly in what is now the northeastern part of the United States, needs a larger scale.

I. Grants for Large Tracts
[PLATE 42]

Grants of the first class are illustrated on Plate 42. In order to save space this map is carried but a little westward of the Mississippi River. Those color lines that stop at the western border of the map are to be understood as extending to the Pacific Ocean (with the possible exception of De Monts' grant).

Grant to De Monts by Henry IV, 1603. This is a grant, by the French king Henry IV, of powers of government and not of title to lands. De Monts was authorized, however, to take for his own use such lands as he wished. The area covered by the grant is thus described:

... "the countries, territories, coasts, and confines of La Cadie [Acadia], commencing from the fortieth degree unto the forty-sixth; and within the said limits or any part of them, as far and to such distance inland as may be possible" (W. L. Grant and H. P. Biggar, *History of New France by Marc Lescarbot*, Toronto, 1911, Vol. 2, pp. 212 and 490).

The limits of this grant are represented by *lines 1*—dot-and-dash blue lines.

Grants to the Virginia Companies by James I, 1606. These grants, which are found in the first charter of Virginia, were made to two companies, one consisting of "certain Knights, Gentlemen, Merchants, and other Adventurers of our City of London and elsewhere," and the other of a similar class of Englishmen residing in Bristol, Exeter, Plymouth, and other places. These companies were empowered to plant colonies in "Virginia," and the first of them, here designated as the "Virginia Company (London)," settled Jamestown, Va., in 1607. The grant to this company in respect to lands is in the following language:

... "and they shall and may begin their said first Plantation and Habitation at any Place upon the said Coast of Virginia or America, where they shall think fit and convenient, between the said four and thirty, and one and forty Degrees of said Latitude; and that they shall have all the Lands ... from the said first Seat of their Plantation and Habitation by the Space of fifty Miles of English Statute Measure, all along the said Coast of Virginia and America, towards the West and Southwest, as the Coast lyeth ... and also all the lands ... from the said Place of their first Plantation and Habitation for the Space of fifty like English Miles, all along the said Coast of Virginia and America, towards the East and Northeast or towards the North, as the Coast lyeth ... and also all the Lands ... from the same fifty Miles every way on the Sea Coast,

---

[8] John Haywood, *Civil and Political History of the State of Tennessee*, Nashville, 1891, pp. 154-155; W. W. Henry, *Patrick Henry*, New York, 1891, pp. 276-277. Respecting the meridian of the mouth of Little River, see above, note 5. The Laurel Mountain was crossed by the Great Kanawha River near the mouth of the Greenbrier and to the south corresponded with the range now known as Cumberland Mountain (F. Hutchins, "Map of Western Parts of Virginia, Pennsylvania, Maryland, and North Carolina," 1778). The provision "down the Tennessee to the most southerly part or bend in said river" is disregarded, since the "most southerly part or bend" lies up the Tennessee from the mouth of Elk River. The Hightower River is one of the upper branches of the Coosa. From the mouth of this river the line is drawn northwardly to the summit of the Alleghenies and not "south," since the summit does not lie in that direction. The line is drawn along the crest of the Alleghenies in preference to the watershed—see above, note 5.

directly into the main Land by the Space of one hundred like English Miles" (William Stith, *History of First Discovery and Settlement of Virginia*, New York, 1865, Appendix, p. 2).

From this language it is plain that the Virginia Company (London) might plant a colony anywhere between the thirty-fourth and forty-first parallels. Should they plant a colony on the thirty-fourth parallel they could secure lands fifty miles southward thereof, and should they plant a colony on the forty-first parallel they could secure lands fifty miles northward thereof. The area on the coast within which they might secure lands lay therefore between a point fifty miles southward of the thirty-fourth parallel and a point fifty miles northward of the forty-first parallel. This area extended inland one hundred miles.

The limits within which the Virginia Company (London) might secure lands are represented by *line 2*—a short-dash red line. In mapping the westward limits only the general contour of the coast was regarded. The limits at the northward and southward are drawn at right angles to the general trend of the coast.

The grant in respect to lands to the second of these companies, here designated as the "Virginia Company (Plymouth)," is in the following language:

... "they shall and may begin their said Plantation and Seat of their first Abode and Habitation at any Place upon the said Coast of Virginia and America, where they shall think fit and convenient, between eight and thirty Degrees of the said Latitude and five and forty Degrees of the same Latitude; and that they shall have all the Lands ... from the first Seat of their Plantation and Habitation by the Space of fifty like English Miles, as is aforesaid, all alongst the said Coast of Virginia and America towards the West and Southwest or towards the South, as the Coast lyeth ... and also all the Lands ... from the said Place of their first Plantation and Habitation for the Space of fifty like Miles all alongst the said Coast of Virginia and America towards the East and Northeast or towards the North, as the Coast lyeth ... and also all the Lands ... from the same fifty Miles every way on the Sea Coast, directly into the main Land, by the Space of one hundred like English Miles" (*ibid.*, Appendix, pp. 2–3).

The limits within which the Virginia Company (Plymouth) might secure lands are represented by *line 3*—a dotted blue line. In mapping these limits the same principles were observed as in the case of the Virginia Company (London), described above.

The limits of the territory within which either company might secure lands are represented by *line 4*—a short-dash yellow line.

Grants to the Virginia Company (London) by James I, 1609. Since the first charter to the Virginia Company (London) proved unsatisfactory, in 1609 a more liberal charter was granted the company under the name of the "Treasurer and Company of Adventurers and Planters of the City of London for the first Colony in Virginia." The territory granted is described as follows:

... "all those Lands, Countries, and Territories situate, lying, and being in that Part of America called Virginia, from the Point of Land called Cape or Point Comfort all along the Sea Coast to the Northward two hundred Miles, and from the said Point of Cape Comfort all along the Sea Coast to the Southward two hundred Miles, and all that Space and Circuit of Land lying from the Sea Coast of the Precinct aforesaid, up into the Land, throughout from Sea to Sea, West and Northwest" (*ibid.*, Appendix, p. 15; this grant included all islands within one hundred miles of the coast. Point Comfort is the present Old Point Comfort).

This is the first grant of territory in America extending from sea to sea, that is from the Atlantic Ocean to the Pacific Ocean or South Sea. The words "up into the Land, throughout from Sea to Sea, West and Northwest" are open to different constructions. Virginia never specifically construed them. Her claim to western lands, however, can best be explained by a construction that gives her a western line for a boundary on the south and a northwest line for a boundary on the north (for the interpretation of these words see below, p. 35). This construction is here adopted. The limits of this grant are represented by *lines 5*—long-dash blue lines.

Grant to the Council for New England by James I, 1620. The Virginia Company (Plymouth) failed to establish a permanent colony. In 1620 it was reorganized under the name of "The Council established at Plymouth in the County of Devon for the planting, ruling, ordering, and governing of New England in America." The grant of territory to the new company is as follows:

... "all that Circuit, Continent, Precincts, and Limitts in America, lying and being in Breadth from Fourty Degrees of Northerly Latitude from the Equinoctiall Line, to Fourty-eight Degrees of the said Northerly Latitude, and in Length by all the Breadth aforesaid throughout the Maine Land, from Sea to Sea" (Ebenezer Hazard, *Historical Collections*, Philadelphia, 1792, Vol. 1, p. 105).

The limits of this grant are represented by *lines 6*—solid blue lines. The Council for New England surrendered its patent in 1635 but continued to survive in a fashion thereafter for several years. Its most important grants are illustrated below (see pp. 27–28).

Grant to the Massachusetts Bay Company by Charles I, 1629. This grant, which is found in the first Massachusetts charter, was made to Sir Henry Roswell and twenty-five other English gentlemen, who were constituted a corporate body under the name of the "Governor and Company of the Massachusetts Bay in New England." It confirmed to Roswell and his associates a grant of territory which they had obtained in 1628 from the Council for New England. This territory was described as follows:

... "all that Parte of Newe England in America which lyes and extendes betweene a greate River there, comonlie called Monomack River, alias Merrimack River, and a certen other River there, called Charles River, being in the Bottome of a certen Bay there comonlie called Massachusetts ... Bay, and also all ... those Landes ... lying within the Space of Three Englishe Myles on the South Parte of the saide River, called Charles River or of any or every Parte thereof; and also all ... the Landes ... lying and being within the Space of Three Englishe Miles to the southward of the southermost Parte of the said Baye ... and also all those Landes ... which lye and be within the Space of Three English Myles to the Northward of the saide River called Monomack, alias Merrimack, or to the Northward of any and every Parte thereof, and all Landes ... lying within the Lymitts aforesaide ... throughout the mayne Landes there, from the Atlantick and Westerne Sea and Ocean on the East Parte to the South Sea on the West Parte" (*ibid.*, Vol. 1, p. 243; this grant was repeated in the second charter of Massachusetts, 1691).

The location of the northern boundary line of Massachusetts under this grant was long disputed (see Pl. 97A and pp. 72–73, below). Massachusetts claimed that her charter line on the north was the parallel of a point three miles north of the source of the most northerly branch of the Merrimac River. This line is shown as the northern boundary of this grant. The southern boundary was also disputed but within narrower limits. The present southern boundary of Massachusetts is based upon the official survey of Woodward and Saffery made in 1642. The parallel of a point three miles south of the Charles River as determined by this survey is shown as the southern boundary of the grant. (A map of the survey of Woodward and Saffery will be found in C. W. Bowen, *Boundary Disputes of Connecticut*, Boston, 1882, between pp. 18 and 19.) The limits of this grant are represented by *lines 7*—short-dash blue lines.

Grant to Sir William Alexander by Charles I, 1629. This large grant to the founder of Nova Scotia includes a part of the original grant of that country made to him by James I in 1621 (see below, p. 27). The grant was of little value to Alexander, although it was ratified by the Parliament of Scotland. As may be seen, it conflicts with various other grants. The territory granted is described as follows:

... "fifty leagues of bounds on both sides of the foresaid river Canada [St. Lawrence] from the said mouth and entrance to the said head, fountain, and source thereof; also on both sides of the said other rivers flowing into the same; as also on both sides of the said lakes, arms of the sea, or waters through which any of the said rivers have their course or in which they terminate; and ... from the foresaid head, fountain, and source of (the river) Canada ... down to the foresaid Gulf of California ... with fifty leagues altogether on both sides of the said passage before the said head of (the river) Canada, and Gulf of California" (E. F. Slafter, *Sir William Alexander and American Colonization* (Prince Soc. Publs., Vol. 8), Boston, 1873, pp. 241–242).

The limits of this grant are represented by *lines 8*—dotted red lines. The description permits only an approximate location. The grant extends beyond the western border of the map in a southwesterly direction to the Gulf of California.

Grant to Sir Robert Heath by Charles I, 1629. Heath, who was a friend of Charles I and attorney-general of England, was granted the province of Carolina, or Carolana, which is thus described:

... "all that River or Rivulet of St. Mattheo [St. Marys] on the South Part and all that River or Rivulet of Passo Magno [Albemarle Sound] on the North Part, and all Lands ... extending between and within the said two Rivers ... unto the Ocean on the Eastern and Western Parts, so far forth and as much as the Continent there extends itself ... all which lie within 31 and 36 Degrees of Northern Latitude inclusively" (Daniel Coxe, *Description of the English Province of Carolana*, London, 1741, p. 110).

The River of St. Mattheo has been identified as the St. Marys of Florida, and the River of Passo Magno as Albemarle Sound (Woodbury Lowery, *Spanish Settlements within Present Limits of the United States*, New York and London, 1905, p. 34, map, and p. 392; Hugh Williamson, *History of North Carolina*, Philadelphia, 1812, Vol. 1, p. 84).

The parallel of the most southerly point of the St. Marys River is shown as the southerly boundary of the grant; and the parallel of the most northerly source of the Roanoke River, the principal tributary of Albemarle Sound, as the northern boundary. The provision of the description respecting the two rivers calls for boundaries that differ slightly from those called for by the provision respecting the two degrees of latitude.

The limits of the grant are represented by *lines 9*—solid red lines.

Grant to the Connecticut Company by Charles II, 1662. This grant is found in the Connecticut charter of 1662, from which the title of Connecticut to her present territory is derived. It constituted John Winthrop and his associates a corporate body under the name of the "Governor and Company of the English Colony of Connecticut in New England." The territory granted to the governor and company is described as follows:

... "all that parte of our Dominions in Newe England in America bounded on the East by Norrogancett River, commonly called Norrogancett Bay, where the said River falleth into the Sea, and on the North by the lyne of the Massachusetts Plantation, and on the South by the Sea, and in longitude as the lyne of the Massachusetts Colony, runinge from East to West, (that is to say) from the said Norrogancett Bay on the East to the South Sea on the West parte" (*Public Records of Colony of Connecticut*, Hartford, 1852, Vol. 2, p. 10).

As this description does not fix the southern boundary of the grant to the westward of what is now the present state of Connecticut, the parallel of the southwest corner of the state, approximately the 41st parallel, is shown as the westward extension of the southern boundary. This is the line claimed by Connecticut in her controversy over western lands.[9]

The limits of this grant are represented by *lines 10*—dot-and-dash red lines.

Grants to the Proprietors of Carolina by Charles II, 1663, 1665. In 1663 Heath's grant was declared void by an Order in Council, although claims under it were made many years later. In the same year Charles II, in the first Carolina charter, granted to the Earl of Clarendon and seven British gentlemen associated with him under the name of the "Lords Proprietors of Carolina" a large territory located similarly to that of Heath. It was described as follows:

... "extending from the north end of the island called Lucke island, which lieth in the southern Virginia seas, and within six and thirty degrees of the northern latitude, and to the west as far as the south seas, and so southerly as far as the river St. Matthias [St. Marys] which bordereth upon the coast of Florida, and within one and thirty degrees of northern latitude, and so west in a direct line as far as the south seas aforesaid" (*Colonial Records of North Carolina*, Raleigh, 1886, Vol. 1, p. 21).

The limits of this grant are represented by *lines 11*—solid yellow lines. Lucke Island lay at the entrance of Albemarle Sound. Its northern end was a little north of the 36th parallel (Nicholas Comberford, "Map of Northern Part of North Carolina," 1657; J. S. Bassett, *Writings of Colonel William Byrd*, New York, 1901, p. 21).

In 1665 a second charter was granted to Clarendon and his associates, enlarging their province. The new boundaries were described as follows:

... "extending north and eastward as far as the north end of Currituck river or inlet, upon a strait westerly line to Wyonoak creek, which lies within or about the degrees of thirtysix and thirty minutes, northern latitude; and so west in a direct line as far as the south seas; and south and westward as far as the degrees of twenty-nine, inclusive, of northern latitude; and so west in a direct line as far as the south seas" (*Colonial Records of North Carolina*, Vol. 1, pp.102-103).

This grant is represented by *lines 12*—dotted yellow lines. Currituck Inlet was an opening in the sand barrier off the coast of North Carolina, which connected the Atlantic Ocean with Currituck Sound. It no longer exists. It is doubtful what stream was meant by the designation "Wyonoak Creek." In 1728 the Virginia-North Carolina Boundary Commission resolved the doubt in favor of Nottoway River (Bassett, *op cit.*, pp. 24 and 88).

Grant to the Trustees of Georgia by George II, 1732. This grant was made in the Georgia charter of 1732 to the "Trustees for establishing the colony of Georgia in America," consisting of James Oglethorpe and nineteen gentlemen associated with him. The territory granted is thus described:

... "all those lands, countries, and territories situate, lying, and being in that part of South Carolina in America which lies from the Northern stream of a river there commonly called the Savannah, all along the sea coast to the Southward unto the most Southern stream of a certain other great water or

river called the Alatamacha [Altamaha], and Westward from the heads of the said rivers respectively in direct lines to the South Seas, and all that space, circuit, and precinct of land lying within the said boundaries" (*Charters of ... Provinces of North America*, London, 1766, "Charter of Georgia," p. 4).

The limits of this grant are represented by *lines 13*—dot-and-dash yellow lines. The most southern stream of the Altamaha is the Ocmulgee River.

II. Grants for Small Tracts
[PLATE 43A]

Grant to Sir William Alexander by James I, 1621. This is the grant of Nova Scotia to its founder, Sir William Alexander. The territory granted is described as follows:

... "the lands of the continent and islands situated and lying in America, within the head or promontory called Cape of Sable, lying near the forty-third degree of north latitude or thereabouts: from this Cape stretching along the shores of the sea westward to the roadstead of St. Mary, commonly called Saint Mary's Bay, and thence northward by a straight line crossing the entrance or mouth of that great roadstead which runs toward the eastern part of the land between the countries of the Suriqui and Etechemini, commonly called Suriquois and Etechemines, to the river generally known by the name of St. Croix, and to the remotest springs or source from the western side of the same, which empty into the first mentioned river; thence by an imaginary straight line which is conceived to extend through the land or run northward to the nearest bay, river, or stream emptying into the great river of Canada [St. Lawrence]: and going from the eastward along the low shores of the same river of Canada to the river, harbor, port, or shore commonly known and called by the name of Gathepe or Gaspie, and thence south-southeast to the isles called Bacalaos, or Cape Breton, leaving the said isles on the right, and the mouth of the said great river of Canada, or large bay, and the territory of Newfoundland, with the islands belonging to the same lands, on the left: thence to the headland or point of Cape Breton aforesaid lying near latitude 45°, or thereabouts; and from the said point of Cape Breton toward the south and west to the above-mentioned Cape Sable, where the boundary began" (E. F. Slafter, *Sir William Alexander and American Colonization* (Prince Soc. Publs. Vol. 8), Boston, 1873, pp. 129-130; this grant included a considerable area of sea adjoining the coasts, with the islands therein).

The limits of this grant are represented by *line 1*—a solid red line. Saint Mary's Bay is the large bay in southwestern Nova Scotia near the entrance to the Bay of Fundy. The "great roadstead" is the Bay of Fundy. The country southward of the Bay of Fundy was occupied by the Souriquois Indians, and the country northward by the Etechemins (W. F. Ganong, *Monograph of the Evolution of the Boundaries of the Province of New Brunswick*, maps on pp. 216 and 217). What stream was the St. Croix River and where were "the remotest springs or source from the western side of the same" are mooted questions. The decision of the British-American Boundary Commission in 1798 was in favor of the stream now known as the St. Croix River, and this is taken to be the St. Croix for the purposes of this map (see below, p. 58). Since the nearest tributary of the St. Lawrence to the source of the St. Croix is the Kamouraska River, "the imaginary straight line" of the description is taken to be a line connecting the source of the St. Croix with the nearest point on the Kamouraska. The forty-third and forty-fifth degrees of north latitude referred to in the description are shown on contemporary maps somewhat farther northward than on modern ones.

Grant to Gorges and Mason by the Council for New England, 1622. This grant to Sir Ferdinand Gorges and Captain John Mason, both members of the Council for New England, is the first grant of the province of Maine. The territory granted is thus described:

... "all that part of the Maine land in New England lying upon the Sea Coast betwixt the rivers of Merimack and Sagadahock [Kennebec], and to the furthest heads of the said Rivers, and Soe forwards up into the land westward untill threescore Miles be finished from the first entrance of the aforesaid rivers" (*New Hampshire State Papers*, Vol. 29, Concord, 1896, p. 25).

This grant is represented by *line 2*—a dotted blue line. As both the Merrimac and the Kennebec rivers are longer than sixty miles, the courses described as "forwards up into the land westward" are disregarded, and the river lines are stopped sixty miles from the mouths of the streams. The early drafters of British patents for New England did not know that a few miles inland the Merrimac River bends sharply to the east from a southward course. As a result of this bend the grants to Gorges and Mason, 1622, and to Mason, 1629 (see below), are somewhat diminished in area.

Grant to Mason by the Council for New England, 1629. This is the grant of the province of New Hampshire to Captain John Mason. The territory granted is described as follows:

---
[9] See below, p. 34. The southern boundary is more specifically described in the "Old Patent of Connecticut, 1631," in Ebenezer Hazard, *Historical Collections*, Philadelphia, 1792, Vol. 1, p. 318.

... "all that part of the Maine land in New England lying upon the sea Coaste begining from the Middle part of Merrimack River, and from thence to proceed Northwards along the Sea coaste to passcattaway [Piscataqua] river, and soe forwards up within the said river to the furthest head thereof, and from thence Northwestwards untill Threescore miles be finished from the First entrance of passcattaway river, and also from Merrimacke through the said River and to the furthest head thereof, and soe forward up into the land West-wards untill Threescore miles be finished, and from thence to cross over land to the Threescore miles end accounted from passcattaway river" (*ibid.*, Vol. 29, p. 30).

The limits of this grant are represented by *line 3*—a short-dash red line. As the Merrimac River is more than sixty miles long, the part of the description which prescribes a westward course from the head of that river is disregarded. The line along the Merrimac is stopped sixty miles from the mouth of the river.

Grant to Plymouth Colony by the Council for New England, 1630. This grant, which fixed the boundaries of the colony of Plymouth, was made to "William Bradford, his heirs, associates, and assigns." Bradford was governor of the colony. The territory granted is thus described:

... "[1] all that part of New-Englande in America ... and tractes of land that lye within or betweene a certaine rivolet or rundlett there commonly called Coahassett alias Conahassett towards the north, and the river commonly called Naragansets river towards the south; and the great westerne ocean towards the east, and betweene and within a straight line directly extendinge upp into the maine land towards the west from the mouth of the said river called Naragan-setts river to the utmost limits and bounds of a cuntry or place in New Eng-lande called Pokenacutt alias Sowamsett westward, and another like straight line extendinge itself directly from the mouth of the said river called Coahassett alias Conahassett towards the west so farr up into the maine lande westwardes as the utmost limitts of the said place or cuntry commonly called Pokencutt alias Sowamsett doe extend, togeather with one half of the said river called Naragansett's and the said rivolett or rundlett called Coahassett ... [2] and ... all that tracte of lande or parte of New England in America aforesaid which lyeth within or betweene and extendeth itself from the utmost limitts of Cob-biseconte alias Comasee-Conte which adjoineth to the river of Kenebeke alias Kenebekike towards the westerne ocean and a place called the falls att Mequam-kike in America aforesaid, and the space of fifteene Englishe miles on each side of the said river commonly called Kenebek river, and all the said river called Kenebek that lies within the said limitts and bounds" (William Brigham, *Compact with Charter and Laws of Colony of New Plymouth*, Boston, 1836, pp. 22–23).

This is a grant of two tracts, one, a relatively large tract in south-eastern Massachusetts, generally known as Plymouth Colony, and the other, a small tract in Maine. The description of the first tract is faulty and if literally followed gives two lines for parts of the boundary. If instead of "mouth," "source" be read, the description is greatly im-proved. The intended boundaries are, however, reasonably clear. Cohas-set Rivolet is a little stream between Cohasset and Scituate, Massa-chusetts (*Massachusetts Hist. Soc. Colls.*, Ser. 2, Vol. 4, Boston, 1816, p. 223). In early documents "Narragansett River" was often used inter-changeably with "Narragansett Bay." Pokanoket comprised the region now occupied by the towns of East Providence, Barrington, Warren, and Bristol in Rhode Island and portions of the towns of Seekonk, Swansea, and Rehoboth in Massachusetts (*Rhode Island Hist. Soc. Publs.*, Vol. 2, new ser., Providence, 1894, p. 197).

The location of the Maine tract was long disputed. Plymouth con-tended that it extended southward to the sea. Its limits are mapped in accordance with a decision of the General Court of Massachusetts, appointed under a resolve of October 28, 1783. The committee decided that "the utmost limitts of Cobbiseconte" was the southern bend of the Cobbosseecontee River and that the "place called the falls att Mequam-kike" was some sixteen miles above the mouth of that river (*Statement of Kennebeck Claims*, Boston, 1786, pp. 15–16).

The limits of this grant are represented by *lines 4*—short-dash blue lines.

Grant to Lord Baltimore by Charles I, 1632. This grant is found in the charter of Maryland, 1632, which incorporated the province of Maryland and made Baltimore "the true Lord and Proprietary" thereof. The territory granted is thus described:

... "all that Part of the Peninsula, or Chersonese, lying in the Parts of America between the Ocean on the East and the Bay of Chesopeake on the West, divided from the Residue thereof by a Right Line drawn from the Promontory, or Head-Land, called Watkin's Point, situate upon the Bay aforesaid, near the River of Wighco, on the West, unto the Main Ocean on the East; and between that Boundary on the South, unto that Part of the Bay of Delaware on the North, which lieth under the Fortieth Degree of North Latitude from the Aequinoctial, where New-England is terminated; and all the Tract of that Land within the Metes underwritten (that is to say) passing from the said Bay,

called Delaware Bay, in a right Line, by the Degree aforesaid, unto the true Meridian of the first Fountain of the River of Pattowmack, thence verging towards the South, unto the further Bank of the said River, and following the same on the West and South unto a certain Place called Cinquack situate near the Mouth of the said River where it disembogues into the aforesaid Bay of Chessopeake, and thence by the shortest Line unto the aforesaid Promontory or Place called Watkin's Point" (Thomas Bacon, *Laws of Maryland*, Annapolis, 1765, "Charter of Maryland," p. 3).

For the location of the Wighco River, now the Pocomoke River, and Cinquack see Plate 100 D, "Chesapeake Bay Line." In colonial docu-ments "Delaware Bay" often includes "Delaware River." The location of the first fountain or source of the Potomac River was for many years disputed by Maryland and Virginia and later by West Virginia (see Pl. 51A and below, pp. 38 and 78–79). The source as it was finally agreed upon is taken to be the "first Fountain of the River of Pattow-mack."

The limits of this grant are represented by *lines 5*—long-dash blue lines.

Grant to Lord William Alexander by the Council for New Eng-land, 1635. Lord William Alexander was the son of Sir William Alexander, first Earl of Stirling. His grant is an enlargement of the grant of 1621 to his father (see above, p. 27). The territory granted is described as follows:

..."all that part of the Maine Land of Newe England aforesaid, beginninge from a certain place called or knowne by the name of Saint Croix next adjoin-inge to New Scotland in America aforesaid, and from thence extendinge alonge the sea coaste unto a certaine place called Pemaquid, and soe upp the River thereof to the furthest head of the same as it tendeth Northwarde, and extend-inge from thence att the nearest unto the River of Kinebequi and soe upwards alonge by the shortest course which tendeth unto the River of Canada [St. Lawrence River]."[10]

There is a gap in the description in respect to the boundary along the St. Lawrence River and from that river to the St. Croix River. The intention to grant Lord William a tract of land adjacent to that granted to his father in 1621 is clear, and the boundary of the new grant on the east evidently follows that of the old on the west. Pemaquid and Pema-quid River are near the Maine coast, somewhat east of the lower Kenne-bec River.

The limits of this grant are represented by *line 6*—a long-dash red line.

Grant to Gorges by Charles I, 1639. Having agreed with Mason to a division of their lands with the Piscataqua River as a boundary line, Gorges in 1639 obtained from the king a charter for Maine with en-larged limits. The territory granted is described as follows:

... "all that Parte ... of the Mayne Lande of New England aforesaid beginning att the entrance of Pascataway Harbor, and soe to passe upp the same into the River of Newichewanocke, and through the same unto the furthest heade thereof, and from thence Northwestwards till one hundred and twenty miles bee finished, and from Pascataway Harbor mouth aforesaid Northeast-wards along the Sea Coasts to Sagadahocke, and upp the River thereof to Kynybequy River, and through the same unto the heade thereof, and into the Lande Northwestwards untill one hundred and twenty myles bee ended, being accompted from the mouth of Sagadahocke, and from the period of one hundred and twenty myles aforesaid to crosse over Lande to the one hundred and twenty myles end formerly reckoned upp into the Lande from Pascataway Harbor through Newichewanocke River" (B. P. Poore, *Federal and State Con-stitutions*, Washington, 1878, Vol. 1, p. 775).

The northern branch of the Piscataqua River was formerly called the Newichewanocke River. Sagadahoc was an early settlement at the mouth of the Sagadahoc River, the early name for the lower Kennebec River. The Kennebec River line is stopped one hundred and twenty miles from the mouth of the river.

The limits of this grant are represented by *line 7*—a dotted yellow line.

Grant to Providence Plantations by the Governor and Com-missioners of Parliament, 1643. In 1643 Roger Williams, the founder of Rhode Island, obtained a patent from the governor and commissioners of Parliament, at that time charged with the administration of the colonies in America, incorporating the inhabitants of the towns of Provi-dence, Portsmouth, and Newport under the name of "the Providence Plantations in the Narragansett Bay in New England." The patent granted liberal powers of government but no territory. However, it

---

[10] E. F. Slafter, *Sir William Alexander and American Colonization* (Prince Soc. Publs., Vol. 8), Boston, 1873, pp. 252–253. Lord Alexander's grant included also Long Island. In 1638 the council made an addition to the grant, which comprised the territory between the Pemaquid and Kennebec rivers, and, thus augmented, granted the whole to the Earl of Stirling (Sir William Alexander) (*ibid.*, p. 253, note).

described specifically the territory over which the powers of government were to be exercised. The description is as follows:

... "a Tract of Land in the Continent of America aforesaid, called by the Name of the Narranganset-Bay; bordering Northward and Northeast on the Patent of Massachusetts, East and Southeast on Plymouth Patent, South on the Ocean, and on the West and Northwest by the Indians called Nahigganneucks, alias Narranganssets; the whole Tract extending about Twenty-five English Miles unto the Pequot River and Country" (*Records of Colony of Rhode Island and Providence Plantations*, Vol. 1, Providence, 1856, p. 144). Another version of this grant reads "twenty-seven" instead of "twenty-five" miles (*Rhode Island Hist. Soc. Publs.*, Vol. 2, new ser., Providence, 1894, p. 260).

The boundary line between the Narraganset and Pequot Indians near the seacoast was the Pawcatuck River (F. W. Hodge, *Handbook of American Indians*, Washington, 1912, Vol. 2, p. 29). Farther northward it is not possible to define it so specifically. The phrase "unto the Pequot River and Country" is inconsistent with itself, as the Pequot River (the modern Thames River) lies some fourteen miles westward of the eastern boundary of the Pequot Country.

The limits of this grant are represented by *line 8*—a dotted red line.

Grant to Lord Hopton and others by Charles II, 1649. This grant was made by Charles II, soon after the execution of his father, in the year 1649, officially styled the first year of his reign. As Lord Fairfax many years later acquired title to the grant, it is usually known as the Fairfax grant. The original grantees were Lord Hopton and six other British gentlemen. No powers of government were conferred. The territory granted is thus described:

... "all that intire tract, territory, or parcel of land, situate, lying, and being in America, and bounded within the head of the rivers Rappahannock and Quiriough, or Patomack rivers, the courses of said rivers as they are commonly called and known by the inhabitants and descriptions of those parts and Chesapeak Bay; together with the rivers themselves" (W. W. Hening, *Virginia Statutes at Large*, Vol. 4, Richmond, 1820, p. 515).

The limits of this grant are represented by *line 9*—a dot-and-dash yellow line. The part of the line connecting the heads of the two rivers is drawn as claimed by Lord Fairfax (see Pl. 51A).

Grant to La Tour and others by Cromwell, 1656. This is a grant to Charles Amador de La Tour, Thomas Temple, and William Crowne. La Tour was of French extraction, Temple and Crowne were Englishmen. The limits of the grant are thus described:

... "the country and territory called Acadia, and part of the country called Nova Scotia, from Merliguesche on the east coast to the port and cape of La Have, continuing along the sea coast to Cape Sable; and from thence to a certain port called Port Latour, and now named Port L'Esmeron; and from thence continuing along the coast and islands to Cape Fourchu; and from thence to the Cape and River St. Mary, continuing along the sea coast to Port Royal; and from thence continuing along the coast to the extremity of the bay; and from thence continuing along the said bay to the fort St. John; and from thence continuing all along the coast to Pentagoet and the River St. George in Mescourus, on the borders of New England on the west coast, and into the lands throughout the said coaste to one hundred leagues of depth" (W. F. Ganong, *Monograph of Evolution of Boundaries of Province of New Brunswick*, London, 1901, pp. 182–183; *Memorials of English and French Commissioners concerning Limits of Nova Scotia or Acadia*, London, 1755, pp. 727–728).

The limits of this grant are represented by *line 10*—a dot-and-dash blue line. Owing to the doublings of the coast no mapping of this grant is entirely satisfactory. In accordance with the method of mapping that was followed, "one-hundred-league" lines were drawn at right angles to the general trend of the coast described above, and of these, two exterior lines and parts of two others were taken for boundary lines. The parts of the coast line cut by the one-hundred-league lines were disregarded, and the three remaining parts were taken. The northerly boundary line passes through the most northerly termini of the one-hundred-league lines.

Several of the names of places found in the description are now obsolete. Merliguesche was near the site of the present town of Lunenberg, Nova Scotia. Port Latour or Port L'Esmeron was on the southern coast of Nova Scotia north of Cape Sable. Cape Fourchu was near the site of the present town of Yarmouth. The River St. Mary is the present St. Marys Bay. The cape of that name is at the southern entrance of the bay. "The bay" of the description is the present Bay of Fundy. Pentagoet was on the eastern shore of Penobscot Bay—the modern Castine. By Mescourus is meant the Muscongus or Waldo grant, extending from the Penobscot River westward to the Muscongus River.

Grant to Rhode Island and Providence Plantations by Charles II, 1663. This grant is found in the Rhode Island charter of 1663. It

was made to the "Governor and Company of the English Colony of Rhode Island and Providence Plantations in New England in America." The territory granted is thus described:

... "all that parte of our dominiones in New England, in America, conteyneing the Nahantick and Nanhyganset Bay and countryes and partes adjacent, bounded on the west or westerly to the middle or channel of a river there commonly called and known by the name of Pawcatuck, alias Pawcawtuck river, and soe along the sayd river as the greater or middle streame thereof reacheth or lyes upp into the north countrye, northward, unto the head thereof, and from thence by a streight lyne drawne due north untill itt meets with the south lyne of the Massachusetts Collonie; and on the north or northerly by the aforesayd south or southerly lyne of the Massachusetts Collony or Plantation; and extending towards the east or eastwardly three English miles to the east and northeast of the most eastern and northeastern parts of the aforesayd Narragansett Bay, as the sayd bay lyeth or extendeth itself from the ocean on the south or southwardly, unto the mouth of the river which runneth towards the towne of Providence, and from thence along the eastwardly side or banke of the sayd river (higher called by the name of Seacuncke river), up to the Falls called Patuckett Falls, being the most westwardly lyne of Plymouth Collony, and soe from the sayd Falls in a streight lyne due north untill itt meete with the aforesayd lyne of the Massachusetts Collony; and bounded on the south by the ocean" (*Records of Colony of Rhode Island and Providence Plantations*, Vol. 2, Providence, 1857, pp. 18–19); for Rhode Island's disputes over her eastern and western boundaries, see Pl. 97, maps C and D, and pp. 510–518, below).

The limits of this grant are represented by *line 11*—a full yellow line.

Grant to the Duke of York by Charles II, 1664. This grant was made by Charles II to his brother, the Duke of York, several months before New Netherland was surrendered to the English by the Dutch. The territory granted is described as follows:

... "[1] all that part of the maine Land of New England beginning at a certain place called or known by the name of St. Croix next adjoining to New Scotland in America, and from thence extending along the Sea Coast unto a certain place called Petuaquine or Pemaquid and so up the River thereof to the furthest head of the same as it tendeth Northwards and extending from thence to the River Kinebequi and so Upwards by the Shortest course to the River Canada [St. Lawrence] Northward ... [2] together also with the said River called Hudsons River and all the Land from the West side of Connecticut [River] to the East side of Delaware Bay."[11]

This is a grant of two tracts. The description of the first follows with slight variations that of the grant of 1635 to Lord Alexander (see above, p. 28) and calls for the same territory. Since often in early documents "Delaware Bay" and "Delaware River" are used interchangeably and are thus used by the Duke of York in interpreting his grant, the western boundary is drawn from the source of the Hudson River to the source of the Delaware River and thence down the east side of the river and bay to the ocean.

The limits of this grant are represented by *lines 12*—long-dash yellow lines.

Grant to Berkeley and Carteret by the Duke of York, 1664. A little more than three months after the Duke of York received the grant described above, and before he was in possession of his property, he granted to two of his friends, Lord Berkeley and Sir George Carteret, the southwestern part thereof under the name of New Ceaserea or New Jersey. The territory granted is thus described:

... "all that Tract of Land adjacent to New-England, and lying and being to the Westward of Long-Island and Manhitas Island, and bounded on the East part by the main Sea, and part by Hudson's River, and hath upon the West Delaware Bay or River, and extendeth Southward to the Main Ocean as far as Cape May at the mouth of Delaware Bay; and to the Northward as far as the Northermost Branch of the said Bay or River of Delaware, which is forty one Degrees and forty Minutes of Latitude, and crosseth over thence in a strait Line to Hudson's River in forty one Degrees of Latitude" (Aaron Leaming and Jacob Spicer, *Grants, Concessions, and Original Constitutions of the Province of New Jersey*, Philadelphia, 1758, p. 10).

The limits of this grant are represented by *line 13*—a solid blue line. The northern boundary, which was long disputed by New York and New Jersey (see Pl. 97F and pp. 76–77, below), is drawn as finally settled.

Grant to William Penn by Charles II, 1681. This grant is found in the Pennsylvania charter. The territory granted is thus described:

... "all that tract or parte of land in America ... as the same is bounded on the East by Delaware River, from twelve miles distance Northwarde of New

---

[11] E. B. O'Callaghan, *Documents relating to Colonial History of State of New York*, Vol. 2, Albany, 1858, pp. 295–296. This grant included Long Island, Marthas Vineyard, and Nantucket. The second grant to the Duke of York, 1674, repeats the description of boundaries found in the first grant.

Castle Towne, unto the three and fortieth degree of Northern latitude if the said River doth extend soe farre Northwards; but if the said River shall not extend soe farre Northward, then by the said River soe farr as it doth extend, and from the head of the said River, the Easterne bounds are to bee determined by a meridian line to bee drawn from the head of the said River unto the said three and fortieth degree; the said lands to extend Westwards five degrees in longitude to be computed from the said Easterne Bounds; and the said lands to bee bounded on the North by the beginning of the three and fortieth degree of Northern latitude; and on the south by a circle drawn at twelve miles distance from New Castle Northwards and Westwards unto the beginning of the fortieth degree of Northerne Latitude, and then by a streight line Westwards to the limitt of Longitude above mencioned" (*Pennsylvania Archives*, Ser. 4, Vol. 1, Harrisburg, 1900, pp. 4–5).

The limits of this grant are represented by *line 14*—a dot-and-dash red line. The provision of the grant making part of the southern boundary "a circle drawn at twelve miles distance from New Castle" is disregarded, since the circle does not touch the fortieth parallel. For the dispute over the southern boundary see Plate 100C and pp. 84–85, below; for the dispute over the western boundary of Pennsylvania, see Plate 97G and pp. 77–78, below.

Grants to William Penn by the Duke of York, 1682. These grants were made in two deeds of feoffment, both dated August 24, 1682. They conveyed the territory comprising the present state of Delaware. The first grant is as follows: "all that the town of New Castle, otherwise called Delaware, and all that tract of land lying within the compass or circle of twelve miles about the same, situate, lying, and being upon the River Delaware" (Samuel Hazard, *Annals of Pennsylvania*, Philadelphia, 1850, p. 588).

The second grant is as follows: "all that tract of land upon Delaware River and Bay, beginning twelve miles south from the town of New Castle, otherwise called Delaware, and extending south to the Whorekills, otherwise called Cape Henlopen" (*ibid.*, p. 591).

The limits of this grant are represented by *line 15*—a short-dash yellow line. As the extent of the second grant to the westward is not specifically described and as its extent both westward and southward was disputed, the western and southern lines are drawn as finally settled.[12] For the dispute over these lines, see Plate 100 C and pp. 84–85, below.

ALLOTMENTS OF LAND, DORCHESTER, MASSACHUSETTS, 1660

[PLATE 43B]

This is a map of the part of Dorchester that was incorporated as Milton in 1662. It illustrates the allotments of land made by New England towns during the early colonial period (see also Pl. 41D). The tracts to the right of the "sixth division" were granted by Dorchester before 1660, chiefly to some of the early proprietors. The tract labeled "church lands" was set apart for the use and maintenance of the ministry.

To facilitate the allotments the sixth division was divided into two parts by a range line, and each part was laid off into lots. Those who owned lots in the first or original division of Dorchester were assigned lots in the new division. The acreage that each proprietor received was governed either by the amount that he paid into the company as a proprietor or by the amount of his taxable property. For this reason the lots vary greatly in size, the smallest containing ten acres and the largest four hundred and fifty-seven acres. On the left are shown a "church lot" and "common land"—the latter devoted to the use of the proprietors of the town.

Plate 43B is a reproduction of a map found in A. K. Teele, *History of Milton, Massachusetts*, Boston, 1887, opposite p. 16.

DIVISIONS OF LAND IN MAINE, 1795

[PLATE 44A]

This map is a reproduction of a part of Osgood Carleton's "Map of the district of Maine," published as the frontispiece of James Sullivan, *History of the District of Maine*, Boston, 1795. It shows chiefly town divisions. Early towns are designated by names, and later ones by numbers. The early towns vary in size and shape, while the later ones approximate the same size and shape—a square. The range lines do not run due north and south but roughly at right angles to the coast.

"The Lottery Land" on the right of the map comprised fifty towns that were disposed of by the state in 1786–1788 by means of a lottery. Two large tracts are shown, one the Waldo Patent, in the lower central part of the map, and the other Bingham's Purchase, near the upper

left-hand corner. South of Bingham's Purchase are several towns that were granted by Massachusetts for educational purposes: "B" to the Taunton Academy, "D" to the Berwick Academy, and "E" to the Hallowell Academy. The two towns designated "A" were granted to the sufferers of Portland whose property was burned by the British in 1775. "C" was granted to the proprietors of Warren and Groton. Part of an Indian reserve, under the designation "Land reserved for the [Indians]," is shown in the upper central part of the map.

FARM OF GOVERNOR JOHN ENDICOTT, 1668

[PLATE 44B]

As the colonial governments possessed much land and but little money, they often granted lands to civilians as rewards for services or in payment of debts or for the promotion of industries. The grant in 1657 of one thousand acres to Governor John Endicott by the General Court of Massachusetts "in lieu of seventy-five pounds paid by him and his wife in the general adventure" is a specimen of this sort of grant. In 1668, three years after Endicott's death, five hundred acres of his grant were laid off in what is now the city of Concord, N. H. Plate 44B is reproduced from a plan of the farm found in the *New Hampshire State Papers*, Vol. 24, Concord, 1894, p. 63.

GRANTS IN MAINE TO PLYMOUTH COLONY, LAKE, AND OTHERS, 1753

[PLATE 44C]

This map illustrates early land grants. For the grant to Plymouth Colony see above, p. 28, and Plate 43A. The representation of Plymouth's possessions is not favorable to her claim, which extended to the seashore. The lands of Sir Bibye Lake and others are also shown. Lake held the land under the title of his grandfather, Thomas Lake, who purchased the land from Christopher Lawson, the original owner. Lawson's title was based on deeds from the Indians. The dates of the grants preceded by a good many years the date of the map, 1753.

This map also illustrates the colonial practice of purchasing lands from the Indians. It is a reproduction of a map found in the Division of Maps, Library of Congress.

MEREDITH, NEW HAMPSHIRE, 1770

[PLATE 44D]

This is a typical plan of a New England town founded near the close of the colonial period (for a plan of an early New England town, see Pl. 41D). Its principal features are the three main divisions of the town (the first in the middle and lower part of the map, the second on the left of the first, and the third on the right of the first), the lot assigned to each proprietor in each division, and the lots reserved in each division for the minister and parsonage, the school, and the proprietors in their corporate capacity. In the first division a reservation of common land is also shown. The lots in the first division contain one hundred acres, in the second one hundred and twenty acres, and in the third ninety-five acres.

Plate 44D is a reproduction of a map found in the *New Hampshire State Papers*, Vol. 27, Concord, 1896, p. 488.

GRANTS OF WESTERN LANDS BY GEORGIA TO LAND COMPANIES, 1789, 1795

[PLATE 45A]

Much speculation has accompanied the disposition of the public lands. Large tracts have often been purchased, not for settlement or permanent possession but for sale at a profit. Plate 45A illustrates one of the most important of these speculative enterprises.

In 1789 Georgia granted to three speculative land companies more than twenty-five million acres in the present states of Mississippi and Alabama and within the territory then claimed by her (C. H. Haskins, *Yazoo Land Companies*, New York, 1891, p. 8; see p. 35, below). The companies were allowed two years in which to pay for the land. The first of these companies, known as the South Carolina Yazoo Company, was granted a tract which is thus described:

... "beginning at the mouth of Cole's creek on the Mississippi, continuing to the head spring or source thereof; from thence a due east course to the Tom or Don Bigby river, then continuing along the middle of the said river up to the latitude thirty-three; thence down along the latitude thirty-three, bounding on the territory of the Virginia Yazoo company, a due west course to the middle of the Mississippi; thence down the middle of the Mississippi to the mouth of Cole's creek aforesaid" (*Georgia Acts*, Dec. 21, 1789).

---

[12] The grants to the Duke of York of 1664 and 1674 did not include Delaware. He claimed it as part of the territory captured from the Dutch. In 1683, subsequent to his deed to Penn, he received a grant of Delaware from Charles II. In this some of the boundaries are described with considerable detail (*Maryland Archives*, Vol. 5, Baltimore, 1887, p. 426).

This grant is represented on the map by perpendicular shading. A second company, the Virginia Yazoo Company, received a grant of land which is described thus:

... "beginning at the mouth of Bear creek on the south side of the Tennessee river, running thence up the said creek to the head or source; thence a due west course to the Tom or Don Bigby, or Twenty mile creek; thence down the same to the latitude thirty-three; thence along the said latitude, bounding on the South Carolina Yazoo company's line, a due west course to the middle of the Mississippi; thence up the said river, in the middle thereof, to the northern boundary of this state; thence along the said boundary line a due east course to the Tennessee river; thence up the middle of the said river to the beginning thereof" (*ibid.*).

This grant is represented on the map by diagonal shading running in a northeast-southwest direction.

The grant to the third company, the Tennessee Company, was as follows:

... "beginning at the mouth of Bear creek on the south side of the Tennessee river in the latitude of thirty-four degrees, forty-three minutes, running thence up Bear creek to the head or source; thence a due west course to the Tom Bigby or Twenty mile creek; thence down the said Bigby, or Twenty mile creek, to the latitude thirty-four degrees; thence a due east course one hundred and twenty miles; thence a due north course to the northern boundary line of this state; thence a due west course along the northern boundary line to the Great Tennessee river; thence up the middle of the said river Tennessee to the place of beginning" (*ibid.*).

This grant is represented on the map by diagonal shading running in a southeast-northwest direction.

Title under the acts of 1789 never passed from the state, as the companies failed to pay for the land within the prescribed time. In 1795 Georgia made a second grant, which included the larger part of the land granted in 1789 together with much additional land, in all some 35,000,000 acres, comprising the greater parts of the present states of Mississippi and Alabama (Haskins, *op. cit.*, p. 24; P. J. Treat, *National Land System, 1785-1820*, New York, 1910, p. 357). For this munificent territory four land companies agreed to pay a total sum of five hundred thousand dollars. The first of these companies, known as the Georgia Company, was granted a tract which is described as follows:

... "beginning on the Mobille bay where the latitude thirty-one degrees north of the Equator intersects the same, running thence up the said bay to the mouth of lake Tensaw; thence up the said lake Tensaw to the Alabama river ... thence up the said river Alabama to the junction of the Coosa and Oakfuskee rivers; thence up the Coosa river above the Big Shoals to where it intersects the latitude of thirty-four degrees north of the Equator; thence a due west course to the Mississippi river; thence down the middle of the said river to the latitude of thirty-two degrees, forty minutes; thence a due east course to the Don or Tombigby river; thence down the middle of the said river to its junction with the Alabama river; thence down the middle of the said river to the Mobille bay; thence down the said Mobille bay to the place of beginning" (*Georgia Acts*, Jan. 7, 1795).

This grant is represented on the map by a violet color. As Mobile Bay and Lake Tensaw lie farther south than was supposed, the courses along these bodies of water are disregarded.

A second company, the Georgia Mississippi Company, was granted lands which are thus described:

... "beginning on the river Mississippi at the place where the latitude of thirty-one degrees and eighteen minutes north of the Equator intersects the same; thence a due east course to the middle of Don or Tombigby river; thence up the middle of the said river to where it intersects the latitude of thirty-two degrees and forty minutes north of the Equator; thence a due west course along the Georgia Company line to the river Mississippi; thence down the middle of the same to the place of beginning" (*ibid.*).

This grant is represented on the map by a red color.

A third company, the Upper Mississippi Company, was granted a tract which is described as follows:

... "beginning at the Mississippi river where the northern boundary line of this state strikes the same; thence along the said northern boundary line due east to the Tennessee river; thence along the said Tennessee river to the mouth of Bear Creek; thence up Bear Creek to where the parallel of latitude twenty-five British statute miles south of the northern boundary of this state intersects the same; thence along the said last mentioned parallel of latitude, across Tombigby or Twenty Mile creek, due west to the Mississippi river; thence up the middle of the said river to the beginning" (*ibid.*).

This grant is represented on the map by a yellow color. The slight discrepancy between the limits as depicted and as described is caused by ignorance of the drainage in 1795.

A fourth grant was to the Tennessee Company, whose lands were thus described:

... "beginning at the mouth of Bear Creek on the south side of the Tennessee river; thence up the said creek to the most southern source thereof; thence due south to the latitude of thirty-four degrees, ten minutes, north of the Equator; thence a due east course one hundred and twenty miles; thence a due north course to the Great Tennessee river; thence up the middle of the said river to the northern boundary line of this state; thence a due west course along the said line to where it intersects the Great Tennessee river below the Mussel Shoals; thence up the said river to the place of beginning" (*ibid.*).

This grant is represented on the map by a green color. Since the "Great Tennessee River" lies westward and southward of its supposed location, the courses along this river are disregarded.

In 1796 Georgia rescinded the grants of 1795. Thereupon the claimants under the grants turned for relief to Congress, which body in 1814 passed an act that satisfied most of them. A half-century elapsed, however, before the last of the claims were finally decided (Haskins, *op. cit.*, p. 44).

MILITARY RESERVES, 1778-1816

[PLATE 45B]

The practice of granting public lands to soldiers as bounties or as rewards for service was adopted during the colonial period and followed during the Revolution (A. C. Ford, *Colonial Precedents of our National Land System*, Madison, 1910, pp. 103-107). The practice of setting apart large tracts known as military reserves, to satisfy these grants, arose during the Revolution. The acts under which these tracts were reserved emanate from both federal and state governments. The federal government was the first to offer lands for military service, but since it possessed no public domain until after the states had ceded to it their western lands (see Pl. 47B-E and pp. 34-36, below) it fell to the states that owned lands to make the first provision for satisfying the offers of the federal government. During the years 1778-1784 New York, Pennsylvania, Maryland, Virginia, North Carolina, South Carolina, and Georgia created military reserves. In 1787 the federal government established a military reserve for Revolutionary soldiers. In the first year of the War of 1812 an act was passed establishing reserves for the soldiers of that war. The system of military reserves came to an end in 1842 with the passage of an act permitting persons holding military land warrants to locate any public lands, subject to private entry, wherever situated (*U. S. Statutes at Large*, Vol. 5, Boston, 1848, p. 497). Previous to this date they could locate lands only within the reserves.

Virginia Military Reserves, 1778-1781, 1784. The first of the military reserves was that created by a resolution of the Virginia legislature dated December 19, 1778, which reserved for "the officers and soldiers in the Virginia line" a tract described as follows:

... "bounded by the Green river and a south east course from the head thereof to the Cumberland mountains, with the said mountains to the Carolina line, with the Carolina line to the Cherokee or Tennessee river, with the said river to the Ohio river, and with the Ohio river to the said Green river" (W. W. Hening, *Virginia Statutes at Large*, Vol. 10, Richmond, 1810, p. 55).

On surveying the Virginia-North Carolina boundary line in 1779 it was discovered that a part of the lands reserved the previous year lay in North Carolina. In lieu of these lands the Virginia legislature in 1781 added to the reserve "all that tract of land included within the rivers Mississippi, Ohio, and Tenissee, and the Carolina boundary line" (*ibid.*, pp. 465-466).

The reserve as finally established lay entirely in what is now the state of Kentucky. Providing against a possible exhaustion of the lands of this reserve, Virginia in her act of cession of 1784 (see below, p. 35) included the following provision:

... "in case the quantity of good lands on the southeast side of the Ohio, upon the waters of Cumberland river, and between the Green river and Tennessee river which have been reserved by law for the Virginia troops upon continental establishment should, from the North Carolina line bearing in further upon the Cumberland lands than was expected, prove insufficient for their legal bounties, the deficiency should be made up to the said troops in good lands, to be laid off between the rivers Scioto and Little Miami on the northwest side of the river Ohio" (*Journs. Cont. Cong.*, Vol. 4, Washington, 1823, p. 343).[13]

In 1790, agents for the Virginia troops having reported that there was an insufficiency of good land in the Virginia reserve in Kentucky, Congress opened up the Virginia reserve in Ohio. All this reserve was eventually located for the Virginia troops, with the exception of about one hundred and twenty square miles, which Congress in 1871 ceded to Ohio (*U. S. Statutes at Large*, Vol. 1, Boston, 1845, pp. 182-183; Vol. 16, Boston, 1871, p. 416).

---

[13] Virginia also reserved 150,000 acres (not shown because of the small size of the tract) to satisfy a promise of lands made to George Rogers Clark and his troops (see below, p. 38 and Pl. 50C).

South Carolina Military Reserve, 1778. In 1778 South Carolina established a military reserve for the soldiers of the South Carolina regiments on the continental establishment and for the heirs of those soldiers who were slain or who died during the war. The tract reserved is described as "all the lands in the forks between Tugaloo and Keowee rivers up to the new Cherokee boundary line" (Thomas Cooper, *South Carolina Statutes at Large*, Vol. 4, Columbia, 1838, p. 411). The new Cherokee boundary was established by the treaty of South Carolina and Georgia with the Cherokees, May 20, 1777.

This reserve is shown on the map in northwestern South Carolina.

North Carolina Military Reserves, 1780, 1783. In 1780 North Carolina created for "the officers and soldiers of its continental battalions" a military reserve in what is now eastern Tennessee. The tract is thus described:

... "situate between the Virginia line and the rivers Tenasee and Holston, as far up as the mouth of French Broad river; thence a direct course to the mouth of Powell's river; thence a direct course to a great gap in Cumberland mountain, about twenty miles southwest of the Kentucky road where it strikes Cumberland mountain; thence a north course to the Virginia line" (*North Carolina State Records*, Vol. 24, Goldsboro, 1905, p. 338).

In 1783 North Carolina created a second reserve, whose limits were described as follows:

... "beginning in the Virginia line where Cumberland river intersects the same, thence south fifty miles, thence west to the Tenasee river, thence down the Tenasee to the Virginia line, thence with the said Virginia line east to the beginning" (*ibid.*, p. 483).

This land was reserved for the continental officers and soldiers in the service of North Carolina, for the heirs or assigns of such of these as should fall in the defense of their country, and for General Nathanael Greene and his heirs and assigns. The two North Carolina reserves lay in the present state of Tennessee.

Maryland Military Reserve, 1781. In 1781 Maryland reserved for her officers and soldiers all the unappropriated lands in Washington County, Maryland, westward of Fort Cumberland that were necessary to satisfy the offers of land that had been made (*Laws of Maryland*, Ch. 20, Sect. 2, November, 1781).

New York Military Tract, 1782. In 1782 New York created a military reserve whose limits are as follows:

... "all the Lands situate ... in the County of Tryon, bounded on the North by Lake Ontario, the Onondago [Oswego] River, and the Oneida Lake; on the West by a Line drawn from the Mouth of the Great Sodus or Asorodus Creek thro' the most westerly Inclination of the Seneca Lake; on the South by an East and West Line drawn thro' the most southerly Inclination of the Seneca Lake; and on the East by a Line drawn from the most westerly Boundary of the Oneida or Tuscarora Country on the Oneida Lake thro' the most westerly Inclination of the West Bounds of the Oneida or Tuscarora Country" (*New York Session Laws*, Ch. 11, July 25, 1782).

This tract was reserved for the major-generals and brigadier-generals who at the time of their entering the military service resided in New York, for the troops of New York serving in the army of the United States and their legal representatives, and for such other persons as New York in the future should provide for on account of military service in the army of the United States.

Pennsylvania Donation and Depreciation Lands, 1783. In 1783 Pennsylvania reserved for her officers and privates in the federal army a tract which was described as follows:

... "beginning at the mouth of Mogulbughtiton creek; thence up the Allegheny river to the mouth of Cagnawaga creek; thence due north to the northern boundary of this state; thence west by the said boundary to the northwest corner of the state; thence south by the western boundary of the state to the northwest corner of lands appropriated by this act for discharging the certificates herein mentioned; and thence by the same lands east to the place of beginning" (Charles Smith, *Laws of Pennsylvania*, Vol. 2, Philadelphia, 1810, pp. 63–64).

This tract is known as the Pennsylvania Donation Lands.

In 1780 Pennsylvania passed an act providing for the settlement, upon a basis of gold and silver, of the depreciation in the pay of the officers and privates of the Pennsylvania line. Under this act the soldiers received certificates specifying the sums due them. In 1783 an act (the same act that provided for the Donation Lands) was passed making these certificates receivable at the state land office in payment for unlocated lands within a tract whose limits are as follows:

... "beginning where the western boundary of this state crosses the Ohio river; thence up the said river to Fort Pitt; thence up the Allegheny river to the mouth of the Mogulbughtiton creek; thence by a west line to the western boundary of this state; thence south by the said boundary to the place of beginning" (*ibid.*, pp. 62–63; *Pennsylvania Archives*, Ser. 3, Vol. 3, Harrisburg, 1894, pp. 761–771).

Two small areas within this tract were not included in the reserve. This tract is known as the Pennsylvania Depreciation Lands.

Georgia Military Reserve, 1784. In 1784 Georgia created a military reserve for the "officers, and seamen, and soldiers who are entitled to land in this state by any resolve of Congress or act or resolve of this state, refugees and other militia excepted." The tract reserved was described as "all the lands between the North and South fork of the Okoney [Oconee River] up to the present temporary line."[14] It was reserved for the term of twelve months. This reserve lay in northeastern Georgia.

United States Military Reserves, 1787–1816. In 1787 Congress, having come into possession of the lands northwest of the Ohio River, reserved a million acres in what is now eastern Ohio "for the purpose of satisfying the military bounties." The limits of this tract are described thus: "bounded east by the 7th range of townships, south by the land contracted for by Cutler and Sargent, and to extend north as far as the ranges of townships, and westward so far as to include the above quantity" (*Journs. Cont. Cong.*, Vol. 4, Washington, 1823, p. 801). "The land contracted for by [Manasseh] Cutler and [Winthrop] Sargent" is the land of the Ohio Company (see below, p. 38). A reserve in what is now southwestern Illinois between the Ohio and Mississippi rivers was also authorized but was never made.

In 1796 the reserve of 1787 was enlarged so as to include more than two million five hundred thousand acres. The bounds of the enlarged reserve are thus described:

... "beginning at the northwest corner of the seven ranges of townships, and running thence fifty miles due south along the western boundary of the said ranges; thence due west to the main branch of the Scioto river; thence up the main branch of the said river to the place where the Indian boundary line crosses the same; thence along the said boundary line to the Tuscaroras branch of the Muskingum river at the crossing place above Fort Lawrence; thence up the said river to the point where a line run due west from the place of beginning will intersect the said river; thence along the line so run to the place of beginning" (*U. S. Statutes at Large*, Vol. 1, Boston, 1845, p. 490).

Soon after the outbreak of the War of 1812, on May 6 of that year, Congress reserved six million acres of public land for the purpose of satisfying the bounties to "the non-commissioned officers and soldiers of the United States," promised to them under the acts of December 24, 1811, and January 11, 1812 (*ibid.*, Vol. 2, Boston, 1845, pp. 728–729). Later, state troops and volunteers were given the benefit of the bounty laws (P. J. Treat, *National Land System, 1785–1820*, New York, 1910, pp. 246–247). The six million acres were to be distributed and located as follows: two million acres in Michigan Territory, two millions in Illinois Territory north of the Illinois River, and two millions in Louisiana Territory (later Arkansas Territory) between the St. Francis and Arkansas rivers. The reserve in Michigan Territory was never made, but in lieu thereof, in May, 1816, five hundred thousand acres were reserved in Missouri Territory, and one million five hundred thousand acres were added to the reserve in Illinois Territory (*U. S. Statutes at Large*, Vol. 3, Boston, 1846, p. 332). In April, 1816, a reservation of two million acres was authorized, but it was never made (*ibid.*, p. 287; Treat, *op. cit.*, p. 249, note 39).

These three reserves lay, respectively, in western Illinois, north-central Missouri, and east-central Arkansas.

BRITISH POSSESSIONS IN EASTERN NORTH AMERICA AFTER THE QUEBEC ACT, 1774

[PLATE 46A]

The object of this map is to show the changes in the boundary of Quebec and the Indian Reserve effected by the Quebec Act. Incidentally it also shows the new northern boundary of West Florida, established in 1764. All other boundary lines are the same as those of Plate 41A. By the Quebec Act the Labrador coast, Anticosti, Magdalen, and certain other islands were detached from Newfoundland and attached to Quebec.

---

[14] A. D. Candler, *Colonial Records of State of Georgia*, Vol. 19, Part II, Atlanta, 1911, p. 299. By "the present temporary line" is meant the line established by the treaty of Georgia with the Cherokee Indians, May 31, 1783 (*American State Papers, Indian Affairs*, Vol. 1, Washington, 1832, p. 23). In February, 1785, a second reserve was made conditionally, but the condition was not fulfilled (*Colonial Records*, etc., p. 440; *Amer. State Papers*, etc., p. 17).

The enlarged Quebec embraced a vast territory, extending from the Atlantic Ocean southwestward to the Ohio and Mississippi rivers, and including what later became the Old Northwest Territory. On the north it was bounded by the possessions of the Hudson's Bay Company; and on the south the limits, as described in the act, were as follows:

... "bounded on the south by a line from the bay of Chaleurs along the highlands which divide the rivers that empty themselves into the river St. Lawrence from those which fall into the sea, to a point in forty-five degrees of northern latitude on the eastern bank of the river Connecticut, keeping the same latitude directly west through the lake Champlain, until in the same latitude it meets the river St. Lawrence; from thence up the eastern bank of the said river to the lake Ontario; thence through the lake Ontario and the river commonly called Niagara, and thence along by the eastern and southeastern bank of lake Erie, following the said bank until the same shall be intersected by the northern boundary granted by the Charter of the Province of Pennsylvania, in case the same shall be so intersected; and from thence along the said northern and western boundaries of the said province, until the said western boundary strike the Ohio ... and along the bank of the said river westward to the banks of the Mississippi, and northward to the southern boundary of the territory granted to the merchants adventurers of England trading to Hudson's Bay" (*North-Eastern Boundary Arbitration Papers*, Washington, 1829, Appendix to Two Statements of United States, p. 169; *British Statutes*, 14 George III, Ch. 83, sect. 1).

This line as shown on the map follows the northern and western charter boundaries of Pennsylvania as finally established. A late edition of John Mitchell's map of North America shows this line following the forty-third parallel as the northern boundary of Pennsylvania, and a line lying five degrees westward of the Delaware River and corresponding to the meanderings thereof as the western boundary of Pennsylvania. The omitted part of the description describes an alternative line to be followed in case the northern boundary of Pennsylvania should not intersect Lake Erie. The latter part of the description is concise, but its meaning is clear.

A new northern boundary of West Florida was established by the commission of George Johnstone as governor of West Florida, dated June 6, 1764. It is thus described: "a line drawn from the mouth of the river Yasous [Yazoo] where it unites with the Mississippi, due east to the river Apalachicola" (*North-Eastern Boundary Arbitration Papers*, Washington, 1829, p. 262; *Amer. State Papers*, *Public Lands*, Vol. 1, Washington, 1832, pp. 65-66).

PROPOSED STATES ACCORDING TO ORDINANCE OF 1784

[PLATE 46B]

On March 1, 1784, the day upon which Virginia completed her cession of western lands (see below, p. 35), Thomas Jefferson, chairman of a committee appointed "to prepare a plan for the temporary government of the Western Territory," reported to Congress a set of resolutions dealing with this subject (H. S. Randall, *Life of Thomas Jefferson*, Philadelphia, 1888, Vol. 1, p. 397). These after being variously amended were adopted on April 23, 1784. They contain the following provisions respecting proposed states:

"That so much of the territory ceded or to be ceded by individual states to the United States ... shall be divided into distinct states in the following manner, as nearly as such cessions will admit: that is to say, by parallels of latitude, so that each state shall comprehend from north to south two degrees of latitude, beginning to count from the completion of 45 degrees north of the equator; and by meridians of longitude, one of which shall pass through the lowest point of the rapids of Ohio, and the other through the western cape of the mouth of the great Kenhaway [Great Kanawha]; but the territory eastward of the last meridian between the Ohio, lake Erie, and Pennsylvania shall be one state whatsoever may be its comprehension of latitude; that which may lie beyond the completion of the 45th degree between the said meridians shall make part of the state adjoining it on the south; and that part of the Ohio which is between the same meridians coinciding nearly with the parallel of 39° shall be substituted so far in lieu of that parallel as a boundary line" (*Journs. Cont. Cong.*, Washington, 1823, Vol. 4, p. 379).

The proposed states here described are shown on Plate 46B and are numbered from 1 to 14.

Jefferson's original resolution contained a provision naming the states northwest of the Ohio River and describing their boundaries somewhat specifically (P. L. Ford, *Writings of Thomas Jefferson*, New York, 1894, Vol. 3, pp. 407-410). Its division of the western territory was similar to that adopted by Congress.

TERRITORIAL ACQUISITIONS, 1783-1853

[PLATE 46C]

This map is self-explanatory. For the boundary of the Unites States as fixed by the Treaty of Paris see Pls. 89-90, line 13, and the text below,

pp. 54-55; for the boundary of the Louisiana Purchase, Pl. 95A, line 15, and below, p. 68; of the Florida Purchase, Pl. 93E, F, and below, pp. 62-63; of Texas and of the Mexican Cession, Pls. 93H, 94A, 95B, and below, pp. 63-66 and 68-69; of the Gadsden Purchase, Pl. 94B and below, p. 66. For the extinguishment of the British claims to the Oregon Country, see the text below, pp. 36-37 and 61.

INDIAN CESSIONS, 1750-1890

[PLATE 47A]

During the early part of the colonial period neither the European nor the colonial governments pursued a settled or well-defined policy respecting the right of the Indians to the lands they claimed or occupied. Many of the early colonial grants ignored the Indians and by implication denied that they possessed any rights of ownership or occupancy. At times, however, the governments purchased their lands or made treaties with them respecting their lands, thus recognizing that they possessed some sort of right to the soil. Private persons also by purchasing lands of the Indians recognized this right.

By the end of the colonial period certain rules or principles respecting Indian lands had become pretty well established. These may be summarized as follows: The Indians possess a usufruct or right of occupancy to the soil. In alienating this right by a cession of lands the Indian chiefs can bind their tribe. The terms of cession should be set forth in a written document or treaty signed by the chiefs and the representatives of the government or governments taking part in the cession. Purchases by private persons are not legal unless validated by the government. (For the general subject of the policy of governments toward the Indians see *Eighteenth Ann. Rept. Bur. of Amer. Ethnology*, Washington, 1899, Part II, pp. 527-643.)

These rules established during the colonial period were accepted by the government of the United States, and until 1871 were regularly observed by it. In an act passed on March 3 of that year Congress provided "that hereafter no Indian nation or tribe within the territory of the United States shall be acknowledged or recognized as an independent nation, tribe, or power with whom the United States may contract by treaty" (*U. S. Statutes at Large*, Vol. 16, Boston, 1871, p. 566). Thereafter "agreements" were made with the Indians. In the later years not infrequently the federal government took possession of Indian land without entering into either a treaty or an agreement with them. The Indians were collected and removed to reservations set apart for their use. In 1862 the federal government extinguished the title of the Sioux Indians in Minnesota to some of their lands on the ground of conquest (*Rept. Commissioner of Indian Affairs*, Washington, 1890, p. xxix).

Since the policy of the government in the early part of the colonial period was not well defined, and since many of the documents relating to early purchases are not extant, no attempt was made to map the cessions before 1750, and that year was taken as the beginning date. By 1890 all Indian titles to large tracts were extinguished with the exception of those to a few reservations, and that year was therefore taken as the concluding date. The 140 years between 1750 and 1890 were divided into six periods.

The first period, 1750-1783, includes all cessions made to British, colonial, and state governments during those years.[15] The second period, 1784-1810, begins with the year of the first cession made to the federal government, 1784, and ends with the census year, 1810. All the cessions of this period were made to the federal government with the exception of a few made to New York by the Iroquois Indians. The four remaining periods, covering the eighty years 1811-1890, are each of twenty years length. All the cessions for these periods were made to the federal government. The number of cessions for the first period, 1750-1783, was about twenty, and for the last five periods, 1784-1890, several hundred. The cessions and "reservations" for the last five periods number more than seven hundred. The number of treaties made with the Indians by the federal government during the years 1778-1871 was 372 (*Eighteenth Ann. Rept. Bur. of Amer. Ethnology*, Washington, 1899, Part II, pp. 648-939; *Rept. Commissioner of Indian Affairs*, 1890, p. xxix).

The territory ceded during each period is represented on the map by a distinguishing color: 1750-1783, blue; 1784-1810, red; 1811-1830, yellow; 1831-1850, green; 1851-1870, violet; and 1871-1890, orange. The small blank areas in the western part of the map are Indian reservations or parts of reservations to which the Indians in 1890 had an original title. Since that year these have been diminished by cession. The large blank areas on the Atlantic seaboard or the Gulf of Mexico are either lands acquired by the colonists before 1750 or lands acquired later by the United States in Louisiana and Texas without Indian cession.

[15] The purchases of the Transylvania Company of 1775 are included, since Virginia and North Carolina claimed the benefits arising therefrom as the successors of the royal prerogative within their respective limits (*Fifth Ann. Rept. Bur. of Amer. Ethnology*, Washington, 1887, p. 149).

A single map of small scale, such as that here employed, is quite sufficient to give a general view of Indian cessions. It necessitates, however, certain rules of exclusion. In ceding their lands the Indians often retained a part of them, and by successive cessions the parts retained became exceedingly small. These small areas, known as reservations and quite numerous, are disregarded. Not infrequently a tribe ceded all its lands and accepted government lands elsewhere. Thus the Five Civilized Tribes ceded their lands in the Southern States and accepted lands in what is now Oklahoma. Subsequently a tribe might cede the lands thus acquired. Such subsequent cessions are disregarded, as the map illustrates the extinguishment of original titles only. When several tribes claim the same land and cede it on different dates, the date of the last cession is taken as the date of the extinguishment of title. In a few cases, however, when the succeeding cession was one of a more or less indefinite claim, it was disregarded. Those cases are treated as cessions in which a tribe relinquished lands and accepted a reservation without entering into a treaty or agreement. The date of the formation of the reservation is taken as the date of the extinguishment of title. There are still many small tracts, either reservations or lands held in severalty by the Indians, to which the Indian titles have not been extinguished. To these the map gives no clue. As the eastern boundary of some of the early cessions in New York, Maryland, and West Virginia is not specifically described, it is located approximately and its location represented by a dotted line.

The principal references to sources for the period 1750–1883 are as follows:

For the Iroquois and other northern Indians: E. B. O'Callaghan, *Documentary History of State of New York*, Vol. 1, Albany, 1849, pp. 586 (map) and 589–590; J. R. Brodhead and E. B. O'Callaghan, *Documents relative to Colonial History of State of New York*, Vol. 8, Albany, 1857, pp. 135–137; C. Smith, *Laws of Pennsylvania*, Vol. 2, Philadelphia, 1810, pp. 119–123; W. R. Shepherd, *History of Proprietary Government in Pennsylvania*, New York, 1896, pp. 103–107; *Minutes of Provincial Council of Pennsylvania*, Vol. 9, Harrisburg, 1852, pp. 554–555; Charles Thomson, *Causes of Alienation of Delaware and Shawanese Indians from British Interest*, Philadelphia, 1867, p. 184 (map). For Cherokee and other southern Indians: C. C. Royce, "Cherokee Nation of Indians," *Fifth Ann. Rept. Bur. of Amer. Ethnology*, Washington, 1887, pp. 130–131, 144–151, and 564 (map); idem, "Indian Land Cessions in United States," *Eighteenth Ann. Rept. Bur. of Amer. Ethnology*, Washington, 1899, Part II, pp. 558–561 and 624–639; U. B. Phillips, *Georgia and State Rights*, Washington, 1902, p. 40 (map); *Laws of the United States ... relative to Public Lands*, Washington, 1836, Vol. 2, Appendix I, pp. 274–277; A. Fortier, *Louisiana*, Atlanta, 1909, Vol. 1, pp. 572–582.

For the years 1784–1890 the principal source is C. C. Royce's maps, sixty-seven in number, found at the end of the *Eighteenth Ann. Rept. Bur. of Amer. Ethnology*, Part II. These have been used in connection with the Schedules of Indian Land Cessions, pp. 648–939 of this volume. While Royce's lines are occasionally located with greater precision than is warranted by the language of the treaties, they have in the main been followed, as his work shows much painstaking care and research. Areas in California (maps 7 and 8) and the Dakotas (map 11) left blank by Royce have been treated as Indian lands (for the claims of the Indians to this territory see *Rept. Commissioner of Indian Affairs*, 1866, p. 168, and 1875, pp. 50 and 76; F. W. Hodge, *Handbook of American Indians*, Washington, 1912, Vol. 2, pp. 1010 and 1011). Use was also made of the map "Indian Cessions in Georgia," in U. B. Phillips, *Georgia and State Rights*, Washington, 1902, opposite p. 40. Additional sources for this period are: *U. S. Statutes at Large*, Vol. 7, Boston, 1846 (*Indian Treaties for 1778–1842*); C. J. Kappler, *Indian Affairs: Laws and Treaties*, 2 vols. (*Senate Doc. No. 452, 57th Cong., 1st Sess.*); F. B. Hough, *Proceedings of Commissioners of Indian Affairs in State of New York*, Albany, 1861; F. W. Hodge, *op. cit.*

Respecting the extent of territory claimed by the Iroquois Indians, evidence was found in: Brodhead and O'Callaghan, *op. cit.*, Vol. 7, Albany, 1856, p. 576; F. B. Hough, *History of Jefferson County in State of New York*, Albany, 1854, p. 38; idem, *History of St. Lawrence and Franklin Counties, New York*, Albany, 1853, pp. 140–141 and 147–148; and in other county histories of New York. In locating the eastern boundary of these claims use was made of these histories and of the maps found in E. B. O'Callaghan, *Documentary History of State of New York*, Vol. 1, Albany, 1849, p. 774, and Vol. 4, Albany, 1851, p. 530, and also of Amos Lay, "Map of the Northern Part of the State of New York," Newark, 1812.

CLAIMS AND CESSIONS OF WESTERN LANDS, 1776–1802

[PLATE 47B–E]

During the period 1776–1802 seven of the original states, Massachusetts, Connecticut, New York, Virginia, North Carolina, South Carolina, and Georgia, claimed western lands and ceded or relinquished them to the federal government or to one of the original states. The remaining six states made no claims.[16] The western lands lay for the most part between the Allegheny Mountains and the Mississippi River.

Part of the western lands claimed by Massachusetts, Connecticut, and New York lay, however, east of the Allegheny Mountains. The term "western lands" as here used and as applied to each state means the lands claimed by a state westward of its western boundary as finally fixed during the period 1776–1802. The western lands that lay in the western part of a state after its boundary was "finally fixed" are not counted as "western lands" for that state. Thus the territory comprising what is now West Virginia is not included in the "western lands" of Virginia, although it formed a part of Virginia's western lands.

The claims and cessions of the seven states named above are illustrated by the maps of this series. To avoid overlapping, four maps, each of which has the same base, were required, and a selection of states for each map that departs from the order of cession to the United States was rendered necessary. The cessions to the United States were in the following order: New York, 1782; Virginia, 1784; Massachusetts, 1785; Connecticut, 1786; South Carolina, 1787; North Carolina, 1790; and Georgia, 1802.

Each of the seven claimant states, with the exception of New York, based its claim upon its "from sea to sea" grant. The grants of the six states making no claims were for limited areas on the Atlantic seaboard (see Pls. 42–43A). These non-claimant states were greatly interested in a movement to make the western country federal territory, and one of them, Maryland, led in the movement. On October 15, 1777, she proposed that Congress should have the right to fix the western boundary of the claimant states and to erect new states from the territory westward of that boundary. On February 19, 1780, New York, whose claims were weakest, offered to cede her western lands, and on September 6 of that year Congress requested the six remaining states to take similar action (H. B. Adams, *Maryland's Influence upon Land Cessions to the United States* (Johns Hopkins Univ. Studies No. 3), Baltimore, 1885, pp. 22–23; *Journs. Cont. Cong.*, Vol. 17, Washington, 1910, pp. 806–807; Vol. 19, Washington, 1912, pp. 208–209). In 1782 the first cession, that of New York, was consummated. Not until twenty years later, 1802, was the last cession, that of Georgia, completed. Beginning with the Maryland resolution of 1777, a quarter of a century elapsed before the question of western land cessions was finally settled. During the early years the general policy and the rights of the states respecting western lands were the most fruitful subjects of discussion, and during the later years the terms and conditions of cession. The adjustment of terms necessitated much negotiation and legislation. (For a general account of western land claims and cessions see P. J. Treat, *National Land System, 1785–1820*, New York, 1910, pp. 1–13 and 319–369; B. A. Hinsdale, *The Old Northwest*, New York, 1888, pp. 192–254.)

Connecticut and South Carolina
[PLATE 47B]

Connecticut based her claim to western lands on the grant to the Connecticut Company by Charles II in 1662 (*Journs. Cont. Cong.*, Vol. 23, Washington, 1914, p. 488; see Pl. 42, lines 10, and above, p. 27). She claimed the territory lying between the Delaware and Mississippi rivers and between the southern and northern boundaries of her grant, the latitude of which she stated to be, respectively, 41° and 42° 2' N. (*ibid.*, Vol. 4, Washington, 1823, pp. 133–137 and 697). During the quarter of a century which preceded the Revolutionary War she settled the part of this territory that lay in eastern Pennsylvania and organized it as the county of Westmoreland. Her intrusion within the charter limits of Pennsylvania brought her into conflict with that colony, which vigorously disputed her claims. The controversy was finally referred to a "court of commissioners" organized under the Articles of Confederation, which in 1782 rendered a decision in favor of Pennsylvania (*ibid.*, p. 140). As a result of this decision Connecticut relinquished her claim to lands between the Delaware River and the western boundary of Pennsylvania (tract 3).

In 1786 Connecticut deeded to the United States title and jurisdiction to all the lands claimed by her west of a line "beginning at the completion of the 41st degree of north latitude, 120 miles west of the western boundary line of the commonwealth of Pennsylvania, as now claimed by said commonwealth, and from thence by a line to be drawn north, parallel to, and 120 miles west of the said west line of Pennsylvania, and to continue north until it comes to 42 degrees and 2 minutes north latitude" (tract 1) (*ibid.*, pp. 697–698) and retained title and jurisdiction to all the lands claimed by her east of that line (tract 2).[17] The tract

---

[16] The claim of New Hampshire to Vermont (see Pl. 97B and p. 73, below), which was decided adversely in 1764 by the King in Council, is assimilated to the later claims to western lands. Massachusetts had a large tract of unoccupied land in Maine.

[17] Connecticut's act of cession was dated May 11 and her deed of cession September 13, 1786. An earlier act of conditional cession was passed October 10, 1780 (B. A. Hinsdale, *The Old Northwest*, New York, 1888, p. 219).

On May 30, 1800, Connecticut also ceded title and jurisdiction to a fourth tract claimed by her and known as "The Gore" but too narrow to be shown on the map. This tract, which was about 2½ miles wide and 220 miles long, lay in what is now New York, between the Delaware River and the western boundary of New York and between the northern boundary of Pennsylvania (42° N.) and the northern charter line of Connecticut (42° 2' N.) (A. C. Bates, "The Connecticut Gore Land Company," *Ann. Rept. Amer. Hist. Assn.*, Washington, 1898, pp. 141–162).

retained by Connecticut lay between the western boundary of Pennsylvania and a meridian one hundred and twenty miles westward thereof and is known as the Connecticut, or Western, Reserve (see Pl. 61E). During the years 1788–1795 she sold the lands of the reserve but retained jurisdiction over them. Finally on May 30, 1800, she ceded the jurisdiction to the United States (B. A. Hinsdale, *The Old Northwest*, New York, 1888, pp. 368–386; *U. S. Statutes at Large*, Vol. 2, Boston, 1845, pp. 56–57).

South Carolina based her claims to western lands on the grants to the proprietors of Carolina by Charles II in 1663 and 1665 (*Journs. Cont. Cong.*, Vol. 23, Washington, 1914, p. 489; see Plate 42 and p. 27, above). She conceded that her original territory was reduced by the grant to Georgia of 1732. The extent of this reduction was a matter of dispute between her and Georgia. She claimed two tracts. The first lay between her western boundary and the Mississippi River and between the southern boundary of North Carolina and the parallel of the mouth of the Tugaloo River (tract 4), and the second (tract 5) embraced all the lands of the United States east of the Mississippi River and south of the Altamaha River and the parallel of its head (*ibid.*, Vol. 4, Washington, 1823, pp. 769–771). The Tugaloo and Keowee rivers unite to form the Savannah River (see Pl. 100B). By the terms of the Beaufort Convention of 1787 (see pp. 83–84, below) she relinquished these claims to Georgia.

Believing that she possessed a narrow belt of territory some fifteen or twenty miles wide, extending from the Allegheny Mountains to the Mississippi River and lying northward of the southern boundary of North Carolina, South Carolina in 1787 "ceded" it to the United States. It is thus described:

... "all the territory or tract of country included within the river Mississippi and a line beginning at that part of the said river which is intersected by the southern boundary line of the State of North Carolina, and continuing along the said boundary line until it intersects the ridge or chain of mountains which divides the eastern from the western waters, then to be continued along the top of the said ridge of mountains, until it intersects a line to be drawn due west from the head of the southern branch of Tugaloo river, to the said mountains, and thence to run a due west course to the river Mississippi" (Cooper, *South Carolina Statutes at Large*, Vol. 5, Columbia, 1839, p. 5).

Since the southern boundary of North Carolina (which colony then included what is now Tennessee) lies south of the source of the southern branch of the Tugaloo River and not north, as was generally believed at the time, this description encloses no territory, and the "cession" therefore ceded nothing.[18]

New York, 1776–1802
[PLATE 47C]

New York derived her claim from treaties with the Six Nations or Iroquois Indians, which made them her dependents and allies. She claimed "all the lands belonging to the Six Nations of Indians and their tributaries" (*Journs. Cont. Cong.*, Vol. 22, Washington, 1914, pp. 225–226; Vol. 23, Washington, 1914, p. 488) but conceded that some of these lands lay within the just boundaries of several of the principal colonies to the southward. From this general statement it is fair to conclude that her claim included, in addition to the "Erie Triangle" (tract 2), a territory bounded by Lakes Erie, Huron, and Michigan, the Illinois, Mississippi, Ohio, and Tennessee rivers, the Allegheny Mountains, and the western boundaries of Maryland and Pennsylvania (tract 1) (L. H. Morgan, *League of the Ho-dé-no-sau-nee or Iroquois*, New York, 1904, pp. 12–14; F. W. Hodge, *Handbook of American Indians*, Washington, 1912, Vol. 1, p. 618; John Mitchell, "Map of North America," 1755 (see Pl. 89); B. A. Hinsdale, *The Old Northwest*, New York, 1888, p. 198; Henry Gannett, *Boundaries of United States*, Washington, 1904, pp. 81–82).

New York's deed of cession, which was accepted by Congress on October 29, 1782, fixed her western boundary between the Pennsylvania

line and Lake Erie on the meridian of "the most westerly bent" of Lake Ontario and ceded to the United States the title and jurisdiction to all lands claimed by her to the westward thereof (tracts 1 and 2) (*Journs. Cont. Cong.*, Vol. 23, Washington, 1914, p. 694). New York's act of cession was dated February 19, 1780, and her deed of cession March 1, 1781 (*ibid.*, Vol. 19, Washington, 1912, pp. 208–213).

Virginia and Georgia
[PLATE 47D]

Virginia based her claim to western lands on the grant of 1609 (see Pl. 42 and p. 26, above).[19] She never precisely defined the bounds of her claim nor did she specifically construe the words of her grant "up into the land, throughout from sea to sea, west and northwest," upon the construction of which depended the bounds. The grant of 1609 gave Virginia a frontage of four hundred miles on the seacoast—two hundred miles north and south of Old Point Comfort. According to Thomas Paine, who wrote a pamphlet on the subject, "the advocates for the Virginia claim" argued that the words "west and northwest" gave Virginia a boundary on the south drawn westerly from her most southerly point on the seacoast and a boundary on the northeast drawn northwesterly from her most northerly point on the seacoast (M. D. Conway, edit., *Writings of Thomas Paine*, New York and London, 1894–1896, Vol. 2, p. 39). Since Virginia specifically asserted a claim to territory as far south as the southern boundary thus drawn, and almost as far north as the northeastern boundary thus drawn, the construction of the grant of 1609 made by "the advocates for the Virginia claim" has been adopted for the purpose of representing her claims and cessions (Virginia Constitution of 1776, par. XXI; W. W. Hening, *Virginia Statutes at Large*, Vol. 10, Richmond, 1822, p. 527).[20]

Virginia's deed of cession which was accepted by Congress on March 1, 1784, ceded both title and jurisdiction to "the territory or tract of country within the limits of the Virginia charter, situate, lying, and being to the northwest of the river Ohio" (*ibid.*, Vol. 11, Richmond, 1822, p. 574).[21] This description does not give the precise bounds of the territory ceded. It has been interpreted to include the lands northwest of the Ohio River and southwest of the northwest line of the grant of 1609 (tract 1), that is, all of the Old Northwest Territory, with the exception of a small area in the eastern part of the Upper Peninsula of Michigan.

On June 1, 1792, Virginia relinquished to Kentucky the title and jurisdiction of the district of Kentucky, which on that date was admitted into the Union as the state of Kentucky—tract 2.[22]

Georgia based her claim on the grant to the trustees of Georgia by George II in 1732 (*Journs. Cont. Cong.*, Vol. 23, Washington, 1914, p. 489; see Pl. 42 and p. 27, above). Her claim conflicted with the claim of South Carolina. This conflict was settled by the Beaufort Convention of 1787 (see p. 83, below). In her controversy with the United States over western lands Georgia claimed the territory between her western boundary and the Mississippi River and between the southern boundary of North Carolina (which included what is now Tennessee) and the international boundary line on the south—tract 3.

On April 24, 1802, commissioners appointed by the United States and Georgia agreed to three "articles of agreement and cession," which went into force on June 16 of that year, when they were ratified by Georgia. By their terms Georgia ceded to the United States both title and jurisdiction to the lands west of her western boundary as it was fixed by the "articles"—the present boundary (*Message from the President, April 26, 1802, accompanying Certain Articles of Agreement and Cession*, Washington, 1804(?); *Acts of Georgia for 1802*, Louisville, 1803, pp.

---

[18] Until the southern boundary of western North Carolina was precisely determined in 1811–1812 (see p. 84, below) it was not known that the South Carolina cession was not a true cession. In 1802 the United States ceded to Georgia what claim it might have to lands acquired from South Carolina eastward of the western boundary of Georgia as described in the Georgia cession (*Articles of Agreement and Cession entered into by Commissioners of United States and Georgia*, pp. 7–8). There were no such lands. The error was a natural one, as the location of the southern boundary of North Carolina and that of the thirty-fifth parallel were generally believed to be northward of the sources of the Tugaloo River and were thus shown on contemporary maps (see maps of United States by William Faden 1783 and 1785, John Reid 1783, C. Bowles 1783, and William McMurray 1784; also pp. 82–84, below). McMurray's map makes clear the terms of the cession, shows why such terms were used and why the southern branch of the Tugaloo River was specified, and helps to identify the southern branch. That the description of the cession should specify the southern branch of the Tugaloo, and the description of the Beaufort Convention (see p. 83, below) the northern branch, has been considered puzzling. Since they emanate from different authorities, which may not have been working in complete concert, this difference might readily arise.

[19] Virginia Constitution for 1776, par. XXI; W. W. Hening, *Virginia Statutes at Large*, Vol. 10, Richmond, 1822, p. 527; *Journs. Cont. Cong.*, Vol. 23, Washington, 1914, p. 489; K. M. Rowland, *Life of George Mason*, New York and London, 1892, Vol. 2, pp. 31–32; Gaillard Hunt, edit., *Writings of James Madison*, Vol. 1, New York, 1900, p. 187. Virginia not only did not assert a right to territory northwest of the Ohio River based upon the conquests of George Rogers Clark, but she laid down a rule that excluded it (Hening, *op. cit.*, Vol. 10, p. 558).

[20] The Virginia boundary commissioners of 1779 (see p. 77, below) construed the grant of 1609 so as to give Virginia a northeast boundary passing through the state of Pennsylvania "with a west north west course" and emerging therefrom "about the beginning of the forty-second degree of northern latitude" (Hening, *Statutes at large of Virginia*, vol. 10, p. 527). This may or may not mean a west-northwest line. If it does, it would deprive Virginia of a considerable part of the area of the Old Northwest Territory. A west-northwest line on the south, a logical counterpart to such a line on the north, would deprive Virginia of a part of Kentucky. To such a construction she would never have agreed.

[21] Virginia's first act of cession was dated January 2, 1781. This was modified to meet the views of Congress at the October session of her legislature, 1783 (*Journs. Cont. Cong.*, Vol. 4, Washington, 1823, pp. 265–267 and 342–344). In 1784 Virginia laid no claim to lands in Maryland, Pennsylvania, Delaware, New Jersey, and New York to which she was entitled under the construction made by "the advocates of the Virginia claim" (see Pl. 42 and pp. 77–78, below).

[22] The movement which culminated in the separation of Kentucky began in 1782 (see p. 24, above). The consent of Virginia to the creation of the new state was given on December 18, 1789, and of Congress on February 4, 1791 (R. H. Collins, *History of Kentucky*, Covington, 1894, Vol. 1, pp. 21–23; Hening, *op. cit.*, Vol. 13, Philadelphia, 1823, p. 17; *U. S. Statutes at Large*, Vol. 1, Boston, 1845, p. 189).

3–8).[23]   The cession of 1802 is represented by tract 3 (*Journs. Cont. Cong.*, Vol. 4, Washington, 1823, pp. 834–835).

Massachusetts and North Carolina
[PLATE 47E]

Massachusetts based her claim upon the grant of 1629 to the Massachusetts Bay Company by the Council for New England and its confirmation in the following year by Charles I (*Journs. Cont. Cong.*, Vol. 4, Washington, 1823, pp. 444–445; see Pl. 42 and p. 26, above). She claimed the territory lying between the Hudson and Mississippi rivers and between the southern and northern boundaries of her grant, respectively, the parallels of 42° 2′ and 44° 15′ N.—tracts 1, 2, 3, 4, 5, and 6 (*ibid.*, pp. 445 and 503).[24] On April 19, 1785, Congress accepted a deed of cession from Massachusetts conveying both title and jurisdiction to the lands west of the western boundary of New York—tracts 1, 2, and 3 (*Journs. Cont. Cong.*, Vol. 4, Washington, 1823, pp. 503–504). Massachusetts authorized the cession on November 13, 1784 (*ibid.*, p. 503). Her right to the rest of the lands claimed by her (tracts 4, 5, and 6) was contested by New York. On December 16, 1786, agents of the two states concluded an agreement according to which Massachusetts ceded to New York jurisdiction over all the disputed lands and title to all such lands, with the exception of the title to two tracts (4 and 5), which New York ceded to Massachusetts (*ibid.*, pp. 787–790).[25] During the years 1786–1791 Massachusetts sold tracts 4 and 5 to private persons. The larger of the two (tract 4) consisted of that part of the state of New York which lies west of the meridian of a point eighty-two miles westward of the northeast corner of Pennsylvania on the Delaware River (with the exception of a small area near the Niagara River, too small to be shown on the map). The smaller of the two (tract 5) consisted of 230,400 acres of land lying between the Owego and Chenango rivers (*ibid.*, p. 789; *Massachusetts Laws and Resolves, 1786–1787*, Boston, 1893, p. 370, and *1790–1791*, Boston, 1895, p. 416; *Rept. Regents' Boundary Commission upon New York and Pennsylvania Boundary*, Albany, 1886, pp. 415–417; H. P. Smith, *History of Broome County, New York*, Syracuse, 1885, p. 90).

North Carolina based her claim on the grants to the proprietors of Carolina by Charles II in 1663 and 1665 (*Journs. Cont. Cong.*, Vol. 23, Washington, 1914, p. 489; see Pl. 42 and p. 27, above). She claimed the territory lying within her "chartered limits" between her western boundary and the Mississippi River (*U. S. Statutes at Large*, Vol. 1, Boston, 1845, pp. 106–107), that is the present state of Tennessee —tract 7. On February 25, 1790, she deeded this land to the United States, and on April 2 of that year the U. S. Congress accepted the deed (*ibid.*, pp. 106–109). This deed was authorized by an act of the legislature of December, 1789. On June 2, 1784, North Carolina had passed an earlier act of cession, which she had repealed on November 20 of that year (*North Carolina State Records*, Vol. 24, Raleigh, 1905, pp. 561–563 and 678–679; Vol. 25, Goldsboro, 1906, pp. 4–6; *Journs. Cont. Cong.*, Vol. 4, Washington, 1823, pp. 523–525).

SYSTEM OF SURVEY OF PUBLIC LANDS
UNDER ACT OF 1796
[PLATE 48A]

The public lands of the United States have been surveyed according to either the systematic plan or the indiscriminate location plan (see above, p. 25, and Pl. 41E). The systematic plan divides the land into squares of equal area by means of parallel lines, equidistant from each other and running from east to west and from north to south. The squares are described by reference to a principal parallel or base line and a principal meridian.

There have been three systematic systems of surveys of the public lands. Provision for the first of these was made by the ordinance of May 20, 1785, according to which townships were to be six miles square and lots were to be numbered from south to north (P. J. Treat, *National Land System, 1785–1820*, New York, 1910, pp. 396–397). Under this system only the Seven Ranges of Townships (see Pl. 41B) were surveyed. By an act of June 1, 1796, Congress directed that the United States Military District in Ohio should be laid off into townships five miles

square (*U. S. Statutes at Large*, Vol. 1, Boston, 1845, p. 490). A few days before this, on May 18, Congress had provided for a system of survey for certain lands lying northwest of the Ohio River and above the mouth of the Kentucky River (*ibid.*, p. 466). In the history of the public lands this act is designated as the Act of 1796. With the exceptions named above, all the public lands have been surveyed under the system established by it.

Diagram 1 shows the method of numbering townships. These are six miles square and contain thirty-six square miles. Sections are one mile square and contain six hundred and forty acres. Diagram 2 shows the legal subdivisions of a section. Diagram 3 shows the plan of designating townships. The heavy line running east and west is a base line, and the heavy line crossing it at right angles and running north and south is a principal meridian. These are the first lines established. The light lines running east and west, six miles apart, are township lines and divide the tract into "townships," which are numbered north and south from the base line. The light lines crossing the township lines at right angles are range lines and divide the tract into ranges, which are numbered east and west from the principal meridian. Each township is designated by its appropriate township and range number. Thus, the upper right-hand township of the diagram would be designated township 5 north, range III east.

PLAN OF LYSTRA, KENTUCKY, 1795
[PLATE 48B]

This plan, which is a reproduction of a map found in William Winterbotham, *Historical, Geographical, Commercial, and Philosophical View of the American United States*, London, 1795, Vol. 3, opposite p. 141, illustrates a western "boom" or speculative town. A company of land speculators, who promoted their enterprise from an office in Threadneedle Street, London, purchased fifteen thousand acres in central Kentucky, on the Rolling Fork, a branch of Salt River, and laid out on South Creek, a branch of the Rolling Fork, the town of Lystra "on a very eligible plan combining everything necessary for utility and ornament." The town was divided into 188 lots, several of which were reserved—among others, one for the first schoolmaster, one for the first minister of the first church, and one for the first member of Congress residing in Nelson County and chosen after 1794 (Winterbotham, *op. cit.*, Vol. 3, pp. 141–144). The ambitious plans of the promoters were never realized.

FOUR TOWNSHIPS IN MARENGO COUNTY, ALABAMA, GRANTED TO FRENCH EMIGRANTS, 1817
[PLATE 48C]

Occasionally grants were made to settlers of the same nationality or European stock. Thus arose such settlements as those of the Scotch in New Scotland, in Conway, N. H., the Germans in Germantown, Pa., and the French in Gallipolis, Ohio. Plate 48C, which is a reproduction of a map found in *American State Papers, Public Lands*, Vol. 5, Washington, 1860, opposite p. 466, illustrates a grant of this kind. The grant was made in 1817 by Congress to some French emigrants, to encourage the cultivation of the vine and the olive. It comprised four townships on the Black Warrior River, in Marengo County, Alabama.

TERRITORIAL CLAIMS AND LIMITS ON THE NORTHWEST COAST OF AMERICA, 1790–1846
[PLATE 49]

During the sixteenth, seventeenth, and eighteenth centuries four states, Spain, Great Britain, Russia, and the United States, through discovery, exploration, or settlement, established territorial claims to parts of the northwest coast of America. Not until toward the end of the eighteenth century did they begin to state definitely the limits of their claims. Such statements, however, did not specify an eastern limit, which therefore cannot be mapped. In order that the northern and southern limits might be mapped, all claims were arbitrarily assumed to extend eastward as far as the continental divide.

The drainage and projection of Plate 49 are taken from a map of North America published by the U. S. Geological Survey (no date) and measuring 17 by 23 inches.

During the years 1790–1846 several boundary lines were established by treaties between two of the claimant states. These lines are shown upon the map in black. They are as follows:

Limits of Area Open to British-American Joint Occupation, 1819–1846.—The third article of the Convention of 1818 between the United States and Great Britain provided that a certain specified territory "together with its harbors, bays, and creeks, and the navigation of all rivers within the same be free and open ... to the vessels, citizens,

---

[23] The movement which resulted in the cession of 1802 began in 1786 and lasted more than fifteen years. An act of cession of Georgia dated February 1, 1788, was not accepted by Congress.

[24] The agreement of 1786 (*Journs. Cont. Cong.*, Vol. 4, Washington, 1823, pp. 787–790) included within the disputed tract the territory between the western boundary of Massachusetts and the Hudson River. This inclusion was merely formal, as Massachusetts did not claim that territory (D. J. Pratt, *Boundaries of State of New York*, Albany, 1884, pp. 177–180).

[25] As a result of a petition of Massachusetts of May 27, 1784, a federal court was instituted to settle the dispute. After the agreement of December 16, 1786, the court was no longer needed, and it was dissolved by Congress, October 8, 1787 (*Journs. Cont. Cong.*, Vol. 4, pp. 444–445, 536, and 787–791).

and subjects" of the United States and Great Britain. This agreement, which was for the term of ten years, was in 1827 continued indefinitely. The territory to which it applied was described as "any country that may be claimed by either party on the northwest coast of America, westward of the Stony [Rocky] Mountains" (W. M. Malloy, edit., *Treaties, Conventions, International Acts, Protocols, and Agreements between the United States of America and Other Powers, 1776–1909*, Washington, 1910, Vol. 1, pp. 632 and 644). The eastern limit of this territory is the summit of the Rocky Mountains or the continental divide; the northern limit is the northern boundary claimed by the United States under the Spanish-American Treaty of 1819 (line 3); and the southern limit is the southern boundary claimed by Great Britain, which she stated in 1826 to be the thirty-eighth parallel (line 7).

Spanish-American Boundary, 1819.—This is the western part of the boundary between the possessions of the United States and Spain fixed by the treaty of 1819 between those two countries (see below, p. 68). It follows the forty-second parallel, the meridian of the source of the Arkansas River, and the Arkansas River (*ibid.*, Vol. 2, p. 1653).

Russian-American Boundary, 1824.—This line was established by the third article of the Convention of 1824 between the United States and Russia. By this article the United States agreed not to form "any establishment upon the Northwest coast of America ... to the north of fifty-four degrees and forty minutes of north latitude," and Russia agreed to form none south of that parallel (*ibid.*, Vol. 2, p. 1513).

British-Russian Boundary, 1825.—This boundary was established by the third and fourth articles of the Convention of 1825 between Great Britain and Russia (*ibid.*, pp. 1521–1522). It is described with considerable detail, and its description has been quoted in another connection (see pp. 69–70, below). Its location east and south of the one hundred and forty-first meridian was long disputed. It is shown on the map as finally settled in 1903 and 1905 by Great Britain and the United States, which latter country in 1867 succeeded to the rights of Russia.

British-American Boundary, 1846.—This line was established by the treaty of 1846 between Great Britain and the United States (*ibid.*, Vol. 1, p. 657). It follows the forty-ninth parallel to the channel between the continent and the island of Vancouver and passes thence through this channel and the strait of Juan de Fuca to the Pacific Ocean (see Pls. 93C and 96C and pp. 61 and 71–72, below).

In 1790 Count Fernan Nuñez, the Spanish ambassador to France, in a statement to the French government on the subject of the detention of two British vessels seized in Nootka Sound, claimed that Spain possessed "all the coast to the north of the western America, on the side of the South Sea, as far as beyond what is called Prince William's Sound, which is in the sixty-first degree" (*Amer. State Papers, Foreign Relations*, Vol. 5, Washington, 1858, p. 445).

As this description is not entirely specific, it is possible to represent Spain's claim only approximately. This has been accomplished by connecting the meridian of the most westerly point of Prince William Sound with the parallel of its most northerly point and extending the parallel to the Rocky Mountains. The northern limit claimed by Spain is represented by *line 1*—a solid blue line.

By reason of the discoveries and explorations of Captain Robert Gray in 1792 and of Lewis and Clark in 1805–1806 and of the settlement of Astoria in 1811 the United States claimed a territory on the northwest coast bounded on the north by the parallel of the most northerly point of the Columbia River or its tributaries and on the south by the most southerly point of the same (*ibid.*, pp. 446 and 554). The United States did not state its claim quite so specifically as here given, but this is what its claim amounted to. The northern and southern limits claimed by the United States are represented by *lines 2*—dot-and-dash yellow lines.

By the treaty of 1819 between the United States and Spain the United States acquired all the rights, claims, and pretensions of Spain to the territories north of the boundary line established by the treaty (Malloy, *Treaties*, Vol. 2, p. 1653; see p. 68, below). As the successor of Spain, the claim of the United States on the north extended therefore "as far as beyond what is called Prince William's Sound, which is in the sixty-first degree." On the south she claimed the forty-second parallel, the line established by the treaty between the Pacific Ocean and the meridian of the source of the Arkansas River (*Amer. State Papers, Foreign Relations*, Vol. 5, Washington, 1858, pp. 446 and 554; J. D. Richardson, *A Compilation of the Messages and Papers of the Presidents, 1789–1897*, Washington, 1899, Vol. 4, p. 258).[26]

[26] In 1823 Secretary of State J. Q. Adams, in instructions to Richard Rush, American plenipotentiary to England, claimed all the rights of Spain north of the forty-second parallel. In his negotiations with the British, Rush claimed "as high up as 60°"—which may be regarded as a rough statement of the claims of the United States (*Amer. State Papers, Foreign Relations*, Vol. 5, Washington, 1858, pp. 446 and 554).

These claims of the United States are represented by *lines 3*—short-dash red lines.

During the controversy with Great Britain over the Oregon question in 1843–1846 Presidents Tyler and Polk claimed as a northern limit the parallel of 54°40', the line established in 1824 as the boundary between the claims of the United States and Russia (Richardson, *op. cit.*, pp. 258 and 395; J. S. Reeves, *American Diplomacy under Tyler and Polk*, Baltimore, 1907, pp. 245 and 249–250). This claim is represented by *line 4*—a dot-and-dash blue line.

In 1821 the Russian minister of finances claimed the fifty-first degree of north latitude as the southern limit of the Russian possessions on the northwest coast (*Amer. State Papers, Foreign Relations*, Vol. 4, Washington, 1834, pp. 857 and 861). This claim is represented by *line 5*—a short-dash blue line.

In the course of the negotiations that led to the Convention of 1825 between Russia and Great Britain Sir Charles Bagot, British ambassador to Russia, stated that his government had always claimed the fifty-ninth degree of north latitude as the northern limit of its possessions (*Proceedings of Alaska Boundary Tribunal*, Washington, 1904, Vol. 2, p. 127). This claim is represented by *line 6*—a dotted yellow line.

During the negotiations between the United States and Great Britain that resulted in the Conventions of 1827 Great Britain claimed the right to make settlements anywhere north of the thirty-eighth parallel and to navigate all rivers emptying into the Pacific Ocean north of that line (*Amer. State Papers, Foreign Relations*, Vol. 6, Washington, 1859, p. 656). This claim is represented by *line 7*—a dotted blue line.

During the negotiations between the United States and Great Britain that resulted in the Convention of 1818 the British plenipotentiaries proposed that an area of joint occupation should be established on the northwest coast, and an article providing for such an area was incorporated in the convention (see above, pp. 36–37) but with limits varying greatly from those proposed by the British. The limits as originally proposed were the forty-fifth and forty-ninth parallels (*ibid.*, Vol. 4, Washington, 1834, p. 391, article B). These limits are represented by *lines 8*—short-dash yellow lines.

When in 1824 the respective claims of the United States and Great Britain were again the subject of negotiations between the two countries the American plenipotentiaries proposed, first, that the third article of the Convention of 1818 should be extended to a second term of ten years, and, secondly, that Great Britain should stipulate that her citizens make no settlements south of the fifty-first parallel or north of the fifty-fifth parallel and that the United States should stipulate that her citizens make no settlements north of the fifty-first parallel. On the refusal of Great Britain to accept this proposal the American plenipotentiaries made a more liberal one, which the British also refused. By the second proposal the southern line was to be the forty-ninth parallel instead of the fifty-first (*ibid.*, Vol. 5, Washington, 1858, pp. 554, 557, and 582).

The northern limit of area open to settlement by the United States and the southern limit of area open to settlement by Great Britain according to the first proposal is represented by *line 9*—a solid yellow line. The northern limit of area open to settlement by Great Britain according to the first and second proposals is represented by *line 10*—a dot-and-dash red line. The northern limit of area open to settlement by the United States and the southern limit of area open to settlement by Great Britain according to the second proposal are represented by *line 11*—a solid red line.

LANDS GRANTED TO STATES FOR EDUCATIONAL AND OTHER PURPOSES, 1785–1919

[PLATE 50A]

This map, the original of which was made for the *Atlas*, is based upon the manuscript materials of the General Land Office. Among the principal grants made for other than educational purposes are the grants for internal improvements, public buildings, and charitable, penal, and reformatory institutions. Large grants of swamp lands and small grants of salt lands were also made to many of the states. In most of the states the grants for educational purposes exceeded all other grants. In seven states, however, the swamp lands constituted more than one half of the total grant. These states with the acreage of the total grant are as follows: Arkansas, 7,700,000 acres; Florida, 21,959,000; Louisiana, 9,400,000; Michigan, 5,700,000; Minnesota, 4,700,000; Mississippi, 3,300,000; and Wisconsin, 3,300,000. It is the swamp lands that give these states their darker shading on the map. The largest acreage of swamp lands was received by Florida—20,200,000.

Since many of the eastern states had no public lands within their borders they received script, which in the hands of purchasers could be exchanged for public lands. For the purposes of this map the script is treated as if it were a grant of lands. The grants made to those states which received less than 500,000 acres were chiefly for agricultural colleges. Delaware received the smallest acreage—90,000.

LAND OF THE OHIO COMPANY, ABOUT 1787
[PLATE 50B]

From about the middle of the eighteenth century until its close various companies were organized to acquire western lands. Plate 50B, which is a reproduction of a map in the possession of the Western Reserve Historical Society, Cleveland, Ohio, illustrates the activities of one of these companies. It is a sketch map of the first purchase of the Ohio Company. This purchase was made in 1787 and called for 1,500,000 acres. The large squares are townships. The small shaded squares in each township are sections 16 and 29, reserved by Congress for public schools and religious purposes, respectively. The three small unshaded squares are the sections reserved by Congress for future sale. In the lower left-hand corner of the map is shown a proposed plan for Marietta.

GEORGE ROGERS CLARK GRANT, ABOUT 1785
[PLATE 50C]

This is a specimen of a grant of land made as a reward for military services rendered during the Revolutionary War. In 1781 Virginia voted 150,000 acres to George Rogers Clark and the troops who had taken part in the reduction of the western posts of the British; and in 1784, when she ceded her western lands to the federal government, she reserved that number of acres northwest of the Ohio for the use of Clark and his troops (see p. 31). About 1785 a tract was located on the north side of the Ohio near the falls of that river and was laid off into lots.

Plate 50C is reproduced from a map of the survey of this tract found in W. H. English, *Conquest of the Country Northwest of the River Ohio, 1778–1783*, Indianapolis, 1896, Vol. 2, pp. 852–853.

GRANT TO DARTMOUTH COLLEGE AND PRESIDENT WHEELOCK, 1771
[PLATE 50D]

This map illustrates the granting of land for higher education, a practice well established during the colonial period. The tract granted to Dartmouth College and President Wheelock lay in the southwestern part of the town of Hanover, N. H., on the Connecticut River (shown at the top of the map). Plate 50D is reproduced from a map found in the *New Hampshire State Papers*, Vol. 25, Concord, 1895, p. 89.

LANDS GRANTED IN 1828 FOR THE CONSTRUCTION OF THE COLUMBUS AND SANDUSKY TURNPIKE
[PLATE 50E]

One of the earliest grants of alternate sections of land in aid of the construction of wagon roads was made by the federal government in 1828 to the Columbus and Sandusky Turnpike Company of Ohio. The grant is in the following language:

... "forty-nine sections of land to be located in the Delaware land district in the following manner, to wit: every alternate section through which the road may run, and the section next adjoining thereto on the west so far as the said sections remain unsold, and if any part of the said sections shall have been disposed of, then a quantity equal thereto shall be selected ... from the vacant lands in the sections adjoining on the west of those appropriated" (*U. S. Statutes at Large*, Vol. 4, Boston, 1846, p. 263).

Plate 50E is a reproduction of a map found in W. E. Peters, *Ohio Lands and their Subdivision*, Athens, 1918, p. 313.

A SURVEY OF THE NORTHERN NECK OF VIRGINIA (FAIRFAX LANDS), 1736–1737
[PLATE 51A]

This map illustrates an early survey of a large grant. The lands were first granted to Lord Hopton and six other British gentlemen by Charles II in 1649 (see p. 29, above, and Pl. 43A). In 1688 the title to them was vested in Lord Culpepper and later it passed, through his daughter, who married the fifth Lord Fairfax, into the possession of the Fairfaxes. In 1733 the sixth Lord Fairfax petitioned the king for a commission to ascertain its boundaries. The petition was granted, and an order in Council was issued directing the lieutenant governor of Virginia to appoint three or more commissioners, who in conjunction with a like number to be appointed by Lord Fairfax were "to survey and settle the marks and boundaries." In 1736 six commissioners were appointed, three by the lieutenant governor and three by Lord Fairfax, and under their direction the tract was surveyed and mapped.

The two sets of commissioners disagreed as to the location of the heads of the Rappahannock and Potomac rivers and made separate reports. In 1738 these were referred to the lords of the committee of the Council for plantation affairs, who in 1745 decided that the source of the Rappahannock was the first spring of the southern branch of that river, and that the source of the Potomac was the first spring of the western branch of the Potomac River. In 1745 this decision was confirmed by the King in Council (*Transcript of Record, Maryland vs. Virginia*, 1909, Vol. 2, pp. 1208–1243 and 1288–1299; Justin Winsor, *Narrative and Critical History of America*, Vol. 5, Boston, 1887, p. 276). The map here reproduced shows both the original survey and the line between the heads of the two rivers as finally determined. The reproduction is from a map in the Division of Maps, Library of Congress.

GRANT TO WASHINGTON FOR MILITARY SERVICES, 1774
[PLATE 51B]

The practice of granting lands as a reward for military services was followed by both the colonial and British governments during the seventeenth and eighteenth centuries. Before 1775 a considerable amount of land had been thus granted. Plate 51B is a specimen survey of such a grant.

The royal proclamation of 1763 commanded the colonial governments to make liberal grants of land to the officers, soldiers, and seamen who had served in North America in the French and Indian War and prescribed the number of acres to be granted, which varied with the rank of the grantee (*Annual Register*, London, 1763, p. 211). A field officer was to receive 5000 acres. As Washington had this rank, he received a warrant for 5000 acres, which was signed by the governor of Virginia. A part of this grant, consisting of 2950 acres, was located on the Great Kanawha River near the present city of Charlestown, W. Va., and was surveyed in 1774 by Samuel Lewis. From Lewis's data Washington drew a plan of the tract. Plate 51B is a copy of Washington's drawing, the original of which is in the Division of Maps, Library of Congress.

A FRENCH SETTLEMENT: KASKASKIA, ILLINOIS
[PLATE 52]

1. **Plan of Settlement, 1807** [*Plate 52A*]. This is a general map of the settlement, and shows the location of the village, the commons, and the common field or fields. The map is a copy of one found in *American State Papers, Public Lands*, Vol. 2, Washington, 1834, between pp. 182 and 183. The settlement was established about 1698.

2. **Specimen of Common Fields, about 1809** [*Plate 52B*]. This map illustrates the allotment of the common fields among the residents of the village. It is a copy of part of a map found in *American State Papers, Public Lands*, Vol. 2, Washington, 1834, between pp. 182 and 183. The original is based upon a survey made about 1809 with a view to the settlement of claims.

A SOUTHERN PLANTATION: MOUNT VERNON, VIRGINIA
[PLATE 53A and B]

1. **Mansion House Grounds, about 1787** [*Plate 53A*]. This map is a reproduction of part of a map found in the Division of Maps, Library of Congress. The plan of the grounds is very much reduced.

2. **The Farms, 1793** [*Plate 53B*]. This map is found in the Division of Maps, Library of Congress, and was published at Philadelphia in 1876 by S. W. F. Weaver.

The Mount Vernon estate contained more than 8000 acres. Of this acreage more than half was comprised in the Mansion House farm and the woodlands. The cultivable land of the four remaining farms was distributed as follows: Union farm 928 acres, Dogue Run farm 650 acres, Muddy Hole farm 476 acres, and River farm 1207 acres—a total of 3261 acres (W. C. Ford, edit., *Writings of George Washington*, New York, 1889–1891, Vol. 12, pp. 362–363). Each farm had its own buildings and slave quarters. The location of the larger buildings is shown.

A COLONIAL MANOR: LIVINGSTON MANOR, NEW YORK
[PLATE 53C and D]

1. **Plan of Manor, 1714** [*Plate 53C*]. This is a general map of the manor. The manor house and the mill are shown in the lower left-hand corner. "Gov. Hunter's Land" was purchased by Hunter in 1710 for the use of the Palatines. The manor was patented in 1684–1686 and contained 160,240 acres.

Plate 53C is a reproduction of a map found in E. B. O'Callaghan, *Documentary History of the State of New York*, Vol. 3, Albany, 1850, opposite p. 690.

2. **Distribution of Tenants, 1798** [*Plate 53D*]. This is a map of the northwest part of the manor and shows the location of the houses of the tenants, the manor house, gristmills, sawmill, churches, and roads. It is a reproduction of part of a map found in E. B. O'Callaghan, *op. cit.*, opposite p. 834.

A MODERN CITY: SPRINGFIELD, ILLINOIS

[PLATES 54-55B]

1. **Plan of City, 1915** [*Plate 54*]. This is a reproduction of a map of Springfield, Ill., published by the Sangamon County Abstract Company in 1915. It shows blocks, streets, churches, schools, fire department buildings, other main public buildings, public parks, railroads, street-car lines, etc. House numbers for corresponding blocks are shown.

2. **Ward Map, 1914** [*Plate 55A*]. This is a reproduction of a map found in Franz Schneider, *Public Health in Springfield, Illinois*, published by the Russell Sage Foundation, New York, 1915, p. 6.

3. **Specimen Blocks, 1914** [*Plate 55B*]. This is a copy of part of a map found in the *Plat Book of Sangamon County, Illinois*, 1914, Springfield, p. 150. It shows the lots and streets of a part of the Harvard Park addition of Springfield. The larger numbers are the numbers of the lots, and the smaller the width of the lots or streets.

LARGE LAND HOLDINGS IN SOUTHWESTERN WASHINGTON, 1914

[PLATE 55C]

This map illustrates the concentration of landownership that has resulted from the land policy of the federal government. The holdings of the Northern Pacific Railway Company are derived from the federal grant of alternate sections. The Weyerhaeuser Timber Company derived most of its holdings from the Northern Pacific Railway Company. The "group of large holders" derived their titles from both the railway company and private holders. It comprises the Milwaukee Land Company, the St. Paul and Tacoma Lumber Company, the Puget Mill Company, and thirty other companies. The areas left blank belong to "small holders," many of whom, however, own tracts of considerable size.

Plate 55C is a reproduction of part of a map found in *The Lumber Industry*, Part II, published by the U. S. Bureau of Corporations, Washington, 1914, opposite p. 44.

DONATION LANDS UNDER ACT OF 1850

[PLATE 55D]

Under preëmption, homestead, and donation acts the federal government has given away or sold for a nominal sum a considerable part of the public domain. In 1919 the total acreage disposed of under the homestead act alone amounted to 185,000,000 acres (*Rept. Commissioner of General Land Office*, Washington, 1919, p. 76).

Plate 55D shows part of the donation lands in Marion County, Oregon, located under the donation act of September 27, 1850. This act, which applied only to the territory of Oregon, granted to those persons who had become settlers before December 1, 1850, and who had resided on and had cultivated their lands for four consecutive years, 320 acres of land if they were single and 640 acres if married; and to those persons who should become settlers between December 1, 1850, and December 1, 1853, 160 acres if they were single and 320 acres if married (*U. S. Statutes at Large*, Vol. 9, Boston, 1851, pp. 497-498).

This map is a copy of part of a map found in Frank Strong and Joseph Schafer, *Government of the American People*, Cambridge, 1901, opposite p. 260.

A WESTERN TOWN: CARROLL, NEBRASKA, 1918

[PLATE 56A]

This map is from the *Standard Atlas of Wayne County, Nebraska*, Chicago, 1918, p. 15. It shows the original town, additions, a few lots adjacent to the town, the town lots, streets, principal industries and business houses, churches, public school, railroad, railroad station, some of the residences, a corner of the federal survey, etc. In 1920 the population of Carroll was 448.

A WESTERN TOWNSHIP: PILOT KNOB TOWNSHIP, HARPER COUNTY, KANSAS, 1919

[PLATE 56B]

This is a reproduction of a map found in the *Standard Atlas of Harper County, Kansas*, Chicago, 1919, p. 31. It shows farms, with acreage, names of owners, residences, roads, rural free delivery routes, railroads, public schools, a church, the town of Harper at the crossing of the railroads, section numbers, lines of the federal survey, etc. Pilot Knob Township is designated in the federal survey as township 32 south, range VI west of the 6th principal meridian.

SPECIMEN PRIVATE LAND CLAIMS, 1835

[PLATE 56C]

Grants made in good faith by foreign governments of land within territories possessed by them but later acquired by the United States are considered valid by the United States. Claimants, however, must prove their titles and have their claims confirmed. In 1920 private land claims amounting to more than 33,000,000 acres had been confirmed by the federal government (statement based upon typewritten information furnished by officials of the General Land Office).

Plate 56C, which is a reproduction of a map found in *American State Papers, Public Lands*, Vol. 8, Washington, 1861, opposite p. 22, shows the private land claims in parts of St. Charles and Lincoln counties, Missouri. The townships and sections (numbered from 1 to 36) of the federal survey are also shown. Owing to the private land claims many of the sections are not of full size, and some of them are omitted.

FEDERAL LAND GRANTS FOR THE CONSTRUCTION OF RAILROADS AND WAGON ROADS, 1823-1871

[PLATE 56D]

This map was redrawn for the *Atlas* from a much larger map found in *The Lumber Industry*, Part I, published by the U. S. Bureau of Corporations, Washington, 1913, opposite p. 222.

The practice of granting public lands for the construction of railroads was established during the decade 1850-1859. Some thirty years earlier similar grants had been made for wagon roads. According to their usual form, the grants to the railroads gave to the roads, or to the states as their trustees, alternate sections (640 acres), within a specified number of miles on each side of the road, of those lands that had not been disposed of, reserved, or otherwise appropriated. The width of the tract within which the alternate sections might be selected varied with different grants. For the railroads the minimum was ten miles and the maximum eighty miles—that is, five in the one case and forty in the other on each side of the road. For wagon roads the tract was generally narrower than for railroads. The parallel lines bounding this tract were called the "primary limits." In case some of the alternate sections were already taken the roads according to most grants were permitted to make up their "losses" from the alternate sections of certain "indemnity" tracts, the limits of which lay usually from five to ten miles beyond the "primary limits."

On Plate 56D the lines denoting the limits are plainly shown. Where these are not too numerous the line representing the road may be seen. The first lines on each side of the road are the "primary limits," and the second lines are the "indemnity limits." For a part of the Northern Pacific Railway "second indemnity limits" are shown. These are the limits of the tracts to be drawn upon when the lands of the "first indemnity" tracts should be exhausted. Not all roads were given indemnity lands (see the Union Pacific Railway in the Rocky Mountain states). In case there was not enough land within the indemnity tracts to make up for "losses" the road "lost" some of its land. Thus in Iowa, where much land had been disposed of before the roads were built, the roads received only one-fourth as much as they would have received had all the land been unappropriated government land.

The grants for railroads number sixty-four and cover the years 1850-1871, and the grants for wagon roads thirteen and cover the years 1823-1869. A few unimportant grants, however, are not represented, as information respecting them is not available. The grants for most of the wagon roads lay in Michigan and Oregon. The two earliest grants, which lay in Ohio, are not shown (see Pl. 50E). No federal land grants were made in Texas, since this state "was an independent sovereignty before its admission to the Union and the treaty of union provided that the State should retain the ownership of all public lands within its boundaries. It has given to railroads grants amounting to approximately 32,400,000 acres, over one sixth of the area of the State" (quotation from legend appearing on original map).

The total number of acres granted for railroads by the federal government has been estimated at 190,000,000, and of wagon roads at more than 3,000,000. Of the 190,000,000 acres some 35,000,000 acres have been forfeited because of failure to construct the roads. The principal forfeitures were in New Mexico, Arizona, and California. These are indicated on the map by brown and white bands (*The Lumber Industry*, Part I, Washington, 1913, pp. 219–225, and map at p. 222; *Statement showing Land Grants made by Congress to aid in the Construction of Railroads* ..., Washington, 1915, pp. 2–23).

OIL LAND WITHDRAWALS IN CALIFORNIA, 1915
[PLATE 56E]

The practice of reserving mineral lands was established by the ordinance of May 20, 1785, which reserved "one-third part of all gold, silver, lead, and copper mines (*Journs. Cont. Cong.*, Washington, 1823, Vol. 4, p. 521). An act of 1796 reserved each section of land that contained a salt spring (*U. S. Statutes at Large*, Vol. 1, Boston, 1845, p. 466). Various acts since that date have authorized mineral reservations or withdrawals.

Plate 56E shows the oil land withdrawals in California outstanding November 1, 1915. It is based upon a map that accompanies M. W. Ball, *Petroleum Withdrawals and Restorations affecting the Public Domain*, Washington, 1916.

PUBLIC LANDS OF THE UNITED STATES, 1790–1929
[PLATES 57–59]

Owing to lack of information it is not possible to show the distribution by counties of the public lands except for recent years. For this reason they are represented by states and territories for the years 1790, 1810, 1830, 1850, 1890, and 1910 by means of cartograms. For 1929 their distribution is shown by counties.

Public Lands of the United States, 1790–1910 [*Plates 57–59A*]. These maps are based upon calculations made from statistics found chiefly in the volumes of the *American State Papers, Public Lands*, the annual reports of the General Land Office, and the *Statistical Abstracts* published first by the Treasury Department and later by the Department of Commerce (see especially: *Amer. State Papers, Public Lands*, Vol. 3, Washington, 1834, pp. 459–460 and 533; Vol. 6, Washington, 1860, pp. 315–316, 448, 468–469, 488, and 628; P. J. Treat, *National Land System, 1785–1820*, New York, 1910, pp. 401–402 and 406–411; W. E. Peters, *Ohio Lands and their Subdivision*, Athens, 1918, pp. 192–193; *Ann. Repts. General Land Office*, for 1850, pp. 37–38; for 1870, pp. 504–507; for 1890, p. 121; for 1903, p. 493; for 1910, pp. 17–27; *Statistical Abstract of United States*, for 1879, p. 148; for 1882, p. 146; for 1892, p. 248; for 1910, pp. 26–28). These statistics are often inaccurate and incomplete and are frequently at variance with one

another. Some of them are no more than rough estimates. What was included under "lands sold or otherwise disposed of" at one time may be excluded at another. Thus, in the earlier tables lands appropriated by the federal government for public schools and other purposes are treated as "lands sold or otherwise disposed of" from the date of appropriation, while in the later tables they are not so treated until actually selected. In respect to school lands it is not possible to reduce the statistics to uniformity. In respect to certain other lands the following rules are as far as possible observed: national forests are treated as public lands; Indian reservations also are thus treated, with the exception of the permanent possessions in the Indian Territory of the Five Civilized Tribes, which are treated as lands disposed of from the date when they came into the possession of these tribes; railroad lands are treated as public lands until "approved" or selected; private land claims, with some exceptions, are treated as public lands until "confirmed."

Dealing with such imperfect statistics, no two persons would deduce from them quite the same results. Fortunately, owing to the small scale of the maps, a considerable inexactitude is negligible. In the larger states a difference of 5,000,000 acres can scarcely be detected by the eye.

The method of representation is that of the cartogram. For each state and territory the relative areas of public lands and of "lands sold or otherwise disposed of" are shown arbitrarily without reference to their actual location—the public lands at the westward, colored red, and the "lands sold or otherwise disposed of" at the eastward, colored blue. Acreages too small to map are disregarded. States whose lands never belonged to the public domain are left blank. Of this class are the lands of the thirteen original states and of Vermont, Kentucky, and Texas. Tennessee, while nominally a public-land state, was not actually so (Treat, *op. cit.*, pp. 105–106). The Connecticut Reserve and the Virginia Military Reserve in Ohio, while never parts of the public domain, are treated for purposes of representation as if they belonged to "lands sold or otherwise disposed of." The "Erie Triangle" was public land until sold by the federal government to Pennsylvania in 1790.

The identification of the boundary lines of the territories will be facilitated by referring to the maps of the series "States, Territories, and Cities" (Pls. 61E–67A).

Public Lands of the United States, 1929 [*Plate 59B*]. This map, which shows the public lands by counties, is based on statistics showing the area of "unappropriated and unreserved land" by counties published in "Vacant Public Lands on July 1, 1929" (*Circular No. 1197*, General Land Office, Department of the Interior, Washington, D. C.) and on the areas of the counties as given in *United States Census of Agriculture, 1925*, 3 vols., Washington, 1927. No public lands are known to the General Land Office as "remaining undisposed of in the States of Illinois, Indiana, Iowa, Missouri, and Ohio. Small areas remain in the States of Alabama, Kansas, Louisiana, Michigan, Mississippi, Oklahoma, and Wisconsin, in widely scattered tracts, and no descriptive lists thereof are available." The largest acreage (9,671,374) is found in Nye County, Nevada. Several counties contain less than five acres.

SETTLEMENT, POPULATION, AND TOWNS, 1650-1790

[PLATES 60–61D]

Settled Areas and Population, 1660–1790

[PLATE 60]

THIS series illustrates the spread of settlement and the increase in population between 1660 and 1790. The settled areas in 1660, 1700, 1760, 1775, and 1790 are derived from a map prepared under the direction of J. R. H. Moore and published in Edward Channing, *A History of the United States*, Vol. 3, New York, 1920, p. 528. The populations of the several colonies in 1660, 1700, 1750, and 1775, and of the several states in 1790, are depicted by symbols representing globes. The relative volumes of these globes are proportional to the estimated population. The figures for population were derived from Franklin B. Dexter, *Estimates of Population in the American Colonies*, in *Proc. Amer. Antiquarian Society*, New Series, Vol. 5, 1888, pp. 22–50. From a critical study of available data Dexter constructed graphs showing the trends in population decade by decade for each colony, each graph culminating with the population determined by the United States Census in 1790. From Dexter's text and by interpolation from these graphs the population for the years 1660, 1700, 1750, and 1775 was estimated approximately in round numbers. Table 1, below, shows in column (a) the figures for population as thus calculated and represented by the volumes of the globes, and in column (b) the estimated population as given in Bureau of the Census, *A Century of Population Growth*, Washington, 1909, Table 1, p. 9. Slightly different sizes of globes would in some instances have resulted had the latter estimates been used as the basis of calculation.

Although census figures by townships and counties exist for several of the colonies for different dates (*ibid.*, pp. 3–15, 149–185) they are scattered, often inaccurate, and not comparable. It would, therefore, be impossible to construct for all the colonies a series of uniform maps similar to those based on the United States Census reports for 1790–1930 (Pls. 76B–79), showing in detail the density of population.

On Plate 60 globe symbols instead of circles are used because of the extreme variations in the figures that had to be graphically represented.

Colonial Towns, 1650–1775

[PLATE 61A-D]

This series of four maps shows the towns for the years 1650, 1700, 1750, and 1775 in the thirteen original colonies and Florida and in the western country lying between these colonies and the Mississippi River (including the west bank of that river). It is supplemented by a succeeding series (see p. 45, below). Each town is indicated by a dot. The contemporary boundary lines are shown when they aid in identifying the colonies. When disputed or uncertain they are indicated by broken lines and are drawn as finally established. Disputes involving small areas are disregarded. In respect to boundary lines this series is introductory to the succeeding one (see p. 43, below, also pp. 25–30, above, and Pls. 42, 43A).

The colonial town in New England and parts of eastern New York and New Jersey differs somewhat from the colonial town farther southward, and consequently the maps for the two regions are unfortunately not strictly comparable. In the northern region a town is an incorporated area containing settlers organized for purposes of local government. In the southern region it may be defined as a collection of houses, more or less compactly built, constituting a center of population of relative importance. It may or may not be incorporated. The difference is not so great as it appears to be, since a northern town as a rule contains an "urban area" that corresponds pretty closely to a southern town. In other words, a northern town usually contains, in addition to a large rural area, a "collection of houses, more or less compactly built, constituting a centre of population of relative importance."

In the case of the northern towns the date of incorporation, with some exceptions, is taken as determining the year of the beginning of the town. The exceptions are the towns of Vermont that were incorporated before they were settled and organized, and the towns in other colonies that were never incorporated. In these the date of the first town meeting or other action indicative of organization is taken as decisive. In listing the northern towns their size and importance are disregarded.

In listing the southern towns the work is by no means so simple. Many southern places that in books and on maps are called towns are not towns in the sense in which the term "town" is here used but are crossroads, taverns, insignificant hamlets, names of localities, or proposed or projected towns. Before deciding whether a place is or is not a town it is therefore necessary to obtain some notion of its size and importance. Unfortunately, information respecting many places is exceedingly slight, and decisions often have had to be based upon meager evidence. As there were no colonial censuses in the years covered by the maps, and as in other years there were but few that enumerated the inhabitants of towns, it is not possible to ascertain with precision the population of many colonial towns. An estimate of population based upon the number of houses can, however, sometimes be made. Often in forming a judg-

TABLE 1

POPULATION, 1660–1790

	1660		1700		1750		1775	1780	1790	
	a	b	a	b	a	b	a	b	a	b
Maine	(1)	(1)	(1)	(1)	(1)	(1)	(1)	55,500	(1)	96,643
New Hampshire	5,000	2,300	8,000	6,000	35,000	31,000	82,100	84,500	141,800	141,899
Vermont						(3)		40,000		85,341
Massachusetts	22,000[1]	25,000[1]	69,000[1]	70,000[1]	173,000[1]	180,000[1]	340,000[1]	307,000	475,000[1]	378,556
Rhode Island	5,000	1,500	9,000	6,000	38,000	35,000	60,000	52,000	68,800	69,112
Connecticut	8,000	8,000	26,000	24,000	119,000	100,000	200,000	203,000	237,900	237,655
New York	5,000	6,000	19,000	19,000	82,000	80,000[3]	191,000	200,000	340,000	340,241
New Jersey	5,000		13,000	14,000	70,000	66,000	125,000	137,000	184,000	184,139
Pennsylvania			28,000[2]	20,000[2]	150,000[2]	150,000[2]	300,000[2]	335,000	493,000[2]	433,611
Delaware			(2)	(2)	(2)	(2)	(2)	37,000	(2)	59,096
Maryland	8,000	8,000	30,000	31,000	140,000	137,000	240,000	250,000	319,700	319,728
Virginia	30,000	33,000	68,000	72,000	250,000	275,000	522,000	520,000	820,000[4]	747,610
North Carlina		1,000	6,000	5,000	85,000	80,000	278,000	300,000	429,000[5]	395,005
South Carolina			13,000	8,000	70,000	68,000	189,000	160,000	249,000	249,073
Georgia					10,000	5,000	45,000	55,000	82,000	82,548

[1] Maine included with Massachusetts.
[2] Delaware included with Pennyslvania.
[3] Vermont included with New York.
[4] Including Kentucky.
[5] Including Tennessee County.

ment it is necessary to rely upon the miscellaneous information recorded by travelers and local historians. Clues to the importance of a town are sometimes found in its geographical position, in its location within a settlement, in its trade and industries, in its formal incorporation or establishment, and in the layout of streets and lots. The possession of a seat of government, a church, a school, a fort, or a post office is regarded as significant. Forts, churches, missions, and courthouses when standing alone or virtually alone are, however, excluded. Many insignificant hamlets apparently containing a population of about one hundred people or less are also excluded. A few hamlets of no more than one hundred people, when important, may have been included.

In applying criteria of so general and indefinite a character as these probably no two persons would always agree. It may also be true that a larger knowledge of local history would necessitate a few slight modifications in the maps. The details, however, are as accurate as they can be made under the circumstances, after a considerable study of local history. Slight changes of details would not affect the general appearance of the maps.

The number of colonial towns lying within the areas of the present states, for each of the four years, is shown in table 2:

The towns having 5000 or more inhabitants, for each of the four years, are as follows: 1650, none; 1700, Boston and Philadelphia; 1750, Boston, Newport, Middletown, Norwich, New York, and Philadelphia; 1775, Salem, Boston, Newport, Norwich, New Haven, New London, Farmington, Stratford, New York, Philadelphia, Baltimore, and Charleston. The population of the most populous city was as follows: in 1700, Boston 7000; in 1750, Boston 16,000; and in 1775, Philadelphia (including suburbs) 34,000.

This series is based chiefly upon information found in town and local histories, state registers and manuals, and *A Century of Population Growth*, Washington, 1909, pp. 11–14 and 149–185.

TABLE 2

COLONIAL TOWNS WITHIN THE PRESENT LIMITS OF THE UNITED STATES

	1650	1700	1750	1775
Maine	2	7	11	34
New Hampshire	4	8	43	128
Vermont				37
Massachusetts	41	81	146	221
Rhode Island	4	12	24	29
Connecticut	12	36	67	73
New York	11	35	52	64
New Jersey		12	19	21
Pennsylvania		3	11	27
Delaware		2	4	4
Maryland	1	2	13	16
District of Columbia				1
Virginia	1	2	17	30
West Virginia				2
North Carolina			6	14
South Carolina		3	6	10
Georgia			5	6
Florida	1	1	2	2
Alabama			1	1
Louisiana			1	1
Mississippi				1
Missouri			1	2
Illinois			3	3
Indiana			1	1
Michigan		1	2	2
Total	77	205	435	730

STATES, TERRITORIES, AND CITIES, 1790-1930
[PLATES 61E–67A]

THIS series of maps shows (1) state and territorial boundary lines and (2) the principal cities for each census year during the period 1790–1930. Boundary lines and cities are shown together, not because they are closely connected but because their combination effects a saving of space. The state and territorial boundaries are discussed in the immediately following paragraphs, the cities on p. 45, below.

States and Territories, 1790–1920
[PLATES 61E–66]

The state and territorial boundary lines are shown upon either the main maps of the series or upon "additional maps," combined with the main maps as insets or, as in the case of the years 1845–1868 (Pl. 64C), brought together in a collection in the place of a main map. The additional maps are drawn on the same scale as the main maps. The boundaries for census years are shown upon the main maps and for the intermediate years, when they differ from those of census years, upon the additional maps. When a change of boundary is made during a census year following a change made during the nine preceding years, the latest boundary is shown upon the main map, and the one immediately preceding is shown upon an additional map. When more than one change in the boundary of a territory is made during a single year (which has happened rarely) only the first and the final boundary for that year are shown. Small and relatively unimportant changes are not shown.

The names of the territories are on the maps, as also are the names of the states when the states have been enlarged or reduced in area or when it is necessary to indicate their admission into the Union. The dates of admission are in parentheses. The period during which a territory had the boundary shown upon a given map is indicated below the name of the territory by means of inclusive dates. The successive forms assumed by a territory or a state on account of reduction or enlargement are indicated by the numerals 1, 2, 3, etc. The final form is numbered when it appears but not thereafter.

Boundaries are generally represented by full black lines. Disputed and uncertain boundaries, however, when the dispute or the uncertainty is of relative importance, are represented by short-dash or broken lines. Occasionally in representing such boundaries it has been necessary to make a choice of lines. Thus, as the international boundary between the most northwestern point of the Lake of the Woods and the Mississippi River, 1790–1803, a due south line from the point as determined by the Commissioners under the seventh article of the Treaty of Ghent is chosen (see p. 57, below). Such a line strikes the Mississippi River near its source. As the western boundary of Spanish Florida, 1810–1821, the Perdido River, the line claimed by the United States, is chosen (see Pl. 93F and p. 63, below). As the international boundary line in 1850 between the Rio Grande and the first branch of the Gila River, the line agreed upon by the American and Mexican boundary commissioners is shown (see Pl. 93H and pp. 63–64, below). For the practice of the Census Office respecting these lines see *Census Reports, Twelfth Census,* 1901, Vol. I, pp. ccxxiii-ccxxv.

The state and territorial boundary lines are drawn from the descriptions found in *U. S. Statutes at Large*, Vols. 1–37. The state and territorial lines in the Great Lakes, not usually shown upon maps, are thus derived. Specific references to these descriptions will be found in the indexes to the *Statutes* under the names of the states and territories. Most of the descriptions will be found in E. M. Douglas, *Boundaries, Areas, Geographic Centers, and Altitudes of the United States and the Several States* (U. S. Geol. Survey, *Bull.* 817), Washington, 1930, pp. 74–244. The international boundary lines are drawn from the descriptions found in the treaties and conventions of the United States and the reports of international boundary commissions. References to these descriptions will be found on pp. 54–69, below.

States and Territories, 1790 [*Plate 61E*]. Before the end of 1790 all the original states had ratified the Constitution and were incorporated into the Union. Maine at this time belonged to Massachusetts. Vermont, while not yet admitted into the Union, had had her rights to a

separate existence recognized by New York, which had long disputed them (see Pl. 97B and p. 73, below). The Erie Triangle, which lay between southwestern New York and northwestern Pennsylvania, was federal territory. The Connecticut, or Western, Reserve in Ohio was claimed by Connecticut. Virginia included the present states of Virginia, West Virginia, and Kentucky. Georgia claimed the Mississippi River as her western boundary. The Territory Northwest of the River Ohio (1st form) was organized in 1787, and the Territory Southwest of the River Ohio in 1790.

States and Territories, 1791–1800 [*Plate 61F*]. During the years 1791–1800 the most important territorial changes and settlements were as follows:

1791.   Admission of Vermont.
1792.   Admission of Kentucky and reduction of Virginia (see Pl. 41C and p. 24, above); conveying of Erie Triangle to Pennsylvania (see Pl. 47C and p. 35, above).
1795.   Settlement of Spanish-American boundary (see Pl. 93E and pp. 62–63, below).
1796.   Admission of Tennessee.
1798.   Organization of Mississippi Territory (1st form); settlement of St. Croix River boundary (see Pl. 91C and p. 58, below).
1800.   Reduction of the Territory Northwest of the River Ohio (2d form) and organization of Indiana Territory (1st form); cession of jurisdiction over Western Reserve by Connecticut (see Pl. 47B and pp. 34–35, above).

States and Territories, 1801–1810 [*Plate 61G*]. During the years 1801–1810 the most important territorial changes were as follows:

1803.   Admission of Ohio; purchase of Louisiana; enlargement of Indiana Territory (2d form).
1804.   Enlargement of Mississippi Territory (2d form); organization of Orleans Territory (1st form); formation of Louisiana District and extension of government of Indiana thereto.
1805.   Organization of Michigan Territory (1st form) and reduction of Indiana Territory (3d form); change of name of Louisiana District to Louisiana Territory and organization of a separate government therefor.
1809.   Organization of Illinois Territory and reduction of Indiana Territory (4th form).
1810.   Enlargement of Orleans Territory (2d form).

In 1802 Georgia ceded to the federal government the lands claimed by her lying between her present western boundary and the Mississippi River (see Pl. 47D and p. 35, above). In 1798 the southern part of this area had been organized as Mississippi Territory, and in 1804 the northern part was annexed to that territory. Between 1802 and 1804 the northern part was unorganized federal territory. Between 1809 and 1816 Indiana possessed a detached land area in what is now the upper peninsula of Michigan. In 1810 President Madison by proclamation attached West Florida to Orleans Territory (for disputed boundary, see Pl. 93F and p. 63, below).

The northern and western boundaries of the Louisiana Purchase (Louisiana District and Orleans Territory) are shown as uncertain. The northern boundary (as shown) is the forty-ninth parallel; and the western boundary, the line of the Adams-Onis treaty of 1819 as far as the summit of the Rocky Mountains and thence the continental divide to the forty-ninth parallel.

States and Territories, 1811–1820 [*Plate 62A*]. During the years 1811–1820 the most important territorial changes and settlements were as follows:

1812.   Admission of Louisiana (1st form); enlargement of Louisiana (2d form); enlargement of Mississippi Territory (3d form); change of name of Louisiana Territory to Missouri Territory.
1816.   Admission of Indiana and reduction of Michigan Territory (2d form).
1817.   Admission of Mississippi (1st form); organization of Alabama Territory.

1818. Admission of Illinois; enlargement of Michigan Territory (3d form); settlement of international boundary between Lake of the Woods and Rocky Mountains (see Pl. 93B and pp. 60–61, below); convention with Great Britain for joint occupation of the Oregon Country.

1819. Admission of Alabama (1st form); organization of Arkansas Territory; treaty with Spain settling southwest boundary (see Pl. 95A and p. 68, below); completion of settlement of northern boundary of Georgia (see p. 84, below).

1820. Admission of Maine; enlargement of Mississippi (2d form) and reduction of Alabama (2d form).

Louisiana was enlarged in 1812, a few months after her admission, by the addition of that part of the present state lying northeast of the line of Lake Pontchartrain and the Iberville and Mississippi rivers. From the admission of Indiana in 1816 to the enlargement of Michigan Territory in 1818 the small detached land area in the upper peninsula formerly belonging to Indiana Territory was "unorganized." The act admitting Indiana gave that state a northern boundary ten miles north of the territorial boundary, thereby enlarging Indiana at the expense of Michigan Territory. In 1820 a bend was made in the southern part of the Mississippi-Alabama boundary line, thereby enlarging Mississippi and reducing Alabama.

The Oregon Country is now shown for the first time, since the claims of the United States to it had been strengthened by the convention with Great Britain of 1818 and by the treaty with Spain of 1819. Its northern and southern boundaries are shown as uncertain, since the area claimed by the United States extended north of the northern boundary and the area claimed by Great Britain extended south of the southern boundary (see Pl. 49 and pp. 36–37, above).

States and Territories, 1821–1830 [*Plate 62B*]. During the years 1821–1830 the most important territorial changes and settlements were as follows:

1821. Admission of Missouri (1st form); cession of Florida.
1822. Organization of Florida Territory; settlement of international boundary in Lakes Ontario and Erie (see p. 71, below).
1824. Reduction of Arkansas Territory (2d form).
1828. Reduction of Arkansas Territory (3d form).

Florida was unorganized from 1821 to 1822. Missouri was admitted in 1821, with the meridian of the mouth of the Kansas River as her western boundary.

States and Territories, 1831–1840 [*Plate 63A*]. During the years 1831–1840 the most important territorial changes and settlements were as follows:

1834. Enlargement of Michigan Territory (4th form).
1836. Organization of Wisconsin Territory (1st form) and reduction of Michigan Territory (5th form); admission of Arkansas; settlement of Ohio-Michigan boundary (see Pl. 98B and pp. 79–80, below).
1837. Admission of Michigan; enlargement of Missouri (2d form).
1838. Organization of Iowa Territory and reduction of Wisconsin Territory (2d form).
1840. Settlement of Texas-United States boundary (see Pl. 93G and p. 63, below).

In 1837 Missouri was enlarged by the addition of the area lying between the Missouri River and the meridian of the mouth of the Kansas River.

States and Territories, 1841–1850 [*Plate 63B*]. See also Plate 64C, Additional Maps, 1845–1868. During the years 1841–1850 the most important territorial changes and settlements were as follows:

1842. Settlement of international boundary from St. Croix River to St. Lawrence River and from the Neebish Channels to Lake of the Woods (see Pls. 91A–B, 93A–D, and pp. 55–62, below).
1845. Admission of Florida; admission of Texas (1st form). In 1849 the eastern boundary of Texas was moved from the western bank to the middle of the Sabine River, Lake, and Pass (*Laws of Texas*, Austin, Nov. 24, 1849).
1846. Settlement of northwest international boundary (see Pl. 93C and p. 61, below); settlement of Illinois-Wisconsin boundary (see Pl. 99C and p. 82, below); admission of Iowa.
1848. First Mexican cession (see p. 65, below); organization of Oregon Territory; admission of Wisconsin.
1849. Organization of Minnesota Territory; settlement of northern boundary of Missouri (see Pl. 98C and p. 80, below).
1850. Admission of California; reduction of Texas (2d form); organization of Utah and New Mexico territories.

In 1846, on the admission of Iowa, the northern part of Iowa Territory was reduced to the status of "unorganized territory"; and in 1848, on the admission of Wisconsin, this area was enlarged by the admission of a considerable area lying northwest of Wisconsin. In 1849 the whole of this area was organized as Minnesota Territory. From 1846 to 1848 the area that became Oregon Territory was unorganized; and from 1848 to 1850 California, Utah, and most of New Mexico had the same status.

States and Territories, 1851–1860 [*Plate 64A*]. See also Plate 64C, Additional Maps, 1845–1868. During the years 1851–1860 the most important territorial changes were as follows:[1]

1853. Purchase of territory in the southwest by Gadsden (see Pl. 94B and p. 66, below); organization of Washington Territory (1st form) and reduction of Oregon Territory (2d form).
1854. Incorporation of Gadsden Purchase with New Mexico (2d form); organization of Kansas Territory; organization of Nebraska Territory (1st form).
1858. Admission of Minnesota.
1859. Admission of Oregon and enlargement of Washington Territory (2d form).

The Gadsden Purchase from the date of the purchase in 1853 until it was incorporated with New Mexico in 1854 was unorganized.

States and Territories, 1861–1870 [*Plate 64B*]. See also Plate 64C, Additional Maps, 1845–1868. During the years 1861–1870 the most important territorial changes were as follows:[2]

1861. Admission of Kansas; organization of Colorado Territory; reduction of New Mexico Territory (3d form); reduction and enlargement of Nebraska Territory (2d form); organization of Nevada Territory (1st form); reduction of Utah Territory (2d form); organization of Dakota Territory (1st form); reduction of Washington Territory (3d form).
1862. Enlargement of Nevada Territory (2d form) and reduction of Utah Territory (3d form).
1863. Organization of Idaho Territory (1st form); reduction of Washington Territory (4th form); reduction of Dakota Territory (2d form); organization of Arizona Territory (1st form) and reduction of New Mexico Territory (4th form); reduction of Nebraska Territory (3d form); admission of West Virginia (1st form); enlargement of West Virginia (2d form).
1864. Admission of Nevada (1st form); organization of Montana Territory,[3] enlargement of Dakota Territory (3d form); and reduction of Idaho Territory (2d form).
1866. Enlargement of Nevada (2d form); reduction of Utah Territory (4th form); reduction of Arizona Territory (2d form).
1867. Admission of Nebraska (1st form).
1868. Organization of Wyoming Territory; reduction of Dakota Territory (4th form); reduction of Idaho Territory (3d form); reduction of Utah Territory (5th form).

In 1861 Nebraska Territory was reduced by the formation of Colorado and Dakota territories, and in the same year it was enlarged by the addition of a small area lying westward of the Rocky Mountains and belonging to Utah and Washington territories. West Virginia was admitted into the Union on June 20, 1863. It was enlarged by the addition of Berkeley County on August 5 and of Jefferson County on November 2 of the same year. These additions were confirmed by the U. S. Supreme Court in 1871. In 1864 an area comprising a large part of the present state of Wyoming was temporarily incorporated with Dakota Territory, an arrangement which lasted until 1868, when Wyoming Territory was organized.

States and Territories (Additional Maps), 1845–1868 [*Plate 64C*]. See text on Plates 63B, 64A–B, above, and also p. 43.

States and Territories, 1871–1880 [*Plate 64D*]. During the years 1871–1880 the most important territorial changes and settlements were as follows:[4]

1872. Settlement of the San Juan water boundary (see Pl. 96C and pp. 71–72, below).
1876. Admission of Colorado.

---

[1] In 1855 Massachusetts ceded a small area in the southwest corner of that state to New York.
[2] In 1862 the boundary between Massachusetts and Rhode Island was changed, each state receiving a small area from the other (see Pl. 97C and p. 74, below).
[3] The parallel of 44° 30′ cuts the meridian of 34° west of Washington south of the crest of the Rocky Mountains and not north, as was believed by Congress when the boundaries of Montana were defined in 1864 (*U. S. Statutes at Large*, Vol. 13, Boston, 1866, p. 86). Still laboring under this misconception, Congress in 1873 passed a law attaching to Montana a small area that did not exist (*ibid.*, Vol. 17, Boston, 1873, p. 464; E. M. Douglas, *Boundaries, Areas,...of United States* (U. S. Geol. Survey, *Bull.* 817), Washington, 1930, p. 220);
[4] In 1880 New York ceded a small area to Vermont.

States and Territories, 1881–1890 [*Plate 65A*]. During the years 1881–1890 the most important territorial changes were as follows:

1882. Enlargement of Nebraska (2d form) and reduction of Dakota Territory (5th form).
1889. Admission of Washington, Montana, North Dakota, and South Dakota.
1890. Admission of Idaho and Wyoming; organization of Oklahoma Territory.

States and Territories, 1891–1900 [*Plate 65B*]. During the years 1891–1900 the most important territorial changes and settlements were as follows:[5]

1893. Enlargement of Oklahoma Territory.
1896. Admission of Utah; settlement of Texas-Oklahoma boundary (see Pl. 97H and p. 78, below).

States and Territories, 1901–1910 [*Plate 66A*]. During the years 1901–1910 the most important territorial changes and settlements were as follows:

1907. Admission of Oklahoma.
1910. Settlement of Maryland-West Virginia boundary (see Pl. 98A and pp. 78–79, below).

States and Territories, 1911–1920; States, 1930 [*Plates 66B and 67A*]. During the years 1911–1930 the most important territorial changes and settlements were as follows:

1912. Admission of New Mexico and Arizona.
1923. Settlement of Oklahoma-Texas boundary along the Red River (see Pl. 101C and p. 87, below).
1926. Settlement of Michigan-Wisconsin boundary (see Pl. 101A and p. 86, below).

Cities, 1790–1930
[PLATES 61E–67A]

This series supplements the series illustrating colonial towns, 1650–1775 (see Pl. 61A-D and pp. 41–42, above). It shows, for each census year from 1790 to 1930, the cities containing 5000 or more inhabitants. The term "cities" includes all urban places known as cities, towns, villages, or boroughs, and a few urban "districts" near Philadelphia.

---

[5] In 1892 the U. S. Supreme Court decided that a small part of Iowa lay west of the Missouri River (see Pl. 101B and pp. 86–87, below).

It also includes New England towns, which usually contain both urban and rural areas. Since the census statistics for New England are by towns, it is impossible to ascertain what was the population of the urban areas of most towns, and consequently it is necessary to treat the New England town as a "city." Nearly every town of 5000 or more inhabitants, however, contains an urban area. Nevertheless, the application of the rule makes the urban area in New England on some of the maps appear somewhat excessive.

Since the censuses before 1870 did not always give the population of urban places it is sometimes necessary for those earlier years, in ascertaining the population of cities of about 5000 inhabitants, to rely upon secondary sources and careful estimates based upon all available information. With this exception the maps are based upon the publications on population of the U. S. Census Office (or Bureau). The volumes used are the following:

1st Census, *Return of Whole Number of Persons within the Several Districts of the United States*, 1791, octavo.
2d Census, *Return of Whole Number of Persons within the Several Districts of the United States*, 1801, folio.
3rd Census, *Aggregate Amount of Each Description of Persons within the United States*, 1811, folio.
4th Census, *Census for 1820*, 1821, folio.
5th Census, *Enumeration of the Inhabitants of the United States*, 1832, folio.
6th Census, *Compendium of the Enumeration of the Inhabitants and Statistics of the United States*, 1841, folio.
7th Census, *Seventh Census of the United States*, 1853, quarto.
8th Census, *Population of the United States in 1860*, 1864, quarto.
9th Census, *Statistics of the Population of the United States*, 1872, quarto.
10th Census, *Statistics of the Population of the United States 1883*, quarto.
11th Census, *Compendium of the Eleventh Census*, Part I, *Population*, 1892, quarto.
12th Census, Vol. 1, *Population*, Part I, 1901, quarto.
13th Census, Vols. 1–3, *Population*, 1913, quarto.
14th Census, Vol. 1, *Population*, 1921, quarto.
15th Census, *Population Bulletins*, First Series, 1930; Second Series, 1930–1931 (one bulletin for each state). Since the maps were engraved, Vol. 1, *Population*, 1931, has been published.

Cities containing from 5000 to 100,000 inhabitants are represented by a small dot, and cities containing 100,000 inhabitants or more by a large dot. In several of the eastern states the dots are so numerous they are partially superimposed. As a result a congestion of cities appears on the map as an irregular black spot. Occasionally the number of dots is reduced by the division of a "city" (usually a New England town) or by the consolidation of cities. A reduction thus caused does not signify a reduction of population.

POPULATION, 1790-1930
[PLATES 67B–80A]

THIS series illustrates the following subjects: slaves, free negroes, colored population, European sources of emigration to the colonies and to the United States, foreign-born population, German, Irish, and Swedish-Norwegian population, density of population, and centers of population. Not until the First Census, 1790, are the statistics of population adequate for the construction of comparable maps covering the whole of the territory comprising the thirteen original colonies (see, however, Plate 60 and p. 41, above).

Slaves, Free Negroes, and Colored Population, 1790–1930
[PLATES 67B–70B]

This series shows the negro population, by counties, during the period 1790–1930. There are some statistics of the number of negroes for the period 1698–1786, but they are not sufficiently numerous or specific to afford adequate materials for a series of maps (*A Century of Population Growth*, Washington, 1909, pp. 149–185). Beginning with 1790 the statistics of the U. S. Census are available, and it is upon these that the maps of Plates 67B–70B are based. The Census statistics are found in the publications of the several censuses relating to population (for a list of the most important of these volumes see the preceding page. Especial use has been made of *Statistics of the Population of the United States*, Ninth Census, 1872, Vol. 1, pp. 11–74, which contains in concise form the statistics of negro population for the first nine censuses. When discrepancies between earlier and later publications are discovered the figures deemed most trustworthy are used. Such discrepancies, however, are infrequent.

This series contains thirteen maps, of which eight show slaves, two show free negroes, and three show negro population. In the cases of slaves and negro population percentages are shown; and in the case of free negroes, numbers. Whether percentages or numbers should be shown has been determined in large part by trying out the two methods with a view to discovering the one that would make the best maps. The advantages and limitations of each method have also been considered. When the percentages are relatively large the percentage method, and when relatively small the number method, is likely to produce the best results. By the percentage method the figures for counties of widely varying populations are made more comparable. This is one of its advantages. On the other hand, by this method counties may be shifted from one group to another at different censuses, not because of changes in the negro population but because of changes in the white population. This method is sometimes misleading in respect to new counties containing but few people. Collingsworth County, Texas, is a case in point. In 1880 it contained six persons, three of whom were negroes; and it is therefore on the map for that year given the heaviest shading. In 1900 it contained 1233 persons, two of whom were negroes, and on the map for that year it is given the lightest shading.

The number method makes no adjustment on account of differences in the total population of counties. By this method counties may be given the heaviest shading when they have relative to the white population fewer negroes than other counties which are given the lightest shading. Some limitations are common to both methods. Thus, a very slight change in the negro population of a county as returned by successive censuses may be sufficient to shift a county from one group to another if the percentage or number for that county is close to the percentage or number that separates two groups. An area may shift from one group to another not because of a change in population but because of the creation of new counties or because of a modification of boundary lines.

Some of the large counties of the Western States contain unsettled areas which are shaded, since it was not possible to separate them from the settled areas. Many large unsettled areas, however, have been cut off from their counties often more or less arbitrarily and appear on the maps as blank areas.

In conformity with the practice of some of the census compilations Baltimore is treated as if it were a part of Baltimore County, and the Virginia cities that form independent municipalities are treated as if they were a part of the respective counties to which they geographically belong. These cities are too small for separate treatment. The shading of Monroe County, Florida, the larger part of which lies on the mainland, is chiefly determined by the population of its most populous part, the city of Key West, which lies on an island at the southern extremity of the state.

Slaves, 1790–1860 [*Plates 67B–68B*]. The states in which no slaves were reported are as follows: 1790 and 1800, Maine (part of Massachusetts until 1820), Massachusetts, and Vermont; 1810 and 1820, Maine, Massachusetts, Vermont, New Hampshire, and Ohio; 1830, Vermont; 1840, Maine, Massachusetts, Vermont, and Michigan; 1850, Maine, Massachusetts, Vermont, New Hampshire, Rhode Island, Connecticut, New York, Pennsylvania, Ohio, Indiana, Illinois, Michigan, Wisconsin, and Iowa; 1860, the same states as for 1850, with the addition of Minnesota. The large blank areas in the Southern States, which disappear on the map for 1850, are unsettled areas. The blank areas in the west and northwest are chiefly unsettled areas, although they are in part settled areas without slaves. Indian Territory, for which there are no statistics, is shown as a blank area. There were, however, some slaves there in 1860 and earlier (A. H. Abel, *The American Indian as Slaveholder and Secessionist*, Cleveland, 1915, Vol. 1, pp. 22 and 292). In 1850 twenty-six slaves were reported in Utah "en route for California" (*Seventh Census of the United States*, 1850, Washington, 1853, p. 993).

Free Negroes, 1810 and 1860 [*Plates 68C and 69A*]. The large blank areas on these maps are chiefly unsettled areas, and the small blank areas are chiefly settled areas containing no free negroes. The blank area on Plate 68C in eastern North Carolina is Pitt County, for which no free negroes were returned in 1810. This may be an error, as this county returned 32 free negroes in 1800 and 29 in 1820.

Colored Population, 1880–1930 [*Plates 69B–70B*]. For 1880 there are no returns for the Indian Territory, which therefore is left blank on the map for that year. The Indian nations and reservations in Oklahoma and Indian Territory for which there are returns for 1900 are treated as counties. Two negroes that were returned in 1880 for "unorganized territory" in Nebraska, two that were returned in the same year for Fort Sisseton, Dakota, and four that were returned in 1900 for Indian reservations in South Dakota are disregarded. Some of the areas in Texas and the Dakotas left blank on the maps for 1880 and 1900 are unsettled areas.

Emigration to the Colonies and to the United States, 1607–1929
[PLATES 70C–O]

Plate 70, maps C and D, illustrate a small part of the emigration to the colonies. Information respecting additional emigrants for the colonial period was too slight to furnish adequate materials for additional maps. Plate 70E–O illustrate the larger part of the emigration to the United States for the period covered by the statistics on this subject.

English and Welsh Emigration to Virginia and New England, 1607–1700 [*Plate 70C–D*]. These two maps show, by counties, the emigration to Virginia and New England, before 1701, of all adult English and Welsh settlers whose counties of origin could be discovered. The number of such settlers for Virginia from England was 629 and from Wales 8; for New England from England 1276 and from Wales 5. The number of settlers from London for New England was 193, or 15 per cent; for Virginia 179, or 28 per cent. The counties (with numbers) sending the most settlers to New England are as follows: Norfolk 125, Suffolk 116, Kent 106, Essex 100, Devon 76, and Wiltshire 69; to Virginia, Gloucester 44, Kent 42, Yorkshire 30, and Lancaster 22. Of the emigrants from Gloucester both to New England and Virginia more than half came from Bristol. Of the Norfolk emigrants to New England half came from Hingham and Norwich.

While the maps are based upon only a small percentage of the total number of settlers, it is believed that they show roughly the relative numbers coming from each county or section of England and Wales. The list of New England settlers was compiled chiefly from the following sources: James Savage, *Genealogical Dictionary of the First Settlers of New England*, Boston, 1860–1862, Vols. 1–4; C. H. Pope, *Pioneers of Maine and New Hampshire, 1623 to 1660*, Boston, 1908; *New England Historical and Genealogical Register*, Boston, 1847–1919, Vols. 1–73. The list of Virginia settlers was compiled from W. G. and M. N. Stanard, *Colonial Virginia Register*, Albany, 1909, and from manuscript lists supplied by Mr. Stanard.

The county lines were taken from a modern map.

Only for New England and Virginia was the available information on the origin of emigrants sufficient to give satisfactory results.

Sources of Emigration to the United States, 1831–1929 [*Plate 70E-O*].

This series illustrates the emigration to the United States from the countries of Europe. The emigration from other countries is of relatively little importance. During the period covered by the immigration statistics of the United States government, 1820–1929, Europe has supplied more than ninety per cent of all immigrants.

The total number of emigrants from each country is indicated for each decade by a black disc. The relative areas of the discs are proportional to the number of emigrants (see key on Pl. 70G).

The maps of this series through 1920 are based chiefly upon the statistical tables of immigrants found in Vol. 3 of the *Reports of the Immigration Commission (Senate Doc. No. 756, 61st Cong., 3rd Sess., 1911)*, pp. 17–44; in the monograph *Immigration into the United States*, published in 1903 by the Bureau of Statistics, Treasury Department, pp. 4338–4340; and in the *Annual Report of the Commissioner General of Immigration*, 1920, pp. 184–185. These tables have been occasionally corrected and supplemented by the annual reports on immigrants that have been published by the United States government beginning with the year 1820. The map for 1921–1929 is based on tables in the *Annual Reports of the Commissioner General of Immigration* covering those years.

The series covers the years 1831–1929 and contains ten maps, one for each decade until 1920, and one for the nine years 1921–1929. Statistics are available for the years 1821–1830. It was convenient, however, not to include a map for this decade; nor was its inclusion especially desirable, since it would not differ greatly from the map for 1831–1840.

The statistics are not altogether uniform and occasionally are less detailed than one would wish. For 1831–1867 they are for "alien passengers arriving," 1868–1903 for "immigrants arriving," 1904–1906 for "aliens admitted," and for 1907–1929 for "immigrant aliens admitted" (*Reports of the Immigration Commission*, 1911, Vol. 3, p. 4). The figures for Spain include those for the Canary and Balearic islands; and the figures for Portugal those for the Azores and Cape Verde islands. These inclusions cannot affect the earlier maps. They might affect the maps for 1871–1929 in respect to Portugal and the map for 1901–1910 in respect to Spain. Norway and Sweden are treated as a single country through 1870. Separate statistics are given for Poland for the period 1831 to 1900 although Poland was not at that time an independent nation. The outline of Poland, shown on the maps by a broken line, represents the approximate area from which emigrants are believed to have claimed Polish birth and accordingly to have been listed as Poles. On the map for 1901–1910 emigrants from Poland are divided among Austria Hungary, Germany, and Russia. The Balkan States are shown separately when the statistics permit. In ascertaining the number of immigrants from Serbia, Bulgaria, and Montenegro for 1891–1900, 1901–1910, and 1911–1920 these countries were treated as a single state, since the statistics do not give the figures for them separately. The discs representing these immigrants are placed in Bulgaria. The map for 1911–1920 shows the boundaries existing in 1911 in solid lines, and the 1914 boundaries in broken lines. In this decade statistics for 1920 only are given for Finland, Poland, Czechoslovakia, and Jugoslavia. These have been divided proportionally among the nations to which these areas belonged in 1914.

Immigrants from the United Kingdom of Great Britain and Ireland listed as "not specified" are apportioned between Great Britain and Ireland according to the relative numbers of immigrants that are specified. (For estimates of Irish emigration from British ports between 1846 and 1850 see Frances Morehouse, *Irish Migration of the 'Forties*, in *Amer. Hist. Rev.*, Vol. 33, 1928, pp. 579–592.)

Immigrants listed under the heading "countries not specified" are disregarded. Occasionally during the early years these were considerable, but in general their number is negligible. When the statistics are not for calendar years they are reduced to that basis. The country of an immigrant is determined by his place of birth or origin.

Foreign-Born Population, 1860–1930

[PLATES 71–76A]

This series of maps shows, by counties, for the years 1860, 1880, 1900, and 1930, the population of the United States that was born in foreign countries, and for the years 1880, 1900, and 1930 the population that was born in Germany, Ireland, and Norway-Sweden, respectively. The maps are based upon information derived chiefly from the published reports of the U. S. Census (see p. 45, above) supplemented for 1900 by manuscript information derived from the Census Bureau. As the statistics for 1930 are for "foreign-born white," Plate 72A is not strictly comparable with the earlier maps, particularly in the southwest, since foreign-born Chinese, Japanese, and Mexicans not definitely returned as white are not included.

The Census statistics of foreign-born population distributed by counties begin with the year 1860, and of foreign-born population distributed by counties and by racial stocks with the year 1870. The year 1860 was therefore chosen as the beginning year of the maps showing total foreign-born population. The year 1880 instead of 1870 was chosen as the beginning year of the maps showing population born in Germany, Ireland, and Norway-Sweden in order to make the dates of these maps correspond with the dates of the maps for total foreign-born.

The foreign-born population of the United States is derived from a great number of national and racial stocks. That derived from three stocks, the German, Irish, and Swedish-Norwegian, is mapped. These three were chosen because their representatives in the United States are numerous and well distributed and tend to preserve their stock characteristics and to form distinct political and social classes. No other stocks satisfy equally well these conditions.

The series contains thirteen maps, four of which illustrate total foreign-born population, three population born in Germany, three population born in Ireland, and three population born in Norway and Sweden. The four maps illustrating total foreign-born population show percentages, and the remaining nine show numbers. For the advantages and limitations of these two methods of representation see the preceding page.

Baltimore is treated as if it were a part of Baltimore County, and the Virginia cities as if they were parts of the counties to which they geographically belong. Indian reservations when they do not form a part of a county and the several tribal lands of the Indian Territory are treated as counties.

The four maps (Pls. 71–72) entitled "Foreign-Born Population," covering the years 1860–1930, show in five groups the per cent of foreign-born population in the total population. The areas that have no foreign-born population, as well as those that are unsettled, are unshaded. Since a foreign-born population of less than 1 per cent is practically negligible, areas of less than 1 per cent are also unshaded.

On the map for 1860 the large unshaded areas in the south are chiefly areas of less than 1 per cent (there being only a few counties with no foreign-born population), while the large unshaded areas in the west are chiefly unsettled areas. There are no returns for the Indian Territory, nor for three counties in Mississippi, two in Iowa, and one in Louisiana, all of which are unshaded. A small foreign-born population in what is now Colorado and the Dakotas is not shown, since the statistics do not distribute it by counties.

In 1860 there were forty-one counties in which one half or more of the population was foreign-born. These counties are distributed as follows: Minnesota 9, California 8, Texas 8, Michigan 6, Wisconsin 5, Nebraska 3, Missouri 1, and New Mexico 1. The most counties containing no foreign-born population in any state, with the exception of Texas, were in Kentucky and were five in number.

On the map for 1880 unsettled areas are shown in Dakota and western Texas. There are no returns for the Indian Territory. In thirty-five counties the foreign-born population constituted 50 per cent or more of the population. These are distributed as follows: Texas 11, Dakota 5, Michigan 5, Minnesota 3, Idaho 3, Nevada 2, Arizona 1, California 1, Florida 1, Oregon 1, Washington 1, and Wisconsin 1. The most counties containing no foreign-born population in any state, with the exception of Texas, were in Kansas and were four in number.

Some of the unshaded areas in western Texas on the map for 1900 are unsettled areas. In four counties the foreign-born population for this year was 50 per cent or more of the total population. Three of these were in North Dakota and one in Texas. The most counties containing no foreign-born population in any state were in Texas and were eight in number.

In 1930 in no county was the foreign-born white population 50 per cent or more of the total population. Nineteen counties had no foreign-born. These counties are distributed as follows: Georgia 7, Kentucky 5, Tennessee 4, North Carolina 2, and Texas 1.

The nine maps (Pls. 73-76A) illustrating the population born in Germany, Ireland, and Norway-Sweden show numbers of population in four groups, as follows: 1 to 10, 10 to 100, 100 to 1000, and 1000 and over. Areas without population born in these countries and unsettled areas are unshaded. On the maps for 1880 large unsettled areas are shown in western Texas and Dakota. There were no returns for the Indian Territory. On the maps for 1900 unsettled areas are shown in western Texas. The census returns for 1930 give no data for Norwegian and Swedish-born for West Virginia.

The following table shows for each of the years 1860, 1880, 1900, and 1930 the total population of the United States, the total population born in foreign countries, and the population born in Germany, Ireland and Norway-Sweden.

TABLE 1

FOREIGN-BORN POPULATION OF THE UNITED STATES

	TOTAL POPULATION	FOREIGN-BORN	GERMAN-BORN	IRISH-BORN	NORWEGIAN AND SWEDISH-BORN
1860	31,443,000	4,136,000	1,301,000	1,611,000	63,000
1880	50,156,000	6,680,000	1,967,000	1,855,000	376,000
1900	76,149,000	10,357,000	2,667,000	1,619,000	910,000
1930[1]	122,775,000	13,366,000[2]	1,609,000	745,000[3]	1,123,000[4]

[1] Figures for 1930 based on U. S. Census, press release dated Sept. 18, 1931.
[2] Foreign-born white only.
[3] Irish Free State only.
[4] Includes Denmark.

Density and Centers of Population, 1790–1930
[PLATES 76B-80A]

Density of Population, 1790–1930 [*Plates 76B–79*]. This series, except for the map for 1930, is based upon the maps, chiefly colored, published by the U. S. Census Office (or Bureau) during the years 1874-1925. The map for 1930 was compiled for the *Atlas* directly from the statistics by counties in *Population Bulletins*, First Series, of the Fifteenth Census of United States, Washington, 1930. The Census maps were redrawn and adapted to the needs of the *Atlas*. Since the *Atlas* maps are black and white, a different scheme of shading was followed. The *Atlas* maps show the density of the total population, while the Census maps, with the exception of those for 1910 and 1920, show the density of the rural population. This change made it necessary to recalculate the density of population of many urban counties (counties containing cities whose population was in excess of 8000) and not infrequently of counties adjacent thereto. Some of the very small areas on the Census maps, chiefly in the West, were omitted. A few obvious errors in the Census maps were corrected. Usually the Census calculations of density were accepted. It was apparent, however, that the more accurate determination in recent years of the area of counties would sometimes change the Census results.

The geographical unit employed by the Census as the basis of its calculations was usually the county but by no means always. The maps of the first nine censuses, 1790–1870, were made during the years 1870-1874, and the method followed in their compilation is thus described in the *Census Atlas* for the Ninth Census, published in 1874:

"The county has ordinarily been taken as the unit of treatment. Its population at the period to which the individual map has reference having been ascertained ... the number of inhabitants was divided by the number of square miles in the county, the quotient representing the average density of settlement. Where, however, any county was of unusual extent, or there was reason known to the compiler for suspecting that various portions of it might be found in very different stages of settlement, the county was no longer taken entire, but the investigation was carried down to sections of the county and even to its several townships. The number of counties thus broken up for the purposes of this compilation, would naturally vary much. At some censuses they would amount to several hundreds; at others, to scarcely as many score ... The plan of grouping has been to make as large groups as could be done without merging any appreciable proportion of counties in groups of a markedly different grade. Thus, if a single county of small extent belonging to Group III. [18 to 45] should appear surrounded by numerous counties of Group IV. [45 to 90], or of Group II. [6 to 18], it would not be preserved distinct, but would take the shading of its general section. If, however, a county of Group IV. or V. [90 and over] should appear among counties of Group I. [2 to 6] or II., the distinction would be regarded as of sufficient importance to be maintained. Again, a county whose average brought it within Group IV. might come between III.'s and V.'s, appearing thus to belong to a group distinct from both. Yet the resolution of the county into its constituent townships might develop the fact that those parts of the county which bordered on the III.'s were themselves of that grade, while the parts bordering on the V.'s were of that degree of density. In such a case, the division of the county by a central line, and the throwing of the parts, on the one side and on the other, into the adjacent groups, would not only dispense with the necessity of preserving a troublesomely small group upon the map, but would even better represent the facts of the case" (*Statistical Atlas of the United States*, Washington, 1874, Part II, "Progress of the Nation," p. 1).

In adapting the Census maps to the needs of the *Atlas* considerable regard was shown for county lines. The maps for 1910, 1920, and 1930 are based wholly on the county as a unit, and their lines are located with precision. Much less refinement was employed by the Census in locating the lines of the earlier maps. The Census maps for 1910, 1920, and 1930 show the density of the total population. Differences in what is shown and in methods of construction make these three maps not strictly comparable with the earlier ones. Imperfect in details, the Census maps for 1790–1900 and the *Atlas* maps based upon them are fairly reliable in respect to the general picture presented by them. More than this can hardly be said.

The Census maps are of varying sizes. The maps for 1850 and 1860 do not extend west of the meridian of central Texas. Each census from the tenth to the thirteenth has republished the maps of the previous censuses. The maps of the *Atlas of Historical Geography* are based upon the maps found in the volumes of the *Statistical Atlas of the United States*, published by the Census Bureau in 1874, 1898, 1903, 1914, and 1925, respectively. The specific references to these volumes are as follows: for 1790–1870, *Atlas of the Ninth Census*, Pls. 16, 16(a), 17, 17(a), 18, and 19; for 1880 and 1890, Eleventh Census, Pl. 5, No. 19, and Pl. 6; for 1900, Twelfth Census, Pl. 13; for 1910, Thirteenth Census, Pl. 68; for 1920, Fourteenth Census, Pl. 68.

Centers of Population, 1790–1930 [*Plate 80A*]. This map is based upon Plate 121 of the *Statistical Atlas of the United States*, published by the Census Bureau in 1925. The center of the total population of the United States, 1930, is added from a press release of the Census Bureau, Aug. 27, 1931.

COLLEGES, UNIVERSITIES, AND CHURCHES, 1775-1890
[PLATES 80B–88]

Colleges and Universities, 1775–1890
[PLATES 80B–81]

THIS series of five maps illustrates the colleges and universities for the years 1775, 1800, 1830, 1860, and 1890. The year 1775 was chosen as the beginning year because it marks the close of the colonial period, and the year 1890 as the final year because relatively few colleges have been founded since that date.

Since the terms "college" and "university" are used to designate schools of different kinds and varying standards, it was necessary to exclude many institutions in order to obtain some degree of uniformity among those included. Technological schools and professional schools (including normal and military schools) were excluded. As the first colleges for women, usually designated "female seminaries" or "female colleges," were essentially secondary or "finishing" schools, none of them was admitted to the lists for 1830 and 1860. All those given first rank by the Bureau of Education (*Rept. U. S. Commissioner for Education*, 1904, Vol. 2, pp. 1526–1527) were admitted to the list for 1890. Of the colleges for men and the coeducational institutions the less substantial ones were excluded. In separating the more substantial from the less substantial, consideration was given to the curriculum, the faculty, the general reputation of the institution, the rank assigned it by others, its capacity to survive, and its possession of the right to grant academic degrees. It was not possible to apply these criteria mechanically or objectively. The best that could be done was to estimate each institution in a somewhat general way in accordance with the evidence available. In respect to colleges for men and coeducational institutions the presumption was in favor of inclusion. No well known institution was excluded. All the institutions that were mapped, with one exception (Clark University, which in 1890 had no undergraduate school), possess a department of arts and sciences. The best of the colleges for negroes were admitted to the list for 1890.

The variations in successive maps are caused chiefly by the creation of new institutions, but occasionally they are caused by the discontinuance of an institution or by its removal from one place to another. The date taken as decisive for purposes of mapping is the date of charter, the date of opening, or the date of the attainment of collegiate rank.

Of the published lists of colleges those found in the annual reports of the Bureau of Education, 1870–1920, were chiefly used. The lists found in the *American Almanac*, Boston, 1860 (pp. 204–206), in Nicholas Murray Butler, *Education in the United States*, Albany, 1910 (Vol. 1, pp. 243–249), and in various church almanacs and histories were also used. The series of *Contributions to American Educational History*, edited by Herbert B. Adams and published by the U. S. Bureau of Education in 1887–1903, were exceedingly serviceable, as were also the excellent collections of college catalogues and local histories found in the Library of Congress.

The total numbers of institutions for each of the years are as follows: 1775, 9; 1800, 22; 1830, 56; 1860, 203; and 1890, 370. The only state with twenty or more institutions before 1890 was Ohio, with twenty-one in 1860. Five states were in this class in 1890: Illinois 23, Iowa 22, New York 24, Ohio 29, and Pennsylvania 29.

Churches, 1775–1890
[PLATES 82–88]

Owing to the great difficulty of discovering and locating the colonial churches no maps of the churches before 1775–1776 were made. The task of finding and collecting information for maps between 1776 and 1860, when the Census statistics begin, was given up because of its magnitude. Changes made since 1890 are not sufficient to justify additional maps. The increase in the number of churches by 1860 made it necessary to change the scale of mapping.

Churches, 1775–1776
[PLATE 82]

This plate shows the churches in the thirteen original colonies for the period January 1, 1775–July 4, 1776, the period of the beginning of the American Revolution. The early churches that were discontinued before January 1, 1775, and the later ones that were established after July 4, 1776, obviously are not shown. Indian churches (see Pl. 37, "Indian Missions, 1567–1861") are excluded.

Sources of Information. The sources of information upon which the maps are based are many and varied. The principal original sources may be classified as follows: (a) records of individual churches, church books, minutes of meetings, letters, and other documents, commonly found among the archives of a church; (b) records of groups of churches organized as an association, presbytery, conference, council, coetus, ministerium, synod, etc.; (c) letters, diaries, journals, etc., particularly of the clergy or of others directly concerned with the work of a church or group of churches.

Many of the original sources are in manuscript, and a large use was made of manuscript sources. They are described in William H. Allison, *Inventory of Unpublished Material for American Religious History in Protestant Church Archives and Other Depositories*, Carnegie Institution of Washington, 1910. The manuscript materials are now generally deposited with the central organizations governing the several denominations, with religious and historical societies, and with the libraries and archives of theological seminaries. A few lists of church records, based on personal investigation, are in print. Illustrations of such lists are those found in Stephen B. Weeks, *Southern Quakers and Slavery*, Baltimore, 1896, and William Nelson, *Church Records in New Jersey*, Paterson, 1904. The correspondence and reports of the missionaries of the Society for the Propagation of the Gospel in Foreign Parts, transcripts of which are in the Library of Congress, were found useful for the Protestant Episcopal and other denominations.

The records of the central organizations governing the denominations usually list delegates to meetings and the churches that they represent, mention congregations applying for "supplies," and name the "supplies" and the congregations that they serve. Such records are valuable for the congregations on the frontier. There are published collections of some of the records. Among such publications are the following: W. M. Engles, *Records of the Presbyterian Church in the United States of America*, 1706–1778, Philadelphia, 1841; *Documentary History of the Evangelical Lutheran Ministerium of Pennsylvania and Adjacent States*, 1748–1821, Philadelphia, 1898; *Minutes and Letters of the Coetus of the German Reformed Congregations in Pennsylvania*, 1734–1792, Philadelphia, 1903; *Minutes of the Methodist Conferences Annually held in America, from 1773 to 1813*, Vol. 1, New York, 1813; *Acts and Proceedings of the General Synod of the Reformed Protestant Dutch Church in North America*, 1738–1812, Vol. 1, New York, 1859; *Minutes of the Philadelphia Baptist Association, 1707–1807*, Philadelphia, 1851.

Several lists of churches dating from about the time of the American Revolution were found useful. They are based in part on personal observation and knowledge and in part on conversations and correspondence. Some of them are in manuscript, while others have been printed in whole or in part. The compilations of Ezra Stiles on the Congregationalists, now in the library of Yale University, have been printed in part in his *Literary Diary*, New York, 1901, and in *Extracts from the Itineraries and other Miscellanies of Ezra Stiles*, New Haven, 1916—both works edited by F. B. Dexter. The names of many early Baptist churches will be found in Morgan Edwards, *Materials towards a History of the American Baptists*. His work, which is the result of extensive travels, is in print for Pennsylvania (Philadelphia, 1770), New Jersey (Philadelphia, 1792), and Rhode Island (*R. I. Hist. Soc. Colls.*, Vol. 6, Providence, 1867, pp. 301–370), and in manuscript for other colonies south of New England. Some important lists of colonial churches, such as the list of the Episcopal churches of Virginia in the *Virginia Almanack*, Williamsburg, 1776, were printed contemporaneously. There is an extensive list of the Baptist churches in John Asplund, *Annual Register of the Baptist Denominations in North-America, to the First of November, 1790* (n. p., 1792).

There are a few histories of denominations by authors who were living in or about 1775–1776 and who often had first-hand knowledge or had access to materials no longer extant. Among these is Robert B. Semple, *History of the Rise and Progress of the Baptists in Virginia*, Richmond, 1810, with elaborate lists of Baptist churches in Virginia.

Many later writers have published lists of churches, often in denominational registers or manuals, or histories of individual denominations, or histories of all the denominations in a state. These authorities often disagree respecting the date of the organization of a church or congregation or of its existence in 1775–1776. Among their important books are the following: I. M. Allen, *Triennial Baptist Register*, Philadelphia, 1836; Rufus M. Jones, *Quakers in the American Colonies*, London, 1911; E. T. Corwin, *Manual of the Reformed Protestant Dutch Church in North America*, New York, 1859; J. S. Clark, *Historical Sketch of the Congregational Churches in Massachusetts*, Boston, 1858; R. F. Lawrence, *New Hampshire Churches*, Claremont, 1856; George Howe, *History of the Presbyterian Church in South Carolina*, Columbia, 1870–1883; William Meade, *Old Churches, Ministers, and Families of Virginia*, Philadelphia, 1857; W. H. Foote, *Sketches of North Carolina*, New York, 1846, and *Sketches of Virginia*, Philadelphia, 1850–1856. Meade is excellent for the Episcopalians, and Foote for the Presbyterians. The published histories of the various presbyteries of the Presbyterian Church are valuable, and they supplement the original manuscript records, which are the principal source used for this church.

Much valuable information was obtained from the biographies of clergymen. Use was made of the collections of religious biographies and especially of William B. Sprague's *Annals of the American Pulpit*, 9 vols., New York, 1857–1869.

Information supplemental to that derived from religious sources was obtained from histories of counties, towns, and parishes and from publications of the secular historical societies. Since there are many such books for New England, the supplemental information for that section was considerable. Gazetteers of the early nineteenth century were found helpful in identifying the names of churches.

The Problem of Mapping Churches. Plate 82 shows the distribution of churches for 1775–1776 by denominations. The term "church" is here used in a special sense. It may be defined as a congregation of people who meet periodically for religious services. The maximum interval between meetings is generally not more than several months. A temporary congregation, such as often came together on short notice to listen to the preaching of an itinerant minister or missionary, is not a "church." In contemporary writings a "church" may be so called or it may be designated as a congregation, meeting, conference, mission, branch, station, or charge. The meeting place may be a church building, chapel, schoolhouse, public building, private house, barn, or tent, or may be under a tree, in a field, or by a roadside. A "church" may have no church building and be without a formal organization. It may have neither pastor nor officers. Its services may be conducted by a temporary or permanent leader chosen by itself. Its pastor may serve several other congregations.

Obviously the total number of congregations is much larger than the total number of clergymen or of church buildings. The difference is least in the case of the Congregationalists in New England and largest in the case of the Presbyterians and Baptists on the frontiers of Pennsylvania and of the southern colonies.

In respect to completeness and precision the maps have limitations, caused chiefly by a lack of adequate information and by complications in the religious practices. The limitations apply chiefly to the churches of the middle and southern colonies. Some of these will be described.

The names of all the congregations cannot be ascertained, and some of those whose names are known cannot be located. This is especially true for some of the congregations of the Presbyterian and other Protestant denominations on the frontier of the middle and southern colonies and for some of the Catholic congregations in private houses.

It was not unusual for the pastor of a well-established church to visit several small congregations within a radius of thirty miles of his church. Sometimes such congregations were served by itinerant missionaries and preachers. Some of these "mission" churches cannot now be discovered or located. The case of the Presbyterian congregations in middle and western Pennsylvania presented unusual difficulties. They had neither church buildings nor settled pastors but were served by traveling preachers. There is a record of an assignment of fourteen preachers to some seventy-five places. The names of many preaching places are known, but the available information is not sufficient to determine which of them were periodically and which occasionally visited. Only those congregations were listed for which there is good evidence of their having been visited periodically.

The "branch" Baptist churches of the southern colonies are listed as separate churches, although some authorities list only the churches to which the branches belong. Morgan Edwards describes a North Carolina Baptist church as having six branches, with a meetinghouse and an assistant at each place.

Such general names for churches as "New River," "Yadkin River," etc., which were rather usual in the southern colonies, do not always admit of precise location; and such common names as "Sandy Creek," "Mill Creek," etc., may occasionally have resulted in the confusing of two streams of the same name. Local names that were long ago discontinued are often hard to identify.

It is often difficult to determine whether a church, known to have been in existence before or after 1775–1776, was in existence at that date. The authorities may disagree respecting the date of its organization. Some records of congregations were destroyed during the Revolutionary War, and churches were often abandoned. After the war they were revived, and the date of revival was set down as the date of organization. It is not always easy to tell when a temporary or unorganized congregation became a "church." A decision usually depends on whether the meetings were periodical.

Congregations in a state of transition from one denomination to another are sometimes hard to classify. This was true for New England of Presbyterian congregations becoming Congregational, and of Congregational-Separatist congregations becoming Baptist. Independent congregations, with the exception of four "independent" churches in Massachusetts, are not mapped. These congregations were not attached to any denomination and were often short-lived, sporadic, and of a fanatical character.

The problem of union churches was not always easy to solve. Two congregations of different denominations may jointly own or use a church building, meet alternately or together in it, and have the same or different pastors. If each congregation regarded itself as distinct from the other, both are listed; otherwise only one. Several Lutheran and German Reformed congregations used the same building. When a congregation and its minister belonged to different denominations the congregation was classified under its own denomination.

Some of the difficulties that were encountered in listing churches on the frontier may be seen from the following contemporary descriptions by clergymen of religious conditions in a frontier county—Sussex County, New Jersey. In 1770 this county was described as having fifteen hundred families (Presbyterians, Anabaptists, Quakers, and Low Dutch), all very poor, and no settled minister of any denomination in the whole territory. "They have many strolling preachers among them, particularly the Baptists; and they are frequently visited by the Presbyterian ministers of the neighboring counties." In 1776 the Episcopalian missionary of this county writes that he "statedly attends divine service on week days at fifteen different places and on Sundays officiates at four congregations as usual."

Number of Churches. The total number of churches mapped is 3228. Further research in sources not now accessible would probably add some hundred and fifty additional churches. The number of denominations mapped, disregarding four "independent" churches in Massachusetts, is eighteen. The numbers of the churches for the ten leading denominations are as follows: Congregational 668, Presbyterian 588, Episcopal 495, Baptist 494, Friends, 310, German Reformed 159, Lutheran 150, Dutch Reformed 120, Methodist 65, and Catholic 56. For the eight minor denominations: Moravian 31, Congregational-Separatist 27, Dunker 24, Mennonite 16, French Protestant 7, Sandemanian 6, Jewish 5, and Rogerene 3. The total number of churches for the five leading denominations is 2555—79 per cent of all the churches; for the next five denominations 550—17 per cent; and for the eight minor denominations 120—4 per cent.

The numbers of churches by sections are as follows: New England 1021, Middle Colonies 1129, Southern Colonies 1078—about the same number for each section. The distribution of churches by sections and by colonies is shown by the maps. All but seven of the Congregational churches are in New England, and more than half of the Episcopal churches are in the southern colonies. Under "Baptist" are included all the divisions of this denomination—Separate, Six Principle, Seventh Day, etc.; and under "Presbyterian" all of the divisions of that denomination, "New Light," "Old Light," Associate Reformed, etc.

Churches, 1860, 1890

[PLATES 83–88]

The maps for 1860 are based chiefly upon the statistics of churches found in *Mortality and Miscellaneous Statistics, Eighth Census*, pp. 352–496, published by the Census Office in 1866. Unfortunately the statistics are not complete or perfect. There are no returns for some of the territories. The returns for a few counties in several of the states are also missing (see pp. 392, 414, 417, 419, 425, 440, 453, 470, 474, 488, 493–496). To supply these deficiencies a considerable use has been made of the lists of churches published by the denominations. After such additions have been made the statistics for the frontier states and territories are less complete than is desirable.

The maps for 1890 are based upon the *Report on Statistics of Churches*

(*House Misc. Doc. No. 340, 52nd Cong., 1st Sess.*, Part 17), published by the Census Office in 1894.

The census statistics for 1890 are for "organizations" and those for 1860 for "churches." This latter term is ambiguous and it is not possible in any particular case to be certain whether church organizations or church edifices were returned by the census official (*Statistics of Population, Ninth Census*, Vol. 1, Washington, 1872, p. 502).

Those denominations which are regarded as historically the most important are chosen for representation. Several denominations are composed of numerous divisions or branches. Thus, in 1890 the census statistics enumerated thirteen kinds of Baptists, seventeen kinds of Methodists, and twelve kinds of Presbyterians. Before mapping these denominations it was necessary to combine their divisions. In determining what divisions belong to a given denomination the classification of the Census Office was in the main followed. There were, however, a few exceptions to this rule. Thus, the Dunkers, Mennonites, and Winebrenners, classed by the Census Office in 1860 as Baptists, are not so treated. Only the Roman Catholics and Greek Catholics (Uniates) are treated as Catholics.

Under the term "Christian" the Census for 1860 included the Christian Church or Christian Connection, the Christian Church (South), and the Disciples of Christ. As it is not possible to separate these churches, the practice of the Census is followed. Under the term "Reformed" are included both the Dutch and German Reformed churches.

As the average number of communicants to a church of the Catholic denomination greatly exceeds the average number for the Protestant denominations, the maps of the Catholic churches do not adequately show the relative strength of that church.

THE three series constituting this section of the *Atlas* illustrate the most important questions that have arisen since 1607 concerning international, colonial, and state boundary lines. A uniform method of treating these questions has been followed so far as possible. The base maps upon which are shown the drainage, projection, and other geographical features are in black; the lines that were claimed, proposed, and agreed upon are in colors. Lines agreed upon are in general shown in green. In the case of international boundary negotiations lines originating with the United States are in blue and lines originating with other nations in yellow. For the sake of clearness, however, a few departures from this scheme have been made. When only one line of a given color is shown, a solid line has been preferred. Since it is not possible to superimpose color lines on one another, lines occupying the same position are drawn adjacent and parallel to one another. Only lines that were officially claimed, proposed, or agreed upon are shown.

NEGOTIATIONS FOR PEACE, 1779–1783
[PLATES 89 and 90]

Negotiations for Peace (Complete Map), 1779–1783
[PLATE 89]

The object of this map is to represent the various lines officially claimed, proposed, or agreed upon during the peace negotiations of 1779–1783. As the geographical features shown upon modern maps differ so greatly from the corresponding features shown upon maps in use at the time of the negotiations, it is not possible to represent on modern maps the boundary lines as they were understood by the negotiators. A contemporary map (John Mitchell, "Map of the British and French Dominions in North America," 2nd edit., London, 1755) has therefore been chosen as the base map. This was selected because it was the chief map used by the peace commissioners and the one upon which they marked the boundary lines, and because the boundary lines can be better represented on it than on any other map.[1] The Mitchell map that was reproduced is one found in the Department of State, upon the back of which are the words "Mitchell's Map—the copy used by the framers of the treaty of 1783" (the correctness of this statement is questioned). This was preferred to other copies because it contains no color lines, which tend to appear in photographic reproductions and greatly detract from their value as bases for representing boundary lines. Since the original is in only a fair condition, a touching-up of the print in places was rendered necessary in order to remove stains and restore mutilated lines. The title, text and scales found in the lower right-hand corner have been removed to make room for the new explanation. Certain names of interest in connection with the boundary negotiations have been rewritten in order that they may be legible. They are spelled as on the original map. The size of the original is about 6 feet 4 inches by 4 feet 4 inches. The reduction is about two-thirds and the map has been trimmed on all edges.

The first official statement respecting the boundaries of the United States was made by a committee of the Continental Congress appointed February 17, 1779, and presided over by Gouverneur Morris as chairman. On February 23 this committee reported to Congress, recommending that in the event of negotiations for peace the foreign ministers of the United States should insist on the following boundaries:

"Northerly by the ancient limits of Canada, as contended for by Great Britain, running from Nova Scotia, southwesterly, west, and northwesterly, to lake Nepissing, thence a west line to the Mississippi; easterly by the boundary settled between Massachusetts and Nova Scotia; southerly by the boundary settled between Georgia and East and West Florida; and westerly by the river Mississippi" (*Journs. Cont. Cong.*, Vol. 13, Washington, 1909, p. 241).

The boundary proposed by the committee is represented by *line 1*—a short-dash blue line. For the northeastern part of this line represented on Mitchell's map, reduced one-third, see Plate 90. See also the same for other lines lying wholly or partly in the northeastern section.

"The ancient limits of Canada" are represented on Mitchell's map by a short-dash black line. The short-dash blue line follows this, with the exception of a short section of line eastward of Lake Nipissing, where it follows the west branch of the Ottawa River instead of the northwest branch. This slight departure from the "ancient limits" was made in order to satisfy the condition of running to Lake Nipissing.

"The boundary settled between Massachusetts and Nova Scotia" is interpreted to mean the western boundary of Nova Scotia as defined in the commissions of Governors William Campbell (1765) and Francis Legge (1773), namely, a line drawn from the mouth of the St. Croix River to its source and thence due north to the southern boundary of Quebec. As the Royal Proclamation of 1763 made the southern boundary of Quebec the "highlands" south of the St. Lawrence River, there is a small gap in the line described by the committee between the "highlands" and the St. Lawrence.[2] Since before the proclamation Nova Scotia extended to the St. Lawrence River and is thus shown on Mitchell's map, the gap has been filled by extending the line of the committee to the St. Lawrence.

"A west line to the Mississippi" is interpreted to mean a due west line. "The boundary settled between Georgia and East and West Florida" is interpreted to mean the line established by the Royal Proclamation of 1763 and modified by letters patent of June 6, 1764, changing the northern boundary of West Florida (*North-Eastern Boundary Arbitration Papers*, Washington, 1829, "Appendix to Two Statements on the Part of the United States," pp. 262–263; see also pp. 22–23 and 33, above).

Congress, sitting as a committee of the whole, amended and elaborated the report of February 23 (*Journs. Cont. Cong.*, Vol. 13, Washington, 1909, pp. 263–265 and 329–331) and on March 19 "agreed to the following ultimata:"

"That the thirteen United States are bounded, north, by a line to be drawn from the north-west angle of Nova Scotia, along the high lands which divide those rivers which empty themselves into the river St. Lawrence from those which fall into the Atlantic ocean, to the north-westernmost head of Connecticut river; thence down along the middle of that river to the forty-fifth degree of north latitude; thence due west in the latitude forty-five degrees north from the equator, to the north-westernmost side of the river St. Lawrence, or Cadaraqui; thence strait to the south end of lake Nepissing; and thence strait to the source of the river Mississippi: west, by a line to be drawn along the middle of the river Mississippi from its source to where the said line shall intersect the latitude of thirty-one degrees north: south, by a line to be drawn due east from the termination of the line last mentioned in the latitude thirty-one degrees north from the equator to the middle of the river Apalachicola, or Catahouchie; thence along the middle thereof to its junction with the Flint river; thence straight to the head of St. Mary's river; thence down along the middle of St. Mary's river to the Atlantic ocean: and east, by a line to be drawn along the middle of St. John's from its source to its mouth in the bay of Fundy."[3]

---

[1] Consult the following for evidence respecting the use of Mitchell's map: *Amer. State Papers, Foreign Relations*, Vol. 1, Washington, 1833, p. 91; *Mass. Hist. Soc., Proc.*, Ser. 2, Vol. 3, Boston, 1888, p. 89; Jared Sparks, edit., *Works of Benjamin Franklin*, Vol. 10, Boston, 1840, p. 448; Justin Winsor, *Narrative and Critical History of America*, Vol. 7, Boston and New York, 1888, pp. 180–181; *Works of John Adams*, Vol. 8, Boston, 1853, pp. 392 and 398; D. A. Mills, "British Diplomacy in Canada," *United Empire*, Vol. 2 (N.S.), 1911, pp. 698–700; Lawrence Martin, *Noteworthy Maps . . . Accessions, 1925–26*, published by the Library of Congress, Washington, 1927, pp. 20–22. The Convention of 1827 between the United States and Great Britain refers to Mitchell's map as the map "by which the framers of the treaty of 1783 are acknowledged to have regulated their joint and official proceedings" (W. M. Malloy, *U. S. Treaties and Conventions*, Washington, 1910–1923, Vol. 1, p. 648). With the exception of the maps of Popple and Bowen, which are referred to by a committee of Congress in 1782, it is not known what maps were used by Congress (*Journs. Cont. Cong.*, Vol. 23, Washington, 1914, pp. 492 and 509).

[2] For the commissions of Campbell and Legge see *North-Eastern Boundary Arbitration Papers*, Washington, 1829, "Appendix to Two Statements on the Part of the United States," pp. 144–156. See also *Amer. State Papers, Foreign Relations*, Vol. 6, Washington, 1859, p. 917. In 1779–1783 the boundary line between Nova Scotia and Massachusetts was disputed (but see W. F. Ganong, "Monograph of the Evolution of the Boundaries of the Province of New Brunswick," *Royal Soc. of Canada Proc. and Trans.*, Ser. 2, Vol. 7, 1901, pp. 223–224; for the Royal Proclamation of 1763, see William Macdonald, *Select Charters*, New York and London, 1899, pp. 267–272).

[3] *Journs. Cont. Cong.*, Vol. 13, Washington, 1909, pp. 339–341. The description of that part of the northern line of Congress lying to the eastward of Lake Nipissing is similar to the description of the southern boundary of Quebec in that region, described in the Royal Proclamation of 1763 and in the Quebec Act of 1774. The following extract is from the Royal Proclamation: "to the south end of Lake Nipissin, from whence the said line crossing the river St. Lawrence and the Lake Champlain in forty-five degrees of North latitude passes along the High Lands which divide the Rivers that empty themselves into the said River St. Lawrence from those which fall into the Sea." The Quebec Act reads thus, "along the highlands which divide the rivers that empty themselves into the river St. Lawrence from those which fall into the Sea, to a point in forty-five degrees of northern latitude, on the eastern bank of the river Connecticut, keeping the same latitude directly

The line of the Continental Congress is represented by *line 2*—a solid blue line. It is necessary to break this line in the region of the head-waters of the Mississippi River, owing to the inset map of Hudson Bay which occupies the northwest corner of Mitchell's map.

The northwest angle of Nova Scotia in accordance with the terms of the Royal Proclamation of 1763 and the commissions of Governors Campbell and Legge, 1765, 1773 (see p. 52, above), is the angle in Nova Scotia made by the meridian of the source of the St. Croix River and the line of the "highlands." This is the northwest angle as usually defined and represented in the years 1763-1783. Since Congress proposed to make the St. John River the western boundary of Nova Scotia, the eastern line described by Congress cannot be represented literally without representing a new northwest angle. By following the main branch of the upper St. John River of Mitchell's map to its source the new northwest angle is shifted a considerable distance southwestward of the usual one. However, by following the northern branch of the upper St. John to its source the new northwest angle is shifted westward only a few miles. If, however, the northwest angle be regarded as a fixed angle, it is not possible to represent the east line of the vote of Congress literally and satisfy the condition respecting this angle. This condition may be satisfied without a wide departure from the condition respecting the St. John River by drawing the line up the northern branch of the upper St. John to the point where it is crossed by the meridian of the St. Croix River, near the northwest corner of Lake Medousa, and up that meridian to the "fixed angle." All three interpretations are shown upon Plate 89. On John Jay's copy of Mitchell's map the boundary line is drawn according to the second of these interpretations (Albert Gallatin, "Memoir on the North-Eastern Boundary," with map, in *N. Y. Hist. Soc. Proc.*, 1843).

The "highlands" are interpreted to mean the highlands referred to in the Royal Proclamation of 1763 and in the Quebec Act of 1774 as contemporaneously represented (for the Quebec Act see *North-Eastern Boundary Arbitration Papers*, Appendix, etc., p. 169; see also p. 33, above). "The northwesternmost head of Connecticut River" is assumed to be the lake shown upon Mitchell's map in about latitude 45° 40′ N., longitude 71° 05′ W. "The source of the river Mississippi" is assumed to be in about latitude 50° N., longitude 106° W., which is the supposed source according to a legend on Mitchell's map found below the inset map of Hudson Bay. Since the St. Marys River is not shown upon Mitchell's map, the boundary along this river is represented as shown in color on King George III's copy of Mitchell's map, now in the British Museum. The junction of the Flint and Apalachicola rivers, which is a few miles southward of the thirty-first parallel, is on Mitchell's map and many other maps of this period a few miles northward of this parallel.

As an alternative to the line of the St. John River the vote of Congress proposed "a line to be settled and adjusted between that part of the State of Massachusetts Bay, formerly called the province of Maine, and the colony of Nova Scotia, agreeably to their respective rights." The vote also contained the provision "that if the line to be drawn from the mouth of Lake Nepissing to the head of the Mississippi cannot be obtained without continuing the war for that purpose, then, that a line or lines may be drawn more southerly, so as not to be southward of a line in latitude forty-five degrees north" (*Journs. Cont. Cong.*, Vol. 13, Washington, 1909, pp. 340-341).

On August 14, 1779, the Continental Congress agreed on a draft of instructions for a peace commissioner, in which were incorporated, with a few unimportant changes of phraseology, the boundaries adopted on March 19; and on September 27 John Adams of Massachusetts was chosen to this office with the title of minister plenipotentiary (*ibid.*, Vol. 14, 1909, pp. 958-959; Vol. 15, 1909, p. 1113). Several years elapsed after this appointment before an occasion for beginning negotiations presented itself.

In the meantime Spain, supported by France, undertook to circumscribe the bounds of the United States on the west. Her views were presented to the Continental Congress by the French minister Count Luzerne, who in January, 1780, stated to a committee of Congress that the Spanish cabinet held "that the United States extend to the westward no farther than settlements were permitted by the royal proclamation bearing date the 7th day of October, 1763." The Royal Proclamation prohibited settlements by the colonies "westward of the sources of

the rivers which fall into the sea from the west and northwest" (*ibid.*, Vol. 16, 1910, p. 115; William Macdonald, *Select Charters*, New York and London, 1899, p. 271). The west line according to this proposal is represented by *line 3*—a solid yellow line.

Having decided to increase the number of peace commissioners, Congress on June 13, 1781, chose John Jay and on the following day Benjamin Franklin, Henry Laurens, and Thomas Jefferson, to serve with John Adams. On June 15 instructions for the commissioners were adopted, in which they were referred as to boundaries to the previous instructions of August 14, 1779.[4] Since Jefferson declined the appointment as peace commissioner, and since Laurens did not arrive in Paris until a few days before the provisional treaty was signed, the negotiations on the part of the United States fell almost entirely to Franklin, Jay, and Adams. The early preliminary negotiations on the part of the United States were conducted entirely by Franklin. Jay did not arrive in Paris until June 23, and Adams until October 26, 1782. The British peace commissioner was Richard Oswald. His first commission was dated August 7; and his second, issued to meet the objections of the American commissioners to the first, September 21. During the preliminary negotiations, beginning in April, Oswald was merely the confidential agent of Lord Shelburne, secretary of state for home, Irish, and colonial affairs. From October 20 to November 30 Henry Strachey assisted Oswald as the confidential agent of Shelburne and Shelburne's successor, Thomas Townshend.

The preliminary negotiations began in April 1782, with informal conversations between Franklin and Oswald, during which little or nothing was said about boundaries. Franklin, however, proposed that Great Britain should give up the whole of Canada.[5] On April 28 Shelburne furnished Oswald with memoranda of genera instructions in which Oswald was informed that the "Penobscot [was] to be always kept" (*Proceedings in North Atlantic Coast Fisheries Arbitration, Senate Doc. No. 870, 61st Cong., 3rd Sess.*, Vol. 7, Washington, 1912-1913, p. 56). The northeast line according to these instructions is represented by *line 4*—a short-dash red line.

On August 3 Count Aranda, the Spanish ambassador at Paris, proposed to Jay the following west line:

[from] ... "the point of the Lakes beginning with Lake Superior, and then along the shore of part of them as far as the point of Lake Erie or Oswego ... [then] down to the junction of the Great Kanawa and Ohio, thence to proceed toward the farthest entering bend of South Carolina in order to continue the line toward a lake in the land of the Apalaches or the George River, but without striking it ... leaving the line without running it as it neared the boundaries of Georgia and Florida" (J. F. Yela Utrilla, *España ante la independencia de los Estados Unidos*, Lérida, 1925, Vol. 2, pp. 356-357. There is an abridged description of this line in Francis Wharton, edit., *Revolutionary Diplomatic Correspondence of the United States*, Washington, 1889, Vol. 6, p. 23).

This line is represented by *line 5*—a short-dash yellow line.

On August 25 Vergennes, the French minister for foreign affairs, proposed to Aranda the line of the Wabash River as a substitute for the part of Aranda's line that lay between Lake Erie and the junction of the Great Kanawha and the Ohio. Replying to Vergennes, Aranda proposed as a compromise a line between these two, extending from Lake Erie to the Ohio and passing between the two lakes designated "Etang Castor" (Yela Utrilla, *op. cit.*, p. 360). Vergennes' line is represented by *line 6*—a long-dash line, Aranda's by *line 7*—a dot-and-dash yellow line.

On September 6 Rayneval, the principal secretary of Vergennes, sent Jay a memoir in which he proposed that the territory between the Mississippi and the Alleghenies south of the Ohio should constitute a neutral area, the Indians in the eastern part of which should be under the protection of the United States and those in the western part under the protection of Spain. He described the line of division as follows:

"A right line should be drawn from the eastern angle of the Gulf of Mexico, which makes the section between the two Floridas, to Fort Toulouse, situated in the country of the Alabamas; from thence the river Loneshatchi should be

---

west, through the lake Champlain, until, in the same latitude, it meets the river St. Lawrence" (*North-Eastern Boundary Arbitration Papers*, Washington, 1829, Appendix, etc., pp. 165 and 169).

In the Papers of the Continental Congress there is a paper in the handwriting of Gouverneur Morris, without date and endorsed, "Relative to Committee of the Whole," which describes a boundary similar to that of Congress, with the exception of the west and northwest line, which is described as follows: "Thence up the River Mississippi along the middle thereof to the River Illinois, thence up along the middle thereof to the source thereof, thence to the southwesternmost part of Lake Michigan or Illinois, thence due north to the northern shore of the waters of the Lakes Superior and Huron, thence along the said shore eastwardly up the River called the Rivière des François to the mouth of Lake Nipissing" (*Journs. Cont. Cong.*, Vol. 13, Washington, 1909, p. 341).

---

[4] *Journs. Cont. Cong.*, Vol. 20, Washington, 1912, pp. 638, 648, and 651. On June 8, 1781, the Virginia delegates moved that the peace commissioners should not recede from the ultimatum respecting boundaries of August 14, 1779, "except with respect to so much of the said ultimatum as delineates the boundary from the intersection of the forty-fifth degree of north latitude with the river St. Lawrence to the mouth of the Ilionois river, from which you are authorised to recede so far as to agree that the boundary of the states between these two points shall run from the intersection aforesaid, through the middle of the said rivers, of Lake Ontario, of the Strait of Niagara, and of Lake Erie, to the mouth of the Miami river, thence in a direct line to the source of the river Ilionois, and thence down the middle of the said river to its confluence with the Mississippi" (*ibid.*, pp. 611-612). This motion by a large negative vote failed of passage.

[5] John Bigelow, edit., *Works of Benjamin Franklin*, Vol. 8, New York, 1888, p. 15. On July 10 Franklin communicated to Oswald a rough outline of a treaty of peace, which was divided into "necessary" and "advisable" articles. Number 3 of the necessary articles referred to boundaries and as reported by Oswald was as follows: "A confinement of the boundaries of Canada, at least to what they were, before the last Act of Parliament ... in 1774, if not to a still more contracted State, on an ancient footing." Number 4 of the advisable articles suggested that Great Britain should give up "every part of Canada" (*ibid.*, p. 80). "The last Act of Parliament ... in 1774" refers to the Quebec Act of that year (see p. 33, above).

ascended, from the mouth [source?] of which a right line should be drawn to the Fort or Factory Quenassee; from this last place, the course of the river Euphaseè is to be followed till it joins the Cherokee; the course of this last river is to be pursued to the place where it receives the Pelisippi; this last to be followed to its source, from whence a right line is to be drawn to Cumberland River, whose course is to be followed until it falls into the Ohio" (William Jay, *Life of John Jay*, New York, 1833, Vol. 2, p. 479; for a description of Rayneval's line extending it down the Ohio to the Mississippi see Yela Utrilla, *op. cit.*, p. 364).

Rayneval's neutral line is represented by *line 8*—a dotted yellow line. It is assumed that the southern terminus of this line is the apex of the angle made by the eastern and northern coast lines of the Gulf of Mexico.

On October 1 formal negotiations for peace were begun by Franklin, Jay, and Oswald, and on October 8 they agreed to articles of peace in which the boundary was described, with one important omission, in almost the precise words used by Congress in its vote of March 19, 1779. The description of the articles is as follows:

"North by a line to be drawn from the northwest angle of Nova Scotia along the highlands which divide those rivers which empty themselves into the River St. Lawrence from those which fall into the Atlantic Ocean, to the northermost head of Connecticut River; thence down along the middle of that river to the forty fifth degree of north latitude, and thence due West in the Latitude forty five degrees north from the Equator to the northwesternmost side of the River St. Lawrence or Cadaraqui, thence straight to the south-end of the Lake *Nipissing*, and then straight to the source of the River Mississippi; *West*, by a line to be drawn along the middle of the River Mississippi from its source to where the said line shall intersect the thirty first degree of north latitude. South, by a line to be drawn due east from the termination of the line last mentioned in the latitude of thirty one degrees north of the Equator to the middle of the River Appalachicola or Catahouchi, thence along the middle thereof to its junction with the Flint River, thence straight to the head of St. Mary's River; and thence down along the middle of St. Mary's River to the Atlantic Ocean" (*Proceedings in North Atlantic Coast Fisheries Arbitration*, Vol. 7, Washington, 1912-1913, p. 119).

This line is represented by *line 9*—a short-dash green line. For the method of representing the northwest angle of Nova Scotia, the "highlands," the source of the Mississippi River, and St. Marys River, see what was said in connection with line 2 (p. 53, above). Note that the phrase "northermost head of Connecticut River" is used.

The original drafts of the agreement included the following description of the east line, taken from the vote of Congress: "East by a line to be drawn along the middle of St. John's River from its source to its mouth in the bay of Fundy." On Oswald's objecting to this line it was agreed that the east line, or the boundary between the United States and Nova Scotia, should be settled by commissioners after the war (*ibid.*, pp. 119, 120, and 121; Library of Congress, Peace Transcripts, Oswald to Townshend, Oct. 8, 1782).

The British government declined to accept the articles agreed to by Oswald and, having decided to insist on more favorable terms of peace, sent Henry Strachey to Paris to confer with Oswald and to assist him with the negotiations. Strachey's instructions, dated October 20, required him to obtain a "favorable boundary of Nova Scotia, extending it if possible, so as to include the Province of Maine; if that cannot be, the Province of Sagadahock, or at the very least to include Penobscott." Respecting British claims in the northwest, west, and southwest his instructions were as follows: "Urge our right to all Backlands, the claim of the Provinces having been bounded by the Proclamation of 1763, and acquiesced in ... Urge the French boundary of Canada. Urge the boundary established by the Quebec Act, which was acquiesced in ... Urge the just boundaries of West Florida" (*Proceedings in North Atlantic Coast Fisheries Arbitration*, Vol. 7, Washington, 1912-1913, p. 124. See also *Works of John Adams*, Boston, 1850-1856, Vol. 1, p. 665; Vol. 8, pp. 18 and 210; Justin Winsor, *Narrative and Critical History of America*, Vol. 7, Boston and New York, 1888, p. 171. As may be seen, these instructions proposed three alternative northeast lines, the west and northwest boundary of Maine, the west boundary of Sagadahoc, and the Penobscot River; three alternative west and northwest lines, the line of the Royal Proclamation of 1763 (see pp. 22-23, above), the French boundary of Canada, and the line of the Quebec Act of 1774; and one southwest line, the northern boundary of West Florida established by letters patent of 1764. All these lines, with the exception of the French boundary of Canada, which because of its uncertainty is not shown, are represented by *lines 10*—solid red lines.

The line of the Quebec Act as represented follows the northern and western boundary of Pennsylvania shown on Mitchell's map, which is quite different from the boundary as finally fixed. This line is stopped at the forty-fifth parallel, since the context of Oswald's instructions shows that it was proposed only as a west and northwest line. The line of the Quebec Act (southern boundary of Quebec) is thus described in the act:

... "from the bay of Chaleurs, along the highlands which divide the rivers that empty themselves into the river St. Lawrence from those which fall into the Sea, to a point in forty five degrees of northern latitude, on the eastern bank of the river Connecticut, keeping the same latitude directly west, through the lake Champlain, until, in the same latitude, it meets the river St. Lawrence: from thence up the eastern bank of the said river to the lake Ontario: thence through the lake Ontario, and the River commonly called Niagara, and thence along by the eastern and south-eastern bank of lake Erie, following the said bank, until the same shall be intersected by the northern boundary, granted by the Charter of the Province of Pennsylvania, in case the same shall be so intersected: and from thence along the said northern and western boundaries of the said province, until the said western boundary strikes the Ohio ... and along the bank of the said river, westward, to the banks of the Mississippi" (*North-Eastern Boundary Arbitration Papers*, Washington, 1829, Appendix, etc., p. 169).

On November 5 the British and American commissioners agreed upon the following line:

"From the north-west angle of Nova Scotia, viz., that angle which is formed by a line drawn due north from the source of St. Croix River to the High lands, along the said High lands which divide those rivers that empty themselves into the River St. Lawrence from those which fall into the Atlantic Ocean to the north-westernmost head of Connecticut River; thence down along the middle of that river to the 45th degree of north latitude, from thence by a line due west on said latitude, until it strikes the River Iroquois or Cataroquy, thence along the middle of said river into Lake Ontario, through the middle of said lake, until it strikes the communication by water between that lake and Lake Erie, thence along the middle of said communication into Lake Erie, through the middle of said lake until it arrives at the water communication between that lake and Lake Huron, thence along the middle of said water communication into Lake Huron, thence through the middle of said lake to the water communication between that lake and Lake Superior, thence through Lake Superior northward of the Isles Royal and Philipeaux to the Long Lake, thence through the middle of said Long Lake and the water communication between it and the Lake of the Woods to the said Lake of the Woods, thence through the said lake to the most northwestern point thereof, and from thence on a due western course to the River Mississippi, thence by a line to be drawn along the middle of the said River Mississippi until it shall intersect the northernmost part of the 31st degree of north latitude; south, by a line to be drawn due east from the determination of the line last mentioned in the latitude of 31 degrees north of the Equator, to the middle of the River Apalachicola or Catahouche, thence along the middle thereof to its junction with the Flint River, thence straight to the head of St. Mary's River, and thence down along the middle of St. Mary's River to the Atlantic Ocean; east, by a line to be drawn along the middle of the River St. Croix from its mouth in the Bay of Fundy to its source, and from its source directly north to the aforesaid High lands which divide the rivers that fall into the Atlantic Ocean from those which fall into the River St. Lawrence."[6]

As an alternative to part of this line the commissioners agreed on a line continuing along the forty-fifth parallel from the St. Lawrence River to the Mississippi River.[7] The British government was to choose between the line through the Great Lakes and the line along the forty-fifth parallel. These lines are represented by *lines 11*—dot-and-dash green lines. For the method of representing the northwest angle of Nova Scotia, the "highlands," the northwesternmost head of Connecticut River, the source of the Mississippi River, and St. Marys River, see what was said in connection with line 2 (p. 53, above).

The agreement of November 5 contained the following "separate article," which is also to be found in the Provisional Treaty of November 30:

"It is hereby understood and agreed, that in case Great Britain, at the conclusion of the present war, shall recover or be put in possession of West Florida, the line of North boundary between the said province and the United States, shall be a line drawn from the mouth of the River Yassous where it unites with the Mississippi, due east to the River Apalachicola" [and thence to the mouth of the Flint River]" (*Proceedings in North Atlantic Coast Fisheries Arbitration*, Vol. 7, Washington, 1912-1913, pp. 143, 181-182).

The conditional line of the "separate article" is represented by *line 12*—a dotted green line.

The British government chose the line through the Great Lakes. The line agreed upon is described in the same language in the Provisional Treaty of Peace of November 30, 1782, and the Definitive Treaty of Peace of September 3, 1783. Article 2 of the Definitive Treaty, which relates to boundaries, reads as follows:

---

[6] *Proceedings in North Atlantic Coast Fisheries Arbitration*, Vol. 7, Washington, 1912–1913, p. 143. Long Lake is the first lake in the water communication between Lake Superior and Lake of the Woods.

[7] *Ibid.*, p. 141. The line through the Great Lakes is the line of the "first proposition" of the American commissioners, and the line along the forty-fifth parallel is the line of their "second proposition." The line of the second proposition is described in the draft of the proposed treaty because its description is shorter (*ibid.*, pp. 137 and 139). There are other differences, although unimportant, between the two propositions. In the second proposition the reading is "northwestern head of Connecticut River." It also describes an ocean line "from the mouth of said St. Mary's River to the mouth of the River St. Croix in the Bay of Fundy."

"And that all disputes which might arise in future on the subject of the boundaries of the said United States may be prevented, it is hereby agreed and declared that the following are and shall be their boundaries, viz: From the northwest angle of Nova Scotia, viz. that angle which is formed by a line drawn due north from the source of St. Croix River to the Highlands; along the said Highlands which divide those rivers that empty themselves into the river St. Lawrence from those which fall into the Atlantic Ocean, to the northwest-ernmost head of Connecticut River; thence down along the middle of that river, to the forty-fifth degree of north latitude; from thence, by a line due west on said latitude, until it strikes the river Iroquois or Cataraquy; thence along the middle of said river into Lake Ontario, through the middle of said lake until it strikes the communication by water between that lake and Lake Erie; thence along the middle of said communication into Lake Erie, through the middle of said lake until it arrives at the water communication between that lake and Lake Huron; thence along the middle of said water communication into the Lake Huron; thence through the middle of said lake to the water communication between that lake and Lake Superior; thence through Lake Superior northward of the Isles Royal and Phelipeaux, to the Long Lake; thence through the middle of said Long Lake, and the water communication between it and the Lake of the Woods, to the said Lake of the Woods; thence through the said lake to the most northwestern point thereof, and from thence on a due west course to the river Mississippi; thence by a line to be drawn along the middle of the said river Mississippi until it shall intersect the northermost part of the thirty-first degree of north latitude. South, by a line to be drawn due east from the determi-nation of the line last mentioned, in the latitude of thirty-one degrees north of the Equator, to the middle of the river Apalachicola or Catahouche; thence along the middle thereof to its junction with the Flint River; thence strait to the head of St. Mary's River; and thence down along the middle of St. Mary's River to the Atlantic Ocean. East, by a line to be drawn along the middle of the River St. Croix from its mouth in the Bay of Fundy to its source, and from its source directly north to the aforesaid Highlands, which divide the rivers that fall into the Atlantic Ocean from those which fall into the River St. Lawrence; comprehending all islands within twenty leagues of any part of the shores of the United States, and lying between lines to be drawn due east from the points where the aforesaid boundaries between Nova Scotia on the one part, and East Florida on the other, shall respectively touch the Bay of Fundy and the Atlantic Ocean; excepting such islands as now are, or heretofore have been, within the limits of the said province of Nova Scotia" (W. M. Malloy, *U. S. Treaties and Conventions*, Washington, 1910–1923, Vol. 1, pp. 587–588; for omission in this description, see p. 71, below).

The boundary line of the treaties of peace is represented by *line 13*— a solid green line. What has been said respecting certain points and lines in connection with line 2 (p. 53, above) applies to line 13.

Negotiations for Peace (Northeast Section), 1779–1783
[PLATE 90]

The base of the preceding map (Pl. 89) illustrating the negotiations for peace, owing to the large reduction from the original, shows some of the geographical features less distinctly than is desirable. This applies chiefly to the northeast section, the lines of which are especially impor-tant by reason of subsequent boundary disputes. It is therefore thought advisable to show the boundary lines of this section on a reproduction of Mitchell's map (see p. 52, above) reduced about one-third. This is the base used for Plate 90. It has been somewhat touched up in order to remove color stains and the effects of folding. The figures on the southern and western border indicating longitude and latitude have been added.

The color lines of Plate 90 are numbered so as to correspond with those of Plate 89. For the text respecting these lines see pp. 52–53, and above.

INTERNATIONAL BOUNDARY DISPUTES, 1784–1927
[PLATES 91–96]

This series illustrates the most important boundary disputes between the United States and foreign countries involving the continental United States, including Alaska. The boundary lines that are shown are those that were officially claimed, proposed, or agreed upon. For the color scheme see p. 52, above.

The maps used as bases are made from tracings of the drainage and projection of recent or contemporary maps. Recent maps, with their greater accuracy and precision, have been preferred and used in all cases where possible. In a few cases, however, they could not be used because the geographical features conceived by the negotiators differed so widely from those shown on modern maps. Tracings have been preferred to photographs because the originals contain much information not germane to the disputes. The choice of bases is often determined by the need of a map showing drainage on both sides of the boundary line. A few bases are on the same scale as the originals, but most of them are enlargements or reductions of the originals made to meet the needs of illustration or to fit the space available. Occasionally a base is derived

from two or more maps. The lettering on the base maps, which may or may not appear upon the originals, was made solely for the purpose of illustrating the disputes. In the cases where both the modern and the contemporary names are given, the contemporary name is enclosed in parentheses. The scales are calculated from the scales on the originals of the bases.

The dates found in the list of lines printed on each map are usually the dates of the official documents in which a given line was claimed, proposed, or fixed. In a few cases, however, in respect to lines claimed, the history of the claim and not a specific document was relied upon in fixing dates. The beginning of a dispute may antedate the years in the list of lines, since it was necessary to rely upon some specific document for a description of the line precise enough for purposes of representation.

In the text for each dispute given below, pp. 55–72, no attempt is made to present a complete history of the dispute. The limitations of space are such that no more than a brief account giving the main facts of the dispute with an explanation and description of the various lines that figure in it is possible.

The Northwest Angle of Nova Scotia and the Highlands
[PLATE 91A]

The drainage on Plate 91A is taken chiefly from the *Atlas of Canada*, map 14, published by the Department of the Interior of Canada, Toronto, 1906. A slight use has been made of the map of Maine (1910) published by the Water Storage Commission of that state, of G. N. Colby, *Atlas of Maine*, Houlton, 1884, pp. 89–90, and of "Official Map A," in the U. S. Department of State. The projection is from the *Atlas of Canada*, map 14.

There are bibliographies of the literature of the northeast boundary controversy, which is quite extensive, by A. R. Hasse, in the *New York Public Library Bulletin*, Vol. 4, New York, 1900, pp. 391–411; and by R. M. Brown (1915), manuscript copies in the Library of Congress and in the U. S. Coast and Geodetic Survey. Justin Winsor, *Narrative and Critical History of America*, Vol. 7, Boston and New York, 1888, pp. 171–182, and Joseph Williamson, *Bibliography of the State of Maine*, Portland, 1896, may be consulted. The best accounts of the controversy are found in J. B. Moore, *History and Digest of the International Arbitra-tions*, etc., Washington, 1898, Vol. 1, pp. 65–161, and in W. F. Ganong, "Monograph of the Evolution of the Boundaries of the Province of New Brunswick," *Royal Soc. of Canada Proc. and Trans.*, Ser. 2, Vol. 7, 1901, pp. 295–358.

The chief dispute in the northeast boundary controversy was over the location of the northwest angle of Nova Scotia and of the "highlands." Three other disputes of somewhat less importance were involved in the controversy: one over the location of the meridian of the source of the St. Croix River (not illustrated in this *Atlas*); another over the north-westernmost source of the Connecticut River (see Pl. 93A and pp. 59–60, below); and the third over the line of the forty-fifth parallel (see Pl. 93D and pp. 61–62, below). The controversy began with the dispute over the northwest angle and the highlands, finally embraced the three lesser disputes, and involved the boundary line from the source of the St. Croix River to the intersection of the forty-fifth parallel with the St. Lawrence River. The measures taken or proposed for the settlement of the controversy often related to two or more of these disputes.

The Treaty of Peace of 1783 described part of the boundary line in terms of the northwest angle of Nova Scotia and of the highlands. This description is as follows:

"From the northwest angle of Nova Scotia, viz. that angle which is formed by a line drawn due north from the source of Saint Croix River to the Highlands; along the said Highlands which divide those rivers that empty themselves into the river St. Lawrence, from those which fall into the Atlantic Ocean, to the northwesternmost head of Connecticut River ... East, by a line to be drawn along the middle of the river St. Croix, from its mouth in the Bay of Fundy to its source, and from its source directly north to the aforesaid Highlands, which divide the rivers that fall into the Atlantic Ocean from those which fall into the river St. Lawrence" (W. M. Malloy, *U. S. Treaties and Conventions*, Washington, 1910–1923, Vol. 1, pp. 587–588; see p. 54, above).

Attempts to interpret these words and to locate the angle and the highlands described by them gave rise to the dispute. That they were susceptible of different interpretations was recognized by both the United States and Great Britain before 1800 (Ganong, *op. cit.*, pp. 304, 307, and 377–378). In 1802 the American government officially recog-nized the dispute, and in the immediately succeeding years several attempts to settle it were made by representatives of the two countries. Both the Hawkesbury-King convention of 1803 and the proposed con-vention of 1807 contained provisions for determining the northwest angle and for running the boundary line from the source of the St. Croix River to that angle (Moore, *op. cit.*, Vol. 1, pp. 45–46; *Amer. State Papers*,

Foreign Relations, Vol. 2, Washington, 1832, p. 584, Vol. 3, 1832, p. 164). As neither of these conventions became a law the dispute remained unsettled. Finally, in 1814, the negotiators of the Treaty of Ghent agreed on a plan of settlement. The fifth article of that treaty relates to the northeast boundary controversy and reads in part as follows:

"Whereas neither that point of the highlands lying due north from the source of the river St. Croix, and designated in the former treaty of peace between the two Powers as the northwest angle of Nova Scotia, nor the northwesternmost head of Connecticut River, has yet been ascertained; and whereas that part of the boundary line between the dominions of the two Powers which extends from the source of the river St. Croix directly north to the above-mentioned northwest angle of Nova Scotia, thence along the said highlands which divide those rivers that empty themselves into the river St. Lawrence from those which fall into the Atlantic Ocean to the northwesternmost head of Connecticut River, thence down along the middle of that river to the forty-fifth degree of north latitude; thence by a line due west on said latitude until it strikes the river Iroquois or Cataraquy [St. Lawrence], has not yet been surveyed: it is agreed that for these several purposes two Commissioners shall be appointed" (Malloy, *op. cit.*, Vol. 1, p. 615).

The article further provided that one of the two commissioners should be appointed by the United States and the other by Great Britain. The American commissioner was Cornelius P. Van Ness, of Vermont, and the British commissioner Thomas Barclay, who had served on the St. Croix River commission in 1796–1798. The commission held its first meeting at St. Andrews, New Brunswick, on September 23, 1816, and continued to hold sessions at various places during a period of almost six years. On October 4, 1821, each commissioner made a written statement of his claim. Van Ness was of the opinion that the northwest angle of Nova Scotia "ought to be fixed at a place about one hundred and forty-four miles due north from the source of the River St. Croix, and about sixty-six miles north of the River St. John." According to Barclay's statement, the northwest angle of Nova Scotia was "at or near a mountain or hill called Mars Hill distant about forty miles on a due north line from the source of the River St. Croix, and about thirty-seven miles south of the River St. John" (Moore, *op. cit.*, Vol. 1, pp. 81–82; Department of State, Journal of Commission under Art. V of the Treaty of Ghent, pp. 199–202). The northwest angle of Van Ness, or the eastern terminus of his line of the "highlands," lay one hundred miles north of of the northwest angle and eastern terminus of Barclay. The western terminus of the line of the "highlands" of each commissioner was located in the headwaters of the Connecticut River. The line of the "highlands" of Van Ness lay between the headwaters of the southern tributaries of the St. Lawrence River and the northern or western tributaries of the Restigouche, St. John, Penobscot, Kennebec, and Androscoggin rivers. The line of the "highlands" of Barclay lay for the most part between the southern tributaries of the Aroostook, St. John, and St. Lawrence rivers and the northern or western tributaries of the Penobscot, Kennebec, and Androscoggin rivers. To the northwestward of the headwaters of the Connecticut River the two lines were identical. Farther eastward, one lay to the north of the northern tributaries of the St. John River, and the other to the south of the southern tributaries. Van Ness's line is represented by *line 1*—a solid blue line, and Barclay's by *line 2*—a solid red line. Van Ness's line was claimed by the Americans and Barclay's by the British, until the dispute was settled in 1842.

The commissioners disagreed in respect to each of the disputes referred to them. They met in final session at New York in April, 1822, and, after filing disagreeing opinions and presenting their respective reports, adjourned on the 13th of that month.

The fifth article of the Treaty of Ghent provided that in case of a failure to render a decision the two governments should refer the reports of the commissioners to "some friendly sovereign or state," who should decide the points of difference (Malloy, *op. cit.*, Vol. 1, p. 616). Each government delayed action under this provision. In 1826 Albert Gallatin, the American minister in London, made an attempt to have the controversy referred to Washington for direct negotiation, but failed. Finally, in 1827, he negotiated with Great Britain a convention providing for the submission of the northeast boundary controversy to arbitration. The two governments chose as arbitrator the King of the Netherlands and in 1830 submitted to him lengthy statements of their cases. The statements of the case of the United States were prepared by Albert Gallatin and William Pitt Preble (Moore, *op. cit.*, Vol. 1, pp. 85–91). The arbitrator rendered an award on January 10, 1831. He did not attempt to determine the northwest angle of Nova Scotia by interpreting the Treaty of Peace of 1783 but recommended a compromise line which (beginning at the point where the meridian of the source of the St. Croix River intersects the middle of the St. John River) was to be drawn as follows:

... "thence, the middle of the *thalweg* of that river [St. John], ascending it to the point where the river St. Francis empties itself into the river St. John;

thence, the middle of the *thalweg* of the river St. Francis, ascending it to the source of its southwesternmost branch; ... thence, a line drawn due west, to the point where it unites with the line claimed by the United States of America; ... thence, by said line to the point at which ... it concides with that claimed by Great Britain; and thence ... to the northwesternmost source of Connecticut River" (*ibid.*, p. 134).

This line is represented by *line 3*—a solid yellow line.

The British government offered to accept the award, but the United States government declined to accept it. On December 28, 1835, Charles Bankhead, the British minister at Washington, withdrew Great Britain's offer of acceptance and proposed that the boundary from the point where the meridian of the source of the St. Croix River intersected the St. John River "should run up the bed of the St. John's to the southernmost source of that river."[8] On February 29, 1836, John Forsyth, the American secretary of state, replying to Bankhead, proposed as a boundary the "River St. John's from its source to its mouth" (*British and Foreign State Papers*, Vol. 24, London, 1858, p. 1186). Bankhead's line is represented by *line 4*—a short-dash red line, and Forsyth's by *line 5*—a short-dash blue line.

From 1837 until the final settlement in 1842 many projects and counter-projects were suggested, resulting in much correspondence between the two governments. In 1839 the British government directed two commissioners, G. W. Featherstonhaugh and R. Z. Mudge, to make new surveys and to obtain additional information respecting the nature and configuration of the country in dispute. In 1840 they reported that they found a "Line of Highlands, agreeing with the language of the 2nd Article of the Treaty of 1783, extending from the north-westernmost Head of the Connecticut river to the sources of the Chaudière, and passing from thence in a north-easterly direction, South of the Roostuc [Restigouche] to the Bay of Chaleurs"; and they presented this line, which they called the "axis of maximum elevation," as the true highlands of the treaty (*Parliamentary Papers*, London, Sess. 1840, Vol. 32, "North American Boundary," Part II, pp. 40, 57, and maps A and B at end of volume; *ibid.*, 1843, Vol. 61, "Map to Illustrate Boundary Established by Treaty of Washington").

The line of Featherstonhaugh and Mudge is represented by *line 6*—a long-dash red line. Their "axis of maximum elevation," to the eastward of the meridian of the St. Croix River, makes a bend to the northward, ending at Chaleur Bay (about 70 miles northeast of the name Restigouche R. on Plate 91A). This line, while shown upon one of the maps of the British government, was never formally proposed to the United States as a boundary line.

The negotiations that ended the controversy were initiated by Daniel Webster, Secretary of State, in the summer of 1841. Great Britain chose Lord Ashburton as a special minister and gave him full powers to settle the long-standing dispute. Acting on the suggestion of Webster, Maine and Massachusetts appointed commissioners to represent their interests. The negotiations were conducted at Washington during the summer of 1842. No attempt was made to settle the dispute by locating the northwest angle of Nova Scotia. Instead, the plan of finding a compromise line that would be acceptable to both governments was followed.

On June 21 Ashburton proposed to Webster the "line of the St. John, from where the north line from the St. Croix strikes it, up to some one of its sources ... with the exception ... of a settlement formed on both sides of the St. John from the mouth of the Madawaska up to that of the Fish river" (*House Ex. Doc. No. 2, 27th Cong., 3rd Sess.*, 1842–1843, p. 38). This line is represented by line 4—a short-dash red line, with the exception of that part near the Madawaska settlement, which is represented by *line 7*—a dot-and-dash red line.

Since Ashburton's instructions call for the most southerly branch of the St. John River this branch has been followed in representing his line (*Amer. Hist. Rev.*, Vol. 17, 1912, p. 770). The words of his instructions are: ... "the river St. John from its junction with the St. Francis up to its source in the small Lake of St. John, or the oostastagomessis of the Indians." His proposal, however, is more indefinite, as it calls for some one of the sources of the St. John. The Madawaska settlement exceeded the limits specified in Ashburton's proposal. Contemporary maps represent it as extending eastward of the Madawaska River and westward of Fish River.

On June 29 the Maine commissioner proposed the following line:

"Beginning at the middle of the main channel of the river St. John, where the due north line from the source of the river St. Croix crosses the St. John; thence westerly by the middle of the main channel of the St. John to a point three miles

---

[8] *British and Foreign State Papers*, Vol. 24, London, 1858, p. 1183. The line described by Bankhead did not end at the southernmost source of the St. John River but was continued to the head of the Connecticut River. This part of it, however, cannot be represented. It was to be drawn "in such manner as to make the northern and southern allotments of the divided territory as nearly as possible equal to each other in extent; the northern allotment to remain with Great Britain, the southern allotment to belong to the United States" (*ibid.*, pp. 1183–1184).

westerly of the mouth of the river Madawaska; thence, by a straight line to the outlet of Long Lake; thence westerly by a direct line to the point where the river St. Francis empties itself into Lake Pohenagamook; thence, continuing in the same direct line, to the highlands which divide the waters emptying themselves into the river Du Loup, from those which empty themselves into the river St. Francis" [thence along the highlands to the northwesternmost head of the Connecticut River] (*House Ex. Doc. No. 2, 27th Cong., 3rd Sess.*, 1842–1843, p. 76).

This line was accepted by Webster and on July 8 proposed by him to Lord Ashburton. It is represented by *line 8*—a dot-and-dash blue line. The Webster-Ashburton Treaty was signed on August 9, 1842. The boundary which it established from the point of intersection in the St. John River to Halls Stream is thus described:

... "thence, up the middle of the main channel of the said river St. John, to the mouth of the river St. Francis; thence, up the middle of the channel of the said river St. Francis, and of the lakes through which it flows, to the outlet of the Lake Pohenagamook; thence, southwesterly, in a straight line, to a point on the northwest branch of the river St. John, which point shall be ten miles distant from the main branch of the St. John, in a straight line, and in the nearest direction; but if the said point shall be found to be less than seven miles from the nearest point of the summit or crest of the highlands that divide those rivers which empty themselves into the river St Lawrence from those which fall into the river St. John, then the said point shall be made to recede down the said northwest branch of the river St. John, to a point seven miles in a straight line from the said summit or crest; thence, in a straight line, in a course about south, eight degrees west, to the point where the parallel of latitude of 46° 25′ north intersects the southwest branch of the St. John's; thence, southerly, by the said branch, to the source thereof in the highlands at the Metjarmette portage; thence, down along the said highlands which divide the waters which empty themselves into the river St. Lawrence from those which fall into the Atlantic Ocean, to the head of Hall's Stream" (*Malloy, op. cit.*, Vol. 1, pp. 651–652).

This line is represented by *line 9*—a solid green line. Its length is about 400 miles. On a map of small scale it is not possible to show many of the irregularities in the line of the "highlands." There are nearly 3150 turning points in the line between Halls Stream and the Metgermette Portage. Its length is about 175 miles (data furnished by Mr. E. C. Barnard, U. S. boundary commissioner).

Isle Royal to Lake of the Woods

[PLATE 91B]

The drainage of this map is taken chiefly from Edward Stanford, *Atlas of Universal Geography*, London, 1904, Pl. 85. A considerable use, however, was made of the Ontario Map, English River Sheet and Rainy River Sheet, published by the Department of the Interior of Canada in 1914, and of the Map of the State of Minnesota, published by the U. S. General Land Office in 1905. The projection is from Pl. 85 of Stanford's *Atlas*.

The Treaty of Peace of 1783 described the most westerly part of the northern boundary of the United States as follows:

... "thence through Lake Superior northward of the Isles Royal and Phelipeaux, to the Long Lake; thence through the middle of said Long Lake and the water communication between it and the Lake of the Woods, to the said Lake of the Woods; thence through the said lake to the most northwestern point thereof, and from thence on a due west course to the river Mississippi" (W. M. Malloy, *U. S. Treaties and Conventions*, Washington, 1910–1923, Vol. 1, p. 587).

Since doubts arose soon after 1783 whether the Mississippi River extended as far north as the Lake of the Woods, no attempt was ever made to locate a line due west of the most northwestern point of that lake. Not until 1822, when the commissioners under the seventh article of the Treaty of Ghent (see p. 71, below) began their survey, was an attempt made to locate the boundary line westward of Lake Superior. Without much difficulty the commissioners agreed upon a line from a point near the head of Rainy Lake to the most northwestern point of the Lake of the Woods. Since their description of this line is more or less detailed and mentions many islands that cannot be shown on a map of small scale, the whole of it need not here be quoted. The following is an abridgment:

"Beginning at a point in Lac la Pluie [Rainy Lake] ... below the Chaudière Falls of Lake Namecan ... thence through the middle of said lake to its sortie, which is the head of Rivière la Pluie [Rainy River] ... thence down the middle of said river to its entrance ... into the Lake of the Woods ... thence [to] ... the most northwestern point of the Lake of the Woods ... being in latitude 49° 23′ 55″ north of the equator, and in longitude 95° 14′ 38″ west from the observatory at Greenwich" (*British and Foreign State Papers*, 1866–1867, Vol. 57, London, 1871, pp. 808–809; J. B. Moore, *History and Digest of the International Arbitrations*, etc., Washington, 1898, Vol. 1, pp. 187–188).

This line is represented by *line 1*—a short-dash green line.

The commissioners disagreed on the boundary from a point one hundred yards north and east of Chapeau Island, near Isle Royale, to the point near the head of Rainy Lake described above. Commissioner Porter was of the opinion that the line between these two points ought to take the following course:

... "to proceed from the said point in Lake Superior, and passing to the north of the island named on the map Paté, and the small group of surrounding islands which he supposes to be the islands called Phillipeaux in the Treaty of 1783, in a direction to enter the mouth of the River Kamanistiguia, to the mouth of said river; thence up the middle of the river to the lake called Dog Lake, but which the American Commissioner supposes to be the same water which is called in the Treaty of 1783 Long Lake; thence through the middle of Dog or Long Lake and through the middle of the river marked on the maps Dog River until it arrives at a tributary water which leads to Lac de l'Eau Froide; thence through the middle of said tributary water to its source in the highlands which divide the waters of Lake Superior from those of Hudson's Bay near Lac de l'Eau Froide; thence across the height of land, and through the middle of the lakes and rivers known and described as the Old Road of the French, viz.: To the River Savannah, and thence through the middle of the Savannah to Mille Lacs, through the middle of Mille Lacs and its water communication with Lac Dorade, through the middle of Lac Dorade and its water communication with Lake Winedago, through the middle of Lake Winedago, and its water communication with Sturgeon Lake to Sturgeon Lake, through the middle of Sturgeon Lake and the Rivière Maligne to Lac à la Croix, through the middle of Lac à la Croix and its water communication with Lake Namecan to Lake Namecan; thence through the middle of Lake Namecan and its water communication with Lac la Pluie to the point in Lac la Pluie where the two routes assumed by the Commissioners again unite" (*British and Foreign State Papers*, 1866–1867, Vol. 57, p. 805; Moore, *op. cit.*, pp. 185–186).

This line is represented by *line 2*—a short-dash blue line. For the position of Long Lake as understood by the framers of the Treaty of 1783, see p. 54, above.

Commissioner Barclay claimed a more southerly line, which he described at great length. By omitting many references to islands and portages, his description may be abridged as follows:

... "from the before-mentioned point of agreement in Lake Superior ... to the west end of the said Ile Royale ... thence through the middle of Lake Superior, passing north of the islands, called the Apostles; thence through the middle of the Fond du Lac, to the middle of the sortie or mouth of the estuary or lake of St. Louis River ... thence up the middle of the said River St. Louis to its junction with the Rivière des Embarras ... thence up the middle of the Rivière des Embarras ... to the portage of the height of land ... thence through the middle of the portage of the height of land to the ... Vermilion River ... thence down the middle of the said river to the Great Vermilion Lake; thence through the middle of this said lake ... thence down the middle of Vermilion River ... into Crane Lake; thence through the middle of this said lake ... to the Sand Point Lake; thence through the middle of this said lake ... thence down the middle of its strait or river to its entrance into Lake Namecan; thence through the middle of said lake ... thence ... to Lac la Pluie" (*British and Foreign State Papers*, 1866–1867, Vol. 57, pp. 805–808; Moore, *op. cit.*, pp. 186–187; a manuscript map of the commission under Art. VII of the Treaty of Ghent, in the Department of State, shows the lines claimed by the commissioners).

This line is represented by *line 3*—a short-dash red line. Barclay identified the mouth of the St. Louis River as the Long Lake of the Treaty of 1783.

Since the commissioners were desirous of reaching an agreement, each of them proposed a "compromise line"; but neither would accept the compromise line of the other. The two compromise lines follow the same general course and do not vary greatly from the line finally adopted by Webster and Ashburton in 1842 (line 4). Porter's compromise line may be described as the "Pigeon River, Arrow River, and water route," and Barclay's as the "Grand Portage, Pigeon River, and water and portage route." Porter described his line only in general terms, which were as follows: "Beginning at the point in Lake Superior described as 100 yards distant from the island named Chapeau, near the northeast end of Ile Royale, and proceeding thence to the mouth of the Pigeon River on the northwestern shore of the lake, enter and ascend the middle of that river, and leaving it at its junction with Arrow River, proceed to Lake Namecan and Lac la Pluie by the most direct and most continuous water communication" (*British and Foreign State Papers*, 1866–1867, Vol. 57, p. 810; Moore, *op. cit.*, p. 188).

Barclay described his line at great length, enumerating more than thirty portages over which it passed, and more than two hundred islands which lay near it. It proceeded by way of the Grand Portage to Pigeon River and thence "by the most easy and direct route to Lac la Pluie ... from water to water, overland, through the middle of the old and accustomed portages" (*British and Foreign State Papers*, 1866–1867, Vol. 57, pp. 811–816; Moore, *op. cit.*, p. 189).

Owing to the small scale of Plate 91 these compromise lines are not shown on it.

Inasmuch as the commissioners under the seventh article of the Treaty of Ghent disagreed, the boundary that was referred to them remained in dispute after their final adjournment in 1827. It was not settled until 1842, when Webster and Ashburton agreed upon a line. The part lying to the westward of Chapeau Island they described as follows:

... "southwesterly, through the middle of the sound between Ile Royale and the northwestern main land, to the mouth of Pigeon River, and up the said river, to and through the north and south Fowl Lakes, to the lakes of the height of land between Lake Superior and the Lake of the Woods; thence, along the water communication to Lake Saisaginaga, and through that lake; thence, to and through Cypress Lake, Lac du Bois Blanc, Lac la Croix, Little Vermillion Lake, and Lake Namecan, and through the several smaller lakes, straits, or streams, connecting the lakes here mentioned, to that point in Lac la Pluie, or Rainy Lake, at the Chaudière Falls, from which the Commissioners traced the line to the most northwestern point of the Lake of the Woods; thence, along the said line, to the said most northwestern point, being in latitude 49° 23' 55" north, and in longitude 95° 14' 38" west from the observatory at Greenwich" (Malloy, op. cit., Vol. 1, p. 652).

This line is represented by *line 4*—a solid green line. The length of the line from the mouth of Pigeon River to the northwestern point of the Lake of the Woods is about 409 miles. After the survey of this line in 1822–1827 no survey of it was made until recent years, when it has surveyed and monumented by the International Boundary Commission. For the curved line in Lake Superior the International Waterways Commission in 1915 substituted a series of connecting straight lines.

St. Croix River
[PLATE 91C]

The drainage and projection of this map are taken from the New Brunswick Map, St. John Sheet (1905), published by the Department of the Interior of Canada, and from the Map of Maine (1910), published by the Water Storage Commission of that state.

The Treaty of Peace signed September 3, 1783, described part of the eastern boundary as a "line to be drawn along the middle of the river St. Croix from its mouth in the Bay of Fundy to its source" (W. M. Malloy, U. S. Treaties and Conventions, Washington, 1910–1923, Vol 1, p. 588; see p. 55, above). Before the end of 1783 a dispute had arisen over the identity of the St. Croix River. Maps of the region in dispute showed three rivers, each named St. Croix, emptying into Passama-quoddy Bay, an inlet of the Bay of Fundy. The Indian names of these rivers, also found on maps, were respectively (beginning on the east) Magaguadavic, Schoodic, and Cobscook (Amer. State Papers, Foreign Relations, Vol. 1, Washington, 1833, p. 91). For the St. Croix named in the treaty the Americans claimed the Magaguadavic, the most easterly of the three rivers; and the British, the Schoodic, the middle river. The claim of the Americans is represented by *line 1*—a solid blue line; that of the British by *line 2*—a solid red line.

One of the earliest statements of the American claim will be found in a report to the governor of Massachusetts, dated October 19, 1784, and made by Generals Benjamin Lincoln and Henry Knox, who had been appointed by that state as "agents" to investigate the encroachments of the British (ibid., p. 91). The claim to the Schoodic River was made by the British government in a letter of Lord Sydney, secretary of state for the home department, to the governor of New Brunswick, dated March 8, 1785 (W. F. Ganong, "Monograph of the Evolution of the Boundaries of the Province of New Brunswick," Royal Soc. of Canada Proc. and Trans., Ser. 2, Vol. 7, 1901, p. 247).

In 1785 the American secretary for foreign affairs proposed that Congress should enter into an arrangement with Great Britain for settling the dispute, and in 1790 President Washington sent a message to the Senate treating of the same subject (Amer. State Papers, Foreign Relations, Vol. 1, 1833, pp. 90 and 94). Four years later a plan of adjustment was agreed upon and was incorporated in the Jay Treaty, 1794. The fifth article of that treaty provided for the appointment of three commissioners, one by Great Britain, one by the United States, and a third by the two commissioners thus appointed, to decide "what river is the river St. Croix, intended by the treaty" [of 1783] (Malloy, op. cit., pp. 593–594). The United States appointed David Howell, of Providence, R. I., as commissioner; Great Britain appointed Thomas Barclay, of Annapolis, Nova Scotia; and Howell and Barclay chose Egbert Benson, of New York City, as the third commissioner. The commission was formally organized at St. Andrews, New Brunswick, on October 4, 1796, and soon thereafter proceeded to explore the river in dispute. Owing to the time consumed in making surveys, collecting evidence, and listening to arguments, more than two years elapsed before it completed its work (J. B. Moore, History and Digest of the International Arbitrations, etc., Washington, 1898, Vol. 1, pp. 6–24).

A memorial was presented to the commission by James Sullivan, the American agent, claiming the Magaguadavic River, and another by Ward Chipman, the British agent, claiming the Schoodic River (ibid., p. 15). For a time Howell supported the claim for the Magagua-davic but finally accepted the view of the other two commissioners that the Schoodic was the true St. Croix River (T. C. Amory, Life of James Sullivan, Boston, 1859, Vol. 1, pp. 330–331). The decision of the commission in favor of the Schoodic River is represented by *line 2*—a solid red line.

As to what was the Upper St. Croix River, that is the St. Croix from the confluence of its northern and western branches to its source, the commissioners differed. Howell held that it was the northern branch, or Chiputneticook, and that its source was in the outlet of First Lake, the first or more southerly lake on that branch. Barclay, supporting the claim of Chipman, held that it was the western branch and that its source was the "most remote western spring" of that branch. Benson held that it was the western branch and that its source was the outlet of Lake Genesagernagumsis, the first or most easterly lake of that branch (G. L. Rives, Selections from Correspondence of Thomas Barclay, New York, 1894, p. 91; Amory, op. cit., Vol. 1, pp. 331–332). Howell's claim is represented by *line 3*—a short-dash blue line, Barclay's by *line 4*—a short-dash yellow line, and Benson's by *line 5*—a short-dash green line.

In the end, by way of compromise, the commissioners agreed that the northern branch, or the Chiputneticook, was the upper St. Croix River and that its source was the most northern source lying to the northward of the Schoodic Lakes. This source was definitely described in the "declaration of the commission," which also fixed the mouth of the St. Croix, "in Passamaquoddy Bay, at a point of land called Joe's Point" (Moore, op. cit., Vol. 1, pp. 29–31). The decision of the commissioners respecting the upper St. Croix River is represented by *line 6*—a short-dash red line. The red line partly solid and partly broken represents the entire line agreed upon by the commission. The length of this line is about 116 miles.

The Treaty of Peace of 1783 did not mention Passamaquoddy Bay. The negotiators of the treaty seem to have considered this bay as either a part of the Bay of Fundy or as the mouth of the St. Croix River (Amer. State Papers, Foreign Relations, Vol. 1, Washington, 1833, p. 93; Moore, op. cit., p. 45).

Islands in Bay of Fundy
[PLATE 92A]

The drainage, projection, and coast lines of this map are taken chiefly from the "Map of New Brunswick" (1912), published by the Department of the Interior of Canada. A slight use was made of the Map of Washington County in G. N. Colby, Atlas of Maine, Houlton, 1884, pp. 89–90.

According to the second article of the Treaty of Peace of 1783 the United States was to possess "all islands within twenty leagues of any part of the shores of the United States," lying between two due east lines, one to be drawn from the mouth of the St. Croix River in the Bay of Fundy, and the other from the mouth of the St. Mary's River (Florida) in the Atlantic Ocean, "excepting such islands as now are, or heretofore have been, within the limits of ... Nova Scotia" (W. M. Malloy, U. S. Treaties and Conventions, Washington, 1910–1923, Vol. 1, p. 588; see also p. 55, above). In 1798 the St. Croix River Commission decided that the mouth of the St. Croix River was opposite Joe's Point in Passamaquoddy Bay (see above). Since the treaty described the mouth of the river as in the Bay of Fundy, Passamaquoddy Bay must be regarded as an inlet of the Bay of Fundy. Soon after the treaty was concluded conflicting claims of sovereignty and jurisdiction arose in regard to some of the islands near the mouth of the river, and the fixing of the boundary in this region became highly desirable (J. B. Moore, History and Digest of the International Arbitrations, etc., Washington, 1898, Vol. 1, pp. 45–46). With a view to preparing the way for a settlement Secretary of State Madison, in a letter to Rufus King, American minister in London, dated July 28, 1801, stated that it was believed that the following line would be satisfactory to both nations:

... "beginning in the middle of the channel of the river St. Croix, at its mouth; thence direct to the middle of the channel, between Pleasant point and Deer island; thence to the middle of the channel between Deer island on the east and north, and Moose island and Campo Bello island on the west and south; and round the eastern point of Campo Bello island, to the bay of Fundy" (Amer. State Papers, Foreign Relations, Vol. 2, Washington, 1832, p. 585).

This line is represented by *line 1*—a short-dash blue line.

On June 8, 1802, Madison, having decided to authorize King to settle all outstanding boundary disputes with Great Britain, gave him his instructions. For his guidance in respect to the line in the Bay of Fundy, King was referred to the letter of July 28, 1801. Madison, however, now regarded Campobello Island as a possession of Great Britain. The boundary agreed upon by King and the British negotiator, Lord Hawkesbury, is described in article 1 of their convention, signed on May 12, 1803, which reads as follows:

"The line hereinafter described shall and is hereby declared to be the boundary between the mouth of the river St. Croix and the bay of Fundy; that is to say, a line beginning in the middle of the channel of the river St. Croix, at its mouth, as the same has been ascertained by the commissioners appointed for that purpose; thence through the middle of the channel between Deer island on the east and north, and Moose island, and Campo Bello island on the west and south, and round the eastern point of Campo Bello island, to the bay of Fundy; and the islands and waters northward and eastward of the said boundary, together with the island of Campo Bello, situated to the southward thereof, are hereby declared to be within the jurisdiction and part of His Majesty's province of New Brunswick; and the islands and waters southward and westward of the said boundary, except only the island of Campo Bello, are hereby declared to be within the jurisdiction and part of Massachusetts, one of the said United States" (*ibid.*, p. 584).

The boundary agreed upon is represented by *line 1*—a short-dash blue line. The agreement involves the absurdity of drawing an American boundary line between two British islands— Deer Island and Campobello Island.

As the Hawkesbury-King convention failed to become a law, negotiations were renewed in 1807, and British and American commissioners reached a tentative agreement respecting the boundary. They accepted the line of the Hawkesbury-King convention but avoided the inconsistencies of its description. The new description, as phrased by the British commissioners, was as follows:

"The line hereinafter described shall, and is hereby declared to be, the boundary between the mouth of the river St. Croix and the Bay of Fundy; that is to say, a line beginning in the middle of the channel of the river St. Croix, at its mouth, as the same has been ascertained by the commissioners appointed for that purpose; thence through the middle of the channel, between Deer island, Marvel island, and Campo Bello island on the east, and Moose island, Dudley island, and Frederick island on the west; and round the south point of Campo Bello island to the Bay of Fundy; and the islands and waters eastward of the said boundary are hereby declared to be within the jurisdiction and part of His Majesty's province of New Brunswick, and the islands and waters westward of the said boundary are declared to be within the jurisdiction and part of Massachusetts, one of the said United States" (*ibid.*, Vol. 3, Washington, 1832, p. 164).

The line of the agreement of 1807 is represented by *line 2*—a broken green line. Subsequently Marvel Island was named Indian Island.

The negotiations of 1807 also failed. Finally, in 1814, provision for the settlement of the dispute was made in the Treaty of Ghent. The fourth article of that treaty provided for the appointment of two commissioners to decide upon the claims of the two nations to the "several islands in the Bay of Passamaquoddy, which is part of the Bay of Fundy, and the island of Grand Menan in the said Bay of Fundy" (Malloy, *op. cit.*, Vol. 1, pp. 614-615). The American commissioner was John Holmes of Maine, and the British commissioner Thomas Barclay of Nova Scotia; the American agent was J. T. Austin, and the British agent Ward Chipman. To the agents fell the duty of presenting before the commission the claims of their respective governments. Austin claimed that all the islands in Passamaquoddy Bay south of a line drawn due east from Joe's Point, together with the island of Grand Manan, belonged to the United States. Chipman claimed that the "several islands in the Bay of Passamaquoddy ... and the island of Grand Menan" belonged to Great Britain (Department of State, Memorial of American Claim, Art. IV of the Treaty of Ghent, pp. 1-23, Memorial of British Claim, p. ix; Moore, *op. cit.*, Vol. 1, p. 53). The line indicating the claim of Austin is represented by *line 3*—a solid blue line, and the line indicating the claim of Chipman, by *line 4*—a solid red line.

The decision of the commissioners, rendered November 24, 1817, was that

"Moose Island, Dudley Island, and Frederick Island, in the Bay of Passamaquoddy, which is part of the Bay of Fundy, do each of them belong to the United States of America; and that all the other islands in the Bay of Passamaquoddy, and the Island of Grand Menan, in the Bay of Fundy, do each of them belong to His Britannic Majesty, in conformity with the true intent of the second article of the treaty of peace of one thousand seven hundred and eighty-three" (Malloy, *op. cit.*, Vol. 1, p. 619).

The line indicating the decision of the commission is represented by *line 5*—a solid green line. Dudley Island is at the present time Treat Island, and Frederick Island is Dudley Island.

Definition of Boundary in Bay of Fundy
[PLATE 92B]

The coast lines and projection of this map are taken from the chart

"Calais to Little River" (1912), published by the U. S. Coast and Geodetic Survey.

The decision of the commissioners under the fourth article of the Treaty of Ghent, in 1817, partitioning the islands in the Bay of Fundy (see above), did not define the boundary, and for almost a century it remained undefined. The train of events that led to its definition began in 1891, with the seizure of several American fishing boats by the Canadians near Cochran's Ledge, opposite Eastport, Maine. A serious controversy ensued, the merits of which involved the location of the boundary line. To avoid future troubles of this kind the United States and Great Britain agreed in 1892 to a boundary convention that provided for the appointment of two commissioners, "to determine upon a method of more accurately marking the boundary line between the two countries in the waters of Passamaquoddy Bay in front of and adjacent to Eastport, in the state of Maine, and to place buoys or fix such other boundary marks as they may determine to be necessary" (W. M. Malloy, *U. S. Treaties and Conventions*, Washington, 1910-1923, Vol. 1, pp. 764-765). The American commissioner was T. C. Mendenhall, of Washington, D. C., and the British commissioner, W. F. King, of Ottawa, Canada. The commissioners interpreted the words "adjacent to Eastport" so as to include the whole of the boundary southward of Joe's Point—about twenty miles in length. They agreed upon a line except at three places. One of these places was at Cochran's Ledge, opposite Eastport; another at Pope's Folly Island; and a third between Lubec and Quoddy Roads (T. C. Mendenhall, *Twenty Unsettled Miles in the Northeast Boundary*, Worcester, 1897, pp. 17-24, with map; Final Report of T. C. Mendenhall, Mar. 24, 1896, and Mendenhall-King, "Map of International Water Boundary between United States and Dominion of Canada, 1893," both in office of International Boundary Commission). At these three places each commissioner claimed different line. The sections of line agreed upon (with the exception of the northern part of the northern section, which in order to save space is not shown) are represented by *lines 1*—short-dash green lines. The lines claimed by Commissioner Mendenhall at the places of disagreement are represented by *lines 2*—short-dash blue lines; and the lines claimed by Commissioner King by *lines 3*—short-dash red lines.

Since the commissioners could not agree upon the whole line, they decided to make separate reports and adjourned finally in April, 1895.

No further attempt to define the boundary was made until 1908, when a provision was included in the general boundary treaty with Great Britain of that year for the appointment of two commissioners for the purpose "of more accurately defining and marking the international boundary line between the United States and the Dominion of Canada in the waters of Passamaquoddy Bay from the mouth of the St. Croix River to the Bay of Fundy." In defining and marking the boundary the commissioners were to adopt and follow "as closely as may be" the line agreed upon by Commissioners Mendenhall and King.[9] The American commissioner was O. H. Tittmann, of Washington, D. C., and the British commissioner was W. F. King. These two commissioners agreed upon a line which was accepted and ratified by the two governments in the "treaty concerning the boundary line in Passamaquoddy Bay," signed at Washington, May 21, 1910 (Garfield Charles, *Supplement to U. S. Treaties and Conventions*, Washington, 1913, pp. 47-50). This line (with the exception of the northern part) is represented by *line 4*—a solid green line.

Northwesternmost Head of the Connecticut River
[PLATE 93A]

The drainage of this map is taken chiefly (and the projection entirely) from H. F. Walling and C. H. Hitchcock, *Atlas of the State of New Hampshire*, New York, 1877, pp. 60-61, and partly from the Quebec Map, Quebec and Montreal Sheet (1914), published by the Department of the Interior of Canada. The most southerly bend of the Connecticut River southeast of Halls Stream is drawn according to the maps of Estcourt and Smith, whose survey of this region made in 1843-1847 is the most reliable. Many maps show the Connecticut River at this point touching the forty-fifth parallel or bending south of it.

In the region of northern New Hampshire the Treaty of Peace of 1783 called for a line passing "along the said Highlands, which divide those rivers that empty themselves into the river St. Lawrence from those which fall into the Atlantic Ocean, to the northwesternmost head of Connecticut River; thence, down along the middle of that river to the forty-fifth degree of north latitude" (W. M. Malloy, *U. S. Treaties and Conventions*, Washington, 1910-1923, Vol. 1, p. 587).

---

[9] Malloy, *op. cit.*, pp. 815-817. The framers of the treaty were under the impression that Mendenhall and King differed in respect to the line at only two places. Mendenhall's article, referred to above, makes it clear that they differed at three places.

A dispute arose over the location of the "northwesternmost head of Connecticut River." By referring to a map of northern New Hampshire it will be seen that four branches of the Connecticut River extend from the "highlands," namely Halls Stream, Indian Stream, Perrys Stream, and the main branch of the Connecticut. Since each of these four streams has several branches rising in the "highlands," the possibilities of the dispute were numerous.

The settlement of the controversy over the source of the Connecticut River was provided for in the fifth article of the Treaty of Ghent (see p. 56, above). The American agent under this article was William C. Bradley of Vermont. As the northwesternmost head of the Connecticut River, Bradley claimed the source of the "middle branch of Halls Stream" (*North-Eastern Boundary Arbitration Papers*, Washington, 1829, Appendix, pp. 394–395; Dept. of State, Records of Commission under Art. V. of the Treaty of Ghent, Claims of Agents, p. 66; J. B. Moore, *History and Digest of the International Arbitrations*, etc., Washington, 1898, Vol. 1, p. 80; Department of State, Atlas of Exploring Surveys, maps 11 and 12). American Commissioner Van Ness claimed the source of the "west branch of Indian Stream" (*North-Eastern Boundary Arbitration Papers*, Appendix, p. 395; Dept. of State, Records of Commission under Art. V of the Treaty of Ghent, Report of Commissioner Van Ness, pp. 57 and 58; Moore, *op. cit.*, p. 82). British Commissioner Barclay claimed the source of the "northwesternmost stream which empties into the third lake of Connecticut River" (*ibid.*, p. 81). The claim of Barclay was contended for by the British until 1842. The line claimed by Bradley is represented by *line 1*—a solid blue line; the line claimed by Van Ness by *line 2*—a short-dash blue line; and the line claimed by the British by *line 3*—a solid red line.

Since Van Ness made no claim respecting the line of the forty-fifth parallel the southern terminus of line 2 is uncertain. It was terminated at the Vallentine and Collins line (see p. 61, below), the line of the forty-fifth parallel claimed by Bradley. It may be assumed that Van Ness was more likely to support the claim respecting the forty-fifth parallel of Bradley, than that of Barclay, the true forty-fifth parallel (see p. 62, below).

In their statement presented to the King of the Netherlands in 1830 the British again claimed the line of the main branch of the Connecticut. The Americans in their official statement claimed the west branch of Indian Stream, but on the official map of the arbitration they claimed the middle branch of Halls Stream (*ibid.*, p. 105 and map opposite p. 85). The arbiter decided in favor of the British claim (line 3) (*ibid.*, p. 135).

In 1842 Webster and Ashburton settled the dispute by agreeing that the boundary should run along the highlands "to the head of Hall's Stream; thence, down the middle of said stream till the line thus run intersects the old line of boundary surveyed and marked by Valentine and Collins" (Malloy, *op. cit.*, Vol. 1, p. 652). This line is represented by *line 4*—a solid green line.

The locating and marking of the "head of Hall's Stream" fell to boundary commissioners whose appointment was provided for by the Webster-Ashburton Treaty. The American commissioner was Albert Smith, and the British commissioner J. B. B. Estcourt. Of the two northerly branches of Halls Stream the commissioners decided that the most northwesterly one was the boundary line and that its source was the "head of Hall's Stream." Smith and Estcourt's report, made in 1847, is in J. D. Richardson, *Compilation of the Messages and Papers of the Presidents*, 1789–1897, Washington, 1899, Vol. 4, pp. 171–177. The length of the Halls Stream line is about twenty-four miles.

Southward and Westward of Lake of the Woods
[PLATE 93B]

The drainage of this map is taken from Edward Stanford, *Atlas of Universal Geography*, London, 1904, Pl. 85. Use was also made of the Ontario Map, Rainy River Sheet (1914), published by the Department of the Interior of Canada, and of the Map of the State of Minnesota (1905), published by the U. S. General Land Office. The projection is from Pl. 85 of Stanford's *Atlas*.

Before the cession of Louisiana in December, 1803, proposals for the extension of the boundary line from the most northwestern point of the Lake of the Woods had reference to connecting that point with the Mississippi River, and after the cession they had reference to establishing a boundary between the Louisiana Purchase and the British possessions. It is for this reason that lines 1 and 2 differ greatly in direction from line 3. In drawing the color lines the position of the most northwestern point of the Lake of the Woods is assumed to be that agreed upon by the commissioners under the seventh article of the Treaty of Ghent in 1826 and adopted by Webster and Ashburton in 1842.

In 1794 Lord Grenville made two proposals regarding a revision of the boundary westward of Lake Superior, but as these are based upon misconceptions respecting the drainage they cannot be shown on a modern map. The next official proposal for remedying the defect in the Treaty of Peace of 1783 respecting the line between the Lake of the Woods and the Mississippi River was made by James Madison, Secretary of State, in his instructions of June 8, 1802, to Rufus King, the American minister in London, who was authorized to settle with the British government all the boundaries between the two nations that remained in dispute. The instructions to King respecting a line southward of the Lake of the Woods were as follows:

"It is now well understood that the highest source of the Mississippi is south of the Lake of the Woods; and, consequently, that a line due west from its most northwestern point would not touch any part of that river. To remedy this error, it may be agreed that the boundary of the United States in that quarter shall be a line running from that source of the Mississippi which is nearest to the Lake of the Woods, and striking it, westwardly, as a tangent, and, from the point touched, along the water-mark of the lake to its most northwestern point, at which it will meet the line running through the lake."[10]

The proposal of Madison is represented by *line 1*—a solid blue line. The representative of Great Britain in its negotiations with King was Lord Hawkesbury, principal secretary of state for foreign affairs. On May 12, 1803, King and Hawkesbury signed a convention, in which the line between the Lake of the Woods and the Mississippi River is thus described: "the boundary of the United States in this quarter shall, and is hereby declared to be the shortest line which can be drawn between the northwest point of the Lake of the Woods and the nearest source of the river Mississippi" (*Amer. State Papers*, *Foreign Relations*, Vol. 2, p. 584). This line is represented by *line 2*—a short-dash green line.

On February 9, 1804, the Senate assented to the convention on the condition that article 5 be expunged (*Senate Ex. Journ.*, Vol. 1, Washington, 1828, pp. 463–464). The ratifications were never exchanged and the convention did not become a law. The cession of Louisiana had rendered the line to the Mississippi undesirable to the United States.

As early as January, 1804, the United States showed a disposition to regard the forty-ninth parallel as the boundary between the Louisiana Purchase and the British possessions (*Amer. State Papers*, *Foreign Relations*, Vol. 2, p. 574). In 1807, during the negotiations in London which resulted in the drafting of a "supplemental convention," James Monroe and William Pinkney, the American commissioners, proposed this parallel as a boundary line, and it was accepted by the British commissioners. Article 5 of the proposed convention, which relates to the boundary westward of the Lake of the Woods, is, in the form that the British accepted it, as follows:

"It is agreed that a line drawn due north or south (as the case may require) from the most northwestern point of the Lake of the Woods until it shall intersect the forty-ninth parallel of north latitude, and from the point of such intersection, due west, along and with the said parallel, shall be the dividing line between his Majesty's territories and those of the United States to the westward of the said lake, as far as their said respective territories extend in that quarter; and that the said line shall, to that extent, form the southern boundary of his Majesty's said territories and the northern boundary of the said territories of the United States: provided that nothing in the present article shall be construed to extend to the northwest coast of America, or to the territories belonging to or claimed by either party on the continent of America to the westward of the Stony [Rocky] mountains (*ibid.*, Vol. 3, 1832, p. 165).

The effect of the proviso is to terminate the line at the Rocky Mountains. The line of the supplemental convention is represented by *line 3*—a solid green line. In order to save space, map B is not extended as far westward as the Rocky Mountains, and line 3 therefore stops short of its western terminus.

The supplemental convention of 1807 was not concluded. In 1814 an attempt of the commissioners at Ghent to settle the line westward of the Lake of the Woods also failed (J. B. Moore, *History and Digest of the International Arbitrations*, etc., Washington, 1898, Vol. 1, p. 202). Finally, in 1818 an agreement satisfactory to both governments was reached. The convention of that year, signed on October 20 by Albert Gallatin and Richard Rush, plenipotentiaries for the United States, and Frederick John Robinson and Henry Goulburn, plenipotentiaries for Great Britain, contained the following article on this subject:

"It is agreed that a line drawn from the most northwestern point of the Lake of the Woods, along the forty-ninth parallel of north latitude, or, if the said point shall not be in the forty-ninth parallel of north latitude, then that a line drawn from the said point due north or south as the case may be, until the said line

---

[10] *Amer. State Papers, Foreign Relations*, Vol. 2, Washington, 1832, p. 585. On June 3, 1792, Thomas Jefferson, Secretary of State, in a conversation with George Hammond, the British minister, proposed that the gap in the boundary line, if found to exist, should be filled by a "line running due north from the northernmost source of the Mississippi till it should strike the western line from the Lake of the Woods" (P. L. Ford, edit., *Writings of Thomas Jefferson*, Vol. 1, New York, 1892, p. 195). This line cannot be drawn, since the "northernmost source" lies eastward of the northwestern point of the Lake of the Woods.

shall intersect the said parallel of north latitude, and from the point of such intersection due west along and with the said parallel, shall be the line of demarcation between the territories of the United States, and those of His Britannic Majesty, and that the said line shall form the northern boundary of the said territories of the United States, and the southern boundary of the territories of His Britannic Majesty, from the Lake of the Woods to the Stony [Rocky] Mountains."[11]

This line is represented by *line 3*—a solid green line. The length of the boundary from the northwestern point of the Lake of the Woods to the summit of the Rocky Mountains is about 887 miles.

Rocky Mountains to Pacific Ocean
[PLATE 93C]

The drainage and projection of this map are taken from the Base Map of North America (1912), published by the U. S. Geological Survey.

Before 1818 the United States, while claiming territory west of the Rocky Mountains, made no specific proposal respecting a boundary line in that quarter. In 1818, at the negotiations in London which resulted in the convention of that year, Albert Gallatin and Richard Rush, the American plenipotentiaries, submitted the following proposition:

"It is agreed that a line drawn due north or south, as the case may require, from the most northwestern point of the Lake of the Woods, until it shall intersect the forty-ninth parallel of north latitude, and from the point of such intersection, due west, along and with the said parallel, shall be the line of demarcation between the territories of the United States and those of His Britannic Majesty to the westward of the said lake; and that the said line shall form the northern boundary of the said territories of the United States, and the southern boundary of His Britannic Majesty's said territories, from the said lake to the Pacific ocean; it being, however, distinctly understood that, with respect to the territories situated on the northwest coast of America, or westward of the Stony mountains, the two high contracting parties intend hereby to define the extent of their respective claims so far only as relates to the two parties, and without reference to the claims of any other nation" (*Amer. State Papers, Foreign Relations*, Vol. 4, Washington, 1834, p. 384).

Since the British plenipotentiaries would not agree to the extension of the line of the forty-ninth parallel west of the Rocky Mountains, the Convention of 1818 left this part of the northern line unsettled (see above). From 1818 until 1846, when a line was agreed upon, American negotiators frequently expressed a willingness to accept the forty-ninth parallel (*ibid.*, Vol. 6, Washington, 1859, pp. 644–645 and 652; George Bancroft, *Memorial on the Canal de Haro*, Berlin, 1872?, pp. 10–11, Appendix, pp. 16 and 18; *House Doc. No. 2, 29th Cong., 1st Sess.*, 1845–1846, p. 169; *House Ex. Doc. No. 1, 42nd Cong., 3rd Sess.*, 1872–1873, Part II, Vol. 5, p. 222). The line of this parallel is represented by *line 1*—a solid blue line.

In 1824, during the negotiations at London in which Richard Rush represented the United States, and W. Huskisson and Stratford Canning Great Britain, the British plenipotentiaries proposed that a line should be drawn from the Rocky Mountains "due west along the 49th parallel of north latitude to the point where that parallel strikes the great northeasternmost branch of the Oregon or Columbia river, marked in the maps as McGillivray's river, thence down along the middle of the Oregon or Columbia to its junction with the Pacific Ocean" (*Amer. State Papers, Foreign Relations*, Vol. 5, Washington, 1858, p. 582). Subsequently the same proposal was made by other British negotiators (*House Doc. No. 2, 29th Cong., 1st Sess.*, 1845–1846, p. 157; *House Ex. Doc. No. 1, 42nd Cong., 3rd Sess.*, 1872–1873, Part II, Vol. 5, p. 219). This line is represented by *line 2*—a solid red line.

During the negotiations over the northwestern boundary in 1826, W. Huskisson and H. U. Addington, the British plenipotentiaries, proposed to Albert Gallatin, the American plenipotentiary, the line offered in 1824, with the addition of certain territory northward thereof. This proposal was as follows:

"That, considering that the possession of a safe and commodious port on the Northwest Coast of America, fitted for the reception of large ships, might be an object of great interest and importance to the United States, and that no such port was to be found between the 42d degree of latitude and the Columbia River, Great Britain, in still adhering to that river as a basis, was willing so far to modify her former proposal as to concede, as far as she was concerned, to the United States the possession of Port Discovery, a most valuable harbor on the southern coast of De Fuca's inlet, and to annex thereto all that tract of country comprised within a line to be drawn from Cape Flattery, along the southern shore of De Fuca's inlet, to Point Wilson, at the northwestern extremity of Admiralty inlet; from thence along the western shore of that inlet, across the

entrance of Hood's inlet, to the point of land forming the northeastern extremity of the said inlet; from thence along the eastern shore of that inlet to the southern extremity of the same; from thence direct to the southern point of Gray's harbor; from thence along the shore of the Pacific to Cape Flattery, as before mentioned" (*Amer. State Papers, Foreign Relations*, Vol. 6, Washington, 1859, p. 660).

In 1844 Richard Pakenham, the British minister in Washington, made the same proposal to John C. Calhoun, the American secretary of state (*House Doc. No. 2, 29th Cong., 1st Sess.*, 1845–1846, p. 157; *House Ex. Doc. No. 1, 42nd Cong., 3rd Sess.*, 1872–1873, Part II, Vol. 5, pp. 220–221). The territory comprised in these proposals is inclosed by *line 3*—a short-dash red line.

The instructions given to Lord Ashburton in 1842 covered the northwestern as well as the northeastern boundary dispute. In respect to the northwestern boundary, he was authorized to propose to the government of the United States a "line of boundary commencing at the mouth of the Columbia River, thence by a line drawn along the middle of that river to its point of confluence with the Great Snake River, thence by a line carried due east to the Rocky or Stony Mountains, and thence by a line drawn in a northerly direction along the said mountains until it strikes the forty-ninth parallel of north latitude" (*ibid.*, pp. 218–219). This line is represented by *line 4*—a dot-and-dash red line.

In case Lord Ashburton found it impracticable to obtain the line described above he was to accept the line of the forty-ninth parallel and the Columbia River (line 2) (*ibid.*, p. 219).

After conferring over the northwestern boundary Webster and Ashburton, apprehensive that its consideration at that time might interfere with the settlement of the northeastern boundary, decided not to attempt to reach an agreement respecting the less important dispute (*Parliamentary Papers, Correspondence relative to ... Oregon Territory*, Vol. 52, London, 1846, p. 2). In 1843 negotiations for the settlement of the northwestern boundary were begun in London but were shortly removed to Washington, where they were finally terminated in 1846 by the treaty concluded on June 15 of that year by James Buchanan, the American secretary of state, and Richard Pakenham, the British minister to the United States. The first article of that treaty reads in part as follows:

"From the point on the forty-ninth parallel of north latitude, where the boundary laid down in existing treaties and conventions between the United States and Great Britain terminates, the line of boundary between the territories of the United States and those of Her Britannic Majesty shall be continued westward along the said forty-ninth parallel of north latitude to the middle of the channel which separates the continent from Vancouver's Island; and thence southerly through the middle of said channel, and of Fuca's Straits, to the Pacific Ocean" (W. M. Malloy, *U. S. Treaties and Conventions*, Washington, 1910–1923, Vol. 1, p. 657).

This line is represented by *line 5*—a solid green line. The part of the water line from the forty-ninth parallel to the Strait of Juan de Fuca, which was subsequently disputed (see p. 71, below), is drawn as finally settled. The length of the line from the Rocky Mountains to the Pacific Ocean is about 559 miles.

The Forty-Fifth Parallel
[PLATE 93D]

The drainage of this map is taken chiefly, and the projection entirely, from the Quebec Map, Montreal and Quebec Sheet (1914), published by the Department of the Interior of Canada, and partly from the Base Map of New York (1913) and the Base Map of New Hampshire and Vermont (1914), both published by the U. S. Geological Survey. For the region north of the boundary line near the St. Lawrence River some of the drainage was taken from the U. S. Post Route Map of New York (1916).

The Treaty of Peace of 1783 described the line of the forty-fifth parallel as follows: ... "thence down along the middle of that river [Connecticut] to the forty-fifth degree of north latitude; from thence, by a line due west on said latitude, until it strikes the river Iroquois or Cataraquy [St. Lawrence]" (W. M. Malloy, *U. S. Treaties and Conventions*, Washington, 1910–1923, Vol. 1, p. 587).

In 1783 the boundary between New York and Quebec was the line of the forty-fifth parallel as surveyed and marked in 1771–1774 by the two provinces. This is known as the "Vallentine and Collins line," named for the principal surveyor for Quebec, Thomas Vallentine, and the principal surveyor for New York, John Collins (D. H. Pratt, *Boundaries of State of New York*, Albany, 1884, Vol. 2, pp. 7–43). As early as 1802 it was known that the Vallentine and Collins line was not accurately run (Douglas Brymner, *Report on Canadian Archives, 1885*, Ottawa, 1886, p. xcv). In 1818 Ferdinand R. Hassler and Dr. J. C. Tiarks, respectively

---

[11] W. M. Malloy, *U. S. Treaties and Conventions*, Washington, 1910–1923, Vol. 1, p. 632. The Webster-Ashburton Treaty defines this line more briefly: "thence [from the most northwestern point of the Lake of the Woods] according to existing treaties, due south to its intersection with the 49th parallel of north latitude, and along that parallel to the Rocky Mountains" (*ibid.*, p. 652).

the American and the British astronomers under the fifth article of the Treaty of Ghent, reported that at Lake Champlain near Rouses Point the Vallentine and Collins line was about three fourths of a mile north of the true forty-fifth parallel and that the American fort in that locality was about one fourth of a mile north of the true parallel. Observations at other points showed that the old line lay for the most part north of the true line (G. L. Rives, *Selections from Correspondence of Thomas Barclay*, New York, 1894, pp. 402–404; Joseph Bouchette, *British Dominions in North America*, London, 1832, Vol. 1, pp. 17–18). Since the adoption of the true line would result in a considerable loss of territory to the United States and in much inconvenience to the settlers thereon and would give the Canadians a valuable fort, it was not to be expected that the Americans would favor it. Moreover, there were other grounds for claiming the old line, which need not be here stated.

In 1821 American Agent Bradley, in his argument before the commissioners under the fifth article of the Treaty of Ghent, claimed the Vallentine and Collins line, and thereafter this line was generally claimed by Americans.[12] American Commissioner Van Ness declined to report any opinion on this part of the northeast boundary (J. B. Moore, *History and Digest of the International Arbitrations*, etc., Washington, 1898, Vol. 1, p. 82). British Commissioner Barclay claimed the true forty-fifth parallel (*ibid.*, p. 81), and this line was claimed by the British until 1842. The line claimed by the Americans is represented by **line 1**—a short-dash black line, and the line claimed by the British by **line 2**—a solid red line.

Halls Stream is made the eastern terminus of line 1. This is its terminus according to Bradley's claim in 1821, according to the official map laid before the King of the Netherlands under the convention of 1827, and according to the claim of Webster in 1842. Albert Gallatin, the principal American agent under the convention of 1827, while claiming Halls Stream on the official map, thought it safer to insist on Indian Stream in his written statement of the American case (*ibid.*, p. 105). In order therefore to represent the claim of Gallatin to the Vallentine and Collins line made in his written statement it would be necessary to extend line 1 from Halls Stream to the Connecticut River. The eastern terminus of the Vallentine and Collins line is the Connecticut River (Pratt, *op. cit.*, p. 22).

At the arbitration of 1829–1831 before the King of the Netherlands, the Americans, as stated above, claimed the Vallentine and Collins line and the British claimed the true forty-fifth parallel (Moore, *op. cit.*, pp. 106 and 112). The king decided in favor of the British claim, with one exception, as may be seen from his opinion, which was as follows:

"That it will be suitable to proceed to fresh operations to measure the observed latitude in order to mark out the boundary from the river Connecticut along the parallel of the 45th degree of north latitude to the river St. Lawrence, named in the Treaties Iroquois or Cataraquy, in such manner however that, in all cases, at the place called Rouse's Point, the territory of the United States of America, shall extend to the fort erected at that place, and shall include said fort and its Kilometrical radius (*rayon Kilometrique*)" (*ibid.*, p. 136).

The departure from the true forty-fifth parallel at Rouses Point made by the king in order to run the line north of the American fort near that place cannot be shown on Plate 93D, owing to its small scale. With this exception, the king's line is represented by **line 2**—a solid red line.

Early in the negotiations of 1842 Lord Ashburton expressed a willingness to accept, as a part of a general compromise, the Vallentine and Collins line (*House Doc. No. 2, 27th Cong., 3rd Sess.*, pp. 39–40), and this was the line agreed upon (**line 1**). The boundary from the head of Halls Stream is described in the Webster-Ashburton Treaty as follows:

... "thence, down the middle of said stream, till the line thus run intersects the old line of boundary surveyed and marked by Vallentine and Collins, previously to the year 1774, as the 45th degree of north latitude, and which has been known and understood to be the line of actual division between the States of New York and Vermont on one side, and the British province of Canada on the other; and from said point of intersection, west, along the said dividing line, as heretofore known and understood, to the Iroquois or St. Lawrence River" (Malloy, *op. cit.*, p. 652).

Line 1 is copied from the Index Map of Estcourt and Smith, joint commissioners for mapping and marking the northeast boundary, who were appointed in accordance with a provision of the Webster-Ashburton Treaty. (The copy of the Index Map that was used is the one published

in 1908 by the British Ordnance Survey.) The precise location of the line with respect to the true forty-fifth parallel differs slightly with different determinations of the parallel. According to Estcourt and Smith the western terminus at the St. Lawrence River is a few rods north of the parallel. A more recent calculation of its position, in terms of the "North American datum," places it several rods south of the parallel (*Report of International Waterways Commission*, in Dept. of State, 1915, p. 25). The length of the line of the forty-fifth parallel (Halls Stream to St. Lawrence River) is about 154 miles.

Old Southern Boundary

[PLATE 93E]

The drainage and projection of this map are taken from La Tour's map, "L'Amérique Septentrionale, 1783." The longitude is measured eastward from the meridian of the Island of Ferro, which is about eighteen degrees west of the meridian of Greenwich. The meridians are numbered consecutively around the whole circumference of the earth. The junction of the Flint and Appalachicola rivers, which is a few miles southward of the thirty-first parallel, is, on La Tour's map, Mitchell's map, and many other maps of this period, a few miles north of this parallel. What was formerly the upper Appalachicola River is now the Chattahoochee River.

The southern boundary of the United States is described in the Treaty of Peace of 1783 as follows:

"South, by a line to be drawn due east from the determination of the line last mentioned [line of the Mississippi River] in the latitude of thirty-one degrees north of the Equator, to the middle of the river Apalachicola or Catahouche; thence along the middle thereof to its junction with the Flint River; thence strait to the head of St. Mary's River; and thence down along the middle of St. Mary's River to the Atlantic Ocean" (Malloy, *U. S. Treaties and Conventions*, Washington, 1910–1923, Vol. 1, p. 588; see also p. 55, above).

Spain accepted the eastern part of the boundary thus described (the northern boundary of East Florida), but she disputed the western part, that is the part lying west of the Appalachicola and Flint rivers. The United States claimed the line established by the Treaty of Peace of 1783 and frequently asserted its right to this line during the negotiations with Spain for a treaty, 1785–1795. On August 25, 1785, the Continental Congress instructed John Jay, secretary of state for foreign affairs, who represented the United States in the negotiations with the Spanish envoy, Gardoqui, "particularly to stipulate the right of the United States to their territorial bounds ... as established in their treaties with Great Britain" (*Secret Journs. Cont. Cong.*, Vol. 3, Boston, 1821, p. 586). The government under the Constitution reasserted this right in the instructions to William Carmichael and William Short, 1792, and to Thomas Pinckney, 1794 (*Amer. State Papers, Foreign Relations*, Vol. 1, Washington, 1833, pp. 252–253 and 534; see p. 63, below). The claim of the United States is represented by **line 1**—a solid blue line.

On July 25, 1784, the Spanish government issued instructions to Gardoqui respecting the treaty which he was authorized to negotiate with the United States. In these Spain accepted the boundary east of the Appalachicola and Flint rivers as described in the Treaty of Peace, but claimed a large territory lying southwestward of a line drawn from the junction of these rivers up the Flint River to its source, thence in a straight line to the Euphasee River, down this river to its junction with the River of the Cherokees (Tennessee River), thence down the River of the Cherokees to its junction with the Ohio River, and down the Ohio to its junction with the Mississippi River (Gardoqui Despatches, University of Chicago Library, Vol. 5, pp. 205–210). This line is represented by **line 2**—a solid red line.

On April 28, 1785, Count Bernardo de Galvez, captain general of Cuba, Louisiana, and the Floridas, residing in Havana, instructed Gardoqui that in case the line of his instructions of 1784 could not be obtained he should use strong efforts to secure the line of the thirty-fifth parallel between the Mississippi and the "Cherokee, the Euphasee, or the Flint" and the line of the Flint to the line connecting with the St. Mary's River; as a last resort he might accept the parallel of the mouth of the Yazoo River. The first of these concessions is represented by **line 3**—a long-dash red line, and the second by **line 4**—a short-dash red line.[13] The gap in the description of line 3 between the Euphasee and the Flint is filled with a straight line.

[12] Dept. of State, Records of Commission under Art. V of the Treaty of Ghent, Claims of Agents, pp. 68–85. Bradley said that, in case the Vallentine and Collins line did not prove acceptable to the commissioners, he proposed to claim the forty-fifth parallel as determined by the principles of "geocentric latitude." Thus determined, the line would fall thirteen miles north of the true parallel (J. B. Moore, *History and Digest of the International Arbitrations*, etc., Washington, 1898, Vol. 1, pp. 80–81 and 112). It may be added that Bradley had the erroneous impression that a small part of the line between New York and Quebec east of the St. Lawrence River had not been surveyed by Vallentine and Collins.

[13] S. F. Bemis, *Pinckney's Treaty*, Johns Hopkins University, 1926, pp. 77–78, and map D, opposite p. 77. Professor Bemis' maps are based chiefly on the Gardoqui Despatches. For corrections respecting the "Proposed Spanish-American Boundary Lines, 1782," see Bemis, "Communication," *Hisp. Amer. Hist. Rev.*, Vol. 7, 1927, pp. 386–389.

Galvez also suggested a line beginning at the mouth of the Yazoo River and running in such a way as to include to the southward the territory of the Chickasaws, Alibamous, and Choctaws, and the greater part of the territory of the Talapuches and Creeks (Gardoqui Despatches, Vol. 6, pp. 149–156).

On September 1, 1786, Floridablanca, the Spanish foreign minister, drafted a treaty which was sent to Gardoqui for his guidance. It provided for a "neutral Indian territory" extending from the northern boundary of West Florida, now provisionally fixed as a line drawn from the mouth of the Yazoo River to the confluence of the Flint River and Apalachicola (or Chattahooche) River, to the line of Spain's maximum claims (line 2). The boundary of the "neutral Indian territory" is represented by *line 5*—a broken black line (Bemis, *op. cit.*, p. 118, and map E, opposite p. 77).

In September, 1787, Floridablanca issued new instructions for Gardoqui, conceding the American claim to the 31st parallel, with the exception of a tract between the Mississippi and the Pearl rivers and the 31st and 32nd parallels. He was authorized, however, to recede from this if necessary and accept the parallel of a point "two, three, or more leagues" north of Natchez and the line of the Amite River. The first concession is represented by *line 6*—a dot-and-dash red line, and the second by *line 7*—a dotted red line (*ibid.*, pp. 121–122, and map F, opposite p. 77; Manuel Serrano y Sanz, *El Brigadier Jaime Wilkinson*, Madrid, 1915, p. 15). The gap in the description of line 7 has been filled by a straight line drawn from the parallel of a point two leagues above Natchez to the Amite River.

Inasmuch as Jay and Gardoqui failed to agree upon a treaty, new negotiations were begun in Madrid in 1792, at which the United States was represented by William Carmichael and William Short, commissioners plenipotentiary. They also failed, and in 1794 the task of renewing negotiations fell to Thomas Pinckney, American envoy extraordinary to Spain. On October 27, 1795, Pinckney concluded with Spain a "treaty of friendship, boundaries, commerce, and navigation," in which the boundary between the United States and West Florida was described as follows: "a line beginning on the River Mississippi at the northernmost part of the thirty-first degree of latitude north of the equator, which from thence shall be drawn due east to the middle of the River Apalachicola, or Catahouche, thence along the middle thereof to its junction with the Flint" (*Amer. State Papers, Foreign Relations*, Vol. 1, Washington, 1833, pp. 257 and 533; Malloy, *op. cit.*, Vol. 2, p. 1641). This is the line claimed by the United States and is represented by *line 1*—a solid blue line.

Southeastern Boundary of Louisiana Purchase

[PLATE 93F]

The drainage and projection of this map are taken from the Base Map of the United States (1911), scale 1:7,000,000, published by the U. S. Geological Survey.

The treaty of 1803 for the cession of Louisiana did not prescribe the metes and bounds of the territory acquired by the United States. It ceded the territory which France acquired from Spain by the Treaty of San Ildefonso (1800) and adopted from that treaty the following description of the territory ceded by Spain:

... "the Colony or Province of Louisiana, with the same extent that it now has in the hands of Spain, and that it had when France possessed it; and such as it should be after the Treaties subsequently entered into between Spain and other States" (W. M. Malloy, *U. S. Treaties and Conventions*, Washington, 1910–1923, Vol. 1, p. 509).

So general a description made disputes over boundary lines inevitable. As a matter of fact the whole of the boundary of the Louisiana Purchase, with the exception of a part of the line of the Mississippi River, was disputed. One of the principal disputes was over the southeastern boundary, or the line separating the Purchase from Spanish Florida. The United States claimed the Perdido River from its mouth to the "old southern boundary" on the 31st parallel (see Pl. 93E, line 1). (For the genesis of the American claim see P. L. Ford, edit., *Writings of Thomas Jefferson*, Vol. 8, New York, 1897, pp. 242–245 and 261–263; Henry Adams, *History of the United States*, Vol. 2, New York, 1898, pp. 68–73.) Spain claimed a line extending from the Gulf of Mexico through the middle of lakes Pontchartrain and Maurepas, up the Iberville River to its junction with the Mississippi River, and up the Mississippi River to the "old southern boundary." An early statement of the claim of Spain will be found in a letter of the Spanish first secretary of state, Pedro Cevallos, dated Feb. 24, 1805, to James Monroe and Charles Pinckney, American ministers (*Amer. State Papers, Foreign Relations*, Vol. 2, Washington, 1832, p. 645). This line was established in 1763 as the southeastern boundary between the English and Spanish possessions.

The line claimed by the United States is represented by *line 1*—a solid blue line, and the line claimed by Spain by *line 2*—a solid red line.

The dispute over the southeastern boundary of the Louisiana Purchase came to an end with the cession of Florida to the United States by Spain in 1819. This was provided for in the Adams-Onis Treaty of that year (Malloy, *op. cit.*, Vol. 2, p. 1652 (see p. 68, below)).

Sabine River

[PLATE 93G]

The drainage and projection of this map are taken from the Base Map of the United States (1911), scale 1:7,000,000, published by the U. S. Geological Survey.

The Adams-Onis Treaty of 1819 described the boundary line between the United States and Mexico south of the Red River as follows:

"The boundary line between the two countries west of the Mississippi shall begin on the Gulph of Mexico at the mouth of the river Sabine, in the sea, continuing north along the western bank of that river to the 32d degree of latitude; thence, by a line due north to the degree of latitude where it strikes the Rio Roxo of Natchitoches or Red River ... The whole being as laid down in Melish's map of the United States published at Philadelphia, improved to the first of January, 1818" (W. M. Malloy, *U. S. Treaties and Conventions*, Washington, 1910–1923, Vol. 2, pp. 1652–1653; see also p. 68, below).

Notwithstanding this explicit description, which admits of no doubt as to the river intended, the United States during the years 1829–1840 advanced the claim that the river emptying into Sabine Lake from the northwest, commonly called the Neches River, was the Sabine River referred to in the Adams-Onis Treaty of 1819 (*Register of Debates in Congress*, Vol. 14, Washington, 1837, Appendix, Part II, p. 128; G. L. Rives, *United States and Mexico, 1821–1848*, New York, 1913, Vol. 1, pp. 237 and 376–377; T. M. Marshall, *History of the Western Boundary of the Louisiana Purchase, 1819–1841*, Berkeley, 1914, pp. 87, 88, 99, 104, 162, 209–210, and 218; *Arkansas Hist. Assn. Publs.*, Vol. 2, Fayetteville, 1908, p. 230; *Senate Doc. No. 199, 27th Cong., 2nd Sess.*, 1841–1842, p. 14; *Texas Diplomatic Correspondence*, in *Ann. Rept. Amer. Hist. Assn.*, Washington, 1907, Vol. 2, Part I, p. 287). The claim of the Neches River involved the claim of a new meridian line between the thirty-second parallel and the Red River, about one hundred miles westward of the meridian line claimed by Spain. The line south of the Red River claimed by the United States is represented by *line 1*—a solid blue line.

Mexico and Texas claimed that the stream that entered Sabine Lake from the north was the true Sabine River (Marshall, *op. cit.*, pp. 99 and 218; *Texas Diplomatic Correspondence*, in *Ann. Rept. Amer. Hist. Assn.*, Washington, 1907, Vol. 2, Part I, p. 138). The line south of the Red River according to their claim is represented by *line 2*—a solid red line.

In 1838 the United States and Texas concluded a convention which authorized the appointment of a commission to mark the boundary between the two nations from the mouth of the Sabine River to the Red River (Malloy, *op. cit.*, Vol. 2, pp. 1779–1780). The commissioner for the United States was John H. Overton, of Louisiana; and for Texas, Memucan Hunt. On October 23, 1839, John Forsyth, secretary of state, issued the following instructions to Overton respecting the determination of the true Sabine River:

"Soon after the conclusion of the treaty for defining the limits between the United States and Mexico, this Government was led to believe that the river Neches, which, as well as the Sabine, flows into the Sabine lake, was the most considerable of those two streams; that it was navigable, while the Sabine was too shallow for that purpose, and that the general direction of the Neches corresponded better than that of the Sabine to the course which, according to the treaty, the boundary line was to take. Recent examinations, however, made under the direction of the Department of War, in the accuracy of which there is reason to confide, tend to show that the information referred to was, at least to some extent, incorrect. In the present state of information, that question is still pending, and requires particular examination by the commission of which you are a member, with a view to its final adjustment. You will, therefore, make the necessary inquiries, note all the facts bearing upon it, and regulate yourself by the result of them" (*Senate Doc. No. 199, 27th Cong., 2nd Sess.*, 1841–1842, pp. 7–8).

After a thorough consideration of the question the commission decided that the more easterly stream was the true Sabine River and that the "River Neches could not have been intended as the river designated by the treaty" (*ibid.*, pp. 60–61). The decision of the commission is represented by *line 2*—a solid red line.

Southern and Western Boundary of New Mexico

[PLATE 93H]

The drainage and projection of this map are taken from the Map of Arizona and New Mexico, *Century Atlas of the World* (1911), No. 55.

The Treaty of Guadalupe Hidalgo provided for the appointment of a commissioner and a surveyor by each government, to run and mark the boundary line between the United States and Mexico (W. M. Malloy, *U. S. Treaties and Conventions*, Washington, 1910–1923, Vol. 1,

p. 1110). Toward the end of 1850, when work was begun on the line extending from the Rio Grande westward, the American commissioner was John R. Bartlett, the American surveyor A. B. Gray, and the Mexican commissioner, P. G. Conde.

According to the treaty, the line was to run up the middle of the Rio Grande "to the point where it strikes the southern boundary of New Mexico; thence westwardly along the whole southern boundary of New Mexico (which runs north of the town called Paso)[14] to its western termination; thence northward along the western line of New Mexico, until it intersects the first branch of the river Gila." The treaty further specified that the southern and western boundaries of New Mexico referred to were those laid down on Disturnell's map of Mexico, published in 1847 (*ibid.*, pp. 1109–1110; see also p. 65, below).

Because of the inaccuracies of Disturnell's map, the commissioners found it difficult to locate on the ground the point at which the Rio Grande crossed the southern boundary of New Mexico and the point at which the southern boundary met the western boundary. Relative to the "town of Paso," the thirty-second parallel of Disturnell's map was more than thirty miles too far south. The location of this town on the map was about 32° 15' N., while its true location was about 31° 45' N. On Disturnell's map the location of the Rio Grande near the southern boundary of New Mexico was about longitude 104° 40' west from Greenwich (27° 40' west from Washington), while it should have been about longitude 106° 40' west from Greenwich—a difference of two degrees. A correct representation of the Rio Grande showed the southern boundary of New Mexico on the west side of that river to be about one degree in length, while on Disturnell's map it was about three degrees (*Senate Ex. Doc. No. 119, 32nd Cong., 1st Sess.*, 1851–1852, pp. 388 and 392).

Mexican Commissioner Conde claimed that the line of the southern and western boundary should begin at a point on the Rio Grande in latitude 32° 22' N.—the latitude of the point of intersection of the southern boundary with the Rio Grande on Disturnell's map; thence about one degree westward—the length of the southern boundary on a map correctly representing the Rio Grande—to the Rio Mimbres; thence up this stream to its source; and thence in a direct line to the Gila River (*ibid.*, pp. 277–279, 387, 391–392, and map at end of volume). The part of this line corresponding to the western boundary was more or less a conventional line. Conde's line is represented by *line 1*—a solid red line.

Commissioner Bartlett agreed to accept the starting point, 32° 22' N., if Conde would agree to run the line three degrees west—the length of the southern boundary according to Disturnell's map. After some hesitation Conde accepted Bartlett's proposal (*ibid.*, pp. 387–388, 391, and map 1).[15] The line agreed upon by the commissioners is represented by *line 2*—a solid green line.

American Surveyor Gray refused to accept the line of the commissioners and claimed a line more favorable to the United States. Gray calculated that the southern boundary on Disturnell's map was about seven minutes north of Paso, the correct position of which town was about 31° 45' N. He therefore started his line at a point on the Rio Grande in latitude 31° 52' N.; thence it ran due west three degrees and thence due north to the Gila River (*ibid.*, pp. 145–146, 280–283, 298–299, and map "B"; G. Schroeter, "Map of Disputed Boundary," New York, 1853). Gray's line is represented by *line 3*—a solid blue line.

Some of the minor officials of the American surveying party supported Gray's claim, and a contention ensued, which soon involved the higher officials at Washington. Congress took a hand in it and inserted in the general appropriation act of 1852 a proviso that the money appropriated by that act for running the boundary line between the Unites States and Mexico should not be expended until the President was convinced "that the southern boundary of New Mexico is not established by the commissioner and surveyor of the United States farther north of the town called 'Paso' than the same is laid down in Disturnell's map" (*U. S. Statutes at Large*, Vol. 10, Boston, 1855, pp. 94–95). In other words, it repudiated the commissioners' line and approved Gray's. The line approved by Congress is represented by *line 3*—a solid blue line.

United States-Mexican Boundary

[PLATE 94A]

The drainage and projection of this map are taken from J. Disturnell's "Mapa de los Estados Unidos de Méjico," revised edition, 1847, published in New York and known as the "treaty map," since it is referred to in the Treaty of Guadalupe Hidalgo (see p. 65, below). The southern

and western boundaries of New Mexico and the northern boundary of Lower California are also taken from this map. It may be noted, however, that Disturnell gave the part of New Mexico east of the Rio Grande the same color as Texas. The longitude is reckoned from the meridian of Washington.

The joint resolution for the annexation of Texas was approved on March 1, 1845, and some months later President Polk decided to send John Slidell to Mexico as envoy extraordinary and minister plenipotentiary, to adjust the questions of difference then pending between the United States and that country. One of the most important of these questions was the boundary between Texas and Mexico. In Slidell's instructions, which were signed by James Buchanan, secretary of state, and were dated November 10, 1845, the right of Texas to the line of the Rio Grande as far as the Paso del Norte was recognized, but some doubt was expressed as to her right to the line (see Pl. 95B, line 3, and p. 69, below) claimed by her to the northward of the Paso del Norte, since it included a part of New Mexico (*Senate Ex. Doc. No. 52, 30th Cong., 1st Sess.*, 1846–1848, pp. 75–77). The Paso del Norte is the great pass of the Rio Grande near "Paso." Since the whole of New Mexico was desired by the United States, Slidell was authorized to assume the payment of all the just claims of American citizens against Mexico and in addition to pay $5,000,000 in case the Mexican government would agree to the following boundary line:

… "from the mouth of the Rio Grande, up the principal stream to the point where it touches the line of New Mexico; thence west of the river along the exterior line of that province, and so as to include the whole within the United States, until it again intersects the river; thence up the principal stream of the same to its source; and thence due north until it intersects the forty-second degree of north latitude" (*ibid.*, p. 78).[16]

Slidell was further instructed that the United States wished California as well as New Mexico, and that if he found there was a good prospect for obtaining both he might, in addition to assuming American claims, offer $25,000,000 for a line running due west from the southern boundary of New Mexico or from any point on the western boundary of New Mexico that would include Monterey; or $20,000,000 for a line running due west from any point on that boundary that would include the bay and harbor of San Francisco (*ibid.*, pp. 78–79). These three alternative lines are represented by *lines 1*—solid blue lines. The proposals respecting Monterey and San Francisco are represented by lines that give the United States a minimum of territory. Somewhat more southerly lines would also satisfy the descriptions.

Slidell's instructions further authorized him to offer, in case Mexico was unwilling to agree to a boundary westward of the Rio Grande, to assume the payment of the claims of American citizens if she would accept the line defined by the act of the Texan Congress, December 19, 1836, namely a line "beginning at the mouth of the Rio Grande, thence up the principal stream of said river to its source, thence due north to the forty-second degree of north latitude" (*ibid.*, p. 78; see also pp. 68–69, below). This line is represented by *line 2*—a short-dash blue line.

The Mexican government refused to receive Slidell as minister of the United States, and as a consequence negotiations for the settlement of the boundary line between the two countries were postponed until toward the end of the Mexican War. After the fall of Vera Cruz, March 29, 1847, President Polk decided to send a commissioner to accompany the army in Mexico and to conclude a treaty of peace whenever the Mexican government should show an inclination to end the war. As commissioner, Polk chose Nicholas P. Trist, chief clerk of the Department of State. Trist's instructions, dated April 15, 1847, authorized him to acquire New Mexico and Upper California and, if possible, Lower California. For the three states he was to pay not more than $25,000,000, and for the two not more than $20,000,000. Should he acquire the three states the boundary line was to be as follows:

… "commence in the Gulf of Mexico, three leagues from the land opposite the mouth of the Rio Grande; from thence up the middle of that river to the point where it strikes the southern line of New Mexico; thence westwardly along the southern boundary of New Mexico to the southwestern corner of the same; thence northward along the western line of New Mexico, until it intersects the first branch of the river Gila; or, if it should not intersect any branch of that river, then to the point on the said line nearest to such branch; and thence in a direct line to the same, and down the middle of said branch, and of the said river, until it empties into the Rio Colorado; thence down the middle of the Colorado, and the middle of the Gulf of California, to the Pacific ocean" (*ibid.*, pp. 82 and 86).

---

[14] The town of Paso, El Paso, Paso del Norte, or El Paso del Norte, was in Mexico (not far from the present El Paso, Texas), near the great pass of the Rio Grande, called the Paso del Norte.

[15] Because of the great difficulty of running and marking the slightly curved lines of the southern and western boundary of New Mexico as shown on Disturnell's map no one proposed to run these lines, and all agreed that in place of them straight lines should be run.

[16] On Disturnell's map the northern boundary of New Mexico intersects the Rio Grande at its source. Buchanan stated that a mountain line north of New Mexico would be preferable to the due north line. This variation is unimportant, as the mountain line would lie but a few miles from the due north line.

Should he fail to acquire Lower California, the boundary line was to pass down the middle of the Gulf of California "to a point directly opposite the division line between Upper and Lower California; thence due west along the said line, which runs north of the parallel of 32 degrees and south of San Miguel, to the Pacific ocean" (*ibid.*, p. 82). These two alternative lines are also represented by *lines 3*—dot-and-dash blue lines.

On July 13 Buchanan, in response to a suggestion of Trist and with a view to including within the United States the Paso del Norte, authorized the instructions of April 15 to be modified in respect to the boundary in that region. According to the new instructions the line was to run from the middle of the Rio Grande along the thirty-second parallel to a point due south of the southwestern angle of New Mexico, and thence due north to said angle (*ibid.*, pp. 90 and 116). This modification is not represented on the map.

On July 19 Buchanan authorized a further modification of Trist's instructions of April 15, according to which, if Lower California could be obtained, the line was to run from the Rio Grande along the thirty-second parallel to the Gulf of California and down the middle of the gulf to the Pacific Ocean. In case, however, Lower California could not be obtained, the line of the thirty-second parallel was to be extended to the Pacific Ocean (*ibid.*, pp. 91 and 117). These modifications were suggested on July 13 but not authorized until July 19. On July 13 a line due west from the southwest angle of New Mexico was also suggested. Buchanan did not intend that Trist should make the thirty-second parallel, instead of the Gila River, a *sine qua non*. He was to obtain it, if practicable. The modifications are represented by *lines 4*—long-dash blue lines.

Late in August Mexico appointed four peace commissioners, and early in September Trist conferred with them on the subject of boundaries. Their instructions required them to insist on the Nueces River as the southwestern boundary between Texas and Mexico and not to cede any part of California or New Mexico.

On September 2, apparently without consulting their government, they suggested a "compromise line," as follows:

. . . "beginning the boundary line on the Pacific at latitude 36° 30′, and running it due east until it passed Santa Fé; then down southward some distance, and again eastward so as to strike the head of the Nueces [and along the Nueces to the Gulf of Mexico]" (*ibid.*, p. 197). The description of this line is taken from Trist's account of the conference of September 2.

This line is represented by *line 5*—a solid red line.

On the same day, September 2, Trist, unauthorized by his government, suggested the following compromise line:

. . . "commence at a point in the Gulf of Mexico three leagues from land opposite to the middle of the southernmost inlet into Corpus Christi bay; thence through the middle of said inlet, and through the middle of said bay, to the middle of the mouth of the Rio Nueces; thence up the middle of said river to the southernmost extremity of Yoke lake, or Laguna de las Yuntas, where the said river leaves the said lake, after running through the same; thence by a line due west to the middle of the Rio Puerco [Pecos River]; and thence up the middle of said river to the parallel of latitude six geographical miles north of the fort at the Paso del Norte [near Paso], on the Rio Bravo [Rio Grande]; thence due west along the said parallel, to the point where it intersects the western boundary of New Mexico; thence northwardly along the said boundary, until it first intersects a branch of the river Gila (or if it should not intersect any branch of that river, then to the point on said boundary nearest to the first branch thereof, and from that point in a direct line to such branch); thence down the middle of said branch and of the said river Gila, until it empties into the Rio Colorado, and down or up the middle of the Colorado, as the case may require, to the thirty-third parallel of latitude; and thence due west along the said parallel, into the Pacific ocean" (*ibid.*, pp. 195 and 201).

This line is represented by *line 6*—a dotted blue line. Since on Disturnell's map the western boundary of New Mexico does not extend as far south as the thirty-second parallel, the line is drawn northward from that parallel along a projection of the western boundary. The American government censured Trist for suggesting this line (*ibid.*, p. 94).

After a consultation with their government, which proved to be less yielding than themselves, the Mexican commissioners on September 6 proposed the following line:

. . . "commence in the gulf of Mexico, three leagues from land, opposite the southern mouth of the bay of Corpus Christi; shall run in a straight line from within the said bay to the mouth of the river Nueces; thence through the middle of that river, in all its course, to its source; from the source of the river Nueces shall be traced a straight line until it meets the present frontier of New Mexico on the east-southeast side; it shall then follow the present boundary of New Mexico on the east, north, and west, until this last touches the 37th degree; which will serve as limit for both republics, from the point in which it

touches the said frontier of the west of New Mexico to the Pacific ocean" (*ibid.*, p. 339).

This line is represented by *line 7*—a short-dash red line.

On September 7 the peace negotiations were discontinued and were not renewed until after the fall of the City of Mexico. In November the government of Mexico chose new peace commissioners and on December 30 instructed them that the boundary line was to follow the Rio Grande to a point two leagues north of the town of Paso del Norte, thence run westward along a parallel to the Sierra de los Mimbres, thence northward along that ridge of mountains as far as the height of the source of the Gila River, or of that branch nearest the Sierra, thence along the Gila River to the Colorado River, and thence along a parallel to the Pacific Ocean, unless that parallel cut the village of the port of San Diego, in which case it should run along the parallel two leagues north of San Diego (J. M. Roa Bárcena, *Recuerdos de la invasion Norte-Americana, 1846–1848*, Mexico, 1883, pp. 595–596). This line is represented by *line 8*—a dot-and-dash red line.

The second period of negotiations, which lasted several weeks, was terminated on February 2, 1848, by the conclusion of the Treaty of Guadalupe Hidalgo, signed by Trist and the Mexican commissioners. Article V of this treaty, which relates to the boundary line, reads in part as follows:

"The boundary line between the two Republics shall commence in the Gulf of Mexico, three leagues from land, opposite the mouth of the Rio Grande . . . from thence up the middle of that river, following the deepest channel, where it has more than one, to the point where it strikes the southern boundary of New Mexico; thence, westwardly, along the whole southern boundary of New Mexico (which runs north of the town called Paso) to its western termination; thence, northward, along the western line of New Mexico, until it intersects the first branch of the river Gila (or if it should not intersect any branch of that river, then to the point on the said line nearest to such branch, and thence in a direct line to the same); thence down the middle of the said branch and of the said river, until it empties into the Rio Colorado; thence across the Rio Colorado, following the division line between Upper and Lower California, to the Pacific Ocean.

"The southern and western limits of New Mexico, mentioned in this article, are those laid down in the map entitled 'Map of the United Mexican States, as organized and defined by various acts of the Congress of said republic, and constructed according to the best authorities. Revised edition. Published at New York, in 1847, by J. Disturnell,' of which map a copy is added to this treaty, bearing the signatures and seals of the undersigned Plenipotentiaries. And, in order to preclude all difficulty in tracing upon the ground the limit separating Upper from Lower California, it is agreed that the said limit shall consist of a straight line drawn from the middle of the Rio Gila, where it unites with the Colorado, to a point on the coast of the Pacific Ocean, distant one marine league due south of the southernmost point of the port of San Diego, according to the plan of said port made in the year 1782 by Don Juan Pantoja, second sailing-master of the Spanish fleet, and published at Madrid in the year 1802, in the atlas to the voyage of the schooners *Sutil* and *Mexicana*" (W. M. Malloy, *U. S. Treaties and Conventions*, Washington, 1910–1923, Vol. 1, pp. 1109–1110).

This line is represented by *line 9*—a solid green line.

The treaty was ratitifed by the Senate on March 10, 1848, by a vote of 38 to 14. During the debate on its ratification Senator Sam Houston of Texas, on February 28, submitted a resolution in which the following boundary line was proposed:

. . . "begin one league south of Tampico, on the sea-shore, and from thence running in a straight line west-northwest [?] from the beginning, and passing one league south of the San Luis Potosi, to the summit of the main ridge of the Sierra Madre, and thence northwest along the said ridge of the Sierra until it strikes the 25th degree of north latitude, and then with said degree or parallel west until it reaches the eastern line of Lower California, thence pursuing said line south and west until it reaches the Pacific Ocean" (*Senate Ex. Journ.*, Vol. 7, Washington, 1887, p. 305).

This line is represented by *line 10*—a blue line consisting of dashes and circles.

On March 6, during this debate, Senator Jefferson Davis of Mississippi moved to insert an article in the treaty which defined the boundary thus:

. . . "commence in the Gulf of Mexico, three leagues from land, opposite a point midway between the mouths of the rivers San Fernando and Santander (Boquillas Cerradas and Barra de Santander); thence westwardly to the town of Labradores, at the head of the mountain pass from the plain of Linares; thence to Agua Nueva; thence to the southwestern angle of the State of Cohahuila; thence northwardly along the highlands of the Balson de Mapimi and Santa Rosa Mountains to the Rio Grande, the line to be so traced as to include the sources of the river Sabinas and to intersect the Rio Grande, above the mouth of the river Puerco [Pecos]; thence up the main channel of the said Rio Grande to the thirty-first parallel of north latitude; thence due west to the thirty-fourth meridian of longitude west of Washington; thence in a direct line to a point on the Rio Colorado of the West, ten miles below the junction of the Gila and Colorado Rivers; thence to a point on the coast of the Pacific Ocean one marine league south of the most southern point of the harbor of San Diego" (*ibid.*, pp. 322-323).

This line is represented by *line 11*—a blue line consisting of dashes and x's.

Gadsden's and Other Lines

[PLATE 94B]

The drainage and projection of this map are taken from the Map of Mexico, *Century Atlas of the World* (1911), No. 64. The line of the Treaty of Guadalupe Hidalgo, shown in black, between the Rio Grande and the Gila River is that agreed upon in 1850 by the Mexican-American Boundary Commission.

In 1853 President Pierce decided to settle the controversy over the boundary line between the Rio Grande and the Gila River (see pp. 63-64, above) by diplomatic negotiations with Mexico and to obtain if possible, through the purchase of territory, a line more favorable to the United States than that established by the Treaty of Guadalupe Hidalgo. To conduct the negotiations he chose James Gadsden of South Carolina, who was appointed minister to Mexico. Gadsden's instructions, dated October 22, 1853, described six lines. For the most desirable line, which would add to the United States an area of about 125,000 square miles, he was authorized to offer, as a maximum sum, $50,000,000. This line was described as follows:

"From a point on the Gulf of Mexico midway between the Boquillas Cerradas and the Barra de Santander, westward along the ridge dividing the waters which flow into the river San Fernando from those which flow into the river Santander to the Coast range of mountains. Thence obliquely across that range on the south side of the Pass of Linares and along the heights which border the desert plains of Durango to a point south of the Lakes de Alamo and Parras. Thence along the highlands on the west side of the said Lakes following the principal ridge which divides the waters flowing into the Rio Conchos and Rio Sabinas up to the mountain ridge contiguous to the Rio Grande. Thence along said ridge and across the Conchos river up to the parallel of San Eliasario, and thence westwardly passing on the South side of Lake Guzman along the highlands or the middle of the plains which divide the waters flowing into the Gulf of California from those flowing into the Rios Grande and Gila until the line so traced shall intersect the 111th degree of longitude West of Greenwich, and thence in a direct course to the Gulf of California at the 31st degree of North latitude. Thence down the middle of said Gulf to its Southern extremity."[17]

This line is represented by *line 1*—a solid blue line.

For the second line mentioned in the instructions, which included an area estimated at 50,000 square miles, Gadsden was to offer, as a maximum sum, $35,000,000. This line was described as follows:

"From a point on the Gulf of Mexico midway between the Rio Grande and the Rio San Fernando, westwardly through the middle of the plain which divides the waters flowing into the Rio Grande and the Rio San Fernando, until the line so drawn shall reach the highlands and thence along the said highlands so as to include the waters flowing into the Rio Grande to the Pass of Los Muertos, thence northwestwardly along the highlands including the waters of the Rio Grande, to a point on said river between the mouth of the Rio Pecos and the Presidio del Norte, where the highlands thus defined are intersected by the Rio Grande. Thence along said river to the 31st degree of north latitude. Thence from the canyon of the Rio Grande below San Eliasario, north latitude thirty-one, along the mountain ridge which is contiguous to the Rio Grande, up to the parallel of the Presidio San Eliasario. Thence westwardly passing on the south side of Lake Guzman along the highlands or the middle of the plains which divide the waters flowing into the Gulf of California from those flowing into the Rios Grande and Gila until the line so traced shall intersect the 111th of longitude west of Greenwich. Thence in a direct course to the Gulf of California at the 31st degree of north latitude. Thence west to the middle of the Gulf of California. Thence up the centre of the said Gulf and the channel of the Rio Colorado to the present boundary of the United States."

This line is represented by *line 2*—a short-dash blue line.

For the third line, which included an area estimated at 68,000 square miles, Gadsden was to offer, as a maximum sum, $30,000,000. This line began at the thirty-first parallel, at the canyon of the Rio Grande, and followed the course of the second line to the middle of the Gulf of California and thence the course of the first line to the Pacific Ocean. This line is represented by *line 3*—a dot-and-dash blue line.

For the fourth line, which included an area estimated at 18,000 square miles, Gadsden was to offer, as a maximum sum, $20,000,000. This line also began at the thirty-first parallel, at the canyon of the Rio Grande below San Elizario, and followed the course of the second line to the boundary between the United States and Mexico. This line is represented by *line 4*—a long-dash blue line.

In case Mexico would agree to none of these four lines, Gadsden was to acquire a suitable route for a railroad to California by obtaining the parallel of 30° 48′ N. as the boundary between the Rio Grande and the Gulf of California. For this line and certain other advantages he was to offer, as a maximum sum, $15,000,000. This line is represented by *line 5*—a dotted blue line. As an alternative to this line the parallel of 32° N. was proposed.

The line obtained by Gadsden and described in the treaty that he signed with Mexico on December 30, 1853, is similar to the fourth line of his instructions. It began on the Rio Grande at latitude 31° 47′ 30″ N., passed thence by a right line to the intersection of the 31st parallel with the 111th meridian, thence by a right line to a point in the Colorado River two marine leagues north of the most northern part of the Gulf of California, and thence up the middle of that river to the boundary fixed by the Treaty of Guadalupe Hidalgo (*Senate Confidential Doc. No. 15, 33rd Cong., 1st Sess.*, 1853-1854; *Senate Ex. Journ.*, Vol. 9, Washington, 1887, p. 278). This line is represented by *line 6*—a short-dash green line.

After various amendments had been offered to the Gadsden Treaty, the Senate on April 17, 1854, made considerable changes in it, and on June 29 the President ratified the amended treaty. As ratified the article relating to boundaries provided for a line beginning at the middle of the Rio Grande, latitude 31° 47′ N., running thence "due west one hundred miles, thence south to the parallel 31° 20′ north latitude, thence along the said parallel of 31° 20′ to the 111th meridian of longitude west of Greenwich, thence in a straight line to a point on the Colorado River twenty English miles below the junction of the Gila and Colorado Rivers, thence up the middle of the said river Colorado until it intersects the present line between the United States and Mexico" (W. M. Malloy, *U. S. Treaties and Conventions*, Washington, 1910-1923, Vol. 1, p. 1122). This line is represented by *line 7*—a solid green line.

The administration at Washington was not satisfied with the extent of territory acquired under the Gadsden Treaty and for several years after that treaty was concluded tried to obtain additional lands from Mexico. On July 17, 1857, Lewis Cass, secretary of state, instructed John Forsyth, American minister to Mexico, to offer $12,000,000 for a line beginning at the middle of the Rio Grande on the thirtieth parallel and running thence "due west to the intersection of that parallel with the easternmost tributary of the Rio Chico or Rio Hiaqui (Yaqui), thence down the middle of the said Rio Chico to a point due west of the same in the middle of the Gulf of California, thence down the middle of said gulf to its mouth" ("Mexico, Instructions, 1854-1857," pp. 156-157, in U. S. Dept. of State; J. M. Callahan, "Mexican Policy of Southern Leaders under Buchanan's Administration," *Ann. Rept. Amer. Hist. Assn.*, Washington, 1910, p. 138). This line is represented by *line 8*—a blue line consisting of dashes and x's.

On March 7, 1859, Cass instructed R. M. McLane, the American minister who had succeeded Forsyth, to pay $10,000,000 for Lower California, the right to a transit across the Isthmus of Tehuantepec, and other privileges ("Mexico, Instructions, 1854-1857," p. 214). The line of this proposal is represented by *line 9*—a line consisting of dashes and circles.

Western Boundary of Louisiana Purchase

[PLATE 95A]

The drainage and projection of this map are taken from John Melish's "Map of the United States ... improved to the 1st of January 1818." This is the map used by the negotiators of the Spanish-American Treaty of 1819, and is referred to in that treaty. Its drainage is often inaccurate, and its projection does not always give the correct position of geographical features. It should be especially noted that the Multnomah or San Clemente River, the modern Willamette River, extends many miles too far east and that the source of the Arkansas River is too far north. In interpreting descriptions of lines use was made of a few geographical features shown on Melish's map but not on Plate 95A.

The dispute with Spain over the western boundary of the Louisiana Purchase involved to some extent the northern boundary and also a line west of the Rocky Mountains separating the possessions of Spain from the territory claimed by the United States and Great Britain. The enlarged dispute is here illustrated. The general term "western boundary" includes the special term "southwestern boundary."

The negotiations of the United States for the settlement of the

---

[17] For Gadsden's instructions see "Special Missions," in U. S. Dept. of State, Vol. 3, pp. 38-43 and 277-281. Since the positions of some of the geographical features mentioned in the description of this and several other lines on Plate 94B are not shown upon the base and vary somewhat on the maps upon which they are shown, it has not been possible to locate parts of several of the lines with the precision usually employed. See also Pl. 93H, and P. N. Garber, *Gadsden Treaty*, Philadelphia, 1923, pp. 91-93).

boundaries of the Louisiana Purchase covered the years 1803-1808 and 1816-1819 and were participated in by various officials of the two countries, the most important of whom are mentioned below. The question of boundaries was seldom considered alone but was almost always connected with the cession to the United States of Spanish Florida and the settlement of claims. The boundary lines proposed by each country are therefore usually "conventional lines," the acceptance of which was conditioned on the acceptance of the remaining parts of a general agreement or compromise.

Irrespective of other questions of difference between the two countries, the United States claimed, as a right under the treaty of 1803 ceding Louisiana, the Rio Grande—a claim frequently made.[18] This claim is represented by *line 1*—a solid blue line.

On April 13, 1805, Cevallos, the Spanish first secretary of state, in a communication to Charles Pinckney and James Monroe, who had been authorized to negotiate a treaty with Spain, claimed a line "which, beginning at the Gulf of Mexico between the river Caricut or Cascassia [Calcasieu] and the Armenta or Marmentoa [Mermenton], should go to the north, passing between the Adaes and Natchitoches, until it cuts the Red river" (*Amer. State Papers, Foreign Relations*, Vol. 2, Washington, 1832, p. 662).[19] This was the Spanish claim of a western boundary, irrespective of other questions of difference. It was based upon the "*uti possidetis*, or state of possession in 1763" (*ibid.*, Vol. 4, p. 466). There are slight variations in the description of this claim (see below). The line of Cevallos is represented by *line 2*—a solid red line.

On May 12, 1805, Pinckney and Monroe proposed to Cevallos, as a part of a general agreement embracing the cession of Florida and the arbitration of claims, the following line: "the river Colorado ... from its mouth to its source; thence a straight line to the most southwestwardly source of the Red river ... thence, along the ridge of high land which divides the waters belonging to the Mississippi and Missouri from those belonging to the Rio Bravo [Rio Grande]; and thence, a meridian to the northern boundary of Louisiana" (*ibid.*, Vol. 2, pp. 638 and 665; see also P. L. Ford, edit., *Writings of Thomas Jefferson*, Vol. 8, New York, 1897, pp. 379-384). This line is represented by *line 3*—a short-dash blue line. Since the Convention of 1818 (see p. 60, above) fixed the northern limits of the Louisiana Purchase at the forty-ninth parallel, this line is stopped at that parallel.

On March 13, 1806, James Madison, secretary of state, in instructions to John Armstrong, American minister to France, and to James Bowdoin, American minister to Spain, who were authorized to negotiate a convention with Spain by the aid of France, proposed the following line: "the Colorado ... from its mouth to its most northerly source; thence, a right line to the nearest high lands, enclosing all the waters running directly or indirectly into the Mississippi or Missouri, and along the said high lands as far as they border on the Spanish dominions" (from "Project" of a proposed convention; see *Amer. State Papers, Foreign Relations*, Vol. 3, Washington, 1832, p. 540).[20] This line is represented by *line 4*—a dot-and-dash blue line. Since its northern terminus is uncertain it is stopped at the forty-ninth parallel.

On the failure of the mission of Armstrong and Bowdoin in 1808 the first period of negotiations for the settlement of Spanish-American differences came to an end. In 1816 negotiations were renewed both in Washington and Madrid. On August 17, 1817, Pizarro, Spanish minister of state, proposed in a "project of articles of arrangement" sent to George W. Erving, American minister to Spain, that the Mississippi River from its source to its mouth, passing through the "La Fourche" branch of the Mississippi in the delta region, should be the boundary between Spain and the United States, Spain surrendering all her territory to the eastward of the Mississippi River, and the United States all her territory to the westward thereof (*Amer. State Papers, Foreign Relations*, Vol. 4, Washington, 1834, p. 447). This line is represented by *line 5*—a short-dash red line.

On January 16, 1818, John Quincy Adams, secretary of state, proposed to Onis, the Spanish minister in Washington, "the Colorado, from its mouth to its source, and from thence to the northern limits of Louisiana" (*ibid.*, p. 464).[21] Adams' line beyond the source of the Colorado River

is not described specifically; but, since his proposals are based upon those made by Pinckney and Monroe to Cevallos on May 12, 1805, it seems rather more probable that he intended to follow their line than a line drawn due north from the source of the Colorado River. Adams' line may therefore be represented by *line 3*—a short-dash blue line.

On January 24 Onis proposed to Adams (Spain ceding Florida) the Mississippi River from its source to its mouth, passing either through the "La Fourche" or the Atchafalaya branch of the Mississippi. The line through the "La Fourche" branch is the same as that proposed by Pizarro, August 17, 1817, and is represented by *line 5*—a short-dash red line. The alternative line through the Atchafalaya branch would have given to the United States several square miles of territory on the lower Mississippi, as may be seen by reference to the map.

In case this line was not acceptable, Onis offered the following line, Florida remaining in possession of Spain: "the western line of division to be established from the sea at a point between the rivers Carcasa [Calcasieu] and the Mermento, or Mermentao [Mermenton] running thence by Arroyo Hondo, till it crosses the Colorado of Natchitoches [Red River] between that post and Adaes."[22]

The "second line of Onis" is the same as that claimed by Cevallos, April 13, 1805, and is represented by *line 2*—a solid red line.

In July, 1818, giving up the Colorado, Adams made the following proposal to Onis:

... "the Trinity from its mouth to its source, then a line north to the Red River, following the course of that to its source, then crossing to the Rio del Norte [Rio Grande], and following the course of it, or the summit of a chain of mountains northward and parallel to it; there stop, or take a line west to the Pacific" (*Memoirs of John Quincy Adams*, Philadelphia, 1874-1877, Vol. 4, p. 110).

Adams' line along the Trinity and upper Rio Grande to the Pacific Ocean is represented by *line 6*—a long-dash blue line. The alternative proposals of running with the chain of mountains and of stopping at the source of the Rio Grande or opposite thereto are not represented.

On October 24, 1818, Onis proposed to Adams the following line, an extension of his "second line" of January 24, 1818, northward of the Red River:

... "beginning on the Gulf of Mexico, between the rivers Mermento [Mermenton], and Calcasia [Calcasieu], following the Arroyo Hondo, between the Adaes and Natchitoches, crossing the Rio or Red river at the thirty-second degree of latitude, and ninety-third of longitude from London, according to Melish's map, and thence running directly north, crossing the Arkansas, the White, and the Osage rivers, till it strikes the Missouri, and then following the middle of that river to its source" (*Amer. State Papers, Foreign Relations*, Vol. 4, p. 529).

This line is represented by *line 7*—a dot-and-dash red line.

Having decided to give up Texas and to insist on compensation in the Oregon country, Adams on October 31 proposed to Onis the following line:

"Beginning at the mouth of the river Sabine, on the Gulf of Mexico; following the course of said river to the thirty-second degree of latitude ... thence, due north, to the northernmost part of the thirty-third degree of north latitude, and until it strikes the Rio Roxo, or Red river; thence, following the course of the said river to its source, touching the chain of the Snow mountains, in latitude thirty-seven degrees twenty-five minutes north, longitude one hundred and six degrees fifteen minutes west, or thereabouts, as marked on Melish's map; thence to the summit of the said mountains, and following the chain of the same to the forty-first parallel of latitude; thence, following the said parallel of latitude forty-one degrees, to the South sea" (*ibid.*, pp. 530-531). The eastern bank and all the islands in the Sabine River were to belong to the United States, and the western bank to Spain.

This line is represented by *line 8*—a blue line consisting of dashes and x's.

Accepting Adams' line of the Sabine River and the meridian northward thereof to the Red River, Onis, on November 16, proposed to continue this line due northward from the Red River until it intersected the Mississippi River, and thence up that river to its source (*ibid.*, p. 532). This line is represented by *line 9*—a long-dash red line.

After an interruption in the negotiations, Onis, having received new

---

[18] The genesis of this claim may be followed in T. M. Marshall, *History of the Western Boundary of the Louisiana Purchase, 1819-1841*, Berkeley, 1914, pp. 10-14. For a late assertion of it see J. Q. Adams to Luis de Onis, Mar. 12, 1818, in *Amer. State Papers, Foreign Relations*, Vol. 4, Washington, 1834, p. 470.

[19] The limits to the northward of the Red River, Cevallos said, were doubtful and little known, and he proposed that they should be settled by commissioners.

[20] Armstrong and Bowdoin were further instructed to make the boundary the Gaudalupe River instead of the Colorado, "if attainable." The line of the Colorado River was proposed by Talleyrand to Armstrong in 1805 (Henry Adams, *History of the United States*, New York, 1898, Vol. 3, p. 104).

[21] As an alternative to this line Adams proposed to leave the boundary "unsettled for future arrangement."

The Colorado River was proposed by Secretary of State Monroe to Onis in January, 1817 (*Amer. State Papers, Foreign Relations*, Vol. 4, p. 438), and by G. W. Erving to Pizarro in July, 1818 (*ibid.*, p. 517). For the negotiations between Adams and Onis see Marshall, *op. cit.*, pp. 50-63.

[22] *Amer. State Papers, Foreign Relations*, Vol. 4, p. 466. From the Red River the line was to extend "northward to a point to be fixed and laid down by commissioners respectively appointed for the purpose." The Arroyo Hondo was a deep gully or ravine, about eight miles long, between Adaes and Natchitoches, over which passed the road leading to the Sabine River (Amos Stoddard, *Sketches ... of Louisiana*, Philadelphia, 1812, p. 144).

On January 16, 1817, and January 5, 1818, Onis claimed a line which followed the Mermenton River instead of passing between that river and the Calcasieu (*Amer. State Papers, Foreign Relations*, Vol. 4, pp. 438 and 459). This is a variation in the description of the Spanish claim represented by line 2. Onis also maintained that Texas at one time extended to the Mississippi River and that Spain had an "original and indisputable right" to the right bank of that river (*ibid.*, pp. 458-459).

instructions, proposed on January 16, 1819, the following line to the Pacific Ocean: "from the source of the Missouri, westward to the Columbia River, and along the middle thereof to the Pacific Ocean" (*ibid.*, p. 616). This line is represented by *line 10*—a red line consisting of dashes and x's. Whether he expected this line to be joined to that of November 16, 1818, by a line connecting the source of the Mississippi with the source of the Missouri is not clear.

On January 29, 1819, Adams repeated his proposal of October 31, 1818 (*ibid.*, p. 616; for less important proposals and suggestions made by Adams, De Neuville, and President Monroe, see Adams' *Memoirs*, Vol. 4, pp. 234–273).

On February 1 Onis proposed to Adams a line which he described as follows:

"Drawing the boundary line from the Gulf of Mexico, by the river Sabine, as laid down by you, it shall follow the course of that river to its source; thence by the ninety-fourth [ninety-fifth] degree of longitude, to the Red river of Natchitoches and along the same to the ninety-fifth [ninety-sixth] degree; and crossing it at that point, to run by a line due north to the Arkansas, and along it to its source; thence, by a line due west, till it strikes the source of the river San Clemente, or Multnomah, in latitude 41°, and along that river to the Pacific ocean: the whole agreeably to Melish's map" (*Amer. State Papers, Foreign Relations*, Vol. 4, p. 617).

As the source of the Sabine River on Melish's map is on the ninety-fifth meridian, Onis evidently meant ninety-five instead of "ninety-four," and ninety-six instead of "ninety-five." His line of February 1 is represented by *line 11*—a red line consisting of dashes and circles.

On February 6 Adams, in the projet of a treaty sent to Onis, proposed the following line:

"Beginning at the mouth of the river Sabine, on the Gulf of Mexico; following the course of said river to the thirty-second degree of latitude ... thence, due north, to the northernmost part of the thirty-third degree of north latitude, and until it strikes the Rio Roxo, or Red river; thence, following the course of said river, to the northernmost point of the bend between longitude 101° and 102°; thence, by the shortest line, to the southernmost point of the bend of the river Arkansas, between the same degrees of longitude 101° and 102°; thence, following the course of the river Arkansas, to its source, in latitude 41° north; thence, following the same parallel of latitude 41°, to the South sea ... the whole being as laid down in Melish's map of the United States published at Philadelphia, improved to the 1st of January, 1818" (*ibid.*, p. 617).[23]

This line is represented by *line 12*—a blue line consisting of dashes and circles.

On February 9 Onis delivered to Adams the project of a treaty in which the boundary is thus defined:

"The boundary line between the two countries shall begin on the Gulf of Mexico, at the mouth of the river Sabine, in the sea; continuing north, along the middle of that river, to the thirty-second degree of latitude; thence, by a line due north, to the thirty-third degree of latitude, where it strikes the Rio Roxo of Natchitoches (Red river), following the course of the Rio Roxo to the westward, to the one hundredth degree of longitude and thirty-three and one-fourth degree of latitude, where it crosses that river; thence, by a line due north, by the said one hundredth degree of longitude from London, according to Melish's map, till it enters the river Arkansas; thence along the middle of the Arkansas, to the forty-second degree of latitude; thence, a line shall be drawn to the westward, by the same parallel of latitude, to the source of the river San Clemente or Multnomah, following the course of that river to the forty-third degree of latitude; and thence, by a line due west, to the Pacific ocean" (*ibid.*, Vol. 4, pp. 617–618).

This line is represented by *line 13*—a dotted red line. Since the Arkansas River does not extend to the forty-second parallel, the line is drawn due north from the source of the river to the parallel. Thence it is drawn westward along the parallel to a branch of the San Clemente and down this branch to the main stream.

On February 12 President Monroe authorized Adams to accept the one-hundredth meridian and the forty-third parallel, if a better line could not be obtained (Adams' *Memoirs*, Vol. 4, p. 253). Adams, however, was determined to obtain a better line, and on February 13 he sent to Onis a counterproject, which contained the following provision respecting a boundary line:

"The boundary line between the two countries, west of the Mississippi, shall begin on the Gulf of Mexico at the mouth of the river Sabine, in the sea; continuing north, along the western bank of that river, to the thirty-second degree of latitude; thence, by a line due north, to the degree of latitude where it

strikes the Rio Roxo of Natchitoches, or Red river; thence, following the course of the Rio Roxo westward, to the degree of longitude 102° west from London, and 25° from Washington; then, crossing the said Red river, and running thence, by a line due north, to the river Arkansas; thence, following the course of the southern bank of the Arkansas, to its source, in latitude 41° north; and thence, by the parallel of latitude, to the South sea: the whole being as laid down in Melish's map of the United States, published in Philadelphia, improved to the 1st of January, 1818" (*Amer. State Papers, Foreign Relations*, Vol. 4, pp. 619–620).

This line is represented by *line 14*—a dotted blue line. It is less favorable to Spain than line 12.

On February 22, 1819, a "treaty of amity, settlement, and limits" between the United States and Spain was concluded by Adams and Onis, which established the following boundary:

"The boundary line between the two countries, west of the Mississippi, shall begin on the Gulf of Mexico, at the mouth of the river Sabine, in the sea; continuing north, along the western bank of that river, to the thirty-second degree of latitude; thence, by a line due north, to the degree of latitude where it strikes the Rio Roxo of Natchitoches, or Red river; then, following the course of the Rio Roxo westward, to the degree of longitude one hundred west from London, and twenty-three west from Washington; then, crossing the said Red river, and running thence, by a line due north, to the river Arkansas; thence, following the course of the southern bank of the Arkansas, to its source in latitude forty-two degrees north; and thence, by that parallel of latitude, to the South sea: the whole being as laid down in Melish's map of the United States, published at Philadelphia, improved to the 1st of January, 1818. But, if the source of the Arkansas river shall be found to fall north or south of latitude forty-two degrees, then the line shall run from the said source, due south or north, as the case may be, till it meets the said parallel of latitude forty-two degrees; and thence, along the said parallel, to the South sea" (*ibid.*, p. 623; W. M. Malloy, *U. S. Treaties and Conventions*, Washington, 1910–1923, Vol. 2, pp. 1652–1653).

This line is represented by *line 15*—a solid green line.

Texas-Mexican Boundary

[PLATE 95B]

The drainage and projection of this map are taken from the Base Map of the United States (1911), scale 1:7,000,000, published by the U. S. Geological Survey.

Some months elapsed after Texas declared her independence of Mexico on March 2, 1836, before she made a specific statement respecting her boundaries. The first of such statements is to be found in the instructions of W. H. Wharton, Texas minister to the United States, prepared by Stephen F. Austin, Secretary of State, and dated November 18, 1836. This is as follows:

"We claim and consider that we have possession to the Rio Bravo del Norte [Rio Grande]. Taking this as the basis, the boundary of Texas would be as follows. Beginning at the mouth of said River on the Gulf of Mexico, thence up the middle thereof, following its main channel, including the Islands to its most northerly Source, thence in a direct line to the United States boundary under the treaty of De Onis at the head of Arkansas river, thence down said river and following the United States line as fixed by the said De Onis treaty to the Gulf of Mexico at the mouth of Sabine, thence Southwardly along the Shore of said Gulf to the place of beginning" (*Diplomatic Correspondence of the Republic of Texas*, Part I, in *Ann. Rept. Amer. Hist. Assn.*, Washington, 1907, Vol. 2, p. 132).

The part of this line forming the Texas-Mexican boundary is represented by *line 1*—a solid blue line.

Austin's further instructions authorized him, in case it appeared that insistence on the line described above would cause serious embarrassments and delays, to accept a line more favorable to Mexico. This is described as follows:

"Beginning on the West of the Gulf of Mexico, half way between the mouth of the Bravo [Rio Grande] and the inlet of Corpus Christi, which is the main outlet of the Nueces River and bay into the Gulf, thence in a Northwestwardly direction following the dividing ridge of high land that divides the waters of the Nueces river and bay, from those of the river Bravo to the hills or mountains in which the main branch of the said Nueces River has its Source, and thence following said ridge or chain of mountains westerly so as to strike the River Puerco or Pecos five leagues above its mouth ... From the place where the line will strike the Puerco it is to follow the ridge or mountain that divides its waters from those of Rio Bravo, and to continue along said mountains above the head of said Puerco or Pecos to the United States line, at the head of the Arkansas River" (*ibid.*, p. 133).

Austin's second line is represented by *line 2*—a short-dash blue line.

On December 19 the Texas Congress approved an act that defined the boundaries of the new republic as follows:

"Beginning at the mouth of the Sabine river, and running west along the Gulf of Mexico three leagues from land, to the mouth of the Rio Grande, thence

---

[23] On February 3 De Neuville, the French minister in Washington, who took an active interest in the negotiations, proposed to Adams "the course of the Red River to the one hundredth degree of longitude from London, then a line north to the Arkansas, then to the source of that river, thence to the Multnomah, following its course to latitude forty-three, and on that parallel of latitude to the South sea" (Adams' *Memoirs*, Vol. 4, p. 244).

up the principal stream of said river to its source, thence due north to the forty-second degree of north latitude, thence along the boundary line as defined in the treaty between the United States and Spain to the beginning" (*Laws of Republic of Texas*, Vol. 1, Houston, 1838, pp. 133 and 134).

The line of the Texas Congress is represented by *line 3*—a dot-and-dash blue line.

On February 20, 1839, the secretary of state of Texas instructed Barnard E. Bee, envoy to Mexico, to insist on the boundaries as defined in the act of December 19, 1836; and on August 9, 1839, James Treat, and on March 22, 1841, James Webb, envoys of Texas to Mexico, received similar instructions.[24] The line of the Texas envoys is represented by *line 3*.

The "Boundary of Texas, 1816," shown in black on the map, is derived, through copies, from an official map of Mexico of about that year (G. P. Garrison, *Westward Extension, 1841–1850*, New York, 1906 (American Nation Ser., Vol. 17), pp. 104–105 and map). According to this line the boundary of Texas on the southwest near the Gulf of Mexico was the Nueces River. During the years immediately preceding the revolution of 1835–1836 it was generally understood that Texas was bounded on the southwest by that river (*Senate Doc. No. 20, 24th Cong., 2nd Sess.*, 1836–1837, p. 13; *Texas State Hist. Assn. Quart.*, Vol 8, Austin, 1905, p. 233; H. S. Tanner's maps of Texas (1830, 1836), compiled by Stephen F. Austin).

Chamizal Tract

[PLATE 95C]

The drainage and projection of this map are taken from the "treaty map" (1911) of the Mexican-American International Boundary Commission. The channel of the Rio Grande is that of September, 1897.

The Treaty of Guadalupe Hidalgo (1848) and the Gadsden Treaty (1853) provided that the "middle" of the Rio Grande and of the Colorado River should be the boundary line (W. M. Malloy, *U. S. Treaties and Conventions*, Washington, 1910–1923, Vol. 1, pp. 1109–1110 and 1122). Because of changes in the location of the channel of these rivers, and especially in that of the Rio Grande, the location of the boundary line at many points became uncertain. In 1884 the United States and Mexico concluded a convention respecting the boundary along these two rivers, in which it was agreed that the following principles should be applied to shifting channels: (1) when the change in channel is caused by "slow and gradual erosion and deposit of alluvium" the line shifts and follows the channel; (2) in the case of any other change, "wrought by the force of the current," the line does not shift, but continues to follow the old channel (*ibid.*, pp. 1159–1160). In 1889 the two countries concluded a convention establishing an international boundary commission which was authorized to settle questions of difference arising out of changes in the channels of the two rivers (*ibid.*, p. 1167). The American commissioner was Colonel Anson Mills, and the Mexican commissioner, in 1896, F. J. Osorno. One of the first cases that came before the commission, which was organized in 1894, was the Chamizal case. This involved the international title to El Chamizal, a tract of 630 acres, constituting part of the site of El Paso, Texas, and lying on the north side of the channel of the Rio Grande as it now runs, but on the south side of the river as it ran in 1852 when surveyed by Emory and Salazar of the Mexican-American Boundary Commission constituted under a provision of the Treaty of Guadalupe Hidalgo. After considering the case for nearly two years the commissioners disagreed. American Commissioner Mills expressed the opinion that the change in the location of the channel of the Rio Grande had been slow and gradual and that the present (1896) channel of the river was the boundary line. Mexican Commissioner Osorno expressed the opinion that the change or changes had been sudden and violent and that the old channel of 1852 was the boundary line (*Chamizal Arbitration*, Washington, 1911, *Case of the United States*, pp. 15–18). The line claimed by Mills is represented by *line 1*—a solid blue line, and the line claimed by Osorno by *line 2*—a solid red line.

Negotiations begun with a view to effecting a settlement of the Chamizal case failed in 1898. More than ten years later negotiations were renewed. These resulted in the convention of 1910, which provided that the case should be referred to the Mexican-American International Boundary Commission, after that commission had been enlarged by the addition of a presiding commissioner, who should be a "Canadian jurist" (Malloy, *op. cit., Supplement*, 1913, pp. 91–94). The commission thus enlarged consisted of General Anson Mills, F. B. Puga, commis-

sioner for Mexico, and Eugene Lafleur, of Montreal, Canada. As in 1896, Mills was of the opinion that the present channel of the Rio Grande was the boundary line, and Puga agreed with the position taken by his predecessor, Osorno. Yielding his opinion, however, he united with Lafleur in the award, which was as follows:

"The international title to the portion of the Chamizal tract lying between the middle of the bed of the Rio Grande, as surveyed by Emory and Salazar in 1852, and the middle of the bed of the said river as it existed before the flood of 1864, is in the United States of America; and the international title to the balance of the said Chamizal tract is in the United States of Mexico" (*Chamizal Arbitration, Award in Chamizal Case*, pp. 35–36).

Since no one has located the Rio Grande "as it existed before the flood of 1864," the line of the award cannot be shown. General Mills dissented from the award. He said, "nobody knows and nobody ever will know" the course of the river in 1864 (*Hearings before Committee on Foreign Affairs relative to International (Water) Boundary Commission, United States and Mexico*, Washington, 1914, p. 6). The Chamizal case is still pending (1931).

Elimination of Bancos

[PLATE 95D]

The drainage and projection of this map are taken from the Index Map (1911), no. 2, found in the *Proceedings of the International Boundary Commission, United States and Mexico* (Washington, 1910), "American Section, Elimination of Fifty-seven Old Bancos," first series.

"Bancos" may be briefly defined as small tracts of land in the valleys of the Rio Grande and the Colorado which are isolated by the river when it cuts through a sharp bend and forms a new channel. The making of a bend is slow and gradual, and the cutting through sudden and violent. According to the first of the principles of the convention of 1884 (see above) the boundary line follows the channel when the bend is being made, and according to the second principle it remains with the old channel when the bend is cut through. Since the application of these principles to bancos was inconvenient, the United States and Mexico in 1905 agreed to a convention for the elimination of bancos. This provided that the boundary line should follow the "deepest channel" and that bancos on the right bank of the river should belong to Mexico and on the left bank to the United States. From this provision, however, were excepted bancos having an area of over 250 hectares or a population of over 200 souls (Malloy, *op. cit.*, Vol. 1, pp. 1199–1202).

Plate 95D shows a section of the lower Rio Grande in which the bancos are most numerous. *Line 1*—a solid yellow line—represents the boundary, as accurately as it can be ascertained, before the bancos were eliminated. *Line 2*—a solid green line—represents the boundary after the bancos were eliminated (*Proc. International Boundary Commission, United States and Mexico*, etc., Washington, 1910, first series, index map, no. 2). In 1914 eighty-five bancos had been eliminated (*Hearings before Committee on Foreign Affairs relative to International Water Boundary Commission, United States and Mexico*, Washington, 1914, p. 11).

Alaska-Canadian Boundary

[PLATE 96A]

The drainage and projection of this map are taken chiefly from the Index Map of the Alaskan Boundary Tribunal's *Atlas of Award* (1904), published by the United States government. Southward of the southern limit of the Index Map, about latitude 54° 15′ N., the islands and coast line are derived from the Map of British Columbia (1911), published by the Department of the Interior of Canada.

The convention ceding Alaska, concluded by Russia and the United States on March 30, 1867, described the eastern and southeastern boundary of the territory ceded by quoting from the British-Russian convention of 1825. The description was as follows:

"The eastern limit is the line of demarcation between the Russian and the British possessions in North America, as established by the convention between Russia and Great Britain of February 28–16, 1825, and described in Articles III and IV of said convention in the following terms:

" 'Commencing from the southernmost point of the island called Prince of Wales Island, which point lies in the parallel of 54 degrees, 40 minutes, north latitude, and between the 131st and 133d degrees of west longitude (meridian of Greenwich), the said line shall ascend to the north along the channel called Portland channel, as far as the point of the continent where it strikes the 56th degree of north latitude; from this last mentioned point, the line of demarcation shall follow the summit of the mountains, situated parallel to the coast, as far as the point of intersection of the 141st degree of west longitude (of the same meridian); and finally, from the said point of intersection, the said meridian line of the 141st degree, in its prolongation as far as the Frozen ocean.

---

[24] *Diplomatic Correspondence of the Republic of Texas*, Part II, *Ann. Rept. in Amer. Hist. Assn.*, Washington, 1908, Vol. 2, pp. 432–433, 471, and 733–734. Before submitting the line of the Texas Congress as an ultimatum Treat was "to feel the authorities of Mexico" by proposing a line drawn from the mouth of the Rio Grande up that river to the Paso del Norte, thence due west to the Gulf of California, and thence along the southern shore of that gulf to the Pacific Ocean (*ibid.*, p. 471).

" 'IV. With reference to the line of demarcation laid down in the preceding article, it is understood—

" '1st That the island called Prince of Wales Island shall belong wholly to Russia' (now, by this cession, to the United States).

" '2d That whenever the summit of the mountains which extend in a direction parallel to the coast from the 56th degree of north latitude to the point of intersection of the 141st degree of west longitude shall prove to be at the distance of more than ten marine leagues from the ocean, the limit between the British possessions and the line of coast which is to belong to Russia as above mentioned (that is to say, the limit to the possessions ceded by this convention) shall be formed by a line parallel to the winding of the coast, and which shall never exceed the distance of ten marine leagues therefrom.' " (W. M. Malloy, *U. S. Treaties and Conventions*, Washington, 1910-1923, Vol. 2, pp. 1521-1522.) The Portland Channel is now generally called the Portland Canal.

As this line had not been surveyed or marked, and as the region where it lay was largely unexplored, doubts inevitably arose as to its location. The determination of the line of the 141st meridian offered little ground for dispute; but it was quite otherwise with the determination of the line that lay to the southeastward thereof. In respect to the boundary between the 56th parallel and the 141st meridian the convention of 1825 contained alternative provisions, and it was doubtful which should be applied. Whether this boundary should follow a line of mountains, or the ten-marine-league line, or partly one and partly the other could not be determined until the coast region had been carefully surveyed. In case a mountain line was followed it was necessary to determine what mountain line, and such determination was rendered difficult by the absence of a "defined and continuous range" and the presence of "numerous isolated peaks and short ridges running in different directions" (*Proc. Alaskan Boundary Tribunal*, Washington, 1904, Vol. 1, Part II, pp. 85-86). In case a ten-marine-league line was followed the method of locating it had to be decided upon, and there were not a few possibilities. The width of the "lisière" or fringe of coast might be measured from tidewater. It might be measured at all places from the mainland coast of the ocean, or it might be differently measured at the places where the "lisière" was indented by large inlets. At such places it might be measured (1) from the line marking the general trend of the coast, (2) from the line separating the waters of the ocean from territorial waters, or (3) from the heads of the inlets (*ibid.*, Vol. 1, Part I, pp. 30-31). Since the Portland Canal did not extend to the 56th parallel, as was understood by the convention of 1825, the location of the line between the canal and the parallel was doubtful. Finally, the identity of the lower part of the Portland Canal was open to question.

Settlers early established themselves near the mouth of the Stikine River, and as a result the ascertaining of the boundary in that quarter became a matter of considerable importance. In 1877 Joseph Hunter, representing the Canadian government, located this boundary as best he could, and in the following year the United States and Great Britain adopted Hunter's line as a temporary and provisional boundary. It began at Mt. Whipple, crossed the Stikine River 24.74 miles from its mouth, and thence proceeded on a course a little west of north toward the summit of the mountains (*ibid.*, Vol. 3, Part I, pp. 34-37, Part II, pp. 299-305 and 319-321; *British Atlas*, map 26). It is represented by *line 1*—a sort-dash yellow line.

With a view to the settlement of the Alaska-Canadian boundary a joint survey of the region in dispute was made in 1892-1896. Equipped with the information thus obtained, the Joint High Commission of 1898-1899, constituted for the purpose of adjusting pending questions of difference between the United States and Canada, attempted to settle the boundary dispute but failed. The British High Commissioners, Sir Julian Pauncefote and Sir Louis Davies, presented to the commission a map showing the line then claimed by Great Britain.[25] The line claimed by Great Britain is represented by *line 2*—a dot-and-dash red line.

On the discovery of gold in the valley of the Yukon River, in 1896, a considerable commerce was attracted there by way of the Lynn Canal, and the ascertaining of the boundary in the region of the canal became highly desirable. As a temporary measure the United States and Great Britain, on October 20, 1899, concluded a *modus vivendi* fixing a provisional boundary near the head of the canal. This is officially described as follows, omitting references to maps:

"In the region of the Dalton Trail, a line beginning at the peak West of Porcupine Creek ... thence running to the Klehini (or Klaheela) River in the direction of the Peak north of that river ... thence following the high or right bank of the said Klehini river to the junction thereof with the Chilkat River, a mile and a half, more or less, north of Klukwan ... and from said junction to the summit of the peak East of the Chilkat river ...

"On the Dyea and Skagway Trails, the summits of the Chilcoot and White Passes" (Malloy, *op. cit.*, Vol. 1, pp. 777-778).

This provisional boundary consists of three lines: Klehini River line, Chilkoot Pass line, and White Pass line. The last two are quite short. These lines are represented on the map by *lines 3*—solid yellow lines.[26] On January 24, 1903, a convention for the settlement of the Alaskan boundary was signed in Washington by John Hay, secretary of state, and Sir Michael H. Herbert, British ambassador to the United States. This provided for a tribunal of six "impartial jurists of repute," three be appointed by the United States and three by Great Britain. The American members were Elihu Root, Henry Cabot Lodge, and George Turner, and the British members, Baron Alverstone, Sir Louis A. Jetté, and Allen B. Aylesworth.

Since by the terms of the convention of 1903 a series of questions was submitted to the tribunal, the cases presented to the tribunal and its decisions were largely in the form of answers to these questions. The most important questions may be briefly stated as follows: (1) at what point does the line begin, (2) what canal is the Portland Canal, (3) what is the course of the line between the starting point and the Portland Canal, (4) what is the course of the line between the head of Portland Canal and the 56th parallel, (5) does the line cross the large inlets or run around them, and (6) what are the mountains referred to in the convention of 1825 (Malloy, *op. cit.*, Vol. 1, pp. 787-792; *Proc. Alaskan Boundary Tribunal*, Vol. 1, Part I, pp. 30-31).

The United States held that the southern part of the Portland Canal lay to the southward of Wales and Pearse islands, that the line ran around the large inlets, and that the mountains referred to in the convention of 1825 did not exist within ten marine leagues of the coast. It claimed that the boundary

... "began at Cape Muzon and ran thence in an easterly direction to the entrance to Portland Canal between Wales and Compton islands; thence northeasterly along the center of Portland Canal to a point equidistant from Pearse Island and Ramsden Point; thence northerly along the center of Portland Canal until the line touched the mainland at the head of Portland Canal; thence upon the same course continued to the 56th parallel of north latitude; thence northwesterly, always 10 marine leagues from tide water, around the head of Lynn Canal; thence westerly, still following the sinuosities of the coast at a distance therefrom of 10 marine leagues, until the line intersected the 141st meridian of longitude west of Greenwich" (*ibid.*, Vol. 1, Part II, pp. 102-106).

This line is represented by *line 4*—a solid blue line.[27]

Great Britain held that the southern part of the Portland Canal lay northward of Pearse, Wales, Sitklan, and Kanagunut islands, that the line crossed the large inlets, and that the mountains referred to did exist within ten marine leagues of the coast. She claimed a line beginning at Cape Muzon, and, passing to the northward of the islands named above, up the Portland Canal to its head, thence westerly to the point where the fifty-sixth parallel crossed the crest of the mountains identified by her as the mountains referred to in the convention of 1825, and along the crest of these mountains to the one hundred forty-first meridian (*Proc. Alaskan Boundary Tribunal*, Vol. 3, Part I, pp. 47-83). This line is represented by *line 5*—a solid red line. It is taken from the *British Atlas*, map 37, and from the *United States Atlas*, map 26.

The official British map presented to the tribunal shows, in addition to the line described above, two alternative lines, one at Lynn Canal and the other at Glacier Bay. These were the lines claimed by Great Britain in case the tribunal decided that it was necessary to apply at these places the ten-marine-league provision (*Proc. Alaskan Boundary Tribunal*, Vol. 3, Part II, p. 402). These lines are represented on the map by *lines 6*—short-dash red lines (*ibid.*, *British Atlas*, map 37).

The tribunal, its vote usually being four to two (the minority consisting of the Canadian members), held that the Portland Canal passes between Sitklan and Wales islands and to the northward of Wales and Pearse islands, that the line passed around the large inlets, and that the mountains referred to in the convention of 1825 did exist within ten

[25] *Proc. Alaskan Boundary Tribunal*, Vol. 3, Part I, p. 43; Vol. 4, Part I, p. 86; Part II, p. 123; *United States Atlas*, map 27. At one of the conferences the British commissioners proposed a "conventional boundary, by which Canada should receive, by cession or perpetual grant, Pyramid Harbor on Lynn Canal, and a strip of land connecting it with Canadian territory to the northwest, and the remaining boundary line to be drawn in the main conformable to the contention of the United States" (John W. Foster, "The Alaskan Boundary," *Natl. Geog. Mag.*, Vol. 10, 1899, p. 455; a more detailed account of this proposal could not be found).

[26] These lines are drawn according to a map prepared by the U. S. Coast and Geodetic Survey in 1899 to accompany a copy of the *modus vivendi* (see *House Doc. No. 1, 56th Cong., 1st Sess.*, 1899-1900, p. 330). The length of the Chilkoot Pass line and that of the White Pass line are somewhat exaggerated. For the provisional lines as surveyed and marked by Commissioners W. F. King and O. H. Tittmann see the joint report of the commissioners published by the Department of the Interior of Canada in 1901.

[27] Line 4 is copied from map 2, *United States Atlas*. It is there drawn by connecting points situated ten marine leagues (about 34½ statute miles) from the ocean or the heads of inlets. The line as drawn in the *United States Atlas* did not originate with the Alaskan Boundary Tribunal, for it may be found on maps of the U. S. Coast and Geodetic Survey as early as April, 1898. A somewhat more sinuous line would also satisfy the description of the line claimed by the United States (see, for instance, the map accompanying Robert Lansing, "The Questions Settled by the Award of the Alaskan Boundary Tribunal," *Bull. Amer. Geog. Soc.*, Vol. 36, 1904, opp. p. 128).

marine leagues of the coast. It decided that the line began at Cape Muzon and passed up the Portland Canal, as defined above, to its head, thence northerly to the fifty-sixth parallel, and thence by a mountain line to the one hundred forty-first meridian. The whole of the line was laid down upon the maps of the tribunal, with the exception of about 120 miles of the mountain line situated, approximately, between the parallels of 57° 13′ and 58° 44′ N. The evidence before the tribunal was insufficient to enable it to identify the mountains in this region (*Proc. Alaskan Boundary Tribunal*, Vol. 1, Part I, pp. 31–32). In 1905 notes were exchanged in Washington providing for the filling up of this gap (Malloy, *op. cit.*, Vol. 1, pp. 796–798).

The line of the award and the notes is represented by *line 7*—a solid green line (*Proc. Alaskan Boundary Tribunal, Atlas of Award*, index map; International Boundary Commission, organized under Boundary Treaty of 1908, MS. maps). The part completed in accordance with the notes lies between "T" and "P."

The mountain line of the tribunal is a zigzag line joining peaks and lies between the mountain line claimed by Great Britain and the ten-marine-league line claimed by the United States. It follows Hunter's line (line 1) and touches two of the provisional lines of 1899 (Chilkoot and White Pass lines) and passes to the northward and westward of the third (Klehini River line). The length of the boundary from Cape Muzon to the 141st meridian is about 887 miles.

Horseshoe Reef

[PLATE 96B]

The drainage and projection of this map are taken from the New York, Buffalo Topographical Quadrangle (1901), published by the U. S. Geological Survey.

The boundary line from the intersection of the forty-fifth parallel with the St. Lawrence River to the western end of Lake Superior, "the river and lake line," is described in the Treaty of Peace of 1783 as follows:

... "thence along the middle of said river [St. Lawrence] into Lake Ontario, through the middle of said lake until it strikes the communication by water between that lake and Lake Erie; thence along the middle of said communication into Lake Erie, through the middle of said lake until it arrives at the water communication between that lake and Lake Huron; thence along the middle of said water communication into the Lake Huron; thence through the middle of said lake to the water communication between that lake and Lake Superior[28]; thence through Lake Superior northward of the Isles Royal and Phelipeaux to the Long Lake" (W. M. Malloy, *U. S. Treaties and Conventions*, Washington, 1910–1923, Vol. 1, p. 587; see also p. 55, above).

Soon after the signing of the treaty doubts arose as to the location of the middle of the river, lakes, and water communications mentioned and as to the ownership of certain islands therein that lay near the boundary line. Provision for the settlement of these doubtful points was accordingly made in the Treaty of Ghent of 1814. The sixth article of that treaty authorized the appointment of two commissioners to determine the boundary and to settle the ownership of the islands as far westward as the water communication between Lake Huron and Lake Superior; and the seventh article authorized the commissioners under the sixth article to fix the boundary farther westward (*ibid.*, pp. 616–617). The commissioner for the United States under the sixth article was Peter B. Porter, of New York. The first commissioner for Great Britain was John Ogilvy, of Montreal. He was succeeded some months after his death in 1819 by Anthony Barclay, of Annapolis, Nova Scotia, a son of Thomas Barclay. The commission was in session during the years 1816–1822 (J. B. Moore, *History and Digest of the International Arbitrations*, etc., Washington, 1898, Vol. 1, pp. 163–166). In its final report, dated June 18, 1822, it described the boundary that it fixed and in a series of twenty-five maps laid it down with considerable precision (Malloy, *op. cit.*, Vol. 1, pp. 620–623; copies of the maps are in Moore, *op. cit.*, Vol. 6, maps 1–25). The line of the commission near the present Horseshoe Reef Lighthouse, opposite the city of Buffalo, N. Y., is represented by *line 1*—a short-dash green line (*ibid.*, maps 16 and 17).

In 1850, after a local survey had disclosed that Horseshoe Reef was the most eligible site for a lighthouse at the mouth of the Niagara River, the United States and Great Britain signed a protocol providing for the cession to the United States of "such portion of the Horseshoe Reef as may be found requisite for the intended lighthouse," and in 1851 the cession was made (Malloy, *op. cit.*, Vol. 1, pp. 663–664). No provision for changing the boundary line at this point was made until one was included in the boundary treaty of 1908. The fourth article of that

treaty, which authorized the International Waterways Commission to reëstablish the location of the boundary from the intersection of the forty-fifth parallel with the St. Lawrence River to the mouth of Pigeon River, directed the commission to make such deviation from the old line as might be required by the cession of 1851 (*ibid.*, pp. 821–822). The line fixed by this commission is represented by *line 2*—a solid green line (Dept. of State, Report of International Waterways Commission, Apr. 29, 1915, p. 79; Maps of International Waterways Commission, 1913, sheet 12).

San Juan Water Boundary

[PLATE 96C]

The drainage and projection of this map are taken from the Map of the State of Washington (1909), published by the U. S. General Land Office.

The Buchanan-Pakenham Treaty of 1846 called for a line extending from the forty-ninth parallel southerly through the "middle of the channel which separates the continent from Vancouver's Island" (see p. 61, above). Soon after the treaty was signed a dispute arose over the location of the middle of the channel. No effective steps toward settling it were taken until 1856, when provision was made for the appointment of two boundary commissioners. The American commissioner was Archibald Campbell, of New York, and the British commissioner, James C. Prevost, a captain in the Royal Navy. During 1857 the commission held several formal meetings and after disagreeing adjourned finally on December 3 of that year (J. B. Moore, *History and Digest of the International Arbitrations*, etc., Washington, 1898, Vol. 1, pp. 213–214).

Commissioner Campbell maintained that the line should pass through Canal de Haro, and Commissioner Prevost, that it should pass through Rosario Strait (*Senate Ex. Doc. No. 29, 40th Cong., 2nd Sess.*, 1867–1868, pp. 48–49).[29] On November 24 Prevost proposed a compromise line, which he described in the following words, addressed to Campbell:

"In contemplating your view that all the channels between the continent and Vancouver's Island, from the termination of the Gulf of Georgia to the eastern termination of the Straits of Fuca, are but a continuation of the channel of the Gulf of Georgia, I see a way by which I can in part meet your views without any gross violation of the terms of the treaty. I am willing to regard the space above described as one channel, having so many different passages through it, and I will agree to a boundary line being run through the middle of it, in so far as islands will permit" (*Senate Ex. Doc. No. 29, 40th Cong., 2nd Sess.*, 1867–1868, p. 34).

The line through the Canal de Haro claimed by the United States is represented by *line 1*—a solid blue line; the line through the Rosario Strait claimed by Great Britain by *line 2*—a solid red line; the compromise line of Commissioner Prevost by *line 3*—a short-dash red line.[30]

It should be noted that line 1, which also represents the boundary as finally fixed, is located with more precision than could be done from the description of the claim of the United States, namely, "a line passing through Canal de Haro."

During the years 1859–1872 several attempts were made to settle the dispute. In March and April, 1871, the Joint High Commission, sitting in Washington, held several conferences on this subject, at which the respective claims of the two governments were reasserted. On its failure to reach a settlement the commission included an article in the Treaty of Washington that provided for the submission of the dispute to the "arbitration and award" of the German Emperor (W. M. Malloy, *U. S. Treaties and Conventions*, Washington, 1910–1923, Vol. 1, p. 714). The American case was presented to the emperor by George Bancroft, American minister in Berlin, and the British case by James C. Prevost, at this time a rear admiral. Bancroft claimed the Canal de Haro, and Prevost the Rosario Strait. Agreeing with Bancroft, the emperor decided that the "boundary line between the territories of Her Britannic Majesty and the United States should be drawn through the Haro Channel" (Moore, *op. cit.*, p. 230).

This decision fixed the general course of the line but not its precise position. The latter was settled by a protocol dated March 10, 1873, and signed in Washington by Hamilton Fish, secretary of state, Edward Thornton, British minister, and James C. Prevost, British boundary commissioner (*ibid.*, pp. 231–235). The protocol defined the boundary by means of a chart showing the line and by a description giving courses

---

[28] There is an omission in the description of the treaty that may be supplied by adding the following words after "Lake Superior": "thence along the middle of said water communication into Lake Superior."

[29] As early as 1846 United States officials showed a disposition to claim the Canal de Haro (J. B. Moore, *History and Digest of the International Arbitrations*, etc., Washington, 1898, Vol. 1, pp 213–214). The Canal de Haro is now generally called Haro Strait and the Gulf of Georgia, Georgia Strait.

[30] On April 19, 1871, the British members of the Joint High Commission sitting in Washington proposed a compromise line identical with, or similar to, Prevost's line. The commissioners' line was to run through the "Middle Channel (generally known as the Douglas Channel)" (*House Ex. Doc. No. 1, 43rd Cong., 1st Sess.*, 1873–1874, Part II, p. 405). Since the Middle Channel and the Douglas Channel are represented as different bodies of water, the precise location of the line is in doubt (see map in Moore, *op. cit.*, Vol. 1, p. 231).

and distances. The line established by the award of the emperor and the protocol is represented by *line 1*—a solid blue line (*ibid.*, pp. 231 (map) and 234). The length of the water boundary from the eastern shore of the Gulf of Georgia to the Pacific Ocean is about 149 miles. Under a provision of the boundary treaty of 1908, straight lines were substituted for the curved line in the Gulf of Georgia near the one hundred and twenty-third meridian (Malloy, *op. cit.*, pp. 825–826).

COLONIAL AND STATE BOUNDARY DISPUTES, 1607–1930

[PLATES 97–101]

The maps of this series illustrate the most important disputes between the American colonies and states over their boundaries that occurred during the years 1607–1930. The twenty-one disputes that are illustrated are a selection from more than forty. In making a selection the principal factors considered were the historical importance of the dispute, its magnitude, the length of the period covered by it, the rank of the court or authority that settled it, and the value of the territory, property, and rights involved. Some consideration was also given to the desirability of making the series representative of the several sections of the Union, of the whole period of American history, and of all the varieties of controversy.

The method of representation is the same as that used in illustrating "Negotiations for Peace" and "International Boundary Disputes" (see pp. 52 and 55, above). The lines that were claimed, proposed, or agreed upon are shown in colors on base maps that delineate the drainage, projection, and other geographical features in black. The lines emanating from one of the two disputing colonies or states are in blue, and from the other in red, and the lines agreed upon are in green. Occasionally, however, for the sake of clearness, a black line is used when the rule requires a green one. Explanatory lines and adjacent state boundaries are also in black. Color lines that occupy the same position upon the earth's surface, since they cannot be superimposed, are drawn parallel to each other.

The base maps are made from tracings of the original maps or of reduced or enlarged copies of them. When, as in a few cases, the geographical features of the bases differ so widely from those conceived by the disputants that they affect the illustration of the dispute, attention is called to the fact in the text.

Massachusetts-New Hampshire Boundary

[PLATE 97A]

The drainage, projection, and coast line of this map are taken from the maps of Maine, Vermont and New Hampshire, and Massachusetts, numbers, 6, 7, and 8, found in the *Century Atlas* (1902). The boundary line between New Hampshire and Maine, shown in black, was established in 1740.

The dispute between Massachusetts and New Hampshire over their boundary, which began in the first half of the seventeenth century, soon after the colonies were settled, lasted for more than two centuries. Until 1740 the chief point at issue was the interpretation of the words of the Massachusetts charter of 1629 describing the northern limits of the colony. These words are as follows:

... "all those lands and hereditaments whatsoever, which lye and be within the space of three English myles to the northward of the saide river called Monomack, alias Merrymack, or to the norward of any and every parte thereof ... [and extending] from the Atlantick ... to the south sea" (*Records of ... Massachusetts Bay*, Boston, 1853–1854, Vol. 1, p. 7; see Pl. 42 and p. 26, above).

Massachusetts early construed these words so as to make her northern boundary a parallel passing through a point three miles north of the most northerly part of the Merrimac River.[31] In 1652 two commissioners appointed by Massachusetts, Symon Willard and Edward Johsnon, located the most northerly part of the Merrimac at Aquedahian (now The Weirs), where the river flows out of Lake Winnepesaukee, and reported that the boundary was in the lake, three miles northward of Aquedahian, latitude 43° 43′ 12″ N. In 1654 two other commissioners, Jonas Clarke and Samuel Andrews, located the boundary on the seacoast where it was found to strike Casco Bay near Upper Clapboard Island, a short distance north of the present city of Portland (*ibid.*, Vol. 3, pp. 274, 278, 288, 329, and 361–362). Because of the crude methods of determining latitude then in use the points located by the two sets of commissioners were not on the same parallel, and as a con-

sequence the line fixed by their survey does not run due east and west. The line of the Massachusetts survey of 1652–1654 is represented by *line 1*—a short-dash blue line. This line and all other lines on this map are terminated at the Connecticut River, the western boundary of the state of New Hampshire as finally determined.

The claim of Massachusetts to the line of 1652–1654 was disputed by Gorges and Mason, proprietors of New Hampshire, in petitions to King Charles II, who referred the dispute to his lords chief justices. In 1677 the justices decided that the boundary was not to extend "further northwards along the river Merrimack than three English miles," that it was to extend as far as the river goes, and that thence it was to follow westward an imaginary line (*ibid.*, Vol. 5, pp. 108–116; *New Hampshire State Papers*, Vol. 1, Concord, 1867, pp. 321–339; Vol. 19, Manchester, 1891, pp. 303–307). In the same year, 1677, this decision was confirmed by the King in Council. Since it is somewhat ambiguous and is open to varying interpretations it is not represented on the map.

The decision of 1677 put a quietus to the claim of Massachusetts that her northern boundary followed a parallel of latitude from the seacoast westward. The dispute over the eastern part of the boundary was henceforth concerned with the location of a line in respect to the Merrimac River. Beginning with 1693, several attempts were made to settle the controversy by means of commissioners representing each colony (*ibid.*, Vol. 19, pp. 180–232). After repeated failures, the king in 1737 appointed a commission of twenty men, chosen from the councils of New York, New Jersey, Nova Scotia, and Rhode Island, to determine the boundary (*ibid.*, pp. 274–282). On August 1 of 1737 the commission held its first meeting at Hampton, N. H., four commissioners being present, and on the same day a committee of the General Court of New Hampshire laid before it a statement of the claims of that colony. The line claimed is thus described:

... "the Southern boundary of Said Province should begin at the end of three Miles North from the Middle of the Channel of Merrimack River where it runs into the Atlantick Ocean, and from thence should run on a Straight Line West up into the Main Land (towards the South Sea) until it meets with His Majesty's other Governments" (*ibid.*, pp. 283–284).

This line is represented by *line 2*—a solid red line.

The committee of the General Court of Massachusetts, which presented the case of that colony, claimed the following line:

... "beginning at the Sea three English miles North from the black Rocks So called, at the Mouth of the River Merrimack as it Emptied it Self into the Sea Sixty years agoe, thence running Parralel with the River as farr Northward as the Crotch or parting of the River, thence due North as far as a certain Tree Commonly known for more than Seventy Years past, by the name of Indicots [Endicott's] Tree, Standing three English miles Northward of said Crotch or parting of Merrimack River, And from thence due West to the South Sea" (*ibid.*, p. 291).[32]

This line is represented by *line 3*—a solid blue line.

Evading the issue, the commission rendered a decision in alternative form. It decided that if the Massachusetts charter of 1691 granted to Massachusetts all the lands granted by the charter of 1629 the line (no. 3) claimed by Massachusetts was the true boundary, and if it did not, the line (no. 2) claimed by New Hampshire was the true boundary (*ibid.*, pp. 391–392).[33] The charter of 1691 omitted the words "or to the norword of any and every parte thereof," found in the first charter (see above). Both colonies were dissatisfied with this decision and appealed to the king. In 1740 the King in Council decided that the boundary was

... "a similar Curve line pursueing the course of Merrimack River at three miles distance on the North side thereof, beginning at the Atlantick Ocean and ending at a Point due North of a place ... call'd Pantucket [Pawtucket] Falls, and a strait Line drawn from thence due West cross the said River till it meets with his Majestys other Governments" (*ibid.*, p. 478; W. L. Grant and J. Munro, *Acts of Privy Council, Colonial Series*, Vol. 3, 1720-1745, Hereford, 1910, p. 599).

Astounded at the decision which gave New Hampshire a much better line than she had asked for, and which deprived Massachusetts of thirty or more towns or parts of towns settled by her, the Massachusetts legislature took no part in surveying the new line. With money appropriated by New Hampshire, Jonathan Belcher, governor of both provinces, caused a survey to be made by George Mitchell from the ocean to a point three miles north of Pawtucket Falls, since known as the "Bound-

---

[31] In 1638 the Massachusetts General Court voted to pay Nathaniel Woodward and John Stretton "to lay out the line 3 mile northward of the most northermost part of Merrimack" (*Records of Massachusetts Bay*, Boston, 1853-1854, Vol. 1, pp. 237 and 261). Precisely what Woodward and Stretton did is not known (see, however, *Report of Commission for Protection of Endicott Rock*, Concord, 1893, p. 7).

[32] The New Hampshire committee had no knowledge of "Indicots Tree" (*ibid.*, p. 294). "The Crotch" is the junction of the two streams that form the Merrimac River southwest of Lake Winnepesaukee.

[33] The decision was signed by seven members—one from New York, three from New Jersey, and three from Rhode Island.

ary Pine," and another survey by Richard Hazzen from this point to the Hudson River (*Report of New Hampshire Boundary Commissioners*, Manchester, 1887, p. 6; *Mass. House Doc. No. 150*, 1887, p. 3; *New Hampshire State Papers*, Vol. 19, pp. 484–505). The line decided upon by the King in Council and surveyed by Mitchell and Hazzen is represented by *line 4*—a solid green line (for Mitchell's and Hazzen's maps see *Rept. N. H. Commissioners*, Manchester, 1889).

In time Massachusetts accepted the Mitchell-Hazzen line, and New Hampshire became dissatisfied with it. New Hampshire discovered that Hazzen made an allowance for the variation of the compass in excess of what it should have been and that consequently his line ran somewhat north of west instead of due west. She raised objections also to Mitchell's line and proposed that in place of it a new line should be run conforming more closely to the decree of 1740. In 1825–1827 commissioners attempted to settle the dispute but failed, and little further was done for many years (*ibid.*, 1887, pp. 7–8; *Mass. House Doc. No. 490*, 1889, pp. 59–64). Massachusetts monumented the line in 1827. Finally, in 1885, it was agreed that each state should appoint three commissioners "for the purpose of ascertaining and establishing the true jurisdictional boundary line." The commissioners were duly appointed, but upwards of a decade elapsed before they succeeded in settling the dispute. The Massachusetts commissioners claimed the Mitchell-Hazzen line as then monumented. The New Hampshire commissioners claimed that east of the Boundary Pine the true boundary was a line every part of which lay three miles due north of the corresponding part of the Merrimac River and that west of the Boundary Pine the true boundary was the true parallel of the Boundary Pine (*Rept. N. H. Commissioners*, 1887, p. 8; 1889, p. 4; Concord, 1895, p. 11; *Mass. House Doc. No. 490*, 1889, p. 4). The claim of Massachusetts is represented by line 4, and of New Hampshire by *line 5*—a short-dash red line.

As the two claims were irreconcilable, and an end of the troublesome controversy was desired, the New Hampshire commissioners finally, in 1888, entered into an agreement with the Massachusetts commissioners to recommend to their respective legislatures the adoption of the Mitchell line as then monumented (with a few unimportant exceptions). In 1894 they entered into a similar agreement respecting the Hazzen line (*Rept. N. H. Commissioners*, 1889, pp. 4–10, Concord, 1895, pp. 12–30).[34] The two legislatures accepted the first agreement in 1889–1890, and the second in 1895 (*New Hampshire Laws*, 1889, p. 143; 1895, p. 488; *Massachusetts Acts and Resolves*, 1890, pp. 557–558; 1895, pp. 688–689). The line of the agreement is represented by *line 4*—a solid green line.

New York-New Hampshire and Vermont Boundary
[PLATE 97B]

The drainage and projection of this map are taken from the Map of New Hampshire and Vermont (1914) and the Map of New York (1913), published by the U. S. Geological Survey. The northern boundary of Massachusetts, shown in black, was established in 1740 (see p. 72, above). The boundary northward of the disputed territory is the boundary established by the Royal Proclamation of 1763 and surveyed by Vallentine and Collins in 1771–1777, the present boundary between the United States and Canada (see p. 61, above).

The dispute illustrated by this map arose in 1749. At first the disputants were New York and New Hampshire. Later Vermont took the place of New Hampshire. New York claimed the Connecticut River, basing her claim on the grant to the Duke of York in 1664, of "all the Land from the West side of the Connecticut [River] to the East side of Delaware Bay" (E. B. O'Callaghan, *Documents Relative to Colonial History of the State of New York*, Vol. 2, Albany, 1858, p. 296; see Pl. 43A and p. 29, above). This claim is represented by *line 1*—a solid blue line. In 1674, after the temporary occupation of New York by the Dutch, the grant of New York was again made to the duke.

New Hampshire claimed a line lying about twenty miles eastward of the Hudson River and a territory extending as far westward as that of Connecticut and Massachusetts (*ibid.*, Vol. 4, 1851, pp. 533, 538, and 554). More specifically than this she did not describe the boundary claimed by her. It is represented approximately by the line finally established, *line 2*—a solid red line.

The dispute over jurisdiction between the two colonies was brought to an end in 1764 by an Order of the King in Council establishing the boundary on "the Western Banks of the River Connecticut, from where it enters the Province of the Massachusetts Bay, as far North as the forty-fifth Degree of Northern Latitude" (*ibid.*, p. 574). This line is represented by line 1.

The Order of the King in Council of 1764 ended the dispute between New York and New Hampshire over jurisdiction, but it did not end the dispute that had arisen over the ownership of lands granted by New Hampshire within the disputed area. New York claimed that the order of the king annulled the grants and that the titles of the grantees were therefore invalid. The grantees claimed that the order did not affect the validity of their titles. This dispute led, in 1777, to the formation of the state of Vermont and to the renewal of the old dispute over jurisdiction, Vermont taking the place of New Hampshire as one of the disputants. New York again claimed the Connecticut River as her eastern boundary (line 1), and Vermont claimed as her western boundary the line formerly claimed by New Hampshire (approximately line 2). Vermont first stated her claim, "a twenty mile line from Hudson's river," in her declaration of independence of 1777 (William Slade, *Vermont State Papers*, Middlebury, Vt., 1823, p. 70).[35]

In February, 1781, the Vermont legislature voted to make a more extensive claim of territory and to establish as a western boundary the Hudson River north of its point of intersection with a projection of the northern boundary of Massachusetts, and the meridian of its source as far north as the 45th parallel (Slade, *op. cit.*, p. 131). This line is represented by *line 3*—a short-dash red line.

On June 22, 1781, the legislature of Vermont appointed three delegates to go to Philadelphia and arrange for the admission of the state into the Union. On August 18 they made a statement to a committee of the Continental Congress in which they proposed a line following the western boundary of the New Hampshire Grants and the deepest channel of the Poultney River and Lake Champlain—almost precisely the line (no. 2) agreed upon in 1790—but reserved for future adjudication the claim of their state to a district west of the proposed line (*ibid.*, p. 156; *Vermont Hist. Soc. Colls.*, Vol. 2, 1871, pp. 164–165). Two days later Congress resolved as one of the preliminaries to admission that Vermont should accept the following western boundary:

"Beginning at the northwest corner of the State of Massachusetts, thence running twenty miles east of Hudson's river, so far as the said river runs northeasterly in its general course; then by the west bounds of the townships granted by the late government of New Hampshire, to the river running from South Bay to Lake Champlain, thence along the said river to Lake Champlain, thence along the waters of Lake Champlain to the latitude 45 degrees north, excepting a neck of land between Missiskoy Bay and the waters of Lake Champlain" (*Journs. Cont. Cong.*, Vol. 21, Washington, 1912, p. 887).

The line varies slightly from that proposed by the delegates and is represented approximately by line 2. In the final settlement the peninsula between Missiquoi Bay and Lake Champlain was given to Vermont (see below).

On February 23, 1782, Vermont accepted the conditions of admission specified by Congress and agreed that her western boundary should be a line "twenty miles east of Hudson's river, as specified in the resolutions of August last" (Slade, *op. cit.*, p. 169) (approximately line 2). Having accepted the terms of Congress she expected to be admitted forthwith into the Union, but she was disappointed and was not admitted until 1791. In 1789 New York decided to consent to her admission, and in the following year commissioners representing both states agreed upon the following boundary line:

. . . "beginning at the northwest corner of the state of Massachusetts, thence westward along the south boundary of Pownall to the southwest corner thereof, thence northerly along the western boundaries of the townships of Pownall, Bennington, Shaftsbury, Arlington, Sandgate, Rupert, Pawlet, Wells, and Poultney, as the said townships are now held or possessed, to the river commonly called Poultney river, thence down the same, through the middle of the deepest channel thereof, to East Bay, thence through the middle of the deepest channel of East Bay and the waters thereof to where the same communicates with Lake Champlain, thence through the middle of the deepest channel of Lake Champlain, to the eastward of the islands called the Four Brothers, and the westward of the islands called Grand Isle and Long Isle, or the Two Heroes, and to the westward of the Isle La Mott, to the forty-fifth degree of north latitude" (*ibid.*, p. 193; Hiland Hall, *History of Vermont*, Albany, 1868, pp. 444–449; *Vermont Governor and Council Records*, Vol. 3, Montpelier, 1875, pp. 457–463; *Vermont Hist. Soc. Colls.*, Vol. 2, 1871, pp. 482–498).

This line is represented by *line 2*. Its description follows in the main that of the Vermont delegates, although it is somewhat more detailed.

---

[34] At a few places Mitchell's line varies slightly from the line claimed by Massachusetts and from the line finally agreed upon. These variations cannot be shown on a map of small scale.

[35] In 1774 several Vermont leaders had projected the establishment of a royal colony that would include not only the New Hampshire grants but also the country north of the Mohawk River and east of the St. Lawrence River and Lake Ontario (*Vermont Hist. Soc. Colls.*, Vol. 1, Montpelier, 1870, p. 360).

Eastern Boundary of Rhode Island
[PLATE 97C]

The drainage, projection, and coast line of this map are taken from the Topographic Map of Massachusetts and Rhode Island (1915), published by the U. S. Geological Survey. The northern boundary of Rhode Island, shown in black, was run in 1719.

On the granting of the Rhode Island charter of 1663 a boundary dispute arose between that colony and Plymouth. The charter described the territory of Rhode Island as extending

... "three English miles to the east and northeast of the most eastern and northeastern parts of the aforesayd Narragansett Bay, as the sayd bay lyeth or extendeth itself from the ocean on the south, or southwardly, unto the mouth of the river which runneth towards the towne of Providence, and from thence along the eastwardly side or banke of the sayd river (higher called by the name of Seacunck river) up to the Falls called Patuckett Falls, being the most westwardly lyne of Plymouth Colony, and soe from the sayd Falls in a streight lyne, due north, untill itt meete with the aforesaid lyne of the Massachusetts Colony" (*Rhode Island Colony Records*, Providence, 1856-1859, Vol. 2, pp. 18-19; see Pl. 43A and pp. 189-190, above).[36]

Basing her claim on this description, Rhode Island claimed that her territory extended three miles to the eastward of Narrangansett Bay (*R. I. Colony Records*, Vol. 2, p. 128). Plymouth claimed that her territory extended to the Narragansett Bay and the Pawtucket (or Seekonk) River (*New Plymouth Colony Records*, Vol. 11, Boston, 1861, p. 186). Her patent of 1630 made the Narragansett River (or Bay) her boundary, and gave her one half of that river (Ebenezer Hazard, *Historical Collections*, Philadelphia, 1792, Vol. 1, p. 300). In the early colonial documents "Narragansett River" is sometimes used as synonymous with "Narragansett Bay." In 1665 the king's commissioners (see p. 75, below) considered the dispute and "appointed the water, the natural bounds of each colony, to be their present bounds until his Majesty's pleasure be further known." In other words, they established the Narragansett Bay and Pawtucket (or Seekonk) River as a provisional and temporary boundary. In 1666 the king postponed the establishment of a permanent boundary (*R. I. Colony Records*, Vol. 2, p. 128; Thomas Hutchinson, *History of Colony of Massachusetts Bay*, Vol. 1, London, 1765, p. 548; *Narragansett Club Publs.*, Vol. 6, Providence, 1874, p. 342). These early claims are not shown on the map since they are made in somewhat general terms and cannot be represented with precision.

After the union of Plymouth with Massachusetts in 1691 Massachusetts became one of the two parties to the dispute. Several attempts were made to settle the controversy in the latter part of the seventeenth and the early part of the eighteenth century (many references to the dispute will be found in Arnold, *op. cit.*, and in the *R. I. Colony Records*, Vols. 3-5). For many years the northern boundary of Rhode Island was also disputed, and the two disputes are more or less connected. Attempts at settlement failing, Rhode Island in 1738 made a representation to the king praying him to determine the disputed bounds. Accordingly, in 1740, the king appointed a commission consisting of five commissioners from each of the colonies of New York, New Jersey, and Nova Scotia to fix the eastern boundary of Rhode Island. The commission tried the case at Providence, R. I., in April-June, 1741. Eight members attended, four from New York and four from Nova Scotia (*Mass. Senate Doc. No. 128*, 1848, pp. 10-12 and 21; *Acts of Privy Council, Colonial Series*, Vol. 3, pp. 1720-1745, Hereford, 1910, 436-439). In accordance with a vote of her general assembly, Massachusetts presented a claim to the following line:

... "the middle of the Narragansett River, between the end of Rhode Island and Little Compton, where the said river runs into the main ocean; and from thence along the middle of said river to the mouth of Seaconk River; and from thence up the said river, called Seaconk River below, and Patucket River above, till we come against a heap of stones on the east bank of that river [and on the northern boundary of Rhode Island run in 1719]" (*Mass. Senate Doc. No. 128*, 1848, pp. 12-13; for a contemporary representation of lines 1, 2, and 3 see map in Arnold, *op. cit.*, Vol. 2, p. 132).

The line claimed by Massachusetts is represented by *line 1*—a solid blue line.

Rhode Island claimed

... "all the lands lying within and bordering on the Narragansett Bay, from three English miles east-northeast from a place called Assonet, the same being the most eastern and northeastern part of the aforesaid bay, and from the extent of the said three miles, a due south course to the ocean, and also from the extent of the said three miles, a west or westerly course, unto a place called Fox Point, being the mouth or entrance of the river that runneth unto the town of Provi-

dence, and from thence, along the easterly side or bank of said river, higher called by the name of Seaconk River, up to the falls called Pawtucket Falls; and so from the said falls in a straight line due north, until it meet with the aforesaid line of the Massachusetts Colony" (*Mass. Senate Doc. No. 128*, 1848, p. 15).

The line claimed by Rhode Island is represented by *line 2*—a solid red line.

After a thorough consideration of the case the commission decided that the eastern boundary of Rhode Island was the meridian of Pawtucket Falls, the eastern bank of the Seekonk and Providence Rivers, and a line three miles distant from certain specified points on the northern and eastern shores of Narragansett Bay (*ibid.*, pp. 18-20; *Acts Privy Council*, Vol. 3, pp. 445-447; see these references for a full description of the line). The decision was signed by six commissioners, three from New York and three from Nova Scotia. This line is represented by *line 3*—a short-dash green line. In 1746 the award of the commission was confirmed by the King in Council, and in the same year Rhode Island ran the line (*Mass. Senate Doc. No. 128*, 1848, pp. 33-34 and 78-80).

In time a dispute arose over the location of the line of 1746, each state claiming that the line encroached on its territory. In 1791 an attempt at settlement by a joint commission resulted in disagreement. Finally, action taken by Rhode Island in 1844 for the preservation of oysters in some of the disputed waters led to a movement for the establishment of the boundary, which several years later attained its object (*ibid.*, pp. 35-37). In 1847 a joint commission agreed upon a line that differed but little from the line of 1746. In the following year the Massachusetts legislature declared the proceedings of the commission null and void, and a second joint commission was appointed, whose efforts also proved fruitless. In 1852 Massachusetts instituted a suit in the U. S. Supreme Court for a final adjustment of the boundary. In 1859, while this suit was pending, Congress passed an act authorizing the Attorney-General to give the consent of the United States to the adoption of a conventional line. In 1860-1861 such a line was agreed upon by the two states, and in the latter year the Supreme Court issued a decree confirming it, to take effect March 1, 1862 (*ibid.*, pp. 38-40; *Mass. House Doc. No. 1230*, 1899, pp. 3-8; *U. S. Statutes at Large*, Vol. 11, Boston, 1859, p. 382; *R. I. Acts and Resolves*, January session, 1860, pp. 139-141, May session, 1861, pp. 3-4; *Mass. Acts and Resolves*, 1861, pp. 496-499; a detailed description of the line is given in *Mass. House Doc. No. 1230*, 1899, pp. 5-8). By this agreement Massachusetts received from Rhode Island a part of the present town of Fall River, and Rhode Island from Massachusetts parts of her present towns of Pawtucket and East Providence. The line of the agreement is represented by *line 4*—a solid green line.

Connecticut-Rhode Island Boundary
[PLATE 97D]

The drainage, projection, and coast line of this map are taken from the Map of Connecticut and Rhode Island found in the *Century Atlas* (1902), map no. 10. The northern boundary of Rhode Island was run in 1719, and the northeastern boundary in 1746 (see above), both of which are shown in black.

Connecticut and Rhode Island soon after their settlement became rival claimants of the Narragansett country, which lay to the westward of Narragansett Bay. On the granting to these colonies of the charters of 1662-1663 the dispute over this territory assumed a more definite form, since these documents described their boundaries with considerable detail. The Connecticut charter of 1662 bounded Connecticut on the east by the Narragansett River or Bay, on the south by the Atlantic Ocean, and on the north by the southern boundary of Massachusetts (*Connecticut Colony Public Records*, Vol. 2, Hartford, 1852, p. 10; see Pl. 42 and p. 27, above). Connecticut accordingly claimed the Narragansett River or Bay as her western boundary (*ibid.*, p. 527; C. W. Bowen, *Boundary Disputes of Connecticut*, Boston, 1882, pp. 32-36). Her claim is represented by *line 1*—a solid blue line.

The Rhode Island charter described the western boundary of Rhode Island as follows:

... "the middle or channel of a river there, commonly called and known by the name of Pawcatuck, alias Pawcawtuck river, and soe along the sayd river, as the greater or middle streame thereof reacheth or lyes upp into the north countrye, northward unto the head thereof, and from thence, by a streight lyne drawne due north, untill itt meets with the south lyne of the Massachusetts Collonie" (*R. I. Colony Records*, Providence, 1856-1859, Vol. 2, p. 18; see Pl. 43A and p. 29, above).[37]

---

[36] Previous to 1663 Plymouth had claimed territory that now forms a part of Rhode Island (references in S. G. Arnold, *History of Rhode Island*, Providence, 1859-1860, Vol. 1, p. 569; see below).

[37] The charter also contained the substance of an agreement entered into by the agents of the two colonies in London to the effect that the Pawcatuck River should be called the Narragansett River, and that in order to prevent future disputes it should be deemed to be the Narragansett River (*R. I. Colony Records*, Providence, 1856-1859, Vol. 1, p. 518; Vol. 2, p. 20).

Early in 1665 a royal commission which had been appointed by the king to settle questions of difference between several of the colonies in America established as an adjunct of Rhode Island a territory called the King's Province, which it bounded on the west by the Pawcatuck River from its mouth to "the ford near to Thomas Shaw's house," and thence by a north line extending to the southern boundary of Massachusetts (*ibid.*, Vol. 2, pp. 59–60, 93–95, 127–128, and 229–230; I. B. Richman, *Rhode Island, its Making and its Meaning*, New York and London, 1902, Vol. 2, p. 241). Basing her claim upon her charter of 1663 and upon the work of the royal commission in 1665, Rhode Island claimed as her western boundary the western boundary of the King's Province.[38] This claim is represented by *line 2*—a solid red line.

In the course of the dispute numerous letters respecting it were exchanged by the officials of the two colonies, various colonial commissions considered it but failed to find a solution, and several appeals were made to the government in London (the details of the dispute may be best followed in Bowen, *op. cit.*, pp. 31–49; there are many references to it in the published colonial documents of the two colonies). In 1683 a commission appointed by the king decided in favor of the claim of Connecticut (line 1), but neither this decision nor a similar one made by the Attorney-General of England in 1696 was considered binding by Rhode Island (*ibid.*, pp. 41–44). In 1677 Connecticut had proposed by way of a compromise that Cowesett, now East Greenwich, R. I., should be the boundary (*R. I. Colony Records*, Vol. 2, pp. 584 and 597; S. G. Arnold, *History of Rhode Island*, Providence, 1859–1860, Vol. 1, p. 427). Finally in 1703, while the case was pending before the British Board of Trade, commissioners representing the two colonies agreed upon a line which was described as follows:

... "the middle channel of Pawquatuck River, alias Narragansett River, as it extendeth from the salt water upwards, till it come to the mouth of Ashaway River where it falls into the said Pawquatuck River, and from thence to run a straight line till it meet with the southwest bounds or corner of Warwick grand purchase ... and from the said southwest bounds or corner of said purchase, to run upon a due north line till it meet with the south line of the Province of the Massachusetts Bay" (*R. I. Colony Records*, Vol. 3, p. 474).

This line is represented by *line 3*—a solid green line. The last course, bearing slightly west of north, is drawn as surveyed in 1728.

Since this agreement was not satisfactory to Connecticut she imposed delays in respect to the survey of the line. In 1720 she reasserted her right to the line of Narragansett Bay (line 1) and proposed a line running up the Pawcatuck River to one of its heads in a pond lying a few miles westward of the mouth of Narragansett Bay and running thence northward to the Massachusetts boundary (Bowen, *op. cit.*, pp. 46–47; *R. I. Colony Records*, Vol. 4, pp. 275–277). This proposal is represented by *line 4*—a short-dash blue line.

In 1720 Rhode Island petitioned the king to establish the line of 1665 (line 2). In 1724 she instructed her boundary commissioners to obtain this line if possible; if not, to obtain the line of 1703 (line 3), with the exception that a due north-and-south line from the mouth of the Ashaway River to the Massachusetts boundary should be substituted for the corresponding part of the old line (*ibid.*, pp. 279–285 and 355–356). In 1727 the King in Council confirmed the line of 1703 (line 3), and in the following year that line, the present boundary, was surveyed and monumented (*ibid.*, pp. 370–373; *Acts Privy Council*, Vol. 3, p. 16; Bowen, *op. cit.*, pp. 47–48).

New York-Connecticut Boundary

[PLATE 97E]

The drainage, projection, and coast line of this map are taken from the maps of Connecticut, New York, and New Jersey, scale 1:500,000, published by the U. S. Geological Survey, 1913–1914. The northern boundary of Connecticut, shown in black, was run in 1801–1803 and in 1826. The northern boundary of New Jersey, also shown in black, was run in 1774 (see p. 77, below).

In the second quarter of the seventeenth century a controversy arose between New England and New Netherland over their territorial limits. Suggestions respecting a settlement were early made, but nothing came of them. Finally, in 1650, Peter Stuyvesant, director-general of New Netherland, met the Commissioners of the United Colonies of New England at Hartford for the purpose of establishing a boundary line and adjusting other matters of difference. Somewhat uncertain as to the eastern limits of New Netherland, Stuyvesant at one time named Cape Cod and at another Cape Judith as the extreme point on the northeast coast of the Dutch colony (*New Plymouth Colony Records*, Vol. 9,

Boston, 1859: *Acts of Commissioners of United Colonies of New England*, Vol. 1, p. 184). The commissioners claimed the Connecticut region but did not give its bounds. After several conferences it was agreed that the questions at issue should be referred to four arbitrators, two to be appointed by Stuyvesant and two by the commissioners. Such a reference was made, and the arbitrators agreed upon a provisional line which they described as follows:

"The bounds upon the mayne to begine at the West side of Greenwidge bay, being about 4 miles from Stanford, and soe to Runne a Northerley lyne twenty miles up into the Cuntry, and after as it shalbee agreed by the two goverments of the Duch and of Newhaven, provided the said lyne Com not within 10 miles of hudsons River" (*ibid.*, p. 189).

The arbitrators' line is represented by *line 1*—a short-dash green line (for a representation of lines 1, 3, and 5, made in 1857, see diagram in D. J. Pratt, *Boundaries of State of New York*, Vol. 2, Albany, 1884, p. 408). In 1656 the agreement was ratified by the States General (E. B. O'Callaghan, *Documents Relative to Colonial History of State of New York*, Vol. 1, Albany, 1853, p. 611). It was never ratified by the British government and was not regarded as binding by the Duke of York, who obtained possession of New Netherland on its capture by the English in 1664.

Both the grants of 1664 and 1674 of New Netherland to the Duke of York conveyed to him all the land "from the West side of Connecticut [River] to the East side of Delaware Bay" (Aaron Leaming and Jacob Spicer, *Grants, Concessions, and Original Constitutions of New Jersey*, Philadelphia, 1758, pp. 4 and 42; see Pl. 43A and p. 29, above). While disposed to compromise with Connecticut, the duke and his officials more than once claimed the Connecticut River as the eastern boundary of New York (O'Callaghan, *op. cit.*, Vol. 3, 1853, pp. 230, 235, 236, 238, and 247). This claim is represented by *line 2*—a short-dash blue line.

Connecticut was greatly concerned over the grant to the Duke of York since it conflicted with her charter of 1662, which gave her a domain stretching from Narragansett River or Bay to the Pacific Ocean (*Public Records of Colony of Connecticut*, Vol. 2, Hartford, 1852, p. 10; see Pl. 42 and p. 27, above). In the fall of 1664 the conflicting claims of the two colonies were thoroughly considered at New York by the king's commissioners (see above), commissioners of Connecticut appointed for the purpose, and the governor of that colony. These officials agreed that the western boundary of Connecticut should be

... "the Creeke or River called Momoronock ... and a Line drawne from the East point or side where the Fresh water falls into the Salt at high water Marke, North North West to the Line of the Massachusetts" (Pratt, *op. cit.*, p. 230; according to the original draft of an agreement that was drawn up but never executed, the boundary was to be a line twenty miles east of the Hudson River—*ibid.*, p. 229).

The line agreed upon is represented by *line 3*—a dot-and-dash green line.

The agreement of 1664 was not confirmed by the king, and New York declined to abide by it. In 1682 the dispute was revived, and in the following year New York claimed a line twenty miles east of the Hudson River, basing her claim upon the unexecuted agreement of 1664 and upon an alleged statement of Connecticut that the Mamaroneck River was everywhere twenty miles from the Hudson (*ibid.*, p. 241; C. W. Bowen, *Boundary Disputes of Connecticut*, Boston, 1882, pp. 70–71). This line is represented by *line 4*—a solid blue line. It is drawn parallel to the general course of the Hudson.

Both colonies appointed commissioners to settle the dispute. Connecticut instructed her commissioners to claim the Mamaroneck River and the rest of the line of 1664 (line 3), except at those places where it ran westward of such a line as New York would agree to. On November 28, 1683, the commissioners agreed upon a line beginning at the mouth of the Byram River and running up that river to the "wading place," thence north-northwest about eight miles, thence eastward about twelve miles parallel to Long Island Sound, and thence northward parallel to the Hudson River and twenty miles therefrom to the southern boundary of Massachusetts. It was provided, however, that if lands within twenty miles of the Hudson River lying along the southern part of this line should fall to Connecticut, then Connecticut should set off to New York an equal area lying along the part of the line that was parallel to the Hudson River. As a result of this provision the northern part of the line was shifted eastward a little more than a mile and three-quarters, and New York received a considerable area, long known as the "Oblong" or "Equivalent Tract" (Pratt, *op. cit.*, pp. 243–245; Bowen, *op. cit.*, pp. 72–74).

The line of the agreement of 1683 as finally run is represented by *line 5*—a solid green line. The survey of this line, which was long a

---

[38] For a statement of this claim in 1668, see the same, Vol. 2, p. 230; for a representation of it see John Mumford's map of the Connecticut-Rhode Island boundary dispute, 1720 (original in the John Carter Brown Library, Providence, R. I.); see also map in *Acts of Privy Council, Colonial Series*, Vol. 3, 1720–1745, Appendix V).

subject of contention, was not completed until 1731. The parts of the line parallel to Long Island Sound and the Hudson River correspond to the general course of those waters and not to their minute windings. The southern area north of Long Island Sound bounded by the solid green and solid blue lines is the area lying less than twenty miles from the Hudson River that fell to Connecticut, and the northern area similarly bounded and extending to the Massachusetts line is the area lying more than twenty miles from the Hudson River that was set off to New York.

After a century and a quarter had elapsed the controversy was reopened in 1856 by the disagreement of commissioners appointed by New York and Connecticut to ascertain the boundary line between the two states, an undertaking rendered necessary by the disappearance of many of the old monuments. The disagreement was only in respect to the northern part of the line—the last course which runs a little east of north and parallel to the Hudson River. The New York commissioners wished to reëstablish the old line of 1731, which owing to imperfections in the survey was quite crooked. The crooks are small and cannot be shown on a map of small scale (see diagram in Bowen, *op. cit.*, p. 74). The Connecticut commissioners wished to establish a new straight line, which would add to their state several square miles of territory. In 1859 new commissioners were appointed, and on their disagreement New York ran the old line. Finally in 1879 a new joint commission agreed on the old line. In 1880 this agreement was confirmed by the two states, and in the following year it was approved by Congress (Pratt, *op. cit.*, pp. 385–597; Bowen, *op. cit.*, pp. 78–79; *U. S. Statutes at Large*, Vol. 21, 1881, pp. 351–352). The line as finally settled is represented by **line 5**. As a compensation for yielding, Connecticut received a favorable line in Long Island Sound.

Northern Boundary of New Jersey

[PLATE 97F]

The drainage, projection, and coast line of this map are taken from the maps of New Jersey, New York, Pennsylvania, and Connecticut, published by the U. S. Geological Survey, 1913–1914.

In June, 1664, the Duke of York, a few months after he was granted New York by the king, conveyed the southern part of his colony, under the name of New Jersey (see Pl. 43A and p. 29, above), to Lord Berkeley and Sir George Carteret. The northern limits of New Jersey are described in the grant to Berkeley and Carteret as follows:

... "to the Northward as farre as the Northermost Branch of the said Bay or River of Delaware which is in fourtie one degrees and fourtie Minutes of Latitude, and Crosseth over thence in a Straight Line to Hudsons River in fourty one degrees of Lattitude" (*New Jersey Archives*, Ser. 1, Newark, 1880–1886, Vol. 1, pp. 9 and 12; see Pl. 43A and p. 29, above).

In 1686 the point of intersection on the Hudson River of the parallel of 41° and the point of intersection on the Delaware River of the parallel of 41° 40′ were determined by surveyors appointed for that purpose by New York and East Jersey. The point on the Hudson was described as "one minute and twenty-five Seconds to the Northwards of Younckers Milne" (*ibid.*, pp. 520–552; D. J. Pratt, *Boundaries of State of New York*, Vol. 2, Albany, 1884, pp. 601–602). The point on the Delaware cannot be ascertained from contemporary documents, as there is extant no contemporary description of it. In course of time New York laid claim to a boundary line connecting these two points, and in 1769 she described the point on the Delaware as lying north 62° west from the point on the Hudson River. The terminus of the line on the Delaware is sometimes said to have been Minisink Island (*ibid.*, p. 763; two manuscript maps (1769) illustrating the dispute, in Library of Congress; *Report of Commissioners on New York-New Jersey Boundary Line*, Albany, 1884, pp. 115 and 117). The line claimed by New York under the survey of 1686 is represented by **line 1**—a solid blue line.

As no line was run under the survey of 1686, the location of the boundary remained in doubt. During the succeeding third of a century many proposals for a settlement were made; but nothing came of them until 1719, when commissioners were appointed by New York and East Jersey to ascertain and run the line of division. Proceeding first to the Delaware River, the commissioners fixed the partition point "upon the Low Land in the Indian Town called Cashieglitonk," on the Fishkill Branch of the Delaware, latitude 41° 40′ N. They were less successful in locating the partition point on the Hudson River. After several observations had been made at Corbets on that river the New York surveyor raised objections to the astronomical instrument, declaring that a larger one was required for accuracy and refusing to complete the survey with the one in use. This action of the New York surveyor was closely connected with certain vigorous complaints made by New York landholders whose lands, bordering on the partition line, would have fallen to New

Jersey had the surveyors completed their task. No determination of the partition point on the Hudson was made by the commission (Pratt, *op. cit.*, pp. 606–642). The East Jersey surveyor, however, made a determination which placed it 89 chains and 60 links—somewhat more than a mile—south of Corbets (*ibid.*, p. 665; two manuscript maps (1769), illustrating the dispute, in Library of Congress; *Report of Commissioners on New York-New Jersey Boundary Line*, map at end). Later this position proved to be a trifle south of the true forty-first parallel. Under the survey of 1719 New Jersey claimed a line passing through these two partition points. It is represented by **line 2**—a solid red line.

For twenty years after the survey of 1719 the controversy was more or less quiescent. In 1740, however, it was actively revived and for a quarter of a century numerous attempts were made in both England and America to settle it. In 1757 the Lords of Trade reported favorably on a petition of the East Jersey proprietors asking that a royal order be issued making the line of 1719 (no. 2) the line of jurisdiction until the true line should be established (*N. J. Archives*, Ser. 1, Vol. 8., Part II, pp. 225–228 and 243–247; E. J. Fisher, *New Jersey as a Royal Province* (Columbia Univ. Studies in Hist., Econ. and Public Law, Vol. 41), New York, 1911, pp. 211–226; J. Munro, *Acts of Privy Council, Colonial Series*, Vol. 4, 1745–1766, London, 1910, pp. 214–215). Many delays ensued; and finally, after several acts for the settlement of the line had been passed by the two colonies, the king in 1767 appointed a commission consisting of thirteen commissioners, all resident in America, to establish the boundary. In August, 1769, six of these commissioners—Charles Stewart, surveyor-general of customs for the district of Quebec, Andrew Elliot, receiver-general of quit-rents in New York, Samuel Holland, surveyor-general of lands for the northern colonies, Andrew Oliver, secretary of Massachusetts, Charles Morris, surveyor of lands in Nova Scotia, and Jared Ingersoll, of Connecticut—met in the city of New York and proceeded to try the case (Pratt, *op. cit.*, pp. 752–754; *N. J. Archives*, Ser. 1, Vol. 9, pp. 624–625 and 630–636). New Jersey claimed a line drawn from a point on the Delaware in latitude 41° 40′ to a point on the Hudson in latitude 41° (Pratt, *op. cit.*, pp. 764–769; *Report of Commissioners on New York-New Jersey Boundary Line*, map at end; manuscript maps (1769) illustrating the dispute, in Library of Congress). This claim, according to the determination of these points in 1719, is represented by line 2.

New York claimed conditionally several lines. In case the commission decided that the survey of 1686 was binding, she claimed the line of that survey as defined by her. In case it decided that the survey of 1686 was not binding and that the Duke of York could not have granted to Berkeley and Carteret territory north of the north line of his grant literally construed, namely a line drawn from the head of the Connecticut River to the head of the Delaware Bay, she claimed a line beginning at a point on the Hudson River in latitude 41° N. and running on a direct course toward the "Forks of the Delaware" until it intersected the duke's north line and thence along this line to the head of Delaware Bay at Reedy Island. In case the commission decided that the duke's grant embraced all the territory between the Connecticut and Delaware rivers, she claimed a line beginning at a point on the Hudson River, latitude 41° N., and running to the Forks of the Delaware (Pratt, *op. cit.*, pp. 756–763; *N. J. Archives*, Ser. 1, Vol. 10, pp. 119–130; the "Forks of the Delaware" are the forks made by the upper Delaware and the Lehigh River). These three lines are represented by **lines 3**—short-dash blue lines. The second of these lines, which according to its description terminated at Reedy Island, is stopped at the Delaware River, since the duke's north line passes through Pennsylvania.

On October 7, 1769, the commissioners decided that the boundary between the two colonies was a straight line running from the Mahackamack Fork of the Delaware, latitude 41° 21′ 37″ N., to a rock on the west bank of the Hudson River in latitude 41° N., 79 chains and 27 links south of Corbets, about one mile. In determining the partition point on the Delaware the commissioners were governed by Nicholas John Vischer's map, which they regarded as the most correct map of the disputed region in 1664, when Berkeley and Carteret were granted New Jersey. On this map the Mahackamack Fork was laid down in latitude 41° 40′ N. (Pratt, *op. cit.*, pp. 769–770; the Mahackamack Fork is the fork made by the Neversink River and the Fishkill Branch of the Delaware). The line of the decision (as run in 1774) is represented by **line 4**—a solid green line.

The decision was not unanimous, as two members of the commission, Holland and Morris, declined to concur in it. They held that both partition points should be determined by Vischer's map and that, thus determined, the partition point on the Hudson was opposite the upper part of Manhattan Island. The true line, in their opinion, was a line connecting this point with the Mahackamack Fork. This line is represented by **line 5**—a short-dash green line. Since this line would work an injustice to New Jersey, they proposed, as more equitable, a line beginning on the Hudson River at the partition point of 1686 and running thence to the Mahackamack Fork (*ibid.*, pp. 771–772). This line is represented by *line 6*—a dot-and-dash green line.

Both colonies were dissatisfied with the decision of the commission, but in 1771 New York and in the following year New Jersey approved it. In 1773 these acts were confirmed by the King in Council. The line of the decision, the present boundary, was finally run and monumented in 1774 (*ibid.*, pp. 773–801; *N. J. Archives*, Ser. 1, Vol. 10, pp. 416 and 501; *Acts of Privy Council, Colonial Series*, Vol. 5, 1766–1783, London, 1912, pp. 45–46). Owing to imperfections in the survey it bends to the southwest.

Pennsylvania-Virginia Boundary

[PLATE 97G]

The drainage and projection of this map are taken from the Map of the United States, scale 1:2,500,000, published by the U. S. Geological Survey in 1914. The western boundary of Maryland, shown in black, is that finally established (for the dispute over this boundary see Pl. 98A and pp. 78–79, below). The northern boundary of Pennsylvania, the forty-second parallel, is not shown. It was first surveyed in 1786–1787.

A need for the establishment of the western boundary of Pennsylvania did not arise until about the middle of the eighteenth century, when Virginia granted lands and began to build forts in the territory claimed by Pennsylvania. As a result of these acts of Virginia proposals were made by both colonies for a settlement of boundaries, but they proved fruitless (*Pennsylvania Provincial Council Minutes*, Harrisburg, 1851–1852, Vol. 5, pp. 423–425; Vol. 6, p. 8; Boyd Crumrine, *History of Washington County, Pennsylvania*, Philadelphia, 1882, pp. 164–165).

The claims of Virginia to the disputed region were based on her charter of 1609, which granted her, in addition to territory along the seacoast, the backlands thereof extending "from Sea to Sea, West and Northwest" (see Pl. 42 and pp. 26 and 35, above). The claim of Pennsylvania was based on the charter of 1681, which granted to William Penn a tract of land bounded on the east by the Delaware River, on the north by the beginning of the forty-third degree of latitude, on the south by the beginning of the fortieth degree of latitude, and extending westward "five degrees in longitude to bee computed from the said Easterne Bounds" (F. N. Thorpe, *Federal and State Constitutions*, Washington, 1909, Vol. 5, p. 3036; Vol. 7, p. 3795; see Pl. 43A and pp. 29–30, above).[39] Virginia did not deny the validity of the Pennsylvania charter. The point in controversy was the location of the boundary described in the charter.

About 1771 the controversy which had been quiescent since 1754 was reopened, and early in 1774 Governor John Penn of Pennsylvania began a correspondence with Lord Dunmore, governor of Virginia, with a view to effecting a settlement. Penn claimed a line beginning at the southwest corner of Maryland and running thence southward to "the beginning of the fortieth degree," or thirty-ninth parallel (his interpretation of the words quoted), thence westward on this parallel a distance of five degrees from the Delaware River, and thence a line northward corresponding to the meanderings of that river, to the forty-second parallel (*Pennsylvania Provincial Council Minutes*, Vol. 10, pp. 150 and 161; N. B. Craig, *The Olden Time*, Pittsburgh, 1846, Vol. 1, pp. 448–450 and 463). Penn's line is represented by *line 1*—a solid blue line.

In May, 1774, Governor Penn sent two commissioners, James Tilghman and Andrew Allen, to Williamsburg to treat with Lord Dunmore respecting boundaries and the preservation of peace in the disputed region. As a provisional boundary, pending a permanent settlement by royal authority, the commissioners proposed to Dunmore the extension westward of Mason and Dixon's Line to a point five degrees from the Delaware River and from that point a line northward to the Ohio River corresponding to the meanderings of the Delaware (*Pennsylvania Provincial Council Minutes*, Vol. 10, pp. 182–183). This temporary boundary was not to prejudice Pennsylvania's claims to lands southward of the extension of Mason and Dixon's Line. It is represented by *line 2*—a short-dash blue line.

Declining to accept the proposal of the commissioners and their construction of the charter of 1681, which gave them a line corresponding to the meanderings of the Delaware, Lord Dunmore proposed as a western boundary a meridian line beginning at a point on the forty-second parallel five degrees from the Delaware River, and running thence

southward to the southern boundary of Pennsylvania (*ibid.*, p. 184). This proposal is represented by *line 3*—a solid red line. Since it is not clear how Dunmore proposed to draw the southern boundary, line 3 is a terminated in the latitude of Mason and Dixon's Line.

Lord Dunmore was under the impression that his line lay some fifty miles eastward of Fort Pitt, at the confluence of the Allegheny and Monongahela rivers. As a matter of fact it lay more than twenty miles westward thereof. Under a similar impression the Pennsylvania commissioners declined his offer and proposed a western boundary less favorable to themselves, "the river Monongahela from the Line of Dixon and Mason downward" (*ibid.*, pp. 187–188). This proposal is represented by *line 4*—a dotted blue line.

Since the proposal of the commissioners involved the loss of Fort Pitt, Lord Dunmore declined it, and the negotiations shortly came to an end (*ibid.*, pp. 188–191).

On June 15, 1776, the Virginia convention proposed to Pennsylvania that the two colonies should agree on a temporary boundary, which it described with considerable detail. This line began on the meridian of the head fountain of the Potomac River and followed for a considerable part of its course Braddock's Road and the Youghiogeny River, passed eastward of Fort Pitt, and terminated northward thereof on the Allegheny River (for a full description of this line see Peter Force, *American Archives*, Ser. 4, Vol. 6, Washington, 1846, p. 1576). It is represented by *line 5*—a short-dash red line.

On December 18, 1776, the Virginia legislature instructed her delegates in the Continental Congress to propose to Pennsylvania a permanent boundary beginning at the northwest corner of Maryland and running due north to the fortieth parallel, thence along that parallel to a point five degrees from the Delaware River, and thence northward along a line corresponding to the meanderings of the Delaware (*Revised Code of Virginia*, Vol. 1, Richmond, 1819, pp. 51–52; N. B. Craig, *Lecture upon Controversy between Pennsylvania and Virginia about Boundary Line*, Pittsburgh, 1843, p. 19).[40] The line proposed by Virginia is represented by *line 6*—a dotted red line.

In 1779 commissioners were appointed by each state to "adjust the boundary," and on August 27 of that year they met at Baltimore for that purpose. On the following day the Pennsylvania commissioners addressed a lengthy communication to the Virginia commissioners in which they claimed the thirty-ninth parallel (their interpretation of "the beginning of the fortieth degree"), between the Potomac River and a point five degrees from the Delaware, as the southern boundary of Pennsylvania (W. W. Hening, *Virginia Statutes at Large*, Vol. 10, Richmond, 1822, pp. 521–524).[41] The claim of Pennsylvania is represented by *line 7*—a long-dash blue line.

In order to effect an amicable settlement the Pennsylvania commissioners, however, were willing to recede from their "just rights." They therefore proposed a line beginning at the head spring of the north branch of the Potomac River and running along its meridian to the thirty-ninth parallel and thence to the western boundary of Pennsylvania (*ibid.*, p. 524). This proposal is represented by *line 8*—a dot-and-dash blue line. It is the same as the southern part of line 1.

Refuting the claim and declining the proposal of the Pennsylvania commissioners, the Virginia commissioners, on August 30, claimed the territory westward of Maryland and as far northward as the parallel of a point on the Delaware River twelve miles northward of Newcastle (*ibid.*, pp. 524–528). This claim is represented by *line 9*—a long-dash red line.

The Virginia commissioners, however, proposed as a compromise the extension of Mason and Dixon's Line to the western limits of Pennsylvania (*ibid.*, p. 528). This proposal is represented by *line 10*—a dot-and-dash red line. The line is the same as the southern part of line 2.

Replying on the same day, the Pennsylvania commissioners expressed a willingness to accept an extension of Mason and Dixon's Line, provided it was extended:

... "so far beyond the limits of Pennsylvania, as that a meridian drawn from the western extremity of it to the beginning of the forty-third degree of north latitude, shall include as much land as will make the state of Pennsylvania what it was originally intended to be, viz., three degrees in breadth and five degrees in length, excepting so much as has been heretofore relinquished to Maryland" (*ibid.*, p. 529).

This proposal is represented by *line 11*—a blue line composed of dashes and x's. The description admits only of an approximate location of the western part of the line.

---

[39] In the Pennsylvania charter "the three and fortieth degree" and "the beginning of the three and fortieth degree" are used synonymously. William Penn regarded "the beginning of the fortieth degree" and "the fortieth parallel" as synonymous (Samuel Hazard, *Annals of Pennsylvania*, Philadelphia, 1850, p. 482; *Pennsylvania Archives*, Ser. 2, Vol. 16, Harrisburg, 1890, pp. 397–399).

[40] The legislature proposed that the line corresponding to the meanderings of the Delaware should be either a curved line or a series of connecting straight lines. The Virginia constitution of 1776 "ceded, released, and forever confirmed" to Pennsylvania the territory described in the Pennsylvania charter of 1681 (Thorpe, *op. cit.*, Vol. 7, p. 3818).

[41] The commissioners for Pennsylvania were George Bryan, John Ewing, and David Rittenhouse, and for Virginia, James Madison, Robert Andrews, and Thomas Lewis. Madison was later a bishop of the Episcopal Church. Lewis did not attend the meetings in Baltimore.

Declining to accept the last proposal, the Virginia commissioners offered the Pennsylvanians as a southern boundary the parallel of 39° 30′ to a point five degrees from the Delaware River (*ibid.*, pp. 530–531). This proposal is represented by *line 12*—a red line composed of dashes and x's.

On August 31 the Pennsylvania commissioners agreed to accept the line of 39° 30′, provided the Virginia commissioners would accept the meridian of the terminus of that line as the western boundary of Pennsylvania (*ibid.*, p. 531). This proposal is represented by *line 13*—a blue line composed of dashes and o's.

This last proposal was declined by the Virginia commissioners, who now made a proposal that proved acceptable. The final agreement, dated August 31, was as follows:

"To extend Mason and Dixon's line due west five degrees of longitude, to be computed from the river Delaware, for the southern boundary of Pennsylvania, and that a meridian drawn from the western extremity thereof to the northern limit of the said state be the western boundary of Pennsylvania forever" (*ibid.*, p. 533).

This line, the present boundary, is represented by *line 14*—a solid green line. In 1779–1780 it was ratified by the two states. In 1784 it was surveyed to the southwest corner of Pennsylvania, and in the following year continued northward (*ibid.*, pp. 534–537; *Report of Pennsylvania Secretary of Internal Affairs ... containing Reports of Surveys ... of Boundary Lines*, Harrisburg, 1887, pp. 291–328; C. V. C. Mathews, *Andrew Ellicott*, New York, 1908, pp. 16–46).

Texas-Oklahoma Boundary: Portion Near Forks of Red River

[PLATE 97H]

This map illustrates a dispute over that portion of the Texas-Oklahoma boundary which is located near the forks of the Red River and which involved the possession of Greer County. (For the dispute of 1921–1923 relating to the boundary along the Red River, see Pl. 101C and below, p. 87.) The drainage and projection are taken from the Map of the United States, scale 1:2,500,000, published by the U. S. Geological Survey in 1914.

In the controversy between the United States and Texas over the portion of the boundary of Texas near the forks of the Red River both parties asserted title under the treaty of 1819 between the United States and Spain (see p. 68, above). This treaty described in the following words the international boundary line along the Red River and the hundredth meridian, beginning at the point where that river is intersected by a due north line drawn from the point of intersection of the Sabine River and the thirty-second parallel:

... "following the course of the Rio Roxo [Red River] westward to the degree of longitude 100 west from London, and 23 from Washington; then crossing the said Red River, and running thence by a line due north ... the whole being as laid down in Melish's map of the United States, published at Philadelphia, improved to the first of January, 1818" (W. M. Malloy, *U. S. Treaties and Conventions*, Washington, 1910–1923, Vol. 2, p. 1653).

It was the western part of the line thus described, south of the parallel of 36° 30′, whose location was disputed. The boundary of Texas west of the intersection of the hundredth meridian with the parallel of 36° 30′ was established by the Compromise of 1850. The beginning of this boundary is represented by a dot-and-dash black line.

In 1858 a joint commission, consisting of one commissioner appointed by the United States and one by Texas, began the survey of the Texas boundary between the Rio Grande and the Red River. Before reaching the hundredth meridian the Texas commissioner withdrew from the survey, and the United States commissioner, John H. Clark, completed it. In 1860 Clark surveyed the line of the hundredth meridian. For the southern part of it he adopted a line run in 1859 by the Indian Office beginning at the point of intersection of the hundredth meridian with the South Fork of the Red River and running northward (*Senate Ex. Doc. No. 70, 47th Cong., 1st Sess.*, 1881–1882, pp. 2, 268, 291, 300; *House Ex. Doc. No. 635, 57th Cong., 1st Sess.*, 1901–1902, pp. 14–15). Clark's survey was a formal assertion of the claim of the United States to the South Fork of the Red River and the true hundredth meridian. The boundary according to this claim is represented by *line 1*—a solid blue line.

On April 28, 1860, the governor of Texas instructed the Texas commissioner to insist upon the North Fork as the true boundary line (*Papers of United States and Texas Boundary Commission*, Austin, 1886, Exhibit A, pp. 59–60). This claim of Texas is represented by *line 2*—a solid red line.

On February 8, 1860, Texas passed an act erecting the territory between the forks of the Red River east of the hundredth meridian into the county of Greer. This county contained somewhat more than a

million and a half acres. By 1890 the number of its inhabitants was several thousand. It voted as a part of Texas in the presidential elections of 1888 and 1892.

During and immediately after the Civil War the dispute received little or no attention. In 1886 a joint commission, appointed under an act of Texas of 1882 and an act of Congress of 1885, tried to effect a settlement but failed. The United States commissioners claimed the South Fork (line 1), and the Texas commissioners the North Fork (line 2). The Texas commissioners also offered evidence and advanced arguments to prove that the boundary was the hundredth meridian as laid down on Melish's map, which shows it some seventy miles east of the forks of the Red River. In the previous year the governor of Texas had expressed the same view (*ibid.*, pp. 99 and 107; *ibid.*, "First Argument of Texas Commission," p. 39; *ibid.*, "Report of Proceedings of Joint Commission," pp. 45–46). The claim of Texas to the hundredth meridian as laid down on Melish's map is represented by *line 3*—a short-dash red line.

On December 30, 1887, President Cleveland issued a proclamation asserting the title of the United States to the disputed region. A similar assertion of title was made by the United States in the act of May 2, 1890, organizing the territory of Oklahoma. This act also provided for the settlement of the dispute by means of a suit in equity in the U. S. Supreme Court against Texas. In pursuance of this act the U. S. Attorney-General instituted such a suit, and the case was heard upon its merits in October, 1895. The counsel for Texas claimed unconditionally the hundredth meridian as laid down on Melish's map (line 3). They also claimed, as an alternative line in case Melish's map was disregarded, the North Fork of the Red River (line 2).[42] The Supreme Court rendered its decision in 1896, which in every respect was in accordance with the claims of the United States. It held that the South Fork was the continuation of the Red River of the treaty of 1819, that the hundredth meridian of that treaty must be interpreted as the true hundredth meridian, and that Greer County belonged to Oklahoma (*U. S. Supreme Court Reports*, Vol. 143, Oct. term, 1891, p. 621; Vol. 162, pp. 1–2, 20–21, and 76; *U. S. Statutes at Large*, Vol. 25, Washington, 1889, p. 1484; Vol. 26, 1891, pp. 92–93). The boundary according to this decision is represented by *line 1*.

Western Boundary of Maryland
[PLATE 98A]

The drainage and projection of this map are taken from the maps of West Virginia, Virginia, and Maryland, scale 1:500,000, published by the U. S. Geological Survey, 1913–1914. The northern boundary of Maryland, part of which is shown, was run in 1763–1767 (see p. 85, below).

According to the Maryland charter of 1632 the boundary of Maryland ran along the fortieth degree of latitude "unto the true meridian of the first Fountain of the River of Pattowmack, thence verging toward the South, unto the further Bank of the said River (F. N. Thorpe, *Federal and State Constitutions*, Washington, 1909, Vol. 3, p. 1678; see Pl. 43A and p. 28, above). From this description it may be seen that the location of the western boundary of Maryland depended largely upon the location of the source of the Potomac River. No effort was made to locate the source of the Potomac until 1733, when Lord Fairfax, who inherited a large tract of land in Virginia between the Rappahannock and Potomac rivers, petitioned the king to appoint commissioners to determine the boundaries. The petition was granted, and in 1736 commissioners, appointed by Fairfax and the state of Virginia, decided that the North Branch of the Potomac River was the main branch of that stream, and directed their surveyors to survey it (see Pl. 51A and p. 38, above). In 1746 a second survey of the Fairfax tract authorized by the King in Council was made, and the source of the North Branch was marked by a stone called the Fairfax Stone (*Transcript of Record, Maryland v. West Virginia*, U. S. Supreme Court, 1909, Vol. 2, pp. 1208–1243; *Acts of Privy Council, Colonial Series*, Vol. 3, 1720–1745, Hereford, 1910, pp. 385–391). In 1753 Lord Baltimore asserted a claim to the South Branch of the Potomac River and the meridian of its head. In 1771 Maryland marked the source of the South Branch and surveyed a north line therefrom (*Transcript of Record, Maryland v. West Virginia*, U. S. Supreme Court, 1909, Vol. 1, pp. 541–542; Vol. 2, pp. 1301–1306; *Documents Relating to Western and Southern Boundary of States of Maryland and Virginia*, Richmond, 1874, pp. 66–67). The line of the South Branch and the meridian of its source was claimed by Maryland at various times until 1910, when the dispute was finally settled. It is represented by *line 1*—a solid blue line.

After the surveys of 1736 and 1746 Virginia accepted as her boundary

---

[42] The Texas commissioners stated that in case the court decided against both of their claims they would insist on an accurate determination of the one hundredth meridian (*U. S. Supreme Court Reports*, Vol. 162, Oct. term, 1895, p. 20). Such a determination was made in 1902, when the true meridian was found to lie 3700 feet east of Clark's line (*House Doc. No. 395, 57th Cong., 2nd Sess.*, 1901–1902, p. 115)).

the North Branch of the Potomac and the meridian of its head, and passed various laws based on this view of her limits (*West Virginia Brief in Maryland v. West Virginia*, U. S. Supreme Court, 1909, pp. 30–36; *Transcript of Record, Maryland v. West Virginia*, U. S. Supreme Court, 1909, Vol. 2, pp. 1252–1281). In 1787 Francis Deakins, under orders from Maryland to lay off bounty lands westward of Fort Cumberland, ran a meridian line from the Fairfax Stone northward to the Pennsylvania boundary, which afterwards proved to be not a true north-and-south line. In the following year Maryland passed a law in which she stated that the Deakins line lay far within her rightful boundary, that is within the line of the South Branch and the meridian of its head (line 1) (*ibid.*, Vol. 1, p. 366; Vol. 2, pp. 1307–1308). In course of time, however, the Deakins line was generally accepted as the boundary. The western boundary of Maryland according to the surveys of 1736, 1746, and 1787 is represented by *line 2*—a solid red line. The part of this line north of the Fairfax Stone is the Deakins line. It runs slightly east of north.

From 1795 to 1863, when West Virginia became a state, Maryland and Virginia made many attempts to establish permanently their boundary. In 1818 and 1852 Maryland passed laws that conceded the North Branch of the Potomac to be the boundary. In 1832, however, she reasserted her right to the South Branch and the meridian of its head (line 1). Virginia claimed the North Branch and the meridian of the Fairfax Stone. In 1852 Maryland conceded the meridian of the Fairfax Stone to be her boundary (W. H. Browne and A. Ritchie, *Report of Committee of Maryland Hist. Soc. on Western Boundary of Maryland*, Baltimore, 1890, pp. 15–26; *Transcript of Record, Maryland v. West Virginia*, U. S. Supreme Court, 1909, Vol. 2, pp. 1317–1363).

In 1858, in accordance with a Virginia act of that year and a Maryland act of 1852, N. W. McDonald of Virginia and T. J. Lee of Maryland were appointed commissioners to settle the whole of the disputed boundary between the two states. In the following year McDonald advanced the claim that the western boundary of Maryland was a line drawn from the point of intersection of the meridian of the Fairfax Stone with the Pennsylvania boundary to the nearest point on the Potomac River (*ibid.*, Vol. 1, pp. 433–434). This claim is represented by *line 3*—a short-dash red line.

Acting under the orders of Lee and McDonald, Lieutenant N. Michler of the U. S. Topographic Corps in 1859 ran a true meridian from the Fairfax Stone. This intersected the Pennsylvania line about three fourths of a mile west of the corresponding intersection made by the Deakins line (*Report relative to Boundary Line between Maryland and Virginia*, January 9, 1860, Richmond, 1874, p. 21). The Michler line is represented by *line 4*—a short-dash black line.

In 1860 Maryland passed an act confirming the Michler line. Virginia, however, did not confirm it. In 1863 West Virginia became a state and soon after the Civil War took steps to effect a settlement of the disputed boundary. In 1887 she confirmed conditionally the Michler line. The condition was that Maryland should confirm all the Virginia patents to land between the Michler and Deakins lines (Browne and Ritchie, *op cit.*, pp. 25–30). Instead of meeting this condition, Maryland in 1891 began a suit in equity in the U. S. Supreme Court to obtain a final settlement of the dispute. In her bill of complaint she asserted her right to the South Branch of the Potomac River and the meridian of its source (line 1), and prayed that this boundary be established. In 1893 West Virginia filed a cross bill, in which she claimed the North Branch of the Potomac and the Deakins line (line 2) (*Transcript of Record, Maryland v. West Virginia*, U. S. Supreme Court, 1909, Vol. 1, pp. 2 and 76).

When the case was tried in 1909 each state presented extensive briefs and arguments. Maryland did not at this time press her claim to the South Branch, but, assuming that the North Branch was the main stream of the Potomac, she claimed a new western line, the meridian of the "Potomac Stone," which was about a mile and a quarter westward of the meridian of the Fairfax Stone. The Potomac Stone was set in 1897 by a Maryland surveyor to mark a source of the North Branch lying to the westward and northward of the Fairfax Stone (*Maryland Brief in Maryland v. West Virginia*, U. S. Supreme Court, 1909, p. 24; *U. S. Supreme Court Reports*, Vol. 217, 1909, p. 29). The claim of Maryland to the meridian of the Potomac Stone is represented by *line 5*—a short-dash blue line.

In 1910 the Supreme Court decided that the Deakins line was the western boundary of Maryland and by this decision established the North Branch as the main stream of the Potomac (*ibid.*, p. 46)[43] The line established by the decision of the court is represented by *line 2*.

---

[43] In her cross bill West Virginia claimed the northern bank of the Potomac River as her boundary. The court decided against this claim. A few months later, when the settlement of the decree in the original suit was before the court, Maryland claimed the high-water mark and West Virginia the low-water mark on the southern bank of the Potomac. The court decided that the low-water mark was the boundary (*U. S. Supreme Court Reports*, Vol. 217, pp. 46 and 577–585).

Ohio-Michigan Boundary
[PLATE 98B]

The drainage and projection of this map are taken from the map found in the *Final Report on the Ohio-Michigan Boundary*, Vol. 1, published by the state of Ohio, Mansfield, 1916. The boundary between Ohio and Indiana was established in 1803, and the boundary between Indiana and Michigan and between Indiana and Illinois in 1816. These lines are shown in black. The parallel of the most southerly extreme of Lake Michigan between that lake and Lake Erie, and a line connecting the most southerly extreme of Lake Michigan with the most northerly cape of Maumee Bay, are represented by dotted black lines (see Pls. 61G and 62A).

The Ohio-Michigan boundary dispute had its origin in the early measures partitioning the Old Northwest Territory. The first of these measures, the ordinance of 1787, provided that there should be formed out of this territory not less than three nor more than five states. If only three states were formed, the territory was to be divided into three parts by two north-and-south lines extending from the Ohio River to the international boundary. The easterly of these lines was the meridian of the mouth of the Great Miami River, and the westerly, the Wabash River to Post Vincents and thence the meridian of Post Vincents. If four or five states were formed, the additional state or states were to be made out of the territory which lay north of an "east and west line drawn through the southerly bend or extreme of Lake Michigan" (*U. S. Revised Statutes*, 1878, p. 16).

The ordinance further provided that the territory for purposes of temporary government should form one district until divided into two districts. A division into two districts was made in 1800, when the territory of Indiana was created. On April 30, 1802, an act of Congress was approved to enable the eastern district, shortly named Ohio, to be admitted into the Union. This act prescribed the boundaries of Ohio with considerable detail. The northern boundary between Lake Erie and the Indiana line was to be the easterly part of an "east and west line drawn through the southerly extreme of Lake Michigan"—the line of division prescribed in the ordinance of 1787 (*U. S. Statutes at Large*, Vol. 2, Boston, 1845, p. 173).

In November, 1802, the Ohio constitutional convention embodied in the constitution of the state the clause relating to boundaries found in the enabling act but, fearing that the meridian of the southerly extreme of Lake Michigan would not give the state the frontage on Lake Erie that was desired, added the following proviso:

"That if the southerly bend or extreme of Lake Michigan should extend so far south that a line drawn due east from it should not intersect Lake Erie, or if it should intersect the said Lake Erie east of the mouth of the Miami River of the Lake [Maumee River] then and in that case, with the assent of the Congress of the United States, the northern boundary of this State shall be established by, and extending to, a direct line running from the southern extremity of Lake Michigan to the most northerly cape of the Miami [Maumee] Bay, after intersecting the due north line from the mouth of the Great Miami River [that is, the western boundary of Ohio]" (F. N. Thorpe, *Federal and State Constitutions*, Washington, 1909, Vol. 5, p. 2909).

On February 19, 1803, an act of Congress was approved by the President providing for the execution of the laws of the United States within the state of Ohio. By this act the United States accepted the constitution of Ohio. Whether so general an acceptance included the proviso respecting boundaries was open to differences of opinion. On January 11, 1805, Congress passed an act for the organization of the territory of Michigan "north of a line drawn east from the southerly bend or extreme of Lake Michigan, until it shall intersect Lake Erie," and east of a line drawn through the middle of Lake Michigan northward to the international boundary (*U. S. Statutes at Large*, Vol. 2, Boston, 1845, pp. 201 and 309).

The varying provisions respecting the northern boundary of Ohio contained in the Ohio constitution and the act creating Michigan Territory were certain to cause a boundary dispute should it be found that the parallel of the southern bend of Lake Michigan passed south of the most northerly cape of Maumee Bay. In 1807 it was generally believed that such a line would pass south of Lake Erie. In that year, under this impression, Ohio instructed her senators and representatives in Congress to obtain the passage of a law ascertaining and defining the northern boundary of the state and fixing it according to the proviso. In 1809 and 1811 she issued similar instructions, and in 1812 Congress acceded to Ohio's importunities, in terms, however, far from satisfactory, by passing an act authorizing the surveyor-general of the United States to mark the northern boundary of Ohio according to the Ohio enabling act of 1802 (*Ohio Laws*, 1806–1807, pp. 143–144; 1808–1809, p. 225; 1811–1812, pp. 191–192; *U. S. Statutes at Large*, Vol. 2, Boston, 1845,

p. 741).[44] Owing to the war of 1812, steps were not taken for carrying out the enabling act until 1816, when Edward Tiffin, the surveyor-general, ordered William Harris, deputy surveyor, to ascertain the position of the parallel of the southern bend of Lake Michigan with relation to the north cape of Maumee Bay. If the parallel passed north of the cape Harris was to mark the line of the parallel as the boundary, and if it passed south he was to mark the line connecting the cape and the southern bend of Lake Michigan as the boundary. Harris found that the parallel passed a little more than seven miles south of the cape, and he accordingly, in 1817, marked the line of the cape and the bend (*line 1*—a blue line). The surveyor-general was doubtless favorably disposed toward the claim of Ohio, since he had been president of the constitutional convention of 1802, the first governor of Ohio, and later one of that state's senators. In 1818 the Ohio legislature adopted a resolution declaring the Harris line (line 1) to be the Ohio-Michigan boundary (*House Ex. Doc. No. 7, 24th Cong., 1st Sess.*, 1835–1836, pp. 232–233 and 236–239).

Both the federal government and the territorial government of Michigan declined to accept the Harris line, and the Secretary of the Treasury directed the Commissioner of the General Land Office to survey a line in conformity with the provisions of the act of 1812. Accordingly John A. Fulton, deputy surveyor, was employed to perform this work, which he did in 1818 by running and marking the line of the parallel of the southerly bend of Lake Michigan (*House Rept. No. 380, 24th Cong., 1st Sess.*, 1835–1836, pp. 69–70). The Fulton line (*line 2*—a solid red line) was claimed by Michigan as the boundary. Until the dispute was settled she exercised jurisdiction to this line.

For a decade and a half after the running of the Harris and Fulton lines numerous proposals for a settlement of the boundary were made, all of which proved fruitless. In 1831 Michigan adopted a resolution authorizing her governor to adjust the dispute with the governor of Ohio "on the basis of a cession of all the territory in dispute situate east of the Maumee river, and the acceptance by Michigan of an equivalent cession of territory west of said stream" (*Michigan Legislative Council Journal*, Detroit, 1831, p. 137). In 1834 Senator Tipton of Indiana made a similar proposal (*Register of Debates in Congress*, Vol. 12, Part I, 1835–1836, p. 1009). If the "equivalent cession" be given a uniform width and be located along the whole of the northern boundary west of the Maumee River, the most natural shape and location, the proposal of Michigan may be represented by *line 3*—a short-dash red line.

In 1833 the territory of Michigan petitioned Congress for admission into the Union, and from that time until the territory was admitted the question of the settlement of the boundary was complicated with that of the admission of the territory. The two questions were inseparably connected, since Michigan could not be admitted without fixing her boundaries. In Congress there was a diversity of opinion respecting the true boundary line. A majority of the Senate favored the claim of Ohio. Early in 1835 Ohio proceeded to enforce her claim by extending her jurisdiction over the disputed region and by remarking the Harris line. Michigan took steps to prevent these acts, and both states assembled a force of militia on the border (A. M. Soule, "Southern and Western Boundaries of Michigan," *Mich. Pioneer and Hist. Soc. Colls.*, Vol. 27, Lansing, 1897, pp. 354–378; W. V. Way, *Facts and Historical Events of the Toledo War of 1835*, Toledo, 1869, pp. 9–50; *House Rept. No. 380, 24th Cong., 1st Sess.*, 1835–1836, pp. 81–90). More than a year elapsed before Congress ended the dispute by the passage of the act of June 15, 1836, "to establish the northern boundary line of the state of Ohio, and to provide for the admission of the state of Michigan into the Union" (*U. S. Statutes at Large*, Vol. 5, Boston, 1848, p. 49). This act established the line (*line 1*) claimed by Ohio and gave Michigan as a recompense for her loss the upper peninsula of that state.

Missouri-Iowa Boundary

[PLATE 98C]

The drainage and projection of this map are taken from the Map of the United States, scale 1:2,500,000, published by the U. S. Geological Survey in 1914.

In 1837 a controversy over the northern boundary of Missouri arose between the state of Missouri and the territory of Wisconsin, whose area then included what is now the state of Iowa. The territory of Iowa on its organization in 1838 and the state of Iowa on its admission into the Union in 1846 in turn inherited the dispute.

The official description of the disputed line is found in the Missouri

enabling act of March 6, 1820. This act provided that the boundary of Missouri should run westward until it intersected

... "a meridian line passing through the middle of the mouth of the Kansas river where the same empties into the Missouri river, thence ... north along the said meridian line to the intersection of the parallel of latitude which passes through the rapids of the river Des Moines, making the said line to correspond with the Indian boundary line; thence east, from the point of intersection last aforesaid, along the said parallel of latitude to the middle of the channel of the main fork of the said river Des Moines; thence down and along the middle of the main channel of the said river Des Moines to the mouth of the same where it empties into the Mississippi river" (*U. S. Statutes at Large*, Vol. 3, Boston, 1846, p. 545).

The Indian boundary line referred to is the line run in 1816 by John C. Sullivan, U. S. deputy surveyor, to mark the boundary of the lands north of the Missouri River ceded to the United States by the Osage Indians in 1808. The Sullivan line began on the Missouri River opposite the mouth of the Kansas River, ran northward 100 miles, and thence, making a right angle, eastward to the Des Moines River. Because of a lack of precision in the survey, the eastward line bore slightly north of east (*House Ex. Doc. No. 128, 25th Cong., 3rd Sess.*, 1838–1839, p. 3; F. E. Landers, "Southern Boundary of Iowa," *Annals of Iowa*, Ser. 3, Vol. 1, Des Moines, 1893–1895, pp. 642–643). The Sullivan line is represented by *line 4*—a dotted black line.

In 1836 Congress passed an act providing for the extension of the limits of Missouri westward to the Missouri River, and in the same year Missouri took steps to establish her northern boundary between the Des Moines and Missouri rivers by passing an act providing for the appointment of commissioners to locate "the rapids of the river Des Moines" and to survey westward to the Missouri River the parallel of these rapids. In the following year, under this act, certain rapids near the Big Bend of the Des Moines River, some ten miles north of the Indian boundary line, were located as the true rapids, and their parallel was surveyed as the northern boundary of Missouri. In 1839 the Missouri legislature passed an act declaring the line of 1837 to be the northern boundary of the state (*Missouri Laws*, 1836–1837, pp. 28–29; 1838–1839, p. 14). The boundary claimed by Missouri under the survey of 1837 is represented by *line 1*—a solid blue line.

In 1837 the governor of Wisconsin objected to the boundary surveyed that year by Missouri and brought forward evidence to prove that "the rapids of the river Des Moines" were the Des Moines Rapids of the Mississippi River near the mouth of the Des Moines River. The officials of the territory of Iowa, 1838–1846, were of the same opinion. They claimed, however, not the parallel of these rapids, but the east-and-west course of the Sullivan line, to which they exercised jurisdiction, and, by implication, the protraction of this line to the Missouri River (B. F. Shambaugh, *Messages and Proclamations of the Governors of Iowa*, Vol. 1, Iowa City, 1903, pp. 21–23, 120–121, 147–149, 172–173, 217–241, 282, and 353). This claim is represented by *line 2*—a solid red line.

In 1838 and again in 1844 the U. S. government tried to settle the dispute but failed (*U. S. Statutes at Large*, Vol. 5, Boston, 1848, pp. 248 and 677). In 1839 both Missouri and Iowa ordered out militia to enforce their claims, and hostilities were narrowly averted. In 1840 a committee of the U. S. House of Representatives reported that the boundary described in the Missouri enabling act of 1820 was the parallel of the center of the Des Moines Rapids of the Mississippi River (line 3). It recommended, however, the adoption of the Indian boundary line of 1816 (line 2) (*House Rept. No. 2, 26th Cong., 1st Sess.*, 1839–1840, p. 11). Finally in 1847, soon after the admission of Iowa into the Union, the two states agreed to settle the controversy by means of an amicable suit in the U. S. Supreme Court, and such suit was accordingly brought that year (Shambaugh, *op. cit.*, p. 398; *U. S. Supreme Court Reports*, Vol. 48, 1849, pp. 665–666). In her bill of complaint Missouri claimed the parallel of the rapids near the Great Bend of the Des Moines River. The boundary according to this claim is represented by line 1. In her cross bill Iowa claimed the parallel of the middle of the Des Moines Rapids in the Mississippi River. These rapids began about three miles above the mouth of the Des Moines River and extended thence eleven miles up the Mississippi River (*ibid.*, pp. 666 and 674; Map of Des Moines Rapids, Washington, 1837). The boundary according to this claim is represented by *line 3*—a short-dash red line.

In 1849 the Supreme Court decided that eastward of the northwest corner established by Sullivan in 1816 the boundary to the middle of the Des Moines River was the Indian boundary line, and that westward of the corner it was a due west line to the Missouri River (*U. S. Supreme Court Reports*, Vol. 48, 1849, p. 679). The boundary established by the court is represented by *line 2*. Under the decree of 1849 the line was marked by a commission appointed by the Supreme Court, and was remarked under a decree of 1896 (*ibid.*, Vol. 51, 1850, p. 1; Vol. 160, 1895, p. 688; Vol. 165, 1896, p. 118).

[44] The early maps show the southern extreme of Lake Michigan some miles north of its true location with respect to Lake Erie. Ohio laid considerable stress on this fact in arguing her claim (A. M. Schlesinger, "Basis of the Ohio-Michigan Boundary Dispute," in *Final Report on Ohio-Michigan Boundary*, Mansfield, 1916, Vol. 1, pp. 59–70).

Virginia-Tennessee Boundary

[PLATE 99A]

To save space only the western part of the Virginia-Tennessee boundary is mapped. The drainage and projection are taken from the Cumberland Gap, Jonesville, Maynardville, and Morristown topographic sheets, published by the U. S. Geological Survey, 1897-1903. The boundary between Tennessee and Kentucky (near the Cumberland Gap) is the Walker line, which was agreed upon by the two states in 1820. The boundary between Virginia and Kentucky was run in 1799. Both of these lines are shown in black.

The line between Virginia and Tennessee was until 1790, when North Carolina ceded her western lands to the United States government, a part of the Virginia-North Carolina boundary. From 1790 to 1796, when Tennessee was admitted to the Union, it was the eastern part of the northern boundary of the Southwest Territory, officially called the Territory South of the River Ohio.

According to the Carolina charter of 1665 the northern boundary of Carolina was a line beginning at

"the north end of Currituck river or inlet, [running thence] upon a strait westerly line to Wyonoak creek, which lies within or about the degrees of thirty-six and thirty minutes, northern latitude; and so west in a direct line as far as the south seas" (*North Carolina Colonial Records*, Vol. 1, Raleigh, 1886, pp. 102-103; see Pl. 42 and p. 27, above).

An early dispute over this line led in 1728 to a survey by Virginia and Carolina commissioners of the eastern portion lying between Currituck Inlet and Peter's Creek, a distance of 241 miles. The line of this survey began at the mouth of the Currituck River and ran westward to the Blackwater River, thence down that river to its junction with the Nottaway River, and thence westward to Peter's Creek. It lies some two or three miles north of the parallel of 36° 30′. In 1749 a second joint commission extended this line westward 88 miles to Steep Rock Creek, a few miles westward of the eastern terminus of the Virginia-Tennessee line (*U. S. Supreme Court Reports*, Vol. 148, 1892, pp. 504-508; W. R. Garrett, *History of South Carolina Cession and Northern Boundary of Tennessee*, Nashville, 1884, pp. 16-19; William Byrd, *History of the Dividing Line Betwixt Virginia and North Carolina*, Richmond, 1866, pp. 16, 25, and 66). In 1778 Virginia and North Carolina passed acts providing for a further extension of the line westward, and in September of the following year Thomas Walker and Daniel Smith, commissioners for Virginia, and Richard Henderson, John Williams, and William Bailey Smith, commissioners for North Carolina, met at Steep Rock Creek and began a third survey of the Virginia-North Carolina boundary. When some forty-five miles west of Steep Rock Creek, the commissioners disagreed over the location of the line, and as a consequence two lines were run between Steep Rock Creek and Cumberland Mountain. The Virginia commissioners continued the line that had been begun, while the North Carolina commissioners ran a new line a little more than two miles north of the old one. The North Carolina commissioners discontinued their survey at the Cumberland Mountain, while the Virginia commissioners continued their survey, with two considerable gaps, to the Mississippi River (W. W. Hening, *Virginia Statutes at Large*, Vol. 9, New York, 1823, pp. 561-564; *North Carolina State Records*, Vol. 14, Winston, 1896, pp. 353-355; Vol. 24, Goldsboro, 1905, pp. 223-224; *U. S. Supreme Court Reports*, Vol. 148, 1892, pp. 508-509; St. G. L. Sioussat, *Journal of Daniel Smith*, Nashville, 1915, pp. 45-48). Because of the imperfections in the surveys both lines bore slightly north of west. The line of the Virginia commissioners is known as Walker's line, and the line of the North Carolina commissioners as Henderson's line.

Not until several years after the completion of the Henderson-Walker surveys did Virginia and North Carolina take action respecting them. At the October session of the Virginia legislature (1787) a resolution was passed proposing to North Carolina the adoption of Walker's line, and in 1789 and again in 1790 the North Carolina legislature concurred in a report recommending the confirmation of this line. In 1791 Virginia passed an act establishing Walker's line (*North Carolina State Records*, Vol. 21, Goldsboro, 1903, pp. 11, 350-351, 353, 441, and 1033; Hening, *op. cit.*, Vol. 13, Philadelphia, 1823, p. 258; John Haywood, *Civil and Political History of the State of Tennessee*, Nashville, 1891, pp. 483-485). Soon after the organization of the Territory South of the River Ohio, in 1790, William Blount, the governor of the territory, declining to be bound by the acts of North Carolina and Virginia, asserted the right of the territory to Henderson's line (*ibid.*, pp. 276-278). A dispute ensued in which the Territory South of the River Ohio, and later Tennessee, claimed Henderson's line, and Virginia, Walker's line. On the map, which shows a section of the Virginia-Tennessee boundary from the Cumberland Mountain eastward, the claim of the Territory South of the River Ohio and of Tennessee is represented by *line 1*—a solid blue line, and the claim of Virginia by *line 2*—a solid red line.

In 1800 Virginia, and in the following year North Carolina, made provision for the appointment of commissioners to establish the disputed boundary. In 1802 three commissioners from **each state** met at Cumberland Gap and, not being able to unite on the **establishment** of either Walker's or Henderson's line, agreed unanimously to run a new line between the old lines equally distant from each. Accordingly a new line was run from the summit of White Top Mountain in the northeast corner of Tennessee to the Cumberland Mountain in the southwest corner of Virginia. In 1803 both states confirmed this line (*U. S. Supreme Court Reports*, Vol. 148, 1892, pp. 510-516; *Amer. Hist. Mag.*, Vol. 2, Nashville, 1897, pp. 337-339).[45] The Virginia-Tennessee boundary of 1802 is represented by *line 3*—a solid green line.

After accepting the line of 1802 for more than half a century Virginia became dissatisfied with it and in 1889 began a suit in the U. S. Supreme Court praying for the establishment by a judicial decree of the true boundary between the two states. In her bill of complaint Virginia claimed the parallel of 36° 30′. This claim is represented by *line 4*—a short-dash red line. Tennessee claimed the line of 1802 (line 3). In 1893 the Supreme Court decided that the line claimed by Tennessee (*line 3*) was the true boundary (*U. S. Supreme Court Reports*, Vol. 148, 1892, pp. 503-528).

In 1901-1902 commissioners appointed by the Supreme Court retraced and remarked the line of 1802, and in 1903 their work was confirmed by the court (*ibid.*, Vol. 190, 1902, pp. 64-68). They found several irregularities in the line of 1802, the chief of which was a considerable offset about twenty miles west of the eastern terminus. These irregularities are not shown on the map.

Louisiana-Mississippi Boundary

[PLATE 99B]

The drainage of this map is taken chiefly from the Map of Louisiana published by the U. S. General Land Office in 1916. A slight use was made of the topographic sheets of the U. S. Geological Survey for the region covered. The projection is from the map of the General Land Office.

The boundary dispute between Louisiana and Mississippi grew out of the enforcement of legislation respecting the oyster industry of Louisiana passed by that state in the latter part of the nineteenth century. Valuable oyster beds lay within the disputed area. The enforcement of the oyster laws disclosed that the two states differed respecting the location of the boundary beginning at the mouth of the Pearl River and extending to the Gulf of Mexico. This line had not been surveyed. In 1901 a joint commission met at New Orleans to determine the boundary. The claims of the two sets of commissioners proved irreconcilable, and finally the Mississippi commissioners suggested that the only hope of settlement lay in a friendly suit in the U. S. Supreme Court (*U. S. Supreme Court Reports*, Vol. 202, 1905, pp. 33-34; *Transcript of Record, Louisiana v. Mississippi*, 1905, p. 15). Accordingly in 1902 Louisiana instituted such a suit. In her bill of complaint Louisiana claimed

"the deep-water channel through the upper corner of Lake Borgne, following said channel, north of Half Moon Island, through Mississippi Sound to the north of Isle à Pitre, through the Cat Island channel southwest of Cat Island, into the Gulf of Mexico" (*U. S. Supreme Court Reports*, Vol. 202, 1905, p. 3).

She based her claim on the clause of the act of 1812 admitting her into the Union, which gave her all islands within three leagues of her coast (*U. S. Statutes at Large*, Vol. 2, Boston, 1845, pp. 702 and 708). Her claim is represented by *line 1*—a solid blue line.

In her answer and cross bill Mississippi claimed a line extending southward through Lake Borgne and along the Louisiana mainland to a point six leagues from her coast and thence eastward to the Gulf of Mexico, following the general trend of her coast. She based her claim on the clause of the act of 1817 admitting her into the Union, which gave her all islands within six leagues of her coast (*U. S. Supreme Court Reports*, Vol. 202, 1905, pp. 16 and 20 (map); *U. S. Statutes at Large*, Vol. 3, Boston, 1846, p. 348). Her claim is represented by *line 2*—a solid red line. The line is copied from a map prepared by Mississippi to illustrate her claim. She was rather generous to herself in measuring the distance of six leagues from her coast.

In 1906 the U. S. Supreme Court decided that the line claimed by Louisiana was the boundary. It described the line in almost the same words used by Louisiana in describing her claim, and it delineated the line on a map accompanying the decision (*U. S. Supreme Court Reports*, Vol. 202, 1905, p. 58 and map). This line is represented by *line 1*.

---

[45] The Kentucky-Tennessee boundary, in respect to which there was a long controversy, follows Walker's line to the Tennessee River. West of this river it approximates the parallel of 36° 30′.

Illinois-Wisconsin Boundary

[PLATE 99C]

The drainage and projection of this map are taken from the Map of the United States, scale 1:2,500,000, published by the U. S. Geological Survey in 1914.

When Indiana was admitted into the Union in 1816 and Illinois in 1818 the proviso of the ordinance of 1787 establishing the parallel of the southern extreme of Lake Michigan as a partition line (see p. 79, above) was disregarded in order to give the new states a frontage on Lake Michigan. No serious objection was made to the northward extension of Indiana, but it was quite otherwise with the northward extension of Illinois. The northern boundary of Illinois established by the enabling act of that state was the parallel of 42° 30', from the middle of Lake Michigan to the middle of the Mississippi River (*U. S. Statutes at Large*, Vol. 3, Boston, 1846, p. 429). Ten years after the passage of this act residents of Illinois north of the partition line of the ordinance of 1787 and residents of the territory of Michigan (which at this time included Wisconsin) west of Lake Michigan expressed in a petition to Congress their dissatisfaction with the northern boundary of Illinois and their right to insist on the parallel of the most southerly bend of Lake Michigan (*line 2*—a blue line) as the true boundary. In 1836 Wisconsin Territory was organized with the parallel of 42° 30' as its southern boundary. Two years later in a petition to Congress Wisconsin protested against this line and claimed as her southern boundary the parallel of the southern extreme of Lake Michigan (line 2). For several years thereafter she continued to protest against the northern line and to claim the southern one. In 1840 delegates representing northern Illinois met at Rockford in that state and declared that northern Illinois properly belonged to Wisconsin (William Radebaugh, "Boundary Dispute between Illinois and Wisconsin," *Chicago Hist. Soc. Proc.*, Vol. 2, 1903-1906, pp. 123-140; A. H. Sanford, "State Sovereignty in Wisconsin," *Ann. Rept. Amer. Hist. Assn.*, Washington, 1891, pp. 183-189).

Illinois claimed the line (*line 1*—a red line) established by her enabling act of 1818 (Radebaugh, *op. cit.*, p. 145). Since she was in possession of the disputed region she viewed with more or less indifference the action of Wisconsin and of her own dissatisfied residents. In 1846 Congress put a quietus to the dispute by admitting Wisconsin into the Union with the parallel of 42° 30' as her southern boundary (line 1) (*U. S. Statutes at Large*, Vol. 9, Boston, 1851, pp. 56-57). The distance between the two lines is about 61 miles, and the area of the disputed region about 8500 square miles. Within the disputed region lay Chicago, at present the second city of the Union.

North Carolina-South Carolina Boundary

[PLATE 100A]

The drainage and projection of this map are taken from the Map of the United States, scale 1:2,500,000, published by the U. S. Geological Survey in 1914.

Not until the Carolinas were transferred to the crown in 1729 did the establishment of a definite boundary between the northern and the southern colony receive much attention. From this date, however, until 1815 it was a fertile source of controversy. In the course of the dispute North Carolina claimed that the ancient line of division between the two colonies was the Santee River (*North Carolina Colonial Records*, Vol. 2, Raleigh, 1886, pp. vii-viii; Vol. 3, 1886, p. 154), and South Carolina claimed that it was the Cape Fear River (*ibid.*, Vol. 8, 1890, p. 565; Vol. 11, Winston, 1895, pp. 127 and 147); North Carolina was described officially before 1720 as lying north and east of Cape Fear (*ibid.*, Vol. 1, Raleigh, 1886, p. 841; Vol. 2, 1886, p. 395). The claim of North Carolina is represented by *line 1*—a solid blue line, and the claim of South Carolina by *line 2*—a solid red line.

In 1730 the British Board of Trade and Plantations, after consultations with the governors of North and South Carolina, reached the following decision respecting a boundary, which was incorporated in instructions of the king to the governors:

... "that a line shall be run (by Commissioners appointed by each Province) beginning at the sea thirty miles distant from the mouth of Cape Fear River on the South West thereof, keeping the same distance from the said River as the course thereof runs, to the main source or Head thereof, and from thence the said Boundary line shall be continued West as far as the South Seas; but, if Waggamaw river runs within thirty miles of Cape Fear River, then that river to be the Boundary from the sea to the Head thereof, and from thence to keep the distance of 30 miles parallel from Cape Fear River to the head thereof, and from thence a due West course to the South Seas" (*ibid.*, Vol. 3, 1886, pp. 84 and 115; Vol. 5, 1887, pp. xxxv-xxxvi and 376; Vol. 11, Winston, 1895, pp. 128-129).

The line corresponding to the meanderings of the Cape Fear River and the alternative line along the Waccamaw River are represented by *lines 3*—green lines composed of dashes and x's. The upper part of the Waccamaw River is less than thirty miles and the lower part more than thirty miles from the Cape Fear River.

Governor Burrington of North Carolina raised objections to the decision of the Board of Trade and Plantations and in 1731 and again in 1733 proposed the Peedee River as a boundary (*ibid.*, Vol. 3, 1886, pp. 154 and 435). The Burrington proposal is represented by *line 4*—a short-dash blue line. In 1735 Burrington, after he retired as governor, repeated his proposal (*ibid.*, Vol. 4, 1886, p. 28). Later the lower Peedee was frequently proposed by North Carolina as a boundary (*ibid.*, Vol. 5, 1887, p. 358; Vol. 6, 1888, pp. 611 and 1024; Vol. 7, 1890, p. 155).

In 1732 a dispute arose between the two governors over the interpretation of the instructions of 1730. Governor Burrington was of the opinion that since the upper Waccamaw River was less than thirty miles from the Cape Fear River the alternative provision respecting the Waccamaw should be applied. Governor Johnson of South Carolina was of the opinion that it should not be applied, since the mouth of the Waccamaw was more than thirty miles from the Cape Fear River—the word "mouth," according to him, having been inadvertently omitted from the instructions (*ibid.*, Vol. 5, 1887, pp. xxxvi-xxxvii; Vol. 11, Winston, 1895, pp. 18-21). A memorandum of Johnson proposing the Waccamaw line as an alternative does not contain the word "mouth" (*ibid.*, Vol. 3, 1886, p. 84).

Disregarding in part the instructions of 1730, commissioners representing the two colonies agreed in 1735 upon a line beginning at the sea thirty miles from the west side of the Cape Fear River, running thence northwest to the thirty-fifth parallel, and thence along that parallel to the South Sea. They further agreed upon two provisos, namely, that if the northwest line should approach within five miles of the Peedee River the boundary should depart from that line and run parallel with the river at a distance of five miles from it; and if the west line should cut the lands of the Catawba Indians those lands should be included within South Carolina (*ibid.*, Vol. 5, 1887, pp. 374-375). The northwest line near the thirty-fifth parallel approached within five miles of the Peedee River, and the west line cut the lands of the Catawbas. The line agreed upon by the commissioners is represented by *line 5*—a green line composed of dashes and circles. The irregularity in the west line is caused by the inclusion in South Carolina of the northern part of the Catawba lands.

In 1735-1737 the commissioners ran the northwest line, stopping it at its supposed intersection with the thirty-fifth parallel, which later proved to be some eleven miles south of that parallel (Thomas Cooper, *South Carolina Statutes at Large*, Vol. 1, Columbia, 1836, p. 409). This line, a part of the present boundary, is represented by *line 6*—a solid green line.

In 1764 after ten years of agitation during which South Carolina asserted a right to a line running parallel to the Cape Fear River at a distance of thirty miles therefrom, and the Board of Trade and Plantations questioned the validity of the survey of 1735-1737, commissioners of the two colonies, whose appointment had been authorized by the king, ran a west line from the northern terminus of the line of 1735-1737 to the Charles Town-Salisbury Road, near the lands of the Catawba Indians (*North Carolina Colonial Records*, Vol. 5, 1887, pp. 740 and 1105; Vol. 6, 1888, pp. 1002-1003; *Acts of Privy Council, Colonial Series*, Vol. 4, 1745-1766, London, 1910, pp. 552-553; Cooper, *op. cit.*, pp. 409-410). Because of imperfections in the survey this line bears slightly north of west. It is represented by *line 7*—a short-dash green line. In 1763 the line of 1735-1737 and in 1765 the line of 1764 were declared by the British government to be provisional boundary lines (*Acts of Privy Council*, Vol. 4, p. 553; *North Carolina Colonial Records*, Vol. 7, 1890, p. 142).

Soon after the completion of the survey of 1764 the colonies began to dispute over an extension of the line of this survey. North Carolina proposed that it be extended due westward to the east line of the Cherokee Hunting Grounds (*ibid.*, pp. 877 and 880; Vol. 8, 1890, pp. 210 and 458). The North Carolina proposal is represented by *line 8*—a dotted blue line. The line of the Cherokee Hunting Grounds is represented by a dotted black line. The Cherokee line was surveyed in 1766-1767 from the Savannah River to White Oak or Tryon Mountain. Thence it was to run on a direct course to "Chiswell's mines" on the Great Kanawha River (*ibid.*, Vol. 7, 1890, pp. 207-208, 268, 469, 502, and 509; Vol. 11, Winston, 1895, pp. 80 (map) and 208).

In 1768 South Carolina proposed that the line of 1764 should be extended along the Salisbury Road to the Catawba lands, around the eastern bounds of these lands to the Catawba River, up that river to the South Branch of the Catawba, and up that branch to the Cherokee Mountains (*ibid.*, Vol. 8, Raleigh, 1890, p. 563). Later she proposed that the line should follow the North Branch instead of the South Branch (*ibid.*, pp. 560–561 and 572–573). These proposals are represented by *lines 9*—dotted red lines.

In 1771 the Board of Trade and Plantations, to which the papers relating to the controversy were referred, recommended that the governor of each colony should be instructed to appoint commissioners to continue the boundary

"from the Salisbury road, where it now ends, along said road to where it enters the Catawba Lands, from thence along the Southern, Eastern, and Northern Boundary of said Lands, to where the Catawba River enters the said Lands on the North, from thence to follow the middle stream of that river northerly to the confluence of the northern and southern branches thereof, and from thence due west until it reaches the line agreed upon with the Cherokee Indians" (*ibid.*, p. 573).

Instructions embodying these recommendations were accordingly issued by the king, and in 1772 commissioners surveyed a line from the point of termination of the line of 1764 on the Charles Town-Salisbury Road to a point near Tryon Mountain (Cooper, *op. cit.*, p. 410). The line of this survey is represented by *line 10*—a dotted green line. The last course was run slightly north of west. The instructions of 1771 established this line and the lines of 1735–1737 and 1764 as a permanent boundary between the two colonies, *Acts of Privy Council, Colonial Series*, Vol. 5, 1766–1783, London, 1912, pp. 201–202).

In her bill of rights of 1776 North Carolina claimed as her southern boundary the line surveyed in 1735–1737 (line 6) and the thirty-fifth parallel to the South Sea (*North Carolina State Records*, Vol. 23, Raleigh, 1904, p. 978). The framers of the bill of rights were under the impression that the line of 1735–1737 terminated at the thirty-fifth parallel. In 1786 South Carolina passed an ordinance providing for the appointment of boundary commissioners, but North Carolina declined to avail herself of this opportunity to settle the dispute (*ibid.*, Vol. 17, 1899, pp. 552 and 578; Vol. 18, Goldsboro, 1900, p. 675; Vol. 20, Raleigh, 1902, p. 762). Finally in 1808 commissioners representing the two states signed an agreement providing for the extension of the line of 1772 to the western extremity of South Carolina. In 1813 a second commission, finding itself unable to carry out the agreement of 1808, entered into a second agreement; and in 1815 a third commission, on discovering that it was impossible to carry out the second agreement, ran the present boundary line, which for the most part follows the summit of the mountains that form the watershed between the Green River and the Saluda River and between the French Broad River and the Saluda River (Cooper, *op. cit.*, pp. 415–424). The last course, however, is a straight line drawn from the mountains to the intersection of the Tugaloo River with the thirty-fifth parallel (see Pl. 100B). The agreements of 1808 and 1813 were similar to that of 1815 but could not be executed as they were based upon an imperfect knowledge of the geography of the region. The line of the survey of 1815 is represented by *line 11*—a long-dash green line. The entire boundary between the two states is represented by lines 6, 7, 10, and 11.

Northern Boundary of Georgia

[PLATE 100B]

In order to save space only the eastern part of the northern boundary of Georgia is shown. The drainage and projection are taken from the maps of North Carolina, South Carolina, and Georgia, scale 1:500,000, published by the U. S. Geological Survey, 1912–1913. The boundary between North and South Carolina established by the survey of 1815 (see above) is represented by *line 8*—a dotted black line.

According to the Georgia charter of 1732, the northern boundary of Georgia was a line running westerly from the head of the Savannah River to the South Sea (F. N. Thorpe, *Federal and State Constitutions*, Washington, 1909, Vol. 2, p. 771; see Pl. 42 and p. 27, above). On the spread of settlement into the back country a dispute arose between South Carolina and Georgia over the location of the head of the Savannah River and of the northern and northeastern boundaries of Georgia depending thereon. South Carolina claimed that the head of the Savannah River was at the confluence of the Tugaloo and Keowee rivers and that the northern boundary of Georgia was a line drawn due west therefrom. Georgia claimed that the source of the Keowee River was the head of the Savannah River and that her northern boundary was a line drawn due west from the source of the Keowee (Cooper, *South Carolina Statutes at Large*, Vol. 1, Columbia, 1836, pp. 411–412; *Journs. Cont. Cong.*, Vol. 4, Washington, 1823, pp. 529–530 and 769–770; for an early statement of Georgia's claim, see act of February, 1783, in Watkins, *Digest of Laws of Georgia*, 1800, pp. 264 and 749). The claim of South Carolina is represented by *line 1*—a solid blue line, and the claim of Georgia by *line 2*—a solid red line.

Since the Articles of Confederation made the Continental Congress the "last resort on appeal" in boundary disputes between states, South Carolina in 1785 petitioned Congress to settle her differences with Georgia. In 1786 Congress selected a court to try the case, but before the court convened commissioners representing the two states signed at Beaufort, S. C., on April 28, 1787, a boundary convention, which in the same year was ratified by Congress and in the following year by the legislatures of the two states (*Journs. Cont. Cong.*, Vol. 4, pp. 529–530, 691–693, 695, and 696). This convention provided that the boundary from the confluence of the Tugaloo and Keowee rivers should be

"the most northern branch or stream of the said river Tugoloo till it intersects the northern boundary line of South Carolina, if the said branch or stream extends so far north [and thence the northern boundary line of South Carolina westward to the Mississippi River] ... but if the head spring or source of any branch or stream of the said river Tugoloo does not extend to the north boundary line of South Carolina, then a west line to the Mississippi to be drawn from the head spring or source of the said branch or stream of Tugoloo river, which extends to the highest northern latitude" (Cooper, *op. cit.*, p. 413; *Journs. Cont. Cong.*, Vol. 4, p. 770).

At this time the geography of the region of the upper Tugaloo River was not well known. The northern boundary of South Carolina had been surveyed only to the neighborhood of Tryon Mountain, some fifty miles north-by-east of the head of the most northerly branch of the Tugaloo. Farther westward the boundary between North and South Carolina had not been surveyed nor even agreed upon, unless it be held that the agreement of 1735 (see p. 82, above) establishing the thirty-fifth parallel as the boundary between the two colonies applied to this region. Such was the claim of North Carolina. The opinion, however, was current in South Carolina that the line of division lay north of the headwaters of the Tugaloo, and this was strengthened by the fact that in the region of Tryon Mountain, where it had been fixed, it did lie north of the latitude of those headwaters. If the thirty-fifth parallel be taken as the northern boundary of South Carolina, the line claimed by North Carolina, the first alternative of the Beaufort convention would be applicable, and the northern boundary of Georgia established by that convention would be the thirty-fifth parallel. If, however, a line north of the source of the most northern branch of the Tugaloo River be taken as the northern boundary of South Carolina, the line according to the current view in South Carolina, the second alternative of the Beaufort Convention would be applicable, and the northern boundary of Georgia established by that convention would be the parallel of the source of that branch. These two alternatives are represented by *lines 3*—short-dash green lines.

Believing that she owned a narrow tract of land lying north of the parallel of the headwaters of the Tugaloo River and extending from the Appalachian Mountains to the Mississippi River, South Carolina on March 8, 1787, passed a law authorizing her delegates in Congress to cede this tract to the United States (see Pl. 47B and p. 35, above). The lands ceded were thus described:

"All the territory or tract of country included within the river Mississippi and a line beginning at that part of the said river which is intersected by the southern boundary line of the State of North Carolina, and continuing along the said boundary line until it intersects the ridge or chain of mountains which divides the eastern from the western waters, then to be continued along the top of the said ridge of mountains, until it intersects a line to be drawn due west from the head of the southern branch of Tugoloo river, to the said mountains, and thence to run a due west course to the river Mississippi" (Cooper, *op. cit.*, Vol. 5, Columbia, 1839, p. 5).

On August 9, 1787, the South Carolina delegates in Congress executed a deed of cession conveying this land to the United States. The northern boundary of Georgia according to the South Carolina cession is the parallel of the head of the southern branch of the Tugaloo River (*Journs. Cont. Cong.*, Vol. 4, pp. 771–772). The line of cession is represented by *line 4*—a short-dash blue line. The framers of the law authorizing the cession believed that the "ridge of mountains" lay west of the Tugaloo River. As a matter of fact it lay east (see Wm. McMurray's "Map of the United States," 1784).

In 1802 the United States and Georgia entered into an agreement according to which Georgia ceded to the United States her western lands, and the United States ceded to Georgia whatever "claim, right, or title" she received to lands along the northern boundary of Georgia south of the southern boundary of North Carolina and Tennessee (*President's Message, with Articles of Agreement and Cession*, Apr. 26, 1802, p. 7). Accepting the thirty-fifth parallel as her northern boundary, Georgia soon after the cession of 1802 sent her surveyor-general to locate that parallel. He reported that the boundary line passed near the mouths of the Davidson and Little rivers (D. R. Goodloe, "The North Carolina and Georgia Boundary," *North Carolina Booklet*, Vol. 3, Raleigh, 1903–

1904, No. 12, p. 16). Georgia therefore claimed this line as her northern boundary and as the true thirty-fifth parallel. This claim is represented by *line 5*—a short-dash red line. The line reported by the surveyor-general satisfied the expectation of Georgia respecting her northern boundary. It later proved to be about eighteen miles north of the true thirty-fifth parallel and about fifteen miles north of the line described in the South Carolina cession.

In 1803 Georgia organized Walton County in the eastern part of the disputed territory which in 1791 had been organized by North Carolina as a part of Buncombe County. Riots and dissensions resulted from the conflicting jurisdictions. In 1805 Georgia memorialized Congress to ascertain the boundary line. Both states were disposed to settle the dispute, but differences arose respecting the disposition of the lands that had been already granted to settlers. After considerable correspondence and legislation commissioners representing the two states met at Buncombe Court House in 1807 and, as a preliminary to surveying the boundary, entered into "articles of conventional agreement" in which it was mutually agreed and admitted that the two states were separated by the thirty-fifth parallel (Henry Potter, *Laws of the State of North Carolina*, Vol. 2, Raleigh, 1821, p. 1110; *Memorial of Legislature of Georgia*, Washington, 1806, pp. 1–45; *Annals of Congress*, Vol. 15, 1805–1806, pp. 456–457). The line agreed to by Georgia and North Carolina commissioners is represented by *line 6*—a dotted green line.

After entering into the "articles of conventional agreement" the commissioners proceeded to locate the thirty-fifth parallel, which was found, greatly to the surprise of the Georgia commissioners, to lie about eighteen miles south of the line (line 5) located by the surveyor-general of the state (Goodloe, *op. cit.*, p. 17). The Georgia commissioners accepted the survey as conclusive, but the Georgia legislature repudiated it and asked for a new survey. North Carolina declined to accede to this proposal, and Georgia again memorialized Congress to establish the boundary. Finally, proceeding alone, Georgia in 1811–1812 employed Andrew Ellicott, a surveyor of national reputation, to locate the thirty-fifth parallel. Ellicott made a survey which showed that the survey of 1807 was substantially correct, and Georgia accepted his work as conclusive (*ibid.*, p. 19; T. R. R. Cobb, *Digest of Laws of Georgia*, Athens, 1851, Vol. 1, p. 151; A. S. Clayton, *Compilation of Laws of Georgia*, Augusta, 1813, pp. 682–683, 690–691, and 695; C. V. C. Mathews, *Andrew Ellicott*, New York, 1908, pp. 220–226).

In 1818 the northern boundary of Georgia was surveyed eastward from the Alabama-Georgia line to a point thirty miles from the Tugaloo River, and in the following year a second survey, beginning at the Tugaloo River and running westward thirty miles, completed the boundary (Potter, *op. cit.*, pp. 1487–1488; *North Carolina Session Laws*, 1821, p. 40; C. E. Battle, *Georgia-Tennessee Boundary Dispute*, Columbia, 1902, pp. 20–21). The line of these surveys, the present boundary, is represented by *line 7*—a solid green line. Because of a lack of precision in the surveys it lies south of the true thirty-fifth parallel.

Maryland-Pennsylvania and Delaware Boundary

[PLATE 100C]

The drainage, projection, and coast line of this map are taken from the post route map of Maryland and the adjacent region published by the U. S. Post Office Department in 1896. To save space only the eastern part of the northern boundary of Maryland is shown.

According to the Maryland charter of 1632 the northern boundary of Maryland began at "that Part of the Bay of Delaware ... which lieth under the Fortieth Degree of North Latitude," and ran thence "in a right Line, by the Degree aforesaid, unto the true meridian of the first Fountain of the River Pottowmack" (F. N. Thorpe, *Federal and State Constitutions*, Washington, 1909, Vol. 3, p. 1678; see Pl. 43A and p. 28, above). Basing their claim upon this description, the Lords Baltimore insisted that the fortieth parallel was the northern boundary of Maryland. Their claim is represented by *line 1*—a solid blue line.

The charter issued to William Penn on March 4, 1681 (see Pl. 43A and pp. 29–30, above), described the southern boundary of Pennsylvania as follows:

"on the South by a Circle drawne at twelve miles distance from New Castle Northward and Westward unto the beginning of the fortieth degree of Northern Lattitude, and then by a streight Line Westward to the Limit of Longitude above-mentioned"—five degrees (Thorpe, *op. cit.*, Vol. 5, p. 3036; see p. 77, above).

At this time the precise location of the fortieth degree or parallel was not known. Penn was of the opinion that it was some miles farther south than it proved to be (Samuel Hazard, *Annals of Pennsylvania*, Philadelphia, 1850, pp. 482–483). Realizing the importance of settling his southern boundary he authorized William Markham, deputy gover-

nor of Pennsylvania, to treat on that subject with Lord Baltimore. In 1681–1682 Baltimore and Markham held several conferences, and finally separated in ill humor without reaching an agreement, after having proved by observations that the fortieth parallel was considerably more than twelve miles north of Newcastle (*Report on Resurvey of Maryland-Pennsylvania Boundary*, Baltimore, 1908, pp. 126–130 and 239–244). In December, 1682, and May, 1683, Penn, who arrived in Pennsylvania in the former year, also conferred with Lord Baltimore. In accordance with a letter of Charles I to Lord Baltimore, dated August 19, 1682, Penn proposed to locate the boundary by measuring two degrees northward from Watkins Point, allowing 60 miles to a degree instead of 70—approximately the true length of a degree (*ibid.*, pp. 131, 245, and 248; *Maryland Archives*, Vol. 5, Baltimore, 1887, pp. 371–372 and 381; *Pennsylvania Archives*, Ser. 2, Vol. 16, Harrisburg, 1890, pp. 396–397). Watkins Point is situated on the southern boundary of Maryland opposite the mouth of the Potomac River (see Pl. 100D). The boundary thus derived is represented by *line 2*—a short-dash red line. This line was located by measuring two degrees from the most southerly part of Watkins Point, allowing 60 miles to a degree.

Penn made several other proposals of a more or less similar character. One proposal was that the capes of the Chesapeake were to be the starting point (*Maryland Archives*, Vol. 5, p. 381), and all of them aimed by shortening the length of a degree to obtain a boundary favorable to Pennsylvania. Claiming the fortieth parallel (line 1), Lord Baltimore would accept none of these proposals.

In 1682 Colonel George Talbot, under orders from Lord Baltimore, ran a "temporary line" from the mouth of Octorara Creek to the Delaware River. While the two colonies never agreed that this line should be their provisional boundary, they at times thus regarded it, and it was thus accepted at various places by the residents near it. Talbot tried to run it due east and west but failed owing to a lack of refinement in his survey (*Pennsylvania Archives*, Ser. 2, Vol. 16, pp. 529–538, and Map of Parts of Provinces of Pennsylvania and Maryland, 1740, opposite p. 1; *Pennsylvania Provincial Council Minutes*, Vol. 3, Philadelphia, 1852, p. 223; *Maryland Archives*, Vol. 17, Baltimore, 1898, pp. 235–236; Vol. 25, 1905, pp. 404–409; *Report on Resurvey of Maryland-Pennsylvania Boundary*, pp. 135–137 and 158–160). It is represented by *line 3*—a short-dash green line.

Previous to the conferences of Penn and Baltimore the dispute was complicated by the execution of two deeds of feoffment by the Duke of York, dated August 24, 1682, and conveying Delaware to Penn. By one of the deeds Penn was given the town of Newcastle and all the land lying within the compass or circle of twelve miles about that town, and by the other all the land on the Delaware River or Bay beginning twelve miles south of Newcastle and "extending south to the Whorekills, otherwise called Cape Henlopen" (Hazard, *op. cit.*, pp. 588–593; see Pl. 43A and p. 30, above). This territory, as it lay south of the fortieth parallel, was claimed as a part of Maryland by Lord Baltimore. Penn claimed that it was not included in the grant to the Baltimores, since their charter conveyed only lands "hitherto uncultivated," and that Delaware had been early "cultivated" by the Dutch, to whom he traced his title. The controversy was transferred to England, and in 1685 the king approved a report of the Committee for Trade and Plantations recommending that the tract of land lying between the Delaware Bay and River and the Chesapeake Bay should be divided into "two equall parts by a line from the latitude of Cape hinlopen to the 40th degree of Northern latitude"—the western half to belong to Baltimore and the eastern half to Penn (*Maryland Archives*, Vol. 5, pp. 455–456). Two interpretations of this line, depending on the location of Cape Henlopen, are shown upon the map. They are represented by *lines 4*—long-dash green lines. Some of the contemporary maps show one location, and some the other (*Report on Resurvey of Maryland-Pennsylvania Boundary*, pp. 165–166). The Penns claimed the more southerly cape, and the Baltimores the more northerly one—the present Cape Henlopen. The line of 1685 was never run.

For upwards of half a century little advance toward the settlement of the controversy was made, although the need of a settlement became more important with the growth of the colonies and the consequent increase of strife in the disputed region. Finally, in 1732, the sons of William Penn and the great-grandson of the first Lord Baltimore executed in London articles of agreement stipulating that the boundary should be a line beginning at the more southerly Cape Henlopen and running thence due west to the middle of the "Peninsula," thence along a tangent to a circle twelve miles from Newcastle to the tangent point, thence along a meridian to a parallel fifteen miles south of the most southerly part of Philadelphia, and thence westward along that parallel. There was, however, a proviso that if the meridian cut the boundary from the tangent point to the point at which it cut the circle should be the arc of the circle (*Pennsylvania Archives*, Ser. 2, Vol. 16, pp. 449–460). The line of the agreement is represented by *line 5*—a solid green line. Since the meridian cut the circle the part of the line between the tangent point and the upper cutting point is the arc of the circle.

The agreement of 1732 by no means ended the controversy. Commissioners who were appointed to run the line disagreed in 1733, and two years later the Penns filed a bill in chancery asking for the specific execution of the agreement. While this suit was pending the Penns and Lord Baltimore in 1738, with a view to quieting the strife in the disputed territory, agreed to a temporary and provisional boundary westward of the meridian of the tangent point. On the east side of the Susquehanna River the provisional line was to be 15¼ miles, and on the west side 14¾ miles, "south of Philadelphia" (*ibid.*, p. 503). It is represented by *line 6*—a dot-and-dash green line.

In 1750 the case in chancery was decided by Hardwicke, the lord high chancellor, in favor of the Penns, and a decree was issued requiring the specific performance of the agreement of 1732. Hardwicke also settled several questions in respect to which the commissioners of 1732–1733 had disagreed. He decided that the more southerly Cape Henlopen should be taken as the point of beginning, that the center of the town of Newcastle was the center of the circle, and that the distance of twelve miles was to be measured as a radius and not as a circumference (*Report on Resurvey of Maryland-Pennsylvania Boundary*, pp. 170–175). In accordance with the decree of Hardwicke new commissioners were appointed, who, after running the transpeninsular line, disagreed. Long delays ensued, and in 1760 the Penns and Lord Baltimore executed a second agreement confirming the first, and under this the controversy was finally closed. In 1763 the work of surveying, which had been resumed in 1760, was placed in charge of Jeremiah Mason and Charles Dixon, who four years later reached the western limits of Maryland (*ibid.*, pp. 175–189). The line of the agreement of 1732 as confirmed by Hardwicke and as finally surveyed is represented by *line 5*—a solid green line. The latitude of that part of the boundary west of the meridian of the tangent point—the part known as Mason and Dixon's Line—is about 39° 43′ 20″ N.

Chesapeake Bay Line

[PLATE 100D]

The drainage, projection, and coast line of this map are taken from the Map of Chesapeake Bay, sheet 3, published by the U. S. Coast and Geodetic Survey in 1907.

According to the Maryland charter of 1632 the boundary of Maryland extended westward along the fortieth degree of north latitude

... "unto the true meridian of the first Fountain of the River of Pattowmack, thence verging toward the South, unto the further Bank of the said River, and following the same on the West and South, unto a certain Place called Cinquack, situate near the mouth of the said River, where it disembogues into the aforesaid Bay of Chesapeake, and thence by the shortest Line unto the aforesaid Promontory or Place called Watkin's Point" (F. N. Thorpe, *Federal and State Constitutions*, Washington, 1909, Vol. 3, p. 1678; see Pl. 43A and p. 28, above).

From Watkins Point, situated opposite the mouth of the Potomac River on the "Eastern Shore," the southern boundary ran on a right line to the Atlantic Ocean.

At one time or another the whole of the southern boundary of Maryland was disputed. The first to be disputed was the part on the Eastern Shore. This was run in 1668, beginning at the "westernmost angle" of Watkins Point, by Philip Calvert, representing Maryland, and Edmund Scarburgh, representing Virginia. They marked only the parts between the Pocomoke River and the Atlantic Ocean (*Maryland Archives*, Vol. 5, Baltimore, 1887, pp. 44–45; T. J. Lee, *Report on Southern Boundary of Maryland*, Annapolis(?), 1860, pp. 10–12). The Calvert-Scarburgh line is shown on the map in black—the part west of the Pocomoke River as a solid line, and the part east (the present boundary) as a dot-and-dash line.

According to the Calvert-Scarburgh survey the westernmost angle of Watkins Point is the western terminus of the Eastern Shore boundary, but according to a later contention of Maryland (see below) the southernmost angle is the true terminus. Two interpretations are therefore possible of the Chesapeake Bay line described in the charter of 1632 as the shortest line between Cinquack and Watkins Point. Both interpretations are shown on the map by means of *lines 1*— dotted black lines.

During the seventeenth and eighteenth centuries the establishment of the Chesapeake Bay line received but little attention. The line is mentioned, however, in the compact of 1785 between Maryland and Virginia, which treats of navigation and jurisdiction on the waters between the two states. In a provision for the punishment of crimes the boundary

line in Chesapeake Bay is stated to extend from "the south point of Potowmack river (now called Smith's Point) to Watkins's point, near the mouth of Pocomoke river" (W. W. Hening, *Virginia Statutes at Large*, Vol. 12, Richmond, 1823, pp. 52–53; *Report of Joint Commissioners to Adjust Boundary Line of States of Maryland and Virginia*, Annapolis, 1874, p. 127). Two interpretations of this line are represented on the map by means of *lines 2*—short-dash black lines.

Not until a few years before the Civil War did the establishment of the Chesapeake Bay line become a matter of importance. With it was connected the establishment of the Potomac River line, over which the two states had long disputed, and also of the Pocomoke River line. The whole controversy involved the possession of valuable riparian rights, the ownership of a considerable territory, including the main seed beds of oysters in the Chesapeake Bay, and the title to numerous small islands. The property and rights in dispute were estimated to be worth $20,000,000 (L. N. Whealton, *Maryland and Virginia Boundary Controversy*, New York, 1904, p. 41). As usual in boundary disputes, statutes were passed providing for boundary commissions, commissioners were appointed, who disagreed, and the controversy dragged on from year to year. In 1860 the Maryland legislature claimed that the true boundary line ran from Smith's Point at the mouth of the Potomac River to the southernmost angle of Watkins Point (*Maryland Laws*, 1860, Ch. 385). This claim is represented by *line 3*—a solid blue line.

After two commissions had failed to agree upon a line W. H. C. Lovitt, chief oyster inspector of Virginia, and Hunter Davidson, commander of the oyster police force of Maryland, on December 11, 1868, established, with a view to preserving peace in the disputed region, "an oyster boundary line" which for several years was recognized by both states as a temporary boundary. This line ran from Smith's Point to the southern extremity of Smith's Island, thence to Horse Hammock, and thence to the southern extremity of Watkins Point (*Baltimore Sun*, Oct. 13, 1870). It is represented by *line 4*—a dot-and-dash green line.

In 1872 Maryland and Virginia commissioners made lengthy statements respecting the disputed boundary between the two states, which included both the Chesapeake Bay and Potomac River lines. The Maryland commissioners proposed a line that should follow the low-water mark on the south bank of the Potomac River to Smith's Point, run thence to the center of Cedar Strait, thence to the channel of Pocomoke Sound, and up the channel of Pocomoke Sound and Pocomoke River to the Calvert-Scarburgh line (this and other lines proposed in 1872 are described in the *Report of Joint Commissioners*, etc., 1874, pp. 53–58, 60–62, 140–141, and 329). This proposal is represented by *line 5*—a short-dash blue line.

Declining to accept Maryland's proposal the Virginia commissioners proposed a boundary following the low-water mark on the north bank of the Potomac River to Point Lookout, running thence to the westernmost angle of Watkins Point, and thence by the Calvert-Scarburgh line to the Pocomoke River. This line is represented by *line 6*—a short-dash red line.

Attempting to reach an agreement each set of commissioners made concessions, but none of the lines proposed by one side was satisfactory to the other. The principal concession was made by the Virginia commissioners, who offered to accept the main channel of the Potomac River. The commission adjourned finally on November 20, 1873.

Since there was no likelihood of obtaining a settlement through a joint commission the states decided to try a board of arbitration, and in 1874 they referred the dispute to Jeremiah S. Black of Pennsylvania, William A. Graham of North Carolina, and a third person to be selected by these two. Black and Graham chose Charles A. Jenkins of Georgia. In 1876 James B. Beck of Kentucky was selected to succeed Graham, who in the meantime had died (Whealton, *op. cit.*, pp. 41–42; *Maryland Laws*, 1874, Ch. 247; *Virginia Acts of Assembly*, 1874, Ch. 135). After a thorough consideration of the case a majority of the commission, consisting of Black and Jenkins, decided, January 16, 1877, that the true boundary followed the low-water mark of the Potomac River from the line of division between Virginia and West Virginia to Smith's Point, thence ran to Sassafras Hammock on Smith's Island, thence to Horse Hammock, thence to the middle of Tangier Sound, thence through the middle of the sound to the line connecting Smith's Point and the most southerly angle of Watkins Point, thence along that line to that angle, thence to the middle of Pocomoke Sound, and thence up Pocomoke Sound and Pocomoke River to the Calvert-Scarburgh line (*Opinions and Award of Arbitrators on Maryland and Virginia Boundary Line*, Washington, 1877, pp. 29–31).[46] The line of the award is represented by *line 7*—a solid green line.

Beck agreed with his colleagues respecting only the Potomac River

---

[46] The award is much more detailed than the description given above. The low-water mark was to be measured from one headland to another. The southern part of Smith's Island was awarded to Virginia in recognition of her right to it by long possession.

line. From Smith's Point the true line in his opinion ran to the point of intersection of a protraction of the Calvert-Scarburgh line with the western coast of Smith's Island and followed the protraction and the Calvert-Scarburgh line to the Pocomoke River (*ibid.*, p. 97). Beck's line is represented by *line 8*—a short-dash green line.

In 1878 the award was approved by Maryland and Virginia, and in the following year it was ratified by Congress (*Maryland Laws*, 1878, Ch. 274; *Virginia Acts of Assembly*, 1878, Ch. 246; *U. S. Statutes at Large*, Vol. 20, 1879, pp. 481–483).

Michigan-Wisconsin Boundary

[PLATE 101A]

The drainage and projection of this map are taken from U. S. Geological Survey base maps of Michigan, 1916, and Wisconsin, 1928, scale 1:1,000,000.

In 1923 Michigan brought a Bill of Complaint before the Supreme Court of the United States charging that Wisconsin was illegally holding certain areas of land and water (1291 square miles) belonging to Michigan. While the population of the contested area was small (6900) the present and potential value of the land, forests, water power, recreational resources, and fisheries contained within it was considerable. The litigation was unusually intricate; its many points of detail and the mass of evidence, both historical and geographical, that was brought forward cannot be discussed here. The whole matter is treated at length by Lawrence Martin, "The Michigan-Wisconsin Boundary Case in the Supreme Court of the United States, 1923-1926" (*Annals Assn. Amer. Geogrs.*, Vol. 20, 1930, pp. 105–163).

By act of Congress, April 20, 1836, the eastern and northern boundaries of the territory of Wisconsin were defined as follows:

"Bounded on the east, by a line drawn from the northeast corner of the State of Illinois, through the middle of Lake Michigan, to a point in the middle of said lake, and opposite the main channel of Green Bay, and through said channel and Green Bay to the mouth of the Menomonie river; thence through the middle of the main channel of said river, to that head of said river nearest to the Lake of the Desert; thence in a direct line, to the middle of said lake; thence through the middle of the main channel of the Montreal River, to its mouth; thence with a direct line across Lake Superior, to where the territorial line of the United States last touches said lake northwest..." (*U. S. Statutes at Large*, Vol. 5, Boston, 1846, pp. 10–16).

A subsequent act of Congress approved June 15, 1836, defined the boundaries of Michigan in similar terms (*ibid.*, pp. 49–50).

The dispute of 1923-1926 may be discussed in its relation to three segments of the disputed boundary: (1) from Lake Michigan through Green Bay; (2) from Green Bay to the "Lake of the Desert" (Lac Vieux Desert); and (3) from the "Lake of the Desert" to the headwaters of the Montreal River.

(1) From Lake Michigan through Green Bay. Michigan contended that the "main channel" (or the "most usual ship channel")[47] of 1836 followed the Porte des Morts Passage from Lake Michigan into Green Bay, thence passing through the Strawberry Passage east of Chambers Island and the Strawberry Islands, and that the boundary should be drawn accordingly (*line 1*—a red line). Wisconsin produced evidence to show that sailing vessels in 1836 used the Rock Island Passage and kept to the westward of Chambers Island (*line 2*—a blue line). Wisconsin's contention was substantially upheld by the Supreme Court's opinion dated March 1, 1926 (*U. S. Supreme Court Reports*, Vol 270, pp. 295–320, Michigan v. Wisconsin in Equity. No. 19, Original. Argued January 5, 1926). *Line 4*, a broken green line shows the boundary as probably intended. In the Court's decree dated November 22, 1926 (*U. S. Supreme Court Reports*, Vol. 272, pp. 398–399. Michigan v. Wisconsin in Equity. No. 9, Original), however, the boundary was defined with reference to "the course and distances ... of modern steamships and power launches of 1926 rather than the course of sailing vessels of 1836 which had to tack; thereby Michigan wins a broader fishing grounds than she may have previously administered" (Martin, *op. cit.*, p. 144–145). Furthermore, an error in the wording of the decree whereby "north by east" was substituted for "northeast," is pointed out by Martin (*ibid.*, pp. 157–158). If taken literally, this would give to Michigan not only the islands north of Rock Island Passage but a small tip of the mainland of Michigan, as shown by *line 3*—a solid green line.

(2) From Green Bay to the "Lake of the Desert." A survey of this segment was carried out by Captain T. J. Cram in 1840, under the direction of Congress. The Menominee River and its main tributary, the Brule (or Bois Brulé), were found to contain many islands. Cram suggested that all the islands above Pe-me-ne Falls be assigned to Michigan and all the islands below the falls to Wisconsin. In the law passed by Congress

August 6, 1846, authorizing the people of Wisconsin to form a state government, Cram's suggestion was adopted in part. Wisconsin, however, was given all the islands below the Quinnesec Falls, about 23 miles upstream from the Pe-me-ne Falls. The pertinent portions of the law are as follows:

... "the mouth of the Menomonie River; thence up the channel of said river to the Brulé River; thence up said last mentioned river to Lake Brulé; thence along the southern shore of Lake Brulé in a direct line to the centre of the channel between Middle and South Islands, in the Lake of the Desert; thence in a direct line to the head-waters of the Montreal River, as marked upon the survey made by Captain Cramm; thence down the main channel of the Montreal River to the middle of Lake Superior...

"Sec. 2. And be it further enacted, That, to prevent all disputes in reference to the jurisdiction of the islands in the said Brulé and Menomonie Rivers, the line be so run as to include within the jurisdiction of Michigan all the islands in the Brulé and Menomonie Rivers, (to the extent in which said rivers are adopted as a boundary), down to, and inclusive of, the Quinnesec Falls of the Menomonie; and from thence the line shall be so run as to include within the jurisdiction of Wisconsin all the islands in the Menomonie River, from the falls aforesaid down to the junction of said river with Green Bay; Provided, That the adjustment of boundary, as fixed in this act, between Wisconsin and Michigan shall not be binding on Congress, unless the same shall be ratified by the State of Michigan on or before the first day of June, one thousand eight hundred and forty-eight" (*U. S. Statutes at Large*, Vol. 9, Boston, 1851, pp. 48–49).

Wisconsin was admitted as a State on May 29, 1848, under a law which confirmed her boundaries (*line 3*) as thus defined (*ibid.*, pp. 233–235). The act of August 6, 1846, however, was never ratified by Michigan, and it was on these grounds that she laid claim in 1923-1926 to 130 islands below the Quinnesec Falls and incidentally to valuable water-power sites (*line 1*). The Supreme Court in 1926, however, apportioned the islands as originally provided in the act of August 6, 1846 (*line 3*).[48] Owing to the small scale of Plate 101A the islands in dispute cannot be shown.

(3) From the "Lake of the Desert" to the "headwaters" of the Montreal River. The issue here hinged upon the identification of these two waters. In a survey of 1841 Captain Cram had assumed that Lac Vieux Desert was the lake in question. He also found that the Montreal River has an eastern and a western branch and placed the "head proper" of this river at the point where the Balsam and the Pine rivers join to make the eastern branch. Accordingly, when the boundary was subsequently surveyed and marked by W. A. Burt in 1847, a straight line was run from Lac Vieux Desert to Cram's "head proper" of the Montreal (*line 3*). This demarcation was planned by Lucius Lyon, a former United States senator from Michigan, provided for by Congress, and apparently acquiesced in by Michigan until 1907–1908. At that time, however, when Michigan adopted a new constitution, she defined this segment of her boundary as follows: "... through the middle of the main channel of the Montreal River to Island Lake, the headwaters thereof; thence in a direct line to the center of the channel between Middle and South Islands in the Lake of the Desert ..." (Martin, *op. cit.*, p. 134). This line is shown by the northern branch of *line 1*—a red line.

This new Michigan boundary appears to have been submitted neither to Wisconsin nor to Congress (*ibid.*). In the litigation of 1923-1926 attorneys for Michigan claimed even more territory on the ground that Island Lake and not Lac Vieux Desert may have been the "Lake of the Desert" mentioned in the laws of 1836 and that therefore the line should be drawn directly from the headwaters of the Brulé River to Island Lake (southern branch of *line 1*—a red line). This contention was not upheld by the Supreme Court, which declared that "the straight line boundaries [were to] follow the Burt survey of 1847" (*ibid.*, p. 144), as shown by *line 3*.

Iowa-Nebraska Boundary

[PLATE 101B]

This map illustrates a dispute over a small part of the Iowa-Nebraska boundary, near Omaha. The drainage is taken from the Omaha and Vicinity topographic sheet, published by the U. S. Geological Survey in 1906, and from the Map of Omaha and Environs, published by M. H. La Douceur in 1914. The projection is from the Omaha and Vicinity topographic sheet.

---

[47] Wording of act of June 15, 1836.

[48] It was the intention of the Supreme Court to make an exception in the case of "Sugar Island," a name used to designate certain islands of considerable industrial importance lying north of the channel of the Menominee River opposite the city of Menominee, Mich. The court decreed that "the land known as Sugar Island ... is determined to be part of the mainland of Michigan." However, in actually defining the boundary at this point with reference to the lots established by the "Michigan Public Survey" (Michigan meridian) the court appears inadvertently to have given "Sugar Island" to Wisconsin and to have assigned to Michigan only the eastern half of the neighboring Grassy Island. See Lawrence Martin, "The Michigan-Wisconsin Boundary Case," *Annals Assn. Amer. Geogrs.*, Vol. 20, 1930, pp. 145–157.

The boundary line between Iowa and Nebraska is defined by the acts of Congress of 1846 and 1864, preparatory to the admission of the states into the Union, as the middle of the "channel," or "main channel," of the Missouri River (*U. S. Statutes at Large*, Vol. 9, Boston, 1851, p. 52; Vol. 13, Boston, 1866, p. 47). Certain changes in this channel near Omaha made during the years 1851–1877 led to a controversy over the boundary line. The principal change was made in 1877, when the Missouri River suddenly cut through the "Saratoga Bend" and established its present channel at the neck of the bend. In 1890, with a view to effecting a settlement, Nebraska brought a suit in equity in the U. S. Supreme Court. The case was argued in 1892. Nebraska claimed that all the changes had been made gradually or by accretion, with the exception of the change of 1877, which she conceded was made suddenly or by avulsion. She therefore claimed as a boundary the middle of the channel as it lay in 1877 before the avulsion of that year (*Transcript of Record, Nebraska v. Iowa*, on Bill and Cross-bill, U. S. Supreme Court, 1891, p. 5). Her claim is represented by *line 1*—a solid blue line.[49]

Iowa claimed that all the changes were made suddenly or by avulsion, and that the boundary was the middle of the channel as it lay in 1846, when Iowa was admitted into the Union (*ibid.*, pp. 20–21; Brief for Iowa, pp. 2–3). Her claim is represented by *line 2*—a solid red line.

On February 29, 1892, the Supreme Court decided that the rule of accretion and avulsion which it had previously applied in respect to lands of private parties should be applied in respect to boundaries between states, that the changes before 1877 were by accretion and that of 1877 by avulsion, and that the boundary was the middle of the channel as it lay in 1877 before the avulsion of that year. In other words, the court decided that the line claimed by Nebraska (*line 1*) was the boundary (*U. S. Supreme Court Reports*, Vol. 143, 1891, pp. 359–370; the rule of accretion and avulsion is that the line is changed by accretion but not by avulsion—see below). The court did not specifically describe the boundary, but directed the states to agree upon a boundary in accordance with its decision. This they did, and on May 16, 1892, the court by decree established the boundary agreed upon (*ibid.*, Vol. 145, 1891, pp. 519–521). It will be noted that the decision awarded to Iowa a tract of land west of the Missouri River.

Oklahoma-Texas Boundary along the Red River
[PLATE 101C]

This map shows the valley of the Red River south of Grandfield, Oklahoma. It illustrates on a large scale a small segment of the important area involved in the boundary dispute of 1921–1923 between Texas and Oklahoma. The green line indicating the boundary as finally surveyed in 1923 by order of the U. S. Supreme Court is derived from Map No. 3, scale 1:6000, accompanying Supreme Court of the United States, October Term, 1923, No. 15, Original, The State of Oklahoma, Complainant, vs. The State of Texas, Defendant, The United States, Intervener, *First Report of the Boundary Commissioners*, Washington, D. C., 1924. The remaining features of the map are adapted from two maps dated Washington, April 27, 1921, based on surveys made for the Department of Justice by R. W. Livingston of the General Land Office. These maps will be found in Supreme Court of the United States, October Term, 1921, No. 20, Original, The State of Oklahoma, Plaintiff, v. The State of Texas, Defendant, U. S. and Oklahoma Map Exhibits, pp. 25 and 27. They are also reproduced in somewhat modified form by Isaiah Bowman, "An American Boundary Dispute: Decision of the Supreme Court of the United States with Respect to the Texas-Oklahoma Boundary," *Geogr. Rev.*, Vol. 13, 1923, pp. 161–189, Pl. 1, opposite p. 166, and Fig. 25, p. 188.

The dispute was over a narrow but extremely long strip of land (539 miles by river, 321 miles in a direct line) confined wholly to the flood plain of the river between the bluffs enclosing it on the north and south. Because of this circumstance only a section of the disputed area is illustrated. Owing to the presence of oil, however, the most critical issues at stake were found in the portion of the valley shown on Plate 101C; furthermore, the physiographic character of the flood plain in this part of the valley is more or less typical of the western half of the flood plain under dispute, the part that is under the control of a "flash" stream. The eastern half of the disputed zone is marked by strongly developed meanders and other normal flood-plain features.

The treaty between the United States and Spain signed in 1819 and ratified in 1821 established along the Red River a portion of the boundary between the territory of the two nations (see above, pp. 68 and 78). The Red River line became in turn the boundary between the United States and Mexico, the United States and the republic of

Texas, and the states of Texas and Oklahoma. Although the text of the treaty is not altogether clear in the matter, it was agreed between John Quincy Adams and Luís de Onis, the Spanish minister, "that the southern bank of the Red River was the boundary and that *not only the river but all of the islands* were the property of the United States" (*ibid.*, p. 166).

This interpretation was never accepted by Texas. The precise location of the boundary, however, remained for ninety-seven years a matter of little consequence. No serious conflict arose until oil was discovered in 1918 under the bed of the river at several points. Land values were raised enormously at these critical locations, which led to such intensity of feeling that the Texas militia was sent to the Big Bend in 1920 and "armed conflicts between rival aspirants for the oil and gas [were] but narrowly averted" (U. S. Supreme Court, Decision of May 1, 1922, p. 2, quoted in Bowman, *op. cit.*, p. 171).

Attorneys for Texas in presenting their case before the Supreme Court in 1921 claimed as the boundary the "medial line of the stream," which they interpreted in the Great Bend area to be the medial line of the northernmost water channel. Oklahoma and the United States government, which also had a part in the controversy (as will be explained below), sought to have the steep bluffs at the southern edge of the valley made the boundary, *line 1*—a red line.

A principle of the law holds that where the channel of a river moves gradually by the processes of erosion on one side and of accretion on the other, property and political boundaries are carried with the stream; but that where there is a sudden shift, by avulsion, the boundaries follow the old course of the channel (see above). Physiographic, ecologic, and historical evidence was presented by experts representing the parties to the Red River dispute with a view to determining the original course of the south bank of the river in 1821 and its subsequent changes due to erosion and accretion. The peculiar physiographic conditions in the Red River Valley, where channels, banks, and islands shift with every flood, rendered definite proof of the former location of the banks nearly everywhere out of the question. "The trouble with the avulsive principle is that it can only be applied in those cases where the change in the course of the river is a matter of historical record or can be proved by the testimony of living witnesses" (Bowman, *op. cit.*, p. 183). Such cases were very rare. "If we attempt to fix the date on which the river left a given channel and occupied another by the freshness of the topographic forms, the limits of error are exceedingly wide, so wide in fact that the Court felt in this case it could not accept the judgment of the experts even though their conclusions fell well within the limit of one hundred years, the time that has elapsed since the treaty of 1821 with Spain" (*ibid.*, pp. 183–184).

Accordingly, in settling the dispute the Supreme Court did not follow the line of 1821, "in spite of the declaration that 'the boundary as it was in 1821, when the treaty became effective, is the boundary of today, subject to the right application of the doctrines of erosion and accretion and of avulsion to any intervening changes'" (*ibid.*, pp. 182–183).

The dispute was settled by the Supreme Court in three decisions:

"By the first decision, that of April 11, 1921, the court found 'the south bank of Red River' the true boundary between the two states, and not 'the medial line of the stream, as claimed by Texas.' By the second decision, that of May 1, 1922, the court found that 'no part of the [Red] river within Oklahoma is navigable and therefore that the title to the bed did not pass to the state on its admission to the Union.' Any claim by Oklahoma to a part of the bed was declared incidental to ownership of riparian lands on the northern bank. The rights of riparian owners on the northern bank to the bed were to extend only to the medial line between the 'cut banks' of the river [shown by a dash-and-dot black line]. Finally, by the decree of January 15, 1923, the southerly cut bank *line 2*—a green line) was made the boundary between Texas and Oklahoma so far as surface jurisdiction and use are concerned. . . .

"The last decision has one feature of curious interest: *It establishes ownership by the United States of a narrow strip of land on the bed of a stream between the medial line of that bed and the southern cut bank, a strip that shifts its position from flood to flood by two distinct processes (avulsion and erosion) one of which leaves the boundary unchanged while the other alters the boundary.* It excludes not only Oklahoma but also private claimants from ownership of the 'soil' in the southern half of the river bed. Private claimants, relying upon placer mining laws, had entered and developed lands in the southern half of the bed. The court held that they had no rights because by the laws and treaties controlling the disposition of lands in Oklahoma the mining laws were excluded. The court recognized the constitutional rule of equality among the states whereby each new state, like the original states, became the owner of the beds of its navigable streams; but by declaring the Red River unnavigable it, in effect, held that the title remained in the United States subject to the Indian rights and then further held that the title to the northern half of the river bed passed from the United States and the Indians to the riparian owners of the north shore, as the lands fronting on the north bank were sold or allotted" (*ibid.*, pp. 163 and 165).

---

[49] Line 1 is drawn not from the description of Nebraska's claim, which is somewhat general but from the more detailed description of the decree of the Supreme Court.

POLITICAL PARTIES AND OPINION, 1788–1930
[PLATES 102–122]

THIS series covers the years 1788–1930. It consists of thirty-six maps illustrating "Presidential Elections" and of an equal number of maps illustrating "Congressional Measures."

The principal object of the series is to show the geographical distribution of political parties and political sentiment—more briefly, sectionalism in politics. This is attained by mapping the vote at Presidential elections and the vote in the House of Representatives on the leading measures voted upon by that body. These two sets of votes were regarded as on the whole the best adapted for achieving the object in view. No votes before 1788 were sufficiently "national" in scope to furnish materials for a similar set of maps. Many of the votes of the Continental Congress are not recorded, and political conditions during the years of its existence were so chaotic that only occasionally do the recorded votes reveal sectionalism.

PRESIDENTIAL ELECTIONS, 1788–1928
[PLATES 102–111]

In constructing a series of political maps it is self-evident that the materials upon which they are based should be as uniform as possible. This rule was observed in constructing the maps of this series, but unfortunately for some of the maps, chiefly the early ones, the materials are of considerable diversity. Uniformity in the vote illustrated is prevented by differences in the method of choosing electors, by the loss or the inaccessibility of some of the early returns, and by variations in the vote that is published (see below).

The maps of this series are of three classes: (1) maps showing the electoral vote for President, 1789–1796; (2) maps showing the vote at Presidential and other elections, 1800–1816; and (3) maps showing the vote at Presidential elections, 1820–1928.

Character of Available Election Returns. For the first three elections, 1788–1789, 1792, and 1796, the political statistics still in existence are too few and scattering to admit of the construction of maps based upon the vote of the people and of the legislatures for electors. The maps for these three elections are therefore based upon the vote of the Presidential electors. With a few exceptions in connection with the election of 1796 (see pp. 92–93, below) the vote that is mapped is by states.

For the five elections covering the years 1800–1816, owing to the loss or inaccessibility of some of the returns for Presidential elections, the returns of other elections were used to fill the gaps. The maps for these years are therefore based only in part, though chiefly, upon the vote at Presidential elections. With a few exceptions the vote that is mapped is the popular vote, by counties. The exceptions comprise a few cases in which the vote for Presidential electors of one or both houses of some of the state legislatures was used.

The maps covering the years 1820–1928 are based entirely upon the vote at Presidential elections. With a few exceptions they are based upon the popular vote, by counties. The exceptions comprise a few cases for the earlier part of the period in which the vote of one or both houses of the state legislatures was used.

A larger use of the votes of legislatures for electors was prevented by the lack of records giving the vote of each member of the legislature. New York is the only state for which such a vote was found. In several other states it was sometimes possible to ascertain the vote of the members by computation and comparison. According to the New York practice, the election of electors began with the nomination by each house of as many persons as there were electors to be appointed. The two houses then met in joint session and compared nominations. Those persons nominated by both houses were declared to be chosen electors. In case of a disagreement deficiencies were supplied by means of a joint ballot of the two houses (*New York Statutes*, Apr. 12, 1792, Ch. 72; *N. Y. Constitution of 1777*, Section 30). For New York, during the years 1800–1824, the vote mapped is the first vote of the assembly nominating electors. By reason of the small number of counties in Delaware and of their political consistency the vote of the members of the legislature of that state could generally be ascertained. The vote of legislatures when unanimous presented no difficulty.

The published statistics for Presidential elections, except in some recent state publications, do not give the vote for all the electors. They rarely state what vote they give. Comparisons show that as a rule they give the vote for the leading elector on each ticket—that is, the elector who received the most votes in the state. Sometimes they give the vote for the first elector, who generally is the leading elector; sometimes the average vote for all the electors; and sometimes the vote for the leading elector in each county. The vote for electors at large is more likely to be given than that for other electors.

All the several kinds of votes found in the election statistics were used. As a rule no selection was possible. In recent years, however, when the vote for all the electors is occasionally given, close contests were sometimes decided by averaging the vote. Fortunately the political complexion of a county was rarely changed by using one vote rather than another. It was the same whether derived from the vote for the leading elector, the vote for the first elector, or the average vote.

When more than one return for the same election was accessible comparisons were often made with a view to correcting typographical or other errors. Occasionally, in the case of Texas and a few other states, when returns for a county were lacking, its habitual way of voting or the politics of the surrounding area was permitted to determine its political complexion, and the county was mapped accordingly. In general, however, counties for which there were no returns have been left blank. Returns for some of the minor parties, such as the Prohibition party, were sometimes less complete than was desirable; but it is believed that all cases in which minor parties carried a county have been discovered. Several of the minor parties have never carried a county.

Choice of Electors. In the early Presidential elections no uniform method of choosing electors was followed either in the several states or in any one state (with an exception or two). The three most usual methods were: (1) election by the legislature, (2) election by the people in districts, and (3) election by the people on a general ticket. Occasionally two of these methods were combined, as may be seen from the table below. By 1836 all the states except South Carolina, in which the election was by the legislature until the Civil War, had adopted the method that now prevails, that of a popular election on a general ticket. Since that year, with the exception given above, there have been but three instances of an election other than by general ticket. These are Florida in 1868 and Colorado in 1876, in which the elections were by the legislature; and Michigan in 1892, in which the election was by the people in districts, with the exception of two electors who were chosen at large. When the election is by districts the state is divided into electoral districts. Occasionally the electoral and Congressional districts of a state are identical, as was the case in New York in 1828. States in which the election was by general ticket were sometimes divided into districts, with a view to securing a geographical distribution of electors.

Table I, which gives the method of choosing electors during the years 1788–1836, has been compiled chiefly from state statutes and contemporary newspapers.

Geographical Units Used in Constructing the Maps. With a few exceptions the geographical unit employed in constructing the maps for 1789–1796 was the state and in the maps for 1800–1928, the county (or parish, in Louisiana). In mapping the electoral vote for Maryland, Virginia, and North Carolina for 1796 the electoral district was used; and occasionally in mapping the popular vote for the years 1800–1828, when county returns were missing, the electoral or Congressional district was the unit employed. Occasionally the combined vote of some two or three counties, when it was impossible to separate their vote, was mapped.

The county is as a rule the best unit for political purposes. It is common to all the states (except Louisiana, in which the parish corresponds to the county in other states) and is the unit for which election statistics are usually recorded. In New England, however, the town is the more important political unit, but it cannot be shown on maps of small scale. Cities are often more important political units than the counties in which they are situated, but with two exceptions it was not feasible nor desirable to treat them separately from counties. The two exceptions are Baltimore after 1854 and St. Louis after 1876. As these two cities since those years have constituted urban areas distinct from the counties bearing the same names they have been treated separately from their corresponding counties. Boston was treated as a part of Suffolk County; New York, of New York County; Brooklyn, of Kings County; Philadelphia, of Philadelphia County; Baltimore, of Baltimore County for 1800-1852; Chicago, of Cook County; St. Louis, of St. Louis County for 1820-1876; and San Francisco, of San Francisco County. The Virginia cities that form distinct political divisions have been treated as a part of the counties to which they naturally belong.

The counties of the United States vary considerably in size. Wide differences of area will be found by comparing with each other the counties of a given state or of different parts of the Union at any one time, or the same counties of a given state or part of the Union at different times. The area of most counties is between 100 and 1000 square miles. A few fall below the former figure, and a considerable number exceed the latter. In 1920 the average area of the counties of the United States was about 990 square miles. In 1800 the average size of the counties of the thirteen original states was not far from that figure, being a little under 1000 square miles. In 1920 the counties of these thirteen states were about half that size. In the same year the average area of the counties in the Pacific and Rocky Mountain states, in which are found most of the large counties of the Union, was about 2960 square miles; while the average area of the counties of New England, exclusive of those of Maine, was about 630 square miles. There have been no great changes since 1920. In 1930 the smallest county in the Union was New York County, New York, with an area of 22 square miles; and the largest, San Bernardino County, California, with

TABLE 1
METHOD OF ELECTING ELECTORS, 1788–1836

	1788–1789	1792	1796	1800	1804	1808	1812	1816	1820	1824	1828	1832	1836
New Hampshire..	G.T. and L.[1]	G.T.[4]	G.T. and L.[1]	L.	G.T.	G.T.	G.T.	G.T.	G.T.	G.T.	G.T.	G.T.	G.T.
Massachusetts....	D.(8) and L.[2]	D.(4) and L.[5]	D.(14) and L.[7]	L.	D.(17) and A.(2)	L.	D.(6)[11]	L.	D.(13) and A.(2)	G.T.	G.T.	G.T.	G.T.
Rhode Island.....	....	L.	L.	G.T.	G.T.	G.T.	G.T.	G.T.	G.T.	G.T.	G.T.	G.T.	G.T.
Connecticut......	L.	L.	L.	L.	L.	L.	L.	L.	G.T.	G.T.	G.T.	G.T.	G.T.
New York........	....	L.	L.	L.	L.	L.	L.	L.	L.	L.	D.(30) and E.[13]	G.T.	G.T.
New Jersey.......	L.	L.	L.	L.	G.T.	G.T.	L.	G.T.	G.T.	G.T.	G.T.	G.T.	G.T.
Pennsylvania.....	G.T.	G.T.	G.T.	L.	G.T.	G.T.	G.T.	G.T.	G.T.	G.T.	L.	G.T.	G.T.
Delaware........	D.(3)[3]	L.	L.	L.	L.	L.	L.	L.	L.	L.	L.	G.T.	G.T.
Maryland........	G.T.	G.T.	D.(10)	D.(10)	D.(9)[9]	D.(9)[9]	D.(9)[9]	D.(9)[9]	D.(9)[9]	D.(9)[9]	D.(9)[9]	D.(4)[14]	G.T.
Virginia.........	D.(12)	D.(21)	D.(21)	G.T.	G.T.	G.T.	G.T.	G.T.	G.T.	G.T.	G.T.	G.T.	G.T.
North Carolina...	....	L.[6]	D.(12)	D.(12)	D.(14)	D.(14)	L.	G.T.	G.T.	G.T.	L.	L.	L.
South Carolina...	L.	L.	L.	L.	L.	L.	L.	L.	L.	L.	L.	L.	L.
Georgia.........	L.	L.	G.T.	L.	L.	L.	L.	L.	L.	G.T.	G.T.	G.T.	G.T.
Vermont.........		L.	L.	L.	L.	L.	L.	L.	L.	L.	G.T.	G.T.	G.T.
Kentucky........		D.(4)	D.(4)	D.(4)	D.(2)[10]	D.(2)[10]	D.(3)[10]	D.(3)[10]	D.(3)[10]	D.(3)[12]	D.(12)	G.T.	G.T.
Tennessee........			E.[8]	E.[8]	D.(5)	D.(5)	D.(8)	D.(8)	D.(8)	D.(11)	D.(11)	G.T.	G.T.
Ohio............					G.T.	G.T.	G.T.	G.T.	G.T.	G.T.	G.T.	G.T.	G.T.
Louisiana........							L.	L.	L.	L.	G.T.	G.T.	G.T.
Indiana.........								L.	G.T.	G.T.	G.T.	G.T.	G.T.
Mississippi......									G.T.	G.T.	G.T.	G.T.	G.T.
Illinois.........									D.(3)	D.(3)	G.T.	G.T.	G.T.
Alabama........									L.	G.T.	G.T.	G.T.	G.T.
Maine..........									D.(7) and A.(2)	D.(7) and A.(2)	D.(7) and A.(2)	G.T.	G.T.
Missouri........									L.	D.(3)	G.T.	G.T.	G.T.
Arkansas........													G.T.
Michigan........													G.T.

Explanation: L. = by legislature; G. T. = by people, on a general ticket; D. = by people, in districts; A. = by people, in the state at large; E. = by electors. The number in parentheses following the abbreviation "D." is the number of districts into which the state was divided. As a rule each district elected one elector. Exceptions to the rule that are not obvious are given in the notes. The number in parentheses following the abbreviation "A." is the number of electors elected at large.

[1] A majority of the popular vote was necessary for a choice. In case of a failure to elect the legislature supplied the deficiency.

[2] Each of the eight districts chose two electors, from which the General Court (i.e., the legislature) selected one. It also elected two electors at large.

[3] Each qualified voter voted for one elector. The three electors who received most votes in the state were elected.

[4] A majority of votes was necessary for a choice. In case of a failure to elect one or more electors a second election was held by the people, at which choice was made from the candidates in the first election who had the most votes. The number of candidates in the second election was limited to twice the number of the electors wanted.

[5] Two of the districts voted for five members each, and two for three members each. A majority of votes was necessary for a choice. In case of a failure to elect by popular vote the General Court supplied the deficiency. In the election of 1792 the people chose five electors and the General Court eleven.

[6] The state was divided into four districts, and the members of the legislature residing in each district chose three electors.

[7] A majority of votes was necessary for a popular choice. Deficiencies were filled by the General Court, as in 1792. It also chose two electors at large. In 1796 it chose nine electors, and the people seven.

[8] In 1796 and 1800 Tennessee chose three Presidential electors—one each for the districts of Washington, Hamilton, and Mero. Three "electors" for each county in the state were appointed by the legislature, and the "electors" residing in each of the three districts chose one of the three Presidential electors.

[9] During the years 1804-1828 Maryland chose eleven electors in nine districts, two of the districts electing two members each.

[10] Each district elected four electors.

[11] One district chose six electors; one, five; one, four; two, three each; and one, one.

[12] Two districts chose five electors each, and one chose four.

[13] One district elected three electors; two, two electors each; and twenty-seven, one elector each. The thirty-four electors thus elected chose two electors.

[14] One district chose four electors; one, three; one, two; and one, one.

an area of 20,175 square miles. There are eight states any one of which is smaller than San Bernardino County. Its area exceeds by 4000 square miles the combined area of Massachusetts, Rhode Island, Connecticut, and Delaware.

When a state is being settled the older or eastern counties are generally smaller than the newer or western ones. The more populous regions as a rule have the smaller counties. The counties in which Boston, New York, Brooklyn, Jersey City, Denver, and San Francisco are situated are exceptionally small—less than 75 square miles. Because of the creation of new counties the average size of counties in most sections of the Union is always decreasing—rapidly when the sections are new, and slowly, later. In New England, however, no new county has been created since 1860. On the other hand, in Georgia, one of the thirteen original states, eleven counties were created between 1905 and 1912.

In three states, Connecticut, Rhode Island, and Delaware, no new counties have been created since the eighteenth century.

Counties vary greatly in population. In 1930 most of the counties had a population of from 5000 to 50,000, although there was a considerable number with less than 5000 or with more than 50,000. The counties with less than 5000 people were rural counties and were situated chiefly in the Rocky Mountain and Pacific states. The counties with more than 50,000 people usually contained a large urban population and were situated chiefly in the Eastern and North Central states. In 1930 the most populous county was Cook County, Illinois, with a population of 3,982,000; and the least populous was Armstrong County, South Dakota, with a population of 80. Next to Cook County in population was Kings County, New York, with a population of 2,560,000. Los Angeles County, California, was third, with a population of 2,208,000.

Only nine states had total populations greater than that of Cook County. Erie County, New York, was more populous than the states of Arizona, Nevada, and Wyoming combined.

In 1800 the population of most of the counties of the Northern states was from 5000 to 50,000; and of the Southern and Western states, from 1000 to 25,000. In the less populous regions of the West, counties below 1000 were not infrequent. There were a few counties above 50,000. Philadelphia County was the largest, with a population of 81,000.

In 1930 the population was most dense in New York County, where there were 84,878 people to the square mile, and least dense in some of the counties of the Pacific and Rocky Mountain states and Western Texas, where there were fewer than two persons to the square mile. Most counties had a density of from 10 to 100 people to the square mile, although there were many counties below the former figure, chiefly rural counties west of the Mississippi; and not a few counties above the latter figure, chiefly urban counties in the thickly populated regions of the Eastern and North Central states. In 1800, as in 1930, the density of population in most counties was from 10 to 100 to the square mile. Many counties in the West, however, had a density of less than 10 and a few in the East of more than 100 to the square mile. New York County had the greatest density, about 1400 to the square mile. For further information on this subject see p. 48, above, and Plates 76B–79.

Representation of Votes on Maps. The vote that is represented on the maps is the vote for candidates and not necessarily the vote for parties. The vote represented for each of the three classes of maps is as follows: (1) 1789–1796, the electoral vote for Presidential candidates; (2) 1800–1816, the vote for each Presidential or other candidate who carried a county; and (3) 1820–1924, the vote for each Presidential candidate who carried a county. When only two candidates are running the vote represented is a majority vote. When there are more than two candidates running the plurality vote is represented, which may or may not be a majority.

On each map the vote for candidates is represented by two or more of the six following colors: blue, yellow, red, green, violet, and black. All the territory carried by a candidate at any one election is given the same color. Should a candidate run at more than one election, the territory carried by him at subsequent elections is given the color first assigned to him, unless there is a good reason for changing it, which is the case when he runs as the candidate of a different party. Thus, on the map for 1904 the Roosevelt territory is blue, while on the map for 1912 it is red.

While the vote mapped is that for candidates, care was taken to show as far as possible the vote for parties. Each party therefore has a distinctive color. In the case of party factions which support different Presidential candidates the minor factions, or those which from the point of view of party regularity are "irregular," are represented by some color other than the party color. If for a given election one party accepts the candidates of another party, it has no distinctive color for that election. Parties that do not carry counties are not represented.

Inasmuch as a party with a new name often derives its principles and personnel largely from one or more old parties, it is not always easy to decide whether it is a new or an old party. In reaching a decision no hard and fast rule was applied; appeal to usage and expert opinion were deemed the appropriate method rather than minute investigation.

The principal parties and their corresponding colors are as follows: Federalist, blue; Democratic-Republican, red; Democratic, yellow; National Republican, violet; Anti-Masonic, blue; Whig, green; Free Soil Democratic, red; Know-Nothing, or "American," violet; Republican, blue; Greenback-Labor, green; Populist, green; Socialist, black; and Progressive, red.

Cases of fusion, coalition, party factions, and confusion in party lines sometimes arise which render the representation of votes somewhat difficult. Such cases have been treated in accordance with the following principles:

1. When two or more parties or party factions support the same Presidential candidate their vote is united and is represented by the color of that candidate. They may support the same or different Vice-Presidential candidates, and the same or different electoral tickets.

2. When one party or faction accepts unconditionally the electoral candidates of another party or faction its vote is represented by the color of the Presidential candidate of the party whose electoral candidates it accepted.

3. When each of two or more party factions supports different Presidential candidates the vote of each faction is represented by the color of its candidate.

4. When two or more parties or party factions, supporting different Presidential candidates, enter into an agreement to divide the Presidential electors and support a fusion electoral ticket their combined vote is represented by a combination of the colors of the candidates of the several parties entering into the agreement. The vote for fusion tickets and the vote for "straight" tickets (see, for instance, p. 99, below) are not combined.

5. When two or more parties or party factions, supporting different Presidential candidates, vote for the same electoral ticket with the understanding that the electors, guided by the results of the election, will cast their ballots unanimously for one or the other of the candidates the combined vote of those parties or factions is represented by a combination of the colors of their candidates.

6. When the party allegiance or preference of the electoral candidates on any ticket is divided or uncertain, and when such division or uncertainty causes support for the ticket to be drawn from more than one faction or party, the vote for those candidates is represented by a combination of colors.

The method followed in mapping the vote of members of legislatures was to give the county or other geographical unit represented by the member the color of the candidate for whom he voted. In the case of "plural districts," that is, districts represented by more than one member, the vote of the majority was mapped. Members of plural districts who did not vote were disregarded.

All tie votes, whether occurring in popular elections or elections by the legislature, were decided for purposes of mapping in favor of one or the other of the candidates and were represented on the maps in accordance with such decisions. The tie and the decision are noted in the text below. Ties were sometimes decided by an appeal to the average of the votes for all the electors. When this could not be computed, or was not decisive, they were decided more or less arbitrarily. Sometimes the decision turned on the political complexion of the adjacent territory.

Islands, both those near the seaboard and those in the interior lakes, were not colored unless they formed counties, or unless they were unusually important. In accordance with these principles the following islands were colored: Nantucket; Marthas Vineyard, or Dukes County; Long Island; Staten Island, or Richmond County; Key West Island, on which Key West, Florida, the county seat of Monroe County, is situated; the islands in Lake Champlain, forming for the most part Grand Isle County, Vermont; Isle Royale, Michigan, in Lake Superior, for the years 1876–1896, when it was a county; North Manitou Island and Beaver Island, in Lake Michigan, for the years 1856–1892, when with the adjacent islands they formed Manitou County, Michigan; and the principal islands forming San Juan and Island counties, Washington. The proper color of relatively unimportant islands that do not form counties may be ascertained from the color of the counties to which they belong. Thus, the proper color of Block Island is the color of Newport County, Rhode Island; and of Mackinac Island, the color of Mackinac County, Michigan.

Frequently in the early years of a state's history many anomalous conditions respecting counties arise, such as the inclusion within their boundaries of large areas of unsettled territory, the attaching of one county to another, and the creation of a county for a considerable period before its organization. Such anomalies have been dealt with in accordance with the information available. Unsettled or unorganized areas, when of considerable size and admitting of somewhat definite location, have been cut off from the color areas and appear as blank areas on the maps. Occasionally such blank areas include a few scattering voters, and occasionally color areas include considerable unsettled territory. Non-voting areas are also left blank.

Interpretation of the Maps. When making comparisons users of the *Atlas* should note the complications that arise from variations in the size of counties, in the density of population, in the number of candidates, and in the majority or pluralities received by them.

Since the smaller the unit the larger the showing made on the maps by the minority candidates, those states or parts of states that have small counties, other things being equal, show a relatively larger area for such candidates. The same principle holds in respect to the earlier and the later maps for those states that have decreased the size of their counties. The relation between small units and minority parties may be seen by comparing maps based on counties with maps based on states. Thus a map of the Presidential election of 1912 based on states would show but two states, Vermont and Utah, for Taft, while the map for this election (see Pl. 110B) based on counties shows a much larger area. This relation might also be seen by a comparison of maps of New England based on towns with maps based on counties.

Because of variations in the density of population the larger vote is often represented on the maps by the smaller area. This may be illustrated by the Bryan territory in Massachusetts and Kansas shown on the map for 1900 (see Pl. 109A). The Bryan territory in Massachusetts is that of Suffolk County, in which Boston is situated. The Bryan territories in Kansas cover twenty-two counties, the smallest of which is more than eleven times as large as Suffolk County. Bryan's vote in Suffolk County was 48,000 (plurality 7000), while his vote in the twenty-two Kansas counties was 29,000 (plurality 3000). This is an extreme case, but the disproportion is not so great as a comparison of New York County, in which New York City is situated, with the counties of some of the Western states would show. In making comparisons between eastern and western, or urban and rural, areas account should always be taken of differences in density of population.

Since degrees of majority or plurality are disregarded, the majority or plurality that is represented on the maps may vary considerably. In the case of two candidates the majority may vary from a small fraction over 50 per cent to a small fraction under 100 per cent of the entire vote. In the case of three candidates the plurality represented on the maps may vary from a small fraction over 33⅓ per cent to a small fraction under 100 per cent. In the case of four candidates the lower limit is a small fraction over 25 per cent. The larger the number of parties and the more nearly equal their votes, the better is the chance that a county will be carried by a plurality that is relatively small in comparison with the total vote. The larger the number of major candidates and the more nearly equal their votes, the better chance has a minor candidate of carrying counties. For instance, in 1912, when there were three major candidates, Debs (Socialist) carried Burke County, North Dakota (see Pl. 110B), by a vote that was but 29 per cent of the total vote cast in that county. In an election such as that of 1904, in which one of the major candidates received many more votes than the other, the chance of a county being carried by a minor candidate is relatively small.

The variations in majorities and pluralities are as a rule much less than these considerations would lead one to expect. When there are but two major candidates, which with a few exceptions has been the case in Presidential elections, the successful candidate generally receives a majority of all the votes cast in a county. When there are more than two major candidates, however, as in 1912, the successful candidate often receives less than a majority. "Two-party" maps are not strictly comparable with "three-party" maps. In the case of only two major candidates the average county plurality of one major candidate is not likely to vary widely from that of another. The large pluralities of one candidate in some states are likely to be matched by similar pluralities for the other candidate in other states. The great preponderance of the Democratic party in the Southern states, however, tends to raise its average plurality over that of other parties.

As a rule the candidate with the most votes in a state carries most of the counties of that state. In close elections, however, he may carry fewer counties than his opponents. Thus, in 1884 Cleveland, with a plurality of 1047 votes in the state of New York, carried but fifteen out of the sixty counties of that state. In 1912 Taft, with a total vote in Tennessee of 59,400, carried six counties, while Roosevelt, with a total vote of 53,700, carried seventeen counties.

By referring to the special text for the several Presidential elections (see pp. 92-104, below) users of the *Atlas* may ascertain from statements respecting the electoral vote the states carried by each candidate, which, together with other information there found, will often enable them to correct some of the erroneous impressions given by the maps.

Boundary Lines. The international, state, and county boundary lines shown upon the maps are, with a few unavoidable exceptions, contemporary lines—that is, the lines as they were in the year for which the map is constructed. In respect to disputed lines no invariable rule of representation was applied. Those parts of the northern and northeastern boundary line between the United States and Canada that were disputed are shown on all maps as they were finally settled and as they are today. On the maps for 1789 and 1792 the southern international boundary line of the United States, which was disputed, is that claimed by the United States and defined in the treaty with Spain of 1795. On the maps for 1804 and 1808 the boundary between Louisiana and Spanish Florida is that claimed by Spain. On the maps of 1812 and 1816 the southeastern boundary of Louisiana is that fixed in the acts of 1812 admitting the state and enlarging its limits, and the western boundary of Spanish Florida is that claimed by the United States in Madison's proclamation of 1810 taking possession of West Florida. On the maps for 1789-1800 the northern, western, and southern boundaries of Georgia are those claimed by Georgia, with one exception—namely, on the map for 1800 part of her western and southern boundaries are the lines established by the United States in the act of 1789 organizing Mississippi Territory. Small changes in boundary lines between states, such as those made in the line between Rhode Island and Massachusetts in 1862, are disregarded. For further information respecting boundary lines users of the *Atlas* are referred to the text above, pages 43-45, to the references there given, and to the corresponding maps of the *Atlas*.

The lines within the states separating one color area from another are county boundary lines. These were derived for the most part from contemporary maps of states and occasionally from the statutes establishing or changing county lines. In deriving some of the early lines, however, considerable use was made of modern maps, since these are often based on more detailed and precise surveys and show the lines more accurately than the early maps. In the present state of our knowledge of county boundary lines no method of deriving them is free from occasional inaccuracies. These, however, on maps of small scale are so slight and trifling that they may be disregarded.

The lines within the states separating "unsettled areas" (appearing blank on the maps) from colored or voting areas may be county lines, Indian treaty lines, lines of Indian reservations, or other lines. Often they are drawn arbitrarily and may not appear on other maps.

Sources of Information. The three principal sources of information are as follows: (1) returns of elections, in manuscript, to be found in state archives; (2) returns printed in the official publications of the states; and (3) all other published returns.

A considerable use was made of manuscript returns, especially those of the New England states. It was not possible or feasible, however, to make them the chief source. Many of the early manuscript returns for the Southern and Western states have been lost or destroyed. In respect to the use of such manuscript returns as are still preserved many difficulties presented themselves, not the least of which were the great labor and cost required to explore thoroughly the state archives and to make the necessary copies. Moreover, unless such copies were made with discriminating care they were likely to prove inferior to returns readily accessible in printed form.

A large use was made of the returns found in the official state publications, but it was not possible, had it been desirable, to rely wholly or even chiefly upon them, for not until about 1870 did any considerable number of states begin to publish their election statistics. Neither was it possible nor desirable to rely wholly upon the state publications for the years covered by them, since not all of them are readily accessible and many of their election statistics contain inaccuracies.

The third class of returns are those found in the standard newspaper almanacs or political registers, Matthias's *Politician's Register* (1835), *Niles' Register* (Baltimore, 1811-1849), and contemporary newspapers. These publications are readily accessible in Washington, and the larger part of the returns that were used have been derived from them. By way of supplementing the returns thus derived, especially for purposes of comparison with a view to eliminating inaccuracies, a large use was made of the returns of the other two classes.

So prone are compilers of figures to make errors that it was impossible to place complete reliance on any one source of information or on any one publication. In respect to accuracy the *Tribune Almanac* (New York, 1856-1914) was found to compare favorably with the state publications. An attempt was made to correct the blunders of copyists and typographers by comparing returns, when two or more sets for the same election were available. It was impossible, however, to eliminate all inaccuracies. Fortunately, errors that did not change the political complexion of a county were negligible.

For different periods the sources of information varied somewhat. For the period 1800-1828 the chief sources were: the contemporary newspapers of the several states and of the District of Columbia, for election years; *Niles' Register*, October-December, 1812, 1816, 1820, 1824, and 1828 (Vols. 3, 11, 19, 27, and 35); journals of state legislatures; and state archives, the last-named being frequently drawn upon for the New England states. The information for this period was exceedingly scattering, and not a few returns of elections are no longer in existence. No collection of returns by counties for the several states was found except one for the election of 1828, which was printed in the *United States Telegraph* (Washington, D. C.), March 27-April 1, 1829. *Niles' Register* for this period contains much important election news and some scattering returns by counties. All the newspapers in the Library of Congress and a few in other depositories were thoroughly searched. Of those most serviceable the following may be mentioned:

Cahawba Press and Alabama State Intelligencer; *Alabama Republican* and *Southern Advocate* (Huntsville); *Connecticut Courant* (Hartford); *Connecticut Journal* and *Columbian Weekly Register* (New Haven); *Delaware Gazette* and *Delaware State Journal and Statesman* (Wilmington); *National Intelligencer* and *United States Telegraph* (Washington); *Augusta Chronicle and Georgia Advertiser*; *Savannah Republican*; *Edwardsville* (Ill.) *Spectator*; *Illinois Gazette* (Shawneetown); *Indiana Gazette* (Corydon and Bloomington); *Indiana Journal* (Indianapolis); *Argus of Western America* and *The Kentuckian* (Frankfort); *Kentucky Gazette* and *Kentucky Reporter* (Lexington); *Louisville Public Advertiser*; *Louisiana Courier* (New Orleans); *American Advocate* (Hallowell, Me.); *Eastern Argus* (Portland, Me.); *Maryland Gazette* and *Maryland Republican* (Annapolis); *Federal Gazette and Baltimore Daily Advertiser*; *Baltimore Patriot and Mercantile*

Advertiser; *Easton* (Md.) *Star*; *Columbian Centinel, Independent Chronicle and Universal Advertiser, New England Palladium and Commercial Advertiser, Patriot and Daily Mercantile Advertiser* (Boston); *Salem* (Mass.) *Gazette*; *Massachusetts Spy* (Worcester); *Southern Luminary* (Jackson, Miss.); *Missouri Intelligencer* (Franklin); *Independent Patriot* (Jackson, Mo.); *Missouri Gazette and Public Advertiser* and *Missouri Republican* (St. Louis); *New Hampshire Journal* and *New Hampshire Patriot and State Gazette* (Concord); *New Hampshire Constitutionalist and Weekly Magazine* (Exeter); *New Hampshire Sentinel* (Keene); *New Hampshire Gazette* and *Portsmouth Oracle* (Portsmouth); *Fredonian* (New Brunswick, N. J.); *True American* (Trenton); *Albany Argus*; *New York Daily Advertiser, New York American, New York Herald, National Advocate* (New York); *Catawba Journal* (Charlotte, N. C.); *Carolina Sentinel* (Newbern, N. C.); *Raleigh Register and North Carolina Gazette*; *The Supporter and Scioto Gazette* (Chillicothe, Ohio); *Cincinnati Daily Gazette*; *Liberty Hall and Cincinnati Mercury*; *Harrisburg Republican*; *Poulson's American Daily Advertiser, Aurora and General Advertiser, Relf's Philadelphia Gazette and Daily Advertiser, Democratic Press* (Philadelphia); *Newport Mercury* and *Rhode Island Republican* (Newport); *Charleston* (S. C.) *Daily Courier*; *Knoxville Register*; *Nashville Whig, Tennessee Gazette, Nashville Republican and State Gazette, Impartial Review and Cumberland Repository* (Nashville); *Vermont Gazette* (Bennington); *Vermont Watchman and State Gazette* (Montpelier); *The Washingtonian* (Windsor, Vt.); *Alexandria Herald*; *Norfolk Gazette and Public Ledger* and *Norfolk Herald*; *Virginia Argus, Richmond Enquirer*, and *Virginia Patriot* (Richmond).

For the year 1832 the sources for 1800–1828 mentioned above were used, but the principal source was the *Politician's Register* (Philadelphia, 1835), by Benjamin Matthias. This contains one of the earliest collections of votes by counties for the several states and, with that for 1828 in the *United States Telegraph*, supplements those in the *Whig Almanac*, which begin with 1836.

For the years 1836–1928 the principal sources were the newspaper almanacs or registers, state publications, state archives, *Niles' Register* (1836–1848), and contemporary newspapers. Of these the source most used was the annual publication that was first issued in 1838 by Horace Greeley under the title *The Whig Almanac and Politician's Register*. The title for 1839–1841 was *The Politician's Register*, and for 1843–1855 *The Whig Almanac and United States Register*. The publication did not appear in 1842. From 1856 to 1914, when it was discontinued, it was issued under the title *The Tribune Almanac and Political Register*. This annual, as its title indicates, specialized in political information, and its election statistics are exceedingly complete, though not without inaccuracies. In using these statistics it is well to remember that the politics of the annual were for the early years Whig and for the later years Republican.

Of other newspaper almanacs the most helpful were the *World Almanac and Encyclopedia* (New York), 1868–1929, the *Chicago Daily News Almanac and Year Book*, 1890–1929, the *Evening Journal Almanac* (Albany), 1861–1896, and the *American Almanac and Treasury of Facts* (New York and Washington), 1880–1889. Of these four the *World Almanac* was most used. It was the principal source for the elections of 1916–1928. It is necessary to remember that its politics are Democratic. The information in these almanacs often supplements that found in the *Tribune Almanac*.

The election statistics of a given Presidential election will first be found as a rule in the almanacs for the year succeeding the year of the election —statistics for the election of 1860 in the almanacs for 1861, of 1864 in the almanacs for 1865, etc. Occasionally, however, they are not published until the second year succeeding the year of the election. Each series of almanacs republishes election statistics for purposes of comparison in the years immediately succeeding the year of their first appearance.

Before 1870 Maine, Massachusetts, Pennsylvania, Wisconsin, Minnesota, and a few other states began the publication of their election returns. Since that date all or nearly all of the remaining states have established this excellent practice. The form of publication is not uniform in the several states nor always in the same state. In general the returns are to be found in legislative manuals, state registers, official directories, year books, blue books, and reports of secretaries of state. Sometimes they are issued separately under the title of election statistics, abstract of votes, returns of general elections, etc. Occasionally states print their election returns for a given year in more than one state publication, and occasionally they fail to print them in any publication, with the result that there is a hiatus in the series. Often they print a given return several times in the same publication. In general the returns appearing in the year of the election or in the following year were used.

Some of the early state manuals and registers must be regarded as only semi-official, since they were privately copyrighted and sold. The returns in the state publications are sometimes less accurate than those in the almanacs. Occasionally, however, they are superior to those in the almanacs and for recent years sometimes more complete since they may give the vote for each elector. The New England states frequently

publish returns both by counties and by towns. All the state publications from their earliest date to 1914 accessible in Washington and a few found in other depositories have been used.

Several of the states have published collections of their election statistics, as may be seen from the following list of those that were used: *Connecticut State Register and Manual*, Hartford, 1889, pp. 394–409— returns for 1856–1888; W. W. Admire, *Political and Legislative Hand-Book of Kansas*, Topeka, 1891, pp. 224–356 —returns for 1864–1888; *Michigan Official Directory and Legislative Manual*, Lansing, 1913, pp. 672–691—returns for 1836–1912; *Nebraska Blue Book*, Lincoln, 1901–1902, pp. 173–177 —returns for 1868–1900; *New Hampshire Manual of Useful Information*, Manchester, 1889, pp. 240–295 —returns for 1852–1888; *South Dakota Legislative Manual*, Pierre, 1913, pp. 293–506 —returns for 1892–1912 (same in *Official Vote of South Dakota by Counties*, 1889–1912); and R. D. W. Connor, *North Carolina Manual*, Raleigh, 1913, pp. 983–992 —returns for 1836–1912.

Electoral Vote for President, 1789
[PLATE 102A]

Ten of the thirteen original states took part in the Presidential election of 1788–1789. Rhode Island and North Carolina had not yet entered the Union, and New York failed to choose electors because of a disagreement of the two branches of her legislature over the method of choice.

With an exception or two, the electors were chosen on January 7, 1789 (the first Wednesday in January), the date fixed by the Continental Congress. In New Hampshire the people voted for electors in December, 1788. Since a majority of votes was required there was a failure to elect, and the legislature of that state chose electors on January 7. In Maryland the election was held during the week of January 7 and extended over a period of several days. At this time the practice of holding elections on more than one day was not uncommon. For details respecting the choice of electors see table above, p. 89.

The electors voted on February 4, 1789 (the first Wednesday in February), and their votes were counted by Congress on April 6. The electoral vote was Washington 69, not voting 4, total 73. Two Maryland and two Virginia electors did not vote. Washington was the only candidate for President. In many of the states, however, there were both Federalist and anti-Federalist electoral tickets.

A map of the election of 1788–1789 based on county returns in the states that chose electors by the people and on the vote of members of the legislature in the states that chose electors by the legislature would in all probability not differ from the map based on the electoral vote.

Electoral Vote for President, 1792
[PLATE 102B]

Fifteen states—the thirteen original states, Vermont, and Kentucky— took part in the Presidential election of 1792. The date of the election, fixed by Congress on March 1, 1792, was within the period November 1 –December 4, 1792 (34 days preceding the first Wednesday in December). For details respecting the method of choosing electors see table above, p. 89.

The electors voted on December 5, 1792 (the first Wednesday in December), and their votes were counted by Congress on February 13, 1793 (the second Wednesday in February). The electoral vote was Washington 132, not voting 3, total 135. One elector in Vermont and two in Maryland did not vote. Washington was the only candidate for President. There were, however, contests between the Federalists and anti-Federalists over electoral tickets and the Vice-Presidency.

What was said above in respect to a map of the election of 1788–1789 based on county returns would be true of a similar map of the election of 1792.

Electoral Vote for President, 1796
[PLATE 102C]

Sixteen states took part in the Presidential election of 1796, one more than in 1792, the additional state being Tennessee. The date of the election was within the period November 3–December 6. For details respecting the method of choosing electors, see table, p. 89, above.

The electors voted on December 7, 1796, and their votes were counted by Congress on February 8, 1797. The Federalist candidate for President was John Adams, of Massachusetts; and the Democratic-Republican candidate was Thomas Jefferson, of Virginia.

The electoral vote was Adams 71, Jefferson 68, total 139. Adams received all the electoral votes of Vermont, New Hampshire, Massachusetts, Rhode Island, Connecticut, New York, New Jersey, and Delaware, seven votes of Maryland, and one vote each of Pennsylvania, Virginia, and North Carolina. Jefferson received all the electoral votes of South Carolina, Georgia, Kentucky, and Tennessee, fourteen votes of Pennsylvania, four of Maryland, twenty of Virginia, and eleven of

North Carolina. Adams carried seven states, Jefferson four, and four states were divided. Since Maryland, Virginia, and North Carolina chose electors in districts the electoral vote in these states is mapped by districts. In Maryland one elector, who voted for both Adams and Jefferson, has been treated as a Federalist, and his district mapped for Adams. South Carolina's electors voted unanimously for Jefferson and for Thomas Pinckney of that state, the Federalist candidate for Vice-President. Since the Electoral vote of Pennsylvania is divided between the two candidates, and since her electors were chosen on a general ticket, her vote is represented by a combination of the colors of the candidates. Pennsylvania chose two Federalist electors, but one of them voted for Jefferson. The popular vote for electors in Pennsylvania, not quite complete, was: highest Adams elector 12,217, highest Jefferson elector 12,306. Full, though not complete, returns give Adams ten counties and Jefferson eleven counties, including Philadelphia city (*Claypoole's American Daily Advertiser*, Philadelphia, Nov. 19 and 28, 1796). In Georgia, which chose electors on a general ticket, the Federalists carried out of twenty-one counties Richmond County, in which Augusta is situated, and three other up-state counties (U. B. Phillips, *Georgia and State Rights*, Washington, 1902, p. 91). In the New York assembly all the votes, except a few scattering ones, were given for the Adams electors (*N. Y. Assembly Journ.*, Nov. 8, 1796).

Presidential and Other Elections, 1800
[PLATE 102D]

Sixteen states took part in the Presidential election of 1800, the same number as in 1796. Two states (Rhode Island and Virginia) chose Presidential electors by general ticket, three (Maryland, North Carolina, and Kentucky) by districts, one (Tennessee) by special electors, and ten (New Hampshire, Massachusetts, Connecticut, New York, New Jersey, Pennsylvania, Delaware, South Carolina, Georgia, and Vermont) by the legislature (see p. 89, above).

The map for 1800 is based on the vote at the Presidential election in eight states (Rhode Island, New York, Delaware, Maryland, Virginia, North Carolina, Kentucky, and Tennessee) and on the vote at some other election in the eight remaining states. The following elections were used to supplement the Presidential election: gubernatorial elections in New Hampshire and Massachusetts, election for members of the lower house of the legislature in Pennsylvania, and Congressional elections in Connecticut, New Jersey, South Carolina, Georgia, and Vermont. In several states (Maryland, North Carolina, Kentucky, Tennessee, South Carolina, Georgia, and Vermont) county returns, owing to their incompleteness, were supplemented with returns for electoral or Congressional districts. In mapping these states, therefore, considerable use was made of geographical units larger than the county.

For New York the vote is that of the assembly (nominating electors), for Delaware that of the legislature, for Tennessee that of special electors, and for the remaining states that of the people. The dates of the several elections are as follows: March, New Hampshire; April, Massachusetts; September, Connecticut and Vermont; October, Pennsylvania, South Carolina, and Georgia; December, New Jersey; and November (Presidential election), the rest of the states.

The Federalist candidate for President was John Adams of Massachusetts; and the Democratic-Republican candidate, Thomas Jefferson of Virginia. The candidates for governor in New Hampshire were John T. Gilman (Federalist) and Timothy Walker (Democratic-Republican); and in Massachusetts, Caleb Strong (Federalist) and Elbridge Gerry (Democratic-Republican). At the Congressional election in Connecticut the leading candidates were Samuel W. Dana (Federalist) and Gideon Granger (Democratic-Republican); and in New Jersey, D. Vroom (Federalist) and James Mott (Democratic-Republican). In South Carolina the successful Federalist candidates for Congress were Benjamin Huger, Thomas Lowndes, and John Rutledge; the successful Democratic-Republican candidates, William Butler, Thomas Moore, and Thomas Sumter. The successful Congressional candidates in Vermont were Lewis R. Morris (Federalist) and Israel Smith (Democratic-Republican). In Georgia the Democratic-Republican candidates had little opposition. Connecticut, New Jersey, and Georgia elected members of Congress by general ticket, and South Carolina and Vermont by districts.

The vote in the New York Assembly was Adams 39, Jefferson 64, not voting 5, total 108 (*N. Y. Assembly Journ.*, Nov. 6, 1800); and in the Delaware legislature, Adams 20, Jefferson 9, not voting 1, total 30 (*Delaware House Journ.*, Nov. 5, 1800).

In the South Carolina legislature the vote for the highest and the lowest elector on each ticket was as follows: Federalist 69 and 63; Democratic-Republican 87 and 82 (*Amer. Hist. Rev.*, Vol. 4, New York, 1899, p. 120). The popular vote in those states for which it was ascertained is shown in the following table:

TABLE 2
POPULAR VOTE IN PRESIDENTIAL AND OTHER ELECTIONS, 1800

STATES	FEDERALIST	DEMOCRATIC-REPUBLICAN	SCATTERING
New Hampshire[1].....	10,362 (Gilman)	6,039 (Walker)	361
Massachusetts[2].......	19,630 (Strong)	17,019 (Gerry)	2,410
Rhode Island[3]........	1,941 (Adams)	1,684 (Jefferson)	
Connecticut[4].........	6,273 (Dana)	3,012 (Granger)	
New Jersey[5].........	14,118 (Vroom)	14,726 (Mott)	
Virginia[6]...........	5,950 (Adams)	21,000 (Jefferson)	

[1] *Massachusetts Spy*, June 18, 1800; [2] *Columbian Centinel*, May 31, 1800; [3] *Poulson's American Daily Advertiser*, Dec. 4, 1800; [4] *Connecticut Courant*, Oct. 20, 1800; [5] *Aurora*, Jan. 10, 1801; [6] *Virginia Argus*, Dec. 2, 1800 (returns not quite complete).

The electoral vote was Jefferson 73, Adams 65, total 138. Adams received all the votes of Vermont, New Hampshire, Massachusetts, Rhode Island, Connecticut, New Jersey, and Delaware, seven votes of Pennsylvania, five votes of Maryland, and four votes of North Carolina. Jefferson received all the votes of New York, Virginia, South Carolina, Georgia, Kentucky, and Tennessee, eight votes each of Pennsylvania and North Carolina, and five votes of Maryland. Adams carried seven states, Jefferson six, and three states were divided.

Presidential and Other Elections, 1804
[PLATE 102E]

Seventeen states took part in the Presidential election of 1804, one more than in 1800, the additional state being Ohio. Six states (New Hampshire, Rhode Island, New Jersey, Pennsylvania, Virginia, and Ohio) chose electors by general ticket, four (Maryland, North Carolina, Kentucky, and Tennessee) by districts, one (Massachusetts) by districts and at large, and six (Connecticut, New York, Delaware, South Carolina, Georgia, and Vermont) by the legislature (see p. 89, above).

The map for 1804 is based on the vote at the Presidential election in all the states except Connecticut, South Carolina, Georgia, and Vermont. For Connecticut the vote at the election for the nomination of state assistants, and for the other three states the vote at the Congressional election, was used. The returns are by electoral districts for Tennessee, partly by electoral districts for Maryland, and partly by Congressional districts for South Carolina and Vermont. There are no detailed returns for Ohio. It was mapped for Jefferson because he received eight-ninths of the votes. The county returns for Georgia are not complete.

For New York the vote is that of the Assembly (nominating electors), for Delaware that of the legislature, and for the remaining states, that of the people. The dates of the several elections are as follows: September, Connecticut and Vermont; October, South Carolina and Georgia; and November (Presidential election), the rest of the states.

The Federalist candidate for President was Charles Cotesworth Pinckney of South Carolina; and the Democratic-Republican candidate, Thomas Jefferson of Virginia. In Vermont the successful candidates for Congress were Martin Chittenden, William Chamberlain, and James Elliot (Federalists) and Gideon Olin (Democratic-Republican); and in South Carolina, William Butler, Levi Casey, Elias Earle, Robert Marion, Thomas Moore, O'Brien Smith, David R. Williams, and Richard Wynn (Democratic-Republican). In Georgia there was little opposition to the Congressional candidates of the Democratic-Republican party. In Connecticut the leading Federalist candidate for state assistant was William Edmond; and the leading Democratic-Republican candidate, E. Kirby.

In Rhode Island, New Jersey, Virginia, North Carolina, and Kentucky there was little or no opposition to the Democratic-Republican electoral ticket. The vote in the New York Assembly was Pinckney 15, Jefferson 75, not voting 10, total 100 (*N. Y. Assembly Journ.*, Nov. 9, 1804); and in the Delaware legislature, Pinckney 18, Jefferson 5, not voting 7, total 30 (*Delaware House Journ.*, Nov. 12, 1804). The popular vote in those states for which it has been ascertained was as follows:

TABLE 3
POPULAR VOTE IN PRESIDENTIAL AND OTHER ELECTIONS, 1804

STATES	FEDERALIST	DEMOCRATIC-REPUBLICAN
New Hampshire[1].............	8,364 (Pinckney)	9,088 (Jefferson)
Massachusetts[2]...............	25,777 (Pinckney)	29,310 (Jefferson)
Connecticut[3]...............	12,543 (Edmond)	7,990 (Kirby)
New Jersey[4]................	19 (Pinckney)	13,119 (Jefferson)
Ohio[4]...................	364 (Pinckney)	2,593 (Jefferson)
Pennsylvania[5]...............	1,179 (Pinckney)	22,103 (Jefferson)

[1] *New Hampshire Gazette*, Dec. 4, 1804; [2] *Independent Chronicle*, Nov. 22, 1804; [3] *Connecticut Courant*, Oct. 24, 1804 (the vote is for the highest candidate for assistant on each ticket); [4] *Aurora*, Dec. 1, 1804; [5] *Ibid.*, Nov. 23, 1804.

Oneida County, New York, for which there was a tie vote (Pinckney 2, Jefferson 2) is shown as Democratic-Republican area. A "no return" area is shown in New York.

The electoral vote was Jefferson 162, Pinckney 14, total 176. Pinckney received all the votes of Connecticut and Delaware and two votes of Maryland. Jefferson received nine votes of Maryland and all the votes of the remaining states. Pinckney carried two states, Jefferson fourteen, and one state was divided.

Presidential and Other Elections, 1808
[PLATE 102F]

Seventeen states took part in the Presidential election of 1808, the same number as in 1804. Six states (New Hampshire, Rhode Island, New Jersey, Pennsylvania, Virginia, and Ohio) chose electors by general ticket, four (Maryland, North Carolina, Kentucky, and Tennessee) by districts, and seven (Massachusetts, Connecticut, New York, Delaware, South Carolina, Georgia, and Vermont) by the legislature (see p. 89, above).

The map for 1808 is based on the vote at the Presidential election in all the states except Massachusetts, Connecticut, South Carolina, Vermont, and Ohio. For these states the following votes were used: Massachusetts, vote at the gubernatorial election; Connecticut and Vermont, vote for members of the lower house of the legislature; and South Carolina and Ohio, vote at the Congressional election. The returns for Maryland, North Carolina, South Carolina, and Tennessee are partly by electoral or Congressional districts. The returns for Connecticut and Vermont consist of statements of the number of members of the lower house of the legislature elected by each party from each county.

For New York the vote is that of the Assembly (nominating electors); for Delaware and Georgia, that of the legislature; and for the remaining states, that of the people. The dates of the several elections are as follows: April, Massachusetts and Connecticut; September, Vermont; October, Ohio and South Carolina; and November (Presidential election), the rest of the states.

The Federalist candidate for President was Charles Cotesworth Pinckney of South Carolina. The regular Democratic-Republican candidate was James Madison of Virginia. In New York a Democratic-Republican faction favored George Clinton of that state, and in Virginia a Democratic-Republican faction voted for their fellow Virginian James Monroe. Pinckney was also voted for in Virginia, but he carried no counties. In the New York Assembly the two Democratic-Republican factions voted for a mixed ticket, which, if we may judge from the vote for President in the electoral college, was composed of thirteen Madisonians and six Clintonians. The gubernatorial candidates in Massachusetts were Christopher Gore (Federalist) and James Sullivan (Democratic-Republican). The Congressional candidates in Ohio were Philemon Beecher (Federalist) and Jeremiah Morrow (Democratic-Republican). The successful Congressional candidates in South Carolina, all Democratic-Republicans, were Lemuel J. Alston, William Butler, Joseph Calhoun, Robert Marion, Thomas Moore, John Taylor, Richard Wynn, and Robert Witherspoon.

The vote in the New York Assembly was Pinckney 46, Madison and Clinton 64, scattering 1, not voting 1, total 112 (*N. Y. Assembly Journ.*, Nov. 7, 1808); and in the Delaware legislature, Pinckney 18, Madison 9, not voting 3, total 30 (*Delaware House Journ.*, Nov. 15, 1808). There was little or no regular opposition to Madison in Georgia. The number of Federalist and Democratic-Republican members, respectively, elected to the lower house of the legislature in Connecticut was 139 and 61 (*Connecticut Courant*, Apr. 20, 1808); and in Vermont 109 and 94 (*Public Advertiser*, Oct. 1, 1808). The vote in the Massachusetts legislature for the Pinckney electors was 269. One hundred and thirty Republican members who were present declined to vote (*Aurora*, Nov. 28, 1808). The vote in the Connecticut legislature was Pinckney 149, Madison 44 (*Poulson's American Daily Advertiser*, Nov. 12, 1808). The popular vote in Ohio was Pinckney 1174, Madison 3644 (*Public Advertiser*, Dec. 13, 1808). The popular vote in several of the states was as follows:

TABLE 4
POPULAR VOTE IN PRESIDENTIAL AND OTHER ELECTIONS, 1808

STATES	FEDERALIST	DEMOCRATIC-REPUBLICAN	SCATTERING
New Hampshire[1]..	13,945 (Pinckney)	13,644 (Madison)	
Massachusetts[2]...	39,643 (Gore)	41,193 (Sullivan)	311
Rhode Island[3]....	3,070 (Pinckney)	2,692 (Madison)	
New Jersey[4].....	14,639 (Pinckney)	18,644 (Madison)	
Pennsylvania[5]....	11,649 (Pinckney)	42,318 (Madison)	
Virginia[6].......	750 (Pinckney)	15,400 (Madison)	3,450 (Monroe)
Ohio[7]..........	4,505 (Beecher)	10,309 (Morrow)	

[1] New Hampshire Archives; [2] *Columbian Centinel*, June 1, 1808; [3] *Newport Mercury*, Nov. 26, 1808; [4] *Public Advertiser*, Nov. 23, 1808; [5] *Aurora*, Dec. 16, 1808; [6] *Richmond Enquirer*, Nov. 8–25, Dec. 2, 1808 (the returns are not quite complete); [7] *Aurora*, Nov. 24, 1808.

Since part of the electors on the Democratic-Republican ticket in the New York Assembly were for Madison and part for Clinton the area carried by that ticket is striped with the colors of these two candidates (see p. 90, above). A tie in Orange County, Vermont, was decided in favor of the Federalists, and a tie in Addison County in favor of the Democratic-Republicans.

The electoral vote was Madison 122, Pinckney 47, Clinton 6, not voting 1, total 176. One Madison elector in Kentucky did not vote. Pinckney received all the votes of New Hampshire, Massachusetts, Rhode Island, Connecticut, and Delaware, two votes of Maryland, and three votes of North Carolina. Madison received all the votes of Vermont, New Jersey, Pennsylvania, Virginia, South Carolina, Georgia, Tennessee, Kentucky, and Ohio, thirteen votes of New York, nine votes of Maryland, and eleven votes of North Carolina. Clinton received six votes of New York. Pinckney carried five states, Madison nine, and three states were divided.

Presidential and Other Elections, 1812
[PLATE 102G]

Eighteen states took part in the Presidential election of 1812, one more than in the election of 1808, the new state being Louisiana. Five states (New Hampshire, Rhode Island, Pennsylvania, Virginia, and Ohio) chose electors by general ticket, four (Massachusetts, Maryland, Kentucky, and Tennessee) by districts, and nine (Connecticut, New York, New Jersey, Delaware, North Carolina, South Carolina, Georgia, Vermont, and Louisiana) by the legislature (see p. 89, above).

The map for 1812 is based on the vote at the Presidential election in New Hampshire, Massachusetts, Rhode Island, New York, New Jersey, Pennsylvania, Delaware, Maryland, Virginia, Tennessee, and Kentucky; on the vote at the Congressional election in South Carolina and Georgia; and on the vote at the gubernatorial elections in Connecticut and Vermont. No returns for North Carolina, Ohio, and Louisiana were found. The returns for Maryland and Tennessee are chiefly by electoral districts, and those for South Carolina chiefly by Congressional districts.

For New York the vote is that of the Assembly (nominating electors), for New Jersey and Delaware that of the legislature, and for the remaining states that of the people. The dates of the several elections are as follows: April, Connecticut; September, Vermont; October, South Carolina and Georgia; and November (Presidential election) for the rest of the states.

DeWitt Clinton, the leader of a Democratic-Republican faction in New York, was the "regular" Federalist candidate for President. In Virginia the Federalists did not support Clinton but nominated Rufus King of New York, the "straight" Federalist candidate, and voted for him. The regular Democratic-Republican candidate was James Madison of Virginia. In New York a Democratic-Republican faction supported DeWitt Clinton, and in other states he received the support of not a few anti-administration Democratic-Republicans. In contemporary newspapers the Clinton electoral ticket is variously designated as the Federalist, "coalition," or "peace" ticket. The Madison electoral ticket is often called the "war" ticket. On Plate 102G the vote in the New York Assembly of the "straight" Federalists and the vote of the Clinton Democratic-Republicans are shown. For this state the Clinton vote that is mapped is the vote of the Democratic-Republican factionists, for the other states it is the "coalition" vote. The vote of the "straight" Federalists in the New York Assembly is represented on the map by green, the color of King. The Clinton electors were chosen by the legislature as the result of a combination of Federalists and Democratic-Republican factionists.

The candidates for governor in Connecticut were Roger Griswold (Federalist) and Elijah Boardman (Democratic-Republican), and in Vermont, Martin Chittenden (Federalist) and Jonas Galusha (Democratic-Republican). In South Carolina the successful Congressional candidates, all Democratic-Republicans, were John C. Calhoun, John J. Chappell, Langdon Cheves, Elias Earle, David R. Evans, Samuel Farrow, Theodore Gourdin, John Kershaw, and William Lowndes.

There was little opposition to the Democratic-Republican candidates for Congress in Georgia. The vote in the New York Assembly, nominating electors, was "straight" Federalist (King) 58, regular Democratic-Republican (Madison) 23, Democratic-Republican faction (Clinton) 28, not voting 3, total 112 (*N. Y. Assembly Journ.*, Nov. 9, 1812). In the Delaware legislature the vote for electors was Clinton 19, Madison 6, not voting 5, total 30; and in the New Jersey legislature, Clinton 29, Madison 23, not voting 1, total 53 (*Delaware House Journ.*, Nov. 10, 1812; *Minutes of Joint Meeting of N. J. Council and Assembly*, Nov. 6, 1812). In the Presidential election in Pennsylvania the total Federalist majority in the Federalist counties was 2819, and the total Democratic-Republican majority in the Democratic-Republican counties 23,641 (*Aurora*, Nov. 20, 1812).

The vote at the Presidential election in Ohio was Clinton 3301, Madison 7420 (*Federal Gazette and Baltimore Daily Advertiser*, Nov. 21, 1812). The vote of the North Carolina legislature for electors was Clinton 60, Madison 130 (*Charleston Courier*, Nov. 26, 1812). The vote in the Louisiana legislature was 23 to 16 in favor of the Madison electors (*Niles' Register*, Vol. 3, p. 288). The popular vote in several of the states was as follows:

TABLE 5

POPULAR VOTE IN PRESIDENTIAL AND OTHER ELECTIONS, 1812

STATES	FEDERALIST	DEMOCRATIC-REPUBLICAN	SCATTERING
New Hampshire[1]......	18,958 (Clinton)	15,842 (Madison)	
Massachusetts[2].......	50,254 (Clinton)	27,003 (Madison)	
Rhode Island[3].......	4,032 (Clinton)	2,084 (Madison)	
Connecticut[4]........	11,721 (Griswold)	1,487 (Boardman)	487
Virginia[5]............	4,650 (King)	15,050 (Madison)	

[1] *New Hamsphire Sentinel*, Nov. 21, Dec. 5, 1812 (the figures given are based partly upon calculation; the same is true of several other figures for the years 1800-1816); [2] *Columbian Centinel*, Dec. 9, 1812; [3] *Newport Mercury*, Nov. 28, 1812; [4] *Connecticut Courant*, May 19, 1812; [5] *Richmond Enquirer*, Nov. 6, 10, 12, 14, 17, 20, 27, 1812 (the returns are not quite complete).

In the vote of the New York Assembly there were several ties, which have been treated as follows: Westchester County, tie between King and Madison, and Schenectady County, tie between King and Clinton—both shown as King area; Schoharie County, tie between Clinton and Madison—shown as Madison area; Sullivan and Ulster counties, tie between Clinton and Madison—shown as Clinton area.

The electoral vote was Madison 128, Clinton 89, not voting 1, total 218. One Madison elector in Ohio did not vote. Clinton received all the votes of New Hampshire, Massachusetts, Rhode Island, Connecticut, New York, New Jersey, and Delaware, and five votes of Maryland. Madison received six votes of Maryland and all the votes of the remaining states. Clinton carried seven states, Madison ten, and one state was divided.

Presidential and Other Elections, 1816

[PLATE 102H]

Nineteen states took part in the Presidential election of 1816, one more than in the election of 1812, the additional state being Indiana. Seven states (New Hampshire, Rhode Island, New Jersey, Pennsylvania, Virginia, North Carolina, and Ohio) chose electors by general ticket, three (Maryland, Kentucky, and Tennessee) by districts, and nine (Massachusetts, Connecticut, New York, Delaware, South Carolina, Georgia, Vermont, Louisiana, and Indiana) by the legislature (see p. 89, above).

The map for 1816 is based on the vote at the Presidential election in all the states except Massachusetts, Connecticut, and Vermont. For these states the vote at gubernatorial elections was used. The returns of Maryland are chiefly by electoral districts. In the absence of detail returns for several Southern and Western states general statements to the effect that there was no opposition to Monroe have been depended upon.

For New York the vote is that of the Assembly (nominating electors); for Delaware, South Carolina, Georgia, Louisiana, and Indiana that of the legislature; and for the remaining states that of the people. The dates of the several elections are as follows: April, Massachusetts and Connecticut; September, Vermont; December, South Carolina; and November, the rest of the states. The last two dates are of Presidential elections.

The candidate for the Presidency supported by the Federalists was Rufus King of New York. The regular Democratic-Republican candidate was James Monroe of Virginia. In Pennsylvania a Democratic-Republican faction called the "Old School Democrats" nominated and supported an electoral ticket consisting of men who were opposed to the prevailing method of nominating Presidential candidates by caucus, and a part of whom were unfriendly to Monroe. This ticket, which received Federalist support, was unpledged as to candidates (*Aurora*, Oct. 28, 29, Nov. 1, 22, 1816; *Virginia Patriot*, Nov. 6, 1816). In Massachusetts the candidates for governor were John Brooks (Federalist); and Samuel Dexter (Democratic-Republican); in Connecticut, John Cotton Smith (Federalist) and Oliver Wolcott (Democratic-Republican); and in Vermont, Samuel Strong (Federalist) and Jonas Galusha (Democratic-Republican).

There was little or no opposition to Monroe in Rhode Island, New Jersey, Virginia, North Carolina, South Carolina, Georgia, Louisiana, Tennessee, Kentucky, Ohio, and Indiana. In Maryland also there was little opposition to him, although three Federalist electors were chosen.

The vote in the New York Assembly nominating electors was King 35, Monroe 83, not voting 8, total 126 (*N. Y. Assembly Journ.*, Nov. 8, 1816). In the Delaware legislature the vote for electors was King 18, Monroe 7, not voting 5, total 30 (*Delaware House Journ.*, Nov. 12, 1816). The popular vote in those states for which it has been ascertained was as follows:

TABLE 6

POPULAR VOTE IN PRESIDENTIAL AND OTHER ELECTIONS, 1816

STATES	FEDERALIST	DEMOCRATIC-REPUBLICAN	SCATTERING
New Hampshire[1].	13,180 (King)	15,178 (Monroe)	
Massachusetts[2]..	49,578 (Brooks)	47,384 (Dexter)	122
Connecticut[3]....	11,386 (Smith)	10,170 (Wolcott)	203
Pennsylvania[4]...		25,749 (Monroe)	17,597 (Rep. faction)
Vermont[5].......	13,883 (Strong)	17,162 (Galusha)	102

[1] *Portsmouth Oracle*, Nov. 30, 1816; [2] *Columbian Centinel*, June 1, 1816; [3] *Connecticut Journal*, May 14, 1816; [4] *Aurora*, Nov. 23, 1816; [5] *Reporter* (Brattleborough, Vt.), Oct. 22, 1816.

Since several of the electors on the Independent Democratic-Republican ticket in Pennsylvania would have voted for Monroe, the area carried by this ticket is striped with the colors of the two Democratic-Republican tickets (see p. 90, above). The area carried by the three Federalist electors in Maryland is given the color of King. They did not vote in the electoral college.

The electoral vote was Monroe 183, King 34, not voting 4, total 221. One Federalist elector in Delaware and three in Maryland did not vote. King received the votes of Massachusetts, Connecticut, and Delaware, and Monroe the votes of the remaining sixteen states.

Presidential Election, 1820

[PLATE 103A]

Twenty-four states took part in the Presidential election of 1820, five more than in 1812, the additional states being Mississippi, Illinois, Alabama, Maine, and Missouri. Nine states (New Hampshire, Rhode Island, Connecticut, New Jersey, Pennsylvania, Virginia, North Carolina, Ohio, and Mississippi) chose electors by general ticket, four (Maryland, Kentucky, Tennessee, and Illinois) by districts, two (Massachusetts and Maine) by districts and at large, and nine (New York, Delaware, South Carolina, Georgia, Vermont, Louisiana, Indiana, Alabama, and Missouri) by the legislature (see p. 89, above).

The map for 1820 is based wholly on the vote at the Presidential election—and the same is true of all subsequent maps in this series. There are returns, or other information, respecting the election of 1820 for all the states. For New York the vote is that of the Assembly (nominating electors); for Delaware, South Carolina, Georgia, Vermont, Louisiana, Indiana, Alabama, and Missouri that of the legislature; and for the remaining states that of the people.

In the absence of a detailed vote for several states general statements to the effect that Monroe had no opposition have been depended upon. The election was held on different days in November and early December, 1820. The date in most of the states fell within the first half of November.

James Monroe, with a few exceptions, was supported by both Federalists and Democratic-Republicans. In Rhode Island and New Jersey and in many of the Southern and Western states the successful Democratic-Republican electors had no opposition. In some states or electoral districts rival Democratic-Republican candidates contended for the honor of voting for Monroe. In Massachusetts, Delaware, Maryland, and several other states both Federalist and Democratic-Republican candidates were for Monroe. In Massachusetts a majority of the electors were Federalists, in Delaware the electors were chosen by the Federalist members of the legislature, and in Maryland one Federalist elector was chosen. In two states, Pennsylvania and New York, electors were supported who were opposed to Monroe. The movement against Monroe in these states was in the interest of the candidacy of DeWitt Clinton of New York, and in behalf of anti-slavery principles. For the movement in Pennsylvania see J. B. McMaster, *History of the People of the United States*, Vol. 4, New York, 1895, pp. 516–517, and *Albany Argus*, Oct. 31, 1820; in New York, see *Albany Argus*, Oct. 24, Nov. 10, 1820, *National Advocate*, Nov. 15, 1820, and *Ontario Messenger* (Canandaigua), Nov. 14, 1820.

The vote in the New York Assembly nominating electors was Clinton electoral ticket 53, Monroe 72, not voting 1, total 126 (*N. Y. Assembly Journ.*, Nov. 9, 1820). In Pennsylvania the opposition to Monroe received but little support outside of Philadelphia city and county. The vote in Philadelphia city and its environs was Clinton 1226, Monroe 2430 (*Democratic Press*, Nov. 4, 1820; *Niles' Register*, Vol. 19, p.

190). Outside of Pennsylvania the popular vote possesses little of interest compared with previous elections, as it was all for Monroe and everywhere light. In New Hampshire the average vote for the Democratic-Republican ticket was about 9300, and the scattering vote about 1600 (*New Hampshire Gazette*, Dec. 5, 1820). In Rhode Island the whole number of votes cast was 723 (*Newport Mercury*, Nov. 25, 1820). In Connecticut the highest elector on the Democratic-Republican ticket received 3870 votes; and on the "Federal Caucus Nomination" ticket, 728 votes (*Columbian Register*, New Haven, Dec. 2, 1820).

Since several electors on the Clinton electoral ticket in New York would have voted for Monroe the area carried for these electors is striped with the colors of Clinton and Monroe. Ties between the Clinton and Monroe tickets in the two New York Assembly districts, composed, respectively, of Allegany and Steuben counties and of Cattaraugus, Chautauqua, and Niagara counties, were decided for the purpose of mapping in favor of the Clinton ticket.

Because of the dispute whether Missouri was or was not a state of the Union for the purposes of the Presidential election, the president of the Senate announced the result of the election in alternative form, that is, with Missouri included and with Missouri excluded. With Missouri included, the electoral vote was Monroe 231, John Quincy Adams 1, not voting 3, total 235. One elector from each of the states of Pennsylvania, Tennessee, and Mississippi did not vote. There is no record of the popular vote.

The vote for John Quincy Adams was cast by William Plumer of New Hampshire, chairman of the electoral college of that state. In a letter to his son dated January 8, 1821, he gives his reasons for not supporting the Democratic-Republican candidates in the following words: "I was obliged from a sense of duty and a regard to my own reputation to withhold my vote from Monroe and Tompkins; from the first because he had discovered a want of foresight and economy, and from the second because he grossly neglected his duty" (*Amer. Hist. Rev.*, Vol. 21, 1916, pp. 318–319).

Since Plumer ran upon a Monroe ticket, and since his vote was an expression of his own preference and not that of the electorate, New Hampshire is colored on Plate 103A solidly for Monroe.

Presidential Election, 1824

[PLATE 103B]

Twenty-four states took part in the Presidential election of 1824, the same number as in 1820. Twelve states (New Hampshire, Massachusetts, Rhode Island, Connecticut, New Jersey, Pennsylvania, Virginia, North Carolina, Ohio, Indiana, Mississippi, and Alabama) chose electors by general ticket, five (Maryland, Kentucky, Tennessee, Illinois, and Missouri) by districts, one (Maine) by districts and at large, and six (New York, Delaware, South Carolina, Georgia, Vermont, and Louisiana) by the legislature (see p. 89, above).

For South Carolina, Georgia, and Louisiana there are no returns of the vote of the legislature by members. For New York the vote is that of the Assembly (nominating electors), for Delaware and Vermont that of the legislature, and for the remaining states that of the people. The election was held on different days between October 28 and November 30. In most of the states it was held in the first half of November.

There were four Presidential candidates, John Quincy Adams of Massachusetts, Henry Clay of Kentucky, William H. Crawford of Georgia, and Andrew Jackson of Tennessee. Because of the dissolution of the old parties it is not possible to designate each candidate by a distinctive party name. Not all the candidates ran in every state. Coalition and unpledged tickets were rather common. The following summary, in which a few relatively small or scattering votes are disregarded, shows the candidates in each state: Adams, Jackson, Crawford, and Clay in New York, Pennsylvania, Maryland, Virginia, and Illinois; Jackson, Adams, and Crawford in Tennessee, Alabama, South Carolina, North Carolina, New Jersey, and Delaware; Clay, Jackson, and Adams in Ohio, Indiana, Missouri, and Louisiana; Adams and Crawford in Maine, Massachusetts, Rhode Island, and Connecticut; Jackson and Adams in Mississippi; Crawford and Jackson in Georgia; Clay and Jackson in Kentucky; and Adams in Vermont and New Hampshire.

The vote in the New York Assembly nominating electors was Adams 50, Crawford 43, Clay 32, Jackson 1, not voting 2, total 128 (*N. Y. Assembly Journ.*, Nov. 10, 1824). All the votes cast by the Vermont legislature were for Adams (*Vermont Gazette*, Nov. 9, 1824). On the convening of the Delaware legislature, in November, 1824, the strength of the candidates was as follows: Adams 14, Crawford 11, Jackson 5 (*New York American*, Nov. 15, 1824). Since the Delaware electors were chosen by a combination of Adams and Crawford members, this state is striped with the colors of these two candidates. In North Carolina a coalition

ticket was supported by the friends of Jackson and Adams, with the understanding that the electors should vote for the candidate who had the best chance of success. The vote in the South Carolina legislature was Jackson 132, Adams 15, Crawford 10 (*Catawba Journal*, Dec. 14, 1824; *Charleston Courier*, Nov. 29, 1824). The vote in the Georgia legislature was Crawford 121, Jackson 45 (*Augusta Chronicle*, Nov. 10, 1824). The vote in the Louisiana legislature was Jackson and Adams ticket 30, Clay ticket 28. Clay was defeated by a combination of the Jackson and Adams members (*Richmond Enquirer*, Dec. 25, 1824).

Tie votes are shown as follows, New York: Steuben County, tie between Clay and Jackson, for Jackson; Wayne County, tie between Adams and Crawford, for Crawford; Schoharie County, tie between Adams and Crawford, for Adams; Tioga County, tie between Adams and Clay, for Adams; Suffolk County, tie between Adams and Clay, for Clay; and Oneida County, tie between Crawford and Clay, for Crawford; Virginia: Accomac County, tie between Jackson and Adams, and Wood County, tie between Crawford and Adams, for Adams.

Returns were found for only a few counties of Missouri, and the returns for Kentucky, Tennessee, Virginia, and Illinois, are not complete.

The electoral vote was Jackson 99, Adams 84, Crawford 41, Clay 37, total 261. Jackson received all the votes of New Jersey, Pennsylvania, North Carolina, South Carolina, Tennessee, Mississippi, Alabama, and Indiana, one vote of New York, seven votes of Maryland, three of Louisiana, and two of Illinois. Adams received all the votes of Maine, New Hampshire, Vermont, Massachusetts, Rhode Island, and Connecticut, twenty-six votes of New York, one of Delaware, three of Maryland, two of Louisiana, and one of Illinois. Crawford received all the votes of Virginia and Georgia, five votes of New York, two of Delaware, and one of Maryland. Clay received all the votes of Kentucky, Ohio, and Missouri, and four votes of New York. The division of votes among the candidates occurred in those states in which the electors were chosen by districts or by the legislature. The popular vote for the eighteen states in which the people voted was as follows: Jackson 156,000, Adams 105,000, Clay 47,000, and Crawford 44,000, total 352,000. In determining the popular vote for this and succeeding elections the *Tribune Almanac*, New York, 1856–1914; T. H. McKee, *National Conventions and Platforms*, Baltimore, 1901; *U. S. Statistical Abstract* (1912–1930); A. C. McLaughlin and A. B. Hart, *Cyclopedia of American Government*, New York and London, 1914 (Vol. 3, pp. 19–46); and other standard sources have been used. While additional research and more precise computations might slightly change the results, the figures here given are accurate enough for the purpose in view, namely, the indication of the relative strength of candidates and parties. Numerous discrepancies are found in the various published tables of popular votes. Many of these no doubt are caused by taking the vote of different electors to represent the vote for President. In this text the total votes are given in round numbers, and the "scattering vote" is disregarded.

Presidential Election, 1828

[PLATE 103C]

Twenty-four states took part in the Presidential election of 1828, the same number as in 1820 and 1824. All the states except New York, Delaware, Maryland, South Carolina, Tennessee, and Maine chose electors on a general ticket. Maryland and Tennessee elected by districts. Maine chose seven electors by districts and two at large. New York chose thirty-four electors by districts, and the thirty-four thus chosen chose two electors. In Delaware and South Carolina the election was by the legislature (see p. 89, above).

The map for 1828 is based upon the popular vote in all the states except Delaware and South Carolina, for which states the vote of the legislature was used. The vote of the Delaware legislature was Adams 19, Jackson 11, total 30 (*Delaware House Journ.*, Nov. 10, 1828). The vote in the South Carolina legislature was unanimous for Jackson, with the exception of the vote for one elector (*Charleston Courier*, Dec. 5, 1828). In Georgia there were two Jackson tickets of nine electors each and an Adams ticket of two or three electors. There was but little opposition to the Jackson tickets. One of the successful electors on one of the Jackson tickets, however, favored Adams and, rather than vote for Jackson, resigned. The legislature filled the vacancy with a Jackson man (*Augusta Chronicle*, Nov. 1, 8, 29, Dec. 17, 1828). There was relatively little opposition to Jackson in Tennessee and Alabama. The elections were held late in October, in November, and early in December but chiefly in the first half of November.

The candidates for the Presidency were John Quincy Adams of Massachusetts and Andrew Jackson of Tennessee. Adams was the candidate of the National Republican party, and Jackson of the "Jackson men," who later were called Democrats and to whom are traced the beginnings of the Democratic party.

Counties or parishes in which there were tie votes are shown as follows: Grant County, Kentucky, for Jackson; and Elizabeth City County, Virginia, and Ascension and Assumption parishes, Louisiana, for Adams.

The electoral vote was Jackson 178, Adams 83, total 261. Jackson received all the votes of Pennsylvania, Virginia, North Carolina, South Carolina, Georgia, Kentucky, Tennessee, Alabama, Louisiana, Mississippi, Ohio, Indiana, Illinois, and Missouri, one vote of Maine, twenty votes of New York, and five votes of Maryland. Adams received all the votes of Vermont, New Hampshire, Massachusetts, Rhode Island, Connecticut, New Jersey, and Delaware, eight votes of Maine, sixteen of New York, and six of Maryland. Jackson carried fourteen states, Adams seven, and three states were divided. The popular vote for the twenty-two states in which the people voted was as follows: Jackson 643,000, Adams 507,000, total 1,150,000.

Presidential Election, 1832

[PLATE 103D]

Twenty-four states took part in the Presidential election of 1832, the same number as in 1820-1828. All the states chose electors by general ticket except Maryland, in which the election was by districts, and South Carolina, in which the election was by the legislature (see p. 89, above). The elections were held within the period November 1-December 4, but chiefly in the first half of November.

The map for 1832 is based wholly upon the popular vote. Since the vote of South Carolina legislature by members is wanting, that state is left blank. The vote of the legislature by parties was Nullifiers' ticket (also called Anti-Jackson, or Floyd ticket) 99, Union Jackson ticket 32, and State Rights' Dissenters ticket (also for Jackson) 25 (*Southern Patriot*, Dec. 5, 6, 1832).

The candidates for the Presidency were Henry Clay (National Republican) of Kentucky, Andrew Jackson (Democrat) of Tennessee, and William Wirt (Anti-Masonic party) of Maryland. Jackson's popular vote came from all the states in which the election was by the people, and Clay's vote from all such states except Georgia, Alabama, and Mississippi. Wirt's vote came from nine northern states—Vermont, Maine, Massachusetts, Rhode Island, Connecticut, New York, New Jersey, Pennsylvania, and Ohio. The South Carolina electors voted for John Floyd of Virginia.

In New York, Pennsylvania, and Ohio the National Republicans and the Anti-Masons supported coalition tickets (Charles McCarthy, "Anti-Masonic Party," *Ann. Rept. Amer. Hist. Assn.*, Vol. 1, Washington, 1902, pp. 415-416, 451-452, 528-530, and 550). In Ohio the fusion was not complete, and a few votes were cast for a "straight" Wirt ticket.

Fayette County, Indiana, in which Clay and Jackson received the same number of votes, is shown as Clay area. The returns for a part of Missouri and for several counties in other states are missing.

On the regular Jackson ticket Martin Van Buren of New York was the candidate for Vice-President. In Pennsylvania, however, the Vice-Presidential candidate of the Democrats was William Wilkins of that state. Jackson's running mate on a third ticket was Philip P. Barbour of Virginia. This was a rival of the regular ticket in Virginia, North Carolina, Georgia, Mississippi, and Baltimore County, Maryland. In most counties, outside of Georgia, the Barbour ticket received but few votes. In determining the vote for Jackson the votes for the Van Buren and the Barbour tickets were united.

The electoral vote was Jackson 219, Clay 49, Floyd 11, Wirt 7, not voting 2, total 288. The two electors who did not vote were Clay electors, in Maryland. The vote of South Carolina was for Floyd, and the vote of Vermont for Wirt. Clay received all the votes of Massachusetts, Rhode Island, Connecticut, Delaware, and Kentucky, and five votes of Maryland. Jackson received three votes of Maryland and all the votes of the remaining sixteen states. The popular vote (twenty-three states) was Jackson 707,000, Clay 329,000, and Wirt 255,000, total 1,291,000 (Benjamin Matthias, *The Politician's Register*, Philadelphia, 1835, p. 7). The figures for Alabama and Missouri are incomplete.

Presidential Election, 1836

[PLATE 104A]

Twenty-six states took part in the Presidential election of 1836, two more than in the election of 1832, the two additional states being Arkansas and Michigan. All the states chose electors by general ticket except South Carolina, in which state the election was by the legislature. The elections were held within the period November 3-December 6 but chiefly in the first half of November. In many states the date of election was November 7.

The map for 1836 is based entirely upon the popular vote. Since we do not have the vote of the South Carolina legislature by members, this state is left blank. The legislature instructed the electors to vote for Willie P. Mangum of North Carolina. In a legislative caucus a motion to nominate Van Buren was rejected without a dissenting vote, a motion to nominate Harrison was rejected with one dissenting vote, and a motion to nominate White was rejected by a considerable majority (*Southern Patriot*, Charleston, Dec. 7, 1836). A resolution in the house of representatives instructing the electors not to vote for Harrison, White, or Van Buren was adopted by a vote of 89 to 28 (*Charleston Courier*, Dec. 9, 1836).

The candidate of the Democratic party for the Presidency was Martin Van Buren of New York. The Whig party, which consisted of a combination of factions opposed to Jackson and Van Buren, had three candidates, William Henry Harrison of Ohio, Hugh L. White of Tennessee, and Daniel Webster of Massachusetts. Van Buren's vote came from every state in the Union except South Carolina. Harrison's vote came from Maine, New Hampshire, Vermont, Connecticut, New York, New Jersey, Pennsylvania, Delaware, Maryland, Virginia, Kentucky, Ohio, Indiana, and Missouri; White's, from Virginia, North Carolina, Georgia, Alabama, Mississippi, Louisiana, Arkansas, Tennessee, Missouri, and Illinois; and Webster's, from Massachusetts. The South Carolina electors voted for Willie P. Mangum of North Carolina.

In Virginia, Illinois, and Missouri the Harrison and White factions supported coalition tickets. In Michigan there was a Van Buren ticket and an "unpledged or Whig" ticket, which carried Genesee, Oakland, and Monroe counties. On the strength of a statement in the *Detroit Daily Advertiser* to the effect that the unpledged or Whig electors were brought forward by the friends of Van Buren and that it was known they would vote for him, these three counties are given to Van Buren (Henry M. Utley to J. F. Jameson, April 10, 1912). In Maine the electors opposing Van Buren were "unpledged." Since they doubtless would have voted for Harrison had they been elected, the area carried by them has been colored for Harrison. Partly with a view to uniting the opponents of Van Buren, the Whig ticket in several states was not designated by the name of the candidate for President but by the name "Whig" or "Opposition."

Livingston Parish, Louisiana, for which there was a tie between White and Van Buren, and Richmond County, New York, for which there was a tie between Harrison and Van Buren, are shown as Van Buren area.

Owing to the dispute whether Michigan was or was not a state of the Union for the purposes of the Presidential election of 1836, Congress announced the result of the election in alternative form. With Michigan included, the electoral vote was, Van Buren 170, Harrison 73, White 26, Webster 14, Mangum 11, total 294. Mangum received the vote of South Carolina; Webster the vote of Massachusetts; White the vote of Georgia and Tennessee; Harrison the vote of Vermont, New Jersey, Delaware, Maryland, Kentucky, Ohio, and Indiana; and Van Buren the vote of Maine, New Hampshire, Rhode Island, Connecticut, New York, Pennsylvania, Virginia, North Carolina, Louisiana, Mississippi, Illinois, Alabama, Missouri, Arkansas, and Michigan. Van Buren carried fifteen states, Harrison seven, White two, and Webster and Mangum one each. The popular vote (twenty-five states) was Van Buren 762,000, Harrison 549,000, White 146,000, Webster, 41,000, total, 1,498,000.

Presidential Election, 1840

[PLATE 104B]

Twenty-six states took part in the Presidential election of 1840, the same number as in 1836. All the states chose electors by general ticket except South Carolina, in which the election was by the legislature. The election was held within the period October 29-December 1, but chiefly early in November.

The map for 1840 is based upon the popular vote in all the states except South Carolina. For South Carolina the vote is that of the legislature, which was for Van Buren, "without dissent" (*Charleston Courier*, Dec. 7, 1840). However, there were eight Whigs in the legislature (of more than one hundred and sixty members), chiefly from Pendleton and Marion counties (*Niles' Register*, Vol. 59, pp. 217-218).

The principal candidates for the Presidency were William Henry Harrison (Whig) of Ohio and Martin Van Buren (Democrat) of New York. A minor candidate was James G. Birney (Liberty party) of New York. The popular vote was Harrison 1,275,000, Van Buren 1,129,000, Birney 7000, total 2,411,000. Harrison's and Van Buren's popular vote came from every state in the Union except South Carolina. Since Birney carried no counties his vote is not represented on the map. It came from the New England states, New York, New Jersey, Pennsylvania, Ohio, Illinois, and Michigan.

Tie votes are shown as follows: Jasper County, Georgia, and Ascension Parish, Louisiana, for Harrison; and Lowndes County, Mississippi, for Van Buren.

The electoral vote was Harrison 234, Van Buren 60, total 294. Van Buren received the vote of seven states—New Hampshire, Virginia, South Carolina, Alabama, Arkansas, Missouri, and Illinois; and Harrison the vote of the remaining nineteen states. Harrison had a majority of the popular vote.

Presidential Election, 1844

[PLATE 104C]

Twenty-six states took part in the Presidential election of 1844, the same number as in 1836 and 1840. All the states chose electors by general ticket except South Carolina, in which the election was by the legislature. The popular elections were held within the period November 1–12 but chiefly on November 4 (the first Monday of the month). South Carolina chose electors on December 3. In New Jersey the election extended over a period of two days. New Jersey was one of the last states to abandon the practice of holding elections on more than one day (*Niles' Register*, Vol. 67, p. 139). In Virginia the election was *viva voce*, and at some of the polling places all the votes were not polled on the same day (*Congressional Globe*, Vol. 14, p. 15).

The map for 1844 is based upon the popular vote in all the states except South Carolina. Since the strength of parties in the South Carolina legislature is stated to have been Democrats 166, Whigs none (*Niles' Register*, Vol. 67, p. 165), this state is colored solidly for Polk. The vote in the legislature for the successful electors was about 149, varying slightly for different electors (*Charleston Mercury*, Dec. 5, 1844).

The principal candidates for the Presidency were Henry Clay (Whig) of Kentucky and James K. Polk (Democrat) of Tennessee. A minor candidate was James G. Birney (Liberty party) of New York. The popular vote was Clay 1,299,000, Polk 1,337,000, Birney 62,000, total 2,698,000. Clay's and Polk's popular vote came from every state except South Carolina. Birney's vote came from the same states as in 1840, with the addition of Indiana.

Gates County, North Carolina, in which the vote was a tie between Clay and Polk, is shown as Clay area.

The electoral vote was Polk 170, Clay 105, total 275. Clay received the electoral votes of eleven states—Massachusetts, Rhode Island, Connecticut, Vermont, New Jersey, Delaware, Maryland, North Carolina, Tennessee, Kentucky, and Ohio, and Polk the votes of the fifteen remaining states. Polk had a plurality of the popular vote.

Presidential Election, 1848

[PLATE 104D]

Thirty states took part in the Presidential election of 1848, four more than in 1844, the new states being Florida, Texas, Iowa, and Wisconsin. The election was by general ticket in all the states except South Carolina, in which it was by the legislature. A Massachusetts requirement, however, that the successful electors should receive a majority of the votes cast devolved the choice of electors on the legislature, after a popular vote had failed to elect. The vote mapped for that state is the popular vote. By an act of January 23, 1845, Congress fixed the date of Presidential elections on the first Tuesday next after the first Monday in November. In 1848 the date fell on November 7, and for the first time the election was held on the same day in all the states. On the failure of the people to make a choice in Massachusetts the legislature of that state chose electors on November 23.

The map for 1848 is based upon the popular vote. As the vote of the South Carolina legislature, by members, is wanting, that state is left blank. The vote of the legislature, by candidates, was Cass 129, Taylor 27, blanks 8, total 164 (*Charleston Mercury*, Nov. 8, 1848). The vote of the Massachusetts legislature was Taylor 196, Cass 65, Van Buren 37, scattering 1, total 299 (*Massachusetts Spy*, Nov. 29, 1848).

The Whig candidate for the Presidency was Zachary Taylor of Louisiana, and the Democratic candidate Lewis Cass of Michigan. The candidate of the Free Soil Democratic party, successor of the Liberty party, was Martin Van Buren of New York. Two principal factions supported Van Buren—a large faction of the anti-slavery men and a faction composed of anti-administration Democrats. The latter resided chiefly in New York, where they were known as "Barnburners." Gerritt Smith of New York, a fourth Presidential candidate, was supported by two organizations, namely, the Liberty League, an anti-slavery faction standing for the abolition of slavery, and the Industrial Congress, representing organized labor.

The popular vote was Taylor 1,360,000, Cass 1,221,000, Van Buren 291,000, and Smith 3000, total 2,875,000. Taylor's and Cass's popular vote came from every state except South Carolina. Van Buren's vote

came chiefly from the fifteen free states. He received a few scattering votes from the slave states of Delaware, Maryland, Virginia, North Carolina, Louisiana, and Texas. He carried one county in Massachusetts, one in Vermont, seven counties in New York, six in Ohio, six in Wisconsin, and ten in Illinois. Smith received a few votes in New York and Ohio.

Marion County, Arkansas, Lewis and Dunklin counties, Missouri, and Poweshiek County, Iowa, in which the vote was tied by Cass and Taylor, are shown as Cass area. In Texas a few counties for which there are no returns are given to Cass.

The electoral vote was Taylor 163, Cass 127, total 290. Taylor received the vote of fifteen states—Massachusetts, Rhode Island, Connecticut, Vermont, New York, New Jersey, Pennsylvania, Delaware, Maryland, North Carolina, Georgia, Kentucky, Tennessee, Louisiana, and Florida. Cass received the vote of the remaining fifteen states. Van Buren carried no states, and Smith carried no counties. Taylor had a plurality of the popular vote.

Presidential Election, 1852

[PLATE 105A]

Thirty-one states took part in the Presidential election of 1852, one more than in 1848, the additional state being California. The electors were chosen on a general ticket in all the states except South Carolina, in which they were chosen by the legislature. The election was held in all the states on November 2.

The map for 1852 is based wholly upon the popular vote. Since the vote of the South Carolina legislature, by members, is wanting, that state is left blank. The legislature cast 135 votes for Pierce—total number of members about 165 (*Savannah Republican*, Nov. 3, 1852).

The principal candidates for the Presidency were Winfield Scott (Whig) of New Jersey and Franklin Pierce (Democrat) of New Hampshire. The minor candidates were John P. Hale (Free Soil Democrat) of New Hampshire, Daniel Webster (Independent Whig) of Massachusetts, George M. Troup (Southern Rights party) of Georgia, and Jacob Broom (Native American party) of Pennsylvania.

The popular vote was Scott 1,387,000, Pierce 1,601,000, Hale 156,000, Webster 7000, Broom 2700, Troup 2300, total 3,156,000. Hale's vote came from the sixteen free states and from the slave states of Delaware, Maryland, North Carolina, and Kentucky; Webster's vote, from Georgia and Massachusetts; Troup's, from Alabama and Georgia; and Broom's, from Pennsylvania, New Jersey, and Massachusetts. The popular vote of Scott and Pierce came from every state except South Carolina. In Georgia there were two Pierce tickets, known as the regular ticket and the independent or "Tugaloo" ticket. Their votes have been combined.

Ties between Scott and Pierce were decided as follows: Orange County, Florida, Mercer County, Missouri, and Richland County, Wisconsin, for Pierce; and Warren County, Missouri, and Gates County, North Carolina, for Scott. In Texas a few counties for which there were no returns are colored for Pierce.

The electoral vote was Pierce 254, Scott 42, total 296. Scott received the vote of four states—Massachusetts, Vermont, Kentucky, and Tennessee, and Pierce the vote of the remaining twenty-seven states. Pierce had a majority of the popular vote.

Presidential Election, 1856

[PLATE 105B]

Thirty-one states took part in the Presidential election of 1856, the same number as in 1852. The choice of electors was by the legislature in South Carolina and by general ticket in the rest of the states. The election was held on November 4.

The map for 1856 is based in the popular vote in all the states except South Carolina. This state is given to Buchanan, since its legislature unanimously resolved that its electoral vote should be cast for that candidate (*Charleston Daily Courier*, Nov. 5, 1856). The vote of the legislature for electors is not known.

The candidates for the Presidency were John C. Frémont (Republican) of California, James Buchanan (Democrat) of Pennsylvania, and Millard Fillmore (Know-Nothing, or "American," and Whig) of New York. Frémont was also supported by one faction of the Know-Nothing party.

The popular vote was Frémont 1,341,000, Buchanan, 1,838,000, and Fillmore 875,000, total 4,054,000. Buchanan's and Fillmore's popular vote came from every state except South Carolina; Frémont's vote came from the sixteen free states and from the slave states of Delaware, Maryland, Virginia, and Kentucky, in which four states he received about 1200 votes.

In Pennsylvania there was a fusion or "Union" Frémont-Fillmore ticket and a "straight" Fillmore ticket. The area carried by the fusion ticket is striped with the colors of the fusion candidates. The "straight" Fillmore ticket carried no counties. If its vote is combined with that for the fusion ticket, the combination carried, in addition to the fusion area shown upon the map, the counties of Chester, Huntingdon, Wayne, and Wyoming. Coffee County, Georgia, which cast the same number of votes for Fillmore and Buchanan, is shown as Buchanan area.

Including the vote of the Wisconsin electors, which was cast on December 4 instead of December 3, the date prescribed by law, the electoral vote was Buchanan 174, Frémont 114, Fillmore 8, total 296. Fillmore received the vote of Maryland; Frémont the vote of the New England states, New York, Ohio, Michigan, Iowa, and Wisconsin; and Buchanan the vote of New Jersey, Pennsylvania, Indiana, Illinois, California, and the slave states, with the exception of Maryland. Buchanan carried nineteen states, Frémont eleven, and Fillmore one. Buchanan had a plurality of the popular vote.

Presidential Election, 1860
[PLATE 105C]

Thirty-three states took part in the Presidential election of 1860, two more than in 1856, the new states being Minnesota and Oregon. In South Carolina the electors were chosen by the legislature and in all the other states by general tickets. The election was held on November 6.

The map for 1860 is based on the popular vote in all the states except South Carolina. Since the house of representatives of that state resolved unanimously that the electoral vote should be cast for Breckinridge (*S. C. House Journ.*, Nov. 6, 1860), South Carolina is colored for that candidate. The vote of the legislature for the successful electors varied from 142 to 159—total vote 161 (*Charleston Mercury*, Nov. 7, 1860).

The candidates for the Presidency were Abraham Lincoln (Republican) of Illinois, Stephen A. Douglas (Democrat) of Illinois, John C. Breckinridge (Democrat) of Kentucky, and John Bell (Constitutional Union party) of Tennessee. The popular vote was Lincoln 1,866,000, Douglas 1,377,000, Breckinridge 850,000, and Bell 589,000, total 4,682,000. According to this count, the fusion vote is credited as follows: in New Jersey, New York, and Rhode Island to Douglas; in Pennsylvania to Breckinridge; and in Connecticut and Texas to Bell. Splitting the fusion vote into its component parts, one may say that the popular vote for Douglas, for Breckinridge, and for Bell came from every state except South Carolina. Lincoln's popular vote came from every state except Alabama, Arkansas, Florida, Georgia, Louisiana, Mississippi, North Carolina, South Carolina, Tennessee, and Texas. Less than 3000 votes were polled: by Lincoln in each of the states of Kentucky, Maryland, and Virginia; by Douglas in each of the states of Delaware, Florida, and North Carolina; by Breckinridge in each of the states of Illinois, Iowa, Michigan, Minnesota, New Hampshire, Vermont, and Wisconsin; and by Bell in each of the states of Iowa, Maine, Michigan, Minnesota, New Hampshire, Oregon, Vermont, and Wisconsin.

In Connecticut there were "straight" Douglas, Bell, and Breckinridge tickets and also a fusion ticket made up of two names from each of these three "straight" tickets, which, however, was voted for in only a few towns. In Rhode Island and New York the friends of Douglas, Bell, and Breckinridge united in the support of fusion tickets composed of candidates drawn from each of the three parties. The New York fusion ticket consisted of eighteen Douglas men, ten Bell men, and seven Breckinridge men. In New Jersey there was both a fusion ticket and a "straight" Douglas ticket. The fusion ticket consisted of three Douglas men, two Bell men, and two Breckinridge men. The "straight" Douglas ticket adopted the three Douglas men on the fusion ticket. In Pennsylvania there was a fusion ticket made up of Douglas and Breckinridge men and also a "straight" Douglas ticket, which adopted about half of the names on the fusion ticket. In Texas the Bell and Douglas men supported a fusion ticket.

The "straight" Douglas tickets in New Jersey and Pennsylvania received a relatively small vote and carried no counties. In New Jersey the three Douglas men who ran on both tickets were elected. They carried Camden County in addition to the fusion area shown upon the map. In Pennsylvania the Douglas men who ran on both the "straight" Douglas and fusion tickets carried, in addition to the fusion area shown upon the map, the counties of Lehigh, Montgomery, and Montour.

The fusion vote in several of the states apportioned according to the estimated strength of the several contributing parties is, New York: Douglas 203,000, Breckinridge 50,000, and Bell 50,000; New Jersey: Douglas 30,000, Breckinridge 30,000, and Bell 3000; Pennsylvania: Douglas 79,000 and Breckinridge 100,000; Texas: almost entirely Bell (Horace Greeley, *The American Conflict*, Hartford, 1864–1866, Vol. I, p. 328). The vote for the "straight" Douglas ticket in New Jersey was about 5000 and in Pennsylvania about 17,000.

Counties for which the vote is tied are shown as follows: Sutter County, California, tie between Douglas and Breckinridge, and Wood County, Virginia, tie between Bell and Breckinridge, for Breckinridge; Marion County, Georgia, tie between Bell and Breckinridge, for Bell; and Beuna Vista County, Iowa, tie between Lincoln and Douglas, for Lincoln.

The electoral vote was Lincoln 180, Breckinridge 72, Bell 39, Douglas 12, total 303. Douglas received the vote of Missouri and three votes of New Jersey; Bell the vote of Virginia, Kentucky, and Tennessee; Breckinridge the vote of all the slave states except the four carried by Bell and Douglas; and Lincoln the vote of the free states with the exception of three of New Jersey's seven votes. Lincoln carried seventeen states and divided one, Breckinridge carried eleven states, Bell carried three states, and Douglas carried one state and divided one. Lincoln had a plurality of the popular vote.

Presidential Election, 1864
[PLATE 105D]

Twenty-five states voted at the Presidential election of 1864. The eleven Southern states that seceded in 1860–1861 did not take part in the election. Three of the twenty-five states (Kansas, West Virginia, and Nevada) were admitted to the Union after 1860 and now for the first time voted for President. The election, which took place on November 8, was by general ticket in all the states.

The map for 1864 is based upon the popular vote, exclusive of the "soldiers' vote." The latter is the vote of those soldiers who were absent from their home states with the army at the time of the election. About half of the states of the Union passed laws permitting their absent soldiers to vote.

The candidates for the Presidency were Abraham Lincoln (Republican, "Union," or "National Union") of Illinois and George B. McClellan (Democrat) of New Jersey. The popular vote, exclusive of the "soldiers' vote," was Lincoln 2,214,000, McClellan 1,802,000, total 4,016,000.

The electoral vote was Lincoln 212, McClellan 21, not voting (in Nevada) 1, total 234. McClellan received the vote of New Jersey, Delaware, and Kentucky; and Lincoln the vote of the twenty-two remaining states. Lincoln had a majority of the popular vote.

In consequence of the death of one of the Lincoln electors in Nevada, the vote of that state was one short of its full electoral strength. According to the usual practice at this time, the electoral colleges filled vacancies in their membership and in 1864 Connecticut and Pennsylvania each thus supplied a deficiency. Nevada, being a new state, had made no provision for an emergency of this kind.

Presidential Election, 1868
[PLATE 106A]

Thirty-four states took part in the Presidential election of 1868, nine more than in 1864, the additional states being eight of the seceding states, and Nebraska, admitted in 1867. The three seceding states that did not take part in the election were Virginia, Mississippi, and Texas. The election was by general ticket in all the states except Florida, in which state the legislature chose the electors by a *viva voce* vote. The election was held on November 3.

The map for 1868 is based on the popular vote. Since the vote of the Florida legislature, by members, is not known, that state is left blank. The vote of the legislature, by candidates, was Grant 39, Seymour 9, scattering 2, total members in legislature 77 (*Florida Union*, Nov. 7, 1868).

The candidates for the Presidency were Ulysses S. Grant (Republican, "National Republican," "National Union," or "National Union Republican") of Illinois and Horatio Seymour (Democrat) of New York. The popular vote was Grant 3,013,000, Seymour 2,703,000, total 5,716,000.

Counties for which the vote is tied are shown as follows: Audubon County, Iowa, and Nye County, Nevada, for Grant; Churchill County, Nevada, and Douglas County, Wisconsin, for Seymour.

Because of objections to counting the electoral vote of Georgia, Congress announced the result of the election in alternative form. With Georgia included, the electoral vote was Grant 214, Seymour 80, total 294. Seymour received the vote of eight states—New York, New Jersey, Delaware, Maryland, Georgia, Louisiana, Kentucky, and Oregon; and Grant the vote of the remaining twenty-five states. Grant had a majority of the popular vote.

Presidential Election, 1872
[PLATE 106B]

Thirty-seven states took part in the Presidential election of 1872, three more than in 1868, the additional states being Virginia, Mississippi, and Texas, now reconstructed. All the states chose electors by general ticket. The election was held on November 5.

The map for 1872 is based on the popular vote in all of the states. For Louisiana there are two sets of returns, known as the "Warmoth count," and the "Kellogg count" or "Custom House count." The counts were made by rival returning boards, each of which manipulated the figures to meet the needs of its own party. The vote of the state according to the Warmoth count was Greeley 66,467, Grant 59,975; according to the Kellogg count, Greeley 57,029, Grant 71,663. Since the Warmoth returning board was more nearly regular and its figures more nearly official, its count has been mapped. By the Kellogg count, Grant carried, in addition to the area shown upon the map, the parishes of Assumption, Avoyelles, East Baton Rouge, Bossier, Caddo, Catahoula, De Soto, Grant, Jackson, Lafourche, Natchitoches, Rapides, St. Bernard, St. James, St. Tammany, Tangipahoa, Terrebonne, Union, and Webster. By the Warmoth count three of these parishes were without returns and on the map are shown as blank areas. The Warmoth electors voted for Greeley, and the Kellogg electors for Grant. Both returns were sent to Congress.

The principal candidates for the Presidency were Ulysses S. Grant (Republican) of Illinois and Horace Greeley (Democrat and Liberal Republican) of New York. The minor candidates were Charles O'Conor ("straight" Democrat and Labor Reform party) of New York and James Black (Prohibitionist) of Pennsylvania.

The popular vote was Grant 3,597,000, Greeley 2,834,000, O'Conor 29,000, and Black 6000, total 6,466,000. The votes for the major candidates came from every state in the Union. The vote for the minor candidates was insignificant, and they probably in no county held the balance of power. O'Conor's vote came from twenty-four states—California, Connecticut, Delaware, Georgia, Illinois, Indiana, Iowa, Kansas, Kentucky, Maine, Maryland, Michigan, Missouri, New Hampshire, New Jersey, New York, Ohio, Oregon, South Carolina, Texas, Vermont, Virginia, West Virginia, and Wisconsin. Black's vote came from six states—Connecticut, Michigan, New Hampshire, New York, Ohio, and Pennsylvania.

Counties in which the vote was a tie between Grant and Greeley are shown as follows: Clark County, Illinois, for Grant; and Colquitt County, Georgia, and Culpepper County, Virginia, for Greeley.

In consequence of the death of Greeley, which took place between the date of the election and the date of the meeting of the electoral colleges, the Democratic electors, except three from Georgia, did not vote for him but voted for some other distinguished Democrat or Liberal. The men who were thus complimented were B. Gratz Brown of Missouri, Thomas A. Hendricks of Indiana, Charles J. Jenkins of Georgia, and David Davis of Illinois. Congress rejected the vote of Arkansas because of an informality in its certification, the vote of Louisiana because of the double returns, and the three votes of Georgia because they were cast for a man who was dead. If the vote of Arkansas be counted for Grant, and the rejected votes of the other two states for his opponent, the electoral vote may be stated thus: Grant 292, Democratic and Liberal opposition 74, total 366. According to this count the Democratic and Liberal opposition carried seven states—Georgia, Kentucky, Louisiana, Maryland, Missouri, Tennessee, and Texas, and Grant the thirty remaining states. Grant had a majority of the popular vote.

Presidential Election, 1876

[PLATE 107A]

Thirty-eight states took part in the Presidential election of 1876, one more than in 1872, the additional state being Colorado. The electors were chosen on a general ticket in all the states except Colorado, in which state they were chosen by the legislature. The date of the election was November 7.

The map for 1876 is based on the popular vote in all the states except Colorado. For this state the vote mapped is that of the legislature. The vote was Hayes 50, Tilden 25, not voting 1, total 76. It followed strictly party lines (*Rocky Mountain News*, Oct. 31, Nov. 8, 1876).

In South Carolina, Florida, and Louisiana, "disputed states," there were several counts or returns. The returns in each of these states that are most nearly regular and official have been mapped. For South Carolina the returns chosen for mapping are those made by the counties to the South Carolina Canvassing Board and reported by the board to the supreme court of the state. Somewhat different figures, which were reported by a committee of the U. S. House of Representatives appointed to investigate the South Carolina election, do not change the political complexion of any counties (*House Rept. No. 175, 44th Cong., 2nd Sess.*, 1876–1877, Part II, p. 2; *House Misc. Doc. No. 31, 44th Cong., 2nd Sess.*, 1876–1877, Part I, appendix, pp. 2 and 36).

For Florida the "first count," or the count officially declared by the

Florida Canvassing Board, was mapped. The figures of a convassing board subsequently organized and composed wholly of Democrats give to Tilden, in addition to the Tilden area shown on the map, the counties of Jackson, Manatee, and Monroe (*House Misc. Doc. No. 35, 44th Cong., 2nd Sess.*, 1876–1877, Part III, pp. 58 and 79). By the figures of the first board the state was carried for Hayes, and by the figures of the second board for Tilden.

For Louisiana the count of the Louisiana Returning Board was mapped. The count of the Democratic Committee on Returns gives to Tilden, in addition to the Tilden area shown upon the map, the parishes of East Baton Rouge, De Soto, East Feliciana, West Feliciana, Grant, Lafayette, Morehouse, Ouachita, and Webster (*Tribune Almanac*, 1877, pp. 128–129). By the count of the board the state was carried for Hayes, and by the count of the committee for Tilden.

The principal candidates for the Presidency were Rutherford B. Hayes (Republican) of Ohio and Samuel J. Tilden (Democrat) of New York. The minor candidates were Peter Cooper (Greenback, "Independent," or "Independent National") of New York, Green Clay Smith (Prohibitionist or "Prohibition Reform") of Kentucky, and James B. Walker (American National or "Anti-Secret Society party") of Illinois.

The popular vote was Hayes 4,285,000, Tilden 4,034,000, Cooper 82,000, Green 10,000, Walker 500, total 8,411,000. The popular votes for the two major candidates came from every state except Colorado. In but few counties was the combined vote of the minor candidates larger than the plurality of the stronger major candidate; or, in other words, in but few counties did the minor candidates hold the balance of power. Cooper's vote came from twenty-four states—Arkansas, California, Connecticut, Illinois, Indiana, Iowa, Kansas, Kentucky, Maine, Maryland, Massachusetts, Michigan, Minnesota, Missouri, Nebraska, New Hampshire, New Jersey, New York, Ohio, Oregon, Pennsylvania, Rhode Island, West Virginia, and Wisconsin; Green's vote from seventeen states—Connecticut, Illinois, Iowa, Kansas, Kentucky, Maryland, Massachusetts, Michigan, Minnesota, Missouri, Nebraska, New Jersey, New York, Ohio, Pennsylvania, Rhode Island, and Wisconsin; and Walker's vote from five states—Illinois, Kansas, Michigan, Ohio, and Pennsylvania.

White Pine County, Nevada, for which there was a tie between Hayes and Tilden, is shown as Hayes area. Manatee County, Florida, and East Feliciana and Grant parishes, Louisiana, which are shown blank on the map because their votes were rejected by the returning boards, gave Tilden a plurality on the "face of the returns." Several counties in Texas for which there were no returns are colored for the Democratic candidate, and on subsequent maps a few Texas counties have been treated in the same manner.

The electoral vote as declared by Congress was Hayes 185, Tilden 184, total 369. Tilden received the electoral vote of seventeen states—Arkansas, Alabama, Connecticut, Delaware, Georgia, Indiana, Kentucky, Maryland, Mississippi, Missouri, New Jersey, New York, North Carolina, Tennessee, Texas, Virginia, and West Virginia; and Hayes the vote of the remaining twenty-one states. Hayes had a plurality of the popular vote.

Presidential Election, 1880

[PLATE 107B]

Thirty-eight states took part in the Presidential election of 1880, the same number as in 1876. All the states chose electors by general ticket. The election was held on November 2.

The map for 1880 is based on the popular vote in all the states, and the same is true of all subsequent maps. In Louisiana there were two Garfield electoral tickets, known as the "regular" and "Beattie" tickets, and in Virginia there were two Hancock electoral tickets, known as the "regular" or "debtpayer" and the "readjuster" tickets. In each case the votes were added, and the combined result is mapped. In Maine there was a fusion electoral ticket composed of three Democrats and four Greenbackers, and also a "straight" Greenback ticket. The "straight" Greenback ticket polled a light vote and carried no counties. In the counties carried by Garfield its vote was never equal to Garfield's plurality.

The principal candidates for the Presidency were James A. Garfield (Republican) of Ohio and Winfield Scott Hancock (Democrat) of Pennsylvania. The minor candidates were James B. Weaver (Greenback-Labor party) of Iowa, Neal Dow (Prohibitionist or "Prohibition Reform party") of Maine, and John W. Phelps (American or "Anti-Secret Society party") of Vermont.

The popular vote was Garfield 4,454,000, Hancock 4,445,000, Weaver 309,000, Dow 10,000, Phelps 700, total 9,219,000. In this and in all subsequent elections the Republican and the Democratic vote came from every state in the Union. Weaver's vote came from every state except Florida and Nevada. In not a few counties carried by one of the major candidates Weaver held the balance of power. Dow's vote came from seventeen states—Connecticut, Illinois, Iowa, Kansas, Kentucky, Maine, Massachusetts, Michigan, Minnesota, New Hampshire, New Jersey, New York, Ohio, Pennsylvania, Rhode Island, Tennessee, and Wisconsin; Phelps's vote came from seven states—Illinois, Michigan, New York, Ohio, Pennsylvania, Rhode Island, and Wisconsin.

Noble County, Indiana, for which there was a tie between Garfield and Hancock, is shown as Hancock area.

With the votes of Georgia, which were cast on December 8 instead of December 1, the proper date, the electoral vote was Garfield 214, Hancock 155, total 369. Hancock received five votes of California and all the votes of eighteen states—Alabama, Arkansas, Delaware, Florida, Georgia, Kentucky, Louisiana, Maryland, Mississippi, Missouri, Nevada, New Jersey, North Carolina, South Carolina, Tennessee, Texas, Virginia, and West Virginia; and Garfield one vote of California and all the votes of the remaining nineteen states. Garfield had a small plurality of the popular vote.

Presidential Election, 1884
[PLATE 108A]

Thirty-eight states took part in the Presidential election of 1884, the same number as in 1876 and 1880. Electors were chosen on a general ticket in all the states. The election was held on November 4.

There were fusion tickets in five states—Iowa, Michigan, Nebraska, Missouri, and West Virginia. The composition of these tickets was as follows: Iowa, seven Democrats and six Greenbackers; Michigan, for twelve places on the ticket, six Democrats and six Greenbackers, while for the thirteenth place each party had a candidate; Nebraska, two Democrats, two Anti-Monoplists, and one Greenbacker; Missouri, eight Republicans and eight Greenbackers; and West Virginia, four Republicans and two Greenbackers. In West Virginia the agreement between the parties called for an equal division of the electors, but it was not carried out (*Wheeling Daily Intelligencer*, Sept. 3, Nov. 15, 1884). In addition to the fusion tickets there was a "straight" Greenback ticket in both Michigan and West Virginia, which received but a few hundred votes in each state. No change is made in the party complexion of counties by combining the "straight" and the fusion vote.

The principal candidates for the Presidency were James G. Blaine (Republican) of Maine and Grover Cleveland (Democrat) of New York. The minor candidates were Benjamin F. Butler (Greenback-Labor, or "National," and Anti-Monopolist) of Massachusetts and John P. St. John (Prohibitionist) of Kansas. Minor candidates whose names do not appear in returns of elections are not mentioned in the text. Of this class are the candidates of such parties as the Equal Rights party, which in 1884 nominated Mrs. Belva A. B. Lockwood for the Presidency. Belonging to it also are those persons, considerable in number, for whom the "scattering vote" is cast.

The popular vote was Blaine 4,855,000, Cleveland 4,915,000, Butler 134,000, St. John 152,000, total 10,056,000. In this statement of Butler's vote his fusion vote is disregarded. The fusion vote in Iowa, Michigan, and Nebraska is counted for Cleveland, and in Missouri and West Virginia for Blaine. Outside of the five fusion states the Butler vote was relatively small and was not sufficient to carry any counties. He received no votes in Florida, Mississippi, North Carolina, South Carolina, or Virginia. In the fusion states there were a considerable number of Greenbackers. In Michigan they cast a little more than one-fifth of the fusion vote in that state, or about 41,500 votes. St. John's vote came from every state with the exception of Arkansas, Mississippi, Nevada, and South Carolina. He carried no counties. The vote for Butler and St. John, singly or combined, in but few counties equaled the plurality of the successful major candidate. In other words, had there been no minor candidates the political complexion of the counties outside of the fusion states would have been, with a possible exception or two, the same.

McDonough County, Illinois, for which there was a tie between the major candidates, is shown as Blaine area.

The electoral vote was Blaine 182, Cleveland 219, total 401. Blaine received the votes of eighteen states—California, Colorado, Illinois, Iowa, Kansas, Maine, Massachusetts, Michigan, Minnesota, Nebraska, Nevada, New Hampshire, Ohio, Oregon, Pennsylvania, Rhode Island, Vermont, and Wisconsin; and Cleveland the votes of the twenty remaining states. Cleveland had a plurality of the popular vote.

Presidential Election, 1888
[PLATE 108B]

Thirty-eight states took part in the Presidential election of 1888, the same number as in 1876–1884. All the states chose electors on a general ticket. The election was held on November 6.

The principal candidates for the Presidency were Benjamin Harrison (Republican) of Indiana and Grover Cleveland (Democrat) of New York. The minor candidates were Clinton B. Fisk (Prohibitionist) of New Jersey, Anson J. Streeter (Union Labor party) of Illinois, Robert H. Cowdrey (United Labor party) of Illinois, and James Langdon Curtis (American party) of New York.

The popular vote was as follows: Harrison 5,444,000, Cleveland 5,540,000, Fisk 250,000, Streeter 147,000, Cowdrey 3000, Curtis 1600, Socialist party (no candidate for the Presidency) 2100, total 11,388,000. Fisk's vote came from every state except South Carolina; Streeter's from every state except Alabama, California, Delaware, Florida, Maryland, Massachusetts, Nevada, New Jersey, South Carolina, Vermont, and Virginia; Cowdrey's from New York and Illinois; Curtis's from California and Pennsylvania; and the vote of the Socialist party from New York. With the exception of Arenac County, Michigan, and Walker County, Texas, in which Streeter had a plurality, the minor parties carried no counties. In but few counties did they hold the balance of power.

"Greer County," situated in what is now Oklahoma but was for several years claimed by Texas (see Pl. 97H), voted in 1888 as a part of Texas. Its vote is shown upon the map.

The electoral vote was Harrison 233, Cleveland 168, total 401. Cleveland received the vote of eighteen states—Alabama, Arkansas, Connecticut, Delaware, Florida, Georgia, Kentucky, Louisiana, Maryland, Mississippi, Missouri, New Jersey, North Carolina, South Carolina, Tennessee, Texas, Virginia, and West Virginia; and Harrison the vote of the twenty remaining states. Cleveland had a plurality of the popular vote.

Presidential Election, 1892
[PLATE 108C]

Forty-four states took part in the Presidential election of 1892, six more than in 1888, the new states being North Dakota, South Dakota, Montana, Washington, Idaho, and Wyoming. All the states chose electors by general ticket except Michigan, which chose twelve electors by districts and two at large. The election was held on November 8.

The principal candidates for the Presidency were Benjamin Harrison (Republican) of Indiana, Grover Cleveland (Democrat) of New York, and James B. Weaver (Populist) of Iowa. The minor candidates were John Bidwell (Prohibitionist) of California and Simon Wing (Socialist Labor party) of Massachusetts.

The popular vote was Harrison 5,191,000; Cleveland 5,554,000, Weaver 1,027,000, Bidwell 271,000, Wing 22,000, total 12,065,000. In this statement of the popular vote the fusion vote in Alabama and North Dakota is credited to Weaver, and the fusion vote in Louisiana to Harrison. The vote for Bidwell came from every state except Louisiana, South Carolina, and South Dakota. Wing's vote came from Connecticut, Maine, Maryland, Massachusette, New Jersey, New York, and Pennsylvania.

The Democrats had a "straight" electoral ticket in all the states except Colorado, Idaho, Kansas, and Wyoming, in which states they supported the Populist ticket, and in North Dakota, in which state they supported a fusion ticket composed of two Populists and one Democrat. The Republicans had a "straight" electoral ticket in all the states except Florida, in which they supported the Populist ticket, and in Louisiana, in which they supported a fusion ticket made up of five Harrison and three Weaver men. In Alabama one Republican faction supported a "straight" Republican ticket and the other, the larger faction, a fusion ticket made up of five Harrison and six Weaver men. The Populists had a "straight" electoral ticket in all the states except Alabama, Louisiana, and North Dakota, in which they supported fusion tickets. In not a few counties of the Union Weaver held the balance of power, that is, his vote exceeded the difference between the votes of Harrison and Cleveland. He carried one or more counties, on a "straight" or fusion ticket, in Alabama, Colorado, Georgia, Idaho, Kansas, Louisiana, Michigan, Minnesota, Mississippi, Nebraska, Nevada, North Carolina, North Dakota, Oregon, South Dakota, Texas, and Wyoming—all Southern or Western states with the exception of Michigan.

If the "straight" Republican vote in Alabama, which was relatively small, is combined with the fusion vote, the combination carried, in addition to the fusion area shown on the map, the counties of Crenshaw, Shelby, and Talladega. The Harrison vote in Texas shown on the map is the combined vote of the two Republican factions known as the "Regulars" and the "Lily Whites." Since the vote of the Lily Whites was light, the same result is obtained by mapping the vote of the Regulars. In mapping the vote of Oregon and Minnesota certain complications in the vote of the Democrats and Populists were disregarded. In Oregon the Democratic ticket was composed of three Cleveland electors, and of one of the four Weaver electors, who was elected. The vote for this Weaver elector is not mapped. He carried, in addition to the Cleveland and Weaver areas shown upon the map, the counties of Clackamas, Grant, and Morrow. In Minnesota four electoral candidates out of a total of nine were common to both the Democratic and Populist tickets. The votes for the five Democratic and for the five Populist electors not common to both tickets are mapped. The four common electors failed to receive the full strength of both parties and were not elected. They carried all the counties carried by either the five Cleveland or the five Weaver electors, which are shown upon the map, except Benton and McLeod counties. Of the Harrison counties shown upon the map they carried the following: Beltrami, Clay, Hubbard, Meeker, Murray, Norman, Otter Tail, Renville, Swift, Todd, Traverse, and Wilkin. In South Dakota a fusion of the Democrats and Populists was attempted but failed. In Nevada the Democrats voted largely for the Populist electors. "Greer County," situated in what is now Oklahoma, voted in 1892 as a part of Texas.

The electoral vote was Cleveland 277, Harrison 145, Weaver 22, total 444. Weaver received the votes of Colorado, Idaho, Kansas, and Nevada, and one vote of each of the states of North Dakota and Oregon. Harrison received the votes of Iowa, Maine, Massachusetts, Minnesota, Montana, Nebraska, New Hampshire, Pennsylvania, Rhode Island, South Dakota, Vermont, Washington, and Wyoming, and one vote of California, nine of Michigan, one of North Dakota, twenty-two of Ohio, and three of Oregon. Cleveland received eight of the votes of California, five of Michigan, one of North Dakota, and one of Ohio, and all the votes of the remaining states. Cleveland carried twenty-two states and divided four; Harrison carried thirteen and divided five; and Weaver carried four and divided two. Cleveland had a plurality of the popular vote.

Presidential Election, 1896
[PLATE 108D]

Forty-five states took part in the Presidential election of 1896, one more than in 1892, the additional state being Utah. All the states chose electors on a general ticket, and the same is true for all subsequent elections. The election was held on November 3.

The principal candidates for the Presidency were William McKinley (Republican) of Ohio and William J. Bryan (Democrat, Populist, and National Silver party) of Nebraska. The minor candidates were Joshua Levering (Prohibitionist) of Maryland, John M. Palmer (Gold Democrat) of Illinois, Charles H. Matchett (Socialist Labor party) of New York, and Charles E. Bentley (Nationalist party) of Nebraska.

The popular vote was McKinley 7,036,000, Bryan 6,468,000, Palmer 132,000, Levering 131,000, Matchett 36,000, Bentley 14,000, total 13,817,000. The vote for the minor candidates was light and, even when combined, in but five counties exceeded the plurality of the successful major candidate. No counties were carried by a minor candidate. Levering's vote came from all the states except Louisiana, Nevada, South Carolina, and Utah; Palmer's vote from all the states except Arkansas, Idaho, Montana, Nevada, North Dakota, South Dakota, and Wyoming. Matchett's vote came from twenty states—California, Colorado, Connecticut, Illinois, Indiana, Iowa, Maryland, Massachusetts, Michigan, Minnesota, Missouri, Nebraska, New Hampshire, New Jersey, New York, Ohio, Pennsylvania, Rhode Island, Virginia, and Wisconsin; Bentley's vote from eighteen states—California, Colorado, Connecticut, Illinois, Indiana, Iowa, Kansas, Maryland, Michigan, Missouri, Nebraska, New Hampshire, North Carolina, Ohio, Pennsylvania, Rhode Island, Washington, and Wisconsin.

There was a McKinley electoral ticket in every state of the Union. In Louisiana, Mississippi, and South Carolina there were two McKinley tickets. Their designations were as follows: Louisiana, "Regulars" and "Sugar Planters"; Mississippi, "Hill faction" and "Lynch faction"; and South Carolina, "Lily Whites" and "Black and Tans." The combined McKinley vote of each of these states is mapped. There were one or more Bryan electoral tickets in every state. The vote shown on the map is always the total Bryan vote. There were two principal Bryan tickets, which may be designated as the Bryan and Sewall and Bryan and Watson tickets, Sewall being the Vice-Presidential candidate of the Democratic and National Silver parties, and Watson of the Populist, or People's party.

By reason of factions and fusions there are many complications in the Bryan vote. Bryan and Watson were chiefly supported by a faction of the Populist party known as the Middle-of-the-Road Populists, while many members of the other faction of the Populists supported Bryan and Sewall. In several of the states the supporters of Bryan were divided into more than two groups. Thus in Colorado no less than six parties supported him—People's, National Silver, Silver Populist,

Democratic, National People's, and Silver Republican parties. Fusion electoral tickets composed of both Bryan and Sewall and Bryan and Watson electors were supported by both factions in more than half the states—namely, in Arkansas, California, Connecticut, Illinois, Indiana, Iowa, Kentucky, Louisiana, Massachusetts, Michigan, Minnesota, Missouri, Montana, Nebraska, New Jersey, North Carolina, Ohio, Oregon, Pennsylvania, South Dakota, Utah, Washington, West Virginia, Wisconsin, Wyoming, and possibly a few other states (see *World Almanac*, 1897, p. 423). In several states there were both "straight" Bryan and Sewall and "straight" Bryan and Watson tickets. In Kansas the Bryan and Watson faction supported the Bryan and Sewall ticket with the understanding that if Watson received more votes than Sewall outside of Kansas he should receive also the electoral vote of that state. In North Dakota the Populist electors were supported by the Democrats. In Virginia, South Carolina, Delaware, Rhode Island, and possibly a few other states there were no Bryan and Watson electors. In several states in which there were fusion electors there were two Bryan tickets, one headed with the names of Bryan and Sewall and the other with the names of Bryan and Watson, the electors being of course the same on each ticket.

The total vote for Bryan and Sewall may be estimated at more than 6,000,000, and the total vote for Bryan and Watson at less than 500,000. It is of course not possible to give the two votes with precision. In those states in which there were both a Bryan and Sewall and a Bryan and Watson ticket, with different sets of electoral candidates, the total Bryan vote was in excess of the "effective" Bryan vote. Inasmuch as the vote for the Bryan and Sewall ticket in such states was relatively insignificant, those who voted it threw away their votes since they did not increase Bryan's chance of success.

Counties for which the vote of the principal candidates was tied are shown as follows: San Joaquin County, California, and Crawford County, Michigan, for McKinley; and Richmond County, Virginia, for Bryan.

The electoral vote was McKinley 271, Bryan 176, total 447. Bryan received one vote of California, one of Kentucky, and all the votes of Alabama, Arkansas, Colorado, Florida, Georgia, Idaho, Kansas, Louisiana, Mississippi, Missouri, Montana, Nebraska, Nevada, North Carolina, South Carolina, South Dakota, Tennessee, Texas, Utah, Virginia, Washington, and Wyoming. McKinley received the remaining votes of California and Kentucky and all the votes of the remaining states. McKinley carried twenty-one states and divided two, and Bryan carried twenty-two states and divided two. McKinley had a majority of the popular vote.

Presidential Election, 1900
[PLATE 109A]

Forty-five states took part in the Presidential election of 1900, the same number as in 1896. The election was held on November 6. The principal candidates were William McKinley (Republican) of Ohio and William J. Bryan (Democrat, Fusion Populist, and Silver Republican) of Nebraska. The minor candidates were John G. Wooley (Prohibitionist) of Illinois, Eugene V. Debs (Social Democrat) of Indiana, Wharton Barker (Middle-of-the-Road Populist) of Pennsylvania, Joseph F. Malloney (Socialist Labor party) of Massachusetts, Seth H. Ellis (Union Reform party) of Ohio, and Jonah F. R. Leonard (United Christian party) of Iowa.

The popular vote was McKinley 7,220,000, Bryan 6,358,000, Wooley 209,000, Debs 95,000, Barker 50,000, Malloney 33,000, Leonard 5500, Ellis 1000, total 13,971,000. The minor parties polled a light vote and in but few counties held the balance of power. They carried no counties. Wooley's vote came from all the states except Louisiana, Mississippi, Nevada, South Carolina, and Wyoming; and Debs's from all the states except Alabama, Georgia, Idaho, Louisiana, Mississippi, Nevada, North Carolina, Rhode Island, South Carolina, and Wyoming. Barker's vote came from Alabama, Arkansas, Colorado, Florida, Georgia, Idaho, Illinois, Indiana, Iowa, Kentucky, Michigan, Mississippi, Missouri, Montana, Nebraska, New Jersey, North Carolina, North Dakota, Ohio, Oregon, Pennsylvania, South Dakota, Tennessee, Texas, Vermont, Virginia, and West Virginia; Malloney's from Colorado, Connecticut, Illinois, Indiana, Iowa, Kentucky, Maryland, Massachusetts, Michigan, Minnesota, Missouri, Montana, New Jersey, New York, Ohio, Pennsylvania, Rhode Island, Texas, Utah, Virginia, Washington, and Wisconsin; Ellis's from Arkansas, Illinois, Indiana, Maryland, and Ohio; and Leonard's from Illinois and Iowa.

Counties for which the vote of the major candidates was tied are shown as follows: Marion County, Iowa, for McKinley; and Hanson County, South Dakota, for Bryan. Several counties in Texas for which the returns are missing are shown for Bryan since they are regularly Democratic in politics.

The electoral vote was McKinley 292, Bryan 155, total 447. Bryan received the vote of seventeen states—Alabama, Arkansas, Colorado, Florida, Georgia, Idaho, Kentucky, Louisiana, Mississippi, Missouri, Montana, Nevada, North Carolina, South Carolina, Tennessee, Texas, and Virginia; and McKinley the vote of the remaining twenty-eight states. McKinley had a majority of the popular vote.

Presidential Election, 1904

[PLATE 109B]

Forty-five states took part in the Presidential election of 1904, the same number as in 1896 and 1900. The election was held on November 8. The principal candidates for the Presidency were Theodore Roosevelt (Republican) of New York and Alton B. Parker (Democrat) of New York. The minor candidates were Eugene V. Debs (Socialist) of Indiana, Silas C. Swallow (Prohibitionist) of Pennsylvania, Thomas E. Watson (Populist) of Georgia, Charles H. Corregan (Socialist Labor party) of New York, and Austin Holcomb (Continental party) of Georgia.

The popular vote was Roosevelt 7,629,000, Parker 5,084,000, Debs 402,000, Swallow 259,000, Watson 115,000, Corregan 34,000, Holcomb 1000, total 13,524,000. Roosevelt carried every county in several northern and western states. Watson carried a few counties in Georgia. With this exception none of the minor candidates carried a county—a feat rendered unusually difficult by the relatively large pluralities of Roosevelt. In but few counties did they hold the balance of power. Debs's vote came from every state; Swallow's vote from every state except Louisiana, Mississippi, Nevada, South Carolina, and Utah; and Watson's vote from every state except California, Louisiana, Maryland, Pennsylvania, Rhode Island, Utah, Vermont, and Wyoming. Corregan's vote came from Colorado, Connecticut, Illinois, Indiana, Kentucky, Massachusetts, Michigan, Minnesota, Missouri, Montana, New Jersey, New York, Ohio, Pennsylvania, Rhode Island, Texas, Virginia, Washington, and Wisconsin; and Holcomb's vote from Illinois. In Pennsylvania an independent Parker ticket received about 2500 votes.

Counties for which the vote was tied are shown as follows: Scott County, Arkansas, tie between Roosevelt and Parker, for Parker; Forsyth County, Georgia, tie between Parker and Watson, for Watson. Several counties in Texas for which there are no returns, or which are unorganized, are shown as Democratic; and the same is true for the two subsequent maps.

The electoral vote was Roosevelt 336, Parker 140, total 476. Parker received seven votes of Maryland and all the votes of twelve states—Alabama, Arkansas, Florida, Georgia, Kentucky, Louisiana, Mississippi, North Carolina, South Carolina, Tennessee, Texas, and Virginia; Roosevelt received one vote of Maryland and all the votes of the remaining thirty-two states. Roosevelt had a majority of the popular vote.

Presidential Election, 1908

[PLATE 110A]

Forty-six states took part in the Presidential election of 1908, one more than in 1904, the new state being Oklahoma. The election was held on November 3. The principal candidates for the Presidency were William H. Taft (Republican) of Ohio and William J. Bryan (Democrat) of Nebraska. The minor candidates were Eugene V. Debs (Socialist) of Indiana, Eugene W. Chafin (Prohibitionist) of Illinois, Thomas L. Hisgen (Independence party) of Massachusetts, Thomas E. Watson (Populist) of Georgia, August Gillhaus (Socialist Labor party) of New York, and Daniel B. Turney (United Christian party) of Illinois.

The popular vote was Taft 7,679,000, Bryan 6,409,000, Debs 421,000, Chafin 253,000, Hisgen 84,000, Watson 28,000, Gillhaus 14,000, Turney 500, total 14,888,000. Watson carried a few counties in Georgia. With this exception, the minor candidates carried no counties. Debs's vote came from every state; Chafin's vote from every state except Louisiana, Mississippi, Nevada, North Carolina, Oklahoma, South Carolina, and Utah; and Hisgen's vote from every state except Colorado, Mississippi, Nebraska, North Carolina, and Wisconsin. Watson's vote came from Alabama, Arkansas, Florida, Georgia, Illinois, Indiana, Iowa, Kentucky, Mississippi, Missouri, Ohio, Oklahoma, Tennessee, Texas, Virginia, and West Virginia; Gillhaus's vote from Connecticut, Illinois, Indiana, Kentucky, Massachusetts, Michigan, Missouri, New Jersey, New York, Ohio, Pennsylvania, Rhode Island, Texas, Virginia, and Wisconsin; and Turney's vote from Illinois and Michigan. Many voters who in 1904 voted for Watson (Populist) in 1908 voted for Bryan (Democrat). The Populists of Nebraska endorsed Bryan.

The electoral vote was Taft 321, Bryan 162, total 483. Bryan received six votes of Maryland and all the votes of sixteen states—Alabama, Arkansas, Colorado, Florida, Georgia, Kentucky, Louisiana, Mississippi, Nebraska, Nevada, North Carolina, Oklahoma, South Carolina, Tennessee, Texas, and Virginia. Taft received two votes of Maryland and all the votes of the twenty-nine remaining states. Taft had a majority of the popular vote.

Presidential Election, 1912

[PLATE 110B]

Forty-eight states took part in the Presidential election of 1912, two more than in 1908, the new states being New Mexico and Arizona. The election was held on November 5. The principal candidates for the Presidency were William H. Taft (Republican) of Ohio, Woodrow Wilson (Democrat) of New Jersey, and Theodore Roosevelt (Progressive, Washington, and Bull Moose parties) of New York. The minor candidates were Eugene V. Debs (Socialist) of Indiana, Eugene W. Chafin (Prohibitionist) of Arizona, and Arthur Reimer (Socialist Labor party) of Massachusetts.

The popular vote was Taft 3,484,000, Wilson 6,286,000, Roosevelt 4,126,000, Debs 897,000, Chafin 209,000, Reimer 29,000, total 15,031,000. Debs's vote came from every state, and Chafin's from every state except Alabama, Kansas, Louisiana, Mississippi, Nevada, New Mexico, South Carolina, and Utah. Reimer's vote came from Colorado, Connecticut, Illinois, Indiana, Kentucky, Maryland, Massachusetts, Michigan, Minnesota, Missouri, New Jersey, New York, Ohio, Pennsylvania, Rhode Island, Texas, Utah, Virginia, Washington, and Wisconsin. Debs carried Crawford County, Kansas; Beltrami and Lake counties, Minnesota; and Burke County, North Dakota. With the exception of Debs the minor candidates carried no counties.

There were both regular Taft and Roosevelt electoral tickets in every state except California, South Dakota, and Oklahoma. In California there was no regular Taft ticket. In order to vote for Taft in that state it was necessary to write the names of his thirteen electors on the ballot. Under these circumstances his vote in California, about 3000, was negligible.

In South Dakota there was no Taft ticket, but there was a "republican" ticket made up of Roosevelt electors. Before the day of election they issued the following statement: "If Roosevelt can not be elected, and it should become a contest between Mr. Taft and Mr. Wilson, and our votes should thereby defeat Democratic principles and free trade policies, we should vote for Mr. Taft" (*Daily Argus Leader*, Oct. 21, 1912). In Oklahoma there was no "straight" Roosevelt ticket. The electors on the Republican ticket were partly for Taft and partly for Roosevelt (*McAlester News-Capital*, Oct. 19, Nov. 4, 1912). In tables of the popular vote for 1912 the Republican vote in South Dakota is generally credited to Roosevelt, and that in Oklahoma to Taft. The Roosevelt vote mapped for Pennsylvania is the combined vote of the Progressive, Washington, and Bull Moose parties.

Since there were three major candidates in 1912, while there were only two in 1908, the maps for these years are not strictly comparable. In 1912 the successful candidate carried many counties with a vote considerably less than one-half the total vote of the major candidates. Wilson carried many counties with a smaller vote than that with which Bryan lost them in 1908.

The electoral vote was Wilson 435, Roosevelt 88, Taft 8, total 531. Taft received the votes of Utah and Vermont; Roosevelt the eleven votes of California and all the votes of Michigan, Minnesota, Pennsylvania, South Dakota, and Washington; and Wilson the two remaining votes of California and all the votes of the forty remaining states. Wilson had a plurality of the popular vote.

Presidential Election, 1916

[PLATE 111A]

Forty-eight states took part in the Presidential election of 1916, the same number as in 1912. The election was held on November 7. The principal candidates were Charles E. Hughes (Republican) of New York and Woodrow Wilson (Democrat) of New Jersey. The minor candidates were Allan J. Benson (Socialist) of New York, J. Frank Hanly (Prohibitionist) of Indiana, and Arthur E. Reimer (Socialist Labor party) of Massachusetts. In several states there was a Progressive ticket, the electors of which were for Hughes, with the partial exception of those in Louisiana, some of whom were for Hughes and others for Wilson.

The popular vote was Hughes 8,577,000, Wilson 9,129,000, Benson 591,000, Hanly 221,000, Reimer 14,000, Progressive 45,000, total 18,583,000. Benson's vote came from every state, and Hanly's vote from every state except Georgia, Louisiana, Mississippi, Montana, and South Carolina. Reimer's vote came from Connecticut, Illinois, Indiana,

Kentucky, Maryland, Massachusetts, Michigan, Minnesota, Missouri, New Jersey, New York, Pennsylvania, Rhode Island, Utah, Virginia, and Washington. The Progressive vote came chiefly from New York, Georgia, Louisiana, and Indiana.

The Progressive vote in Louisiana is mapped as a separate vote. The Progressive vote in other states is added to the Republican vote, since both were for Hughes. Outside of Louisiana the Progressives carried no counties except in Georgia, where they carried three—Fannin, Gilmer, and Paulding. The vote in Washington County, Kentucky, which was a tie, is given to Wilson.

The electoral vote was Wilson 277, Hughes 254, total 531. Hughes received all the votes of Connecticut, Delaware, Illinois, Indiana, Iowa, Maine, Massachusetts, Michigan, Minnesota, New Jersey, New York, Oregon, Pennsylvania, Rhode Island, South Dakota, Vermont, and Wisconsin, and seven votes of West Virginia. Wilson received one vote of West Virginia and all the votes of the remaining thirty states. Wilson had a plurality of the popular vote.

Presidential Election, 1920

[PLATE 111B]

The election of 1920 was held on November 2. The principal candidates were Warren G. Harding (Republican) of Ohio and James M. Cox (Democrat) of Ohio. The minor candidates were Eugene V. Debs (Socialist) of Indiana, Parley P. Christensen (Farmer-Labor party) of Utah, Aaron P. Watkins (Prohibitionist) of Ohio, W. W. Cox (Industrialist or Socialist Labor party) of Missouri, Robert C. Macauley (Single Tax party) of Pennsylvania, and James E. Ferguson (American party) of Texas.

The popular vote was Harding 16,180,000, J. M. Cox 9,147,000, Debs 920,000, Christensen 265,000, Watkins 189,000, Ferguson 48,000, W. W. Cox 31,000, Macauley 6000, total 26,786,000. The Socialist vote came from every state except Louisiana, Montana, New Mexico, South Dakota, and Vermont; and the Prohibitionist vote from every state except Arkansas, Kansas, Louisiana, Maine, Maryland, Massachusetts, Mississippi, Montana, Nevada, New Hampshire, New Mexico, North Dakota, Oklahoma, South Carolina, Tennessee, Texas, and Utah. The Farmer-Labor vote came from twenty-one states, the Socialist Labor vote from fifteen states, the Single Tax vote from nine states, and the American party vote from one state—Texas.

The electoral vote was Harding 404, Cox 127, total 531. Cox received the electoral vote of eleven states—Alabama, Arkansas, Florida, Georgia, Kentucky, Louisiana, Mississippi, North Carolina, South Carolina, Texas, and Virginia, and Harding the electoral vote of the remaining thirty-seven states. Harding had a plurality of 7,033,000 votes.

Presidential Election, 1924

[PLATE 111C]

The election was held on November 4. The principal candidates were Calvin Coolidge (Republican) of Vermont, John W. Davis (Democrat) of New York, and Robert LaFollette (Progressive) of Wisconsin. The minor candidates were Herman P. Faris (Prohibitionist) of Missouri, William Z. Foster (Workers and Farmer-Labor parties) of Illinois, Frank T. Johns (Socialist Labor party) of Oregon, Gilbert O. Nations (American party) of Washington, D. C., and William J. Wallace (Commonwealth Land party) of New Jersey.

The popular vote was Coolidge 15,725,000, Davis 8,386,000, La Follette 4,822,000, Faris 58,000, Foster 36,000, Johns 36,000, Nations 24,000, Wallace 2000, total 29,089,000. The votes for each of the three major candidates came from every state. The Prohibitionist vote came from sixteen states, the Socialist-Labor vote from fifteen states, the Farmer-Labor vote from fourteen states, the vote of the American party from eight states, and the vote of the Commonwealth Land party from six states.

The electoral vote was Coolidge 382, Davis 136, LaFollette 13, total 531. Davis received the electoral votes of twelve states—Alabama, Arkansas, Florida, Georgia, Louisiana, Mississippi, North Carolina, Oklahoma, South Carolina, Tennessee, Texas, and Virginia; LaFollette the vote of one state—Wisconsin; and Coolidge the vote of the remaining thirty-five states. Coolidge had a plurality of 7,339,000 votes.

Jefferson County, Montana, for which there was a tie between Coolidge and LaFollette, is shown as Coolidge territory.

Presidential Election, 1928

[PLATE 111D]

The election was held on November 6. The principal candidates were Herbert C. Hoover (Republican) of California and Alfred E. Smith (Democrat) of New York. The minor candidates were Norman Thomas (Socialist) of New York, William Z. Foster (Workers party) of Illinois, Verne L. Reynolds (Socialist-Labor party) of Michigan, William F. Varney (Prohibitionist) of New York, and Frank E. Webb (Farmer-Labor party) of California.

The popular vote was Hoover 21,392,000, Smith 15,016,000, Thomas 267,000, Foster 49,000, Reynolds 22,000, Varney 20,000, Webb 6000, total 36,772,000. The votes for each of the two major candidates came from every state. The Socialist vote came from every state except Arizona, Louisiana, Nevada, North Carolina, Rhode Island, and Vermont. The Workers vote came from thirty-three states, the Socialist-Labor from eighteen states (in Maryland Reynolds ran as the Labor candidate, in Minnesota as the Industrial candidate, and in Pennsylvania as the Industrialist candidate), the Prohibitionist from eight states, and the Farmer-Labor from four states. A Hoover-anti-Smith party carried a number of counties in Georgia.

The electoral vote was Hoover 444, Smith 87, total 531. Smith received the electoral votes of eight states—Alabama, Arkansas, Georgia, Louisiana, Massachusetts, Mississippi, Rhode Island, and South Carolina; and Hoover the electoral vote of the remaining states. In the popular vote Hoover had a plurality of 6,424,000. The total vote cast exceeded that of the previous Presidential election by 6,600,000.

CONGRESSIONAL MEASURES, 1790–1930

[PLATES 112–122]

Choice of Measures Mapped. The many hundreds of votes taken and recorded by the U. S. House of Representatives since it first convened in 1789 constitute a wealth of materials out of which numerous political maps might be constructed. The relatively small number of maps based upon such materials that could be included in the *Atlas* fixed definitely the number of measures to be selected and greatly limited the possibilities of selection. Choice was further limited by several criteria which it was agreed should serve as a guide in making selections. These were as follows:

1. The measures chosen should be among the most important that have been considered by Congress and should be of national interest.

2. They should relate to such general subjects as the tariff, finance, taxation, slavery, internal improvements, public lands, organization of the government, peace and war, and international relations.

3. They should be distributed more or less evenly over the period 1789–1930.

4. Preference should be given to measures that best illustrate sectionalism.

5. Preference should be given to measures for which the vote was more or less evenly divided, and for which the number of members not voting was relatively small.

6. Other things being equal, measures that involve simple issues should be chosen.

7. Due consideration should be given to the special series to which any given measure belongs. Thus, in choosing a tariff measure, consideration should be given to the tariff series.

With these criteria as a guide, and with the advice of several of the leading writers and teachers of American history, thirty-six measures were chosen. Doubtless equally good lists, varying somewhat from this one, could be prepared but none that would not include most of its measures. Several measures that one might expect to see included were for good reasons rejected. Thus, the Wilmot Proviso could not be used because the yea-and-nay vote was not recorded. Several important measures passed during Roosevelt's administration relating to interstate commerce or to colonial government were rejected because the vote was either one-sided or was relatively small, many members not voting. The Dingley Tariff Act was preferred to the somewhat more famous McKinley Tariff Act because it marked a culmination of the high tariff movement and was longer-lived than any other general tariff act.

In the case of many measures more than one vote was recorded, and a selection of votes was rendered necessary. No invariable rule of selection was followed. In general the vote chosen was the one that best represented the division of the House upon the issues involved and that was also best adapted for mapping.

Election and Apportionment of Representatives. The three usual methods that have been followed by the states in electing members to the U. S. House of Representatives are as follows: (1) by districts, (2) on a general ticket, and (3) partly by districts and partly at large. The case of states that choose but a single representative is a little peculiar, and may possibly be regarded as constituting a fourth class. In both text and maps the phrase "at large" is applied to the additional representative or representatives elected by the entire electorate of a state that elects part of its representatives in districts. It is not applied to the sole representative of states that are allotted but one representative, nor is it applied to states that elect two representatives and are not districted. In these two latter cases, recent Congressional directories follow a different practice.

Before 1842 each state prescribed the manner of choosing its representatives. Most of the states showed a preference for the method of election by districts; but several states, especially New Hampshire, Connecticut, New Jersey, and Georgia, were partial to the method of election by general ticket. In the apportionment act of 1842 Congress prescribed that representatives should be chosen in districts. After each succeeding census, with a few exceptions it has reënacted this provision. Occasionally, however, it has made or permitted a few exceptions to the rule. Several states did not readily accept the act of 1842, and three of them (New Hampshire, Missouri, and Mississippi) continued to elect by general ticket until 1846, in which for the first time all representatives were chosen by districts. Since that year, in the case of states electing a small number of representatives, there has been a limited use of the method of election by general ticket. Thus by a federal law California was permitted to choose in this manner her representatives for several years immediately after her admission into the Union. South Dakota from 1889 to 1911, North Dakota from 1902 to 1911, and Washington from 1892 to 1907 were also permitted to follow the same practice.

Since apportionment acts are not as a rule passed until the first or second year following census years, it is often difficult or impossible for states, especially if their legislatures meet biennially, to pass districting acts before the election of the Congress whose term begins on March 4 of the third year succeeding census years, that is, March 4, 1793, 1803, etc. This led Congress to insert in the apportionment act of 1872 (*U. S. Statutes at Large*, Vol. 17, Boston, 1873, p. 28) and in several succeeding acts the provision that in case a state is allowed an increased number of representatives the additional representative or representatives for the first Congress after the passage of the apportionment act might be elected at large, unless the state should otherwise provide before the day of election. The first Congress after a new apportionment act is therefore likely to contain an unusual number of representatives elected at large. In 1882, for the first time, an apportionment act contained the provision that if the number of representatives of any state should be reduced the whole number of representatives to which the state was entitled should be elected at large until the state should otherwise provide (*ibid.*, Vol. 22, 1883, p. 6).

When a new apportionment act changes the number of representatives of a state it is usual for the legislature of that state to create new districts as soon as practicable. Most of the state districting acts are therefore passed in the first or second year succeeding census years. This is the rule, but the exceptions to it are numerous. A state districting act may be passed any year. The acquiring of an additional representative does not invariably result in the passage of a new law, as may be seen from the practice of Colorado, 1902-1912. In 1901 the number of that state's representatives was increased from two to three and in 1911 from three to four. In 1902-1910 she chose one representative at large, in 1912 two, and throughout the whole period two representatives by districts, under a districting act of 1891. Occasionally states are dissatisfied with their districting acts and remodel them. Thus the Arkansas act of 1875 was remodeled in 1879, the Massachusetts act of 1872 in 1876, the Indiana act of 1872 in 1879, and the Ohio act of 1882 in 1886 and again in 1890. If successive apportionment acts make no changes in a state's quota a state may choose representatives for twenty or thirty years or even longer under the same districting act. The members of the House of Representatives of any given Congress are therefore likely to be chosen under districting acts of widely varying dates.

When the states fixed the mode of election they occasionally created a "plural district," that is, one electing two or more members. New York, Pennsylvania, and Maryland showed some liking for this device. In the apportionment act of 1842 Congress provided that each district should elect one representative and in subsequent apportionment acts has frequently repeated this provision. In the Congress of 1841-1843 the three states named above had one or more plural districts. With the passing of this Congress the use of plural districts came to an end.

Until 1872 each state fixed the date of the election of its representatives, with the result that the dates of election throughout the Union were far from uniform. The variation between extreme dates was usually from six months to a year. Thus New York chose her members to the Tenth Congress (the one that first assembled in October, 1807, and voted on the Embargo Act) on April 29, 30, and May 1, 1806, the election lasting three days in that state; while Virginia chose her members in April, 1807. Long before 1872, however, many of the states fixed on a date in the fall of the year preceding the March in which the term of the

new Congress began. The apportionment act of 1872 contained a provision establishing a uniform date of election (beginning with the election of 1876), namely, the Tuesday next after the first Monday of November —the same as that selected in 1845 for the Presidential election (see p. 98, above). In 1875, however, Congress excepted from the operation of this provision the states whose constitutions fixed some other day. In 1930 all the states except Maine, which votes in September, were choosing representatives on the date established by Congress.

States vary in their treatment of new counties created after the passage of one districting act and before the passage of the next succeeding act. Sometimes by statutory provision they attach the new county to a Congressional district. More frequently they do not. In the latter case it is to be inferred that if the new county is composed of territory belonging to a single district it still belongs to that district, and that if it is composed of territory belonging to several districts the several parts still belong to their respective districts.

Congressional Districts. The geographical unit employed in constructing the maps illustrating Congressional measures is, with a few exceptions, the Congressional district. The exceptions comprise those cases in which the Congressmen of a state are chosen on a general ticket (see preceding paragraphs). In these cases the geographical unit employed is the state.

As a rule Congressional districts consist of several counties. In densely populated regions, especially in the larger cities, they may consist of single counties or cities, or of parts of counties or cities. In New England, and occasionally in some of the other Northern states, towns and cities as well as counties are used in forming Congressional districts. In a few states the township, the borough, or the village is occasionally used. Maryland has sometimes made use of election districts in connection with counties. In her first apportionment act North Carolina formed her Congressional districts out of judicial districts, a practice also followed for a time by South Carolina. The first Congressional districts in Louisiana were made from "counties," which were composed of parishes, and the later districts were made from parishes, the political unit in that state most nearly corresponding to counties elsewhere.

In New York and other large cities Congressional districts are often made from wards and parts of wards or from assembly districts, but not infrequently they consist of parts of cities corresponding to no established political unit or combination of political units but are formed with more or less artificial boundaries for the single purpose of electing members of Congress. It is not unusual for small parts of the larger cities to be joined to adjacent rural or extra-urban territory to form a Congressional district. Thus the Massachusetts districting act of 1912 joined the twenty-fifth ward of Boston to parts of Norfolk, Middlesex, and Worcester counties to form the thirteenth Massachusetts district and joined the twenty-sixth ward of Boston to parts of Bristol, Norfolk, and Plymouth counties to form the fourteenth district.

As a rule the states have created Congressional districts from contiguous territory. It is unavoidable, however, that occasionally considerable bodies of water should separate the parts of districts. This is notably the case with the Nantucket and Marthas Vineyard district, which has always included a part of the Massachusetts mainland, and with the Accomac-Northampton district of the "eastern shore" of Virginia, which has always included a part of the Virginia mainland.

In the early years the rule of creating districts from contiguous territory was occasionally broken. Thus in 1808 New York created a district out of Clinton, Franklin, Essex, and Saratoga counties, the two counties last named being separated from each other by what is now Warren County (see Pls. 112D and 113A). In 1822 New York created a district out of Kings County on Long Island, Richmond County or Staten Island, and Rockland County lying north of New Jersey. To prevent this practice a provision was included in the apportionment act of 1842 requiring Congressional districts to be composed of "contiguous territory" (*U. S. Statutes at Large*, Vol. 5, Boston, 1848, p. 491). This provision again appeared in 1862 and in each apportionment act since that date with the exception of that of 1929. Some of the states have similar requirements. Thus the Iowa constitution of 1857 provides that when a Congressional district shall be composed of two or more counties it shall not be entirely separated by a county belonging to another district (Art. III, sect. 37).

Speaking generally, one may say that Congressional districts have been more or less compact in area, fairly regular in shape, and in the main bounded by well-established political lines. There have been, however, many departures from the rule. Not infrequently considerations of party advantage, leading often to the gerrymandering of states, have resulted in the creation of irregular and unnatural districts. Some of the irregularities are quite extraordinary, as are indicated by such nicknames as the "shoe-string" district, the "dumb-bell" district, and the "saddlebag" district. A few of the irregular districts are shown on the maps illustrating Congressional Measures. The blue area in Mississippi (Pl. 117D) is the shoe-string district. An extraordinarily irregular district is the blue area in South Carolina (Pl. 118B), and another is the blue area in Alabama (Pl. 119A).

To prevent such irregularities as these a provision was included in the apportionment act of 1901 requiring Congressional districts to be composed of "compact territory"—a provision that was repeated in the act of 1911 (*U. S. Statutes at Large*, Vol. 31, 1901, p. 734; Vol. 37, 1913, Part I, p. 14). These acts, however, have not prevented gerrymandering and the introduction of more irregularities than are unavoidable (J. R. Commons, *Proportional Representation*, 2nd edit., New York, 1907, p. 52; R. E. Andrews, "The Grip of the Gerrymander," *The Independent*, Vol. 70, New York, 1911, pp. 1002–1006).

The variation in the size of Congressional districts is much greater than that in the size of counties (see pp. 88–89, above). They vary from less than five square miles in the case of some of the districts in the largest cities to more than 100,000 square miles in the case of some of the districts in the Rocky Mountain region, which consist of entire states.

Population of Congressional Districts. The variation in the population of Congressional districts is much less than that in the population of counties (see pp. 89–90, above). The population of Congressional districts has gradually increased since 1789 until at the present time it is seven or eight times what it was then. Since the ratio of population to each representative as fixed by the several federal apportionment acts is roughly proportional to the average population of the Congressional districts under the several acts, a table such as that given below shows with a fair degree of accuracy the relative increase in the population of Congressional districts. This table also shows the increase in the number of representatives.

TABLE 7

RATIO OF APPORTIONMENT AND NUMBER OF MEMBERS
U. S. HOUSE OF REPRESENTATIVES, 1789–1930

	RATIO	DATE OF ACTS	NUMBER OF REPRESENTATIVES	CONGRESSES AND PERIOD
Constitution........			59–68	1–2 ; 1789–1793
First Census........	33,000	Apr. 14, 1792	105–106	3–7 ; 1793–1803
Second Census......	33,000	Jan. 14, 1802	141–143	8–12; 1803–1813
Third Census.......	35,000	Dec. 21, 1811	182–187	13–17; 1813–1823
Fourth Census......	40,000	Mar. 7, 1822	213	18–22; 1823–1833
Fifth Census........	47,700	May 22, 1832	240–242	23–27; 1833–1843
Sixth Census.......	70,680	June 25, 1842	223–233	28–32; 1843–1853
Seventh Census.....	93,407	{May 23, 1850, July 30, 1852	234–238	33–37; 1853–1863
Eighth Census......	126,823	Mar. 4, 1862	241–243	38–42; 1863–1873
Ninth Census.......	134,022	{Feb. 2, 1872 May 30, 1872	292–293	43–47; 1873–1883
Tenth Census.......	151,911	Feb. 25, 1882	325–332	48–52; 1883–1893
Eleventh Census....	173,901	Feb. 7, 1891	356–357	53–57; 1893–1903
Twelfth Census.....	194,182	Jan. 16, 1901	386–391	58–62; 1903–1913
Thirteenth Census...	211,877	Aug. 8, 1911	433–435	63–72; 1913–1933

This table is based upon figures found in various publications of the government. The figures for several of the ratios as given in different documents vary slightly. The variation in the number of representatives for each decade is caused by the admission of new states. No apportionment act based on the figures of the fourteenth census (1920) was passed.

The gradual increase in the average population of Congressional districts has not been so regular as this table indicates. Because of the increase of the population of the United States the average population of districts is always greater than the ratio shown in the table, which is based on the population of census years. Thus the average population of the districts in 1905 was somewhat in excess of the ratio 194,182, based on the census of 1900. Since each increase in the number of representatives tends to decrease the average population of districts the adoption of a new number and a new ratio may decrease the average population. Thus in 1910 the average population of the 391 districts then existing was 233,000, considerably in excess of the ratio of 1911 (211,877) based on a membership of 433 representatives. It will be noted that each apportionment act given in Table 7, with the exception of that of 1842, increased the number of representatives. The act of 1842 decreased the number from 242 to 223. An act passed in 1929 fixing the number under the fifteenth census made no change in the number, 435.

The population of Congressional districts in different parts of the Union or of a state, for any one year, often varies considerably. The method of apportionment of course makes some variation inevitable.

The practice followed by Congress of allotting an additional representative for each major fraction of the ratio of apportionment and of disregarding minor fractions is responsible for some of the inequalities. The uneven rates of increase or decrease of population in the different parts of the Union or of a state sometimes cause districts that were fairly equal in population when created to be unequal before the passage of a new districting act. The inequality was unusually large during the decade 1920–1930, when representatives were elected under the apportionment act of 1911. The Constitutional provision that each state must have at least one representative guarantees a representative to Nevada, which for many years contained less than 50,000 people. The Constitutional provision that in apportioning representatives a slave should count for three-fifths of a white person caused the Southern districts before the Civil War to have a relatively smaller electorate than the Northern districts. The practice of gerrymandering produces unnecessary inequalities.

Each federal apportionment act beginning with that of 1872 has required Congressional districts to contain "as nearly as practicable an equal number of inhabitants" (*U. S. Statutes at Large*, Vol. 17, Boston, 1873, p. 28), but this requirement has not prevented states from creating districts with considerable variations in population. Thus, after the federal apportionment act of 1891 Michigan created twelve districts with populations varying from 149,000 to 192,000; California seven, varying from 148,000 to 229,000; Arkansas six, varying from 148,000 to 220,000; New Jersey eight, varying from 126,000 to 222,000; and New York thirty-four, varying from 115,000 to 228,000. That at least some of these variations exceed what was inevitable may be inferred from the work of Minnesota, which created seven districts, varying from 184,000 to 188,000, and of Massachusetts, which created thirteen districts, varying from 169,000 to 175,000. These figures are based upon those of the census of 1890 (*Congressional Directory*, *53rd Cong.*, *1st Sess.*, 1893, 2nd edit., pp. 161–208). In 1911–1912 New York and New Jersey improved upon their work of twenty years earlier. New York created forty-three districts, varying in population from 195,000 to 230,000, and New Jersey twelve, varying from 198,000 to 230,000.

Representation of Votes on Maps. The general rules respecting the use of color are as follows: the districts represented by members who voted yea are colored blue, the districts represented by members who voted nay are colored yellow, and the districts unrepresented or represented by members who did not vote are shaded. Plural districts, that is, districts electing more than one member, are treated thus: (1) when the yeas and nays were unequal the vote of the majority is shown, and the vote of the minority is listed in the legend under the heading "votes not shown"; (2) in case of a tie one vote is shown and the other is listed as not shown (see, however, p. 122, below); and (3) in case only a part of the members vote the members who do not vote are disregarded. In choosing the vote to be shown in the case of a tie, weight was given to other votes of the district in respect to the measure that was being mapped, to the vote of the adjoining districts, and to the treatment of other ties in the same state.

States which elect their representatives on a general ticket, and New York and other large cities which elect several representatives from districts so small that the votes cannot be shown on the maps, are treated in the same way as plural districts, in accordance with the three rules given above. Representatives at large who do not vote are disregarded. When the vote of a state electing both representatives at large and district representatives is unanimous the state is given its proper color, and the vote of the representatives at large may be regarded as shown. When the vote is divided the vote of the representatives at large is not shown but is listed in the legend.

In the text below, under each measure, will be found the names of the states that elected representatives by general ticket and those that elected representatives at large. Since representatives often reflect the predominating sentiment of the section of the state in which they reside, the residence of representatives elected on a general ticket are, as a rule, given when the vote of a state is divided. The residences also of representatives at large are sometimes given.

Districts whose members did not vote, or which were unrepresented when the vote was taken, are shown, with the exception of small urban districts, by means of shading. With the exception of "live pairs," members who are "paired" are treated as not voting. In recent years members are often paired in such a way as to express a preference for or against a measure, such pairs having received the designation of "live pairs." Since, as a rule, the speaker does not vote, his district is generally shaded. By ascertaining his party affiliation the proper color for his district can often be interpolated on the map. The speaker and his district are noted in the text.

Unsettled and unorganized areas are left blank, and what was said in respect to such areas in the text of the maps illustrating Presidential elections applies for the most part to the maps illustrating Congressional measures (see p. 104, above). The "non-voting areas" on the Congressional maps, however, are not blank but are shaded. Unimportant islands are disregarded. Their proper color may be ascertained from the color of the counties or Congressional districts to which they belong.

Interpretation of the Maps. Because of variations in the size of districts, votes in the House are represented on the maps by color areas of widely varying sizes. Thus the vote of a New York city member is represented by a point of color, while the vote of some of the members from the Rocky Mountain states is represented by a square inch of color. The variation in the size of even rural districts in the same state is often quite considerable. Thus, on Plate 117C the nay area in Minnesota which represents one vote is larger than the yea area in that state which represents two votes. When all the votes are not mapped the "face" of the map is to be corrected by referring to "votes not shown," listed in the legend. Reference to the text, for each measure below, and especially to the tables there found, will also serve to correct misleading impressions. In comparing one map with another it should be remembered that some of the differences that exist may be the result of changes made by different apportioning or districting acts.

It is not to be expected that the color areas always represent accurately the preponderating sentiment in a given district or locality for or against a measure—certainly not with nice precision as respects location. This is prevented, not to speak of other obstacles, by the practice of gerrymandering, by the impossibility of creating uniform districts, by the failure of elections always to gauge accurately public opinion, and by the frequent lack of accord between a representative and his constituents. Votes of different members may represent somewhat different things. Each user of the *Atlas* is expected to make his own interpretation.

Boundary Lines. What was said respecting boundary lines in connection with the maps illustrating Presidential elections (see p. 91, above) applies for the most part to the maps illustrating Congressional measures. This difference, however, should be noted: On the Presidential maps the lines within states separating color areas are county lines, while on the Congressional maps the lines within states separating color areas (or a color area from a shaded area) are sometimes, in New England and other populous regions, not county lines but town, township, borough, city, or assembly district lines. Most of the lines, however, are county lines. The lines within the states bounding "unsettled areas" may be county lines, Indian treaty lines, Indian reservation lines, or other lines. Often they are drawn arbitrarily, and will not be found on other maps.

Sources of Information. Since the *Journal* of the House of Representatives is more authoritative than the *Annals of Congress* and the later proceedings which succeeded the *Annals*, all votes were taken from the *Journal* with the exception of those for a few of the latest measures, which were taken from the *Congressional Record*, since the *Journal* for the later Congresses has not been published. Occasionally the vote given by the *Journal* and that given by the proceedings of Congress differ slightly.

For descriptions of Congressional districts the districting acts found in the session laws of the states or in collections of state statutes were used. Descriptions more accessible, though sometimes inaccurate or abridged, are to be found in the *Congressional Directory*, beginning with the issue for the first session of the Twenty-second Congress, 1831-1832. Reference may be here made to the maps of Congressional districts under each apportionment act since that of 1882, found in several volumes of the *Congressional Directory*, and beginning with the *Supplement* of 1891. These, while probably accurate enough for some purposes, have not been used, since their lines are somewhat generalized and occasionally inaccurate.

In identifying representatives with their districts, the *Congressional Directory*, beginning with the second session of the Fourteenth Congress, 1816-1817, was chiefly relied upon. For the earlier period contemporary newspapers and biographical books were used. A few knotty questions of identification were referred to local historians and antiquarians. It should be noted that several of the early South Carolina representatives did not reside in their districts.

Assumption of State Debts, July 26, 1790
[PLATE 112A]

The vote is by the representatives of the First Congress, second session, on agreeing to an amendment of the Senate to a "bill making provision for the payment of the debt of the United States." The amend-

ment provided for the assumption of state debts by the federal government to the amount of $21,500,000 and apportioned this sum among the several states. The material part of the Senate amendment is section 13 of the act for the payment of the debt of the United States, approved by the President on August 4, 1790 (*U. S. Statutes at Large*, Vol. 1, Boston, 1845, pp. 142-143; *Senate Journ.*, Vol. 1, 1789-1793, p. 185).

The vote in the House on the amendment was yeas 34, nays 28, not voting 3, total 65. The vote by states, thirteen in number, is shown in the following table (*House Journ.*, Vol. 1, 1789-1793, p. 281):

TABLE 8
ASSUMPTION OF STATE DEBTS, 1790

STATE	YEAS	NAYS	NOT VOTING	TOTAL VOTES
Connecticut	5			5
Delaware	1			1
Georgia		3		3
Maryland	2	4		6
Massachusetts	8			8
New Hampshire	1	2		3
New Jersey	4			4
New York	3	3		6
North Carolina		5		5
Pennsylvania	3	4	1	8
Rhode Island			1	1
South Carolina	5			5
Virginia	2	7	1	10
Total	34	28	3	65

The representatives of the First Congress were elected under the apportionment fixed by the Constitution. Delaware and Rhode Island each chose a single representative. In New Hampshire, Connecticut, New Jersey, Pennsylvania, Maryland, and Georgia the election was by general ticket, and in the remaining states—Massachusetts, New York, Virginia, North Carolina, and South Carolina—by districts. Maryland required that one representative should reside in each of the six districts created by her (*Maryland Laws*, Dec. 22, 1788, Ch. 10). The vote was taken after Rhode Island was admitted to the Union and before she chose a representative.

The vote in three states electing representatives by general ticket was divided, and part of it therefore cannot be shown on the map. The votes that cannot be shown are as follows: New Hampshire, 1 yea; Pennsylvania, 3 yeas; and Maryland, 2 yeas. The New Hampshire representative who voted yea came from Canterbury, in the south-central part of the state, and the two representatives who voted nay, from Holderness and Exeter respectively, in the central and the southeastern part. Of the three Pennsylvania representatives who voted yea, two came from Philadelphia and one from Bucks County, all in the southeastern part of the state; the four representatives voting nay resided in Berks, Montgomery, York, and Washington counties respectively, all west of the residences of the members voting yea. The residences of the Maryland representatives and the sections of the state from which they came were as follows: two yeas, Somerset County, southeastern, and Montgomery County, southern; four nays, Baltimore City and Queen Annes County, northeastern, and Prince Georges and Charles counties, southern.

When the vote was taken Tennessee no longer formed a part of North Carolina. The North Carolina member for the Tennessee district, however, was still in Congress. Since he voted nay, the settled part of Tennessee is colored yellow. Kentucky formed a part of Virginia, and Vermont had not been admitted to the Union. The one Pennsylvania member who did not vote was Frederick A. Muhlenberg, speaker of the House.

Act Incorporating the United States Bank, February 8, 1791
[PLATE 112B]

The vote is by the representatives of the First Congress, third session, on the passage of an "act to incorporate the subscribers to the Bank of the United States." This act, which passed the Senate on January 20, was passed by the House without amendment on February 8 and was approved by the President on February 25. It is found in *U. S. Statutes at Large*, Vol. 1, Boston, 1845, pp. 191-196.

The vote was yeas 39, nays 20, not voting 6, total 65. The vote by states, thirteen in number, is shown in the following table (*House Journ.*, Vol. 1, 1789-1793, pp. 372-373):

TABLE 9
ACT INCORPORATING THE UNITED STATES BANK, 1791

STATE	YEAS	NAYS	NOT VOTING	TOTAL VOTES
Connecticut...............	5	....	....	5
Delaware..................	1	....	....	1
Georgia...................	....	3	....	3
Maryland.................	2	4	....	6
Massachusetts............	7	1	....	8
New Hampshire...........	3	....	....	3
New Jersey...............	4	....	....	4
New York................	6	....	....	6
North Carolina...........	2	3	....	5
Pennsylvania.............	7	....	1	8
Rhode Island.............	1	....	....	1
South Carolina...........	1	2	2	5
Virginia..................	....	7	3	10
Total..................	39	20	6	65

For the method of electing representatives to the First Congress, see page 107, above. Maryland is the only state electing representatives by general ticket whose vote was divided. The two yea votes, which are not shown on the map, came, respectively, from Baltimore City and Queen Annes County, both in the northeastern part of the state, and the four nay votes from Montgomery, Prince Georges, Charles, and Somerset counties, all in the southern part of the state.

The vote of the member from the Tennessee district of North Carolina, although this district no longer formed a part of the older state, is shown. Kentucky formed a part of Virginia, and Vermont had not been admitted to the Union. The Pennsylvania member who did not vote was Frederick A. Muhlenberg, speaker of the House.

Alien and Sedition Acts, February 25, 1799

[PLATE 112C]

Two votes, precisely alike, are mapped. The first is on agreeing to the resolution "that it is inexpedient to repeal the act passed the last session, entitled 'an act concerning aliens,'" and the second on agreeing to the resolution "that it is inexpedient to repeal the act passed the last session, entitled 'an act in addition to the act entitled an act for the punishment of certain crimes against the United States.'" The Alien Act was passed on June 25, and the Sedition Act on July 14, 1798 (U. S. Statutes at Large, Vol. 1, Boston, 1845, pp. 570–572 and 596–597). The resolutions, which failed of passage, originated in the House.

The votes, which were by the representatives of the Fifth Congress, third session, were yeas 52, nays 48, not voting 6, total 106. The vote by states, sixteen in number, is shown in the following table (House Journ., Vol. 3, 1797–1801, pp. 493–495):

TABLE 10
ALIEN AND SEDITION ACTS, 1799

STATE	YEAS	NAYS	NOT VOTING	TOTAL VOTES
Connecticut...............	7	....	....	7
Delaware..................	1	....	....	1
Georgia...................	....	1	1	2
Kentucky.................	....	2	....	2
Maryland.................	5	3	....	8
Massachusetts............	11	3	....	14
New Hampshire...........	4	....	....	4
New Jersey...............	4	....	1	5
New York................	6	4	....	10
North Carolina...........	1	7	2	10
Pennsylvania.............	4	8	1	13
Rhode Island.............	2	....	....	2
South Carolina...........	3	2	1	6
Tennessee................	....	1	....	1
Vermont.................	1	1	....	2
Virginia..................	3	16	....	19
Total..................	52	48	6	106

The representatives of the Fifth Congress were elected under the apportionment act of April 14, 1792. Delaware and Tennessee each chose a single representative. New Hampshire, Rhode Island, Connecticut, New Jersey, and Georgia elected representatives on a general ticket. In the remaining states the election was by districts. The vote of none of the states that chose representatives by general ticket was

divided. One representative from New Jersey and one from Georgia did not vote. The representative from New Jersey who did not vote was Jonathan Dayton, speaker of the House. The fourth Pennsylvania district, composed of the counties of Montgomery, Bucks, and Northampton, elected two members, one of whom voted yea and one nay. The nay vote is not shown.

Embargo Act, December 21, 1807

[PLATE 112D]

The vote was by the representatives of the Tenth Congress, first session, on the passage of an "act laying an embargo on all ships and vessels in the ports and harbors of the United States." The act, which was passed by the Senate on December 18, was amended by the House, and the Senate agreed to the House amendments. It was approved by the President on December 22. It is found in the form in which it passed the House in U. S. Statutes at Large, Vol. 2, Boston, 1845, pp. 451–453.

The vote was yeas 82, nays 44, not voting 16, total 142. The vote by states, seventeen in number, is shown in the following table (House Journ., Vol. 6, 1807–1809, pp. 320–321):

TABLE 11
EMBARGO ACT, 1807

STATE	YEAS	NAYS	NOT VOTING	TOTAL VOTES
Connecticut...............	....	7	....	7
Delaware..................	....	....	1	1
Georgia...................	1	3	....	4
Kentucky.................	4	2	....	6
Maryland.................	4	4	1	9
Massachusetts............	10	6	1	17
New Hampshire...........	5	....	....	5
New Jersey...............	5	....	1	6
New York................	7	6	4	17
North Carolina...........	6	5	1	12
Ohio.....................	1	....	....	1
Pennsylvania.............	11	5	2	18
Rhode Island.............	2	....	....	2
South Carolina...........	7	....	1	8
Tennessee................	3	....	....	3
Vermont.................	2	2	....	4
Virginia..................	14	4	4	22
Total..................	82	44	16	142

The election of representatives to the Tenth Congress was under the apportionment act of January 14, 1802. Delaware and Ohio each chose a single representative. New Hampshire, Rhode Island, Connecticut, New Jersey, and Georgia elected representatives by general ticket, and the rest of the states by districts. Georgia was the only state electing by general ticket whose vote was divided. One New Jersey member failed to vote. The following votes are not shown on the map: Georgia, 1 yea; Pennsylvania, 2 nays. The one yea vote from Georgia is that of G. M. Troup, who resided in Savannah about the time he was elected to Congress. (Because of the frequency with which some of the early representatives moved from place to place it is difficult to be sure of their residence.) The three Georgia representatives who voted nay resided respectively in Richmond, Elbert, and Houston counties, lying to the north and west of Savannah. Two districts in Pennsylvania, composed respectively of Montgomery, Bucks, Northampton, Wayne, and Luzerne counties, and of Chester, Lancaster, and Berks counties, were represented by three members each. Two of the representatives of each district voted yea and one nay. The nay votes are not shown.

One of the three members representing a Pennsylvania district, composed of the city and county of Philadelphia, and one of the two members representing a New York district, composed of the city and county of New York and of Kings and Richmond counties, both of whom did not vote, are disregarded. The non-voting area in Massachusetts is the district of J. B. Varnum, speaker of the House. The two non-voting areas in northeastern New York are the discontiguous parts of the same district.

Declaration of War, June 4, 1812

[PLATE 113A]

The vote was by the representatives of the Twelfth Congress, first session, on the passage of an "act declaring war between the United Kingdom of Great Britain and Ireland and the dependencies thereof, and the United States of America and their territories." After passing the House the act was slightly amended by the Senate, and the amendments were concurred in by the House. The act as passed by the House is found in *Senate Journ.*, Vol. 5, 1811–1813, p. 153, and, as approved by the President on June 18, 1812, in *U. S. Statutes at Large*, Vol. 2, Boston, 1845, p. 755.

The vote was yeas 79, nays 49, not voting 15, total 143. The vote by states, eighteen in number, is shown in the following table (*House Journ.*, Vol. 8, 1811–1813, pp. 469–470):

TABLE 12
DECLARATION OF WAR, 1812

STATE	YEAS	NAYS	NOT VOTING	TOTAL VOTES
Connecticut	. . . . .	7	. . . . .	7
Delaware	. . . . .	1	. . . . .	1
Georgia	3	. . . . .	1	4
Kentucky	5	. . . . .	1	6
Louisiana	. . . . .	. . . . .	1	1
Maryland	6	3	. . . . .	9
Massachusetts	6	8	3	17
New Hampshire	3	2	. . . . .	5
New Jersey	2	4	. . . . .	6
New York	3	11	3	17
North Carolina	6	3	3	12
Ohio	1	. . . . .	. . . . .	1
Pennsylvania	16	2	. . . . .	18
Rhode Island	. . . . .	2	. . . . .	2
South Carolina	8	. . . . .	. . . . .	8
Tennessee	3	. . . . .	. . . . .	3
Vermont	3	1	. . . . .	4
Virginia	14	5	3	22
Total	79	49	15	143

The representatives of the Twelfth Congress were elected in the same manner as those of the Tenth Congress (see p. 108, above). The vote of two states electing by general ticket, New Hampshire and New Jersey, and of two plural districts, both in Pennsylvania, was divided. The votes not shown from these states are as follows: New Hampshire, 2 nays; New Jersey, 2 yeas; Pennsylvania, 2 nays.

The two New Hampshire representatives voting nay resided at Stratham and Exeter, in the southeastern part of the state, near the seacoast; and the three voting yea resided inland—one at Keene, in southwestern New Hampshire, and the other two respectively at Meredith and Bartlett, near the central part of the state. The two New Jersey representatives voting yea resided in Middlesex and Morris counties in northeastern New Jersey; of the four voting nay, one resided in Bergen County, in northeastern New Jersey; and the others respectively in Hunterdon, Burlington, and Salem counties in western or southern New Jersey. Each of the two Pennsylvania representatives voting nay resided in a district that elected three members, two of whom voted yea. The districts were composed respectively of Philadelphia and Delaware counties and the city of Philadelphia, and of Montgomery, Bucks, Northampton, Wayne, and Luzerne counties.

The non-voting member from Georgia was Howell Cobb, who in 1812 resigned from Congress to accept a captain's commission in the army. One non-voting member from the second New York district, consisting of the city and county of New York and of Richmond and Rockland counties, and one non-voting member from the sixth New York district, consisting of Columbia, Rensselaer, and Washington counties, each of which districts elected two members, are disregarded. The non-voting area in Kentucky is the district of Henry Clay, speaker of the House. Louisiana was admitted to the Union in April, 1812, but her representative did not take his seat until December. The two yea areas in northeastern New York are the discontiguous parts of one district.

General Tariff Act, April 8, 1816
[PLATE 113B]

The vote was by the representatives of the Fourteenth Congress, first session, on the passage of an "act to regulate the duties on imports and tonnage." This act increased duties about twenty per cent on the average, and contained some new protective provisions (F. W. Taussig, *Tariff History of the United States*, 6th edit., New York and London, 1914, pp. 18–19). The act passed by the House was slightly amended by the Senate, and the House concurred in the Senate amendments. The act as approved by the President on April 27, 1816, is found in *U. S. Statutes at Large*, Vol. 3, Boston, 1846, pp. 310–314.

The vote was yeas 88, nays 54, not voting 40, total 182. The vote by states, eighteen in number, is shown in the following table (*House Journ.*, *14th Cong., 1st Sess.*, 1815–1816, pp. 610–612):

TABLE 13
GENERAL TARIFF ACT, 1816

STATE	YEAS	NAYS	NOT VOTING	TOTAL VOTES
Connecticut	2	2	3	7
Delaware	. . . . .	. . . . .	2	2
Georgia	3	3	. . . . .	6
Kentucky	6	1	3	10
Louisiana	. . . . .	1	. . . . .	1
Maryland	2	5	2	9
Massachusetts	7	4	9	20
Ohio	4	. . . . .	2	6
New Hampshire	1	3	2	6
New Jersey	5	. . . . .	1	6
New York	20	2	5	27
North Carolina	. . . . .	11	2	13
Pennsylvania	17	3	3	23
Rhode Island	2	. . . . .	. . . . .	2
South Carolina	4	3	2	9
Tennessee	3	2	1	6
Vermont	5	1	. . . . .	6
Virginia	7	13	3	23
Total	88	54	40	182

The representatives of the Fourteenth Congress were elected under the apportionment act of December 21, 1811. One state, Louisiana, chose a single representative. All the other states chose representatives by districts, except Vermont, New Hampshire, Rhode Island, Connecticut, New Jersey, Delaware, and Georgia, in which the election was by general ticket. The vote of Vermont, New Hampshire, Connecticut, and Georgia, and of a plural district in Pennsylvania was divided. The following votes from these states are not shown on the map: Vermont, 1 nay; New Hampshire, 1 yea; Connecticut, 2 yeas; Georgia, 3 yeas; and Pennsylvania, 1 nay.

The Vermont representative who voted nay came from Grand Isle County, in the northwestern part of the state; and the five voting nay, respectively from Caledonia, Addison, Rutland, Windsor, and Windham counties, to the southward and eastward of Grand Isle County. The one New Hampshire representative voting yea came from Amherst, in the southern part of the state; and the three voting nay respectively from Dover, Orford, and Walpole, all farther northward than Amherst. The two Connecticut representatives voting yea came from Stamford and Hartford, respectively in the southwestern and north central part of the state; and the two voting nay, from East Haddam and New London, in the southeastern part of the state. Of the three Georgia representatives voting yea, one came from Savannah, in southeastern Georgia, and two respectively from Baldwin and Oglethorpe counties, in the northwestern part of the settled area of the state; of the three voting nay, one came from Savannah and two from Augusta. The nay vote from Pennsylvania which is not shown came from the sixth district, composed of Bucks, Northampton, Lehigh, and Pike counties, electing two members.

Two members not voting from New Hampshire, three from Connecticut, and one from New Jersey are disregarded. One member not voting from each of the three following plural districts is also disregarded: wards 3–10 in New York City (2nd N. Y.), the counties of Ontario, Allegany, Genesee, Niagara, Cattaraugus, and Chautauqua, in New York State (21st N. Y.), and Baltimore City and County in Maryland (5th Md.). Part of the non-voting area in Kentucky is the district of Henry Clay, speaker of the House.

"Bonus" Bill, February 8, 1817
[PLATE 113C]

The vote was by the representatives of the Fourteenth Congress, second session, on the passage of a "bill to set apart and pledge as a permanent fund for internal improvement the bonus of the National Bank, and the United States' share of its dividends." Section 1 of the bill, the most important section, reads as follows:

"That the sum to be paid to the United States by the twentieth section of the 'act to incorporate the subscribers to the Bank of the United States' and the dividends which shall arise from their shares in its capital stock, during the present term of twenty years, for which the proprietors thereof have been incorporated, be, and the same are hereby, set apart, and pledged as a fund for constructing roads and canals, and improving the navigation of water-courses, in order to facilitate, promote, and give security to internal commerce among the several States, and to render more easy and less expensive the means and provisions necessary for their common defence" (*Annals of Congress*, Vol. 30, 1816–1817, p. 1061).

The sum to be paid to the United States in accordance with the twentieth section of the Bank Act amounted to $1,500,000. The shares of the United States in the stock of the bank amounted to $7,000,000. The Senate amended the bill passed by the House, and the House concurred in the Senate amendments. On March 3, 1817, the President vetoed the bill, and on the same day the House failed to pass it over his veto—yeas 60, nays 50 (*House Journ., 14th Cong., 2nd Sess.*, 1816–1817, pp. 368, 507, and 539–540). The bill as introduced in the House is found in the *Annals of Congress*, Vol. 30, p. 362, and the bill in the form in which it was finally passed by Congress, *ibid.*, p. 1061.

The vote in the House on the passage of the bill, February 8, 1817, was yeas 86, nays 84, not voting 13, total 183. The vote by states, nineteen in number, was as follows (*ibid.*, pp. 369–371):

TABLE 14
"BONUS BILL," 1817

STATE	YEAS	NAYS	NOT VOTING	TOTAL VOTES
Connecticut	....	6	1	7
Delaware	....	2	....	2
Georgia	5	1	....	6
Indiana	1	....	....	1
Kentucky	4	5	1	10
Louisiana	....	1	....	1
Maryland	2	6	1	9
Massachusetts	4	16	....	20
New Hampshire	1	5	....	6
New Jersey	3	3	....	6
New York	25	2	....	27
North Carolina	6	6	1	13
Ohio	5	....	1	6
Pennsylvania	17	4	2	23
Rhode Island	....	2	....	2
South Carolina	6	3	....	9
Tennessee	1	3	2	6
Vermont	....	5	1	6
Virginia	6	14	3	23
Total	86	84	13	183

For method of electing representatives to the Fourteenth Congress, see p. 109, above. Indiana, which was admitted to the Union in 1816, chose a single representative. The vote of New Hampshire, New Jersey, and Georgia, states electing representatives on a general ticket, and of a plural district in each of the states of Pennsylvania and Maryland, was divided. The following votes from these states are not shown: New Hampshire, 1 yea; New Jersey, 3 nays; Georgia, 1 nay; Pennsylvania, 1 nay; and Maryland, 1 nay.

The one New Hampshire representative voting yea came from Portsmouth; the five voting nay respectively from Amherst, Nottingham, Dover, Walpole, and Orford, all to the westward or northward of Portsmouth. The three New Jersey representatives voting nay came from Monmouth, Somerset, and Essex counties respectively, in the northeastern part of the state; of the three representatives voting yea, one came from Morris County, in northern New Jersey, and two respectively from Burlington and Cumberland counties, in southern New Jersey. The single representative in Georgia voting nay came from Clark County, in the northwestern part of the settled area of the state; of the five yea votes, two came from Augusta, one from Savannah, and one each respectively from Oglethorpe and Baldwin counties, in the northwestern part of the settled area. The nay vote from Pennsylvania that is not shown came from the district (10th) consisting of the counties of Northumberland, Luzerne, Bradford, Susquehanna, Lycoming, Tioga, Potter, and Columbia. The nay vote from Maryland that is not shown came from the district (5th) composed of Baltimore city and county. Each of these districts elected two members. One member not voting from Vermont, one from Connecticut, and one from Philadelphia are disregarded. The non-voting area in Kentucky is the district represented by Henry Clay, speaker of the House.

Missouri Compromise, March 2, 1820

[PLATE 113D]

The vote is by the representatives of the Sixteenth Congress, first session.

On March 1, 1820, the House of Representatives passed a "bill to authorize the people of the territory of Missouri to form a constitution and state government, and for the admission of such state into the Union on an equal footing with the original states" (*House Journ.,*

16th Cong., 1st Sess., 1819–1820, pp. 269–270). On the following day the Senate amended the fourth section of the bill by striking out certain lines respecting slavery, the most significant of which restricted slavery in the state of Missouri. The lines were as follows:

"And shall ordain and establish that there shall be neither slavery nor involuntary servitude in the said state, otherwise than in the punishment of crimes, whereof the party shall have been duly convicted: Provided always, That any person escaping into the same from whom labor or service is lawfully claimed in any other state, such fugitive may be lawfully reclaimed, and conveyed to the person claiming his or her labor or service, as aforesaid: Provided, nevertheless, That the said provision shall not be construed to alter the condition or civil rights of any person now held to service or labor in the said territory" (*Senate Journ., 16th Cong., 1st Sess.*, 1819–1820, p. 201).

On March 2 a conference committee of the two houses recommended that these lines be struck out, and on the same day the House voted on concurring with the Senate in striking them out. It is this vote that is mapped. The act from which the lines were stricken out was approved by the President on March 6, 1820 (*U. S. Statutes at Large*, Vol. 3, Boston, 1846, pp. 545–548). The vote on striking out the lines was yeas 90, nays 87, not voting 9, total 186. The vote by states, twenty-two in number, is shown in the following table (*House Journ., 16th Cong., 1st Sess.*, 1819–1820, pp. 276–277):

TABLE 15
MISSOURI COMPROMISE, 1820

STATE	YEAS	NAYS	NOT VOTING	TOTAL VOTES
Alabama	1	....	....	1
Connecticut	2	4	1	7
Delaware	1	....	1	2
Georgia	6	....	....	6
Illinois	....	1	....	1
Indiana	....	1	....	1
Kentucky	8	....	2	10
Louisiana	1	....	....	1
Maryland	9	....	....	9
Massachusetts	4	16	....	20
Mississippi	1	....	....	1
New Hampshire	....	6	....	6
New Jersey	3	3	....	6
New York	2	22	3	27
North Carolina	12	....	1	13
Ohio	....	6	....	6
Pennsylvania	2	21	....	23
Rhode Island	1	1	....	2
South Carolina	9	....	....	9
Tennessee	6	....	....	6
Vermont	....	6	....	6
Virginia	22	....	1	23
Total	90	87	9	186

The representatives of the Sixteenth Congress were elected in the same manner as those of the Fourteenth Congress (see p. 109, above). Each of five states—Alabama, Illinois, Indiana, Louisiana, and Mississippi—chose a single representative. The vote of three of the states that elected representatives by general ticket—Rhode Island, Connecticut, and New Jersey—and of a plural district in each of two states—New York and Pennsylvania—was divided. The vote of Rhode Island and New Jersey was evenly divided. The following votes are not shown on the map: Rhode Island, 1 yea; Connecticut, 2 yeas; New Jersey, 3 yeas; New York City, 1 yea; and Pennsylvania, 1 nay.

The Rhode Island representative voting nay was from Middletown, in the southern part of the state, and the representative voting yea from Providence, in the northern part of the state. Of the two Connecticut representatives who voted yea, one came from Stamford, in southwestern Connecticut, and the other from Cheshire, in south central Connecticut; of the four who voted nay, two came respectively from Hartford and Simsbury, in the north-central part of the state, one from East Haddam, in the south-central part, and one from Fairfield, in the southwestern part. The residences of the New Jersey representatives and the sections of the state from which they came were as follows: yeas, Bergen County (northeastern), Middlesex County (eastern), and Burlington County (western); and nays, Sussex County (northwestern), Somerset County (northern), and Cumberland County (southern). The yea vote from New York that is not shown is from the second district, comprising wards 3–10 of New York City, and electing two members. The nay vote from Pennsylvania that is not shown is from the fifth district of that state, comprising Cumberland, Franklin, and Adams counties, and electing two members. The most northerly of the non-voting areas in Kentucky is the district represented by Henry Clay, speaker of the House.

General Tariff Act, April 22, 1828

[PLATE 114A]

The vote was by the representatives of the Twentieth Congress, first session, on the passage of an "act in alteration of the several acts imposing duties on imports." This act, sometimes called the "tariff of abominations," was a protectionist measure, which by means of "minimum valuations" considerably increased the duty on several staple articles. The act passed by the House was amended by the Senate, and the House concurred in the Senate amendments. For the act as it passed the House see *H. R. Bill No. 132, 20th Cong., 1st Sess.,* 1827-1828; as approved by the President on May 19, 1828, see *U. S. Statutes at Large,* Vol. 4, Boston, 1846, pp. 270-275.

The vote in the House was yeas 105, nays 94, not voting 14, total 213. The vote by states, twenty-four in number, was as follows (*House Journ., 20th Cong., 1st Sess.,* 1827-1828, pp. 607-609; several members who did not vote on the passage of the bill voted on its third reading, *ibid.,* pp. 577-580):

TABLE 16
GENERAL TARIFF ACT, 1838

STATE	YEAS	NAYS	NOT VOTING	TOTAL VOTES
Alabama		3		3
Connecticut	4	2		6
Delaware	1			1
Georgia		7		7
Illinois	1			1
Indiana	3			3
Kentucky	12			12
Louisiana		3		3
Maine		7		7
Maryland	1	5	3	9
Massachusetts	2	11		13
Mississippi		1		1
Missouri		1		1
New Hampshire	4	2		6
New Jersey	5		1	6
New York	27	6	1	34
North Carolina		13		13
Ohio	13		1	14
Pennsylvania	23		3	26
Rhode Island	1	1		2
South Carolina		8	1	9
Tennessee		9		9
Vermont	5			5
Virginia	3	15	4	22
Total	105	94	14	213

The representatives of the Twentieth Congress were elected under the apportionment act of March 7, 1822. In each of four states—Delaware, Illinois, Mississippi, and Missouri—a single representative was chosen. All the remaining states elected representatives by districts except New Hampshire, Rhode Island, Connecticut, New Jersey, and Georgia, in which states the election was by general ticket. In the three states first named the vote was divided, and part of it is therefore not shown on the map. The votes not shown are as follows: New Hampshire, 2 nays; Rhode Island, 1 yea; and Connecticut, 2 nays.

The two New Hampshire representatives who voted nay came respectively from Portsmouth and Rochester, both in the southeastern part of the state; the four who voted yea came respectively from Francestown, Sutton, Washington, and Wentworth, towns situated in western or southwestern New Hampshire. The Rhode Island representative voting yea came from Providence, and the representative voting nay from Newport. The two Connecticut representatives voting nay came respectively from Stratford and New Haven, towns on the coast; and the four voting yea, from New Milford, Simsbury, Windham, and Groton, all inland towns except Groton.

Five members from plural districts, who did not vote, are disregarded. These districts are as follows: twenty-sixth New York, comprising Seneca, Ontario, Yates, and Wayne counties; seventh Pennsylvania, comprising Berks, Schuylkill, and Lehigh counties; eighth Pennsylvania, comprising Bucks, Northampton, Pike, and Wayne counties; ninth Pennsylvania, comprising Union, Northumberland, Columbia, Luzerne,

Susquehanna, Bradford, Lycoming, Tioga, Potter, and McKean counties; and fifth Maryland, comprising Baltimore city and county. Each of these districts elected two members except the ninth Pennsylvania, which elected three. The western part of the most easterly of the non-voting areas in Virginia is the district of Andrew Stevenson, speaker of the House.

Maysville Road Bill, April 29, 1830

[PLATE 114B]

The vote was by the representatives of the Twenty-first Congress, first session, on the passage of a "bill authorizing a subscription of stock in the Maysville, Washington, Paris, and Lexington turnpike road company." The bill directed the Secretary of the Treasury to subscribe for fifteen hundred shares of the stock of this company. The legislature of Kentucky had incorporated the company for the purpose of building a section of a road planned to run from the Cumberland Road at Zanesville, Ohio, to Florence, Ala., on the Tennessee River (William MacDonald, *Jacksonian Democracy* (American Nation Ser., Vol. 15), New York and London, 1906, p. 139). The Senate passed the bill on May 15, the President vetoed it on May 27, and the House failed to pass it over his veto on May 28, 1830—yeas 96, nays 92. For the text of the bill see *H. R. Bill No. 285, 21st Cong., 1st Sess.,* 1829-1830.

The vote was yeas 102, nays 87, not voting 24, total 213. The vote by states, twenty-four in number, is shown in the following table (*House Journ., 21st Cong., 1st Sess.,* 1829-1830, pp. 586-587):

TABLE 17
MAYSVILLE ROAD BILL, 1830

STATE	YEAS	NAYS	NOT VOTING	TOTAL VOTES
Alabama	2	1		3
Connecticut	4		2	6
Delaware	1			1
Georgia		7		7
Illinois	1			1
Indiana	2		1	3
Kentucky	11	1		12
Louisiana	1	1	1	3
Maine	3	2	2	7
Maryland	6	1	2	9
Massachusetts	10	2	1	13
Mississippi		1		1
Missouri	1			1
New Hampshire		6		6
New Jersey	5		1	6
New York	9	19	6	34
North Carolina	1	12		13
Ohio	12		2	14
Pennsylvania	18	5	3	26
Rhode Island	2			2
South Carolina		9		9
Tennessee	4	5		9
Vermont	5			5
Virginia	4	15	3	22
Total	102	87	24	213

The representatives of the Twenty-first Congress were elected in the same manner as those of the Twentieth (see above). The vote of none of the states that chose representatives by general ticket was divided. The vote of the twenty-sixth New York and the eighth Pennsylvania districts, each electing two members, was evenly divided, and the yea votes are not shown on the map.

Two members not voting from Connecticut, one from New York, one from New Jersey, and two from Pennsylvania are disregarded. The New York member came from the twentieth district of that state, which elected two members and was composed of Oswego, Jefferson, Lewis, and St. Lawrence counties. The two Pennsylvania members came from the fourth (Delaware, Chester, and Lancaster counties) and the ninth (see above) districts. The non-voting area in eastern Virginia is the district of Andrew Stevenson, speaker of the House.

General Tariff Act, June 28, 1832

[PLATE 114C]

The vote was by the representatives of the Twenty-second Congress, first session, on the passage of an "act to alter and amend the several acts imposing duties on imports." This was a protective measure which did away with the minimum valuations and other "abominations" of the act of 1828. The act passed by the House was amended by the Senate, and subsequently several of the Senate amendments were amended by the House. The differences between the two houses were adjusted by a conference committee. For the act as passed by the House see *H. R. Bill No. 584, 21st Cong., 1st Sess.*, 1829-1830, and as approved by the President on July 14, 1832, see *U. S. Statutes at Large*, Vol. 4, Boston, 1846, pp. 583-594.

The vote was yeas 132, nays 65, not voting 16, total 213. The vote by states, twenty-four in number, is shown in the following table (*House Journ., 22nd Cong., 1st Sess.*, 1831-1832, pp. 1023-1024):

TABLE 18

GENERAL TARIFF ACT, 1832

STATE	YEAS	NAYS	NOT VOTING	TOTAL VOTES
Alabama.................	2	1	....	3
Connecticut.............	2	3	1	6
Delaware................		1		1
Georgia.................	1	6	....	7
Illinois................	1			1
Indiana.................	3		....	3
Kentucky...............	9	3	....	12
Louisiana..............	1	2		3
Maine..................	6	1	....	7
Maryland...............	8		1	9
Massachusetts..........	4	8	1	13
Mississippi............	1			1
Missouri...............	1			1
New Hampshire..........	5		1	6
New Jersey.............	3	3	....	6
New York..............	27	2	5	34
North Carolina.........	8	4	1	13
Ohio...................	13		1	14
Pennsylvania...........	14	12	....	26
Rhode Island...........		2		2
South Carolina.........	3	6		9
Tennessee..............	9		....	9
Vermont................		3	2	5
Virginia...............	11	8	3	22
Total..............	132	65	16	213

The representatives of the Twenty-second Congress were elected in the same manner as those of the Twentieth (see p. 111, above). The vote of Connecticut, New Jersey, and Georgia, states choosing representatives on a general ticket, and of three plural districts in Pennsylvania was divided. The following votes from these states are not shown on the map: Connecticut, 2 yeas; New Jersey, 3 nays; Georgia, 1 yea; and Pennsylvania, 1 yea and 2 nays.

One of the Connecticut representatives voting yea came from New Haven, in the southern part of the state, and the other from Killingly Center, in the eastern part; and the three voting nay respectively from Middletown, Hartford, and Litchfield, in middle or northwestern Connecticut. The three New Jersey representatives voting nay came respectively from Morris County, in the northern part of the state, and from Gloucester and Cape May counties, in the southern part; the three voting yea came respectively from Essex, Middlesex, and Somerset counties, in the northeastern part. The one Georgia representative voting yea came from Savannah, near the seacoast; and the six voting nay respectively from Augusta, Macon, Athens, Greensboro, Elberton, and McDonough, all situated inland and well up the state. The yea vote from Pennsylvania not shown is from the seventh district, composed of the counties of Berks, Schuylkill, and Lehigh, electing two members. The two nays from this state not shown are from the districts composed respectively of Delaware, Chester, and Lancaster counties (electing three members), and of Allegheny, Beaver, Butler, and Armstrong counties (electing two members).

One member who did not vote from New Hampshire, one from Connecticut, and one from the twenty-sixth district of New York, composed of the counties of Seneca, Ontario, Yates, and Wayne and electing two members, are disregarded. The non-voting area in eastern Virginia is the district of Andrew Stevenson, speaker of the House.

Independent Treasury Act, June 30, 1840

[PLATE 114D]

The vote was by the representatives of the Twenty-sixth Congress, first session, on the passage of an "act to provide for the collection, safe-keeping, transfer, and disbursement of the public revenue." This act was passed by the Senate on January 23, was passed by the House

without amendment on June 30, and was approved by the President on July 4, 1840. It is found in *U. S. Statutes at Large*, Vol. 5, Boston, 1848, pp. 385-392. The most important part of the act is section 1, establishing an independent treasury, which reads as follows:

"That there shall be prepared and provided within the new Treasury building now erecting at the seat of government, suitable and convenient rooms for the use of the Treasurer of the United States, his assistants, and clerks, and sufficient and secure fire-proof vaults and safes for the keeping of the public moneys in the possession and under the immediate control of the said Treasurer; which said rooms, vaults, and safes, are hereby constituted and declared to be the Treasury of the United States. And the said Treasurer of the United States shall keep all the public moneys, which shall come to his hands, in the Treasury of the United States as hereby constituted, until the same are drawn therefrom according to law."

The vote was yeas 124, nays 107, not voting 11, total 242. The vote by states, twenty-six in number, is shown in the following table (*House Journ., 26th Cong., 1st Sess.*, 1839-1840, pp. 1175-1177):

TABLE 19

INDEPENDENT TREASURY ACT, 1840

STATE	YEAS	NAYS	NOT VOTING	TOTAL VOTES
Alabama................	3	2	....	5
Arkansas...............	1			1
Connecticut............		5	1	6
Delaware...............	1		....	1
Georgia................	3	6		9
Illinois...............	1	2		3
Indiana................	3	3	1	7
Kentucky..............	2	9	2	13
Louisiana.............		3		3
Maine.................	6	2		8
Maryland..............	5	3	....	8
Massachusetts.........	2	9	1	12
Michigan..............	1		....	1
Mississippi...........	2			2
Missouri..............	2			2
New Hampshire.........	5		....	5
New Jersey............	5	1	....	6
New York.............	19	19	2	40
North Carolina........	7	5	1	13
Ohio..................	11	7	1	19
Pennsylvania..........	17	11	....	28
Rhode Island..........		2		2
South Carolina........	7	2	....	9
Tennessee.............	6	7		13
Vermont...............	2	3	....	5
Virginia..............	13	6	2	21
Total.............	124	107	11	242

The representatives of the Twenty-sixth Congress were elected under the apportionment act of May 22, 1832. Each of three states—Arkansas, Delaware, and Michigan—chose a single representative. All the remaining states elected representatives by distircts except New Hampshire, Rhode Island, New Jersey, Georgia, Mississippi, and Missouri, which states elected by general ticket. The vote of Georgia and New Jersey was divided. The following votes from these states are not shown on the map: Georgia, 3 yeas, and New Jersey, 1 nay. The three Georgia representatives who voted yea came from Jacksonboro, Gainesville, and Columbus respectively, in the eastern, northeastern, and western part of the state; the six representatives who voted nay came respectively from the following towns or counties, the section of the state being given in parentheses: Clarkesville (northeastern), Macon and Greensboro (north-central), Lagrange (western), Sumter County (southwestern), and Glynn County (southeastern). The one New Jersey representative who voted nay came from Middlesex County, in the eastern part of the state; the five who voted yea came respectively from the following counties: Passaic (northeastern), Somerset and Monmouth (eastern), and Salem and Gloucester (southwestern). The vote of the third Pennsylvania district (yea), consisting of a part of Philadelphia County, is not shown on the map owing to the small size of the district. A part of the non-voting area in Virginia is the district of Robert M. T. Hunter, speaker of the House.

Public Land Act, July 6, 1841

[PLATE 114E]

The vote was by the representatives of the Twenty-seventh Congress, first session, on the passage of an "act to appropriate the proceeds of the sales of the public lands and to grant pre-emption rights." This is the "general pre-emption law." It authorized settlers upon public lands to enter with the register of the land office any number of acres of land, not exceeding 160, and including the residence of the claimant, on the payment of the minimum price of such land. It also authorized the division among the states of certain proceeds arising from the sale of the public lands. The act as approved by the President on September 4, 1841, included several unimportant amendments made by the Senate and concurred in by the House. It is found in *U. S. Statutes at Large*, Vol. 5, Boston, 1848, pp. 453-458.

The vote was yeas 117, nays 108, not voting 17, total 242. The vote by states, twenty-six in number, is shown in the following table (*House Journ., 27th Cong., 1st Sess.*, 1841, pp. 222-223):

TABLE 20
PUBLIC LAND ACT, 1841

STATE	YEAS	NAYS	NOT VOTING	TOTAL VOTES
Alabama		5		5
Arkansas			1	1
Connecticut	6			6
Delaware	1			1
Georgia		8	1	9
Illinois			3	3
Indiana	6	1		7
Kentucky	9	2	2	13
Louisiana	2	1		3
Maine	4	4		8
Maryland	6	2		8
Massachusetts	11	1		12
Michigan			1	1
Mississippi			2	2
Missouri		2		2
New Hampshire		5		5
New Jersey	6			6
New York	18	20	2	40
North Carolina	5	8		13
Ohio	12	7		19
Pennsylvania	13	12	3	28
Rhode Island	2			2
South Carolina		9		9
Tennessee	5	7	1	13
Vermont	5			5
Virginia	6	14	1	21
Total	117	108	17	242

The representatives of the Twenty-seventh Congress were elected in the same manner as those of the Twenty-sixth (see p. 112, above). No vote of a plural district, or of a state in which the election was by general ticket, was divided. One member from Georgia who did not vote is disregarded. When the vote was taken Illinois and Mississippi were not represented in Congress, their Congressional elections being held later. The non-voting area in southeastern Kentucky is the district of John White, speaker of the House.

Annexation of Texas, January 25, 1845
[PLATE 114F]

The vote was by the representatives of the Twenty-eight Congress, second session, on the passage of a "joint resolution for annexing Texas to the United States." The Senate amended the act by adding section 3, which gave the President the option of submitting the resolution to Texas as an offer of admission or of negotiating with Texas for admission. On February 28 the House concurred in the amendment—yeas 134, nays 77 (*House Journ., 28th Cong., 2nd Sess.*, 1844-1845, pp. 527-529). For resolution as passed by the House (without section 3) see the same, pp. 259-260. The resolution as approved by the President on March 1, 1845, is found in *U. S. Statutes at Large*, Vol. 5, Boston, 1848, pp. 797-798.

The vote was yeas 120, nays 98, not voting 5, total 223. The vote by states, twenty-six in number, is shown in table 21 (*House Journ., 28th Cong., 2nd Sess.*, 1844-1845, pp. 264-265),

The representatives of the Twenty-eighth Congress were elected under the apportionment act of June 25, 1842. Arkansas and Delaware each elected one representative. All the rest of the states elected representatives by districts except Georgia, Mississippi, Missouri, and New Hampshire, which states elected by general ticket. Of these, New Hampshire was the only state whose vote was divided. Two yea votes from this state and two yea votes from New York City are not shown

TABLE 21
ANNEXATION OF TEXAS, 1845

STATE	YEAS	NAYS	NOT VOTING	TOTAL VOTES
Alabama	7			7
Arkansas	1			1
Connecticut	3	1		4
Delaware		1		1
Georgia	8			8
Illinois	6	1		7
Indiana	8	2		10
Kentucky	5	5		10
Louisiana	4			4
Maine	1	6		7
Maryland		5	1	6
Massachusetts	1	9		10
Michigan	1	2		3
Mississippi	4			4
Missouri	5			5
New Hampshire	2	2		4
New Jersey	3	2		5
New York	9	24	1	34
North Carolina	5	4		9
Ohio	9	12		21
Pennsylvania	10	13	1	24
Rhode Island		2		2
South Carolina	7			7
Tennessee	10		1	11
Vermont		4		4
Virginia	11	3	1	15
Total	120	98	5	223

on the map. The two New Hampshire representatives voting yea came respectively from Newport, in the western part of the state, and Pittsfield in the south-central part; and the two voting nay, from Dover, in the eastern part, and Haverhill, in the western part. One of the two New York City representatives voting yea came from the fourth district (wards 6, 7, 10, and 13), and one from the fifth district (wards 8, 9, and 14). The non-voting area in Virginia is the district of John W. Jones, speaker of the House.

Walker Tariff Act, July 3, 1846
[PLATE 114G]

The vote was by the representatives of the Twenty-ninth Congress, first session, on the passage of an "act reducing the duties on imports, and for other purposes." This act effected a reduction of duties and put into operation, as far as was possible under the circumstances, the principle of free trade. Nevertheless it afforded no small amount of protection to several staple articles of manufacture (F. W. Taussig, *Tariff History of the United States*, 6th edit., New York and London, 1914, p. 156).

An unimportant amendment to the act made by the Senate was agreed to by the House on July 29. The act as approved by the President on July 30 is found in *U. S. Statutes at Large*, Vol. 9, Boston, 1851, pp. 42-49.

The vote was yeas 114, nays 95, not voting 17, total 226. The vote by states, twenty-eight in number, is shown in the following table (*House Journ. 20th Cong., 1st Sess.*, 1845-1846, pp. 1029-1030):

TABLE 22
WALKER TARIFF ACT, 1846

STATE	YEAS	NAYS	NOT VOTING	TOTAL VOTES
Alabama	7			7
Arkansas			1	1
Connecticut		4		4
Delaware		1		1
Florida	1			1
Georgia	5	2	1	8
Illinois	5		2	7
Indiana	5	2	3	10
Kentucky	3	7		10
Louisiana	3	1		4
Maine	6	1		7
Maryland	1	2	3	6
Massachusetts		9	1	10
Michigan	3			3

TABLE 22 (*Concluded*)

WALKER TARIFF ACT, 1846

STATE	YEAS	NAYS	NOT VOTING	TOTAL VOTES
Mississippi	4	....	....	4
Missouri	4	....	1	5
New Hampshire	3	....	1	4
New Jersey	....	5	....	5
New York	16	16	2	34
North Carolina	6	3	....	9
Ohio	12	8	1	21
Pennsylvania	1	23	....	24
Rhode Island	....	2	....	2
South Carolina	7	....	....	7
Tennessee	6	5	....	11
Texas	2	....	....	2
Vermont	....	3	1	4
Virginia	14	1	....	15
Total	114	95	17	226

Arkansas, Delaware, and Florida each elected one representative to the Twenty-ninth Congress. Of the remaining states all elected representatives by districts except New Hampshire, Mississippi, and Missouri, in which states the election was by general ticket. In none of these three states was the vote divided. The vote of the member from the fourth district of New York (wards 6, 7, 10, and 13 of New York City), a yea, is not shown on the map. One representative from New Hampshire who did not vote and one from Missouri are disregarded. Wards 12-14 of Baltimore city belonged to the third district of Maryland, whose representative did not vote; the rest of Baltimore city constituted the fourth district, whose representative voted yea. The northern part of the non-voting area in southwestern Indiana is the district of John W. Davis, speaker of the House.

Compromise of 1850, September 6, 1850

[PLATE 114H]

The measures of the Compromise of 1850 are embodied in five acts of Congress, as follows: (1) act fixing the boundaries of Texas and establishing a territorial government for New Mexico; (2) act admitting California into the Union; (3) act establishing a territorial government

TABLE 23

COMPROMISE OF 1850

STATE	YEAS	NAYS	NOT VOTING	TOTAL VOTES
Alabama	3	4	....	7
Arkansas	....	1	....	1
Connecticut	....	3	1	4
Delaware	1	....	....	1
Florida	1	....	....	1
Georgia	3	2	3	8
Illinois	4	2	1	7
Indiana	7	3	....	10
Iowa	1	....	1	2
Kentucky	10	....	....	10
Louisiana	....	2	2	4
Maine	3	3	1	7
Maryland	4	....	2	6
Massachusetts	3	4	3	10
Michigan	1	2	....	3
Mississippi	....	4	....	4
Missouri	4	1	....	5
New Hampshire	3	1	....	4
New Jersey	1	3	1	5
New York	14	17	3	34
North Carolina	5	3	1	9
Ohio	5	14	2	21
Pennsylvania	13	7	4	24
Rhode Island	1	1	....	2
South Carolina	....	7	....	7
Tennessee	11	....	....	11
Texas	2	....	....	2
Vermont	....	4	....	4
Virginia	8	6	1	15
Wisconsin	....	3	....	3
Total	108	97	26	231

for Utah; (4) act for reclaiming fugitive slaves; and (5) act suppressing the slave trade in the District of Columbia. It is the first of these acts whose vote is mapped. Its full title is "an act proposing to the state of Texas the establishment of her northern and western boundaries, the relinquishment by the said state of all territory claimed by her exterior to said boundaries, and of all her claims upon the United States, and to establish a territorial government for New Mexico."

The vote was by the representatives of the Thirty-first Congress, first session. The act originated in the Senate, was amended by the House, and the Senate agreed to the House amendments. The act as passed by the House and approved by the President on September 9, 1850, is found in *U. S. Statutes at Large*, Vol. 9, Boston, 1851, pp. 446-452.

The vote was yeas 108, nays 97, not voting 26, total, 231. The vote by states, thirty in number, is shown in table 23 (*House Journ., 31st Cong., 1st Sess.*, 1849-1850, pp. 1412-1413):

Delaware, Arkansas, and Florida each elected one representative to the Thirty-first Congress. All the rest of the states chose two or more representatives, by districts. The vote from the third Pennsylvania district (part of Philadelphia County), a nay, is not shown on the map. The northeastern part of the non-voting area in Georgia is the district of Howell Cobb, speaker of the House.

Kansas-Nebraska Act, May 22, 1854

[PLATE 115A]

The vote was by the representatives of the Thirty-third Congress, first session, on the passage of an "act to organize the territories of Nebraska and Kansas." The most noteworthy part of the act was that which "repealed the Missouri Compromise" by providing that the states formed from these two territories should be received into the Union, "with or without slavery, as their constitution may prescribe at the time of their admission." The act passed the Senate without amendment and was approved by the President on May 30, 1854. It is found in *U. S. Statutes at Large*, Vol. 10, Boston, 1855, pp. 277-290.

The vote was yeas 113, nays 100, not voting 21, total 234. The vote by states, thirty-one in number, is shown in the following table (*House Journ., 33rd Cong., 1st Sess.*, 1853-1854, pp. 923-924):

TABLE 24

KANSAS-NEBRASKA ACT, 1854

STATE	YEAS	NAYS	NOT VOTING	TOTAL VOTES
Alabama	7	....	....	7
Arkansas	2	....	....	2
California	2	....	....	2
Connecticut	1	3	....	4
Delaware	1	....	....	1
Florida	1	....	....	1
Georgia	6	2	....	8
Illinois	3	5	1	9
Indiana	7	3	1	11
Iowa	1	....	1	2
Kentucky	8	....	2	10
Louisiana	3	1	....	4
Maine	1	5	....	6
Maryland	4	....	2	6
Massachusetts	....	10	1	11
Michigan	2	2	....	4
Mississippi	4	....	1	5
Missouri	5	1	1	7
New Hampshire	1	2	....	3
New Jersey	2	3	....	5
New York	9	22	2	33
North Carolina	6	2	....	8
Ohio	4	15	2	21
Pennsylvania	11	14	....	25
Rhode Island	....	2	....	2
South Carolina	3	....	3	6
Tennessee	6	4	....	10
Texas	2	....	....	2
Vermont	....	3	....	3
Virginia	11	1	1	13
Wisconsin	....	2	1	3
Total	113	100	21	234

The representatives of the Thirty-third Congress were elected under the apportionment acts of May 23, 1850, and July 30, 1852. California was the only state that elected representatives by general ticket. Two states, Delaware and Florida, each chose a single representative. The vote from the sixth district of New York (wards 11, 15, and 17 of New York City) and from the second district of Pennsylvania (part of Philadelphia), both nays, are not shown on the map. The most westerly of the two non-voting areas in Kentucky is the district of Linn Boyd, speaker of the House.

General Tariff Act, March 2, 1857

[PLATE 115B]

The vote was by the representatives of the Thirty-fourth Congress, third session, on agreeing to the report of a conference committee respecting an "act reducing the duties on imports, and for other purposes." This act brought the general level of tariff duties to the lowest point reached by them since 1815.

On February 20, 1857, the House, which was controlled by the opposition to the Democrats, passed an act framed in the interest of the manufacturers (James Schouler, *History of the United States of America*, Vol. 5, New York, 1894, p. 363). This was radically amended by the Senate, which was controlled by the Democrats. The House disagreed to the Senate amendments, and a committee of conference was appointed to adjust the differences. It is the vote of the House on the report of this committee that is mapped. Both the House and the Senate agreed to the report. The report is found in the *House Journal, 34th Cong., 3rd Sess., 1856-1857*, pp. 606-609; and the act as approved by the President in *U. S. Statutes at Large*, Vol. 11, Boston, 1859, pp. 192-195.

The vote was yeas 122, nays 72, not voting 40, total 234. The vote by states, thirty-one in number, is shown in the following table (*House Journ., 34th Cong., 3rd Sess., 1856-1857*, pp. 614-615):

TABLE 25

GENERAL TARIFF ACT, 1857

STATE	YEAS	NAYS	NOT VOTING	TOTAL VOTES
Alabama	7			7
Arkansas	2			2
California	2			2
Connecticut	4			4
Delaware		1		1
Florida	1			1
Georgia	4		4	8
Illinois	4	4	1	9
Indiana	3	8		11
Iowa	1	1		2
Kentucky	6	2	2	10
Louisiana	4			4
Maine	6			6
Maryland	4	1	1	6
Massachusetts	9		2	11
Michigan	1	3		4
Mississippi	4		1	5
Missouri		3	4	7
New Hampshire	1	1	1	3
New Jersey	2	1	2	5
New York	16	11	6	33
North Carolina	6		2	8
Ohio	5	14	2	21
Pennsylvania	3	16	6	25
Rhode Island	1	1		2
South Carolina	4		2	6
Tennessee	7		3	10
Texas	1		1	2
Vermont		3		3
Virginia	13			13
Wisconsin	1	2		3
Total	122	72	40	234

The members of the Thirty-fourth Congress were elected in the same manner as those of the Thirty-third (see p. 114, above). The vote from the first district of Pennsylvania (part of Philadelphia), a yea, is not shown on the map. The district of one member from New York City who did not vote is disregarded. The non-voting area in northeastern Massachusetts is the district of Nathaniel P. Banks, speaker of the House.

Thirteenth Amendment, January 31, 1865

[PLATE 116A]

The vote was by the representatives of the Thirty-eighth Congress, second session, on the passage of a "resolution submitting to the legislatures of the several states a proposition to amend the Constitution of

the United States." The first section of the resolution, the most important one, reads as follows: "Neither slavery nor involuntary servitude, except as a punishment for crime whereof the party shall have been duly convicted, shall exist within the United States, or any place subject to their jurisdiction."

On April 8, 1864, the resolution passed the Senate. On May 31 it was rejected by the House (yeas 76, nays 55), and again on June 15 (yeas 95, nays 66) (*House Journ., 38th Cong., 1st Sess., 1863-1864*, pp. 728 and 812). On January 31, 1865, the House reconsidered the vote of June 15 and passed the resolution by the narrow margin of three votes—a two-thirds majority, or 117 votes, being necessary to pass it. The resolution, which was approved by the President on February 1, is found in *U. S. Statutes at Large*, Vol. 13, Boston, 1866, p. 567.

The vote was yeas 119, nays 56, not voting 9, total 184. The vote by states, twenty-five in number, is shown in the following table (*House Journ., 38th Cong., 2nd Sess., 1864-1865*, pp. 170-171):

TABLE 26

THIRTEENTH AMENDMENT, 1865

STATE	YEAS	NAYS	NOT VOTING	TOTAL VOTES
California	3			3
Connecticut	4			4
Delaware	1			1
Illinois	5	9		14
Indiana	4	5	2	11
Iowa	6			6
Kansas	1			1
Kentucky	4	5		9
Maine	4	1		5
Maryland	4	1		5
Massachusetts	10			10
Michigan	6			6
Minnesota	2			2
Missouri	7	2		9
Nevada	1			1
New Hampshire	2		1	3
New Jersey	1	2	2	5
New York	20	10	1	31
Ohio	6	11	2	19
Oregon	1			1
Pennsylvania	15	8	1	24
Rhode Island	2			2
Vermont	3			3
West Virginia	3			3
Wisconsin	4	2		6
Total	119	56	9	184

The representatives of the Thirty-eighth Congress were elected under the apportionment acts of March 4 and July 14, 1862. Each of four states—Delaware, Kansas, Nevada, and Oregon—chose a single representative. California elected representatives on a general ticket. Illinois elected thirteen representatives by districts and one at large. With these exceptions the election was by districts.

The votes not shown are as follows: a yea vote from the seventh New York district (part of New York City), a yea vote from the third New York district (part of Brooklyn), a nay vote from the first Pennsylvania district (part of Philadelphia), and a nay vote from the Illinois representative at large, who came from Palestine, Crawford County, in the eastern part of the state. The northern part of the yea area in northern Indiana is the district of Schuyler Colfax, speaker of the House.

Reconstruction Act, March 2, 1867

[PLATE 116B]

The vote was by the representatives of the Thirty-ninth Congress, second session, on the passage over the President's veto of an "act to provide for the more efficient government of the rebel states." The act was first passed by the House on February 13—yeas 109, nays 55, not voting 26 (*House Journ., 39th Cong., 2nd Sess., 1866-1867*, p. 376). It is found in *U. S. Statutes at Large*, Vol. 14, Boston, 1868, pp. 428-429. It provided for the establishment and administration of a rigorous and comprehensive military government in the ten states not restored to the Union and declared that the restoration of these states should be effected only after reorganization on the basis of the enfranchisement of the negroes and the limited disfranchisement of the Confederates (W. A. Dunning, *Reconstruction, Political and Economic* (American Nation Ser., Vol. 22), New York, 1907, p. 93).

The vote was yeas 138, nays 51, not voting 4, total 193. The vote by states, twenty-seven in number, is shown in the following table (*House Journ., 39th Cong., 2nd Sess.,* 1866–1867, p. 574):

TABLE 27
RECONSTRUCTION ACT, 1867

STATE	YEAS	NAYS	NOT VOTING	TOTAL VOTES
California	3			3
Connecticut	4			4
Delaware		1		1
Illinois	9	4	1	14
Indiana	8	3		11
Iowa	6			6
Kansas	1			1
Kentucky	1	7	1	9
Maine	5			5
Maryland	2	3		5
Massachusetts	10			10
Michigan	6			6
Minnesota	2			2
Missouri	7	2		9
Nebraska	1			1
Nevada	1			1
New Hampshire	3			3
New Jersey	2	3		5
New York	19	12		31
Ohio	17	2		19
Oregon	1			1
Pennsylvania	15	7	2	24
Rhode Island	2			2
Tennessee	3	5		8
Vermont	3			3
West Virginia	2	1		3
Wisconsin	5	1		6
Total	138	51	4	193

Each of five states—Delaware, Kansas, Nebraska, Nevada, and Oregon—elected a single representative to the Thirty-ninth Congress. Illinois chose one representative at large. With these exceptions all the representatives were elected in districts. The votes from three New York City districts (6th, 8th, and 9th), all yeas, the vote from one Philadelphia district (1st Pa.), a nay, and the vote of the Illinois representative at large, a yea, are not shown on the map. The last-named came from Shelbyville, Shelby County, in the central part of the state. Schuyler Colfax of Indiana, speaker of the House, voted yea. Of the Confederate states only Tennessee was represented in this Congress.

Enforcement Act, April 6, 1871

[PLATE 117A]

The vote was by the representatives of the Forty-second Congress, first session, on the passage of an "act to enforce the provisions of the fourteenth amendment of the Constitution of the United States, and for other purposes"—commonly called the Ku-Klux act. The purpose of this act was to make it a duty of the United States government "to secure life, liberty, and property, and the enforcement of the law" within the several states and most especially within the Southern states.

The Senate amended the bill passed by the House, the House disagreed to several of the Senate amendments, and the differences between the two Houses were resolved by two conference committees. The bill in the form in which it was introduced into the House is found in the *Congressional Globe, 42nd Cong., 1st Sess.,* 1871, Part II, appendix, p. 138; and in the form in which it finally passed Congress and was approved by the President on April 20, 1871, in *U. S. Statutes at Large,* Vol. 17, Boston, 1873, pp. 13–15.

The vote was yeas 118, nays 91, not voting 34, total 243. The vote by states, thirty-seven in number, is shown in table 28 (*House Journ., 42nd Cong., 1st Sess.,* 1871, pp. 133–134).

The representatives of the Forty-second Congress were elected under the apportionment acts of 1862. Each of six states—Delaware, Florida, Kansas, Nebraska, Nevada, and Oregon—chose a single representative. Illinois elected one representative at large. With these exceptions all the representatives were elected in districts. California, Connecticut, and Texas did not hold their Congressional elections until after March 4, 1871, and were unrepresented in Congress when the vote was taken. The one member from Illinois who did not vote was the representative at large. John A. Logan had been elected to this office but had resigned it on being chosen senator. The vote of one Philadelphia district (1st Pa.),

a nay, is not shown on the map. The southern part of the most easterly of the non-voting areas in Maine is the district of James G. Blaine, speaker of the House.

TABLE 28
ENFORCEMENT ACT, 1871

STATE	YEAS	NAYS	NOT VOTING	TOTAL VOTES
Alabama	2	3	1	6
Arkansas	2	1		3
California			3	3
Connecticut			4	4
Delaware		1		1
Florida	1			1
Georgia	2	3	2	7
Illinois	7	6	1	14
Indiana	6	5		11
Iowa	6			6
Kansas	1			1
Kentucky		8	1	9
Louisiana	3		2	5
Maine	2		3	5
Maryland		4	1	5
Massachusetts	9		1	10
Michigan	4	1	1	6
Minnesota	1		1	2
Mississippi	4		1	5
Missouri	4	4	1	9
Nebraska	1			1
Nevada			1	1
New Hampshire		3		3
New Jersey	3	2		5
New York	14	14	3	31
North Carolina	2	4	1	7
Ohio	14	5		19
Oregon		1		1
Pennsylvania	12	11	1	24
Rhode Island	2			2
South Carolina	4			4
Tennessee	1	6	1	8
Texas			4	4
Vermont	3			3
Virginia	3	5		8
West Virginia	1	2		3
Wisconsin	4	2		6
Total	118	91	34	243

Resumption of Specie Payments, January 7, 1875

[PLATE 117B]

The vote was by the representatives of the Forty-third Congress, second session, on the passage of an "act to provide for the resumption of specie payments." The principal provisions of this act may be summarized as follows: (1) resumption of specie payments on January 1, 1879, (2) a system of free banking, (3) retirement of greenbacks, (4) substitution of silver coin for paper fractional currency, and (5) removal of the charge for coinage of gold (D. R. Dewey, *Financial History of the United States*, New York, 1903, pp. 372–373).

The act passed the Senate on December 22, 1874. It passed the House without amendment and was approved by the President on January 14, 1875. It is found in *U. S. Statutes at Large*, Vol. 18, 1875, p. 296.

The vote was yeas 136, nays 98, not voting 58, total 292. The vote by states, thirty-seven in number, is shown in table 29 (*House Journ., 43rd Cong., 2nd Sess.,* 1874–1875, p. 138).

The representatives of the Forty-third Congress were elected under the apportionment acts of February 2 and May 30, 1872. Because of the short time intervening between the dates of these acts and the dates of election, several states held elections under their old districting acts and chose at large the additional representatives allotted to them. Each of four states—Delaware, Nebraska, Nevada, and Oregon—chose a single representative. Two states—Florida and Kansas—elected their representatives on a general ticket. Nine states—Alabama, Arkansas, Indiana, Louisiana, New York, Pennsylvania, South Carolina, Tennessee, and Texas—chose at large their additional representatives.

The following votes, the first three from districts and all nays, and the rest at large and all yeas, are not shown on the map: one, third Massachusetts (part of Boston); two, first and fourth Pennsylvania (parts of Philadelphia); two, Alabama; one, Arkansas; two, Indiana; one, New York; two, Pennsylvania; one, South Carolina; and one, Tennessee.

TABLE 29
RESUMPTION OF SPECIE PAYMENTS, 1875

STATE	YEAS	NAYS	NOT VOTING	TOTAL VOTES
Alabama	4	3	1	8
Arkansas	2	1	1	4
California	3	....	1	4
Connecticut	2	1	1	4
Delaware	....	....	1	1
Florida	1	....	1	2
Georgia	2	6	1	9
Illinois	10	3	6	19
Indiana	9	3	1	13
Iowa	9	....	....	9
Kansas	2	....	1	3
Kentucky	....	8	2	10
Louisiana	....	....	6	6
Maine	3	....	2	5
Maryland	2	3	1	6
Massachusetts	2	7	2	11
Michigan	6	1	2	9
Minnesota	1	....	2	3
Mississippi	4	2	....	6
Missouri	1	9	3	13
Nebraska	1	....	....	1
Nevada	....	....	1	1
New Hampshire	2	1	....	3
New Jersey	4	1	2	7
New York	19	9	5	33
North Carolina	1	6	1	8
Ohio	9	9	2	20
Oregon	....	1	....	1
Pennsylvania	18	6	3	27
Rhode Island	2	....	....	2
South Carolina	3	....	2	5
Tennessee	4	4	2	10
Texas	....	6	....	6
Vermont	2	1	....	3
Virginia	3	4	2	9
West Virginia	....	2	1	3
Wisconsin	5	1	2	8
Total	136	98	58	292

TABLE 30
SILVER PURCHASE ACT, 1878

STATE	YEAS	NAYS	NOT VOTING	TOTAL VOTES
Alabama	8	....	....	8
Arkansas	3	....	1	4
California	3	1	....	4
Colorado	1	....	....	1
Connecticut	2	1	1	4
Delaware	....	1	....	1
Florida	1	1	....	2
Georgia	9	....	....	9
Illinois	18	1	....	19
Indiana	13	....	....	13
Iowa	9	....	....	9
Kansas	3	....	....	3
Kentucky	10	....	....	10
Louisiana	3	1	2	6
Maine	....	5	....	5
Maryland	3	....	3	6
Massachusetts	1	10	....	11
Michigan	7	2	....	9
Minnesota	2	1	....	3
Mississippi	6	....	....	6
Missouri	13	....	....	13
Nebraska	1	....	....	1
Nevada	1	....	....	1
New Hampshire	....	3	....	3
New Jersey	1	4	2	7
New York	6	26	1	33
North Carolina	8	....	....	8
Ohio	16	1	3	20
Oregon	1	....	....	1
Pennsylvania	12	9	6	27
Rhode Island	....	2	....	2
South Carolina	4	1	....	5
Tennessee	10	....	....	10
Texas	5	1	....	6
Vermont	....	3	....	3
Virginia	6	....	3	9
West Virginia	2	....	1	3
Wisconsin	8	....	....	8
Total	196	73	24	293

The two representatives at large from Texas voted nay. One representative at large from Pennsylvania and one from Louisiana did not vote. One member from Florida and one from Kansas, who did not vote, are disregarded. The following districts, whose members did not vote, are also disregarded: third Maryland (part of Baltimore), and the second, fifth, and seventh New York (parts of New York City). The southern part of the non-voting area in Maine is the district of James G. Blaine, speaker of the House.

The representatives of the Forty-fifth Congress were elected under the apportionment acts of February 2 and May 30, 1872. Each of five states —Colorado, Delaware, Nebraska, Nevada, and Oregon—chose a single representative. With this exception the election was by districts. One yea vote from a New York City district (6th N. Y.) and one from a Philadelphia district (4th Pa.) are not shown on the map. The third Pennsylvania district (part of Philadelphia), represented by Samuel J. Randall, speaker of the House, who did not vote, is disregarded.

Silver Purchase Act, February 28, 1878

[PLATE 117C]

The vote was by the representatives of the Forty-fifth Congress, second session, on the passage over the President's veto of an "act to authorize the coinage of the standard silver dollar, and to restore its legal-tender character"—commonly known as the Bland-Allison Silver Purchase Act. The most important provisions of this act may be summarized as follows: (1) authorization of the purchase of not less than $2,000,000 nor more than $4,000,000 worth of silver bullion a month and the coinage of the same into silver dollars; (2) restoration of the legal-tender character of the silver dollar; and (3) provision for the issuing of silver certificates.

A bill introduced by Richard P. Bland of Missouri and passed by the House on November 5, 1877, provided for the free and unlimited coinage of silver—yeas 164, nays 34, not voting 92 (*House Journ., 45th Cong., 1st Sess.*, 1877, pp. 143–144). Under the leadership of Senator William B. Allison of Iowa the Senate amended the bill by limiting the volume of coinage, and by adding some new provisions of considerable importance. The House agreed to the amendments of the Senate, the President vetoed the bill on February 28, 1878, and on the same day the House and the Senate passed it over his veto. The act is found in *U. S. Statutes at Large*, Vol. 20, 1879, pp. 25–26.

The vote in the House on February 28 was yeas 196, nays 73, not voting 24, total 293. The vote by states, thirty-eight in number, was as follows (*House Journ., 45th Cong., 2nd Sess.*, 1877–1878, pp. 549–550):

General Tariff Act, March 3, 1883

[PLATE 117D]

The vote was by the representatives of the Forty-seventh Congress, second session, on agreeing to the report of a conference committee appointed to adjust the differences between the two Houses arising in respect to an "act to reduce internal revenue taxation, and for other purposes." On June 27, 1882, the House passed a bill for the reduction of internal revenue taxes. To this the Senate tacked on, as an amendment, a tariff bill, based in the main on the recommendations of the Tariff Commission of 1882. The House disagreed to the amendment, and a committee of conference was appointed, which finally settled the details of the act, making changes that as a rule increased the protection to industries. The act effected the first general revision of the tariff, with the exception of the "abortive horizontal reduction of 1872," since the Civil War. It has been described as a "half-hearted attempt on the part of those wishing to maintain a system of high protection, to make some concession to a public demand for a moderate tariff system. Some duties were increased, some lowered; nor was any consistent policy followed" (F. W. Taussig, *Tariff History of the United States*, 6th edit., New York and London, 1914, pp. 230–233, and 249). The act as reported by the conference committee and as approved by the President on March 3, 1883, is found in *U. S. Statutes at Large*, Vol. 22, 1883, pp. 488–526.

The vote of the House on agreeing to the report of the conference committee was yeas 152, nays 116, not voting 25, total 293. The vote by states, thirty-eight in number, is shown in the following table (*House Journ.*, 47th Cong., 2nd Sess., 1882–1883, pp. 612–613):

TABLE 31
GENERAL TARIFF ACT, 1883

STATE	YEAS	NAYS	NOT VOTING	TOTAL VOTES
Alabama	1	4	3	8
Arkansas		3	1	4
California	2	2		4
Colorado	1			1
Connecticut	3		1	4
Delaware		1		1
Florida	1	1		2
Georgia	1	7	1	9
Illinois	13	5	1	19
Indiana	8	5		13
Iowa	7	1	1	9
Kansas	3			3
Kentucky	1	8	1	10
Louisiana		5	1	6
Maine	4	1		5
Maryland		6		6
Massachusetts	9		2	11
Michigan	8	1		9
Minnesota	3			3
Mississippi	1	4	1	6
Missouri	4	8	1	13
Nebraska	1			1
Nevada		1		1
New Hampshire	3			3
New Jersey	7			7
New York	21	8	4	33
North Carolina	1	6	1	8
Ohio	7	11	2	20
Oregon	1			1
Pennsylvania	20	5	2	27
Rhode Island	2			2
South Carolina	2	3		5
Tennessee	3	7		10
Texas		5	1	6
Vermont	3			3
Virginia	4	4	1	9
West Virginia	1	2		3
Wisconsin	6	2		8
Total	152	116	25	293

The representatives of the Forty-seventh Congress were elected in the same manner as those of the Forty-fifth (see p. 117, above). Two votes from New York City districts (8th and 9th N. Y.), both yeas, and one from a Brooklyn district (2nd N. Y.), a nay, are not shown on the map. A New York City district (5th N. Y.) whose member did not vote, is disregarded. The non-voting area in western Ohio is the district of J. Warren Keiffer, speaker of the House.

Reagan Interstate Commerce Bill, January 8, 1885

[PLATE 118A]

The vote was by the members of the Forty-eighth Congress, second session, on the passage of a "bill to regulate interstate commerce, and to prohibit unjust discriminations by common carriers." This bill was brought before the House by John H. Reagan of Texas, chairman of the Committee on Commerce, on December 2, 1884, when he moved to substitute it for a "bill to establish a board of commissioners of interstate commerce and to regulate such commerce." Two weeks later the House accepted the Reagan bill and on January 8 passed it. On February 3 the Senate, by amendment, substituted a bill of its own for the Reagan bill and on the following day passed it. On February 7 and also on February 27 Reagan asked unanimous consent to take from the speaker's table the bill passed by the Senate, with a view to securing the non-concurrence of the House in the Senate amendments and to the appointment of a committee of conference; but on both occasions an objection was raised, and the measure failed of passage. The Reagan bill is found in the *Congressional Record*, 48th Cong., 2nd Sess., Vol. 16, Part I, pp. 535–536.

The vote was yeas 161, nays 75, not voting 89, total 325. The vote by states, thirty-eight in number, is shown in the following table (*House Journ.*, 48th Cong., 2nd Sess., 1884–1885, pp. 205–206):

TABLE 32
REAGAN INTERSTATE COMMERCE BILL, 1885

STATE	YEAS	NAYS	NOT VOTING	TOTAL VOTES
Alabama	6	1	1	8
Arkansas	3		2	5
California	6			6
Colorado			1	1
Connecticut		4		4
Delaware	1			1
Florida	1	1		2
Georgia	5	4	1	10
Illinois	8	7	5	20
Indiana	9		4	13
Iowa	7	1	3	11
Kansas	7			7
Kentucky	6		5	11
Louisiana	4		2	6
Maine		2	2	4
Maryland	4	1	1	6
Massachusetts	2	7	3	12
Michigan	5	4	2	11
Minnesota	4	1		5
Mississippi	4	1	2	7
Missouri	9		5	14
Nebraska	1		2	3
Nevada	1			1
New Hampshire	1		1	2
New Jersey	2	4	1	7
New York	11	9	14	34
North Carolina	4	2	3	9
Ohio	10	2	9	21
Oregon	1			1
Pennsylvania	12	13	3	28
Rhode Island		1	1	2
South Carolina	1	4	2	7
Tennessee	8	1	1	10
Texas	7		4	11
Vermont			2	2
Virginia	5	3	2	10
West Virginia	3		1	4
Wisconsin	3	2	4	9
Total	161	75	89	325

The representatives of the Forty-eighth Congress were elected under the apportionment act of February 25, 1882. Each of four states—Colorado, Delaware, Nevada, and Oregon—chose a single representative. Maine elected representatives on a general ticket. Eight states—Arkansas, California, Georgia, Kansas, New York, North Carolina, Pennsylvania, and Virginia—chose one or more representatives at large. With these exceptions the method of election was by districts.

The votes here noted are not shown on the map. From districts: three nays, eight, tenth, and eleventh New York (parts of New York City); one yea, third Pennsylvania (part of Philadelphia); and one nay, third Maryland (part of Baltimore). At large: one yea, Arkansas; one nay, Georgia; one nay, Pennsylvania; and one nay, Virginia. The two California and the four Kansas representatives at large voted yea. One representative at large from New York, one representative at large from North Carolina, and two representatives from Maine, who did not vote, are disregarded. The fourth Massachusetts district (part of Boston), the seventh New York (part of New York City), and the second New York (part of Brooklyn), whose members did not vote, are also disregarded. The most northwesterly part of the non-voting area in eastern Kentucky is the district of John G. Carlisle, speaker of the House.

Bland Free Coinage Bill, March 24, 1892

[PLATE 118B]

The vote was by the representatives of the Fifty-second Congress, first session, on laying on the table a "bill for the free coinage of gold and silver, for the issue of coin notes, and for other purposes." With this vote the movement for the free coinage of silver reached its maximum in the House. The bill was introduced in the House on January 21, 1892, by Richard P. Bland of Missouri, chairman of the Committee on Coinage, Weights, and Measures. The motion to lay the bill on the table was made, March 24, by Julius C. Burrows of Michigan, an opponent of the measure. It took the Speaker's vote to defeat this motion. The opponents next resorted to filibustering, and the bill was finally dropped without coming to a vote on its passage. It is found in the *Congressional Record, 52nd Cong., 1st Sess.,* 1891-1892, Vol. 23, Part III, p. 2323.

The vote was yeas 148, nays 149, not voting 35, total 332. The vote by states, forty-four in number, is shown in the following table (*House Journ., 52nd Cong., 1st Sess.,* 1891-1892, p. 113):

TABLE 33
BLAND FREE COINAGE BILL, 1892

STATE	YEAS	NAYS	NOT VOTING	TOTAL VOTES
Alabama		6	2	8
Arkansas		4	1	5
California	4	2		6
Colorado		1		1
Connecticut	4			4
Delaware	1			1
Florida		2		2
Georgia		10		10
Idaho		1		1
Illinois	8	7	5	20
Indiana	2	9	2	13
Iowa	9	2		11
Kansas		6	1	7
Kentucky	1	9	1	11
Louisiana	2	3	1	6
Maine	4			4
Maryland	4		2	6
Massachusetts	11		1	12
Michigan	7	4		11
Minnesota	3	2		5
Mississippi		5	2	7
Missouri	1	12	1	14
Montana		1		1
Nebraska		3		3
Nevada		1		1
New Hampshire	2			2
New Jersey	6	1		7
New York	28	1	5	34
North Carolina		8	1	9
North Dakota	1			1
Ohio	8	10	3	21
Oregon		1		1
Pennsylvania	26	1	1	28
Rhode Island	2			2
South Carolina	1	4	2	7
South Dakota		2		2
Tennessee	1	7	2	10
Texas		11		11
Vermont	2			2
Virginia		8	2	10
Washington	1			1
West Virginia	1	3		4
Wisconsin	8	1		9
Wyoming		1		1
Total	148	149	35	332

The representatives of the Fifty-second Congress were elected under the apportionment act of February 25, 1882, six states being admitted after the passage of the act. Each of nine states—Colorado, Delaware, Idaho, Montana, Nevada, North Dakota, Oregon, Washington, and Wyoming—chose a single representative. South Dakota elected her representatives on a general ticket. With these exceptions the method of election was by districts.

The vote of one of the St. Louis districts (9th Mo.), which was yea, is not shown on the map. One New York City district (8th N. Y.) and one Chicago district (3rd Ill.) whose members did not vote, are disregarded. The Speaker of the House, Charles F. Crisp of Georgia, voted nay. His district is situated in the southwestern part of the state.

Dingley Tariff Act, March 31, 1897

[PLATE 119A]

The vote was by the representatives of the Fifty-fifth Congress, first session, on the passage of an "act to provide revenue for the government, and to encourage the industries of the United States." This act is especially significant in two respects: (1) it is the longest-lived of all the general tariff acts, and (2) it marks the maximum point reached by the policy of a protective tariff before 1921 (F. W. Taussig, *Tariff History of the United States,* 6th edit., New York and London, 1914, pp. 358 and 361).

The Senate made many amendments to the act passed by the House, and the differences were adjusted by a conference committee. For the act as it passed the House see *H. R. Bill No. 379, 55th Cong., 1st Sess.,* 1897; for the act as it was approved by the President July 24, 1897, see *U. S. Statutes at Large,* Vol. 30, 1899, pp. 151-213.

The vote was yeas 205, nays 122, not voting 30, total 357. The vote by states, forty-five in number, is shown in the following table (*House Journ., 55th Cong., 1st Sess.,* 1897, pp. 57-58):

TABLE 34
DINGLEY TARIFF ACT, 1897

STATE	YEAS	NAYS	NOT VOTING	TOTAL VOTES
Alabama	1	8		9
Arkansas		6		6
California	3	4		7
Colorado			2	2
Connecticut	4			4
Delaware		1		1
Florida		2		2
Georgia		11		11
Idaho			1	1
Illinois	17	5		22
Indiana	9	4		13
Iowa	11			11
Kansas	1	2	5	8
Kentucky	4	7		11
Louisiana	3	3		6
Maine	3		1	4
Maryland	6			6
Massachusetts	10	1	2	13
Michigan	10	2		12
Minnesota	7			7
Mississippi		7		7
Missouri	3	11	1	15
Montana			1	1
Nebraska	2		4	6
Nevada			1	1
New Hampshire	2			2
New Jersey	8			8
New York	29	4	1	34
North Carolina	3	1	5	9
North Dakota	1			1
Ohio	15	6		21
Oregon	2			2
Pennsylvania	26	3	1	30
Rhode Island	2			2
South Carolina		7		7
South Dakota			2	2
Tennessee	2	8		10
Texas	3	9	1	13
Utah		1		1
Vermont	2			2
Virginia	2	8		10
Washington			2	2
West Virginia	4			4
Wisconsin	10			10
Wyoming		1		1
Total	205	122	30	357

The representatives of the Fifty-fifth Congress were elected under the apportionment act of February 7, 1891. Each of seven states—Delaware, Idaho, Montana, Nevada, North Dakota, Utah, and Wyoming—chose a single representative. South Dakota and Washington elected representatives on a general ticket. Kansas chose one, and Pennsylvania two representatives at large. With these exceptions the method of election was by districts. One vote from a Boston district (9th Mass.), one from a Philadelphia district (3rd Pa.), and one from a San Francisco district (4th Cal.), all nays, and four votes from New York City districts (8th, 13th, 14th, and 15th N. Y.) and the two votes of the Pennsylvania representatives at large, all yeas, are not shown on the map.

One New York City district (10th N. Y.), whose member did not vote, is disregarded. The Kansas representative at large did not vote. The speaker of the House, who voted yea, was Thomas B. Reed of Maine. The representatives of Colorado, Idaho, Montana, Nevada, South Dakota, and Washington, none of whom voted, were present when the vote was taken, with the exception of J. H. Lewis of Washington. Four representatives from Nebraska and four from Kansas were present but did not vote.

Gold Standard Act, December 18, 1899

[PLATE 119B]

The vote was by the representatives of the Fifty-sixth Congress, first session, on the passage of an "act to define and fix the standard of value, to maintain the parity of all forms of money issued or coined by the United States, to refund the public debt, and for other purposes." For the bill passed by the House on December 18 the Senate substituted one of its own, which it passed, and the differences between the two houses were adjusted by a committee of conference. For the act as passed by the House on December 18, see *H. R. Bill No. 1, 56th Cong., 1st Sess.*, 1899–1900. For the act as signed by the President on March 14, 1900, see *U. S. Statutes at Large*, Vol. 31, 1901, pp. 45–50.

The vote was yeas 190, nays 150, not voting 17, total 357. The vote by states, forty-five in number, was as follows (*House Journ., 56th Cong., 1st Sess.*, 1899–1900, pp. 108–109):

TABLE 35
GOLD STANDARD ACT, 1899

STATE	YEAS	NAYS	NOT VOTING	TOTAL VOTES
Alabama		7	2	9
Arkansas		6		6
California	6	1		7
Colorado		2		2
Connecticut	4			4
Delaware	1			1
Florida		2		2
Georgia		11		11
Idaho		1		1
Illinois	14	8		22
Indiana	9	4		13
Iowa	10		1	11
Kansas	7	1		8
Kentucky	2	8	1	11
Louisiana		3	3	6
Maine	4			4
Maryland	5		1	6
Massachusetts	11	2		13
Michigan	11		1	12
Minnesota	7			7
Mississippi		6	1	7
Missouri	2	12	1	15
Montana			1	1
Nebraska	2	4		6
Nevada		1		1
New Hampshire	2			2
New Jersey	6	2		8
New York	22	10	2	34
North Carolina	2	6	1	9
North Dakota	1			1
Ohio	15	6		21
Oregon	2			2
Pennsylvania	20	9	1	30
Rhode Island	2			2
South Carolina		7		7
South Dakota	2			2
Tennessee	2	8		10
Texas	1	12		13
Utah			1	1
Vermont	2			2
Virginia		10		10
Washington	2			2
West Virginia	3	1		4
Wisconsin	10			10
Wyoming	1			1
Total	190	150	17	357

The representatives of the Fifty-sixth Congress were elected in the same manner as those of the Fifty-fifth (see p. 119, above). One vote from a Brooklyn district (6th N. Y.), a nay; two votes from New York City districts (13th and 15th N. Y.), both yeas; and three votes from Chicago districts (3rd, 4th, and 5th Ill.), all nays; the vote of the two Pennsylvania representatives at large, a yea and a nay; and the vote of the Kansas representative at large, a yea, are not shown on the map. Parts of Boston and Buffalo were in districts voting yea, but the principal parts in districts voting nay. A St. Louis district (11th Mo.) and a Philadelphia district (5th Pa.), whose members did not vote, are disregarded. The non-voting area in Iowa is the district of David B. Henderson, speaker of the House.

Payne-Aldrich Tariff Act, July 31, 1909

[PLATE 120A]

The vote was by the representatives of the Sixty-first Congress, first session, on agreeing to the report of a conference committee in respect to an "act to provide revenue, equalize duties, and encourage the industries of the United States, and for other purposes." This act is significant in its showing a tendency toward the enactment of lower duties and in its marking a halt in the upward movement of the tariff, which movement began with the Morrill Tariff Act of 1861.

On April 9 the House passed an act (yeas 217, nays 161) which made several significant reductions in the tariff and which effected a considerable measure of "real" revision. This was extensively amended by the Senate, chiefly by way of an increase of duties (F. W. Taussig, *Tariff History of the United States*, 6th edit., New York and London, 1914, pp. 372 and 375). The details of the act were finally settled by a conference committee, which in the main accepted the views of the Senate (*American Year Book*, New York, 1910, p. 322). The report of this committee is found in the *House Journ., 61st Cong., 1st Sess.*, 1909, pp. 278–299. The act as approved by the President on August 5, 1909, is found in *U. S. Statutes at Large*, Vol. 36, 1911, Part I, pp. 11–118.

The vote in the House on agreeing to the report of the conference committee was yeas 195, nays 183, not voting 13, total 391. The vote by states, forty-six in number, was as follows (*House Journ., 61st Cong., 1st Sess.*, 1909, p. 301):

TABLE 36
PAYNE-ALDRICH TARIFF ACT, 1909

STATE	YEAS	NAYS	NOT VOTING	TOTAL VOTES
Alabama		7	2	9
Arkansas		7		7
California	8			8
Colorado		3		3
Connecticut	4		1	5
Delaware	1			1
Florida		3		3
Georgia		11		11
Idaho	1			1
Illinois	17	7	1	25
Indiana	2	11		13
Iowa	6	5		11
Kansas	7	1		8
Kentucky	3	8		11
Louisiana	2	5		7
Maine	4			4
Maryland	2	3	1	6
Massachusetts	10	3	1	14
Michigan	12			12
Minnesota	1	8		9
Mississippi		8		8
Missouri	6	10		16
Montana	1			1
Nebraska	3	2	1	6
Nevada			1	1
New Hampshire	2			2
New Jersey	7	3		10
New York	25	12		37
North Carolina	3	7		10
North Dakota	1	1		2
Ohio	12	9		21
Oklahoma	3	2		5
Oregon	2			2
Pennsylvania	26	5	1	32
Rhode Island	2			2
South Carolina		6	1	7
South Dakota	2			2
Tennessee	2	8		10
Texas		15	1	16
Utah	1			1
Vermont	2			2
Virginia	1	9		10
Washington	1	1	1	3
West Virginia	5			5
Wisconsin	7	3	1	11
Wyoming	1			1
Total	195	183	13	391

The representatives of the Sixty-first Congress, first session, were elected under the apportionment act of January 16, 1901. Each of six states—Delaware, Idaho, Montana, Nevada, Utah, and Wyoming—

chose a single representative. North Dakota and South Dakota elected representatives on a general ticket. Colorado and Connecticut each chose at large one additional representative. With these exceptions the method of election was by districts. The vote from North Dakota was one yea and one nay. The representative who voted yea, and whose vote is not shown on the map, came from Fargo, in the southeastern part of the state; the representative voting nay came from Lakota, in the northeastern part of the state. A yea vote from a Baltimore district (3rd Md.), two nay votes from Brooklyn districts (2nd and 7th N. Y.), three yea votes from New York City districts (13th, 15th, and 17th N. Y.), four nay votes from Chicago districts (2nd, 4th, 5th, and 8th Ill.), and one nay vote from a St. Louis district (11th Mo.) are not shown on the map. One Chicago and Cook County district (6th Ill.), whose member did not vote, is disregarded. The representative at large from Connecticut voted yea, and the one from Colorado nay. Joseph G. Cannon, speaker of the House, representing an eastern Illinois district (18th Ill.), voted yea.

Canadian Reciprocity Act, April 21, 1911

[PLATE 120B]

The vote was by the representatives of the Sixty-second Congress, first session, on the passage of an "act to promote reciprocal trade relations with the Dominion of Canada, and for other purposes." This act provided for free trade between the United States and Canada in grain, vegetables, domestic animals, fish, and other primary food products, and for a mutual lowering of duties on several manufactured articles and on meat, flour, and other secondary food products.

The act passed the Senate on July 22 and four days later was signed by the President. It is found in *U. S. Statutes at Large*, Vol. 37, 1913, Part I, pp. 4–12.

The vote was yeas 268, nays 89, not voting 34, total 391. The vote by states, forty-six in number, is shown in table 37 (*House Journ., 62nd Cong., 1st Sess.*, 1911, pp. 140–141).

The representatives of the Sixty-second Congress were elected in the same manner as those of the Sixty-first (see pp. 120–121, above). One vote from a Philadelphia district (3rd Pa.), a nay, and the vote of the representative at large for Colorado, a yea, are not shown on the map. The Connecticut representative at large voted yea. Two Brooklyn districts (2nd and 5th N. Y.), one Philadelphia district (2nd Pa.), and one San Francisco district (4th Cal.), whose members did not vote, are disregarded. Champ Clark, speaker of the House, representing a district in eastern Missouri (9th), voted yea.

Underwood Tariff Act, May 8, 1913

[PLATE 120C]

The vote was by the representatives of the Sixty-third Congress, first session, on the passage of an "act to reduce tariff duties and to provide revenue for the government, and for other purposes." This act began a policy of "much moderated protection" and effected the most radical revision of the tariff made in half a century (F. W. Taussig, *Tariff History of the United States*, 6th edit., New York and London, 1914, p. 448).

The act was amended by the Senate, and the differences between the two Houses were adjusted by a conference committee. For the act as it

TABLE 37
CANADIAN RECIPROCITY ACT, 1911

STATE	YEAS	NAYS	NOT VOTING	TOTAL VOTES
Alabama	8	....	1	9
Arkansas	7	....	....	7
California	5	1	2	8
Colorado	2	1	....	3
Connecticut	4	....	1	5
Delaware	1	....	....	1
Florida	2	....	1	3
Georgia	9	....	2	11
Idaho	....	1	....	1
Illinois	16	8	1	25
Indiana	12	....	1	13
Iowa	2	8	1	11
Kansas	4	4	....	8
Kentucky	9	2	....	11
Louisiana	5	1	1	7
Maine	2	2	....	4
Maryland	6	....	....	6
Massachusetts	13	1	....	14
Michigan	4	8	....	12
Minnesota	3	6	....	9
Mississippi	7	....	1	8
Missouri	15	....	1	16
Montana	....	1	....	1
Nebraska	2	3	1	6
Nevada	1	....	....	1
New Hampshire	1	1	....	2
New Jersey	7	1	2	10
New York	20	9	8	37
North Carolina	7	3	....	10
North Dakota	....	2	....	2
Ohio	17	4	....	21
Oklahoma	3	2	....	5
Oregon	1	1	....	2
Pennsylvania	22	6	4	32
Rhode Island	2	....	....	2
South Carolina	7	....	....	7
South Dakota	....	2	....	2
Tennessee	9	....	1	10
Texas	14	....	2	16
Utah	....	1	....	1
Vermont	....	2	....	2
Virginia	10	....	....	10
Washington	....	3	....	3
West Virginia	4	....	1	5
Wisconsin	5	4	2	11
Wyoming	....	1	....	1
Total	268	89	34	391

TABLE 38
UNDERWOOD TARIFF ACT, 1913

STATE	YEAS	NAYS	NOT VOTING	TOTAL VOTES
Alabama	10	....	....	10
Arizona	1	....	....	1
Arkansas	7	....	....	7
California	5	6	....	11
Colorado	4	....	....	4
Connecticut	5	....	....	5
Delaware	1	....	....	1
Florida	4	....	....	4
Georgia	12	....	....	12
Idaho	....	2	....	2
Illinois	18	6	3	27
Indiana	12	....	1	13
Iowa	3	8	....	11
Kansas	5	3	....	8
Kentucky	9	2	....	11
Louisiana	4	4	....	8
Maine	1	3	....	4
Maryland	6	....	....	6
Massachusetts	8	8	....	16
Michigan	2	11	....	13
Minnesota	1	9	....	10
Mississippi	8	....	....	8
Missouri	14	2	....	16
Montana	2	....	....	2
Nebraska	3	3	....	6
Nevada	....	1	....	1
New Hampshire	2	....	....	2
New Jersey	10	1	1	12
New Mexico	1	....	....	1
New York	28	13	2	43
North Carolina	10	....	....	10
North Dakota	....	3	....	3
Ohio	18	3	1	22
Oklahoma	6	2	....	8
Oregon	....	3	....	3
Pennsylvania	13	23	....	36
Rhode Island	2	1	....	3
South Carolina	6	....	1	7
South Dakota	....	3	....	3
Tennessee	7	2	1	10
Texas	18	....	....	18
Utah	....	2	....	2
Vermont	....	2	....	2
Virginia	9	1	....	10
Washington	1	4	....	5
West Virginia	2	3	1	6
Wisconsin	5	6	....	11
Wyoming	....	1	....	1
Total	283	141	11	435

passed the House on May 8, see *H. R. Bill No. 3321, 63rd Cong., 1st Sess.*, 1913. For the act as approved by the President see *U. S. Statutes at Large*, Vol. 38, 1915, Part I, pp. 114–202.

The vote in the House on the passage of the act, including "live pairs" (see p. 106, above), was yeas 283, nays 141, not voting 11, total 435. The vote by states, forty-eight in number, is shown in table 38 (*House Journ., 63rd Cong., 1st Sess.*, 1913, pp. 138–139).

The representatives of the Sixty-third Congress were elected under the apportionment act of August 8, 1911. Each of five states—Arizona, Delaware, Nevada, New Mexico, and Wyoming—chose a single representative. In three states—Idaho, Montana, and Utah—the election was by general ticket. Representatives at large were chosen as follows: Alabama 1, Colorado 2, Florida 1, Illinois 2, Michigan 1, Minnesota 1, Ohio 1, Oklahoma 3, Pennsylvania 4, Texas 2, Washington 2, and West Virginia 1. With these exceptions the election was by districts.

A nay vote from a New York City district (19th N. Y.), a nay vote from a Brooklyn district (6th N. Y.), a yea vote from a Philadelphia district (6th Pa.), three nay votes from Chicago districts (1st, 2nd, and 9th Ill.), a yea vote from a St. Louis district (11th Mo.), and a yea vote from a district consisting of a part of San Francisco city and county (5th Cal.) are not shown on the map. The votes of representatives at large which cannot be shown are as follows: Illinois, 2 yeas; Michigan, 1 nay; Minnesota, 1 nay; Ohio, 1 yea; Oklahoma, 3 yeas; Pennsylvania, 1 yea and 3 nays; Washington, 1 yea; and West Virginia, 1 nay. Two New York City districts (13th and 21st N. Y.), whose members did not vote, are disregarded. The Speaker of the House was Champ Clark of Missouri, who voted yea.

War Resolution, April 5, 1917

[PLATE 120D]

The vote was by the representatives of the Sixty-fifth Congress, first session, on the passage of a joint resolution "declaring that a state of war exists between the Imperial German Government and the Government and the people of the United States, and making provision to prosecute the same." The resolution was passed by the Senate on April 4, passed by the House without amendment on April 5, and approved by the President on April 6. It is found in the *Congressional Record*, Vol. 55, Part I, p. 305, and in *U. S. Statutes at Large*, Vol. 40, 1919, Part I, p. 1.

The vote on the passage of the resolution, including "live pairs," was yeas 376, nays 53, not voting 6, total 435. The vote by states, forty-eight in number, is shown in the following table: (*Cong. Record, 65th Cong., 1st Sess.*, 1917, pp. 412–413):

TABLE 39
WAR RESOLUTION, 1917

STATE	YEAS	NAYS	NOT VOTING	TOTAL VOTES
Alabama	8	2	....	10
Arizona	1	....	....	1
Arkansas	7	....	....	7
California	8	3	....	11
Colorado	2	2	....	4
Connecticut	5	....	....	5
Delaware	1	....	....	1
Florida	4	....	....	4
Georgia	12	....	....	12
Idaho	2	....	....	2
Illinois	21	6	....	27
Indiana	13	....	....	13
Iowa	8	3	....	11
Kansas	6	2	....	8
Kentucky	9	2	....	11
Louisiana	8	....	....	8
Maine	4	....	....	4
Maryland	6	....	....	6
Massachusetts	16	....	....	16
Michigan	12	1	....	13
Minnesota	6	4	....	10
Mississippi	8	....	....	8
Missouri	11	4	1	16
Montana	1	1	....	2
Nebraska	3	3	....	6
Nevada	....	1	....	1
New Hampshire	1	....	1	2
New Jersey	11	....	1	12
New Mexico	1	....	....	1
New York	41	1	1	43
North Carolina	8	2	....	10

TABLE 39 (*Concluded*)
WAR RESOLUTION, 1917

STATE	YEAS	NAYS	NOT VOTING	TOTAL VOTES
North Dakota	2	....	1	3
Ohio	21	1	....	22
Oklahoma	8	....	....	8
Oregon	3	....	....	3
Pennsylvania	35	....	1	36
Rhode Island	3	....	....	3
South Carolina	6	1	....	7
South Dakota	1	2	....	3
Tennessee	10	....	....	10
Texas	17	1	....	18
Utah	2	....	....	2
Vermont	2	....	....	2
Virginia	10	....	....	10
Washington	3	2	....	5
West Virginia	6	....	....	6
Wisconsin	2	9	....	11
Wyoming	1	....	....	1
Total	376	53	6	435

The representatives of the Sixty-fifth Congress were elected under the apportionment act of August 8, 1911. Five states, as in the Sixty-third Congress (see above), chose a single representative. In two states, Idaho and Montana, the election was by general ticket. In order to show the divided vote of Montana, the state is striped with the yea and the nay colors—a practice not elsewhere followed in this series. Representatives at large were chosen as follows: Illinois 2, Pennsylvania 4, and Texas 2.

A nay vote from a New York City district (12th N. Y.), cast by Meyer London, Socialist, a nay vote from a Chicago (9th Ill.) and a nay vote from a St. Louis district (11th Mo.) are not shown. The following votes of representatives at large could not be shown: Illinois, 1 yea and 1 nay; and Texas, 1 nay. One New York City district (5th N. Y.), in which there was a vacancy, is disregarded. The district in Missouri not voting was represented by Champ Clark, speaker of the House.

Prohibition Resolution, December 17, 1917

[PLATE 121A]

The vote was by the representatives of the Sixty-fifth Congress, second session, on the passage of a joint resolution proposing an amendment to the Constitution prohibiting the "manufacture, sale, or transportation of intoxicating liquors ... for beverage purposes." The resolution originated in the Senate and was passed by that body on August 1, 1917. It was amended by the House, and the House amendments were concurred in by the Senate. The resolution is found in *U. S. Statutes at Large*, Vol. 40, 1919, Part I, p. 1050. The vote, including "live pairs," was yeas 289, nays 134, and not voting 12, total 435. The vote by states is shown in the following table (*Cong. Record, 65th Cong., 2nd Sess.*, 1917–1918, pp. 469–470):

TABLE 40
PROHIBITION RESOLUTION, 1917

STATE	YEAS	NAYS	NOT VOTING	TOTAL VOTES
Alabama	5	5	....	10
Arizona	1	....	....	1
Arkansas	7	....	....	7
California	5	5	1	11
Colorado	4	....	....	4
Connecticut	....	5	....	5
Delaware	1	....	....	1
Florida	4	....	....	4
Georgia	12	....	....	12
Idaho	2	....	....	2
Illinois	17	7	3	27
Indiana	13	....	....	13
Iowa	10	1	....	11
Kansas	8	....	....	8
Kentucky	8	3	....	11
Louisiana	4	4	....	8
Maine	4	....	....	4
Maryland	2	4	....	6

TABLE 40 (*Concluded*)

PROHIBITION RESOLUTION, 1917

STATE	YEAS	NAYS	NOT VOTING	TOTAL VOTES
Massachusetts	6	8	2	16
Michigan	11	2	....	13
Minnesota	8	2	....	10
Mississippi	8	....	....	8
Missouri	12	3	1	16
Montana	2	....	....	2
Nebraska	6	....	....	6
Nevada	....	1	....	1
New Hampshire	2	....	....	2
New Jersey	2	10	....	12
New Mexico	1	....	....	1
New York	14	28	1	43
North Carolina	8	2	....	10
North Dakota	3	....	....	3
Ohio	12	8	2	22
Oklahoma	8	....	....	8
Oregon	2	1	....	3
Pennsylvania	18	18	....	36
Rhode Island	1	2	....	3
South Carolina	6	1	....	7
South Dakota	3	....	....	3
Tennessee	10	....	....	10
Texas	8	8	2	18
Utah	2	....	....	2
Vermont	1	1	....	2
Virginia	10	....	....	10
Washington	5	....	....	5
West Virginia	6	....	....	6
Wisconsin	6	5	....	11
Wyoming	1	....	....	1
Total	289	134	12	435

For the election of representatives to the Sixty-fifth Congress see p. 122, above.

A yea vote from a New York City district (6th N. Y.) and two yea votes from Philadelphia districts (5th and 6th Pa.) are not shown. Of the votes of representatives at large, four nays in Pennsylvania, one yea in Illinois, and one yea and one nay in Texas are not shown. A Boston district (11th Mass.) and a Chicago district (2nd Ill.), whose members did not vote, and a Chicago district (4th Ill.) in which there was a vacancy are disregarded. One of the Illinois representatives at large did not vote. The non-voting area in Missouri is the district of Champ Clark, speaker of the House.

Woman Suffrage Resolution, May 21, 1919

[PLATE 121B]

The vote was by the representatives of the Sixty-sixth Congress, first session, on the passage of a joint resolution "proposing an amendment to the Constitution extending the right of suffrage to women." The resolution was passed by the Senate on June 4, 1919. It is found in *U. S. Statutes at Large*, Vol. 41, Part I, p. 362. The vote, including "live pairs," was yeas 308, nays 92, not voting 35, total 435. The vote by states is shown in the following table (*Cong. Record, 66th Cong., 1st Sess.*, 1919, pp. 93–94):

TABLE 41

WOMAN SUFFRAGE RESOLUTION, 1919

STATE	YEAS	NAYS	NOT VOTING	TOTAL VOTES
Alabama	1	7	2	10
Arizona	1	....	....	1
Arkansas	6	....	1	7
California	10	....	1	11
Colorado	4	....	....	4
Connecticut	3	1	1	5
Delaware	1	....	....	1
Florida	3	1	....	4
Georgia	1	9	2	12
Idaho	1	....	1	2
Illinois	27	....	....	27
Indiana	13	....	....	13

TABLE 41 (*Concluded*)

WOMAN SUFFRAGE RESOLUTION, 1919

STATE	YEAS	NAYS	NOT VOTING	TOTAL VOTES
Iowa	10	1	....	11
Kansas	8	....	....	8
Kentucky	9	1	1	11
Louisiana	1	5	2	8
Maine	4	....	....	4
Maryland	3	3	....	6
Massachusetts	8	5	3	16
Michigan	11	1	1	13
Minnesota	9	....	1	10
Mississippi	....	6	2	8
Missouri	15	....	1	16
Montana	2	....	....	2
Nebraska	6	....	....	6
Nevada	1	....	....	1
New Hampshire	2	....	....	2
New Jersey	8	3	1	12
New Mexico	1	....	....	1
New York	37	3	3	43
North Carolina	2	8	....	10
North Dakota	3	....	....	3
Ohio	19	2	1	22
Oklahoma	7	....	1	8
Oregon	3	....	....	3
Pennsylvania	22	8	6	36
Rhode Island	3	....	....	3
South Carolina	....	7	....	7
South Dakota	3	....	....	3
Tennessee	7	3	....	10
Texas	10	7	1	18
Utah	2	....	....	2
Vermont	....	1	1	2
Virginia	1	8	1	10
Washington	5	....	....	5
West Virginia	6	....	....	6
Wisconsin	8	2	1	11
Wyoming	1	....	....	1
Total	308	92	35	435

The representatives of the Sixty-sixth Congress were elected under the apportionment act of August 8, 1911. Illinois elected two representatives at large, and Pennsylvania four.

A yea vote from a Boston district (10th Mass.), a nay vote from a New York City district (11th N. Y.), a nay vote from a Philadelphia district (3rd Pa.), a yea vote from a Baltimore district (4th Md.), a nay vote from a Detroit district (1st Mich.), and a yea and a nay vote of two Pennsylvania representatives at large are not shown. A Boston district (12th Mass.), two New York City districts (2nd and 15th N. Y.), a Jersey City district (12th N. J.), a Philadelphia district (4th Pa.), and a San Francisco district, whose members did not vote, and a Milwaukee district (5th Wis.), in which there was a vacancy, are disregarded. Two Pennsylvania representatives at large did not vote. The non-voting area in western Massachusetts is the district of F. H. Gillett, speaker of the House.

Fordney Tariff Act, July 21, 1921

[PLATE 122A]

The vote was by the representatives of the Sixty-seventh Congress, first session, on the passage of an act "to provide revenue, to regulate commerce with foreign countries, to encourage the industries of the United States, and for other purposes." This act reversed the policy of the Underwood Tariff Act of 1913 and established rates "higher than any in the long series of protective measures" (F. W. Taussig, *Tariff History of the United States*, 7th edit., New York, 1923, p. 453).

In the Senate many amendments were adopted generally raising duties. The differences between the two Houses were adjusted by a conference committee, and the act was signed by the President on September 21, 1922. For the act as it passed the House on July 21, 1921, see *H. R. Bill No. 7456, 67th Cong., 1st Sess.*, 1921; and for the act as it was approved by the President see *U. S. Statutes at Large*, Vol. 42, 1923, Part I, pp. 858–990.

The vote, including "live pairs," was yeas 292, nays 131, not voting 12, total 435. The vote by states is shown in the following table (*Cong. Record, 67th Cong., 1st Sess.*, pp. 4197–4198):

TABLE 42
FORDNEY TARIFF ACT, 1921

STATE	YEAS	NAYS	NOT VOTING	TOTAL VOTES
Alabama		10		10
Arizona		1		1
Arkansas		7		7
California	11			11
Colorado	2		2	4
Connecticut	5			5
Delaware	1			1
Florida		3	1	4
Georgia		12		12
Idaho	2			2
Illinois	23	3	1	27
Indiana	13			13
Iowa	10		1	11
Kansas	8			8
Kentucky	2	8	1	11
Louisiana	4	4		8
Maine	4			4
Maryland	4	2		6
Massachusetts	11	2	3	16
Michigan	13			13
Minnesota	9	1		10
Mississippi		8		8
Missouri	14	2		16
Montana	2			2
Nebraska	6			6
Nevada	1			1
New Hampshire	2			2
New Jersey	11	1		12
New Mexico	1			1
New York	33	10		43
North Carolina		10		10
North Dakota	2	1		3
Ohio	20	2		22
Oklahoma	5	3		8
Oregon	3			3
Pennsylvania	35		1	36
Rhode Island	2		1	3
South Carolina		7		7
South Dakota	3			3
Tennessee	5	5		10
Texas	1	16	1	18
Utah	2			2
Vermont	2			2
Virginia	1	9		10
Washington	5			5
West Virginia	6			6
Wisconsin	7	4		11
Wyoming	1			1
Total	292	131	12	435

The representatives of the Sixty-seventh Congress were elected under the same laws as those of the Sixty-sixth (see p. 123, above).

The following votes are not shown: a yea from a Boston district (11th Mass.), 8 nays from New York city districts (3rd, 4th, 11th, 12th, 13th, 16th, 18th, and 22nd N. Y.), a nay from a Jersey City district (12th N. J.), a nay from a Baltimore district (4th Md.), a nay from a Cleveland district (21st Ohio), three nays from Chicago districts (4th, 5th, and 8th Ill.), and a nay from a St. Louis district (11th Mo.). There was a vacancy in the representatives at large of Pennsylvania and of Illinois. The non-voting area in western Massachusetts is the district of F. H. Gillett, speaker of the House.

Smoot-Hawley Tariff Act, June 13, 1930

[PLATE 122B]

The vote was by the representatives of the Seventy-first Congress, second session, on the passage of an act "to provide revenue, to regulate commerce with foreign countries, to encourage the industries of the United States, to protect American labor, and for other purposes." This act established rates higher than those of previous protective measures.

The bill was debated and amended in the House and later by the Senate. The House disagreed with the Senate amendments. Finally, conference reports were approved by the Senate (Concurrent Resolution no. 31). The House approved the conference reports on June 13 (*Cong. Record, 71st Cong., 2nd Sess.,* 1929–1930, pp. 10691–10848), and the act (*H. R. 2667*) was signed by the President on June 17, 1930. For the act as it was approved by the President see *U. S. Statutes at Large,* 1930, Part I, pp. 590–763.

The vote, including "live pairs," was yeas 245, nays 176, not voting 14, total 435. The vote by states is shown in the following table:

TABLE 43
SMOOT-HAWLEY TARIFF ACT, 1930

STATE	YEAS	NAYS	NOT VOTING	TOTAL VOTES
Alabama		10		10
Arizona		1		1
Arkansas		7		7
California	9	1	1	11
Colorado	4			4
Connecticut	4		1	5
Delaware	1			1
Florida	3		1	4
Georgia		12		12
Idaho	2			2
Illinois	18	6	3	27
Indiana	10	3		13
Iowa	10	1		11
Kansas	5	3		8
Kentucky	7	4		11
Louisiana	7	1		8
Maine	4			4
Maryland	1	4	1	6
Massachusetts	13	3		16
Michigan	12		1	13
Minnesota	2	8		10
Mississippi		8		8
Missouri	9	7		16
Montana	1	1		2
Nebraska	4	2		6
Nevada	1			1
New Hampshire	2			2
New Jersey	9	2	1	12
New Mexico	1			1
New York	18	25		43
North Carolina	2	8		10
North Dakota	2		1	3
Ohio	18	3	1	22
Oklahoma	2	6		8
Oregon	3			3
Pennsylvania	36			36
Rhode Island	2		1	3
South Carolina		7		7
South Dakota	1	2		3
Tennessee	2	8		10
Texas	2	16		18
Utah	1		1	2
Vermont	2			2
Virginia	3	7		10
Washington	5			5
West Virginia	4	1	1	6
Wisconsin	2	9		11
Wyoming	1			1
Total	245	176	14	435

The representatives of the Seventy-first Congress were elected under the same laws as those of the Sixty-sixth (see p. 123, above).

The following votes are not shown: a nay from a Boston district (12th Mass.), a nay from a Buffalo district (42nd N. Y.), three nays from Chicago districts (4th, 5th, and 8th Ill.), a yea from a New York City district (25th N. Y.), a nay from a St. Louis district (11th Mo.), and a nay from a San Francisco district (5th Cal.).

There were vacancies in the following districts: Connecticut (5th), Illinois (15th and 24th), Rhode Island (3rd), Utah (2nd), West Virginia (4th). The non-voting area in southern Ohio (1st) is the district of Nicholas Longworth, speaker of the House.

POLITICAL, SOCIAL, AND EDUCATIONAL REFORMS, 1775-1931

[PLATES 123-132]

THE maps in this section illustrate the progress of some of the more important political, social, and educational reform movements in American history as effected primarily through legislation enacted by state governments. The following movements are covered: (1) abolition of slavery, 1777-1865; (2) property qualifications for suffrage, 1775-1920; (3) woman suffrage, 1838-1920; (4) prohibition, 1845-1920; (5) public elementary and secondary school education, 1852-1930; and (6) labor legislation, 1883-1931.

When changes affecting the classification were made during the year given in a title, conditions as they existed at the close of the year are illustrated. Areas for which there was no legislation are left blank.

Abolition of Slavery, 1800-1865

[PLATES 123 and 124A]

These six maps illustrate the abolition of slavery, which began in 1777 with the prohibitory clause in the Vermont constitution of that date, and ended on December 18, 1865, with the proclamation of the Secretary of State declaring that the Thirteenth Amendment had become a part of the Constitution of the United States.

Measures respecting abolition were passed by the states, the territories, or the federal government and were embodied in constitutions, statutes, ordinances, proclamations, or amendments. They provided for unconditional abolition, gradual abolition, or reference of the question of slavery to territories for decision. The legislation providing for gradual abolition deprived slavery of its hereditary element by freeing the children of slave mothers at specified ages or on specified dates.

The states and territories in which slavery was abolished or prohibited are designated "free" and are colored blue. The states and territories in which slavery was not abolished or prohibited are designated "slave" and are colored yellow. The states which were under a scheme of gradual abolition are colored green; and the territories to which the federal government left the decision in respect to slavery are shaded. The dates on the maps are those on which states or territories became "free."

The classification of a state as "free" means that slavery had been abolished in it. Since abolition might not be strictly enforced, might be evaded, or might be inapplicable to excepted classes of slaves, such a state often contained a few slaves. The Emancipation Proclamation of 1863 did not immediately do away with slavery in the states or parts of states to which it applied.

The maps are based chiefly on information derived from federal statutes and state constitutions.

Abolition of Slavery, 1800 [*Plate 123A*]. This map illustrates the early progress of the abolition movement within the original territory of the United States. Slavery in Vermont was abolished by the Vermont declaration of rights of 1777 (*Vermont Const. of 1777*, Ch. 1, Art. 1); in Massachusetts (which included Maine) by the Massachusetts declaration of rights of 1780 as interpreted by the courts of the state in 1781-1783 (*Massachusetts Const. of 1780*, Part I, Art. 1; G. H. Moore, *Notes on the History of Slavery in Massachusetts*, New York, 1866, pp. 210-215). The Maine declaration of rights of 1820 contains a clause similar to that of Massachusetts (*Maine Const. of 1820*, Art. 1, sect. 1). In New Hampshire slavery was abolished by the New Hampshire bill of rights of 1783 (*New Hampshire Const. of 1783*, Part I, Arts. 1 and 2; *New Hampshire State Papers*, Vol. 9, Concord, 1875, pp. 896-898). Gradual abolition acts were passed by Pennsylvania in 1780 (*Pennsylvania Statutes at Large*, Vol. 10, Harrisburg, 1904, pp. 67-73), by Connecticut and Rhode Island in 1784 (G. M. Stroud, *Sketch of Laws relating to Slavery in the Several States*, Philadelphia, 1827, p. 137), and by New York in 1799 (*New York Laws*, Mar. 29, 1799, Ch. 62). Slavery was prohibited in the Northwest Territory by the Ordinance of 1787 (*Ordinance of 1787*, Art. 6).

Abolition of Slavery, 1820 [*Plate 123B*]. This map illustrates the status of abolition after the passage of the Missouri Compromise of 1820, which prohibited slavery north of the parallel of 36° 30', with the exception of the state of Missouri (*U. S. Statutes at Large*, Vol. 3, Boston, 1846, p. 548). In 1804 New Jersey passed a gradual abolition act (*New Jersey Laws*, Feb. 14, 1804, Ch. 103). The Ohio constitution of 1802 (Art. 8, sect. 2) and the Indiana constitution of 1816 (Art. 11, sect. 7) contain the provision prohibiting slavery found in the Ordinance of 1787. The Illinois constitution of 1818 (Art. 6, sect. 1) does not contain this provision, but contains another forbidding slavery "hereafter."

Abolition of Slavery, 1850 [*Plate 123C*]. The principal measures dealing with slavery between 1821 and 1850 were the act of 1848 establishing the territorial government of Oregon, which imposed upon that territory the prohibition of slavery found in the Ordinance of 1787 (*U. S. Statutes at Large*, Vol. 9, Boston, 1851, p. 329; a constitution for a provisional government of Oregon adopted in 1843 prohibited slavery—G. P. Garrison, *Westward Extension* (American Nation Series, Vol. 17), New York, 1906, p. 166), and the compromise acts of 1850, which admitted California as a free state, reduced the area of Texas, and left to the new territories of Utah and New Mexico the decision as to whether they should become slave or free states (*U. S. Statutes at Large*, Vol. 9, Boston, 1851, pp. 446, 447, 452, and 453). A constitution adopted by New Mexico in 1850 prohibited slavery (H. H. Bancroft, *Arizona and New Mexico*, San Francisco, 1888, p. 447). Slavery was prohibited by the Michigan constitution of 1835 (Art. 11), the Iowa constitution of 1846 (Art. 1., sect. 23), the Wisconsin constitution of 1848 (Art. 1, sect. 2), and the California constitution of 1849 (Art. 1, sect. 18). In accordance with an act passed by New York in 1817, slavery came to an end in that state in 1827 (*New York Laws*, Mar. 31, 1817, Ch. 137). Slavery was abolished in Rhode Island in 1842 (*Rhode Island Const. of 1842*, Art. 1, sect. 4), in New Jersey in 1846 (*Revised Statutes of New Jersey*, Trenton, 1847, p. 382; under this statute the "slaves" became "apprentices"; the censuses of 1850 and 1860, however, list them as "slaves"—H. S Cooley, *A Study of Slavery in New Jersey*, Trenton, 1847, p. 31), and in Connecticut in 1848 (*Connecticut Public Acts*, June 12, 1848, Ch. 79). In 1845 slavery was prohibited in the part of Texas that lay northward of the line of 36° 30'—the Missouri Compromise line (*U. S. Statutes at Large*, Vol. 5, Boston, 1848, p. 798). After the compromise legislation of 1850 this prohibition applied only to three small areas bordering on Utah and New Mexico territories, the locations of which are roughly indicated on the map by the three "1845's." Since Pennsylvania had no slaves according to the census of 1850, that state is classified as "free," having become such between 1840 and 1850 under the operation of the gradual abolition act of 1780. Pennsylvania had sixty-four slaves according to the census of 1840 (*Population and Social Statistics*, Ninth Census, Vol. 1, p. 59).

Abolition of Slavery, 1854 [*Plate 123D*]. This map illustrates the status of abolition after the passage of the Kansas-Nebraska Act of 1854, which repealed the Missouri Compromise of 1820 and left the decision respecting slavery in Kansas and Nebraska to those territories (*U. S. Statutes at Large*, Vol. 10, Boston, 1855, pp. 283 and 284).

Abolition of Slavery, 1863 [*Plate 123E*]. The most important changes respecting abolition between 1854 and 1863 were two. The first was effected by the act of 1862, forbidding slavery in the territories (Washington, Idaho, Dakota, Nebraska, Nevada, Utah, Colorado, and New Mexico) (*U. S. Statutes at Large*, Vol. 12, Boston, 1863, p. 432). This act did not apply to the Indian Territory. This was the view taken in the Senate when the act was on its passage through that body (*Congressional Globe, 37th Cong., 2nd Sess.*, 1861-1862, p. 2618). The second and most important change was effected by the Emancipation Proclamation of 1863, which freed the slaves in Alabama, Arkansas, Florida, Georgia, Mississippi, North Carolina, South Carolina, Texas, and the larger parts of Louisiana and Virginia (*U. S. Statutes at Large*, Vol. 12, pp. 1268-1269). Kansas Territory prohibited slavery in 1859 (*Kansas Const. of 1859*, Bill of Rights, sect. 6). The Minnesota constitution of 1857 (Art. 1, sect. 2) prohibited slavery. An act of Congress of 1863 to provide a temporary government for Arizona forbade slavery (*U. S. Statutes at Large*, Vol. 12, p. 665). In 1859 New Mexico passed an "act to provide for the protection of slaves in this territory" (*New Mexico Laws, 1858-1859*, pp. 64-80, Ch. 26). Nebraska Territory prohibited slavery in 1861 (*Laws of Nebraska, 1860–1861*, pp. 43–44). This act was passed over the governor's veto. A similar act was vetoed by the governor in 1860. In 1862 an act of Congress abolished slavery in the District of Columbia (*U. S. Statutes at Large*, Vol. 12, pp. 376–378). In 1863 West Virginia and Missouri provided for the gradual abolition of slavery (*W. Va. Const. of 1861–1863*, Art. 11, sect. 7; H. A. Trexler, *Slavery in Missouri, 1804–1865*, Baltimore, 1872, 1914, pp. 236–237).

The date 1862, the year that slavery was forbidden in the territories, is given on the maps as the date that Dakota, Idaho, and Colorado became "free," although large parts of this territory are covered by the prohibitions of the Missouri Compromise of 1820, by the act of 1848 establishing Oregon, by the abolition clause of the Kansas constitution of 1859, and by the abolition statute of Nebraska of 1861.

Abolition of Slavery, 1865 [*Plate 124A*]. The abolition of slavery was completed on December 18, 1865, when the Thirteenth Amendment went into effect (*U. S. Statutes at Large*, Vol. 13, Boston, 1866, pp. 774–775). In 1864 Louisiana and Virginia abolished slavery, making "free" the areas not covered by the Emancipation Proclamation (*Louisiana Const. of 1864*, Title 1, Art. 1; *Virginia Const. of 1864*, Art. 4, sect. 19). Six other states to which the Emancipation Proclamation applied abolished or prohibited slavery before December 18, 1865: Arkansas (*Const. of 1864*, Art. 5, sect. 1), Alabama (*Const. of 1865*, Art. 1, sect. 34), Florida (*Const. of 1865*, Art. 16, sect. 1), Georgia (*Const. of 1865*, Art. 1, sect. 20), Mississippi (*Amend. to Const.*, Art. 8, ratified Aug. 21, 1865), North Carolina (*Ordinance*, ratified Oct. 9, 1865), and South Carolina (*Const. of 1865*, Art. 9, sect. 11). The Texas constitution of 1866 (Art. 8, sect. 1) and the Nevada constitution of 1864 (Art. 1, sect. 17) prohibited slavery.

Slavery was abolished in 1864 by Maryland (*Maryland Const. of 1864*, Declaration of Rights, Art. 24). In 1865 Missouri, Tennessee, and West Virginia abolished slavery (*Missouri Const. of 1865*, Art. 1, sect. 2; *Amendment to Tennessee Const.*, ratified Feb. 22, 1865; *West Virginia Laws*, Feb. 3, 1865, Ch. 10). When the Thirteenth Amendment went into effect slavery was legal only in Delaware, Kentucky, and the Indian Territory. In 1866 representatives of each of the Five Civilized Tribes negotiated treaties with the federal government abolishing slavery within their respective tribes (*U. S. Statutes at Large*, Vol. 14, Boston, 1868, pp. 756, 769, 786, and 801). In 1863 the Cherokee National Council passed an act abolishing slavery (*ibid.*, p. 801).

Property Qualifications for Suffrage, 1775–1920

[PLATES 124B–126B]

This series of maps illustrates property qualifications for suffrage during the years 1775–1920. The map for 1775 illustrates property qualifications at the beginning of the Revolutionary War. A map for an earlier date would not differ essentially from this one, since the rule during the colonial period was to base voting on property qualifications. The map for 1800 illustrates property qualifications a few years after the close of the Revolution. The dates of the four remaining maps are at intervals of thirty years. The series shows first the discontinuance of property qualifications and later their restoration in the Southern states as a means of restricting the voting of the negro. The series also illustrates tax-paying qualifications.

As a rule the property qualifications of electors for all offices in a given state are uniform. In cases where they are not so the qualifications of electors for the lower house of the state legislature are mapped, since these are most representative of the election laws of a state. Exceptions under the general election laws are disregarded.

The states colored blue have no property qualifications. Those colored yellow have property qualifications without an alternative thereto. Those colored green have property qualifications with an alternative thereto. Alternative qualifications may be of a tax-paying, educational, residential, or other character. The dates on the maps are those on which property qualifications were discontinued.

States marked "T" have tax-paying qualifications. Such qualifications are usually required in states that have no property qualifications, as a less severe requirement, but they may be required in addition to property qualification or as an alternative thereto. The taxes required may be either poll or property taxes. In recent years they are chiefly poll taxes. The amount required is usually a small sum, such as one or two dollars.

Information for the colonial period was derived chiefly from A. E. McKinley, *The Suffrage Franchise in the Thirteen English Colonies in America*, Philadelphia, 1905. For the later period large use was made of state constitutions, statutes, and election laws. Use was also made of the well known compilations of charters and constitutions made by

Poore and by Thorpe, and of the compilation made by L. C. Kendrick and H. P. Salisbury, *General Constitutional and Statutory Provisions Relative to Suffrage*, Providence, 1912.

Property Qualifications for Suffrage, 1775 [*Plate 124B*]. In 1775 all the colonies based the exercise of the suffrage on the ownership of property (A. E. McKinley, *op. cit.*, pp. 41, 70–74, 111, 120, 162, 172, 211–212, 254–255, 270, 282–283, 354–355, 377, 413–414, and 461). South Carolina, however, prescribed as an alternative to the possession of a freehold estate the payment of a tax of ten shillings (Cooper, *Statutes at Large of South Carolina*, Vol. 4, Columbia, 1838, p. 99). While the property qualifications varied, the most usual ones were the possession of fifty acres of land or of other property worth forty pounds. Possession of land valued at forty pounds or land yielding forty shillings annual income were not unusual. (A summary of the property qualifications in 1775 will be found in K. H. Porter, *History of Suffrage in the United States*, Chicago, 1918, p. 12.)

On the map for 1775 the western territory, which was claimed by several of the colonies, is cut off arbitrarily from the eastern colonies. In 1775 Vermont, which was claimed by both New York and New Hampshire, was not organized.

Property Qualifications for Suffrage, 1800 [*Plate 124C*]. Property qualifications were discontinued by Pennsylvania and North Carolina in 1776, by New Hampshire in 1784, by Georgia in 1789, and by Delaware in 1792 (*Pennsylvania Const. of 1776*, sect. 6; *North Carolina Const. of 1776*, sect. 8; "New Hampshire Constitution of 1784," in B. P. Poore, *Charters and Constitutions*, Washington, 1878, pp. 1284 and 1286; *Georgia Const. of 1789*, Art. 4, sect. 1; *Delaware Const. of 1792*, Art. 4, sect. 1). The North Carolina constitution of 1776, which did not require the electors of members of the lower house to possess property, required the electors of state senators to possess fifty acres of land (sect. 7). This qualification was not discontinued until 1856 (F. N. Thorpe, *Charters and Constitutions*, Washington, 1909, Vol. 5, p. 2799). Vermont came into the Union in 1791, and Kentucky in 1792, without property qualifications for suffrage (*Vermont Const. of 1793*, Ch. 2, sect. 21; *Kentucky Const. of 1792*, Art. 3). The Vermont constitution of 1777 contained no property qualifications (Ch. 2, sect. 6). The part of Virginia that became the state of Kentucky in 1792 possessed property qualifications previous to that date. The New York constitution of 1777 stipulated, as an alternative to the possession of a freehold of the value of twenty pounds, the renting of a tenement of the yearly value of forty shillings and the paying of taxes. These were the qualifications for the electors of state representatives. The electors of state senators were required to possess a freehold of the value of one hundred pounds (*New York Const. of 1777*, sects. 7 and 10). The Tennessee constitution of 1796 required voters to possess a freehold (*Tennessee Const. of 1796*, Art. 3, sect. 1). In the three territories (Indiana, Mississippi, and the Territory Northwest of the River Ohio) the possession of fifty acres of land was necessary to qualify one for voting (*Ordinance of 1787*, sect. 9; *U. S. Statutes at Large*, Vol. 2, Boston, 1845, p. 59; Dunbar Rowland, *Mississippi Territorial Archives*, Vol. 1, Nashville, 1905, p. 254). There were tax-paying qualifications in Delaware, Georgia, New York, North Carolina, Pennsylvania, and South Carolina (Poore, *op. cit.*, Vol. 1, pp. 283 and 394; Vol. 2, pp. 1334, 1411, 1560, and 1628). There were also tax-paying qualifications in New Hampshire in 1784–1792 and in Georgia in 1777–1789 (*ibid.*, Vol. 1, p. 379; Vol. 2, pp. 1285–1286).

Property Qualifications for Suffrage, 1830 [*Plate 125A*]. Maryland discontinued property qualifications in 1810, and Massachusetts and New York in 1821 (*Amendment of 1810 to Maryland Const. of 1776*, Art. 14; *New York Const. of 1821*, Art. 2, sect. 1; *Amendment of 1821 to Massachusetts Const. of 1780*, Art. 3). In 1818 Connecticut and in 1830 Virginia adopted alternatives to property qualifications. In Connecticut the alternative was the payment of a state tax (*Connecticut Const. of 1818*, Art. 6, sect 2). In Virginia the alternative was the same but applied only to a housekeeper and head of a family (*Virginia Const. of 1830*, Art. 3, sect. 14). Ohio in 1803, Louisiana in 1812, Mississippi in 1817, Alabama in 1819, and Missouri in 1821 were admitted into the Union without property qualifications (*Ohio Const. of 1802*, Art. 4, sect. 1; *Louisiana Const. of 1812*, Art. 2, sect. 8; *Mississippi Const. of 1817*, Art. 3, sect. 1; *Alabama Const. of 1819*, Art. 3, sect. 5; *Missouri Const. of 1820*, Art. 3, sect. 10). There was a property qualification in Orleans Territory (*Orleans Territory Laws*, 1806, p. 82). Such qualifications were discontinued in Indiana Territory in 1811, Illinois Territory in 1812, and Michigan Territory in 1819 (*U. S. Statutes at Large*, Vol. 2, Boston, 1845, pp. 659 and 741; Vol. 3, 1846, pp. 483 and 769). Arkansas was organized in 1819 without property qualifications (B. P. Poore, *Charters and Constitutions*, Washington, 1878, Vol. 1, p. 100; Vol. 2, p.

1098). Florida did not require voters to possess property (*Florida Laws*, 1822–1825, p. 154; 1828, p. 256). Between 1801 and 1830 tax-paying was made a requisite for voting in Arkansas, Connecticut, Louisiana, Massachusetts, Michigan, Mississippi, Ohio, and Virginia (Poore, *op. cit.*, Vol. 1, pp. 100, 263, 701, and 973; Vol. 2, pp. 1056, 1459, and 1917; *U. S. Statutes at Large*, Vol. 3, 1846, pp. 483 and 769). Indiana had a tax-paying qualification in 1811–1816, Illinois in 1812–1818, and Missouri in 1812–1820 (*ibid.*, Vol. 2, 1845, pp. 659 and 741; Poore, *op. cit.*, Vol. 1, pp. 442 and 507; Vol. 2, pp. 1098 and 1106). In 1810 South Carolina and in 1826 New York discontinued tax-paying requirements (*ibid.*, Vol. 2, pp. 1350 and 1635). From 1810 to 1865 the alternative in South Carolina to property qualifications was six months' residence in an election district.

Property Qualifications for Suffrage, 1860 [*Plate 125B*]. Between 1831 and 1860 property qualifications were discontinued by Connecticut, New Jersey, Virginia, and Tennessee (*Amendment of 1845 to Connecticut Const. of 1818*, Art. 8; *New Jersey Const. of 1844*, Art. 2, sect. 1; *Virginia Const. of 1850*, Art. 3, sect. 1; *Tennessee Const. of 1834*, Art. 4, sect. 1), and tax-paying qualifications by Arkansas, Connecticut, Louisiana, Michigan, Mississippi, Ohio, and Virginia (Poore, *op. cit.*, Vol. 1, pp. 104, 267, 713, and 984; Vol. 2, pp. 1069, 1472, and 1922). In the new states and territories of California, Iowa, Kansas, Minnesota, Nebraska, New Mexico, Oregon, Texas, Utah, and Washington neither property nor tax-paying qualifications were required (*ibid.*, Vol. 1, pp. 196, 554, and 636; Vol. 2, pp. 1023 and 1493; *Nebraska Laws*, 1855, p. 176; *New Mexico Laws*, 1851, p. 200; *Utah Acts*, 1851–1852, p. 107; *Washington Laws*, 1854, p. 64). In 1842 Rhode Island adopted a residential and tax-paying qualification as an alternative to the possession of real estate worth one hundred and thirty-four dollars or renting for seven dollars a year (*Rhode Island Const. of 1842*, Art. 2, sects. 1 and 2). The alternative did not apply to foreign-born citizens.

Property Qualifications for Suffrage, 1890 [*Plate 126A*]. In 1865 South Carolina discontinued property qualifications for suffrage (*South Carolina Const. of 1865*, Art. 4). Between 1861 and 1890 the new states and territories of Arizona, Colorado, Idaho, Montana, Nevada, North Dakota, Oklahoma, South Dakota, and Wyoming made neither the possession of property nor the payment of taxes a requisite for the exercise of the suffrage (*Arizona Revised Statutes*, 1887, p. 31; F. N. Thorpe, *Charters and Constitutions*, Vol. 1, p. 492; Vol. 2, p. 907; Vol. 4, pp. 2321 and 2404; Vol. 5, pp. 2868 and 2942; Vol. 6, p. 3372; Vol. 7, p. 4132). North Carolina in 1868 and Rhode Island in 1888 discontinued their tax-paying requirements (*ibid.*, Vol. 5, p. 2814; Vol. 6, p. 3236). The alternative to the property qualification in Rhode Island was a residential one. There was a tax-paying requirement for some of the local elections. Florida in 1889, Mississippi in 1890, and Tennessee and Virginia in 1870 established tax-paying requirements (*Florida Laws*, 1889, p. 13; Thorpe, *op. cit.*, Vol. 4, p. 2120; Vol. 6, p. 3460; Vol. 7, pp. 3901–3902). Virginia had a tax-paying requirement in 1864–1870 (Poore, *op. cit.*, Vol. 2, pp. 1939 and 1955).

Property Qualifications for Suffrage, 1920 [*Plate 126B*]. During 1891–1920 Alabama, Georgia, Louisiana, South Carolina, and Virginia established a small property qualification as an alternative to educational and other qualifications (*Alabama Const. of 1901*, Art. 8, sect. 181; *Amendment of 1908 to Georgia Const. of 1877*, Art. 2, sect. 1; *Louisiana Const. of 1898*, Art. 197, sect. 4; *South Carolina Const. of 1895*, Art. 2, sect. 4; *Virginia Const. of 1902*, Art. 2, sect. 19). Tax-paying qualifications were established in Alabama, Arkansas, Louisiana, North Carolina, South Carolina, and Texas (F. N. Thorpe, *Charters and Constitutions*, Washington, 1909, Vol. 1, pp. 209 and 373; Vol. 3, pp. 1563–1564; Vol. 6, p. 3310; *North Carolina Laws*, 1901, p. 247; *Texas Laws*, 1903, p. 133). Massachusetts discontinued tax-paying requirements in 1891, and Delaware in 1897 (Thorpe, *op. cit.*, Vol. 1, p. 620; Vol. 3, pp. 1921 and 1923).

Woman Suffrage, 1875–1920

[PLATES 126C–128A]

This series illustrates the movement for woman suffrage, which began with the granting by Kentucky of school suffrage to women in 1838 and ended with the adoption of the Nineteenth Amendment in 1920. The dates chosen for mapping, with the exception of 1920, are those that are best adapted to illustrate the granting of full state suffrage to women. The map for 1920 illustrates the culmination of the national movement for woman suffrage.

The states (or territories) colored blue have full suffrage, those colored green have partial suffrage, and those colored yellow have no suffrage.

In the states colored green and marked "Pr" the women have, in addition to other forms of suffrage, the Presidential suffrage, that is, the right to vote for Presidential electors. Before 1915 "partial suffrage" was generally school suffrage. In a few cases small local grants of suffrage (some of which are specified below) were disregarded. The dates are those on which full suffrage went into effect.

The chief sources of information are the statutes and constitutions of the states and territories. Use was also made of Bertha Rembaugh's *Political Status of Women in the United States*, New York and London, 1911; *History of Woman Suffrage*, edited by E. C. Stanton and others, New York, 1902, 1922, Vols. 4 and 6; and the *American Year Book* for 1919, pp. 227–229.

Woman Suffrage, 1875 [*Plate 126C*]. Full suffrage was granted to women in Wyoming in 1869 and in Utah in 1870 (*Wyoming Laws*, Dec. 10, 1869, Ch. 31; *Utah Laws*, 1870, p. 8). Between 1838 and 1875 limited school suffrage was granted to women by eight states or territories. These, with the date of the initial law, were as follows: Kentucky 1838, Washington 1854, Kansas 1861, Oregon 1864, Idaho and Michigan 1867, Nebraska 1869, and Indiana 1873 (*Kentucky Laws*, Feb. 16, 1838, Ch. 898; *Washington Laws*, 1854, p. 325; *Kansas Laws*, 1861, p. 261; *Oregon General Laws*, 1845–1864, p. 641; *Idaho Laws*, 1866–1867, p. 24; *Michigan Laws*, Mar. 26, 1867, No. 110; *Nebraska Laws*, 1869, p. 119; *Indiana Laws*, 1873, p. 73).

Woman Suffrage, 1900 [*Plate 126D*]. During the period 1876–1900 two states granted full suffrage to women—Colorado in 1893 and Idaho in 1896 (*Colorado Laws*, Apr. 7, 1893, Ch. 83; *Proclamation of Governor D. H. Waite*, Dec. 2, 1893; *Amendment of 1896 to Idaho Const.*, Art. 6, sect. 2). The *Colorado Constitution of 1876* granted school suffrage to women (Art. 7, sect. 1). The women of Utah were deprived of the vote by the federal government in 1887. Utah entered the Union as a full suffrage state in 1896 (*U. S. Statutes at Large*, Vol. 24, 1887, p. 639; *Utah Const. of 1895*, Art. 4, Sect. 1). Between 1876 and 1900 eighteen states or territories granted women full or limited (usually limited) school suffrage. These, with dates of the grant, are as follows: Minnesota and Texas 1876, Mississippi and New Hampshire 1878, Dakota and Massachusetts 1879, New York and Vermont 1880, Montana 1883, Wisconsin 1885, Arizona and New Jersey 1887, Oklahoma 1890, Illinois 1891, Connecticut 1893, Iowa and Ohio, 1894, and Delaware 1898 (*Minnesota Laws*, Mar. 1, 1876, Ch. 14; *Texas Const. of 1876*, Art. 11, sect. 10; *Amendment of 1883 to Texas Const.*, Art. 7, sect. 3; *Mississippi Laws*, 1878, p. 102; *New Hampshire Laws*, Aug. 13, 1878, Ch. 46; *Dakota Laws*, 1879, p. 33; *Massachusetts Acts*, Apr. 16, 1879, Ch. 223; *New York Laws*, Feb. 12, 1880, Ch. 9; *Vermont Laws*, Dec. 18, 1880, No. 103; *Montana Laws*, 1883, p. 54; *Wisconsin Laws*, Apr. 1, 1885, Ch. 211; *Arizona Revised Statutes*, 1887, pp. 279–280; *New Jersey Laws*, 1887, p. 149; *Oklahoma Laws*, 1893, p. 1085; *Illinois Laws*, 1891, p. 135; *Connecticut Acts*, 1893, p. 151; *Iowa Laws*, Apr. 13, 1894, Ch. 39; *Ohio Laws*, 1894, p. 182; *Delaware Laws*, 1898, pp. 179–180). In 1898 the tax-paying women of Louisiana were granted limited voting rights (*Louisiana Const. of 1898*, Art. 199). In Delaware, Iowa, Montana, and New York some of the women were given the right to vote in respect to matters involving taxes or finance (*History of Woman Suffrage*, New York, 1902, 1922, Vol. 4, pp. 566 and 869; *Iowa Laws*, Apr. 13, 1894, Ch. 39; *Montana Const. of 1889*, Art. 9, sect. 12). In 1900 the women of Annapolis, Md., were given the right to vote on the question of issuing bonds (*Maryland Laws*, Apr. 7, 1900, Ch. 188).

Woman Suffrage, 1915 [*Plate 127A*]. During the years 1901–1909 there was relatively little change in the suffrage privileges granted to women. Between 1910 and 1914 seven states adopted constitutional amendments granting full suffrage to women—Washington in 1910, California in 1911, Arizona, Kansas, and Oregon in 1912, and Montana and Nevada in 1914 (*Washington Const.*, Art. 6, sect. 1; *California Const.*, Art. 2, sect. 1; *Kansas Const.*, Art. 5, sect. 8; *Arizona Const.*, Art. 7, sect. 2; *Oregon Const.*, Art. 2, sect. 2; *Montana Const.*, Art. 9, sect. 2; *Nevada Const.*, Art. 2, sect. 1; *Amer. Year Book*, 1915, p. 82). In 1913 the women of Illinois were granted the right to vote for Presidential electors and for many state, county, and municipal officers (*Illinois Laws*, 1913, p. 333). In 1910 New Mexico gave conditionally to women the suffrage at school elections (*New Mexico Const. of 1910*, Art. 7, sect. 1). In 1908 the women of Still Pond, Md., were given municipal suffrage (*Maryland Laws*, 1908, p. 893), and in 1911 the women of Wrightsville Beach, N. C., were given the right to vote on a bond issue (*North Carolina Private Laws*, Mar. 6, 1911, Ch. 393).

Woman Suffrage, 1919 [*Plate 127B*]. During the years 1916–1919 four states adopted constitutional amendments granting full suffrage to women—New York in 1917, and Michigan, Oklahoma, and South Dakota in 1918 (*New York Const.*, Art. 2, sect. 1; *Michigan Const.*, Art. 3, sect. 1; *Oklahoma Const.*, Art. 3, sect. 1; *South Dakota Const.*, Art. 7, sect. 1; *Amer. Year Book*, 1919, p. 229). In many states women were granted additional suffrage rights, and in eleven states they were granted a vote for Presidential electors—an important step in the direction of full suffrage. These eleven states, with the date of the grant, were as follows: Nebraska, North Dakota, and Rhode Island, 1917; and Indiana, Iowa, Maine, Minnesota, Missouri, Ohio, Tennessee, and Wisconsin, 1919 (*Nebraska Laws*, Apr. 21, 1917, Ch. 30; *North Dakota Laws*, Jan. 23, 1917, Ch. 254; *Rhode Island Acts*, Apr. 18, 1917, Ch. 1507; *Indiana Laws*, Feb. 6, 1919, Ch. 2; *Iowa Laws*, Apr. 25, 1919, Ch. 353; *Maine Laws*, Mar. 28, 1919, Ch. 120; *Minnesota Laws*, Mar. 24, 1919, Ch. 89; *Missouri Laws*, 1919, p. 335; *Ohio Laws*, 1919, Part I, p. 699; *Tennessee Laws*, Apr. 17, 1919, Ch. 139; *Wisconsin Laws*, Feb. 28, 1919, Ch. 5). Arkansas in 1917 and Texas in 1918 gave women the right to vote at primary elections (*Arkansas Laws*, Mar. 6, 1917, No. 186; *Texas Laws*, Mar. 26, 1918, Ch. 34). Between 1915 and 1920 sixteen Florida towns received charters granting women municipal suffrage (*History of Woman Suffrage*, New York, Vol. 6, 1922, p. 120). The white women of Atlanta, Ga., voted in the city primaries in April, 1919 (*ibid.*, p. 138).

Woman Suffrage, 1920 [*Plate 128A*]. On June 5, 1919, a joint resolution of Congress proposing an amendment to the Constitution extending the right of suffrage to women was deposited in the Department of State; and on August 26, 1920, Secretary of State Colby declared that the amendment had been ratified by three fourths of the states and had become a part of the Constitution (*U. S. Statutes at Large*, Vol. 41, 1921, Part I, p. 362; Part II, p. 1823; see p. 123, above). The amendment was ratified by all but the following ten states: Alabama, Delaware, Florida, Georgia, Louisiana, Maryland, Mississippi, North Carolina, South Carolina, and Virginia. By this amendment the women of the following thirty-three states received full suffrage: Alabama, Arkansas, Connecticut, Delaware, Florida, Georgia, Illinois, Indiana, Iowa, Kentucky, Louisiana, Maine, Maryland, Massachusetts, Minnesota, Mississippi, Missouri, Nebraska, New Hampshire, New Jersey, New Mexico, North Carolina, North Dakota, Ohio, Pennsylvania, Rhode Island, South Carolina, Tennessee, Texas, Vermont, Virginia, West Virginia, and Wisconsin.

Prohibition, 1845–1920

[PLATES 128B–131A]

This series of maps illustrates the movement for the prohibition of the sale and manufacture of intoxicating liquors, which began about the middle of the nineteenth century, when a considerable number of states adopted state-wide prohibition, and which ended in 1920, when the Eighteenth Amendment went into effect. The dates chosen for mapping, with the exception of 1920, are those which best show the advance and recession of the movement for state-wide prohibition. The map for 1920 illustrates the culmination of the movement for national prohibition.

The "dry states," which are colored blue, have state-wide, or national, prohibition. The states of local prohibition, which are colored green, are the states that have local option laws or that have attained local prohibition through other laws granting or permitting it. The "wet states," which are colored yellow, do not have state-wide, national, or local prohibition. The dates on the maps are those on which state-wide, or national, prohibition went into effect. The term "state-wide" is used to cover states, territories (organized and unorganized), and the District of Columbia.

The usual, or typical, state-wide prohibitory law or amendment prohibited the sale and manufacture of intoxicating liquors as a beverage. Some of the earlier laws, however, were less inclusive. Thus, the Connecticut law of 1854 excepted from its provisions sales of five gallons or more of domestic cider or wine by the maker when sold to be taken away at one time (*Connecticut Acts*, June 22, 1854, Ch. 57). Local prohibition was usually obtained through local option laws. Sometimes, however, it was obtained through local laws and sometimes through the action of local authorities empowered by law to grant or withhold licenses. A state might obtain local prohibition through more than one of these methods, or it might by successive laws extend or change its application of the principle of local option. The passage of a local option law was regarded as conclusive that the state had local prohibition. In other cases of local prohibition the number of dry areas was taken into consideration, and when these were negligible the state was classified as "wet."

Information was derived chiefly from the statutes of the states. Considerable use was made of Funk and Wagnalls, *Cyclopaedia of*

Temperance and Prohibition, New York, 1891, pp. 275–360; J. Rowntree and A. Sherwell, *Temperance Problem and Social Reform*, New York, 1891, pp. 255–322; E. H. Cherrington, *Evolution of Prohibition in the United States of America*, Westerville, 1920; and the *Anti-Saloon League Year Book* for 1908, 1911, 1915, and 1919.

Prohibition, 1845 [*Plate 128B*]. In 1845 only Oregon and the "Indian country" were under state-wide prohibition. The Oregon prohibition law was passed in 1844 by the provisional government of that territory (*Oregon Laws*, June 24, 1844; in 1849 the first territorial legislature passed a license act). In 1834 Congress prohibited the sale and manufacture of liquors in the Indian country (*U. S. Statutes at Large*, Vol. 4, Boston, 1846, pp. 732–733). Such "supplies" as should be necessary for the officers and troops of the army might be brought in. Prohibition laws were passed by the Five Civilized Tribes (W. E. Johnson, *Federal Government and the Liquor Traffic*, Westerville, 1911, pp. 217–219). Beginning with 1832 Indiana passed several laws which gave a considerable measure of local prohibition (*Indiana Laws*, 1832, Ch. 170; Funk and Wagnalls, *Cyclopaedia of Temperance and Prohibition*, New York, 1891, pp. 293–294). In 1845 local option laws were passed by Michigan, New York, and Rhode Island (*Michigan Laws*, Mar. 19, 1845, No. 46; *New York Laws*, May 14, 1845, Ch. 300; *Rhode Island Acts*, May, 1845, p. 72). Before 1845 several states had passed and repealed local option laws.

Prohibition, 1855 [*Plate 129A*]. At the close of 1855 ten states and one territory were under state-wide prohibition. These states and the years of the adoption of the prohibitory law were as follows: Maine, 1851; Massachusetts and Vermont, 1852; Rhode Island, 1853; Connecticut, 1854; and Delaware, Iowa, Michigan, New Hampshire, and New York, 1855 (*Maine Acts*, June 2, 1851, Ch. 211; *Massachusetts Acts*, May 22, 1852, Ch. 322; *Vermont Acts*, Nov. 23, 1852, No. 24; *Rhode Island Acts*, Jan., 1853, p. 232; *Connecticut Acts*, June 22, 1854, Ch. 57; *Delaware Laws*, Feb. 27, 1855, Ch. 255; *Iowa Laws*, Jan. 22, 1855, Ch. 45; *Michigan Laws*, Feb. 3, 1855, No. 17; *New Hampshire Laws*, July 14, 1855, Ch. 1658; *New York Laws*, Apr. 9, 1855, Ch. 231). The territory was Nebraska, which passed a prohibitory law in 1855 (*Nebraska Laws*, Mar. 16, 1855). During the years 1851–1855 several states (or territories) passed prohibitory laws which were rendered nugatory by the governor, the courts, or the people.

The following states enacted local option laws: Missouri, 1851; Louisiana, 1852; Illinois, 1853; and Mississippi and Texas, 1854 (*Missouri Laws*, 1850–1851, pp. 216–217; *Louisiana Laws*, Mar. 4, 1852, No. 105; *Illinois Laws*, 1853, p. 91; *Mississippi Laws*, Feb. 17, 1854, Ch. 42; *Texas Laws*, Feb. 11, 1854, Ch. 88). The territory of Kansas enacted a local option law in 1855 (*Kansas Laws*, 1855, Ch. 64).

Maine in 1846, New Hampshire in 1849, and Vermont in 1850 passed less sweeping prohibitory laws than those to which references are given. The Maine law of 1851, the first "regular" prohibitory law, was the model followed by other states.

A state-wide prohibitory law passed by Indiana on February 16, 1855, was declared void by the supreme court of that state at the November term for that year. Illinois had a state-wide prohibitory law during 1851–1853. In 1855 Wisconsin passed a prohibitory law which was vetoed by the governor. A prohibitory law enacted by Minnesota in 1852 failed in a referendum to receive the approval of the people.

Prohibition, 1875 [*Plate 129B*]. At the close of the year 1875 only three states—Maine, New Hampshire, and Vermont—of the ten states that had state-wide prohibition in 1855 still had it. Delaware repealed its prohibitory law in 1857, Rhode Island in 1863, Massachusetts in 1868, Connecticut in 1872, and Michigan in 1875. Nebraska Territory repealed its law in 1858. Iowa largely nullified its law by the "wine and beer" clause of 1858, and the New York court of appeals in 1856 declared the law of that state unconstitutional. Massachusetts in 1869 and Rhode Island in 1874 passed new state-wide prohibitory laws, both of which were repealed in 1875.

Minnesota passed a local option law in 1858, Iowa in 1870, Connecticut in 1872, Arkansas, Kentucky, and North Carolina in 1874, and Rhode Island in 1875 (*Minnesota Laws*, Aug. 12, 1858, Ch. 74; *Iowa Laws*, Apr. 8, 1870, Ch. 82; *Connecticut Acts*, Aug. 1, 1872, Ch. 99; *Arkansas Laws*, May 30, 1874, Ch. 37; *Kentucky Laws*, Jan. 26, 1874, Ch. 117; *North Carolina Laws*, Feb. 16, 1874, Ch. 138; *Rhode Island Acts*, June 25, 1875, Ch. 508). Between 1855 and 1875 Alabama and Georgia obtained a considerable measure of local prohibition by means of local laws. During this period Arkansas and North Carolina also passed many local prohibitory laws (E. H. Cherrington, *Evolution of Prohibition in the United States of America*, pp. 186, 188–190, 192, and 194). In 1856 Texas repealed her local option law of 1854.

Prohibition, 1890 [*Plate 129C*]. Between 1875 and 1890 four new states adopted state-wide prohibition: Kansas in 1881, Iowa in 1884, and North and South Dakota in 1889 (*Kansas Laws*, Feb. 19, 1881, Ch. 128; *Iowa Laws*, Mar. 4, 1884, Ch. 8; *North Dakota Const. of 1889*, Art. 20; *South Dakota Const. of 1889*, Art. 24). Ten states adopted local option: Texas in 1876, Massachusetts in 1881, South Carolina in 1882, Florida and Georgia in 1885, Virginia in 1886, Montana in 1887, Ohio in 1888, and Michigan and Wisconsin in 1889 (*Texas Laws*, June 24, 1876, Ch. 33; *Massachusetts Acts*, Mar. 3, 1881, Ch. 54; *South Carolina Laws*, Feb. 9, 1882, No. 632; *Florida Const. of 1885*, Art. 19; *Georgia Laws*, Sept. 18, 1885, No. 182; *Virginia Laws*, Feb. 26, 1886, Ch. 248; *Montana Compiled Statutes*, 1887, p. 1035; *Ohio Laws*, Mar. 3, 1888, House Bill No. 90; *Michigan Laws*, June 29, 1889, No. 207; *Wisconsin Laws*, Apr. 24, 1889, Ch. 521). Maryland obtained considerable local prohibition through local laws. In Nebraska and West Virginia the local authorities, with whom the granting of licenses was vested, obtained a measure of local prohibition (Funk and Wagnalls, *Cyclopaedia of Temperance and Prohibition*, New York, 1891, p. 310; *Nebraska Laws*, Feb. 28, 1881, Ch. 61; *West Virginia Laws*, 1877, p. 142; *Anti-Saloon League Year Book*, 1908, pp. 182 and 192). Tennessee obtained local prohibition by means of its laws which forbade the sale of liquor within four miles of schools (*Tennessee Laws*, Mar. 20, 1877, Ch. 23; Mar. 26, 1887, Ch. 167). The first legislature of Oklahoma passed a license act (*Oklahoma Laws*, Dec. 25, 1890, Ch. 48; Funk and Wagnalls, *op. cit.*, p. 337).

Prohibition, 1905 [*Plate 129D*]. In 1894 Iowa passed the "mulct law," establishing a system of local option and license instead of prohibition (*Iowa Laws*, Mar. 29, 1894, Ch. 62). In 1896 South Dakota repealed the prohibitory article of its constitution and in the following year passed a license and local option law (*South Dakota Laws*, 1895, Ch. 38; 1897, Ch. 72). In 1903 New Hampshire and Vermont substituted local option for state-wide prohibition (*New Hampshire Laws*, Mar. 27, 1903, Ch. 95; *Vermont Acts*, Dec. 11, 1902, No. 90). Local option went into effect in New York in 1896; in Arizona, 1901; in Oregon, 1904; and in Indiana, 1905 (*New York Laws*, Mar. 23, 1896, Ch. 112; *Arizona Revised Statutes*, 1901, p. 801; *Oregon Laws*, 1905, Ch. 2; *Indiana Laws*, Feb. 15, 1905, Ch. 6).

Prohibition, 1915 [*Plate 130A*]. During the decade 1906–1915 state-wide prohibition went into effect in eight Southern or Southwestern states: Oklahoma in 1907, Georgia in 1908, Mississippi, North Carolina, and Tennessee in 1909, West Virginia in 1914, and Alabama and Arizona in 1915 (*Oklahoma General Statutes*, 1908, pp. 162–163; *Georgia Laws*, Aug. 6, 1907, No. 23; *Mississippi Laws*, Feb. 19, 1908, Ch. 113; *North Carolina Laws*, Jan. 31, 1908, Ch. 71; *Tennessee Laws*, Jan. 21, 1909, Ch. 10; *West Virginia Acts*, 1913, p. 96; *Alabama Laws*, 1915, p. 1; *Arizona Laws*, 1915, p. 1, at end of volume). Alabama was "dry" during the years 1909–1911. Local option laws were passed as follows: Colorado and Delaware in 1907, Idaho and Washington in 1909, California and Utah in 1911, and New Mexico in 1913 (*Delaware Laws*, Mar. 21, 1907, Ch. 65; *Colorado Laws*, Mar. 25, 1907, Ch. 198; *Idaho Laws*, Feb. 20, 1909, Senate Bill No. 62; *Washington Laws*, Mar. 12, 1909, Ch. 81; *California Laws*, Apr. 4, 1911, Ch. 351; *Utah Laws*, 1911, p. 153; *New Mexico Annotated Statutes*, 1915, pp. 857–861). Under a law passed in 1903 Nevada obtained local prohibition through local petitions (*Nevada Laws*, Mar. 10, 1903, Ch. 55). In 1909 Wyoming forbade the sale of liquor outside of incorporated cities and towns (*Wyoming Laws*, Feb. 9, 1909, Ch. 7). By 1905 the local authorities obtained a measure of local prohibition in New Jersey and Pennsylvania (*Anti-Saloon League Year Book*, 1915, pp. 175–176 and 192–193). The District of Columbia is the only "wet" area shown on the map.

Prohibition, 1919 [*Plate 130B*]. During the years 1916–1919 state-wide prohibition went into effect in the District of Columbia (1917—*U. S. Statutes at Large*, Vol. 39, 1917, Part I, p. 1123) and in twenty-one states. These states, with the dates that prohibition became effective, are as follows: Arkansas, Colorado, Idaho, Iowa, Oregon, South Carolina, Virginia, and Washington, 1916; Nebraska, South Dakota, and Utah, 1917; Indiana, Michigan, Montana, Nevada, New Hampshire, New Mexico, and Texas, 1918; and Florida, Ohio, and Wyoming, 1919 (*Arkansas Laws*, Feb. 6, 1915, Art. 30; *Colorado Laws*, Mar. 3, 1915, Ch. 98; *Oregon Laws*, 1915, pp. 12 and 150; *South Carolina Laws*, Feb. 16, 1915, No. 76; *Virginia Acts*, Mar. 10, 1916, Ch. 146; *Washington Laws*, 1915, p. 2; *Nebraska Laws*, Apr. 21, 1917, Ch. 187; *South Dakota Laws*, 1916–1917, p. 488; *Utah Laws*, 1917, p. 152; *Indiana Laws*, Feb. 9, 1917, Ch. 4; *Michigan Laws*, 1917, p. 937; *Montana Laws*, 1917, Ch. 175; *Wyoming Laws*, Feb. 15, 1919, Ch. 25; *Anti-Saloon League Year Book*, 1919, pp. 108, 110, 114, 130, 131, 134, 138, and 149). Kentucky adopted

state-wide prohibition in 1919; which, however, was not to become effective until June 30, 1920 (*World Almanac*, 1920, p. 803). New Jersey adopted a local option law in 1918 (*Anti-Saloon League Year Book*, 1919, p. 132).

Prohibition, 1920 [*Plate 131A*]. The Eighteenth Amendment to the Constitution, which provided for national prohibition, went into effect at midnight of January 16, 1920 (*U. S. Statutes at Large*, Vol. 40, 1919, Part II, p. 1941; *World Almanac*, 1920, p. 787; see p. 122, above). It made prohibition effective in the following sixteen states: California, Connecticut, Delaware, Illinois, Kentucky, Louisiana, Maryland, Massachusetts, Minnesota, Missouri, New Jersey, New York, Pennsylvania, Rhode Island, Vermont, and Wisconsin. Without the amendment prohibition would have become effective in Kentucky on June 30, 1920. All but three states—Connecticut, New Jersey, and Rhode Island—ratified the amendment.

Public Elementary and Secondary Schools, 1852–1930
[PLATE 131B–E]

This series illustrates important phases of the progress of elementary and secondary education, as measured by the sums of money expended on schools, 1870–1928, and as recorded in the passage by the several states of compulsory attendance laws, 1852–1918. The minimum terms of attendance required by law in the different states in 1930 are also shown (map E).

Schools: Expenditures per Capita, 1870–1928 [*Plates 131B–D*]. These three maps show by states the expenditures, per capita of the total population, on public elementary and secondary schools. Maps B and C, for the school years 1870–1871 and 1902–1903 respectively, are based on statistics given in the *Report of the Commissioner of Education for the Year 1903*, Washington, Vol. 1, p. xcvi; and Map D, for 1927–1928, is based on a table in the *Statistical Abstract of the United States, 1930*, Washington, 1931, p. 114. No statistics are given for Arizona Territory and for Indian Territory for 1870–1871, hence these territories are left blank on Map B.

The maps show (1) the expenditures per capita as measured in terms of dollars of the values prevailing at the dates for which each map was drawn. These are the expenditures as actually given in the statistics for the several states and school years. They are indicated by the numbers on each state and by the varying values of the symbols as shown in the legend of each map.

The maps also show (2) the same expenditures as measured in terms of dollars of the value prevailing in 1870–1871. Fourteen symbols appear on the three maps, ranging from widely spaced dots to solid black. These express expenditures per capita in terms of dollars of 1870–1871 as follows: (1) less than $0.50, (2) 0.50–1.00, (3) 1.00–1.50, (4) 1.50–2.00, (5) 2.00–2.50, (6) 2.50–3.00, (7) 3.00–4.00, (8) 4.00–5.00, (9) 5.00–7.50, (10) 7.50–10.00, (11) 10.00–12.50, (12) 12.50–15.00, (13) 15.00–20.00, (14) 20.00 and over. The symbols thus conform to a uniform scheme and render the three maps approximately comparable by eliminating the misleading effect of changes in price levels. In constructing the scheme of symbols it was assumed that the dollar of 1870–1871 was the equivalent of $0.691 in 1902–1903 and the equivalent of $1.21 in 1927–1928, these values being $\frac{85}{123}$ of a dollar and $\frac{148.5}{123}$ of a dollar, respectively, —123 being the index number of wholesale prices for 1870–1871, 85 the same for 1902–1903, and 148.5 the same for 1927–1928. The index numbers employed are averages determined from the series plotted on Plate 135E (see also below, pp. 131–132).

Schools: Compulsory Attendance, 1852–1918, and Minimum Term, 1930 [*Plate 131E*]. This map has been compiled from data furnished by courtesy of the Bureau of Education, U. S. Department of the Interior. The dates are those of the enactment of compulsory attendance laws. The large numbers and corresponding shading indicate the minimum term of required attendance in 1930. In three states, however, there were exceptions to the prevailing rule: in Montana 4 months was required in third-class districts; in Nebraska 6 months in districts with less than 10 pupils; and in South Carolina 3 months in any district where the school tax was less than 8 mills and monthly attendance was less than 15.

Progress of Labor Legislation, 1931
[PLATE 132]

Plate 132 illustrates the progress to January 1, 1931, of nine important reform movements in the field of state legislation relating to conditions of labor and associated problems. The topics were selected and the maps compiled for the *Atlas* by the staff of the American Association for Labor Legislation, under the direction of Mr. John B. Andrews, secretary of the Association.

On the maps for Workmen's Compensation, Vocational Rehabilitation, Old Age Pensions, One Day of Rest in Seven, and Civil Service Requirements for Employees of State Departments of Labor, the dates of enactment of the several laws are given. For the other topics it was impracticable to indicate such dates owing to the fact that over a long period of years there have been fragmentary laws enacted and then later supplemented and in many cases supplanted by new acts.

Workmen's Compensation, 1931 [*Plate 132A*]. On January 1, 1931, all the states except Arkansas, Mississippi, South Carolina, and Florida had workmen's compensation laws. Beginning with 1911 the compensation principle as the modern legislative method of dealing with occupational injuries spread rapidly. North Carolina was added to the list of states having such laws in 1929, bringing the number of workmen's compensation laws in force in the United States and territories up to 51. This number included the laws of Alaska, the Philippine Islands, Hawaii, and Porto Rico, and the three federal laws for civilian employees, longshoremen, and private employees in the District of Columbia. It is estimated that no fewer than 17,000,000 wage earners and their families were thus protected and that the amount paid out yearly under the compensation principle was then about $150,000,000.

The dates of enactment of the original workmen's compensation laws were derived from F. Robertson Jones, *Digest of Workmen's Compensation Laws in the United States and Territories*, 9th edit., New York, 1925, p. 11, and from supplementary data compiled by the American Association for Labor Legislation. Earlier laws which were declared unconstitutional by the courts have been disregarded. The laws of Nebraska and Missouri were held up by a referendum and were approved by the voters during the year following the date given on the map. Federal workmen's compensation laws were enacted as follows: civilian employees, 1908 (this law applied to a very limited number of federal employees; the present law was adopted in 1916); longshoremen's act, 1927; and District of Columbia, 1928.

Vocational Rehabilitation, 1931 [*Plate 132B*]. Since 1920 the Federal government has been offering financial aid for the retraining of cripples to those states that fulfill the requirements of the Vocational Rehabilitation Act. Only four states (Washington, Kansas, Vermont, and Delaware) had failed by January 1, 1931, to take advantage of this plan. Two additional states, Missouri and New Hampshire, were without financial appropriation to carry on the work.

The dates of acceptance by the states of the federal Vocational Rehabilitation Act of 1920 were derived from Federal Board for Vocational Rehabilitation, *Vocational Rehabilitation in the United States*, 1927, p. 17, supplemented by the annual summaries of labor laws of the American Association for Labor Legislation. In Minnesota, Nevada, and New York the laws were passed in anticipation of the federal act.

Mothers' Pensions, 1931 [*Plate 132C*]. Only four states (New Mexico, Alabama, Georgia, and South Carolina) had not by January 1, 1931, given to widows and orphans the protection of mothers' pensions. The first state-wide law was adopted by Illinois in 1911. It was estimated that payments under these laws approximate $30,000,000 annually.

Old Age Pensions, 1931 [*Plate 132D*]. Beginning with 1923 twelve states (shown in white on this map) have adopted laws for old age pensions and old age security by January 1, 1931. They were: Montana and Nevada (1923), Wisconsin (1925), Kentucky (1926), Colorado and Maryland (1927), California, Utah, Wyoming, and Minnesota (1929), New York and Massachusetts (1930). The territory of Alaska enacted such a law in 1915.

Women's Working Hours, 1931 [*Plate 132E*]. This map, based upon data compiled by the Women's Bureau, U. S. Department of Labor, as of January 1, 1931, shows the maximum number of hours per week allowed to women in industry at the beginning of 1931 by the laws of the several states. There was no legal restriction on the length of the working week for women in five states, while in nine the limit was between 60 and 70 hours.

The earliest act that effectively restricted the hours of labor for women was passed by Massachusetts in 1874. Wisconsin in 1867 had passed an ineffective law (L. D. Brandeis and Josephine Goldmark, *Women in Industry*, Decision of the U. S. Supreme Court in Curt Miller vs. State of Oregon, Upholding the Constitutionality of the Oregon Ten Hour Law for Women and Brief for the State of Oregon, Boston, 1908, p. 16).

One Day of Rest in Seven, 1931 [*Plate 132F*]. By January 1, 1931, only three states, Wisconsin, New York, and Massachusetts, had adopted genuine one-day-of-rest-in-seven laws for adult male workers as well as for women and children, although several other states had enacted legislation embodying in some measure the one-day-of-rest-in-seven principle.

Minimum Age for Children in Factories and Stores, 1931 [*Plate 132G*]. This map, from data furnished by the Children's Bureau, U. S. Department of Labor, shows the minimum legal age for child workers in factories and stores in the several states on January 1, 1931. In two states (Montana and Ohio) the minimum was 16 years, and in five states (California, Texas, Michigan, Rhode Island, and Maine) 15 years; Utah and Wyoming had no age restriction, while in the remaining states the minimum was 14 years. Although these laws set up certain age limits as legal standards they did not entirely prohibit work for children below these ages. In many states there were exceptions in the form of laws permitting work outside school and in certain industries and occupations. Thus, Vermont, Delaware, Virginia, and Alabama made exceptions in favor of canneries, and Florida permitted twelve-year-old workers in stores. The Mississippi law, enacted in 1930, forbids work to children between 14 and 16 unless they have complied with the school attendance law. Compulsory school attendance laws frequently interlock with the minimum age requirements and sometimes operate indirectly to produce an age limitation different from that of the law.

In 1836 Massachusetts passed the first child labor law in the United States. It provided that no child under 15 should be employed in any manufacturing establishment unless he had attended school for three months in the preceding year. In 1842 Massachusetts and Connecticut passed more typical laws (R. G. Fuller, "Child Labor," article in E. R. A. Seligman and Alvin Johnson, *Encyclopaedia of the Social Sciences*, Vol. 3, New York, 1930, p. 414).

Civil Service Requirements for Employees of State Departments of Labor, 1931 [*Plate 132H*]. On January 1, 1931, the nine states shown in white on this map had laws requiring civil service standards in the selection of state employees, which include practically all of the employees of state departments of labor. In all of these nine states factory inspectors must meet such requirements. New York and Massachusetts were the pioneers in this type of legislation and were the only states with civil service laws prior to 1905. Most of the other laws were adopted between 1905 and 1913. In November, 1930, a civil service system was inaugurated in the District of Columbia through an executive order signed by the President.

The dates of enactment of the state civil service laws are from data supplied by the National Civil Service Reform League. The Kansas law has been inoperative since 1922 owing to lack of appropriations. Connecticut passed a law in 1913 which was repealed in 1921.

State Public Employment Offices, 1931 [*Plate 132J*]. The twenty-four states shown in white on this map, which was prepared from data contained in *Monthly Labor Review*, Vol. 32, 1931, pp. 10-13, maintained public employment offices as a state service in 1930. Eight states with laws directing the establishment of such offices had no offices in regular operation. Ohio, by a law passed in 1890, was the first state to establish a state placement service. Other early laws were those of New York (1896), Illinois and Missouri (1899), and Connecticut and Wisconsin (1901). Several of these were later repealed and new laws enacted. State employment offices have frequently been handicapped by insufficient appropriations.

In several states that maintain no public employment service the federal government has established seasonal offices dealing in the main with farm labor. Federal authorities have also coöperated in a limited way with states that maintain their own offices. Supplementary to these services is the work done by a few municipal employment exchanges.

INDUSTRIES AND TRANSPORTATION, 1620-1931

[PLATES 133-147]

THE maps of these plates illustrate some of the principal industries. Choice was limited by the space in the *Atlas*, which was restricted, and by the statistics, which are not always available for the early years. Plates 133–134D and 135–137D illustrate Manufacturing Industries; Plates 138–141, Transportation; and Plates 137E and 142–147, Agriculture. Plate 134E is a graph showing changes in wholesale price levels, 1791–1930.

MANUFACTURING INDUSTRIES, 1620–1927
[PLATES 133–137]

These industries are illustrated by means of five series of maps: Principal Manufacturing Cities, 1839–1919; Value Added by Manufacture, 1849–1927; Iron and Steel Works, 1620–1908; Cotton Spinning Industry, 1810–1926; and Manufacture of Motor Vehicles, 1909, 1927.

Principal Manufacturing Cities, 1839–1919
[PLATES 133–134A]

These maps are based upon the publications of the U. S. Census, for the sixth, eight, twelfth, and fourteenth censuses. The source of information for Plate 133A is the *Compendium of the Enumeration of the Inhabitants and Statistics of the United States* (1841), pp. 4–99; for Plate 133B, the *Statistics of the United States including Mortality, Property, etc., in 1860* (1866), pp. xviii–xix; for Plate 133C, *Twelfth Census of the United States* (1902), Vol. 7, pp. ccxxxi–ccxxxv; and for Plate 134A, *Fourteenth Census of the United States* (1923), Vol. 8, pp. 224–238. The figures in the last-named volume under the heading "all other cities" were supplemented by information obtained from officials of the Census Bureau.

The figures for the several years are not strictly comparable. Those for 1889 and 1919 are based upon more accurate and thorough investigations than those for 1839 and 1859. Under the term "employees" are included, for 1839, "persons engaged in manufactures and trades"; for 1859, "hands employed in manufactures"; and for 1889 and 1919, "average number of wage earners employed in manufactures."

The word "cities" of the title includes a few New England "towns." Brooklyn is always treated as a part of New York, and in a few other cases consolidations were anticipated.

Value Added by Manufacture, 1849–1927
[PLATE 134 B–D]

These three maps illustrate the growth of manufacturing by states as indicated by the value added by manufacture. Map B, for the year ending June 1, 1850, is based upon a table in: U. S. Census Office, *Statistical View of the United States ... Being a Compendium of the Seventh Census*, Washington, 1854, p. 179[1]; map C, for the year ending May 1, 1890, on *Report on Manufacturing Industries in the United States at the Eleventh Census: 1890*, Part I, Washington, 1895, p. 8; and map D, for the calendar year 1927, on *Biennial Census of Manufactures, 1927*, Washington, 1930, pp. 1311–1315.

The "value added by manufacture," which represents essentially the value created by the manufacturing processes, is "the difference between cost of materials and value of products." It is a much more accurate measure of the "economic importance of the processes of manufacture" than "the quantity or the value of the products leaving the factories," since the value of the raw materials used and also duplication "due to the use of the products of certain establishments as materials by others," are eliminated (*Biennial Census of Manufactures, 1927*, pp. 9–10).

In all comparative studies of values at different dates changes in prices—or, in other words, in the value of the dollar—ought to be taken into consideration. Owing to higher price levels a dollar in 1927 would not buy as much as a dollar in 1849–1850. On map D, for 1927, the entire area within each outer circle represents the value added by manufacture in terms of dollars of 1927. The black discs represent the same values in terms of dollars of 1849. This correction was made by

using the index numbers of wholesale prices for 1849 and 1927 plotted in the graph shown on Plate 134 E (see below). The index number for 1849 is 92, that for 1927 is 147. The areas of the black discs are approximately $\frac{92}{147}$ of those of the entire areas within the outer circles.

No attempt was made on map C to show 1889 prices in terms of 1849–1850 values, since the price levels in both years were nearly the same. Prices were lower in 1889 than in 1849, the index numbers for these years being 81 and 92 respectively. Discs showing 1889 values in terms of 1849 dollars would therefore be slightly larger than those actually appearing on map C (their diameters would be about one eighteenth longer).

Wholesale Prices, 1791–1930 (graph)
[PLATE 134E]

This graph has been included as an aid to the interpretation of the following series of maps showing values: Schools: Expenditures, 1870–1928 (Pl.131B–D); Value added by Manufacture (Pl.134B–D); Value of Farm Lands and Buildings per Acre of All Lands in Farms (Pl. 147A–D); Value of Farm Machinery and Implements per Acre of All Lands in Farms (Pl. 147E–H); Exports and Imports 1791–1930 (Pls. 148E–151); Wealth (Pls. 152–153); Bank Capital (Pl. 154B, D, F, H, K, and L); and Income and Profits Taxes (Pl. 155).

Owing to changes in price levels—or, in other words, in the value of the dollar—the same dollar value as shown on two maps of different dates does not necessarily represent the same real values. On certain of the maps listed above (Pls. 131B–D, 134D, 147, and 151D–G) schemes of symbols are employed which serve to standardize values. How this is done in each case is explained in the text (see above; and below, p. 132). No such adjustment of the symbols was attempted on the remaining maps. Among these, owing to differences in the basic statistics from which they were compiled, the maps within each chronological series would not be strictly comparable even if the symbols were reduced to a uniform scale of real, as distinguished from money, values.

The graph and Table 1, however, will furnish at least a rough means of checking comparisons that the student may wish to make between values as shown on maps of different dates. Supposing, for example, we wish to compare exports, 1920–1929, as shown on Plate 151C with exports, 1871–1880, as shown on Plate 150A. It is obvious from the graph (Pl. 134E) that the index number representing the average price level for 1871–1880 is somewhere near 118 and that for 1921–1929 somewhere near 142. It follows, therefore, that the values for 1921–1929 would have to be reduced to about $\frac{118}{142}$ or six-sevenths of the amounts actually shown on Plate 151C, if any valid comparison were to be made between these values and those of 1871–1880.

Plate 134E is a plotted curve of the index numbers given in Table 1.

The index numbers for 1791–1924 are from *Report of the Commission of Gold and Silver Inquiry*, United States Senate, European Currency and Finance, Serial 9, Vol. 1, p. 435, Tables 2 and 3. "From 1791 through 1865 the series is based on figures computed by Alvin H. Hansen and Harold V. Roelse, appearing in the quarterly publications of the American Statistical Association, December, 1915, and December, 1917. From 1866 through 1889 the index numbers are based on those of Joseph L. Snider published in the *Review of Economic Statistics*, Harvard University, April, 1924, and ... compiled largely from price data contained in the report of the Senate Committee on Finance, published in 1893, of which Senator Aldrich was chairman. From 1890 to date [*i. e.*, 1924] the index numbers are those of the United States Bureau of Labor Statistics. The entire series has been converted to a 1913 base." The index numbers for 1925–1927 are from *Index Numbers of Wholesale Prices on Pre-War Base, 1890–1927*, U. S. Department of Labor, Bureau of Labor Statistics, Washington, 1928. Those for 1928, 1929, and 1930 are each $\frac{146.8}{95.4}$ of the Bureau of Labor Statistics' index numbers on the 1926 base for each of the three years in question, 146.8 being the Bureau of Labor Statistics' index number for 1927 on the 1913 base, and 95.4 being the same bureau's index number for the same year on the 1926 base. The Bureau has not published index numbers on the 1913 base beyond December, 1927.

---

[1] This table includes in the totals for each state the value of the annual products of mining industries. In the computation of value added by manufacture the figures for gold, iron, and lead mining (from U. S. Census Office, *Abstract of the Statistics of Manufactures According to the Returns of the Seventh Census*, by J. C. G. Kennedy, Washington, 1859, pp. 57, 67, and 70) were subtracted from the value of manufactures for each state where any mining was done.

TABLE 1

(1) INDEX NUMBERS OF WHOLESALE PRICES IN THE UNITED STATES, 1791–1930

1913 = 100

Year	Index	Year	Index	Year	Index
1791	108	1838	122	1885	79
1792	114	1839	127	1886	76
1793	120	1840	109	1887	78
1794	....	1841	108	1888	83
1795	159	1842	100	1889	81
1796	....	1843	94	1890	81
1797	171	1844	95	1891	80
1798	169	1845	96	1892	75
1799	162	1846	99	1893	77
1800	....	1847	99	1894	69
1801	172	1848	94	1895	70
1802	141	1849	92	1896	67
1803	145	1850	95	1897	67
1804	155	1851	98	1898	70
1805	160	1852	95	1899	75
1806	156	1853	101	1900	81
1807	148	1854	105	1901	79
1808	145	1855	105	1902	84
1809	....	1856	105	1903	86
1810	166	1857	105	1904	86
1811	161	1858	95	1905	86
1812	164	1859	93	1906	89
1813	190	1860	93	1907	94
1814	237	1861	94	1908	90
1815	186	1862	110	1909	97
1816	159	1863	138	1910	101
1817	161	1864	177	1911	93
1818	156	1865	202	1912	99
1819	138	1866	170	1913	100
1820	118	1867	159	1914	98
1821	113	1868	153	1915	101
1822	116	1869	146	1916	127
1823	111	1870	125	1917	177
1824	109	1871	121	1918	194
1825	110	1872	126	1919	206
1826	110	1873	121	1920	226
1827	110	1874	117	1921	147
1828	105	1875	113	1922	149
1829	104	1876	102	1923	154
1830	101	1877	101	1924	159
1831	107	1878	86	1925	151
1832	108	1879	83	1926	149
1833	107	1880	96	1927	133
1834	100	1881	99	1928	150
1835	115	1882	105	1929	149
1836	128	1883	93	1930	133
1837	128	1884	85		

(2) WHOLESALE PRICES ON GOLD BASIS, 1862–1878

Year	Price on Gold basis	Year	Price on Gold basis	Year	Price on Gold basis
1862	97.13	1868	109.55	1874	105.18
1863	95.08	1869	109.79	1875	98.31
1864	87.08	1870	108.75	1876	91.60
1865	128.47	1871	108.30	1877	96.35
1866	120.70	1872	112.14	1878	85.31
1867	115.12	1873	106.36		

It must be pointed out that the entire series of index numbers is not strictly consistent throughout, since it is plotted from a composite of different series computed with reference to the prices of different commodities as modified by different systems of weighting. It was, however, the only series of index numbers on a uniform base for the entire period 1791–1927 available at the time the *Atlas* went to press. The forthcoming publication of a new series of index numbers of wholesale prices from 1797 to the present has recently been announced (G. F. Warren and Frank A. Pearson, "A Monthly Index Number of Wholesale Prices in the United States for 135 Years," *Journ. Amer. Statist. Assn.*, Vol. 26, 1931, pp. 244–249).

Iron and Steel Works, 1620–1908

[PLATE 135]

This series illustrates the manufacture of commercial iron and steel, that is of pig iron, bar iron, sheet iron, steel ingots, etc. Under the term "iron and steel works" are included forges, bloomeries, furnaces, rolling-mills, and steel works. With a few exceptions, no attempt was made to improve upon the classification and calculations of the compilers of iron and steel statistics. They do not count the forges and furnaces operated in connection with rolling-mills and steel works. A few slitting-mills that did not also roll iron may have been included in the lists for maps B and C, since the sources of information often enumerate iron mills under the general heading "rolling and slitting mills." Since no steel was made until the eighteenth century, map A illustrates iron works only. The making of steel in large quantities was a development of the last half of the nineteenth century.

All of the early works were small, and many of them crude. Their entire production did not equal that of one of the larger establishments of the present time. In 1810 the production of pig iron was 54,000 tons, while in 1908 it was more than 25,000,000 tons. It will be noted (see below) that for the later years the forges and bloomeries (smaller works) decrease in number and the rolling-mills and steel works (larger works) increase.

In comparing the later maps with the earlier ones and in comparing urban areas on the later maps (such as that of Allegheny County, Pennsylvania) with rural areas (such as that of eastern Tennessee) it is well to remember the variation in the size of the works. The total output of a county generally increases with the size of the works. In comparing the first two maps with later ones allowance should be made for the long period covered by each of the earlier ones.

The dates of the later maps are determined partly by the availability of statistics. The date 1908 is the last date of Swank's *Directory* (see below), and since subsequent compilers have not followed Swank's classification it has been thought advisable to end the series with 1908. The first census of iron and steel works was taken in 1810. The mapping is by counties.

Iron and Steel Works, 1620–1675 and 1725–1775 [*Plate 135A and B*]. The chief sources of information for these two maps are J. M. Swank, *History of the Manufacture of Iron in all Ages*, Philadelphia, 1892, pp. 100–300; J. L. Bishop, *History of American Manufactures*, Philadelphia, 1866, Vol. 1, pp. 469–631; and county and local histories. While the search was not exhaustive it is believed that but few works for which information is available were omitted.

Many of the early works had short lives. This is especially true of the works shown in Connecticut, New Jersey, and Virginia, on map A. Each of the three dots stands for a single work.

Iron and Steel Works, 1810 [*Plate 135C*]. This map is based chiefly upon the statistics of manufactures of the Third Census (1810), which were digested by Tench Coxe. The most available publication of them is in *American State Papers, Finance*, Vol. 2, Washington, 1832, pp. 719–805. Inasmuch as Coxe's digest is not altogether satisfactory it has been supplemented by information derived chiefly from Swank's *History* and from county and other local histories. While the list of works thus obtained contains omissions, it is sufficiently complete to furnish a basis for a fairly accurate view of the iron and steel industry in 1810.

Iron and Steel Works, 1858 [*Plate 135D*]. This map, with an exception or two, is based upon the lists of works found in J. P. Lesley, *Iron Manufacturer's Guide to Furnaces, Forges and Rolling Mills of the United States*, New York and London, 1859, pp. 1–262. Since Lesley's statistics do not extend beyond 1858 the map has been given that date. The total numbers of works listed by Lesley are as follows: furnaces 558, forges and bloomeries 396, rolling-mills 210.

Iron and Steel Works, 1878 [*Plate 135E*]. This map is based upon the lists found in the *Directory to the Iron and Steel Works of the United States*, Philadelphia, 1878, compiled by J. M. Swank. The total numbers of works listed are as follows: furnaces 698, forges and bloomeries 122, rolling-mills and steel works 382.

Iron and Steel Works, 1908 [*Plate 135F*]. This map is based upon the lists found in the *Directory to the Iron and Steel Works of the United States*, Philadelphia, 1908. The total numbers of works (pp. xii–xiv) are as follows: furnaces 448, forges and bloomeries 12, rolling-mills and steel works 598.

Cotton Spinning Industry, 1810–1926

[PLATES 136 and 137A]

This series of maps illustrates the cotton industry conducted under the factory system. Before 1790 cotton was spun exclusively in families. The date 1810 is chosen to show the industry in its infancy, and that of 1926 the industry at the present time. Choice of the two intermediate dates has been determined partly by the availability of statistics.

The mapping is by counties and by spindles. The amount of cotton consumed by a spindle in a day is a fraction of a pound.

The total number of spindles for each of the four years is as follows: 100,000 (partly estimated) in 1810; 2,285,000 in 1840; 10,653,000 in 1880; 37,587,000 in 1926.

Cotton Spinning, 1810 [*Plate 136A*]. This map is based chiefly upon Gallatin's report on mills for spinning cotton, 1809-1810 (*American State Papers, Finance*, Vol. 2, Washington, 1832, pp. 427 and 432-435), and on a list of mills supplemental to those found in Gallatin's report, supplied by Dr. Victor S. Clark, author of the *History of Manufactures in the United States, 1607-1860*, published by the Carnegie Institution of Washington in 1916. Use was also made of the Digest of Manufactures found in the volume of *State Papers* named above (pp. 666-812), first published in 1813 and based upon the census of 1810. Unfortunately the census statistics do not distinguish between mills for spinning and mills for weaving. A few details omitted by Gallatin were partly supplied from local histories. While the full list of mills obtained from these sources is incomplete, it is believed that the omissions are not important. The number of spindles is sometimes estimated. All or nearly all the mills used the Arkwright machinery. They were driven either by water or horse power.

Cotton Spinning, 1840 [*Plate 136B*]. This map is based upon the statistics for cotton manufactures found in the *Compendium of the Enumeration of the Inhabitants and Statistics of the United States*, 1841, pp. 108-324, a publication of the Sixth Census.

Cotton Spinning, 1880 [*Plate 136C*]. This map is based upon the cotton statistics found in the *Textile Manufacturers' Directory of the United States and Canada*, New York, 1880, pp. 199-292, compiled by William C. Wyckoff, secretary of the Silk Association of America. Wyckoff corrected his compilation by means of the returns of the census of 1880. Use has been made of subsequent numbers of the *Directory* to supply missing details. One county, that of Bristol, Massachusetts, had more than a million spindles.

Cotton Spinning, 1926 [*Plate 137A*]. This map is based upon the manuscript sheets in the Bureau of the Census, Department of Commerce, showing the number of spindles (ring or mule) in place on July 31, 1926. In four counties the spindles exceeded a million—Bristol, Mass., 7,500,000; Providence, R. I., 1,700,000; Gaston, N. C., 1,137,000; and Middlesex, Mass., 1,000,400.

Motor Vehicles, Tractors, Horses and Mules

[PLATE 137B-E]

Manufacture of Motor Vehicles, 1909, 1927 [*Plate 137B and C*]. These maps illustrate the growth of the automobile industry between 1909 and 1927 as measured by the number of wage earners employed in the manufacture of motor vehicles and of motor vehicle bodies and parts. Map B is based on U. S. Bureau of the Census, *Thirteenth Census of the United States ... 1910*, Vol. 8, *Manufactures*, Washington, 1913, p. 650; map C on the *Biennial Census of Manufactures*, 1927, Washington, 1930, pp. 1158-1159. Owing to the fact that the Census Bureau is not permitted by law to publish figures that may disclose data reported by individual establishments no statistics are available for the states indicated by small squares, even though some of these states had more wage earners than other states for which the statistics are given.

Tractors on Farms, Increase in Number, 1920-1925 [*Plate 137D*]. **Horses and Mules on Farms, Decrease in Number, 1920-1925** [*Plate 137E*]. These maps, which are reproduced from maps compiled by the Bureau of Agricultural Economics, U. S. Department of Agriculture, illustrate certain effects of the growth of the motor vehicle industry. They might as logically have been placed in the section of the *Atlas* devoted to agricultural history as in that devoted to manufactures and may well be studied in connection with the maps on land utilization (see Pls. 144-147). By replacing horses and mules on farms, the tractor has not only greatly increased the efficiency of farm labor as measured by the output per man, but has also released for other uses large areas of land formerly devoted to the raising of fodder crops. The introduction of the tractor and other farm machinery (see Pl. 147E-H) has contributed to the rise of many critical problems in American agriculture in recent years—problems of overproduction, of land utilization, and of the decrease in farm population.

Maps K and L, Plate 141 (see p. 135, below) also illustrate the growth of the motor vehicle industry.

TRANSPORTATION, 1774-1931

[PLATES 138-141]

Rates of Travel from New York City, 1800-1930

[PLATE 138A-E]

These maps show rates of travel in the United States in 1800, 1830, 1858, and 1930. In constructing them the length of time required to travel from New York City to selected points throughout the United States was plotted on base maps, and isochronic lines were drawn connecting places equally distant in point of time from New York City. The time interval employed is the week. On maps A-D the first week is subdivided into daily intervals; and on the final map, showing the rate of travel by airplane in September, 1930, the interval is further reduced to twelve hours. No effort has been made to estimate the time required to reach sections of the country more than six weeks distant from New York City. On maps A, B, and C the definite information necessary for the construction of the isochronic lines in the more remote sections of the country was often inadequate. In such cases the length of time required to travel to additional selected points was estimated theoretically on the basis of the rate of travel at the time, whether by land or water, and the character of the country traversed.

In 1800 travel by stagecoach was limited to the area bounded by Boston, Bennington, and Albany on the north, Richmond on the south, and the Allegheny Mountains to the west. It required 10 days of sailing to travel from New York City to Charleston and a minimum of 26 to 28 days to reach New Orleans. Buffalo was a 9-day journey via the Hudson-Mohawk route, and the trip over the mountains to Pittsburgh required 10 days. It required 22-25 days to reach Louisville by way of the Ohio and 28-30 days to reach Cairo. In Tennessee and Kentucky travel on horseback was more rapid than water transportation, because of the circuitous courses of the rivers, and several well-defined overland routes such as the Natchez Trail had already developed.

The period between 1800 and 1830 was one of rapid development of water transportation and extension of highways. It marked both the development of the steamboat as a means of transportation and the completion of the Erie Canal. The traveling time from New York to Charleston was reduced to 6 days and to New Orleans to 14 days. To Cleveland was a 10-day and to Detroit a 13-day journey. From Detroit to Chicago was a 6-day trip overland, the much longer trip by water requiring about two weeks.

The chief sources of information for the construction of maps A and B are: Francis Bailey, *Tour of the Unsettled Parts of North America*, London, 1856; Jacob Burnet, *Notes on the Settlement of the Northwest*, New York, 1847; Samuel Cummings, *The Western Pilot*, Cincinnati, 1836; Seymour Dunbar, *History of Travel in America*, Vols. 1-3, Indianapolis, 1915; A. M. Earle, *Stage-Coach and Tavern Days*, New York, 1912; Josiah Gregg, *Commerce of the Prairies*, New York and London, 1844; F. W. Halsey, *Old New York Frontier*, New York, 1901; A. B. Hulbert, *Historic Highways of America*, Vols. 7-14, Cleveland, 1902-1905; A. B. Hulbert, *Paths of Inland Commerce* (Chronicles of America Ser., Vol. 21), New Haven, 1920; Malcolm Keir, *The March of Commerce* (Pageant of America Ser., Vol. 4), New Haven, 1927; Caroline MacGill, *History of Transportation in the United States before 1860* (Carnegie Institution of Washington, Bull. 215C), 1927; Harriet Martineau, "Travels in and around Michigan, 1836," *Michigan History Magazine*, Vol. 7, 1923, Nos. 1 and 2; *Journal of André Michaux, 1793-1796*, and *Travels to the West of the Allegheny Mountains*, by F. A. Michaux (Early Western Travels Ser., edited by R. G. Thwaites, Vol. 3), Cleveland, 1904; *The Navigator*, Pittsburgh, 1801; M. M. Quaife, *Chicago and the Old Northwest*, Chicago, 1913; Thomas Speed, *The Wilderness Road* (Filson Club Publ. 2), Louisville, 1886; H. S. Tanner, *The American Traveler*, Philadelphia, 1838.

The result of the development of railroads in the second quarter of the nineteenth century and their extension westward to the Mississippi River and into southern Wisconsin is shown on map C. Appleton's *Railway and Steam Navigation Guide*, New York, 1858, furnished the basis for determining the rates of travel east of the Mississippi. To the west the rates were based on the speed of the post-riders. The Pacific Northwest could be reached either overland from Salt Lake City or by boat from San Francisco, the latter route requiring less time. Since there were no post routes north of the St. Louis-Salt Lake City-San Francisco line, rates of travel between St. Paul and the Pacific were based upon the speed of the explorers and fur traders. Additional sources of information for this map are: H. M. Chittenden, *The American Fur Trade in the Far West*, 3 Vols., New York, 1902; L. R. Hafen, *The Overland Mail, 1849-1869*, Cleveland, 1926; Granville Stuart, *Forty Years on the Frontier*, Cleveland, 1925; Rufus King, "Milwaukee to St.

Paul in 1855," *Wisconsin Magazine of History*, Vol. 6, 1927, No. 2; J. Q. Thornton, *Oregon and California in 1848*, New York, 1849; G. K. Warren, *Preliminary Report of Explorations in Nebraska and Dakota in the Years 1855-'56-'57*, Washington, 1875 (originally printed as appendix to Report of the Secretary of War, in the President's Message and Documents, December, 1858).

Map D, Rates of Travel by Railroad in 1930, is based entirely upon the *Official Guide of the Railways and Steam Navigation Lines of the United States* for August, 1930. The rates of travel by airplane in 1930, shown by map E, were determined from the *Official Aviation Guide of the Airways* for September, 1930.

Waterways, 1930

[PLATE 138F and G]

Navigable Rivers, 1930 [*Plate 138F*]. This map is based upon data supplied by courtesy of the office of the Chief of Engineers, U. S. War Department.

Canals and Canalized Rivers, 1930 [*Plate 138G*]. As a rule canals less than twelve miles in length are not shown. Abandoned canals are indicated by broken lines, and those still in use in 1930 by solid lines. A few of the latter are used very little. Several canals along the coast of the Southern states are too short to be shown.

This map was first drawn as of 1915 and was based upon information found in the following sources: *United States Census of 1880*, Vol. 4, *Transportation*; *Report of the Commissioner of Corporations on Transportation by Water in the United States*, Washington, 1909, Part I; *Preliminary Report of the Inland Waterways Commission* (*Senate Doc. No. 325, 60th Cong., 1st Sess., 1907-1908*); and N. E. Whitford, *History of the Canal System of the State of New York*, Albany, 1906. The map was revised to 1930 from information furnished by courtesy of the office of the Chief of Engineers, U. S. War Department.

Post Roads and Stage Routes, 1774–1834

[PLATE 138H–K]

These maps show the principal transportation routes on land before the railroads supplanted the turnpikes and other highways. Since information respecting stage roads, turnpikes, and common roads is scattering and incomplete the post roads, for which there is much reliable information, were chosen for representation. It was possible, however, to show the main stage routes for 1774.

The year 1774 was chosen as the date of the first map in preference on 1775 because it was the last full calendar year during which the colonial post was controlled by the British government. An interval of thirty years between the post-route maps proved to be the most satisfactory one. The year 1804 corresponds with the date of Bradley's post-route map; and the year 1834 marks with sufficient precision the beginning of the transportation of the mails by the railroads and is near enough to the date of Burr's post-route maps (1839) to make them a valuable source of information.

Since the sources of information often give only the chief offices or termini of roads, minute precision in relating the roads to the topography of the base map was not always attainable.

Public Post Roads and Main Stage Routes, 1774 [*Plate 138H*]. The public post roads of 1774 were located chiefly by means of the information found in the *Journal kept by Hugh Finlay, Surveyor of the Post Roads on the Continent of North America, 1773-1774*, Brooklyn, 1867, and in contemporary newspapers and almanacs. Between New York and Boston the post went either by way of the "old post road," which passed through New London, Newport, and Providence, or by way of the "upper post road," which passed through Hartford, Springfield, and Worcester. Between New York and Albany post roads are shown on both sides of the Hudson, since in December, 1774, the general post office issued an order that the mail should be carried alternately along these roads (*Boston Gazette*, Dec. 12, 1774). The mail was generally carried on horseback by postrider. Between Boston and Portsmouth it was carried by stagecoach.

Information respecting stage routes for 1774 was found chiefly in the contemporary newspapers and almanacs and in the town histories. Many newspaper advertisements of stage lines in New Jersey are found in the *New Jersey Archives*, first ser., Vols. 24–29. The stage conveyance was a coach, a wagon, or a boat. The lower, or Bordentown, stage between New York and Philadelphia was by boat between New York and South Amboy and between Burlington and Philadelphia. Most of the route between Philadelphia and Baltimore was by water, by way of the Delaware River and Chesapeake Bay.

Main Post Roads, 1804 [*Plate 138J*]. The principal sources of information for this map are *U. S. Statutes at Large*, Vol. 1, Boston, 1845, pp. 354–357, 419–420, and 509–511; Vol. 2, pp. 42–45, 125–127, 189–191, and 275–277; "Proposals for Carrying the Mails," in the *National Intelligencer*, Jan. 5 and 7, Apr. 20, 22, and 25, 1803, and Jan. 2, Feb. 27, May 7 and 9, Nov. 26, and Dec. 5, 1804; *List of Post Offices in the United States*, 1803 and 1805; and Abraham Bradley's "Map of the United States Exhibiting the Post Roads," 1804.

There is no complete list of the post roads for 1804 and 1834. Most roads were established by Congress, some by the Post Office Department, and a few by the War Department. It is therefore impossible to ascertain the location of all the post roads by a study of the statutes. Moreover, there were so many changes in the statutes and so many changes in the routing of the mails by the Post Office Department that it is impossible from the statutes to locate all the roads with precision.

The "main post roads" include the roads connecting important places, the roads along which much mail was carried, and the roads on the frontier in regions where there was but a single post road. In densely populated regions, such as New England, it was possible to show only the most important roads.

Main Post Roads, 1834 [*Plate 138K*]. The map for 1834 is based chiefly upon *U. S. Statutes at Large*, Vol. 2, Boston, 1845, pp. 579–588, 730–732, and 806; Vol. 3, 1846, pp. 130–132, 221–222, 334–338, 363–366, 453–457, 503–508, 577–581, 623–628, 702–707, and 764–767; Vol. 4, 1846, pp. 95–100, 221–226, 315–320, and 535–549; "Proposals for Carrying the Mails," in the *Weekly Globe*, Washington, June 28 and July 5, 1832, and July 25, 1833; and in the *Semi-Weekly Globe*, July 23, 1834; *House Doc. No. 212, 22nd Cong., 1st Sess., 1831-1832; Senate Doc. No. 408* and *No. 422, 23rd Cong., 1st Sess., 1833-1834; House Doc. No. 175* and *No. 176, 23rd Cong., 2nd Sess., 1834-1835*; and D. H. Burr, *American Atlas Exhibiting Post Offices, Post Roads ...*, London, 1839.

In 1804 the mails were carried chiefly on horseback or by stagecoach. By 1834 much mail was carried by sulky. The steamboat was also in use, and two short lines of railroad were carrying mail (*House Ex. Doc. No. 2, 23rd Cong., 2nd Sess., 1834-1835*, p. 389).

Railroads, 1840–1930, and Overland Mail Routes, 1850–1869

[PLATES 138L–141G]

Railroads in Operation, December, 1840 [*Plate 138L*]. This map is based upon many sources of information, only the most important of which are here mentioned. For the New England railroads the *Monthly Chronicle* (Boston, 1840 and 1841), Vols. 1 and 2, was found useful. H. V. Poor, *History of the Railroads and Canals of the United States*, New York, 1860, Vol. 1, is excellent for New England and the Middle states. The progress of the New York railroads in 1832–1859 may be followed in the tables found in Vol. 16 of the *American Railroad Journal*. For the railroads of Pennsylvania the reports of Ludwig Klein, a European engineer, found in the *Journal of the Franklin Institute*, Vol. 30, Philadelphia, 1840, pp. 89–92 and 306, were valuable. The tables of F. A. Gerstner, a railroad engineer, found in the same volume and also in his report on American railroads, are erroneous.

Among the sources that were used for the Southern states are the following: *American Railroad Journal*, 1836–1837, Vols. 5 and 6; U. B. Phillips, *History of Transportation in the Eastern Cotton Belt to 1860*, New York, 1908; *U. S. Census of 1880*, Vol. 4, *Transportation*; H. V. Poor, *op. cit.*; and *Hunt's Merchant Magazine*, 1840-1841, Vols. 2–5. The information for the railroads of the Middle Western states is derived chiefly from state, county, and local histories and from the proceedings of state historical societies. This was checked with the information found in the *U. S. Census of 1880*, Vol. 4.

Railroads in Operation, December, 1850, and Overland Mail Routes, 1850-1859 [*Plate 139A*]. The railroad routes as shown on this map are based chiefly upon the following sources: *U. S. Census of 1880*, Vol. 4; *House Ex. Doc. No. 2, 34th Cong., 3rd Sess.*, 1856–1857, pp. 240 ff.; H. V. Poor, *History of the Railroads and Canals of the United States*, New York, 1860, Vol. 1; *Account of Celebration of Opening of Railroad between Boston and Canada*, Boston, 1852 (for New England); *Hunt's Merchant Magazine*, Vol. 24, pp. 499 and 758 (for Mass.), p. 258 (for Pa.), p. 378 (for N. Y.); Vol. 26, p. 638, Vol. 28, p. 107, and Vol. 30, p. 121 (for U. S.); and the *American Railroad Journal*, Vols. 22, 23, and 24 (especially Vols. 22 and 23).

None of these authorities is free from error. Information found in them was checked with that found in the *American Railway Guide* (C. Dinsmore, New York), May, 1851. The *Guide* gives the time-tables of all railroads that carried passengers, and it was corrected monthly. A few railroads were mapped whose formal opening did not take place until early in 1851. Many lines were in progress of construction.

On the western part of this and the following map the principal Overland Mail Routes shown for the period 1850-1869 are based on L. R. Hafen, *The Overland Mail, 1849-1869*, Cleveland, 1926, supplemented by information furnished by Mr. Hafen. The dates indicate the year or years during which the several routes were in operation, or, when a single date is followed by a hyphen, the year in which operation was begun. In the latter case operation was in nearly every instance continued after 1869. The steamship routes shown on map A were also in operation during and after the period covered by map B.

The first transcontinental railroad (Union Pacific and Central Pacific) follows approximately the route of the Daily Overland Mail from Atchison to Salt Lake City (marked "1860-1869," map B). In 1866 the Union Pacific had reached Manhattan, Kansas, and the eastern terminus of the stage route was transferred to that point. "As the railroad advanced westward along this route the stage terminus accordingly receded" (*ibid.*, p. 317). No attempt is made to show this recession. From Salt Lake City to Sacramento the Central Pacific Railroad was built about 100 miles north of the old stage route, over which service was kept up until a month before the Central and Union Pacific lines were joined on May 10, 1869 (*ibid.*, p. 327).

Railroads in Operation, December, 1860, and Overland Mail Routes, 1860-1869 [*Plate 139B*]. This map is based upon the time-tables of Appleton's *Illustrated Railway and Steam Navigation Guide*, March, 1861. The *Guide* of this date was used because most of the individual time-tables were dated on the closing days of 1860. The lines thus derived were compared with those found on the following maps: "Map of Railroad Lines in actual Operation October, 1860," in T. C. Smith, *Parties and Slavery* (American Nation Ser., Vol. 18, New York, 1906), p. 62; "Map of the United States," December 31, 1860, Pl. 162 in the *Atlas to Accompany the Official Records of the Union and Confederate Armies*; and Pl. 16 of Scribner's *Statistical Atlas of the United States*, New York, 1885.

On the Overland Mail Routes as shown on this map see comment on Plate 139A, above. The Pony Express, 1860-1861, between St. Joseph and San Francisco followed the route subsequently taken by the Daily Overland Mail, 1861-1869, and designated "1860-1869" on the map.

Railroads, 1870 [*Plate 140A*]. This map is based chiefly upon the *Travellers' Official Railway Guide for the United States and Canada* (National Railway Publication Company, New York), October, 1870; and H. V. Poor, *Manual of the Railroads of the United States*, New York, 1870-1871. Use was also made of the local histories and of the collection of state maps found in the Library of Congress. In the thickly populated regions of some of the Northern states the railroads were too numerous for all of them to be shown. Some very short lines also are not shown.

Western Railroads, 1880 [*Plate 141A*]. This and the following map show the progress in the construction of railroads in the Western states. The lines are arbitrarily stopped at the western boundary of the middle tier of states. The map for 1880 is redrawn from the railroad maps accompanying the *Travellers' Official Railway Guide* for that year. This guide was issued periodically, and the maps were regularly revised.

Western Railroads, 1930 [*Plate 141B*]. This map is based upon "Railroad Map of the United States," prepared under the direction of the Chief of Engineers, U. S. Army, Washington, July, 1930. Small branch lines are not shown.

Railroad Systems, 1912-1914, [*Plates 140B and 141C-G*]. One of the most important features of railroad history is the consolidation of lines into systems, six of which cover most of the United States. These six systems which have been chosen for illustration are designated as follows: New England System, New York Central System, Pennsylvania System, Southern Railroad, the James J. Hill Railroads, and the Harriman System. The method of consolidation varied. Sometimes consolidations have been the result of a gradual process of absorption and construction extending over a long period. From 1850 to 1890 this was the prevailing method. More recently consolidations have been brought about in a few years by a railroad builder or promoter, such as James J. Hill or E. H. Harriman.

The six maps illustrating the railroad systems are based upon the official maps accompanying the annual reports of the roads.

The Harriman System, 1912 [*Plate 140B*]. The principal roads of this system, which were consolidated by the late E. H. Harriman, are the Union Pacific, the Southern Pacific, and the Los Angeles, San Pedro, and Salt Lake. The map shows the trackage of 1914 but represents the consolidated system as it was in 1912, before the Union Pacific and the

Southern Pacific were separated by a decision of the United States Supreme Court. The Union Pacific connects Omaha and Kansas City, and the Southern Pacific connects New Orleans and Galveston, with the Pacific Coast.

New England System, 1914 [*Plate 141C*]. This map illustrates the New England system as it existed early in 1914. A few months later it was dissolved by order of the United States government. It comprised the following roads: the New York, New Haven, and Hartford, the Boston and Maine, and the Maine Central. The lines of the system lie chiefly in New England. It had extensions into Canada, New York, and Pennsylvania. These are not shown on this map.

New York Central System, 1914 [*Plate 141D*]. This system, often called the Vanderbilt system, extends from Boston and New York to Chicago and St. Louis. Like the Pennsylvania system it has been built up by a gradual process of absorption and construction. It has extensions into Canada to Montreal and Ottawa.

Pennsylvania System, 1914 [*Plate 141E*]. This system connects New York, Philadelphia, Baltimore, and Washington with many of the chief cities of the Middle West. It is made up largely of lines that formerly belonged to more than two hundred companies. As in the case of the New York Central, the consolidation began about 1850.

Southern Railroad, 1913 [*Plate 141F*]. The Southern Railroad is a consolidation of many lines effected about a quarter of a century ago by the late J. Pierpont Morgan. It covers chiefly the Southern states east of the Mississippi River and extends northward to Washington, Louisville, and St. Louis.

The James J. Hill Railroads, 1914 [*Plate 141G*]. The James J. Hill railroads, while not operated as a unit, are generally regarded as forming a single system. The principal roads in this group are the Great Northern, the Northern Pacific, the Chicago, Burlington, and Quincy, and the Colorado and Southern. In the last-named road there is a small break near Fort Worth. This system connects Chicago, St. Louis, and St. Paul with Seattle and Portland, and Denver with Houston. Its connections with Winnipeg, Vancouver, and other Canadian towns are not shown.

Air Mail Routes in Operation, 1920-1931

[PLATE 141H and J]

These two maps illustrate the rapid growth of aerial transportation during the period 1920-1931. It should be noted that they show mail routes only. The network of routes covered by regular passenger, express, and freight air services was extended even more rapidly during the same period, but strictly comparable data for different dates showing all regularly operated air routes could not be procured. On map H the routes as of 1920 are derived from a map in *Aircraft Yearbook, 1920*, New York, 1920, p. 44; the routes as of 1927 on map H and of 1931 on map J are from maps compiled by the Post Office Department and dated Nov. 15, 1927, and July 1, 1931.

Persons per Motor Vehicle, 1913, 1930

[PLATE 141K and L]

These two maps show by states the number of persons per motor vehicle in 1913[1] and 1930. For maps illustrating the manufacture of motor vehicles see Plate 137B and C.

Maps K and L are based on statistics of motor vehicle registration compiled by the Bureau of Public Roads, U. S. Department of Agriculture. The figures for 1913 are also given in the *World Almanac, 1931*, p. 382.[2]

AGRICULTURE, 1839-1930

[PLATES 142-147]

These maps illustrate certain outstanding developments in the history of agricultural production, land utilization, and land tenure in the United States. Owing to the lack of comparable statistics it was not possible to begin the several series at earlier dates. With the exception of Plates 146N-Q and 147, which were compiled especially for the *Atlas*, the maps are reproductions from prints prepared by the Division of Statistical and Historical Research, U. S. Department of Agriculture.

---

[1] In compiling Plates 141K, 152B and D, 153A and D, and 155B and D the population of each state for certain intercensal years was estimated on the assumption that population tends to increase by geometrical rather than by arithmetic progression.

[2] In the table in the *World Almanac* the figure for Michigan should read 54,366, not 554,366.

The maps of the Division (except Pl. 142A), as well as those especially compiled, are based upon the statistics of the U. S. Census Bureau, the dot maps on statistics by counties and the remainder (*i.e.*, Pls. 146N-Q Tenancy; Pl. 147A-D, Values of Farm Lands and Buildings; and Pl. 147 E-H, Value of Farm Implements and Machinery) on statistics by states. See also Plate 137, maps D and E, and p. 133, above.

Agricultural Regions, 1928

[PLATE 142A]

This map is one of a series of Agricultural Maps published by Dr. O. E. Baker in *Yearbook of Agriculture, 1928*, U. S. Department of Agriculture, 1929, pp. 640–665. The map

"outlines areas characterized for the most part by a dominant crop or system of farming. As agriculture becomes more commercialized the trend is toward the concentration of production in those regions where physical conditions, including distance to market, are most favorable. This map may be helpful in keeping the major agricultural features of the country in mind. . . The United States may be divided agriculturally into two parts, the East and the West. The East has a humid or subhumid climate and the land is devoted principally to crop production. The West is mostly an arid or semiarid climate, except the North Pacific coast and the higher altitudes in the Sierra-Cascade and Rocky Mountains, and most of the land is devoted to grazing. Each of these two parts may be divided into agricultural regions. Each of the eight eastern regions (excluding the Forest and Hay region) is based on the dominance of a certain crop or kind of farming, which in turn is the result largely of latitude and temperature conditions. Each of the four western regions is based principally on the use of the land for crops, for pasture, or for forest, which in turn is determined largely by altitude and rainfall conditions" (*ibid.*, pp. 640 and 641; see also Pls. 3E, 4B, and 5).

For a subdivision of the United States into agricultural regions of smaller area than those shown on Plate 142A, with a detailed description, see O. E. Baker, "Agricultural Regions of North America," *Econ. Geogr.*, Vol. 2, 1926, pp. 459–493; Vol. 3, 1927, pp. 50–87, 309–340, and 447–466; Vol. 4, 1928, pp. 44–73 and 399–433; Vol. 5, 1929, pp. 36–69; Vol. 6, 1930, pp. 166–190 and 278–308.

Agricultural Production, 1839–1924

[PLATES 142B–144B]

Plates 142B–144B illustrate the production of cotton, 1839–1924; of cattle, 1860–1925; of tobacco, 1839–1924; of corn, 1839–1924; and of wheat, 1839–1924. For each of these commodities all the maps except the map for the latest date in each series (two maps in the case of wheat) are comparable, *i.e.*, one dot represents the same quantity of a given commodity on each map for that commodity. Unfortunately, for the period since 1920 maps of production comparable to the maps based on the earlier census reports were not available for reproduction.

Improved Land and Land in Harvested Crops, 1850–1929

[PLATES 144C–146M]

This series of twenty-six maps based on the U. S. Census reports illustrate trends in agricultural land utilization since 1850. Plates 144C–145C show the total acreage of "improved land" in 1850, 1860, 1870, 1880, 1890, 1900, and 1910, and of "land in harvested crops" in 1919 and 1929. The maps for 1919 and 1929 are not comparable with those for 1850–1910, since the Census category "land in harvested crops" does not include acreage of crop failure, of idle or fallow land, or of pasture. The Census of 1920 was the last in which acreage of improved land was reported. Although a map could have been compiled showing improved land for that year, it was thought best to reproduce instead the map showing land in harvested crops in 1919, which may be compared with the map for 1929.

Plates 145D–146B show the increase in acreage of improved land by decades between 1850 and 1920; Plate 146, maps C and D show respectively the increase in acreage of land in harvested crops, 1909–1924 and 1924–1929. Plate 146, maps E–K show the decrease in acreage of improved land by decades between 1850 and 1910; Plate 146, maps L and M show respectively the decrease in acreage of land in harvested crops, 1909–1924 and 1924–1929. Map C is thus comparable with map L and map D with map M, but, owing to the difference in the periods covered, map C is not comparable with map D, nor map L with map M.

Farm Tenancy, 1880, 1900, 1920, 1930

[PLATE 146N–Q]

This series of four maps shows the percentage of all farmers who were tenant farmers in 1880, 1900, 1920, and 1930. The maps for 1880, 1900, and 1920 are based on percentage figures derived from the Census reports for those years as shown on a map illustrating an article by L. C. Gray and others, "Farm Ownership and Tenancy," *Agricultural Yearbook, 1923*, U. S. Department of Agriculture, 1924, pp. 507–600 (map on p. 513). The map for 1930 was compiled from Census information furnished by courtesy of the Bureau of Agricultural Economics. Census statistics on tenure first became available in 1880, in which year 25.6 per cent of all farmers in the United States were tenants; in 1900 35.3 per cent, in 1920 38.1 per cent, and in 1930 42.4 per cent were tenants. "When the percentages are calculated on the basis of persons engaged in agriculture, instead of on the basis of the number of farms operated, it appears that the increase in the percentage of tenant farms was not entirely at the expense of the proportion of owner farmers, but may have been partly at the expense of farm wage laborers" (*ibid.*, p. 512).

Average Value of Farm Lands and Buildings per Acre of All Lands in Farms, 1850, 1880, 1910, 1930

[PLATE 147A–D]

Average Value of Farm Implements and Machinery per Acre of All Lands in Farms, 1850, 1880, 1910, 1930

[PLATE 147E–H]

The maps in these two series were compiled from statistics published in the U. S. Census reports. The symbols on the maps for 1910 and 1930 are adjusted so as to take account of changes in the value of the dollar since 1850. Since the dollar had almost exactly the same value in 1880 as in 1850 a similar adjustment was not deemed necessary for the maps for 1880. In each series a given symbol represents approximately the same value in terms of wholesale prices prevailing in 1850, although it may represent different values in terms of the prices prevailing at the date of the map. This adjustment was made with reference to the index numbers tabulated and discussed on pp. 131–132, above, and plotted on Plate 134 E.

While each series as a whole probably gives a sufficiently accurate general view of comparative values in the several sections of the United States at different dates, caution should be exercised in interpreting the data as shown for any one state. For example, a marked decrease in the average value of farm lands and buildings in any one state between two census dates may have been due to an increase in the total area of land in farms of relatively low value and not necessarily to a decrease in the value of the particular farm lands reported at the first census date. Accordingly, the maps should be compared with those showing increases and decreases in acreage of improved land and of land in harvested crops (Pls. 145D–146M).

FOREIGN COMMERCE, 1701-1929

[PLATES 148-151]

INASMUCH as there are no published statistics of colonial commerce before 1697, and beginning with that date only of the commerce with England, the maps illustrating colonial commerce are confined to the eighteenth century and to England. The initial dates of the two series of maps illustrating United States exports and imports have been fixed by the dates at which the statistics, by states, begin—in the case of exports with 1791, and in the case of imports with 1821. Since there are no statistics of the imports from all countries for 1791-1800, the imports from England for that period have been mapped. No maps illustrating domestic commerce have been included in the *Atlas* because there are no adequate statistics covering this field.

Imports from England, 1701-1800, Exports to England, 1701-1774 [*Plate 148A-E*]. These maps are based upon the tables found in Sir Charles Whitworth, *State of the Trade of Great Britain in its Imports and Exports Progressively from the Year 1697*, London, 1776, Part I, pp. 63-70, 78, and 95. Whitworth's lists of articles exported and imported, while quite inclusive, do not, however, include ships (*ibid.*, pp. xliii-xliv, xlviii-lii, lv-lvi). Since this volume combines the figures for the New England colonies, for Maryland and Virginia, and for North and South Carolina these areas are treated as units. It gives no figures for New Jersey and Delaware, whose trade was negligible. By manuscript additions Whitworth's volume (Library of Congress copy) is carried down to 1801.

Exports, 1791-1929; Imports, 1821-1929 [*Plates 148F-151C*]. For the period through 1880 the maps (Pls. 148F-150A) are based upon the tables found in the following publications of the Treasury Department: *Quarterly Reports of the Chief of the Bureau of Statistics showing the Imports and Exports for the Fiscal Year ending June 30, 1878*, pp. 336-339, 342-345, and 405, and *Annual Statement of the Chief of the Bureau of Statistics on the Commerce and Navigation of the United States for the Fiscal Year ending June 30, 1879* (pp. 25-27), and *June 30, 1880* (pp. 24-25). The maps for 1901-1929 (Pls. 150B-151C) are based upon the following issues of *Foreign Commerce and Navigation of the United States*, published first by the Treasury Department, later by the Department of Commerce and Labor, and later by the Bureau of Foreign and Domestic Commerce of the Department of Commerce: Plates 150B and 151A: issue for 1901, Vol. 1, pp. 52-56; 1902, Vol. 1, pp. 52-56; 1903, Vol. 1, pp. 72-74; 1904, Vol. 1, pp. 130-132; 1905, pp. 40-42; 1906, pp. 46-48; 1907, pp. 44-46; 1908, pp. 48-50; 1909, pp. 52-54; and 1910, pp. 54-56; Plates 151B and C: issue for 1925, Vol. 2, p. xi; for 1928, p. xiv, supplemented by figures for 1929 from *Monthly Summary of Foreign Commerce* for December, 1929, p. 84. The statistics are for fiscal years and are given by states, which in most instances correspond to customs districts.

For 1871-1880 and 1901-1910, however, Jersey City belonged to the New York City customs district, and Camden to the Philadelphia district. Since the statistics for these two New Jersey cities cannot be ascertained and united with those for New Jersey, the figures for New York and Pennsylvania for these years are somewhat too large and for New Jersey somewhat too small. Likewise in 1920-1929 certain ports of entry belonged in customs districts whose headquarters lay in neighboring states. This explains why no exports or imports are shown for certain states on Plate 151B and C even though some foreign trade flowed through their ports of entry. It also accounts for a certain degree of exaggeration or under-representation of the foreign trade of other states. In *Foreign Commerce of the United States* tables are given listing the ports of entry by customs districts. As changes were made in these districts during the decade covered by the maps, it has been deemed impracticable to attempt to show their boundaries.

In comparing any two maps for different decades changes in price levels should be borne in mind (see pp. 131-132, above).

The World, Showing Imports from and Exports to the United States, 1821-1929 [*Plate 151D-G*]. These four maps show the value of imports received from the United States by the different major regions of the world, and the value of exports shipped to the United States from the same regions. They cover the period 1821-1929 inclusive. Maps D, E, and F cover three decades each; map G covers the decade 1911-1920 and the nine years 1921-1929. The values of exports and imports are depicted by symbols representing globes. For each region the globes in the upper row reveal approximately the values of commodities received from the United States, and those in the lower row the values of commodities shipped to the United States. The relative volumes of the globes are proportional to the values represented. As on Plate 60, globe symbols instead of circles are employed on account of the extreme variations in the quantities that have to be shown. In order to eliminate so far as possible the effect of changes in price levels since 1821 the scales upon which the globes have been drawn have been adjusted so that all globes represent values in terms of dollars of 1821 and hence are directly comparable. A separate scale, however, is given for each decade, showing the values in terms of the dollars of that decade. These scales were constructed by using the index numbers of wholesale prices plotted in the graph shown on Plate 134E (see p. 132, above). Averages of the index numbers for each decade of 1821-1920, and for the nine years 1921-1929 were determined and the scales drawn with reference to these averages. For example: the average for the index numbers for 1821-1830, is 108.9; that for the decade 1911-1920, is 142.1. Accordingly, the scale for 1911-1920 has been constructed in such a way as to indicate that the volume of a globe representing any given value for 1911-1920 would be $\frac{108.9}{142.1}$ of the volume of a globe representing the same value for 1821-1830.

The several regions whose trade with the United States is illustrated on these maps correspond to the major regions for which statistics of exports and imports are classified in recent numbers of the *Statistical Abstract of the United States*: *i.e.*, Northern North America, Southern North America (including the West Indies), South America (Caribbean Region), South America (East Coast), South America (West Coast), Northwestern and Central Europe, Northeastern Europe, Southwestern Europe, Southeastern Europe (including Turkey in Asia, 1821-1850), Asia (including the Philippines), Africa, and Oceania (including Australia and New Zealand). Western Asia, Southern and Southeastern Asia, and Eastern Asia (including the Philippines and Soviet Russia in Asia) are differentiated on the map for 1921-1929. The maps are based on totals computed from statistics found in the following publications: Isaac Smith Homans, Jr., *An Historical and Statistical Account of the Foreign Commerce of the United States, 1820-1856*, New York, 1857, pp. 67-181; U. S. Treasury Department, *Quarterly Reports of the Chief of the Bureau of Statistics Showing the Imports and Exports of the U. S. for the Four Quarters of the Year Ending June 30, 1888, and for the Corresponding Quarters of the Fiscal Year 1887*, 1889, pp. 188-193; U. S. Bureau of Statistics (Treasury Department), *Statistical Tables Exhibiting the Commerce of the United States with European Countries from 1790 to 1890*, 1893, pp. xx-xlv; U. S. Bureau of Statistics (Department of Commerce and Labor), *Statistical Abstract of the World . . .*, 1904, pp. 3805-3936; U. S. Bureau of Statistics (Treasury Department), *The Foreign Commerce and Navigation of the United States*, published annually; U. S. Bureau of Statistics, *Statistical Abstract of the United States*, published annually. Through 1842 the fiscal year for which the statistics are given in these publications ended on September 30, from 1843 through 1917 it ended on June 30, and from 1918 through 1929, on December 31.

Besides possible inaccuracies in the basic statistics used, there are two other causes of minor errors in the construction of these maps: (1) the inaccuracy of the average index numbers used in reducing all maps to a uniform scale (see above), and (2) discrepancies in the regions for which the basic statistics were tabulated for different years (for example, in 1869 the figures for British Honduras were included with the figures for other British possessions in North America; since it was not possible to segregate these figures, they had to be included in preparing Plate 151E in the totals for "Northern North America"). It should also be noted that map G is not strictly comparable with the others since the globes for 1921-1929 illustrate the commerce of nine years only as contrasted with the commerce of full decades shown by the other globes. It is believed, however, that despite the errors and inconsistencies due to these causes the series gives a fairly satisfactory general view of the trend of American foreign commerce.

DISTRIBUTION OF WEALTH, 1799-1928

[PLATES 152-155]

THREE criteria have been used for measuring and mapping the distribution of wealth: statistics of wealth, statistics of banks, and statistics of federal income taxes. It would have been highly desirable to show consistently the local distribution of wealth within the several states. Unfortunately this was not possible, except in so far as the maps representing the distribution of banks within the states (Pl. 154A, C, E, G, and J) may be said to reveal the distribution of wealth therein. The other maps are by states. Statistics of wealth as a rule are by states and not by counties, and where county statistics exist they have been prepared on different bases and by different methods. Even the figures for states for different years are not comparable, since here again different bases were used, and there have been marked changes in price levels (see pp. 131-132, above).

Each map showing total wealth (except that for 1912), and each map showing total federal income taxes is accompanied with a corresponding per capita map.

Wealth, 1799-1922 [*Plates 152-153*]. Plate 152, maps A and B, showing Wealth (Houses and Lands), 1799, are based upon the table found in Timothy Pitkin, *Statistical View of the Commerce of the United States of America*, New York, 1817, p. 372. The "houses and lands" were valued for the purpose of levying a direct tax. Plates 152C-153D, Wealth (Taxable Property), 1850, and Wealth (All Property), 1880, 1912, and 1922 are based upon census statistics. These are found in the publication of the Bureau of the Census, *Wealth, Debt, and Taxation, 1922: Estimated National Wealth*, Washington, 1924, pp. 25-27. For what is included under "wealth" for each of these three years see the same volume, pp. 16-20. There were no returns for Minnesota for 1850. The value of slaves is included in the statistics for that year. The specified items of wealth for 1880, 1912, and 1922 differ somewhat, and do not include intangibles. The maps of this series are only roughly comparable.

Banks, 1800-1928 [*Plate 154*]. Maps A, C, and E, showing the number and location of banks in 1800, 1830, and 1850, are based chiefly upon the official registers of the states, local histories, the directories of cities, the statutes, journals, and documents of the states, and histories of banks and banking. For map C use was made of the lists of banks found in Albert Gallatin, *Considerations on the Currency and Banking System of the United States*, Philadelphia, 1831, pp. 97-106; and for map E, of the lists found in the *Bankers' Magazine* (Baltimore) for 1848-1852. The chief source of information for maps G and J, showing the number and location of banks in 1880 and 1910, is the *Bankers' Directory* for 1880 and 1910, respectively, published by Rand McNally and Company.

All banks, whether state, national, or private, doing business under the name of "bank," "trust company," or similar designation are counted. Private banks whose business was not thus designated are not counted. Branch banks when not located in the same town as the parent bank are counted. Since the statistics for 1830 and 1850 are imperfect and scattering, a few banks for those years may not have been discovered.

Since rural banks are on the average much smaller than city banks, maps based on banking capital by counties would show greater differences as between rural and urban areas than do the maps based on the number of banks.

The number of banks for each of the five years is as follows: 32 for 1800, 472 for 1830, 988 for 1850, 4550 for 1880, and 24,600 for 1910.

Baltimore is treated as a part of Baltimore County, St. Louis as a part of St. Louis County, and the Virginia cities as parts of the counties to which they historically belong.

Maps B, D, F, H, K, and L show bank capital by states: Maps B and D, for 1801 and 1830, are based on figures given in *Monthly Summary of Commerce and Finance of the United States, for the Fiscal Year 1899*, New Series, Vol. 6 (House Doc. No. 573, Part I, 55th Cong., 2nd Sess.), Washington, 1899, pp. 208-209. Map F, showing capital stock of state banks in 1850, is based on a table in the same publication, p. 218 ff. Maps H and K, capital of national banks in 1880 and 1910, are based on *Annual Report of the Comptroller of the Currency to the Third Session of the Sixty-First Congress of the United States, 1910* (Treasury Doc. No. 2590), Washington, 1911, pp. 371 ff. Map L, capital of national banks and of "all banks reporting," 1928, is based on tables in *Statistical Abstract of the United States, 1929*, Washington, 1930, pp. 265 and 271. A question mark means that no figure for bank capital was found, although banks existed in the state at the time.

Income Taxes, 1866, 1928 [*Plate 155*]. Maps A and B, showing federal income taxes, 1866, are based upon the income tax receipts found in the *Report of the Commissioner for Internal Revenue* for 1866, p. 272. The year 1866 (fiscal) was selected because the total receipts were at a maximum that year. The first tax on incomes was authorized in 1861, and the last tax was collected in 1873. No data on income taxes are given in the statistics for Dakota Territory, Indian Territory, Arizona Territory, and Florida. Hence these areas are left blank on maps A and B.

Income taxes per capita are not indicated on map B for Montana and Idaho because, owing to lack of census figures for the population of these territories in 1860, it was impossible to estimate the population as of 1866.

Maps C and D, federal income taxes, 1928, are based upon the table of receipts of income and profits taxes found in the *Report of the Secretary of the Treasury* for 1928, p. 1524. The receipts are for the fiscal year.

PLANS OF CITIES, 1775-1803

[PLATES 156–159]

THIS series of seven maps illustrates some of the principal cities of the United States at the close of the colonial or the beginning of the national period of American history. The cities chosen were those of the largest population and greatest historical importance at that time. The maps selected are those best adapted for illustration. With the exception of the one for New York, all the maps have been reduced in size. Those for Boston, Philadelphia, Charleston, New Orleans, and Baltimore have been further reduced by trimming. On the map of Charleston the title and on those of Boston and New Orleans the lists of references have been moved so as to appear on the parts of the maps reproduced. A few of the references on the map of New Orleans (upper right-hand corner) are not shown on the part of the map that is reproduced. The references to these maps are as follows:

A Plan of the Town of Boston, 1775 [*Plate 156*]. Lieutenant Page's map, reproduced from copy in W. Faden, *Atlas of the Battles of the American Revolution*, Bartlett and Welford's edition, New York, *ca.* 1845, No. 18 (Division of Maps, Library of Congress).

Charlestown, South Carolina, 1780 [*Plate 157A*]. From "Plan of the Siege of Charlestown in South Carolina, 1780," in Faden, *op. cit.*, No. 10.

Plan of the City of Philadelphia . . . by Benjamin Easburn, Surveyor General, 1776 [*Plate 157B*]. From original in the Division of Maps, Library of Congress.

Plan of New Orleans . . . (1803) [*Plate 157C*]. From the original of Boquita de Welseri's "Plan of New Orleans, 1803," in the Library of the American Geographical Society, New York. A few of the reference given beneath the title are not shown on the part of the map reproduced.

Plan of the City of Washington . . . (1793) [*Plate 158*]. From reduction of Thackara and Vallance's "engraved and official" map of 1792 in *Universal Magazine*, Vol. 93, London, 1793, p. 41 (Division of Maps, Library of Congress).

Plan of the City of New York Drawn by Major Holland, Surveyor General, 1776 [*Plate 159A*]. Inset of Holland's "Map of the Provinces of New York and New Jersey . . .," in Thomas Jefferys, *American Atlas*, London, 1775 (Division of Maps, Library of Congress).

Warner and Hanna's Plan of the City and Environs of Baltimore . . . 1801 [*Plate 159B*]. From reproduction in C. C. Hall, edit., *Baltimore, its History and its People*, Vol. 1, New York, 1912, facing p. 60.

MILITARY HISTORY, 1689-1918
[PLATES 160–165]

THESE six plates cover the principal wars of the colonies and the United States from 1689 to 1918: the colonial wars with France and Spain, 1689–1763 (Pl. 161); the American Revolution, 1775–1783 (Pl. 160)[1]; the War with France, 1798–1800 (Pl. 160J); the War of 1812, 1812–1815 (Pl. 162 A–H); the Texan Campaigns, 1835–1836 (Pl. 162 J); the Mexican War, 1845–1847 (Pl. 162 K–O); the Civil War, 1861–1865 (Pls. 163–164); the Spanish-American War, 1898 (Pl. 165A–C); and American Participation in the World War, 1917–1918 (Pl. 165D–H). Other maps bearing upon military history are Plate 34A–D, showing the locations of battles with the Indians, and Plate 166A, showing the locations of certain military engagements in which American forces have taken part in the Far East, in Russia, and in Italy.

The present series has been devised primarily to illustrate the progress of campaigns, although in connection with the Civil War two maps (Pl. 164D and E) are included, which show the movements of Secession and Reconstruction. A uniform scheme of symbols, explained on Plate 160, has been employed on all the strictly military maps except those covering the Spanish-American War, 1898, and American Participation in the World War, 1917–1918. For the World War somewhat different treatment was required and is explained below. Detailed plans of battlefields are not included. The maps show the locations of the more important battles, sieges, etc., and the course of the larger strategic operations. To attempt to illustrate complex tactical movements on individual battlefields was not feasible.

The maps are intended so far as possible to tell their own story, and the symbols have been devised with this end in view. Routes of the more important movements of troops and fleets are shown. The symbols for battles, sieges, and other operations are for the most part connected with route lines. The route lines are only approximate. It should be understood that the purpose in indicating them is not to give a precise representation of the lines of march taken by armies and of the courses followed by fleets, but, rather, to make intelligible the progress of events and their chronological sequence. With this end in view liberties were often taken in drawing the routes. In many instances they have been generalized—shown, for example, as running straight where the actual movement included twists and turns. In some cases two route lines have been drawn arbitrarily as crossing one another when the actual routes may not have crossed. This was necessary in order to show at a glance which of two or more movements was the earlier, since on the maps of this series a convention has been adopted requiring that route lines and other symbols for earlier operations be consistently broken so as to appear to pass or lie beneath those representing operations of later date (see explanation on Pl. 160).

Only the principal engagements are shown. In making selections consideration has been given to the number of casualties, the number of troops engaged (shown graphically for the more important Civil War battles),[2] and the importance of the results. The rejections greatly exceed the selections. This is especially true of the Civil War, in which there were between five and ten thousand "actions." In the case of battles known by more than one name the most approved name was chosen.

On Plate 164C, Reconstruction, 1861–1877, the dates given for the establishment of reconstruction governments and for the reëstablishment of conservative governments are the dates of the inauguration of governors, except as follows: those for Virgnia July 1, 1865, and Oct. 5, 1869, and for North Carolina Nov. 21, 1870, are the dates of the convening of the legislature, and that for Tennessee Aug. 5, 1869, is the date of the election of the governor.

The principal sources of information used in the preparation of Plates 160–165C are as follows:

Colonial Wars with France and Spain, 1689–1763 (Pl. 161)—H. E. Bolton, *Arredondo's Historical Proof of Spain's Title to Georgia*, Berkeley, California, 1925; Francis Parkman, *Count Frontenac and the New France*, Boston, 1877;

idem, *Montcalm and Wolfe*, 2 vols., Boston, 1884; idem, *A Half Century of Conflict*, 2 vols., Boston, 1892; H. M. Sylvester, *Indian Wars of New England*, Vols. 2 and 3, Boston, 1920; Justin Winsor, *Narrative and Critical History of America*, Vols. 4 and 5, Boston and New York, 1884, 1887; William Wood and R. H. Gabriel, *The Winning of Freedom* (Pageant of America, Vol. 6), New Haven, 1927; G. M. Wrong, *The Conquest of New France* (Chronicles of America, Vol. 10), New Haven, 1918; and state and local histories of the colonial wars.

The American Revolution, 1775–1783 (Pl. 160)—E. M. Avery, *History of the United States*, Vols. 5 and 6, Cleveland, 1904–1910; F. V. Greene, *The Revolutionary War and the Military Policy of the United States*, New York, 1911; B. J. Lossing, *The Pictorial Field-Book of the Revolution*, New York, 2 vols., 1859; N. A. Strait, *Alphabetical List of Battles, 1754–1900*, Washington, 1914, pp. 225–230; Winsor, *op. cit.*, Vol. 6, 1888; G. M. Wrong, *Washington and His Comrades in Arms* (Chronicles of America, Vol. 12), New Haven, 1921; Wood and Gabriel, *op. cit.*

War of 1812, 1812–1815 (Pl. 162 A–H)—Henry Adams, *History of the United States*, New York, 1890–1891, Vols. 6, 7, and 8; H. B. Dawson, *Battles of the United States*, New York, 1858, Vol. 2, pp. 88–420; B. J. Lossing, *The Pictorial Field Book of the War of 1812*, New York, 1868; C. P. Lucas, *The Canadian War of 1812*, Oxford, 1906; R. D. Paine, *The Fight for a Free Sea* (Chronicles of America, Vol. 17), New Haven, 1920; Strait, *op. cit.*, pp. 231–234.

Texan Campaigns, 1835–1836 (Pl. 162 J).—N. W. Stephenson, *Texas and the Mexican War* (Chronicles of America, Vol. 24), New Haven, 1921; H. Yoakum, *History of Texas*, New York, 2 vols., 1856.

Mexican War, 1846–1847 (Pl. 162)—Dawson, *op. cit.*, Vol. 2, pp. 444–530; G. L. Rives, *The United States and Mexico*, New York, 1913, Vol. 2; Justin H. Smith, *The War with Mexico*, 2 vols., New York, 1919; Stephenson, *op. cit.*

Civil War, 1861–1865: (1) Maps of Campaigns (Pls. 163A–C, 164A–C)—*Battles and Leaders of the Civil War*, New York, Century Company, 1887–1889; C. R. Cooper, *Chronological and Alphabetical Record of the Engagements of the Great Civil War*, Caxton Press, 1903; F. H. Dyer, *A Compendium of the War of the Rebellion*, Des Moines, 1908, pp. 558–991; A. B. Hart and H. E. Bolton, *American History Atlas*, Chicago, 1930, Map 16; T. L. Livermore, *Numbers and Losses in the Civil War*, Boston, 1900; B. J. Lossing, *Pictorial History of the Civil War in the United States of America*, Philadelphia, 3 vols., 1866; *Official Records of the War of the Rebellion*, Washington, 1894–1922; M. F. Steele, *American Campaigns*, Washington, 1909, Vol. 2, pp. 67–298; T. D. Strickler, *When and Where We Met Each Other*, Philadelphia, 1899; U. S. Surgeon General's Office, *Chronological Summary of Engagements and Battles*; William Wood, *Captains of the Civil War* (Chronicles of America, Vol. 31), New Haven, 1921. (2) Progress of Military Conquest of the South (Pl. 163D)—G. W. Colton, "The New Guide Map of the United States and Canada with Railroads . . .", New York, 1861; John Formby, *The American Civil War*, New York, 1910, maps in portfolio; W. P. Hazard, "Railroad and Military Map of the Southern States," Philadelphia, 1862; C. E. MacGill and others, *History of Transportation in the United States Before 1860*, Carnegie Institution of Washington, 1917. (3) Secession, Reconstruction (Pl. 164 D, E).—Hart and Bolton, *op. cit.*, Map 17; the dates are derived from divers histories and monographs on the reconstruction period.

American participation in the World War in France, Belgium, and Germany is shown on Plate 165D–H. For American operations in Italy, Siberia, and northern Russia, see Plate 166A. Since the character of the military operations on the Western Front during the World War differed materially from that of operations in earlier wars of the United States, it was not practicable to use the same symbols on Plate 165D-H as on the preceding maps of the series.

Plate 165D illustrates some of the main features of the organization of the American lines of communication and of other services behind the front. This organization, effected more than 2000 miles from the military base in America, was not only a colossal undertaking in itself but contributed largely to the final collapse of German resistance. German morale was immeasurably lowered when at last it became clear that the Americans were in a position quickly to concentrate men and materials at the battle front. The "lines of communication" shown are railroads. Only the principal ports, locomotive erection stations, storage depots, and base hospitals are indicated. The map is a simplification of a map accompanying "Organization of the Services of Supply, American Expeditionary Forces," *Monograph No. 7*, Prepared in the Historical Branch, War Plans Division, General Staff, Washington, 1921. The original map, which represents the situation in November, 1918, reveals other features, and many additional details concerning the location of American establishments in the zone of the Services of Supply will be found in the monograph referred to above.

---

[1] The maps of the American Revolution were compiled in part by Mr. K. W. Macbeth.
[2] The graphic representation of numbers of troops engaged in certain battles of the Civil War is based on a table in T. J. Livermore, *Numbers and Losses in the Civil War*, Boston, 1900, pp. 140–141.

Plate 165, maps E and F, illustrate American operations on the Western front. With the exception of the front line of March 21, 1918 (taken from an undated map entitled "War Map of the Western Front," scale about 1 inch to 18 miles, W. and A. K. Johnston, Edinburgh) combat operations are represented on the basis of maps accompanying "Final Report of Gen. John J. Pershing," in War Department, *Annual Reports, 1919*, Vol. 1, Part 1, 1920, pp. 547–642. The zones traversed by the American army, November 17–December 1, and held by the American Army of Occupation, December, 1918–January, 1923, are outlined as described in instructions drawn up by Marshal Ferdinand Foch, commander-in-chief of the allied armies, November 16 and December 12, 1918 (see De Chambrun and De Marenches, *The American Army in the European Conflict*, New York, 1919, pp. 311 and 315).

The combat operations of the American Expeditionary Forces were of two kinds: (1) the holding of stationary sectors of the front, and (2) offensive movements. Sectors held are shown by bands ruled in blue in such a way as to indicate approximately the total length of time that each sector was occupied. Offensive movements are shown by solid blue patches representing the ground gained by American forces. The dates have been generalized in some instances to show periods within which American troops were actively engaged rather than the particular days when they were actually in the lines.

Plate 165, maps H and G, respectively, show in some detail the St. Mihiel and Meuse-Argonne offensives. They are based upon two maps accompanying General Pershing's report (cited above), *i.e.*, sheets of the maps published by the French Service Géographique de l'Armée, 1:80,000, upon which are printed lines indicating the daily position of the front. These maps, which were compiled by "G-3," or the operations section of General Headquarters of the American Expeditionary Forces, bear the following statement: "It is thought the lines shown are as near accurate as it will ever be possible to obtain." On the originals the lines are marked for the positions of the front line at each successive midnight. These positions are reproduced on map H only, the map of the St. Mihiel offensive. For the Meuse-Argonne offensive (map G) the lines are so numerous that it would have been confusing to show them all, and hence, for all but the initial and final stages of the offensive when rapid advances were made, the front lines are shown at five-day intervals.

POSSESSIONS AND TERRITORIAL CLAIMS OF THE UNITED STATES; ALSO CERTAIN MILITARY OPERATIONS AND GROUNDS FORMERLY FREQUENTED (ca. 1815–1860) BY AMERICAN WHALERS

[PLATE 166]

THE maps on Plate 166 illustrate a variety of important interests of the government of the United States and activities of its citizens in different parts of the world.

POSSESSIONS, DEPENDENCIES, TERRITORIAL CLAIMS, AND TREATY AGREEMENTS

[PLATE 166]

As is shown by the legend on map A, which applies to all the maps on Plate 166, possessions, territorial claims, and leaseholds of the United States are colored red or in the case of the smaller areas are indicated by red lines beneath their names. In the category "possessions" are classified the areas over which the United States maintains either full and undisputed sovereignty or the equivalent (Canal Zone). Red boundary lines on the sea mark limits within which lands, islands, and adjacent territorial waters (but not, of course, the high seas beyond the three-mile limit from shore) have been ceded to the United States by treaty. There are certain areas to which the United States has claims to sovereignty that are contested but probably valid; the names of these are underlined by thin red lines. The names of certain other areas of doubtful international status that have been claimed for the United States, or in regard to which there appear to be grounds upon which an American claim could be based, are underlined by dotted red lines. The names of leaseholds of the United States are underlined by heavy broken red lines. Areas within which the United States has acquired by international agreement rights to the use of land or adjacent waters are shown in blue. Blue boundary lines mark the limits of areas where pelagic sealing has been prohibited by international agreements in which the United States has taken part. The names of certain republics in Central America and the Caribbean region whose full exercise of sovereignty is to some degree limited by treaty or other agreement with the United States are shown by red rulings. Areas over which the United States has apparently renounced or allowed to lapse any claims that it may formerly have had are underlined by thin black lines. The several possessions, dependencies, claims, and rights will be discussed in geographical order under the following headings: Pacific Ocean, Central America and Caribbean Region, North Atlantic Fisheries Controversy, the Antarctic, and Alaska and the Arctic.

Pacific Ocean

[PLATE 166, A, D, F]

Midway Islands (Map A). These two small islets were discovered by Captain N. C. Brooks of the American ship *Gambia* in 1859. They were surveyed and taken possession of in behalf of the United States by Captain William Reynolds of the U. S. S. *Lackawanna* in 1867 and are now under the jurisdiction of the Hawaiian Islands (see W. T. Brigham, *An Index to the Islands of the Pacific Ocean*, Honolulu, 1900, p. 105; E. M. Douglas, *Boundaries, Areas, Geographic Centers, and Altitudes of the United States* ... (U. S. Geol. Survey Bull. 817), Washington, 1930, pp. 46–47; C. P. Howland, *Survey of American Foreign Relations* [annual], New Haven, 1930, p. 295).

Hawaiian Islands (Map A). Pearl Harbor was leased by the United States as a naval base in 1887. In 1893 the Queen of Hawaii was forced to abdicate as a result of a revolution "fomented largely by American citizens" who attempted "to negotiate a treaty of annexation with the Harrison administration." The American government, however, for several years was reluctant to appropriate the islands. Annexation was finally brought about by joint resolution of Congress, May 4 to July 6, 1898. In April, 1900, Congress authorized the creation of the "Territory of Hawaii" (Howland, *op. cit.*, pp. 298–301).

Philippine Islands (Map D). These islands were ceded to the United States by Spain under the terms of the Treaty of Paris, 1898, which brought the Spanish-American War to a close. The United States paid Spain $20,000,000 for them. Article III of the treaty describes the boundaries within which the islands lie (W. M. Malloy, *Treaties, Conven-*

tions, International Acts ... between the United States of America and Other Powers, Vol. 2, 1910, p. 1691).[1] Owing to an error in the description of the lines in the treaty the islands of Cagayan Sulú and Sibutú were not included. These were ceded by Spain to the United States by treaty in 1900, in consideration for which the United States paid Spain $100,000 (*ibid.*, pp. 1696–1697). By this treaty the Philippine-Borneo boundary has been interpreted to be the line defined by earlier treaties to which Spain was a party, which gave Spain territorial rights up to within nine nautical miles (three leagues) of North Borneo. The fringing reef, however, results in a coast line from which it is exceedingly difficult to measure the three-league line. Hence by a convention between the United States and Great Britain signed January 2, 1930, a more practicable line was defined which approximates very closely the three-league limit (Senate Documents, 71st Cong., 2nd Sess., 1930, Executive D).

Las Palmas (Map D). Although this island lies within the boundaries of the Philippines as delimited by the Treaty of Paris, sovereignty was awarded in 1928 to the Netherlands by an arbiter appointed by the Hague Permanent Court of Arbitration (Douglas, *op. cit.*, p. 49; Howland, *op. cit.*, pp. 266–267).

Guam (Map A). This island was ceded by Spain to the United States by the Treaty of Paris, 1898 (Malloy, *op. cit.*, p. 1691).

Wake Island (Map A). This island was discovered by Lieutenant Charles Wilkes, U. S. N., in 1841 and claimed by him for the United States. Possession was definitely taken for the United States by the U. S. S. *Bennington*, January 17, 1899 (Howland, *op. cit.*, pp. 294 and 304–305; Douglas, *op. cit.*, pp. 50–51).

American Samoa (Map F). In 1878 the United States signed a treaty with the independent government of Samoa which gave to the former, among other privileges, the right to establish a naval station at the port of Pagopago (Malloy, *op. cit.*, p. 1574). A conflict of interests between Great Britain, Germany, and the United States in Samoa was brought to a close in 1899 by the conclusion of a tripartite convention by the three governments. Under this treaty Great Britain and Germany renounced in favor of the United States all rights and claims to the islands of the Samoan group east of longitude 171° west of Greenwich (*ibid.*, p. 1596). Although President Roosevelt in 1904 "accepted the cession of the eastern group ... made by the island chiefs in 1900 ... not until 1929 did the 70th Congress formally accept the cession of the eastern Samoan Islands" (Howland, *op. cit.*, pp. 308–309).

Swain's Island, or Gente Hermosa (Map F). This island was occupied by an American family named Jennings "in 1856 and for many years thereafter." American sovereignty over it was assumed by joint resolution of Congress in 1925, and it was placed under the jurisdiction of American Samoa (Douglas, *op. cit.*, pp. 55–56; Howland, *op. cit.*, p. 305).

Johnston's (or Cornwallis) Island and the Palmyra Islands (Map A). These islands are under the jurisdiction of Hawaii. They have been claimed by Great Britain, Johnston's Island in 1898 and the Palmyra Islands in 1889. Great Britain, however, has withdrawn its claim to Johnston's Island, which "is now acknowledged in official British publications to be an American possession ... Palmyra ... was included by the United States as among the islands belonging to Hawaii in view of claims of annexation by the King of Hawaii in 1862" (Howland, *op. cit.*, p. 295). The subsequent continuous occupation of the Palmyra Islands by American citizens has undoubtedly confirmed the American title to these islands.

Guano Islands (Map A). Various islands have been bonded as guano islands under the terms of an act of Congress of 1856 which provides that:

[Section 5570] "Whenever any citizen of the United States discovers a deposit of guano on any island, rock, or key, not within the lawful jurisdiction of any

---

[1] The northern boundary is defined as "a line running from west to east along or near the twentieth parallel of north latitude, and through the middle of the navigable channel of Bachi, from the one hundred and eighteenth (118th) to the one hundred and twenty-seventh (127th) degree meridian of longitude east of Greenwich" (Malloy, *loc. cit.*). The twenty-first parallel of latitude runs through the Bashi Channel. On Plate 166 D the line has been drawn so as to pass through this channel.

other government, and not occupied by the citizens of any other government, and takes peaceable possession thereof, and occupies the same, such island, rock, or key may, at the discretion of the President, be considered as appertaining to the United States. . . .

[Section 5578] "Nothing in this title contained shall be construed as obliging the United States to retain possession of the islands, rocks, or keys, after the guano shall have been removed from the same." (Douglas, *op. cit.*, p. 54.)

Under Section 5574 the discoverer was required to give bond to deliver the guano to citizens of the United States only.

Between the years 1856 and 1884, inclusive, bonds were filed for about seventy guano islands in the Pacific Ocean and the Caribbean Sea. As many of these as could be identified with reasonable certainty from a list given in J. B. Moore, *A Digest of International Law. . .*, Vol. 1, Washington, 1906, pp. 567–568, are shown on map A, being designated by the letter "G."[1] The status of several islands is still in doubt. Great Britain has laid claim to most of them, and the United States has apparently made no protest. As it is not always practicable to make a definite distinction between the guano islands to which the United States has a doubtful claim and those to which it either has no claim or has apparently allowed its claim to lapse, no attempt was made on Map A to show their status in respect to the claims of the United States, except in a few cases. Howland points out that "the doubt as to sovereignty arises in part from the failure of any nation subsequent to the Guano Act to establish a satisfactory basis for a claim to sovereignty on grounds required by international law" (Howland, *op. cit.*, pp. 291–292). It would seem that, among the guano islands of the Pacific, the United States has valid claims to Swain's Island, Johnston's Island, and the Palmyra Islands, and that its claims to Baker and Howland islands, to Kingman Reef, and possibly to McKean's Island are superior to those of any other country.

Bonin Islands (Map A). Commodore M. C. Perry in 1853 took possession of a part of this group for the United States. The United States, however, made no objection when Japan laid claim to the islands in 1861 (Howland, *op. cit.*, pp. 18 and 30).

Tonga Islands (Map A). By a treaty signed in 1886 with the King of Tonga the United States acquired the privilege (not yet exercised) of establishing a coaling station (Malloy, *op. cit.*, p. 1782; Douglas, *op. cit.*, pp. 57–58).

Yap Island (Map A). By treaty with Japan, 1922, the United States acquired the right to "free access . . . in all that relates to the existing Yap-Guam cable or of any cable which may hereafter be laid or operated by the United States or its nationals connecting with the island of Yap," as well as the right to hold property in Yap (Douglas, *op. cit.*, p. 58; Howland, *op. cit.*, p. 312).

Bering Sea and North Pacific: the Fur Seal Controversy (Map A). The main breeding grounds of the northern fur seal are found on: (1) the Pribilof Islands, which were ceded to the United States by Russia in 1867; (2) the Commander Islands, which have remained under Russian sovereignty; and (3) Robben Island, which belongs to Japan. During most of the year the fur seals range far and wide over the waters of Bering Sea and the North Pacific Ocean; but in late spring, summer, and early autumn they congregate in great herds on the shores of these islands and particularly on the Pribilof Islands. Here many "bachelors," or young males, may be killed under governmental supervision without effects detrimental to the continued propagation of the herds. Sealing operations on the Pribilof Islands from the time of their acquisition by the United States were strictly controlled by the American government with a view to the protection of the herd.

A rapid decline in the Pribilof Islands herd, however, was brought about in the seventies and eighties of the last century by pelagic seal hunters, many of them from Canadian ports. Operating on the high seas both north and south of the Aleutian Islands, these hunters indiscriminately slaughtered females with young, as well as young and old males. In order to check this destruction, the United States instituted a patrol on Bering Sea east of the international boundary and seized several vessels of British registry.

A controversy with Great Britain arose as a result of these seizures and of other measures which the American government wished to take to pro-

tect the Pribilof Islands herd. The points at issue were submitted in 1893 to a Tribunal of Arbitration consisting of representatives of the United States, Great Britain, France, Italy, and Sweden and Norway. The tribunal's award was adverse to the United States. It decided that ". . . the United States has not any right of protection or property in the fur seals frequenting the islands of the United States in Bering Sea, when such seals are found outside the ordinary three mile limit." A series of concurrent regulations, however, were formulated by the tribunal and accepted by Great Britain. Among other things, these regulations forbade pelagic sealing at all times "within a zone of sixty [nautical] miles around the Pribilof Islands, inclusive of the territorial waters," and from May 1 to July 31 inclusive "on the high sea, in the part of the Pacific Ocean, inclusive of the Bering Sea, which is situated to the north of the 35th degree of North latitude, and eastward of the 180th degree of longitude from Greenwich till it strikes the water boundary described in Article 1 of the Treaty of 1867 between the United States and Russia, and following that line up to Bering Straits" (*Fur Seal Arbitration. Proceedings of the Tribunal of Arbitration . . .* Washington, 1895, Vol. 1, *Award of the Tribunal of Arbitration*, p. 79).

The lines as thus defined by the arbitrators are shown on Map A by broken blue lines.

For a variety of reasons, among them the entry of Japanese pelagic seal hunters into Bering Sea, the concurrent regulations formulated by the tribunal were ineffective, and the herds frequenting the Pribilof and other islands continued to decline during subsequent years. In 1911 a quadrilateral convention was concluded by the United States, Great Britain, Russia, and Japan. This prohibited all persons and vessels subject to the laws and treaties of the High Contracting Parties "from engaging in pelagic sealing in the waters of the North Pacific Ocean, north of the thirtieth parallel of north latitude and including the Seas of Bering, Kamchatka, Okhotsk and Japan" (Malloy, *op. cit.*, Vol. 3, p. 2967). This treaty is still in force. The thirtieth parallel is shown on map A by a solid blue line.

Central America and Caribbean Region
[PLATE 166 A, C, E]

Porto Rico (Map E). This island was ceded to the United States by Spain under the terms of the Treaty of Paris, 1898.

Virgin Islands of the United States (Map E). These islands were ceded by Denmark to the United States by a convention concluded in 1916. For them the United States paid Denmark $25,000,000 and also, apparently, renounced any claims that it may have had in Greenland (see below).

Canal Zone (Map C). In 1903 the Republic of Panama concluded a convention with the United States relating to the construction of the Panama Canal. Under Article II Panama granted to the United States "in perpetuity the use, occupation and control of a zone of land and land under water for the construction, maintenance, operation, sanitation and protection of said Canal of the width of ten miles extending to the distance of five miles on each side of the center line of the route of the Canal to be constructed." All islands within the limits of the zone, together with the small islands of Perico, Naos, Culebra, and Flamenco, in the Gulf of Panama, were likewise ceded to the United States, although the cities of Panama and Colon were expressly excluded from the areas so transferred. Panama, moreover, undertook to grant to the United States "any other lands and waters outside of the zone above described" which might become needed in connection with the construction, operation, etc., of the canal. In Article III it is pointed out that Panama grants to the United States "all the rights, power and authority within the zone . . . which the United States would . . . exercise if it were the sovereign of the territory within which said lands and waters are located to the entire exclusion of the exercise by the Republic of Panama of any such sovereign rights." (See Malloy, *op. cit.*, Vol. 2, p. 1350; Vol. 3, pp. 2752–2756.)

Since the convention of 1903 the boundaries of the zone have been readjusted from time to time, and certain tracts outside the zone have been acquired by the United States. Some land on the outskirts of Panama City was given back to Panama in 1914; in the same year the shores of Gatun Lake up to the 100-foot contour and in 1924 the valley of the Chagres River up to the 260-foot contour were taken by the United States (Douglas, *op. cit.*, p. 52; Malloy, *op. cit.*, Vol. 3, pp. 2770–2776; map of the Canal Zone, scale 1:100,000, compiled under the direction of O. E. Malsbury, Section of Surveys, January, 1927).

Navassa and Other Guano Islands (Map A). For a general account of the Guano Islands see above. The following islands in the Caribbean Sea bonded under the terms of the Guano Act of 1865 were declared to be under the exclusive jurisdiction of the United States by presidential proclamations: Navassa Island (January 17, 1916), Quita Sueño and

---

[1] In many instances the names given for the islands in the bonds differ from those that appear on the charts and in the pilot books of the U. S. Hydrographic Office. The latter rather than the former names are shown on map A for the following islands in the Pacific whose identification appeared reasonably sure: Fanning (for America Islands), Kingman Reef (for Dangerous Rock), Nuku Nono (for Clarence), Atafu (for Duke of York), Fakaofu (for Low Islands), Manahiki (for Humphrey's), Palmyra (for Palmyros), Penrhyn (for Penhuyn's), Swain's (for Quiros), Vostok (for Stavers). Canton I. (for Mary's), near Enderbury I., is not shown on the map owing to lack of space. The following islands appear more than once in Moore's list: Caroline (also listed as Anne's), Starbuck or Hero (also as Barren or Starve), Enderbury (also as Enderbury's, though the position of the latter corresponds more closely to that of McKean), Palmyros (also as Samarang), Washington (also as Prospect). No islands appear on the charts sufficiently near the listed positions of the following to warrant definite identification: Barbers, Bauman's, David's, Favorite, Frances, Gallego, Ganges, Groninque, Liderons, Mary Letitia's, Pescado, Rierson's, Rogewein's Islands, Sarah Anne, Walker. See Moore, *A Digest of International Law*, Vol. 1, Washington, 1906, pp. 569–580, for additional notes concerning other guano islands in which American citizens have been interested.

Serrana Banks (February 25, 1919), Roncador Cay (June 5, 1919). The three last named are also claimed by Colombia, but in 1928 by an exchange of notes between the two governments "it was decided to maintain the status quo, the United States to use the islands for maintenance of aids to navigation and Colombia to have fishing rights in the adjacent waters" (Douglas, *op. cit.*, pp. 54–55; R. R. Platt, "A Note on Political Sovereignty and Administration in the Caribbean," *Geogr. Rev.*, Vol. 16, 1926, p. 637). An opinion of the Attorney General states that "the dominion of the United States Government was extended over the Swan Islands ... Feb. 11, 1863." The Swan Islands are also claimed by Honduras (Douglas, *op. cit.*, p. 55), but, as Americans have almost continuously occupied them and as the claims of Honduras are vague, the American title appears well founded.

Guantanamo Bay and Bahia Honda (Map A). By an agreement made in 1903 between the presidents of the two nations, Cuba undertook to lease to the United States for an indefinite period Guantanamo Bay and Bahia Honda for use as naval and coaling stations. The boundaries of the lands leased at Guantanamo Bay are shown on Plate 165 C (Malloy *op. cit.*, Vol. 1, p. 358). By a treaty signed in 1912 but as yet unratified by the United States Senate the United States gave up its rights at Bahia Honda (Howland, *op. cit.*, 1929, p. 24).

Great and Little Corn Island (Map A). Leased for 99 years by a convention with Nicaragua signed in 1914 (Malloy, *op. cit.*, Vol. 3, p. 2741).

Gulf of Fonseca (Map A). By the Convention of 1914 with Nicaragua the United States acquired the right to establish, operate, and maintain a naval base on the Nicaraguan shores of the Gulf of Fonseca (*ibid.*).

Isle of Pines (Map A). The treaty of 1903 between Cuba and the United States incorporates the provisions of the Platt Amendment (see below), one of which is to the effect "that the Isle of Pines shall be omitted from the proposed constitutional boundaries of Cuba, the title thereto being left to future adjustment by treaty" (Malloy, *op. cit.*, Vol. 1, p. 363). In a treaty with Cuba signed in 1904 but not ratified by the United States Senate until 1925 the United States relinquished any claim it may have had to this island (Howland, *op. cit.*, 1929, p. 24).

Carribean Republics (Map A). To Cuba, Haiti, the Dominican Republic, Nicaragua, and Panama the United States stands in a special relation. While nominally independent, each of these republics has concluded with the United States a formal agreement relinquishing to the latter the exercise of certain sovereign rights. Furthermore, the United States at one time or another since 1900 has intervened with military forces in all five of these republics.

Cuba. Relations between the United States and Cuba are governed by the so-called Platt Amendment to the American army appropriation bill of 1901. This empowered the President of the United States to " 'leave the government and control of the island of Cuba to its people' so soon as a government shall have been established in said island under a constitution which ... shall define the future relations of the United States" in accordance with certain principles, the more important of which may be summarized as follows: no treaty with a foreign power may be entered into by the Cuban government which will tend to impair the independence of Cuba; the Cuban government may allow no foreign power to obtain lodgment or control over any part of the island; certain restrictions are placed on Cuban fiscal management; Cuba assents to the right of intervention by the United States for the preservation of its independence and the maintenance of treaty rights acquired by the United States under the terms of the Treaty of Paris; Cuba undertakes to carry out plans already devised for the sanitation of the cities of the island (Howland, *op. cit.*, 1929, pp. 16–17). The provisions of the Platt Amendment were "added as an appendix" to the Cuban Constitution of 1901 and incorporated in a treaty with the United States concluded in 1903 (*ibid.*, p. 21; Malloy, *op. cit.*, Vol. 1, pp. 362–363).

Haiti. By a treaty with the United States concluded in 1915 and ratified in 1916 Haiti undertook, among other things, to place her financial affairs under the administration of an American General Receiver; to surrender no territory to other nations; to make no agreement with other nations that would impair her independence; to permit the United States to direct measures of sanitation and public improvement and to aid in promoting the development of her agricultural, mineral, and commercial resources; and to permit the creation of a native constabulary officered by Americans (Howland, *op. cit.*, 1929, pp. 131–133; Malloy, *op. cit.*, Vol. 3, pp. 2673–2677).

Dominican Republic. By a convention signed in 1907 the United States took over the administration of the Dominican customs. On the ground that the Dominican government had not lived up to the terms of this convention, the United States intervened in 1916 and administered the government until 1924. In that year a new convention was concluded which continued the American receivership of the Dominican customs (Howland, *op. cit.*, 1929, pp. 82–105).

Nicaragua. By a convention signed in 1914 Nicaragua granted to the United States in perpetuity "the exclusive proprietary rights necessary and convenient for the construction, operation and maintenance of an interoceanic canal by way of the San Juan River and the great Lake of Nicaragua or by way of any route over Nicaraguan territory." Under the same treaty Nicaragua leased to the United States the Great and Little Corn islands and granted to the United States the right to build a naval base on the Gulf of Fonseca. In return the United States agreed to pay Nicaragua $3,000,000 (Malloy, *op. cit.*, Vol. 3, pp. 2740–2742).

Panama. Besides ceding the Canal Zone to the United States by the convention of 1903 (see above), Panama in its constitution of 1904 conceded that "in return for the guarantee of Panama's sovereignty and independence the 'Government of the United States of America may intervene in any part of the Republic of Panama to reëstablish public peace and constitutional order in the event of their being disturbed' (Article 136). A close fiscal supervision is maintained, and the expenditure of government loans placed in the United States has been restricted" (Howland, *op. cit.*, 1929, p. 209).

North Atlantic Fisheries Controversy, 1818–1912

[PLATE 166 G]

Under Article III of the Treaty of Paris of 1783, which concluded the War of American Independence, it was agreed that the people of the United States should continue to enjoy the liberty they had enjoyed in colonial times of taking fish on all the coasts of British America. It was also agreed that they should have the right to dry and cure fish on the unsettled shores of Nova Scotia (including what is now New Brunswick), the Magdalen Islands, and Labrador, but not on the shores of Newfoundland (Malloy, *op. cit.*, Vol. 1, p. 588).

These provisions were modified under Article I of the Convention of London concluded with Great Britain in 1818, which contains the following clauses:

"... it is agreed ... that the inhabitants of the said United States shall have forever, in common with the subjects of His Britannic Majesty, the liberty to take fish of every kind on that part of the southern coast of Newfoundland which extends from Cape Ray to the Rameau Islands, on the western and northern coast of Newfoundland, from the said Cape Ray to the Quirpon Islands, on the shores of the Magdalen Islands, and also on the coasts, bays, harbours, and creeks from Mount Joly on the southern coast of Labrador, to and through the Streights of Belleisle and thence northwardly indefinitely along the coast ... And that the American fishermen shall also have liberty forever, to dry and cure fish in any of the unsettled bays, harbours, and creeks of the southern part of the coast of Newfoundland hereabove described, and of the coast of Labrador; but so soon as the same, or any portion thereof, shall be settled, it shall not be lawful for the said fishermen to dry or cure fish at such portion so settled, without previous agreement for such purpose with the inhabitants, proprietors, or possessors of the ground. And the United States hereby renounce forever, any liberty heretofore enjoyed or claimed by the inhabitants thereof, to take, dry, or cure fish on, or within three marine miles of any of the coasts, bays, creeks, or harbours of His Britannic Majesty's dominions in America not included within the abovementioned limits ..." (*ibid.*, Vol. 1, pp. 631–632).

On map G the coasts on which American fishermen were permitted by the convention of 1818 to take, dry, and cure fish are shown by a solid blue band; those on which they were permitted to take but not to dry and cure fish, by a ruled blue band.

During the nineteenth century the fishing industry in Newfoundland and Canada grew with a rapidity that had not been anticipated at the time of the signing of the convention, and many portions of the coast unsettled in 1818 were occupied. Inevitably conflicts arose between American fishermen and the local inhabitants. The authorities in Canada and Newfoundland made and attempted to enforce regulations which the Americans held to be in violation of their treaty rights. "For seventy years a state of irritation ... prevailed, which the two governments ... vainly sought to remove through diplomatic channels" (Robert Lansing, "The North Atlantic Coast Fisheries Arbitration," *Amer. Journ. of Internatl. Law*, Vol. 5, 1911, p. 6). The dispute was brought to a head in 1909, when Great Britain and the United States submitted to five arbitrators selected by the Permanent Court at the Hague seven questions concerning "the true intent and meaning" of Article I of the convention of 1818.

The main purpose of these questions was to obtain a decision as to the extent to which Great Britain, Canada, and Newfoundland were entitled under the convention to impose restrictions upon the activities of the American fishermen. Questions 5 and 6 called for rulings in regard to the particular waters and shores of British America where fish could be taken, dried, and cured by American fishermen. The precise meaning of the text of the convention is not clear in respect to these geographical points. Question 5 asked "From where must be measured the 'three marine miles of any of the coasts, bays, creeks, or harbours' referred to in the said Article?" (*i. e.*, in the last sentence of Article I of the convention as quoted above). Here the essential point at issue was whether the United States had renounced forever the right of its inhabitants to take, dry, or cure fish in certain *bays* on the coasts of British America. Did the convention mean merely bays wholly included within British territorial limits and therefore bays with entrances not more than six marine miles wide, or did it mean bays in the geographical sense, many of which have much wider entrances? The United States contended that the former was the case, Great Britain argued in favor of the latter. The award of the Tribunal of Arbitration was favorable to Great Britain: "In case of bays the 3 marine miles [within which the United States renounced its rights to take, dry, and cure fish] are to be measured from a straight line drawn across the body of water at the place where it ceases to have the configuration and characteristics of a bay." In order that no doubt might in future arise as to precisely which were the bays from which American fishermen were excluded, the tribunal made specific recommendations, and in an agreement between the United States and Great Britain concluded in 1912 these recommendations were adopted with certain modifications (Malloy, *op. cit.*, Vol. 3, pp. 2635–2636). On map G the bays from which American fishermen are excluded under the terms of this agreement are shown in black.

The agreement includes the following clause: "It is understood that the award does not cover Hudson Bay." The Bay of Fundy was not taken into consideration by the tribunal, since it was specified by an exchange of notes between the British and American governments in 1909 that "no question as to the Bay of Fundy considered as a whole apart from its bays or creeks, or as to innocent passage through the Gut of Canso, is included in this question [Question 5] as one to be raised in the present arbitration" (Malloy, *op. cit.*, Vol. 1, pp. 841–844). "This is in effect a permanent arrangement in favor of American fishermen" (Lansing, *op. cit.*, p. 20).

Question 6 asked: "Have the inhabitants of the United States the liberty under the said Article or otherwise to take fish in the bays, harbours, and creeks on that part of the southern coast of Newfoundland which extends from Cape Ray to Rameau Islands, or on the western and northern coasts of Newfoundland from Cape Ray to Quirpon Islands, or on the Magdalen Islands?"

In answer, the tribunal replied: "This Tribunal is of opinion that the American inhabitants are entitled to fish in the bays, creeks and harbours of the Treaty coasts of Newfoundland and the Magdalen Islands and it is so decided and awarded."

The text of the award of the Tribunal of Arbitration is given in U. S. Department of State, *Papers relating to Foreign Relations of United States ... 1910*, Washington, 1915, p. 544; also in Elihu Root, *North Atlantic Coast Fisheries Arbitration at the Hague, Argument on Behalf of the United States*, Cambridge, Mass., 1917, pp. lviii–xciv.

The Antarctic

[PLATE 166 B]

In 1908 and 1917 the British government laid claim to sovereignty over the lands and islands in the area shown as "Falkland Islands Dependency" and in 1923 over the lands and islands in the area shown as "Ross Dependency." "British sovereignty over these two sectors has not, it appears, been officially recognized by either Norway or the United States. The interest of the United States concerns the Falkland sector and is due to the discovery in 1821 by Captain Nathaniel B. Palmer of Stonington, Conn., of what was until Wilkins' flight of 1928 thought to be the mainland of 'Graham Land' and of the islands along this coast that now bear Palmer's name" (W. L. G. Joerg, *Brief History of Polar Exploration since the Introduction of Flying*, 2nd edit., American Geographical Society, New York, 1930, pp. 72–73). The United States government has refrained from definitely renouncing any claims it may have in this area. Marie Byrd Land, which lies outside the Ross Dependency, was claimed for the United States by Rear Admiral R. E. Byrd in 1929 (*ibid.*, p. 12).

Alaska and the Arctic

[PLATE 166 A, H]

Alaska (Map A). Russia ceded Alaska to the United States for a consideration of $7,200,000 by a convention concluded in 1867 (Malloy, *op. cit.*, Vol. 2, pp. 1521–1522). The eastern and western boundary lines within which lie the "territories and dominion" conveyed by Russia are

shown, as described in Article I of the convention, by red lines. The eastern boundary is the same as that defined by the convention of 1825 between Russia and Great Britain. The dispute in which the United States engaged with Great Britain over the southern portion of this line is illustrated on Plate 96 A (see also above, pp. 69–70). Alaska was made a territory of the United States in 1912.

The Arctic (Map H). The western boundary of the Alaska purchase is described in the convention of 1867 with Russia as proceeding along the 169th meridian west from Greenwich due north "without limitation" into the "Frozen Ocean." The eastern boundary is described as following the 141st meridian *as far as* the "Frozen Ocean." In so far as this treaty is concerned, the status of the segment of the Arctic Ocean lying between these two meridians and coming to an apex at the North Pole is left in doubt. The United States government has published no definite statement regarding its attitude toward any lands that may be discovered in this segment. Canada, however, through a declaration made by her Minister of the Interior in 1925 has laid claim to the Arctic islands to the eastward of the 141st meridian, thereby relinquishing, presumably in favor of the United States, any claim she might have to islands, if islands exist, west of the 141st meridian. It is on these grounds that the segment in question is shown on map C as lying under United States sovereignty (D. H. Miller, "Political Rights in the Polar Regions," *Problems of Polar Research*, American Geographical Society, New York, 1928, pp. 235–247). The government of the United States has announced no claim to the Arctic islands between the 141st meridian and Greenland (*ibid.*, p. 239), although some of these in the vicinity of Greenland, in view of their exploration by Americans, have at times been shown on maps as appertaining to the United States. Any possible American claims to northern Greenland arising from Peary's explorations were apparently renounced in a declaration of the American government published on the occasion of the convention of 1916 with Denmark under which the Virgin Islands were ceded to the United States (Malloy, *op. cit.*, Vol. 3, p. 2564).

Possession of Wrangel Island was taken in the name of the United States in 1881, but "no attempt seems to have been made to validate this claim" (Joerg, *op. cit.*, p. 67). The same is apparently true of Bennett, Henrietta, and Jeannette islands discovered by De Long in 1881 and claimed for the United States (Douglas, *op. cit.*, p. 59). These four islands lie in the segment of the Arctic to which the Union of Soviet Socialist Republics has laid claim by a declaration published in 1926 (Joerg, *op. cit.*, p. 64), and Russian sovereignty over them appears to be well established.

MILITARY OPERATIONS. WHALING-GROUNDS

[PLATE 166 A]

American Military Operations. Certain localities where American military forces have been engaged in active military operations outside the limits of the United States and its possessions are shown on map A. Only such operations are indicated as were of substantial historical importance and are not illustrated on other plates in the *Atlas* (Plates 160–165). Naval engagements with pirates, military activities in the Philippines during the pacification of the islands, and skirmishes during the course of American military interventions in Central America and the Caribbean republics are not shown. The following sources of information were used: R. W. Neeser, *Statistical and Chronological History of the United States Navy*, 2 vols., New York, 1909; *Report of the Secretary of War* and *Final Report of Gen. John Pershing*, in: War Department, *Annual Reports*, 1919, Vol. 1, Washington, 1920; *Current History*, published by the *New York Times*, volumes for 1918, 1919, and 1920, *passim*; *Archangel: the American War with Russia*, by a Chronicler, Chicago, 1924.

Whaling-Grounds Frequented by American Whalers, ca. 1815–1860. On map A the word "whaling" designates the whaling-grounds most frequented by American whalers during the early and middle periods of the last century when American whaling was at its height. The primary source of information used is a list of the "well-known cruising grounds" visited by American whalers found in C. M. Scammon, *The Marine Mammals of the North-western Coast of North America ... together with an Account of the American Whale-Fishery*, San Francisco, 1874, pp. 213–215; supplemented by data derived from Alexander Starbuck, "History of the American Whale Fishery from its Earliest Inception to the Year 1876" (U. S. Commission of Fish and Fisheries, Part IV, *Report of the Commissioner for 1875–1876*, Appendix A), Washington, 1878, and from W. S. Tower, *A History of the American Whale Fishery* (Publs. Univ. of Pennsylvania, Series in Polit. Econ. and Public Laws, No. 20), Philadelphia, 1907.

INDEX

INDEX

Bold-face numerals refer to plates, capital letters to maps, letters and Roman numerals in connection with plate references to the marginal reference letters and numerals on the plates. Other numerals refer to text pages, the exact quarter of the page being indicated by the letters a, b, c, d, which refer respectively to the upper and lower halves of the first and second columns. Place names appearing on the reproductions of early maps and the names of campaigns, battles, and commanders on the maps of military history have not as a rule been indexed. For the military maps consult the name of the war in question.

INDEX

PART II. PLATES

NATURAL REGIONS, GLACIATED AREAS, OCEAN CURRENTS AND MARITIME EXPLORERS' ROUTES

A

NATURAL REGIONS ACCORDING TO HERBERTSON

Regions having similar types of natural environments are indicated by the same symbols. Herbertson's designations follow with equivalents in parentheses:—

Cold
1a   Norway (and S. W. Alaska)
1c   Tundra
1d   Yukon
1e   Greenland

Cool
2a   Western Europe (Br. Columbia)
2b   St. Lawrence (Appalachians)
2c   Siberia (Central Canada)
2d   Baikalia (Northern Rocky Mtns.)

Warm
3a   Mediterranean (California)
3b   China (Eastern United States)
3c   Turan (Great Plains)
3d   Iran (Mexico)
3e   Mongolia (Northern Great Basin)

Hot
4a   Sahara (Southern Great Basin)
4b   India (Central America)

REFERENCE

Conjectural Routes of the Norsemen ....
Columbus 1st Voyage 1492-1493 _____
"   2nd   "   1496
"   3rd   "   1498
"   4th   "   1504
Verrazano 1524
Drake   1577-1579
Bering   1741
Warm currents
Cool currents
Thicker arrows denote stronger currents
Limits of Pleistocene glaciations

Drake 1579
Columbus 1493
Columbus 1504
Verrazano 1524
Columbus 1492
Columbus 1496
Columbus 1493
Columbus 1502

MAJOR GEOGRAPHICAL REGIONS OR "LANDSCHAFTSGÜRTEL" according to Passarge

B

Polar Cap
Subpolar
Intermediate Zone
Temperate
Subtropical
Warm Zone
Tropical

Cold
Intermediate
Warm

Steppes and desert
Subpolar meadows
Subpolar forests
Temperate forests
Subtropical-temperate forests
Steppes with woodlands
Steppes

Rain forests
Sclerophyllous vegetation; woodlands and steppes
Humid steppes
Dry steppes
Dry regions
C   Coniferous forests
M   Mixed forests
O   Oceanic forests

CULTIVATED CROPS

C

Potatoes
Oats
Wheat
Corn
Cotton
Citrus fruits

WINDS AND SAILING ROUTES: WINTER

D

WINDS AND SAILING ROUTES: SUMMER

E

Arrows fly with the wind, thickening of arrows denotes stronger winds
Westerly sailing routes
Easterly sailing routes

Copyright by Carnegie Institution of Washington

A. HOEN & CO., INC.

RELIEF

Over 8000 Feet
5000–8000 "
2000–5000 "
1000–2000 "
500–1000 "
Under 500 "

SOIL REGIONS

PREPARED BY
C.F. MARBUT
AND
ASSOCIATES
IN THE
SOIL SURVEY

LIGHT COLORED SOILS

1. Brown gravelly and stony loams
2. Grayish to brownish silt loams and loams, often poorly drained
3. Light brown predominantly silty loams from limestone drift
4. Gray to brown silty soils, compact silty-clay subsoils
5. Gray to brown soils, heavy clay subsoils
6. Brown silt loams
7. Yellowish to reddish silt loams often stony
8. Yellowish silty, sandy to stony loams from sandstone
9. Reddish sandy and clay loams
10. Yellowish sandy loams
11. Yellowish silt loams
12. Yellow brown soils, yellow subsoils
13. Red brown soils, red subsoils
14. Light colored soils, brown subsoils

DARK COLORED SOILS

15. Black soils highly calc. subsoils
16. Very dark brown soils, calcareous subsoils
17. Dark chocolate brown soils, calcareous subsoils
18. Dark brown silty soils, yellowish brown subsoils
19. Dark brown loams, yell. brown heavy subsoils
20. Dark brown soils, clay subsoils
21. Black clays & clay loams from marly limestone
22. Dark colored calcareous soils, poorly drained
23. Shallow, stony soils from limestone
24. Chestnut brown soils, calcareous subsoils
25. Medium, dark yellowish brown soils, calcareous subsoils

OTHER SOILS

P. Brown soils of the Pacific Valleys
D. Gray or brown soils of arid regions
S. Sands & sands resting on clay in Florida
Alluvial soils
Marsh and Swamp
Rough and mountainous

Copyright by Carnegie Institution of Washington

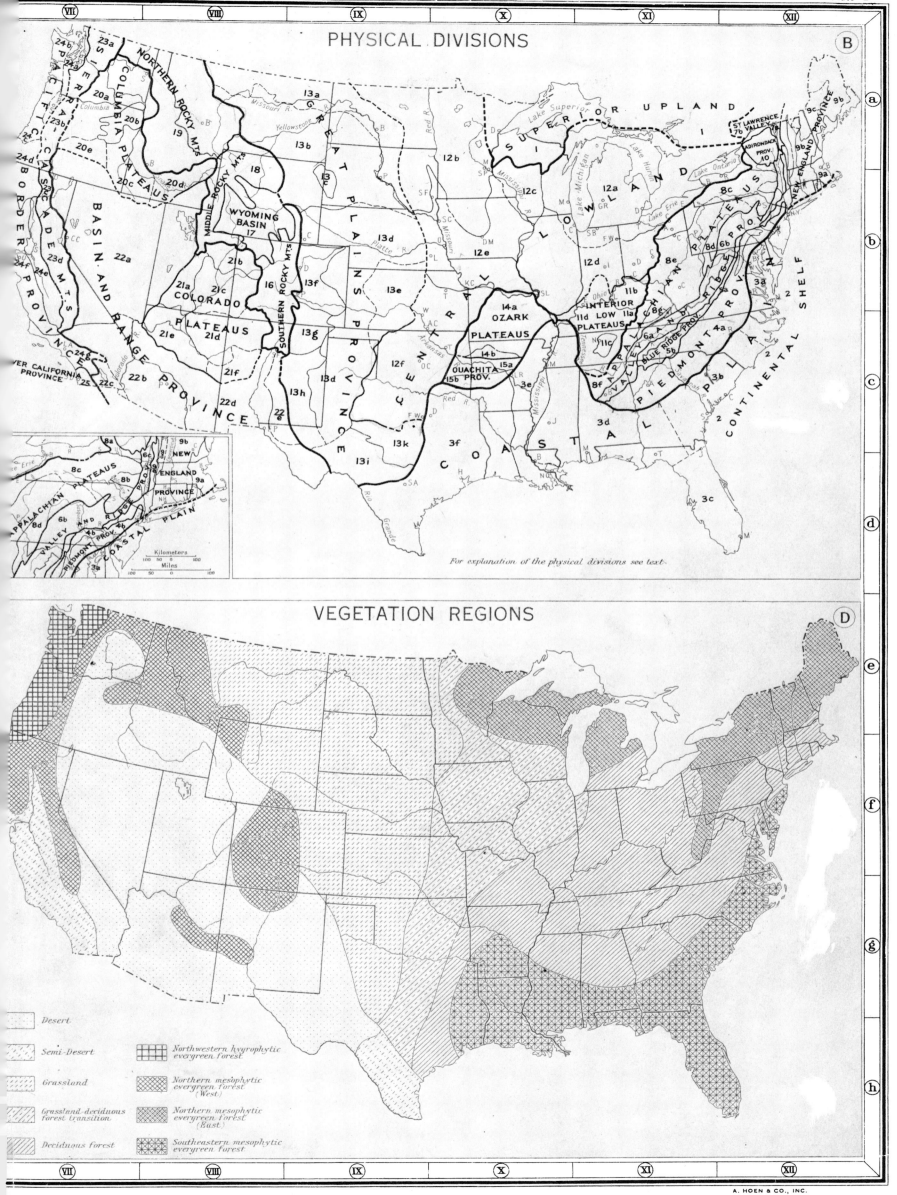

PHYSICAL DIVISIONS

For explanation of the physical divisions see text.

VEGETATION REGIONS

Desert

Semi-Desert

Grassland

Grassland-deciduous
forest transition

Deciduous forest

Northwestern hygrophytic
evergreen forest

Northern mesophytic
evergreen forest (West)

Northern mesophytic
evergreen forest (East)

Southeastern mesophytic
evergreen forest

A. HOEN & CO., INC.

FORESTS; GROWING SEASON

Plate 3

AREA OF VIRGIN FOREST
1620

A

AREA OF VIRGIN FOREST
1850

B

*Each dot represents
25,000 acres*

AREA OF VIRGIN FOREST
1926

C

NATIONAL FORESTS
1930

D

*Each dot represents
25,000 acres*

AVERAGE LENGTH OF GROWING SEASON

E

SCALE OF SHADES

	UNDER 90 DAYS
	90 TO 120 DAYS
	120 TO 150 DAYS
	150 TO 180 DAYS
	180 TO 210 DAYS
	210 TO 240 DAYS
	240 DAYS & OVER

AREA OF FROSTLESS SEASON ZONES

LENGTH OF SEASON WITHOUT KILLING FROST	LAND AREA, ACRES	PER CENT OF LAND AREA OF UNITED STATES
Under 90 days . .	179,127,000	9.4
90 to 120 days . .	308,375,000	16.2
120 to 150 days . .	357,039,000	18.8
150 to 180 days . .	317,831,000	16.7
180 to 210 days . .	317,610,000	16.7
210 to 240 days . .	221,083,000	11.6
Over 240 days . .	202,091,000	10.6

Copyright by Carnegie Institution of Washington

A. HOEN & CO., INC.

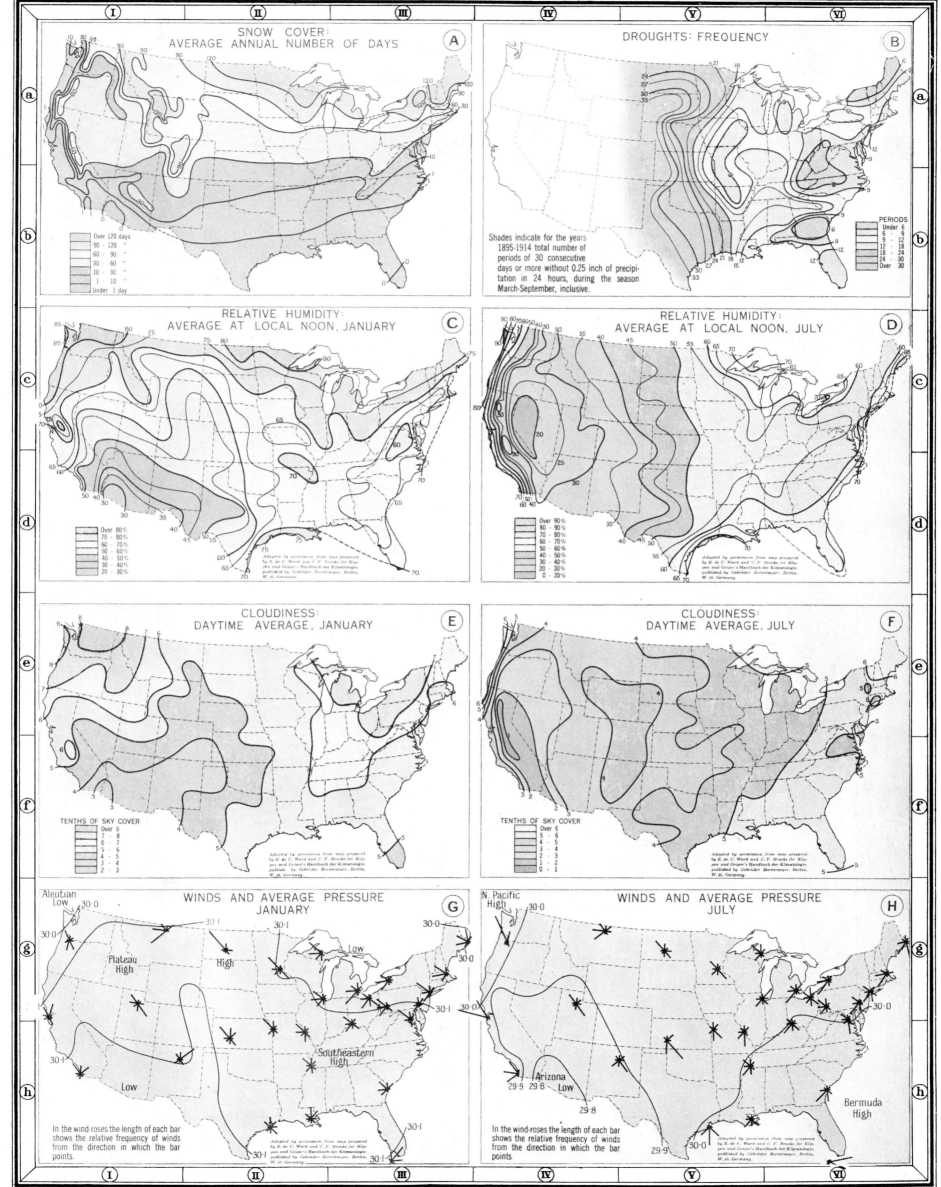

SNOW COVER:
AVERAGE ANNUAL NUMBER OF DAYS

Over 120 days
90 - 120 "
60 - 90 "
30 - 60 "
10 - 30 "
1 - 10 "
Under 1 day

DROUGHTS: FREQUENCY

Shades indicate for the years 1895-1914 total number of periods of 30 consecutive days or more without 0.25 inch of precipitation in 24 hours, during the season March-September, inclusive.

PERIODS
Under 6
6 - 9
9 - 12
12 - 18
18 - 24
24 - 30
Over 30

RELATIVE HUMIDITY:
AVERAGE AT LOCAL NOON, JANUARY

Over 80%
70 - 80%
60 - 70%
50 - 60%
40 - 50%
30 - 40%
20 - 30%

RELATIVE HUMIDITY:
AVERAGE AT LOCAL NOON, JULY

Over 90%
80 - 90%
70 - 80%
60 - 70%
50 - 60%
40 - 50%
30 - 40%
20 - 30%
0 - 20%

Adapted by permission from map prepared by R. de C. Ward and C. F. Brooks for Köppen and Geiger's Handbuch der Klimatologie, published by Gebrüder Borntraeger, Berlin, W. 35, Germany.

CLOUDINESS:
DAYTIME AVERAGE, JANUARY

TENTHS OF SKY COVER
Over 8
7 - 8
6 - 7
5 - 6
4 - 5
3 - 4
2 - 3

CLOUDINESS:
DAYTIME AVERAGE, JULY

TENTHS OF SKY COVER
Over 6
5 - 6
4 - 5
3 - 4
2 - 3
1 - 2
0 - 1

Adapted by permission from map prepared by R. de C. Ward and C. F. Brooks for Köppen and Geiger's Handbuch der Klimatologie, published by Gebrüder Borntraeger, Berlin, W. 35, Germany.

WINDS AND AVERAGE PRESSURE
JANUARY

Aleutian Low
Plateau High
High
Low
Southeastern High
Low

In the wind-roses the length of each bar shows the relative frequency of winds from the direction in which the bar points.

WINDS AND AVERAGE PRESSURE
JULY

N. Pacific High
Arizona Low
Bermuda High

In the wind-roses the length of each bar shows the relative frequency of winds from the direction in which the bar points.

Adapted by permission from map prepared by R. de C. Ward and C. F. Brooks for Köppen and Geiger's Handbuch der Klimatologie, published by Gebrüder Borntraeger, Berlin, W. 35, Germany.

TEMPERATURE: AVERAGE, JANUARY

DEGREES FAHRENHEIT

	Below 0
	0 – 10
	10 – 20
	20 – 30
	30 – 40
	40 – 50
	50 – 60
	60 – 70

TEMPERATURE: AVERAGE ANNUAL MAXIMUM

C

DEGREES FAHRENHEIT

	Below 80
	80 – 90
	90 – 100
	Over 100

Adapted by permission from map prepared
by R. de C. Ward and C. F. Brooks for Köppen and Geiger's Handbuch der Klimatologie,
published by Gebrüder Borntraeger, Berlin,
W. 35, Germany.

TEMPERATURE: AVERAGE ANNUAL MINIMUM

D

DEGREES FAHRENHEIT

	Below 40
	-40 – 30
	-30 – 20
	-20 – 10
	0 – 0
	10 – 20
	20 – 30
	30 – 40
	40 – 50

Adapted by permission from map prepared
by R. de C. Ward and C. F. Brooks for Köppen and Geiger's Handbuch der Klimatologie,
published by Gebrüder Borntraeger, Berlin,
W. 35, Germany.

RAINFALL: AVERAGE, JANUARY.
Including water equivalent of snowfall

E

RAINFALL IN INCHES

	Over 16
	12 – 16
	8 – 12
	6 – 8
	4 – 6
	3 – 4
	2 – 3
	1 – 2
	Under 1

Adapted by permission from map prepared
by R. de C. Ward and C. F. Brooks for Köppen and Geiger's Handbuch der Klimatologie,
published by Gebrüder Borntraeger, Berlin,
W. 35, Germany.

RAINFALL: AVERAGE, JULY

F

RAINFALL IN INCHES

	Over 8
	6 – 8
	4 – 6
	3 – 4
	2 – 3
	1 – 2
	Under 1

Adapted by permission from map prepared
by R. de C. Ward and C. F. Brooks for Köppen and Geiger's Handbuch der Klimatologie,
published by Gebrüder Borntraeger, Berlin,
W. 35, Germany.

ONS, 1567-1861

VII VIII IX X XI XII

a

PASSAMAQUODDY, 1794, C.
PENOBSCOT, 1688, C. +
PENTAGOET, 1645, C. +
ABNAKI, 1646, C. +

b

ST. FRANCIS REGIS, 1760, C.;
LA PRESENTATION, 1748, C.

× CHIPPEWA, 1833, PR.
× L'ANSE, 1833, M.; 1843, C.
SAULT STE. MARIE, 1668, C.;
1828, B.; 1835, M.;
LA POINTE, 1665, C. ×
× CHIPPEWA, 1830, PR.
× CHIPPEWA, 1852, E.; 1853, C.
× WINNEBAGO, 1853, C.
× CHIPPEWA, 1840, M. ×
DAKOTA, 1834, PR. ×
SIOUX, 1842, C. ×
× DAKOTA, 1837, M.
× SIOUX, 1835, PR.
× SIOUX, 1860, E.

MACKINAW, 1671, C.; 1823, PR. ×
× OTTAWA, 1829, C.
OTTAWA, 1838, P.
GREEN BAY, 1671, C.
ONEIDA, 1826, P.; 1832, M. ×
STOCKBRIDGE, 1828, PR. ×
MENOMINEE, 1843, C. ×
× OTTAWA, 1839, PR.
× OTTAWA, 1826, B.; 1838, M.
BROTHERTON, 1842, M. ×
× CHIPPEWA, 1845, L.
× OTTAWA, 1840, E.
LAKEVILLE, 1843, M. ×
NEW GNADENHÜTTEN, 1782, MO. ×

TUSCARORA, 1800, PR.
TONAWANDA, 1820, B.
SENECA, 1811, PR. ×
SENECA, 1868, C.
CAYUGA, 1868, C. ×
ONONDAGA, 1654, C.; 1830, M.
ONEIDA, 1667, C.; 1786, CO.; 1816, E.;
1820, B.; 1825, M.
× MOHAWK, 1667, C.
FORT HUNTER, 1712, E.
NEW STOCKBRIDGE, 1786, CO.
STOCKBRIDGE, 1734, CO. ×
NATICK, 1651, CO. ×
MARTHA'S VINEYARD, 1643, CO.
MASHPEE, 1660, CO.
× NARRAGANSETT, 1721, E.
CATTARAUGUS, 1808, F.; 1822, PR. ×
SENECA, 1798, F.
ALLEGHENY, 1831, PR. ×
SENECA, 1814, P. ×
SHEKOMEKO, 1740, MO. ×
SCHECHSCHIQUANUNK, 1769, MO.
MOHEGAN, 1673, CO. ×
× SCATICOOK, 1742, MO.
× SHINNECOCK, 1741, P.

WINNEBAGO, 1845, C. ×
WINNEBAGO, 1833, PR. ×
× ST. JOSEPH, 1686, C.
× CAREY, 1822, B.
NOTTOWA, 1847, M. ×
MAUMEE, 1822, P. ×
WYANDOT, 1806, M. ×
DETROIT, 1728, C.
NEW SALEM, 1787, MO. ×
FRIEDENSHÜTTEN, 1766, MO. ×
GOSCHGOSCHÜNK, 1767, MO. ×
WECHQUETANK, 1760, MO. ×
GNADENHÜTTEN, 1746, MO. ×
NAIN, 1757, MO. ×
× MUNSEE, 1745, P.

CHICAGO, 1696, C. ×
POTAWATOMI, 1825, M. ×
KASKASKIA, 1674, C. ×
× PEORIA, 1693, C.
× SHAWNEE, 1816, F.
WYANDOT, 1816, M. ×
FRIEDENSTADT, 1770, MO. ×
SCHÖNBRUNN, 1772, MO.
GOSHEN, 1798, MO. ×
GNADENHÜTTEN, 1772, MO. ×
LICHTENAU, 1776, MO. ×

× POTAWATOMI, 1838, C.
1846, P. ×

c

d

× MARYLAND, 1634, C.

IOWA, 1834, P. ×
1833, M.; 1836, C. ×
WYANDOT, 1844, M.
1832, M.; 1833, B.; 1831, B.; 1837, F.
MUNSEE, 1837, MO. × SHAWNEE, 1830, M.
1830, M. × PEORIA, 1833, M.
OTTAWA, 1837, B.
X, 1860, M. × × × WEA, 1834, P.; 1840, B.
7, B., M., 1838, C.
MIAMI, 1847, B. ×
× OSAGE, 1821, PR.
CAHOKIA, 1699, C. ×
VINCENNES, 1750, C.
KASKASKIA, 1700, C. ×

PR.; 1847, C. ×

QUAPAW, 1843, M. ×
SENECA, 1839, M. ×
CHEROKEE, 1832, B. ×
AGE, 1820, PR. ×
M.; 1842, P. × CHEROKEE, 1838, MO.
1829, PR.; 1832, M. ×
CHOCTAW, 1832, B., M. ×
× CHEROKEE, 1820, PR.
P. ×

e

CHEROKEE, 1820, B.; 1830, M.
CHEROKEE, 1803, P.; 1835, B. ×
CHEROKEE, 1817, PR. ×
CHEROKEE, 1801, MO.; 1827, M. ×
CHEROKEE, 1819, PR.; 1821, B. ×
CHICKASAW, 1826, PR. ×
CHEROKEE, 1820, PR.; 1822, M. ×

CHOCTAW, 1846, P. ×
× CHOCTAW, 1832, PR.
ARKANSAS, 1727, C. ×
M. × CHICKASAW, 1821, PR.
× CHICKASAW, 1820, P.
× CHOCTAW, 1818, PR.; 1825, M.

f

× ADAYES, 1717, C.
× YAZOO, 1727, C.
SIX TOWNS, 1825, PR. ×
× CHOCTAW, 1726, C.
ALIBAMU, 1726, C. ×
CREEK, 1822, B. ×
CREEK, 1822, M. ×
IRENE, 1735, MO. ×
GUALE, 1569, C. ×
× NATCHEZ, 1700, C.
× TUNICA, 1699, C.
× APALACHE, 1633, C.
× TIMUCUA, 1567, C.

ASINAI, 1690, C. ×

g

ATACAPA, 1756, C. ×

h

VII VIII IX X XI XII

INDIAN MISSIO

X CHAUDIERE, 1846, C. X

X SNOHOMISH, 1857, C.

FLATHEAD, 1838, PR. X

X PEND D'OREILLE, 1844, C.

X NISQUALLI, 1839, M.
X PUGET SOUND, 1848, C.

X COEUR D'ALENE, 1842, C.   X BLACKFEET, 1859, C.

X CHINOOK, 1851, C.   X PEND D'OREILLE, 1854, C.
X COWLITZ, 1839, C.

X CLATSOP, 1840, M.   X YAKIMA, 1847, C.

CAYUSE, 1836, PR. X

X WASCO, 1838, M.; 1848, C.   X CAYUSE, 1847, C.   X NEZ PERCÉ, 1836, PR.   X FLATHEAD, 1841, C.

X WILLAMETTE, 1834, M.

PEMBINA, 1848, C. X

X CHEYENNE, 1861, L.

OMAHA, 1856, F

PAWNEE, 1834, PR. X

OTOE, 1833, B.:

+ SAN FRANCISCO SOLANO, 1823, C.

+ SAN RAFAEL, 1817, C.

KICKAPOO,
DELAWARE,
M.

+ SAN FRANCISCO, 1776, C.

X SAN JOSE, 1797, C.
X SANTA CLARA, 1777, C.

KANSAS

X SANTA CRUZ, 1791, C.

SAC AND F

X SAN JUAN BAUTISTA, 1797, C.
X SAN CARLOS, 1770, C.

POTAWATOMI, 18

X SOLEDAD, 1771, C.

X SAN ANTONIO, 1771, C.

OSAGE, 182

X SAN MIGUEL, 1797, C.

X SAN LUIS OBISPO, 1772, C.

SAN GABRIEL, 1598-1608?,   SAN JUAN, 1622,
SANTA CLARA, ca. 1608?, C.

X PURISIMA CONCEPCIÓN, 1787, C.   SAN ILDEFONSO, ca. 1617, C.   X TAOS, ca. 1617, C.
X SANTA INÉS, 1804, C.   X PICURIS, ca. 1622, C.
X SANTA BARBARA, 1786, C.   COCHITI, ca. 1622, C.   X X APACHE, 1733, C.   O

HOPI, 1629, C. X   NAMBE, ca. 1622, C.

X SAN FERNANDO, 1797, C.   JEMEZ, ca. 1617, C. X   X X TESUQUE, 1677-1720, C.   OS
X SAN BUENAVENTURA, 1782, C.   X PECOS, ca. 1617, C.   CREEK, 1832, PR., B
X SAN GABRIEL, 1771, C.   ZUÑI, 1629, C. X   SANTA ANA 1677 C   X SAN CRISTOBAL 1677 - ca. 1690, C.   CHEROKEE
                        NAVAHO, 1746, C. X X   X X SANTO DOMINGO, ca. 1617, C.
                        ACOMA, 1629, C. X X LAGUNA, 1699, C.   SAN FELIPE, ca. 1617, C.   SEMINOLE, 1848.
                        PUARAY, ca. 1617, C.   SANDIA, 1580-1581, C.
X SAN JUAN CAPISTRANO, 1776, C.   ISLETA, ca. 1622, C.   SAN DIA, 1617-1680, C.   CHICKASAW, 1852
                        X QUARAI, 1629, C.   CHICKASAW, 1843

X SAN LUIS REY, 1798, C.

X SOCORRO, 1622, C.

X SAN DIEGO, 1769, C.
YUMA, 1780, C. X

X SAN JOSÉ DEL TUCSON, 1776, C.
X SAN XAVIER DEL BAC, 1700, 1732, C.

X SAN CAYETANO DE TUMA CACORI, 1701, 1754, C.
X CUEVAVI, 1701, 173 , C.

APACHE, 1757, C. X   SAN XAVIER, 1746, C. X

B. = BAPTIST
C. = CATHOLIC
CO. = CONGREGATIONALIST
E. = EPISCOPALIAN
F. = FRIENDS
L. = LUTHERAN
M. = METHODIST
MO. = MORAVIAN
P. = PRESBYTERIAN
PR. = PROTESTANT

LA JUNTA, 1683, C

SAN ANTONIO, 1718, C. X

ESPÍRITU SANTO, 1722, C.

Copyright by Carnegie Institution of Washington

A — INDIAN RESERVATIONS, 1900

MAKAH, 1855; OZETTE, 1893; QUILEUTE, 1855; HOH RIVER, 1893; QUINAIELT, 1855; SHOALWATER, 1866; LUMMI, 1855; PORT MADISON, 1855; SWINOMISH, 1855; PUYALLUP, 1854; MUCKLESHOOT, 1857; SQUAXON ISLAND, 1854; CHEHALIS, 1864; SKOKOMISH, 1855; COLVILLE, 1872; SPOKANE, 1881; BLACKFEET, 1873; FORT PECK, 1888; JOCKO, 1855; FORT BELKNAP, 1888; TURTLE MOUNTAIN, 1882; RED LAKE, 1863; DEVILS LAKE, 1867; VERMILLION LAKE, 1881; ONTONAGON, 1854; L'ANSE, 1854; LA POINTE, 1854; LAC DU FLAMBEAU, 1854; ST. REGIS, 1796; YAKIMA, 1855; COEUR D'ALENE, 1867; LAPWAI, 1867; UMATILLA, 1855; CROW, 1868; NORTHERN CHEYENNE, 1884; FORT BERTHOLD, 1870; STANDING ROCK, 1868; CHEYENNE RIVER, 1889; LAC COURTE OREILLE, 1854; WHITE EARTH, 1867; MILLE LAC, 1855; MENOMINEE, 1854; STOCKBRIDGE, 1856; ISABELLA, 1855; TONAWANDA, 1797; ONEIDA, 1788; CATTARAUGUS, 1797; ONONDAGA, 1788; OIL SPRING, 1797; SENECA, 1797; ALLEGANY, 1797; TUSCARORA, 1797; GRANDE RONDE, 1857; WARM SPRINGS, 1855; LEMHI, 1875; KLAMATH, 1864; FORT HALL, 1868; WIND RIVER, 1868; LOWER BRULE, 1889; CROW CREEK, 1889; PINE RIDGE, 1889; ROSEBUD, 1889; SIOUX, 1882; WINNEBAGO, 1865; OMAHA, 1854; SAC AND FOX, 1867; HOOPA VALLEY, 1864; DUCK VALLEY, 1877; ROUND VALLEY, 1854; PYRAMID LAKE, 1874; UINTAH VALLEY, 1861; WALKER RIVER, 1874; KICKAPOO, 1832; SAC & FOX, 1836; POTTAWATOMIE, 1837; MOAPA RIVER, 1873; TULE RIVER, 1873; UTE, 1863; NAVAJO; HOPI, 1882; HAVASUPAI, 1880; HUALPAI, 1883; JICARILLA APACHE, 1874; KANSAS, 1872; PONCA, 1881; OTOE & MISSOURI, 1881; OSAGE; PAWNEE, 1876; PEORIA, 1867; MODOC, 1874; OTTAWA, 1867; SHAWNEE, 1831; WYANDOT, 1867; IOWA, 1883; PUEBLO INDIANS, 1858; ZUNI, 1877; COLORADO RIVER, 1865; MISSION INDIANS, 1875; SALT RIVER, 1879; WHITE MOUNTAIN, 1871; ARAPAHO & CHEYENNE, 1869; WICHITA, 1872; CHEROKEE; CREEK, 1833; SAC & FOX, 1867; EASTERN CHEROKEE, 1874; GILA BEND, 1882; GILA RIVER, 1859; YUMA, 1884; KIOWA & COMANCHE, 1865; CHICKASAW, 1837; CHOCTAW, 1820; SEMINOLE, 1833; PAPAGO, 1874; MESCALERO APACHE, 1873; POTTAWATOMIE, 1867; SEMINOLE, 1894

B — INDIAN RESERVATIONS, 1930

MAKAH, 1855; OZETTE, 1893; QUILEUTE, 1855; HOH RIVER, 1893; QUINAIELT, 1855; SHOALWATER, 1866; COLVILLE, 1872; TULALIP, 1855; KALISPEL, 1914; SPOKANE, 1881; BLACKFEET, 1873; ROCKY BOY, 1916; FORT BELKNAP, 1888; FORT PECK, 1888; FORT BERTHOLD, 1870; DEVIL'S LAKE, 1867; RED LAKE, 1863; VERMILLION LAKE, 1881; WHITE EARTH, 1867; LA POINTE, 1854; LAC DU FLAMBEAU, 1854; ST. REGIS, 1796; YAKIMA, 1855; COEUR D'ALENE, 1867; LAPWAI, 1867; FLATHEAD, 1855; UMATILLA, 1855; WARM SPRINGS, 1855; CROW, 1868; NORTHERN CHEYENNE; CHEYENNE RIVER, 1889; LAC COURTE OREILLE, 1854; TUSCARORA, 1797; TONAWANDA, 1797; ONEIDA, 1788; CATTARAUGUS, 1797; ONONDAGA, 1788; OIL SPRING, 1797; ALLEGANY, 1797; KLAMATH, 1864; FORT HALL, 1868; WIND RIVER, 1868; CROW CREEK, 1889; PINE RIDGE, 1889; ROSEBUD, 1889; SIOUX, 1882; WINNEBAGO, 1865; OMAHA, 1854; SAC AND FOX, 1867; HOOPA VALLEY, 1864; PAIUTE AND SHOSHONE, 1918; DUCK VALLEY, 1877; WINNEMUCCA, 1917; ROUND VALLEY, 1856; PYRAMID LAKE, 1874; SKULL VALLEY, 1912; GOSHUTE, 1914; UINTAH VALLEY, 1861; WALKER RIVER, 1874; KICKAPOO, 1832; PAIUTE, 1912; INDIAN PEAK, 1924; KANOSH, 1929; SHIVWITS, 1916; KAIBAB, 1913; MOAPA RIVER, 1873; NAVAJO; UTE, 1863; JICARILLA APACHE, 1874; OTOE, 1881; PONCA, 1881; OSAGE, 1870; WYANDOT, 1867; TULE RIVER, 1873; HUALPAI, 1883; HAVASUPAI, 1880; CHEMEHUEVI VALLEY, 1907; COLORADO RIVER, 1865; FORT MOJAVE, 1910; HOPI, 1882; CAMP VERDE, 1914; ZUNI, 1877; FORT WINGATE, 1928; PUEBLO INDIANS, 1858; CHEYENNE & ARAPAHO, 1869; WICHITA, 1872; CHOCTAW, 1820; KIOWA & COMANCHE, 1865; EASTERN CHEROKEE, 1874; MISSION INDIANS, 1873; CAMP McDOWELL, 1903; SALT RIVER, 1879; GILA BEND, 1882; FORT APACHE, 1871; SAN CARLOS, 1872; YUMA, 1884; GILA RIVER, 1859; MARICOPA, 1912; SAN XAVIER, 1874; PAPAGO, 1874; MESCALERO APACHE, 1873; ALABAMA AND COUSHATTA, 1928; SEMINOLE, 1894

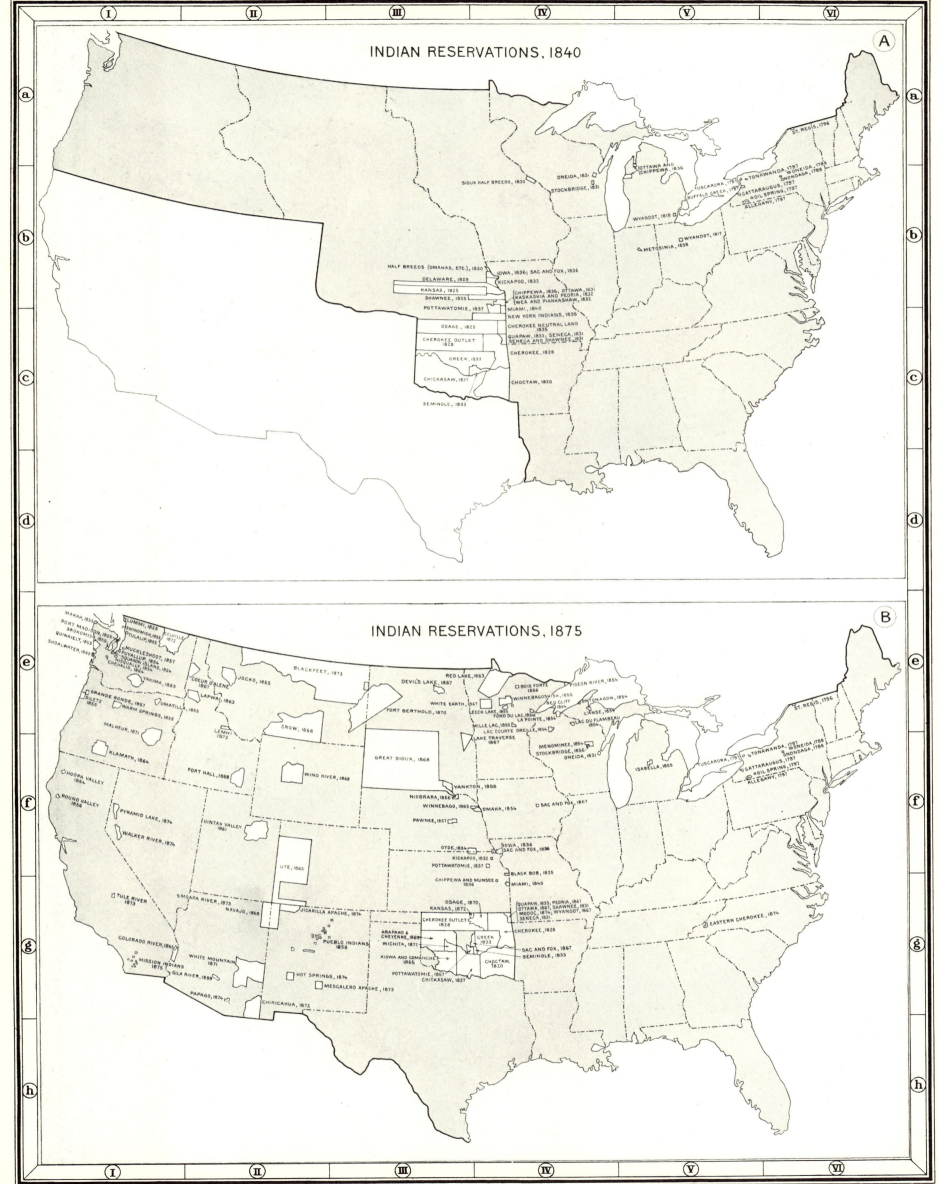

INDIAN RESERVATIONS, 1840

INDIAN RESERVATIONS, 1875

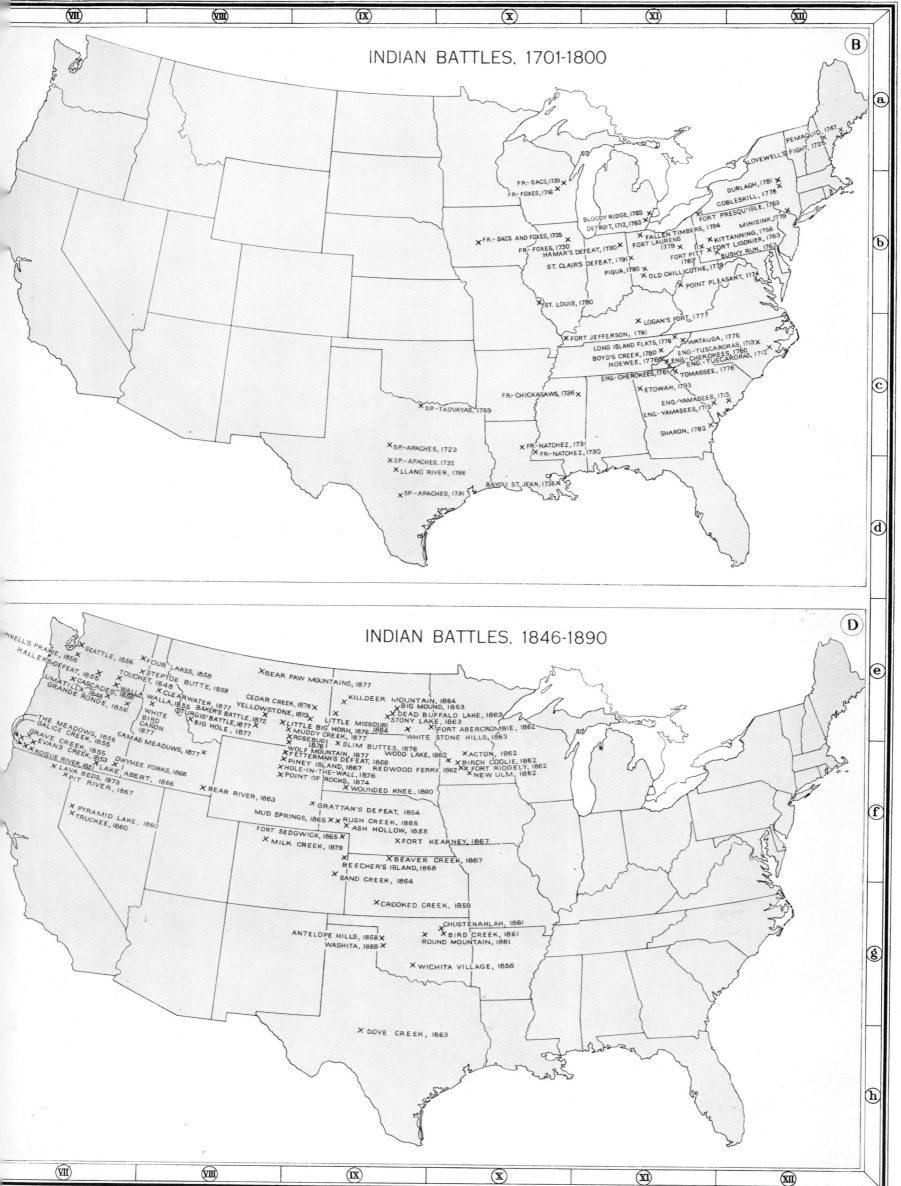

INDIN BATTLES, 1701-1800

INDIAN BATTLES, 1846-1890

Ⓘ   Ⓘ   Ⓘ   Ⓘ   Ⓘ   Ⓘ

INDIAN BATTLES, 1521-1700

PEMAQUID, 1689
FALMOUTH, 1689
FR.-IROQUOIS, 1615
FR.-IROQUOIS, 1609
TURNER'S FALL
SUDBU
FR.-SENECAS, 1687
DUTCH-MOHAWKS, 1626
BLOODY BROOK, 1676
NARRAGANSETT FORT, 1675
GREAT SWAMP, 1637
PEQUOT FO
STRICKLAND PLAINS, 1644

× FORT ST. LOUIS, 1684

PISCATAWAY FORT, 1675 ×
PAMUNKEY, 1624 ×
BLOODY RUN, 1676 × ×
YORK RIVER, 1676 ×

× SP.-ESCANJAQUES, 1601

JEMEZ, 1694 × SAN ILDEFONSO, 1694
SIA, 1688 × × SANTA FÉ, 1680, 1693
CIENEGUILLA, 1694
× × TIGUEX, 1541
ACOMA, 1599
CIBOLA, 1540

× TULLA, 1541

× "STAKED FORT", 1541

× AAYS, 1542 × NAGUATEX, 1542

× MAUILLA, 1540

× SP.-CUITAOS, 1654

ACUERA, 1521 ×

× SP.-CACAXTLES, 1655

INDIAN BATTLES, 1801-1845

× ARICKARA, 1823

× BAD AXE, 1832
WISCONSIN HEIGHTS, 1832 ×
PECATONICA, 1832 ×
APPLE RIVER FORT, 1832 × × KELLOGG'S GROVE, 1832
STILLMAN'S DEFEAT, 1832 × × FORT DEARBORN, 1812
CAMPBELL'S ISLAND, 1814
FORT MADISON, 1812, 1813 × × FORT WAYNE, 1812
× MISSISSINEWA, 1812
TIPPECANOE, 1811
× FORT MASON, 1813 × FORT HARRISON, 1812
× SINK HOLE, 1815

× TALISHATCHEE, 1813
× TALLADEGA, 1813
× ENOTACHAPCO, 1814
× EMUCKFAU, 1814
× HORSESHOE BEND, 1814
× CALEBEE, 1814
× AUTOSSE, 1813
× HOLY GROUND, 1813
FORT SINQUEFIELD, 1813
× NECHES RIVER, 1839 × BURNT CORN, 1813
FORT MIMS, 1813

ENCONFINO, 1818 × × LAKE PITHLACHOKA, 1812
SUWANEE, 1818 ×
CAMP IZARD, 1836 × × DUNLAWTON, 1836
× PLUM CREEK, 1840 WITHLACOOCHEE, 1835 × × FORT MELLON, 1837
WAHOO SWAMP, 1836
DADE MASSACRE, 1835 × LAKE OKEECHOBEE, 1837

Ⓘ   Ⓘ   Ⓘ   Ⓘ   Ⓘ   Ⓘ

Copyright by Carnegie Institution of Washington

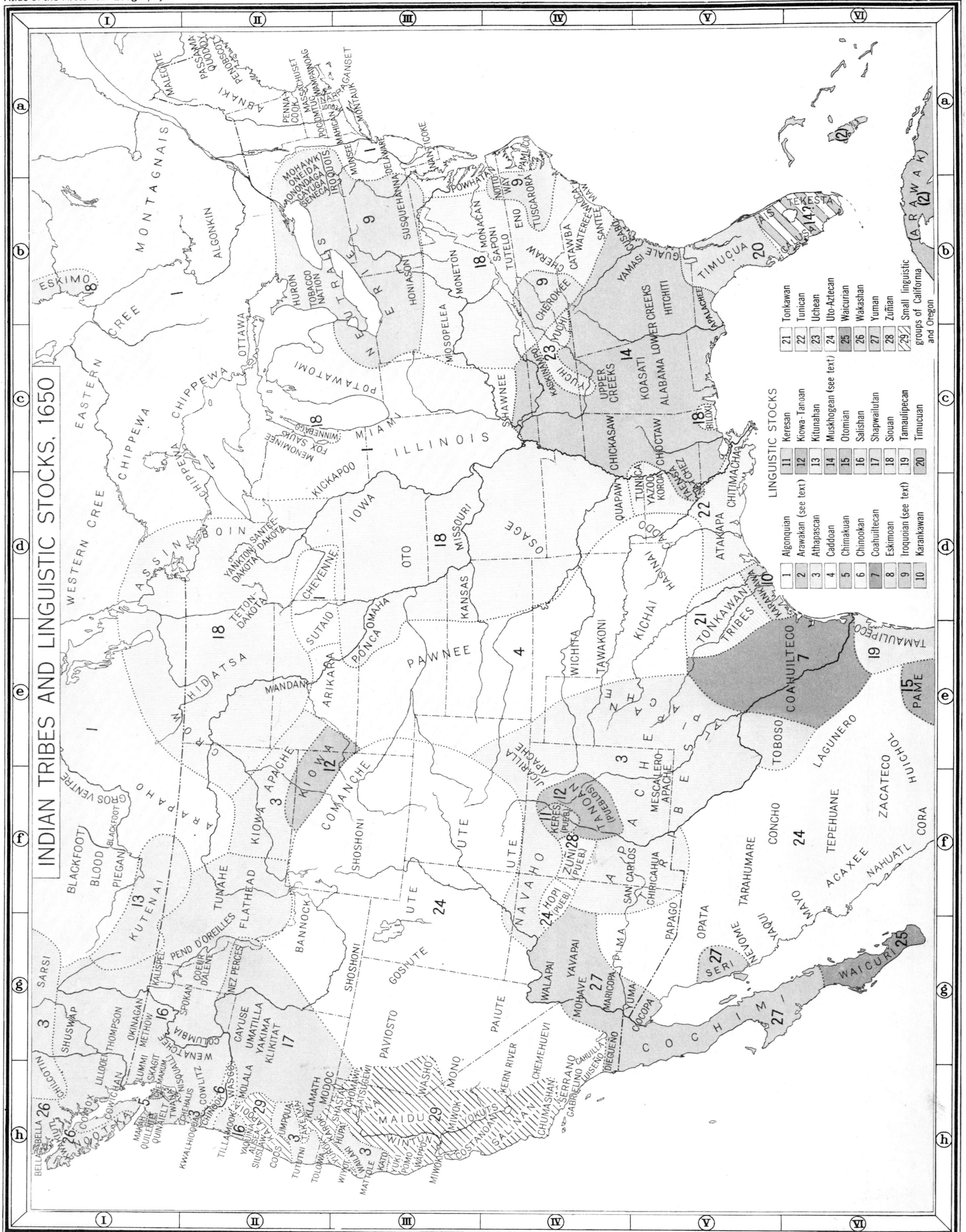

INDIAN TRIBES AND LINGUISTIC STOCKS, 1650

LINGUISTIC STOCKS

1	Algonquian	11	Keresan	21	Tonkawan
2	Arawakan (see text)	12	Kiowa-Tanoan	22	Tunican
3	Athapascan	13	Kitunahan	23	Uchean
4	Caddoan	14	Muskhogean (see text)	24	Uto-Aztecan
5	Chimakuan	15	Otomian	25	Waicurian
6	Chinookan	16	Salishan	26	Wakashan
7	Coahuiltecan	17	Shapwailutan	27	Yuman
8	Eskimoan	18	Siouan	28	Zuñian
9	Iroquoian (see text)	19	Tamaulipecan	29	Small linguistic groups of California and Oregon
10	Karankawan	20	Timucuan		

(Map labels, selected, reading across regions:)

ESKIMO 8 · MONTAGNAIS · CREE · EASTERN CREE · WESTERN CREE · EASTERN CHIPPEWA · CHIPPEWA · ALGONKIN · OTTAWA · POTAWATOMI · MENOMINEE · FOX · SAUK · WINNEBAGO 8 · KICKAPOO · ILLINOIS · MIAMI · SHAWNEE · HURON · TOBACCO NATION · NEUTRALS · IROQUOIS · MOHAWK · ONEIDA · ONONDAGA · CAYUGA · SENECA 9 · ERIE · SUSQUEHANNA · DELAWARE · MUNSEE · MAHICAN · POWHATAN · MONACAN · MONETON · MOSOPELEA · HONIASON · SAPONI · TUTELO · MONAHAN · NOTTOWAY · MEHERRIN · TUSCARORA · ENO · CATAWBA · WATEREE · SANTEE · CHERAW · CHEROKEE 9 · YUCHI 23 · CREEK · UPPER CREEKS · LOWER CREEKS · KOASATI · ALABAMA · HITCHITI · KASKINAMPO · CHICKASAW · CHOCTAW · QUAPAW · NATCHEZ · TAENSA · YAZOO · KOROA · BILOXI 18 · TUNICA 22 · ATAKAPA · CHITIMACHA · CADDO · HASINAI · ADAI · YAMASI · GUALE · AIS · TEKESTA · CALUSA · TIMUCUA 20 · APALACHEE · ARAWAK 2 · AIS 14 · BLOOD · PIEGAN · BLACKFOOT · GROS VENTRE · SARSI · KUTENAI 13 · SHUSWAP · CHILCOTIN · BELLA BELLA 26 · BELLA COOLA · KWAKIUTL · COMOX · COWICHAN · NOOTKA 26 · SONGISH · CLALLAM · QUILLIUTE · QUINAIELT · TWANA · LUMMI · SKAGIT · NISQUALLI · CHEHALIS · COWLITZ · KALISPEL · SPOKAN · COEUR D'ALENE · COLUMBIA · WENATCHEE · OKINAGAN · METHOW · KLIKITAT · YAKIMA · UMATILLA · CAYUSE · NEZ PERCE · FLATHEAD · PEND D'OREILLES · TUNAHE · CHINOOK · TILLAMOOK · ALSEA · SIUSLAW · COOS · UMPQUA · TUTUTNI · TAKELMA · SHASTA · KLAMATH · MODOC · ACHOMAWI · ATSUGEWI · MAIDU 29 · WINTUN · YANA · POMO · WAPPO · YUKI · MIWOK · WASHO · PAVIOTSO · MONO · YOKUTS · COSTANOAN · SALINAN · CHUMASHAN · KERN RIVER · TUBATULABAL · CHEMEHUEVI · SERRANO · GABRIELINO · LUISEÑO · CAHUILLA · DIEGUEÑO · PAIUTE · SHOSHONI · GOSHUTE · UTE · BANNOCK · PAVIOTSO · NAVAHO · HOPI (PUEB.) · ZUÑI 28 (PUEB.) · KERES 11 (PUEB.) · TANOAN 12 (PUEB.) · JICARILLA APACHE · MESCALERO APACHE · CHIRICAHUA · SAN CARLOS · WALAPAI · YAVAPAI · MOHAVE · MARICOPA · YUMA · COCOPA · PIMA · PAPAGO · SERI 27 · OPATA · YAQUI · NEVOME · MAYO · TARAHUMARE · CONCHO · TOBOSO · LAGUNERO · COAHUILTECO 7 · TAMAULIPECO · PAME 15 · TEPEHUANE · ACAXEE · ZACATECO · HUICHOL · CORA · NAHUATL · CAHITA · COCHIMI 27 · WAICURI 25 · COMANCHE · KIOWA 12 · KIOWA APACHE · CHEYENNE · ARAPAHO · SUTAIO · TETON-DAKOTA · YANKTON-DAKOTA · SANTEE-DAKOTA · ASSINIBOIN · MANDAN · HIDATSA · ARIKARA · PAWNEE · PONCA · OMAHA · OTO · IOWA · MISSOURI 18 · KANSAS · OSAGE · WICHITA · TAWAKONI · KICHAI · TONKAWAN TRIBES 21 · KARANKAWAN 10 · PASSAMAQUODDY · PENOBSCOT · MALECITE · ABNAKI · PENNACOOK · MASSACHUSET · NIPMUC · WAMPANOAG · NARRAGANSET · PEQUOT · MONTAUK · MANHATTAN · WAPPINGER

AP. 1810

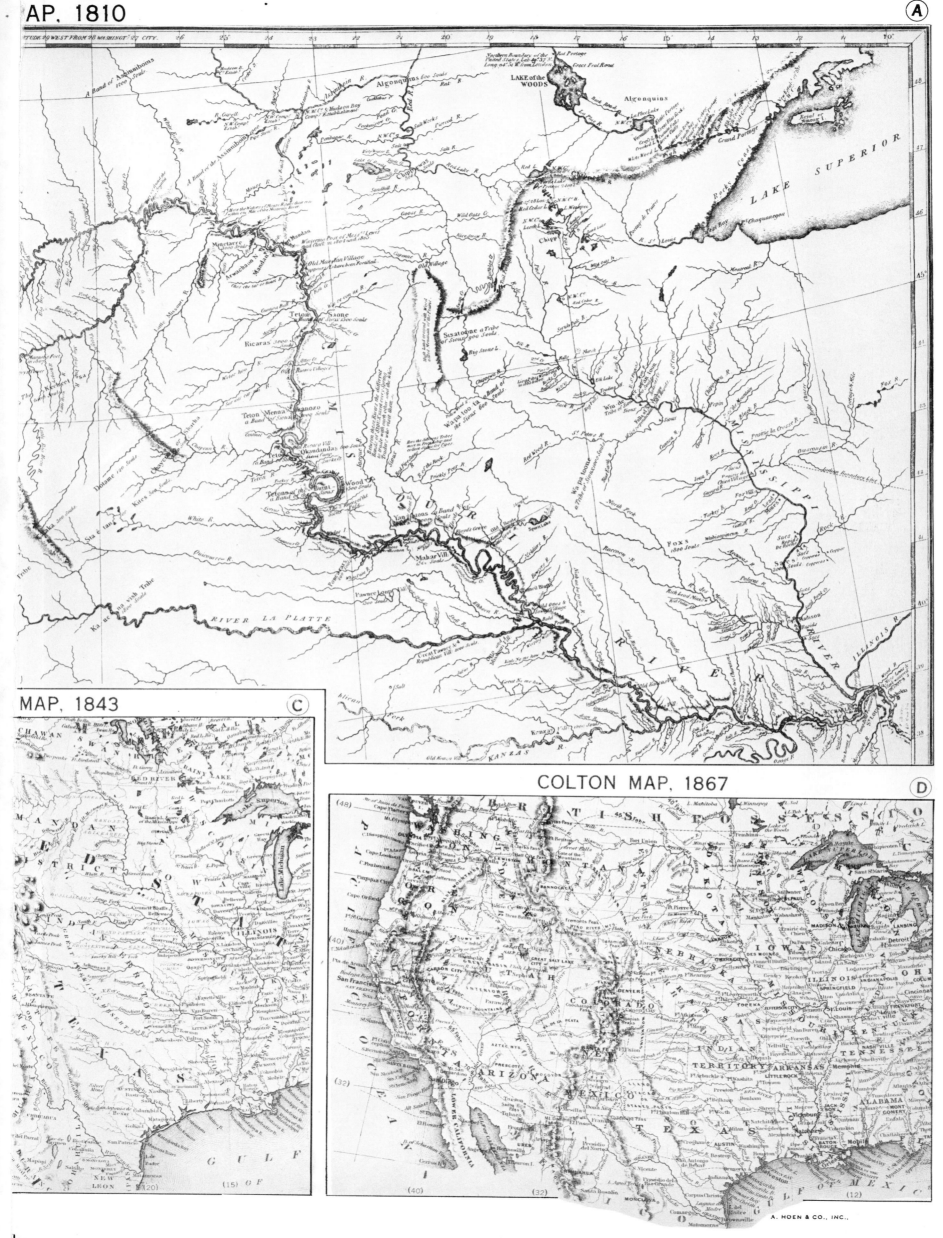

MAP, 1843 ©

COLTON MAP, 1867 ©

A. HOEN & CO., INC.,

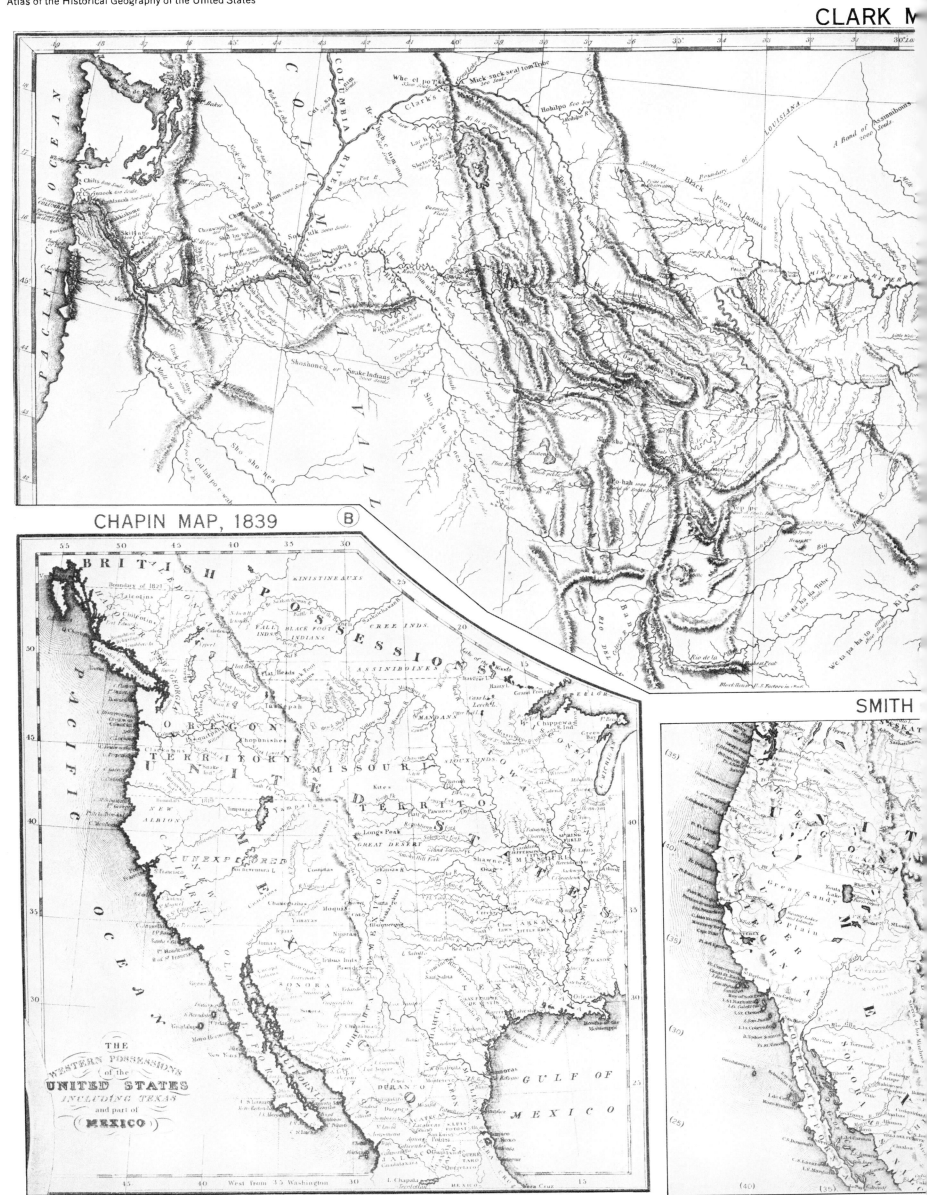

CHAPIN MAP, 1839

SMITH M

THE
WESTERN POSSESSIONS
of the
UNITED STATES
INCLUDING TEXAS
and part of
MEXICO

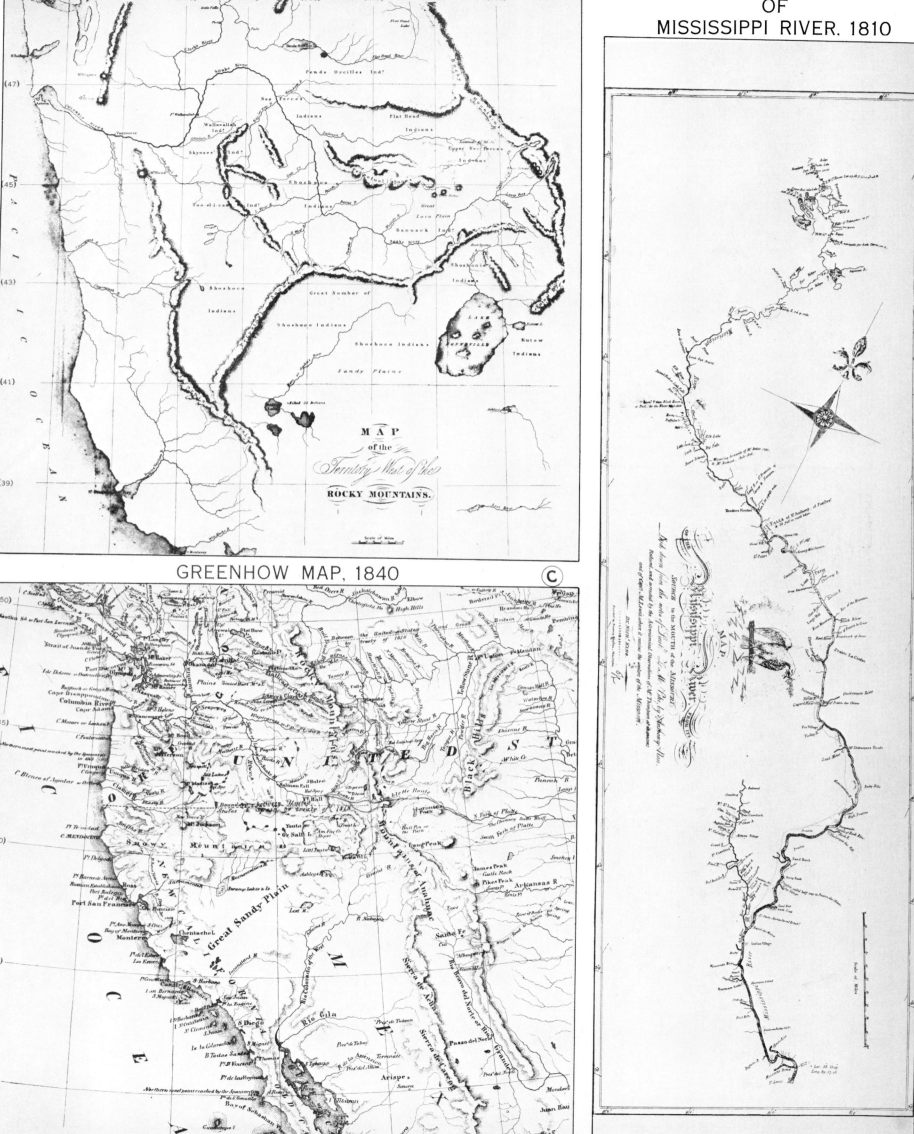

BONNEVILLE MAP, 1837   (A)

PIKE MAP OF MISSISSIPPI RIVER. 1810   (B)

GREENHOW MAP, 1840   (C)

Carnegie Institution of Washington

A. HOEN & CO., INC.,

CARTOGRAPHY, 1492-1867
PIKE MAP, 1810

Plate 30

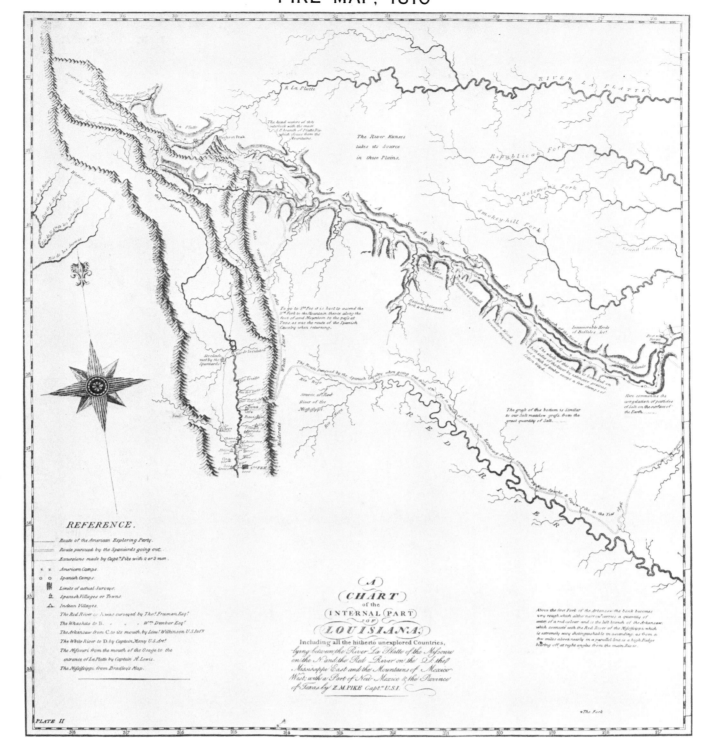

HUMBOLDT MAP, 1811

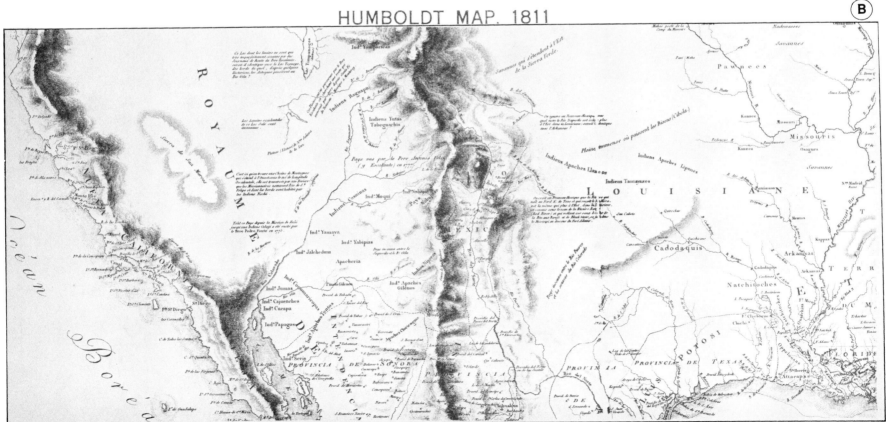

A. HOEN & CO., INC.

H MAP, 1814

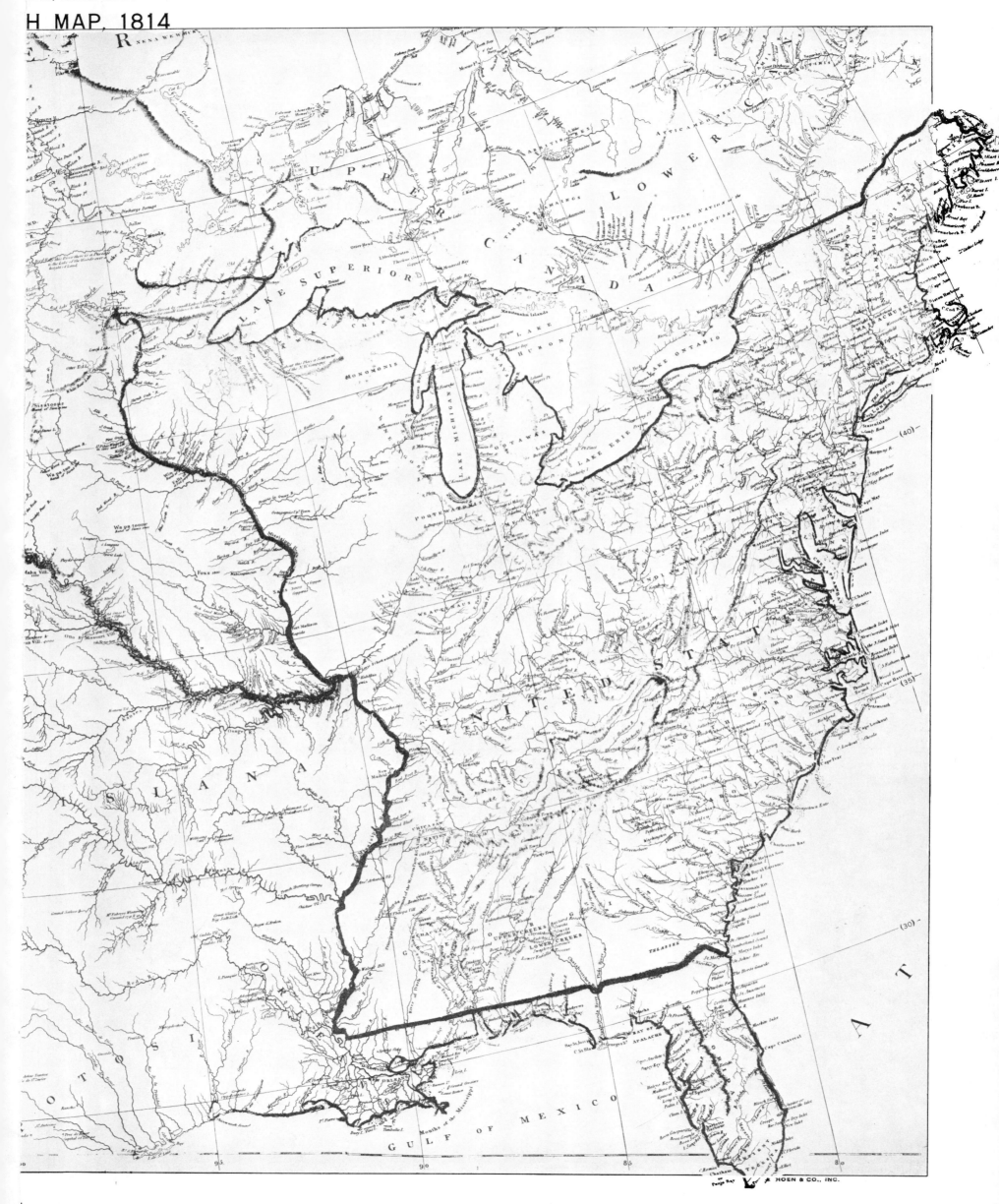

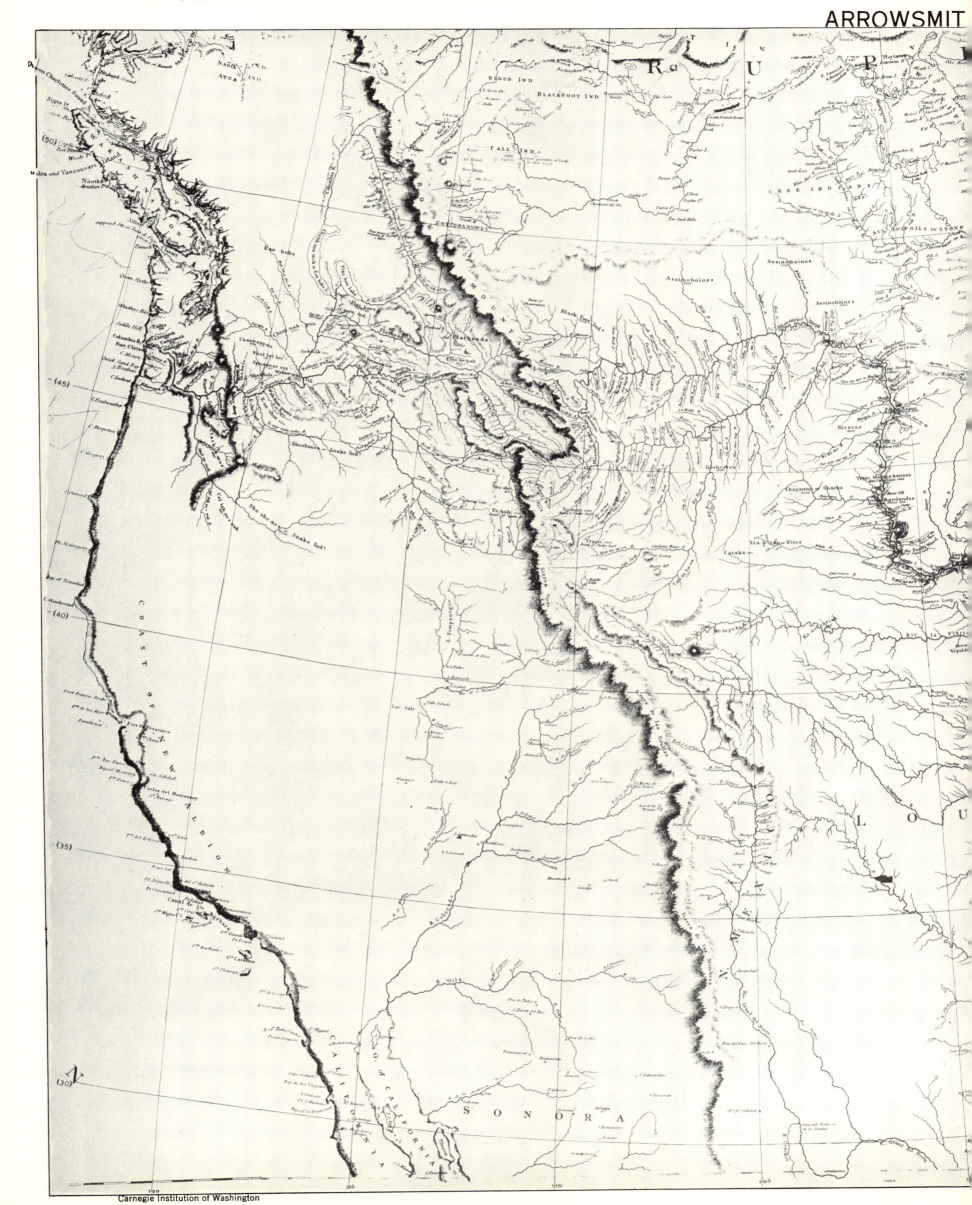

LEWIS MAP, 1804

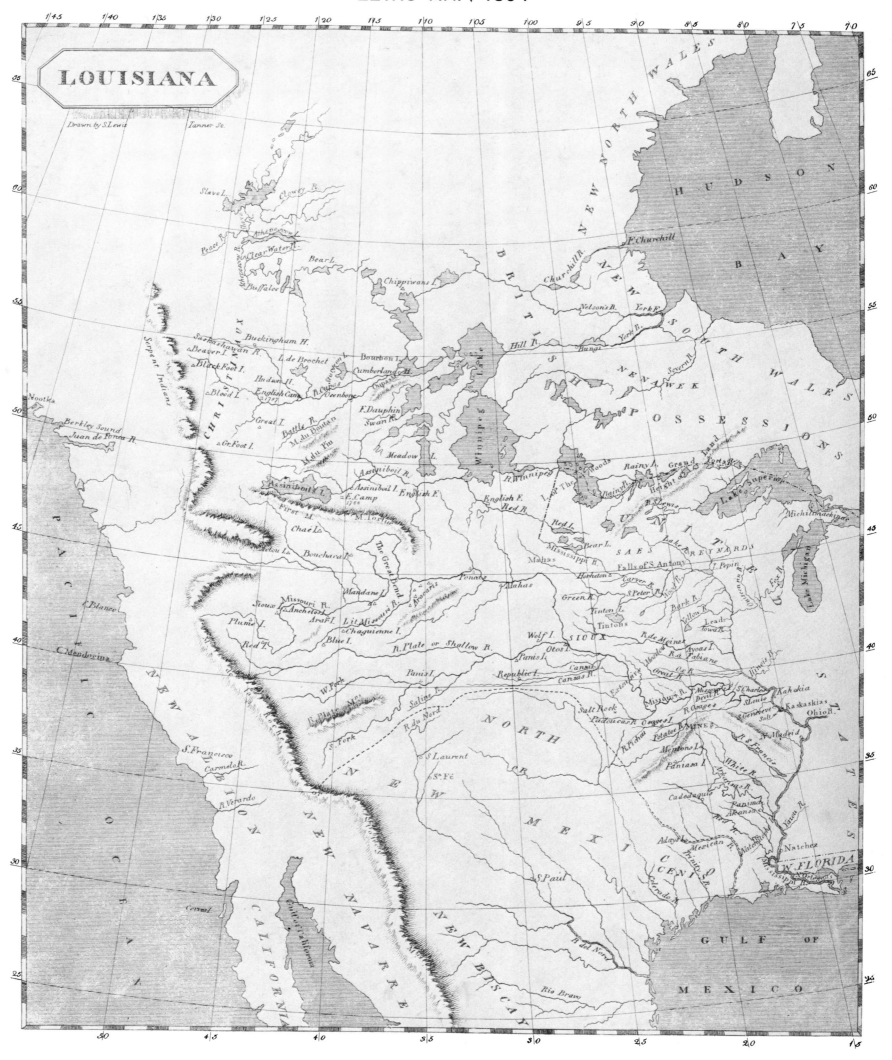

LOUISIANA

Drawn by S. Lewis   Tanner Sc.

A. HOEN & CO., INC.

POPPLE MAP, 1733

Hudson's Bay

TERRA de LABR

CHRISTIANAUX or KILISTINONS

LAKE SUPERIOUR

LAKE HURONS

LAKE ILLINOIS

LAKE ERIE

LAKE ONTARIO or FRONTENAC

QUEBEC

NEW ENGLAND

MASSACHUSETTS BAY

Boston H.

Cape Cod

NEW YORK

PENNSYLVANIA

MARYLAND

VIRGINIA

NORTH CAROLINA

Cape Charles
Cape Henry
Cape Hatteras
Cape Look out
Cape Fear
Charles Town

SOUTH CAROLINA

GEORGIA

St Helena Sound
St Augustine

FLORIDA

LOUISIANA

APALACHEAN MOUNTAINS

R. Mississippi

GULF OF MEXICO

TROPICK OF CANCER

Vera Crux to the Havana to avoid the Trade Winds

GULF OF FLORIDA

Bahama I.

LUCAYOS or LUCAYOS or BAHAMA ISLANDS

Providence

CUBA

The Havana

JUCATAN

BAY OF CAMPECHE

JAMAICA

SPANIOLA

THE WINDWARD PASSAGE

W

A T

TROPI

The Southward Boundary of CAROLINA by the last Charter.

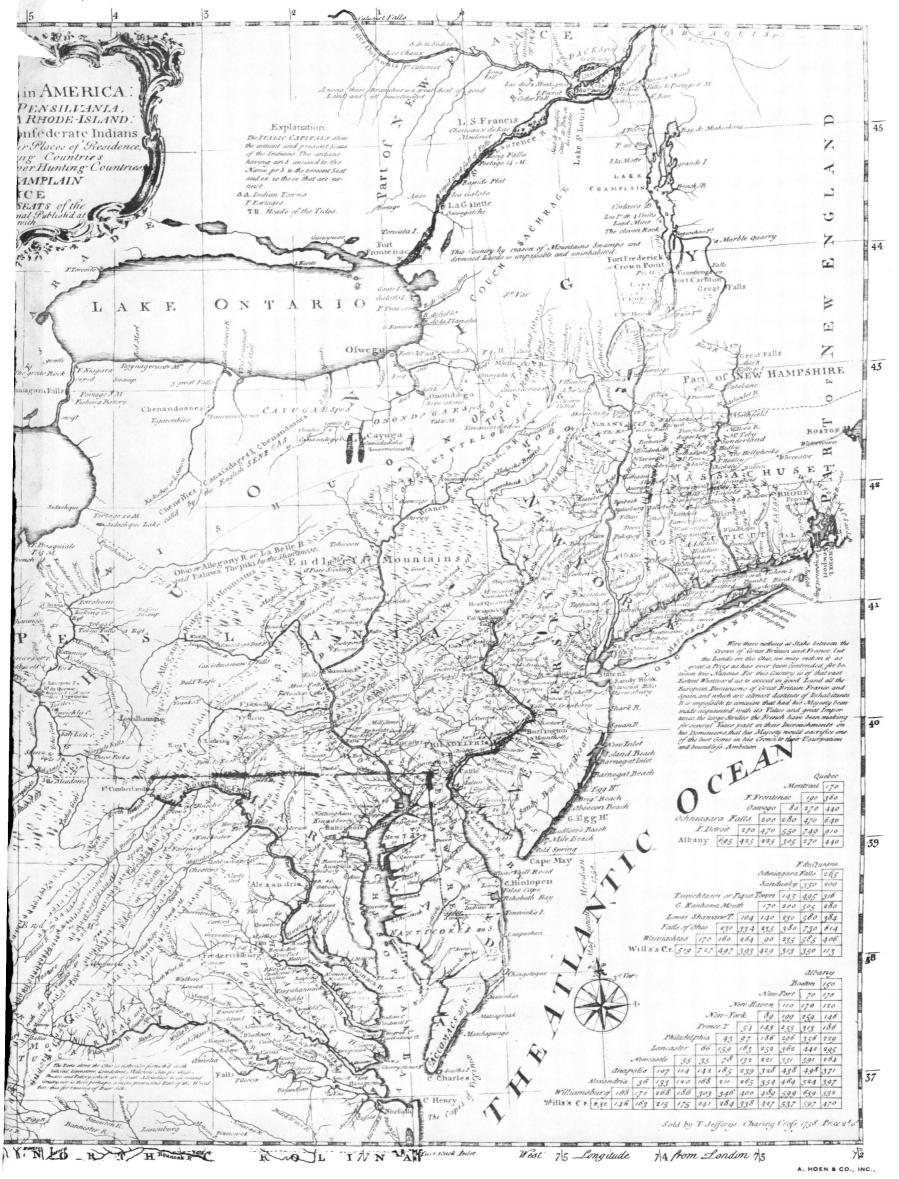

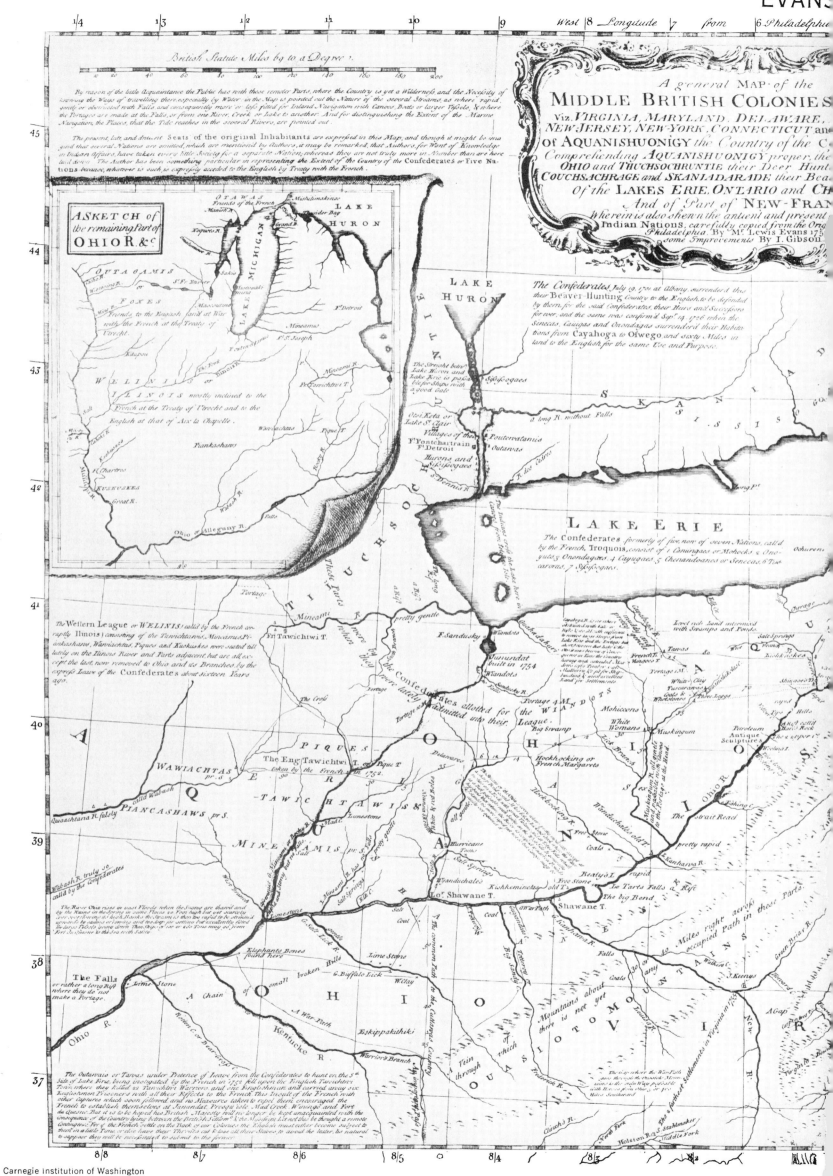

MÜLLER MAP, 1754

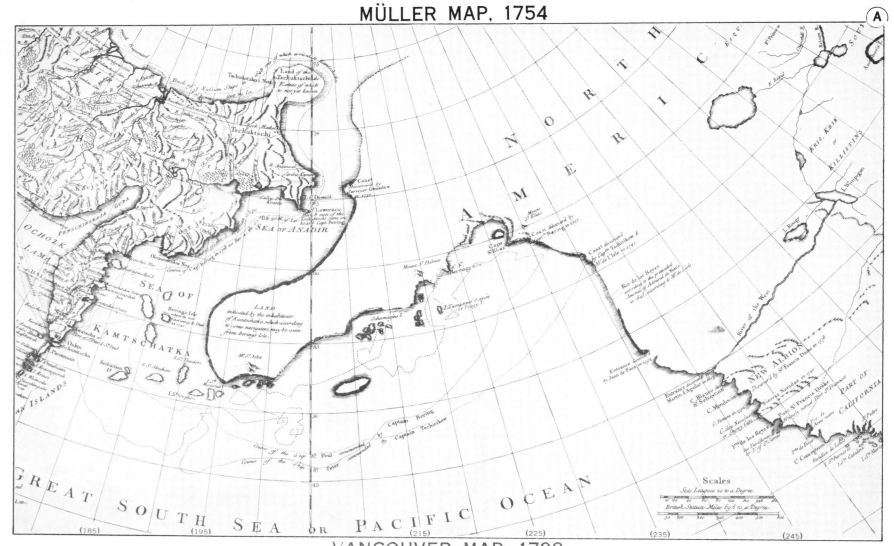

VANCOUVER MAP, 1798

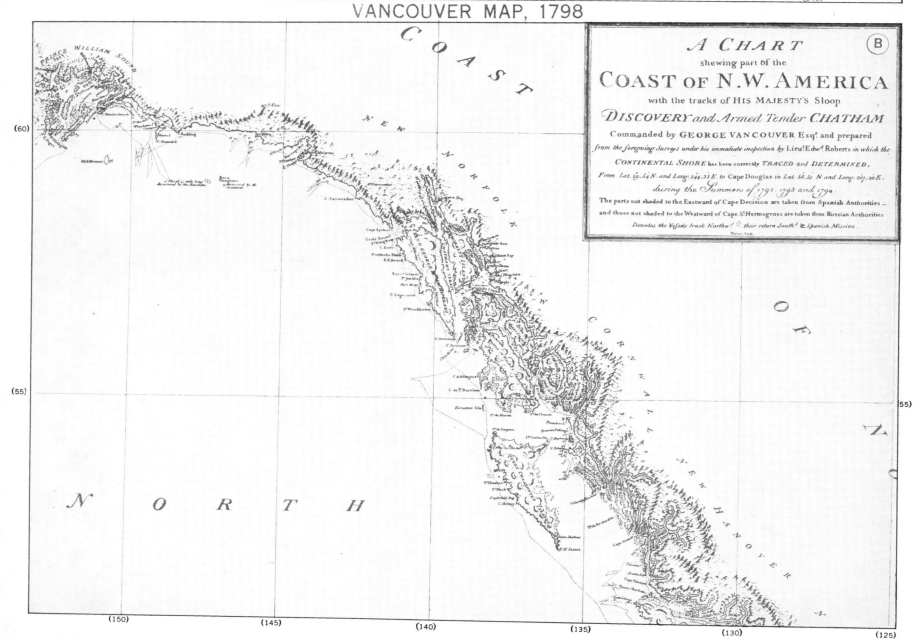

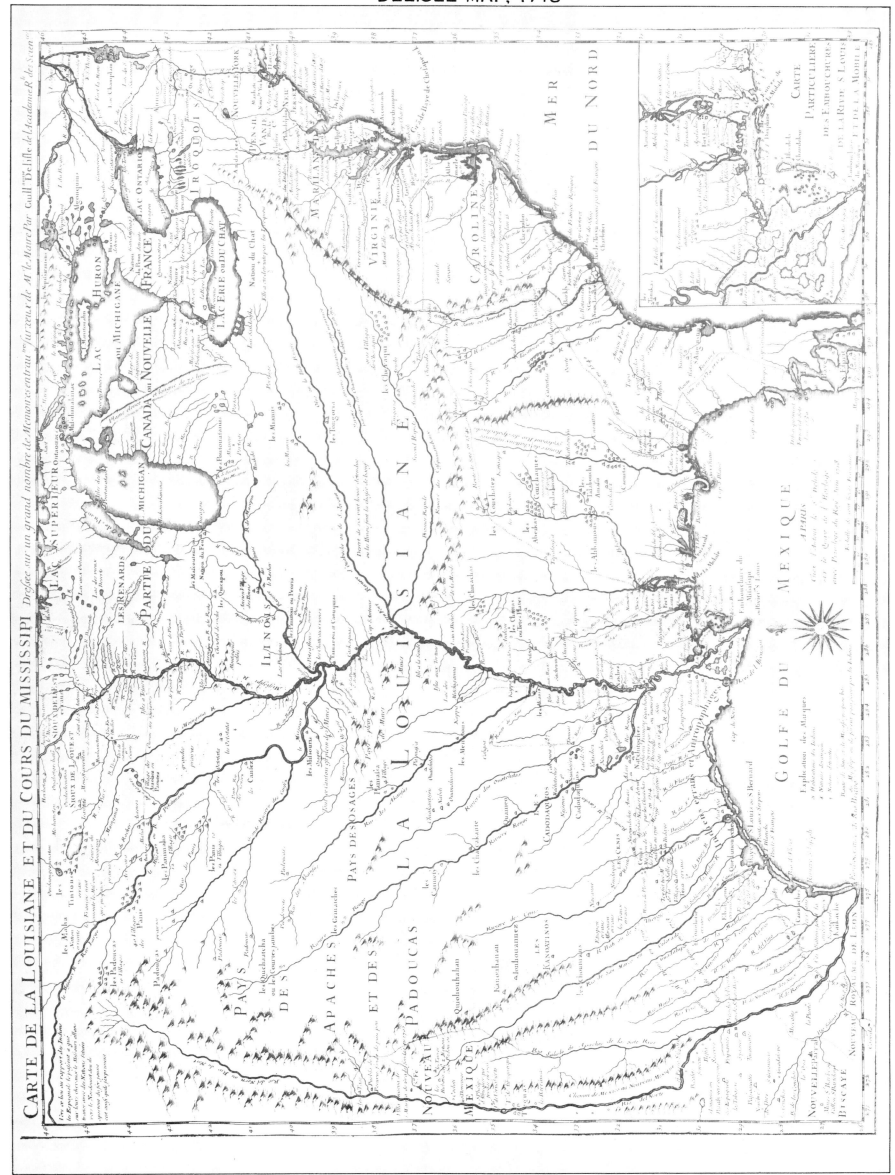

Copyright by Carnegie Institution of Washington

A. HOEN & CO., INC.

MAP, 1703

BELLIN MAP, 1743 Ⓒ

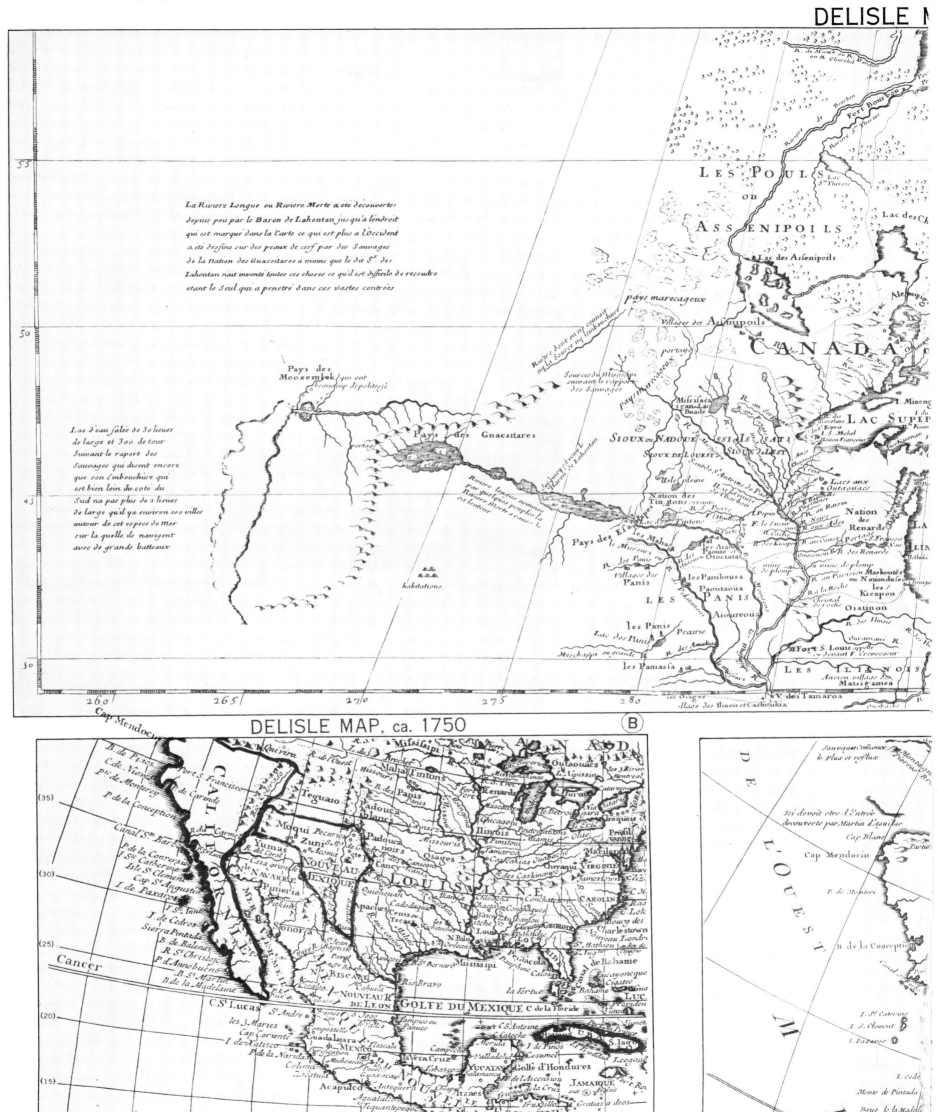

DELISLE MAP, ca. 1750

NDE MER DU SUD

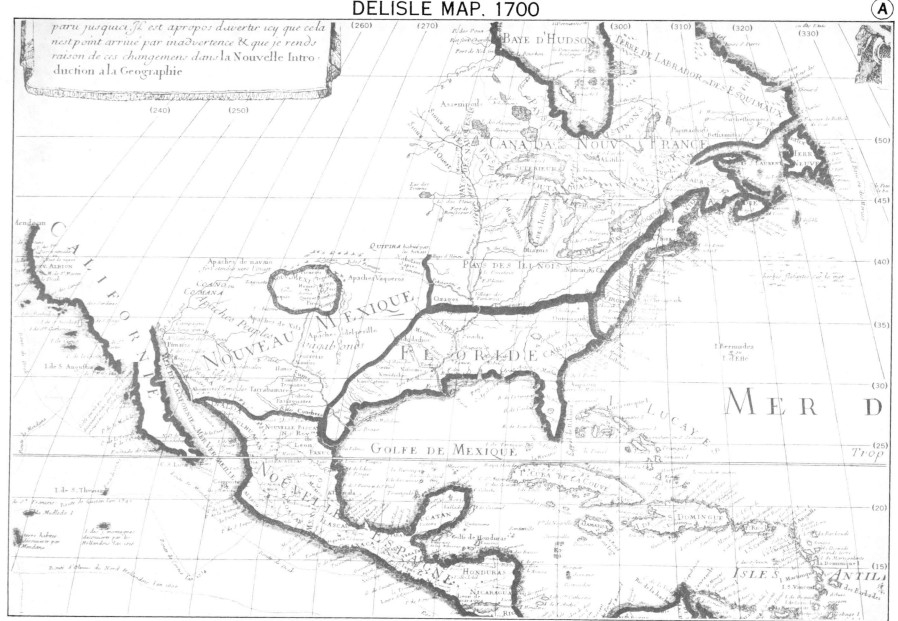

GENTIL MAP, ca. 1700
(B)

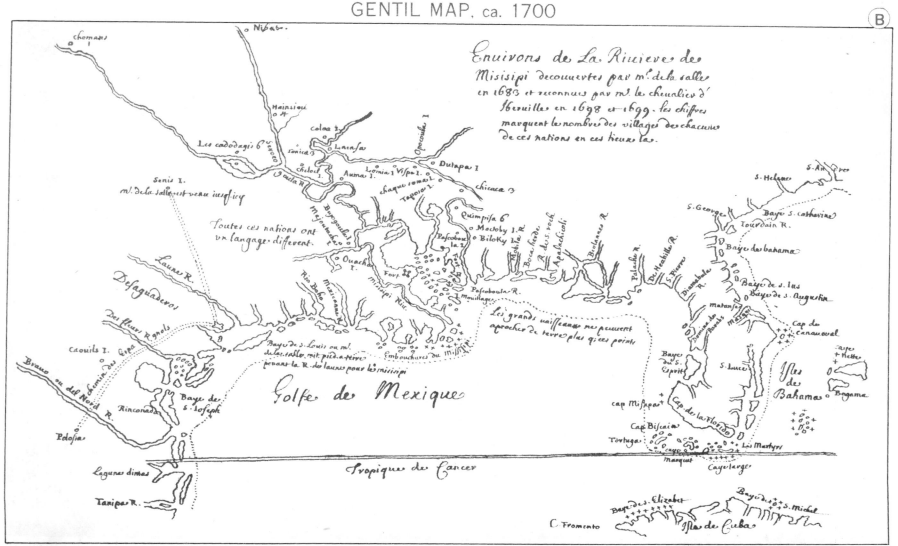

Copyright by Carnegie Institution of Washington

A. HOEN & CO., INC.

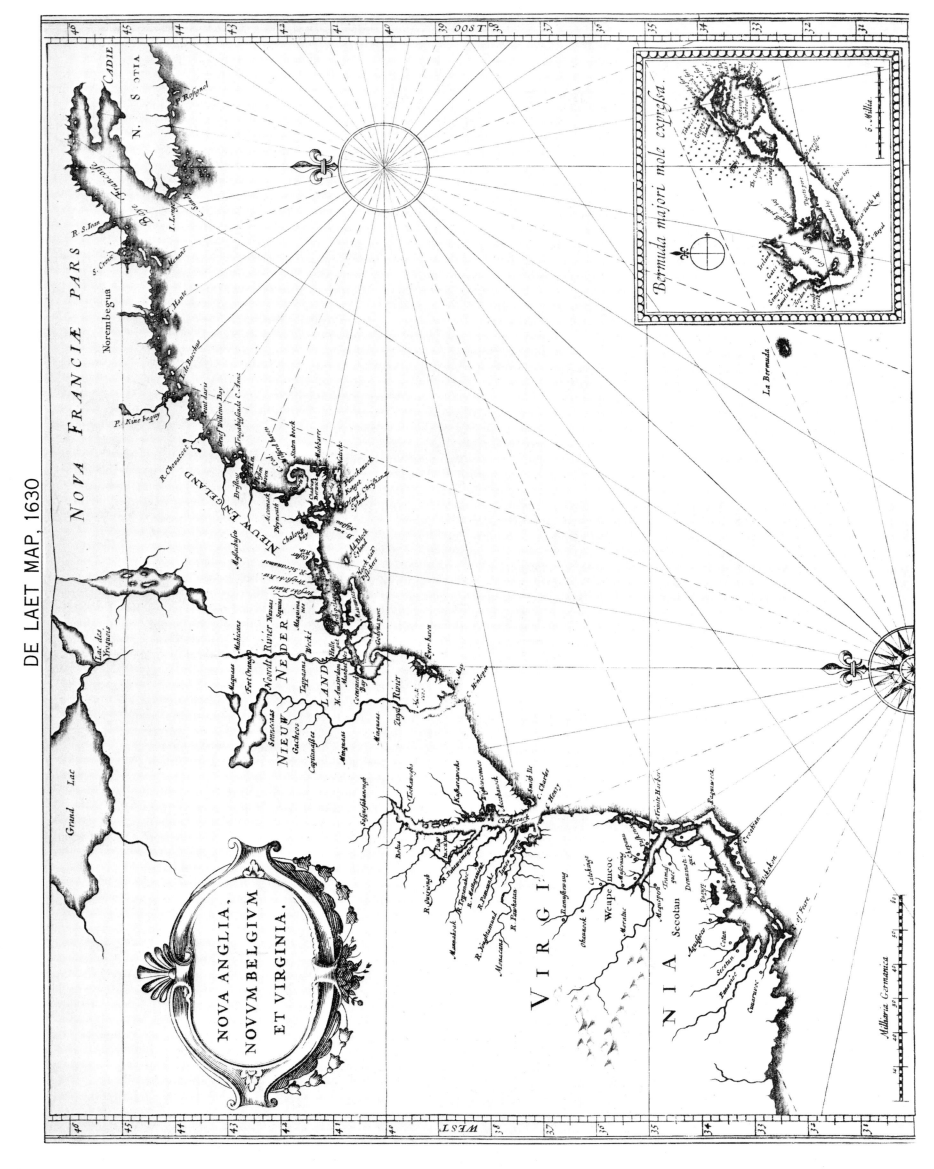

DE LAET MAP, 1630

NOVA ANGLIA.
NOVVM BELGIVM
ET VIRGINIA.

JESUIT MAP, 1672

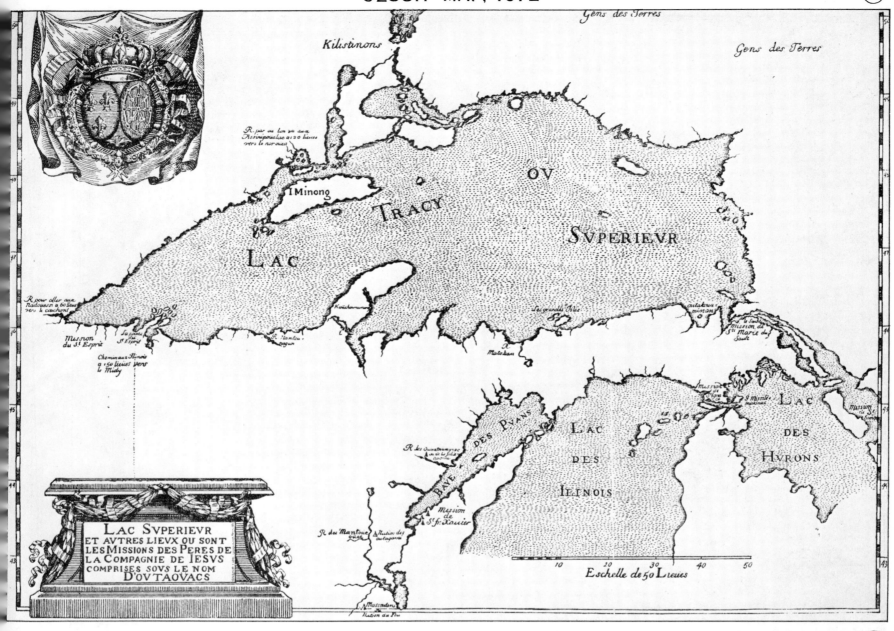

RAFFEIX MAP, 1688

HONDIUS MAP, 1630

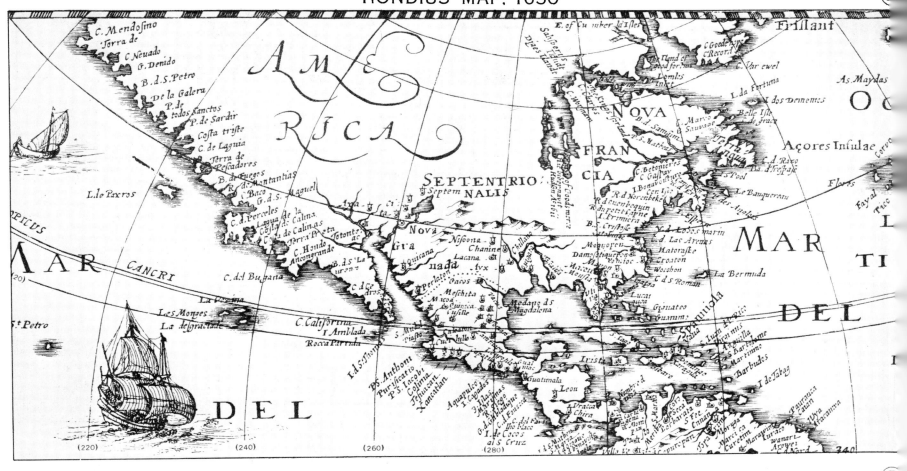

SANSON MAP, 1656

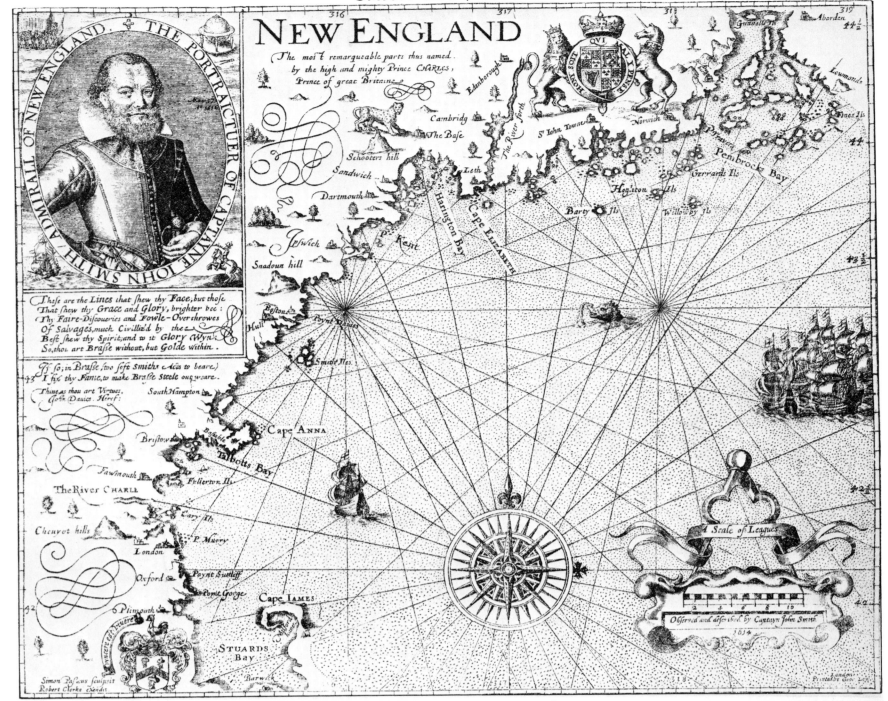

SMITH MAP, 1612

CHAMPLAIN MAP, 1612

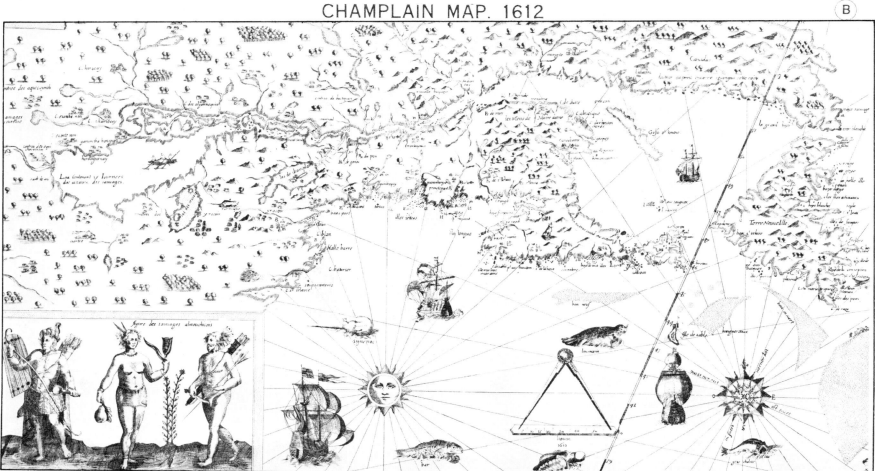

A. HOEN & CO., INC.

...MAP, ca. 1523

VIZCAINO MAP, 1603

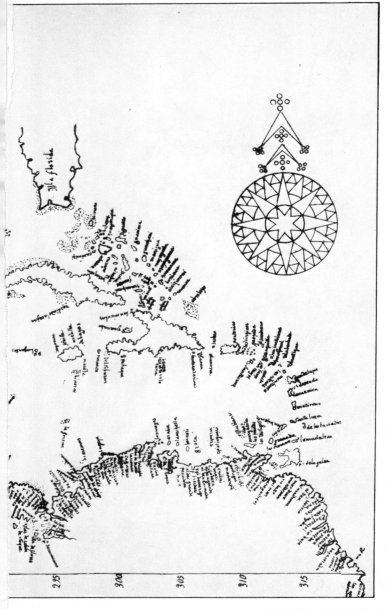

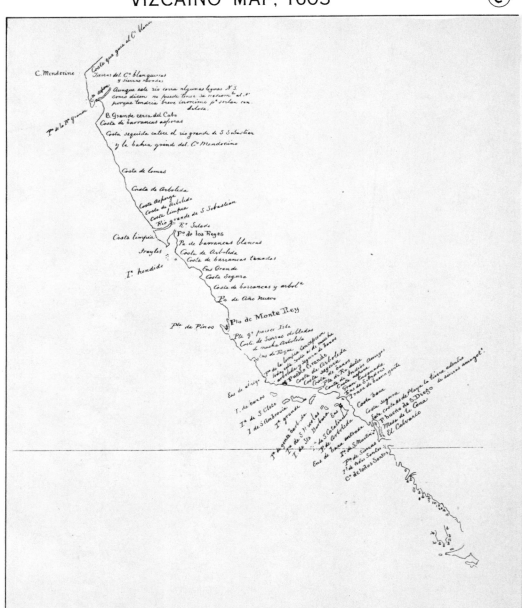

TATTONUS MAP, 1600

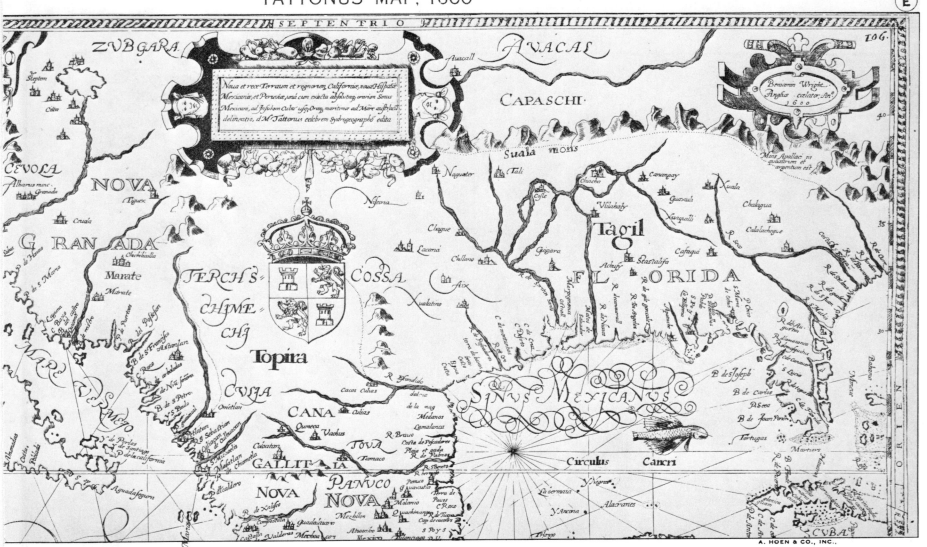

A. HOEN & CO., INC.,

CORTES MAP, 1520

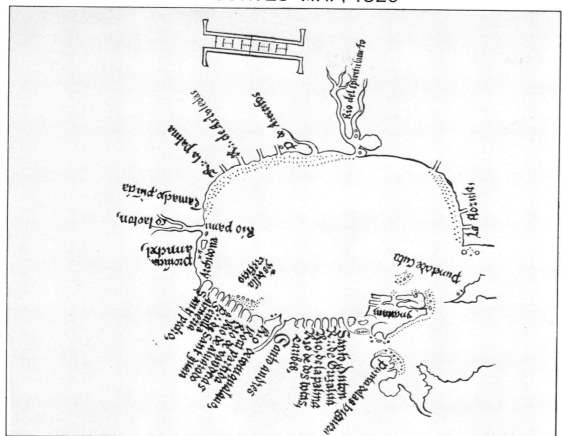

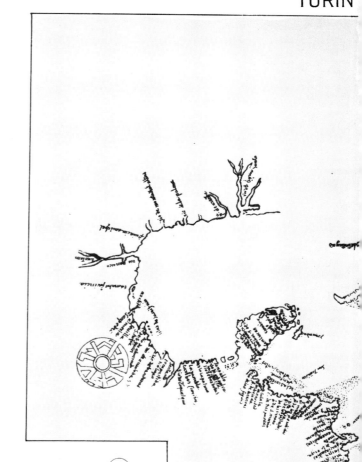

MOLINEAUX-WRIGHT MAP, 1600

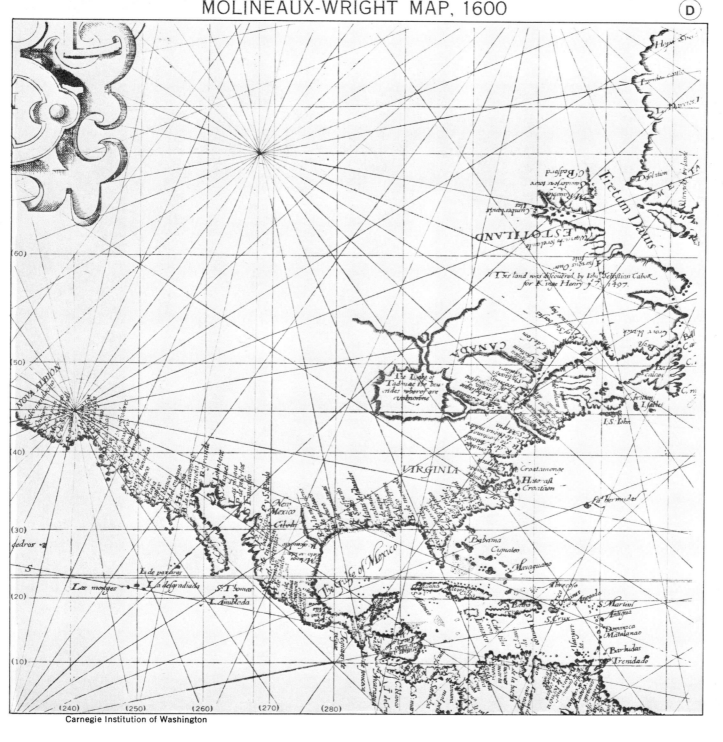

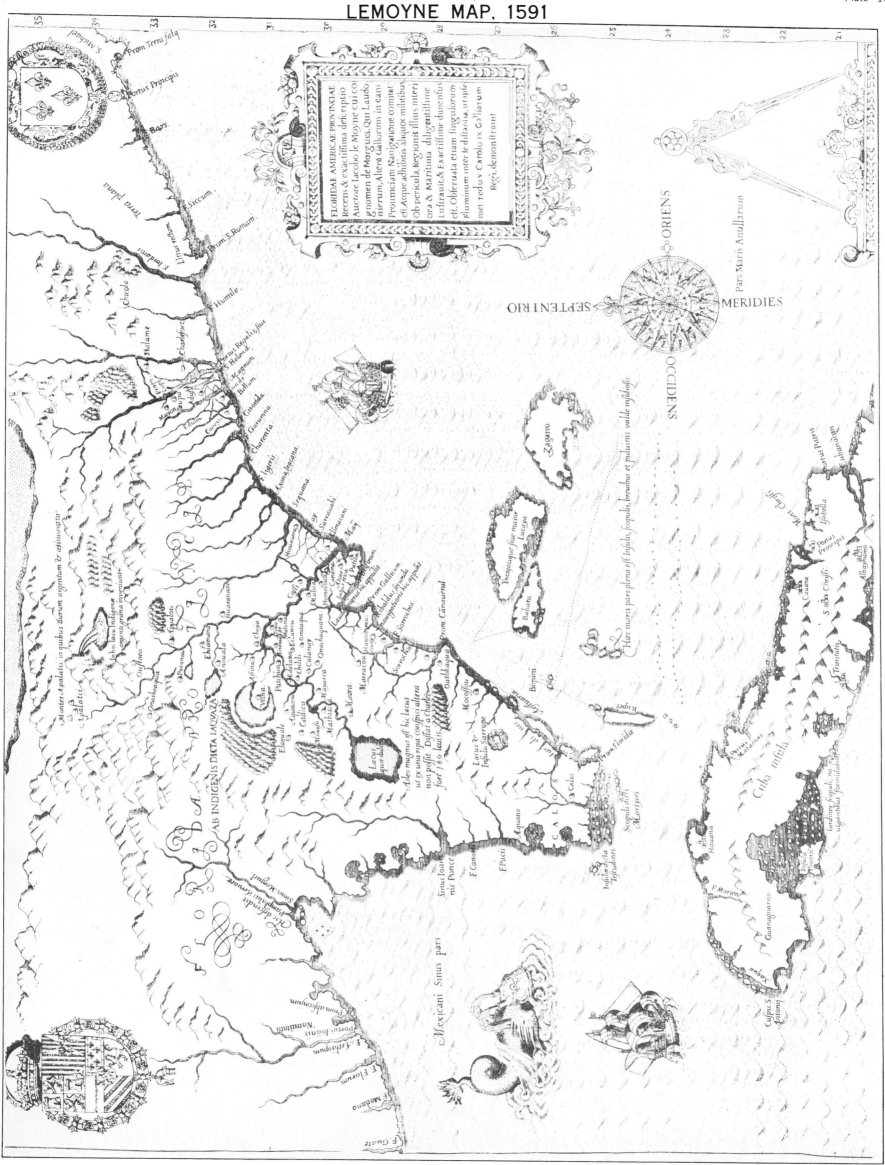

Copyright by Carnegie Institution of Washington

A. HOEN & CO., INC

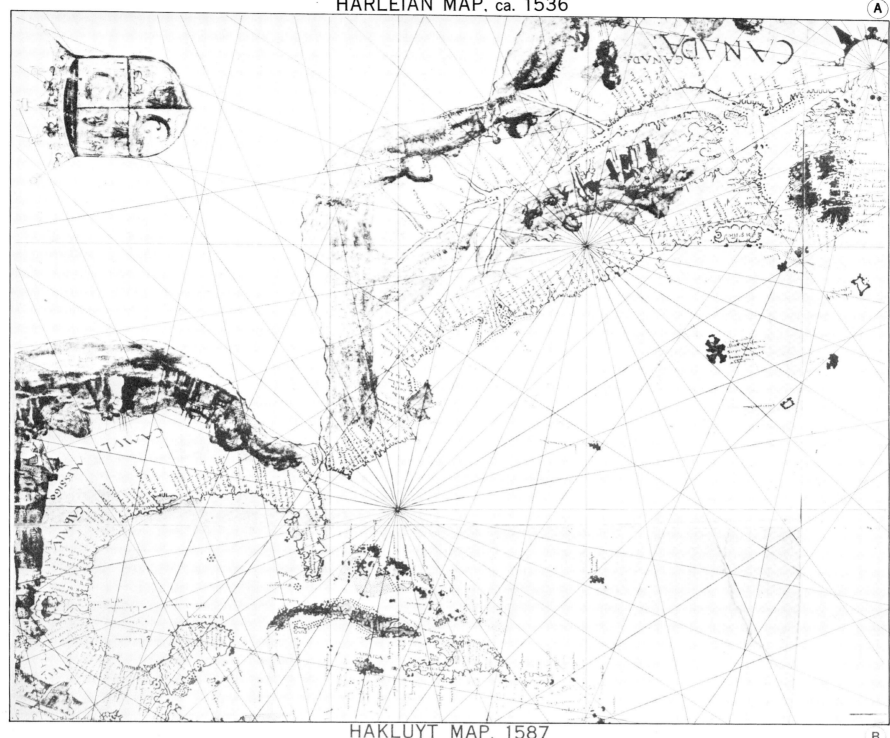

HAKLUYT MAP, 1587

B

Plate 13

MAP. 1529

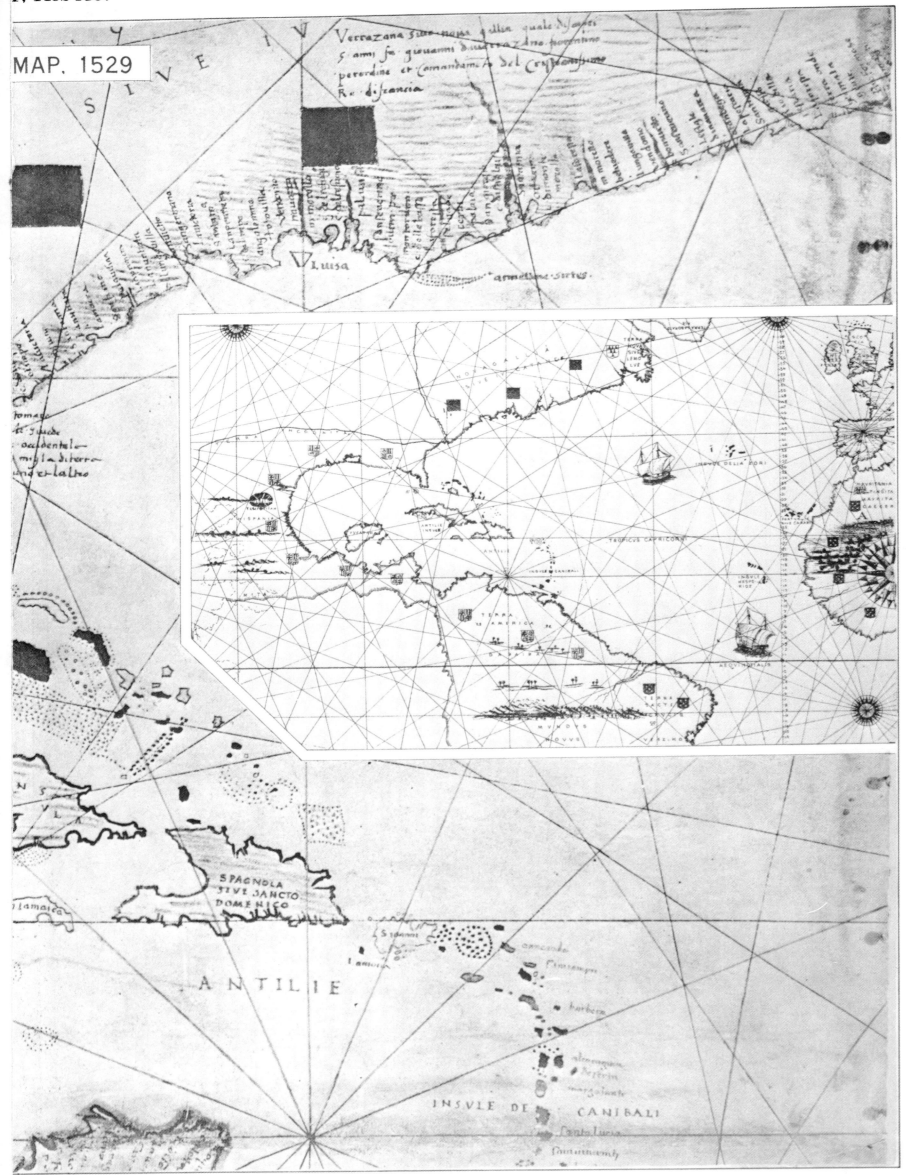

VERRAZANO

COGNITA

TERRA
FLOR
I D
A

SIVE
ISABELA CVBA
ANTILIE
INSVIE

IVCATANA

COLVACANA

CARTOGRAPHY. 1492-1867
DE SOTO MAP, ca. 1544

GASTALDI MAP, 1546

Ⓑ

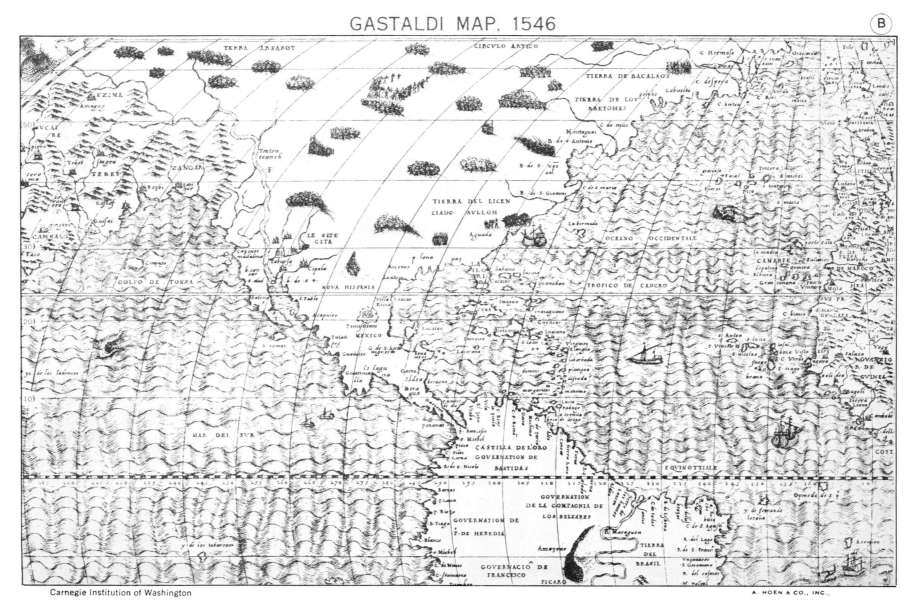

A. HOEN & CO., INC.,

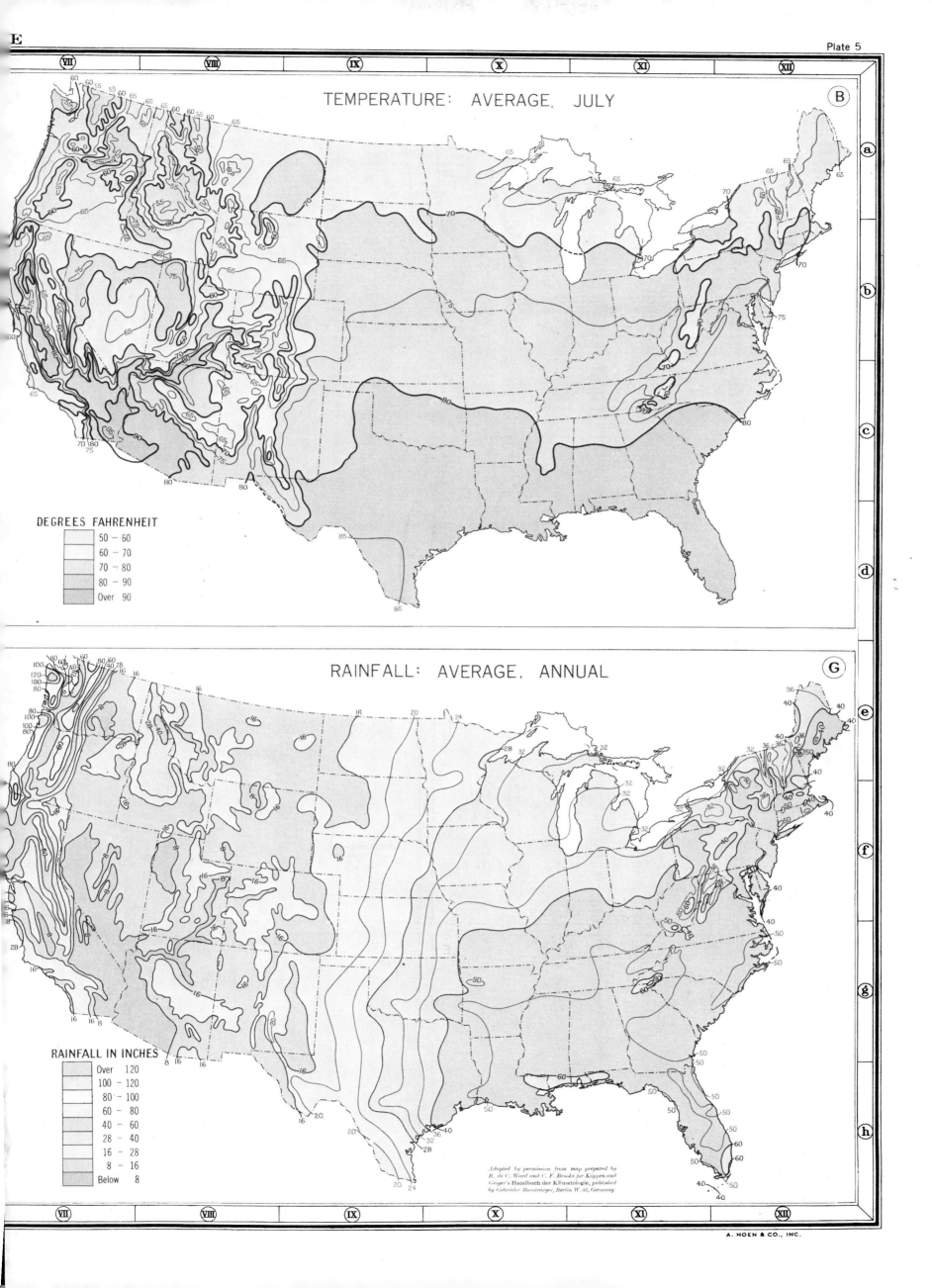

TEMPERATURE: AVERAGE, JULY

DEGREES FAHRENHEIT

50 – 60
60 – 70
70 – 80
80 – 90
Over 90

RAINFALL: AVERAGE, ANNUAL

RAINFALL IN INCHES

Over 120
100 – 120
80 – 100
60 – 80
40 – 60
28 – 40
16 – 28
8 – 16
Below 8

Adapted by permission from map prepared by
R. de C. Ward and C. F. Brooks for Köppen and
Geiger's Handbuch der Klimatologie, published
by Gebrüder Borntraeger, Berlin W. 35, Germany.

COAL FIELDS

A

ANTHRACITE

SEMIBITUMINOUS

BITUMINOUS

SUB-BITUMINOUS

LIGNITE

Dark ruling indicates coal beds of commercial value
Light ruling indicates coal beds of doubtful value
Dots indicate that the coal-bearing rocks are covered

DISTRIBUTION AND PRODUCTION OF IRON ORE

B

Hematite-bearing areas and outcrops

Brown ore-bearing areas

Magnetite-bearing areas

The upper black bar shows, for any state, production for 1929; and the
succeeding bars, for 1919, 1909, 1899, 1889, and 1879, respectively.

0 1 2 3 4 5,000,000 tons

Copyright by Carnegie Institution of Washington

A. HOEN & CO., INC.,

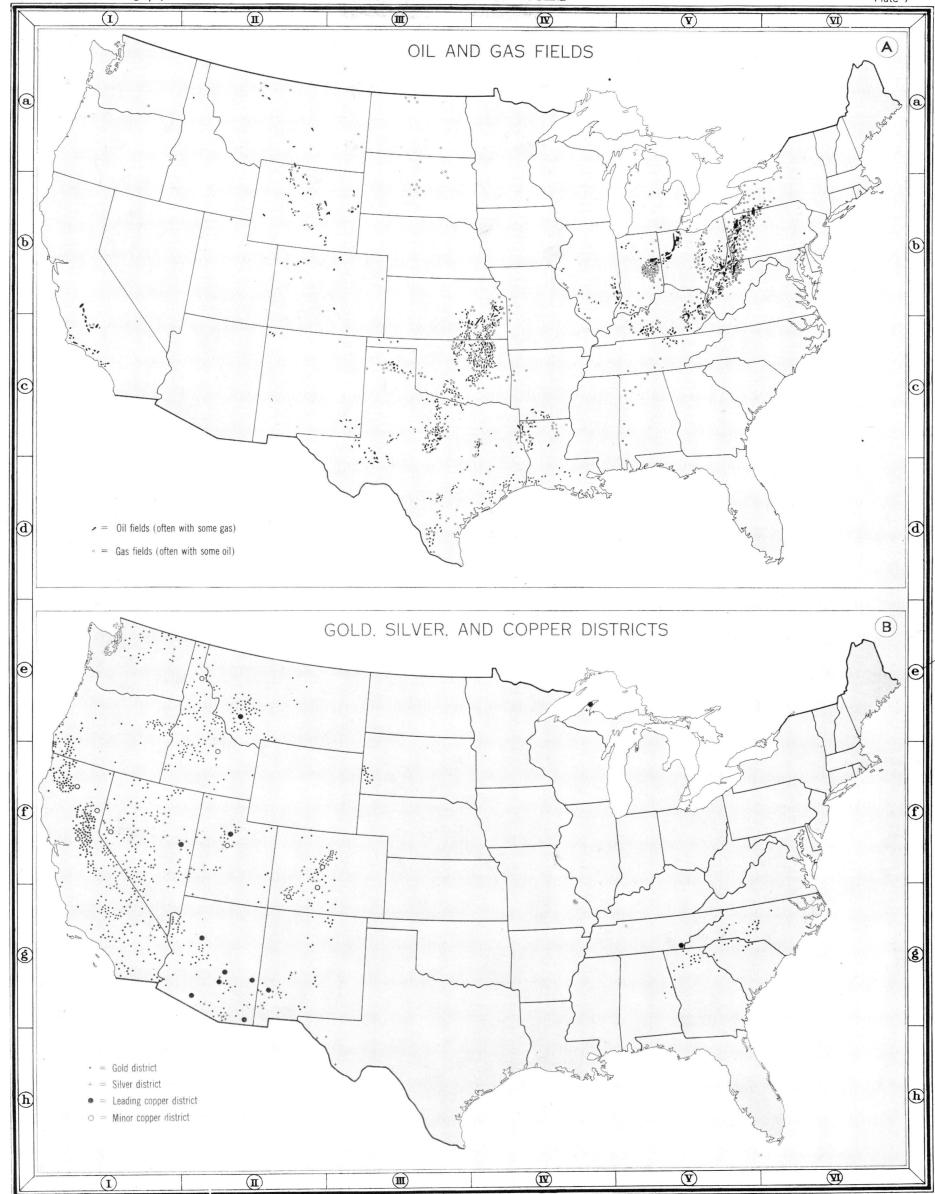

OIL AND GAS FIELDS

A

➴ = Oil fields (often with some gas)

○ = Gas fields (often with some oil)

GOLD, SILVER, AND COPPER DISTRICTS

B

· = Gold district

+ = Silver district

● = Leading copper district

○ = Minor copper district

Copyright by Carnegie Institution of Washington

A. HOEN & CO., INC.

BEHAIM GLOBE

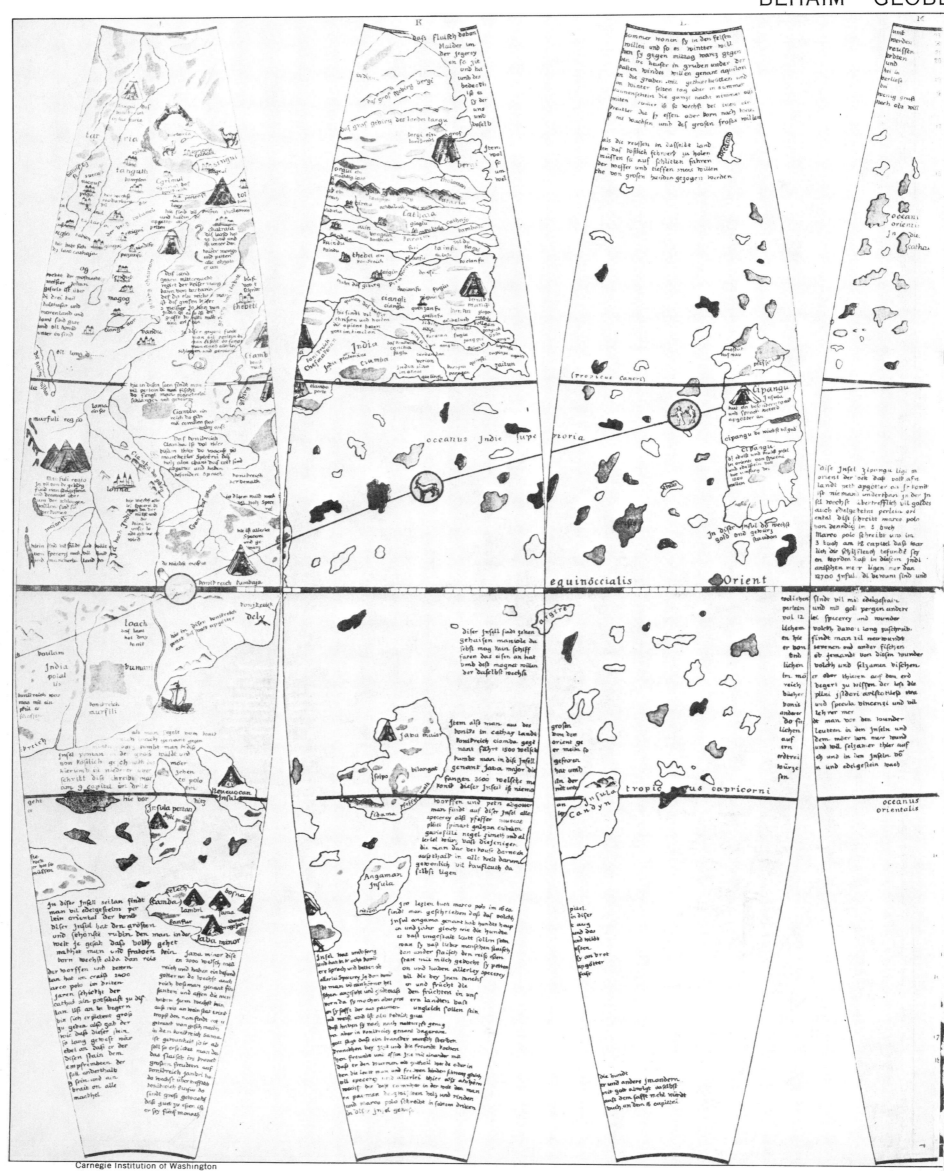

E GORES, 1492

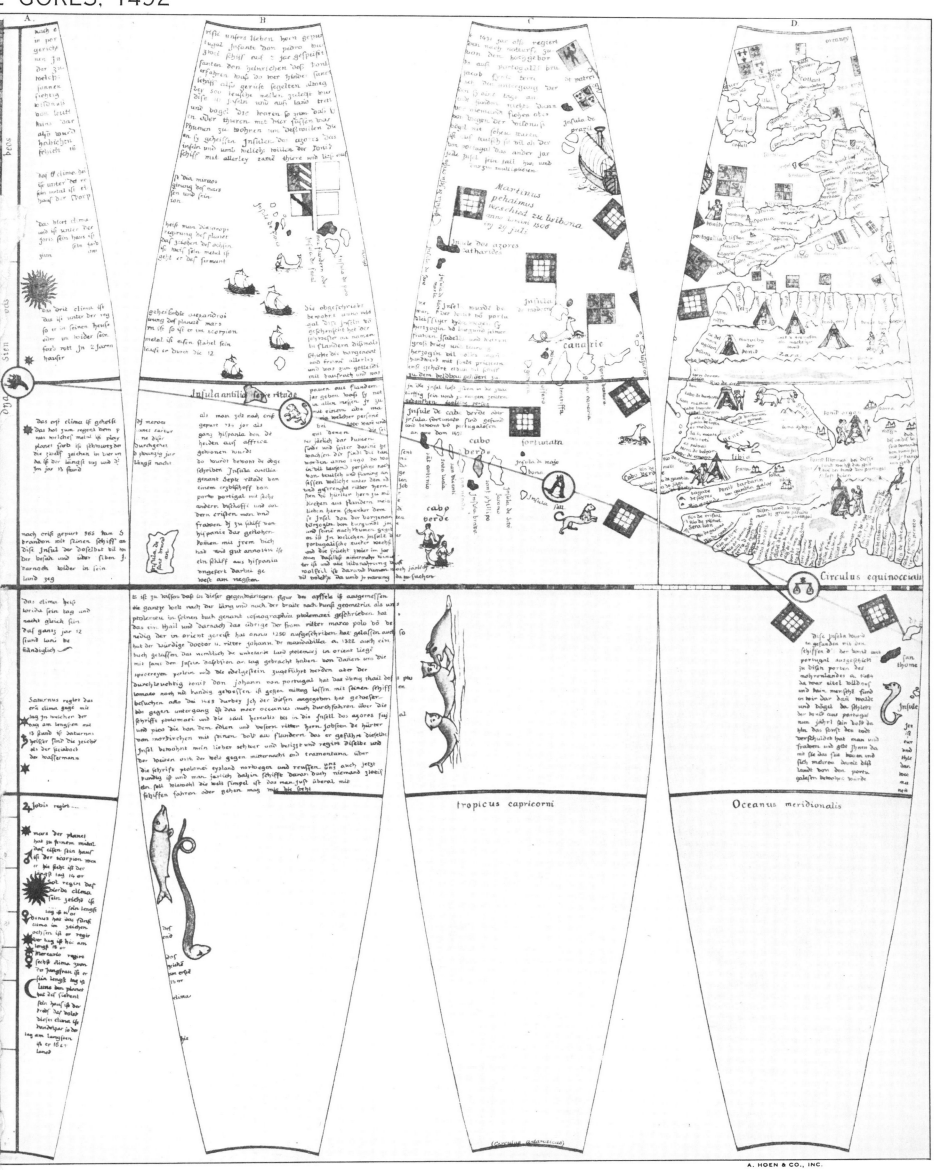

A. HOEN & CO., INC.

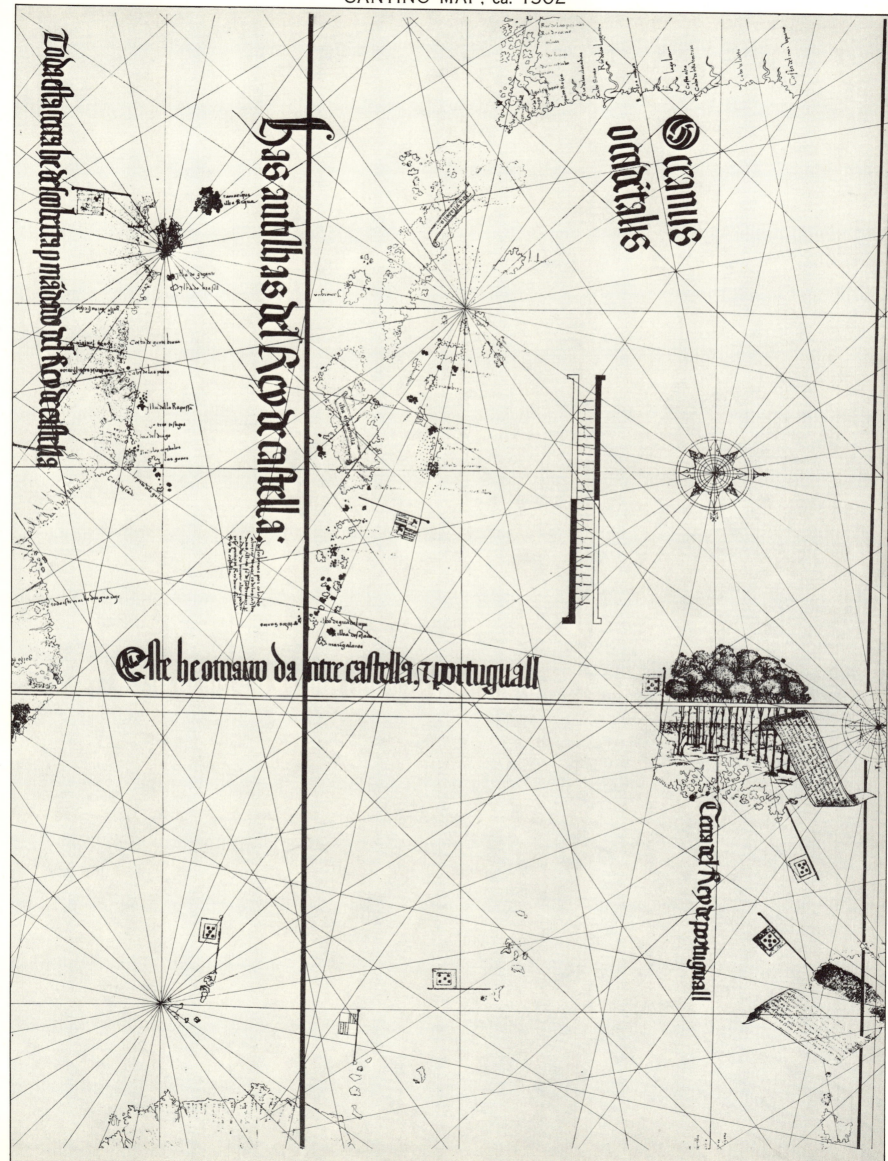

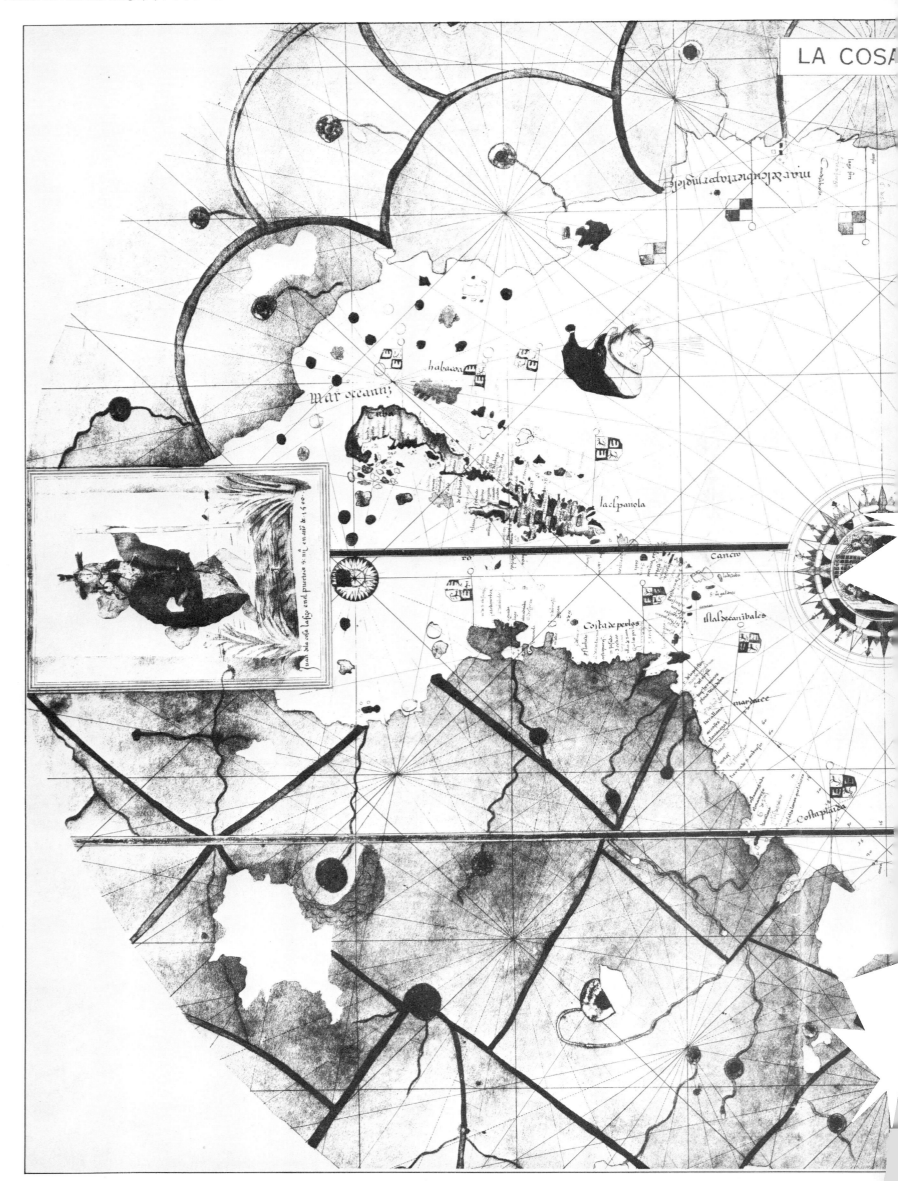

LA COSA

MAP, 1500

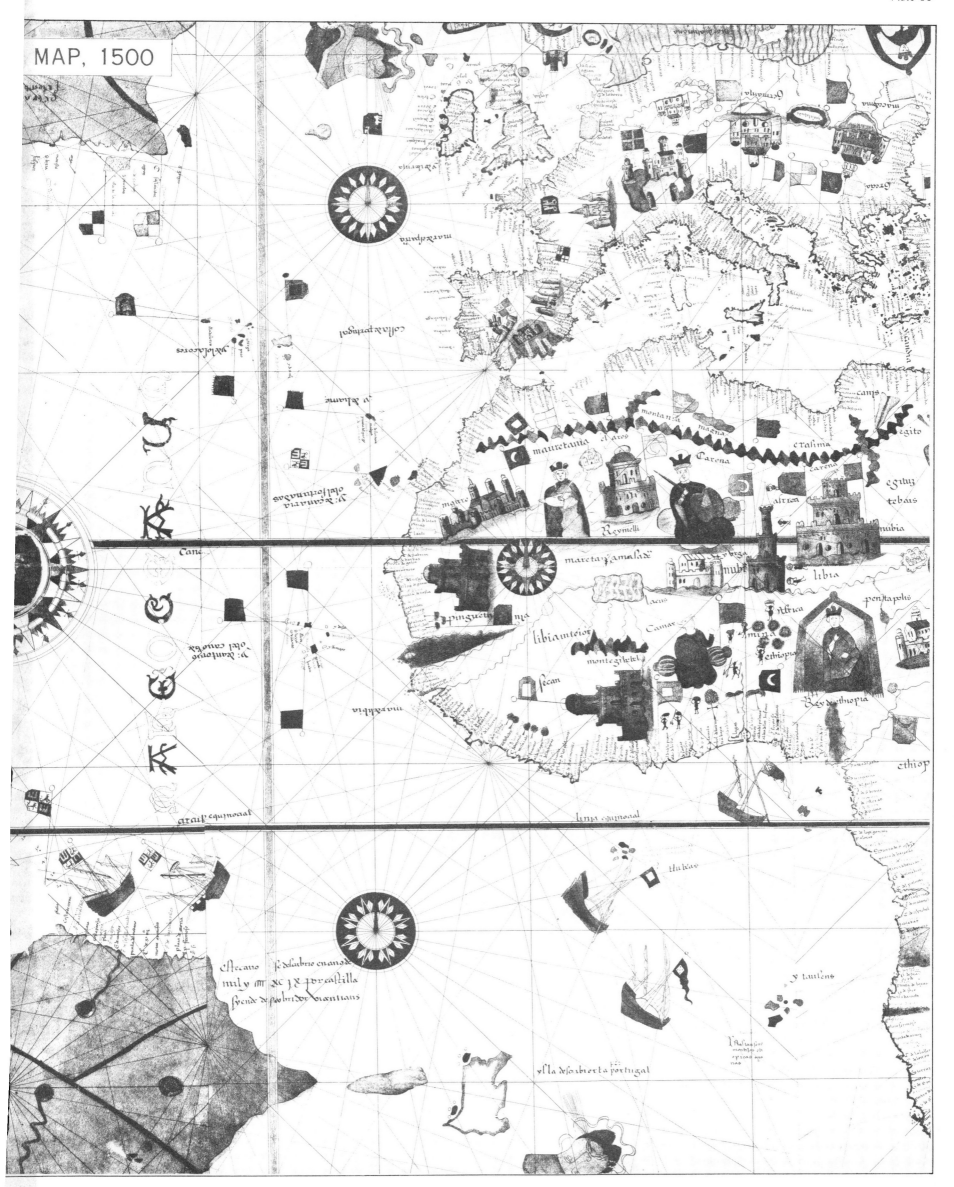

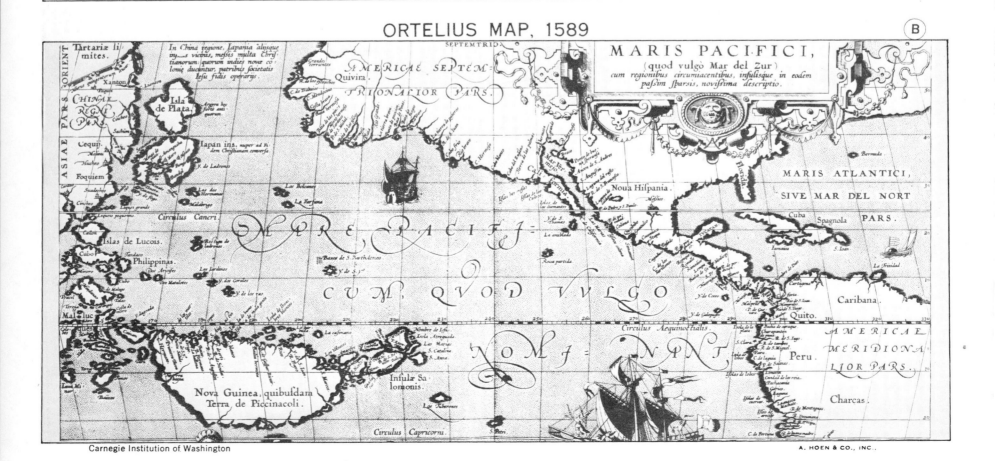

ORTELIUS MAP, 1589

Ⓑ

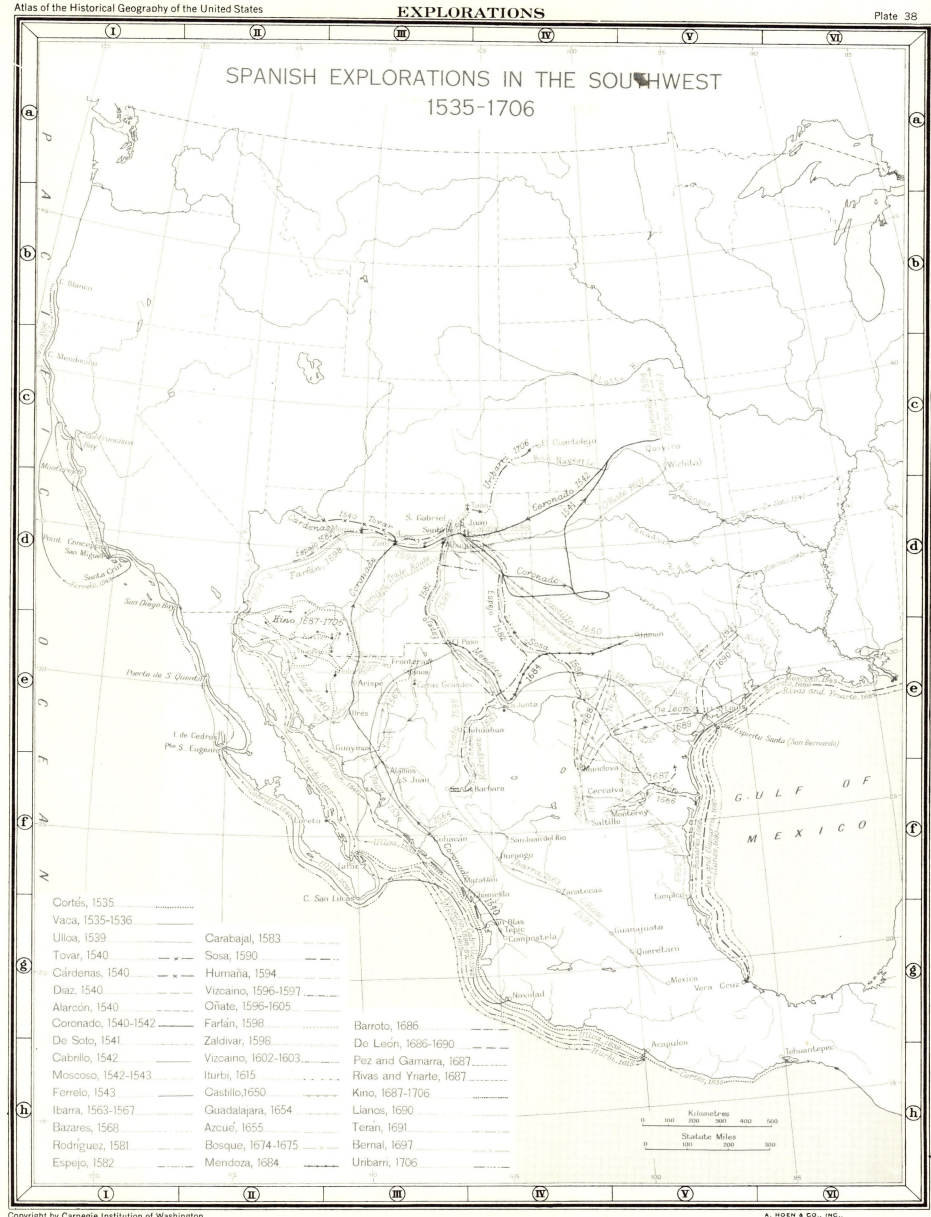

SPANISH EXPLORATIONS IN THE SOUTHWEST
1535-1706

Cortés, 1535
Vaca, 1535-1536
Ulloa, 1539   Carabajal, 1583
Tovar, 1540   Sosa, 1590
Cárdenas, 1540   Humaña, 1594
Diaz, 1540   Vizcaino, 1596-1597
Alarcón, 1540   Oñate, 1596-1605
Coronado, 1540-1542   Farfán, 1598   Barroto, 1686
De Soto, 1541   Zaldivar, 1598   De León, 1686-1690
Cabrillo, 1542   Vizcaino, 1602-1603   Pez and Gamarra, 1687
Moscoso, 1542-1543   Iturbi, 1615   Rivas and Yriarte, 1687
Ferrelo, 1543   Castillo, 1650   Kino, 1687-1706
Ibarra, 1563-1567   Guadalajara, 1654   Llanos, 1690
Bazares, 1568   Azcué, 1655   Terán, 1691
Rodríguez, 1581   Bosque, 1674-1675   Bernal, 1697
Espejo, 1582   Mendoza, 1684   Uribarri, 1706

Kilometres
0 100 200 300 400 500
Statute Miles
0 100 200 300

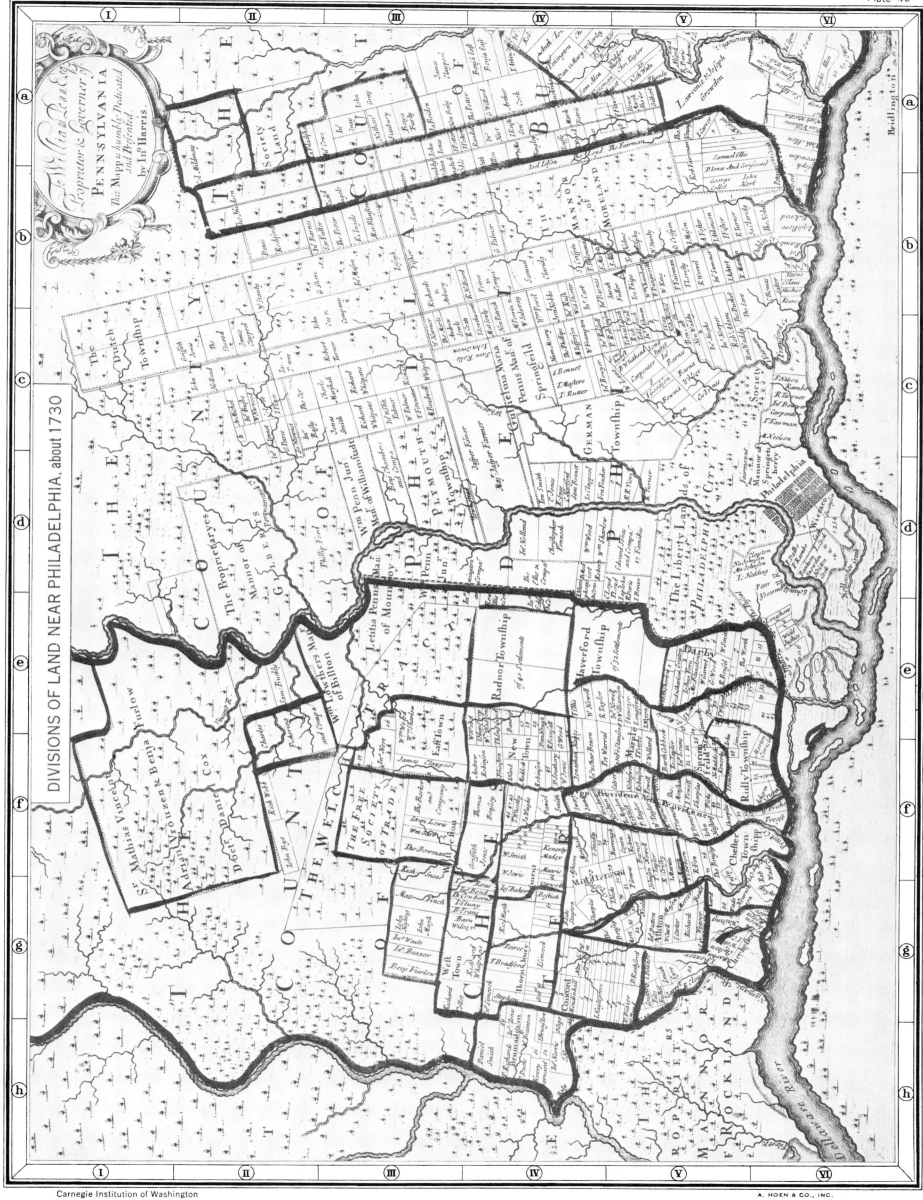

DIVISIONS OF LAND NEAR PHILADELPHIA, about 1730

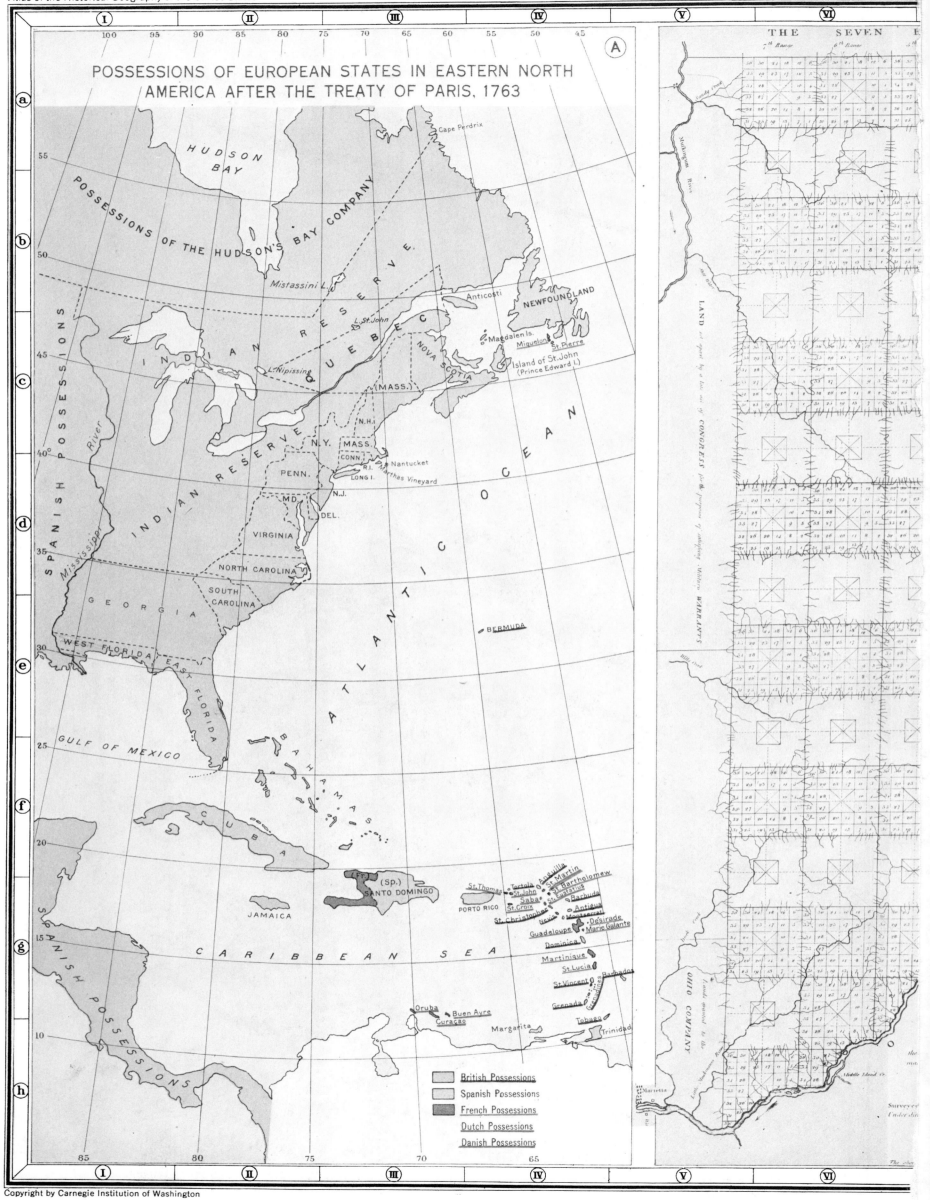

POSSESSIONS OF EUROPEAN STATES IN EASTERN NORTH AMERICA AFTER THE TREATY OF PARIS, 1763

A

HUDSON BAY

POSSESSIONS OF THE HUDSON'S BAY COMPANY

Cape Perdrix

Mistassini L.

Anticosti

NEWFOUNDLAND

L. St. John

QUEBEC

INDIAN RESERVE

L. Nipissing

NOVA SCOTIA

Magdalen Is.
Miquelon
St. Pierre

Island of St. John
(Prince Edward I.)

(MASS.)

N.H.

N.Y.
MASS.
CONN.
R.I.
LONG I.
Nantucket
Martha's Vineyard

PENN.

N.J.

MD.
DEL.

VIRGINIA

INDIAN RESERVE

SPANISH POSSESSIONS

Mississippi River

NORTH CAROLINA

SOUTH CAROLINA

GEORGIA

WEST FLORIDA
EAST FLORIDA

ATLANTIC OCEAN

BERMUDA

GULF OF MEXICO

BAHAMAS

CUBA

JAMAICA

Fr. (Sp.)
SANTO DOMINGO

CARIBBEAN SEA

St. Thomas
St. John
St. Croix
PORTO RICO
Tortola
Saba
St. Eustatius
St. Christopher
Nevis
Antigua
Montserrat
Guadeloupe
Dominica
Martinique
St. Lucia
St. Vincent
Grenada
Anguilla
St. Martin
St. Bartholomew
Barbuda
Désirade
Marie Galante
Barbados
Tobago

Oruba
Curaçao
Buen Ayre
Margarita
Trinidad

DANISH POSSESSIONS

British Possessions
Spanish Possessions
French Possessions
Dutch Possessions
Danish Possessions

Copyright by Carnegie Institution of Washington

THE SEVEN

7th Range   6th Range

LAND sold or opened by a late act of CONGRESS for the purpose of satisfying Military WARRANTS

OHIO COMPANY

Marietta

Surveyed
Under direc.

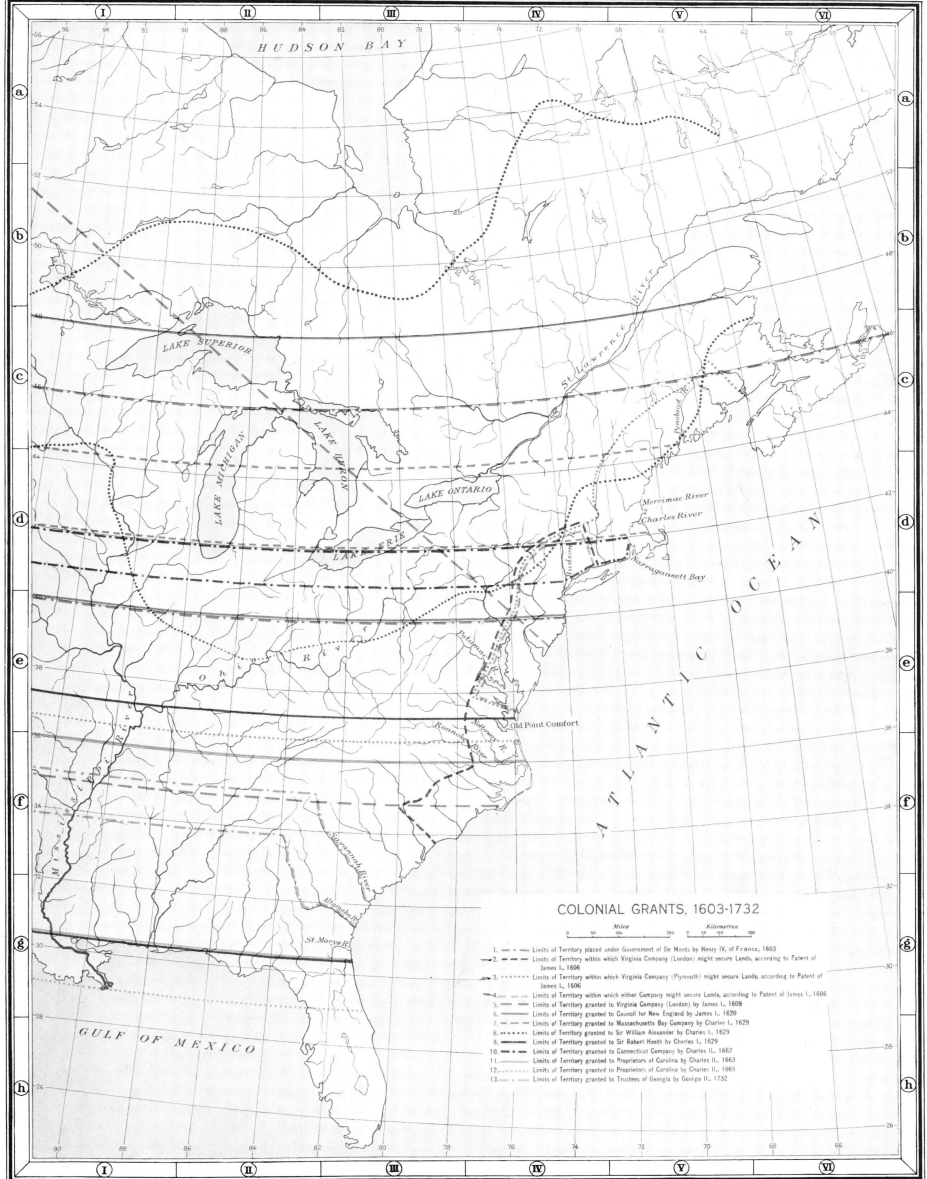

HUDSON BAY

LAKE SUPERIOR

LAKE MICHIGAN

LAKE HURON

LAKE ONTARIO

LAKE ERIE

St. Lawrence River

Penobscot R.

Merrimac River

Charles River

Narragansett Bay

Hudson R.

ATLANTIC OCEAN

Potomac R.

Old Point Comfort

Roanoke River

Nottoway R.

Ohio River

Mississippi River

Savannah River

Altamaha R.

St. Marys R.

GULF OF MEXICO

COLONIAL GRANTS, 1603-1732

Miles | Kilometres
0 50 100 200   0 50 100 200

1. ——·— Limits of Territory placed under Government of De Monts by Henry IV., of France, 1603
2. ——— Limits of Territory within which Virginia Company (London) might secure Lands, according to Patent of James I., 1606
3. ·········· Limits of Territory within which Virginia Company (Plymouth) might secure Lands, according to Patent of James I., 1606
4. ——— Limits of Territory within which either Company might secure Lands, according to Patent of James I., 1606
5. ——— Limits of Territory granted to Virginia Company (London) by James I., 1609
6. ——— Limits of Territory granted to Council for New England by James I., 1620
7. ——— Limits of Territory granted to Massachusetts Bay Company by Charles I., 1629
8. ·········· Limits of Territory granted to Sir William Alexander by Charles I., 1629
9. ——— Limits of Territory granted to Sir Robert Heath by Charles I., 1629
10. ——·—·— Limits of Territory granted to Connecticut Company by Charles II., 1662
11. ——— Limits of Territory granted to Proprietors of Carolina by Charles II., 1663
12. ·········· Limits of Territory granted to Proprietors of Carolina by Charles II., 1665
13. ——·—·— Limits of Territory granted to Trustees of Georgia by George II., 1732

Copyright by Carnegie Institution of Washington

A. HOEN & CO., INC.

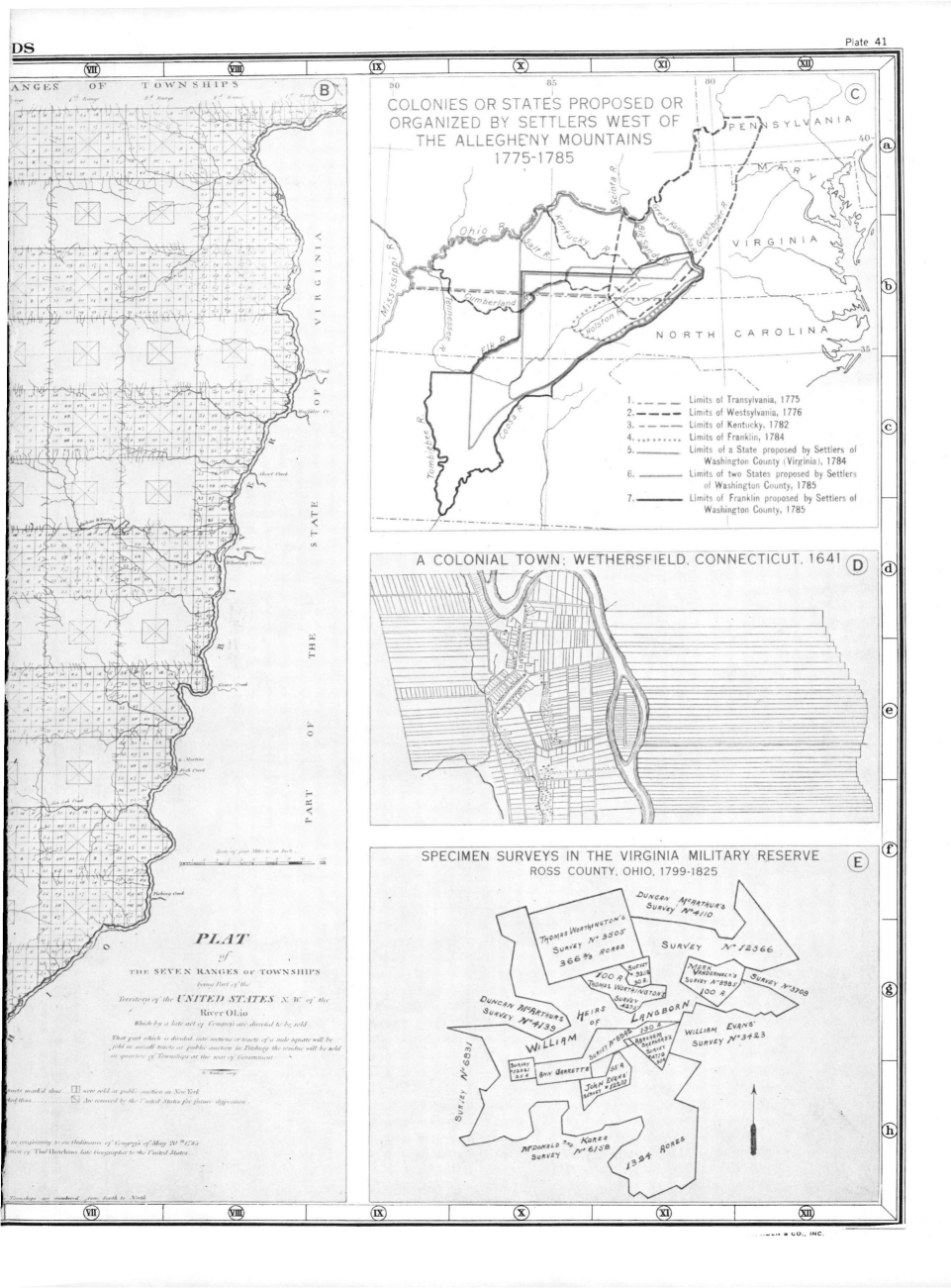

COLONIES OR STATES PROPOSED OR ORGANIZED BY SETTLERS WEST OF THE ALLEGHENY MOUNTAINS 1775-1785

1. Limits of Transylvania, 1775
2. Limits of Westsylvania, 1776
3. Limits of Kentucky, 1782
4. Limits of Franklin, 1784
5. Limits of a State proposed by Settlers of Washington County (Virginia), 1784
6. Limits of two States proposed by Settlers of Washington County, 1785
7. Limits of Franklin proposed by Settlers of Washington County, 1785

A COLONIAL TOWN: WETHERSFIELD, CONNECTICUT, 1641

SPECIMEN SURVEYS IN THE VIRGINIA MILITARY RESERVE
ROSS COUNTY, OHIO, 1799-1825

PLAT
of
THE SEVEN RANGES OF TOWNSHIPS
being Part of the
Territory of the UNITED STATES N.W. of the River Ohio

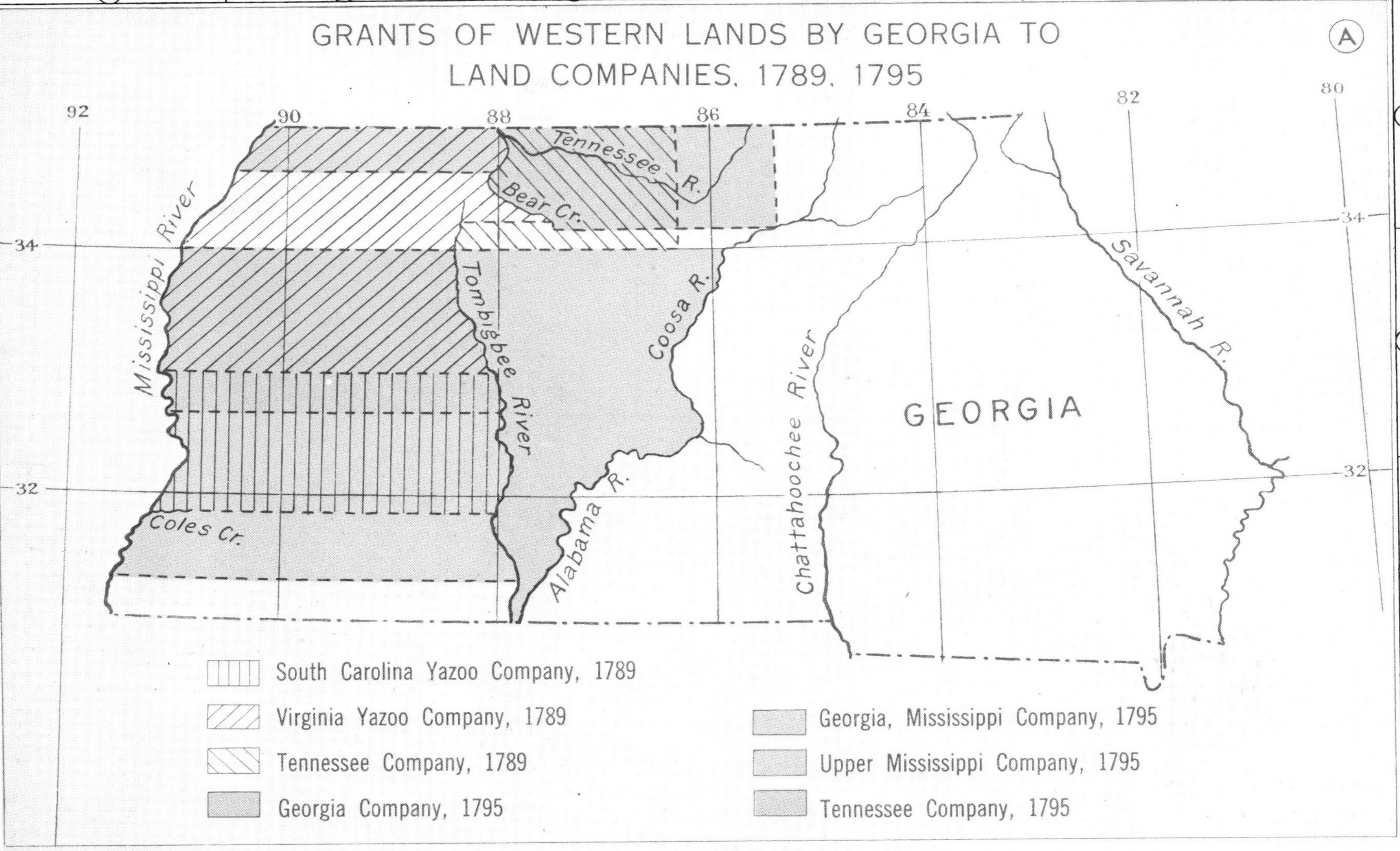

Plate 45

Ⓘ   Ⓘ   Ⓘ   Ⓘ   Ⓘ   Ⓘ

GRANTS OF WESTERN LANDS BY GEORGIA TO LAND COMPANIES, 1789, 1795

Ⓐ

ⓐ

92   90   88   86   84   82   80

Tennessee R.

Bear Cr.

Mississippi River

Tombigbee River

Coosa R.

Savannah R.

34

GEORGIA

ⓑ

Alabama R.

Chattahoochee River

32

Coles Cr.

ⓒ

ⓓ

▦ South Carolina Yazoo Company, 1789	
▨ Virginia Yazoo Company, 1789	▧ Georgia, Mississippi Company, 1795
▨ Tennessee Company, 1789	▧ Upper Mississippi Company, 1795
▨ Georgia Company, 1795	▧ Tennessee Company, 1795

MILITARY RESERVES, 1778–1816
WITH DATES OF CREATION

Ⓑ

LAKE ONTARIO

Oswego R.

N.Y. MIL. TRACT 1782

LAKE MICHIGAN

LAKE ERIE

NEW YORK

ⓔ

PA. DONATION LANDS, 1783

PENNSYLVANIA

PA. DEPRECIATION LANDS, 1783

U.S. BOUNTY LANDS 1812 & 1816

ILLINOIS

INDIANA

OHIO

Lit. Miami R.

Scioto R.

U.S. MIL. DIST. 1787 & 1796

VA. MIL. RESERVE 1784

40

U.S. BOUNTY LANDS 1812 & 1816

ⓕ

MD. MIL. RESERVE 1781

MARYLAND

NEW JERSEY

DEL.

Missouri River

MISSOURI

Illinois R.

Ohio River

Ohio River

KENTUCKY

Green River

VIRGINIA

ATLANTIC OCEAN

ⓖ

Tennessee R.

VA. MIL. RESERVE, 1778 & 1781

Powell R.

N.C. MIL. RESERVE 1783

N.C. MIL. RESERVE 1780

ARKANSAS

U.S. BOUNTY LANDS 1812

TENNESSEE

NORTH CAROLINA

35

Arkansas R.

Mississippi

River

S.C. MIL. RESERVE 1778

SOUTH CAROLINA

ⓗ

ALABAMA

GEORGIA

GA. MIL. RESERVE, 1784

90   85   80   75

Ⓘ   Ⓘ   Ⓘ   Ⓘ   Ⓘ   Ⓘ

Copyright by Carnegie Institution of Washington

A. HOEN & CO., INC

Plate 44

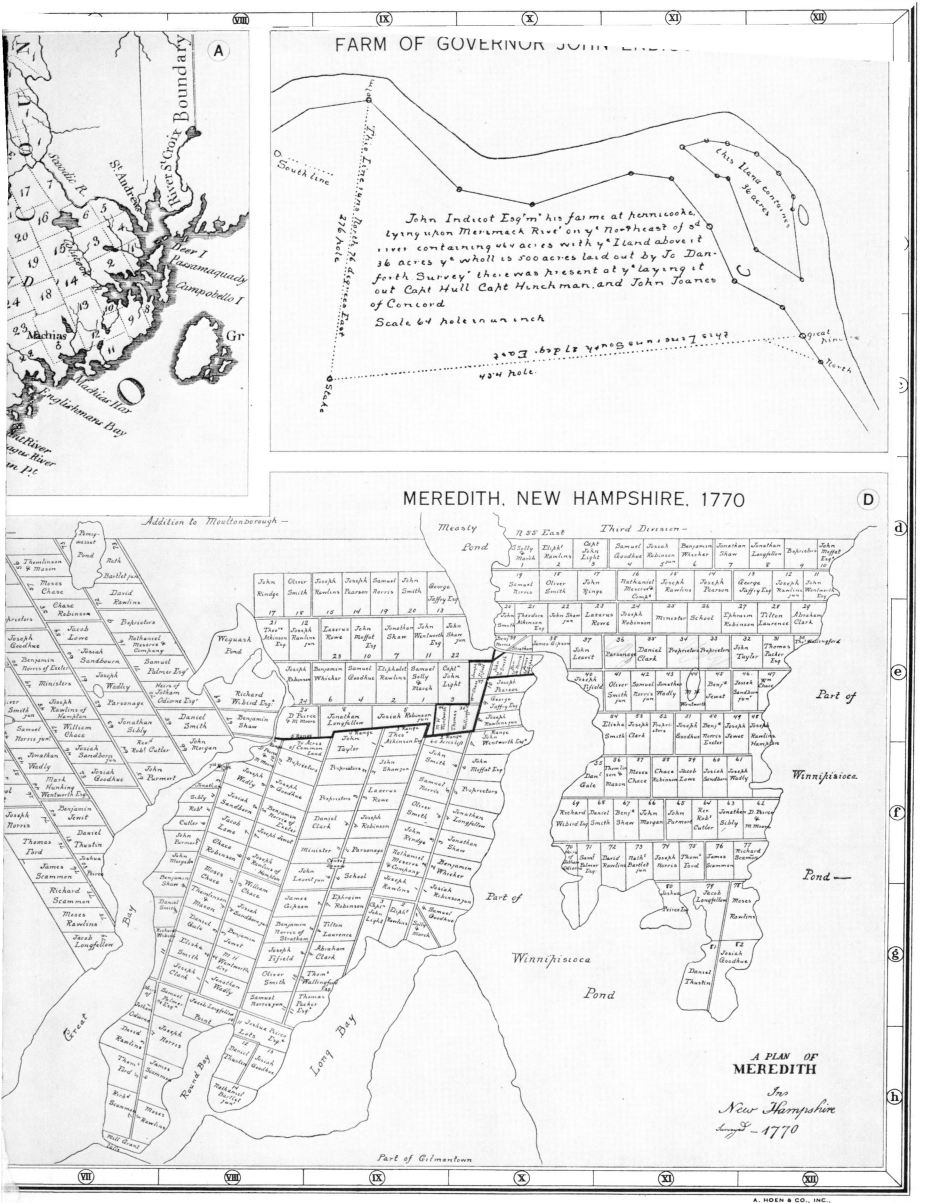

FARM OF GOVERNOR JOHN ENDICOTT

John Indicot Esq'm his farme at pennicooke, lying upon Merrimack River on ye Northeast of sd river containing 464 acres with ye Iland above it 36 acres ye wholl is 500 acres laid out by Jo Danforth Survey' there was present at ye laying it out Capt Hull Capt Hinchman, and John Joanes of Concord

Scale 64 pole in an inch

MEREDITH, NEW HAMPSHIRE, 1770

A PLAN OF
MEREDITH

In
New Hampshire
Surveyed 1770

DIVISIONS OF LAND IN MAINE, 1795

1000000 Acres Sold to Wm Bingham Esqr

Kennebeck River

West branch

Great Carrying place

MOOSE HEAD

Passaghadumkeag River

Penobscot

SCOODIC LAKE

Land reserved for the

Bingham's

Passadumkia R.

Old Town

C U M B E R L A N D

Y O R K

District of Maine

New Hampshire

NEW HAMPSHIRE

Umbagog Lake

Artis Williams

Curtis Williams

Peabody's Patent

East Andover

Curtis

Sudbury Canada

Sudbury Canada

Butterfield slip

Butterfield

Old No 5

Bridgetown Town

Vienna field Redmond

Glover town

New Gloucest

New Sharon

Readi New'utcomb

town Vinyard

Tingstown

Phipps Canada

Chester

Wilmans Plant

Green

Lewiston

Bridgetown

Baker town

Hebron

Turner

Buckstown

Readfield

Winthrop

Livermore

town

Sidney

Mount Vernon

Vassalboro

Pitts town

Bowdoin ham

Pownalsboro

Bowdoin

Topsham

Wool wich

K E N N E B E C

Unity

Fair field

Hancock

Winslow

Norridgewalk

Sandy R.

Sebascook R.

Canaan

Belgrade

W A L D O   P A T E N T

Associates

Union

Warren

Waldoboro

Thomaston

P E N O B S C O T   B A Y

Deer I.

Fial Haven

Newcastle

Edgecomb

Bangor

Hampden

Orington

Buckston

Prospect

Frankfort

Belfast

Penobscot

Belfast

Castine

Sedgwick

Trenton

Golds boro

Sullivan

Narragu

Goldsboro Har

Petit Man

Pleas

C O U N T Y

H A N C O C K   C O U N T Y

L O T T E R Y   L A N D

2
3
1 2 3 4 5 6
39 40 41 42 43
38 34 35 36
32 33
26 27 28 29 30
20 21 22 23 24 25
14 15 16 17 18 19
8 9 10 11 12 13
7 6 5

No 9 No 8 No 7
No 8
No 5 No 4
No 3 No 2 No 1
No 6

GRANTS IN MAINE TO PLYMOUTH COLONY, LAKE AND OTHERS 1753

10 Miles.   15 Miles.
Toconocke Falls   Wesserong R.

Indian Deed to   Lawson May 24th 1653.

Now Owned By Sr Byby Lake & Hitchinson

Nequamkik River

10 Miles.   15 Miles.

Colony of Plymouth Deed to Boyes & others Call'd the Plymouth Compy June 16 1665

Patent to Colony of Plymouth Jany 16, 1629

Indian Deed to ye Colony of Plymouth Aug 5 1648.

Indian Deed to ye Plymouth Company 8 July 1665

Indian Deed to ye Colony by ye Plymo Sep 10 1653

Cobbeseconte Falls.

15 Miles.

Indian Deed to Lawson Oct 10 1649

Sold by Lawson to Lake & Others July 1650

10 Miles.   10 Miles.

Androscoggin Falls.

Androscoggin River

Royalls River

Topsham

Nequasit Purchase of ye Indians Nov 3r 1639

Harrington

Townsend

Pemaquid Pt.

Small Point   Segwin I.

BAY

Second Division 71° 55 E—

| Daniel Gale |
Daniel Clark	Joseph Jewell	Elisha Smith
For the use of the Proprietors	John Leavit jun	Joseph Clark
Proprietors	James Gipson
John Taylor	Benjamin Norris of Stratham
Thomas Packer Esq	Joseph
Thomas Wallingford Esq	Tifield
Abraham Clark
Tilton Laurence
Ephraim Robinson

Sandborton

North 15 West

Part of

all ye lands on both sides of ye River house from Cushenoc upwards to Wesserunset.

all that Tract of land from Cobbeseconte unto a place where I now dwell.

COLONIAL GRANTS, 1603-1732

A

1. ———— Limits of Territory granted to Sir William Alexander by James I., 1621
2. .... Limits of Territory granted to Gorges and Mason by Council for New England, 1622
3. – – – – Limits of Territory granted to Mason by Council for New England, 1629
4. – – – – Limits of Territory granted to Plymouth Colony by Council for New England, 1630
5. –––– Limits of Territory granted to Lord Baltimore by Charles I., 1632
6. –·–·– Limits of Territory granted to Lord Alexander by Council for New England, 1635
7. ········ Limits of Territory granted to Gorges by Charles I., 1639
8. ·········· Limits of Territory placed under Government of Providence Plantations by Governor and Commissioners of Parliament, 1643
9. –·–·– Limits of Territory granted to Lord Hopton and Others by Charles II., 1649
10. –·–·– Limits of Territory granted to La Tour and Others by Cromwell, 1656
11. ———— Limits of Territory granted to Colony of Rhode Island and Providence Plantations by Charles II., 1663
12. ———— Limits of Territory granted to Duke of York by Charles II., 1664
13. ———— Limits of Territory granted to Berkeley and Carteret by Duke of York, 1664
14. –··–··– Limits of Territory granted to William Penn by Charles II., 1681
15. – – – – Limits of Territory granted to William Penn by Duke of York, 1682

Miles   *Kilometres*

ALLOTMENTS OF LAND
B
DORCHESTER, MASSACHUSETTS
1660

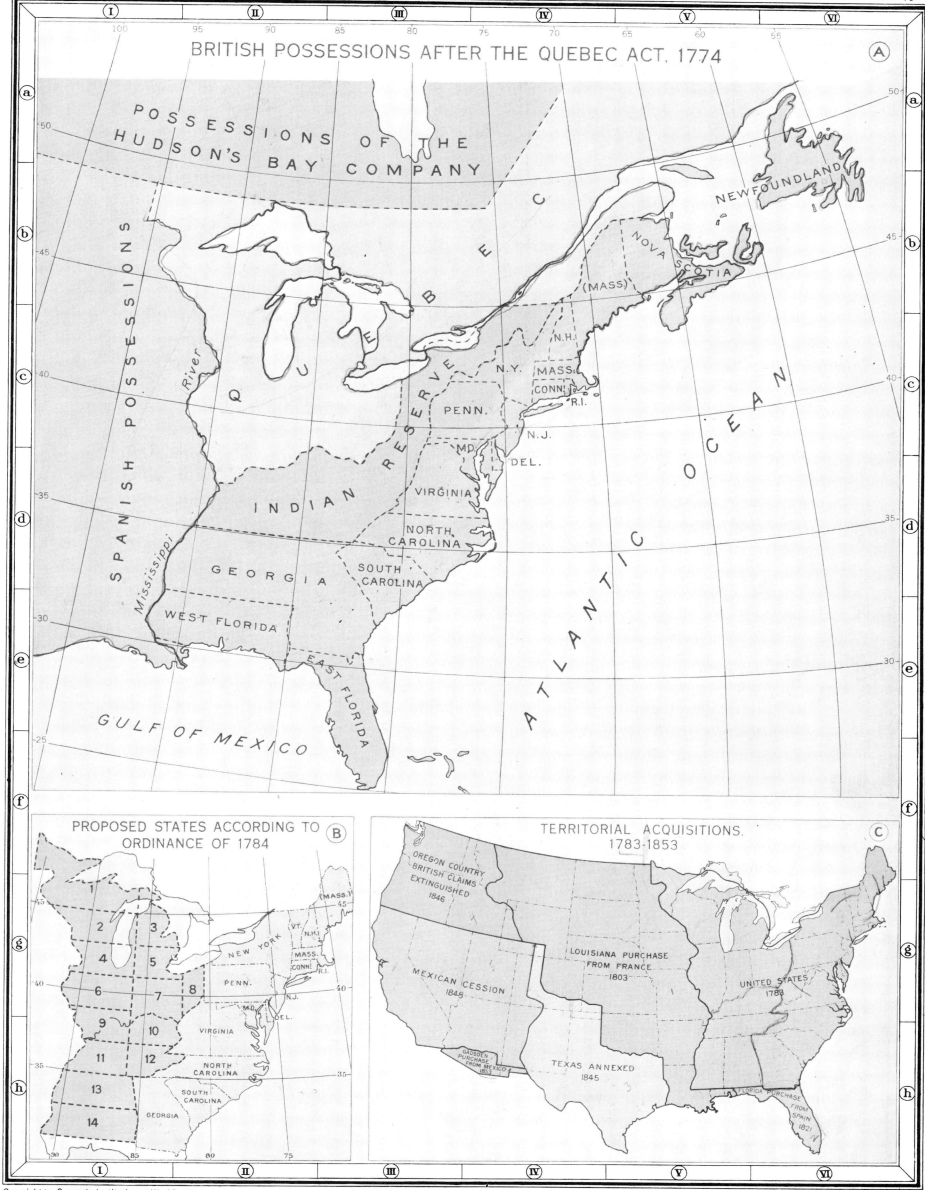

BRITISH POSSESSIONS AFTER THE QUEBEC ACT. 1774

POSSESSIONS OF THE HUDSON'S BAY COMPANY

SPANISH POSSESSIONS

QUEBEC

NEWFOUNDLAND

NOVA SCOTIA

(MASS)

N.H.

N.Y.

MASS.

CONN.

R.I.

PENN.

N.J.

MD.

DEL.

INDIAN RESERVE

VIRGINIA

NORTH CAROLINA

GEORGIA

SOUTH CAROLINA

WEST FLORIDA

EAST FLORIDA

River

Mississippi

ATLANTIC OCEAN

GULF OF MEXICO

PROPOSED STATES ACCORDING TO ORDINANCE OF 1784

1
2 3
4 5
6 7 8
9 10
11 12
13
14

(MASS.)

NEW YORK

VT.

N.H.

MASS.

CONN.

R.I.

PENN.

N.J.

MD.

DEL.

VIRGINIA

NORTH CAROLINA

SOUTH CAROLINA

GEORGIA

TERRITORIAL ACQUISITIONS. 1783-1853

OREGON COUNTRY BRITISH CLAIMS EXTINGUISHED 1846

MEXICAN CESSION 1848

LOUISIANA PURCHASE FROM FRANCE 1803

UNITED STATES 1783

GADSDEN PURCHASE FROM MEXICO 1853

TEXAS ANNEXED 1845

FLORIDA PURCHASE FROM SPAIN 1821

Copyright by Carnegie Institution of Washington

A. HOEN & CO., INC.

Ⓘ   Ⓠ   Ⓡ   Ⓥ   Ⓥ   Ⓦ

INDIAN CESSIONS, 1750–1890

Lands ceded by Indians, 1750–1783
1784–1810
1831–1850
1871–1890

1811–1830
1851–1870
Lands acquired by the colonists before 1750, lands acquired later by the United States in Louisiana and Texas without Indian cession, or Indian reservations not ceded.

CLAIMS AND CESSIONS OF WESTERN LANDS, 1776–1802 Ⓒ
NEW YORK

Lake Superior
Lake Michigan
Lake Huron
L. Ontario
NEW YORK
Lake Erie
2
1
River
Illinois R.
Mississippi
Tennessee River

New York ceded to United States title and jurisdiction to "1" and "2", 1782.

CLAIMS AND CESSIONS OF
VIRGINIA

Lake Superior
Lake Michigan
Lake Huron
Lake
1
River
Ohio River
2
Mississippi
3
GEORGIA

Ⓘ   Ⓠ   Ⓡ   Ⓥ   Ⓥ   Ⓦ

Copyright by Carnegie Institution of Washington

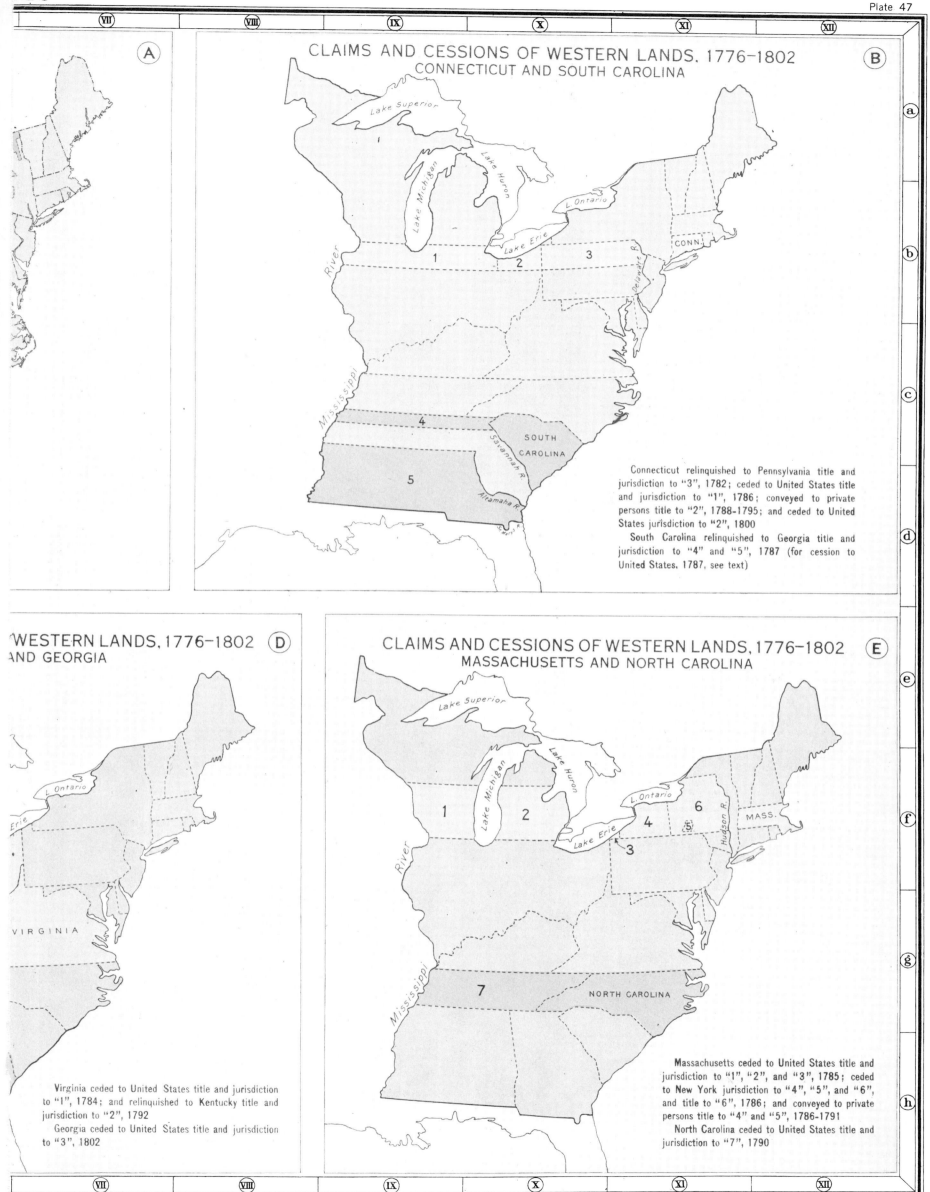

CLAIMS AND CESSIONS OF WESTERN LANDS, 1776–1802
CONNECTICUT AND SOUTH CAROLINA

Ⓑ

Lake Superior

Lake Michigan

Lake Huron

L. Ontario

Lake Erie

CONN.

Delaware R.

River

1   2   3

Mississippi

4

SOUTH CAROLINA

Savannah R.

5

Altamaha R.

Connecticut relinquished to Pennsylvania title and jurisdiction to "3", 1782; ceded to United States title and jurisdiction to "1", 1786; conveyed to private persons title to "2", 1788–1795; and ceded to United States jurisdiction to "2", 1800

South Carolina relinquished to Georgia title and jurisdiction to "4" and "5", 1787 (for cession to United States, 1787, see text)

WESTERN LANDS, 1776–1802 Ⓓ
AND GEORGIA

L. Ontario

Erie

3

VIRGINIA

Virginia ceded to United States title and jurisdiction to "1", 1784; and relinquished to Kentucky title and jurisdiction to "2", 1792

Georgia ceded to United States title and jurisdiction to "3", 1802

CLAIMS AND CESSIONS OF WESTERN LANDS, 1776–1802 Ⓔ
MASSACHUSETTS AND NORTH CAROLINA

Lake Superior

Lake Michigan

Lake Huron

L. Ontario

River

1   2   4   6

Lake Erie   5

3

Hudson R.   MASS.

Mississippi

7

NORTH CAROLINA

Massachusetts ceded to United States title and jurisdiction to "1", "2", and "3", 1785; ceded to New York jurisdiction to "4", "5", and "6", and title to "6", 1786; and conveyed to private persons title to "4" and "5", 1786–1791

North Carolina ceded to United States title and jurisdiction to "7", 1790

A

SYSTEM OF SURVEY OF PUBLIC LANDS UNDER ACT OF 1796

1. SECTIONS OF A TOWNSHIP

6	5	4	3	2	1
7	8	9	10	11	12
18	17	16	15	14	13
19	20	21	22	23	24
30	29	28	27	26	25
31	32	33	34	35	36

A TOWNSHIP IS 6 MILES SQUARE AND CONTAINS 36 SQUARE MILES

2. SUBDIVISIONS OF A SECTION

HALF-SECTION
320 ACRES

QUARTER-SECTION
160 ACRES

HALF QUARTER-SECTION
80 ACRES

QUARTER QUARTER-SECTION
40 ACRES

QUARTER QUARTER-SECTION
40 ACRES

A SECTION IS 1 MILE SQUARE AND CONTAINS 640 ACRES

3. DESIGNATING OF TOWNSHIPS

			T. 5 N.		
			T. 4 N.		
			T. 3 N.		
			T. 2 N.		
			T. 1 N.		

BASE LINE

R. III. W.	R. II. W.	R. I. W.	T. 1 S. R. I. E.	R. II. E.	R. III. E.
			T. 2 S.		
			T. 3 S.		
			T. 4 S.		
			T. 5 S.		

MERIDIAN — PRINCIPAL MERIDIAN

B

PLAN of LYSTRA, in NELSON COUNTY, KENTUCKY.

Orchard Street   Garden Street
Elm Street, Cedar Street, Walnut Street, Sugar Maple Str., Chesnut Street
Edward Street   Pleasant Street
Nelson Street   Jefferson Street
Orange Street   Hill Street   Peckitt Street
Farmer Street   Mee Street
Mulberry Street, Fig Street, Olive Street, Vine Street
Agents Street   Daniel Street

The SOUTH CREEK of the ROLLING FORK

Remarks.
A. The Site of a Church.
B. Dᵒ Collage.
C. Dᵒ Town Hall.
D. Dᵒ Place of Amusement.
a. a. a. a. Dᵒ The Markets.

Note. The Town is divided into 188 Lots.
The Streets 100 feet wide.

C

MAP of FOUR TOWNSHIPS in Marengo County ALABAMA.

Granted to the French Emigrants by Act of Congress 3ᵈ March, 1817.
by
E. PAGUENAUD.

Scale 1¾ Miles to an inch

a. 1 Mile is 80 Chains of 66 feet each, making 5280 feet to a Mile. An Acre is 43560 square feet.

For the explanation of the Map and figures see the printed list of the drage at the Store of the Tombeckbee Company.

Tombeckbee or Black Warrior River
Big Prairie Creek
Tombeckbee River
White Bluff
EAGLEVILLE

RANGE 3 EAST.   RANGE 4 EAST.

TERRITORIAL CLAIMS AND LIMITS ON THE NORTHWEST COAST
OF AMERICA. 1790-1846

Miles

Kilometres

1. ———— Northern Limit claimed by Spain, 1790

2. —·—·— Northern and Southern Limits claimed by United States by reason of Discovery, Exploration, and Settlement in 1792-1811

3. ———— Northern and Southern Limits claimed by United States under Treaty with Spain of 1819

4. —··—··— Northern Limits claimed by United States, 1843-1846

5. ———— Southern Limit claimed by Russia, 1821

6. ·············· Northern Limit claimed by Great Britain, 1823

7. ·············· Southern Limit claimed by Great Britain, 1826

8. ———— Northern and Southern Limits of Area of Joint Occupation according to Proposal of Great Britain, 1818

9. ———— Northern Limit of Area open to Settlement by United States and Southern Limit of Area open to Settlement by Great Britain according to First Proposal of United States, 1824

10. —·—·— Northern Limit of Area open to Settlement by Great Britain according to First and Second Proposals of United States, 1824

11. ———— Northern Limit of Area open to Settlement by United States and Southern Limit of Area open to Settlement by Great Britain according to Second Proposal of United States, 1824

LANDS GRANTED TO STATES FOR EDUCATIONAL
AND OTHER PURPOSES, 1785-1919

A

Under 500,000 acres
500,000 to 3,000,000 acres
3,000,000 to 5,000,000 acres — per state
5,000,000 acres and over

GEORGE ROGERS CLARK GRANT
ABOUT 1785

C

OHIO RIVER

S 64 E 249 Rods
Pine Tree
Lebanon
99 Rods

Copyright by Carnegie Institution of Washington

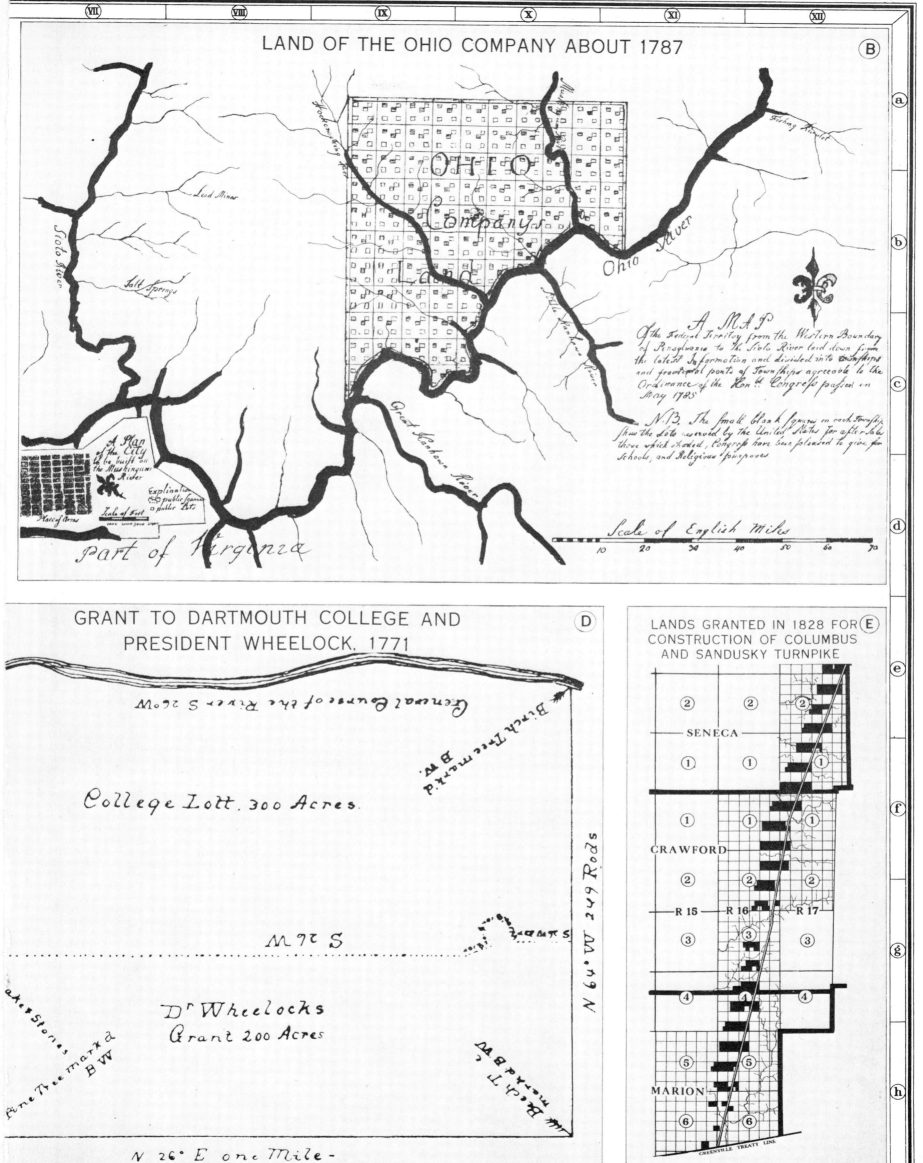

LAND OF THE OHIO COMPANY ABOUT 1787

Ⓑ

OHIO

Company's

Land

Part of Virginia

A Plan of the City to be built on the Muskingum River

Explination of public square a public Lots

Place of Arms

Scale of Feet

Lead Mines

Sciota River

Salt Springs

Ohio River

Great Kanhawn River

A MAP
Of the Federal Territory from the Western Boundary of Pennsylvania to the Scioto River laid down from the latest Information and divided into Townships and fractional parts of Townships agreeable to the Ordinance of the Honble Congress passed in May 1785

N.B. The small blank squares in each Township shew the Lots reserved by the United States for after Sale those which shaded, Congress have been pleased to give for Schools, and Religious purposes

Scale of English Miles
10   20   30   40   50   60   70

GRANT TO DARTMOUTH COLLEGE AND
PRESIDENT WHEELOCK, 1771
Ⓓ

General Course of the River S 26 W

Birch Tree mark'd B W

College Lott 300 Acres

S 26 W

N 64° W 249 Rods

Dr Wheelocks
Grant 200 Acres

Stakes Stones mark'd B W
Pine Tree mark'd B W

Beech T

Beech mark'd B W

N 26° E one Mile

LANDS GRANTED IN 1828 FOR Ⓔ
CONSTRUCTION OF COLUMBUS
AND SANDUSKY TURNPIKE

② ② ②
SENECA
① ① ①

① ① ①
CRAWFORD
② ② ②

R 15   R 16   R 17
③ ③ ③

④ ④ ④

⑤ ⑤

MARION
⑥ ⑥

GREENVILLE TREATY LINE

A. HOEN & CO., INC.,

SURVEY OF THE FAIRFAX LANDS, 1736-1737

A Scale of Miles 69¼ in one Degree of Latitude.

A SURVEY of the NORTHERN NECK
of VIRGINIA, being
The LANDS belonging to the Rt. Honourable
THOMAS LORD FAIRFAX BARON CAMERON, bounded
by & within the Bay of Chesapoyocke and between
the Rivers Rappahannock and Potowmack.
with
The Courses of the Rivers
RAPPAHANNOCK and POTOWMACK,
in
VIRGINIA,
as surveyed according to Order
in the Years 1736 & 1737.

GRANT TO WASHINGTON FOR MILITARY SERVICES, 1774

By Protraction ... N 58 W. 1630 poles

No. 7 .... Containg ... 2950 .. Acres

[Great Kanawha River]

A FRENCH SETTLEMENT
KASKASKIA. ILLINOIS

Map A. Plan of Settlement, 1807
Map B. Specimen of Common Fields about 1809

Map A. Plan of Settlement, 1807 — showing Kaskaskia River, Kaskaskia Village, Cahokia Gate, Common field 8203 Acres, Commons contains 6850 Acres, Road from Kaskaskia to St. Geneviève, Indian Island, Island, Saline Ferry, Obshaus Creek, Mississippi River. Scale of 100 Perches to an Inch.

Map B. Specimen of Common Fields about 1809 — land survey strips along the Kaskaskia River and Mississippi River:

4 Arpt.s Survey No. 278 Clm. 1592 Micheal Danies Heirs who are Charles Micheal & Jerome Danie — 144 As.
A Poles 22 links front Survey No. 277 Unappropriated — 19 As 25 Poles
3 Arpt.s Survey No. 276 Claim No. 791 Jas. Morrison Assee. of Robt. Morrison Assee. of Andrie Faggot — 126 As.
1¾ Arpt. Survey No. 275 Clm. No. 342 Jacob Judy Assee. Antoine Beinvenue — 60 As.
1 Arpt. Survey No. 274 Clm. No. 2184 John Edgar Ass.e of John Cook — 54 As. 27 Po.
1 Arpt. Survey No. 273 Clm. No. 2154 John Edgar Ass.e of Micheal Danie — 52 As.
1½ Arpt. Survey No. 272 Clm. No. 701 Antoine Beinvenue Sen.r — 80 As.
1 Arpt. Survey No. 271 Claim No. 2192 John Edgar Ass.e of Pierre Prevost — 54 As. 27 Po.
½ Arpt. Survey No. 270 Claim No. 2155 John Edgar Ass.e Micheal Danie — 28 As. 13 Po.
1 Arpt. Survey No. 269 Clm. No. 2190 John Edgar Ass.e of Alexis Beauvais — 55 As.
1 Arpt. Survey No. 268 Clm. No. 2532 John Edgar Ass.e of Charles Danie — 55 As. 36 Po.
2 Arpt. Survey No. 267 Clm. No. 2146 John Edgar Ass.e of Barthelemie Richard — 110 As. 64 Po.
3 Arpt.s Survey No. 266 Clm. 2131 John Edgar Ass.e of Ettienne Page — 159¼ As.
1½ Arpt.s Survey No. 265 Clm. No. 1538 Barthelemie Richard Ass.e of Cotteneau & Chenier (Menards) — 74 As.
1½ Arpt.s Survey No. 264 Clm. No. 2193 John Edgar in Right of Daniel McJCDuff Ass.e of Jos.s Bougie — 67¼ As.
1 Arpt. Survey No. 263 Clm. No. 648 Ant. Buyats Heirs in right of Anue Buyat — 40 Acres
½ Arpt. Surv. No. 262 Reputed to be the property of John Edgar in right of Corsete — 18 As 150 Poles
1 Arpt. Survey No. 261 Clm. No. 2187 John Edgar Ass.e of Pierre Degagnie — 36 As. 67 Po.
2⅔ Arpt.s Survey No. 260 Clm. 636 Jas. Kinkaid Ass.e of Louis Brazeau Ass.e of Fra: Javouse — 87¼ As.
2 Arpt. Survey No. 259 Clm. 2200 John Edgar Ass.e of Pierre Allerow — 64 As. 96 Po.
2 Arpt. Surv. No. 258 Clm. 2133 John Edgar Ass.e of Francis Janis — 62 As. 20 Po.
1 Arpt. Surv. No. 257 Clm. 2167 John Edgar Ass.e of Ant. Beinvenne — 30¼ As.
1 Arpt. Surv. No. 256 Clm. No. 2156 John Edgar Ass.e of M Danie — 30 As.
2 Arptds Surv. No. 255 Clm. No. 2533 John Edgar Ass.e of Louis Lamall — 61¼ As.
Survey No. 254 John Edgar Ass.e of Madame Beyatt 68¼ As. 1 Arpt. on Kaskaskia N 78 40 E.
Claim 176 N. 74 10 E. 421 Po. Robt. Reynolds Ass.e of Chas. Danis 77½ As. 1 Arpt. on Kaskaskia
Sur.s No 253 N. 69 40 E. 425 Po. Morrison Ass.e of Robt. Morrison who
Record No. 45 of Andre Faggot
No. 252 130 As. 2 Arpts front on Kaskaskia

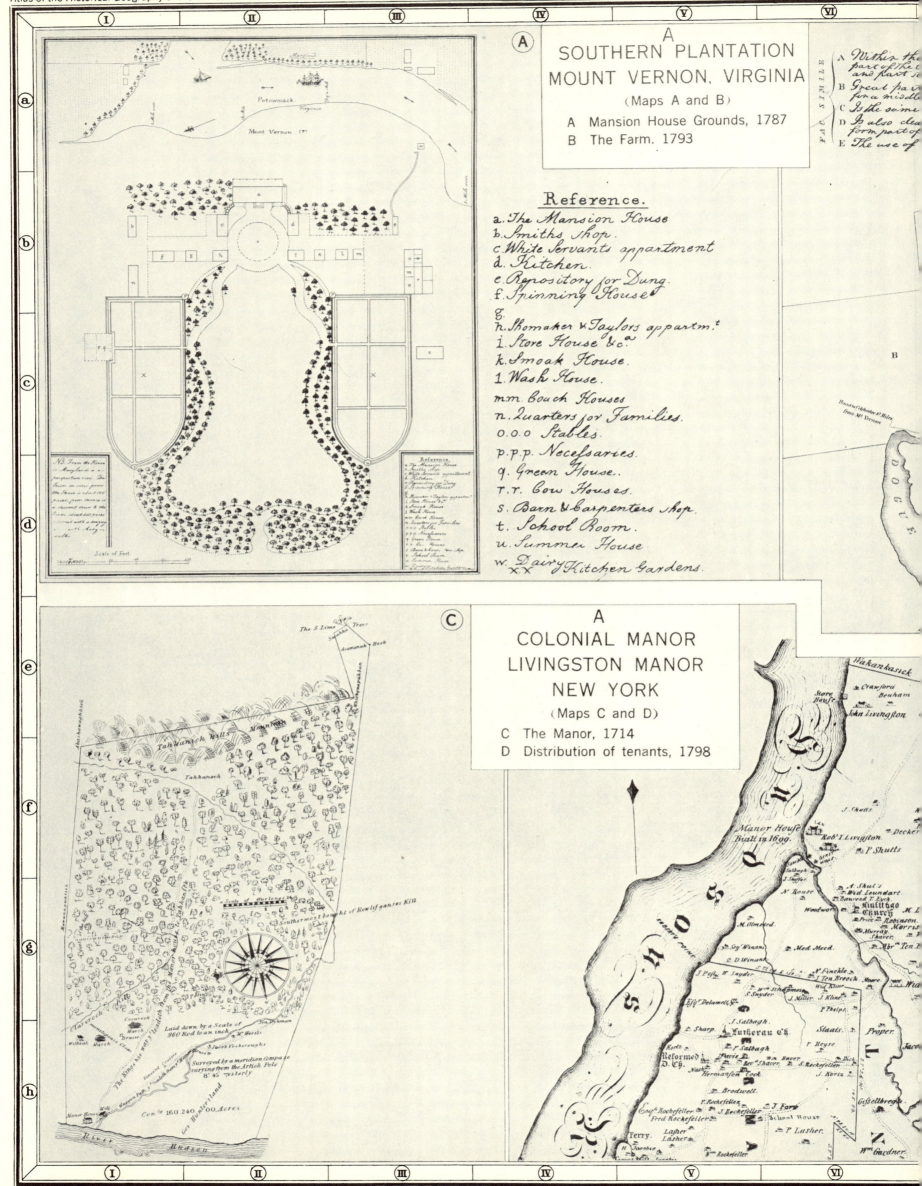

**A
SOUTHERN PLANTATION
MOUNT VERNON, VIRGINIA**
(Maps A and B)
A Mansion House Grounds, 1787
B The Farm. 1793

Reference.
a. The Mansion House
b. Smiths Shop.
c. White Servants appartment
d. Kitchen.
e. Repository for Dung.
f. Spinning House.
g.
h. Shomaker & Taylors appartm.t
i. Store House &c.a
k. Smoak House.
l. Wash House.
mm. Coach Houses
n. Quarters for Families.
o.o.o. Stables.
p.p.p. Necessaries.
q. Green House.
r.r. Cow Houses.
s. Barn & Carpenters Shop.
t. School Room.
u. Summer House.
w. Dairy
x.x. Kitchen Gardens.

**A
COLONIAL MANOR
LIVINGSTON MANOR
NEW YORK**
(Maps C and D)
C The Manor, 1714
D Distribution of tenants, 1798

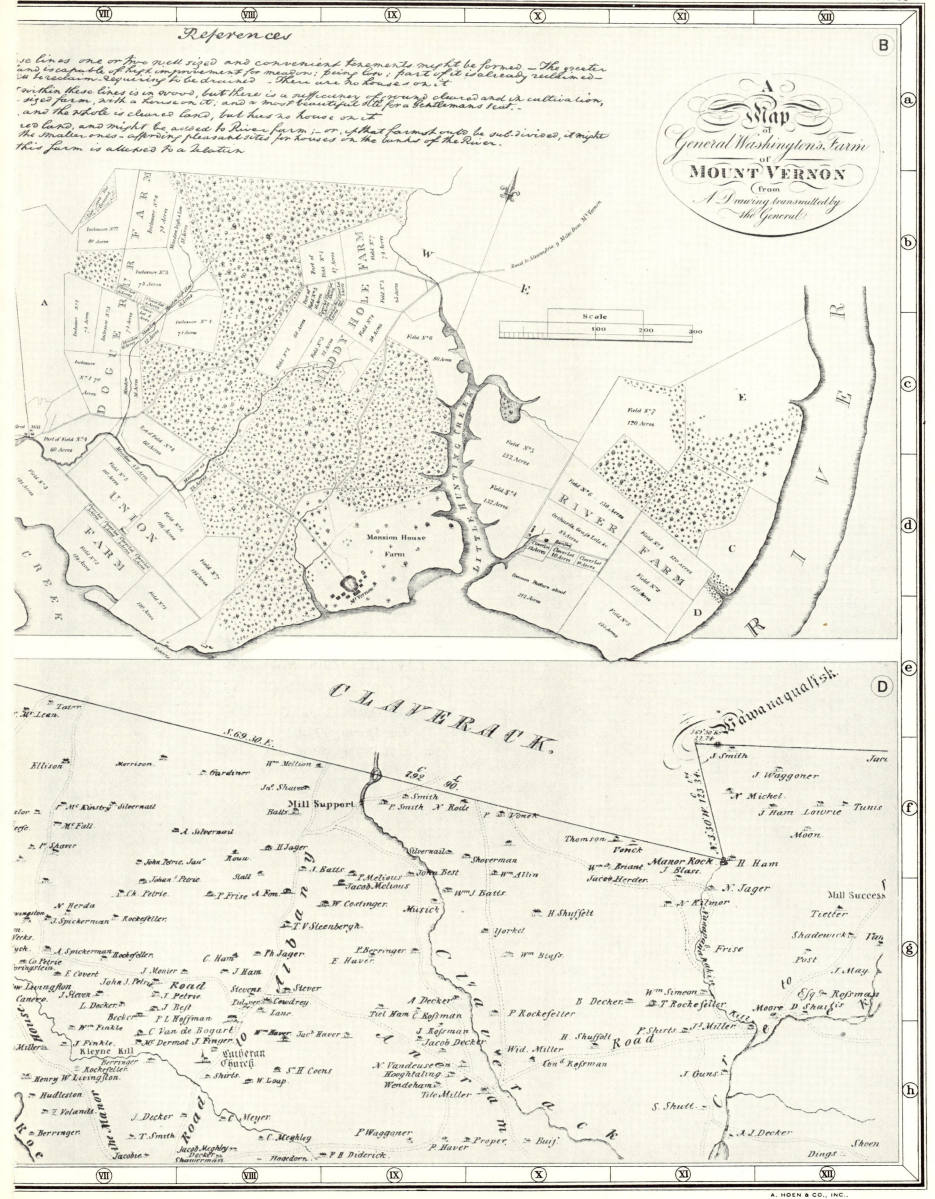

A MODERN CITY
SPRINGFIELD ILLINOIS. 1915

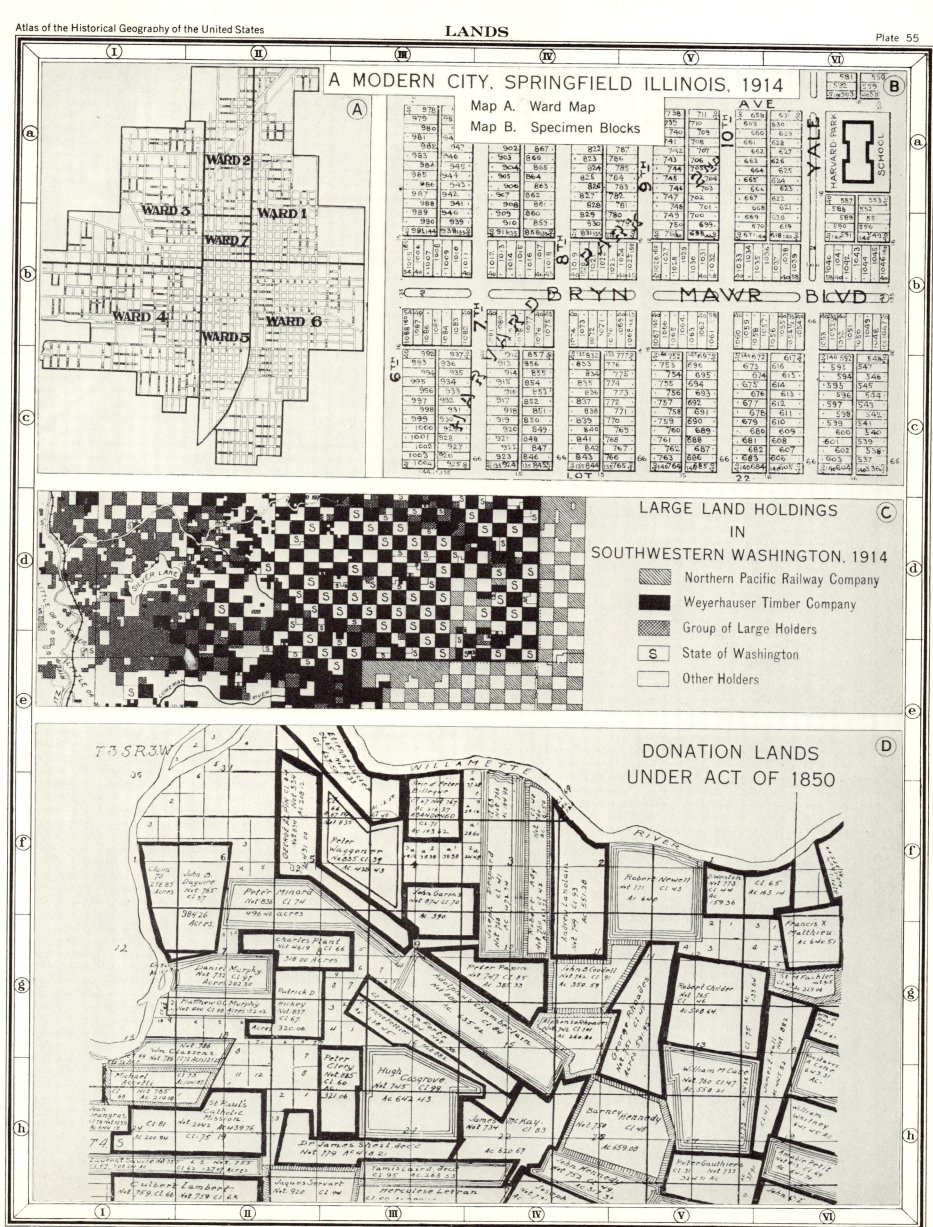

A MODERN CITY, SPRINGFIELD ILLINOIS, 1914

Map A.　Ward Map
Map B.　Specimen Blocks

LARGE LAND HOLDINGS
IN
SOUTHWESTERN WASHINGTON, 1914

Northern Pacific Railway Company
Weyerhauser Timber Company
Group of Large Holders
S　State of Washington
Other Holders

DONATION LANDS
UNDER ACT OF 1850

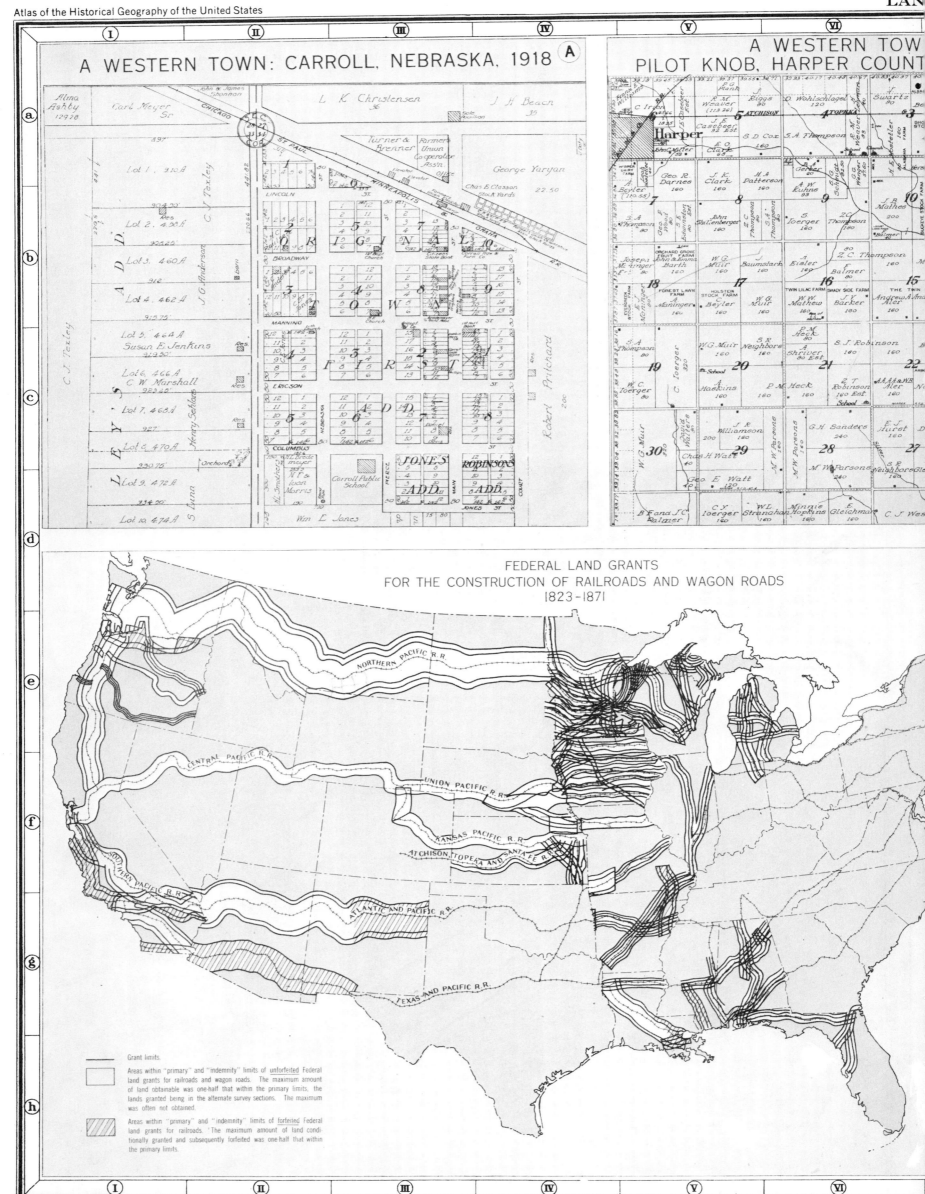

A WESTERN TOWN: CARROLL, NEBRASKA, 1918

A WESTERN TOW
PILOT KNOB, HARPER COUNT

FEDERAL LAND GRANTS
FOR THE CONSTRUCTION OF RAILROADS AND WAGON ROADS
1823–1871

Grant limits.

Areas within "primary" and "indemnity" limits of unforfeited Federal land grants for railroads and wagon roads. The maximum amount of land obtainable was one-half that within the primary limits, the lands granted being in the alternate survey sections. The maximum was often not obtained.

Areas within "primary" and "indemnity" limits of forfeited Federal land grants for railroads. The maximum amount of land conditionally granted and subsequently forfeited was one-half that within the primary limits.

Plate 56

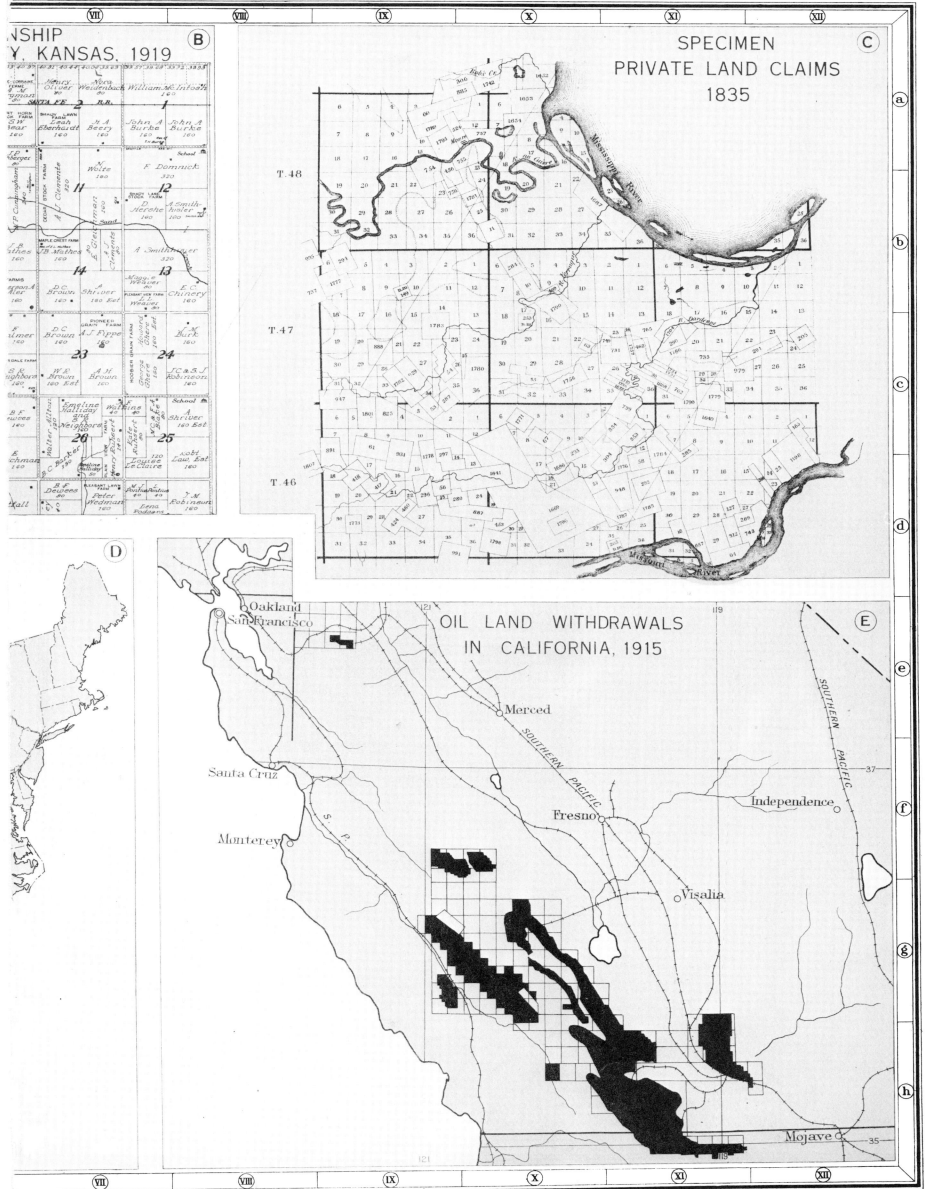

OS

VII VIII IX X XI XII

B NSHIP
Y, KANSAS, 1919

C SPECIMEN
PRIVATE LAND CLAIMS
1835

T.48

T.47

T.46

Mississippi River

Missouri River

D

E OIL LAND WITHDRAWALS
IN CALIFORNIA, 1915

Oakland
San Francisco

Merced

Santa Cruz

Fresno

Monterey

Visalia

Independence

SOUTHERN PACIFIC

Mojave

VII VIII IX X XI XII

A

PUBLIC LANDS OF UNITED STATES, 1830
RELATIVE AREAS ARE SHOWN GRAPHICALLY
FOR EACH STATE AND TERRITORY

Public lands (at the westward)

Lands sold or otherwise disposed of (at the eastward)

Lands not a part of the public domain

C

PUBLIC LANDS OF UNITED STATES 1870
RELATIVE AREAS ARE SHOWN GRAPHICALLY
FOR EACH STATE AND TERRITORY

Public lands (at the westward)

Lands sold or otherwise disposed of (at the eastward)

Lands not a part of the public domain

Copyright by Carnegie Institution of Washington

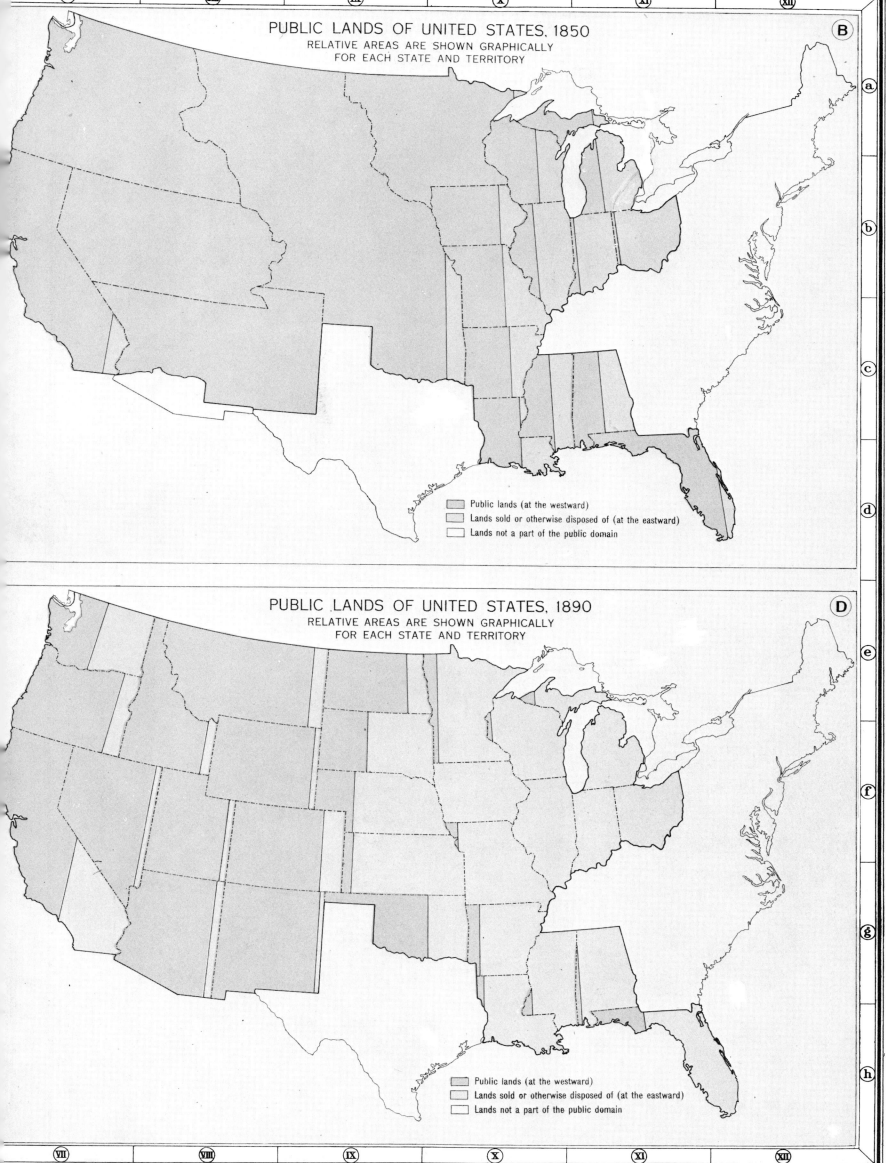

PUBLIC LANDS OF UNITED STATES, 1850
RELATIVE AREAS ARE SHOWN GRAPHICALLY
FOR EACH STATE AND TERRITORY

B

Public lands (at the westward)
Lands sold or otherwise disposed of (at the eastward)
Lands not a part of the public domain

PUBLIC LANDS OF UNITED STATES, 1890
RELATIVE AREAS ARE SHOWN GRAPHICALLY
FOR EACH STATE AND TERRITORY

D

Public lands (at the westward)
Lands sold or otherwise disposed of (at the eastward)
Lands not a part of the public domain

PUBLIC LANDS

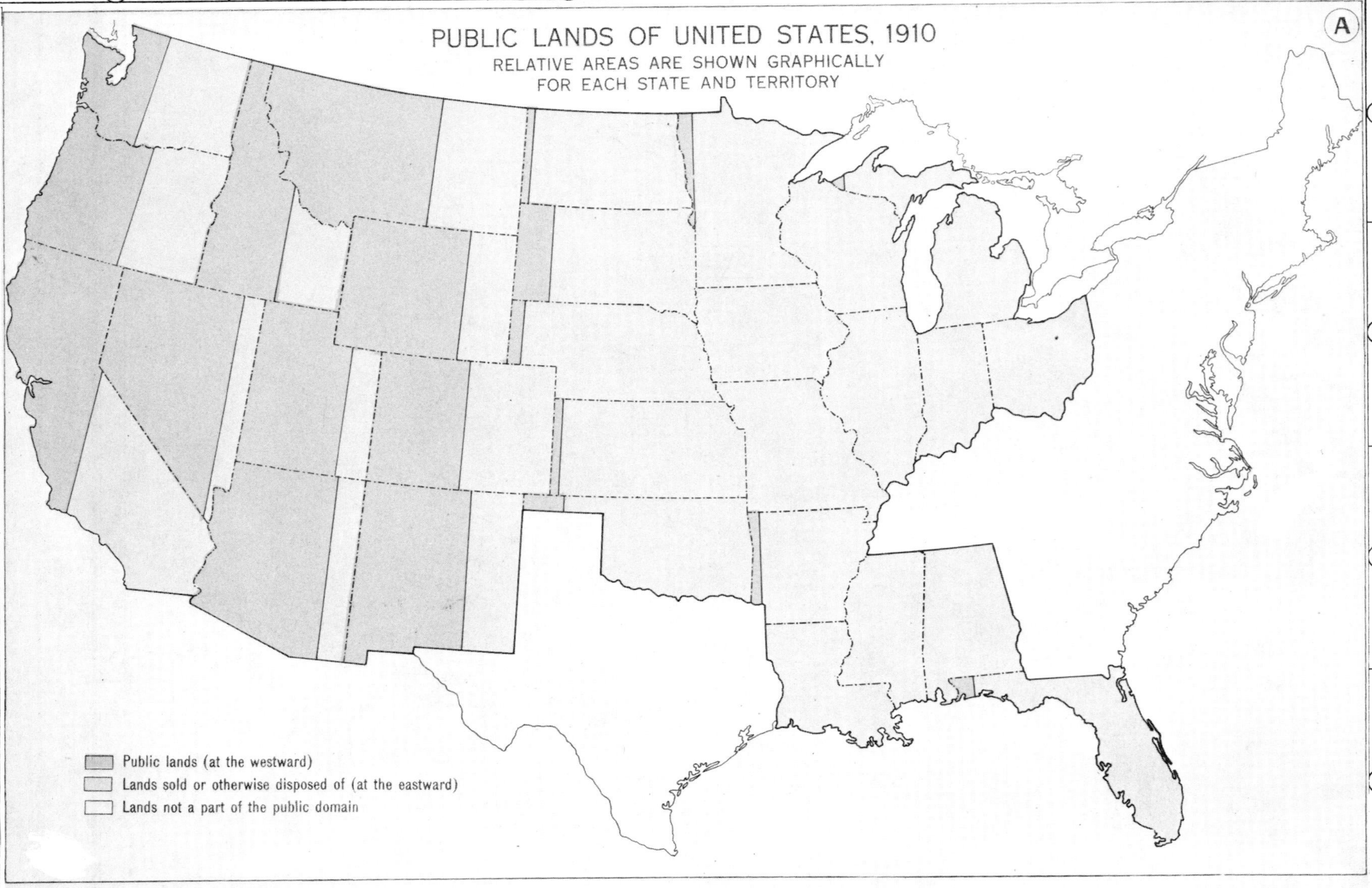

Plate 59

PUBLIC LANDS OF UNITED STATES, 1910
RELATIVE AREAS ARE SHOWN GRAPHICALLY
FOR EACH STATE AND TERRITORY

Public lands (at the westward)

Lands sold or otherwise disposed of (at the eastward)

Lands not a part of the public domain

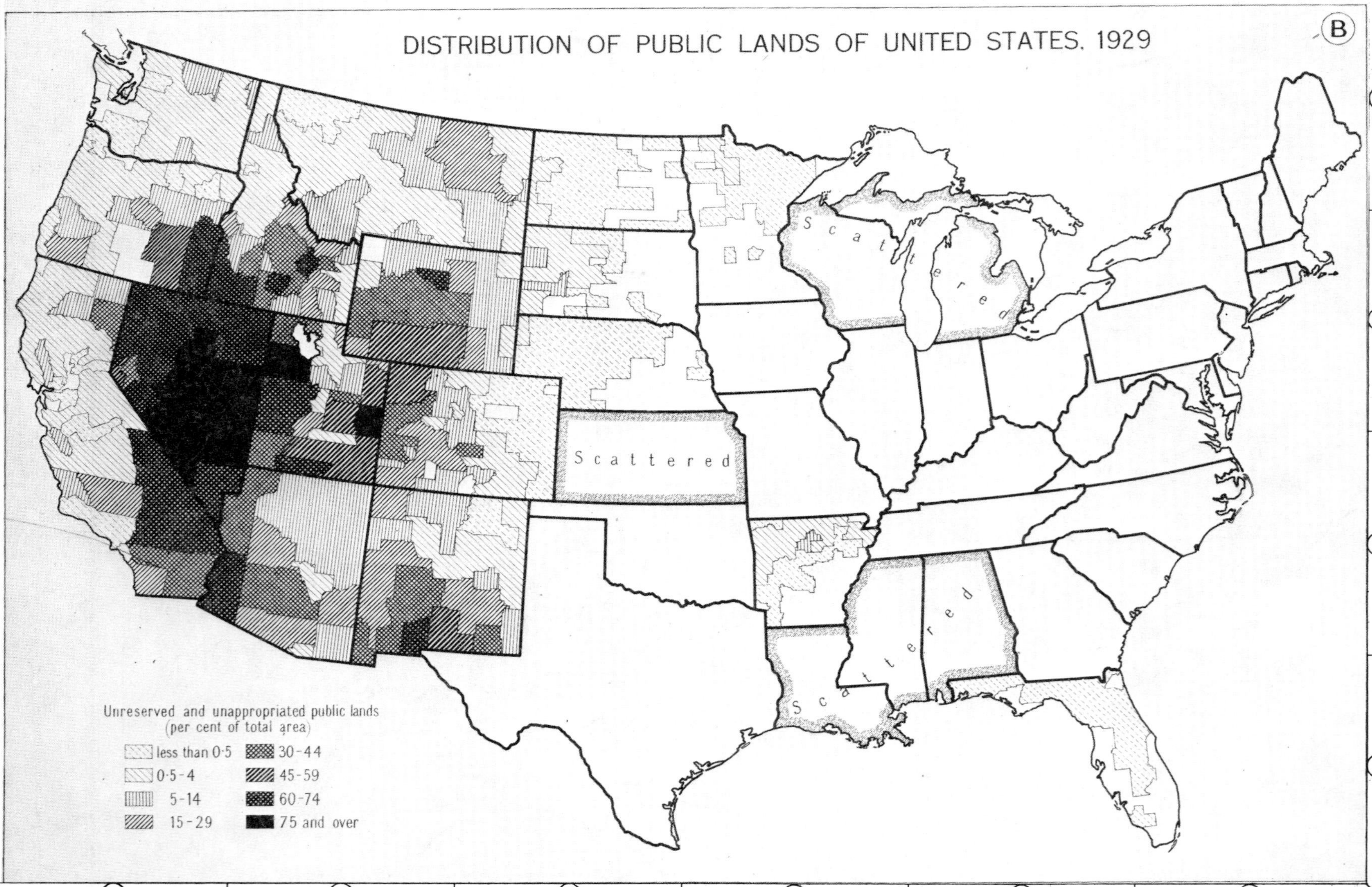

DISTRIBUTION OF PUBLIC LANDS OF UNITED STATES, 1929

Scattered

Scattered

Scattered

Scattered

Unreserved and unappropriated public lands
(per cent of total area)

less than 0·5	30–44
0·5–4	45–59
5–14	60–74
15–29	75 and over

Copyright by Carnegie Institution of Washington

A. HOEN & CO., INC

SETTLEMENT AND POPULATION, 1660-1790

A

SETTLED AREAS
AND
POPULATION
1660

B

SETTLED AREAS
AND
POPULATION
1700

C

SETTLED AREAS, 1760, AND POPULATION, 1750

D

SETTLED AREAS AND POPULATION
1775

E

SETTLED AREAS AND POPULATION
1790

Settled areas

Approximate population of colonies or states

10,000
50,000
100,000
400,000
800,000

Settled areas from map prepared under direction of J. R. H. Moore for
Edward Channing: *History of the United States*, Vol. 3, p. 528.

Copyright by Carnegie Institution of Washington

A. HOEN & CO., INC.,

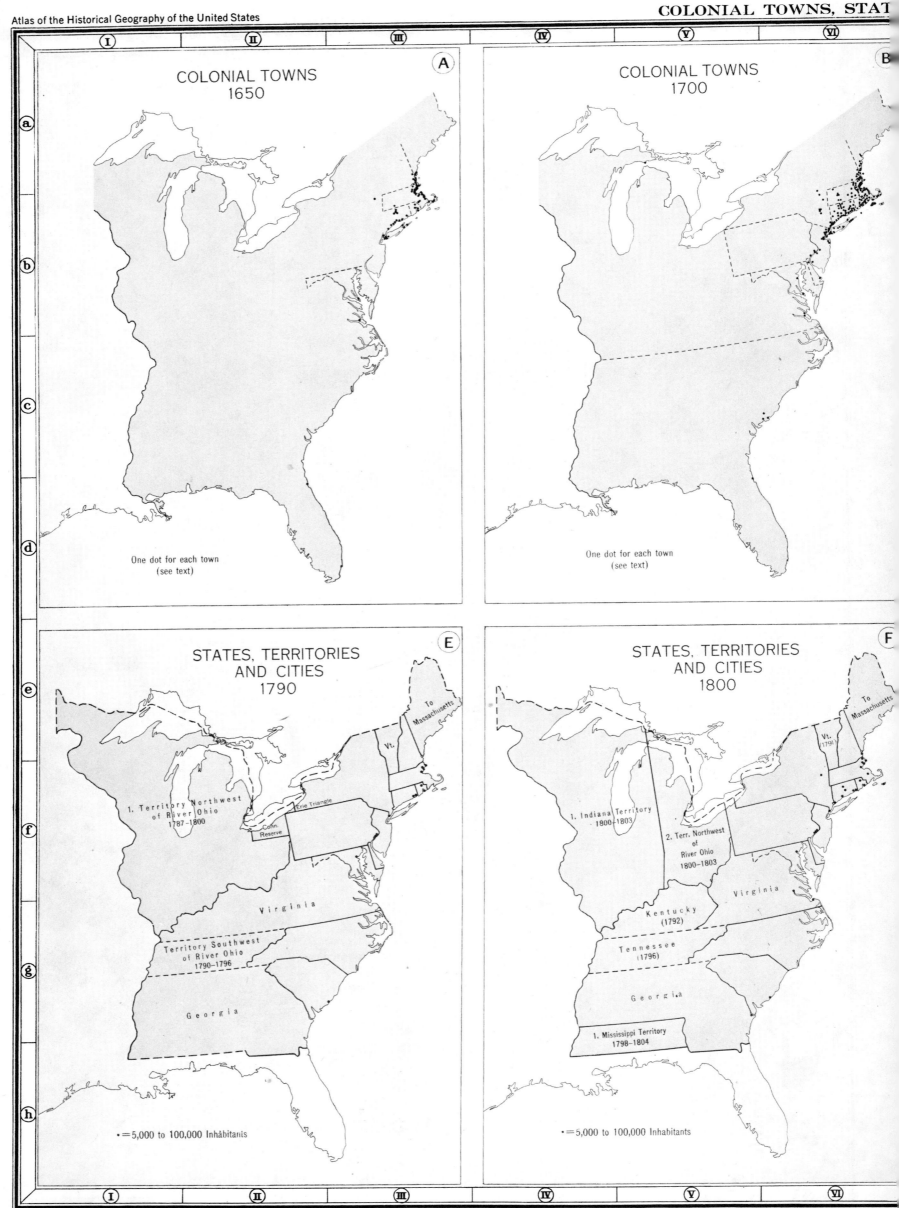

COLONIAL TOWNS
1650

One dot for each town
(see text)

COLONIAL TOWNS
1700

One dot for each town
(see text)

STATES, TERRITORIES
AND CITIES
1790

To
Massachusetts

Vt.

1. Territory Northwest
of River Ohio
1787-1800

Erie Triangle

Conn.
Reserve

Virginia

Territory Southwest
of River Ohio
1790-1796

Georgia

• = 5,000 to 100,000 Inhabitants

STATES, TERRITORIES
AND CITIES
1800

To
Massachusetts

Vt.
(1791)

1. Indiana Territory
1800-1803

2. Terr. Northwest
of
River Ohio
1800-1803

Virginia

Kentucky
(1792)

Tennessee
(1796)

Georgia

1. Mississippi Territory
1798-1804

• = 5,000 to 100,000 Inhabitants

Copyright by Carnegie Institution of Washington

COLONIAL TOWNS
1750

One dot for each town
(see text)

COLONIAL TOWNS
1775

One dot for each town
(see text)

STATES, TERRITORIES, AND CITIES
1810

1. Orleans
Territory
1804-1810

Louisiana District, 1804-1805
(Under Government of Indiana Territory)

Louisiana Territory, 1805-1812

Missouri Territory, 1812-1819

Illinois Terr.
1809-1818

1. Michigan Terr.
1805-1816

4. Indiana Terr.
1809-1816

4. Indiana
Territory
1809-1816

Ohio
(1803)

To
Massachusetts

2. Indiana Territory
1803-1805

3. Indiana Territory
1805-1809

2. Mississippi Territory
1804-1812

2. Orleans
Territory
1810-1812

To Spain

• = 5,000 to 100,000 Inhabitants

STATES, TERRITORIES, AND CITIES
1820

Oregon Country

Missouri Territory
1819–1821

3. Michigan Territory
1818–1834

Illinois
(1818)

Indiana
(1816)

1. Arkansas Territory
1819–1824

2. Mississippi
enlarged
1820

2. Alabama
reduced, 1820

2. Louisiana
enlarged
1812

Maine
(1820)

To Spain

A

1. Louisiana
(1812)

3. Mississippi Territory
1812–1817

1. Mississippi
(1817)

Alabama Terr.
1817–1819
1. Alabama
(1819)

2. Michigan Territory
1816–1818

• = 5,000 to 100,000 Inhabitants
● = 100,000 Inhabitants and over

STATES, TERRITORIES, AND CITIES
1830

Oregon Country

Unorganized

3. Michigan Territory
1818–1834

1. Missouri
(1821)

3. Arkansas Terr.
1828–1836

Florida Territory
1822–1845

B

2. Arkansas Territory
1824–1828

• = 5,000 to 100,000 Inhabitants
● = 100,000 Inhabitants and over

Copyright by Carnegie Institution of Washington

A. HOEN & CO., INC

Ⓐ

STATES, TERRITORIES, AND CITIES
1840

Oregon Country

2. Wisconsin Territory
1838–1848

Iowa Territory
1838–1846

5. Mich. Terr.
1836–1837
Michigan
(1837)

Unorganized

1. Wisconsin Territory
1836–1838

2. Missouri
enlarged, 1837

4. Michigan Territory
1834–1836

Arkansas
(1836)

Florida Territory
1822–1845

• = 5,000 to 100,000 Inhabitants
• = 100,000 Inhabitants and over

Ⓑ

STATES, TERRITORIES, AND CITIES
1850

1. Oregon Territory
1848–1853

Minnesota Territory
1849–1858

Wisconsin
(1848)

1. Utah Territory
1850–1861

Unorganized

Iowa
(1846)

California
(1850)

1. New Mexico Territory
1850–1854

2. Texas
reduced, 1850

Florida
(1845)

• = 5,000 to 100,000 Inhabitants
• = 100,000 Inhabitants and over

Copyright by Carnegie Institution of Washington

A. HOEN & CO., INC.,

STATES, TERRITORIES, AND CITIES
1860

2. Washington Territory
1859–1861

Oregon
(1859)

Unorganized

Minnesota
(1858)

1. Nebraska Territory
1854–1861

1. Utah Territory
1850–1861

Kansas Territory
1854–1861

2. New Mexico Territory
1854–1861

Unorganized

• = 5,000 to 100,000 Inhabitants
● = 100,000 Inhabitants and over

STATES AND TERRITORIES (ADDITIONAL MAPS, 1845–1868)

2. Nebraska Territory
1861–1863

3. Washington Territory
1861–1863

1. Idaho Territory
1863–1864

2. Idaho Territory
1864–1868

2. Utah Territory
1861–1862

1. Texas
(1845)

1. Dakota Territory
1861–1863

3. Dakota Territory
1864–1868

3. Utah Territory
1862–1866

3. New Mexico Territory
1861–1863

1. Arizona Territory
1863–1866

1. Washington Territory
1853–1859

4. Utah Territory
1866–1868

1. West
Virginia
(1863)

2. West
Virginia
enlarged
1863

1. Nevada
Territory
1861–1862

2. Nevada Territory
1862–1864

1. Nevada
(1864)

2. Oregon Territory
1853–1859

Copyright by Carnegie Institution of Washington

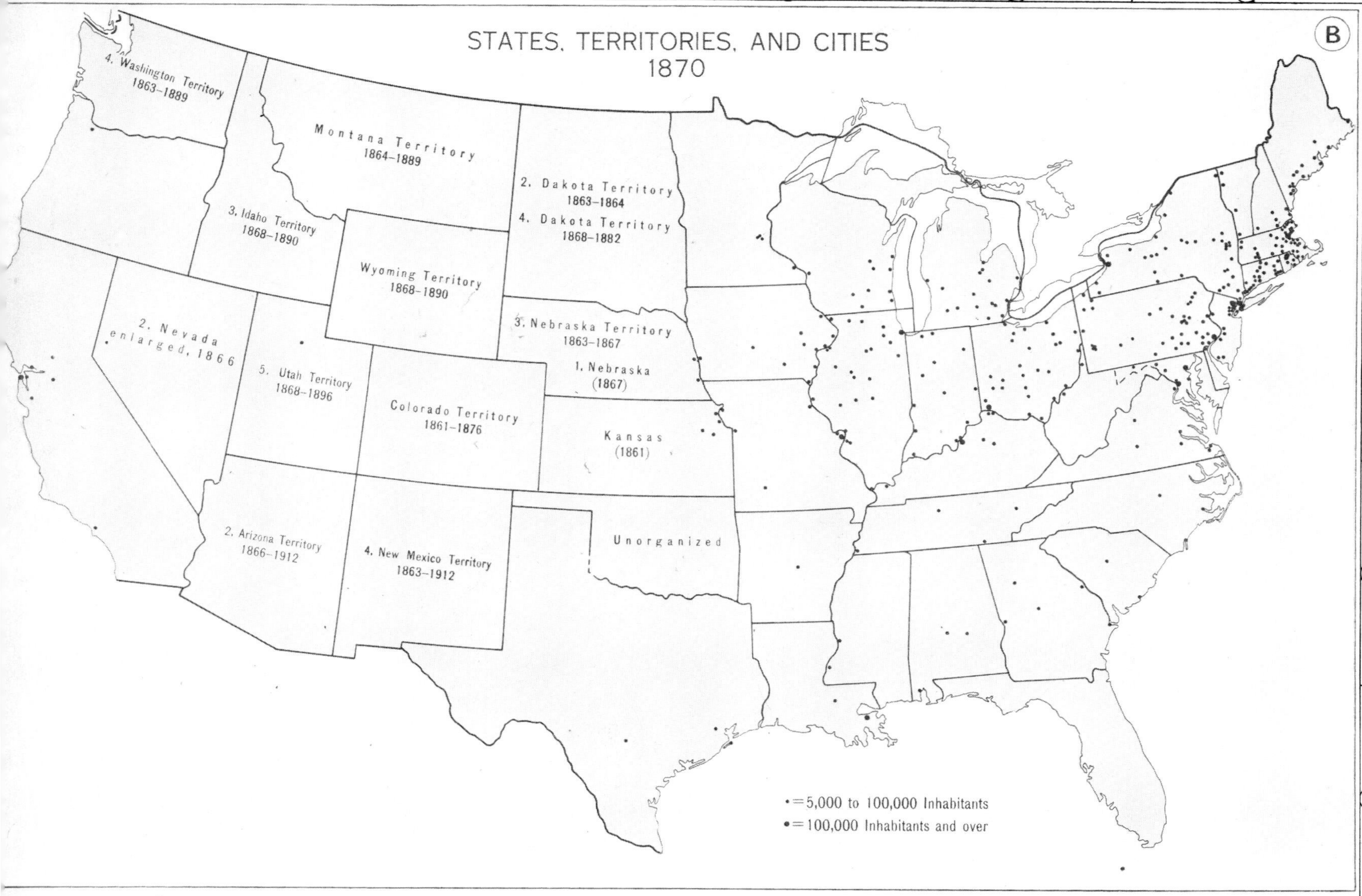

Plate 64

STATES, TERRITORIES, AND CITIES
1870

4. Washington Territory 1863–1889

Montana Territory 1864–1889

3. Idaho Territory 1868–1890

2. Dakota Territory 1863–1864

4. Dakota Territory 1868–1882

Wyoming Territory 1868–1890

2. Nevada enlarged, 1866

5. Utah Territory 1868–1896

3. Nebraska Territory 1863–1867

I. Nebraska (1867)

Colorado Territory 1861–1876

Kansas (1861)

2. Arizona Territory 1866–1912

4. New Mexico Territory 1863–1912

Unorganized

• = 5,000 to 100,000 Inhabitants
● = 100,000 Inhabitants and over

STATES, TERRITORIES, AND CITIES
1880

Washington Territory 1863–1889

Montana Territory 1864–1889

Idaho Territory 1868–1890

4. Dakota Territory 1868–1882

Wyoming Territory 1868–1890

Utah Territory 1868–1896

Colorado (1876)

Arizona Territory 1866–1912

New Mexico Territory 1863–1912

Unorganized

• = 5,000 to 100,000 Inhabitants
● = 100,000 Inhabitants and over

STATES, TERRITORIES, AND CITIES
1890

Washington
(1889)

Montana
(1889)

North Dakota
(1889)

Idaho
(1890)

South Dakota
(1889)

Wyoming
(1890)

2. Nebraska
enlarged, 1882

Utah Territory
1868–1896

To Oklahoma   Unorganized

1. Oklahoma Terr.
1890–1893

Arizona Territory
1866–1912

New Mexico Territory
1863–1912

Unorganized

5. Dakota Territory
1882–1889

• = 5,000 to 100,000 Inhabitants
● = 100,000 Inhabitants and over

STATES, TERRITORIES, AND CITIES
1900

Utah
(1896)

2. Oklahoma Terr.
1893–1907

Arizona Territory
1866–1912

New Mexico Territory
1863–1912

Unorganized

• = 5,000 to 100,000 Inhabitants
● = 100,000 Inhabitants and over

STATES, TERRITORIES, AND CITIES
1910

Arizona Territory
1866-1912

New Mexico Territory
1863-1912

Okla.
(1907)

• = 5,000 to 100,000 Inhabitants
● = 100,000 Inhabitants and over

STATES, TERRITORIES, AND CITIES
1920

Arizona
(1912)

New Mexico
(1912)

• = 5,000 to 100,000 Inhabitants
● = 100,000 inhabitants and over

Copyright by Carnegie Institution of Washington

A. HOEN & CO., INC.,

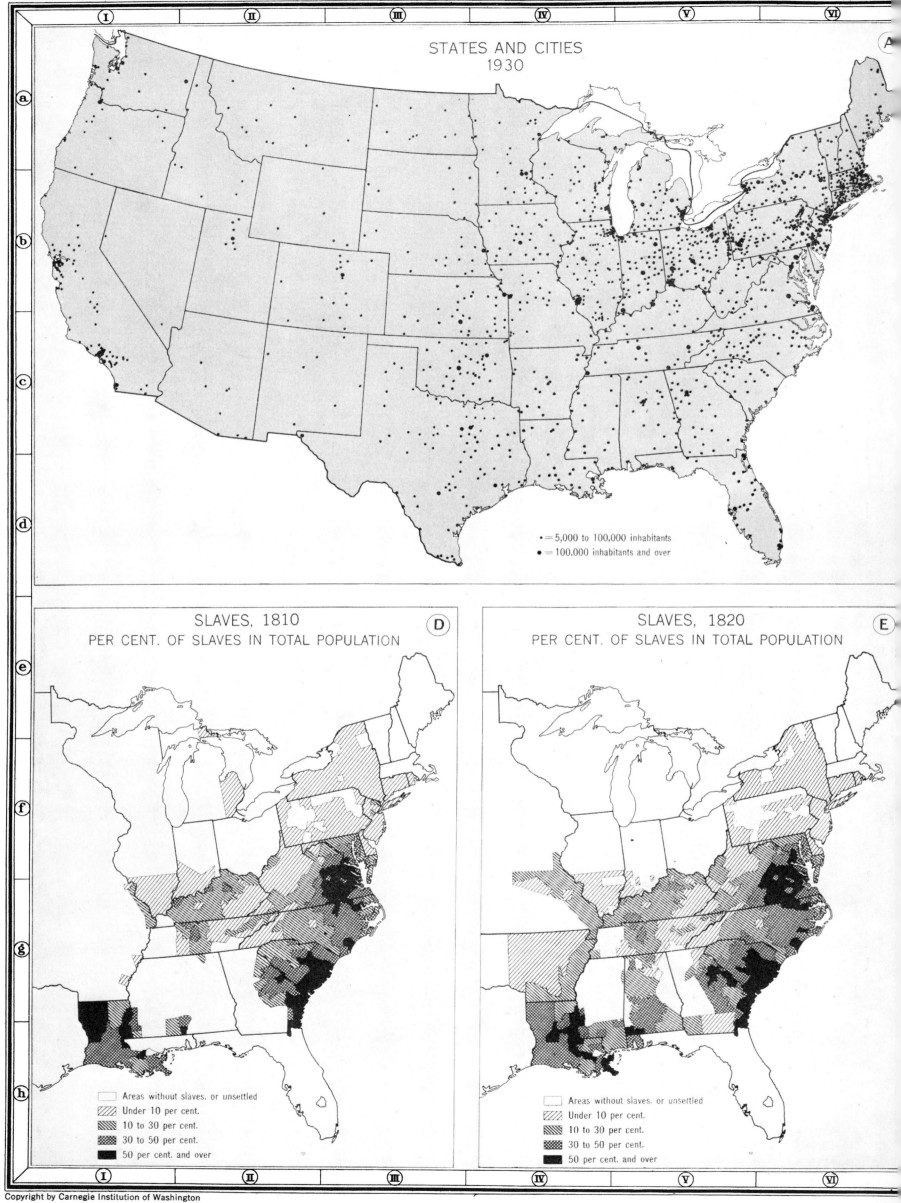

STATES AND CITIES
1930

A

• = 5,000 to 100,000 inhabitants
● = 100,000 inhabitants and over

SLAVES, 1810
PER CENT. OF SLAVES IN TOTAL POPULATION

D

Areas without slaves, or unsettled
Under 10 per cent.
10 to 30 per cent.
30 to 50 per cent.
50 per cent. and over

SLAVES, 1820
PER CENT. OF SLAVES IN TOTAL POPULATION

E

Areas without slaves, or unsettled
Under 10 per cent.
10 to 30 per cent.
30 to 50 per cent.
50 per cent. and over

Copyright by Carnegie Institution of Washington

SLAVES, 1790
PER CENT. OF SLAVES IN TOTAL POPULATION

B

Areas without slaves, or unsettled
Under 10 per cent.
10 to 30 per cent.
30 to 50 per cent.
50 per cent. and over

SLAVES, 1800
PER CENT. OF SLAVES IN TOTAL POPULATION

C

Areas without slaves, or unsettled
Under 10 per cent.
10 to 30 per cent.
30 to 50 per cent.
50 per cent. and over

SLAVES, 1830
PER CENT. OF SLAVES IN TOTAL POPULATION

F

Areas without slaves, or unsettled
Under 10 per cent.
10 to 30 per cent.
30 to 50 per cent.
50 per cent. and over

SLAVES, 1840
PER CENT. OF SLAVES IN TOTAL POPULATION

G

Areas without slaves, or unsettled
Under 10 per cent.
10 to 30 per cent.
30 to 50 per cent.
50 per cent. and over

A. HOEN & CO., INC.,

FOREIGN-BORN POPULATION. 1860
PER CENT. OF FOREIGN-BORN POPULATION
IN TOTAL POPULATION

A

No Returns

No foreign-born population,
  under 1 per cent., or unsettled

1 to 10 per cent.

10 to 20 per cent.

20 to 30 per cent.

30 per cent. and over

FOREIGN-BORN POPULATION. 1880
PER CENT. OF FOREIGN-BORN POPULATION
IN TOTAL POPULATION

B

No Returns

No foreign-born population,
  under 1 per cent., or unsettled

1 to 10 per cent.

10 to 20 per cent.

20 to 30 per cent.

30 per cent. and over

Copyright by Carnegie Institution of Washington

A. HOEN & CO., INC.

FOREIGN-BORN POPULATION, 1900
PER CENT. OF FOREIGN-BORN POPULATION IN TOTAL POPULATION

(A)

No foreign-born population, under 1 per cent., or unsettled

1 to 10 per cent.

10 to 20 per cent.

20 to 30 per cent.

30 per cent. and over

FOREIGN-BORN WHITE POPULATION, 1930
PER CENT. OF FOREIGN-BORN WHITE POPULATION IN TOTAL POPULATION

(B)

No foreign-born white population, under 1 per cent., or unsettled

1 to 10 per cent.

10 to 20 per cent.

20 to 30 per cent.

30 per cent. and over

Copyright by Carnegie Institution of Washington

A. HOEN & CO., INC.,

FOREIGN-BORN POPULATION, GERMAN, 1880
NUMBER OF GERMAN FOREIGN-BORN POPULATION

No Returns

Areas having no German
foreign-born population, or unsettled

1 to 10

10 to 100 } per county

100 to 1000

1000 and over

FOREIGN-BORN POPULATION, GERMAN, 1930
NUMBER OF GERMAN FOREIGN-BORN POPULATION

Areas having no German
foreign-born population, or unsettled

1 to 10

10 to 100 } per county

100 to 1000

1000 and over

Copyright by Carnegie Institution of Washington

(VII) (VIII) (IX) (X) (XI) (XII)

(B)

FOREIGN-BORN POPULATION, GERMAN, 1900
NUMBER OF GERMAN FOREIGN-BORN POPULATION

(a)

(b)

(c)

(d)

Areas having no German
foreign-born population, or unsettled

1 to 10

10 to 100   per county

100 to 1000

1000 and over

(D)

FOREIGN-BORN POPULATION, IRISH, 1880
NUMBER OF IRISH FOREIGN-BORN POPULATION

(e)

(f)

(g)

No Returns

(h)

Areas having no Irish
foreign-born population, or unsettled

1 to 10

10 to 100   per county

100 to 1000

1000 and over

(VII) (VIII) (IX) (X) (XI) (XII)

A. HOEN & CO., INC.

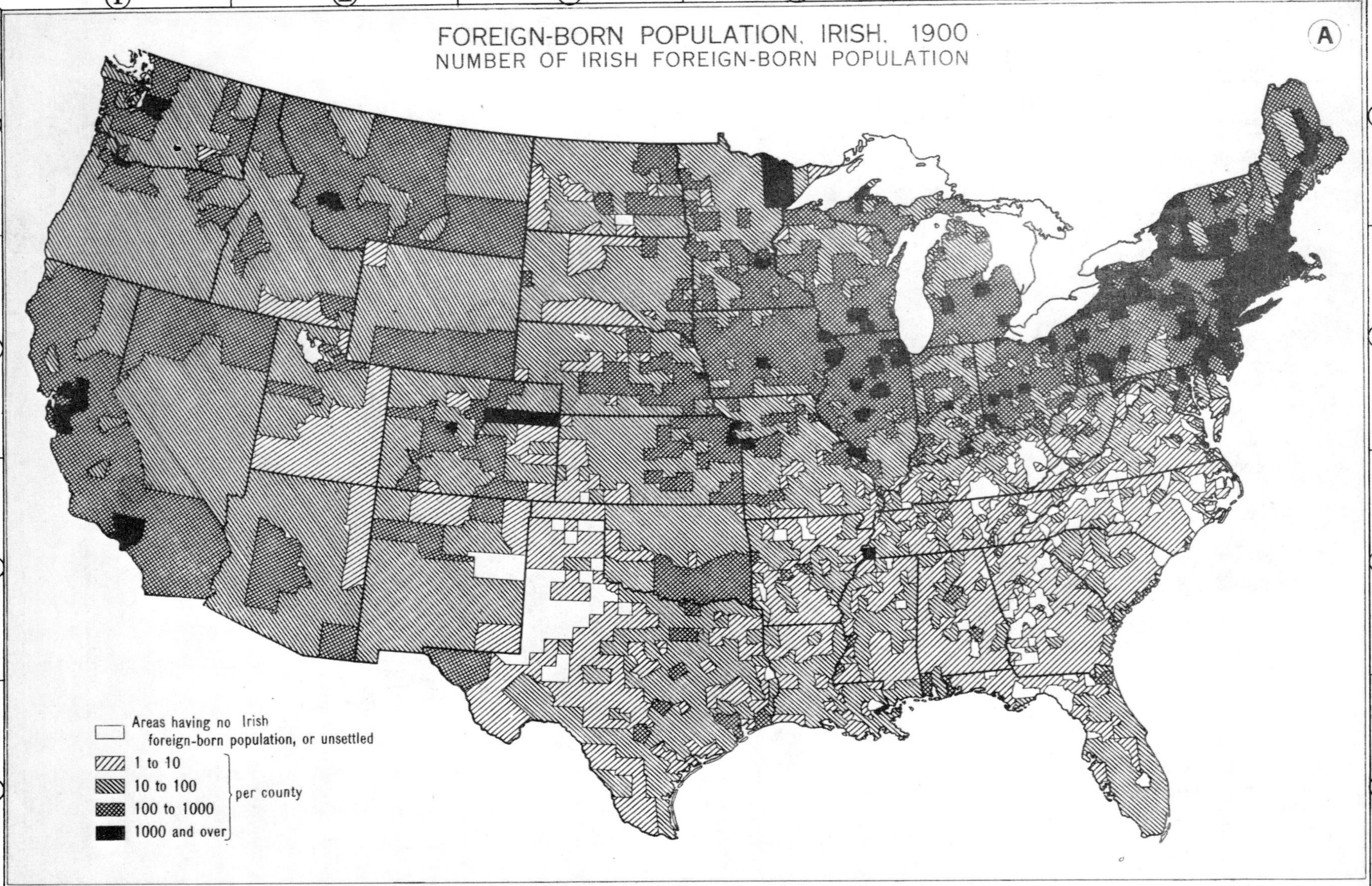

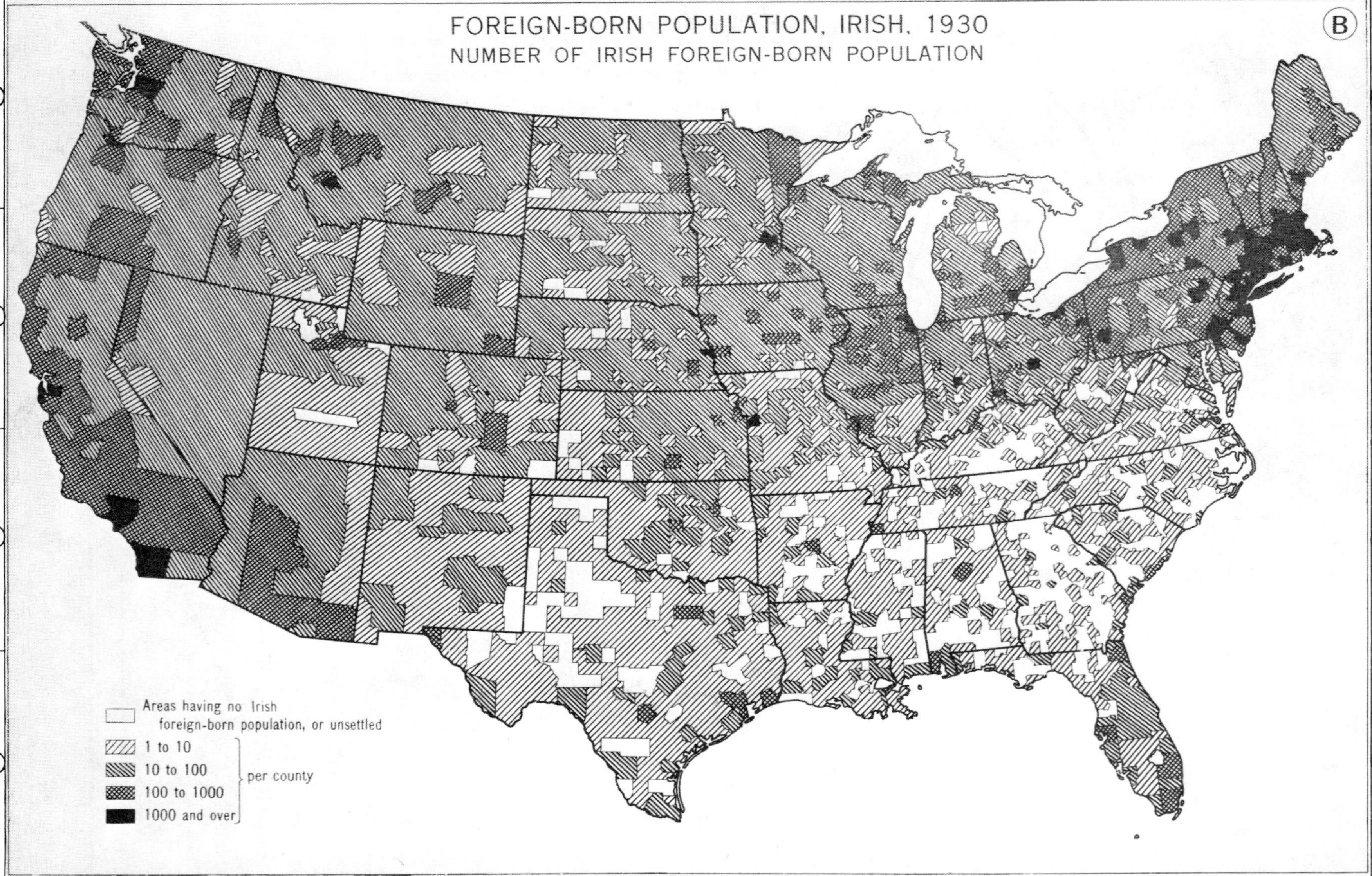

POPULATION

Plate 74

FOREIGN-BORN POPULATION, IRISH, 1900
NUMBER OF IRISH FOREIGN-BORN POPULATION

(A)

Areas having no Irish
foreign-born population, or unsettled
1 to 10
10 to 100   per county
100 to 1000
1000 and over

FOREIGN-BORN POPULATION, IRISH, 1930
NUMBER OF IRISH FOREIGN-BORN POPULATION

(B)

Areas having no Irish
foreign-born population, or unsettled
1 to 10
10 to 100   per county
100 to 1000
1000 and over

Copyright by Carnegie Institution of Washington

A. HOEN & CO., INC.

FOREIGN-BORN POPULATION, SWEDISH AND NORWEGIAN, 1880
NUMBER OF SWEDISH AND NORWEGIAN FOREIGN-BORN POPULATION

Ⓐ

No Returns

Areas having no Swedish and Norwegian foreign-born population, or unsettled
1 to 10
10 to 100
100 to 1000
1000 and over

per county

FOREIGN-BORN POPULATION, SWEDISH AND NORWEGIAN, 1900
NUMBER OF SWEDISH AND NORWEGIAN FOREIGN-BORN POPULATION

Ⓑ

Areas having no Swedish and Norwegian foreign-born population, or unsettled
1 to 10
10 to 100
100 to 1000
1000 and over

per county

Copyright by Carnegie Institution of Washington

A. HOEN & CO., INC.,

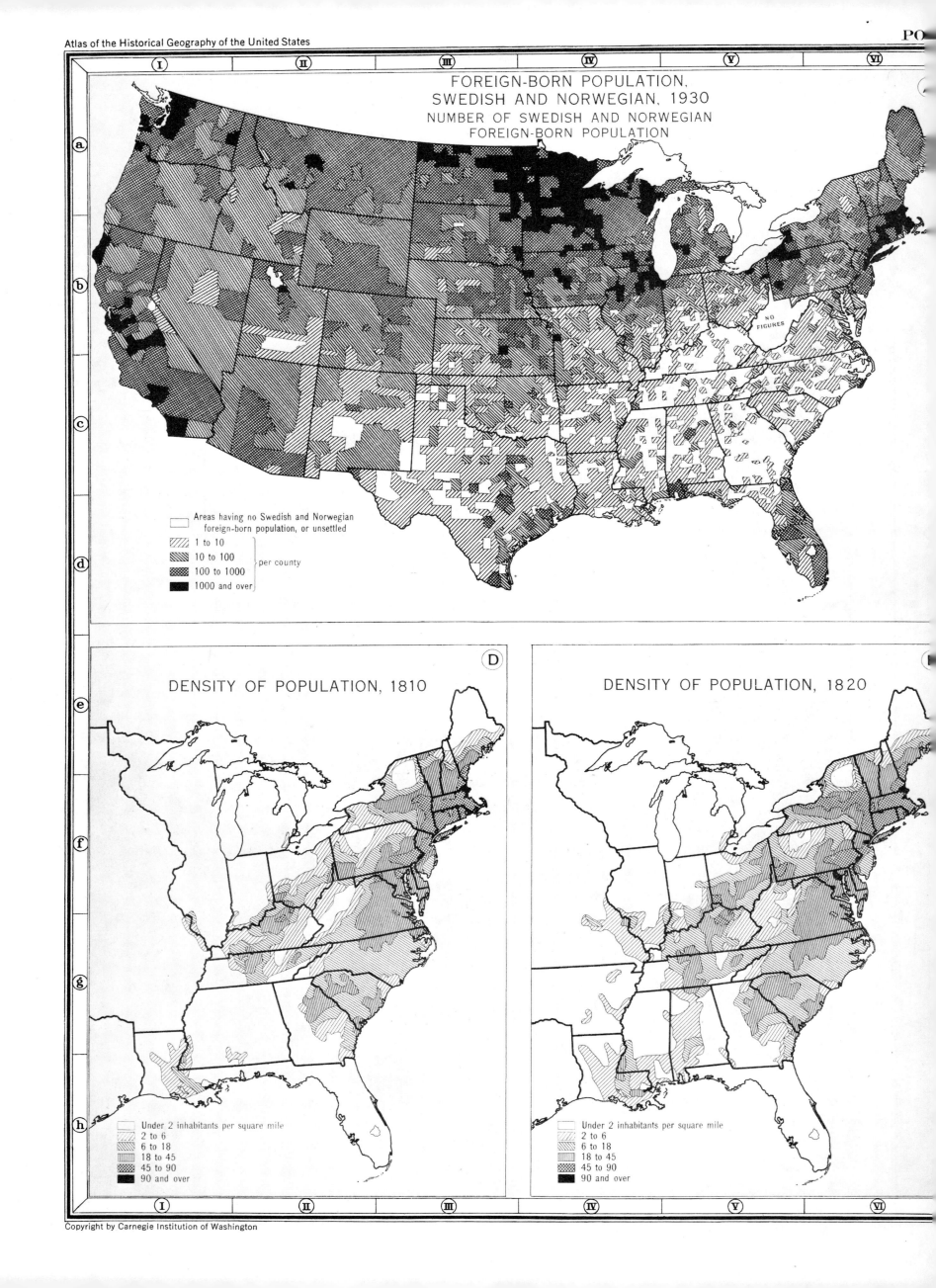

FOREIGN-BORN POPULATION,
SWEDISH AND NORWEGIAN, 1930
NUMBER OF SWEDISH AND NORWEGIAN
FOREIGN-BORN POPULATION

NO
FIGURES

Areas having no Swedish and Norwegian
foreign-born population, or unsettled

1 to 10
10 to 100   per county
100 to 1000
1000 and over

DENSITY OF POPULATION, 1810

DENSITY OF POPULATION, 1820

Under 2 inhabitants per square mile
2 to 6
6 to 18
18 to 45
45 to 90
90 and over

Under 2 inhabitants per square mile
2 to 6
6 to 18
18 to 45
45 to 90
90 and over

Copyright by Carnegie Institution of Washington

Plate 76

DENSITY OF POPULATION, 1790

B

Under 2 inhabitants per square mile
2 to 6
6 to 18
18 to 45
45 to 90
90 and over

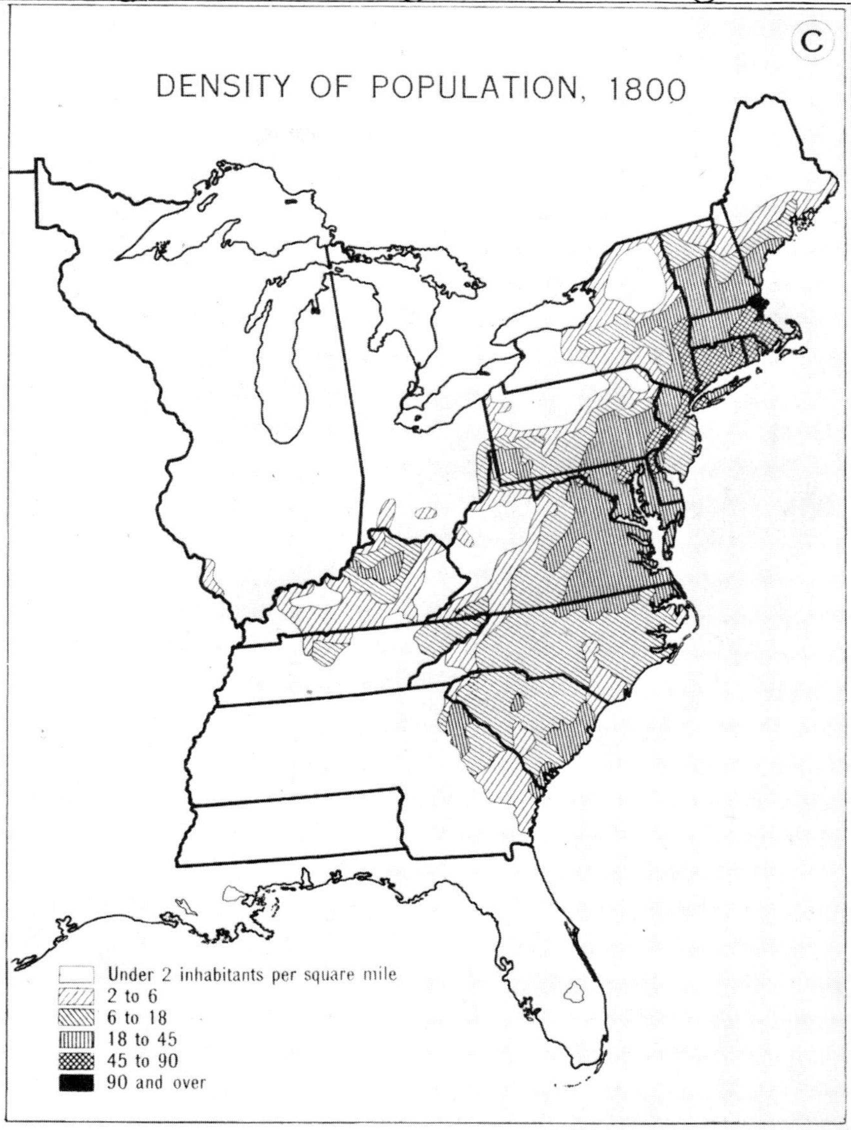

DENSITY OF POPULATION, 1800

C

Under 2 inhabitants per square mile
2 to 6
6 to 18
18 to 45
45 to 90
90 and over

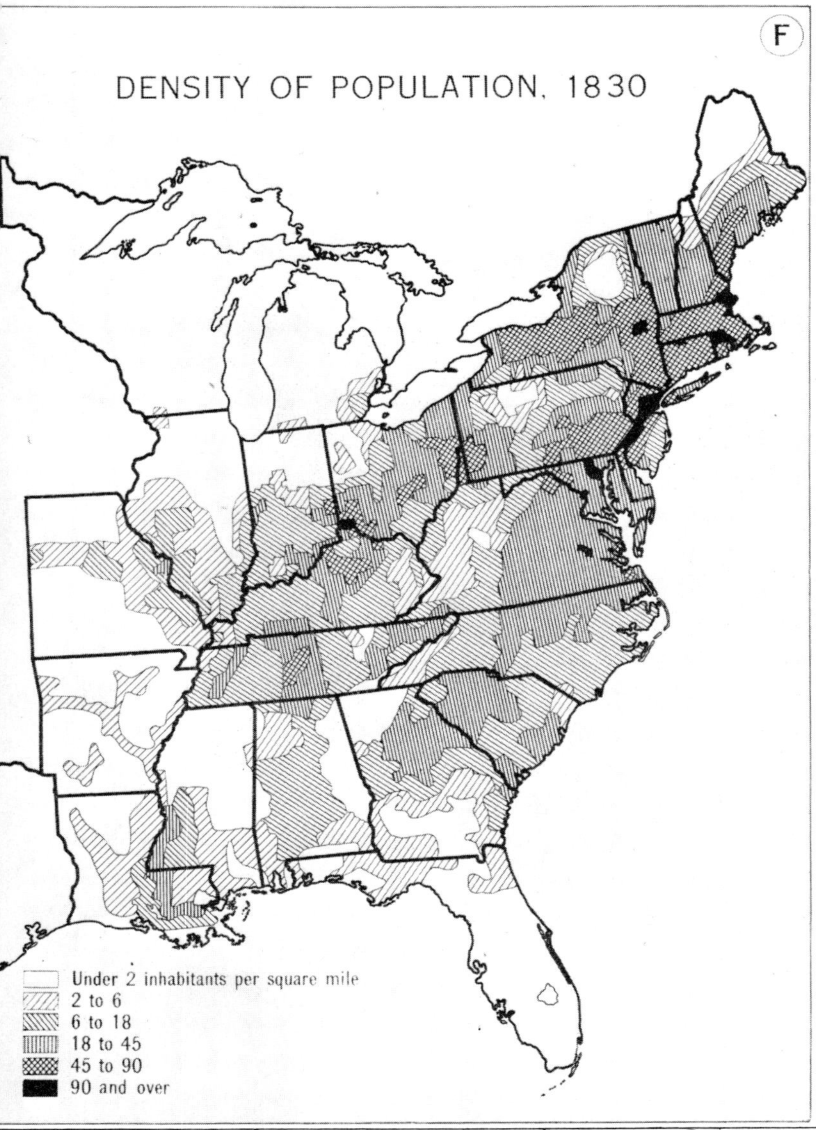

DENSITY OF POPULATION, 1830

F

Under 2 inhabitants per square mile
2 to 6
6 to 18
18 to 45
45 to 90
90 and over

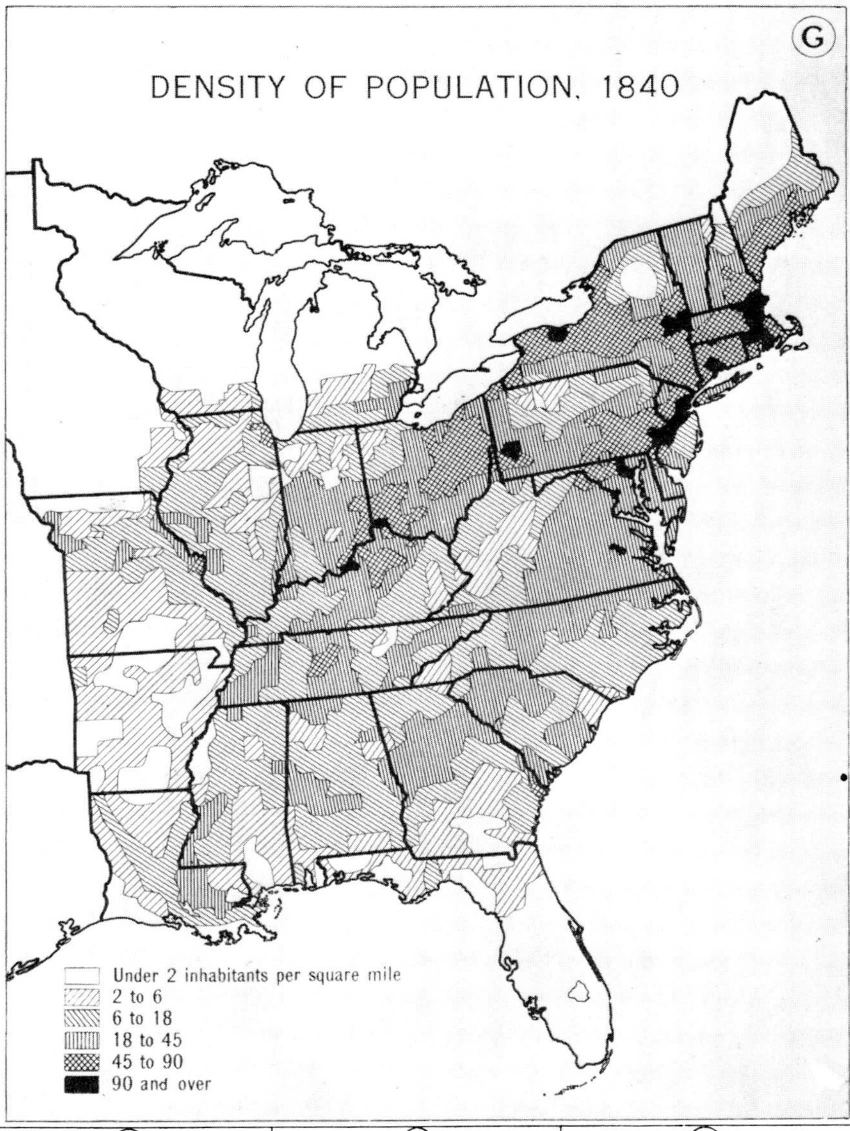

DENSITY OF POPULATION, 1840

G

Under 2 inhabitants per square mile
2 to 6
6 to 18
18 to 45
45 to 90
90 and over

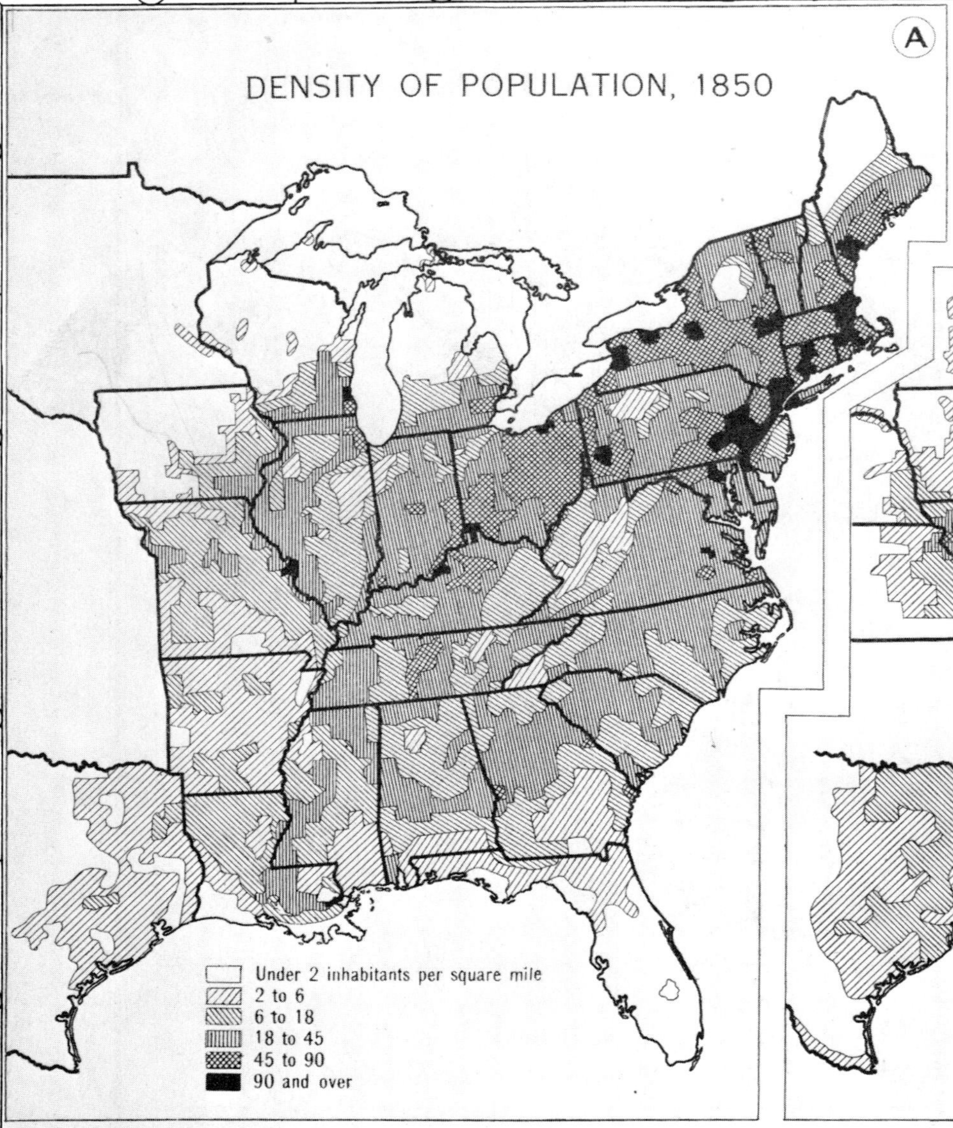

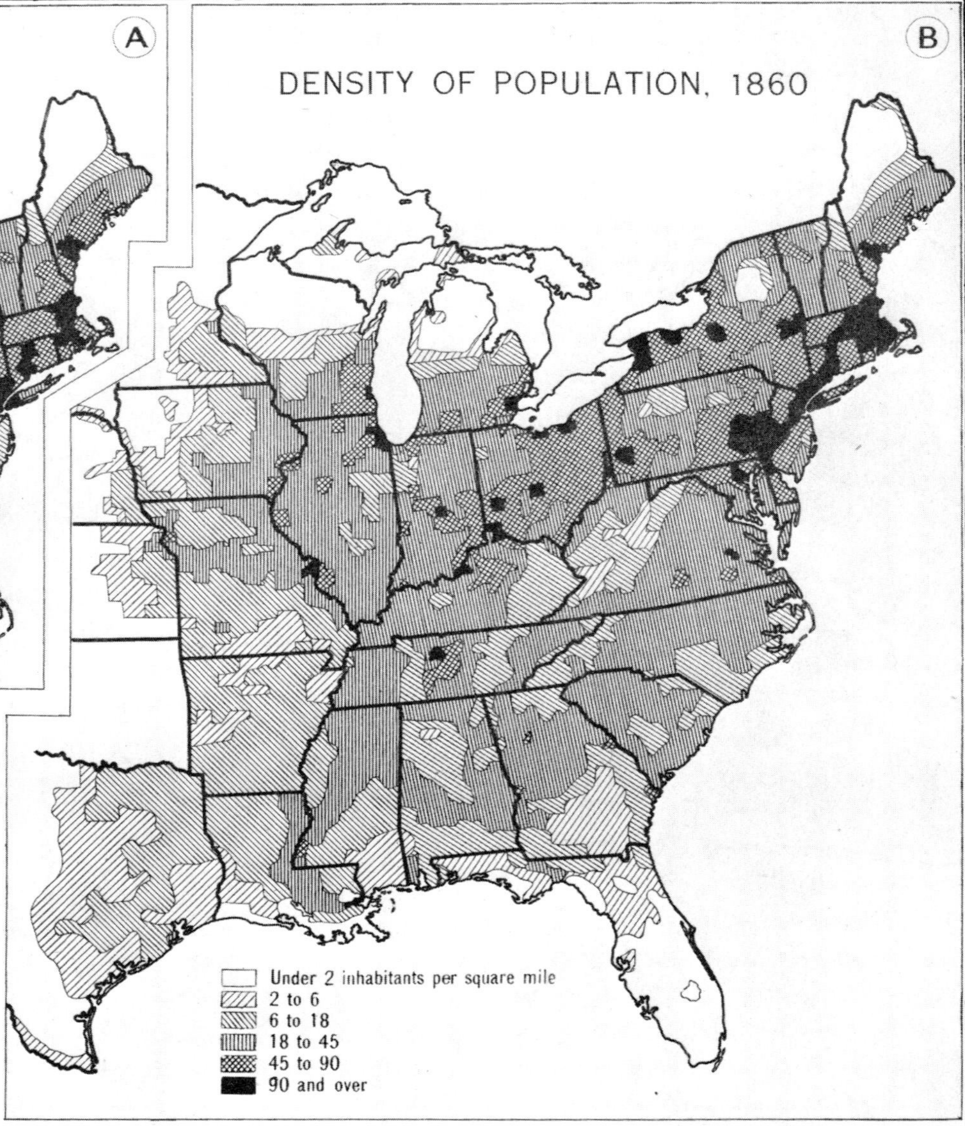

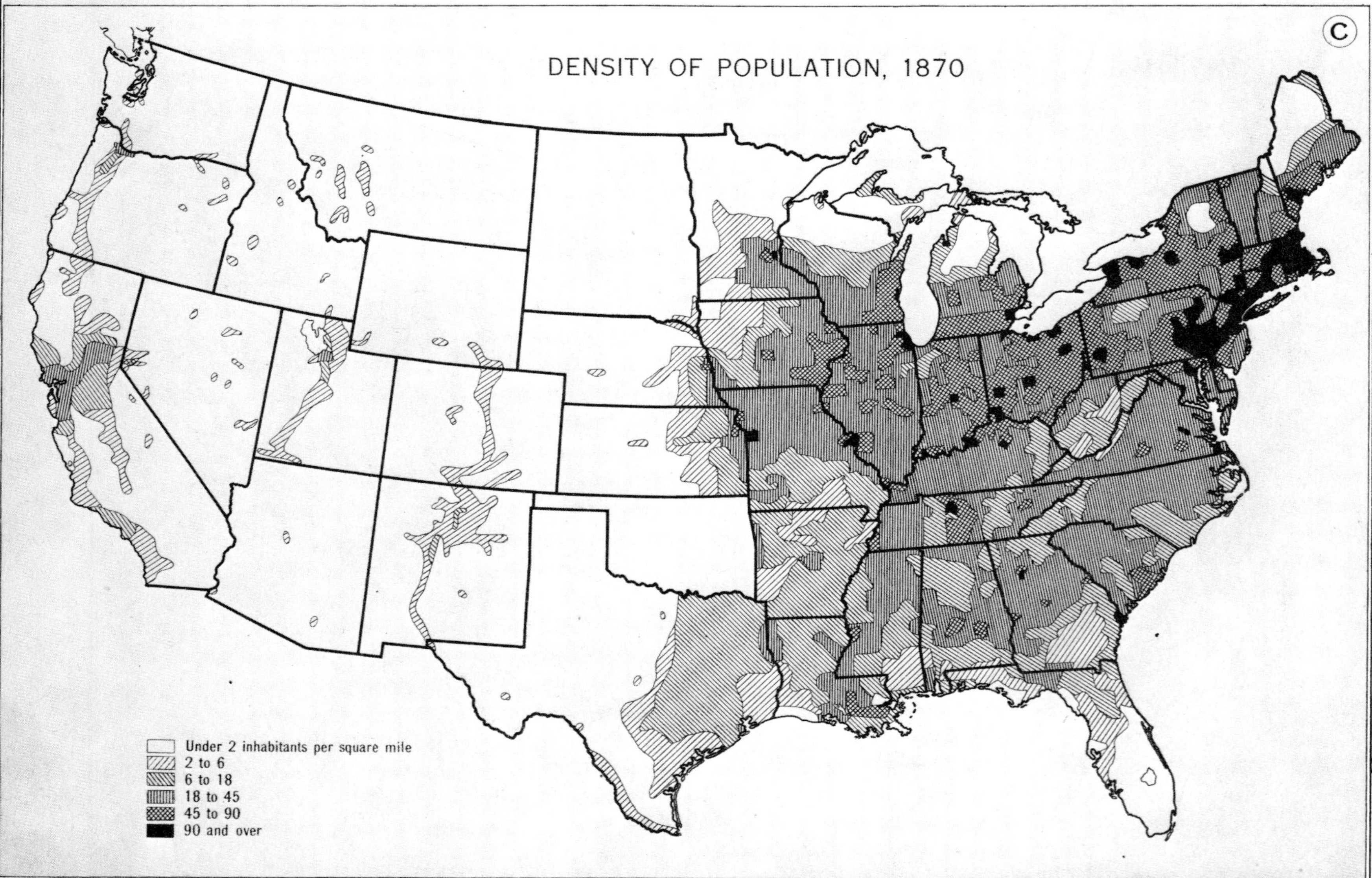

POPULATION

Plate 77

A
DENSITY OF POPULATION, 1850

Under 2 inhabitants per square mile
2 to 6
6 to 18
18 to 45
45 to 90
90 and over

B
DENSITY OF POPULATION, 1860

Under 2 inhabitants per square mile
2 to 6
6 to 18
18 to 45
45 to 90
90 and over

C
DENSITY OF POPULATION, 1870

Under 2 inhabitants per square mile
2 to 6
6 to 18
18 to 45
45 to 90
90 and over

Copyright by Carnegie Institution of Washington

A. HOEN & CO., INC.

DENSITY OF POPULATION, 1880

Under 2 inhabitants per square mile
2 to 6
6 to 18
18 to 45
45 to 90
90 and over

DENSITY OF POPULATION, 1890

Under 2 inhabitants per square mile
2 to 6
6 to 18
18 to 45
45 to 90
90 and over

Copyright by Carnegie Institution of Washington

A. HOEN & CO., INC.,

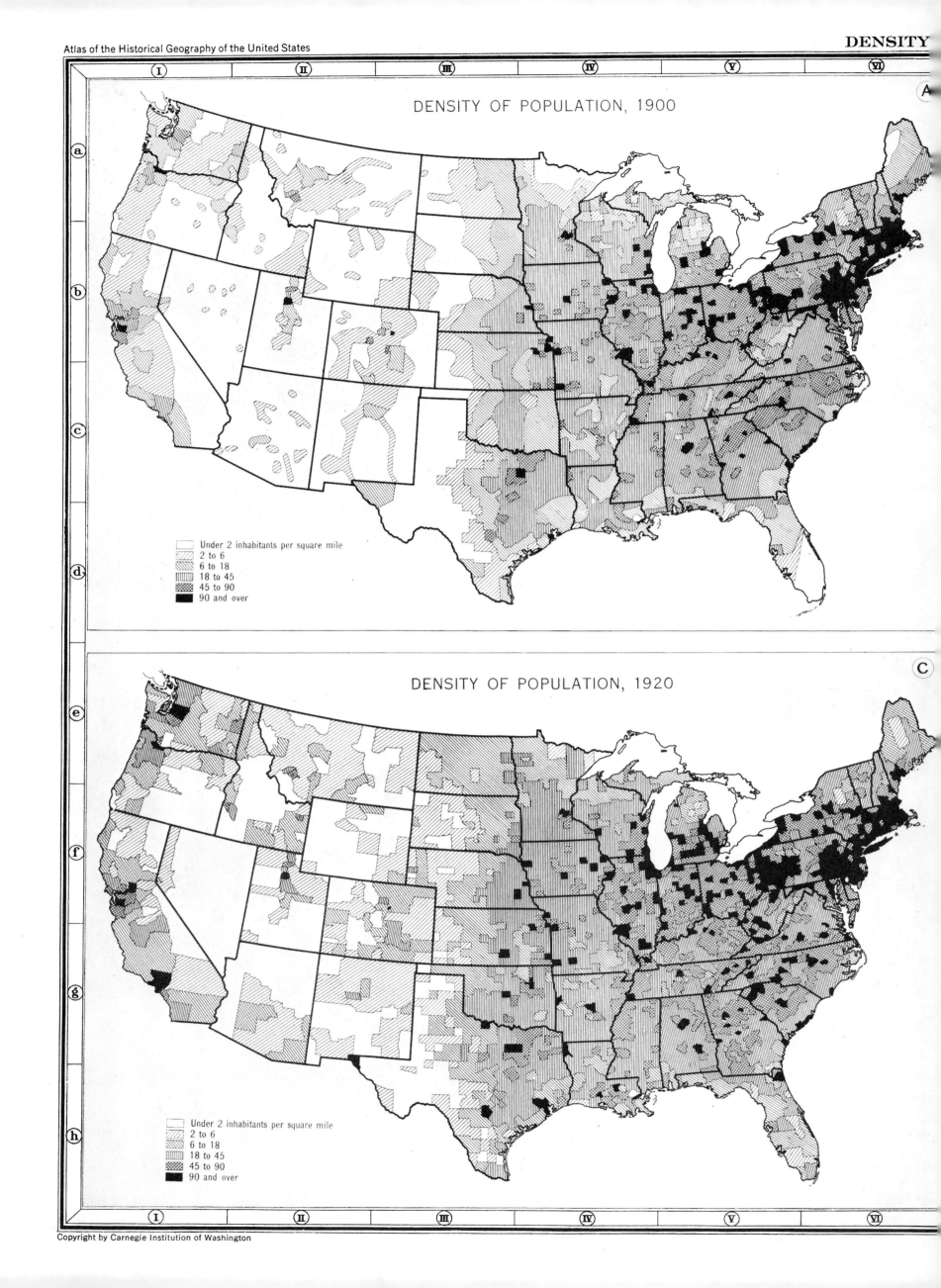

DENSITY OF POPULATION, 1900

Under 2 inhabitants per square mile
2 to 6
6 to 18
18 to 45
45 to 90
90 and over

DENSITY OF POPULATION, 1920

Under 2 inhabitants per square mile
2 to 6
6 to 18
18 to 45
45 to 90
90 and over

Copyright by Carnegie Institution of Washington

DENSITY OF POPULATION, 1910

Under 2 inhabitants per square mile
2 to 6
6 to 18
18 to 45
45 to 90
90 and over

DENSITY OF POPULATION, 1930

Under 2 inhabitants per square mile
2 to 6
6 to 18
18 to 45
45 to 90
90 and over

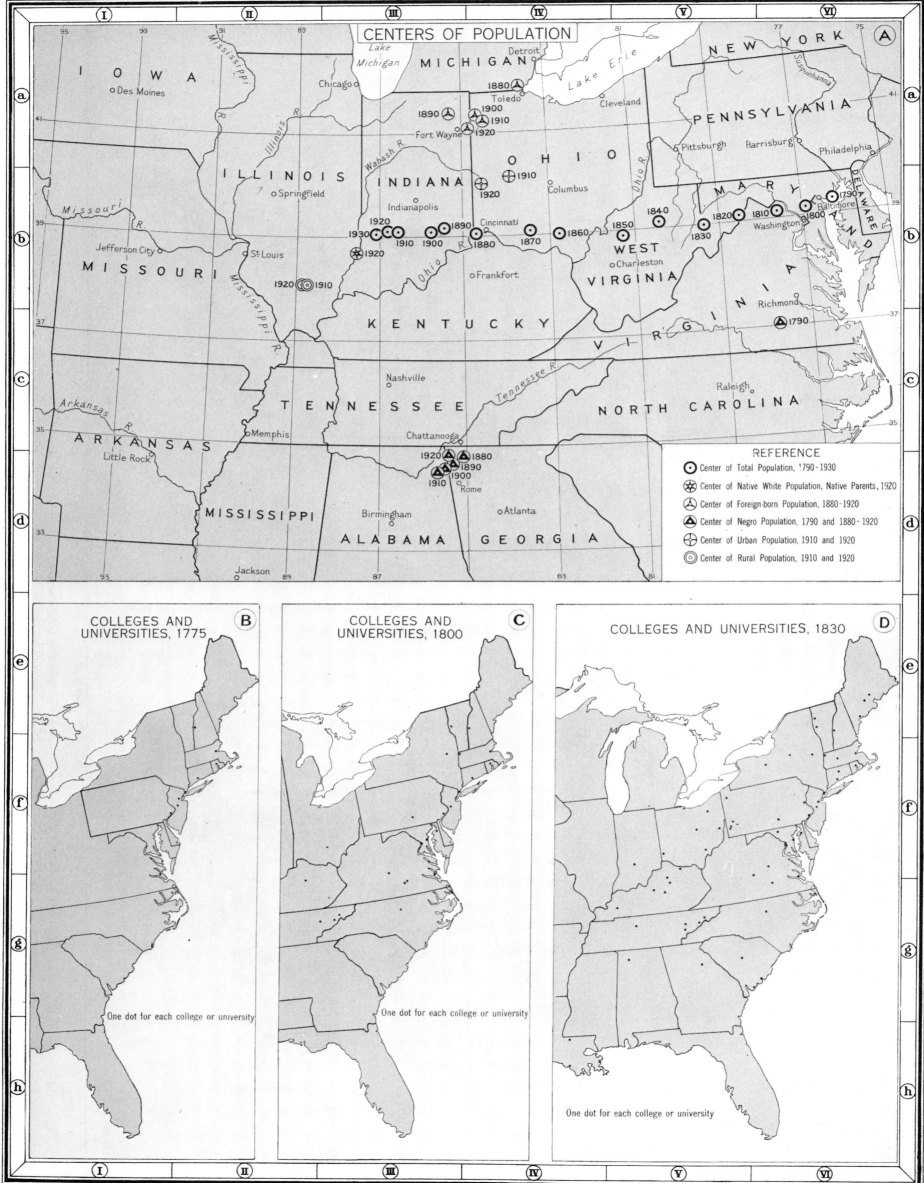

CENTERS OF POPULATION

REFERENCE

⊙ Center of Total Population, 1790-1930

✺ Center of Native White Population, Native Parents, 1920

⟡ Center of Foreign-born Population, 1880-1920

△ Center of Negro Population, 1790 and 1880-1920

⊕ Center of Urban Population, 1910 and 1920

◎ Center of Rural Population, 1910 and 1920

COLLEGES AND UNIVERSITIES, 1775

COLLEGES AND UNIVERSITIES, 1800

COLLEGES AND UNIVERSITIES, 1830

One dot for each college or university

One dot for each college or university

One dot for each college or university

COLLEGES AND UNIVERSITIES, 1860

One dot for each college or university

COLLEGES AND UNIVERSITIES, 1890

One dot for each college or university

Copyright by Carnegie Institution of Washington

A. HOEN & CO., INC.,

CI

I   II   III   IV   V   VI

a

CONGREGATIONALIST
1775-1776

A

One dot for each church (see text)

PRESBYTERIAN
1775-1776

B

N. Y. City ....

One dot for each church (see text)

PROTESTANT-EPISCOPAL
1775-1776

C

N. Y. City ....

One dot for each church (see text)

b

c

d

LUTHERAN, 1775-1776

G

N. Y. City ..

One dot for each church (see text)

DUTCH REFORMED
1775-1776

H

N. Y. City ....

One dot for each church (see text)

METHODIST, 1775-1776

J

N. Y. City .

One dot for each church (see text)

e

f

g

h

I   II   III   IV   V   VI

Copyright by Carnegie Institution of Washington

Plate 82

BAPTIST. 1775-1776   D

One dot for each church (see text)

FRIENDS. 1775-1776   E

N. Y. City

One dot for each church (see text)

GERMAN REFORMED 1775-1776   F

N. Y. City

One dot for each church (see text)

CATHOLIC, 1775-1776   K

One dot for each church (see text)

MINOR DENOMINATIONS 1775-1776   L

N. Y. City × △

One symbol for each church (see text)
× – Moravian
○ – Dunker
• – Mennonite
△ – French Protestant

MINOR DENOMINATIONS 1775-1776   M

N. Y. City △

One symbol for each church (see text)
× – Separatist and Independent
○ – Sandemanian
• – Rogerene
△ – Jewish

A. HOEN & CO., INC.,

CHURCHES

Plate 85

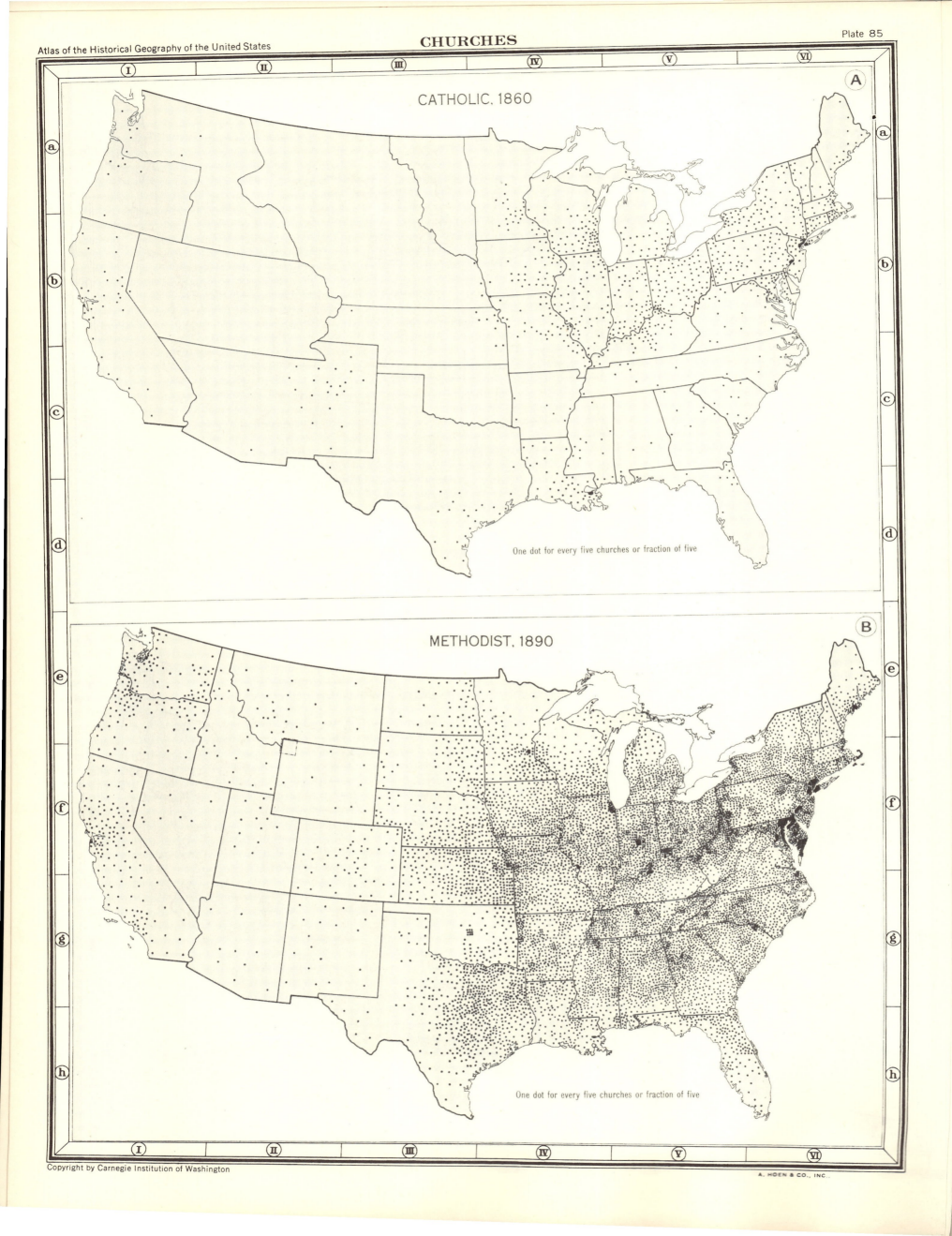

CATHOLIC, 1860

One dot for every five churches or fraction of five

METHODIST, 1890

One dot for every five churches or fraction of five

Copyright by Carnegie Institution of Washington

A. HOEN & CO., INC.

CHURCHES

Plate 86

BAPTIST, 1890

A

One dot for every five churches or fraction of five

PRESBYTERIAN, 1890

B

One dot for every five churches or fraction of five

Copyright by Carnegie Institution of Washington

A. HOEN & CO., INC.,

C

CATHOLIC, 1890

One dot for every five churches or fraction of five

PROTESTANT-EPISCOPAL, 1890

One dot for every five churches or fraction of five

Copyright by Carnegie Institution of Washington

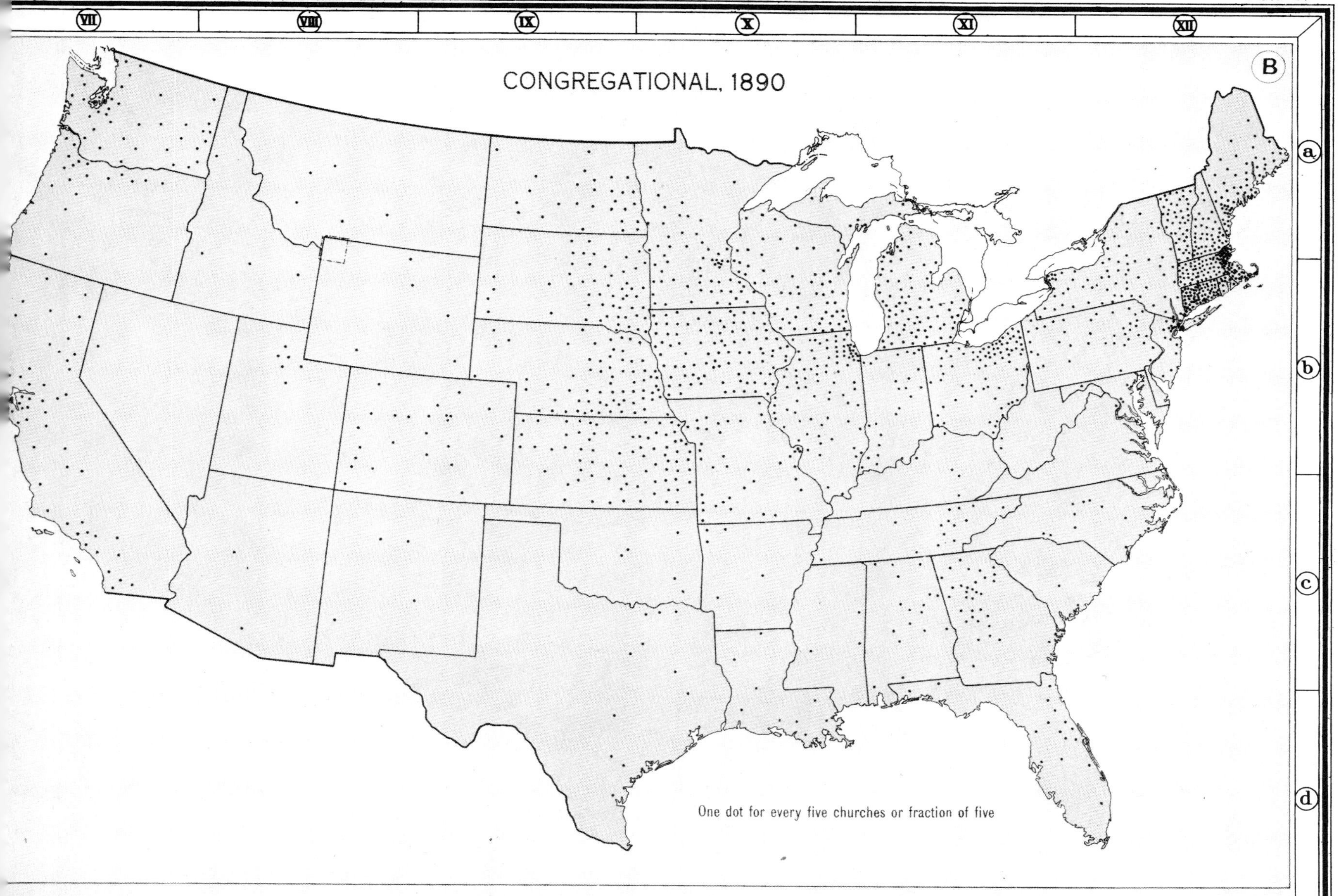

Plate 87

CONGREGATIONAL, 1890

One dot for every five churches or fraction of five

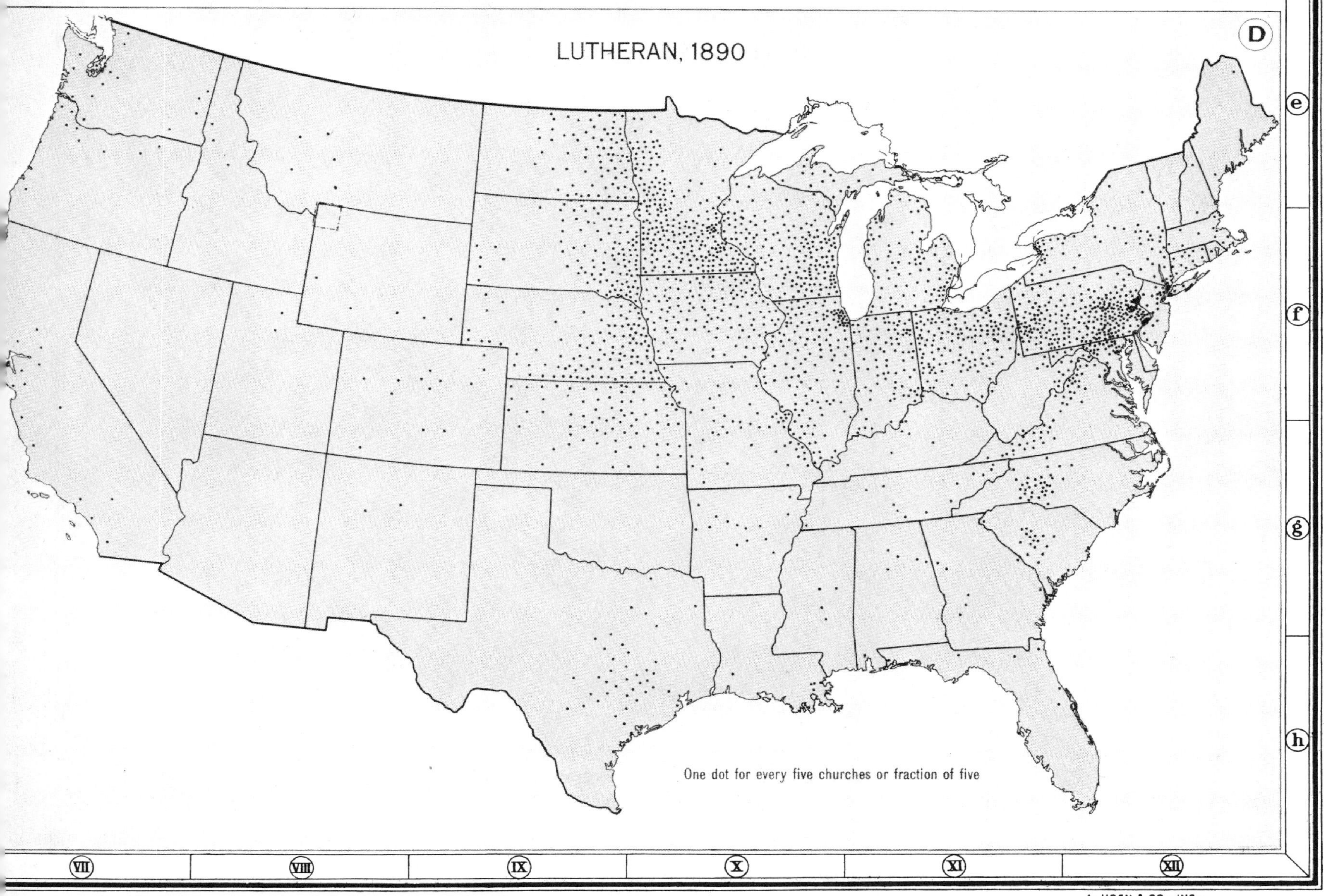

LUTHERAN, 1890

One dot for every five churches or fraction of five

A. HOEN & CO., INC.,

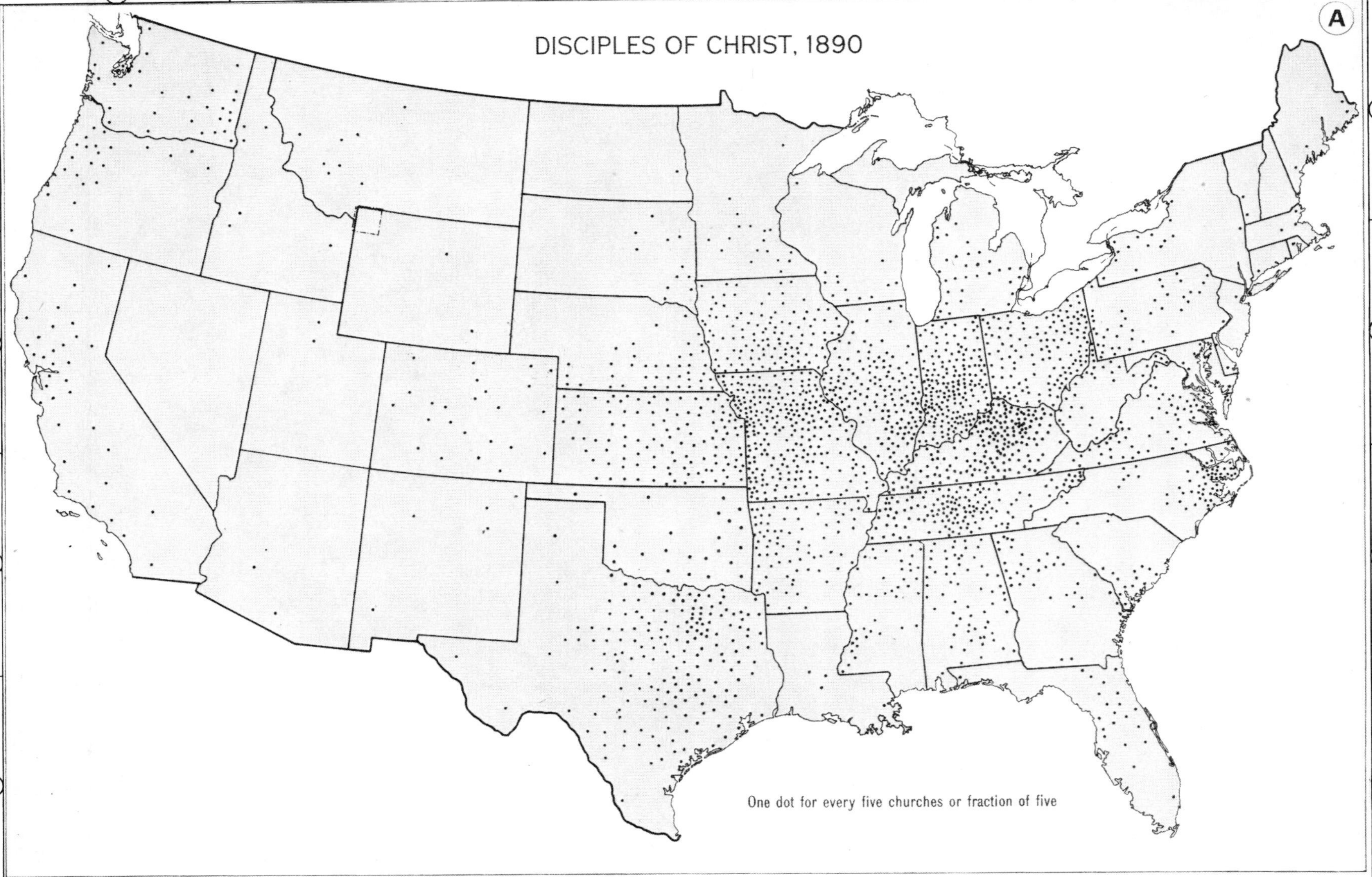

CHURCHES

Plate 88

A

DISCIPLES OF CHRIST, 1890

One dot for every five churches or fraction of five

B

REFORMED, 1890

One dot for every five churches or fraction of five

Copyright by Carnegie Institution of Washington

A. HOEN & CO., INC.,

NEGOTIATIONS I
(Base, Mitchell's Map of North America, 175

NEW FR

LABRADOR
OR
NEW BRITAIN

HUDSONS BAY

EASTERN SIOUX

SIOUX OR NADOUESSIANS

WESTERN SIOUX

SUPERIOR

LAKE HURON

LAKE MICHIGAN

OUTAGAMIS

MASCOUTENS

PANIS

OSAGES

Extensive Meadows

field of Buffaloes

Bounds of Virginia and New England by Charters, May 23, 1609 and Nov.ʳ 3, 1620 extending from Sea to Sea, out of which our other colonies were granted

VIRGINIA

NORTH CAROL

CHER

ARKANSAS

CHICASAWS

SOUTH CAROLIN

LOUISIANA

CREEK INDIAN

CHACTAWS

GEORGIA

COUNTRY THE

Toulouse or Alabama

River Mississippi

CENIS

Copyright by Carnegie Institution of Washington

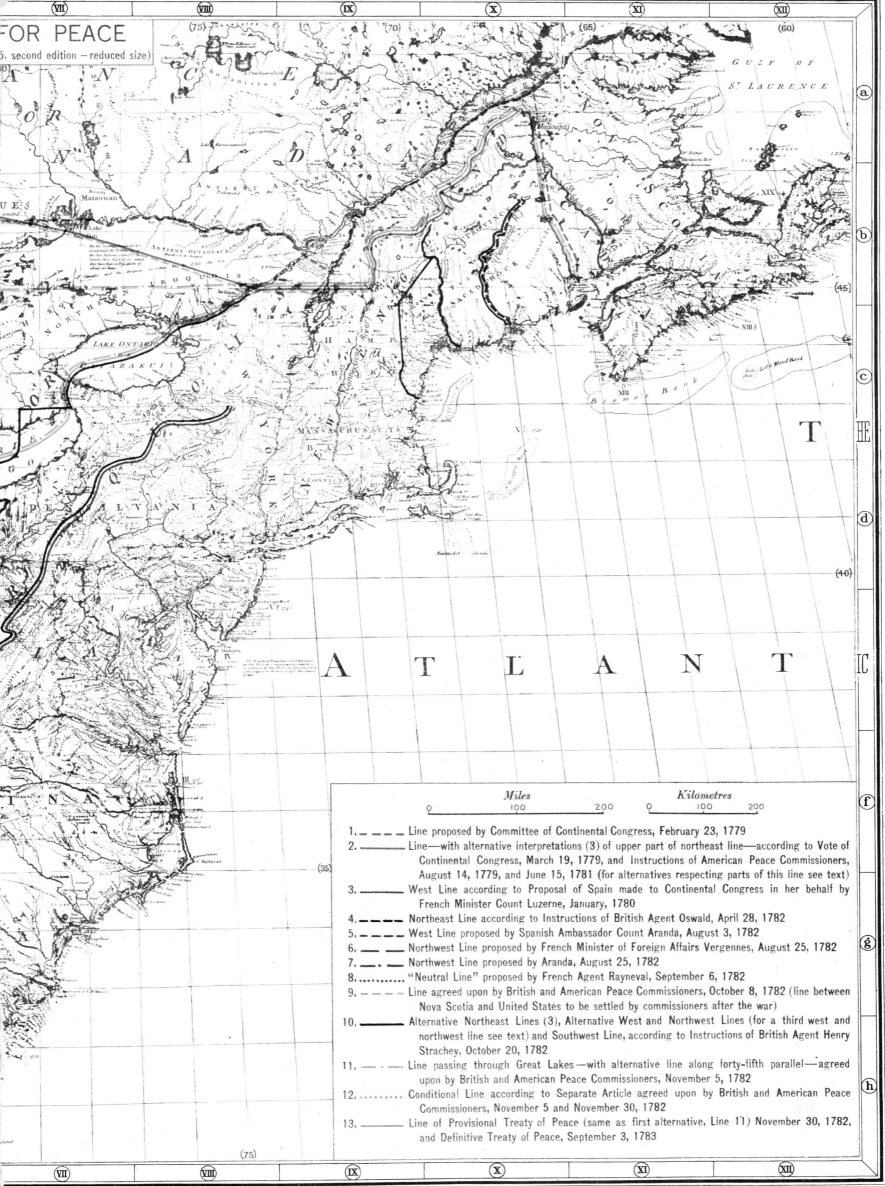

FOR PEACE
5, second edition – reduced size)

Miles   Kilometres

1. ─ ─ ─ ─ Line proposed by Committee of Continental Congress, February 23, 1779
2. ─────── Line—with alternative interpretations (3) of upper part of northeast line—according to Vote of Continental Congress, March 19, 1779, and Instructions of American Peace Commissioners, August 14, 1779, and June 15, 1781 (for alternatives respecting parts of this line see text)
3. ─────── West Line according to Proposal of Spain made to Continental Congress in her behalf by French Minister Count Luzerne, January, 1780
4. ─ ─ ─ ─ Northeast Line according to Instructions of British Agent Oswald, April 28, 1782
5. ─ ─ ─ ─ West Line proposed by Spanish Ambassador Count Aranda, August 3, 1782
6. ── ── ── Northwest Line proposed by French Minister of Foreign Affairs Vergennes, August 25, 1782
7. ─ ∙ ─ ∙ Northwest Line proposed by Aranda, August 25, 1782
8. ∙∙∙∙∙∙∙∙∙∙ "Neutral Line" proposed by French Agent Rayneval, September 6, 1782
9. ─ ─ ─ ─ Line agreed upon by British and American Peace Commissioners, October 8, 1782 (line between Nova Scotia and United States to be settled by commissioners after the war)
10. ─────── Alternative Northeast Lines (3), Alternative West and Northwest Lines (for a third west and northwest line see text) and Southwest Line, according to Instructions of British Agent Henry Strachey, October 20, 1782
11. ── ∙ ── Line passing through Great Lakes—with alternative line along forty-fifth parallel—agreed upon by British and American Peace Commissioners, November 5, 1782
12. ∙∙∙∙∙∙∙∙∙ Conditional Line according to Separate Article agreed upon by British and American Peace Commissioners, November 5 and November 30, 1782
13. ─────── Line of Provisional Treaty of Peace (same as first alternative, Line 11) November 30, 1782, and Definitive Treaty of Peace, September 3, 1783

A. HOEN & CO., INC.

NEGOTIATIONS FOR PEACE (NORTHEAST SECTION)

(Base, Mitchell's Map of North America, 1755, second edition — reduced size.)

Kilometres

Miles

1. — · — · — Line proposed by Committee of Continental Congress, February 23, 1779
2. ——————— Line — with alternative interpretations (3) of upper part of northeast line — according to Vote of Continental Congress, March 19, 1779, and Instructions of American Peace Commissioners, August 14, 1779, and June 15, 1781 (for alternative respecting a part of this line see text)
4. — — — — Northeast Line according to Instructions of British Peace Commissioner Oswald, April 28, 1782
9. ·············· Line agreed upon by British and American Peace Commissioners, October 8, 1782 (line between Nova Scotia and United States to be settled by commissioners after the war)
10. ——————— Alternative Northeast Lines (3), according to Instructions of British Agent Henry Strachey, October 20, 1782
11. —·—·—·— Line agreed upon by British and American Peace Commissioners, November 5, 1782
13. ——————— Line of Provisional Treaty of Peace, November 30, 1782, and Definitive Treaty of Peace, September 3, 1783

Copyright by Carnegie Institution of Washington

A. HOEN & CO., INC.

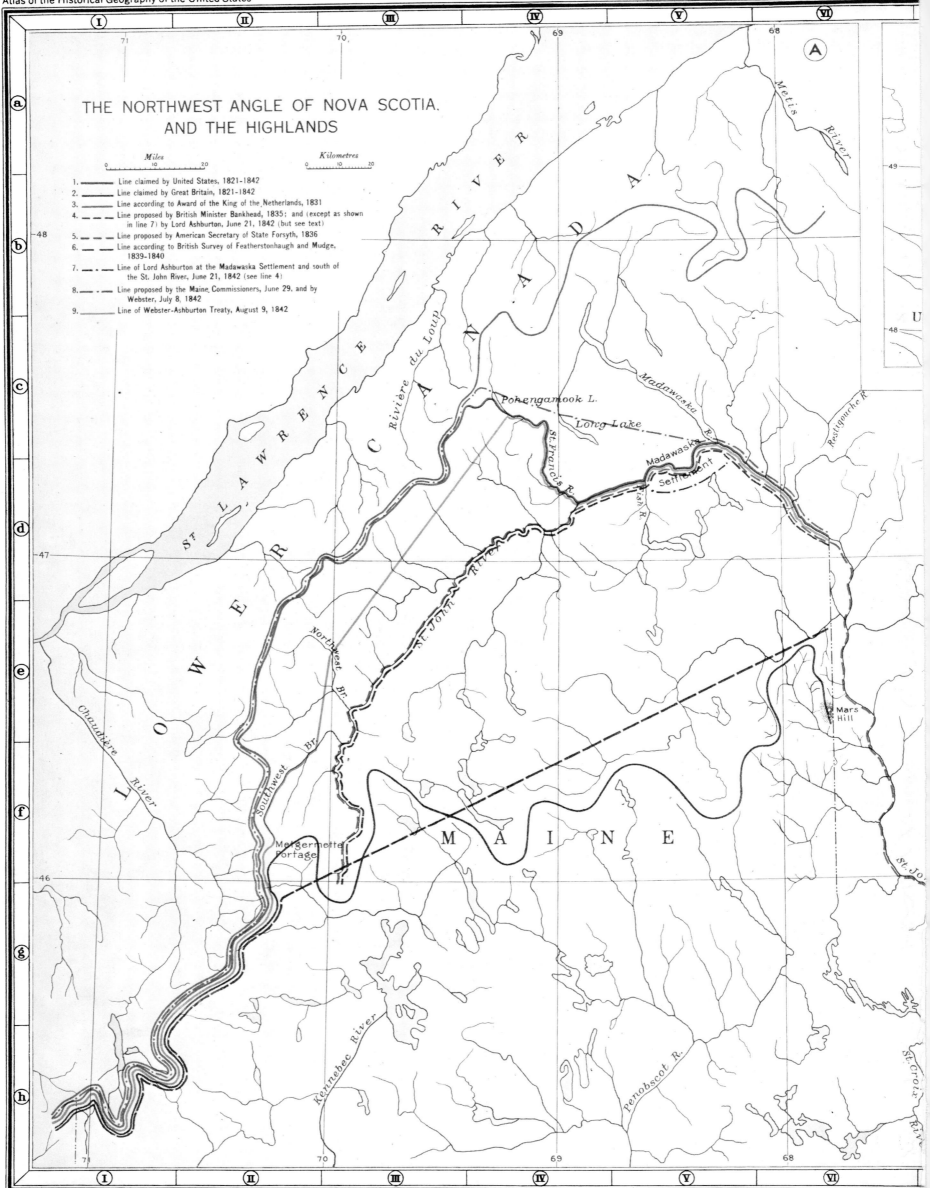

THE NORTHWEST ANGLE OF NOVA SCOTIA,
AND THE HIGHLANDS

Miles   Kilometres

1. —— Line claimed by United States, 1821-1842
2. —— Line claimed by Great Britain, 1821-1842
3. —— Line according to Award of the King of the Netherlands, 1831
4. --- Line proposed by British Minister Bankhead, 1835; and (except as shown in line 7) by Lord Ashburton, June 21, 1842 (but see text)
5. --- Line proposed by American Secretary of State Forsyth, 1836
6. —— Line according to British Survey of Featherstonhaugh and Mudge, 1839-1840
7. -·-· Line of Lord Ashburton at the Madawaska Settlement and south of the St. John River, June 21, 1842 (see line 4)
8. —·—· Line proposed by the Maine Commissioners, June 29, and by Webster, July 8, 1842
9. —— Line of Webster-Ashburton Treaty, August 9, 1842

Copyright by Carnegie Institution of Washington

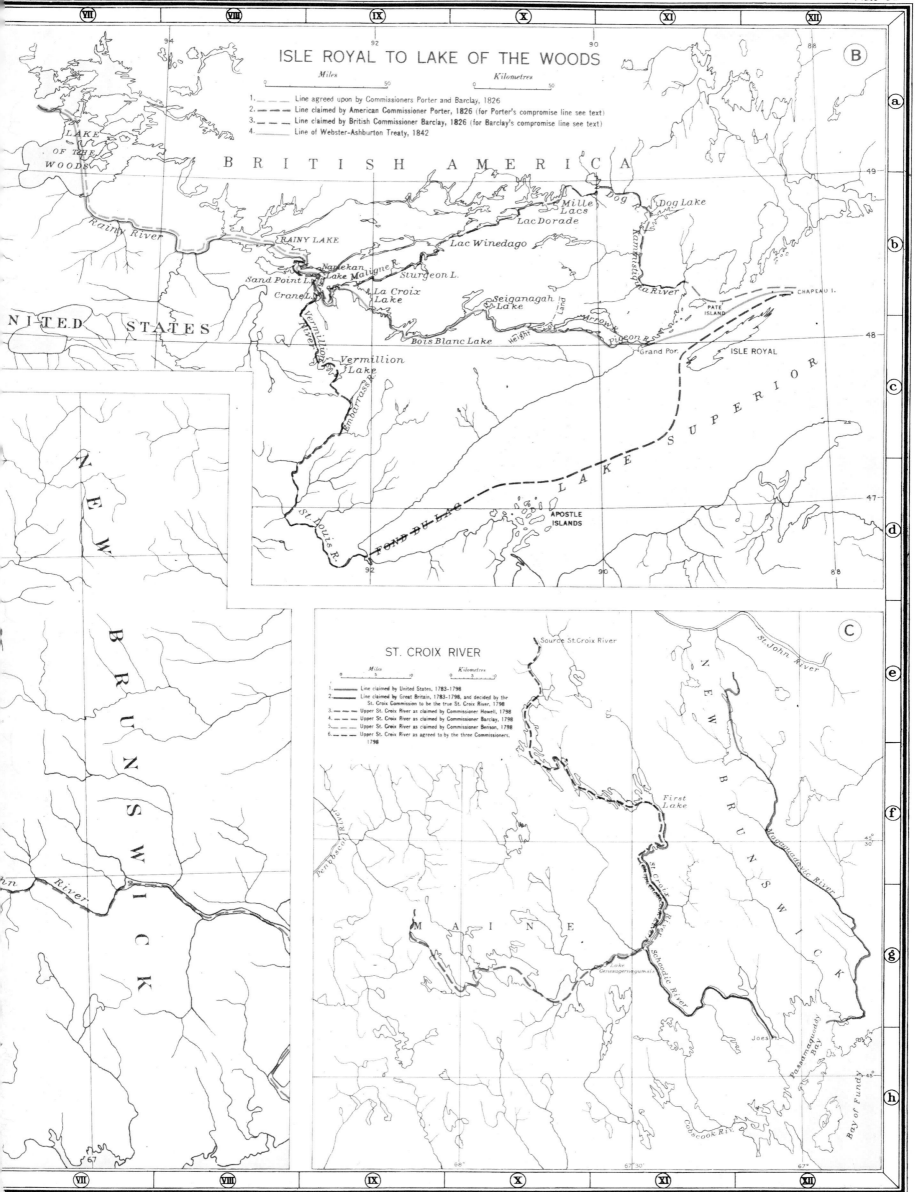

ISLE ROYAL TO LAKE OF THE WOODS

Miles   Kilometres
0   50   0   50

1. ——— Line agreed upon by Commissioners Porter and Barclay, 1826
2. — — — Line claimed by American Commissioner Porter, 1826 (for Porter's compromise line see text)
3. — — — Line claimed by British Commissioner Barclay, 1826 (for Barclay's compromise line see text)
4. ——— Line of Webster-Ashburton Treaty, 1842

ST. CROIX RIVER

Miles   Kilometres
0   5   10   0   5   10

1. ——— Line claimed by United States, 1783-1798
2. ——— Line claimed by Great Britain, 1783-1798, and decided by the St. Croix Commission to be the true St. Croix River, 1798
3. — — — Upper St. Croix River as claimed by Commissioner Howell, 1798
4. — — — Upper St. Croix River as claimed by Commissioner Barclay, 1798
5. — — — Upper St. Croix River as claimed by Commissioner Benson, 1798
6. — — — Upper St. Croix River as agreed to by the three Commissioners, 1798

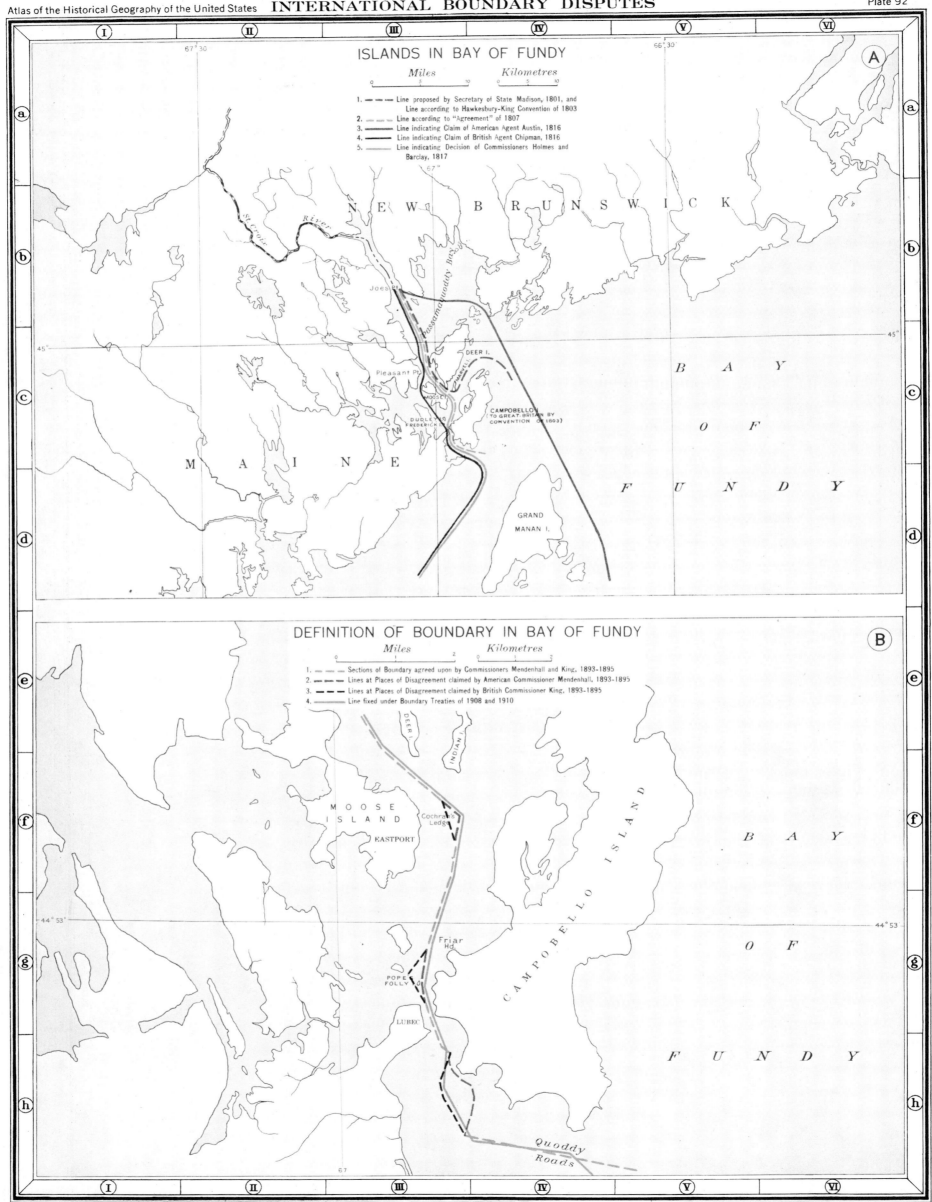

ISLANDS IN BAY OF FUNDY

Miles   Kilometres

1. — · — · — Line proposed by Secretary of State Madison, 1801, and
Line according to Hawkesbury-King Convention of 1803
2. — — — — Line according to "Agreement" of 1807
3. ———— Line indicating Claim of American Agent Austin, 1816
4. ———— Line indicating Claim of British Agent Chipman, 1816
5. ———— Line indicating Decision of Commissioners Holmes and
Barclay, 1817

NEW BRUNSWICK

MAINE

BAY OF FUNDY

CAMPOBELLO I.
(TO GREAT BRITAIN BY
CONVENTION OF 1803)

DEER I.

GRAND MANAN I.

DEFINITION OF BOUNDARY IN BAY OF FUNDY

Miles   Kilometres

1. — — — Sections of Boundary agreed upon by Commissioners Mendenhall and King, 1893-1895
2. — — — Lines at Places of Disagreement claimed by American Commissioner Mendenhall, 1893-1895
3. — — — Lines at Places of Disagreement claimed by British Commissioner King, 1893-1895
4. ———— Line fixed under Boundary Treaties of 1908 and 1910

MOOSE ISLAND

EASTPORT

DEER I.

INDIAN I.

Cochrane's Ledge

CAMPOBELLO ISLAND

BAY OF FUNDY

Friar Hd.

POPE FOLLY I.

LUBEC

Quoddy Roads

Copyright by Carnegie Institution of Washington

A. HOEN & CO., INC

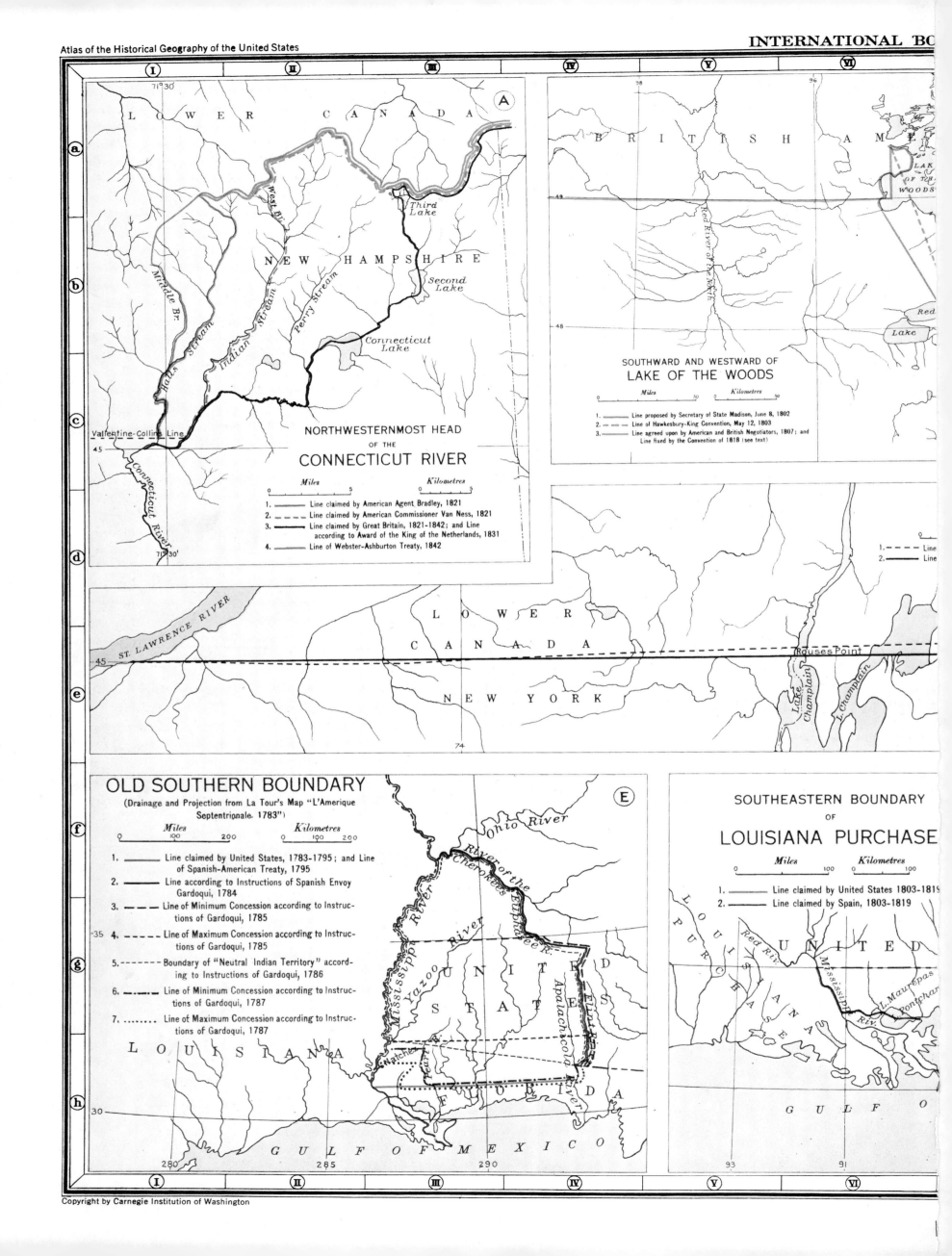

Ⓐ

L O W E R   C A N A D A

71°30'

West Br.

Third
Lake

N E W   H A M P S H I R E

Second
Lake

Middle Br.

Halls Stream

Indian Stream

Perry Stream

Connecticut
Lake

Vallentine-Collins Line

45

Connecticut River

71°30'

NORTHWESTERNMOST HEAD
OF THE
CONNECTICUT RIVER

Miles	Kilometres
0 — 5	0 — 5

1. ——— Line claimed by American Agent Bradley, 1821
2. – – – Line claimed by American Commissioner Van Ness, 1821
3. ▬▬▬ Line claimed by Great Britain, 1821-1842; and Line
   according to Award of the King of the Netherlands, 1831
4. ▬▬▬ Line of Webster-Ashburton Treaty, 1842

B R I T I S H   A M E

98

49

Red River of the North

48

LAKE
OF THE
WOODS

Red

Lake

SOUTHWARD AND WESTWARD OF
LAKE OF THE WOODS

Miles	Kilometres
0 — 50	0 — 50

1. ——— Line proposed by Secretary of State Madison, June 8, 1802
2. – – – Line of Hawkesbury-King Convention, May 12, 1803
3. ▬▬▬ Line agreed upon by American and British Negotiators, 1807; and
   Line fixed by the Convention of 1818 (see text)

1. – – – Line
2. ▬▬▬ Line

ST. LAWRENCE RIVER

L O W E R

C A N A D A

45

Rouses Point

N E W   Y O R K

74

Lake Champlain

L. Champlain

OLD SOUTHERN BOUNDARY

(Drainage and Projection from La Tour's Map "L'Amerique
Septentrionale. 1783")

Miles	Kilometres
0 100 200	0 100 200

1. ——— Line claimed by United States, 1783-1795; and Line
   of Spanish-American Treaty, 1795
2. ▬▬▬ Line according to Instructions of Spanish Envoy
   Gardoqui, 1784
3. – – – Line of Minimum Concession according to Instructions of Gardoqui, 1785
4. – - – Line of Maximum Concession according to Instructions of Gardoqui, 1785
5. - - - - - Boundary of "Neutral Indian Territory" according to Instructions of Gardoqui, 1786
6. – ·· – Line of Minimum Concession according to Instructions of Gardoqui, 1787
7. ········ Line of Maximum Concession according to Instructions of Gardoqui, 1787

Ⓔ

Ohio River

River of the Cherokees

Euphasee R.

Mississippi River

Yazoo River

U N I T E D   S T A T E S

Apalachicola River

Flint River

F L O R I D A

Natchez

-35

L O U I S I A N A

30

G U L F   O F   M E X I C O

280   285   290

SOUTHEASTERN BOUNDARY
OF
LOUISIANA PURCHASE

Miles	Kilometres
0 100	0 100

1. ——— Line claimed by United States 1803-1819
2. ▬▬▬ Line claimed by Spain, 1803-1819

L O U I S I A N A   P U R C H A S E

Red Riv.

Mississippi River

U N I T E D

L. Maurepas

L. Pontchar

G U L F   O F   B O

93   91

Copyright by Carnegie Institution of Washington

Plate 93

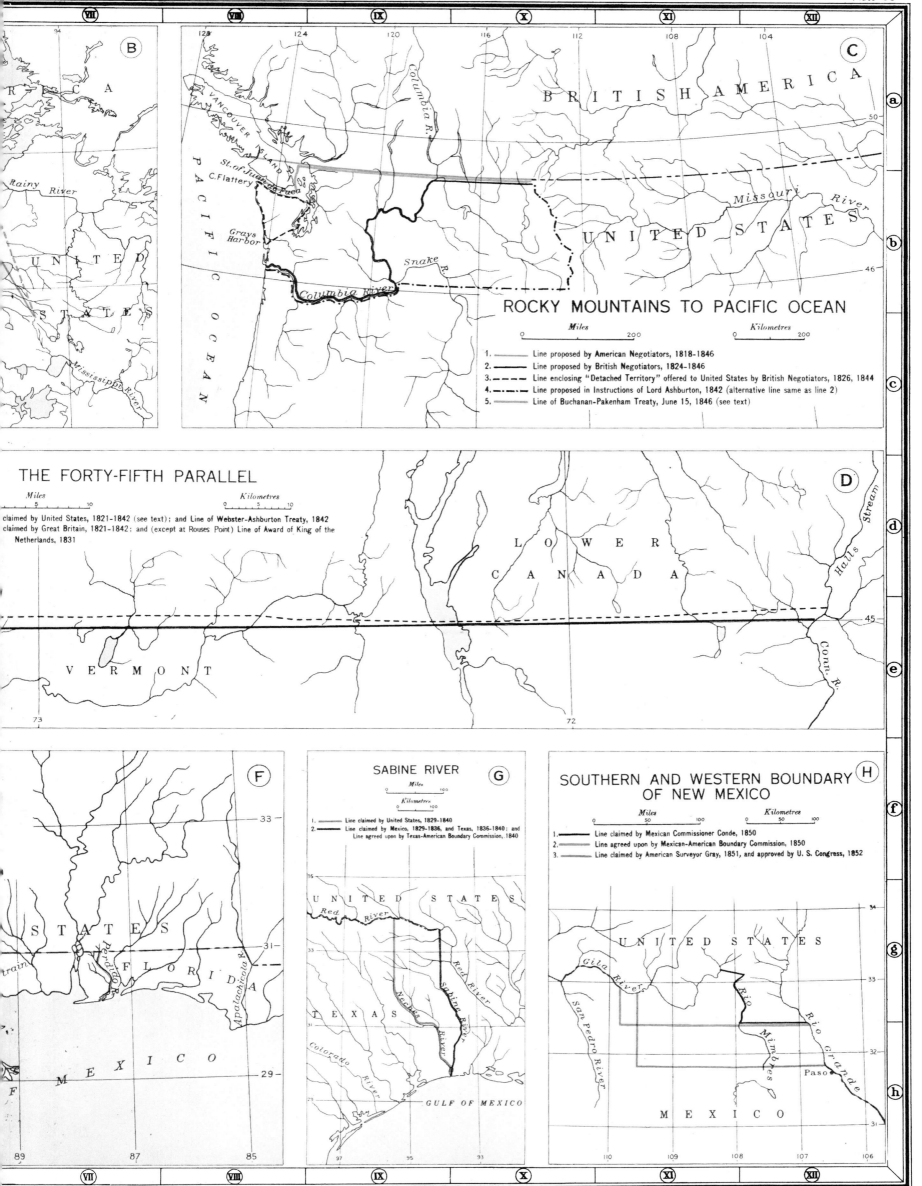

B

C

ROCKY MOUNTAINS TO PACIFIC OCEAN

Miles   200   Kilometres   200

1. ———— Line proposed by American Negotiators, 1818–1846
2. ———— Line proposed by British Negotiators, 1824–1846
3. – – – – Line enclosing "Detached Territory" offered to United States by British Negotiators, 1826, 1844
4. –·–·–·– Line proposed in Instructions of Lord Ashburton, 1842 (alternative line same as line 2)
5. ———— Line of Buchanan-Pakenham Treaty, June 15, 1846 (see text)

THE FORTY-FIFTH PARALLEL

Miles   5   10   Kilometres   5   10

claimed by United States, 1821–1842 (see text); and Line of Webster-Ashburton Treaty, 1842
claimed by Great Britain, 1821–1842; and (except at Rouses Point) Line of Award of King of the
      Netherlands, 1831

D

L O W E R

C A N A D A

V E R M O N T

F

S T A T E S

F L O R I D A

M E X I C O

SABINE RIVER

G

Miles   100

Kilometres   100

1. ———— Line claimed by United States, 1829–1840
2. ———— Line claimed by Mexico, 1829–1836, and Texas, 1836–1840; and
          Line agreed upon by Texas-American Boundary Commission, 1840

U N I T E D   S T A T E S

T E X A S

GULF OF MEXICO

SOUTHERN AND WESTERN BOUNDARY
OF NEW MEXICO

H

Miles   50   100   Kilometres   50   100

1. ———— Line claimed by Mexican Commissioner Conde, 1850
2. ———— Line agreed upon by Mexican-American Boundary Commission, 1850
3. ———— Line claimed by American Surveyor Gray, 1851, and approved by U. S. Congress, 1852

U N I T E D   S T A T E S

M E X I C O

Paso

A. HOEN & CO., INC.,

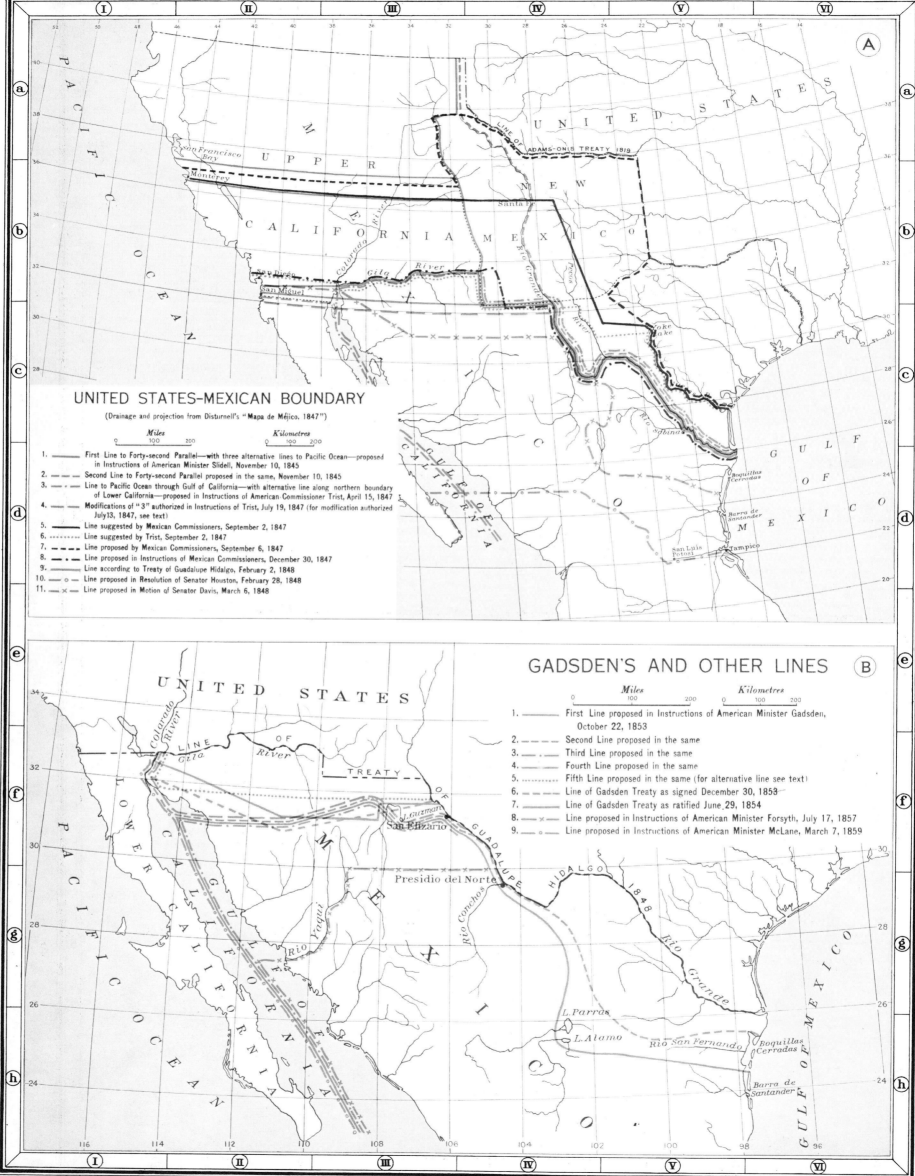

UNITED STATES-MEXICAN BOUNDARY

(Drainage and projection from Disturnell's "Mapa de Méjico, 1847")

Miles
0   100   200

Kilometres
0   100   200

1. First Line to Forty-second Parallel—with three alternative lines to Pacific Ocean—proposed in Instructions of American Minister Slidell, November 10, 1845
2. Second Line to Forty-second Parallel proposed in the same, November 10, 1845
3. Line to Pacific Ocean through Gulf of California—with alternative line along northern boundary of Lower California—proposed in Instructions of American Commissioner Trist, April 15, 1847
4. Modifications of "3" authorized in Instructions of Trist, July 19, 1847 (for modification authorized July 13, 1847, see text)
5. Line suggested by Mexican Commissioners, September 2, 1847
6. Line suggested by Trist, September 2, 1847
7. Line proposed by Mexican Commissioners, September 6, 1847
8. Line proposed in Instructions of Mexican Commissioners, December 30, 1847
9. Line according to Treaty of Guadalupe Hidalgo, February 2, 1848
10. Line proposed in Resolution of Senator Houston, February 28, 1848
11. Line proposed in Motion of Senator Davis, March 6, 1848

GADSDEN'S AND OTHER LINES

Miles
0   100   200

Kilometres
0   100   200

1. First Line proposed in Instructions of American Minister Gadsden, October 22, 1853
2. Second Line proposed in the same
3. Third Line proposed in the same
4. Fourth Line proposed in the same
5. Fifth Line proposed in the same (for alternative line see text)
6. Line of Gadsden Treaty as signed December 30, 1853
7. Line of Gadsden Treaty as ratified June 29, 1854
8. Line proposed in Instructions of American Minister Forsyth, July 17, 1857
9. Line proposed in Instructions of American Minister McLane, March 7, 1859

Copyright by Carnegie Institution of Washington

A. HOEN & CO., INC.

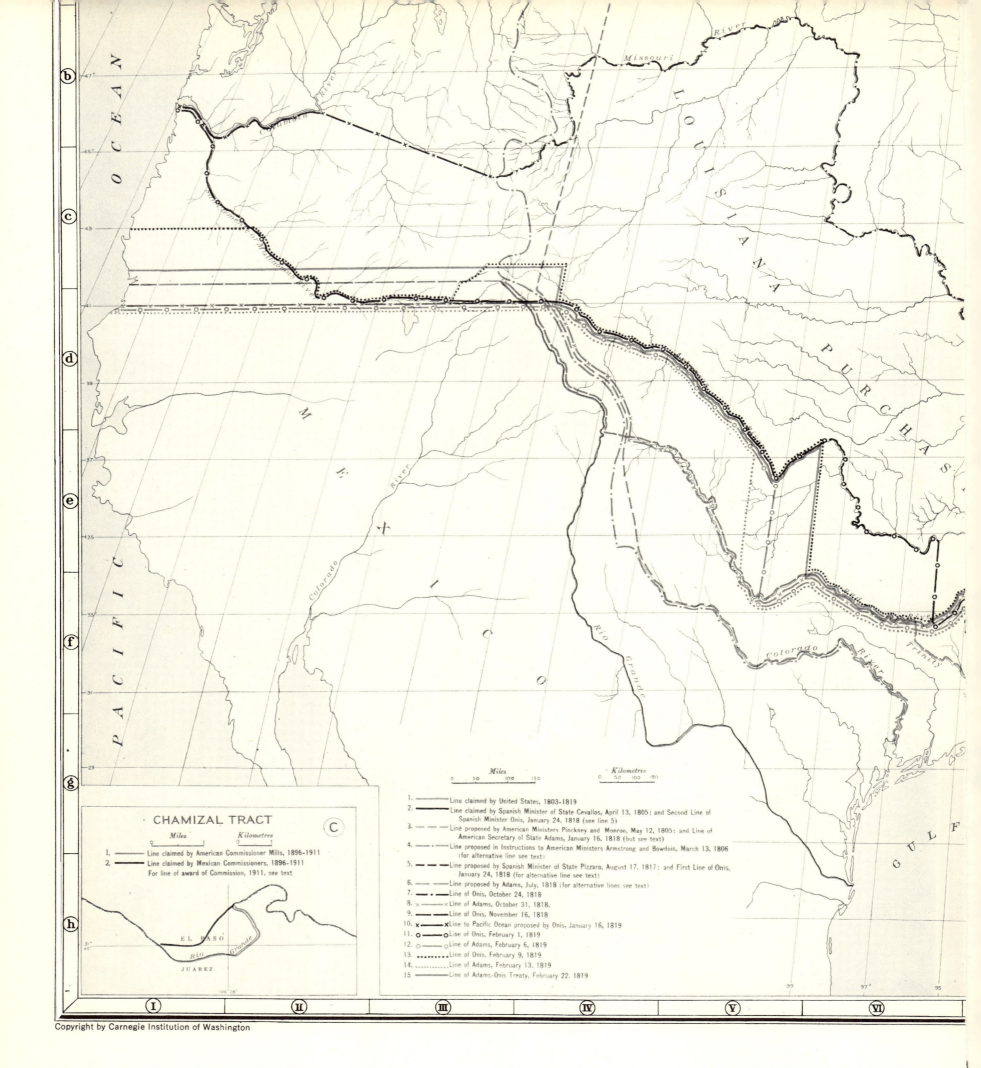

CHAMIZAL TRACT

Miles   Kilometres

1. ——————— Line claimed by American Commissioner Mills, 1896-1911
2. ——————— Line claimed by Mexican Commissioners, 1896-1911
For line of award of Commission, 1911, see text

EL PASO
Rio Grande
JUAREZ

Miles   Kilometres
0   50   100 150   0 50 100 150

1. ——————— Line claimed by United States, 1803-1819
2. ——————— Line claimed by Spanish Minister of State Cevallos, April 13, 1805; and Second Line of Spanish Minister Onis, January 24, 1818 (see line 5)
3. ——————— Line proposed by American Ministers Pinckney and Monroe, May 12, 1805; and Line of American Secretary of State Adams, January 16, 1818 (but see text)
4. ——————— Line proposed in Instructions to American Ministers Armstrong and Bowdoin, March 13, 1806 (for alternative line see text)
5. ——————— Line proposed by Spanish Minister of State Pizzaro, August 17, 1817; and First Line of Onis, January 24, 1818 (for alternative line see text)
6. ——————— Line proposed by Adams, July, 1818 (for alternative lines see text)
7. ——·——·— Line of Onis, October 24, 1818
8. ×————×— Line of Adams, October 31, 1818,
9. ——————— Line of Onis, November 16, 1818
10. ×————×— Line to Pacific Ocean proposed by Onis, January 16, 1819
11. ○————○— Line of Onis, February 1, 1819
12. ○————○— Line of Adams, February 6, 1819
13. •••••••••• Line of Onis, February 9, 1819
14. ············ Line of Adams, February 13, 1819
15. ——————— Line of Adams-Onis Treaty, February 22, 1819

Copyright by Carnegie Institution of Washington

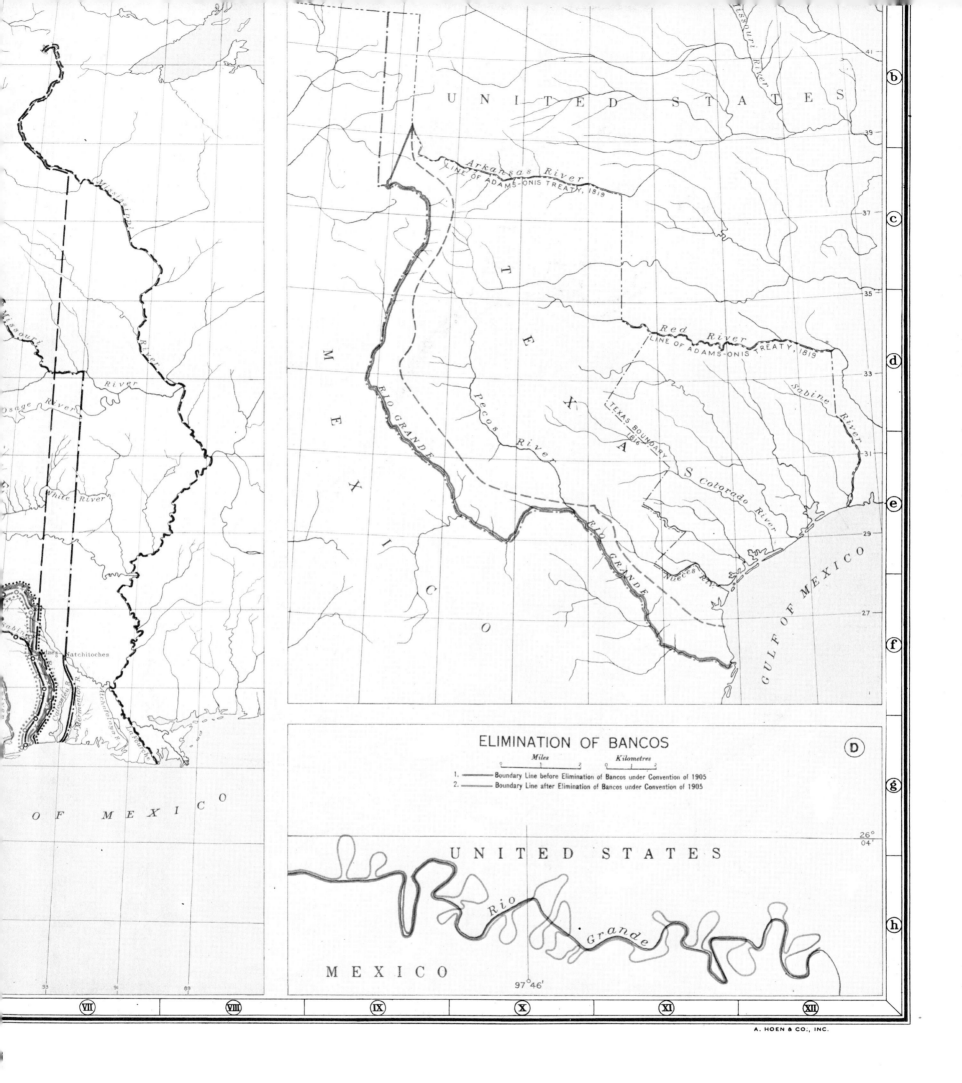

UNITED STATES

MEXICO

TEXAS

Arkansas River
LINE OF ADAMS-ONIS TREATY, 1819

Red River
LINE OF ADAMS-ONIS TREATY, 1819

TEXAS BOUNDARY 1816

RIO GRANDE

Pecos River

Sabine River

Colorado River

Nueces R.

GULF OF MEXICO

Mississippi River

Missouri River

Osage River

White River

Natchitoches

OF MEXICO

ELIMINATION OF BANCOS

Ⓓ

Miles
Kilometres

1. ——— Boundary Line before Elimination of Bancos under Convention of 1905
2. ——— Boundary Line after Elimination of Bancos under Convention of 1905

UNITED STATES

26° 04'

Rio Grande

MEXICO

97° 46'

ⓑ
ⓒ
ⓓ
ⓔ
ⓕ
ⓖ
ⓗ

VII   VIII   IX   X   XI   XII

A. HOEN & CO., INC.

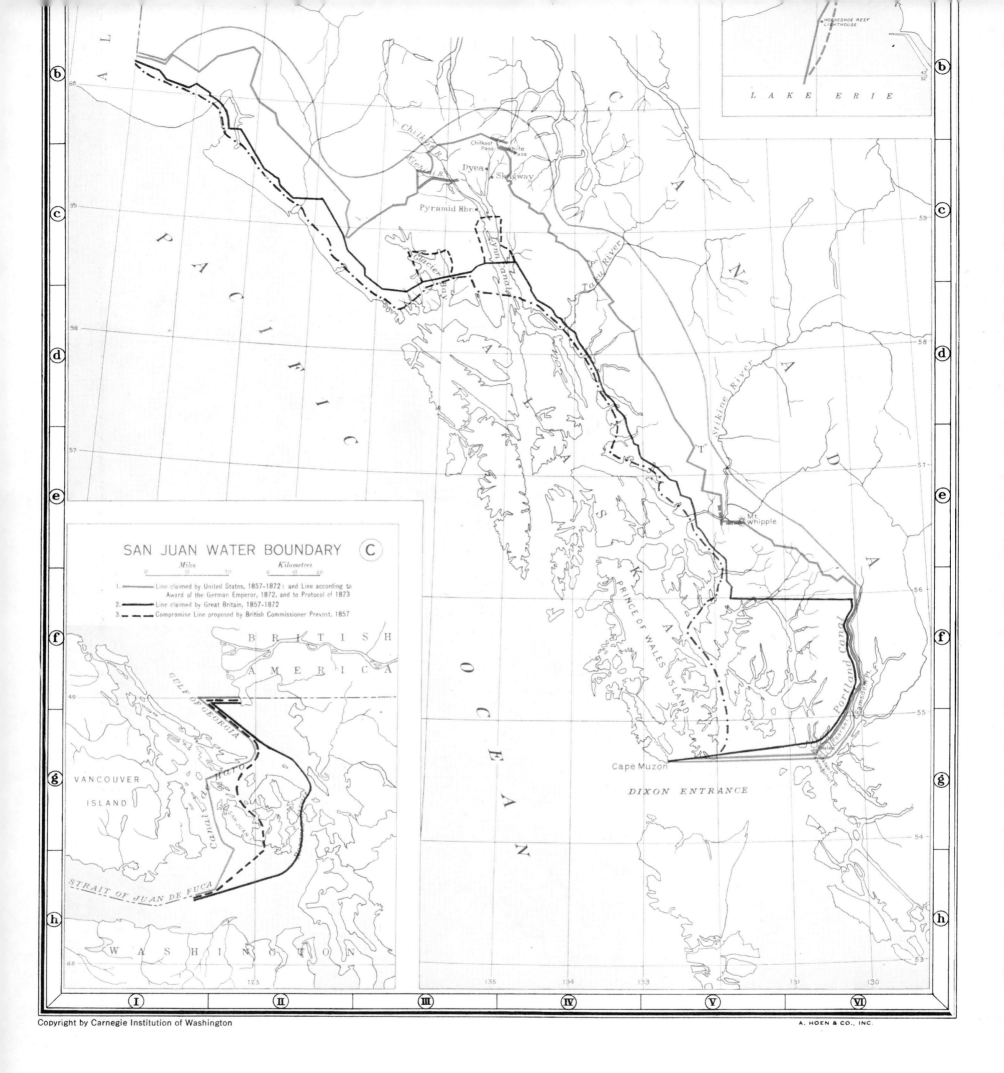

LAKE ERIE

SAN JUAN WATER BOUNDARY   C

Miles   Kilometres

1. ———— Line claimed by United States, 1857-1872 ; and Line according to Award of the German Emperor, 1872, and to Protocol of 1873
2. ———— Line claimed by Great Britain, 1857-1872
3. - - - - Compromise Line proposed by British Commissioner Prevost, 1857

BRITISH

AMERICA

GULF OF GEORGIA

VANCOUVER ISLAND

STRAIT OF JUAN DE FUCA

WASHINGTON

P A C I F I C

A L A S K A

C A N A D A

Chilkat R.

Klehini R.

Chilkoot Pass

White Pass

Dyea

Skagway

Pyramid Hbr.

Glacier Bay

Lynn Canal

Taku River

Stikine River

"T"

Mt. Whipple

PRINCE OF WALES ISLAND

Portland Canal

Cape Muzon

DIXON ENTRANCE

O C E A N

HORSESHOE REEF LIGHTHOUSE

Copyright by Carnegie Institution of Washington

A. HOEN & CO., INC.

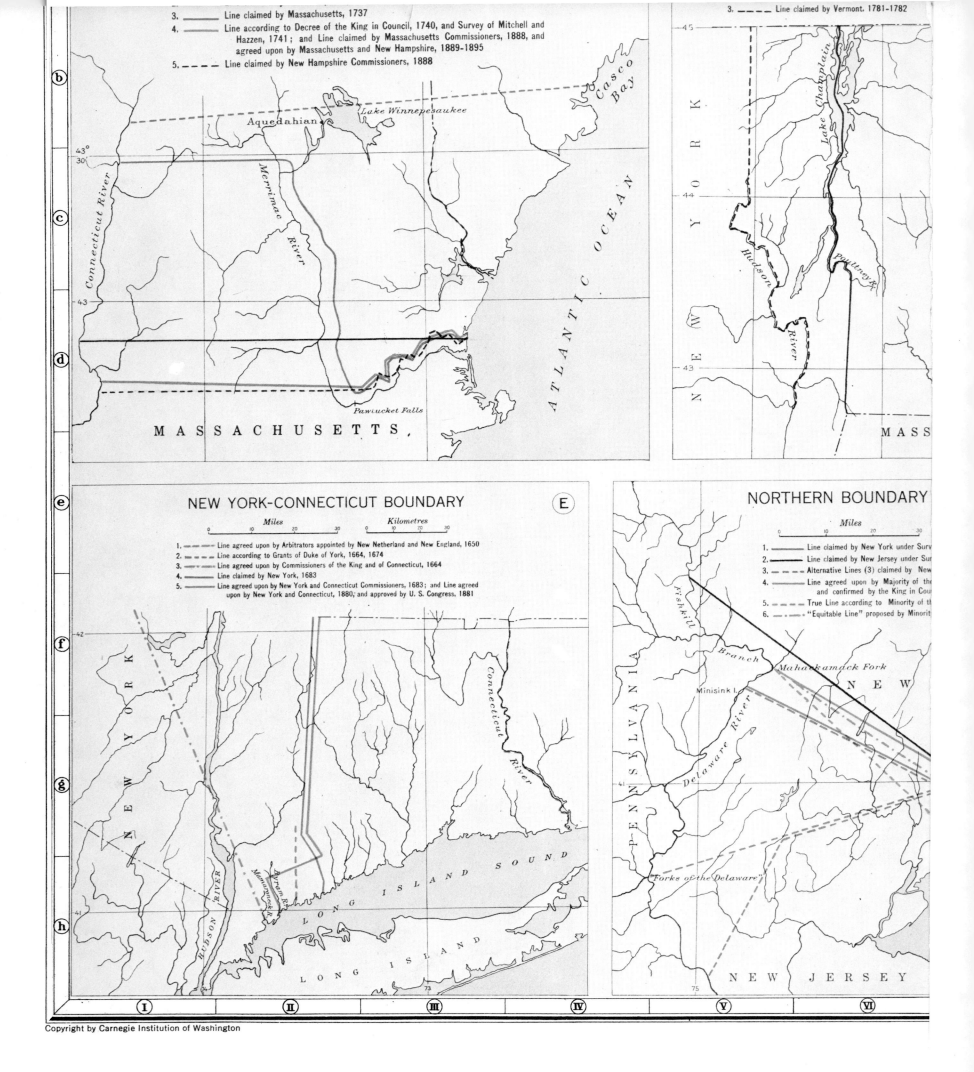

3. ———— Line claimed by Massachusetts, 1737
4. ———— Line according to Decree of the King in Council, 1740, and Survey of Mitchell and
    Hazzen, 1741; and Line claimed by Massachusetts Commissioners, 1888, and
    agreed upon by Massachusetts and New Hampshire, 1889-1895
5. – – – – Line claimed by New Hampshire Commissioners, 1888

3. – – – – Line claimed by Vermont, 1781-1782

Casco Bay

Lake Winnepesaukee
Aquedahtan

Merrimac River
Connecticut River

43° 30'

43

ATLANTIC OCEAN

Pawtucket Falls

M A S S A C H U S E T T S ,

Y O R K

Lake Champlain

Hudson River

Poultney R.

45

44

43

N E W

M A S S

NEW YORK-CONNECTICUT BOUNDARY   ⓔ

Miles   Kilometres

1. –·–·– Line agreed upon by Arbitrators appointed by New Netherland and New England, 1650
2. ———— Line according to Grants of Duke of York, 1664, 1674
3. –·–·– Line agreed upon by Commissioners of the King and of Connecticut, 1664
4. ———— Line claimed by New York, 1683
5. ———— Line agreed upon by New York and Connecticut Commissioners, 1683; and Line agreed
    upon by New York and Connecticut, 1880; and approved by U. S. Congress, 1881

N E W   Y O R K

42

41

HUDSON RIVER
Mamaroneck R.
Byram R.

Connecticut River

L O N G   I S L A N D   S O U N D

L O N G   I S L A N D

73

NORTHERN BOUNDARY

Miles

1. ———— Line claimed by New York under Surv
2. ———— Line claimed by New Jersey under Sur
3. – – – – Alternative Lines (3) claimed by New
4. ———— Line agreed upon by Majority of the
    and confirmed by the King in Cou
5. – – – – True Line according to Minority of th
6. –·–·– "Equitable Line" proposed by Minorit

P E N N S Y L V A N I A

Fishkill
Branch
Mahackamack Fork
Minisink I.
Delaware River

N E W

41

"Forks of the Delaware"

N E W   J E R S E Y

75

Ⓘ   Ⓑⓑ   ⒾⒾ   ⓒⓒ   ⓓⓓ   Ⓘ   ⓔⓔ   Ⓕ   ⓖ   ⓗ   Ⓘ   ⒤   ⒤⒤   ⒤⒤⒤   ⒤Ⓥ   Ⓥ   ⓋⒾ

Copyright by Carnegie Institution of Washington

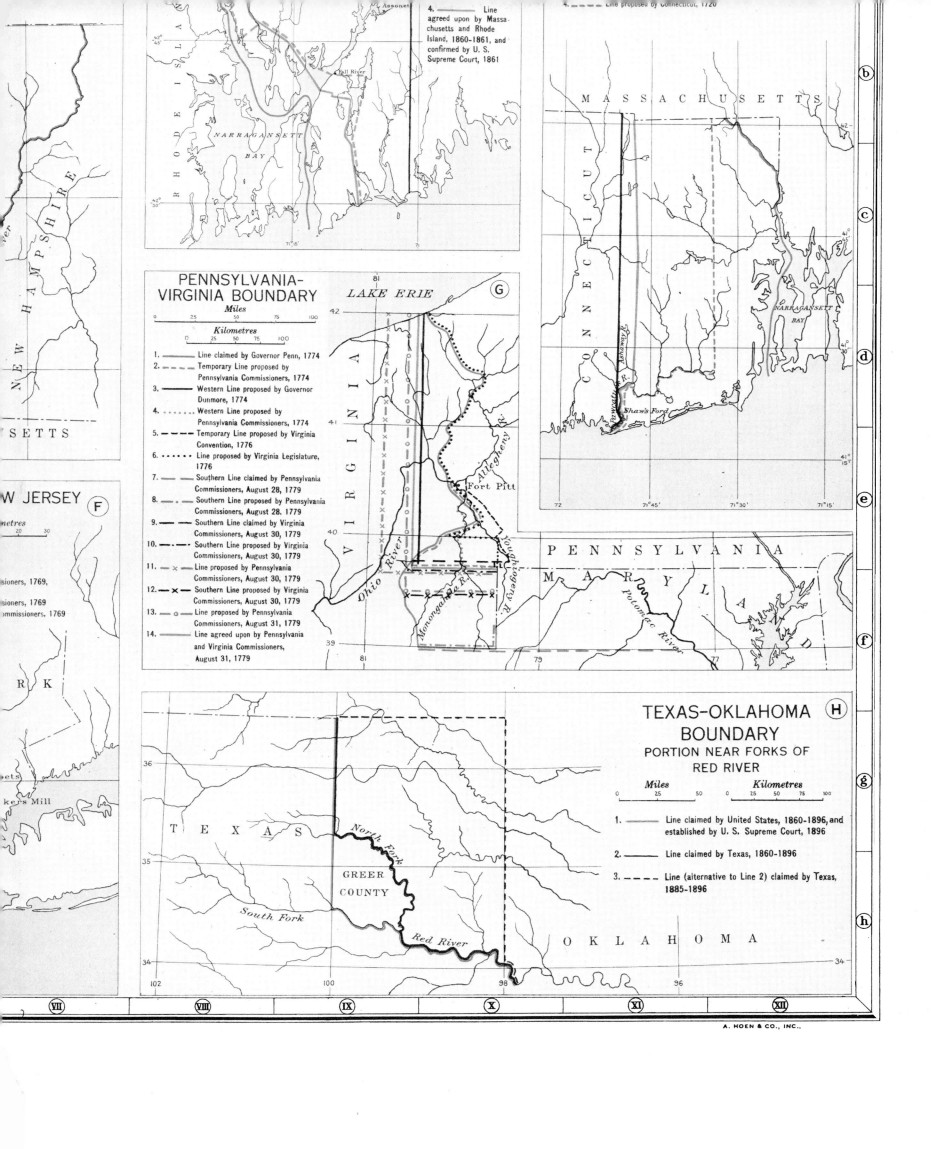

4. — — — Line agreed upon by Massachusetts and Rhode Island, 1860-1861, and confirmed by U. S. Supreme Court, 1861

4. — — — Line proposed by Connecticut, 1720

M A S S A C H U S E T T S

C O N N E C T I C U T

NARRAGANSETT BAY

Shaw's Ford

RHODE ISLAND

NARRAGANSETT BAY

Tall River

Assonet

PENNSYLVANIA-VIRGINIA BOUNDARY

Miles
0   25   50   75   100

Kilometres
0   25   50   75   100

1. ———— Line claimed by Governor Penn, 1774
2. — — — Temporary Line proposed by Pennsylvania Commissioners, 1774
3. ———— Western Line proposed by Governor Dunmore, 1774
4. · · · · · Western Line proposed by Pennsylvania Commissioners, 1774
5. — — — Temporary Line proposed by Virginia Convention, 1776
6. • • • • • Line proposed by Virginia Legislature, 1776
7. — — — Southern Line claimed by Pennsylvania Commissioners, August 28, 1779
8. —·—·— Southern Line proposed by Pennsylvania Commissioners, August 28, 1779
9. ———— Southern Line claimed by Virginia Commissioners, August 30, 1779
10. —··—··— Southern Line proposed by Virginia Commissioners, August 30, 1779
11. —x—x— Line proposed by Pennsylvania Commissioners, August 30, 1779
12. —✕—✕— Southern Line proposed by Virginia Commissioners, August 30, 1779
13. —o—o— Line proposed by Pennsylvania Commissioners, August 31, 1779
14. ———— Line agreed upon by Pennsylvania and Virginia Commissioners, August 31, 1779

LAKE ERIE

G

V I R G I N I A

Ohio River

Monongahela R.

Allegheny R.

Youghiogheny R.

Fort Pitt

P E N N S Y L V A N I A

M A R Y L A N D

Potomac River

NEW HAMPSHIRE

SETTS

W JERSEY

F

RK

ets

kers Mill

TEXAS-OKLAHOMA BOUNDARY
PORTION NEAR FORKS OF RED RIVER

H

Miles
0   25   50

Kilometres
0   25   50   75   100

1. ———— Line claimed by United States, 1860-1896, and established by U. S. Supreme Court, 1896
2. ———— Line claimed by Texas, 1860-1896
3. — — — Line (alternative to Line 2) claimed by Texas, 1885-1896

T E X A S

GREER COUNTY

North Fork

South Fork

Red River

O K L A H O M A

A. HOEN & CO., INC.,

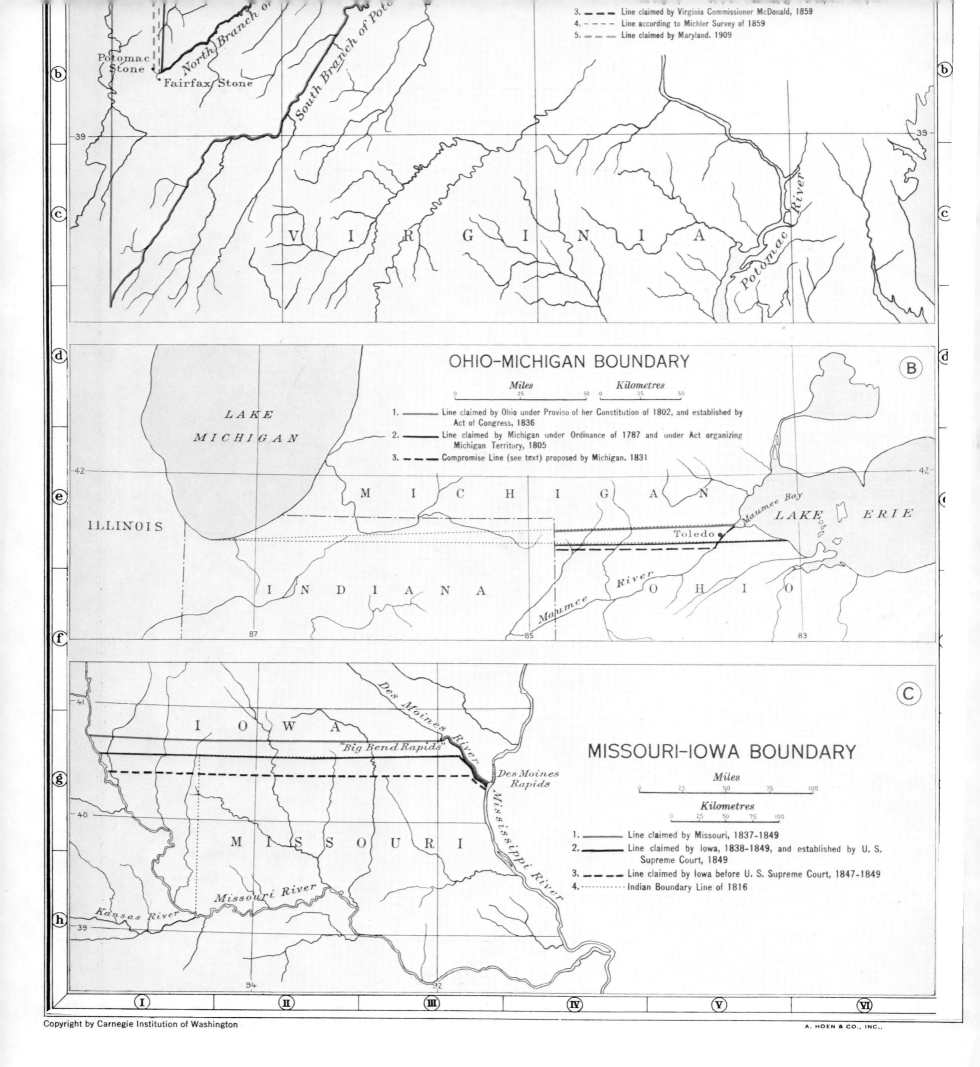

3. ――――― Line claimed by Virginia Commissioner McDonald, 1859
4. ― ― ― ― Line according to Michler Survey of 1859
5. ― · ― · ― Line claimed by Maryland, 1909

Potomac
Stone
Fairfax Stone

North Branch of

South Branch of Poto

Potomac River

V I R G I N I A

OHIO-MICHIGAN BOUNDARY

Miles   Kilometres
0   25   50   0   25   50

1. ――――― Line claimed by Ohio under Proviso of her Constitution of 1802, and established by
   Act of Congress, 1836
2. ――――― Line claimed by Michigan under Ordinance of 1787 and under Act organizing
   Michigan Territory, 1805
3. ― ― ― ― Compromise Line (see text) proposed by Michigan. 1831

LAKE
MICHIGAN

ILLINOIS

M I C H I G A N

Maumee Bay

LAKE ERIE

Toledo

I N D I A N A   Maumee River   O H I O

B

MISSOURI-IOWA BOUNDARY

C

I O W A

Des Moines River

"Big Bend Rapids"

Des Moines
Rapids

Mississippi River

M I S S O U R I

Missouri River

Kansas River

Miles
0   25   50   75   100

Kilometres
0   25   50   75   100

1. ――――― Line claimed by Missouri, 1837-1849
2. ――――― Line claimed by Iowa, 1838-1849, and established by U. S.
   Supreme Court, 1849
3. ― ― ― ― Line claimed by Iowa before U. S. Supreme Court, 1847-1849
4. ··········· Indian Boundary Line of 1816

Copyright by Carnegie Institution of Washington

A. HOEN & CO., INC.,

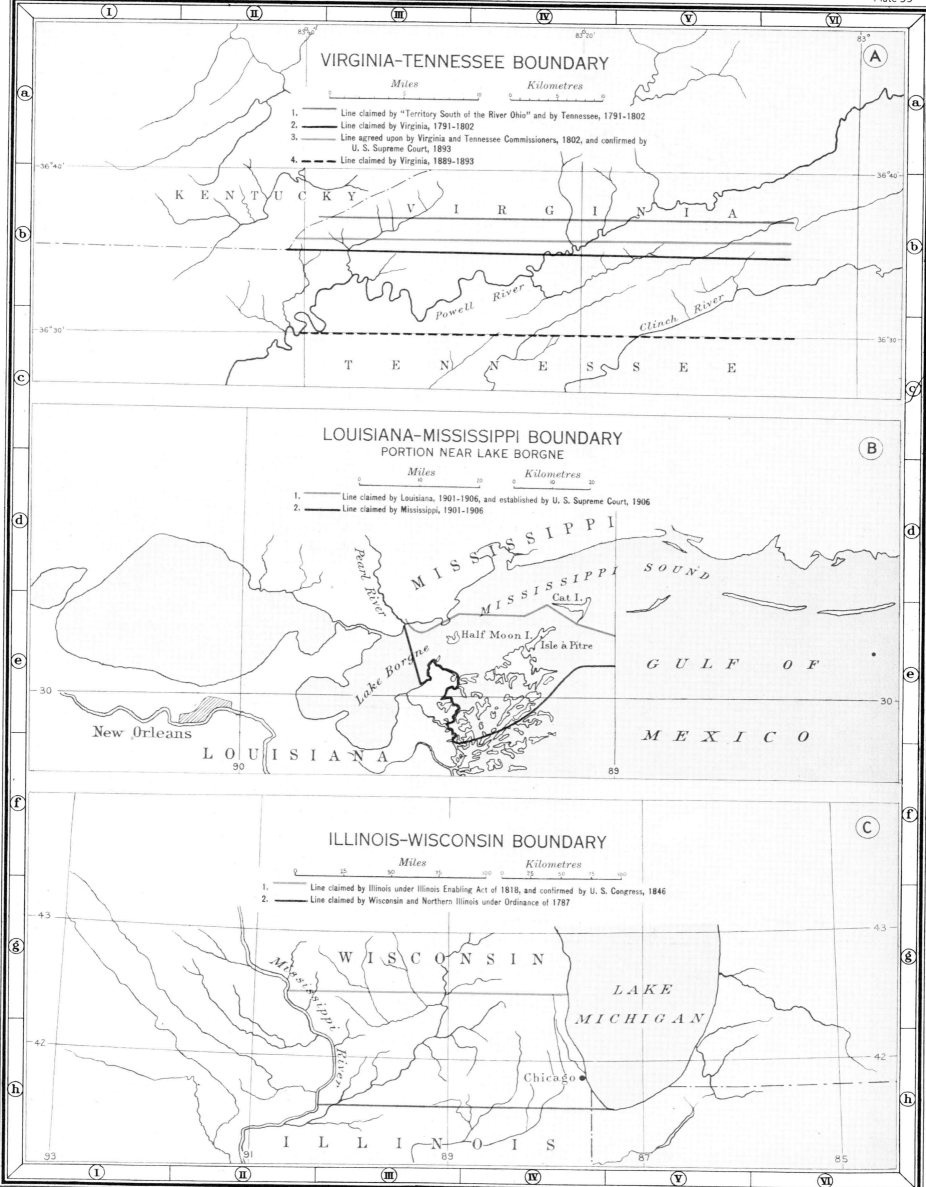

VIRGINIA-TENNESSEE BOUNDARY

Miles   Kilometres

1. —————— Line claimed by "Territory South of the River Ohio" and by Tennessee, 1791-1802
2. —————— Line claimed by Virginia, 1791-1802
3. —————— Line agreed upon by Virginia and Tennessee Commissioners, 1802, and confirmed by U. S. Supreme Court, 1893
4. - - - - - - Line claimed by Virginia, 1889-1893

KENTUCKY   V I R G I N I A

Powell River

Clinch River

T E N N E S S E E

LOUISIANA-MISSISSIPPI BOUNDARY
PORTION NEAR LAKE BORGNE

Miles   Kilometres

1. —————— Line claimed by Louisiana, 1901-1906, and established by U. S. Supreme Court, 1906
2. —————— Line claimed by Mississippi, 1901-1906

M I S S I S S I P P I

Pearl River

MISSISSIPPI   SOUND

Cat I.

Half Moon I.

Isle à Pitre

Lake Borgne

G U L F   O F

New Orleans

L O U I S I A N A

M E X I C O

ILLINOIS-WISCONSIN BOUNDARY

Miles   Kilometres

1. —————— Line claimed by Illinois under Illinois Enabling Act of 1818, and confirmed by U. S. Congress, 1846
2. —————— Line claimed by Wisconsin and Northern Illinois under Ordinance of 1787

W I S C O N S I N

Mississippi River

L A K E
M I C H I G A N

Chicago

I L L I N O I S

Copyright by Carnegie Institution of Washington

A. HOEN & CO., INC.

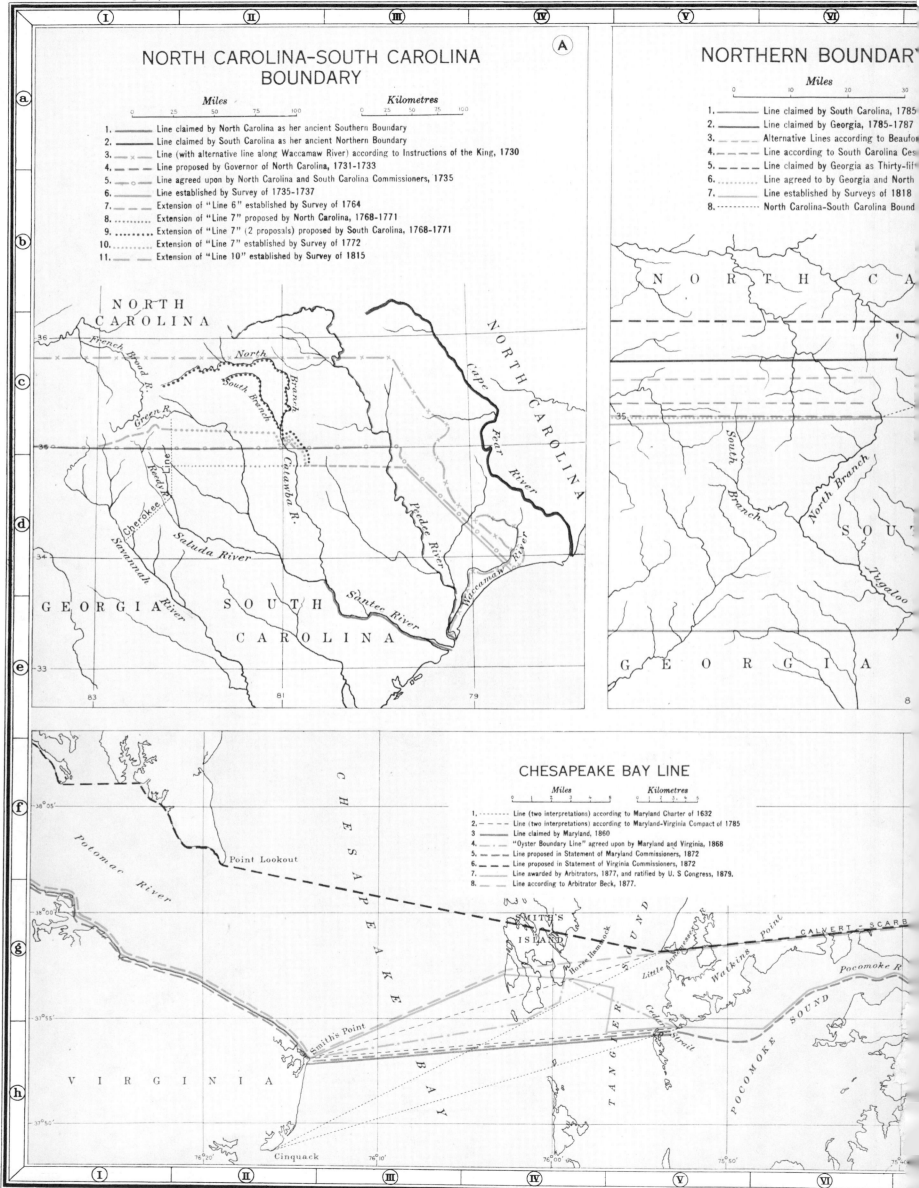

NORTH CAROLINA–SOUTH CAROLINA BOUNDARY

Ⓐ

Miles   Kilometres

1. ——— Line claimed by North Carolina as her ancient Southern Boundary
2. ——— Line claimed by South Carolina as her ancient Northern Boundary
3. —×— Line (with alternative line along Waccamaw River) according to Instructions of the King, 1730
4. —·— Line proposed by Governor of North Carolina, 1731-1733
5. —○— Line agreed upon by North Carolina and South Carolina Commissioners, 1735
6. ——— Line established by Survey of 1735-1737
7. ——— Extension of "Line 6" established by Survey of 1764
8. ········· Extension of "Line 7" proposed by North Carolina, 1768-1771
9. ········· Extension of "Line 7" (2 proposals) proposed by South Carolina, 1768-1771
10. ········· Extension of "Line 7" established by Survey of 1772
11. ——— Extension of "Line 10" established by Survey of 1815

NORTHERN BOUNDARY

Miles

1. ——— Line claimed by South Carolina, 1785
2. ——— Line claimed by Georgia, 1785-1787
3. ——— Alternative Lines according to Beaufo[rt]
4. —— Line according to South Carolina Cess[ion]
5. —·— Line claimed by Georgia as Thirty-fif[th]
6. ········· Line agreed to by Georgia and North
7. ——— Line established by Surveys of 1818
8. ········· North Carolina-South Carolina Bound[ary]

CHESAPEAKE BAY LINE

Miles   Kilometres

1. ········· Line (two interpretations) according to Maryland Charter of 1632
2. —— Line (two interpretations) according to Maryland-Virginia Compact of 1785
3. ——— Line claimed by Maryland, 1860
4. —·— "Oyster Boundary Line" agreed upon by Maryland and Virginia, 1868
5. —·— Line proposed in Statement of Maryland Commissioners, 1872
6. —— Line proposed in Statement of Virginia Commissioners, 1872
7. ——— Line awarded by Arbitrators, 1877, and ratified by U. S Congress, 1879.
8. ——— Line according to Arbitrator Beck, 1877.

Copyright by Carnegie Institution of Washington

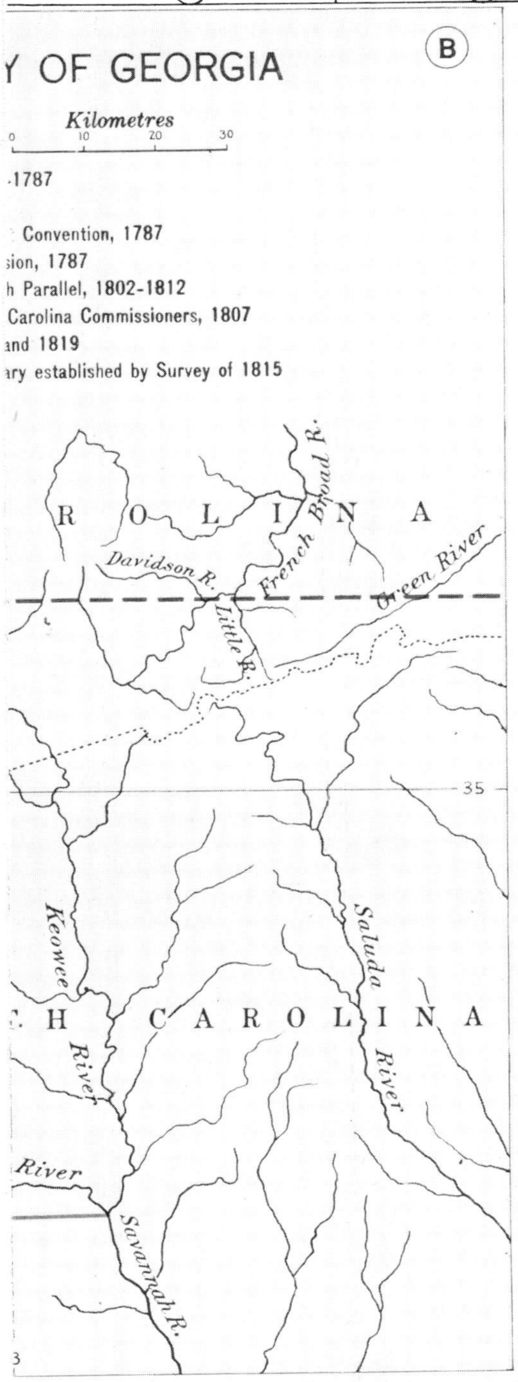

B

Y OF GEORGIA

Kilometres
0   10   20   30

-1787

Convention, 1787
sion, 1787
h Parallel, 1802-1812
Carolina Commissioners, 1807
and 1819
ary established by Survey of 1815

R O L I N A

Davidson R. *French Broad R.* *Green River*
Little R.

35

Keowee River *Saluda River*

H C A R O L I N A

River *Savannah R.*

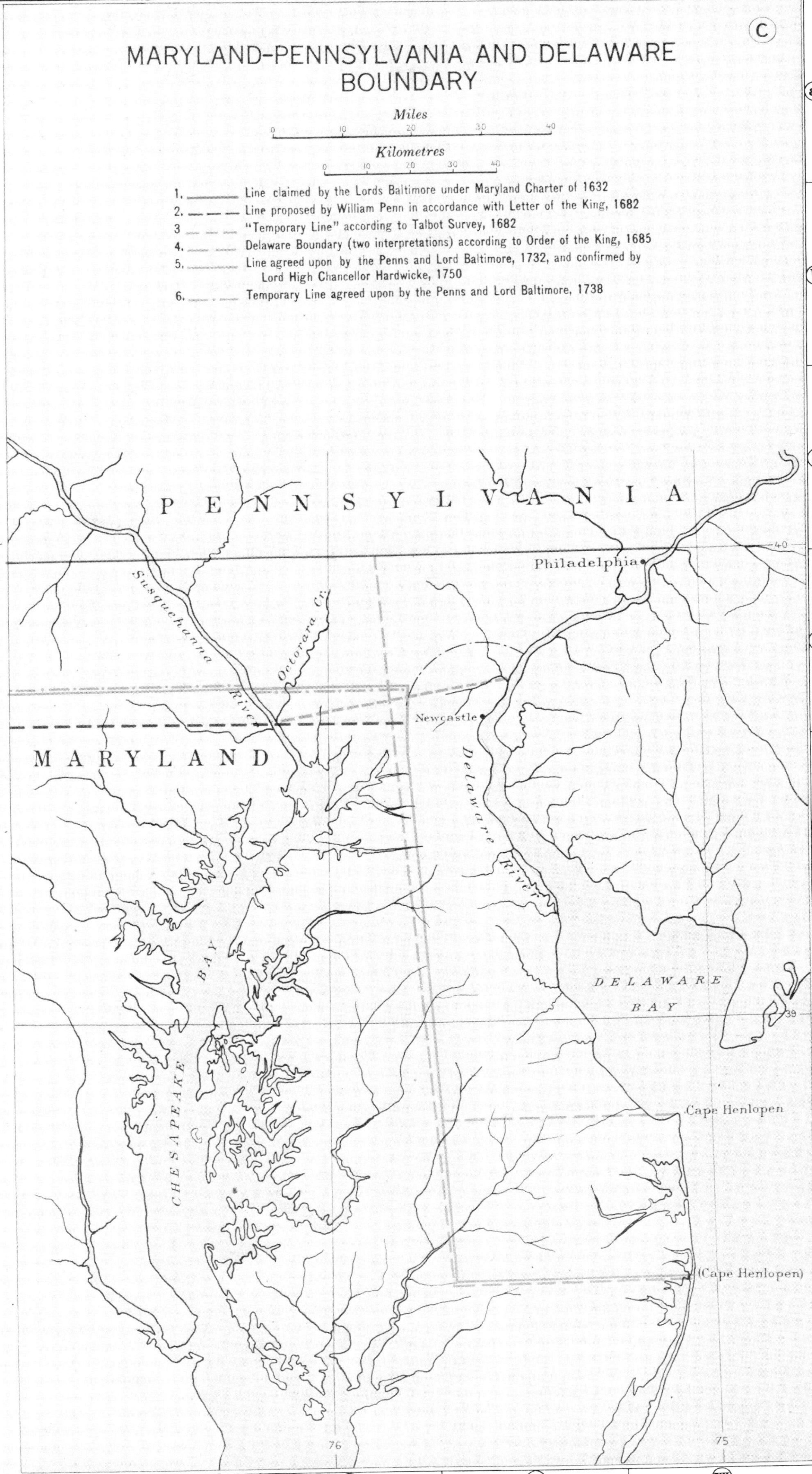

3

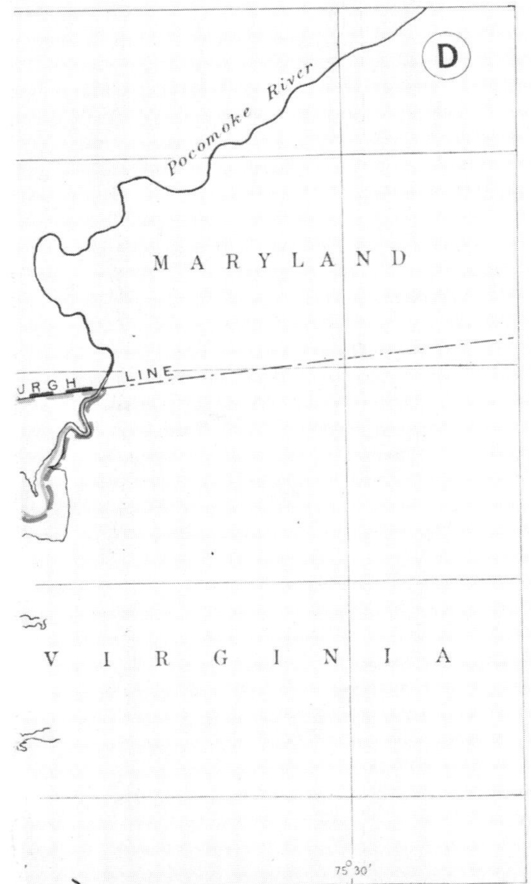

D

Pocomoke River

M A R Y L A N D

URGH   LINE

V I R G I N I A

C

MARYLAND-PENNSYLVANIA AND DELAWARE
BOUNDARY

Miles
0   10   20   30   40

Kilometres
0   10   20   30   40

1. ———————— Line claimed by the Lords Baltimore under Maryland Charter of 1632
2. — — — — Line proposed by William Penn in accordance with Letter of the King, 1682
3. - - - - - - "Temporary Line" according to Talbot Survey, 1682
4. —·—·—·— Delaware Boundary (two interpretations) according to Order of the King, 1685
5. ———————— Line agreed upon by the Penns and Lord Baltimore, 1732, and confirmed by
            Lord High Chancellor Hardwicke, 1750
6. —··—··— Temporary Line agreed upon by the Penns and Lord Baltimore, 1738

P E N N S Y L V A N I A

Philadelphia

40

Susquehanna River *Octorara Cr.*

Newcastle

M A R Y L A N D

Delaware River

C H E S A P E A K E   B A Y

D E L A W A R E
B A Y

39

Cape Henlopen

(Cape Henlopen)

76   75

A. HOEN & CO., INC.,

MICHIGAN-WISCONSIN BOUNDARY

Miles   Kilometres

1. ⎯⎯ Lines claimed by Michigan, 1908-1926
2. ⎯⎯ Line claimed by Wisconsin
   in Green Bay and Lake Michigan, 1836-1926
3. ⎯⎯ Line established by U. S. Supreme Court, Nov. 22, 1926
   (also, between Green Bay and Lake Superior, line
   claimed by Wisconsin)
4. ⎯ ⎯ ⎯ Line probably intended by U. S. Supreme Court, Mar. 1, 1926

A

LAKE SUPERIOR

LAKE SUPERIOR

Montreal River

Island Lake

E. Branch

Brule R.

Lac Vieux Desert

Brule River

Wisconsin River

M I C H I G A N

W I S C O N S I N

Quinnesec Falls

Menominee River

Pe-me-ne Falls

Rock Island Passage

WASHINGTON I.

Porte des Mortes

Menominee

CHAMBERS I.

STRAWBERRY IS.

Marinette

SUGAR I.

G R E E N   B A Y

L A K E

M I C H I G A N

IOWA-NEBRASKA BOUNDARY
PORTION NEAR OMAHA

B

Miles   Kilometres

1. ⎯⎯ Line claimed by Nebraska, 1890-1892, and established by U. S. Supreme Court, 1892
2. ⎯⎯ Line claimed by Iowa, 1890-1892

N E B R A S K A

Cutoff Lake

Missouri River

I O W A

Omaha

OKLAHOMA-TEXAS BOUNDARY ALONG THE RED RIVER

C

One Mile   Kilometre

1. ⎯⎯ Line claimed by Oklahoma and the United States, 1918-1923
2. ⎯⎯ Line established by U. S. Supreme Court, January 15, 1923
3. ······ Medial line between cut banks

   Low water channels, December, 1919
   Exposed bed of river at low water
   Sand drifts, flood plains, islands, and terraces of valley floor

• Oil wells

O K L A H O M A

Bluffs

Cut Bank

Bluffs

Cut Bank

B I G   B E N D
A R E A

GOAT I.

Cut Bank

GRANDFIELD BR.

BURKE
BET.
I.

Bluffs

T E X A S

Copyright by Carnegie Institution of Washington

A. HOEN & CO., INC.

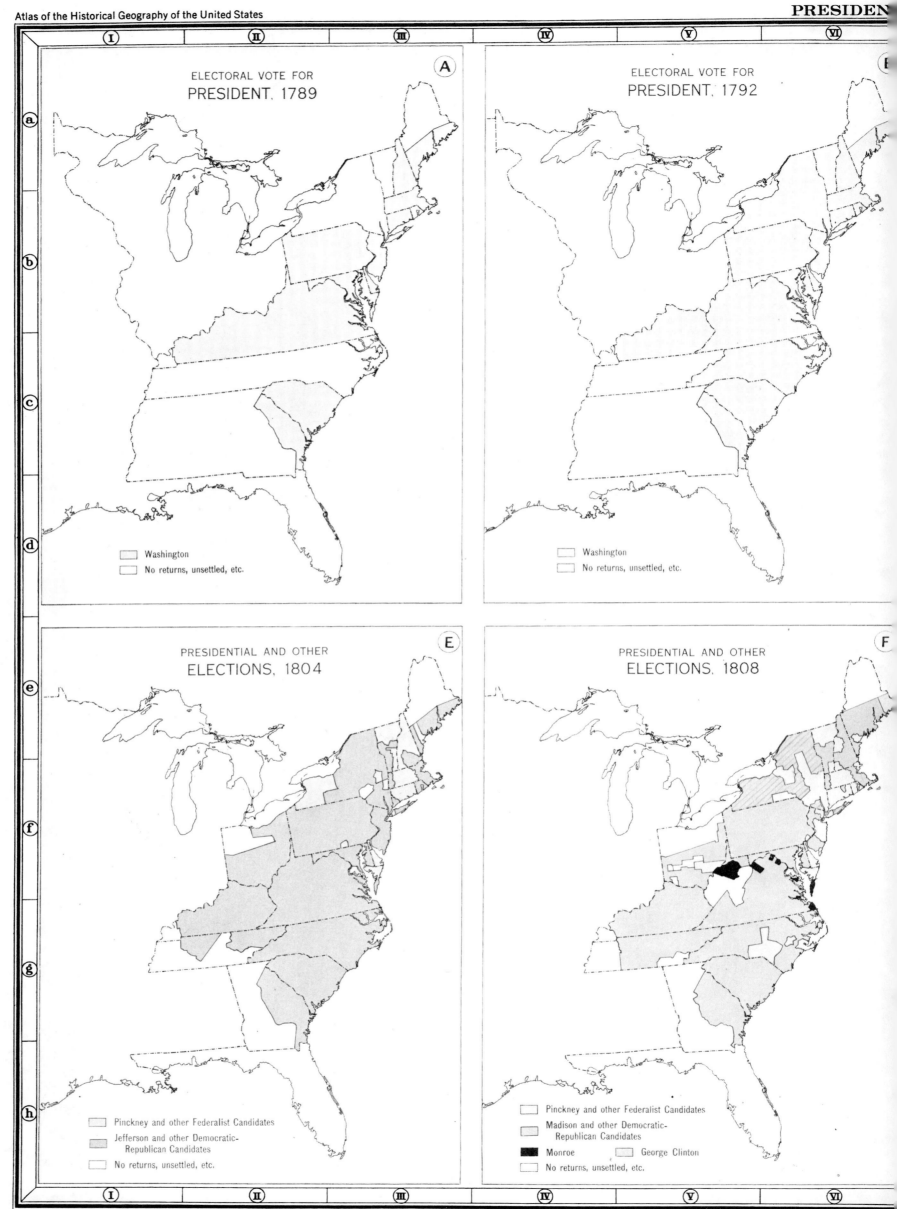

ELECTORAL VOTE FOR
PRESIDENT, 1789

A

☐ Washington
☐ No returns, unsettled, etc.

ELECTORAL VOTE FOR
PRESIDENT, 1792

B

☐ Washington
☐ No returns, unsettled, etc.

PRESIDENTIAL AND OTHER
ELECTIONS, 1804

E

☐ Pinckney and other Federalist Candidates
☐ Jefferson and other Democratic-
Republican Candidates
☐ No returns, unsettled, etc.

PRESIDENTIAL AND OTHER
ELECTIONS, 1808

F

☐ Pinckney and other Federalist Candidates
☐ Madison and other Democratic-
Republican Candidates
■ Monroe   ☐ George Clinton
☐ No returns, unsettled, etc.

Copyright by Carnegie Institution of Washington

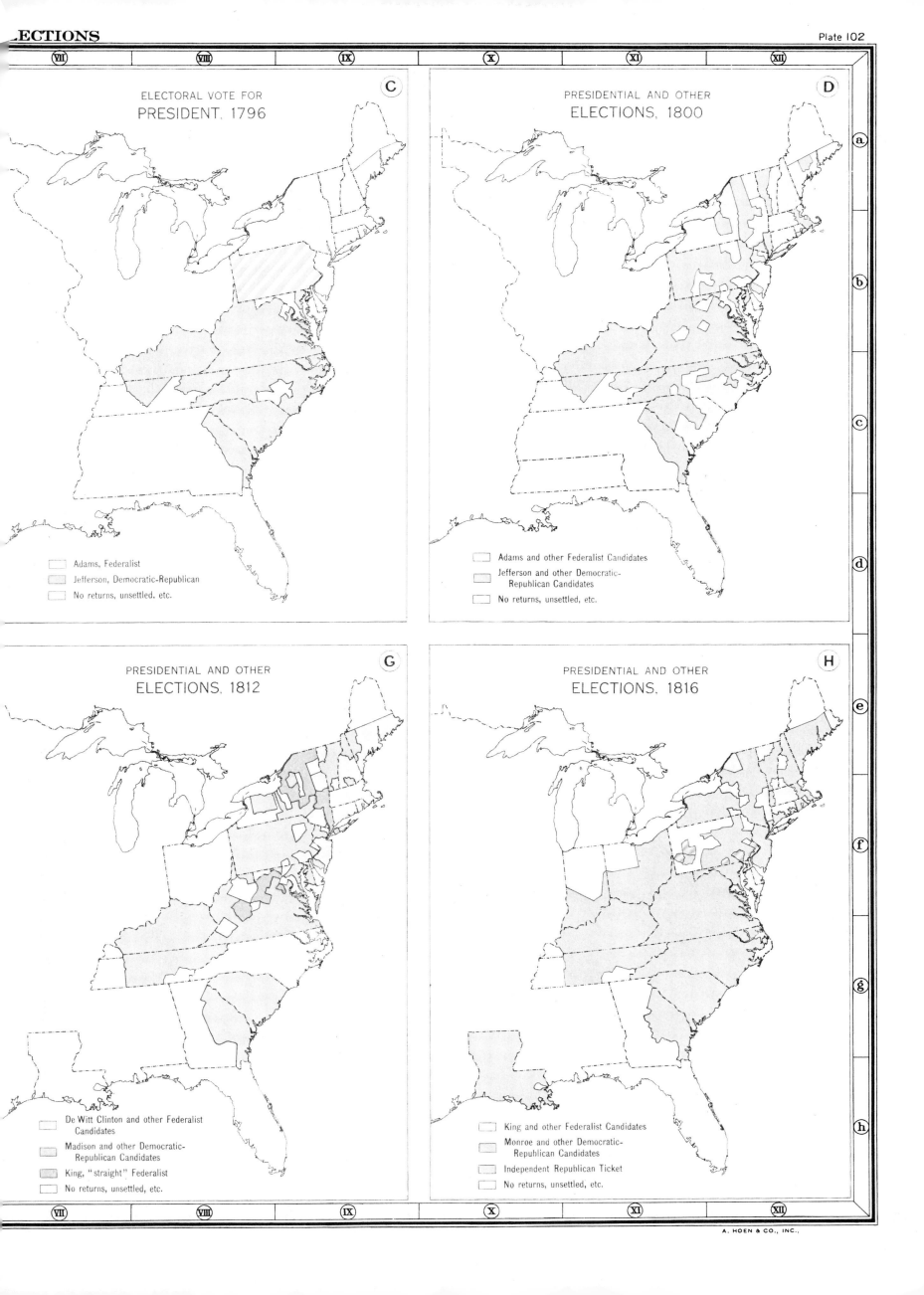

ELECTORAL VOTE FOR
PRESIDENT, 1796

C

Adams, Federalist
Jefferson, Democratic-Republican
No returns, unsettled, etc.

PRESIDENTIAL AND OTHER
ELECTIONS, 1800

D

Adams and other Federalist Candidates
Jefferson and other Democratic-
Republican Candidates
No returns, unsettled, etc.

PRESIDENTIAL AND OTHER
ELECTIONS, 1812

G

De Witt Clinton and other Federalist
Candidates
Madison and other Democratic-
Republican Candidates
King, "straight" Federalist
No returns, unsettled, etc.

PRESIDENTIAL AND OTHER
ELECTIONS, 1816

H

King and other Federalist Candidates
Monroe and other Democratic-
Republican Candidates
Independent Republican Ticket
No returns, unsettled, etc.

PRESIDENTIAL ELECTION
1820

A

Monroe, Democratic-Republican
Clinton, Federalist
No returns, unsettled, etc.

PRESIDENTIAL ELECTION
1824

B

Adams
Jackson
Clay
Crawford
No returns, unsettled, etc.

PRESIDENTIAL ELECTION
1828

C

Adams, National Republican
Jackson, Democrat
No returns, unsettled, etc.

PRESIDENTIAL ELECTION
1832

D

Clay, National Republican
Jackson, Democrat
Wirt, Anti-Masonic
No returns, unsettled, etc.

Copyright by Carnegie Institution of Washington

A. HOEN & CO., INC.,

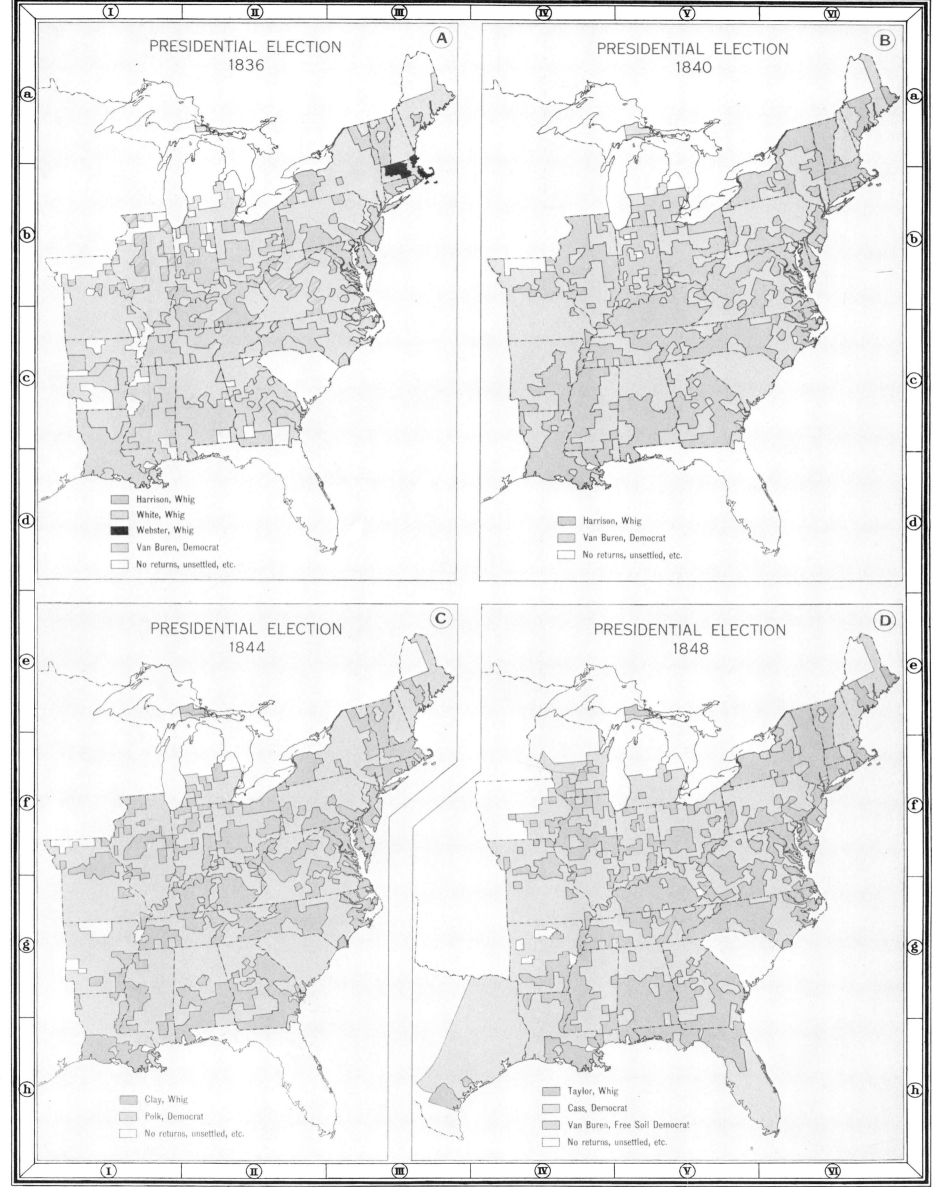

PRESIDENTIAL ELECTION
1836

Harrison, Whig
White, Whig
Webster, Whig
Van Buren, Democrat
No returns, unsettled, etc.

PRESIDENTIAL ELECTION
1840

Harrison, Whig
Van Buren, Democrat
No returns, unsettled, etc.

PRESIDENTIAL ELECTION
1844

Clay, Whig
Polk, Democrat
No returns, unsettled, etc.

PRESIDENTIAL ELECTION
1848

Taylor, Whig
Cass, Democrat
Van Buren, Free Soil Democrat
No returns, unsettled, etc.

Copyright by Carnegie Institution of Washington

A. HOEN & CO., INC.,

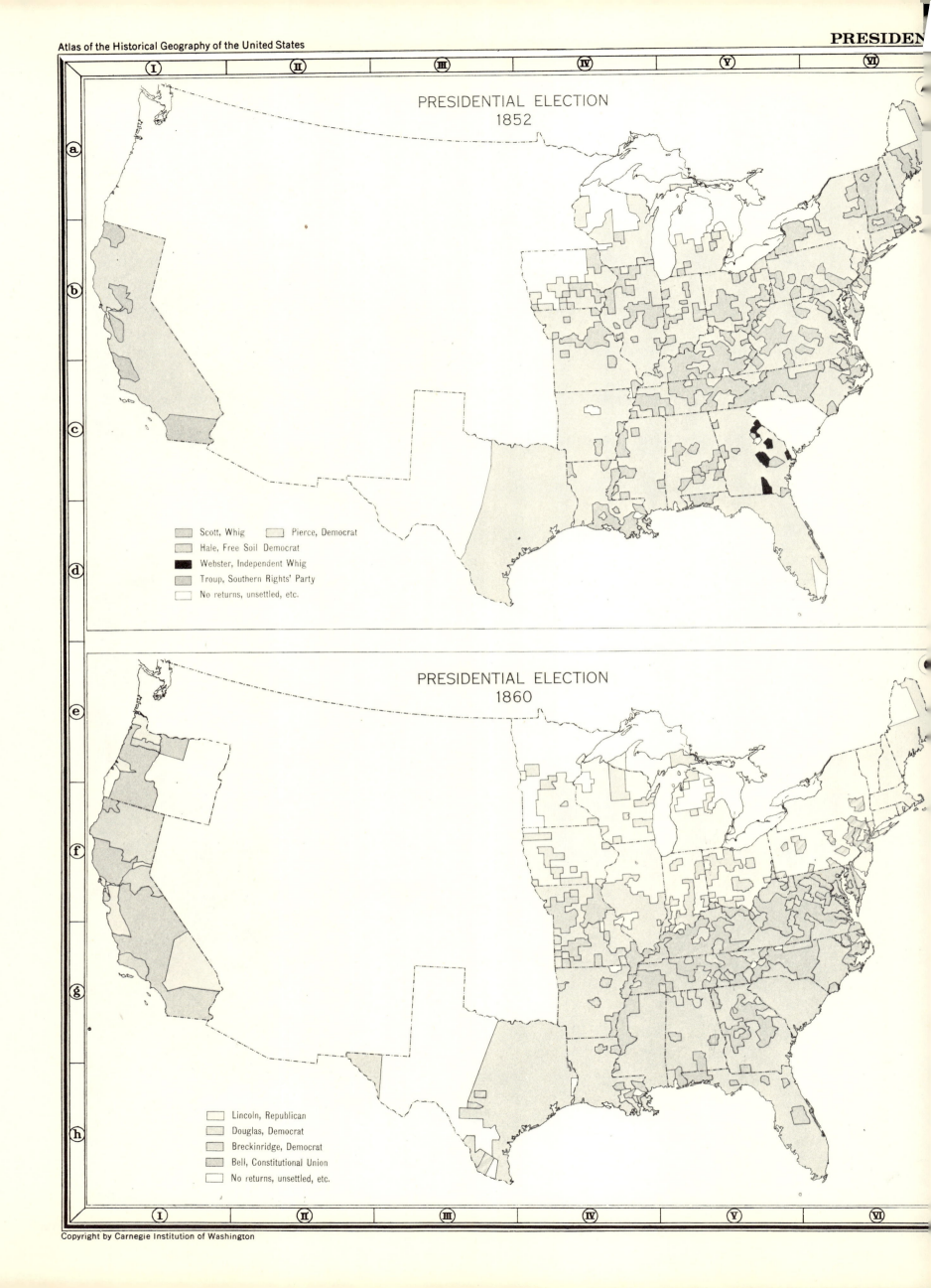

PRESIDENTIAL ELECTION
1852

Scott, Whig   Pierce, Democrat
Hale, Free Soil Democrat
Webster, Independent Whig
Troup, Southern Rights' Party
No returns, unsettled, etc.

PRESIDENTIAL ELECTION
1860

Lincoln, Republican
Douglas, Democrat
Breckinridge, Democrat
Bell, Constitutional Union
No returns, unsettled, etc.

Copyright by Carnegie Institution of Washington

PRESIDENTIAL ELECTION
1856

Fremont, Republican
Buchanan, Democrat
Fillmore, Know Nothing or "American,"
and Whig
No returns, unsettled, etc.

PRESIDENTIAL ELECTION
1864

Lincoln, Republican or "Union"
McClellan, Democrat
Confederate States
Not voting, unsettled, etc.

A. HOEN & CO., INC.,

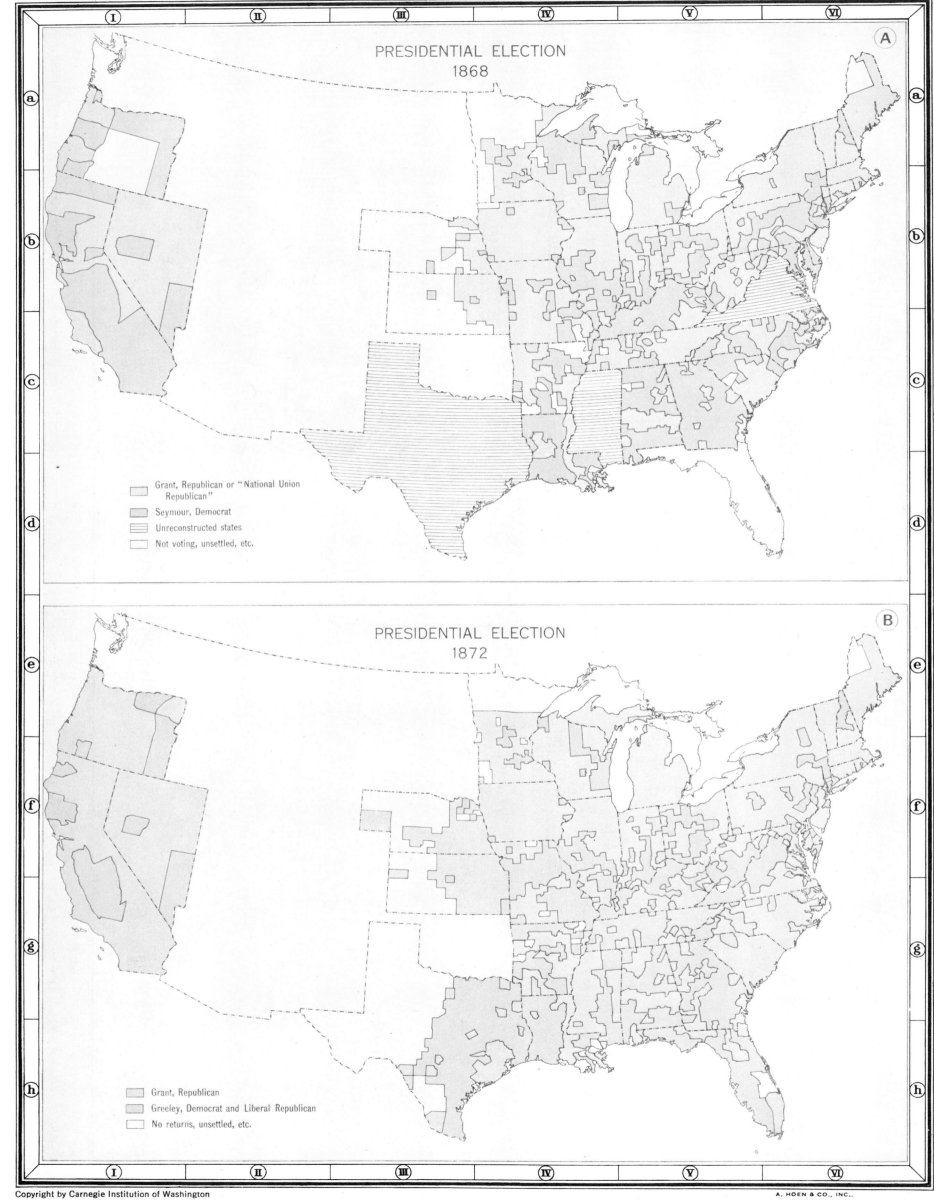

PRESIDENTIAL ELECTION
1868

A

Grant, Republican or "National Union Republican"

Seymour, Democrat

Unreconstructed states

Not voting, unsettled, etc.

PRESIDENTIAL ELECTION
1872

B

Grant, Republican

Greeley, Democrat and Liberal Republican

No returns, unsettled, etc.

Copyright by Carnegie Institution of Washington

A. HOEN & CO., INC.,

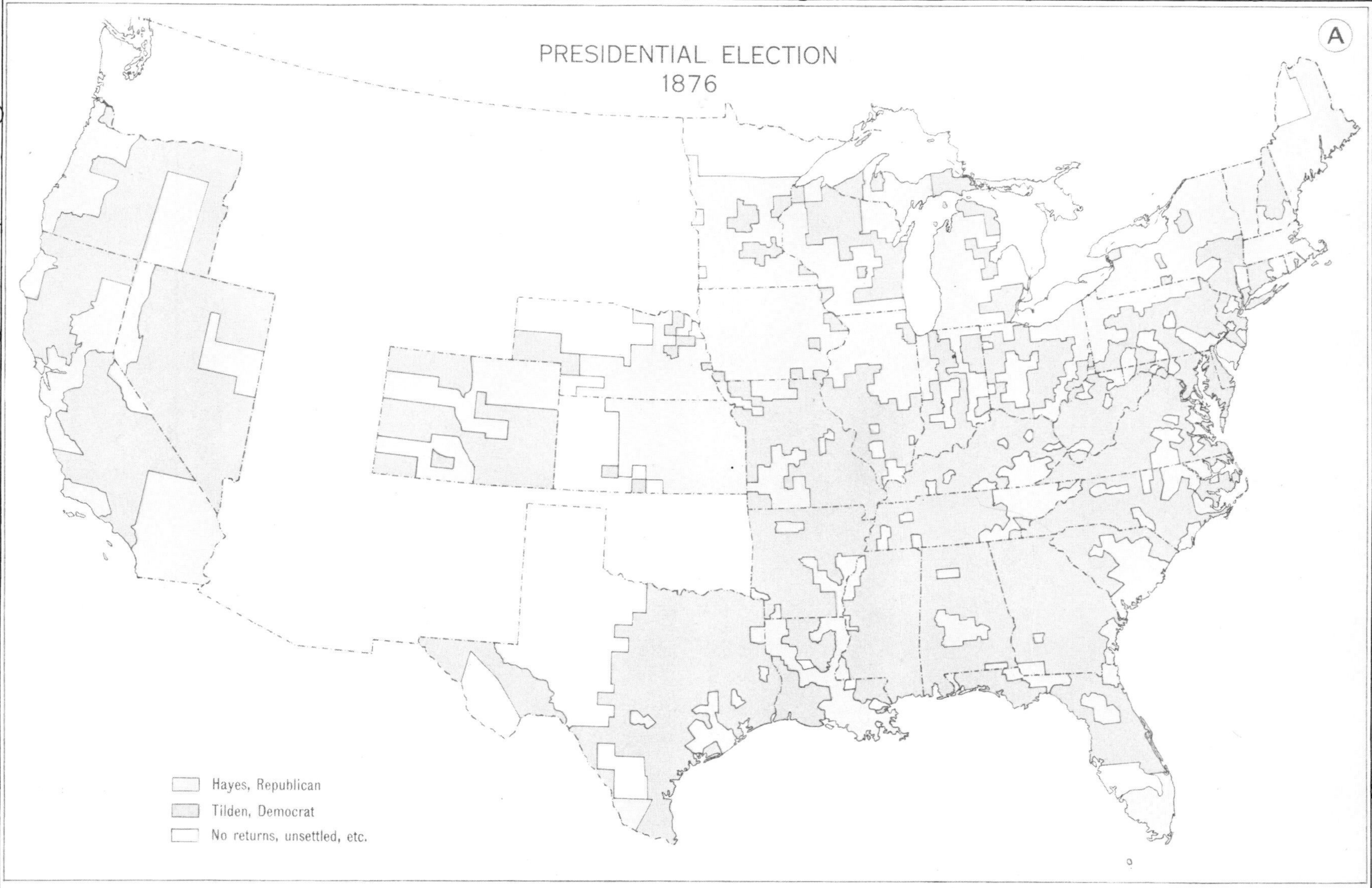
A
PRESIDENTIAL ELECTION
1876
Hayes, Republican
Tilden, Democrat
No returns, unsettled, etc.

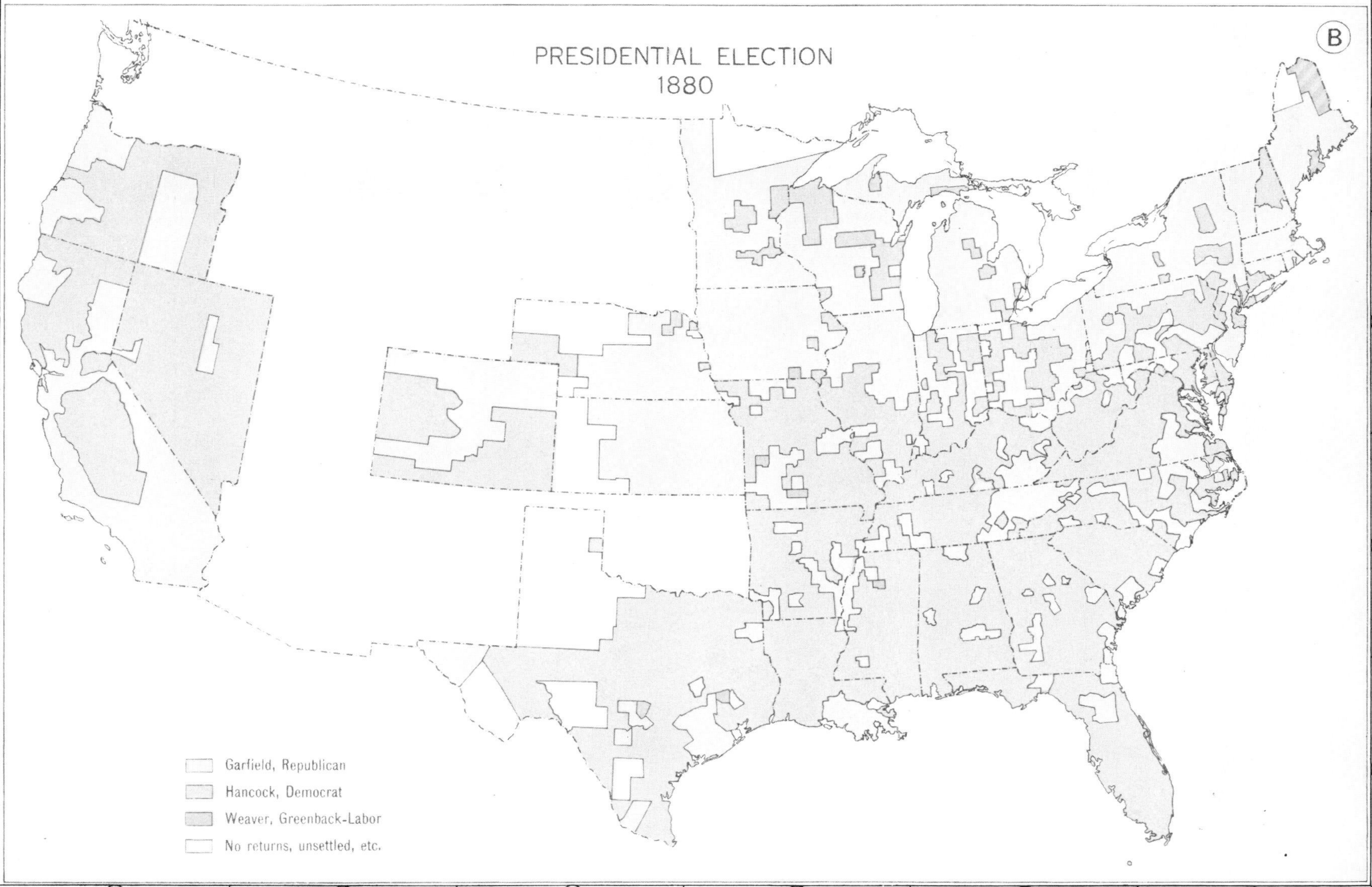
B
PRESIDENTIAL ELECTION
1880
Garfield, Republican
Hancock, Democrat
Weaver, Greenback-Labor
No returns, unsettled, etc.

Copyright by Carnegie Institution of Washington
A. HOEN & CO., INC.

PRESIDENTIAL ELECTION
1884

Blaine, Republican

Cleveland, Democrat

Butler, Greenback-Labor or "National,"
and Anti-Monopolist

No returns, unsettled, etc.

PRESIDENTIAL ELECTION
1892

Harrison, Republican

Cleveland, Democrat

Weaver, Populist

No returns, unsettled, etc.

Copyright by Carnegie Institution of Washington

PRESIDENTIAL ELECTION
1888

Harrison, Republican

Cleveland, Democrat

Streeter, Union Labor

No returns, unsettled, etc.

PRESIDENTIAL ELECTION
1896

McKinley, Republican

Bryan, Democrat, Populist, and
National Silver

No returns, unsettled, etc.

A. HOEN & CO., INC.

PRESIDENTIAL ELECTION
1900

A

McKinley, Republican

Bryan, Democrat, "Fusion Populist,"
and Silver Republican

No returns, unsettled, etc.

PRESIDENTIAL ELECTION
1904

B

Roosevelt, Republican

Parker, Democrat

Watson, Populist

No returns, unsettled, etc.

A

PRESIDENTIAL ELECTION
1908

Taft, Republican

Bryan, Democrat

Watson, Populist

No returns, unsettled, etc.

B

PRESIDENTIAL ELECTION
1912

Taft, Republican

Wilson, Democrat

Roosevelt, Progressive

Debs, Socialist

No returns, unsettled. etc.

Copyright by Carnegie Institution of Washington

A. HOEN & CO., INC.,

PRESIDENTIAL ELECTION
1916

Hughes, Republican
Wilson, Democrat
Hughes and Wilson, Progressive Party
No return, unsettled, etc.

PRESIDENTIAL ELECTION
1924

Coolidge, Republican
Davis, Democrat
La Follette, Progressive
No returns, unsettled, etc.

Copyright by Carnegie Institution of Washington

PRESIDENTIAL ELECTION
1920

Harding, Republican
Cox, Democrat
No returns, unsettled, etc.

PRESIDENTIAL ELECTION
1928

Hoover, Republican
Smith, Democrat
Hoover, anti-Smith Party
No returns, unsettled, etc.

ASSUMPTION OF STATE DEBTS
JULY 26, 1790
Vote on agreeing to Senate Amendment

Yeas   Nays
Not voting   Unsettled, etc.
Votes not shown = (general ticket): N. H., 1 yea;
Pa., 3 yeas; Md., 2 yeas

ACT INCORPORATING U. S. BANK
FEBRUARY 8, 1791
Vote on Passage

Yeas   Nays
Not voting   Unsettled, etc.
Votes not shown = (general ticket): Md., 2 yeas

ALIEN AND SEDITION ACTS
FEBRUARY 25, 1799
Votes on Resolutions for Repeal

Yeas   Nays
Not voting   Unsettled, etc.
Votes not shown = (district): Pa., 1 nay

EMBARGO ACT
DECEMBER 21, 1807
Vote on Passage

Yeas   Nays
Not voting   Unsettled, etc.
Votes not shown = (general ticket): Ga., 1 yea;
(districts): Pa., 2 nays

CONGRESSIONAL MEASURES

Plate 113

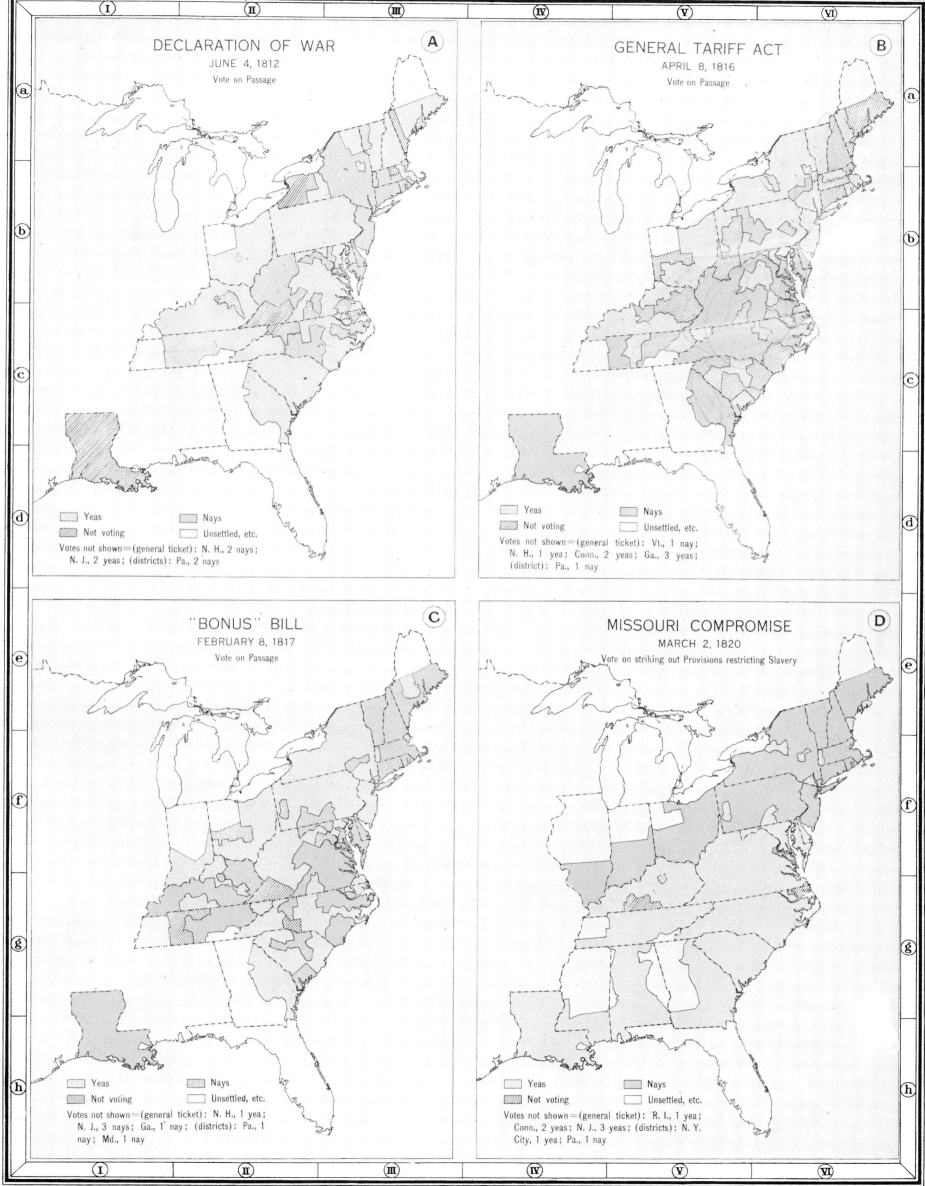

A — DECLARATION OF WAR
JUNE 4, 1812
Vote on Passage

Yeas　　　Nays
Not voting　　　Unsettled, etc.

Votes not shown=(general ticket): N. H., 2 nays;
N. J., 2 yeas; (districts): Pa., 2 nays

B — GENERAL TARIFF ACT
APRIL 8, 1816
Vote on Passage

Yeas　　　Nays
Not voting　　　Unsettled, etc.

Votes not shown=(general ticket): Vt., 1 nay;
N. H., 1 yea; Conn., 2 yeas; Ga., 3 yeas;
(district): Pa., 1 nay

C — "BONUS" BILL
FEBRUARY 8, 1817
Vote on Passage

Yeas　　　Nays
Not voting　　　Unsettled, etc.

Votes not shown=(general ticket): N. H., 1 yea;
N. J., 3 nays; Ga., 1 nay; (districts): Pa., 1
nay; Md., 1 nay

D — MISSOURI COMPROMISE
MARCH 2, 1820
Vote on striking out Provisions restricting Slavery

Yeas　　　Nays
Not voting　　　Unsettled, etc.

Votes not shown=(general ticket): R. I., 1 yea;
Conn., 2 yeas; N. J., 3 yeas; (districts): N. Y.
City, 1 yea; Pa., 1 nay

Copyright by Carnegie Institution of Washington

A. HOEN & CO., INC.

GENERAL TARIFF ACT

APRIL 22, 1828

Vote on Passage

A

Yeas   Nays

Not voting   Unsettled, etc.

Votes not shown = (general ticket): N. H., 2 nays;
R. I., 1 yea; Conn., 2 nays

MAYSVILLE ROAD BILL

APRIL 29, 1830

Vote on Passage

Yeas   Nays

Not voting   Unsettled, etc.

Votes not shown = (districts): N. Y., 1 yea; Pa. 1
yea

PUBLIC LAND ACT

JULY 6, 1841

Vote on Passage

E

Yeas   Nays

Not voting   Unsettled, etc.

ANNEXATION OF TEXAS

JANUARY 25, 1845

Vote on Passage of Joint Resolution

F

Yeas   Nays

Not voting   Unsettled, etc.

Votes not shown = (general ticket): N. H., 2 yeas;
(districts): N. Y. City, 2 yeas

Copyright by Carnegie Institution of Washington

GENERAL TARIFF ACT

JUNE 28, 1832

Vote on Passage

INDEPENDENT TREASURY ACT

JUNE 30, 1840

Vote on Passage

☐ Yeas   ☐ Nays
▨ Not voting   ☐ Unsettled, etc.

Votes not shown = (general ticket): Conn., 2 yeas;
N. J., 3 nays; Ga., 1 yea; (districts): Pa., 1
yea and 2 nays

☐ Yeas   ☐ Nays
▨ Not voting   ☐ Unsettled, etc.

Votes not shown = (general ticket): Ga., 3 yeas;
N. J., 1 nay; (district): Pa. 1 yea

WALKER TARIFF ACT

JULY 3, 1846

Vote on Passage

COMPROMISE OF 1850

SEPTEMBER 6, 1850

Vote on Passage of Texas-New Mexico Provisions

☐ Yeas   ☐ Nays
▨ Not voting   ☐ Unsettled, etc.

Votes not shown = (district): N. Y. City, 1 yea

☐ Yeas   ☐ Nays
▨ Not voting   ☐ Unsettled, etc.

Votes not shown = (district): Pa., 1 nay

CONGRESSIONAL MEASURES

Plate 115

Ⓐ

KANSAS-NEBRASKA ACT
MAY 22, 1854
Vote on Passage

	Yeas		Nays
	Not voting		Unsettled, etc.

Votes not shown = (districts): N. Y. City, 1 nay
Philadelphia, 1 nay

Ⓑ

GENERAL TARIFF ACT
MARCH 2, 1857
Vote on agreeing to Report of Conference Committee

	Yeas		Nays
	Not voting		Unsettled, etc.

Votes not shown = (district): Philadelphia, 1 yea

Copyright by Carnegie Institution of Washington

A. HOEN & CO., INC.

THIRTEENTH AMENDMENT
JANUARY 31, 1865
Vote on Passage of Resolution submitting

Ⓐ

Legend:
- Yeas
- Nays
- Not voting
- Unsettled, etc.
- Confederate States

Votes not shown = (districts): N. Y. City, 1 yea;
Brooklyn, 1 yea; Philadelphia, 1 nay; (at
large): Ill., 1 nay

RECONSTRUCTION ACT
MARCH 2, 1867
Vote on Passage over President's Veto

Ⓑ

Legend:
- Yeas
- Nays
- Not voting
- Unsettled, etc.
- Unreconstructed states

Votes not shown = (districts): N. Y. City, 3 yeas;
Philadelphia, 1 nay; (at large): Ill., 1 yea

Copyright by Carnegie Institution of Washington

A. HOEN & CO., INC.

ENFORCEMENT ACT
APRIL 6, 1871
Vote on Passage

Yeas
Nays
Not voting
Unsettled, etc.
Votes not shown = (district): Philadelphia, 1 nay

SILVER PURCHASE ACT
FEBRUARY 28, 1878
Vote on Passage over President's Veto

Yeas
Nays
Not voting
Unsettled, etc.
Votes not shown = (districts): N. Y. City, 1 yea;
  Philadelphia, 1 yea

Copyright by Carnegie Institution of Washington

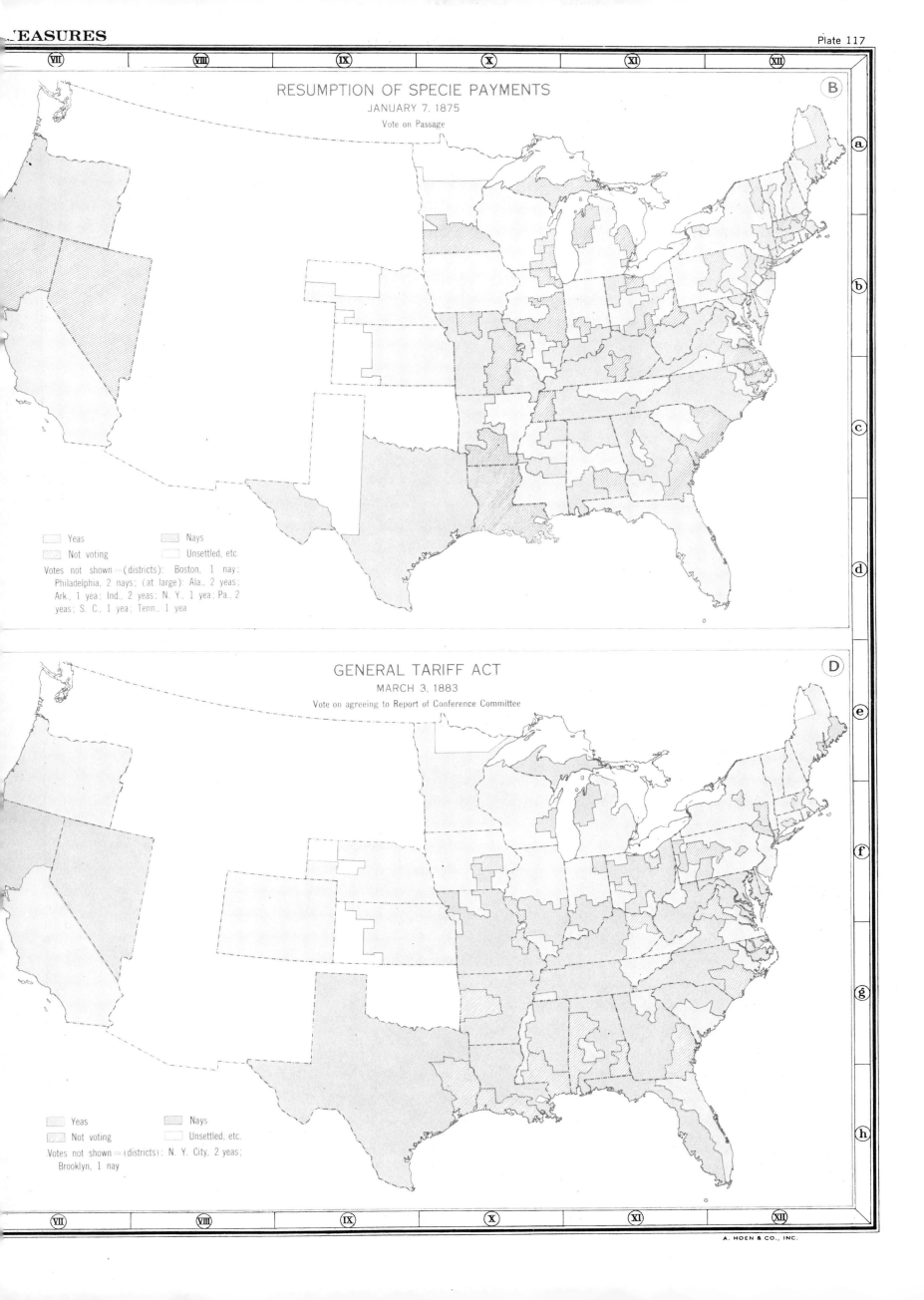

RESUMPTION OF SPECIE PAYMENTS
JANUARY 7, 1875
Vote on Passage

Yeas   Nays

Not voting   Unsettled, etc.

Votes not shown = (districts): Boston, 1 nay;
Philadelphia, 2 nays; (at large): Ala., 2 yeas;
Ark., 1 yea; Ind., 2 yeas; N. Y., 1 yea; Pa., 2
yeas; S. C., 1 yea; Tenn., 1 yea

GENERAL TARIFF ACT
MARCH 3, 1883
Vote on agreeing to Report of Conference Committee

Yeas   Nays

Not voting   Unsettled, etc.

Votes not shown = (districts): N. Y. City, 2 yeas;
Brooklyn, 1 nay

A. HOEN & CO., INC.

Ⓐ

REAGAN INTERSTATE COMMERCE BILL
JANUARY 8, 1885
Vote on Passage

Yeas

Nays

Not voting

Unsettled, etc.

Votes not shown = (districts): N. Y. City, 3 nays;
Philadelphia, 1 yea; Baltimore, 1 nay; (at large)
Ark., 1 yea; Ga., 1 nay; Pa., 1 nay; Va., 1 nay

Ⓑ

BLAND FREE COINAGE BILL
MARCH 24, 1892
Vote on laying Bill on the Table

Yeas

Nays

Not voting

Unsettled, etc.

Votes not shown = (district): St. Louis, 1 yea

Copyright by Carnegie Institution of Washington

A. HOEN & CO., INC.

DINGLEY TARIFF ACT

MARCH 31, 1897

Vote on Passage

(A)

☐ Yeas   ☐ Nays

▨ Not voting   ☐ Unsettled, etc.

Votes not shown = (districts): Boston, 1 nay;
N. Y. City, 4 yeas; Philadelphia, 1 nay; San
Francisco, 1 nay; (at large): Pa., 2 yeas

GOLD STANDARD ACT

DECEMBER 18, 1899

Vote on Passage

(B)

☐ Yeas   ☐ Nays

▨ Not voting   ☐ Unsettled, etc.

Votes not shown = (districts): Brooklyn, 1 nay;
N. Y. City, 2 yeas; Chicago, 3 nays; (at
large) Pa., 1 yea and 1 nay; Kan., 1 yea

Copyright by Carnegie Institution of Washington

A. HOEN & CO., INC.

PAYNE-ALDRICH TARIFF ACT

JULY 31, 1909

Vote on agreeing to Report of Conference Committee

☐ Yeas   ▨ Nays

▨ Not voting   ☐ Unsettled, etc.

Votes not shown = (general ticket): N. Dak., 1 yea;
(districts): Baltimore, 1 yea; Brooklyn, 2 nays;
N. Y. City, 3 yeas; Chicago, 4 nays; St. Louis., 1 nay

UNDERWOOD TARIFF ACT

MAY 8, 1913

Vote on Passage

☐ Yeas   ▨ Nays

▨ Not voting   ☐ Unsettled, etc.

Votes not shown = (districts): N. Y. City, 1 nay;
Brooklyn, 1 nay; Philadelphia, 1 yea; Chicago,
3 nays; St. Louis, 1 yea; San Francisco, 1
yea; (at large—see details in text)

Copyright by Carnegie Institution of Washington

CANADIAN RECIPROCITY ACT
APRIL 21, 1911
Vote on Passage

Ⓑ

Yeas Nays
Not voting Unsettled, etc.
Votes not shown = (district): Philadelphia, 1 nay
(at large): Colo., 1 yea

WAR RESOLUTION
APRIL 5, 1917
Vote on passage

Ⓓ

Yeas Nays
Not voting Unsettled, etc.
Votes not shown = (districts): N. Y. City, 1 nay;
Chicago, 1 nay; St. Louis, 1 nay; (at large):
Illinois, 1 yea and 1 nay; Texas, 1 nay

PROHIBITION RESOLUTION
DECEMBER 17, 1917
Vote on Passage

(A)

Yeas   Nays

Not voting   Unsettled, etc.

Votes not shown=(districts): N. Y. City, 1 yea;
Philadelphia, 2 yeas; (at large): Pa., 4 nays;
Ill., 1 yea; Tex., 1 yea and 1 nay

WOMAN SUFFRAGE RESOLUTION
MAY 21, 1919
Vote on Passage

(B)

Yeas   Nays

Not voting   Unsettled, etc.

Votes not shown=(districts): Boston, 1 yea; N. Y. City, 1 nay;
Philadelphia, 1 nay; Baltimore, 1 yea; Detroit, 1 nay;
(at large): Pa., 1 yea and 1 nay

Copyright by Carnegie Institution of Washington

A. HOEN & CO., INC.

FORDNEY TARIFF ACT

JULY 21, 1921

Vote on Passage

A

Yeas   Nays

Not voting   Unsettled, etc.

Votes not shown = (districts): Boston, 1 yea; N. Y. City,
8 nays; Jersey City, 1 nay; Baltimore, 1 nay;
Cleveland, 1 nay; Chicago, 3 nays; St. Louis, 1 nay

SMOOT-HAWLEY TARIFF ACT

JUNE 14, 1930

Vote on concurring in Conference Reports

B

Yeas   Nays

Not voting   Unsettled, etc.

Votes not shown = (districts): Boston, 1 nay; Buffalo,
1 nay; New York City, 1 yea; Chicago, 3 nays;
St. Louis, 1 nay; San Francisco, 1 nay

Copyright by Carnegie Institution of Washington

A. HOEN & CO., INC.

ABOLITION OF SLAVERY. 1800

1780
1777
1783
1780
1787
1787

Free
Gradual Abolition
Slave
The dates are those on which states or territories became "free"

ABOLITION OF SLAVERY. 1820

1820

Free
Gradual Abolition
Slave
The dates are those on which states or territories became "free"

ABOLITION OF SLAVERY. 1854

Free
Gradual Abolition
Slave
Decision left to territory
The dates are those on which states or territories became "free"

Copyright by Carnegie Institution of Washington

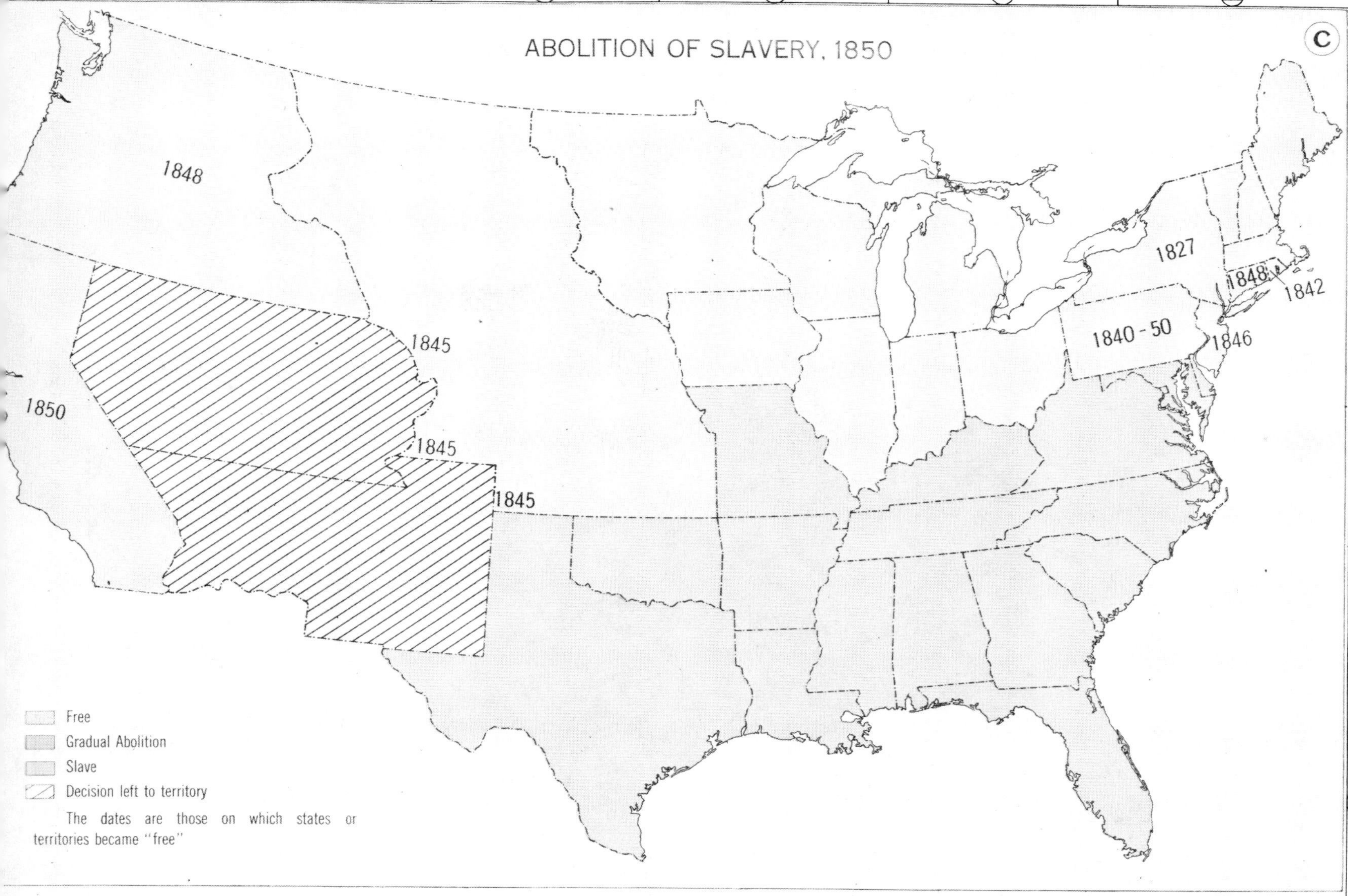

S

Plate 123

VII   VIII   IX   X   XI   XII

ABOLITION OF SLAVERY, 1850

Ⓒ

ⓐ

1848

1827

1848

1842

1840 - 50

1846

1845

ⓑ

1850

1845

ⓒ

1845

ⓓ

Free
Gradual Abolition
Slave
Decision left to territory
The dates are those on which states or
territories became "free"

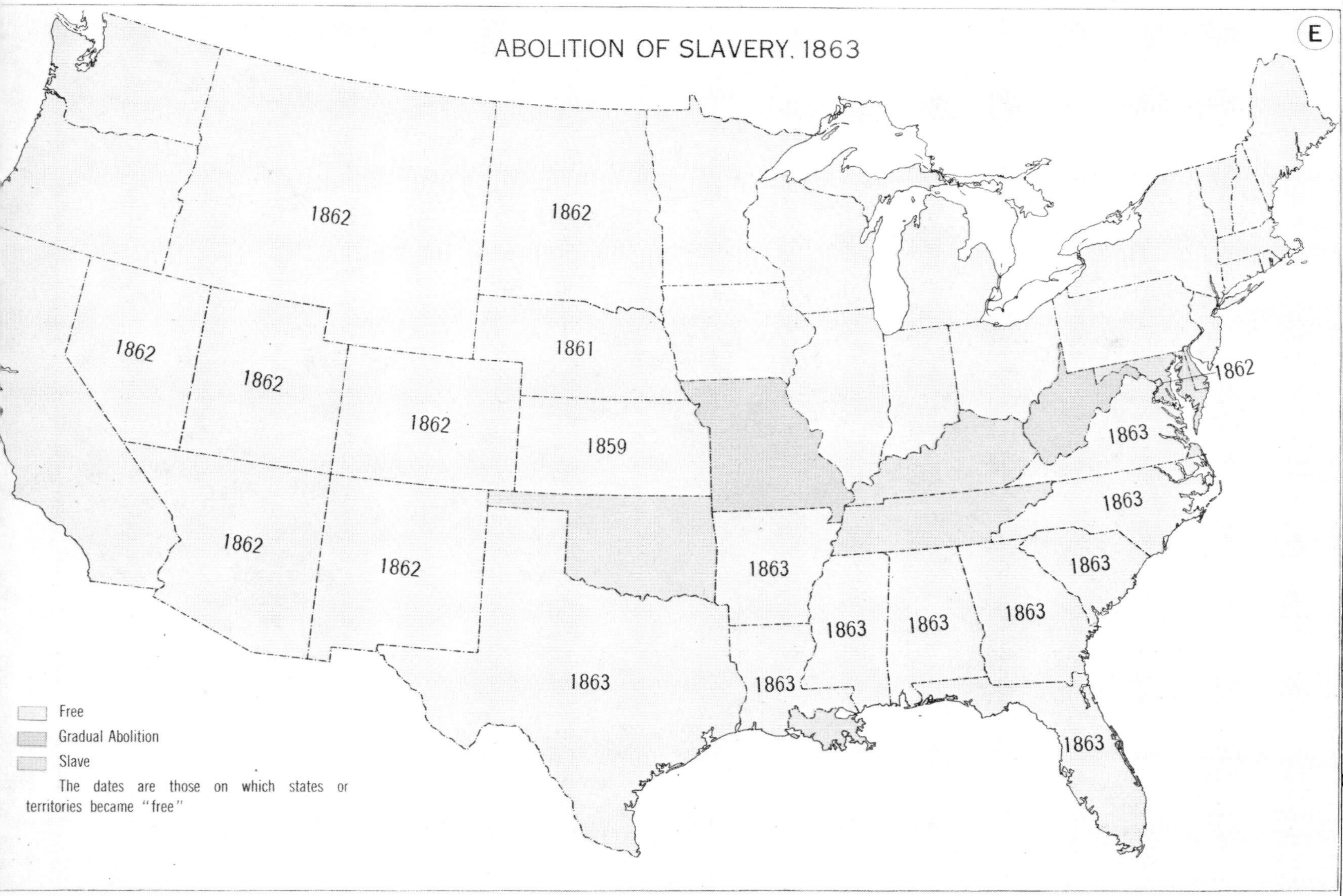

ABOLITION OF SLAVERY, 1863

Ⓔ

ⓔ

1862   1862

1862

1862

1862

1861

1862

1862

1859

1863

1862

ⓕ

1863

1862

ⓖ

1863

1863

1863

1863

1863

1863

1863

1863

1863

1863

ⓗ

Free
Gradual Abolition
Slave
The dates are those on which states or
territories became "free"

VII   VIII   IX   X   XI   XII

A. HOEN & CO., INC.,

REFORMS

Plate 124

A

ABOLITION OF SLAVERY, 1865

1864

1865

1865

1865

1865

1865

1865

1864

1864

1864

Free
Gradual Abolition
Slave

The dates are those on which states or
territories became "free"

B

PROPERTY QUALIFICATIONS
FOR SUFFRAGE, 1775

T

No property qualifications
Property qualifications with an alternative
Property qualifications without an alternative
T = Taxpaying qualifications
The dates are those on which property qual-
ifications were discontinued

C

PROPERTY QUALIFICATIONS
FOR SUFFRAGE, 1800

1784

T

1776
T

1792
T

1776
T

1789
T

T

No property qualifications
Property qualifications with an alternative
Property qualifications without an alternative
T = Taxpaying qualifications
The dates are those on which property qual-
ifications were discontinued

Copyright by Carnegie Institution of Washington

A. HOEN & CO., INC.

PROPERTY QUALIFICATIONS FOR SUFFRAGE, 1830

(A)

1819 T

1821

1821 T

1803 T

1812   1811

1810 T

T

T

1817 T

1819

T

1812 T

T

☐ No property qualifications
▨ Property qualifications with an alternative
▨ Property qualifications without an alternative
T = Taxpaying qualifications
    The dates are those on which property qualifications were discontinued

PROPERTY QUALIFICATIONS FOR SUFFRAGE, 1860

(B)

T

1845

1844

T

1850

1834

T

T

☐ No property qualifications
▨ Property qualifications with an alternative
▨ Property qualifications without an alternative
T = Taxpaying qualifications
    The dates are those on which property qualifications were discontinued

Copyright by Carnegie Institution of Washington   A. HOEN & CO., INC.

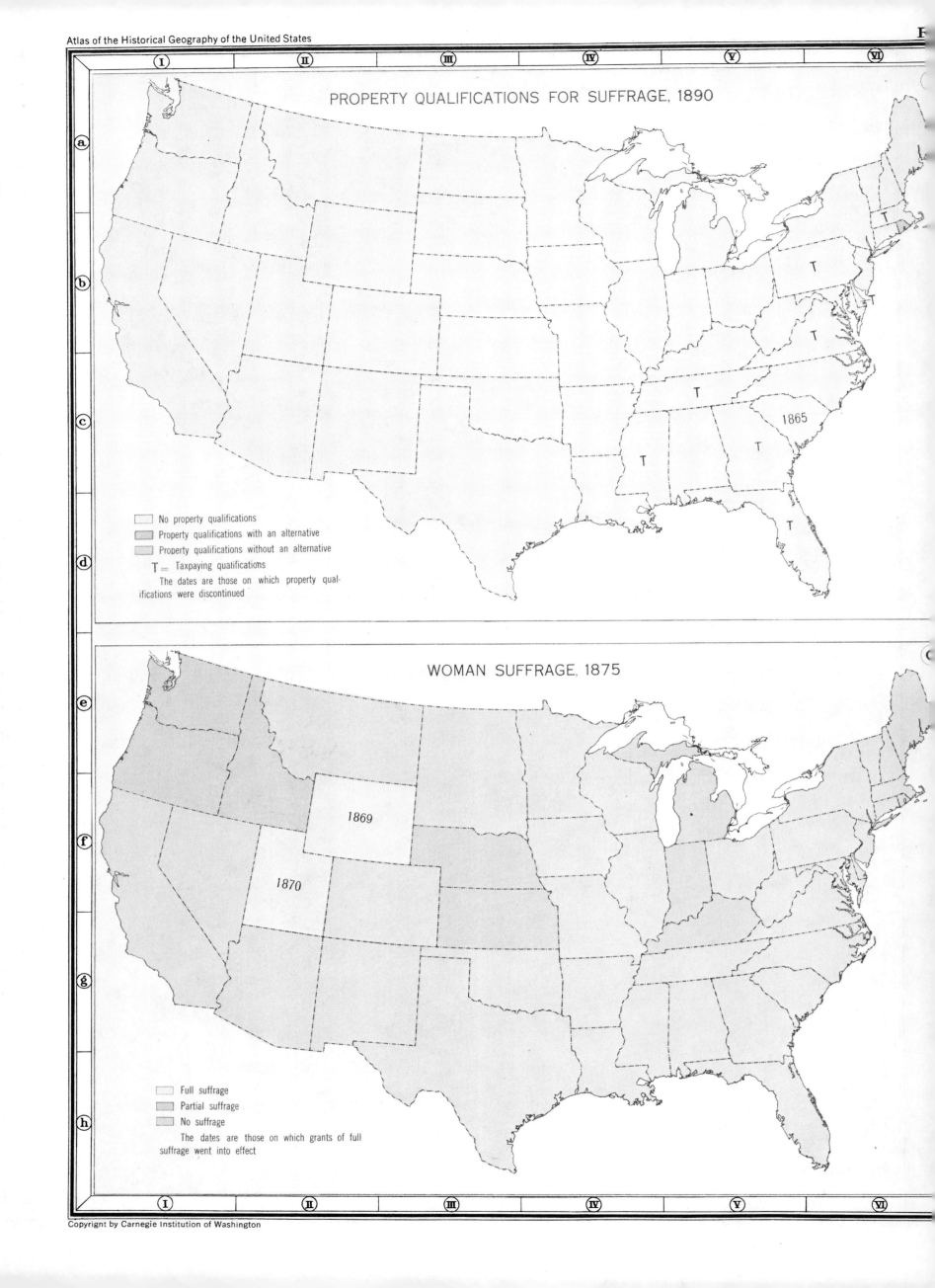

PROPERTY QUALIFICATIONS FOR SUFFRAGE, 1890

1865

No property qualifications
Property qualifications with an alternative
Property qualifications without an alternative
T = Taxpaying qualifications
The dates are those on which property qual-
ifications were discontinued

WOMAN SUFFRAGE, 1875

1869

1870

Full suffrage
Partial suffrage
No suffrage
The dates are those on which grants of full
suffrage went into effect

Copyright by Carnegie Institution of Washington

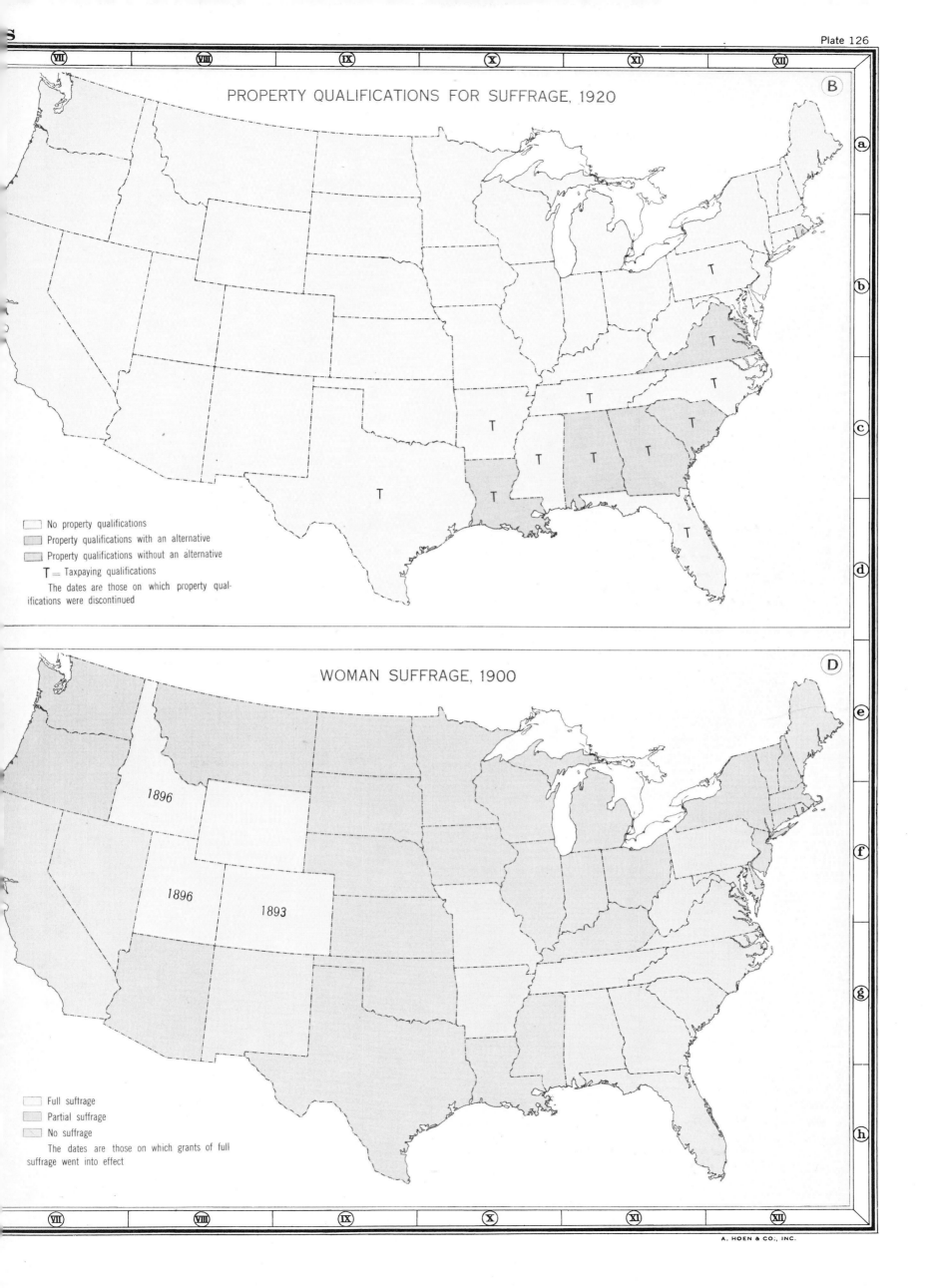

PROPERTY QUALIFICATIONS FOR SUFFRAGE, 1920

No property qualifications
Property qualifications with an alternative
Property qualifications without an alternative
T = Taxpaying qualifications
The dates are those on which property qualifications were discontinued

WOMAN SUFFRAGE, 1900

1896

1896   1893

Full suffrage
Partial suffrage
No suffrage
The dates are those on which grants of full suffrage went into effect

A. HOEN & CO., INC.

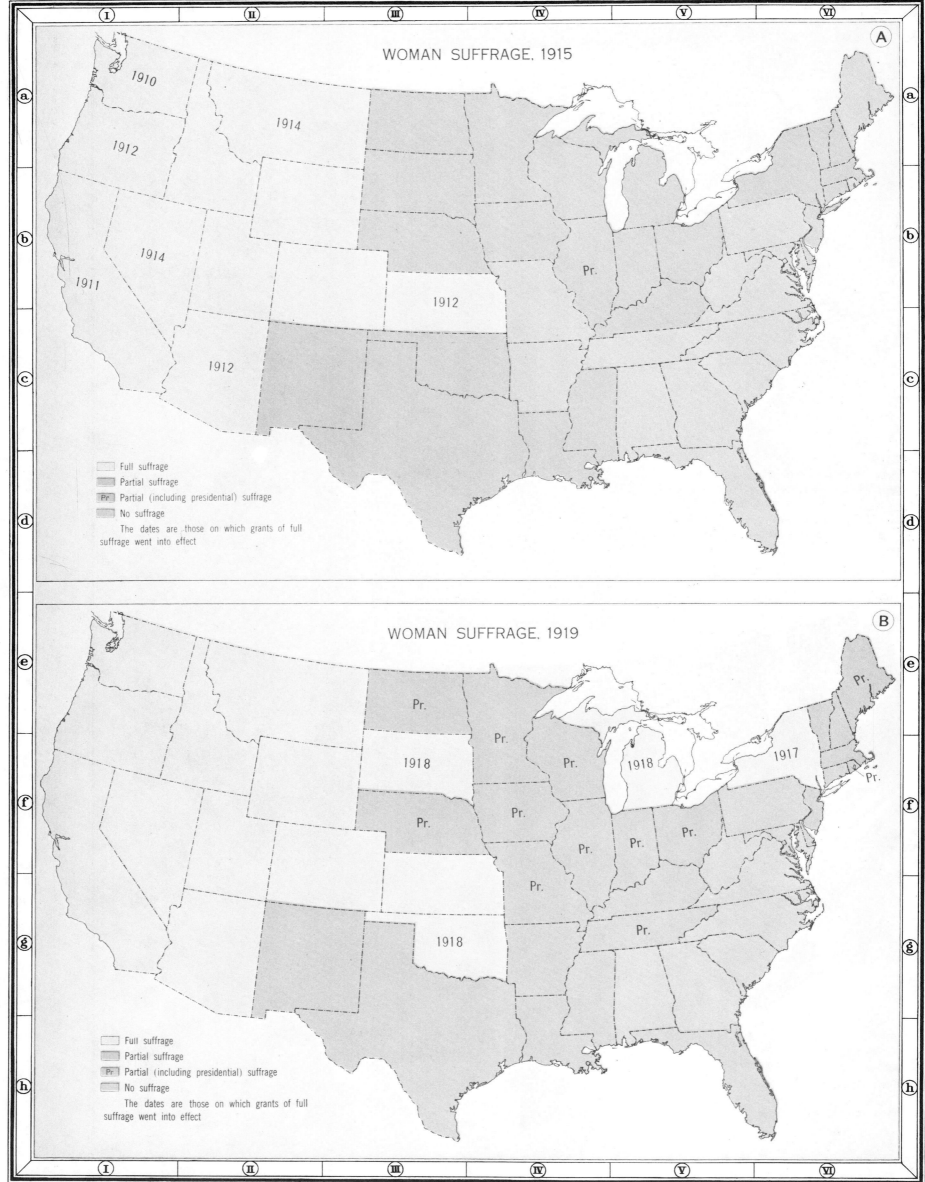

WOMAN SUFFRAGE, 1915

A

1910

1914

1912

1914

1911

1912

1912

Pr.

Full suffrage
Partial suffrage
Pr Partial (including presidential) suffrage
No suffrage

The dates are those on which grants of full
suffrage went into effect

WOMAN SUFFRAGE, 1919

B

Pr.

Pr.

1918

Pr.

1918

1917

Pr.

Pr.

Pr.

Pr.

Pr.

Pr.

Pr.

Pr.

Pr.

1918

Pr.

Full suffrage
Partial suffrage
Pr Partial (including presidential) suffrage
No suffrage

The dates are those on which grants of full
suffrage went into effect

A. HOEN & CO., INC.

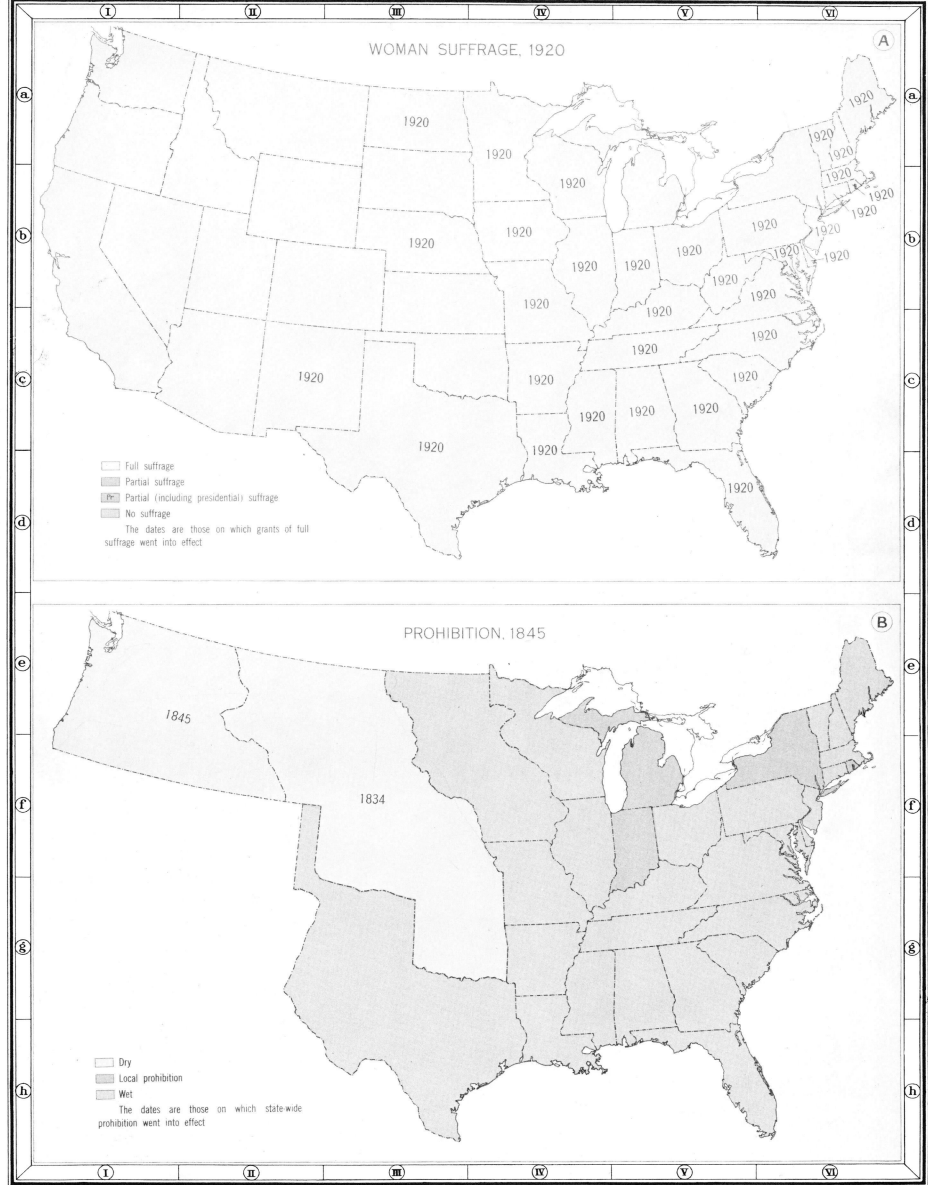

WOMAN SUFFRAGE, 1920

A

Full suffrage

Partial suffrage

Pr Partial (including presidential) suffrage

No suffrage

The dates are those on which grants of full
suffrage went into effect

PROHIBITION, 1845

B

Dry

Local prohibition

Wet

The dates are those on which state-wide
prohibition went into effect

Copyright by Carnegie Institution of Washington

A. HOEN & CO., INC.

PROHIBITION, 1855

1851
1852
1855
1855
1852
1854
1855
1855
1855
1855

Dry
Local prohibition
Wet
The dates are those on which state-wide prohibition went into effect

PROHIBITION, 1890

1889
1889
1884
1881

Dry
Local prohibition
Wet
The dates are those on which state-wide prohibition went into effect

Copyright by Carnegie Institution of Washington

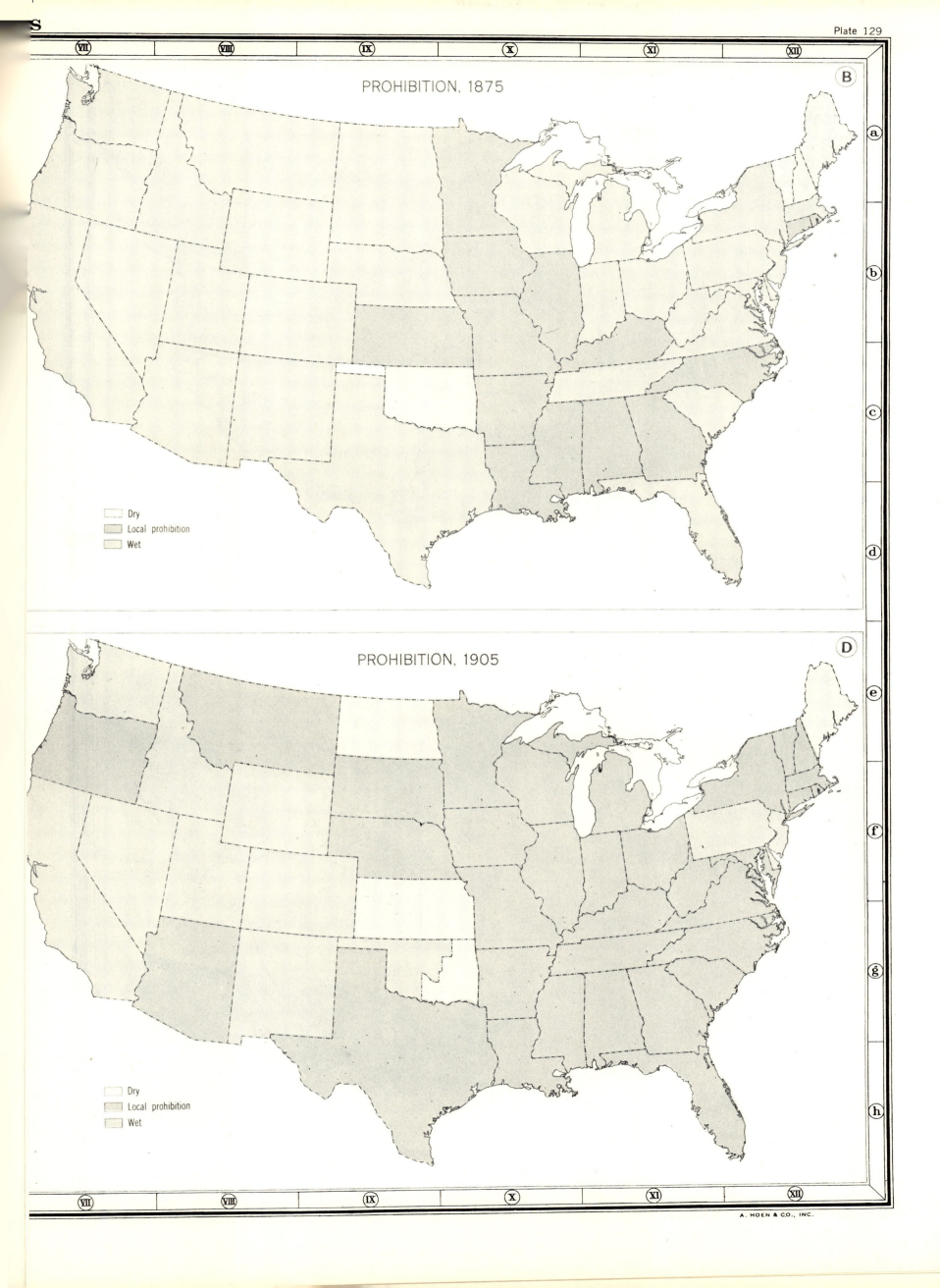

PROHIBITION, 1875

Dry
Local prohibition
Wet

PROHIBITION, 1905

Dry
Local prohibition
Wet

MANU

IRON WORKS, 1620-1675 (A)

IRON AND STEEL WORKS 1725-1775 (B)

- • = 1 to 5 works
- • = 6 to 10
- ● = 11 to 25
- ● = 26 to 50
- ● = 51 to 100
- ● = 100 to 200

IRON AND STEEL WORKS 1810 (C)

- • = 1 to 5 works
- • = 6 to 10
- ● = 11 to 25
- ● = 26 to 50
- ● = 51 to 100
- ● = 100 to 200

IRON AND STEEL WORKS, 1878 (E)

- • = 1 to 5 works
- • = 6 to 10
- ● = 11 to 25
- ● = 26 to 50
- ● = 51 to 100
- ● = 100 to 200

Copyright by Carnegie Institution of Washington

IRON AND STEEL WORKS, 1858

⬤ = 1 to 5 works
● = 6 to 10
● = 11 to 25
● = 26 to 50
● = 51 to 100
⬤ = 100 to 200

IRON AND STEEL WORKS, 1908

⬤ = 1 to 5 works
● = 6 to 10
● = 11 to 25
● = 26 to 50
● = 51 to 100
⬤ = 100 to 200

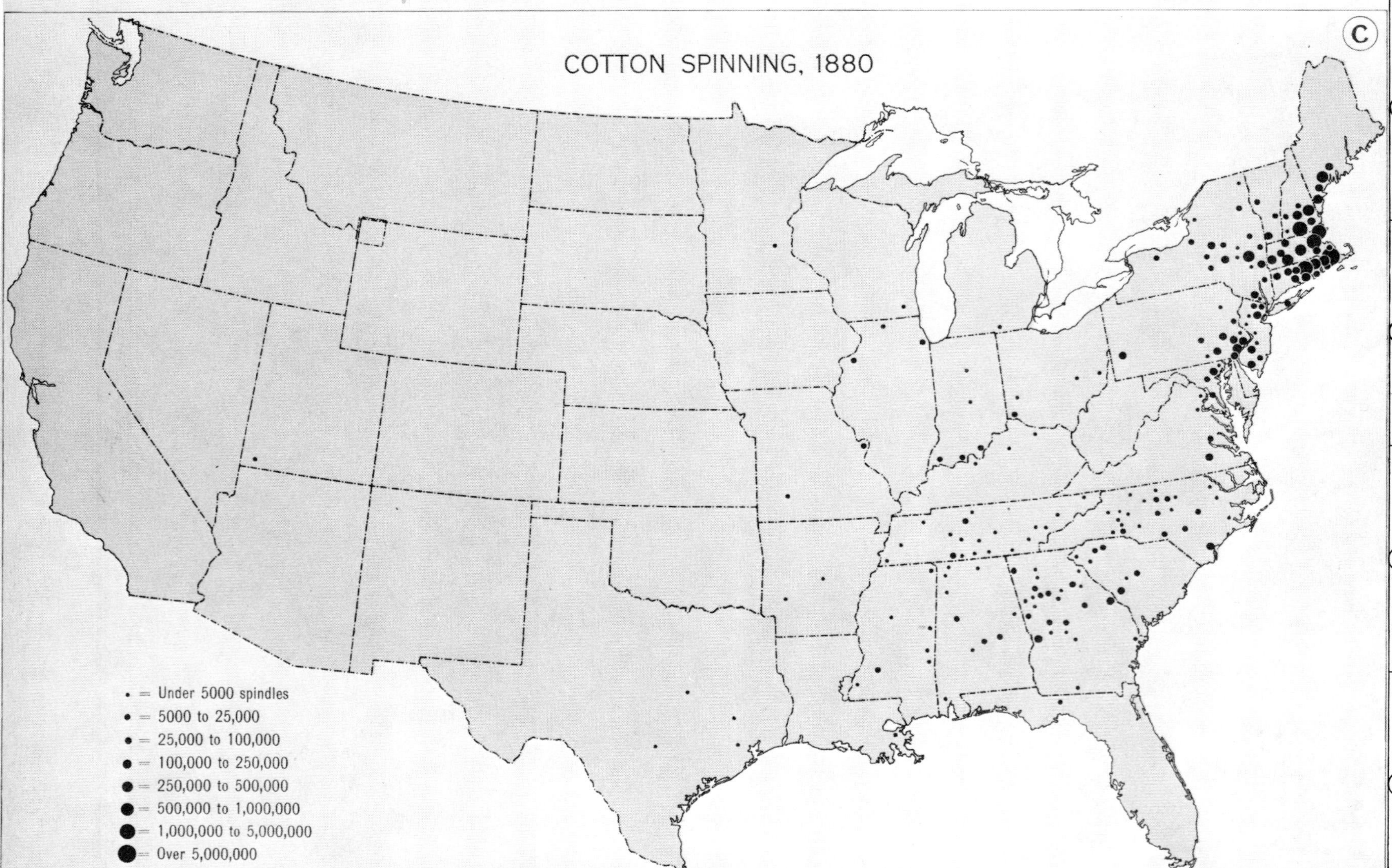

MANUFACTURING

Plate 136

A — COTTON SPINNING, 1810

Legend:
- = Under 5000 spindles
- = 5000 to 25,000
- = 25,000 to 100,000
- = 100,000 to 250,000
- = 250,000 to 500,000
- = 500,000 to 1,000,000
- = 1,000,000 to 5,000,000
- = Over 5,000,000

B — COTTON SPINNING, 1840

Legend:
- = Under 5000 spindles
- = 5000 to 25,000
- = 25,000 to 100,000
- = 100,000 to 250,000
- = 250,000 to 500,000
- = 500,000 to 1,000,000
- = 1,000,000 to 5,000,000
- = Over 5,000,000

C — COTTON SPINNING, 1880

Legend:
- = Under 5000 spindles
- = 5000 to 25,000
- = 25,000 to 100,000
- = 100,000 to 250,000
- = 250,000 to 500,000
- = 500,000 to 1,000,000
- = 1,000,000 to 5,000,000
- = Over 5,000,000

Copyright by Carnegie Institution of Washington

A. HOEN & CO., INC.

COTTON SPINNING, 1926

- = Under 5000 spindles
- = 5000 to 25,000
- = 25,000 to 100,000
- = 100,000 to 250,000
- = 250,000 to 500,000
- = 500,000 to 1,000,000
- = 1,000,000 to 5,000,000
- = Over 5,000,000

MANUFACTURE OF MOTOR VEHICLES, 1909
(INCLUDING BODIES AND PARTS)

Total wage earners in all states marked □ ●

Areas of discs indicate number of wage earners

200,000		
100,000	●	1,000
50,000	●	500
10,000	×	less than 500
5,000	□	Some manufacturing; no statistics by states

MANUFACTURE OF MOTOR VEHICLES, 1927
(INCLUDING BODIES AND PARTS)

Total wage earners in all states marked □ ●

TRACTORS ON FARMS
INCREASE IN NUMBER, JAN. 1, 1920—JAN. 1, 1925

UNITED STATES NET INCREASE 260,000 OR 105.6 PER CENT

Each dot represents 50 tractors

HORSES AND MULES, TWO YEARS OLD AND OVER
DECREASE IN NUMBER, JAN. 1, 1920—JAN. 1, 1925

UNITED STATES NET DECREASE 1,254,000 OR 6 PER CENT

Each dot represents 250 head on farms

Copyright by Carnegie Institution of Washington

A. HOEN & CO., INC

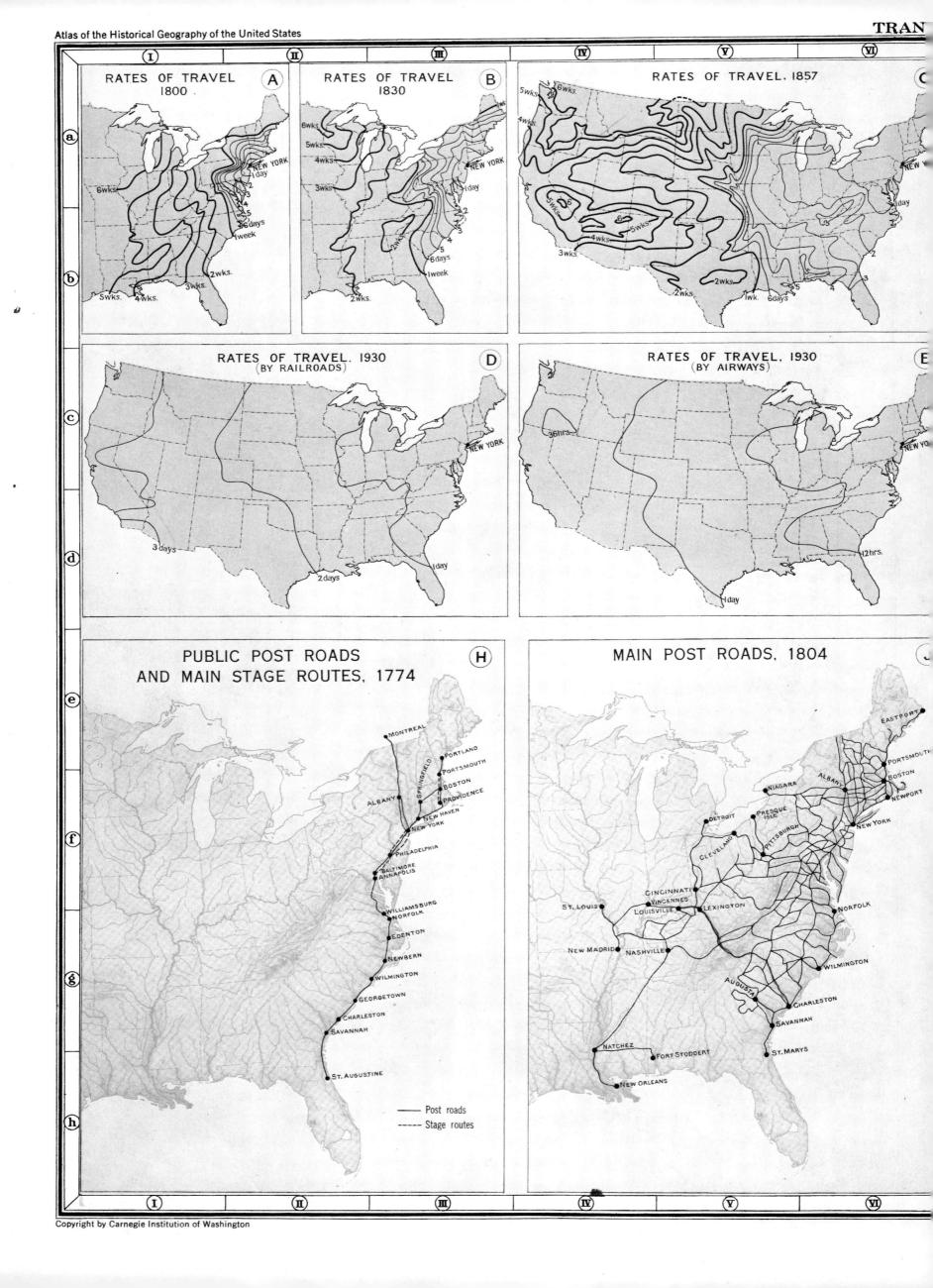

RATES OF TRAVEL 1800

RATES OF TRAVEL 1830

RATES OF TRAVEL, 1857

RATES OF TRAVEL, 1930
(BY RAILROADS)

RATES OF TRAVEL, 1930
(BY AIRWAYS)

PUBLIC POST ROADS
AND MAIN STAGE ROUTES, 1774

Post roads
Stage routes

MAIN POST ROADS, 1804

Copyright by Carnegie Institution of Washington

Plate 138

NAVIGABLE RIVERS, 1930

F

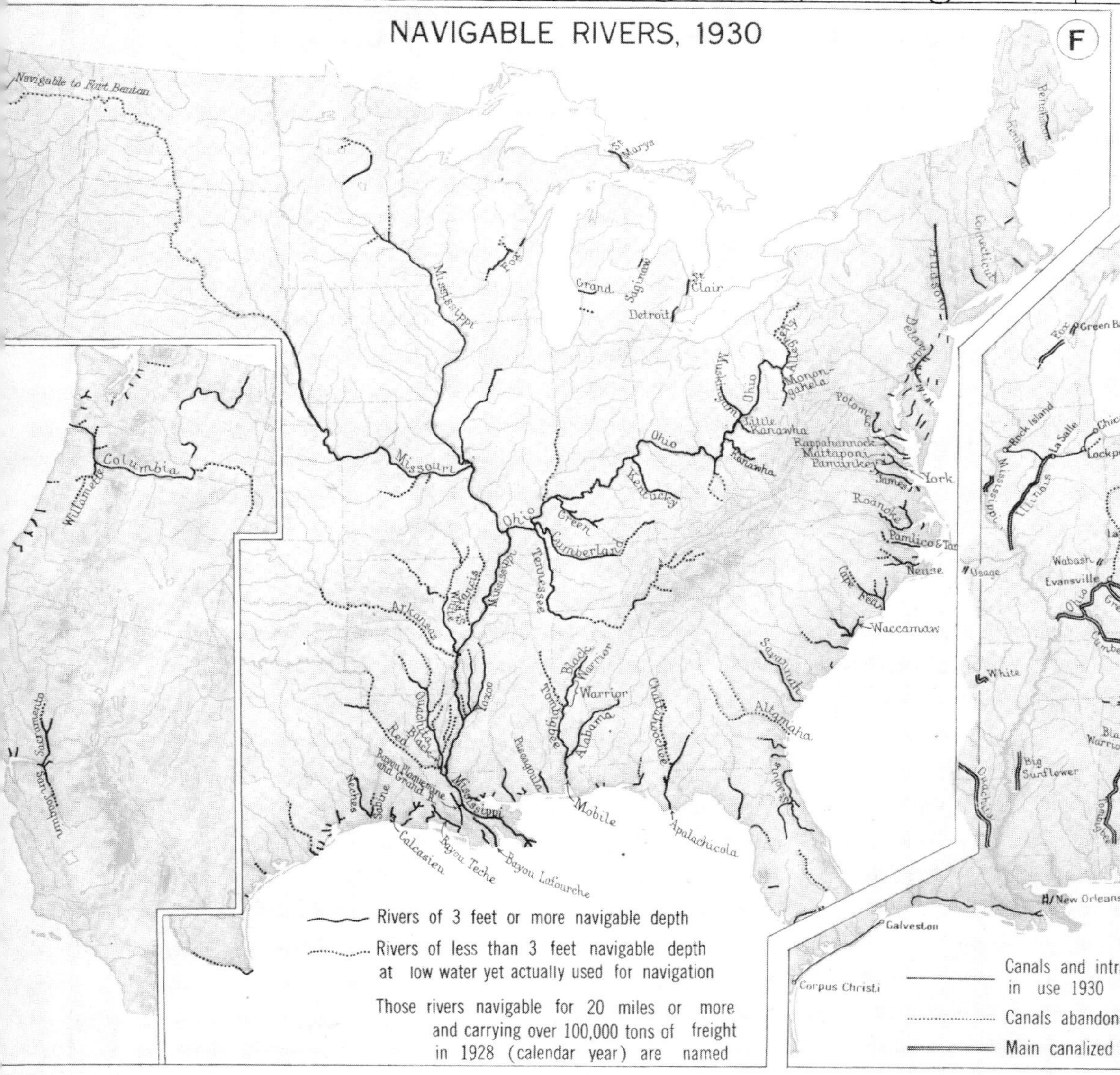

CANALS AND CANALIZED RIVERS 1930

G

Rivers of 3 feet or more navigable depth

Rivers of less than 3 feet navigable depth at low water yet actually used for navigation

Those rivers navigable for 20 miles or more and carrying over 100,000 tons of freight in 1928 (calendar year) are named

Canals and intracoastal waterways in use 1930

Canals abandoned before 1930

Main canalized rivers 1930

MAIN POST ROADS, 1834

K

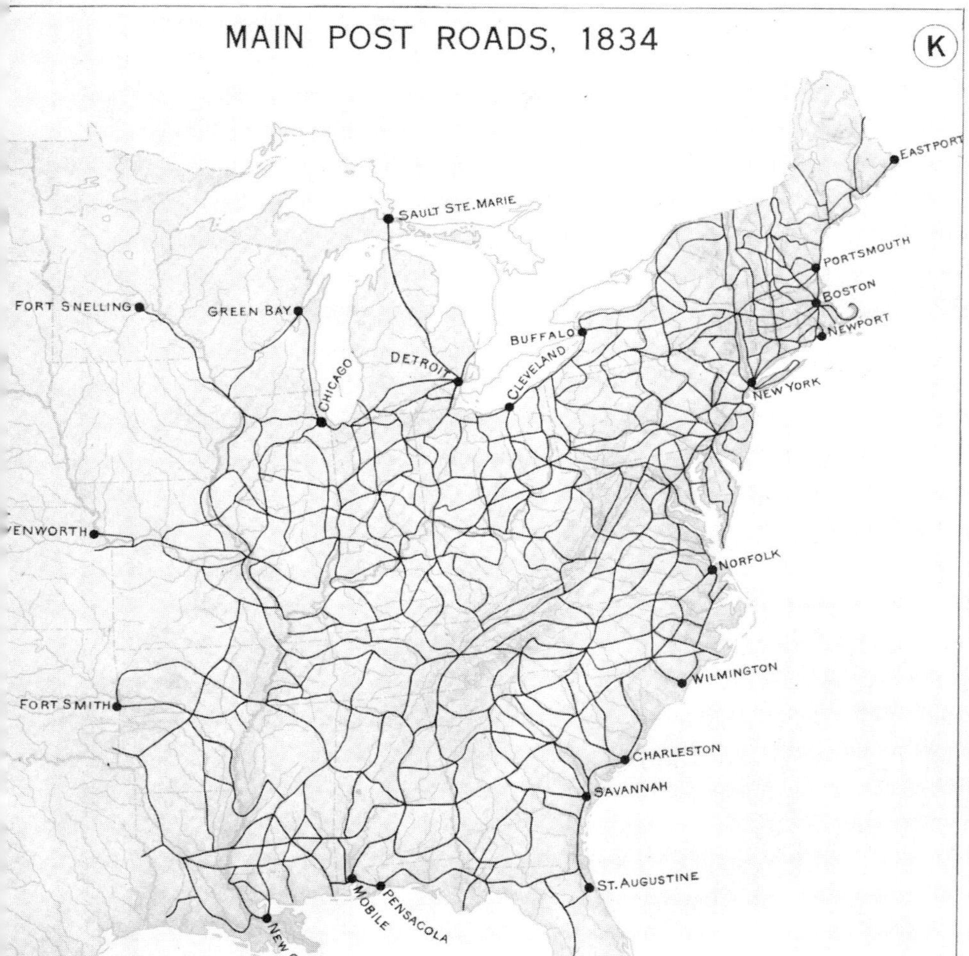

RAILROADS IN OPERATION, DECEMBER, 1840

L

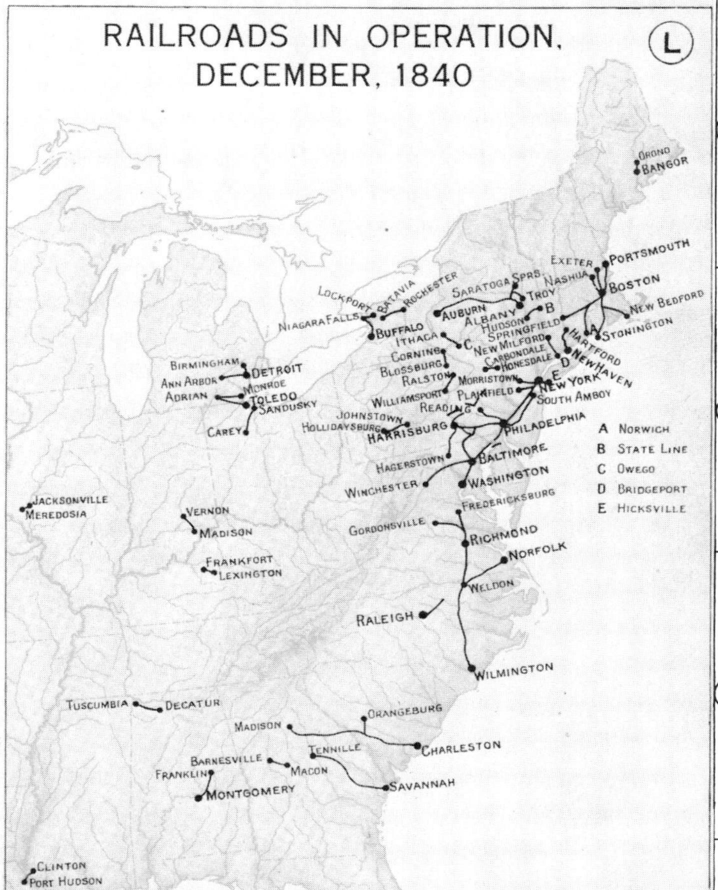

A Norwich
B State Line
C Owego
D Bridgeport
E Hicksville

A. HOEN & CO., INC.,

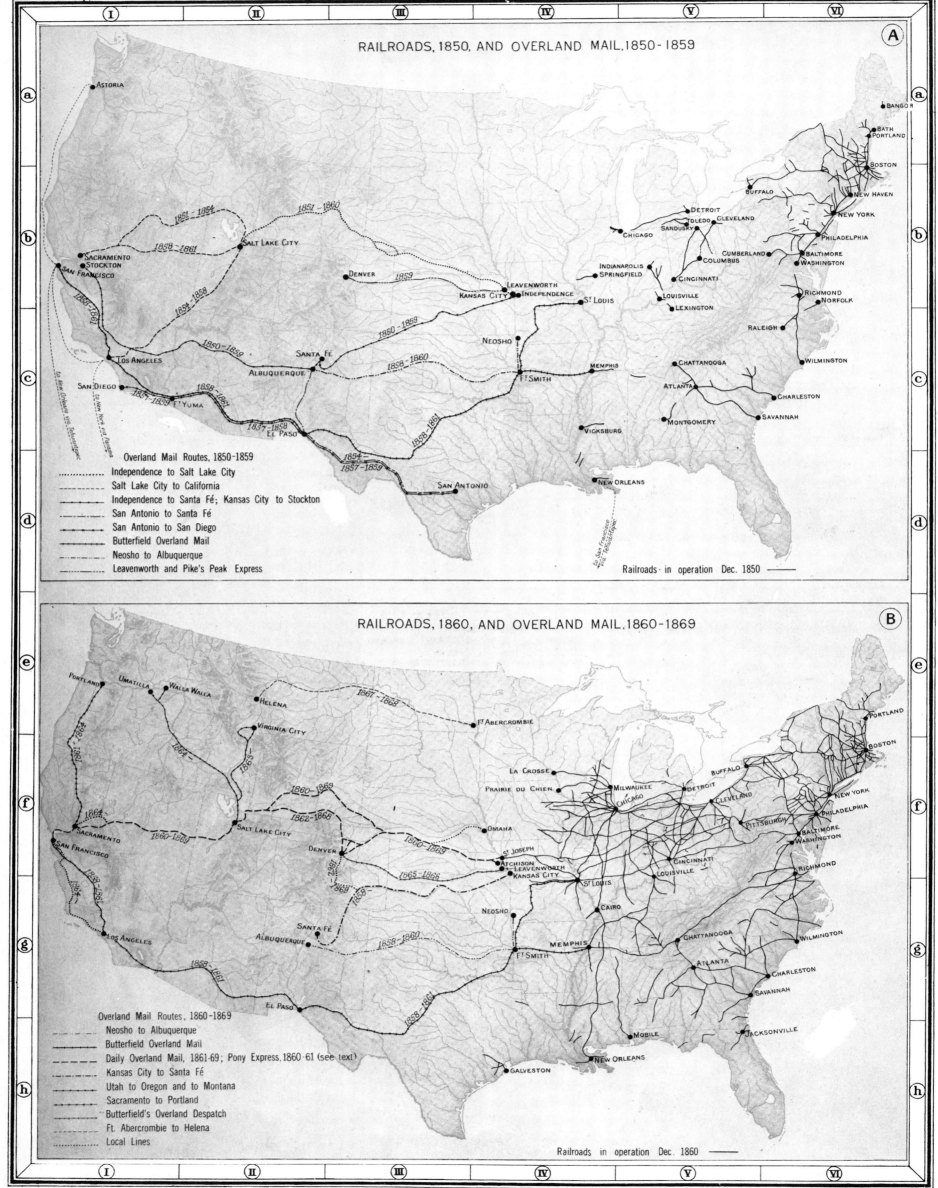

RAILROADS, 1850, AND OVERLAND MAIL, 1850-1859

Overland Mail Routes, 1850-1859
.... Independence to Salt Lake City
- - - - - Salt Lake City to California
━━━━━ Independence to Santa Fé; Kansas City to Stockton
━━━━━ San Antonio to Santa Fé
━━━━━ San Antonio to San Diego
━━━━━ Butterfield Overland Mail
━━━━━ Neosho to Albuquerque
━━━━━ Leavenworth and Pike's Peak Express

Railroads in operation Dec. 1850 ━━━━

RAILROADS, 1860, AND OVERLAND MAIL, 1860-1869

Overland Mail Routes, 1860-1869
.... Neosho to Albuquerque
━━━━━ Butterfield Overland Mail
- - - - - Daily Overland Mail, 1861-69; Pony Express, 1860-61 (see text)
━━━━━ Kansas City to Santa Fé
━━━━━ Utah to Oregon and to Montana
━━━━━ Sacramento to Portland
━━━━━ Butterfield's Overland Despatch
━━━━━ Ft. Abercrombie to Helena
.... Local Lines

Railroads in operation Dec. 1860 ━━━━

TRANSPORTATION

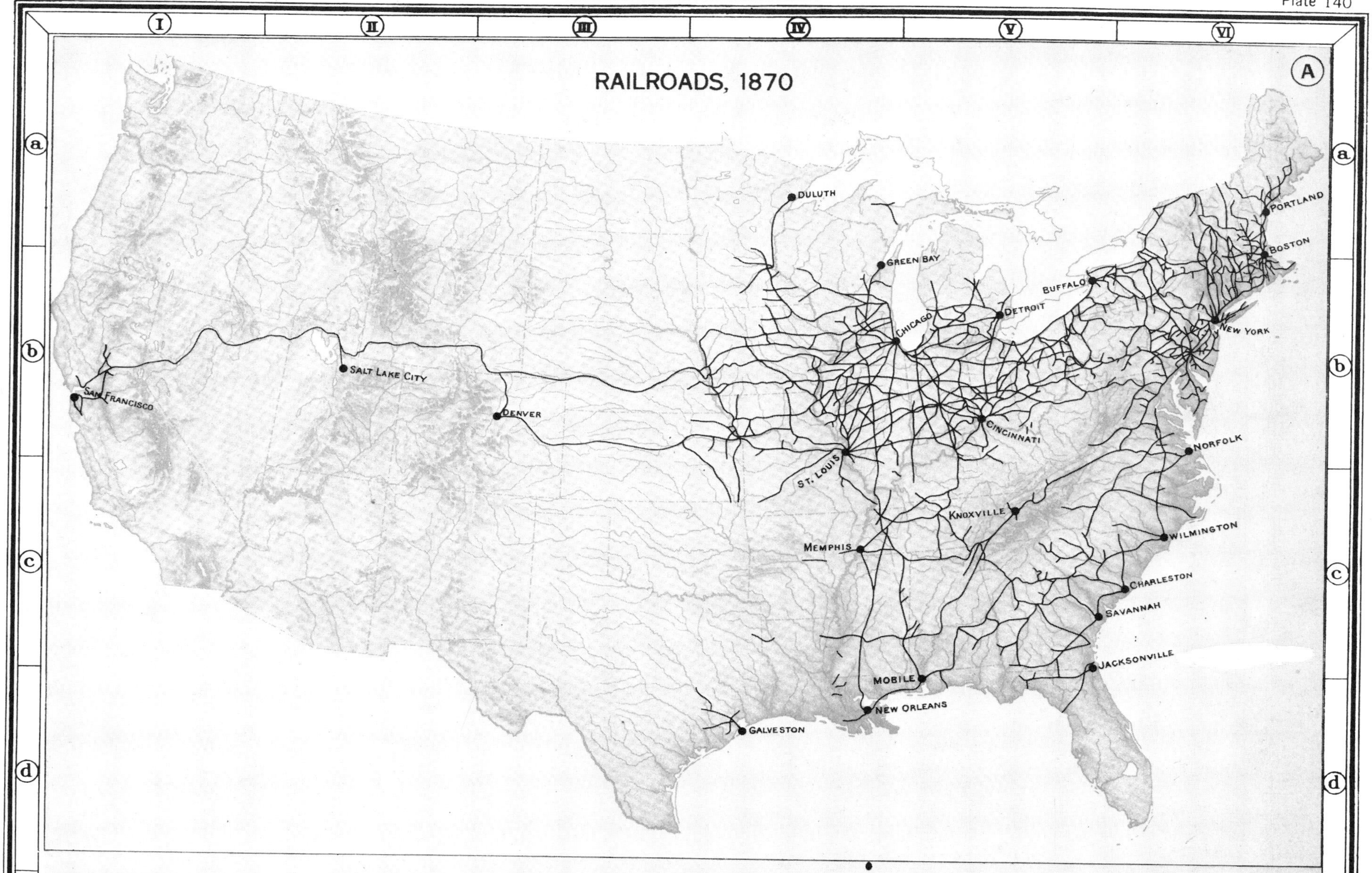

Plate 140

RAILROADS, 1870

A

DULUTH
PORTLAND
BOSTON
GREEN BAY
BUFFALO
DETROIT
CHICAGO
NEW YORK
SALT LAKE CITY
SAN FRANCISCO
DENVER
CINCINNATI
ST. LOUIS
NORFOLK
KNOXVILLE
WILMINGTON
MEMPHIS
CHARLESTON
SAVANNAH
JACKSONVILLE
MOBILE
NEW ORLEANS
GALVESTON

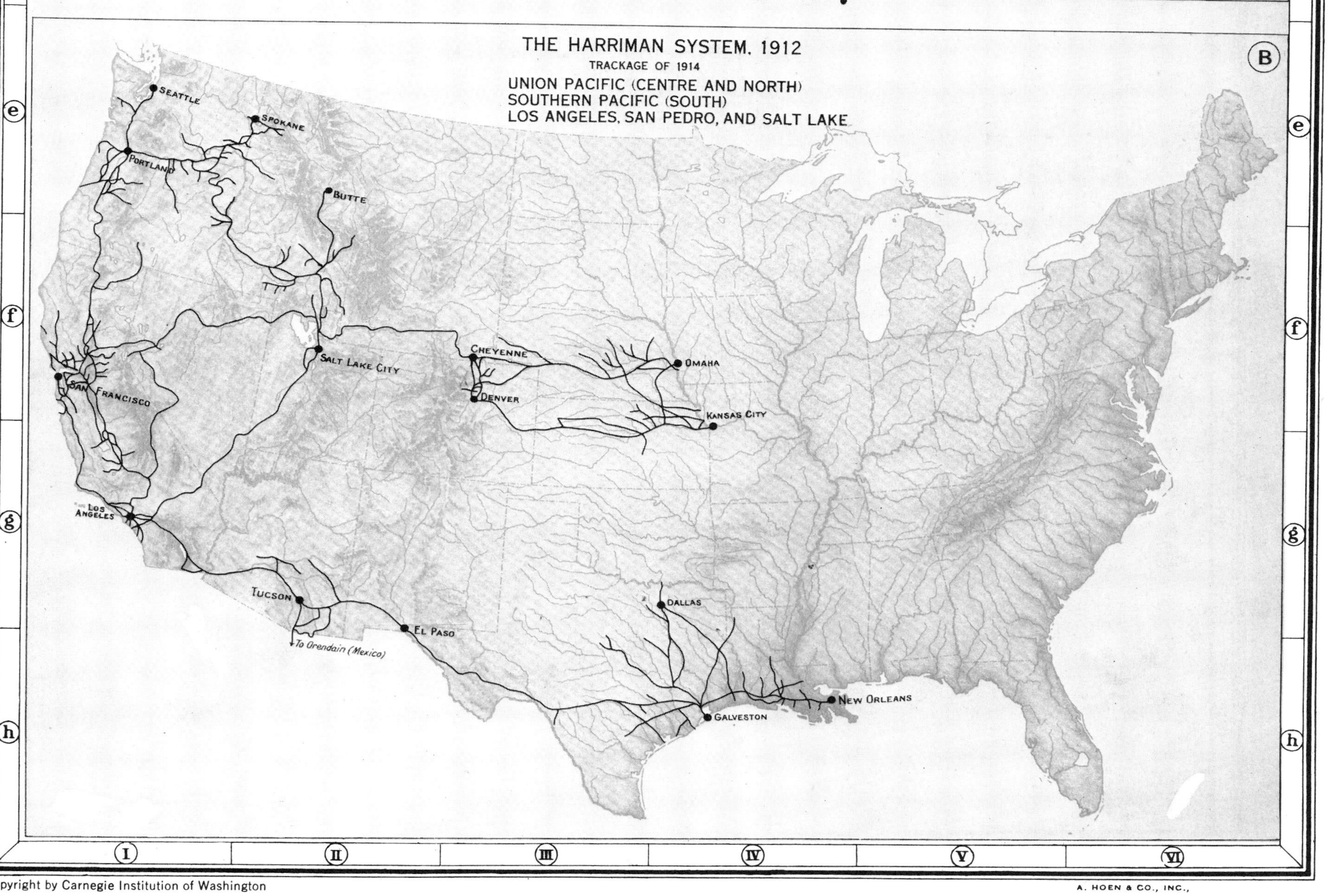

THE HARRIMAN SYSTEM. 1912

TRACKAGE OF 1914

UNION PACIFIC (CENTRE AND NORTH)
SOUTHERN PACIFIC (SOUTH)
LOS ANGELES, SAN PEDRO, AND SALT LAKE

B

SEATTLE
SPOKANE
PORTLAND
BUTTE
SALT LAKE CITY
CHEYENNE
OMAHA
SAN FRANCISCO
DENVER
KANSAS CITY
LOS ANGELES
TUCSON
EL PASO
To Orandain (Mexico)
DALLAS
NEW ORLEANS
GALVESTON

Copyright by Carnegie Institution of Washington

A. HOEN & CO., INC.,

AGRICULTURAL REGIONS
1924

A

COLUMBIA PLATEAU WHEAT REGION

SPRING WHEAT REGION

GRAZING AND IRRIGATED CROPS REGION

HARD WINTER WHEAT REGION

CORN BELT

CORN AND WINTER WHEAT BELT

COTTON BELT

HUMID SUBTROPICAL CROP BELT

HAY AND DAIRY REGION

COTTON PRODUCTION, 1839   **B**
Each dot represents 4000 bales

COTTON PRODUCTION, 1859   **C**
Each dot represents 4000 bales

COTTON PRODUCTION, 1889   **D**
Each dot represents 4000 bales

COTTON PRODUCTION, 1919   **E**
Each dot represents 4000 bales

COTTON PRODUCTION, 1924   **F**
Each dot represents 2000 bales

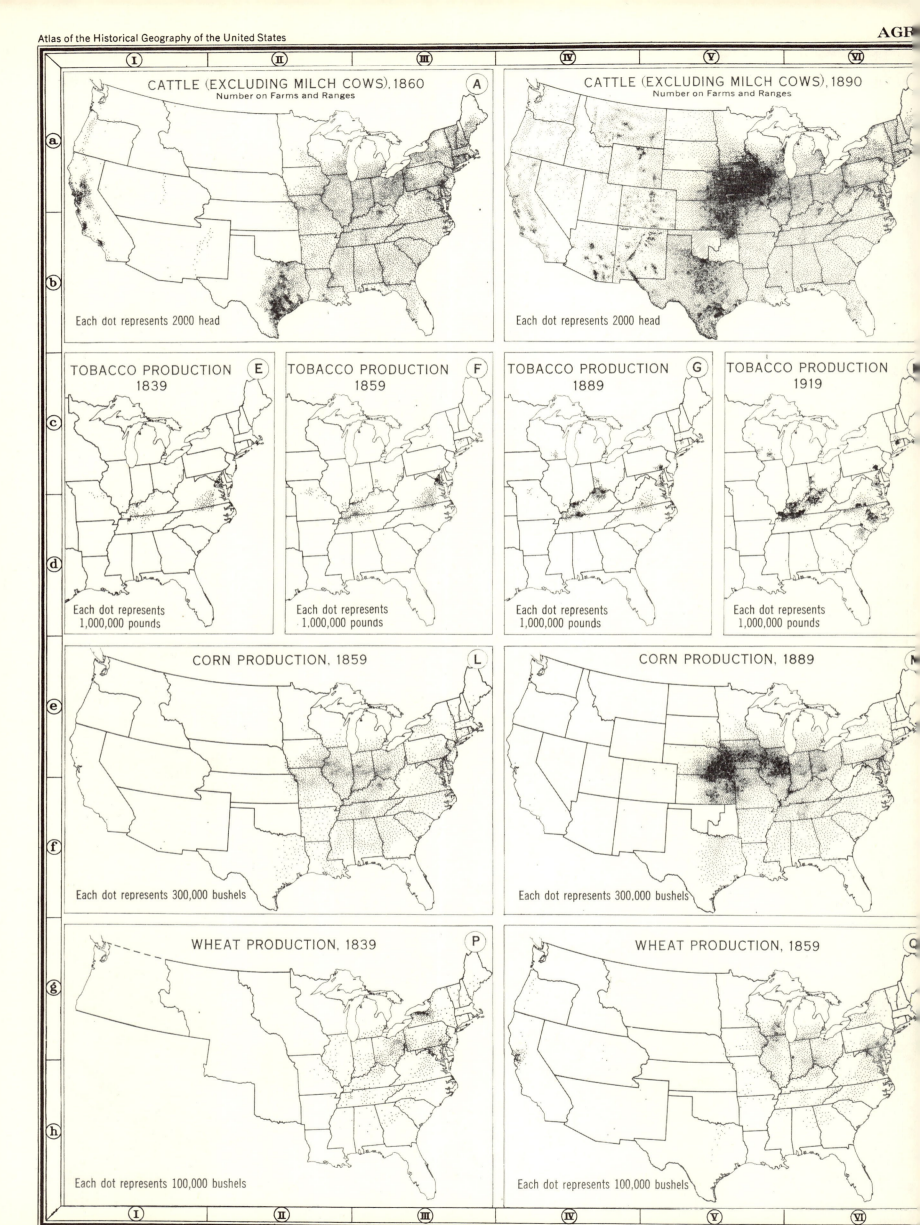

CATTLE (EXCLUDING MILCH COWS), 1860
Number on Farms and Ranges
A

Each dot represents 2000 head

CATTLE (EXCLUDING MILCH COWS), 1890
Number on Farms and Ranges

Each dot represents 2000 head

TOBACCO PRODUCTION
1839
E

Each dot represents
1,000,000 pounds

TOBACCO PRODUCTION
1859
F

Each dot represents
1,000,000 pounds

TOBACCO PRODUCTION
1889
G

Each dot represents
1,000,000 pounds

TOBACCO PRODUCTION
1919

Each dot represents
1,000,000 pounds

CORN PRODUCTION, 1859
L

Each dot represents 300,000 bushels

CORN PRODUCTION, 1889

Each dot represents 300,000 bushels

WHEAT PRODUCTION, 1839
P

Each dot represents 100,000 bushels

WHEAT PRODUCTION, 1859
Q

Each dot represents 100,000 bushels

Carnegie Institution of Washington

CATTLE (EXCLUDING DAIRY COWS), 1920
Number on Farms and Ranges
Each dot represents 2000 head

CATTLE AND CALVES, 1925
Number on Farms
Each dot represents 5000 head

TOBACCO, RICE, AND FLAX, 1924
Each dot represents 2000 acres

CORN PRODUCTION, 1839
Each dot represents 300,000 bushels

CORN PRODUCTION, 1919
ch dot represents 300,000 bushels

CORN FOR GRAIN PRODUCTION, 1924
Each dot represents 500,000 bushels

WHEAT PRODUCTION, 1889
Each dot represents 100,000 bushels

WHEAT PRODUCTION, 1919
Each dot represents 100,000 bushels

SPRING WHEAT PRODUCTION, 1924   Ⓐ

Each dot represents 200,000 bushels

WINTER WHEAT PRODUCTION, 1924   Ⓑ

Each dot represents 200,000 bushels

IMPROVED LAND, 1850   Ⓒ

Each dot represents 25,000 acres

IMPROVED LAND, 1860   Ⓓ

Each dot represents 25,000 acres

IMPROVED LAND, 1870   Ⓔ

Each dot represents 25,000 acres

IMPROVED LAND, 1880   Ⓕ

Each dot represents 25,000 acres

IMPROVED LAND, 1890   Ⓖ

Each dot represents 25,000 acres

IMPROVED LAND, 1900   Ⓗ

Each dot represents 25,000 acres

A. HOEN & CO., INC.

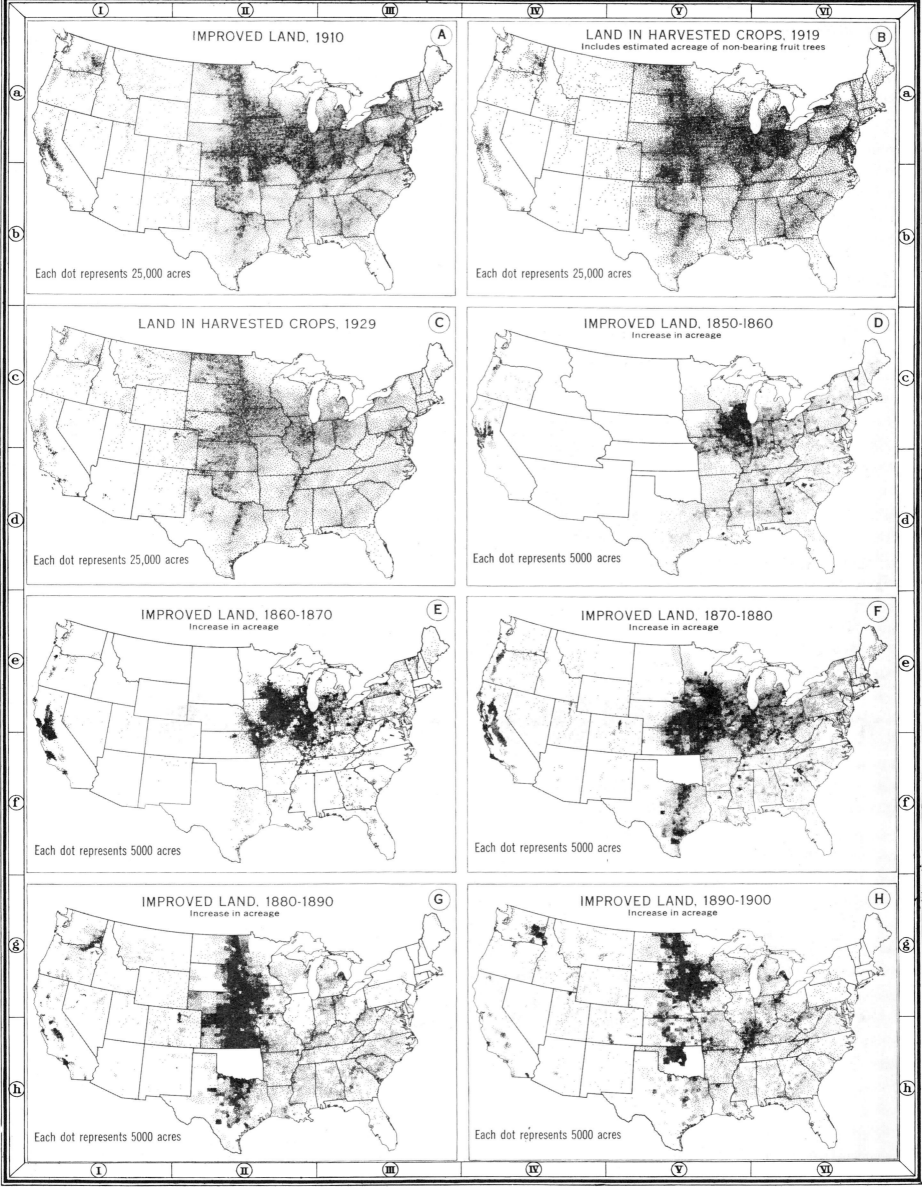

IMPROVED LAND, 1910

Each dot represents 25,000 acres

LAND IN HARVESTED CROPS, 1919
Includes estimated acreage of non-bearing fruit trees

Each dot represents 25,000 acres

LAND IN HARVESTED CROPS, 1929

Each dot represents 25,000 acres

IMPROVED LAND, 1850-1860
Increase in acreage

Each dot represents 5000 acres

IMPROVED LAND, 1860-1870
Increase in acreage

Each dot represents 5000 acres

IMPROVED LAND, 1870-1880
Increase in acreage

Each dot represents 5000 acres

IMPROVED LAND, 1880-1890
Increase in acreage

Each dot represents 5000 acres

IMPROVED LAND, 1890-1900
Increase in acreage

Each dot represents 5000 acres

AGR

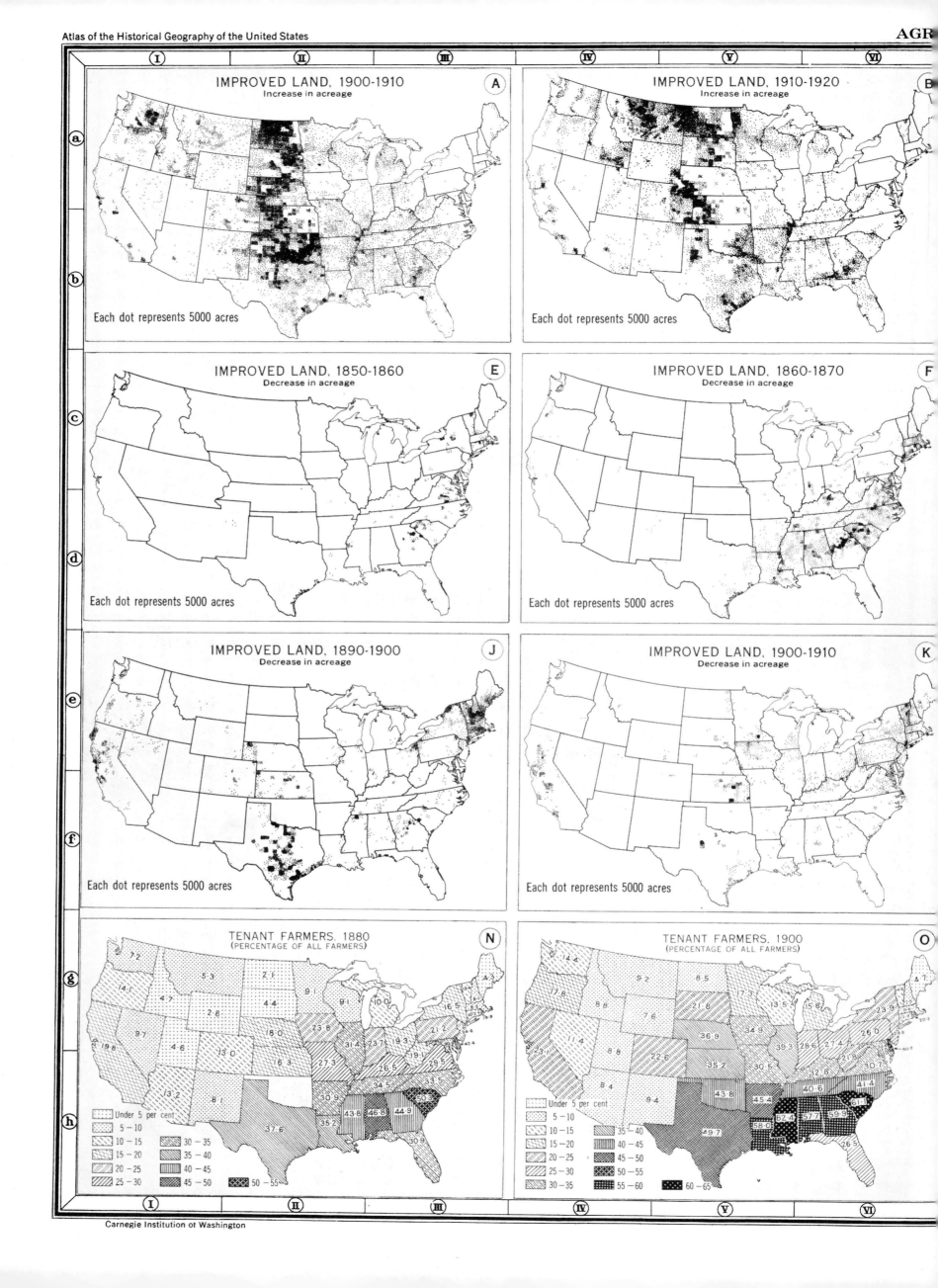

IMPROVED LAND, 1900-1910
Increase in acreage — A

Each dot represents 5000 acres

IMPROVED LAND, 1910-1920
Increase in acreage — B

Each dot represents 5000 acres

IMPROVED LAND, 1850-1860
Decrease in acreage — E

Each dot represents 5000 acres

IMPROVED LAND, 1860-1870
Decrease in acreage — F

Each dot represents 5000 acres

IMPROVED LAND, 1890-1900
Decrease in acreage — J

Each dot represents 5000 acres

IMPROVED LAND, 1900-1910
Decrease in acreage — K

Each dot represents 5000 acres

TENANT FARMERS, 1880
(PERCENTAGE OF ALL FARMERS) — N

Under 5 per cent
5 — 10
10 — 15
15 — 20   30 — 35
20 — 25   35 — 40
25 — 30   40 — 45
               45 — 50
               50 — 55

TENANT FARMERS, 1900
(PERCENTAGE OF ALL FARMERS) — O

Under 5 per cent
5 — 10
10 — 15   35 — 40
15 — 20   40 — 45
20 — 25   45 — 50
25 — 30   50 — 55
30 — 35   55 — 60
               60 — 65

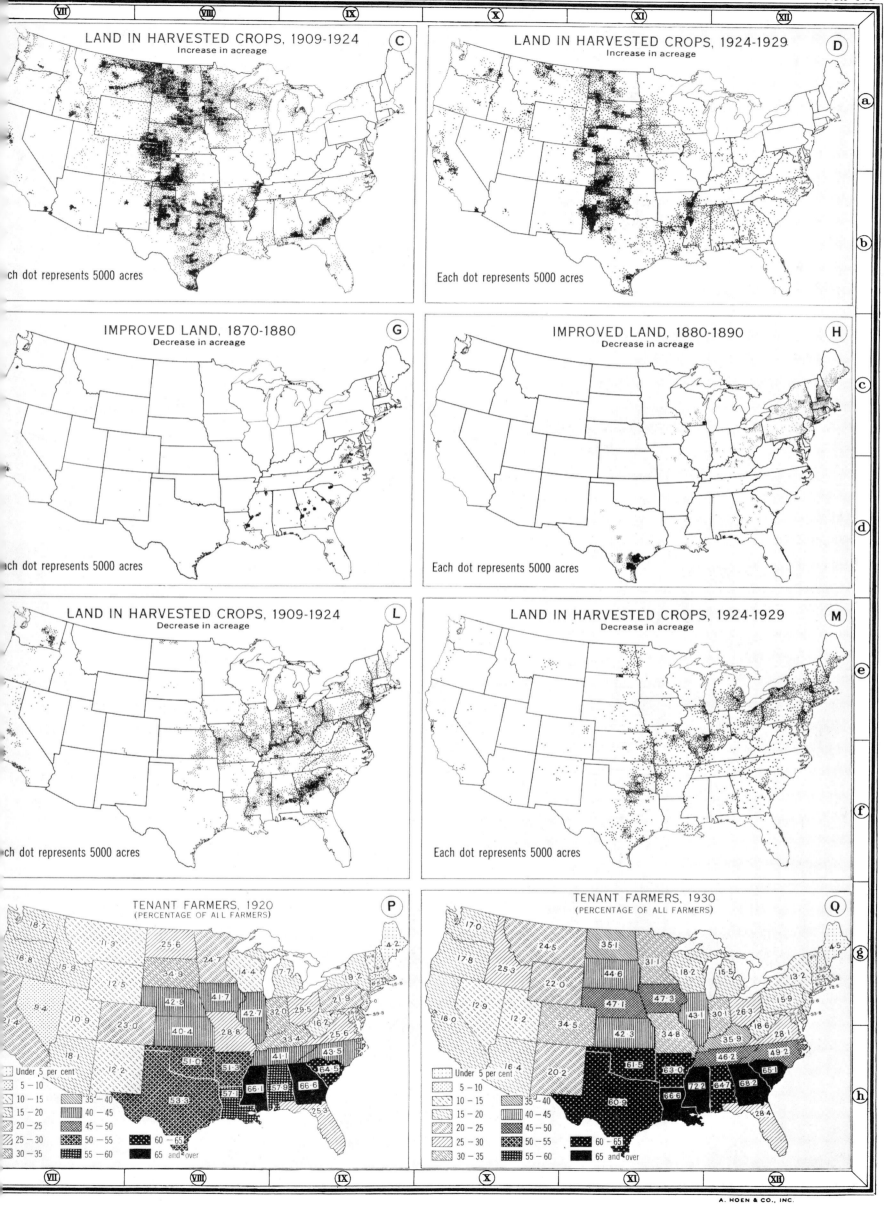

LAND IN HARVESTED CROPS, 1909-1924
Increase in acreage
C

LAND IN HARVESTED CROPS, 1924-1929
Increase in acreage
D

ch dot represents 5000 acres

Each dot represents 5000 acres

IMPROVED LAND, 1870-1880
Decrease in acreage
G

IMPROVED LAND, 1880-1890
Decrease in acreage
H

ch dot represents 5000 acres

Each dot represents 5000 acres

LAND IN HARVESTED CROPS, 1909-1924
Decrease in acreage
L

LAND IN HARVESTED CROPS, 1924-1929
Decrease in acreage
M

ch dot represents 5000 acres

Each dot represents 5000 acres

TENANT FARMERS, 1920
(PERCENTAGE OF ALL FARMERS)
P

TENANT FARMERS, 1930
(PERCENTAGE OF ALL FARMERS)
Q

Under 5 per cent
5 — 10
10 — 15
15 — 20
20 — 25
25 — 30
30 — 35
35 — 40
40 — 45
45 — 50
50 — 55
55 — 60
60 — 65
65 and over

A — FARM LANDS AND BUILDINGS, 1850
(AVERAGE VALUE PER ACRE OF ALL LANDS IN FARMS)

Legend:
- 1 Under $5.00
- 2 5.00 – 10.00
- 3 10.00 – 15.00
- 4 15.00 – 20.00
- 5 20.00 – 30.00
- 6 30.00 – 40.00
- 40.00 and over

B — FARM LANDS AND BUILDINGS, 1880
(AVERAGE VALUE PER ACRE OF ALL LANDS IN FARMS)

Legend:
- 1 Under $5.00
- 2 5.00 – 10.00
- 3 10.00 – 15.00
- 4 15.00 – 20.00
- 5 20.00 – 30.00
- 6 30.00 – 40.00
- 7 40.00 – 50.00
- 50.00 and over

C — FARM LANDS AND BUILDINGS 1910
(AVERAGE VALUE PER ACRE OF ALL LANDS IN FARMS)

Legend:
- 1 $5.30 – 10.60
- 2 10.60 – 15.90
- 3 15.90 – 21.20
- 4 21.20 – 31.80
- 5 31.80 – 42.40
- 6 42.40 – 53.00
- 7 53.00 – 63.60
- 8 63.60 – 74.20
- 9 74.20 – 84.80
- 10 84.80 – 106.00
- 106.00 and over

[$1.06 in 1910 = $1.00 in 1850]

D — FARM LANDS AND BUILDINGS, 1930
(AVERAGE VALUE PER ACRE OF ALL LANDS IN FARMS)

Legend:
- 1 Under $7.00
- 2 7.00 – 14.00
- 3 14.00 – 21.00
- 4 21.00 – 28.00
- 5 28.00 – 42.00
- 6 42.00 – 56.00
- 7 56.00 – 70.00
- 8 70.00 – 84.00
- 9 84.00 – 98.00
- 10 98.00 – 112.00
- 11 112.00 – 140.00
- 140.00 and over

[$1.40 in 1930 = $1.00 in 1850]

E — FARM IMPLEMENTS AND MACHINERY, 1850
(AVERAGE VALUE PER ACRE OF ALL LANDS IN FARMS)

Legend:
- 1 Under $0.25
- 2 0.25 – 0.50
- 3 0.50 – 0.75
- 4 0.75 – 1.00
- 5 1.00 – 1.25
- 6 1.25 – 1.50
- 7 1.50 – 1.75
- 8 1.75 – 2.00
- 2.00 – 3.00

F — FARM IMPLEMENTS AND MACHINERY, 1880
(AVERAGE VALUE PER ACRE OF ALL LANDS IN FARMS)

Legend:
- 1 Under $0.25
- 2 0.25 – 0.50
- 3 0.50 – 0.75
- 4 0.75 – 1.00
- 5 1.00 – 1.25
- 6 1.25 – 1.50
- 7 1.50 – 1.75
- 8 1.75 – 2.00
- 9 2.00 – 3.00

G — FARM IMPLEMENTS AND MACHINERY, 1910
(AVERAGE VALUE PER ACRE OF ALL LANDS IN FARMS)

Legend:
- 2 $0.265 – 0.53
- 3 0.53 – 0.795
- 4 0.795 – 1.06
- 5 1.06 – 1.325
- 6 1.325 – 1.59
- 7 1.59 – 1.855
- 8 1.855 – 2.12
- 9 2.12 – 3.18
- 10 3.18 – 4.24
- $4.24 and over

[$1.06 in 1910 = $1.00 in 1850]

H — FARM IMPLEMENTS AND MACHINERY, 1930
(AVERAGE VALUE PER ACRE OF ALL LANDS IN FARMS)

Legend:
- 2 $0.35 – 0.70
- 3 0.70 – 1.05
- 4 1.05 – 1.40
- 5 1.40 – 1.75
- 6 1.75 – 2.10
- 7 2.10 – 2.45
- 8 2.45 – 2.80
- 9 2.80 – 4.20
- 10 4.20 – 5.60
- 5.60 and over

[$1.40 in 1930 = $1.00 in 1850]

Copyright by Carnegie Institution of Washington

A. HOEN & CO., INC.,

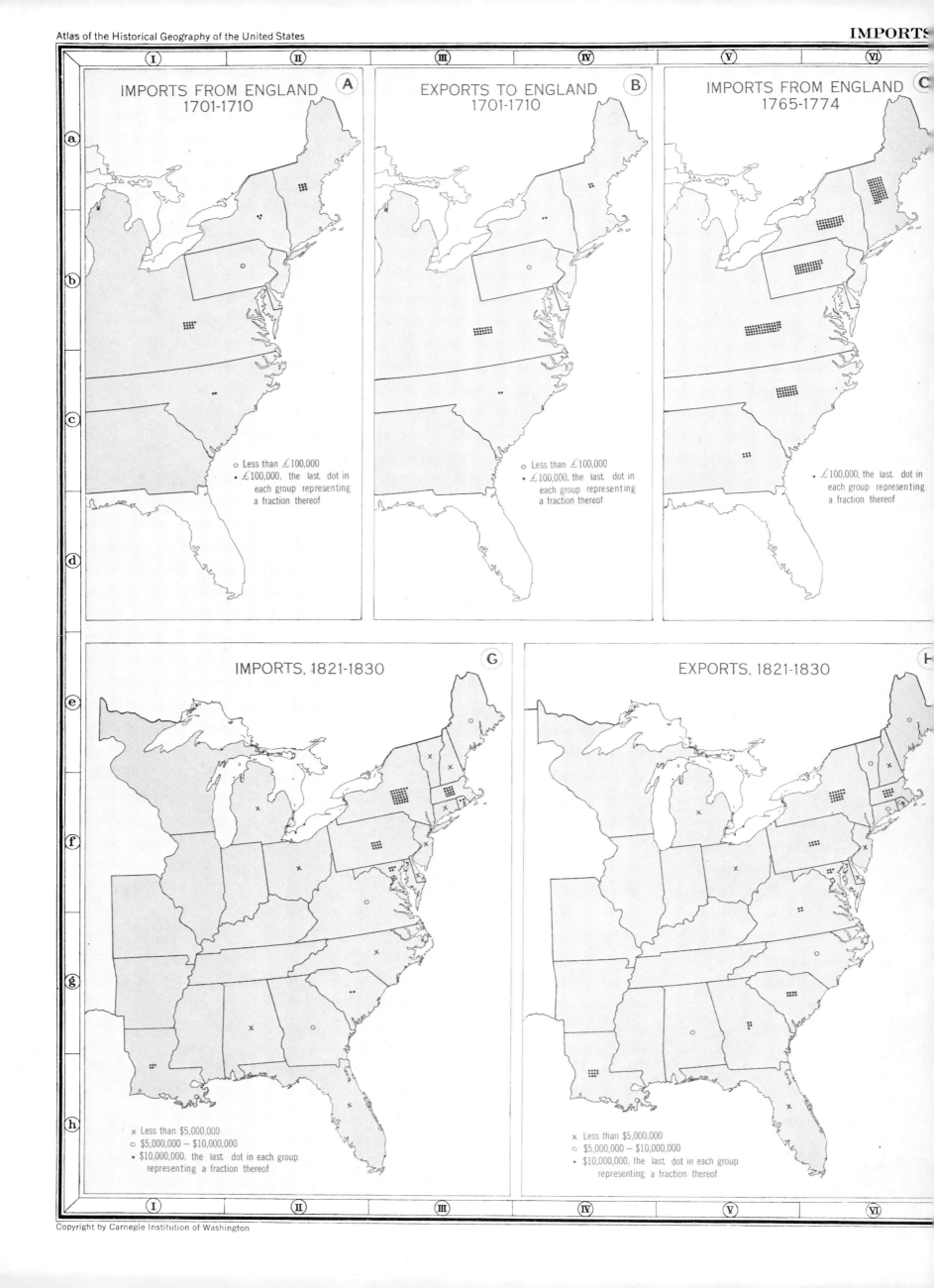

IMPORTS FROM ENGLAND
1701-1710

A

EXPORTS TO ENGLAND
1701-1710

B

IMPORTS FROM ENGLAND
1765-1774

C

○ Less than £100,000
• £100,000, the last dot in
  each group representing
  a fraction thereof

○ Less than £100,000
• £100,000, the last dot in
  each group representing
  a fraction thereof

• £100,000, the last dot in
  each group representing
  a fraction thereof

IMPORTS, 1821-1830

G

EXPORTS, 1821-1830

H

x Less than $5,000,000
○ $5,000,000 − $10,000,000
• $10,000,000, the last dot in each group
  representing a fraction thereof

x Less than $5,000,000
○ $5,000,000 − $10,000,000
• $10,000,000, the last dot in each group
  representing a fraction thereof

Copyright by Carnegie Institution of Washington

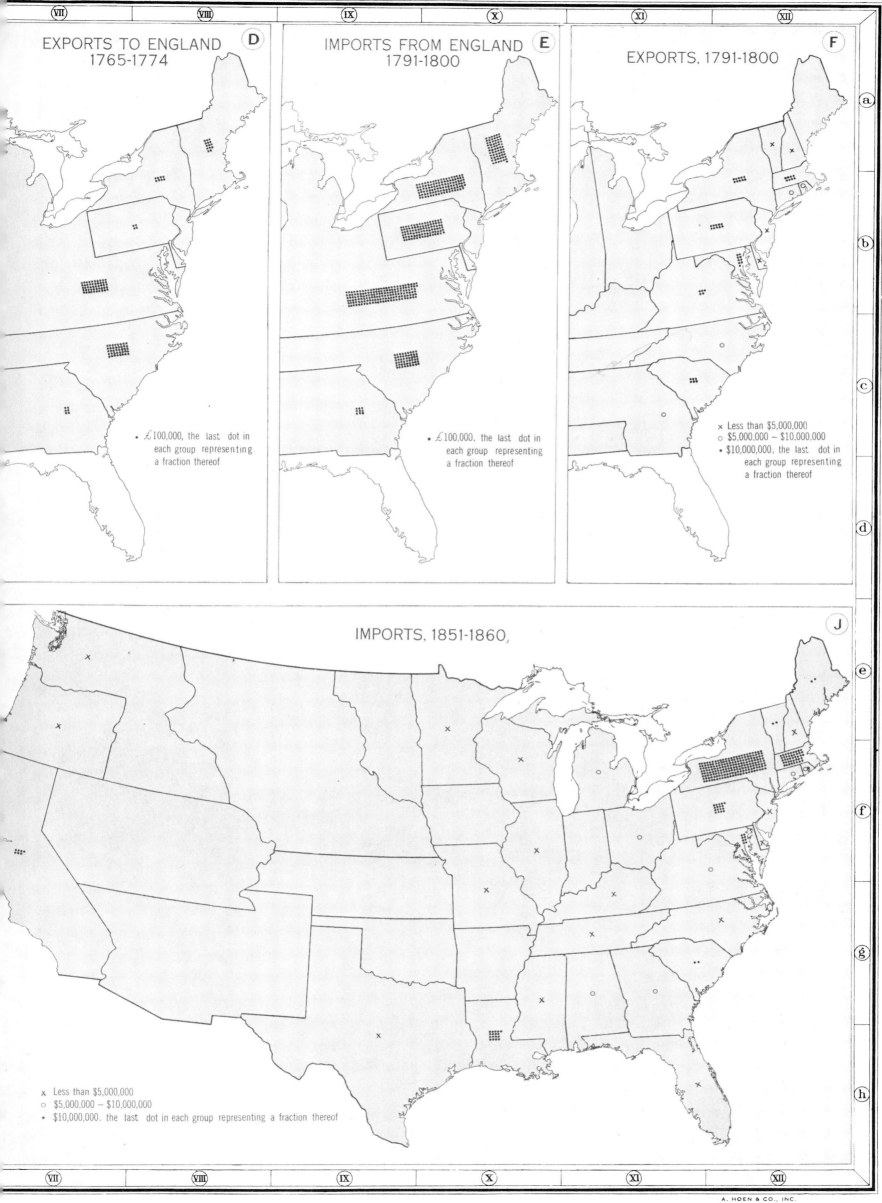

EXPORTS TO ENGLAND
1765-1774 Ⓓ

• £100,000, the last dot in
each group representing
a fraction thereof

IMPORTS FROM ENGLAND
1791-1800 Ⓔ

• £100,000, the last dot in
each group representing
a fraction thereof

EXPORTS, 1791-1800 Ⓕ

× Less than $5,000,000
○ $5,000,000 – $10,000,000
• $10,000,000, the last dot in
each group representing
a fraction thereof

IMPORTS, 1851-1860 Ⓙ

× Less than $5,000,000
○ $5,000,000 – $10,000,000
• $10,000,000, the last dot in each group representing a fraction thereof

EXPORTS, 1851-1860

X Less than $5,000,000

o $5,000,000 — $10,000,000

• $10,000,000, the last dot in each group representing a fraction thereof

IMPORTS, 1871-1880

X Less than $5,000,000

o $5,000,000 — $10,000,000

• $10,000,000, the last dot in each group representing a fraction thereof

Copyright by Carnegie Institution of Washington

A. HOEN & CO., INC.

EXPORTS, 1871-1880

(A)

x   Less than $5,000,000
o $5,000,000 — $10,000,000
• $10,000,000, the last dot in each group representing a fraction thereof

IMPORTS, 1901-1910

(B)

x   Less than $5,000,000
o $5,000,000 — $10,000,000
• $10,000,000, the last dot in each group representing a fraction thereof

Copyright by Carnegie Institution of Washington

A. HOEN & CO., INC.

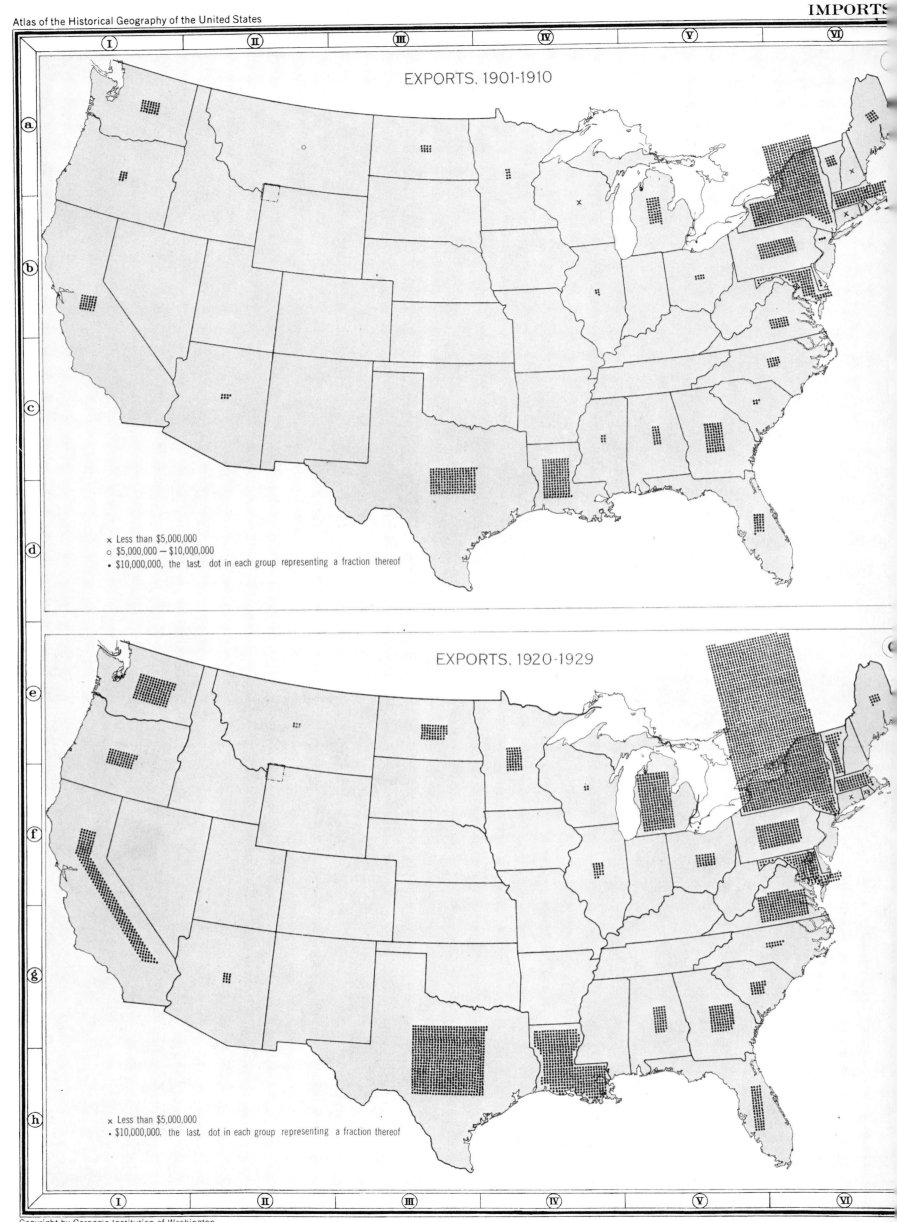

EXPORTS. 1901-1910

x Less than $5,000,000
o $5,000,000 — $10,000,000
• $10,000,000, the last dot in each group representing a fraction thereof

EXPORTS. 1920-1929

x Less than $5,000,000
• $10,000,000, the last dot in each group representing a fraction thereof

Copyright by Carnegie Institution of Washington

IMPORTS. 1920-1929

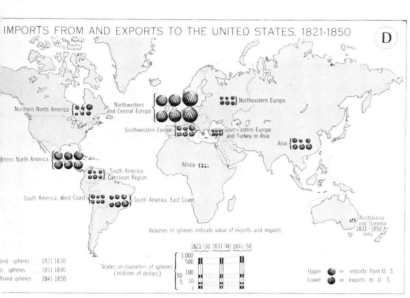

x Less than $5,000,000
• $10,000,000. the last dot in each group representing a fraction thereof

IMPORTS FROM AND EXPORTS TO THE UNITED STATES, 1821-1850 D

Northern North America

Northwestern and Central Europe

Northeastern Europe

Southwestern Europe

Southeastern Europe and Turkey in Asia

Asia

Southern North America

Africa

South America, Caribbean Region

South America, West Coast

South America, East Coast

Australasia and Oceania 1831-1850 only

Volumes of spheres indicate value of exports and imports

1821-30 1831-40 1841-50

Left-hand spheres 1821-1830
Middle spheres 1831-1840
Right-hand spheres 1841-1850

Scales on diameters of spheres
(millions of dollars)

1,000
500
100
50
10
5
1

Upper = imports from U.S.
Lower = exports to U.S.

IMPORTS FROM AND EXPORTS TO THE UNITED STATES, 1851-1880 E

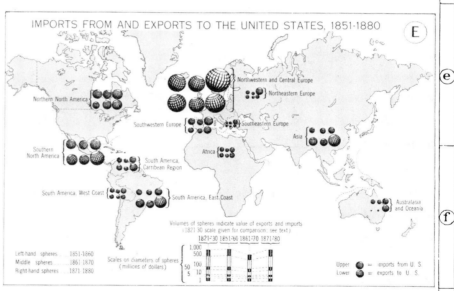

Northern North America

Northwestern and Central Europe

Northeastern Europe

Southwestern Europe

Southeastern Europe

Asia

Southern North America

Africa

South America, Caribbean Region

South America, West Coast

South America, East Coast

Australasia and Oceania

Volumes of spheres indicate value of exports and imports
(1821-30 scale given for comparison; see text)

1821-30 1851-60 1861-70 1871-80

Left-hand spheres 1851-1860
Middle spheres 1861-1870
Right-hand spheres 1871-1880

Scales on diameters of spheres
(millions of dollars)

1,000
500
100
50
10
5
1

Upper = imports from U.S.
Lower = exports to U.S.

IMPORTS FROM AND EXPORTS TO THE UNITED STATES, 1881-1910 F

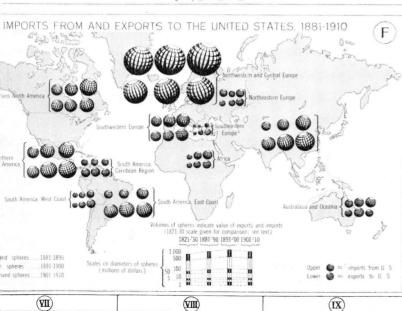

Northern North America

Northwestern and Central Europe

Northeastern Europe

Southwestern Europe

Southeastern Europe

Asia

Northern America

Africa

South America, Caribbean Region

South America, West Coast

South America, East Coast

Australasia and Oceania

Volumes of spheres indicate value of exports and imports
(1821-30 scale given for comparison; see text)

1821-30 1881-90 1891-00 1901-10

Left-hand spheres 1881-1890
Middle spheres 1891-1900
Right-hand spheres 1901-1910

Scales on diameters of spheres
(millions of dollars)

1,000
500
100
50
10
5
1

Upper = imports from U.S.
Lower = exports to U.S.

IMPORTS FROM AND EXPORTS TO THE UNITED STATES, 1911-1929 G

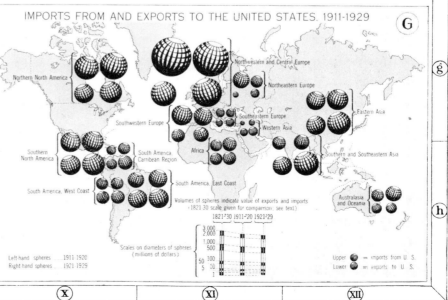

Northern North America

Northwestern and Central Europe

Northeastern Europe

Southwestern Europe

Southeastern Europe

Western Asia

Eastern Asia

Southern North America

Africa

South America, Caribbean Region

Southern and Southeastern Asia

South America, West Coast

South America, East Coast

Australasia and Oceania

Volumes of spheres indicate value of exports and imports
(1821-30 scale given for comparison; see text)

1821-30 1911-20 1921-29

Left-hand spheres 1911-1920
Right-hand spheres 1921-1929

Scales on diameters of spheres
(millions of dollars)

3,000
2,000
1,000
500
100
50
10
5
1

Upper = imports from U.S.
Lower = exports to U.S.

WEALTH (TAXABLE PROPERTY), 1850

Wealth per state
(millions of dollars)
1 Under 10   4 100 — 500
2 10 — 50   5 500 — 1,000
3 50 — 100   6 1,000 — 5,000

WEALTH (ALL PROPERTY), 1880

Wealth per state
(millions of dollars)
2 10 — 50   5 500 — 1,000
3 50 — 100   6 1,000 — 5,000
4 100 — 500 7 5,000 — 10,000

WEALTH (HOUSES AND LANDS) PER CAPITA 1799

Wealth per state in dollars
3 50 — 75   5 100 — 150
4 75 — 100   6 150 — 200

WEALTH (TAXABLE PROPERTY) PER CAPITA 1850

Wealth per state in dollars
(per capita)
1 Under 25   6 200 — 300
2 25 — 50   7 300 — 400
4 50 — 75   8 400 — 500
5 75 — 100   9 500 — 750
              10 150 — 200

WEALTH (HOUSES AND LANDS) 1799

Wealth per state
(millions of dollars)
1 Under 10
2 10 — 50
3 50 — 100
4 100 — 500

Copyright by Carnegie Institution of Washington

A. HOEN & CO. INC.,

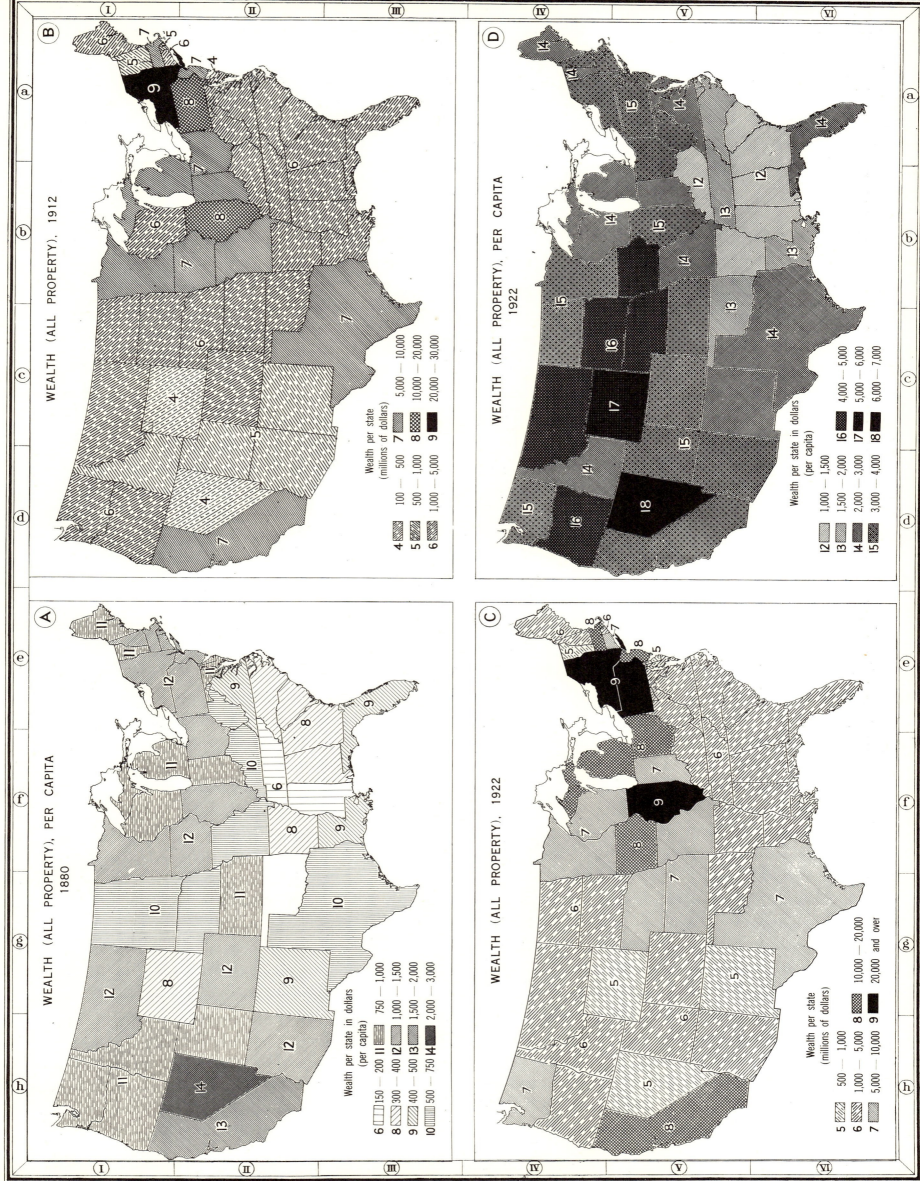

WEALTH (ALL PROPERTY), 1912

Wealth per state
(millions of dollars)

4	100 — 500
5	500 — 1,000
6	1,000 — 5,000
7	5,000 — 10,000
8	10,000 — 20,000
9	20,000 — 30,000

WEALTH (ALL PROPERTY), PER CAPITA 1922

Wealth per state in dollars
(per capita)

12	1,000 — 1,500
13	1,500 — 2,000
14	2,000 — 3,000
15	3,000 — 4,000
16	4,000 — 5,000
17	5,000 — 6,000
18	6,000 — 7,000

WEALTH (ALL PROPERTY), PER CAPITA 1880

Wealth per state in dollars
(per capita)

6	150 — 200
8	200 — 400
9	300 — 400
10	400 — 500
11	500 — 750
11	750 — 1,000
12	1,000 — 1,500
13	1,500 — 2,000
14	2,000 — 3,000

WEALTH (ALL PROPERTY), 1922

Wealth per state
(millions of dollars)

5	500 — 1,000
6	1,000 — 5,000
7	5,000 — 10,000
8	10,000 — 20,000
9	20,000 and over

Copyright by Carnegie Institution of Washington
A. HOEN & CO., INC.,

FEDERAL INCOME TAXES

Plate 155

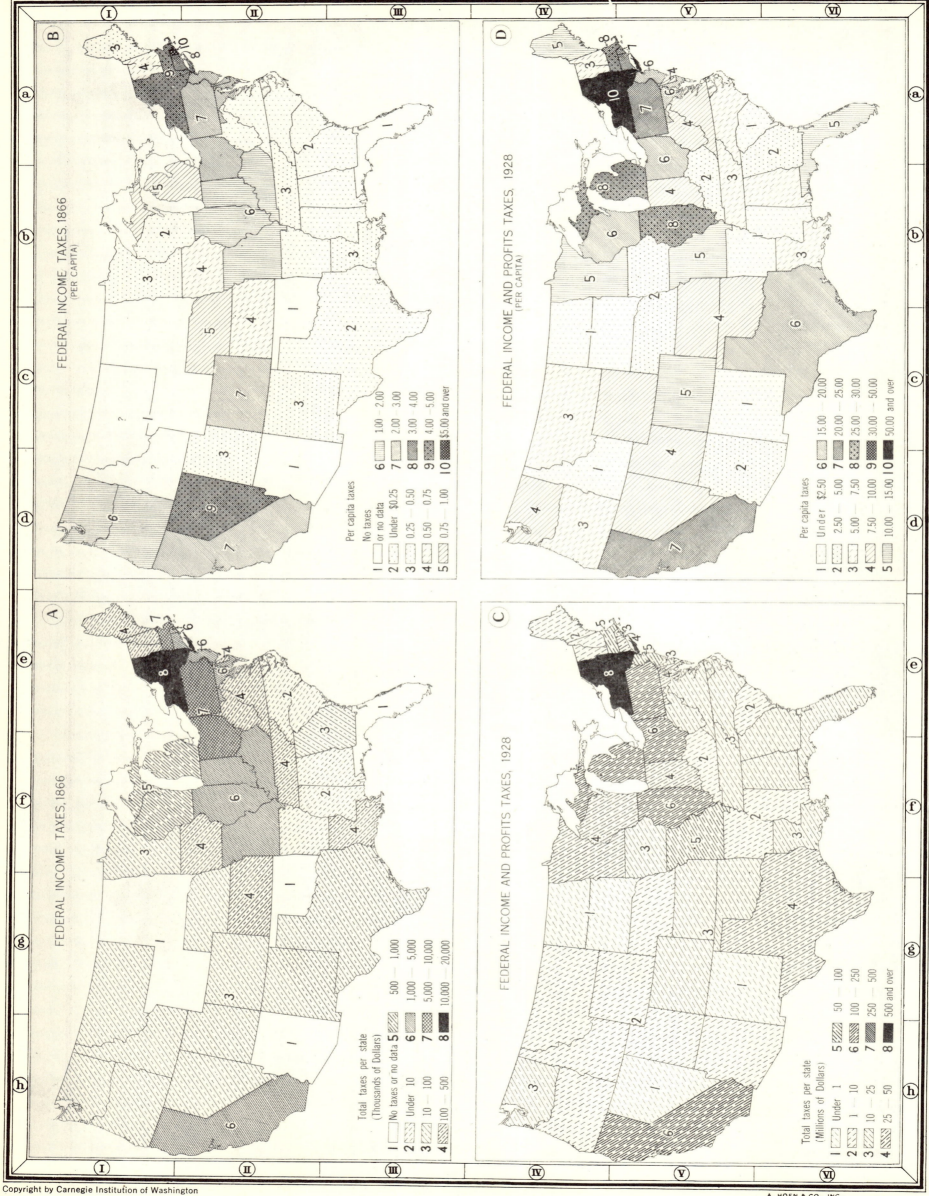

FEDERAL INCOME TAXES, 1866
(PER CAPITA)

FEDERAL INCOME AND PROFITS TAXES, 1928
(PER CAPITA)

FEDERAL INCOME TAXES, 1866

FEDERAL INCOME AND PROFITS TAXES, 1928

Per capita taxes

No taxes
or no data
1
2 Under $0.25
3 0.25 — 0.50
4 0.50 — 0.75
5 0.75 — 1.00
6 1.00 — 2.00
7 2.00 — 3.00
8 3.00 — 4.00
9 4.00 — 5.00
10 $5.00 and over

Per capita taxes

1 Under $2.50
2 2.50 — 5.00
3 5.00 — 7.50
4 7.50 — 10.00
5 10.00 — 15.00
6 15.00 — 20.00
7 20.00 — 25.00
8 25.00 — 30.00
9 30.00 — 50.00
10 50.00 and over

Total taxes per state
(Thousands of Dollars)

1 No taxes or no data
2 Under 10
3 10 — 100
4 100 — 500
5 500 — 1,000
6 1,000 — 5,000
7 5,000 — 10,000
8 10,000 — 20,000

Total taxes per state
(Millions of Dollars)

1 Under 1
2 1 — 10
3 10 — 25
4 25 — 50
5 50 — 100
6 100 — 250
7 250 — 500
8 500 and over

Copyright by Carnegie Institution of Washington

A. HOEN & CO., INC.,

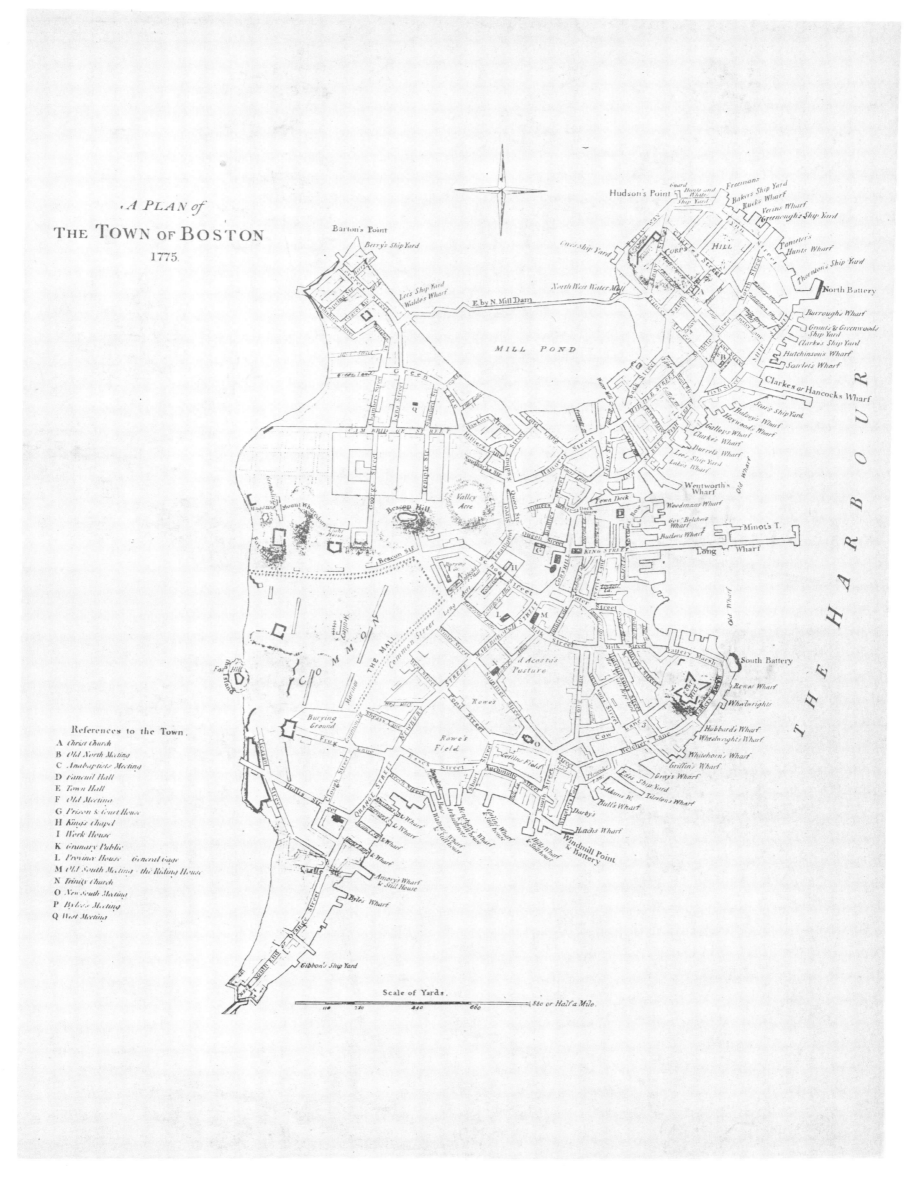

A PLAN of
THE TOWN of BOSTON
1775.

References to the Town.
A Christ Church
B Old North Meeting
C Anabaptists Meeting
D Faneuil Hall
E Town Hall
F Old Meeting
G Prison & Court House
H Kings Chapel
I Work House
K Granary Public
L Province House   General Gage
M Old South Meeting   the Riding House
N Trinity Church
O New South Meeting
P Byles's Meeting
Q West Meeting

Scale of Yards.

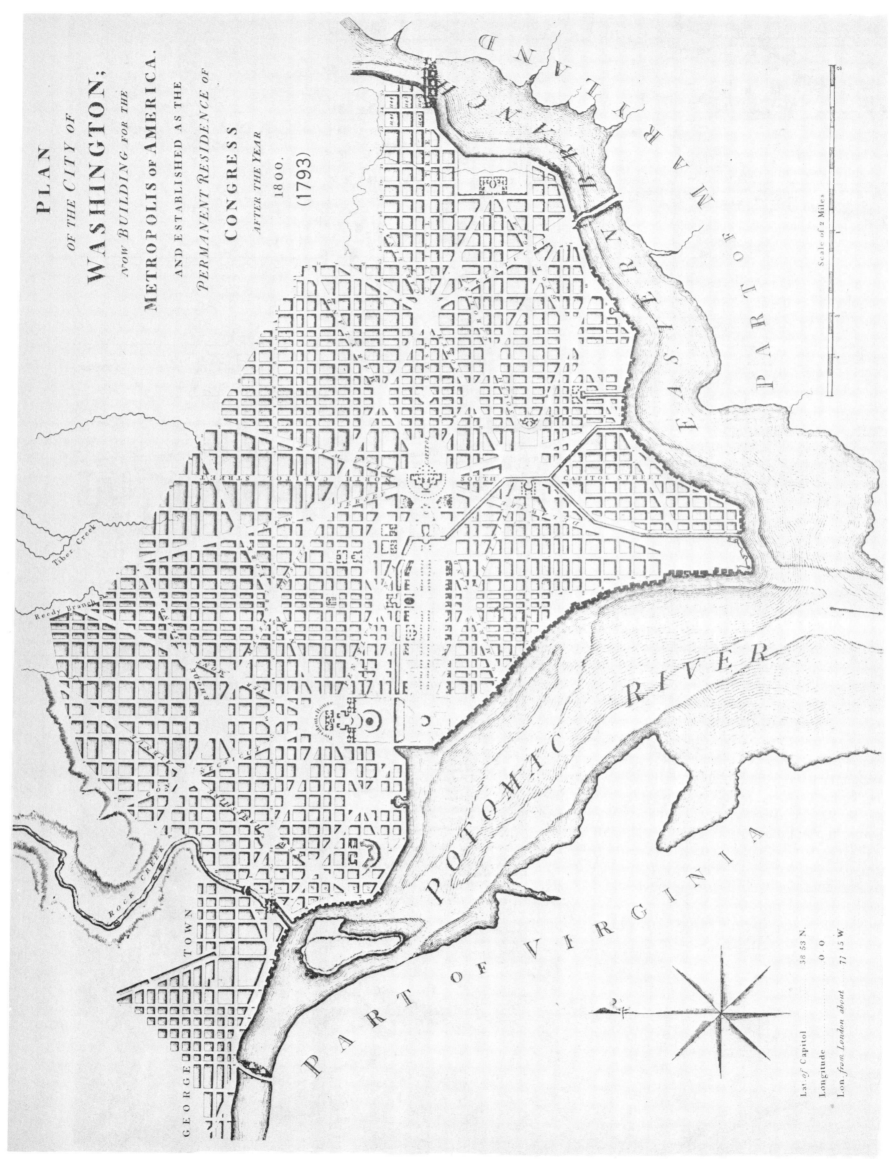

PLAN OF THE CITY OF WASHINGTON; Now BUILDING FOR THE METROPOLIS OF AMERICA. AND ESTABLISHED AS THE PERMANENT RESIDENCE OF CONGRESS AFTER THE YEAR 1800. (1793)

A. HOEN & CO., INC.

NEW YORK, 1776

PLAN OF THE
CITY OF NEW-YORK

Drawn by Major Holland.
SURVEYOR GENERAL.
1776.

Quarter of a Mile

NORTH OR HUDSON RIVER

BROADWAY STREET

COMMON

Fresh Water Pond

Powder Magazine

New Presbyterian Meeting

King George

Jews Burying Ground

CITY HALL

THE FORT

BATTERY

Cherry St

George's Wharf

Craig's Wharf

EAST RIVER OR THE SOUND

Bellevue Square

Division Street

Road to Albany & Kings

Marshy Ground

REFERENCES.

A Military Hospital	O St Pauls
B Governors House	Q St Georges Chapel
C Secretary's Office	R Old Dutch Church
D Custom House	S New Dutch Church
E Fish Market	T Lutheran Church
F Old Slip Market	V Calvinist Church
G Meat Market	W French Protestant Church
H Fly Market	X Quakers Meeting
I Pecks Market	Y Presbyterian Meeting
K Oswego Market	Z Baptist Meeting
L Exchange	u Moravian Meeting
M Dutch Free School	b New Lutheran Meeting
N Engine which suplies the City with Fresh Water	c Jews Synagogue

BALTIMORE, 1801

View of the Market space

Canal

OLD TOWN

FELL POINT

BASON

Public Square

WARNER & HANNA'S
PLAN
of the City and Environs of
Baltimore,

Respectfully dedicated to the Mayor, City Council,
& Citizens thereof, by the Proprietors. 1801.

Scale.

REFERENCES

A. Seminary	P. Hanover Market House
B. Roman Cath¹ Ch.	Q. German Reformed C.
C. S¹ Pauls Church.	R. Christ Church.
D. Menonists Meeting House	S. Baptist M.H.
E. Methodist Church.	T. Methodist C.
F. Baltimore Bank.	V. Quaker M.H.
G. Jail.	W. German Lutheran C.
H. Court House	X. Observatory.
I. English Presb¹ M.H.	Y. Custom H.
K. Maryland Bank.	1. Methodist C. Point.
L. German Calv¹ M.H.	2. Roman Cath. C.
M. Exchange.	3. Market.
N. United States Bank.	4. New Assembly R.S Library.
J. Marsh Market.	5. New Theatre.

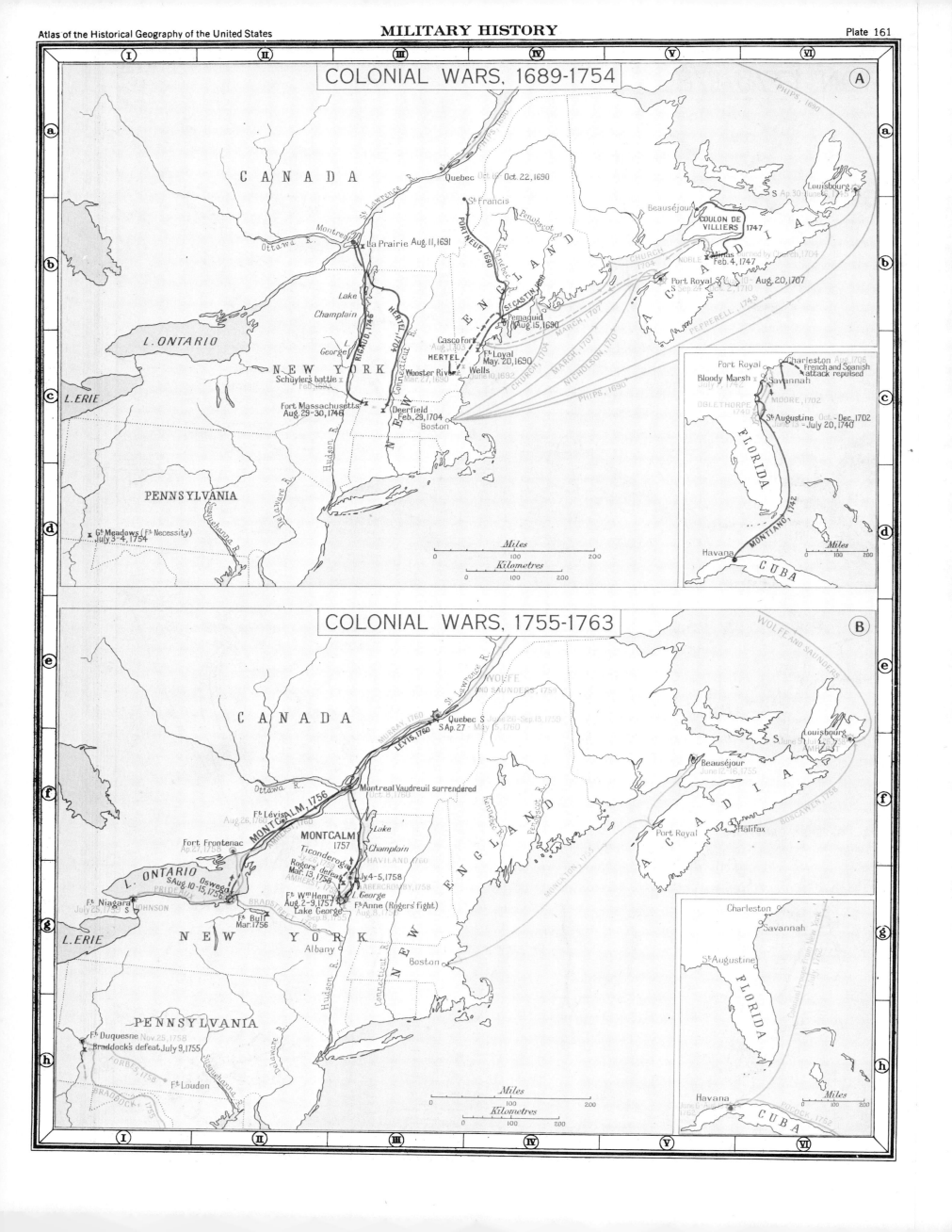

COLONIAL WARS, 1689-1754

A

CANADA

Quebec Oct. 16 - Oct. 22, 1690

St Francis

Montreal
La Prairie Aug. 11, 1691

PORTNEUF, 1690

Beauséjour

Louisbourg
S Ap 30 - June 16, 174

COULON DE VILLIERS 1747

A C A D I A

Minas Feb. 4, 1747

Port Royal S Oct 10 - Aug. 20, 1707
Sep 24 - Oct 27, 1710

Lake Champlain

L. ONTARIO

Lake George

NEW YORK

Schuyler's battle

Fort Massachusetts
Aug. 29-30, 1746

Deerfield
Feb. 29, 1704

Boston

HERTEL

Casco Fort

Ft Loyal
May 20, 1690

Wooster River
Mar. 27, 1690

Wells
June 10, 1692

St CASTIN, 1690

Pemaquid
Aug. 15, 1690

N E W E N G L A N D

L. ERIE

Hudson

Delaware

Susquehanna R.

PENNSYLVANIA

Gt Meadows (Ft Necessity)
July 3-4, 1754

Miles
0   100   200

Kilometres
0   100   200

(inset)

Port Royal

Charleston Aug. 1706
French and Spanish
attack repulsed

Bloody Marsh
July 7, 1742

Savannah

MOORE, 1702

St Augustine Oct. - Dec. 1702
June 13 - July 20, 1740

F L O R I D A

MONTIANO, 1742

Havana

C U B A

Miles
0   100   200

COLONIAL WARS, 1755-1763

B

CANADA

WOLFE AND SAUNDERS

WOLFE
AND SAUNDERS, 1759

Quebec S June 26 - Sep. 13, 1759
S Ap. 27 - May 16, 1760

MURRAY, 1760

LEVIS, 1760

Louisbourg
June - July 26, 1758

Montreal Vaudreuil surrendered
Oct. 8, 1760

Beauséjour
June 12-16, 1755

A C A D I A

Ft Lévis
Aug. 26, 1760

MONTCALM, 1756

Fort Frontenac
Ap. 27, 1758

L. ONTARIO

Oswego
S Aug. 10-15, 1756

Ft Niagara
July 25, 1759 S

PRIDEAUX

JOHNSON

Ft Bull
Mar. 1756

MONTCALM
1757

Ticonderoga

Rogers' defeat
Mar. 13, 1758

HAVILAND 1760

Lake
Champlain

Ft Wm Henry
Aug. 2-9, 1757

Lake George

Ft Anne (Rogers' fight)
Aug. 8, 17

July 4-5, 1758

Halifax

Port Royal

BOSCAWEN, 1758

MONCKTON, 1755

P e n o b s c o t

K e n n e b e c

N E W E N G L A N D

Albany

Boston

AMHERST

BRADSTREET, 1758

ABERCROMBY, 1758

L. ERIE

Hudson

Connecticut

NEW YORK

Delaware

PENNSYLVANIA

Ft Duquesne Nov. 25, 1758
Braddock's defeat, July 9, 1755

FORBES, 1758

BRADDOCK, 1755

Ft Loudon

Susquehanna R.

Miles
0   100   200

Kilometres
0   100   200

(inset)

Charleston

Savannah

St Augustine

F L O R I D A

Colonial troops from New York

Havana
June 7 - Aug. 1762

POCOCK, 1762

C U B A

Miles
0   100   200

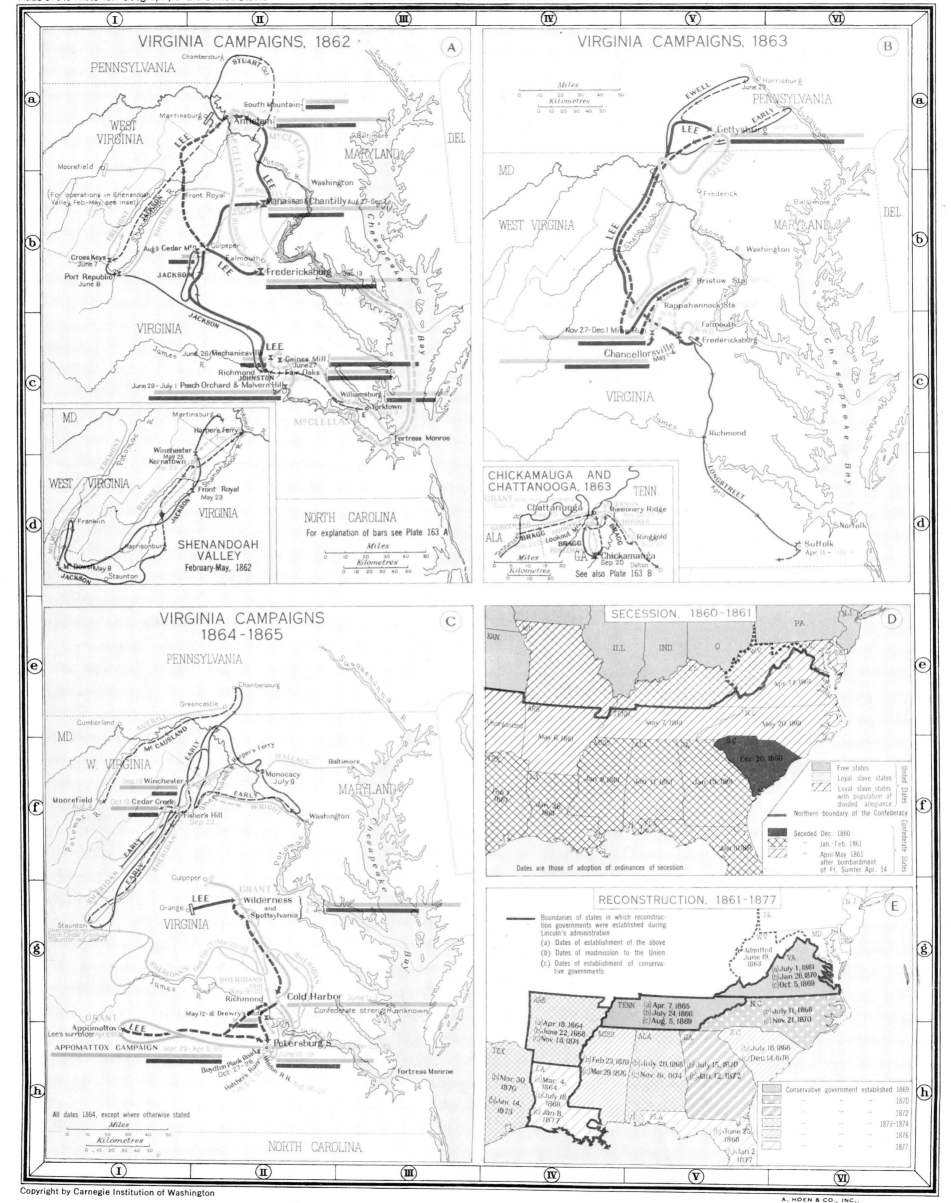

A. HOEN & CO., INC.,

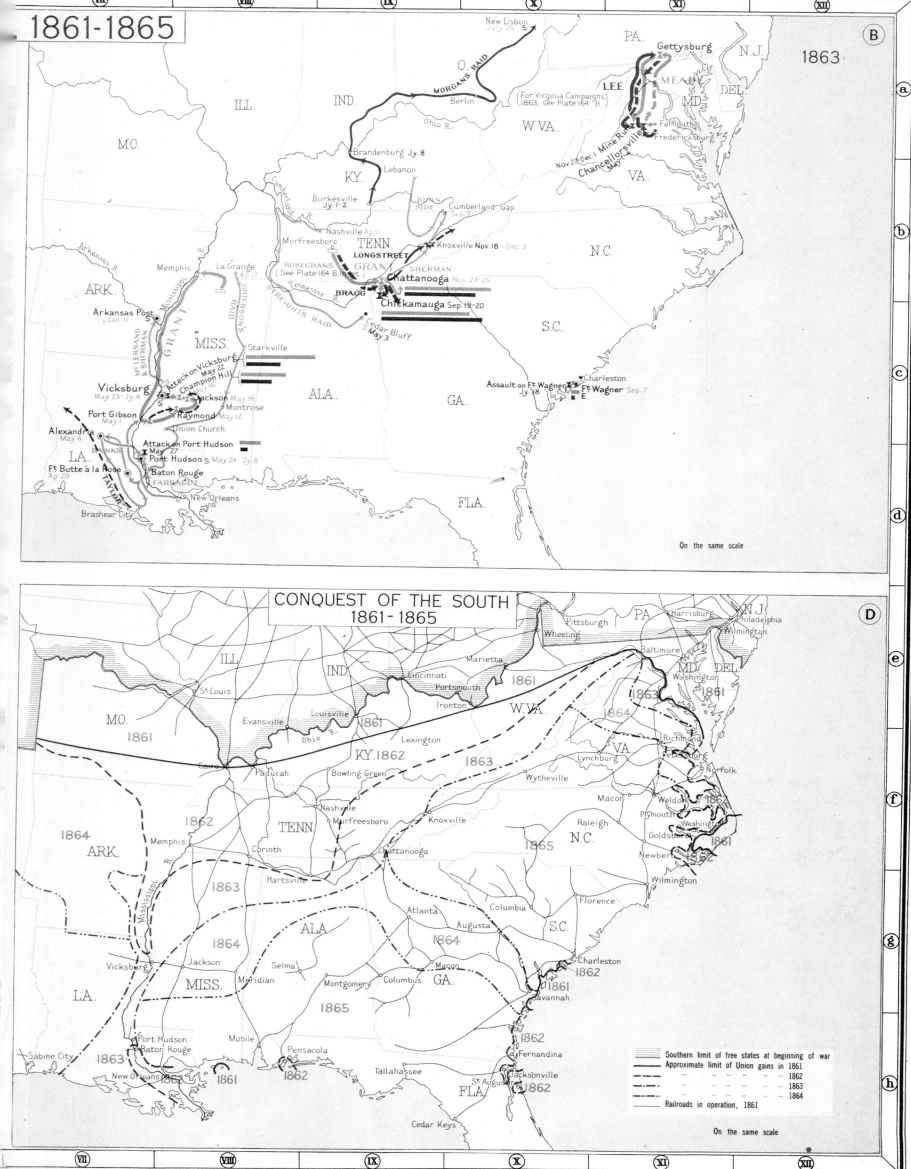

1861-1865

1863

On the same scale

CONQUEST OF THE SOUTH
1861-1865

Southern limit of free states at beginning of war
Approximate limit of Union gains in 1861
" " " " " " 1862
" " " " " " 1863
" " " " " " 1864
Railroads in operation, 1861

On the same scale

A. HOEN & CO., INC.,

CIVIL WAR

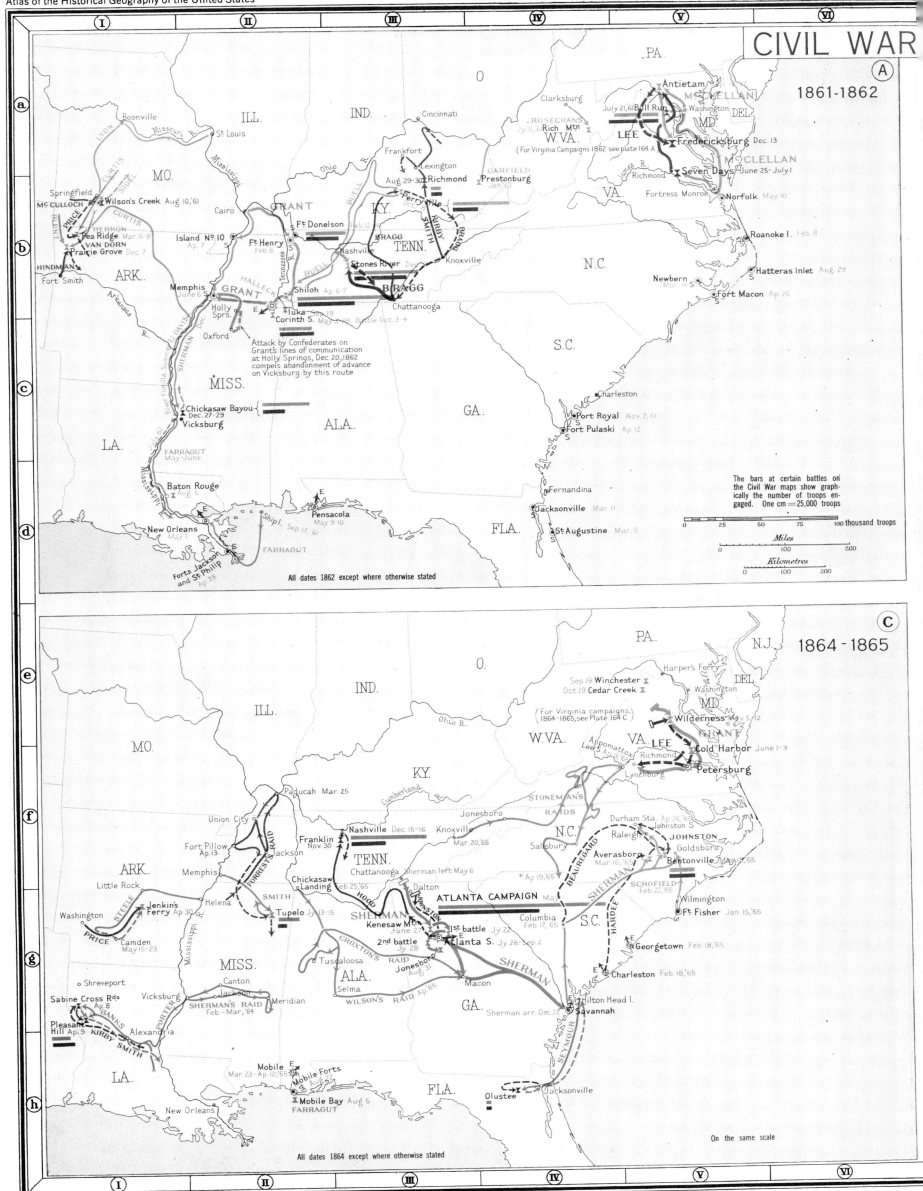

A

1861-1862

(For Virginia Campaigns 1862, see plate 164 A)

Attack by Confederates on Grant's lines of communication at Holly Springs, Dec. 20, 1862 compels abandonment of advance on Vicksburg by this route

The bars at certain battles on the Civil War maps show graphically the number of troops engaged. One cm = 25,000 troops

0   25   50   75   100 thousand troops

Miles
0   100   200

Kilometres
0   100   200

All dates 1862 except where otherwise stated

C

1864-1865

(For Virginia campaigns, 1864-1865, see Plate 164 C)

ATLANTA CAMPAIGN

On the same scale

All dates 1864 except where otherwise stated

Copyright by Carnegie Institution of Washington

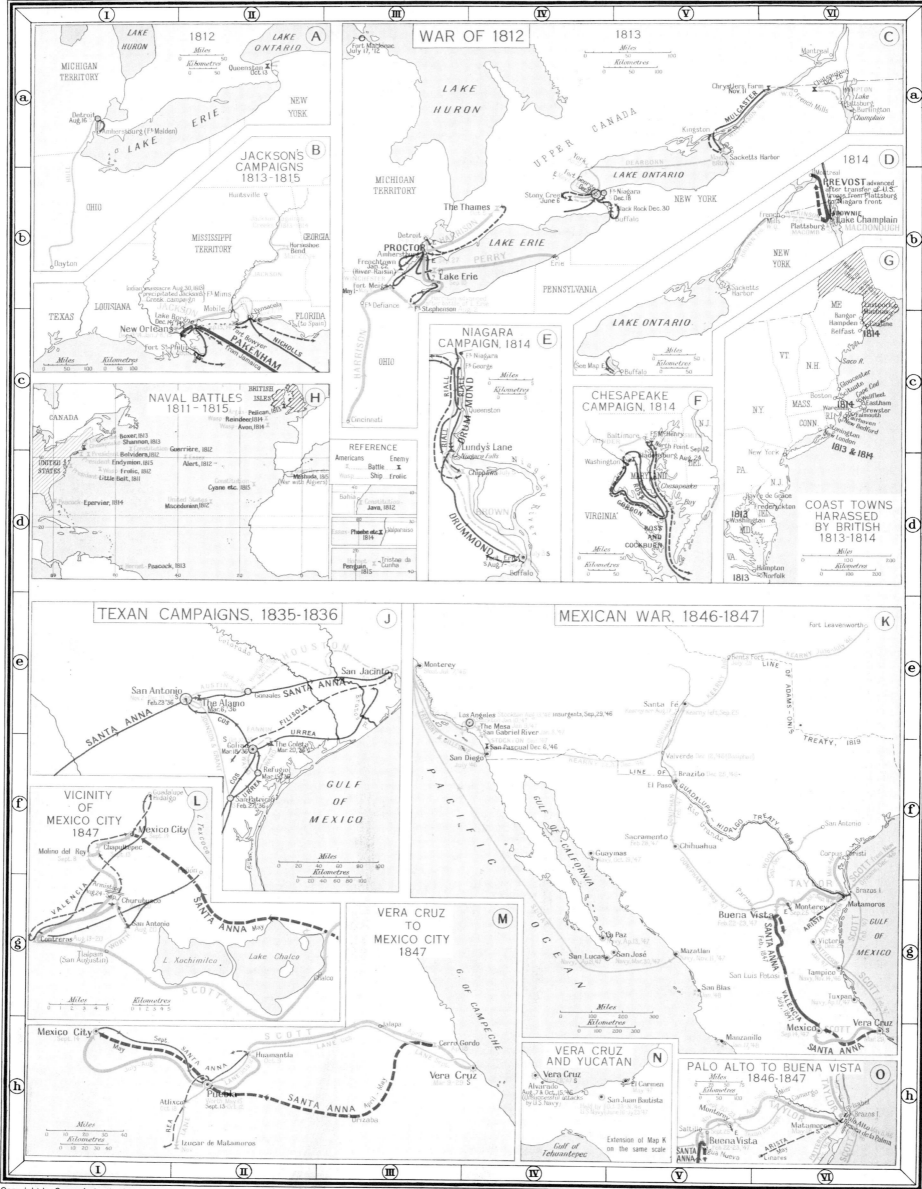

A. HOEN & CO., INC.,

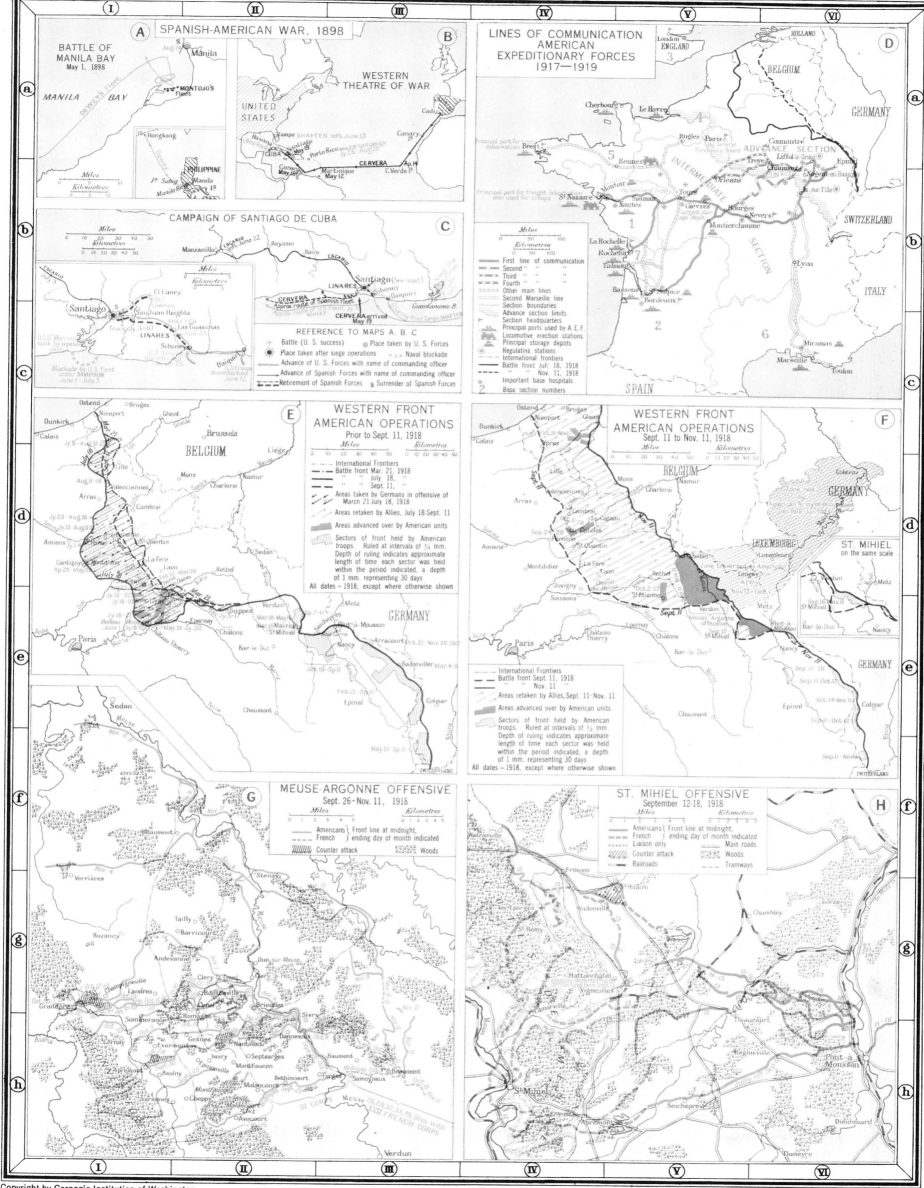

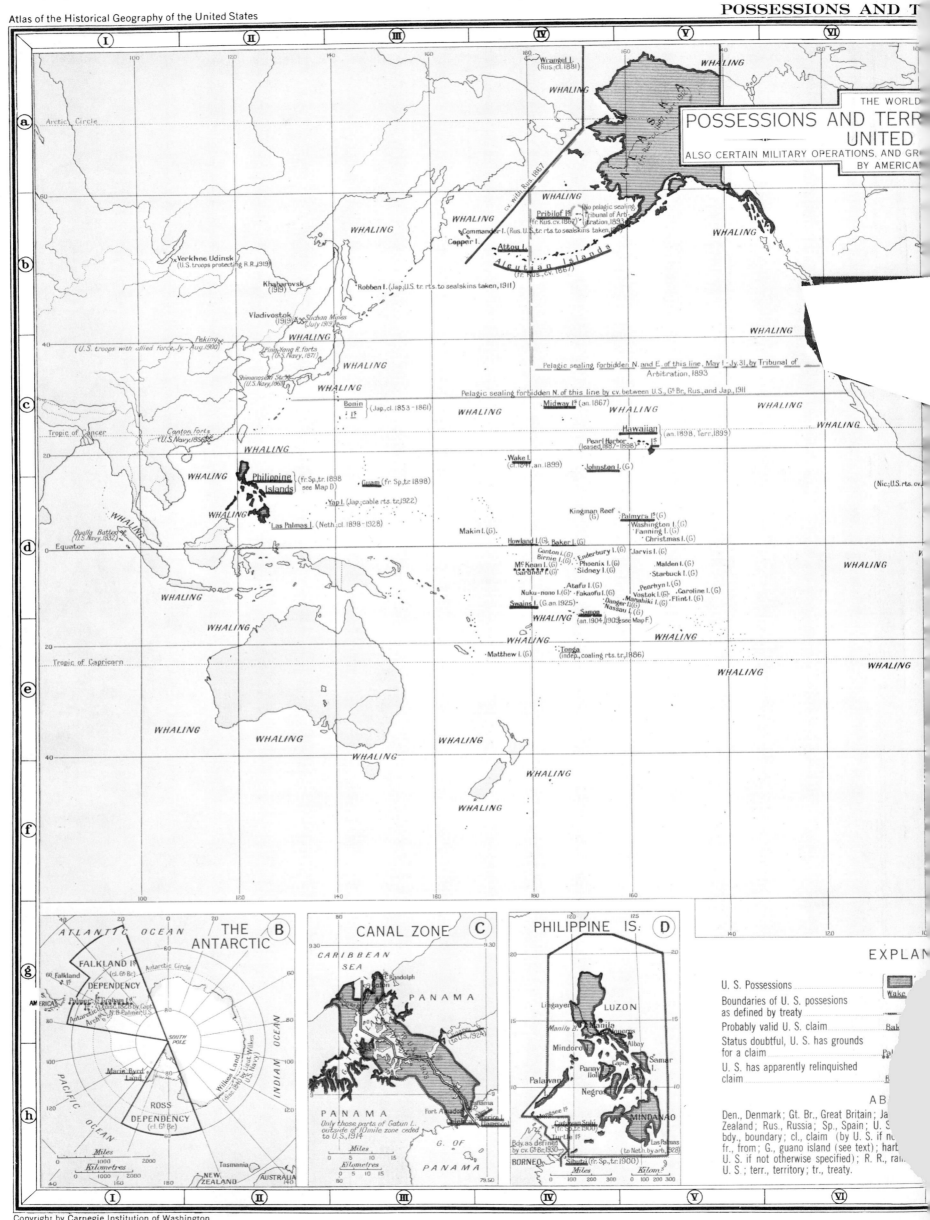

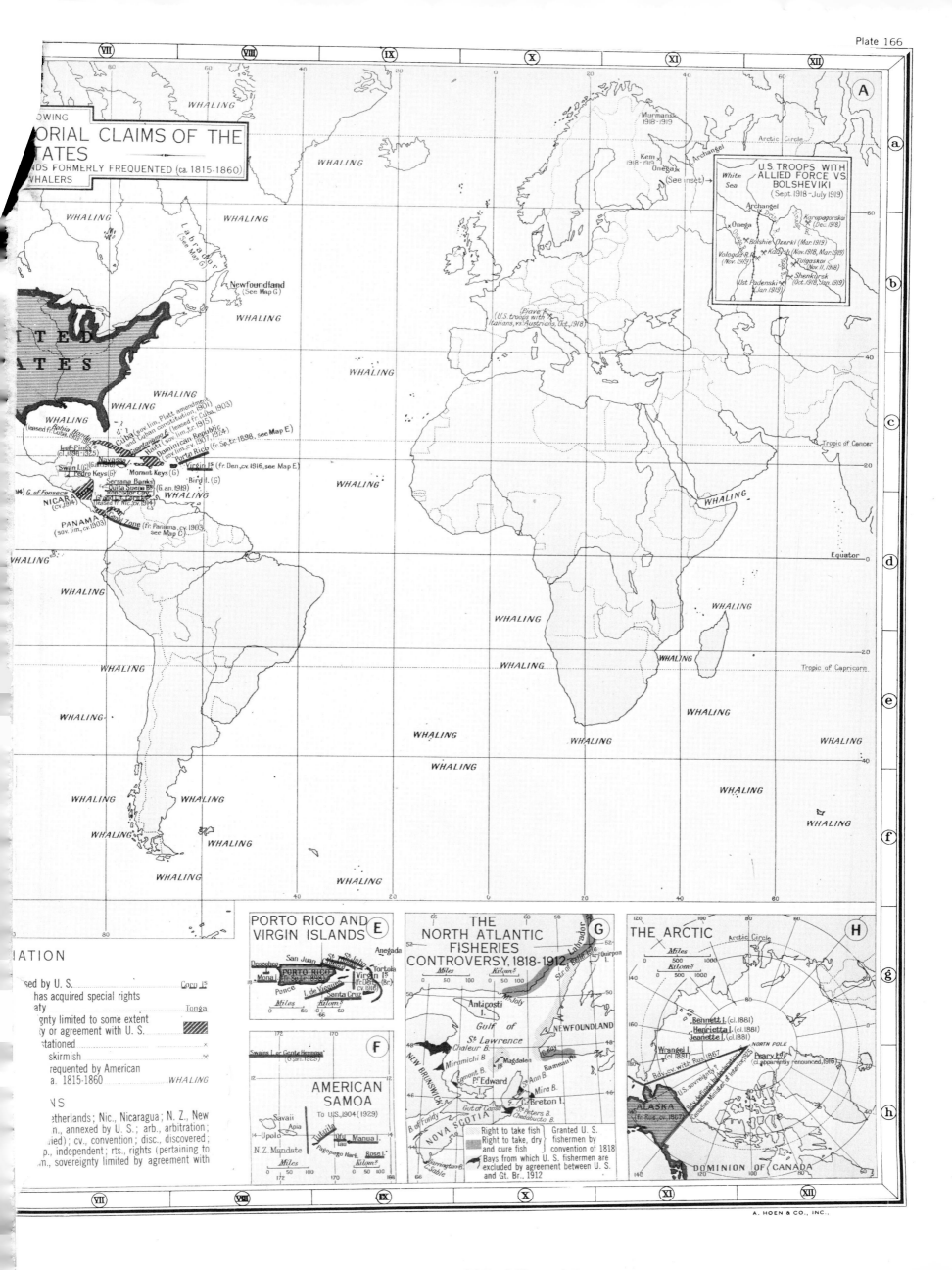

Plate 166

A. HOEN & CO., INC.

COLLEGE OF MARIN

3 2555 00125058 3

REFERENCE